SERMON OUTLINES

BY

CHARLES SIMEON, and others

Formerly published as *Theological Sketchbook, or Skeletons of Sermons*, carefully arranged in systematic order so as to constitute a complete Body of Divinity

Chiefly selected from Simeon's *Horae Homileticae and Skeletons, Sketches of Sermons, Pulpit Assistant, Benson's Plans, Preacher, Pulpit*, and other works

Two Volumes in One

Vol. I

BAKER BOOK HOUSE

Grand Rapids 6, Michigan

1 9 5 4

PHOTOLITHOPRINTED BY CUSHING – MALLOY, INC.
ANN ARBOR, MICHIGAN, UNITED STATES OF AMERICA
1954

PREFACE

~~~~~~~~

This book, entitled SERMON OUTLINES, has an interesting history. The foundation for this work was laid with the appearance of Charles Simeon's *Horae Homileticae* and his volumes of *Skeletons of Sermons*. Later there appeared Hannam's *Pulpit Assistant*, consisting of "skeletons of sermons" selected from the standard sermons of such established and accepted authors as John Tillotson and Isaac Watts. It was in Hannam's work that these so-called "sermon skeletons" were first arranged so as to comprise what was called "a body of Divinity." This rather extended work of Hannam was later telescoped into one volume of selected *Outlines or Skeletons of Sermons*. There next followed a rather large work of nearly four hundred *Sketches of Sermons* from varied authorship, and another selection of "sketches of original sermons" entitled *The Preacher*.

All this culminated in the issuance of the present volume under the imposing title *Theological Sketch-Book, or Skeletons of Sermons; arranged in systematic order to constitute a complete Body of Divinity*. This *Theological Sketch-Book* is, in fact, a systematic selection chiefly from Simeon's Works, with selections from Hannam's *Pulpit Assistant*, the *Sketches of Sermons* and *The Preacher*, so as to form a well-rounded and balanced presentation of Scriptural truth. It is this highly refined volume, originally published as THEOLOGICAL SKETCH-BOOK, etc. which is now reissued under the simpler and more definitive title, SERMON OUTLINES. This brief sketch of its history indicates its purpose and usefulness.

— THE PUBLISHERS

TABLE OF CONTENTS
VOL. I.

CHAPTER I.

THE HOLY SCRIPTURES

CHAPTER II.

TRINITY.

CHAPTER III.

GOD.

CHAPTER IV.

CHRIST.

CHAPTER V.

THE HOLY SPIRIT.

CHAPTER X.

THE MEANS OF GRACE.

TABLE OF CONTENTS
VOL. II.

CHAPTER I.

THE MEANS OF GRACE.

CHAPTER II.

EXHORTATIONS.

CHAPTER III.

THE WORK OF GRACE.

CHAPTER IV.

CHRISTIAN GRACES.

CHAPTER V.

CHRISTIAN DUTIES.

CHAPTER VI.

WARNINGS.

CHAPTER VII.

THE CONSEQUENCES OF SIN.

CHAPTER VIII.

THE BLESSEDNESS OF RELIGION.

INDEX TO THE TEXTS
VOL. I.

INDEX TO THE TEXTS
VOL. II.

CHAPTER I.

THE HOLY SCRIPTURES.

THE BOOK OF THE LORD.

Isaiah xxxiv. 16.—" Seek ye out of the book of the Lord and read." (Sk.)

THE text occurs nearly at the close of one of the most awfully sublime chapters that the language of man ever uttered, or the pen of inspiration ever wrote. A chapter in which JEHOVAH is represented as clothing himself with the garment of vengeance, and coming out of his place to punish the inhabitants of the earth for their iniquities; and a chapter, in which we not only discover the indignation of God displayed against sinners, so as utterly to effect their destruction; but where the very land that had nursed them in their crimes is made a standing monument of Divine vengeance. Can any thing within the whole compass of human language be more awful than the descriptions in ver. 9—16? It is not now necessary to say when these prophecies were fulfilled, or to what particular country they referred: what we have at present to regard is, the advice in the text; and here let us,

I. NOTICE THE OBJECT TO WHICH OUR ATTENTION IS DIRECTED—THE BOOK OF THE LORD. This phrase primarily meant the prophetic writings; but since the canon of Scripture has been filled up, we understand by the "book of the Lord," the whole Bible, consisting of the Old and New Testaments: these are called, "the book of the Lord."

1. *Because they were inspired by the Lord*, 2 Tim. iii. 16, 17. We infer this—from their wonderful preservation—from the exact fulfilment of the prophecies with which they abound—from the most stupendous and indisputable miracles recorded in them—from the grand and elevated subjects on which they treat—and especially from the moral influence of their doctrines in the salvation of mankind.

2. *They abound with the most correct and sublime descriptions of the Lord.* One of the ancients said, 'The Bible is the history of God.' It describes the nature of God—what he is in himself, and what he is to us—what he has been doing, and what he will do. It records the terrible acts of his justice—the grand displays of his mercy—his inviolate faithfulness, immaculate purity, and immutable goodness. There is scarcely a question which a serious mind may be disposed to urge relative to the Divine Being, which cannot be solved from the Old and New Testaments.

3. *They are sanctioned by the Lord, and he has set his seal to their truth,* Isa. lv. 10, 11; Rom. i. 16; 1 Thess. ii. 13. Oh! what great and glorious success attends the doctrines contained in the Bible, when preached in their purity. How many blind eyes are opened! How many hard hearts softened! How many inveterate prejudices subdued! How many wanderers reclaimed! How many penitents cheered! And how many immortal souls made wise unto salvation by the Holy Scriptures!

4. *They lead to the Lord.* They find us out in our state of estrangement and alienation from God; they teach us the way of access unto God, by the blood of the atonement; they mark the steps by which the prodigal returns to his Father; they encourage him by promises, and urge him by threaten-

7

ings; and their most obvious tendency and design is. to lead us "to the rock that is higher than" ourselves.

II. Illustrate the purposes for which we are to seek out of the book of the Lord and read.

1. *To gain instructions* The Bible is a book of knowledge. All the streams of sacred instruction, which have been flowing in every direction through all the Christian world, and fertilizing the waste and desolate places of the earth, have arisen from this source. Do we pant for knowledge? Here it spreads its ample page;

> ' 'Tis revelation satisfies all doubts,
> And solves all mysteries except its own;
> And so illuminates the path of life,
> That fools discover it and stray no more.'

A christian with a Bible in his hand resembles a man standing on the elevated summit of a mountain, "where ether pure surrounds him, and Elysian prospects rise." The dark clouds that hung over the past are all dissipated, and he views the birth of time, the formation of the globe, the origin of evil, and the long train of miracles, prophecies, and wonders, with which the Old Testament abounds. Nor is he less favored in looking through the bright vista of the future years.

2. *To gain examples.* The Bible is a book of models; here we see religion enlivened and embodied. The precepts of the Gospel describe what men ought to be, but in the living characters we see what they were; and there is not a single virtue that can adorn human nature, but what has been exemplified in some living characters, recorded in "the book of the Lord;" such as faith in Abraham, meekness in Moses, patience in Job, &c.

3. *To gain excitements.* The Bible is a book of motives.—Knowledge and practice do not always harmonize. Men know much; but how few live up to what they know! There are no motives equal to those which the Bible presents. Can love allure us? Here is love "no where to be found less than divine." Can terror awe us? Here are the terrors of the Lord most awfully displayed, in the punishments inflicted on the ungodly. Oh, what motives does "the book of the Lord" display! addressed to the understanding, to the conscience, and to the heart.

4. *To gain encouragements.* The Bible is a book of promises and consolations; they suit every case, meet every emergency, redress every grievance, scatter every doubt, and heal every wound; they are pure in their source, satisfying in their nature, and perpetual in their duration.

III. Offer a few thoughts as to the manner, how we should seek out of the book of the Lord and read.

1. *We should do it with deep seriousness and holy awe resting upon our minds.* The very thought that we are about to consult the oracles of eternal truth, which came forth from God, and serve to describe his nature, ought to repress every feeling of levity, and every disposition contrary to serious godliness. Were God again upon earth in human form, and were we to consult him on the great business of our salvation, who can doubt but what we should do it seriously?—So read his word.

2. *We should "seek out of the book of the Lord, and read," with all the attention of which we are capable.* "Search," said our Saviour, "the Scriptures." This is a significant word, and is a metaphor taken from miners, who dig deep, and search for metals in the bowels of the earth. "The book of the Lord" has a rich vein of heavenly wisdom running through it, whose merchandise is better than silver; but this treasure lies deep, and

superficial observers never perceive it: while we read let us seek—bend the whole force of our minds—call in our attention—and repress every wandering thought.

3. *We should do it frequently.* If we cannot spare hours to do it, let us snatch moments; and if we cannot peruse many chapters, let us read single verses, and treasure them up in our memories. "Thy word have I hid in my heart," Psa. cxix. 11. Let our memories be sacred repositories for the words of God.

4. *We should do it with much prayer.* While you *read*, pray—pray for Divine illumination. "Holy men of old spake as they were moved by the Holy Ghost;" we need that same teaching, to understand what they wrote, Psalm cxix. 18; Prov. i. 23.

5. *We should do it practically.* Let us read, not merely to know, but to practise; all knowledge should be influential. "If ye know these things, happy are ye if ye do them," James i. 25.

Infer,

1. *The greatness of our privileges.* We live in a land of Bibles, we have "the book of the Lord;" and by the help of Sunday schools, &c., all may read.

2. *The greatness of our obligations*—to know, love, praise, and obey God.

3. *The greatness of our guilt*, if we abuse our privileges, and violate our obligations to God.

THE DIVINE AUTHORITY AND PERFECTION OF THE SCRIPTURES

2 Tim. iii. 16.—"All scripture is given by inspiration of God, and is profitable for doctrine, for reproof, for correction and instruction in righteousness." (H.)

THERE are but two possible ways of acquiring the knowledge of the mind of God, and these are *reason* and *revelation;* reason is that noble faculty of the soul by which man is distinguished from all inferior orders of creatures, and made capable of moral government. When our first parents were in a state of innocence, this alone was sufficient to acquaint them with every part of their duty; but upon their disobedience it was so far eclipsed, that from this time, the world, with all its wisdom has neither been fully acquainted with the perfections of the true God, nor with the right and acceptable manner of worshipping him; as appears from the history of those ages and nations, which have not had the advantage of revelation. The apostle Paul, speaking of the Gentile world, says, "they changed the glory of the incorruptible God into an image made like corruptible man." Rom. i. 23, &c. He admits they had some little acquaintance with God, but not sufficient to direct their practice; for even at Athens, the most learned city of Greece, there was an altar with this inscription, "To the unknown God." If we look abroad into the barbarous nations at this day, we shall find them buried in ignorance and superstition. How little do they know of the nature and perfections of the one living and true God, and of his reasonable service! and how dim are the remains of natural light, with regard to the terms of acceptance with him! all which demonstrates the necessity and usefulness of a Divine revelation, or of that clear and bright discovery of his will, contained in the scriptures of the Old and New Testament; which, according to the apostle, are given by the inspiration of God, and are profitable for doctrine.

I. THE SCRIPTURES OF THE OLD AND NEW TESTAMENT ARE GIVEN BY THE INSPIRATION OF GOD.

By the scriptures, the apostle, in our text, means chiefly the Old Testament, for the canon of the New was not yet finished ; and by their being inspired, that those ancient prophecies came not by the will of man, but holy men of God spake as they were moved by the Holy Ghost.

In order to judge whether persons are inspired, we must,

1. Inquire into their moral character : Are they virtuous and holy persons ? These dare not deceive, nor deliver any thing as a revelation from God, but what they are fully satisfied they have received from him. If a pretender to inspiration should denounce some remarkable judgment to be inflicted for our vile crimes, and should himself be notoriously guilty of those vices; it is not reasonable to suppose, we should receive him as a prophet sent from God.

2. We must examine into their doctrine. Is the doctrine they teach according to godliness ? A Divine revelation must have a tendency to promote Divine knowledge and virtue, not only by teaching men to deny ungodliness, but also to live soberly, and righteously. Again, do they exalt the Divine glory and majesty, and abase the creature so far, as that no flesh should glory in his sight ?

3. We must consider the credentials, or external proofs of their mission ; which are principally,

1. Miracles. There can be no stronger evidence of a Divine mission than this. When Moses was sent with a massage to Pharaoh, the Lord said to Moses and Aaron, " When Pharaoh shall speak to you, saying, Show a miracle, then take your rod." Ex. vii. 9. By which it appears, that in those early times, miracles were esteemed a convincing proof of a Divine mission. Our Lord appeals, upon all occasions, to his miracles. When John the Baptist sent to inquire of him, " Whether he was the Christ ?" He replies, " Go tell your master, that the blind receive their sight." Matt. xi. 5. How often did he point the scribes and pharisees to his mighty works, as well as his disciples ? (John xiv. 11,) " Believe me that I am in the Father."

2. Fulfilment of prophecy. No mere man can foretell what shall be on the morrow, much less in ages far remote. This is the sole prerogative of the great God ; as he alone searches and tries the reins and the heart, so he only can foretell the end from the beginning. When therefore a prophet speaks in the name of the Lord. Deut. xviii. 20.

Now all these marks and characters of inspiration are no where so conspicuous as in the Holy Scriptures. Moses, David, Solomon, Daniel, and the rest of the prophets, were pious and upright men, and it is no inconsiderable proof of their integrity, that they have left their own faults and infirmities on record. Their doctrines are reasonable, just, and good, tending to promote the glory of God and the happiness of men. What sublime strains of devotion are in the Psalms of David ! What excellent rules for the conduct of life in the writings of Solomon ! and how glorious does the God of Israel shine throughout all the prophets ! how kind and gracious are his promises ! how awful his threatenings ! and how wonderfully is his majesty supported by the numerous representations of the infinite distance and disproportion between him and his creatures ! These holy men believed themselves inspired, for they tell us the word of the Lord came unto them at such a time ; and when they spake, it is with, " Thus saith the Lord."

And with regard to the New Testament, the evidence of its Divine authority is as strong as the nature of things will admit. The apostle tells us, " That God, who at sundry times, and in divers' manners," Heb. i. 1. So that if Jesus Christ be the Son of God, it will certainly follow, that his doctrine could be no other than a Divine revelation. And this appears in many prophecies of the Old Testament. It was prophesied of the Messiah, " that he should be incarnate before the sceptre departed from Judah ; that he should be born of a virgin ; that he should be of the seed of David, and of the tribe of Judah ; that the place of his nativity should be Bethlehem, a village of Judea ; that his name should be Immanuel ; that he should appear in the form of a servant, and after a mean and contemptible life, should be betrayed by one of his own household, and cut off for the sins of the people." It was therefore with the highest reason that our Saviour upbraided his countrymen for their unbelief. " O fools, and slow of heart." Luke xxiv. 25, 26.

Besides, how illustriously do the other characters of inspiration, already mentioned, shine forth in the person of Christ, who was holy, harmless, undefiled ; whose doctrines were so rational and sublime, that the people wondered at the gracious words that proceeded out of his mouth. The miracles which he wrought in confirmation of his doctrine were so clear and surprising, that nothing but the extremest obstinacy and malice could withstand their evidence. But as there were many doctrines necessay to be known, which the apostles of our blessed Saviour could not receive from him in his state of humiliation and suffering ; he therefore promised after his ascension into heaven, to inspire them with the extraordinary gift of the Holy Spirit, whereby they should be led into all truth, and qualified to declare to the Gentiles "the whole counsel of God." Accordingly, on the day of Pentecost, when the apostles were gathered together in one place, "the Holy Ghost came upon them, and enabled them not only to speak divers languages, but to confirm the doctrines they taught with signs and wonders."

II. THE PERFECTION OR SUFFICIENCY OF THE SCRIPTURES.

It is said in the preceding verse, " that they are able to make us wise to salvation ;" and in the text, " that they are profitable for doctrine, for reproof." By the sufficiency of the Holy Scriptures, we mean, that they contain all things necessary to be believed and practised ; the law of Moses was so complete a direction of the faith and obedience of the Jews, that the addition of the Scribes and Pharisees were both useless and vain. Matt. xv. 29. In like manner the writings of the New Testament are a perfect standard to us Christians ; for all things that our blessed Lord heard of his Father, he made known to his apostles, and the apostles to the churches. Acts xx. 26, 27, " I take you to record."

But the perfection of the Holy Scriptures may be farther illustrated from the particulars in my text, as,

1. They are profitable for doctrine ; to acquaint us with our lost and miserable condition by sin, and the train of fatal consequences that attend it, with our recovery by Christ, the covenants of redemption and grace, the offices of Father, Son, and Spirit, in the work of our redemption, and with all those " other mysteries, which were kept secret since the world began." Rom. xvi. 25.

2. For reproof ; or the discovery of our pernicious errors in doctrine and practice. When the gospel was first preached among the idolatrous nations

their dumb idols were thrown down, and their superstitious vanities fled before it, as the shadows of the night before the rising sun. The scriptures are now the standard of truth ; and if men preach not agreeably thereto, it is because there is no light in them. A text of scripture, rightly explained and applied, is as full a confutation of error to a Christian, as a mathematical demonstration to a philosopher.

3. The scriptures are profitable for correction of vice and wickedness ; " wherewithal (says the Psalmist) should a young man cleanse his way ?" Ps. cxix. There we have a collection of all Christian graces and duties, with their opposite vices: the fruits of the Spirit and of the flesh are distinguished with the greatest propriety ; and the most engaging motives to the practice of the one, and awful threatenings against the other, are represented with the greatest strength and advantage.

4. For instruction in righteousness : that is, either in the righteousness of God, which is by faith of Jesus Christ unto all, and upon all, that believe ; or in the practice of moral righteousness, the nature and excellency of which are better explained and illustrated in the sermons of our blessed Saviour, than in all the writings of the ancient philosophers.

The precepts of the Bible are so many excellent rules for a holy life, and the promises are Divine encouragements to it: " Having therefore these promises, dearly beloved," 2 Cor. vii. 1. In a word, the Holy Scriptures are sufficient to all the purposes of religion.

III. THEIR CLEARNESS AND PERSPICUITY.

There are sublime speculations, which may employ the thoughts of the most learned inquirer after truth; as well as the deep things of God, which the angels are desirous to look into : and there are also the principles of the doctrine of Christ; that is, the " milk of the word," or the softest and gentlest food which is fit for babes, as the other is for strong men. The doctrines of the greatest consequence, such as repentance towards God, and faith in our Lord Jesus Christ, the certainty of a future state, of the resurrection of the dead, and of judgment to come, are most clearly revealed. The love of God, and of our neighbour ; together with the necessity of universal holiness, charity, and good works, run through the whole of the New Testament, and are placed in so strong a light, that persons of the meanest capacities cannot but understand them. Besides,

1. The Holy Scriptures are written in the vulgar language, and therefore designed for the use of the common people. The Old Testament was written in the language of the Jewish nation, and a portion of it read in their synagogues every Sabbath-day. The New Testament was written in Greek, which was, at that time, the general language ; and St. Paul's epistles were read in the churches. Now can we suppose, that the scriptures should be read to the common people, and they not capable to understand them ? could not the Spirit of God write clearly ; or would he not ? To say the former is blasphemy ; and to affirm the latter, is in effect to say, the scriptures are no revelation to the churches : for if they cannot understand them after their best inquiries, they might almost as well have been without them.

2. Our Saviour, in his sermons to the people, appeals to the scriptures, and exhorts his countrymen the Jews to search them. " Search the scriptures." John v. 39. The noble Bereans are commended for this practice, Acts xvii. 11 ; and young Timothy appears to have been acquainted with them from his childhood.

Remark,

' Hence we may learn, that the religion of a Christian should be his

Bible; because it contains the whole revealed will of God, and is a perfect rule of faith and practice. It is also a more sure word of prophecy.

2. Let us be thankful that we have the scriptures in the vulgar language. Christianity was professed a thousand years in this island before the Bible was translated into English. This was one of the peculiar blessings of the Reformation.

3. Let us revive this neglected duty of reading the scriptures. It is both a delightful' and useful employment. "Whatsoever things were written aforetime were written for our learning." It was enjoined the Israelites, upon their coming out of Egypt into the land of Canaan, that they should not only love the Lord their God, but " the words which I command thee this day." Deut. vi. 5—7.

4. When we read the scriptures, let us consider them not as the words of men, but as in deed and truth the word of God. If some things are above our capacities, let us remember, " that the foolishness of God is wiser than man." Let us read the scriptures therefore with reverence, and endeavor to understand them, as well as we can, by comparing spiritual things with spiritual.

5. In judging of controversies among Christians, let us not be carried away by the authority of great names or numbers. Councils, and fathers, and synods, may be mistaken in their decrees; but the word of God is infallible. Here we are safe, and no where else.

6. When we read the scriptures, let us pray for the instructions and teachings of the Holy Spirit; for it is not sufficient, that the light of the gospel shines around us, unless the Spirit of God, who once commanded light to shine out of darkness, shines in our hearts. " Then opened he their understandings, that they might understand the scriptures. Lord, open our eyes, that we may behold the wondrous things out of thy law."

ADVANTAGES OF POSSESSING THE SCRIPTURES.

Romans iii. 1, 2.—What advantage then hath the Jew: or what profit is there of circumcision? Much every way: chiefly, because that unto them were committed the oracles of God. (Pr.)

PAUL's leading object in the whole of this epistle is to show that a sinner's justification with God is by faith in Jesus, in opposition to the works of the law. The Jews were for trusting in circumcision as the ground of acceptance; and the apostle admits, that if they had not sinned, circumcision as well as other acts of obedience might be pleaded; but that *having* sinned, their circumcision was nothing, and there was no justification with God on that ground: chap. ii. 25—29.

The words of the text are then introduced as containing an objection; to which the proper answer is given—

I. CONSIDER THE CHARACTER HERE ASCRIBED TO THE HOLY SCRIPTURES: THEY ARE " THE ORACLES OF GOD."

1. Observe, an Oracle is the speech or *answer of a deity*, or of some supposed deity ; as a temple is the residence of a deity, either real or imaginary. — — The heathens had their oracles, which they consulted on every occasion, though they were altogether a delusion, and a mere piece of priestcraft. — — But though all these were counterfeits, yet there were true oracles ; and these are the Word of the true and living God.

The holy Scriptures are called oracles in other passages, as well as in this. In Acts vii. 38, they are denominated " the lively oracles." They are not an old dead history about persons and things long ago, but are what concern the living at this day. They are not like the dead languages, but are themselves a living language, in which every man hears in his own tongue the wonderful works of God.

God's precepts are the same now, as when they were delivered at Sinai. They are not grown obsolete, but are still in force, and are spoken to us as well as to them. Deut. v. 3. — — His threatnings are the same now as then, and God means the same by them as he ever did, and they are all equally in force. — — The promises are all the same : it is God that still invites us, saying, ' Come ye to the waters :' and the invitations are equally addressed to us as to those of old.

2. The Scriptures are called oracles as containing *the first principles* of religion : thus in Heb. v. 12. — — They contain indeed a fund of wisdom and knowledge, as well as first principles, and are therefore to be regarded as the standard of truth. Hence if any one speak or teach, let him do it as the oracles of God speak, and be careful that his doctrine corresponds with that rule. 1 Pet. iv. 11.

3. In some instances the oracles of God are *contrasted with the oracles of the heathen,* as in Isai. xlv. 19. — — The heathen oracles were chiefly distinguished by three things. — — They affected a mysterious concealment : but the oracles of God court examination. — — They disappointed those who trusted in them : but the Lord ' never said to the seed of Jacob seek ye me in vain.' — — They were of an immoral tendency, had no regard to righteousness, but taught and encouraged what was evil, and consulted only the sinful inclinations of the people : but the oracles of God declare ' the things that are right,' without consulting the sinful propensities of men, and whether they would regard it or not.

II. CONSIDER THE ADVANTAGE OF POSSESSING THE SACRED WRITINGS ; THIS IS " MUCH EVERY WAY."

It was the distinguishing privilege of the Jews, that unto them were committed the oracles of God ; and it is also one of our principle advantages. — — We cannot so well estimate the worth of any thing as by considering the condition of those who are without it ; our commonest mercies are all undervalued, because they are common. — — The sun rises every day, and fills the world with light, and we think little of it ; but if we were left in darkness for several months, we should then be taught to estimate its value.

Could we but see the state of the heathen world, and compare it with our own ; could we but compare their general morals with those of christian countries, we should be more fully aware of the advantages which we enjoy. — — The Scriptures have an effect on men in general, who themselves have no love to righteousness ; and they are compelled to act with some degree of decorum and good order. — — David having been driven away among the heathen. by the persecutions of Saul, and obliged to wander in the land of Moab, and among the Philistines, was led from hence to

14

form an idea of the incomparable worth of the holy Scriptures; and then it was, very probably, that he wrote his encomiums in the nineteenth psalm, and also in the cxixth,

Some of the advantages of having the Scriptures will appear, if we consider more particularly the following things—

1. What a flood of light they pour upon that subject *which belongs to our best interests.* — — All men are convinced that they are sinners, for all have a conscience; yet by nature are wholly in the dark, not knowing whither they are going, nor what shall be hereafter. — — Oh the importance of that word, which shineth as a light in a dark place, and shows us the way of life! If heathens ask, what shall we do to be saved; none of their oracles, none of their priests can tell. Neither Greece nor Rome with all their learning, could answer such a question as this. But when the Philippian jailor proposed such a question to Paul and Silas, they could answer and say, Believe on the Lord Jesus Christ, and thou shalt be saved. There is now no need to ascend into heaven, and descend into the deep: the word is nigh us, and it tells us all things. Rom. x. 6—9.

2. Consider **how** plain the directions are which the Scriptures give *on the subject of obedience.* The poor heathens are trying to please God, or rather their idols, in a thousand different ways, yet know not how: but the sacred oracles will tell us at once, and in one word, wherein the whole law is contained. — — God does not require such kind of sacrifices as their idols are supposed to do: his words are, 'My son, give me thy heart.' What does he require, but that we love mercy, and walk humbly with him. The original inhabitants of this island had their wicked idols, like those of Moloch, in which they burned thousands of human beings alive, in honor of their deities.

Whatever use we may make of the oracles of God, and however much they may be abused, they are of the greatest importance in themselves, and it is our chief glory to possess them.

3. They are the principal means which God has used *in the conversion of sinners.* 'The law of the Lord is perfect, converting the soul; sure, making wise the simple.' The *works* of God did not convert men then, any more than they do now, though they declare his glory, and his handy work. Psal. xix.

It is by the truth that we are saved; the gospel is the power of God unto salvation; and whenever the time come that all shall know the Lord, and be made righteous, and when all the people shall praise him; it shall be by his way being made known upon earth, and his saving health among all nations. Psal. lxvii. 2. — — The history of the mission to India confirms this remark: from the time that they translated and circulated the Scriptures, the Lord began to bless them, and not till then.

III. Application of the subject.

1. If the oracles of God were of so much advantage to the Jews, they are *much more so to us.* We have also the New Testament, which is the accomplishment of the Old: such an addition to the sacred oracles is of infinite importance. — — If David could say so much of the five books of Moses, which were nearly all that was extant in his day; what would he have said of the whole Bible as we possess it in our day!

2. What a motive is presented for attempting to *diffuse the knowledge of the Scriptures all around us.* — — If we wish to see mankind blessed and made happy, let us give to them the words of eternal life

The instruction of the children of the poor is in this view a most desirable object. There are many public charities, and also charity schools, which have their use : but Sunday schools in particular have an object in view which distinguishes them from all the rest—that of giving access to the holy Scriptures. — — They give the key of knowledge, which is one of the chief advantages of true religion.

3. Let us remember that the oracles of God will be of no ultimate advantage to us, unless we are brought *truly to believe* and to embrace them, so as to live under their holy influence. — — Without this, they will only be a swift witness against us in the last day.

ON THE PERFECTION OF THE SCRIPTURES.

Psalms cxix. 96.—But thy commandment is exceeding broad. (H.)

By commandment, the Psalmist here means the whole will, word, and law of God, as it is contained in the Holy Scriptures. And I intend from these words to discourse concerning the fulness, perfection, and sufficiency of that word and law.

I. THE PERFECTION OF THE HOLY SCRIPTURES WILL APPEAR, IF WE CONSIDER THEM WITH RESPECT TO THEIR AUTHOR AND ORIGINAL.

This word the almighty God has spoken; this law, or this commandment, the infinite Jehovah has made and given. As the child bears the image of the parent, and the wax receives the impression of the seal, so these sacred oracles breathe forth the spirit of their great Author; and do in every page confess the likeness which they have to their Divine original.

The unparalleled excellence of the Divine nature, the glories of the supreme Majesty, are here expressed, as the features of a man's face are visible in the glass wherein he looks.

These scriptures are not of a common birth; " all scripture is given by the inspiration of God ; and holy men spake as they were moved by the Holy Ghost."

Now there is, in the word and law of God, a perfection of holiness and purity ; of truth and certainty ; of righteousness and justice ; of wisdom and knowledge ; of mercy and goodness ; of perpetuity and duration. Ps. xix. 7—9.

II. IF WE CONSIDER THE SUBJECT MATTER.

It is said of the authority, excellency, and perfection of our Lord's doctrine, that " never man spake like this man." The gospel contains the words which our Lord spake : of which our Lord gives the truest and fairest description, when he says, " The words which I speak, they are spirit and they are life." There is that spirit of heavenly light, life, and love; there is that Divine virtue, and that exquisite beauty, in these sacred writings, that no other composure can parallel.

Here we have the nature of God discovered, the lines of sovereign power and wisdom drawn in the clearest brightness. Much of God may be read in his creatures ; " the invisible things of him." Rom. i. 20.

But the most complete and attractive attributes of God, are nowhere so amply displayed, as in this revelation he has made of himself in his word: from this book do the brightest beams of Divine love break out upon us in the most astonishing manner. The perfection of the scriptures, will appear, if we consider the usefulness of the histories, the certainty of the prophecies, the wisdom of the laws, the sanctity of the morals, the loftiness of the mysteries, the brightness of the examples, the preciousness of the promises on the one hand, and the terror of the judgments on the other.

Here are contained the deep things of God, the unfathomable secrets of infinite wisdom. Here we have discovered to us the adorable mystery of the Trinity, the incarnation of the Son of God, the fall of man, and the corruption of our nature by it, the various windings of Providence, concerning which we have reason to break out with astonishment, " O the depth !"

How important are the discoveries of a future state of inexpressible rewards and punishments, of the solemn and august appearance of the great and last day. How admirable are the rules of life, how strict the precepts of virtue. What a complete treatise of practical religion have we given to us in our Saviour's sermon on the mount. There are such bright images of piety, such refined rules of holy living, such as by far outdo all the former institutions of religion and philosophy. They never taught the duty of loving our enemies, mortifying our anger, abstaining from revenge, the necessity of forgiving injuries. These are some of the peculiar perfections and excellences which belong to the laws of Christ.

III. THE NEXT INSTANCE WHEREIN THE PERFECTION OF THE SCRIPTURES CONSISTS, IS THE MANNER IN WHICH THEY ARE WRITTEN.

In the word of God there is not only a profound treasure of the most excellent matter, but those holy and heavenly truths are also delivered in the most majestic strains of oratory, and with all the ornaments of the most exalted rhetoric. Words are nowhere arranged in a more attractive order, nor do the triumphs of sacred eloquence shine in any author with greater splendour, nor flow with an evener stream. How wonderful and surprising are the descriptions which Job in chaps. xxxvii. xxxviii. and xxxix., gives us of the Divine power and providence ! In how fine and poetical a strain are the songs of Moses and Deborah composed ! and with how much beauty of style, as well as height of devotion, is the book of the Psalms replenished ! How lofty and intricate are some of the prophets ! how pathetical and terrible are others ! and some, again, how mild and gentle ! What refined wisdom, what deep experience, what admirable observations of human policy, have we in the writings of Solomon ! What noble characters, and lively images of things, have we dispersed in those instructive pages ! How inimitably is the passion of grief set forth in the Lamentations of Jeremiah !

" One would think," says Dr. South, " that every letter was wrote with a tear, every word was the sad accent of a breaking heart; that the penman was a man compacted of sorrows, and disciplined to mourning; that he never breathed but in sighs, nor spoke but in a groan."

How awful and dreadful is the account which Moses gives us of the publication of the law : God descended in fire and smoke, and the people did not only fear, but the hill shook, and the mountain did exceedingly quake and tremble. Nothing can give us a juster idea of omnipotent power, than that expression of Moses, when God says, " Let there be light, and there was light. He spake the word, and it was done ; he commanded, and it stood fast."

How exactly, and with how much harmony, have the evangelists written of the life and passion of our Saviour! How strongly do the mysteries of Divine grace and goodness flow in the epistles! What a glorious description have we of the New Jerusalem. Rev. xxi. 23. Indeed, none can describe the excellency and dignity of the whole composition of the New Testament.

IV. THE EXCELLENCY OF THE SCRIPTURES WILL APPEAR, IF WE CONSIDER THE DESIGN FOR WHICH THEY ARE REVEALED.

The intent of their promulgation is glorious. There is no book in the world that is so adapted for the raising our minds, refining our judgments, spiritualizing our affections, and advancing our hearts to the imitation of God.

One great end of this inspired book is, to direct us to the knowledge of God, his being, nature, and attributes. God hath made himself known by his works; but he has done this more perfectly by his word. In the one, he has shown his back-parts, as once he did to Moses; but, in this, he has uncovered his face.

Another end of the Holy Scriptures is to lead us into the knowledge of the providence of God; his various dealings with his church and people in all ages; how he has protected them by his power, corrected them by his judgments, comforted them by his Spirit, ruled them by his laws.

To make us complete and universal in our obedience, that the uprightness which we lost by the fall, may be repaired and restored by the Spirit of grace.

To give us a true and just notion of ourselves, to abate our pride, to show us what we are, and from whom we have received our all.

To give us right thoughts concerning the world, the vanity and uncertainty of every creature.

They do in the best manner direct us to our great end, the glory of God, and the salvation of our souls. In all which particulars, we must say of the law of God,

"Thy commandment is exceeding broad," i. e. it is exceeding perfect, wanting nothing, either to declare the greatness of its Author, or to contribute to the happiness of man.

Observe,

If the scriptures are thus excellent and perfect, in their original composure and design; if we have in them so great and so worthy a rule and direction of life and manners; then from hence it will follow, that we cannot employ our time better than in searching this rule, than in reading and studying the scriptures, which are written for our learning, and which are so exceeding useful and profitable to us in every respect. Let us search, and diligently meditate on these sacred writings; and, since "we have so sure a word of prophecy, we should do well to take heed unto it."

THE WELLS OF SALVATION.

Isaiah xii. 3.—With joy shall ye draw water out of the wells of salvation. (H. H.)

WE wonder not that the Scriptures are read with so little interest by the generality: for, till persons know somewhat of their lost estate, and of the way of salvation provided for them, the Bible is to them a sealed book. But let them once experience a taste of the Redeemer's love, and instantly they will find in the Inspired Volume mines of wealth. Such a storehouse is that blessed book to the godly in this day: and such will it be to the Jewish Church, when once they shall be converted to the faith of Christ. "*In that day* they will say, O Lord, I will praise thee: though thou wast angry with me, thine anger is turned away, and thou comfortedst me." (Such will be the reflections at the time of their first discoveries of God's mercy to them in Christ Jesus. Then they will advance farther to express their full confidence in God.) "Behold, God is my salvation! I will trust, and not be afraid: for the Lord Jehovah is my strength and my song; he also is become my salvation." (Then will they be fully prepared to derive the richest benefit from the Scriptures: and) "*therefore* shall they draw water with joy out of the wells of salvation."

That we may form a just estimate of their privilege, let us consider,

I. THE CHARACTER BY WHICH THE SCRIPTURES ARE HERE DESIGNATED—

The expression, "wells of salvation," is supposed by many to be spoken of Christ: and doubtless it may be very fitly applied to him. But I rather understand it of the Scriptures, from whence, as from an inexhaustible fountain, all true comfort flows. They eminently deserve that name,

1. As containing in themselves all the blessings of salvation—

The whole of salvation as planned in the Divine counsels from all eternity, as executed for us by the Lord Jesus Christ in his incarnate state, as still carrying on by him at the right hand of his Father, and as offered through him to every child of man, is there fully contained. "This mystery of godliness was indeed kept secret since the world began; but now it is made manifest; and by the Scriptures of the Prophets, according to the commandment of the everlasting God, is made known to all nations for the obedience of faith." Rom. xvi. 25, 26.

Now let any one contemplate this mystery, and endeavor to explore the *wisdom*, the *love*, the *mercy*, and the *grace* contained in it: how surpassing all finite comprehension will they be found! Verily, the breadth, and length, and depth, and height of this mystery, and of the wonders contained in it, are utterly unsearchable; and the blessings flowing from it are a plenteous and perennial spring, for the refreshment of all on earth, and of all in heaven.

2. As revealing them for our use—

In the whole world besides, there is not to be found one drop of water to satisfy a thirsty soul. Where can one look that is oppressed with a sense of guilt? Where, one who is mourning over the corruptions of his nature? Go to those who have not the Scriptures: go to even the wisest philosophers of Greece and Rome; and see how vain were all their expedients for pacifying a guilty soul, or purifying a polluted soul. But in the Scriptures we find all that a sinner can desire; an atonement, sufficient for the sins of the whole world; and an Almighty Agent ready to dwell in the heart of all who seek him, and engaged to transform into the Divine image all who commit their souls to him. In them are promises suited to every condition incident to our fallen nature; as suited to refresh the soul, as water is to allay our thirst. Conceive of every want with which a sinner can be oppressed, and the appropriate relief will there be found.

3. As actually imparting them to our souls—

As a spring pours forth its waters, so do the Scriptures impart life, and peace, and strength to all who go to them as God's appointed channel of communication to their souls. They have within themselves a life-giving virtue; John iv. 10; so that, when brought home and applied by the Spirit of God, they quicken the dead, and give a vital energy to all our powers

They are able, not only to "make men wise unto salvation," but to impart salvation itself; being "like fire" to consume dross, Jer. xxiii. 29, and "a hammer to break the rock in pieces," ib., and "a two-edged sword to pierce the very inmost soul," Heb. iv. 12, and "a weapon to destroy every enemy." 2 Cor. x. 4, 5. They have a power to enlighten the darkest mind, Ps. xix. 7, 8, and to sanctify all on whom they operate aright; John xv. 3, and xvii. 19; and so to sanctify them, as to prepare them for the perfect fruition of their God. Eph. v. 26, 27.

Think then of,

II. The blessedness of having access to them—

Truly we should never contemplate them but with joy, on account of,

1. The freeness with which we may approach them—

There is no prohibition to any creature under heaven. About wells that have been dug for a supply of common water, there have been the fiercest contentions: Gen. xxvi. 18—21; but these are public property, and equally accessible to all: none have to "pay for this water," as Israel had: Numb. xx. 19; it is to be had "without money and without price." Isaiah lv. 1. True indeed it is that there are many, Protestants as well as Papists, who would bar our access to them: but God has given to all an equal right to come to them: for his invitation is, "Let him that is athirst come; and whosoever will, let him come and take of the water of life freely." Rev. xxii. 17.

2. The ease with which we may draw from them—

There are those who think it in vain for the poor to come to them, seeing that "the wells are deep, and they have nothing to draw with." John iv. 11. But be it known, that however valuable learning may be for the attaining a *critical* acquaintance with the holy Scriptures, it is not at all necessary for a *spiritual* perception of their truths. It is faith, and not learning, that is wanting for *that* end. All the learning in the universe will not impart to us a spiritual discernment, any more than it will furnish us with any corporeal organs. It is faith alone that will avail us here. That discerns the things which are not visible to mortal eyes; and will go to the very bottom of these wells, and draw from thence the most refreshing consolations.

3. The abundance that we may receive out of them—

When the rock was struck by Moses, the waters gushed out in such abundance, that the whole camp of Israel, with all their cattle, could drink thereof. And, if all the sinners in the universe will go to these wells, they shall find no lack for the supply of their most enlarged necessities. Our Lord says, "If any man thirst, let him come unto me and drink; and out of his belly shall flow rivers of living water." John vii. 37, 38. Indeed, the more intense and ardent your thirst is, the more abundant shall be the blessings which you shall derive from them.

4. The perfect satisfaction that we may find in them—

"Whoever drinks of other waters will thirst again: but whoever drinks of these wells, will never thirst: for the water which he has received will be in him as a well of water springing up into everlasting life." John iv. 13, 14; Isai. xlix. 9, 10. I may appeal to all, whether the most copious draughts of carnal pleasure are ever satisfied? Solomon, who drank as deep of it as a human being could do, pronounced it all to be vanity and vexation of spirit. "The eye was never yet satisfied with seeing, nor the ear with hearing." But he who has obtained the knowledge of Christ, and drunk deep of the promises of the Gospel, has no longer any relish for earthly vanities, nor any desire after them. Give him all the world, and he feels empty : give him the presence of God, and he desires no more.

ADDRESS,

1. Those who are going to broken cisterns—

What is the creature but "a broken cistern that can hold no water?" — — —And will you for this forsake "the fountain of living waters ?" Jer. ii. 13. Let me prevail on every one of you to go to God as your reconciled God in Christ Jesus, and to say with David, "All my fresh springs are in thee." Ps. lxxxvii. 7.

2. Those who are drinking from "the fountain of life"—Ps. xxxvi. 9.

Say whether you have not "a joy with which the stranger intermeddleth not?" Say whether the fountains do not richly supply you; and whether, even on the highest places, which, according to human apprehension, are inaccessible to rivers, the rivers do not follow you? Isai. xli. 17, 18. Yes, till you arrive at heaven itself, the streams shall never fail; and even there shall they run beside you for your comfort to eternal ages. Rev. vii. 17.

THE SPREAD OF THE GOSPEL.

2 Thess. iii. 1. Finally, Brethren, pray for us, that the word of the Lord may have free course and be glorified, even as it is with you. (H. H.)

THE light of the material sun is hailed and welcomed by every nation under heaven : but how much more is the light of the Sun of Righteousness to be desired ! If the one be necessary for our comfort in this life, the other is necessary to guide us in the way to life eternal. Hence the Apostle not only labored to spread the Gospel himself, but endeavored to interest all the Lord's people in its behalf; that by their united supplications they might obtain from God whatever should conduce to its establishment in the world.

In this request of his we see,

I. WHAT WE SHOULD DESIRE FOR THE WORD OF GOD—

1. That it should "have free course"—

It is surprising that any should be averse to the circulation of the Scriptures; or should be jealous of the Scriptures, unless accompanied with human compositions to forestall and determine the judgment of the reader. What is this but to determine the judgment of the reader ? What is this, but to return to Popery ? The Papists locked up the Scriptures in an unknown tongue, and forbade the laity to read them; and sent forth among the people small portions of them only, and counteracted those portions by the most erroneous comments and grossest superstitions. Far be such conduct from Protestants: freely have we received, and freely we should give: nor should we relax our efforts to disseminate the Scriptures, till every human being shall have them in his possession, and be enabled to read in his own native language the wonderful works of God. See Ps. xix. 4, and Rom. x. 18.

II. THAT IT SHOULD "BE GLORIFIED"—

What is implied in this expression, we are at no loss to determine. We have only to see how it was glorified "*with them,*" i. e. the Thessalonian converts, and we have the perfect model of its being glorified amongst ourselves.

In two ways is the word of God glorified; first, *in the conversion of sinners;* and, next, *in the edification and salvation of saints.*

How the Gospel wrought to *the conversion* of the Thessalonians, we are distinctly informed; They received it, "not as the word of man, but as the word of God:" it "came to *them,* not in word only, but in power;" and by it "they were turned from idols to serve the living God" 1 Thess. i. 5, 9, and ii. 13. ——— Similar effects were produced by it in other Churches. Acts vi. 7, and xix. 20. ——— And who must not confess that the word is glorified when such wonders are wrought by it? ——— But that it is so, is expressly affirmed by the voice of inspiration itself. Acts xiii. 48, 49.

Nor was the Gospel less powerful for their continued *edification.* This was greatly advanced among them, as the Apostle himself bore witness, 2 Thess. i. 3, 4, and ii. 13, 14. ——— Yet nothing but the pure word of God was, or could be, effectual for this end. 1 Pet. ii. 2. As the rod of Moses wrought all those miracles in Egypt and the wilderness, so was the Gospel "the rod of God's strength:" and in the production of such miraculous events, both the word itself, and God in it, were greatly glorified: Acts xxi. 19, 20, nor is it possible to see such effects yet produced in the hearts and lives of men, without acknowledging, that "he who hath wrought them to the self-same thing is God." 2 Cor. v. 5. ———

Let us next inquire—

III. How that desire is to be obtained—

The Apostle speaks of himself and all his fellow-laborers, as instruments whereby the Gospel was propagated throughout the world. And the same is true of ministers in all succeeding ages, even to the present day: they are God's Ambassadors to a rebellious world. But the prayers of God's people are no less necessary than the efforts of his ministers: for it is God alone that can give effect to any exertions; and it is prayer alone that can interest him in our behalf—

It is God alone that can raise up ministers, or fit them for the work. Rom. x. 15, and 2 Cor. ii. 15, 16, and iii. 5. ——— Hence we are directed to "pray that *God would send forth* laborers into his harvest." Matt. ix. 38, Eph. iv. 12, 13.

It is God alone that can open places for them to labor in. Men universally of themselves reject the Gospel: but when God opens a door for his servants, no attempts of his enemies can shut it. Acts xviii. 10, 11; 1 Cor. xvi. 9, and Rev. iii. 8.———

It is God alone that can give success to their endeavors. That same divine power, which first opened the understandings of the Apostles, must open the hearts of others to attend to them. Luke xxiv. 45, with Acts xvi. 14 ——— And then only does the word effect any radical change in men, when it comes "in demonstration of the Spirit and of power." 1 Cor. ii. 4, 5, and iii. 5—7.

Hence St. Paul so earnestly intreated the prayers of the Thessalonian Church, and yet more earnestly the intercessions of the saints at Rome. Rom. xv. 30—32. God has in mercy made his servants and his people mutually dependent on each other: the people being quickened by the exertions of their ministers; and ministers being strengthened by the prayers of their people: and thus the builders and the building are advanced together, and all are edified in love.

We conclude this subject with,

1. A word of admonition.

Many who profess a reverence for the Bible, and even display a zeal for conveying the holy Scriptures to Heathen lands, who yet make but little use of it for themselves. But this zeal for the good of others will never be admitted as a substitute for personal religion — — — Many of the religious world also, who study the Bible and profess to love the Gospel of Christ, are far from adorning that Gospel by holy tempers, and by heavenly lives — — — Let such persons look well to themselves; for "not he that saith Lord, Lord, shall enter into the kingdom of heaven; but he that doeth the will of our Father which is in heaven" — — —

2. A WORD OF ENCOURAGEMENT—

Let any one see what was effected in the days of old by a few poor fishermen; and take courage to exert himself for God — — — The same power that wrought effectually in that day will concur with us — — — Let us not then despond, as though our weakness were any obstacle to success; for God will display his own power by means of it, 2 Cor. xii. 9, and " or dain strength in the mouths of babes and sucklings." Whether therefore we address ourselves to the translation of the Scriptures into foreign languages, or labor for the circulation of them at home, let us only implore help from God, and we shall not be permitted to "labor in vain, or run in vain."

CHAPTER II.

THE TRINITY.

THE DOCTRINE OF THE TRINITY VINDICATED.

1 John v. 7.—There are three that bear record in heaven, the Father, the Word, and the Holy Ghost; and these three are one.* (H. H.)

NEVER was there any record so well attested, so worthy of acceptation, so necessary to be believed, as that which God has given of his Son. Upon the receiving or rejecting of it depends the eternal welfare of all mankind. The riches of wisdom, and love, and mercy that are contained in it, surpass all the comprehension of men or angels. With respect to the truth of it, every species of testimony that could be given to it by friends or enemies, by angels from heaven, by men on earth, yea even by devils themselves, has been given in the most abundant degree. But it has been confirmed by other testimony still, even by the Three Persons in the adorable Trinity.

From the words before us, we shall be led to shew,

I. WHO THEY ARE THAT ARE SAID TO " BEAR RECORD"—

We need not wonder at the zeal which has been shewn by the adversaries of the doctrine in our text, to discredit the authenticity of the text itself; since, if the genuineness of the text be admitted, that alone will put an end to all controversy on the subject of the Trinity. On the other hand, we need

---

* Any one who should preach on this subject can use his own discretion about the mode of introducing it. If he be perfectly assured that the words are an interpolation, he can state his views of that matter, and adopt the text, in order to shew, that, *though the words themselves are not authentic, the truths contained in them are truly scriptural, and important :* or he can take ver. 9 for his text.

not be anxious about the validity of this individual passage, as though the doctrine of the Trinity rested upon it; since, if the text were expunged from the Bible, there are a multitude of others which maintain most unequivocally the same important truth.

To establish the mysterious doctrine of a Trinity in Unity, we shall lay down, and substantiate, three positions:

1. There is but one God—

The unity of God may be deduced even from reason itself: but it is repeatedly affirmed in Scripture; compare Deut. vi. 4, with Mark xii. 29; nor must a doubt of it ever be suffered to enter into our minds. It is true, that in a subordinate sense there are gods many, and lords many; because angels, and magistrates, and the idols of heathens, are sometimes called by these names on account of the resemblance they bear to God in the authority vested in them, and the respect paid to them: but there is One Supreme Being, who alone is self-existent, and from whom all other beings, whether in heaven or earth, derive their existence. He, and he only, is God. 1 Cor. viii. 5, 6.

2. Though there is only one God, yet there are three distinct Persons in the Godhead—

In reference to this subject, we use the term *persons*, because there is no other so suitable: but we mean not that these persons are *in all respects* as distinct from each other as Peter, James, and John; but only that *in some respects* they are distinguished from each other, though they subsist together in one undivided essence.

It is certain that *there are three persons mentioned in the Scripture:* for baptism is ordered to be administered, not in the name of God merely, but in the name of "the Father, of the Son, and of the Holy Ghost." Matt. xxviii. 19. *These three are represented as distinct from each other;* for the Son has told us, that "he will send the Holy Spirit from the Father." John xv. 26. *They are moreover spoken of as performing separate offices in the work of redemption;* the Father elects; Eph. i. 4; the Son redeems; Eph. i. 7; the Spirit sanctifies; Rom. xv. 16; and St. Peter, comprising in few words the whole mystery of redemption, ascribes to each of these persons his proper office. 1 Pet. i. 2. *They are also declared to be sources of distinct blessings to the Church;* the Apostle prays, that "the grace of the Lord Jesus Christ, the love of God the Father, and the fellowship of the Holy Ghost, may be with us all. 2 Cor. xiii. 14.

3. Each of these persons is God without any difference or inequality—

We shall not occupy any time with proving the Godhead of the Father; but, taking that for granted, shall establish the Godhead of the Son and of the Holy Ghost.

To each of these belong the same *names* as unto the Father. Is the Father *God?* so is the Word, John i. 1, (as Christ is called in the text.) He is "Emmanuel, God with us," Matt. i. 23; God manifest in the flesh, 1 Tim. iii. 16; the mighty God, Isai. ix. 6; God over all, blessed for evermore. Rom. ix. 5. To Him is also given the incommunicable name, *Jehovah;* for we are to call him, "Jehovah our Righteousness." Jer. xxiii. 6. To the Holy Spirit also these names belong. Ananias, in lying unto the Holy Ghost, lied unto God. Acts v. 3, 4. And we, in being the temples of the Holy Ghost, are the temples of God. 1 Cor. iii. 16. The words also which were confessedly spoken by Jehovah to the prophet Isaiah, Isai. vi. 9, 10; are quoted by St. Paul as spoken by the Holy Ghost. Acts xxviii. 25.

To each of these the same *attributes* also are ascribed as characterize the Father. Is the Father *eternal, omnipresent, omniscient, almighty?* So is the Son (Mic. v. 2, and Heb. xiii. 8.—Matt. xviii. 20, and xxviii. 20.—John ii. 25, and xxi. 17.—John i. 3, and Matt. xxviii. 18.)— — — and so is the Holy Ghost (Heb. ix. 14.—Ps. cxxxix. 7, 8.—1 Cor. ii. 10.—Gen. i. 2, and Job xxvi. 13,)— — —

What now is the conclusion to be drawn from these premises, but that which is asserted in the text, that " there are THREE that bear record in heaven; and that those Three are ONE* ?"

Having shewn that by the Three witnesses we are to understand the Tri-une God, we proceed to shew,

II. WHAT THAT IS CONCERNING WHICH THEY BEAR RECORD—

We may well expect that the importance of the matter to which these Divine witnesses have borne record, is suited to the majesty of the witnesses themselves. Accordingly we find, that

Their testimony relates to the salvation that is in Christ Jesus—

God, who had passed by the angels that fell, has looked in mercy upon fallen man, and has given us eternal life, in and through his Son Jesus Christ. Ver. 11. He sent his dear Son to die in our stead, and, by his own obedience unto death, to work out a righteousness whereby we might be saved. The merit whereby we are to be justified, and the grace whereby we are to be renewed, he treasured up for us in Christ; and he calls all men to receive these blessings out of his fulness. This way of salvation is open for all, and sufficient for all: but, this rejected, no other remains for us.

This is the sum and substance of the Gospel; and this it is to which the sacred Three bear record.

Nor is their testimony at all more than the subject requires—

If God himself had not revealed such things, *who could ever have imagined them?* who could ever have thought of God becoming incarnate, and, by his own death, expiating the guilt of his own creatures? Who could ever have devised a plan so calculated to exalt the perfections of God; so suited to answer the necessities of man; and so efficacious to renew us after the Divine image?— — — Besides, supposing these things to have been reported, *who would ever have believed them*, if they had not been thus Divinely attested? Notwithstanding the testimonies given by the Sacred Three, there is yet reason to adopt that reiterated complaint, " Who hath believed our report?" Isai. liii. 1 ; John xii. 38 ; Rom. x. 16. Professions of faith indeed abound amongst us ; but a true Believer, whose feelings and conduct accord with his professions, is " a sign and a wonder" in Christendom itself. Isai. viii. 18.

It remains yet to be declared,

III. IN WHAT MANNER THEY BEAR RECORD—

Each of these divine persons has borne record at divers times, and in different manners—

The Father thrice bore witness to Christ by an audible voice from heaven ; declaring at the same time his acquiescence in him as the Saviour of men ; and requiring us at the peril of our souls to " hear" and receive him in that

---

*Hence we see how properly we are taught to express our belief of this doctrine in the Athanasian Creed : " We worship one God in Trinity, and Trinity in Unity ; neither confounding the persons, nor dividing the substance ; for there is one person of the Father, another of the Son, and another of the Holy Ghost : but the Godhead of the Father, of the Son, and of the Holy Ghost is all one, the glory equal, the majesty co-eternal . . So that in all things the Unity in Trinity, and Trinity in Unity, is to be worshipped."

character. Matt. iii. 17, and xvii. 5, and John xii. 28. Moreover, in raising Christ from the dead, he yet more emphatically testified, that he had discharged the debt for which he had been imprisoned in the grave, and was "able to save to the uttermost all that should come unto God through him." Rom. i. 4.

The Lord Jesus Christ continually bore witness to himself. When asked, "If thou be the Christ, tell us plainly;" he answered, "I have told you, and ye believe me not." John x. 24, 25. "Before Pontius Pilate he witnessed the same good confession," 1 Tim. vi. 13; though he knew that it would issue in his death. After his resurrection, he called himself "the true and faithful witness," and testified, " am he that was dead and am alive again, and have the keys of death and of hell." Rev. i. 18, and iii. 14.

The Holy Spirit also bore witness to him, when he descended in a bodily shape, like a dove, upon him: And again, when he came down in the likeness of fiery tongues upon the Apostles, and converted three thousand to the faith of Christ. Similar testimonies he still continued to give; Acts x. 44, 45; and at this very day, when any are converted to the faith, it is owing to the testimony which the Holy Spirit bears to Christ; "the Spirit testifies of him," and thereby produces conviction or consolation in the soul. John xv. 26, and xvi. 7—11.

Thus the Sacred Three bear record in heaven, and by their united testimony encourage our acceptance of the salvation offered us in the gospel.

INFER,

1. How unreasonable and dangerous is unbelief!

If only men, who are credible and competent witnesses, attest a thing, we think it right to believe them. What an insult then is it to the Sacred Three to doubt their testimony! Yet this, alas! is the treatment which their record meets with in the world. Some reject it as "a cunningly-devised fable;" while others, professing a regard to it in general, deny the most important part of it, the necessity of being saved by Christ alone. Even those who in their hearts approve the gospel, are too apt to doubt the freeness and sufficiency of the salvation revealed in it. Let every one consider the extreme sinfulness of such conduct, and abhor the thought of "making God a liar,' ver. 9, 10.

2. What obligation lies upon believers to bear an open testimony to the truth!

It is evident how earnestly God desires that his dear Son should be known, and that the salvation wrought out by him should be embraced. Now believers are his witnesses in the midst of a blind deluded world. Ought they then to be ashamed or afraid to bear their testimony for God? What if the world agree to call the gospel a delusion, and to consider all as hypocrites or fanatics who embrace it? Should that deter us from making a public profession of his truth? Should we not rather be the bolder in confessing Christ, in proportion as others are bold in denying him?

But let us not confine our profession to creeds and forms: the best, and most acceptable way of declaring our affiance in Christ, is by manifesting to the world its efficacy on our hearts and lives. *This* will make them think that there is a reality in the gospel; and may contribute to win many who never would obey the written word.

3. How exalted must be the glory which believers still enjoy in heaven!

It cannot be conceived that the Three Persons of the Godhead would have devised and executed such a wonderful plan of salvation, if the end to be accomplished by it were not exceeding glorious. Surely all that the love of the Father can devise, all that the blood of Christ can purchase, all that the Holy Spirit can impart, is prepared for us in the eternal world, and shall be bestowed on us acco ding to our measure and capacity to receive it. Yes, in heaven we shall see God as he is, and have the brightest discoveries of his glory: and, while we have the richest enjoyment of his presence and love, we ourselves shall be witnesses for him, how far his mercy could reach, what astonishing changes it could effect, and what blessedness it can bestow on the most unworthy of mankind.

CHAPTER III.

GOD.

THE SELF-EXISTENCE AND IMMUTABILITY OF GOD.

Exod. iii. 14.—And God said unto Moses, I AM THAT I AM: and He said, Thus shalt thou say unto the children of Israel, I AM hath sent me unto you. (H. H.)

IT is of great importance that ministers should be considered as ambassa dors of God—

And that they should deliver nothing which they cannot enforce with, Thus saith the Lord—

Without this, their word can have but little weight—

But ministrations thus supported will produce the happiest effects—

Moses was commissioned to offer deliverance to the oppressed Israelites—

But he rightly judged that they would ask, From whence he had his authority—

He therefore inquired of God, What answer he should return—

And received from God the direction recorded in the text—

To understand the words aright, we must consider,

I. THE TITLE GOD ASSUMED—

The Deity had hitherto revealed himself to man by the name of God Almighty—

Though he had been called JEHOVAH, he was not fully known by that name, even to his most highly-favored servants—Exod. vi. 3.

He now was pleased to assume a title similar to that; but, if possible, of still plainer import—

The name, I AM THAT I AM, represents him to be

Self-existent—

Creatures have only a derived, and therefore a dependent, existence—

They are now what they once were not, and may again cease to be—

But God from all eternity was precisely what he now is—

To him therefore this august title may be properly applied—

Nor are there wanting other similar descriptions of him to confirm it— Ps. cii. 27; Rev. i. 4.

Immutable—

Every creature in earth and heaven is liable to change—

But "with God there is no variableness, neither shadow of turning"—

He himself claims immutability as his own peculiar prerogative—Mal. iii. 6.

27

And in this view, the title assumed in the text must ever belong to him—
Incomprehensible—

No words can convey, or imagination conceive, an adequate idea of God—
Job. xi. 7; 1 Tim. vi. 16.

Hence God does not endeavor to explain his nature to Moses—

But, by declaring himself to be what he is, intimates, that he is what can
neither be comprehended nor expressed—

His answer, in effect, was similar to that which he afterwards gave to Manoah—Judg. xiii. 17, 18.

The title thus explained, it will be proper to consider,

II. For what end he assumed it—

The Israelites were extremely debased by means of their long bondage—

It was necessary therefore to prepare their minds for the intended deliverance—

Though they groaned under their oppression, they were too much reconciled to their yoke—

They rather affected a mitigation of trouble, than the attainment of liberty—

Though the promises made to their fathers were not wholly forgotten, the
accomplishment of them was not cordially desired—

Indeed, they scarcely conceived it possible that their emancipation should
be effected—

Hence it was necessary to stimulate their desires, renew their hopes, and
confirm their expectations, of a better country—

The title which God assumed was admirably adapted to this end—

If God was so incomprehensible a Being, he could easily devise means
of executing his own sovereign will and pleasure—

If he was the one self-existent, independent Creator of the universe, all
creatures must be wholly subject to his controul—

And if he were absolutely immutable, he could not recede from the covenant entered into with their fathers—

He therefore could not want either inclination or power to deliver them—

Yea, He could not but deliver them for his own great name's sake—

He could not be I AM, if his promised interposition should be either
withheld or defeated—

Thus the declaration of his name must inspire them with confidence—

And induce tnem willingly to put themselves under the direction of Moses—

Infer,

1. What a solemn attention does the Gospel demand!—

The Gospel is a message of mercy to those who are in bondage to sin—

And they who preach it are ambassadors from the great I AM—

Jesus, who sends them forth, assumes to himself this very title—John
viii. 58.

To the same effect also his character is drawn in the Epistle to the Hebrews—Heb. xiii. 8.

He has commissioned his servants to go forth into all the world—Mark
xvi. 15.

And promised (as God did to Moses) to be always with them—Matt.
xxviii. 20.

Shall we then make light of the mercy which He offers to us ! —

Or doubt his power and willingness to fulfil his promises ?—

Shall we thrust away his servants, saying, Why dost thou interfere with
us ?—Acts vii. 27.

Let us remember Who it is that speaks to us in the Gospel—Luke x. 16

Every faithful minister may say, I AM hath sent me unto you—

Nor, though miracles have ceased, shall signs be wanting to confirm the word—

The deaf shall hear, the blind see, the lame walk, the lepers be cleansed—

And blessed is he whosoever shall not be offended at the Redeemer's voice—Matt. xi. 5 6.

2. What encouragement is here afforded to those who are groaning under spiritual bondage!

God brought out his people safely, notwithstanding all their difficulties—

And in due time put them into possession of the promised land—

Shall the spiritual redemption offered by him be less effectual ?—

Are not his power and faithfulness the same as in former ages ?—Isa. lix. 1.

Will he not remove our obstacles, supply our wants, and destroy our enemies ?—

Surely there are none so weak but they shall be made to triumph—Isaiah xlix. 24, 25.

Nor shall the Prince of Darkness oppose with more success than Pharaoh—Rom. xvi. 20.

Behold then, I AM hath sent me to proclaim these glad tidings—

Let all arise, and cast off their yoke, and burst their bands asunder—

Let not unbelief represent the obstacles as insurmountable—

Nor fear induce you to comply with the imperious dictates of the world*—

Behold ! the Pillar and the Cloud are ready to conduct your path—

The great I AM is for you: who then can be against you ?—

Go forth ; and universal nature shall applaud your steps—Isa. lv. 12.

*Pharoah, after many successive plagues, agreed first that they should sacrifice to God in *the land, but not in the wilderness ;* then that they should go *into the wilderness, but not far :* then that *the men* should go, but *without the women or children ;* then that *the women and children, but not the flocks.* Exod. viii. 25, 28, and x. 11, 24. Thus the world would prescribe limits to the service we shall pay to God.

ON THE ETERNITY OF GOD.

Psalm xc. ii.—Before the mountains were brought forth, or ever thou hadst formed the earth, and the world ; even from everlasting to everlasting, thou art God. (H.)

The title of this psalm is a prayer, the author Moses. There are two parts in this psalm ; a complaint of the frailty of man's life in general, verses 3—6; and then a particular complaint of the condition of the church, verses 8—10; a prayer, verse 12. But, before he speaks of the shortness of human life, he fortifies them by the consideration of the refuge they had, and should find in God ; verse 1, "Lord, thou hast been our dwelling-place." God is a perpetual refuge, and security to his people. His providence is not confined to one generation; it is not one age only that tastes his bounty and compassion. His providence is not wearied, nor his care fainting; he never wanted will to relieve us, for he hath been our refuge; nor ever can want power to support us, for he is a God from everlasting to everlasting. The church never wanted a pilot to steer her, and a rock to shelter her, and dash in pieces the waves which threaten her. How worthy is it to remember former benefits, when we come to beg for new. Never were the records of

God's mercies so exactly revised, as when his people have stood in need of new editions of his power; and though so much strength hath been upon various occasions manifested, yet his arm is not weakened: for, "from everlasting to everlasting, thou art God." God is of an eternal duration. The eternity of God is the foundation of the stability of the covenant, the great comfort of a christian.

I. How God is eternal, or in what respects he is so.

Eternity is a negative attribute, and is a denying of God any measure of time, as immensity is a denying of him any bounds of place; as immensity is the diffusion of his essence, so eternity is the duration of his essence.

1. God is without beginning. "In the beginning God created the world." God was then before the beginning of it; and what point can be set wherein God began, if he were before the beginning of created things! God was without beginning, though all other things had time and beginning from him. Gen. i. 1. Whatsoever number of millions of millions of years we can imagine before the creation of the world, yet God was infinitely before those; he is therefore called the Ancient of Days. Dan. vii. 9.

2. God is without end. He always was, always is, and always will be what he is; he remains always the same in being; so far from any change, that no shadow of it can touch him. James i. 17. "The Lord shall endure for ever." As it is impossible he should not be, being from all eternity; so it is impossible that he should not be to all eternity. He is said to live for ever. "The earth shall perish, but God shall endure for ever, and his years shall have no end." Ps. cii. 27. That which had no beginning of duration can never have an end, nor any interruptions in it. Since God never depended upon any, what should make him cease to be what eternally he hath been, or put a stop to the continuance of his perfections.

3. There is no succession in God. God is without succession or change; it is a part of eternity. "From everlasting to everlasting, he is God," *i. e.* the same. God doth not only always remain in being, but he always remains the same in that being. "Thou art the same." The creatures are in a perpetual flux; something is acquired, or something lost, every day. A man is the same in regard of existence, when he is a man, as he was when he was a child; but there is a new succession of quantities and qualities in him. Of a creature it may be said, he was, or he is, or he shall be; of God it cannot be said, but only he is; he is what he always was, and he is what he always will be.

There is no succession in the knowledge of God. The variety of successions and changes in the world make no succession or new objects in the divine mind; for all things are present to him from eternity. "Known unto God are all things from the beginning."

There is no succession in the decrees of God. He doth not decree this now, which he decreed not before. "He chose us in him before the foundation of the world, that we should be holy." Eph. i. 4.

4. God is his own eternity. He is not eternal by grant, and the disposal of any other, but by nature and essence. The eternity of God is nothing else but the duration of God; and the duration of God is nothing else but his existence enduring.

5. Hence all the perfections of God are eternal. In regard of the Divine eternity, all things in God are eternal; his power, mercy, wisdom, justice, knowledge.

II. God is eternal, and must needs be so.

The Spirit of God, in scripture, condescends to our capacities, in signify ing the eternity of God by days and years; but we must not conceive that God is bounded or measured by time. Ps. cii. 27. Though years are ascribed to him, yet they are such as cannot be numbered. "The number of his years cannot be searched out." Job xxxvi. 26, 27. Sometimes this eternity is expressed by parts, as looking backward and forward; by the difference of time, past, present, and to come; "which was, and is, and is to come." Rev. i. 8; and iv. 8. He always was, is now, and always will be.

1. His eternity is evident, by the name God gives himself. "And God said unto Moses, I AM THAT I AM; I AM hath sent me unto you." Ex. iii. 14. God only can be called "I AM;" all creatures have more of not being than being. If God, therefore, be properly "I AM," i. e. being, it follows, that he always was.

2. God hath life in himself. John v. 26. "The Father hath life in himself." He is the living God, therefore steadfast for ever. Dan. vi. 26. He hath life by his essence, not by participation; he is a sun, to give light and life to all creatures, but receives not light nor life from any thing; and therefore he hath an unlimited life: not a drop of life, but a fountain; not a spark of a limited life, but a life transcending all bounds: he hath life in himself: all creatures have their life in him, and from him. Since he hath life in himself, and there was no cause of his existence, he can have no cause of his limitation; and can no more be determined to a time, than he can to a place. What hath life in itself, hath life without bounds, and can never desert it, nor be deprived of it: so that he lives necessarily; all other things "live, and move, and have their being in him." Acts xvii. 28.

3. If God were not eternal, he were not immutable in his nature. It is contrary to the nature of immutability to be without eternity; for whatsoever begins is changed in its passing from not being to being. Mal. iii. 6. "I am the Lord, I change not." Job xxxvii. 23. "Touching the Almighty, we cannot find him out." God is a sun, glittering always in the same glory.

4. God could not be an infinitely perfect being, if he were not eternal. A finite duration is inconsistent with infinite perfection. God hath an unsearchable perfection. Job xi. 7. "Canst thou by searching find out God?" He cannot be found out; he is infinite, because he is incomprehensible. "He is blessed from everlasting to everlasting." Ps. xli. 13. Had he a beginning, he could not have all perfection without limitation; he would have been limited by that which gave him beginning.

5. God could not be omnipotent, almighty, if he were not eternal. The title of Almighty agrees not with a nature that had a beginning; whosoever hath a beginning, was once nothing; and when it was nothing, could act nothing. The almightiness and eternity of God are linked together: "I am Alpha and Omega, the beginning and ending, which was, and which is, and which is to come, the Almighty."

6. God would not be the first cause of all, if he were not eternal. But he is the first, and the last; the first cause of all things, the last end of all things. Rev. i. 8. This power cannot but be eternal; it must be before the world; the founder must be before the foundation; and his existence must be from eternity, or we must say nothing did exist from eternity. Nothing hath no faculties: so that it is necessary to grant some eternal being, or run into inextricable labyrinths and mazes. So then, if God were the cause of all things, he did exist before all things, and that from eternity.

III. Eternity is only proper to God, and not communicable.

It is as great a madness to ascribe eternity to the creature, as to deprive the Lord of the creature of eternity. It is so proper to God, that when the apostle would prove the deity of Christ, he proves it by his immutability and eternity, as well as his creating power. "Thou art the same, and thy years shall not fail." Heb. i. 10—12. Angels and souls have an immortality, but by donation from God, not by their own essence; dependant upon their Creator, not necessary in their own nature. Whatsoever is not God is temporary; whatsoever is eternal is God.

It is a contradiction to say a creature can be eternal; as nothing eternal is created, so nothing created is eternal. Eternity being the essence of God, it would be all one to admit many gods, as many eternals.

1. Creation is a producing something from nothing. What was once nothing, cannot therefore be eternal.

2. There is no creature but is mutable, therefore not eternal. It is as much the essence of a creature to be mutable, as it is the essence of God to be immutable.

3. No creature is infinite, therefore not eternal. To be infinite in duration is all one, as to be infinite in essence. This is the property of the Deity.

4. No effect of an intellectual free agent can be equal in duration to its cause. The producers of natural agents are as ancient often as themselves; the sun produceth a beam as old in time as itself; but who ever heard of a piece of wise workmanship as old as the wise artificer? God only is eternal, the first and the last, the beginning and the end; who, as he subsisted before any creature had a being, so he will eternally subsist, if all creatures were reduced to nothing.

IV. Use.

1. Of information.

1. If God be of an eternal duration, then Christ is God. Eternity is the property of God, but it is ascribed to Christ. "He is before all things," i. e. all created things. "All things were created by him." Col. i. 16. He hath no difference of time; for "he is the same yesterday, to-day, and for ever." Micah v. 2. "Whose goings forth have been of old." As the eternity of God is the ground of all religion, so the eternity of Christ is the ground of the christian religion.

2. If God be eternal, he knows all things as present. All things are present to him in his eternity; for this is the notion of eternity, to be without succession. "Known unto God are all his works, from the beginning." Acts xv. 18.

3. How bold and foolish is it for a mortal creature to censure the counsels and actions of an eternal God, or be too curious in his inquisitions? "Who hath enjoined him his way?" Job xxxvi. 23.

4. What a folly and boldness is there in sin, since an eternal God is offended thereby! All sin is aggravated by God's eternity. The blackness of the heathen idolatry was in changing the glory of the incorruptible God. Rom. i. 23.

5. How dreadful is it to lie under the stroke of an eternal God. His eternity is a great terror to him that hates him, as it is a comfort to him that loves him; because he is the living God, and everlasting king. "The nations shall not be able to abide his indignation." Jer. x. 10. He will "whet his glittering sword," and his "hand shall take hold of judgment," and he will "render vengeance to his enemies, and a reward to them that hate him;" a reward proportioned to the greatness of their offences, and the glory of an eternal God. "I lift up my hand to heaven, and say, I live for ever;" i. e. as surely as I live for ever, I will whet my glittering sword.

2. Of comfort. What foundation of comfort can we have in any of God's attributes, were it not for his infiniteness and eternity; though he be merciful, good, wise, faithful? What support could there be, if they were perfections belonging to a corruptible God?

1. If God be eternal, his covenant will be so. It is founded upon the eternity of God; the oath whereby he confirms it, is by his life: since there is none greater than himself, he swears by himself.

2. If God be eternal, he being our God in covenant, is an eternal good and possession. "This God is our God for ever and ever; he is a dwelling place in all generations." We shall traverse the world awhile, and then arrive at the blessings Jacob wished for Joseph, the blessings of the ever lasting hills.

3. The enjoyment of God will be as fresh and glorious after many ages, as it was at first. God is eternal, and eternity knows no change.

4. If God be eternal: here is a strong ground of comfort against all the distresses of the church, and the threats of the church's enemies. God's abiding for ever is the plea Jeremiah makes for his return to his forsaken church. The first discovery of the name I AM, which signifies the Divine eternity as well as immutability, was for the comfort of the oppressed Israelites in Egypt. Exodus iii. 14, 15. The church's enemies are not to be feared; they may spring as the grass, but soon after do wither by their own inward principles of decay, or are cut down by the hand of God. Psalm xcii. 7—9. They may threaten, but their breath may vanish, as soon as their threatenings are pronounced. Do the prophets and instructers of the church live for ever? No. Shall then the adversaries and disturbers of the church live for ever! They shall vanish as a shadow. He that inhabits eternity is above them that inhabit mortality, who must, whether they will or no, say to corruption, "Thou art my father, and to the worm, Thou art my mother, and my sister."

5. Hence follows another comfort: since God is eternal, he hath as much power as will to be as good as his word. Trust in the Lord for ever

THE OMNIPRESENCE OF GOD.

Psalm cxxxix. 7.—Whither shall I go from thy Spirit? (H.)

God is here; God is every where; veils of flesh and blood prevent our sight of him; these must fall, and we must open the eyes of our spirits, if we would see a God who is a spirit. Hear our prophet; hear his magnificent description of the immensity and omnipresence of God: "Whither shall I go from thy Spirit? or whither shall I flee from thy presence? If I ascend up into heaven, thou art there." 7—12.

In a text less abundant in riches, we might make some remarks on the terms spirit and presence; but we shall content ourselves at present with indicating what ideas we affix to them, by observing, that by the Spirit and presence of God, we understand God himself. The other expressions in our text, heaven, hell, the wings of the morning, are figurative expressions, denoting the rapidity of the light in communicating itself from one end of the world to the other; these expressions need no comment. The presence of God, the Spirit of God, signify then the Divine essence: and this assemblage of ideas, "whither shall I go from thy Spirit? whither shall I flee from thy presence?" means, that God is immense, and that he is present in every place. But wherein consists this immensity and omnipresence. We will content ourselves with giving you some light into the omnipresence of God:

I. By REMOVING THOSE FALSE IDEAS, WHICH, AT FIRST, SEEM TO PRESENT THEMSELVES TO THE IMAGINATION.

II. By ASSIGNING THE TRUE.

I. LET US REMOVE THE FALSE IDEAS.

When we say that God is present in any place, let none suppose we mean, that he is actually contained therein; as if, when we say, that God is in every place, we mean to assign to him a real and proper extension. Neither of these is designed.

1. "God is a Spirit." A spirit cannot be in a place, at least, in the manner in which we conceive of place.

But perhaps God, who is spiritual in one part of his essence, may be corporeal in another. No; for however admirable in man that union may be, and those laws which unite his soul to his body, nothing more fully marks his weakness and dependance, and consequently nothing can less agree with the Divine essence. If God be sometimes represented with feet, with hands, with eyes, these portraits are designed rather to give us emblems of his attributes, than images, properly speaking, of any parts which he possesseth. But there is a very just sense in which it may be said, that the whole universe is the body of the Deity. In effect, as we call this portion of matter our body, which we move, act, and direct, as we please, so God actuates by his will every part of the universe. "He weighs the mountains in scales."

2. But to prove that "God is a Spirit," and that he occupies no place, at least as our imagination conceives, is, in our opinion, to establish the same thesis.

It is difficult to make this consequence intelligible and clear. Yet, I think, whatever difficulty there may be in this system, there is a greater difficulty in the opposite opinion.

II. WHAT NOTIONS THEN MUST WE FORM OF THE IMMENSITY OF GOD? IN WHAT SENSE DO WE CONCEIVE THAT THE INFINITE SPIRIT IS EVERY WHERE PRESENT.

The bounds of our knowledge are so strait, our sphere is so contracted, we have such imperfect ideas of spirits, even of our own spirits, and for a much stronger reason of the "Father of spirits," that no genius in the world. however exalted you may suppose him, after his greatest efforts of meditation, can say to you, "Thus far extend the attributes of God; behold a complete idea of his immensity and omnipresence." Yet by the help of sound reason, above all, by the aid of revelation, we may give you, if not complete, at least distinct ideas of the subject. The omnipresence of God is that universal property by which he communicates himself to all, diffuses himself through all, is the great director of all, or, to confine ourselves to more distinct ideas still, the Infinite Spirit is present in every place:—

1. By boundless knowledge. 2. By a general influence. 3. By a universal direction.

1. The first idea of God's omnipresence is his omniscience. God is every where present, because he seeth all. This the prophet had principally in view. "O Lord, thou hast searched me, and known me," &c.

2. God knows all the effects of matter. He calls into being matter, without motion, and, in some sense, without form. He gives this matter

form and motion. He saw that a certain degree of motion, imparted to a certain portion of matter, would produce water; that another degree of motion, communicated to another portion of matter, would produce fire; that another would produce earth; and so of the rest. He foresaw, with the utmost precision, what would result from this water, from this fire, from this earth, when joined together, and agitated by such a degree of motion as he should communicate. By the bare inspection of the laws of motion, he foresaw fires, earthquakes. He foresaw all the vicissitudes of time; he foresaw those which must put a period to time, when "the heavens shall pass away." 2 Peter iii. 10.

3. But, if God could combine all that would result from the laws of motion communicated to matter, he could also combine all that would result from intelligence, freedom of will, and all the faculties which make the essence of spirits; and, before he had formed those spiritual beings which compose the intelligent world, he knew what all their ideas, all their projects, all their deliberations would be. He says, "he searcheth and knoweth them;" he foresaw, he foretold, the afflictions which Abraham's posterity would endure in Canaan; Gen. xv. 13, the infidelity of the Jews, the faith of the Gentiles, the crucifixion of the Messiah. On this article, we are obliged to exclaim, "Such knowledge is too wonderful for me; it is high, I cannot attain unto it." God is every where, because he veils the most impenetrable; darkness the most thick, distance the most immense, can conceal nothing from his knowledge. Soar to the utmost heights, fly to the remotest climates, wrap thyself in the blackest darkness, every where, every where thou wilt be under his eye. "Whither shall I go from thy Spirit?" But,

2. The knowledge of God is not a bare knowledge, his presence is not an idle presence; it is an active knowledge, it is a presence accompanied with action and motion. We said, just now, that God was every where, because he influenced all, as far as influence agrees with his perfections.

When new beings appear, he is there; he influences their productions. He gives to all life, motion, and being. "Thou, even thou, art Lord alone; thou hast made heaven." Neh, ix. 6. "O Lord, I will praise thee, for I am fearfully and wonderfully made. Ps. cxxxix. 14—16.

When beings are preserved, he is there; he influences preservation. "Thou preservest man and beast. When thou openest thy hands they are filled with good. The eyes of all wait upon thee."

When the world is disordered, he is there. He influences wars, pestilence. If nature refuse her productions, it is because he hath "made the heavens as iron, and the earth as brass." It is he who "makes the winds his messengers, and his ministers flames of fire."

When every thing succeeds according to our wishes, he is there. He influenceth prosperity. "Except the Lord build the house, they labour in vain that build it." Ps. cxxvii. 1.

When our understanding is informed, he is there. He influenceth our knowledge. For "in his light we see light. He enlighteneth every man that cometh into the world."

When our heart disposeth us to our duties, he is there. He influenceth our virtues. It is he who "worketh in us, both to will and to do. Who giveth to all that ask liberally."

When grossest errors cover us, he is there. He influenceth errors. It is God who "sends strong delusions. Go, make the heart of this people fat." Isa. vi. 10.

35

When we live, when we die, he is there. He influenceth life and death, 'Man's days are determined, the number of his months are with him. To God the Lord belong the issues of death. He bringeth down to the grave."

He influenceth the least events, as well as the most considerable. "The hairs of our head are numbered;" even "a sparrow cannot fall to the ground without his will." But,

3. When God communicates himself to all, when he thus acts on all, and diffuseth himself through the whole, he connects all with his own designs. God is present with all, because he directs all.

Doth he call creatures into existence? it is to manifest his perfections; it is to have subjects on whom he may shower his favours; it is, as it were, to go out of himself, and to form through the whole universe, a concert resounding the Creator's existence and glory: For the invisible things of God, even his eternal power and godhead, are understood by the things that are made. The heavens declare the glory of God." Ps. xix. 1—3.

Doth he preserve creatures? it is to answer his own designs; the depth of which no finite mind can fathom; but which we shall one day know, and admire his wisdom.

Doth he send plagues, war, famine? it is to make those feel his justice who have abused his goodness.

Doth he afford prosperity? it is to "draw us with the bands of love."

Doth he impart knowledge to us? it is to discover the snares that surround us, the miseries that threaten us, the origin from which we spring, the course of life we should follow, and the end at which we should aim.

Doth he communicate virtues? it is to animate us in our race; to convince us that there is a mighty arm to raise us from the abyss into which our natural corruption hath plunged us; it is that we may "work out our salvation with fear and trembling; knowing that God worketh in us."

Doth he send error? it is to make us respect that truth which we have resisted.

Doth he prolong our life? it is because he is long-suffering to us. He opens in our favour "the riches of his goodness and forbearance, to lead us to repentance."

Doth he call us to die? it is to open those eternal books in which our actions are registered; it is to gather our souls into his bosom, "to bind them up in the bundle of life;" to mix them with the ransomed armies "of all nations, tongues, and people."

Such are our ideas of the omnipresence of God. Then God seeth all, influenceth all, directeth all. In this sense we are to understand this magnificent language of scripture: "Behold, the heaven of heavens cannot contain thee. Thus saith the Lord, the heaven is my throne, and the earth is my footstool." This was our prophet's meaning throughout the Psalm, "O Lord, thou hast searched me," verse 1, &c.

Inference.

From this idea of God, we see all the virtues issue which religion prescribes.

If such be the grandeur of our God, what ought our repentance to be? who have provoked him to jealousy, as if we had been stronger than he; insulted that majesty which angels adore.

If such be the grandeur of God, what should be our humlity? What are we? a grain of dust, a point, an atom, a nothing.

36

If such be tne grandeur of Goa, what ought our confidence to be? "If God be for us, who can be against us?"

But, above all, if such be the grandeur of God, if God is every where present, what should our vigilance be? What impression should this thought make on reasonable souls, "Thou God seest me?"

THE POWER OF GOD.

Job. xxvi. 14.—Lo! these are parts of his ways: but how little a portion is heard of him? But the thunder of his power who can understand? (H.)

BILDAD had, in the foregoing chapter, entertained Job with a discourse of the dominion and power of God, and the purity of his righteousness; whence he argues an impossibility of the justification of man in his presence, who is no better than a worm. Job, in this chapter, acknowledges the greatness of God's power, and descants more largely upon it than Bildad had done; but both preach it with a kind of ironical speech, as if he had not acted a friendly part, or said little to the purpose. The subject of Job's discourse was the outward prosperity of the wicked, and the afflictions of the godly; and Bildad reads him a lecture of the extent of God's dominion, the number of his armies, and the unspotted rectitude of his nature, in comparison of which the purest creatures are foul. Job therefore taxeth him, verses 1—4, that he had not touched the point, but rambled from the subject in hand: "How hast thou helped him who is without power?" Your discourse is so impertinent, that it will neither strengthen the weak, nor instruct the simple; but, since Bildad would take up the argument of God's power, Job would show that he wanted not his instructions on that subject, that he had more distinct conceptions of it than his antagonist had uttered, and therefore, from verse 5 to the end of the chapter, he treats the subject in a magnificent manner, and concludes in the words of the text, "Lo! these are parts of his ways."

I. THE NATURE OF GOD'S POWER.

Power sometimes signifies authority; but the power of God in the text does not signify his authority, but his strength.

1. The power of God is that ability or strength, whereby he can bring to pass whatsoever he pleaseth, whatsoever his infinite wisdom can direct, and the unspotted purity of his will resolve. His counsel shall stand, and he will do all his pleasure. He hath done whatsoever pleaseth him.

2. The power of God gives activity to all the other perfections of his nature. As holiness is the beauty, so power is the life of his attributes in their exercise. God hath a powerful wisdom to attain his ends without interruption, a powerful mercy to remove our misery, a powerful justice to punish offenders, a powerful truth to perform all his promises.

3. This power is originally and essentially in his nature. The strength and power of princes is originally in their people, and only managed by their authority to command; but the power of God is not derived from any thing without him, but essentially in himself. Power belongeth unto God; and all the power that the creature possesses is derived from him.

4. Hence it follows, that the power of God is infinite, What is the exceeding greatness of his power? According to the working of his mighty

37

power. Nothing can be too difficult for the Divine power to effect. Is any thing too hard for the Lord? A power which cannot be opposed. None can stay his hand.

II. WHEREIN THE POWER OF GOD IS MANIFESTED.

1. In creation. With what majestic lines doth God set forth his power in the works of creation. "The firmament showeth his handy work, and the heavens are the work of his fingers," therefore called the firmament of his power. And he only spake, and it was done; he commanded, and it stood fast. "Let there be light, and there was light."

2. The power of God is made manifest in the government of the world.

1. In preservation or natural government, God is the great Father of the universe, to nourish as well as create it. Thou, Lord, preservest man and beast. As they were created by his word, they are supported by the same. He openeth his hand, and satisfieth the desire of every living creature. It is by his power the heavenly bodies have rolled in their spheres, and the tumultuous elements have persisted in their order. He holds the waters in the hollow of his hand, and weighs the mountains in scales, and the hills in a balance; and in him we live, move, and have our being.

It is no small argument of omnipotence, to keep all the strings of nature in tune; to wind them up to a due pitch for the harmony he intended; and prevent those jarrings which would naturally result from their opposite qualities.

2. This power is evident in moral government.

1. In the restraint of the malicious nature of Satan. Since Satan hath the power of an angel and the malice of a devil, what safety would there be for our persons, did not the Lord restrain his malice? It is a part of the strength as well as the wisdom of God, that the deceived and the deceiver are his. Wisdom to defeat, and power to over-rule, the malicious designs of Satan to his own glory.

2. In the restraint of the wickedness of man, what havoc has this made in the world! "From whence come wars?" But had not the Lord, by his power, restrained these, how would the world be drenched in blood? The Lord not only restrains, but overrules the wickedness of man. "Surely the wrath of man shall praise thee."

3. In his gracious government.

1. In the deliverance of his church. He is the strength of Israel. He hath preserved his little flock in the midst of the wolves, and maintained their standing, when the strongest kingdoms have been sunk, and the best jointed states have been broken in pieces. This power shone forth in the deliverance of his people in the Red Sea; and also in the destruction of their enemies. "He showed strength with his arm; he scattered the proud in the imagination of their hearts."

2. In effecting his purposes by small means. As he magnifies his wisdom, by using ignorant instruments, so he exalts his power by the weak. By the motion of Moses' rod he works wonders in the court of Pharaoh. The walls of Jericho, falling at the sound of the rams' horns, was a more glorious display of the power of God, than if Joshua had battered them with the engines of war. Goliah, a giant, levelled with the ground by the force of a sling from the hand of a stripling, is a more glorious character of the power of God, than if a warlike Israelite in Saul's armour had hewed him to pieces

3. In the work of our redemption. As Christ is called the wisdom of God, so he is called the power of God. The arm of power was lifted up as high

as the designs of wisdom were laid deep; as this way of redemption could not be contrived but by an infinite wisdom, so it could not be accomplished but by infinite power. This will appear,

1. In the person redeeming. The union of the two natures in the person of Christ. "The seed of David according to the flesh," An immortal spirit and dying flesh. Infinite purity and a reputed sinner. Omniscience and ignorance. Immutability and changeableness. Human weakness and almighty power. A God of blessedness and a man of sorrow. "The Word made flesh." When we consider the power of God manifested in this union, we are lost. That God upon a throne should be an infant in a cradle. The thundering Creator be a weeping babe and a suffering man.

2. In the progress of his life. In the miracles he wrought. How did he expel the powers of darkness? By a word and touch, sight is restored to the blind, hearing to the deaf, healing to the sick, life to the dead.

3. In his resurrection. The unlocking the belly of the fish for the deliverance of Jonah, the rescue of Daniel from the den of lions, and the three Hebrew worthies from fire, were signal declarations of his power, yet but faint representations of the resurrection of Jesus. This was an hyperbole of power. The exceeding greatness of power, according to the working of his mighty power, which he wrought in Christ, when he raised him from the dead.

2. In the publication of it.

1. The power of God was manifested in the instruments. Men of a low condition, meanly bred, so far from any splendid estates, that they possessed only their nets; without credit or reputation in the world; without comeliness or strength; as unfit to conquer the world by preaching, as an army of hares were to conquer it by war. Not learned doctors, bred up at the feet of the famous rabbins at Jerusalem, whom Paul calls the princes of this world, nor nursed up in the school of Athens. Not the wise men of Greece, but the fishermen of Galilee, are employed to publish the gospel of Christ. The heavenly treasure was placed in these earthen vessels; as Gideon's lamps in empty pitchers; that the excellency of the power might be of God

2. In the success of their ministry, These poor fishermen, tent makers, ignorent men, without letters, without arms, without power, without intrigues, without human help, without philosophy, without eloquence, contemptible and persecuted people, triumphed over the whole world with the sound of their voice. Idols fell, temples were demolished, oracles were struck dumb, the reign of the devil was abolished, the strongest inclinations of nature were diverted, people's ancient habits were changed, they flocked in crowds to adore Jesus; whole provinces presented themselves at the foot of the cross. This is the finger of God; nay, more, this is the outstretched arm of Jehovah.

To conclude.

1. Here is comfort in all afflictions. Our evils can never be so great to distress us, as his power is to deliver. "If God be for us, who can be against us?"

2. This doctrine teaches us the fear of God. "Who would not fear thee, O thou King of nations?" for, if God be against us, it matters not who they be that are for us. Fear him, therefore, who hath power to cast into hell.

THE WISDOM OF GOD.

Rom. xvi. 27.—To God only wise. (H.

WISDOM is a transcendent excellency of the Divine nature. Most confound the knowledge and wisdom of God together; but there is a manifest distinction between them in our conception.

I. SHOW WHAT WISDOM IS; WISDOM CONSISTS

1. In acting for a right end, and choosing proper means. To shoot at random is a mark of folly. As he is the wisest man that hath the noblest end and the most proper means, so God is infinitely wise; as he is the most excellent being, so he hath the most excellent end. "Of him, and through him, and to him, are all things."

2. Wisdom consists in observing all circumstances for action. He is counted a wise man that lays hold of the fittest opportunities to bring about his designs. God hath all the circumstances of things in one entire image before him. It is impossible he should be mistaken, or miss of the due season of bringing about his own purposes. The time of our Saviour's incarnation is called the fulness of time, the proper season for his coming.

3. In willing and acting according to the right judgment. We never count a wilful man a wise man. The resolves and ways of God are not mere will, but well guided by the reason and counsel of his own infinite understanding. Who worketh all things. Eph. i. 11. All his ways are judgment. Deut. xxxii. 4.

There is an essential and personal wisdom of God. The essential wisdom is the essence of God; the personal wisdom is the Son of God. 1 Cor. i. 24. God is originally wise. "Who hath been his counsellor?" Rom. xi. 34. God is perfectly wise. There is no cloud upon his understanding. Job iv. 18. God is perpetually wise. His counsel stands like an immoveable rock. God is incomprehensibly wise. His thoughts are deep. Ps. xcii, 5. His judgments unsearchable. Depths that cannot be fathomed. Rom. xi. 33. O the depth. Job xi. 6, 7. God is infallibly wise. The wisest men meet with rubs in the way. God always compasses his ends. There is no wisdom. Isa. lv. 11. His word that goeth forth. Isa. xiv. 24, 27. As he thinks, so shall it come to pass.

II. WHEREIN THE WISDOM OF GOD APPEARS.

1. In creation. The whole creation is a poem, every species a stanza, and every individual creature a verse in it. Prov. iii. 19. "The Lord by wisdom, hath founded the earth·" Jer. x. 12. "He hath established the world by his wisdom." There is not any thing so mean, so small, but shines with a beam of Divine wisdom. Ps. civ. 24. "In wisdom hast thou made them all." This wisdom of the creation appears,

1. In the variety. "O Lord, how manifold are thy works!" How great a variety is there of animals, plants, colours. Gen. i. 11, 20, 24.

2. In the beauty and order. Eccles. iii. 11. "He hath made every thing beautiful." All the creatures are as so many pictures, or statues, exactly framed by line. Ps. xix. 4. "Their line is gone."

3. In the fitness of every thing for its end. After the most diligent inspection, there can be found nothing unprofitable. The earth is fitted into his parts; the valleys are appointed for granaries, the mountains to shadow them; the rivers, like veins, carry refreshment. Ps. civ. 14. "There he causes the grass to grow." The sea is fitted for its use; it is a fish pond for

40

the nourishment of man; it joins nations: a great vessel for commerce. Ps. civ. 26. " There go the ships." Showers are appointed, to refresh the bodies, to open the womb of the earth. Ps. civ. 3. " To make it fruitful." Winds are fitted to purify the air, to carry the clouds, to refresh the earth. Ps. civ. 3. " He walketh on the winds." Rivers are appointed to bathe the earth : they are the water pots of the earth. Ps. civ. 10, 12, 13. Trees are for the habitations of birds. The seasons have their uses. The days and nights have also their usefulness. Ps. lxxiv. 16, 17; civ. 23.

4. This wisdom is apparent in the linking all those useful parts together. All parts are exactly suited to one another, and every part to the whole. " The heavens hear the earth." Hos. ii. 21, 22.

III. In his government, especially of man.

I. In his government of him as a rational creature, in the law he gives him.

1. It is suited in the nature of man.

2. To his happiness. " Rejoicing his heart." Ps. xix. 7, 8; Deut. iv. 8.

3. In suiting his laws to his conscience. " The Gentiles do by nature." Rom. ii. 14. Conscience dictates that the law is worthy to be observed.

4. In the encouragement he gives. " In keeping thy commandments." Ps. xix. 11.

II. God's wisdom appears in the government of man as a fallen creature.

1. In the bounding of sin. " The wrath of man." Ps. lxxvi. 10.

2. In overruling it to his own glory and our good. " As sin reigned unto death." Rom. v. 21.

3. In the work of redemption. In which he manifested the greatest hatred to sin, and the greatest love to the sinner. " Herein is love—God so loved the world."

4. In overturning the empire of Satan. " Through death." Heb. ii. 14. Thus the devil ruined his own kingdom, whilst he thought to establish it

5. In the manner of publishing the doctrine of redemption. In the general discoveries of it to Abraham and Moses ; the time and circumstances of the first publication of the gospel by the apostles. Acts ii. 1—12. In the instruments employed: he did not employ philosophers, but fishermen. " The foolishness of God is wiser than men." In the ways and manner: by ways seemingly contrary; by scattering of the disciples, it inflamed their courage, and spread their doctrine. " Many shall run to and fro." Dan. xii. 4. The flames of the martyrs brightened the doctrine. Religion grew stronger by sufferings; making the " wisdom of this world foolishness with God."

To conclude—we may hence see,

1. The right and fitness of God for the government of the world. Power and wisdom are the two arms of authority.

2. That God is a proper object for our trust and confidence. " The Lord knoweth how to deliver." Job v. 13. He taketh the wise.

3. Meditate on the wisdom of God, as manifested in creation. Ps. viii. 4, 5. " When I consider the heavens." In redemption, shall the angels be ravished with it, and bend themselves down to study it, and shall not we admire it ! Prov. ii. 1—6.

4. Let us seek to God for wisdom. " If any man lack wisdom." James i. 17. There is a spirit in man. Job xxii. 8.

Submit to the wisdom of God in all cases; he is a God of judgment.

ON THE HOLINESS OF GOD.

Exodus xv. 11.—Who is like unto thee, O Lord, among the gods? Who is like unto thee, glorious in holiness, fearful in praises, doing wonders? (H.)

THIS verse is one of the loftiest descriptions of the majesty and excellence of God in the whole scripture. It is a part of Moses' triumphant song, after a great, and real, and a typical victory; ir the womb of which all the deliverances of the church were couched. It is the first song upon holy record, and it consists of gratulatory and prophetic matter. It casts a look backward, to what God did for them in their deliverance from Egypt; and a look forward, to what God shall do for the church in future ages.

It consists of, 1. A preface, verse 1—"I will sing unto the Lord."

2. An historical narration of matter of fact, verses 3, 4, "Pharaoh's chariots and his host hath he cast into the Red Sea."

Let these two things be considered. If any, this attribute hath an excellency above his other perfections; none is sounded out so loftily, with such solemnity, and so frequently by angels, as this. Isa. vi. 3. "Holy, holy, holy." Rev. iv. 8. He singles it out to swear by. Ps. lxxxix. 35. "Once have I sworn by my holiness." Amos iv. 2. "The Lord will swear by his holiness;" it is glory and beauty. Power is his hand and arm, omniscience his eye, mercy his bowels, eternity his duration, his holiness is his beauty. 2 Chron. xx. 21. "Should praise the beauty of holiness." It is his very life. So it is called. Eph. iv. 18. "Alienated from the life of God;" that is, from the holiness of God. "Be ye holy, as I am holy."

I. THE NATURE OF DIVINE HOLINESS.

The holiness of God, negatively, is a perfect and unpolluted freedom from all evil; as we call gold pure that is not embased by any dross.

Positively, it is the rectitude or integrity of the Divine nature; or that conformity of it in affection and action of the divine will, whereby he hath a delight and complacency in every thing agreeable to his will.

As there is no darkness in his understanding, so there is no spot in his will. Ps. xi. 7. "The righteous Lord loveth righteousness."

This property of the Divine nature is,

1. An essential and necessary perfection; he is essentially and necessarily holy. His holiness is as necessary as his being.

2. God is only absolutely holy: "There is none holy as the Lord." It is the peculiar glory of his nature; he is not only holy, but holiness. Holiness, in the highest degree, is his sole prerogative.

3. God is so holy, that he cannot possibly approve of any evil done by another, but doth perfectly abhor it; would not else be a glorious holiness. Ps. v. 4. "He hath no pleasure in wickedness."

1. He abhors it necessarily. Holiness is the glory of the Deity, therefore necessarily. The nature of God is so holy, that he cannot but hate it. Hab. i. 13 "Thou art of purer eyes than to behold evil." He is more opposite to it than light to darkness; and therefore it can expect no countenance from him.

2. Therefore intensely. Nothing do men act for more than their glory. He hates the first spark of it in the imagination. Zach. viii. 17. With what variety of expressions doth he repeat his indignation at their polluted services; Amos v. 21, 22; so Isa. i. 14; it is the abominable thing that he hates; Jer. xliv. 4; he is vexed and fretted at it; Isa. lxiii. 10; Ezek. xvi. 43; he abhors it so, that his hatred rebounds upon the person that commits it. Ps. v. 5. "He hates all workers of iniquity."

3. Therefore universally, because necessarily and intensely. He doth not hate it in one, and indulge it in another, but loathes it wherever he finds it; not one worker of iniquity is exempt from it. Ps. v. 5. "Thou hatest all workers of iniquity."

4. Perpetually. This must necessarily follow upon the others. He can no more cease to hate impurity, than he can cease to love holiness. James i. 17. God is always the same, without any shadow of change; and "is angry with the wicked every day," Ps. vii. 11, *i. e.* uninterruptedly.

5. God is so holy, that he cannot but love holiness in others. Not that he owes any thing to his creatures, but from the unspeakable holiness of his nature. Ps. xi. 7. "The righteous Lord loveth righteousness."

6. God is so holy, that he cannot positively will or encourage sin in any. How can he give any encouragement to that which he cannot in the least approve? Light may sooner be the cause of darkness, than he that is the fountain of good should be the source of evil. James iii. 11.

1. God cannot commit any unrighteousness.

2. Nor can God secretly inspire any evil into us.

3. Nor can God necessitate man to sin. Indeed sin cannot be committed by force; there is no sin but is in some sort voluntary.

II. THE DEMONSTRATION OF IT.

1. His holiness appears as he is Creator, in framing man in a perfect uprightness. Angels, as made by God, could not be evil; for God beheld his own works with pleasure, and could not have pronounced them all good, had some been created pure, and others impure; two moral contrarieties could not be good. Human nature was well strung and tuned by God, according to the note of his own holiness. Eccles. vii. 29. "God hath made man upright." Other creatures were his footsteps, but man was his image. "Let us make man in our image, after our likeness;" which, though it seem to imply no more in that place, than an image of his dominion over the creatures, yet the apostle raises it a peg higher, and gives us a larger interpretation. Col. iii. 10. "And have put on the new man, which is renewed in knowledge, after the image of him that created him;" making it to consist in a resemblance to his righteousness.

2. His holiness appears in his laws; and he is a law-giver and a judge. Man was bound to be subject to God, as a creature, and had a capacity to be ruled by the law. Deut. iv. 8. "What nation hath statutes and judgments so righteous?" They are compared to fine gold, that hath no speck nor dross. Ps. xix. 10.

This purity is evident,

In the moral law; which is therefore dignified with the title of holy twice in one verse. Rom. vii. 12. "Wherefore the law is holy."

1. The purity of the law is seen in the matter of it. It prescribes all that becomes a creature towards God, and all that becomes one creature towards another. "Wherefore the law is holy." The purity of this beam and transcript of God, bears witness to a greater clearness and beauty in the sun and original. Undefiled streams manifest an untainted fountain.

2. It is seen in the manner of his precepts. As it prescribes all good, and forbids all evil; so it doth enjoin the one, and banish the other, as such. The laws of men command virtuous things; not as virtuous in themselves, but as useful for human society. But God commands that which is just in itself; enjoins virtues as virtues, and prohibits vices as vices.

3. In the spiritual extent of it. It frowns upon all stains and pollutions of the most retired thoughts; hence the apostle calls it a spiritual law. Rom vii. 14

43

4. In regard to the perpetuity of it. The purity and perpetuity of it are linked together by the Psalmist. Ps. xix. 9. "The fear of the Lord is clean, enduring for ever."

5. This holiness appears in the allurements annexed to the law for keeping it, and the affrightments to restrain from the breaking of it: both promises and threatenings have their fundamental root in the holiness of God. "Having these promises, let us cleanse ourselves from all filthiness of flesh and spirit, perfecting holiness in the fear of God."

6. His holiness appears in the judgments inflicted for the violation of the law. Divine holiness is the root of Divine justice, and Divine justice is the triumph of Divine holiness. Ps. ciii. 6: Dan. ix. 7; Ps. xi. 6, 7.

1. How severely hath he punished his most noble creatures for it?

2. How detestable to him are the very instruments of sin. Gen. iii. 14; Lev. xx. 15; Deut. vii. 25, 26. So contrary is the holy nature of God to every sin, that it curseth every thing that is instrumental in it.

3. How detestable is every thing to him that is in the sinner's possession. The very earth, which God had made Adam the proprietor of, was cursed for his sake." Gen. iii. 17, 18. It lost its beauty, and lies languishing to this day. Rom. viii. 20—22.

4. What design hath God in all these acts of severity and vindictive justice, but to set off the lustre of his holiness?

III. The holiness of God appears in our RESTORATION. It is in the glass of the gospel we behold the glory of the Lord; 2 Cor. iii. 18; that is, the glory of the Lord, into whose image we are changed; but we are changed into nothing, as the image of God, but into holiness. Isa. i. 27.

1. This holiness of God appears in the manner of our restoration, viz. by the death of Christ. Not all the vials of judgments that have, or shall be poured out upon the wicked world, nor the flaming furnace of a sinner's conscience, nor the irreversible sentence pronounced against the rebellious devils, nor the groans of the damned creatures, give such a demonstration of God's hatred of sin, as the wrath of God let loose upon his Son.

It appears the more, if you consider,

1. The dignity of the Redeemer's person. One that had been from eternity, had laid the foundations of the world; had been the object of the Divine delight: he that was "God blessed for ever," becomes a curse. One equal to him in all the glorious perfections of his nature, Phil. ii. 6, dies on a disgraceful cross, and is exposed to the flames of Divine wrath, rather than sin should live.

2. The near relation he stood in to the Father. He was his own Son, that he delivered up. Rom. viii. 32. His essential image, as dearly beloved by him as himself; yet he would abate nothing of his hatred of those sins imputed to one so dear to him.

3. The value he puts upon his holiness appears farther, in the advancement of this redeeming person after his death. Our Saviour was advanced, not barely for his dying, but for the respect he had in his death to this attribute of God. Heb. i. 9. "Thou hast loved righteousness, and hated iniquity."

4. It may be farther considered, that in this way of redemption his holiness in the hatred of sin seems to be valued above any other attribute. He proclaims the value of it above the person of his Son. In this way of redemption the odiousness of sin is equally discovered with the greater of his compassions: an infinite abhorrence of sin, and an infinite love to the world, march hand in hand together Sin is made the chief mark of his displeasure, while the poor creature is made the highest object of Divine pity; in this way mercy and truth, &c. Ps. lxxxv. 10.

II. The holiness of God in his hatred of sin appears in OUR JUSTIFICATION, AND THE CONDITIONS HE REQUIRES OF ALL THAT WOULD ENJOY THE BENEFIT OF REDEMPTION. Our justification is not by the imperfect works of creatures, but by an exact and infinite righteousness. Faith is the condition God requires to justification; but not a dead, but an active faith; such a "faith as purifies the heart." James ii. 20; Acts xv. 9. He calls for repentance, which is a moral retracting our offences. He requires mortification, which is called crucifying; whereby a man would strike as full and deadly a blow at his lusts, as was struck at Christ upon the cross. There is no admittance into heaven of a starting, but a persevering holiness, Rom. ii. 7, "a patient continuance in well-doing."

III. It appears in the ACTUAL REGENERATION OF, AND A CARRYING IT ON TO A FULL PERFECTION. Our pardon is the fruit of his mercy, our knowledge a stream from his wisdom, our strength an impression of his power; so our purity is a beam from his holiness. "Holy Father, keep them through thy own name, and sanctify them through thy truth;" as the proper source whence holiness was to flow to the creature: as the sun is the proper fountain whence light is derived, both to the stars above and bodies here below. Hence he is not only called holy, but the "Holy One of Israel." Isa. xliii. 15.

To conclude.

1. There can be no communion between God and unholy spirits. Can there be any delightful communion between those whose natures are contrary? Darkness and light may as soon kiss each other, and become one nature; God and the devil may as soon enter into an eternal league and covenant together; for God to have pleasure in wickedness, and to admit evil to dwell with him, are things equally impossible to his nature.

2. Hence it will follow, there is no justification of a sinner by any thing in himself. Eph. i. 6. "Who hath made us accepted in the Beloved." The infinite purity of God is so glorious, that it shames the holiness of angels, as the light of the sun dims the light of the fire.

3. This attribute renders God a fit object for trust and dependance. The notion of an unholy, and unrighteous God, is an uncomfortable idea of God, and beats off our hands from laying any hold of him: Isa. xli. 14; "Fear not, thou worm Jacob;" he will be in his actions what he is in his nature.

4. A sense of this will render us humble in the possession of the greatest holiness a creature is capable of. We are apt to be proud with the Pharisee; but let any clap their wings, if they can, in a vain boasting and exaltation, when they view the holiness of this God. "Who can stand before this holy Lord God?"

5. This would make us full of an affectionate reverence in all our approaches to God. By this perfection God is rendered venerable, and fit to be reverenced by his creature; and magnificent thoughts of it in the creature would awaken him to an actual reverence of the Divine Majesty. Ps. cxi. 9. "Holy and reverend is his name." Ps. xlvii. 8.

6. A due sense of this perfection would inflame us with a vehement desire to be conformed to him. Contemplating it as it shines forth in the face of Christ will transform us into the same image.

7. Let us seek for holiness to God, the fountain of it. As he is the author of bodily life in the creature, so he is the author of his own life, the life of

45

God in the soul. By his holiness he makes men holy, as the sun by his light enlightens the air. He is not only the Holy One, but our Holy One. Isa. xliii. 15. The Lord that sanctifies us. Lev. xx. 8. As he hath mercy to pardon us, so he hath holiness to purify us; the excellency of being a sun to comfort us, and a shield to protect us, giving grace and glory. Ps. lxxxiv. 11.

ON THE GOODNESS OF GOD.

Mark x. 18.—And Jesus said unto him, Why callest thou me good? There is none good but one, that is God. (H.)

TRULY "God is good." Ps. lxxiii. 1. All nations in the world have acknowledged this truth. The notion of goodness is inseparable from the notion of a God. We cannot own the existence of God, but we must confess also his goodness.

I. WHAT THIS GOODNESS IS?

There is a goodness of being, which is the natural perfection of a thing; there is the goodness of will, which is the holiness and righteousness of a person; there is the goodness of the hand, which we call liberality, or beneficence, a doing good to others.

1. We mean not by this, the goodness of his essence, or the perfection of his nature. God is thus good, because his name is infinitely perfect; he hath all things requisite to the completing of a most perfect and sovereign being. All good meets in his essence, as all water meets in the ocean.

2. Nor is it the same with the blessedness of God, but something flowing from his blessedness. Were he not first infinitely blessed, and full in himself, he could not be infinitely good and diffusive to us.

Had not the sun a fulness of light in itself, and the sea a vastness of water, the one could not enrich the world with its beams, nor the other fill every creek with its waters.

3. Nor is it the same with the holiness of God. The holiness of God is the rectitude of his nature. The goodness of God is the efflux of his will, whereby he is beneficial to his creatures: "The Lord is good to all."

4. Nor is the goodness of God the same with the mercy of God. Goodness extends to more objects than mercy; goodness stretcheth itself out to all the works of his hands; mercy extends only to a miserable object.

By goodness is meant,

1. The bounty of God. This is the notion of goodness in the world; when we say a good man, we mean either a holy man in his life, or a charitable and liberal man in the management of his goods. As God is great and powerful, he is the object of our understanding; but as good and bountiful, he is the object of our love and desire.

2. The goodness of God comprehends all his attributes. All the acts of God are nothing else but the effluxes of his goodness, distinguished by several names, according to the objects it is exercised about. As the sea, though it be one mass of water, yet we distinguish it by several names, according to the shores it washeth and beats upon. When Moses longed to see his glory, God tells him he would give him a prospect of his goodness. Ex. xxxiii. 19. "I will make all my goodness." The whole catalogue of

"mercy, grace, long-suffering," Ex. xxxiv. 6, all are streams from this fountain. When it confers happiness without merit, it is grace; when it bestows happiness against merit, it is mercy; when he bears with provoking rebels, it is long-suffering; when he performs his promise, it is truth; when it commiserates a distressed person, it is pity; when it supplies an indigent person, it is bounty; when it succours an innocent person, it is righteousness; and when it pardons a penitent person, it is mercy; all summed up in this one name of goodness. Ps. cxlv. 7, 8. "They shall abundantly utter the memory of thy great goodness."

II. THE NATURE OF THIS GOODNESS.

1. He is good by his own essence. God is not only good in his essence, but good by his essence. Hence his goodness must be infinite, and circumscribed by no limits; the exercise of his goodness may be limited by himself, but his goodness, the principle, cannot; for since his essence is infinite, and his goodness is not distinguished from his essence, it is infinite also. He is essentially good by his own essence, therefore good of himself, therefore eternally and abundantly good.

2. God is the prime and chief goodness. Being good by his own essence, he must needs be the chief goodness, in whom there can be nothing but good, from whom there can proceed nothing but good, to whom all good whatso ever must be referred, as the final cause of all good. As he is the chief being, so he is the chief good. Ps. xvi. 2. Our goodness extends not to him; wickedness may hurt a man, as we are, and our righteousness may profit the son of man; but, if we be righteous, "what give we to him, or what receives he at our hands?" Job xxxv. 7, 8. God is all good; other things are good in their kind, as a good man, a good angel. He is no less all good than he is almighty.

3. This goodnes is communicative. None so communicatively good as God. As the notion of God includes goodness, so the notion of goodness includes diffusiveness; without goodness he would cease to be a Deity, and without diffusiveness he would cease to be good. Ps. cxix. 68. "Thou art good and doest good."

4. God is necessarily good. None is necessarily good but God; he is as necessarily good as he is necessarily God. His goodness is as inseparable from his nature as his holiness.

5. Though he be necessarily good, yet he is also freely good. The necessity of the goodness of his nature hinders not the liberty of his actions. It would not be a supreme goodness, if it were not a voluntary goodness. It is agreeable to the nature of the highest good, to be absolutely free, to dispense his goodness in what methods and measures he pleaseth.

6. This goodness is communicated with the greatest pleasure. Moses desired to see his glory, God assures him he should see his goodness; Ex. xxxiii. 18, 19; intimating, that his goodness is his glory, and his glory his delight also. He prevents men with his blessings of goodness. Ps. xxi. 3. He is most delighted when he is most diffusive. He is not covetous of his own treasures. It is the nature of his goodness to be glad of men's solicitations for it.

III. THE MANIFESTATION OF THIS GOODNESS.

1. In creation. His goodness was the cause that he made any thing, and his wisdom was the cause that he made every thing in order and harmony; he pronounced "every thing good."

1. The creation proceeds from goodness. Because God is good, things have a being; if he had not been good, nothing could have been good; nothing could have imparted that which it did not possess.

47

2. Creation was the first act of goodness without himself. Creation was the first efflux of his goodness without himself; and therefore it was the speech of an heathen, "That when God first set upon the creation of the world, he transformed himself into love and goodness."

3. There is not one creature but hath a character of his goodness. The whole world is a map to represent, and a herald to proclaim, this perfection. Ps. cxlv. 9. "He is good to all;" he is therefore good in all; not a drop of the creation, but is a drop of his goodness. These are the colors worn upon the heads of every creature. As in every spark the light of the fire is manifested, so doth every grain of the creation wear the visible badges of this perfection.

But, let us see the goodness of God in the creation of man.

1. How much of goodness is visible in his body? How neatly hath he wrought this "tabernacle of clay, this earthly house?" as the apostle calls it. A curious wrought-piece of needle-work, a comely artifice; an embroidered case for an harmonious lute. It is a cabinet fitted by Divine goodness, for the enclosing a rich jewel; a palace made of dust, to lodge in it the viceroy of the world.

2. But what is this to that goodness which shines in the nature of the soul? Who can express the wonders of that comeliness that is wrapt up in this mask of clay? A soul endued with a clearness of understanding and freedom of will. A soul that excelled the whole world, that comprehended the whole creation. In the ruins of a palace we may see the curiosity displayed, and the cost expended in the building of it; in the ruins of this fallen structure, we still find it capable of a mighty knowledge.

3. Besides this, he did not only make man so noble a creature in his frame, but he made him after his own image in holiness. He imparted to him a spark of his own comeliness, in order to a communion with himself in happiness. He made man after his image, after his own image.

4. The goodness of God appears in the conveniences he provided for, and gave to man.

1. The world was made for man. God put all things under his feet, and gave him a deputed dominion over the rest of the creatures under himself, as the absolute sovereign. Ps. viii. 6. "Thou madest him to have dominion over the works of thy hands."

2. God richly furnished the world for man. He did not only erect a stately palace for his habitation, but provided all kind of furniture, as a mark of his goodness, for the entertainment of his creature man: he arched over his habitation with a bespangled heaven, and floored it with a solid earth. Ps. civ. 14.

3. The goodness of God appears in the laws he hath given to man, and the covenant he hath made with him.

1. In the fitting the law to the nature of man. It was rather below than above his strength; he had an integrity in his nature to answer the righteousness of his precept. Eccles. vii. 29. "God created man upright;" his nature was suited to the law, and the law to his nature.

2. In fitting it for the happiness of man. For the satisfaction of his soul, which finds a reward in the very act of keeping it. Ps. cxix. 165.

3. In engaging man to obedience by promises and threatenings. A threatening is only mentioned, Gen. ii. 17, but a promise is implied.

2. In redemption. The whole gospel is nothing but one entire mirror of Divine goodness: the whole of redemption is wrapt up in that one expression of the angel's song, Luke ii. 14, "Good will towards man."

48

1. Goodness was the spring of redemption. All and every part of it owes only to this perfection the appearance of it in the world. 1 John iv. 8.

2. It was a pure goodness. He was under no obligation to pity our misery, and repair our ruins; he might have stood to the terms of the first covenant and exacted our eternal death, since we have committed an infinite transgression.

3. Hence we may consider the height of his goodness in redemption to exceed that in creation. His goodness in the latter is more astonishing to our belief, than his goodness in creation is visible to our eye. There is more of his bounty expressed in that one verse, John iii. 16, "God so loved the world, that he gave his only begotten Son," than there is in the whole volume of the world. In creation, he formed an innocent creature of the dust of the ground; in redemption, he restores a rebellious creature by the blood of his Son.

4 The goodness of God in his government. That goodness that despised not their creation, doth not despise their conduct. The same goodness that was the head that framed them, is the helm that guides them.

1. This goodness is evident in the care he hath of all creatures. There is a peculiar goodness to his people; but this takes not away his general goodness to the world. Ps. civ. 24. "The earth is full of his riches." The whole world swims in the rich bounty of the Creator. The goodness of God is the river that waters the whole earth. His goodness is seen in preserving all things. Ps. xxxvi. 6. "O Lord, thou preservest man and beast." He visits man every day, and makes him feel the effects of his providence in giving him "fruitful seasons, and filling his heart with food and gladness," Acts xiv. 17, as witnesses of his liberality and kindness to man. "The earth is visited and watered by the river of God; he crowns the year with his goodness."

The goodness of God is seen in taking care of the animals and inanimate things. Divine goodness embraceth in its arms the lowest worm as well as the loftiest cherubim; he provides food for the crying ravens, Ps. cxlvii. 9, and a prey for the appetite of the hungry lion. Ps. civ. 21. He clothes the grass, and arrays the lilies of the field with a greater glory than Solomon, Matt. vi. 26—30.

Again, the Divine goodness is evident in providing a scripture, as a rule to guide us, and continuing it in the world. The scripture was written upon several occasions, yet, in the dictating of it, the goodness of God cast his eye upon the last ages of the world. 1 Cor. x. 11. They are written for our admonition, upon whom the ends of the world are come. It was given to the Israelites, but Divine goodness intended it for the future Gentiles. Thus did Divine goodness think of us, and prepare his records for us, before we were in the world. It is clear, to inform our understandings, and rich, to comfort us in our misery; it is a light to guide us, and a cordial to refresh us; it is a lamp to our feet, and a medicine for our diseases; a purifier of our filth, and a restorer of us in our faintings. He hath by his goodness sealed the truth of it, by its efficacy on multitudes of men: he hath made it the word of regeneration. James i. 18. The Divine goodness doth appear in answering prayers. He delights to be familiarly acquainted with his people, and to hear them call upon him. He indulgeth them a free access to him, and delights in every address of an upright man. Isa. lxv 24. The goodness of God is seen in bearing with the infirmities of his people, and accepting imperfect obedience. He takes notice of a sincere, though chequered obedience, to reward it. The goodness of God is seen in afflictions and persecutions; if it be good for us to be afflicted, for which we have the Psalmist's vote, Ps. cxix. 71. "What is man that thou shouldst magnify him?" Job vii. 17.

To conclude.

1. If God be so good, how unworthy is the contempt or abuse of his goodness. Jer. ii. 5. By a forgetfulness of his benefits, we enjoy the mercies and forget the donor; we take what he gives, and pay not the tribute he deserves. The Israelites forgot God their Saviour, by a distrust of his providence; Num. xiv. 3; thus the Israelites thought their miraculous deliverance from Egypt. In sinning more freely upon the account of his goodness; in ascribing our benefits to other causes than Divine goodness. Thus Israel ascribed her felicity, plenty, and success, to her idols, as rewards which her lovers had given her. Hos. ii. 5, 12. "Thou hast praised the gods of silver, and gold, and brass." Dan. v. 23. This was the proud vaunt of the Assyrian conqueror, for which God threatens to punish the fruits of his stout heart. Isa. x. 11—14. "By the strength of my hand I have done it."

2. It is matter of comfort in afflictions. What can we fear from the conduct of infinite goodness? Can his hand be heavy upon those that are humble before him? They are hands of infinite power indeed, but there is not any motion of it; Ps. lxxxiv. 11. "Grace and glory will he give, and no good thing will he withhold."

3. Imitate this goodness of God. Mat. v. 44, 45. "Do good to them that hate you, that you may be the children of your Father, which is in heaven." Verse 48, "Be not overcome of evil."

ON THE DOMINION OF GOD.

Psalm ciii. 19.—The Lord hath prepared his throne in the heavens, and his kingdom ruleth over all. (H.)

"The Lord hath prepared;" the word signifies established, as well as prepared. Due preparation is a natural way to the establishment of a thing. Hasty resolves break and moulder. This notes,

The infinity of his authority. He prepares it, none else for him. Readiness to exercise it upon due occasions. He hath prepared his throne; he hath all things ready for the assistance of his people. Wise management of it; it is prepared: preparations imply prudence; the government of God is not a rash and heady authority. Successfulness and duration; he hath prepared, or established. It is fixed, not tottering; it is an immoveable dominion, all the struggles of men and devils cannot overturn, nor so much as shake it. As his counsel, so his authority shall stand, and "he will do all his pleasure." Isa. xlvi. 10.

"His throne in the heavens." This is an expression to signify the authority of God; for as God hath no member properly, though he be so represented to us, so he hath properly no throne. It signifies his power of reigning and judging.

"His throne in the heavens," notes,

"The glory of his dominion." The heavens are the most stately and comely pieces of the creation; his majesty is there most visible, his glory most splendid. Ps. xix. 1. The heavens speak out with a full mouth his glory; it is therefore called, "The habitation of his holiness and of his glory" Isa. lxiii. 15. The supremacy of his empire; they are elevated above all earthly empires. Peculiarly of this dominion; he rules in the heavens alone. The vastness of his empire; the earth is but a spot to the heavens. The easiness of managing this government; his being in the heavens renders him capable of doing whatsoever he pleases. Ps. cxv. 3. Duration of it; the heavens are incorruptible. His kingdom rules over all; he hath an absolute right over all things, within the circuit of heaven and earth. 1 Chron. xxix. 11, 12.

Jehovah's dominion is here proclaimed as universal. A dominion over the whole world.

I. I SHALL STATE SOME GENERAL PROPOSITIONS FOR THE CLEARING AND CONFIRMING OF THIS GLORIOUS FACT.

1. We must know the difference between the power of God and his authority. We commonly mean, by the power of God, the strength of God, whereby he is able to effect all his purposes. By the authority of God, we mean the right he hath to act what he pleases. Among men, strength and authority are two distinct things. A subject may be a giant, and be stronger than his prince, but he hath not the same authority. Worldly dominion may be seated, not in a brawny arm, but a sickly and infirm body. A greater strength may be settled in the servant, but a greater authority resides in the master. As God is Lord, he hath a right to enact; as he is almighty, he hath a power to execute. His strength is the executive power belonging to his dominion.

2. All the other attributes of God refer to this perfection of dominion. His goodness fits him for it, because he can never use his authority but for the good of the creatures. His wisdom can never be mistaken in the exercise of it; his power can accomplish the decrees that flow from his absolute authority. Without this dominion, some perfections, as justice and mercy, would lie in obscurity, and much of his wisdom would be hid from our sight.

3. This of dominion, as well as that of power, hath been acknowledged by all. The high-priest was to wave the offering, or shake it to and fro, Ex. xxix. 24, which, the Jews say, was customary from east to west, and from north to south, the four quarters of the world, to signify God's sovereignty over all the parts of the world. And some of the heathens, in their adorations, turned their bodies to all quarters, to signify the extensive dominion of God throughout the whole earth. It is stamped upon the conscience of man, and flashes in his face in every act of self-judgment.

4. This notion of sovereignty is inseparable from the notion of God. To acknowledge the existence of a God and to acknowledge him a rewarder are linked together. Hebrew xi. 6. To acknowledge him a rewarder, is to acknowledge him a governor: rewards being the marks of dominion. We cannot suppose God a Creator, without supposing a sovereign dominion in him. No creature can be made without some law in its nature; if it had not law, it would be created to no purpose. It is so inseparable, that it cannot be communicated to any creature. No creature is able to exercise it, every creature is unable to perform all the offices that belong to this dominion.

II. WHEREIN THE DOMINION OF GOD IS FOUNDED.

1. On the excellency of his nature. God being an incomprehensible ocean of all perfection, and possessing infinitely all those virtues that may lay a claim to dominion, hath the first foundation of it in his own nature. On this account God claims our obedience. Isa. xlvi. 9. "I am God, and there is none like me;" and the prophet Jeremiah on the same account

acknowledgeth it. **Jer. x. 6, 7.** "Forasmuch as there is none like unto thee."

2. In his act of creation. He is the sovereign Lord, as he is the almighty Creator. The relation of an entire Creator induceth the relation of an absolute Lord. His dominion or jurisdiction results from creation. When God himself makes an oration in defence of his sovereignty, Job xxxviii., his chief arguments are drawn from creation, and Ps. xcv. 3—5, "The Lord is a great king above all gods." And so the apostle. As he "made the world and all things therein," he is styled, Lord of heaven and earth. Acts xvii. 24. His dominion also of property stands upon this basis. Ps. lxxxix. 11. "The heavens are thine, the earth also is thine." On this title of forming Israel as a creature, or rather as a church, he demands their service to him as their sovereign. "O Jacob and Israel, thou art my servant: I have formed thee." Isa. xliv. 21.

3. "As God is the final cause, or end of all, he is Lord of all." God, in his actual creation of all, is the sovereign end of all, "for thy pleasure they are and were created. Rev. iv. 11. "The Lord hath made all things for himself." Prov. xvi. 4.

4. "The dominion of God is founded upon his preservation of things." Ps. xcv. 3, 4. The Lord is a great king above all gods. Why? In his hand are all the deep places of the earth. While his hand holds things, his hand hath a dominion over them. The master of this great family may as well be called the Lord of it, since every member of it depends upon him for the support of that being he first gave them. As the right to govern resulted from creation, so it is perpetuated by preservation.

5. The dominion of God is strengthened by the innumerable benefits he bestows upon his creatures. The beneficence of God adds, though not an original right of power, yet a foundation of a stronger upbraiding the creature, if he walk in a violation and forgetfulness of those benefits. Isa. i. 2. "Hear, O heavens, and give ear O earth!" Thus the fundamental right as a creator is made more indisputable by his relation as benefactor. The benefits of God are innumerable. But that benefit of redemption doth add a stronger right of dominion to God; since he not only as a creator gave being, but paid a price of his Son's blood for their rescue from captivity, so that he hath a sovereignty of grace as well as nature. 1 Cor. vi. 19, 20. "Ye are not your own."

III. THE NATURE OF THIS DOMINION.

1. This dominion is independent. His throne is in the heavens; the heavens depend not upon the earth, nor God upon his creatures. Since he is independent in regard of his essence, he is so in his dominion, which flows from the excellency and fulness of his essence.

2. Absolute. If his throne be in the heavens, there is nothing to control him. His authority is unlimited.

1. Absolute in regard of freedom and liberty. Thus creation is a work of mere sovereignty; he created, because it was his pleasure to create. Preservation is the fruit of his sovereignty. Redemption is a fruit of his sovereignty.

2. His dominion is absolute in regard of unlimitedness by any law without him. He is an absolute monarch, that makes laws for his subjects, but receives no rules nor laws from his subjects for the management of his government.

3. In regard of supremacy and uncontrollableness. None can implead him, and cause him to render a reason of his actions. "Who may say unto

him, What doest thou?" Eccles. viii. 4. It is an absurd thing for any to dispute with God. Rom. ix. 20. "Who art thou, O man!" In all the desolations he works, he asserts his own supremacy to silence men. **Ps. xlvi. 10.** " Be still, and know that I am God."

4. In regard of irresistibleness. His word is a law, he commands things to stand out of nothing. "He commands light to shine out of darkness." 2 Cor. iv. 6. There is no distance of time between his word. " Let there be light, and there was light." Gen. i. 3. If the Lord will work. " Who shall let it?" Isa. xliii. 13. He sets the ordinances of the heavens, and the dominion thereof in the earth. And sends lightnings, that they may go, and say unto him, Here we are. Job xxxviii. 35.

5. Yet this dominion, though it be absolute, is not tyrannical. If his throne be in the heavens, it is pure and good. This dominion is managed by the rule of wisdom. What may appear to us to have no other spring than absolute sovereignty, would be found to have a depth of amazing wisdom. His sovereignty is managed according to the rule of righteousness. Worldly princes often fancy tyranny and oppression to be the chief marks of sovereignty, and think their sceptres not beautiful till dyed in blood, nor the throne secure till established upon slain carcasses. But justice and judgment are the foundation of the throne of God. Ps. lxxxix. 14. In all his ways he is righteous. Psalm cxiv. 17. His sovereignty is managed according to the rule of goodness. Some potentates there have been in the world, that have loved to suck the blood and drink the tears of their subjects, that would rule more by fear than love. God's throne is a throne of holiness, so is it a throne of grace. Heb. iv. 16. A throne encircled with a rainbow. Rev. iv. 3. In sight like to an emerald. An emblem of the covenant, that hath the pleasantness of a green color, delightful to the eye betokening mercy. If he bind them in fetters, it is to show them their transgressions, and open their ear to discipline, and renewing commands in a more sensible strain, to depart from iniquity.

6. This sovereignty is extensive. He rules all, as the heavens do over the earth. He is king of worlds, king of ages. Earthly kings may step out of their own country into the territory of God. He hath prepared his throne in the heavens, and his kingdom rules over all. The heaven of angels and other excellent creatures belong to his authority. He is principally called the Lord of Hosts, in relation to his entire command over the angelic legions. And the inanimate creatures in heaven are at his beck, they are his armies in heaven, disposed in an excellent order in their several ranks. Ps. cxlvii. 4. He calls the stars by names. The stars by their influences fight against Sisera. Jud. v. 20. And the sun holds in its reins, and stands still, to light Joshua to a complete victory. Josh. x. 12. They are all marshalled in their ranks, to receive his word of command, and fight in close order. And those creatures which mount up from the earth, and take their place in the lower heavens, vapors whereof hail and snow are formed, are part of the army, and do not only receive, but fulfil his word of command. Ps. cxlviii. 8. These are his stores and magazines of judgment against a time of trouble, and a day of battle and war. Job xxxiii. 22, 23. The hell of devils belong to his authority. They have cast themselves out of the arms of his grace, into the furnace of his justice; they have by their revolt forfeited the treasure of his goodness, but cannot exempt themselves from the sceptre of his dominion. The earth of men and other creatures belong to his authority. Ps. xlvii. 7. God is king of all the earth, and rules to the ends of it.

53

But his dominion extends,

1. Over the least creatures. All the creatures of the earth are listed in Christ's muster-roll, and make up the number of his regiments. He hath a host on earth as well as heaven. Gen. ii. 1. The heavens and the earth were finished, and all the hosts of them. And they are all his servants. Ps. cxix. 91, and move at his pleasure. And he vouchsafes the title of his army, to the locust, caterpillar, and palmer worm. Joel ii. 25. And describes their motions by military words, climbing the walls, marching, not breaking their ranks, ver. 7. He hath the command as a great general over the highest angel, and the meanest worm. Not a spot of earth, nor air, nor water, in the world, but is his possession; not a creature in any element but is his subject.

2. His dominion extends over men. It extends over the highest potentate, as well as the meanest peasant; the proudest monarch is no more exempt than the most languishing beggar. He accepts not the persons of princes, nor regards the rich more than the poor. Job xxxiv. 19.

3. But especially this dominion in the peculiarity of its extent, is seen in the exercise of it over the spirits and hearts of men. Earthly governors have by his indulgence a share with him in a dominion over men's bodies, upon which account he graceth princes and judges with the title of gods. Ps. lxxxii. 6. But the highest prince is but a prince according to the flesh. God is the sovereign; man rules over the beast in man, the body; and God rules over the man in man, the soul.

IV. WHEREIN THIS DOMINION AND SOVEREIGNTY CONSISTS, AND HOW IT IS MANIFESTED.

1. The first act of sovereignty is the making laws. This is essential to God; no creature's will can be the first rule to the creature, but only the will of God. Hence the law is called the royal law. James ii. 8; Isaiah xxxiii. 22. The Lord is our lawgiver, the Lord is our king.

The dominion of God in this regard will be manifest,

1. In the supremacy of it. The sole power of making laws doth originally reside in him. James iv. 12. There is one lawgiver, who is able to save and to destroy.

2. The dominion of God is manifest in the extent of his laws. As he is the governor and sovereign of the whole world, so he enacts laws for the whole. The heavens have their ordinances. Job xxxviii. 33. All creatures have a law imprinted on their beings, rational creatures have Divine statutes copied in their heart. Rom. ii. 15.

3. The dominion of God appears in the moral law, and his majesty in publishing it. As the law of nature was writ by his own fingers in the nature of man, so it was engraven by his own finger in the tables of stone, Ex. xxxi. 18.

4. The dominion of God appears in the obligation of the law, which reacheth the conscience. The laws of every prince are framed for the outward conditions of men. Conscience hath a protection from the King of kings, and cannot be arrested by any human power. The conscience is intelligible to God in its secret motions, and therefore only guidable by God.

2. His sovereignty appears in a power of dispensing with his own laws It is as much a part of his dominion to dispense with his laws, as to enjoin them. Positive laws he hath reversed; as the ceremonial law given to the Jews; the very nature of that law required a repeal, and fell of course. Eph. ii. 14.

54

3. His sovereignty appears in punishing the transgression of the law.

1. This is a breach of God's dominion as lawgiver. As a lawgiver he saves or destroys. James iv. 12.

2. Punishing the transgression of his law. This is a necessary branch of dominion. Surely there is a God that judgeth the earth. Ps. lvii. 9. 11. He reduceth the creature by the lash of his judgments, that would not acknowledge his authority and his precepts.

3. This of punishing was the second discovery of his dominion in the world. His first act of sovereignty was the giving of a law, the next, his appearance in the state of a judge.

4. The means whereby he punisheth shows his dominion. Sometimes he musters up rain and mildew, sometimes he sends regiments of wild beasts; so he threatens Israel. Lev. xxvi. 22. Sometimes he sends out a party of angels, to beat up the quarters of men, and make a carnage among them. 2 Kings xix. 35. Sometimes he mounts his thundering battery, and shoots forth his ammunition from the clouds; as against the Philistines. 1 Sam. vii. 10. Sometimes he sends the slightest creatures to shame the pride, and punish the sin of man; as lice, frogs.

4. The dominion of God is manifested as a governor as well as a lawgiver and proprietor.

1. In disposing of states and kingdoms. Ps. lxxv. 7. God is judge, he puts down one and sets up another. In wars, whereby flourishing kingdoms are overthrown, God hath the chief command. God is called the Lord of Hosts 130 times. It is not the sword of the captain, but the sword of the Lord, bears the first rank. The sword of the Lord and of Gideon. Judges vii. 18. The sword of a conqueror is the sword of the Lord. He looseth the bond of kings, and girdeth their loins with a girdle.

2. The dominion of God is manifested in raising up and ordering the spirits of men according to his pleasure. He doth, as the Father of spirits, communicate an influence to the spirits of men as well as an existence. There are many examples of this part of his sovereignty. God by his sovereign conduct ordered Moses a protectress as soon as his parents had formed an ark of bulrushes, wherein to set him floating on the river. Ex. ii. 3—6. Thus he appointed Cyrus to be his shepherd, and gave him a pastoral spirit for the restoration of the city and temple of Jerusalem. Isa. xliv. 28, and xlv. 5. Tells them in the prophecy, that he had girded him, though Cyrus had not known him.

3. The dominion of God is manifest in restraining the furious passions of men, and putting a block in their way. Sometimes God doth it by a remarkable hand, as the Babel builders were diverted from their proud designs by a sudden confusion; sometimes by ordinary, though unexpected means: as when Saul, like a hawk, was ready to prey upon David, whom he had hunted as a partridge upon the mountains.

4. The dominion of God is manifest in defeating the purposes and devices of men. God often makes a mock of human projects. Job v. 12. He disappointeth the devices of the crafty. The cunningest designs baffled by some small thing intervening, when you see men of profound wisdom infatuated, mistake their way, and grope in the noonday as in the night. Job v. 14.

5. The dominion of God is manifest in the means and occasions of men's conversion. Sometimes one occasion, sometimes another; one word lets a man go, another arrests him, and brings him before God and his own conscience.

6. The dominion of God is manifest in disposing of the lives of men He keeps the key of death, as well as that of the womb, in his own hand; he hath given man a life, but not power to dispose of it, nor lay it down at his pleasure.

To conclude,

1. How great is the contempt of this sovereignty of God? Man naturally would be free from God's empire, to be a slave under the dominion of his own lust. The sovereignty of God as a lawgiver is most abhorred by man. Lev. xxvi. 41; Prov. i. 25. Ye have set at naught all my counsels. All sin is in its nature a contempt of the divine dominion.

2. How dreadful is the consideration of this doctrine to all rebels against God. Punishment is unavoidable. None can escape him. He hath the sole authority over hell and death, the keys of both are in his hand.

3. What matter of comfort and strong encouragement for prayer. My king, was the strong appellation David used in prayer. Ps. v. 2. "Hearken to the voice of my cry." Here is comfort in afflictions. As a sovereign, he is the author of afflictions; as a sovereign, he can be the remover of them. In the severest tempest the Lord that raised the wind against us, which shattered the ship, and tore its rigging, can change that contrary wind for a more happy one, to drive us into the port. It is a comfort to the church in times of public commotions. The consideration of the divine sovereignty may arm us against the threatenings of mighty ones, and the menaces of persecutors. Prov. xxi. 30.

THE LONG–SUFFERING OF GOD.

2 Peter iii. 9.—The Lord is long-suffering to us-ward. (H.)

It is a shocking disposition of mind, which Solomon describes in that well-known passage in Eccles, "Because sentence against an evil work is not executed speedily, therefore the heart of the sons of men is fully set in them to do evil."

It seems, at first sight, as if the wise man had rather exceeded in his portrait of the human heart.

God is patient towards all who offend him; then let us offend him without remorse, let us try the utmost extent of his patience. God lifteth over our head a mighty hand, armed with lightenings and thunderbolts, but his hand is usually suspended awhile before it strikes; then, let us dare it while it delays, and till it moves to crush us to pieces, let us not respect it. What a disposition, what a shocking disposition of mind is this.

Could we have the madness to add sin to sin, if we were really convinced that God entertained the formidable design of bearing with us no longer?

And shall we "despise the riches of the long-suffering of God?" What! because a space to repent, shall we continue in impenitence?

"The Lord is long-suffering to us-ward, not willing that any should perish, but that all should come to repentance."

Consider,

I. The nature of this long-suffering.

1. It is part of the Divine goodness and mercy, yet differs from both The Lord is full of compassion, slow to anger. Long-suffering differs from

mercy in respect to the object; mercy respects the creature as miserable: patience, or long-suffering, respects the creature as criminal: mercy pities him in his misery; long-suffering bears with the sin, and waits to be gracious.

Patience or long-suffering differs also from goodness, in regard to the object. The object of goodness is every creature, from the highest angel in heaven to the meanest creature on earth; goodness respects things in a capacity, or in a state of creation, nurseth and supporteth them as creatures. Long-suffering considers them as already created and fallen short of their duty; goodness respects persons as creatures; long-suffering as transgressors.

2. Since it is a part of goodness and mercy, it is not insensibility. He is slow to anger. The Lord considers every provocation, but is not hasty to discharge his arrows on the offenders; he sees the sin with an eye of abhorrence, but beholds the sinner with an eye of pity; his anger burns against the sin, whilst his arms are open to receive the sinner.

3. As long-suffering is a part of mercy and goodness, it is not constrained or faint-hearted patience. Patience or long-suffering in man, is often a feebleness of spirit and want of strength. But it is not from the shortness of the divine arm, that he cannot reach us, nor from the feebleness of his hand that he cannot strike us. He can soon level us with the dust, dash us in pieces like a potter's vessel, or consume us as a moth.

4. Since it is not for want of power over the creature, it is from a fulness of the power over himself. The Lord is slow to anger, and great in power. As it is the effect of his power, so it is an argument of his power. As the more feeble any man is in reason, the less command he hath over his passions. Revenge is a sign of a childish mind. He that is slow to anger is better than the mighty. The long-suffering of God towards sinners, manifests his power, more than the creation of a world.

5. As long-suffering is a branch of mercy, the exercise of it is founded on the death of Christ. It is in Christ we find the satisfaction of justice; and it is in and through Christ the long-suffering of God is manifested to man

2. How this long-suffering or patience is manifested.

1. To our first parents. The patience or long suffering of God was manifested in not directing his artillery against them, when they first attempted to rebel. He might have struck them dead when they began to hearken to the tempter. And after our first parent had brought his sin to perfection, God did not immediately send that death on him, which he had merited, but continued his life to the space of 930 years.

2. His long-suffering is manifested to the Gentiles. What they were, we need no other witness than the apostle, who sums up many of their crimes, Rom. i. 29—32, being filled with all unrighteousness. And he concludes with these dreadful aggravations, they not only do the same, but have pleasure in them that do them. They were so naturalized in wickedness, that they delighted in nothing else. They were plunged into idolatry and superstition. Yet, did the Lord appear against them with fire and sword? "At the times of that ignorance he winked."

3. The long-suffering of God was manifested to the Israelites. He suffered their manners forty years in the wilderness. He bore with that people above 1500 years from their coming out of Egypt to the destruction of their commonwealth.

In particular this long-suffering of God is manifested,

1. In his giving warning of judgments before they are commissioned to go forth. The Lord speaks before he strikes, and speaks that he may not strike.

Wrath is published before it is executed, and that a long time; the old world were warned 120 years before the deluge came on them.

The Lord does not come unawares. I will chastise them as their congregation hath heard. The Lord summoned by the voice of his prophets, before he confounded by the voice of his thunders. He seldom cuts men down by his judgments, before he hath hewed them by his prophets. Not a remarkable judgment but was foretold; the flood, by Noah; the famine to Egypt, by Joseph; the earthquake, by Amos; Amos i. 1; the storm from Chaldea, by Jeremiah; the captivity of the ten tribes by Hosea; and the total destruction of Jerusalem and the temple, by Christ. And he thus warns, that men may take the warning, and thunders again and again, before he crushes with his thunderbolt.

2. The long-suffering of the Lord is manifested in his unwillingness to execute his threatened judgments, when he can delay no longer. He doth not afflict willingly nor grieve the children of men. He takes no pleasure in it. When he came to reckon with Adam, he walked, he did not run with his sword, and that in the cool of the day. His exercising of judgment, is a coming out of his place. Isa. xxvi. 21; Micah i. 3. Hence every prophecy loaded with a threatening is called the burden of the Lord. When the Lord punishes, he doth it with some regret; when he hurls down his thunders, he seems to do it with a backward hand. He created, saith Chrysostom, the world in six days, but was seven days in destroying one city, Jericho. When the Lord strikes, it is with a sigh. "Ah! I will ease me of my adversaries, and avenge me of my enemies. Oh Ephraim, what shall I do unto thee? How shall I give thee up, oh, Ephraim! And many a time (says the Psalmist) turned he his anger away."

3. His long-suffering is manifested, in that when he begins to send out his judgments, he doth it by degrees. His judgments are as the morning light. He doth not thunder all his judgments at once. First the palmer-worm, then the locust, then the canker-worm, then the caterpillar. Joel i. 4. A Jewish writer says, these came not all in one year, but one year after another.

4. His long-suffering appears, by moderating his judgments. He stirreth not up all his wrath. He doth not empty his quivers, nor exhaust his magazines of thunder. "He rewardeth us not according to our iniquities."

5. His long-suffering farther appears, in giving great mercies after provocations. He is so slow to anger, that he heaps many kindnesses on a rebel; instead of punishment, there is prosperous wickedness. Israel quarrelled with his servant Moses at the Red Sea; yet then the Lord stretched forth his hand and delivered them.

6. The long-suffering of God appears also when we consider the greatness and multitude of our provocations. Men drinking in iniquity like water. Rushing into sin. The imaginations of the thoughts of the heart only evil.

III. THE GROUND AND REASON OF THIS LONG-SUFFERING TO US-WARD.

1. As a testimony of his reconcileable and merciful nature towards sinners. "Howbeit, for this cause I obtained mercy, that in me Jesus Christ might show forth all long-suffering."

2. That sinners may be brought to repentance. "Not knowing," says the apostle, "that the riches of his forbearance and goodness leads thee to repentance." The Lord is long-suffering to us-ward. "The long-suffering of God is salvation," i. e. hath a tendency to salvation.

3. For the continuance of his church. "As the new wine is found in the cluster, and one saith, Destroy it not, for a blessing is in it." Isa. lxv. 8, 9

4. That his justice may be clear when he condemns the impenitent. "I gave her space to repent of her fornication, and she repented not."

5. In answer to the prayers of his people, his long-suffering is exercised towards sinners. "Except the Lord of hosts had left unto us a very small remnant, we should have been as Sodom."

To conclude.

1. How is the long-suffering of God abused! May we not say to the Lord as Saul said to David, "Thou art more righteous than I; thou hast rewarded me with good."

2. Is the Lord long-suffering? How much better, therefore, is it to fall into the hands of God, than into the hands of man: the best of men. Moses, a meek man, once cried, Ye rebels.

3. We may infer from the Lord's long-suffering towards sinners, the value of the soul; he not only died to redeem it, but waits with unwearied patience and forbearance to receive it. "Behold, I stand at the door."

Lastly, If the Lord be thus long-suffering to us-ward, who have so long and repeatedly rebelled against him, ought not christians to exercise forbearance and long-suffering one towards another? "Walk worthy of the vocation wherewith ye are called, with all lowliness and meekness, with long-suffering." Eph. iv. 1—6.

GOD'S COMPASSION.

Hos. xi. 7—9.—My people are bent to backsliding from me: though they called them unto the Most High, none at all would exalt him: [yet] how shall I give thee up, Ephraim? how shall I deliver thee, Israel? how shall I make thee as Admah? how shall I set thee as Zeboim? mine heart is turned within me, my repentings are kindled together. I will not execute the fierceness of mine anger. (S. S.)

THE riches of Divine grace are manifest in all the promises—

But they are more eminently displayed in the manner in which the promises are given—

God often introduces them after an enumeration of his people's sins—

The passage before us well exemplifies this remark—See similar instances, Isa. xliii. 22—25, and lvii. 17, 18.

God has been contrasting his kindness to Israel, and their ingratitude towards him—

In the text he sets forth their wickedness with all its aggravations—

Yet all this is preparatory, not to a heavy denunciation of his wrath, but to the tenderest expressions of paternal love—

I. THE CONDUCT OF MEN TOWARDS GOD.

The ten tribes, since their separation from Judah, had become idolators—

Yet God calls them his people because they had been admitted into cove nant with him, and still professed to be his—

Thus all who call themselves Christians are "God's people"—

But they "are bent to backsliding from him"

The ungodly are justly compared to an unruly heifer—

They will not submit to the yoke of God's laws—

Their whole spirit and temper is like that of Pharoah—Exod. v. 2.

The "bent" and inclination of their hearts is wholly towards sin—

An outward conformity to God's will they may approve—
But they have a rooted aversion to spiritual obedience—
Nor can they by any any means be prevailed on to "exalt and honor him —
They are "called" frequently by God's ministers—
They are exhorted and intreated to return to the Most High—
But neither promises can allure nor threatenings alarm them—
They turn a deaf ear to all admonitions—
They will not "exalt" God in their hearts and lives—
This is almost universally the conduct of mankind
There are a few indeed who desire and delight to serve God—
They wish him to be the sole Lord and Governor of their hearts—
It is their study to exalt him both in their words and actions—
But these are few in every age and place—
So few, that, in comparison of the rebellious, they may be said to be "none at all"—
What might such persons expect at the hand of God?

II. GOD'S CONDUCT TOWARDS THEM

How different are God's ways from the ways of man !—
Instead of executing vengeance in a moment,

He deliberates

Admah and Zeboim were cities destroyed with Sodom and Gomorrah—
And such monuments of wrath do the unregenerate deserve to be—
But God knows not, as it were, how to inflict the deserved punishment—
He calls to mind that they are *his* people*—
He hesitates, like a parent, that is about to disinherit his son—
Thus is he distracted between his affection for them, and his regard for his own honor—Thus also in Hos. vi. 4.

He relents

To accommodate himself to our weak comprehensions he speaks of himself after the manner of men—
He cannot endure the thought of making men the objects of his everlasting displeasure—
Thus did Jesus weep over the murderous Jerusalem—Luke xix. 41.
And thus do the bowels of our Father yearn over us—Jer. xxxi 20.

He resolves

Often has "the fierce anger" of the Lord been kindled against us—
Yet many times has he turned away from his wrathful indignation—Ps. lxxviii. 38.
Often, when his bow was bent, has he forborne to strike—Ps. vii. 11, 12.
He waits, in hope that he may yet return to him—
His language to his rebellious creatures is the same as ever—Jer. ii. 12, 13.

Infer,

1. How precious in the sight of God are the souls of men !—
When it was necessary for man's salvation, God gave his Son—
Nor did he then *deliberate*, "how shall I do this?"—Rom viii. 32.
Neither did he *relent*, when he laid our iniquities on him—Mark xiv. 35, 36
Yea, he was even *pleased* in bruising his own Son for us†—
But when a sinner seems irreclaimable, every tender emotion is excited—

* The repitition of their names, "*thee* Ephraim, and *thee*, Israel," seems to import tenterness and affection towards them.
† This is the proper sense of Isa. liii. 10.

God sustains a conflict in his mind, and cannot give him up—
O that men would duly estimate the worth of their own souls !—
2 How just will be the condemnation of the impenitent !
This compassion of God greatly aggravates their backsliding —
And at last it will give way to wrath and indignation—Gen. vi. 3,
Soon God will not deliberate, but decide; not relent, but laugh at their
calamity ; not resolve to pardon, but swear they shall not enter into his rest—
Then how just will their condemnation appear ?—
May this goodness of God now lead us to repentance !—
3. How certainly shall the returning sinner find mercy !
If God feel thus for the rebellious, how much more for the penitent !—
Let all then seek him with humble confidence in his mercy—
Let them offer their supplications like those of old—Isa. lxiii. 15.
So shall that song of praise succeed their present disquietude—Isa. xii 1

THE MERCY OF GOD.

Micah vii. 18—20.—Who is a God like unto thee, that pardoneth iniquity, and passem oy the transgression of the remnant of his heritage? He retaineth not his anger forever, because he delighteth in mercy. He will turn again, he will have compassion upon us; he will subdue our iniquities; and thou wilt cast all their sins into the depths of the sea. Thou wilt perform the truth to Jacob, and the mercy to Abraham, which thou hast sworn unto our fathers from the days of old. (S. S.)

EVERY work of God should lead our thoughts up to its great author—
The prophet had prayed that the Jews might be restored to their own land—Ver. 14.
God had promised that he would grant them such a deliverance from Babylon as he had before given to their ancestors from Egypt—Ver. 15—17.
The prophet immediately elevates his thoughts from the deliverance to the author of it, and breaks forth in admiration of his mercy—
His devout acknowledgments lead us to consider God's mercy
I. IN ITS RISE
God has had at all times a people in the world
They were very few in the days of Noah, or of Abraham—
In our Lord's day they were but a "little flock"—
The apostle's description of them is still as true as ever—Rom. xi. 5.
These, however, are esteemed as God's "heritage"—Ps. xxxiii. 12.
Towards these he exercises peculiar mercy
He "passes by their transgressions" with much long-suffering—Ps. ciii. 10.
Though he feels anger against them, Ps. vii. 11. "he retains it not for ever"—
He "pardons their iniquities," giving them repentance unto life—
In so doing he is actuated only by his own love and mercy
There is not any thing in his elect that can merit his favor—
But "he delighteth in mercy," and would gladly exercise it towards all*—
The iniquities of the wicked are a burthen to him Isa. i. 14, 24. Amos ii. 13.
He waits to be gracious unto them—Isa. xxx. 18.

*Judgment is called "his *strange* work, his *strange* act." Is. xxviii. 21. Ezek. xxxiii. 11

He deliberates long before he casts them off—Hos. vi. 4.

When he rejects them finally, he does it with reluctance—Luke xix. 41.

He is often so troubled for the obstinate, that he resolves for his own sake to reclaim them by a sovereign exercise of almighty power—Jer. iii. 19.

When he has prevailed on a sinner, he exults for joy—Zeph. iii. 17. See also the parables of the shepherd, the woman, the father, Luke xv.

And thus it is that he saves the remnant of his heritage—Isa. xliii. 25.

What reason then have they to exclaim, "Who is like unto thee?"

The mercy thus freely manifested is worthy of admiration also

II. In its progress.

God continues to act with astonishing forbearance towards them

They are, alas! too prone to backslide from him—

They often provoke him to withdraw himself from them—Deut. xxxii. 20

But he leaves them not eternally to take the fruit of their misconduct—

He has "compassion on them," remembering they are but dust—Ps. ciii. 14

He "turns to them again" after hiding himself for a little season. Isa liv. 7, 8. See a striking declaration to this effect, Isa. lvii. 16—18.

He restores to them the light of his countenance—

How interesting and endearing is this description of his character!—

How must every saint adopt the church's confession!—Lam. iii. 22.

He pledges himself not only to pardon, but to " subdue their iniquities"

He will not suffer sin to have dominion over them—Rom. vi. 14.

He hides his face in order to embitter sin to them—

He turns to them again to encourage their opposition to it—

He renews their strength when they are fainting—Isa. xl. 29—31.

And gradually perfects in them the work he has begun—

Who can survey this progress of mercy, and not exclaim " Who?" &c.—

But the full extent of God's mercy can only be seen

III. In its consummation.

Sin cleaves to the Lord's people as long as they are in the body—

Hence they have daily occasion for renewed forgiveness—

But soon their pardon shall be final and complete

God overthrew the Egyptian host in the Red Sea—

" There was not so much as one of them left"—

So will God " cast his people's sins into the sea"—

He will cast them " all" without one single exception—

And *that* " into the depths" from whence they shall never rise—

If the Israelites so rejoiced in seeing their enemies dead on the shore, how will christians in their final victory over sin—

God will fulfil to them his promises in their utmost extent

The promises as made to Abraham and his seed were " mercy"—

The confirmation of them to Jacob and to the church was " truth"—

They have been established with the sanction of an " oath"—

And these " promises" will be fulfilled " to all the seed"—

Soon will " the head-stone be brought forth with shoutings," &c.— Zech. iv. 7.

How will every glorified soul *then* admire the divine mercy!—

What energy will a sight of sins forgiven, of backslidings healed, of glory bestowed, give to the exclamation in the text!—

May this view of the subject be realized in our experience!—

Application

Let *the careless* consider against whom their sins are committed—

Will they never pause, and exclaim like Joseph—Gen xxxix, 9.

Let *the penitent* reflect on the descriptions given of God in scripture—Neh. ix. 17. Isa. lv. 7.

Nor let them judge of him by the dictates of sense—Isa. lv. 8, 9.

Let *the sincere believer* apply to himself that congratulation—Deut. xxxiii. 29.

And let him adopt that triumphant boast—Isa. xxv. 9.

THE KNOWLEDGE OF GOD BY THE LIGHT OF NATURE.

Acts xiv. 15—17.—The living God, which made heaven and earth, and the sea, and all things that are therein, &c. (H.)

WHEN the apostle Paul gave authority to his ministrations at Lystra, by working a miraculous cure on a man who was born a cripple, the inhabitants imagined that he and Barnabas were gods, and were immediately preparing a sacrifice for them: but to divert this madness and superstition of paying Divine worship to the creatures, the apostles, with holy jealousy and indignation, ran into the midst of them, and preached to them the living and the true God. "We," say they, "are utterly unworthy of these Divine honors; for we are men of such flesh and blood as yourselves, and are liable to the like infirmities: we preach to you, that ye should turn from these vanities to the living God who made heaven and earth," &c.

From which words we may raise the following observations: .

I. THE LIGHT OF NATURE MAY TEACH US, THAT THERE IS ONE SUPREME BEING.

He hath not left himself without witness. The Being which made all things, or the first cause of all. And when I say, God may be known by the light of nature, I mean, that the senses and the reasoning powers, which belong to the nature of man are able to give him so much light in seeking after God, as to find out something of him thereby, or to gain some knowledge of him. Rom. i. 19, 20. "That which may be known of God is manifested."

1. By the light of nature we may come to the knowledge of his existence. It is evident, that nothing could make itself. It is impossible that any thing which once had no being should ever give being to itself. Since, therefore, there is a world with millions of beings in it, which are born and die, it is certain there is some Being who had no beginning. This is the being whom we call God.

Of all the visible beings that we are acquainted with, man is the highest and most noble; but he is forced to confess he is not his own maker. Our parents, or our ancestors, were no more able to make themselves than we are.

Or if some atheist should say, We must run up from son to father, and from father to grandfather, in endless generations without a beginning, and without any first cause. This is impossible; for if ten thousand generations cannot subsist of themselves without dependance on something before them, neither endless generations. Suppose a chain of ten thousand links hung down from the sky, and could not support itself, unless some mighty power upheld the first link; then it is certain, a chain of ten thousand times ten thousand links, or an endless chain, could never support itself. There must be, therefore, some first bird, some first beast, some first man.

2. What God is, viz. that he is a spirit, perfect in wisdom and perfect in power. The amazing work of God in the heavens, the sun, the moon, the stars, their regular and unerring motions, for so many thousand years; the progress of the hours, the changes of day and night, winter and summer, which depend on these motions and revolutions; they all abundantly discover that the maker of them was wise, and skilful beyond all our conceptions. If we observe the operations of a clock or watch, which doth but imitate the motions of these heavenly bodies, and point out to us the day and the hour, we say, it is impossible this curious engine could be made without great wisdom and skill in some artificer who contrived it; and can we be so foolish as to imagine, that this vast and glorious engine of the heavens, with all its bright furniture, which makes times and seasons, day and night, could ever come into being by chance?

The wonderful production of plants, herbs, trees, and flowers, and astonishing operations of living creatures, and their several parts and powers, discover to us the deep wisdom and knowledge of the Being that made them. Let us consider but our own natures, our parts, and powers, what wonders are contained in every sense? Can all these be formed without infinite wisdom? I might demand of the sons of atheism, in the language of the Psalmist, Ps. xciv. 9, 10, " He that planteth the ear, shall not he hear?" And as the wonders of contrivance in the works of God declare his depth of wisdom, so the difficulty of creating them out of nothing argues his almighty power. " When we survey the heavens, the work of his hands," what a glorious and powerful Being must that be, which formed these vast bodies at first, and which upholds their stupendous frame? Man can only change the shapes and qualities of things; he can make a clock, but he must have brass and iron given him, for he cannot create these materials: but God's huge and astonishing engine of the heavens, whereby hours and days, seasons and ages, are made and measured out, were all formed by him without any materials: he made all the materials himself. A creator must be almighty, he must be God.

Again, Let us think within ourselves, what a powerful Being must that be, who can make a soul, a spirit, a thinking being to exist, so nearly like himself, with an understanding capable of knowing the works of God, and of knowing God himself? We are his image, " we are his offspring;" thus sang Aratus the heathen poet, Acts xvii. 28, 29, and spoke like a christian.

And thus it appears beyond all controversy, that the light of nature finds there is a God, and that this God is an all-wise and almighty spirit. If we were in doubt about his existence or being, these reasonings would assure us of it; and if we seek after his nature, and his perfections, these his works discover them.

3. His supreme and absolute dominion over all things, that God is the sovereign lord and possessor of heaven and earth, Gen. xiv. 19, and consequently that he hath a right to dispose of all things as he pleases. Rom. ix. 20. " Who therefore shall say to him, What dost thou?"

4. That though God be the absolute and natural lord of all things that he hath made, yet he is pleased to deal with his rational creatures in a way of moral government. The conscience which he hath formed in man may discover in him so much of the natural law and will of his God, as a righteous governor of the world, if it be properly and wisely employed. Rom. ii. 14, 15. "The Gentiles which have not the written law," which not only teaches them that adoration and worship, prayer and praise, are duties which they owe to God; but it instructs them also to distinguish between vice and virtue. Acts xxviii. 4. " Surely this man is a murderer."

Reason and conscience might teach mankind that since God has given them an understanding and freedom of will to choose or refuse good or evil, he will certainly call them to account for their behaviour. In their own consciences there is a kind of tribunal erected, "their conscience excusing or accusing them."

5. That God is a universal benefactor to mankind, even above and beyond their deserts, and notwithstanding all their provocations. That though they walked in their own idolatrous ways, yet God left them not without witness of his goodness, giving them fruitful seasons.

II. WHAT ARE THE VARIOUS USES OF THIS KNOWLEDGE OF GOD, WHICH IS ATTAINABLE BY THE LIGHT OF NATURE.

In general, it is to bear witness for God in the world. More particularly,

1. This knowledge of God, as our maker and governor, by the light of nature, is useful, not only to show men their duty, but to convince them of sin. The apostle Paul begins with this doctrine in the first chapter of his Epistle to the Romans, where his great design is to show mankind the guilt and wretchedness of their state.

2. As it is a design to awaken men to the practice of their duty. This natural conscience is the candle of their Lord, which he has set up in the heart of man; and though it shines but dimly, yet it has sometimes kept them from being more vile.

3. Gives some encouragement to guilty creatures to repent of their sins, and to return to God by a general hope of acceptance, though they had no promise of pardoning grace. And this was the very principle on which some of the Gentiles set themselves to practise virtue, to worship God, and endeavor to become like him. I do not say, that natural religion can give sinful men a full and satisfying assurance of pardon on their repentance; for the deepest degrees of penitence cannot oblige a prince to forgive the criminal: but still his overflowing goodness may evidently and justly excite in their hearts some hope of forgiving grace. The Ninevites themselves, when threatened with destruction, "repented in sackcloth and ashes." Jonah iii. 5—10. And there is yet a more express text to this purpose. Rom. ii. 4. "Despisest thou the riches of his goodness?"

4. Serves to vindicate the conduct of God as a righteous governor. This will leave them without excuse in "the great day, when God shall judge the secrets of all hearts." Their own consciences will accuse them. Rom. i. 20, 21; ii. 15. "Is God unrighteous, who taketh vengeance on such sinners? God forbid." Rom. ii. 5, 6. In the world to come, not one condemned sinner shall be able to say, God is unjust. "Every mouth shall be stopped, and the heavens and the earth proclaim his righteousness."

5. Prepares the way for preaching and receiving the gospel of grace: and that many ways.

We see the apostle wisely managing his ministry to the Athenians, of which we have but short hints in Acts xvii. 22, &c. By discoursing first on natural religion, and agreeably to this method of propagating the gospel among the heathen nations, we find, in fact, that where there was any thing of the knowledge of the true God, either by the light of nature, or by tradition, there the gospel was soonest received.

III. THE DEFECTS OR IMPERFECTIONS OF IT.

1. It is but a small portion of the things of God, which the bulk of mankind can generally be supposed to learn merely by their own reasonings. This is sufficiently evident by the history of past times and ancient nations, as well as by present observation of the heathen world. Though some of

the philosophers attained considerable knowledge of the nature of God and clearly saw his eternal power and godhead, Rom. i. 20, yet these were but very few in comparison of the rest.

2. It is but dim and feeble, and leaves mankind under many doubts and uncertainties in matters of importance. A short lesson of knowledge in the heathen schools was obtained with long toil and difficulty: their philosophy was rather a feeling after God in the dark, than a sight of him in daylight: so the apostle expresses himself, Acts xvii. 27, "That they should seek the Lord." What feeble words are these! how doubtful a knowledge is represented by them! how generally, and almost, without exception, did their philosophers comply with the idolatry of their country, and "worship God in the form of beasts and birds."

In some countries, the youth and flower of conquered nations were doomed a sacrifice to their idols: and sometimes filthy and abominable lewdness were the ceremonies of their worship. How blind was the eye of their reason, not to see this madness! and how feeble its power, that it made no remonstrance against these lewd and bloody scenes of degenerated piety!

All these instances indeed do not effectually prove, that reason could not possibly teach them better; but the experience of long ages and of whole nations sufficiently shows us, that their reason neither did inform them better, nor was ever likely to do it. 1 Cor. i. 21. "The world by wisdom knew not God."

3. All the knowledge of God which they arrived at, by the light of nature, had actually but little influence to reform the hearts or the lives of mankind. I say, it had but little influence in comparison of what it might or should have had, Acts xiv. 16; Rom. i., "latter end."

4. It doth rather serve to show men their sin and misery, than discover any effectual relief; and in this respect it comes infinitely short of what the revelation of the gospel of Christ hath done.

1. The light of nature of itself gives no assurance or forgiveness to the repenting sinner. "Who can tell but the Lord may turn away from his fierce anger?" is but a feeble motive to repentance and new obedience, in comparison of such a word from God himself, as Ex. xxxiv. 6. "And the Lord passed by before him, and proclaimed, The Lord, the Lord God, merciful and gracious." Prov. xxviii. 13. "He that confesseth and forsaketh."

2. The light of nature discovers no effectual atonement for sin, nor relief to a guilty conscience, by all the costly sacrifice and blood of animals; but the gospel points us to the "Lamb of God that taketh away the sins of the world," John i. 29, and assures us, that if we confess our sins, 1 John, i. 6.

3. The light of nature points us to no effectual mediator, or advocate in heaven; but the gospel leads us to "Jesus the righteous as our advocate with the Father." 1 John ii. 1, 2.

4. The light of nature and our daily experience discover to us our weakness to subdue sin within us, to restrain our unruly appetites, to mortify our corrupt affections, to resist the daily temptations that surround us; but it points us not to the fountain of strength, even the promised aids of the Holy Spirit, these are the peculiar glories and blessings of the gospel of Christ.

5. The light of nature and continual observation show us, that we must die, but give us no clear and certain evidence of happiness after death. But the gospel sets these future glories in a Divine and certain light before every man, who reads or hears it. It encourages us to repentance of sin, to diligence, patience, and perseverance, in the ways of faith and holiness, by the joys unspeakable, which are set before us, and builds our hope of eternal life on the well-attested promises of a God who cannot lie.

Reflections.

1. Since the rational knowledge of God and natural religion had its proper uses, and especially to lay a foundation for our receiving the gospel of Christ, let it not be despised nor abandoned by any of us. There may be some necessary occasions for our recourse to it. St. Paul made glorious use of it in his discourse with the Athenian infidels.

2. Since this knowledge of God, which is attainable by the light of nature, has so many defects, let us never venture to rest in it. Dare not content yourselves with the lessons of the book of nature. The sun in the firmament, with the moon and all the stars, can never give the light to see God, which is derived from the Sun of Righteousness.

What a deplorable thing is it, that multitudes in our nation, where the glory of the blessed gospel shines with such brightness, should be running back to the glimmering light of nature, and satisfy themselves with heathenism and philosophy! that they should choose to walk in twilight, and refuse to be conducted by the blaze of noon. "The God of this world hath blinded the eyes of them that believe not."

3. Since the nations, which have only the light of nature, and forced to feel out their way to God through such dusky glimmerings, let us bless the Lord with all our souls, that we are born in a land of clear light, where the gospel shines in all its beauty. How should we value the Bible as our highest treasure, which gives us such blessed discoveries of God and his wisdom and power, and his mercy in Christ, which infinitely exceed all the doubtful twilight of nature. O, may the blessed Bible lie next our hearts, and be the companion of our bosoms.

4. Pity and pray for the heathen world, the dark corners of the earth, the benighted nations, where the Sun of Righteousness never rose, and were they can but feel after God through the mists of ignorance and error. Let us remember these ancient times, when our forefathers in this nation were led away into the same errors and gross idolatries, and lift up one compassionate groan to heaven for them. When shall the ends of the earth learn to know thee? When shall all nations, people, and languages, begin their songs of salvation to him that sits upon the throne, and to the Lamb?

THE GOSPEL PRODUCTIVE OF GOOD WORKS.

1 Timothy, vi. 3.—The doctrine which is according to godliness. (H. H.)

The objections which men urge against the doctrines of the gospel, originate for the most part in their aversion to its precepts. The restraint which it imposes on their actions is irksome to them. They wish to follow the impulse of their passions, or the dictates of self-interest: and when they are checked in their progress, they complain, that the path marked out for them is too strait, and the yoke which we would put upon them is too heavy.

St. Paul is giving directions for the conduct of masters and servants towards each other: but, however "wholesome his words" were, he foresaw that some would "not consent to" them, notwithstanding they were "the words of Christ himself," and in perfect unison with the gospel, which was in that, as well as in every other respect, "a doctrine according to godliness He then proceeds to animadvert upon such characters, and to shew that their

67

dislike to the injunctions given them was owing only to their own pride, and ignorance, and love of sin.

The expression contained in the text is peculiarly worthy of our attention. It gives a just, and very important view of the gospel; to illustrate and confirm which is the intent of this discourse.

In order to prove that the gospel is indeed "a doctrine according to godliness," let us consult,

I. ITS DOCTRINES,

We might, if our time would admit of it, illustrate this in every one of the doctrines of our holy religion. But we shall confine ourselves to,

1. The representations which it gives us of God—

The systems of religion which obtained among the heathen, were calculated rather to promote, than to repress, iniquity: for even their gods themselves, according to their own representations of them, were monsters of iniquity. But our God is holy and just; so holy, that he cannot look upon sin without the utmost abhorrence of it. Hab. i. 13. And so just, that he will never suffer it to pass unpunished. Exod. xxxiv. 7.

If indeed these were his only attributes, men might set down in despair, and take their fill of sin, because they would have no encouragement to depart from it. But " there is mercy also with him, that he may be feared ;" yea, so "rich is he in mercy," that " none shall ever seek his face in vain."

How must the contemplation of such perfections tend to deter men from the commission of evil, and to foster in them every holy sentiment and desire !

2. The means which it prescribes for our reconciliation with him—

The leading feature of the gospel is, that it proclaims pardon to penitent sinners, through the blood and righteousness of the Lord Jesus Christ.

Let any one reflect on this stupendous mystery, the incarnation and death of the Son of God; let him consider, that no less a sacrifice than that made by our incarnate God was sufficient to atone for sin; and will he then be willing to incur all the penalties of sin, and to bear them in his own person? Will not the tears and agonies of an expiring Savior compel him to exclaim, " If such things were done in the green tree, what shall be done in the dry?" and will not the love of Christ in submitting to such an ignominious death, on purpose that he might redeem him from iniquity, have any influence on his mind? Will he readily trample on the blood that was shed for him, and crucify his Lord afresh by continuing in sin.

Let us prosecute the same inquiry, in relation to,

II. ITS PRECEPTS—

View the precepts relating to God and our neighbor—

The two great commandments of the law are confirmed and ratified by the gospel, "Thou shalt love the Lord thy God with all thy heart, and thy neighbor as thyself," Now can any man love God, and not endeavor to do his will? Or, if he make his own self-love the rule and measure of his love to others, can he willingly injure them in any thing, or forbear to do them good? Would not an unfeigned love to these commands lay the axe to the root of all sin, and transform men into the very image of their God?

View the directions which it gives for self-government—

The gospel does not regulate the actions only, but the heart: it extends its dominion over all the most secret motives and inclinations; and requires every thought to be brought into captivity to the obedience of Christ. It makes no allowance for temptations, as though they extenuated the guilt of sin, or were an excuse for the commission of iniquity; but teaches us to 'heap coals of fire on the head of an enemy" by acts of kindness, and "not to be overcome of evil, but to overcome evil with good." It tolerates no kind or degree of sin, but enjoins us to " cleanse ourselves from all filthiness both of flesh and spirit, and to perfect holiness in the fear of God." It requires us to "be holy as God himself is holy," and "perfect, even as our Father which is in heaven is perfect."

Can any one that considers these precepts, doubt what is the nature and tendency of the gospel?

Let us examine further,

III. ITS EXAMPLES—

It calls us to an imitation of,

1. Our blessed Lord—

He was virtue itself embodied. Neither friends nor enemies could ever find in him the smallest spot or blemish. Under circumstances the most trying that can be imagined, he preserved the same serenity of mind, the same meek and heavenly disposition. While he was suffering the most injurious treatment, he was like a lamb led to the slaughter: and in the very agonies of death, he prayed for nothing but blessings on the head of his cruel murderers. Now we are told, that in all this "he set us an example, that we should follow his steps:" and that all his followers must " walk even as he walked."

2. His holy Apostles—

These were far inferior indeed to their Divine Master; yet were they bright patterns of every thing that was excellent and praise-worthy. As being men of like passions with us, they manifested on some occasions their infirmities: and, in these instances, they are warnings to us, and not examples. But, for the most part, they conducted themselvs in a way that excites our highest admiration. And though, on account of their defects, we cannot follow them in every thing, yet we are called on the whole to tread in their steps, and to " be followers of them, as they were of Christ "

Are not these sufficient proofs of the holy tendency of the gospel?

Infer,

1. How little reason is there for objecting to the gospel as unfriendly to morality!

Men ground this objection upon the doctrine of our being "justified by faith only, without the works of the law." But if they would consider that that faith is always preceded by repentance, and followed by obedience, they would see that there was no foundation at all for their objection. If we said that people might live and die in an impenitent and disobedient state, and yet be saved by their faith, then there were good reason to condemn the gospel which we preach: but while we maintain the character of God as it is exhibited in the gospel, together with the obligation of its precepts, and the purity of its examples, no man need to tremble for the ark of God. A roof is not the less necessary to a house, because it is not to be laid as a foundation: nor are works less necessary because they cannot justify us before God. Let them but stand in their proper place, and they are as necessary as faith itself.

2. How deluded are they who hold the truth in unrighteousness!

There are doubtless many who profess to believe in Christ, while yet by their works they utterly deny him. There was one of this description even in the family of Christ himself. But will the faith which they exercise, be sufficient to save them? No: their faith is dead, being alone: it is no better than the faith of devils: nor will it be productive of any benefit to their souls: yea rather, inasmuch as it argued light and knowledge, it will only enhance their guilt, and aggravate their condemnation. Let those who are not occupied in a careful imitation of their Lord, and an unreserved obedience to his will, know assuredly, that if, on the one hand, he that believeth shall be saved, so, on the other hand, "the unrighteous shall not inherit the kingdom of heaven."

3. How great are the obligations of God's people to walk circumspectly! The world will judge of the gospel, not so much by what they hear, as by what they see. Now, though they have no right to act thus, we should be careful not to lay a stumbling-block before them. We should endeavor rather to make a good impression on their minds, and to give them no occasion from our conduct to speak evil of the truth itself. We should shew them by our lives, that their fears respecting the licentious tendency of the gospel are groundless. By walking as it becometh saints, we should put to silence their ignorant objections, and constrain them to confess, that, however the gospel may be dishonored by its friends, or calumniated by its enemies, it is indeed a doctrine according to godliness.

OF GOD AND HIS NATURAL PERFECTIONS.

John iv. 24.—God is a spirit. (H.)

THE existence of God, and several of his perfections, open themselves with shining evidence in his works, and in his word; but the manner of his existence, and the eminent perfections, as they really exist in him, are wrapped up in thick and awful darkness, as a pavilion round about him. These are far, infinitely far, above our reach; "who by searching can find out God?" Job vi. 7. We can easier say what he is not than what he is. O, may he assist our thoughts, lest we darken counsel by words without knowledge while we speak concerning him!

I. THAT THERE IS BUT ONE GOD, OR ONE DIVINE BEING.

That there is only one God is the concurring language of the genuine light of nature, and of scripture revelation. We are led into this sentiment,

1. By the light of nature.

The very notion it gives us of a God, and the very same arguments by which it proves that there is a God, must, if duly pursued, necessarily lead us into the thought, that there can be no more gods than one; for there can be but one necessarily existent Being, one first Cause, one absolutely infinite, one Supreme. Hence, though the rude, unthinking multitude among the pagans were led, perhaps chiefly by the wild fictions of the poets, into the absurd notion of gods many, and lords many, yet the soberer and wiser of their philosophers had their one supreme God, and all the rest were looked upon but as petty deities. Their most celebrated writers go into this way of representing things; and it is notorious, that Socrates fell a sacrifice to Athenian fury, for asserting the doctrine of one God. But we are still more abundantly assured of this important doctrine.

2. By scripture revelation.

The great and blessed God himself has given us the clearest evidence of his unity in his word. "I, even I, am he. Deut. xxxii. 39. Before me there was no God formed. Isa. xliii. 10. I am the first" Isa. xlvi. 6.

70

And the sacred writers, under Divine inspiration, have said of him, ' The Lord he is God." Deut. iv. 35. And, " Hear, O Israel (Deut. vi. 4 ;) and, Thou art great," says the Psalmist. Ps. lxxxvi. 10.

All this is evidently brought over by our Lord into the doctrine of the New Testament; he told the scribe that came to question him, The first of all the commandments. Mark xii. 29. And he spoke with high approbation of the answer, ver. 32. 34.

II. THAT THIS GOD IS A SPIRIT, OR THAT HE IS A SPIRITUAL BEING.

God is a Spirit. This relates to the nature of God, and as a spirit is the most excellent of beings that we have any notions of, God is represented under this character, to heighten our thoughts of him. We indeed know but little of the nature of spirits. The most natural obvious thought that arises in our minds about a spirit is that it is an incorporeal and invisible being, with life and action, understanding and will.

Let us then a little consider these, as applicable to God.

1. He is incorporeal and invisible.

All corporeal beings consist of parts, and so are in their own nature capable of separation or dissolution, of alterations, additions, or diminutions, and of different figures, sizes, shapes or forms; but all this argues composition and imperfection.

God can indeed, by his infinite power, make what visible appearances he pleases, as he did in various forms under the Old Testament, and at Christ's baptism and transfiguration, in the New ; but these were not appearances of the essence of God itself, they were only outward symbols, which he occasionally formed to notify his presence for special purposes ; but as to his own nature, or essence, he is the " invisible God, whom no man has seen, nor can see." Col. i. 15 ; 1 Tim. vi. 16. Accordingly our Lord says of his Father, " Ye have neither heard his voice. John v. 37.

Whenever therefore we read in scripture of any representations of God, as having eyes, ears; or, as seeing, hearing, we are by no means to imagine, that he hath such bodily organs, or acts by them ; for, " To whom will you liken God ?" Isa. xl. 18.

2. He lives and acts, or is a being that has life and action.

He is usually styled, by way of eminence, the living God : he has life in himself and with him is the fountain of life." John v. 26 ; Ps. xxxvi. 9. All the life of the vegetative, animal and rational world ; the life of nature, and the life of grace here, and the life of glory hereafter, are of him, and derived from him ; and therefore he himself must live,

And as he is a living, so he is an active spirit; he is ever active within himself, in the communion of the sacred Three with each other in the one undivided Godhead, ever active in his purposes and designs to display his own glory, and particularly the riches of his glory in and through a Redeemer. And he is ever capable of acting out of himself. He hath been, is, and ever will be, incessantly active, in upholding, exciting, or restraining, guiding, and governing all that he has made, to the glory of his own great name ; for, " Of him, through him," Rom. xi. 36.

3. He has an understanding and will.

Had not God an understanding, he could never have designed any thing ; and had he not a will, he could never have determined upon the execution of any design. "How manifold are his works !" Ps. civ. 24. "And he works all things," Eph. i. 11. " He is wonderful in counsel," Isa. xxviii. 29. "And he does according to his will." Dan. iv. 35.

III. THAT GOD IS AN INFINITELY PERFECT SPIRIT.

By his being an infinitely perfect Spirit, we may understand, that he is a Spirit, possessed of all possible perfections.

1. God is an infinite Spirit.

Nothing short of infinity can be ascribed to God ; for he can neither limit his own being and perfections, nor can he be limited by any other. The farther our notions go to inquiries after him, the more they lose themselves in solemn wonder at his unsearchable greatness. But, O ! how do we feel ourselves ingulphed, and, as it were, blinded with dazzled light, and lost in our darkness and nothingness, when we read the magnificent accounts the sacred oracles give of him ! " Behold the nations are as a drop of a bucket." Isa. xl. 15. 17.

2. He is a self-sufficient, independent Spirit.

His existence is of himself, not as an effect from its cause ; but he is of himself, as necessarily existing by the essential perfection of his own nature, without dependance on any other being. His name is, "I AM THAT I AM ;" and " He only has immortality, in and of himself." 1 Tim. vi. 16. And as he is, by the perfection of his nature, self-sufficient for his own being, so he is for his own glory and blessedness. He is "exalted in himself above all blessing and praise." Neh. ix. 5. His name is El Shaddai, God all-sufficient, and he is " the Lord that maketh all things." Isa. xliv. 24. " For his pleasure they are and were created. But none can be profitable to God." Rev. iv. 11.

3. He is an eternal Spirit.

His self-sufficiency and independency make it impossible that he should ever begin to be, or cease from being. "Before the mountains were brought forth." Ps. xc. 2. He is without beginning, and without succession, of time or age. " The Lord shall endure for ever." Ps. ix. 7, and cii. 27.

4. He is an unchangeable Spirit.

" With him there is no variableness, nor shadow of turning." James i 17. There can be no change in him, as to posture, situation, or place.

He is unchangeable in his being and perfections.

He is unchangable in his glory. Though the manifestations of his glory, and due ascriptions of it to him, may vary; yet he is, and ever was, infinitely glorious in himself.

His blessedness is as unchangeable as his glory ; for as this consists in the enjoyment of himself, so it neither can be increased nor lessened. "Look into the heavens and see. Job xxxv. 5—7. And it may be said of our Lord's own mediatorial goodness, that it "extendeth not to him," so as that he should be a real gainer by it. Ps. xvi. 2.

He is unchangeable in his decrees. " He is of one mind, who can turn him ? The counsel of the Lord standeth forever." Ps. xxxiii. 11. And he has proclaimed with the majesty of a God, " My counsel shall stand." Isa. xlvi. 10. 11.

And he is unchangeable in his covenant, love and promises, to his people ; for, " The mountains shall depart." Isa. liv. 10. " I am the Lord, I change not." Mal. iii. 6.

Whenever therefore, we read in scripture of God's repenting. and the like. it is not to be understood, of any alteration in his purposes ; but all such expressions are to be understood with relation to his outward dispensations. All those affections of love, joy, grief, and hatred ; that are ascribed to God · these are not properly affections, that take their turns in his heart, as they do in ours ; but they are expressions of the agreeableness, or disagreeableness, of persons and things to his holy nature.

5. He is an omnipresent Spirit.

His infinite essence spreads, in an inconceivaole manner through infinite space, without any parts or bounds : it is intimately near to, and in all creatures, in all places, in heaven, earth and hell, and in all possible space that is between and beyond them. " Do not I fill heaven and earth, says the Lord ? He is not far from any of us, for in him we live. Wherever we are. whatever we do, and whithersoever we go, there is no flying away from God, " Though they dig into hell, thence shall mine hand take them ; though they climb up to heaven, thence will I bring them down." Amos ix. 2, 3. And the Psalmist, in his elegant description of him says, " Whither shall I go from thy Spirit." Ps. cxxxix. 7—10.

Whenever, therefore, we read of God's dwelling in the heavens, coming down from thence, and drawing near to us ; or, of forsaking us, and returning to his place, and the like ; such expressions are not to be understood as if, in his natural being, he were more in one place than another ; but they are to be understood of his actions, and manifestations of himself, in a way of mercy or judgment.

6. He is an all-knowing Spirit.

His omnipresence is with all intelligence attending it, because he is an omnipresent Spirit. " His understanding is infinite. There is not any creature that is not manifest in his sight." Heb. iv. 13. He knows all our works and ways. " His eyes are upon the ways of man, and he seeth all his goings." Job xxxiv, 21, 22. He knows all the secret thoughts of our hearts, all our inmost principles. " The righteous God trieth the hearts and reins." Hence Peter could make this humble appeal to Christ, " Lord, thou knowest all things. John xxi. 17.

And as to all things past, and to come, he challenges the gods of the heathen, as incapable of knowing them like him. " Let them show the former things, what they be." Isa. xli. 22. 23. But known unto the Lord are all his works." Acts xv. 18. And he " calls those things that are not as though they were."

All these things he knows of himself without information from others, and without any external medium to assist him ; for " who has taught him knowledge ? Isa. xl. 14. " He that teacheth man knowledge, shall not he know ?" He knows every thing perfectly and distinctly with the utmost accuracy " Yea, the darkness hideth not from him." Ps. cxxxix. 12. " The very hairs of our head are all numbered." His knowledge is ever the same ; it is perpetual and everlasting. " He neither slumbers nor sleeps ;" and " a thousand years in his sight are but as yesterday." Ps. cxxi. 4 ; xc. 4.

7. He is an almighty Spirit.

He is able to do all that can be the object of power, and that is every thing that does not imply a contradiction, either to his own perfections, or to the nature of things themselves. " By the word of the Lord were the heavens made." Ps. xxxiii. 6. 9. And, " he is able to do exceeding abundantly, above all that we can ask or think." Eph. iii. 20.

Application.

1. How absurd and abominable are all pretended images or pictures of God.

None can draw the figure, or carve the image of his own soul. How monstrously foolish, then, must it be, to offer any visible portraiture of the invisible God. Jer. x. 8—14. It changeth the truth of God into a lie, and degrades the glory of the incorruptible God into the likeness of corruptible creatı res. Rom. i. 23—25. What awful sentiments should we entertain of the gıeat God, and what solemn regards to him!

Wıth what serious attention and spiritual frames of heart, should we worship! with what adoring reverence and profound humility should we ever think and speak of him! With what subjection, resignation and obedience, should we yield up our souls without reserve to him? With what solemnity should we consider ourselves, as his entire dependents, as always in his sight and presence, as accountable to him for all that we think, say, or do.

3. What a dreadful enemy, and what a comfortable friend, must this great God be?

It is a fearful thing to fall into the hands of the living God, Ezek. xxii. 14. "Who can stand before his indignation?" But O, who can rate the happiness of having an interest in the favor of the infinite, eternal, unchangeable, and almighty God! In his favor is life, and his loving kindness is better than life. The eternal God is the people's refuge; and, "If God be for us, who can be against us?"

4. How thankfully should we embrace a gospel revelation, which opens the way of sinful creatures access to God and acceptance with him through a Redeemer.

Without this discovery of him, every thought of his greatness must make creatures, conscious of guilt, tremble before him; but in Christ we may behold him as a Father of mercies, and a God of all consolation.

THE MORAL PERFECTIONS OF GOD.

Matt. v. 48.—Your Father which is in heaven is perfect. (H.)

THE knowledge of God being necessary to the practice of true religion it greatly concerns us to form just apprehensions of him. The natural perfections of the Divine Being have been represented; those that are commonly called moral are the subject of the present. Moral perfections are the same in God and creatures, as to kind, though infinitely different, as to degrees; what we read in the verse of the text plainly supposes this, "Be ye perfect, even as your Father which is in heaven is perfect."

The perfections of the moral sort, which we find ascribed to God in his word, may be reduced to these; wisdom, goodness, holiness, justice, and truth. These shall be now distinctly considered; and under each particular, I shall endeavor to show what practical improvement should be made of it by us; then conclude with some general reflections.

I. GOD IS PERFECTLY WISE.

Wisdom implies knowledge; it is the right use of knowledge; it lies not only in the understanding, but in the will. He acts wisely, whose will is directed by right reason, who does that which is fit to be done. This excelleth folly as far as light excelleth darkness. Nor is it less evident, that wisdom belongs to God. With what brightness does his wisdom shine in his works! How vast are his schemes of creation, providence, and redemption! With what exquisite skill are their various parts contrived and adjusted, to promote his grand design! The Psalmist was thrown into a rapture at the contemplation of some of God's works here below; when he viewed their beautiful order, he cried out, "O Lord, how manifold are thy works! in wisdom hast thou made them all." The consideration of a particular branch of Divine Providence, had the same effect upon the apostle, which he thus expressed: "O the depth of the riches!" How has he abounded towards us in all wisdom and prudence in the contrivance of the method of our redemption by Christ Jesus! The publication of this is spoken of as a discovery of God's manifold wisdom. Eph. iii. 10.

It has pleased the Father of lights to "teach us more than the beasts of the earth." Job xxxv. 11. He has communicated much larger measures of his wisdom to the angels, who dwell in the regions of light; yet the scripture speaks as if the character of wise was peculiar to him: he is styled again and again, "The only wise God, who is wonderful in counsel."

The practical improvement.

1. We should be hereby excited to seek wisdom. To this we are exhorted: "Get wisdom, get understanding." Prov. iv. 5—7. Let this engage our greatest care and most diligent application. There is hardly any thing of which men are more ambitious, than to be thought wise: it would be happy for them if they were as much concerned to obtain true wisdom. The fear of the Lord is the beginning, or the principal part of wisdom; and the knowledge of the holy is understanding.

2. Is God perfectly wise? then we should ask wisdom of him. "If any man lack wisdom, let him ask of God." Would you be made wise unto salvation, apply to Christ Jesus, "in whom are hid all treasures of wisdom. He is made of God wisdom to those that are in him."

3. Is God perfectly wise? then certainly it becomes us to resign to his will, and acquiesce in his appointments. What can be more reasonable than that we leave him to govern the world, who made it so wisely.

II. GOD IS PERFECTLY GOOD.

His other attributes are rendered amiable and engaging to us by his goodness: it is upon the account of this, that he bears the endearing character of Father, in relation to us, which is given him in the text; "Your Father which is in heaven." It was goodness that moved him to create the world; and as the good pleasure of God raised the universe out of nothing, so is his goodness poured out, as it were, upon all his works.. Moses, when he writes the history of the creation, closes his account of every day's work with this expression, "God saw that it was good."

How extensive is the Divine goodness! "The Lord is good unto all. Ps. cxlv. 2—15. The earth is full of the goodness of the Lord." It is said to be great above the heavens. Ps. cviii. 4. It shines in the upper world with amazing lustre; there is no exhausting of this, it endureth for ever.

1. Is God perfectly good? then all our powers ought to be awakened to bless his name. The sense which the Psalmist had of God's goodness, made him press his soul with great earnestness to offer praise unto him upon this account. "Bless the Lord, O my soul." Ps. ciii. How often does he repeat that wish in Ps. cvii. 21. "O that men would praise the Lord for his goodness."

2. Is God perfectly good? how hateful then should sin be unto us. As our sinfulness illustrates the goodness of God, their being committed against an infinitely good God, adds an inconceivable weight to our guilt. The riches of God's goodness leads men to repentance; not only as they encourage their return to God, but as they manifest the great evil of their transgressions.

3. Is God perfectly good? Ought it not to be our ambition to imitate his goodness? "To do good, forget not. Do good to them that hate you."

III. GOD IS PERFECTLY HOLY.

To be holy doth often signify in the scriptures to be set apart from a common and ordinary, to a peculiar and excellent use. In this sense the Sabbath-day is styled holy; and the character of holy may be given to God, to denote the transcendant excellencies of his nature, whereby he is infinitely separated and distinguished from all other beings. Again, by holiness, the word of God frequently means a separation from moral evil. "As he that has called you is holy." 1 Pet. i. 15. Perfecting holiness in the fear of God, stands in opposition to all filthiness both of flesh and spirit. Without doubt, God is infinitely holy in this respect. "God is light, and in him is no darkness at all," *i. e.* no moral imperfection. He is without iniquity. "He is of purer eyes than to behold evil." But there is something positive in God's holiness. The beauty of holiness, which is a description given of God, must needs signify not only a freedom from all blemishes, but the possession of every thing that is excellent and amiable.

The holiness of God is a perfection, for the honor of which he has a very high regard; therefore he swears by it. "Once have I sworn by my holiness." Ps. lxxxix. 35. It is his most distinguishing style, that he is glorious in holiness. The seraphim cried one to another, "Holy, holy, holy, is the Lord of Hosts."

Use.

We should press it on our conscience, as a most powerful argument to induce us to follow after holiness. Thus God condescends to reason with us; "Be ye holy, for I am holy." They and they only are blessed who dwell in his presence; this shall be the felicity of those who are truly sanctified. "Blessed are the pure in heart, for they shall see God." If we would not be debarred a blissful sight of God, let us "follow after holiness." Heb. xii. 14.

IV. GOD IS PERFECTLY JUST.

Justice is commonly distinguished into commutative and distributive. Commutative justice lies in an equal exchange of benefits; and ought to be observed by us in our dealings with each other. But such are the perfections of God, so entire is our dependance upon him, that it is impossible we should lay any obligations on him; therefore this sort of justice can have no place in his transactions with us. "Who hath first given unto the Lord?"

Distributive justice, which ought to be exercised by rulers towards their subjects, consists in the equitable distribution of rewards and punishments. We may be sure, that God is a righteous governor. Men, notwithstanding their most careful inquiries, may be imposed on by false evidence. But all things are naked and open unto God.

Again, the great God cannot be awed by any power to pervert judgment. "Surely the Almighty will not pervert judgment." Job xxxiv. 11, 12.

God cannot be biassed by the prospect of any profit to depart from that which is right; this is a spring of a great deal of injustice among men. But the Most High is infinitely above every temptation of this kind. "The Lord your God is God of gods. Deut. x. 17. He is a righteous lord, and he loveth righteousness."

The judgments of God are a great deep; they cannot be fathomed by us at present: but his righteousness is like the great mountains, very obvious. "Righteous art thou, O Lord." How we ought to be affected with this perfection of God!

1. Should not the consideration of God's justice awaken in us an holy awe of him? The Psalmist declares, that his flesh trembled for the fear of God: he was afraid of his judgments.

2. Is God perfectly just? Is it not then of the greatest concern to us guilty creatures, that we be found in Jesus Christ. Should we not, without delay, apply ourselves to Christ, " whom God hath set forth to be a propitiation through faith in his blood." Rom. iii. 25, 26.

Perfectly true, which is the

V. and last, of the DIVINE PERFECTIONS.

This, as it is a moral virtue, signifies a conformity of words to thoughts, then it is styled veracity; and a conformity of actions to words, then it is called faithfulness. God is perfectly true in each of these respects: as it is impossible for him to be deceived, so it is certain that he will not deceive. "A God of truth. Deut. xxxii. 4. His faithfulness shall never fail. The mountains shall depart. Isa. liv. 10. It is impossible for God to lie." Heb. vi. 18. Nor is God liable to a change of mind. " He is not a man, that he should lie."

1. We may hence learn, that we ought heartily to embrace whatever God has revealed to us : though our reason cannot comprehend it, yet if we have sufficient evidence of its being spoken by God, we may be sure it is true.

2. We may hence infer the reasonableness of a steadfast reliance on God's promises. Great is the guilt of those who will not believe God; they are said to make him a liar.

Reflections.

1. It should yield us great satisfaction to consider, that such a perfect being as God is, governs the world; who is infinitely wise, good, holy, just, and true.

2. We should, in our contemplations of God, and conduct towards him, have a strict regard to the harmony of his attributes. He never displays any one of his excellences, but in a consistence with the honor of the rest.

3. Blessed are they, who upon good grounds can call this perfect Being their Father and their God. That this may be our happiness, let us sincerely give up ourselves to God, through Christ, and take him to be our portion for ever. " Whom have I in heaven but thee?"

THE PROVIDENCE OF GOD IN THE NATURAL WORLD.

Psalm ciii. 19.—The Lord hath prepared his throne in the heavens, and his kingdom ruleth over all. (H.)

THIS is a very grand representation of the majesty of the great God. As an earthly monarch sits upon his throne, and keeps his court in some one capital city, and from thence extends his dominion and government over the whole kingdom ; so, in allusion hereunto, the great and mighty God, who is King of kings, and Lord of lords, is here represented as having prepared his throne in the heavens, and from thence extending his sovereign dominion and influence as wide as universal nature, over all creatures, and over all worlds. By the kingdom of God, we are here to understand his providence, or his preserving and governing all his creatures, and all their actions. The subjects of this universal kingdom may be distinguished into natural and moral :—by the moral world, we mean, the rational part of the creation, or those creatures who are fit subjects of a moral law, as angels and men, considered as reasonable creatures. By the natural world, we understand the whole mass of matter, which is variously disposed into a multitude of shapes and forms, and different sorts of creatures, as sun, moon, and stars, air, earth, and sea; with all the vast variety with which they are stored, and by which they are inhabited. God's providential kingdom is absolutely universal, and over all. But at prevent, consider the providence of God, as the preserver and sovereign disposer of all things, in the natural world only.

I. To prove that there is a PROVIDENCE, which presides over the whole course of nature, and all the world of creatures. This may be argued,

1. From the perfections of God: and of those we need only single out his knowledge and his wisdom, his goodness and his power; for if we believe that God is infinitely possessed of such perfections as these, it will hardly be possible for us to stop short of believing his providence. For will not his wisdom and goodness incline him to take care of his creatures, and govern them in the best manner? Can we suppose the universal Parent of all creatures and worlds, to be like the foolish ostrich? Job xxxix. 16. And since God is almighty, no reasonable doubt can remain of his providence.

2. One may produce many express testimonies out of scripture, for the proof of a Providence. It is said, that God upholdeth all things; and that they continue according to his ordinance. "He appointeth the moon for seasons. Ps. civ. 19. He bringeth the winds out of his treasure." Ps. civ. 24, 25, 27. God is the supreme governor among the nations. This providence of God presides not only over great and important affairs, but it reaches to the minutest creatures. As in Matt. x. 29, 30—"Are not two sparrows sold for a farthing?" But I should transcribe a great part of the Bible, should I collect all the proofs. I will only farther hint to you one article of the doctrine of providence, which we learn from scripture, viz. "That the kingdom of Providence is administered by Christ our Saviour. It is by him that all things consist. Col. i. 17. And to him is all power given." Matt. xxviii. 18. The whole administration of Providence, over all creatures, and all worlds, is committed into the hands of the Mediator, Jesus Christ; which speaks both the dignity of his person, and the safety and happiness of his friends and people. If any farther proof were wanting, one might,

3. Appeal to the appearance of things: to the frame of nature, and the continued order and harmony of the whole creation; where we have as good testimonies to a providence, as to the very being of a God. Can it be only by chance, that day and night, and summar and winter so regularly succeed to one another? Did all things happen by mere chance, it would be altogether uncertain when spring or the autumn season would come; or whether either of them would come any more; nay, it would be ten thousand times more likely, that all things would presently run into confusion and disorder. It is, therefore, most reasonable to ascribe it to the providence of God, that "seed time and harvest." Gen. viii. 22.

II. To explain and illustrate the PROVIDENCE OF GOD IN THE NATURAL WORLD, by some of the principal acts of it.

1. The providence of God is exercised in preserving his creatures.

1. In the preservation of the several species or kinds of animal creatures; so that though all the individuals die, one after another, yet no species, is lost out of the creation, but most probable, and as far as we can learn from the most ancient account of things, there are all sorts of creatures still in the

world, that were at first.   And this is truly wonderful, if we consider what a natural enmity there is betwixt some animals, and others, and with what diligence men have endeavored, in all ages to destroy some whole kinds of them.   The due proportion of the various inhabitants of the world to one another; and especially of the males to the females, which is so constantly preserved throughout the animal creation, is a very sensible instance of providential care.

2. God preserves them by his providence in their individual beings, until the end has been answered for which he made them.   It is God that holdeth our soul in life.   In him we live.   We are the living instances of Divine preservation: hitherto God has helped us.   Nor is God's providential care confined to man.   " He heareth the young raven cry.   Not a sparrow falls to the ground."

2. As God preserves, so he also disposes of, and governs his creatures, and their actions by his providence.

1. The inanimate creatures.   He who fixed the laws of nature in the first creation, does still by his providence continue their force and power.   " He binds the sweet influences of Pleiades, and looses the band of Orion.   Job xxxviii. 31, &c.   He giveth the former, and the latter rain; and he stays the bottles of heaven."   Thus does God keep the springs of universal nature in his own hand, and turns them which way soever he pleaseth.

2. The whole animal creation.   " The beasts of the forest are his, and the cattle upon a thousand hills;" they are all his creatures, and the subjects of his providence.   What but a Providence could direct every beast, bird, and insect, where to seek its food, and its habitation?   Or teach every parent-animal, how to take the properest care of its young?   Or, what is it that conducts those birds, who shift their country and climate at certain seasons of the year, in their passage to some distant land, where multitudes of them never were before?   " The stork in the heavens knoweth her appointed times."   Jer. viii. 7.   Had they reason like men, how little would it help them to find their way through the pathless air, without needle or compass?   What is their guide, but Providence.

III. To lay before you some of the most REMARKABLE PROPERTIES OF GOD'S PROVIDENCE, as it appears in the natural world.

1. The wisdom of Providence.   A property so remarkable, that one may apply those words of the apostle to the mysteries of Providence, as well as those of grace: " O the depth of the riches!"   How is the wisdom of God displayed in his preserving and governing the whole frame of nature!   It is by this the " sparrow is directed to find a house, and the swallow a nest for herself."   How admirably is the wisdom of Providence displayed in the different instinct of the various tribes of animals!   Can we observe these things, and a thousand more of the same kind, and not confess and admire the wisdom of Providence.

Or, if we hearken to the voice even of storms and tempests, they will farther declare to us the admirable wisdom of that God, whose word they obey, and whose designs they execute.   Who, upon a view of the wisdom of Providence in the natural world, can forbear saying, " O Lord, how manifold are thy works!"

2. The goodness and kindness of it.   And we need not go far for instances and proofs of this; for " the earth is full of the goodness of the Lord."   Ps. xxxiii. 5.   There is not a creature that lives in all the world, but bears a testimony to the goodness of Providence.   " These all wait upon God, and he giveth them their meat in due season."   Ps civ 27, 28.   God extends his

kind regard to many thousands of creatures, who have no capacity of knowing and praising their Benefactor. "Shall not I spare Nineveh (saith God,) that great city?" Jonah iv. 11. "He causeth the grass to grow for the cattle." Ps. civ. 14, 15. And as God has plentifully stored the earth with the blessings of his goodness, so his providence kindly directs us to find out the various uses, whether for food or physic, for necessary support, or for convenience, and delight.

3. It is very powerful. God upholdeth all things by the word of his power. The continued harmony of nature and the constant and regular revolutions of seasons, are sensible demonstrations of the power of God. "Thou hast established the earth." Ps. cxix. 90, 91. God brings forth Mazaroth in his season, he guides Arcturus with his sons. He reneweth the face of the earth after the dearth of winter. And the same almighty God, who created this world at first, and still upholds the whole frame of nature, will one day display his mighty power, by dissolving it again, and changing it into another form. "The day of the Lord will come as a thief in the night." 2 Pet. iii. 10—13.

Improvement.

1. To raise our admiring thoughts to the great God. What a great and mighty Being must he be, who is able thus to wield and manage the whole frame of nature! "How large and manifold is his wisdom. He satisfieth the desire of every living thing."

2. We may infer, how terrible the wrath of this great and mighty God must be, and of what importance it is to secure his favor. So Pharoah and the Egyptians found it a very dreadful thing to have that God against them, "whose kingdom ruleth over all;" who had beast and insects, hail and fire, &c., absolutely at his disposal. Only to be without God in the world, to be without his favor, is a very sad circumstance; how much worse to have him for our enemy. How much is it to our interest, while as yet there is hope, to seek after reconciliation and peace with this great and terrible God! And if we return to him, in his appointed way, he will be at peace with us, yea he will "delight over us, to bless us." Rom. viii. 28.

3. Let the reconciled friends and people of God learn from hence to trust and acquiesce in Providence: "It is the Lord that gives, and the Lord that takes away. He that spared not his own Son."

4. Let us learn to observe and adore the providence of God in all that befalls us, and to bless him for all our enjoyments and comforts. What love, and duty, and honor, do all men owe to him, "whose tender mercies are over all his works!"

THE GOVERNMENT OF THE LORD GOD OMNIPOTENT.

Revelation xix. 6.—And I heard as it were the voice of a great multitude, and as the voice of many waters, and as the voice of mighty thunderings, saying, Alleluia: for the Lord God omnipotent reigneth. (Sk.)

THE total overthrow of Babylon, or papal Rome, is predicted in the preceding chapter; and, on the fall of that apostate church, the inhabitants of heaven unite in a song of praise in which they ascribe salvation, and glory, and honor, and power unto the Lord their God, whose judgments are true and righteous. In consequence of that event, the four and twenty elders and the four beasts fall down, and worship God on his throne, saying, "Amen, Alleluia;" and a voice came out of the throne, saying, "Praise our God, all ye his servants, and ye that fear him, both small and great." Then the beloved John heard as it were the voice of a great multitude, and as the voice of many waters resembling the roaring of the sea, and as the voice of mighty thunderings, or loud peals of thunder, saying, "Alleluia: for the Lord God omnipotent reigneth."

I. THE LORD GOD OMNIPOTENT REIGNETH.

1. *The church of Rome reigned over the nations many ages.* Her government was so strong, that no power less than Omnipotence could overthrow it. She ruled with a rod of iron—shed the blood of saints—trampled princes under her feet—and lived in honor, ease, and luxury. Her policy was as deep as hell, her works resembled those of the devil, and her end was a lake of fire, ver. 3.

2. *But the time is at hand when it will be said.* "Babylon the great is fallen, is fallen;" her *power* is *broken*, her *glory* is *faded*, her *wealth* has taken its flight, Prov. xxiii. 5; her oppressions have ceased, and she is now utterly burned with fire, chap. xviii. 8. Thus every thing which exalted itself against God, or against truth and holiness, shall be destroyed, 2 Thess. ii. 4—8.

3. *Then this song shall be sung,—"The Lord God omnipotent reigneth."* He has reigned in the heavenly world, and over the system of nature, ever since he created the holy angels, and the material world; but now he reigneth over men, whose rebellion against his high authority has come to an end. He reigneth in the hearts of believers; in the church, which is his spiritual kingdom; and men of every rank and degree bow down to his authority, Ps. ciii. 19.

4. *It is fit and right that the Lord God omnipotent should reign.* To prove this great truth, let us state, with clearness, the following observations. All things were *created* by the Lord God omnipotent, Rev. iv. 7;—his *wisdom* is a depth which cannot be fathomed, Rom. xi. 33;—his *power* is uncontrollable, Ps. cxxxv. 5. 6;—his *presence* is unlimited, Ps. cxxxix. 7—12; —his *justice* never swerves from what is right, Gen. xviii. 25;—his *purity* is as the light of heaven, 1 John i. 7;—his *goodness* extends to all, Ps. cxlv. 9;—and his *truth* endureth for ever, Ps. c. 5. On a view of these adorable perfections, who would not devoutly pray, "Thy kingdom come!"

5. *The government of the Lord God omnipotent is absolute.* Absolute monarchies among men are *absurd*, because all human beings are *imperfect;* but as every possible perfection meets and unites in Jehovah, it is highly proper that the whole power of government should be placed in his hands. He may employ agents and instruments to carry on his great designs; but he should hold the reigns of government, that he may guide and direct all things in wisdom and goodness, to their proper ends.

6. *And of his government there will be no end.* Mighty empires among men have come to an end. The *Assyrian*, founded by Nimrod, continued about fourteen hundred years; the *Persian*, established by Cyrus, son of Cambyses, continued about two hundred years; the *Grecian*, founded by Alexander the Great, lasted about three hundred years; the *Roman* was more extensive, and endured much longer: but they all "passed away as a flood, or as a tale that is told." Blessed, then, be the Most High, who liveth for ever, and "whose dominion is an everlasting dominion," and whose "kingdom is from generation to generation," Dan. iv. 34; Ps. cxlvi. 10.

II. His subjects should praise him, and sing alleluia.

1. The Hebrew word literally signifies, " Praise ye the Lord." It was often sung by the Jews in the synagogue, but is now transferred to the Christian church. An eminent writer observes, that 'this is the first time the word occurs in the New Testament;' and that 'this word being Hebrew, may be taken for the Christian church's invitation of the Jews, or Hebrews, to join with them in praising God; and being so often used here, implies that Christ shall be praised by the Jews also, now, after Rome's destruction.'

2. *The government of the Lord furnishes matter of praise to all his subjects.* It puts an end to war, and restores *peace* and order among men; it promotes human *happiness* in every possible degree; it puts an end to the *tyranny* of wicked men, sin, and the devil: it places men under the secure *protection* of almighty power: it is a *mild, equitable* and *holy* government; it is *firm* and stable: and its foundations are "righteousness and judgment," Ps. xcvii. 2.

3. *He should be praised for condescending to govern men.* Some men have denied the being of God, Ps. liii. 1, and others, his knowledge of human affairs, Ps. lxiii. 11; but we have indubitable proofs of his being, and comfortable assurances of his watchful care, 1 Pet. iv. 7. We admit that he is *inconceivably* great and glorious, and that it is *infinitely* condescending in him to notice the highest order of celestial spirits; but he is mindful of man, Ps. viii. 4, and he knoweth them that trust in him, Nahum i. 7.— " Praise ye the Lord."

4. *Praise him for receiving you into his kingdom.* You were strangers and foreigners, but are now "fellow citizens with the saints," Eph. ii. 19; you entered into the kingdom by regeneration, which was a work wrought in you by the Spirit of God, John iii. 3, 6; and you now share all the privileges of the kingdom. You are highly honored, and greatly blessed; give God the glory, and praise his holy name, Ps. cxvii.

5. *Endeavor to praise him in lofty and exalted strains.* To this end charge your memory with those Scripture phrases which express the high praises of your God. The inspired songs of Zion far exceed all·other compositions in clearness, strength and sublimity. Angels praise the Lord in lofty strains; try to imitate them, Luke ii. 14; and, ere long, you shall praise him in a higher key, with all the redeemed of the Lord. Isa. lxi. 11.

6. *Employ all your powers in his praise.* Praise him in your *hearts*, by cherishing honorable thoughts of his majesty and glory, by warm affections of love and gratitude, and by inward expressions of his goodness and mercy, Ps. ciii. 1, 2; praise him with your *lips*, by speaking honorably of his attributes, works, and ways, Ps. xxxiv. 1; and praise him in your lives, by living in all things to his honor and glory. The inanimate works of creation may be said to praise God by showing forth his greatness and glory; and when our lives abound in good works, every action speaks his praise, Ps. cxlviii. 4, 8, 9.

7. *Offer up united and loud praises.* Let these resemble "the voice of many waters," and "the voice of mighty thunderings." There is a true sublime in sound. 'The burst of thunder or of cannon, the roaring of winds, the shouting of multitudes, the sound of vast cataracts of water, are all incontestibly grand objects.'* The united praises of *one* large congregation are awfully grand: what then will be the united praises of all the servants of God, both small and great! May the whole earth *ring* with the high praises of this great and glorious Being!

* Blair's Rhetoric.

8. *When the prophecy to which our text refers is accomplished, the church will praise the Lord for the utter destruction of papal tyranny.* That glorious event will put an end to dangerous error and delusion—to degrading superstition—to proud intolerance—and to vile oppression. Then truth will triumph over error, and *Dagon* fall before the ark of God; tormenting fear will be cast out; and persecution, in all its forms, will cease for ever.—"Praise ye the Lord."

9. *But even now let us praise the Lord in every state and circumstance of life.* David said, "I will bless the Lord at all times;" let us follow his example. We may see times of peace, and times of war; times of joy, and times of grief; times of ease, and times of pain; times of wealth, and times of want; and times of honor and times of disgrace. Our circumstances in life are ever varying; but still the Lord God omnipotent reigneth. ALLELUIA.

10. *Thus employed on earth, we shall be prepared to praise the Lord for ever in the realms of light and glory.* Happy spirits in that world may serve the Lord God in ten thousand different ways; but every thing will be begun, carried on, and ended in praise. This exalted work will be an honor to the arch-angel; and the pleasure attending it will be pure and elevated beyond conception.

> "What a rapturous song, when the glorified throng
>   In the spirit of harmony join;
> Join all the glad choirs, hearts, voices and lyres,
>   And the burden, is "Mercy divine!"
> Hallelujah, they cry, to the King of the sky,
>   To the great everlasting I AM;
> To the Lamb that was slain, and that liveth again,—
>   Hallelujah to God and the Lamb!"

GOD'S APPROBATION OF HIS WORKS.

Gen. i. 31.—And God saw every thing that he had made, and behold it was very good. (Sk.)

NOTWITHSTANDING the oppressive load of labor, and care, and sorrow, and temptation, by which we are usually burdened, and the attention we are constrained to bestow on matters which concern food and raiment, and other supplies necessary for ourselves and our dependants, while passing through the present life; the vigorous and immortal mind sometimes disengages herself from her encumbrances, and spurning the low and grovelling pursuits in which she has been detained, plunges into the future; and either anxiously inquires, 'Through what variety of untried being, through what new scenes and changes must I pass?'—or expatiates on the bright and blissful prospects which revelation offers to the eye of faith, and anticipates the period when those prospects shall be realized.

Nor are such excursions confined to the future. Man's future destiny is closely connected with his past and present circumstances. It is therefore natural for us to desire to inform ourselves concerning that part of the history of our species which relates the most important events of former times. Here again revelation comes to our assistance; and in its sacred pages, and particularly in the chapter in which our text is found, carries us back, through a variety of most interesting occurrences, even to the birth of time itself. In this light our text appears to be of considerable consequence: for while it furnishes matter of history the most ancient aud venerable, it asserts some important natural truths, and suggests by way of inference, several others of the moral kind. Let us consider,

I. THE NATURAL TRUTHS ASSERTED. Among these the text asserts,

1st. *The true origin of all things.* "And God saw every thing that *he had made.*" Of this, plain as it may now appear, it is highly probable we should have no conception, but for what the Bible has taught us; for though it may be easily demonstrated, that matter cannot have created itself, yet it will not so easily follow, that it must have had a creator. We acquire our stock of ideas by experience; and a creation out of nothing is so different from all the experience of mankind, that some philosophers, as Aristotle and his followers, supposed the world to have been eternal; while others, as the Epicureans, conjectured that the matter, the atoms only of which it was composed, was eternal, and that they happened by chance to fall into their present form and order. And even to this day, the worshippers of Budhoo, perhaps the most numerous sect of idolators in the world, though they acknowledge "*gods many,*" have no notion of a Supreme Creator. "The world by wisdom knew not God." But the Scripture assures us, that the universe is the production of a Being, who is *infinitely free and powerful:* not overruled by a fatal necessity; but whose will is the *law,* as it was the *cause* of nature, verse 1; Ps. xxxiii. 9: Dan. iv. 35; James i. 18: who is *infinitely wise;* whence those works of design and arrangement we every where perceive, Ps. civ. 24, and even that intellect by which we are capable of the perception, and which is only a feeble emanation from the source of intelligence, Job xxxii. 8; Isa. xl. 28: who is *infinitely good;* not a mere intelligence, wise to design and powerful to execute, yet destitute of every thing like moral excellence, but ever respecting what is *right and holy:* and what is *good,* is *best* for his rational creatures. Agreeably to this, our text asserts,

2d. *The original perfection of all things:*—"And God saw *every thing* that he had made, and behold it was *very good.*"

1. *It was very good, as being well adapted to answer its particular intention.* Instance the suitable instrumentality of the heavenly bodies in the diffusion of light; and the adaptation of the eye to receive, by means of that light, impressions of surrounding objects, ver. 14—17. Instance again, the correspondence between the structure of fishes and the waters in which they are to live; and between that of fowls and the lighter element in which they have to fly, ver. 20, 21; and, in short, we might instance all the numerous subjects of what are called astro and physico theology. In this sense it is said concerning the distribution of almost every day, "*it was good,*" ver. 1, 10, 12, &c.

2. *It was very good, as being conducive to the perfection and welfare of the whole.* Here it may be necessary to distinguish between the world as it now is, and as it came out of its Maker's hands. All its glory, beauty, utility, &c. are *remaining* glory, &c.—all its deformity and disadvantages are superinduced. Sin produced a most disastrous change both in the *constitution* and in the *residence* of man. At first there was nothing parched or dreary in the earth, pestilential or tempestuous in the air, scorching in the sun, ferocious in the animal tribes, &c. but the reverse of this. And man especially, was nobly *free, wise* as needful, *righteous* and truly *holy;* Eph iv. 24; Col. iii. 10. Hence,

3. *It was very good as being well calculated to promote the glory of its Maker.* This was the design of the first, as well as of the *new* creation, Eph. iii. 10; Rev. iv. 11. And in the contemplation of themselves and the universe, God's rational offspring found abundant matter of wonder and praise, Job xxxviii. 7. Even now, in this state of disorder which sin has introduced, to minds rightly disposed, "the things that are made" powerfully declare "the invisible things of God, even his eternal power and Godhead," Ps. xix. 1; Rom. i. 20; and prompt the pious reflection,

> "These are thy glorious works, Parent of good,
> Almighty! thine this universal frame,
> Thus wondrous fair! thyself how wondrous then!"

We are therefore, not surprised that the text asserts,

4. *God's approbation of his work.* He saw it "*very* good;" *superlatively* so. This is affirmed of "*every* thing that he had made." We do not say that all parts of the creation are equally *valuable;* see Matt. x. 29—31; yet God *approves* of what is *good* in its *place and nature;* approves as much of the "green herb" or the tuft of "grass," or even of the rock which furnishes moisture for its support, as of the "living creature" which feeds upon it. He is present to every part of his creation; sees the dependance of the parts on each other; and regards them accordingly. Man, in particular, possessed all the perfections consistent with his nature and his circumstances. And to object on the one hand, that he had better not have been blessed with liberty seeing he has abused it, is to say, in effect, that a mere machine is more excellent than an angel?—and on the other to ask, "Why were not all men made angelic or super-angelic beings?" is to propose a foolish question. In the case proposed, there would have been a different class of entities; but we, as men, should have had no existence at all. When any creature has all its powers and properties in perfection, then it is "very good." Such was creation; and such it was in its Maker's esteem. Let us hear,

II. THE MORAL TRUTHS SUGGESTED. Here we may observe,

1. Seeing that God had done for man the utmost that his case admitted, both as respected himself and as respected the world around him, the blessings of which were given him "richly to enjoy," it follows that *man was under the greatest obligations possible*, in his then present circumstances. He might, indeed, become more indebted for a *continuance* and *increase* of unmerited blessings. And *we* have the obligation of *redemption*, in addition to every other, 1 Cor. vi. 20. Hence,

2. *Sin is at once the vilest injustice and the basest ingratitude, imaginable.* It is an unwarrantable appropriation of *time*, and *talents*, and *property*, not our own but another's, and a foul abuse of favors conferred, to the disadvantage and grief of our best benefactor, Isa. i. 2; Mal. i. 6.

3. *A continuance in sin is the most daring imprudence.* According to that constitution of things which was "very good," holiness and happiness went together. Sin, by violating that constitution, 'brought death into the world, with all our wo.' It is an outrage on the principles of our nature; and the ardent flame might as soon cease to burn, as sin to produce misery. This is abundantly confirmed by the threatenings, Prov. xi. 21; 2 Thess. i, 7, 9;—the entreaties, Ezekiel, xviii. 30—32, and xxxiii. 11 —and even the promises of God's word, Isa. lv. 6, 7; Jer iii. 12, 22.

4. *Reformation is well-pleasing to God.* He approved of things in their original state. He is unchangeable; and therefore must disapprove of the

derangement which sin has occasioned; consequently a restoration to their former order must be highly acceptable in his sight. In proof of this, he has provided ample means of moral renovation.—His Son, John iii. 16; 1 John iii, 3.—His word, Ps. xix. 7—10; John xx. 31.—His ministers, 2 Cor. v. 18—20; Col. i. 25—28.—His Spirit, to convince, intercede, strengthen, comfort, &c. John xvi. 8; Rom. viii. 26; Luke xi. 13.

5. *The text suggests a lesson of humility.* "How is the gold become dim!" the divine image effaced! Humility becomes every rational creature, on account of its *debt* and its *dependance.* Unfallen intelligences feel it; much more should we. "The crown is fallen from our head: wo unto us that we have sinned!" Lam. v. 16; Dan. ix. 7. Yet,

6. *The text furnishes ground of hope and encouragement.* It proclaims the *goodness* of him with whom we have to do; and therefore encourages us to hope in his *mercy.* Let us remember however, that it is to the Gospel we are indebted for improving hope into assurance, Rom. viii. 32. And while we cautiously avoid sin, the pest of happiness and the abhorrence of God, let us gratefully acknowledge, as our surest ground of hope, for grace here, and for "the blissful seat" hereafter, that

> " 'Twas great to speak a world from nought,
> 'Twas *greater* to *redeem !*"

GOD'S DELIGHT IN SAVING SINNERS.

Zeph. iii. 17.—The Lord thy God in the midst of thee is mighty: he will save, he will rejoice over thee with joy; he will rest in his love, he will joy over thee with singing. (S. S.)

A knowledge of ourselves will shew us how much need we have of repentance; and a knowledge of God will encourage us to repent. Many are the descriptions which we have of God in the inspired volume; but none deserves our attention more than that before us. In it we behold

I. God's power to save.

We shall not speak of God's power in general, but as it is manifested in the salvation of his church and people. He dwelt "in the midst" of his people in the wilderness; Exod. xl. 38; and displayed his "power to save them" by delivering them from all their enemies, Exod. xiv. 27, 28, and xvii. 14, and supplying all their wants. Ps. lxxvii. 15, 16, 24, 25. Thus is he in the midst of his church at this time; Matt. xviii. 20, and xxviii. 20; and is as able as ever to save his people. For this end he orders every thing by his providence, Rom. viii. 28, and makes his word effectual through the almighty operations of his Holy Spirit. Heb. iv. 12. 2 Cor. x. 4, 5.

II. His determination to save.

If he should leave us to ourselves none of us would be saved. We all say to him, "Depart from us;" Job xxi. 14, 15; nor do we ever turn effectually to him till he has made us willing in the day of his power. John vi. 44. Ps. cx. 3. On this account he takes the matter into his own hands, and determines to save those whom he has given to his Son. John vi. 37. See this exemplified, Jer. iii. 19. Having bought us with the blood of his Son, he will secure us to himself, by the operation of his Spirit. He does not indeed destroy our free agency; but he overcomes our reluctance, Phil. ii.

13, and draws us to himself by an operation not less powerful than that, which he exerted in raising his Son, Jesus Christ, from the dead. Eph. i. 19, 20.

III. His DELIGHT IN SAVING.

There is not any thing so delightful to God as the work of saving sinners. Nor will he merely feel an inward pleasure; but, as a man, overjoyed at any event, involuntarily expresses his joy by singing, or some other outward token, so will God manifest his pleasure to the returning soul. Luke xv. 23, 24. Man by nature knows no greater happiness than that which a bridegroom feels, when, after long suspense and many fears, he is united to his bride. Yet such is the image which God himself uses, to illustrate his joy over returning sinners. Isai. lxii. 5.

IV. His IMMUTABILITY TOWARDS THOSE WHOM HE INTENDS TO SAVE.

Man is often alienated from the object of his affections, either by means of some unexpected evil he has discovered, or through his own fickleness and inconstancy. But God changeth not. Mal. iii. 6. Jam. i. 17. Whom he loveth he loveth to the end. John xiii. 1. He hateth putting away. Mal. ii. 16. And, as he loved his people from eternity, Jer. xxxi. 3, and chose them without any reference to good either seen or foreseen in them, Deut. vii. 7, 8, and ix. 5, 6; so will he not forsake them on account of their infirmities. Isai. liv. 7—10. He will indeed punish their transgressions with all needful severity; Ps. lxxxix. 30—34; but his gifts and callings are without repentance; Rom. xi. 29; nor will he cast off the people, whom he has chosen in Christ, and given to him. 1 Sam. xii. 22. Hos. ii. 19, 20.

USES—In this glorious character of God we may see

1. The evil of sin

Sin, under whatever circumstances it may be committed, is directly levelled against him. Gen. xxxix. 9. Ps. li. 4. And, if our consciences be not seared as with an hot iron, the thought of having so often committed that, which militates against the honor, the authority, and the very existence of such a God, must render us loathsome in our own eyes, and cause us to abhor ourselves in dust and ashes. Ezek. xxxvi. 28, 31. Job xlii. 6.

2. The danger of dying in an unconverted state.

Those to whom our Lord preached, and amongst whom he wrought his miracles, had a far heavier condemnation than they would have received, if they had never enjoyed such advantages. John xv. 22. Matt. xi. 20—24. And will it be no aggravation of our guilt in the day of judgment to have despised such a loving and gracious God? Surely, he will then shew himself mighty to destroy such obdurate rebels; and will feel an abiding satisfaction in vindicating the honor of his insulted majesty, Luke xii. 20; Prov. i. 24—30; Deut. xxviii. 58, 63; as he now would in displaying the riches of his mercy. It will be "a fearful thing to fall into his hands" under such aggravated guilt.

3. The obligation that lies upon believers to serve the Lord.

Have you been selected by God as objects of his unmerited love? Have you been redeemed with the blood of his dear Son? And have you a good hope, that you shall be made eternal monuments of his power and grace? What should you render to the Lord for such benefits? O love him; rejoice in him with joy unspeakable; and rest in your love to him; having no end, no aim, no wish, but to please and honor the God of your salvation.

87

GOD'S CARE FOR THE RIGHTEOUS.

Prov. x. 3.—The Lord will not suffer the soul of the righteous to famish.   (S. S.)

GOD, who is the author and giver of al good, dispenses his blessings no less to the evil and unjust, than to the good and just.   But he promises to those who seek first his kingdom and his righteousness, that all other things shall be added unto them.   To this effect he speaks also in the passage before us.   But though this be the primary import of the text, we must not exclude its relation also to the concerns of the soul.

To elucidate this blessed promise, we shall shew

I. WHAT REASONS THE RIGHTEOUS HAVE TO APPREHEND THAT THEIR SOULS MAY FAMISH.

A sense of weakness and of guilt may greatly discourage them : for

1. They cannot secure provisions for themselves :—

The word of God, and Christ in the word, is the proper food of the soul : and, if a person can read, he need not be wholly destitute.   But it is by the public ministration of the word that God principally confirms the souls of his people.   Now in many places where Christ should be preached, his name is scarcely heard ; and, instead of children's bread, little is dispensed besides the husks of heathen morality.   Even where some attention is paid to christian doctrines, there is often much chaff mixed with the wheat; and " the trumpet that is blown, gives but an uncertain sound."   Those therefore who by reason of distance, or infirmity, or other insurmountable obstacles, cannot have access to the purer fountains of truth, have great reason to fear that their souls will famish.

2. They cannot, of themselves, feed upon the provisions set before them.

Where all the treasures of the gospel are fully opened, it is God alone that can enrich any soul by means of them : even " Paul may plant, or Apollos may water, but it is God alone that can give the increase."   The very same word is often made a peculiar blessing to one, that was altogether useless to another.   God reserves the times and the seasons in his own hands ; and " gives to every one severally as he will."   When therefore the righteous hear of the effects wrought on others, and feel conscious that they themselves reaped no benefit from the word, they are ready to fear that their souls will famish even in the midst of plenty.

3. They well know that they deserve to be utterly abandoned by their God :—

It is not only for their sins in general, that the righteous find occasion to humble themselves before God, but more particularly for their misimprovement of divine ordinances.   Perhaps there is not any other more fruitful source of self-condemnation to the godly than this.   When therefore they see how many opportunities of improvement they have lost, and how much guilt they have contracted by their deadness and formality in the worship of God, they are sensible that God may justly "remove their candlestick," and leave them to experience " a famine of the word."

But lest a dread of famishing should oppress the minds of the righteous, we shall proceed to shew

II. WHAT GROUNDS THEY HAVE TO HOPE, THAT GOD WILL NEVER SUFFER SUCH A MELANCHOLY EVENT TO HAPPEN.

However great the grounds of fear may be which the righteous feel within themselves, they have abundant reason to "encourage themselves in the Lo:¹ their God"

1. He has bountifully provided even for the ungodly

The gospel is "a feast of fat things full of marrow, and of wines on the lees well refined;" and God has "sent out into all the highways ana neages to invite the poor, the halt, the lame, and the blind," and has commissioned his servants to compel men, by dint of importunity, to accept his invitation. Now has he shewn such concern for the wicked, and will he disregard the righteous? Will he not rather "cause the manna to fall around their tents," and "the water to follow them" through all this dreary wilderness? Yes; he would rather send a raven to feed them, or sustain them by a continued miracle, 1 Kings xvii. 6, 14; than ever suffer their souls to famish.

2. He is peculiarly interested in the welfare of the righteous

The righteous are God's "peculiar treasure above all people;" they are even "his sons and daughters." If they were left to perish, Jesus would lose the purchase of his blood, and the very members of his body. And can we imagine that God will be so unmindful of them as utterly to forsake them? Did he not on many occasions vouchsafe mercy to his chosen people *for his own name sake,* when their backslidings had rendered them fit objects of his everlasting displeasure? Thus then will he still be actuated by a regard for his own honor, and "not forsake his people, because it hath pleased him to make them his people." 1 Sam. xii. 22.

3. He has pledged his word that they shall never want any thing that is good

"Exceeding numerous, great, and precious are the promises which God has given to his people." "He will supply all their wants, according to his riches in glory, by Christ Jesus: he will give them grace and glory; and will withhold no good thing:" their souls "shall be even as a well watered garden:" "bread shall be given them; and their water shall be sure." And will he violate his word? he may leave his people in straits, as he did the Israelites of old: but it shall be only for the more signal manifestation of his love and mercy towards them. Let them only trust in him, and he "will never leave them, never, never forsake them." Heb. xiii. 5; see the Greek.

We shall conclude with a word

1. Of reproof

It is certain that many do not "make their profiting to appear" as they ought. To such therefore we must say, "Wherefore art thou, being a king's son, lean from day to day?" 2 Sam. xiii. 4. Why art thou crying continually, "Woe is me, my leanness, my leanness!" Isai. xxiv. 16; when thou shouldest be "growing up as the calves of the stall?" Mal. iv. 2. Some part of the blame perhaps may attach to him who dispenses the ordinances among you, as wanting more life and spirituality in his ministrations; yet even this would be no excuse to you, since if your hearts were more spiritual, God would render your mean fare as nutritious as the richest dainties. Dan. i. 12—15. If God should even "give you your desire, yet would he also send leanness into your souls," Ps. cvi. 15; while you continued to loathe the heavenly manna. Learn then to come with more eager appetite— — —Be more careful to digest the word afterwards by meditation and prayer— — —And look, not so much to the manner in which the word is preached, as to Christ in the word; since HE is that bread of life which alone can nourish your souls; and which, if eaten by faith, will surely nourish them unto life eternal— — —John vi. 51.

2 Of consolation

Some may put away from them this promise, under the idea that they are not of the character to whom it belongs. Now though we would by no means encourage any to apply the promises to themselves in a presumptuous manner, and thereby to deceive their own souls with ungrounded expectations, yet we would not that any should refuse the consolation that properly belongs to them. Suppose then that any cannot absolutely number themselves among the righteous, yet, " if they hunger and thirst after righteousness, they are blessed, and shall be filled." Matt. v. 6. This is the word of God to their souls ; and we would have them expect assuredly its accomplishment in due season— — —Let them " desire the sincere milk of the word, and they shall grow thereby"— — —1 Pet. ii. 2.

GOD'S TREATMENT OF US AS BRANCHES OF THE TRUE VINE.

John xv. 1, 2.—I am the true vine, and my Father is the husbandman. Every branch in me that beareth not fruit, he taketh away ; and every branch that beareth fruit, he purgeth it, that it may bring forth more fruit. (S. S.)

The union which subsists between Christ and his church is mysterious—
The scripture sets it forth both in figurative and plain expressions—
It is spoken of not as a speculative or doubtful point, but as well known—
John xiv. 20.
It is declared in the text under a beautiful similitude—
Christ is the true vine
If this was a continuation of our Lord's discourse, the idea of a vine might arise from what he had just before said respecting the fruit of the vine—Luke xxii. 18.
If it was spoken in his way to the mount of olives, it might be suggested by his passing through a vineyard—
The representation respects Christ not personally, but as united to his church—
In this view it fitly exhibits *our union with him*
This union is not natural to any—
We are, by nature, plants of a degenerate vine—Jer. ii. 21.
We are, however, separated from it by Almighty power—Eph. i. 19, 20.
And are made willing to be united to Christ—Ps. cx. 3.
We are then engrafted into Christ by the Spirit on God's part, and by faith on ours—Eph. iii. 16, 17.
Thus we become branches of the true vine—
And the union, when formed, is intimate and inseparable—1 Cor. vi. 17. Rom. viii. 35, 39.
It expresses, moreover, *our dependence on him*
A branch derives all its fructifying power from the root—
So believers receive all their grace out of Christ's fulness—John i. 16.
Hence it is that Christ is so precious to them—1 Pet. ii. 7.
Hence, too, they determine to live entirely by faith on him—Gal. ii. 20.
The Father is the husbandman
The husbandman has many offices to perform—
He engrafts the scions, digs about them and dungs them, guards them from the weather, prunes the luxuriant branches, &c.—

The Father performs these offices

He chooses (but not for their superior goodness) what scions he will—

He separates them from their stock by the means he judges best—

He engrafts them, in his own time and manner, into the new stock—

He continues to promote their good by his word, his Spirit, and his providence—

He separate or combines, renews or changes, the various means of culture, as he sees occasion—

His treatment of the branches is suited to their state—

There are "branches in Christ," which are so only in appearance

They have never been thoroughly separated from their old stock—

They have never been truly engrafted into Christ—

The change wrought in them has been only partial—

They bring not forth such fruit as the living branches do—

These the Father " taketh away"—

They are a disgrace to the vine, and to the husbandman himself—

He, however, exercises forbearance towards them—Luke xiii. 8, 9.

His culture of them, in the mean time, shews their unfruitfulness to be of themselves—Isa. v. 4.

But he will ere long separate them from the others—

He will take them away, in order to burn them, ver. 6.—

How fearful should we be lest we be found such branches at last !—

And how carefully should we examine our fruit, in order that we may not be self-deceived !—Matt. vii. 17—20.

There are other branches, which are vitally united to Christ

They manifest that they are so, by the fruits which they produce—

These the husbandman purges and prunes

Notwithstanding their fruitfulness, they need the pruning-knife—

Afflictions have a tendency to make them more fruitful—

God therefore sends them afflictions of various kinds—

This he does to " every one of them"—Heb. xii. 6—8.

He even promises affliction to them as a blessing—Jer. xxx. 11, with Heb. xii. 10, 11.

Let us then enquire whether we be living branches of the true vine—

Let us study to answer the ends of all his care—

If we be indeed fruitful branches, let us welcome affliction as a blessing in disguise—

Let us, above all, seek to be confirmed in our *union to Christ,* and *our dependence on him*—Col. ii. 6, 7.

THE PRESENCE OF GOD WITH HIS PEOPLE.

Exodus xxxiii. 14.—And he said, My presence shall go with thee, and I will give thee rest.
(Sk.)

THE preceding context clearly discovers the deep concern which Moses felt for the children of Israel. Having according, to divine appointment, conducted them from Egyptian bondage to mount Horeb, there the Lord communed with him, and gave him special directions for his future guidance and encouragement. But being ' tremblingly alive' to the awful responsibility of his high and important situation, he was on various accounts greatly perplexed and discouraged. This was particularly the case when he was commanded to proceed on the journey to Canaan; and yet the Lord threatened, that he would not go with them. This deeply affected the tenderest sympathies of his heart, and rendered his prospects exceedingly gloomy and distressing. But he gave himself unto prayer, and obtained, in the text, an assurance that the divine presence would accompany them through the trials of the wilderness, and bring them to the promised rest;—"And he said, My presence," &c. As these words are applicable to the people of God in every succeeding age, they will lead us to observe, The journey they pursue,—The privilege they possess,—and the happiness they enjoy.

1. THE JOURNEY THE PEOPLE OF GOD PURSUE. There is a striking analogy between the *literal* history of the children of Israel, and the *spiritual* history of the members of the Christian church. As the former were delivered from Egyptian bondage, and travelled through the wilderness to the land of Canaan; so the latter are redeemed from sptriual thraldom,—are strangers and pilgrims on the earth,—and are travelling to the land of eternal rest.

1. *They are delivered from sipritual bondage.* Once they were willingly captivated by sin and Satan, and deeply enslaved by the fascinating snares and corruptions of the world. They were the bond slaves of their spiritual enemies, 'tied and bound with the chain of their sins,' John viii. 34. But by the mercy of God, they are happily "delivered from the power of darkness, and stand fast in the liberty wherewith Christ hath made them free," John viii. 36; Gal. v. 1. This glorious emancipation of the soul is eminently the work of God, and is the high calling and common privilege of all his believing people, Luke i. 74, 75: Rom. vi. 22.

2. *They are strangers and pilgrims on the earth.* Such were the children of Israel *literally*, while journeying through the toils of the wilderness; and such is *morally* the state of Christians as travellers to the heavenly Canaan. They are not of the world, but seek "a city which hath foundations, whose builder and Maker is God," Heb. xiii. 14. Like the ancient patriarchs, they desire a better country, for this is not their rest. Heaven is their home, and the world is the house of their pilgrimage. Their portion is above, and they are hastening on to glorious mansions, "not made with hands, eternal in the heavens," John xiv. 1—3; 2 Cor. v. 1.

3. *They are travelling to the land of promise.* The earthly Canaan was, in many respects, a striking emblem of the heavenly rest that remains for the people of God. The former was promised to Abraham and his seed, as a goodly and permanent possession; and the latter is promised as an incorruptible and unfading inheritance, to all the saints, 1 Pet. i. 3—5; 1 John ii. 25. For such characters it is prepared, and kept in reserve. They are heirs of the promises, and "have respect unto the recompense of reward." It is the glorious object of their hope and pursuit: and being faithful unto death, they will receive the crown of life, Rom. ii. 7; Luke xii. 32.—Let us then consider,

II. THE PRIVILEGE THE PEOPLE OF GOD POSSESS. "My *presence* shall go with thee." Not only his *general* or *universal* presence which fills all space; but his *special* and *manifested* presence, to guide, protect, support, and constantly to abide with them.

1. *His guiding presence is with his people.* He led the children of Israel forty years in the wilderness, "that he might bring them to the city of habitation," Deut. viii. 2. He still guides his faithful servants in "the right way," both of providence and of grace. By his word and Spirit, he directs

their steps, and leads them into all truth, Isa. xlii. 16. He is continually **with** them, to instruct them in every difficulty,—encourage them in every trial,— and prepare them for his eternal kingdom, Ps. lxxiii. 24.

2. *His protecting presence is with his people.* Like the Jews, they are travelling through " a terrible wilderness." They are pursued by enemies and beset with snares. But as the Lord led and protected his ancient people, " by day in a pillar of a cloud, and by night in a pillar of fire;" he is still the refuge and strength of them that put their trust in him. Ps. xlvi. 1 ; he is with them in all their troubles, and they are perfectly secure under the sha- dow of his wing. They " shall be as mount Zion, which cannot be moved, but abideth forever, Ps. cxxv. 2 ; 1 Pet. iii. 13.

3. *His sustaining presence is with his people.* They feel their entire dependance upon him ; and as their gracious benefactor and Savior, he richly supplies all their wants, and satisfies them with his goodness, Ps xxxiv. 10. As he anciently fed the Israelites with manna from heaven, and gave them water to drink from the smitten rock ; he will ever continue to spread a table in the wilderness for his beloved people, Exod. xvi. 35, xvii. 6. He grants them the bread and the water of life, " and withholds no good thing from them," Eph. iii. 20; Phil. iv. 19.

4. *His abiding presence is with his people.* "I will *go* with thee." He will not merely send a messenger, or visit them occasionally ; but will continually *abide*, and *go* with them, to the end of their journey, Ps. xlviii. 14. He will be with them in all their afflictions, temptations and trials; and will manifest himself unto them, as he does not unto the world, John xiv. 32. Human friends may fail, and worldly comforts be withdrawn; but God is "a friend that sticketh closer than a brother," and will never leave, nor forsake us, Ps. lxxiii. 26. And hence we may discover,

III. THE HAPPINESS THE PEOPLE OF GOD ENJOY. "And I will give thee *rest.*" This is always the certain result of the divine presence, and is the peculiar privilege and blessedness of the saints.

1. *His presence gives them rest in the present life.* In coming to Christ they find rest for their souls, and have joy and peace in believing. They rest from the terrors of a guilty conscience, and from the painful distractions of an impenitent and unbelieving heart. "We which have believed," says the Apostle, " do enter into rest, and have peace with God through our Lord Jesus Christ," Isa. xxvi. 3. But though they have spiritual rest of mind, it is not perfect and uninterrupted. In the world they have tribulation, and are called to war a good warfare; but in Christ they have peace which pas- seth all understanding, John xvi. 33.

2. *His presence gives them rest in the hour of death.* It was this con- sideration that induced the Psalmist joyfully to anticipate the period of his approaching dissolution, and exclaim with holy confidence, "Though I walk through the valley of the shadow of death, I fear no evil; for thou art with me ; thy rod and thy staff they comfort me." He delivers his people from the fear and sting of death, and enables them to triumph over their last enemy, which shall certainly be destroyed, 1 Cor. xv. 55—57 Though the final exit of the righteous is not *equally* triumphant and glorious, it is *always* peaceful and safe, for they " die in the Lord, and rest from their labors," Ps. xxxvii. 37.

3. *His presence gives them rest in the world to come.* Their bodies shall rest in certain hope of a glorious resurrection to eternal life ; and their spi- rits shall enter into the joy of the Lord, 2 Cor. v. 8. His immediate presence will constitute their perfect and everlasting rest, dignity, and blessed-

ness, Ps xvii. 15.   There they will rest from every enemy, affliction, and trouble; for "in his presence there is fulness of joy, and pleasures for evermore," Rev. vii. 14—17.

From this subject we may learn.

1. The *character* of God's people. They are redeemed and saved by grace, and are heirs of immortal bliss. Rom. viii. 17.

2. The *encouragement* of the saints. It is their ineffable consolation to know, that "the Lord of hosts is with them, and the God of Jacob is their refuge," Deut. xxxiii. 29.

GOD'S CARE FOR HIS PEOPLE.

Isaiah xliii. 2, 3.—When thou passest through the waters, I will be with thee; and through the rivers, they shall not overflow thee: when thou walkest through the fire, thou shalt not be burned; neither shall the flame kindle upon thee: for I am the Lord thy God, the Holy One of Israel, thy Saviour. (S. S.)

God's goodness to his people never appears more wonderful than when contrasted with their conduct towards him

The history of the church in all ages attests the truth of the apostle's assertion—Rom. v. 20.

We have a remarkable instance of this in the passage before us—

The Israelites were utterly incorrigible—Isai. xlii. 24, 25.

Yet God forebore to "make a full end of them"—

On the contrary, to display the riches of his grace, he promised them his continued care and protection, ver. 1, 2.—

The text suggests to our consideration

I. God's care for his people

God's people are subjected to many and great troubles

"Fire and water" are emblems of heavy calamities—

God's people are often brought into them—

All are taught to expect them in their way to heaven—

The most eminent saints have usually the greatest share—Job—Asaph—Heman—David—Paul—

But God takes peculiar care of them in that state

He represents himself as watching them in the furnace like a refiner—Mal. iii. 3.

He has promised they shall not be overwhelmed by temptation—1 Cor x. 13.

He vouchsafes his special presence at those seasons—

Even when he has withdrawn himself apparently from his people, he secretly and imperceptibly upholds them—

The burning bush was intended to teach us this—Exod. iii. 2.

It has been experienced by the saints in all ages—

David bears testimony to this fact—Ps. lxvi. 10—12. "*We went through fire and through water.*"

The history of the Hebrew youths also attests it—Dan. iii. 25, 27.

The passage of the Jews through the Red Sea, and through Jordan, confirms it—Isai. li. 10.

There are also many living witnesses for the truth of it—

However great this mercy is, we are at no loss to assign

II. THE REASON OF IT.

God is the Covenant God and Saviour of his people

God has given himself to his people by covenant—Jer. xxxi. 33.

Hence he assumes the titles "the God of Israel," "the Holy One of Israel"—

This implies that all his perfections shall be employed for their good—

This is the reason of his peculiar care for them

On account of this relation he *feels for* them

God represents himself as tenderly feeling for his people—

His compassion towards them is like that of a parent—Ps. ciii. 13.

He bears them, like a nursing mother, in his arms—Isai. lxiii. 9.

He considers every injury done to them, as done to himself—Zech. ii. **8.**

He sympathizes thus on account of his relation to them—Jer. xxxi. 20.

On this account also he is *interested in* them

He has purchased and redeemed them by the blood of his Son—

Hence he calls them his "purchased possession"—

He regards them as his "peculiar treasure," the "lot of his inheritance"—

He promises to take care of them as *his* vineyard—Isai. xxvii. 3.

Hence Moses made God's interest in his people a plea for his forbearing to destroy them—Exod. xxxii. 11.

Hence David also urged this plea on his own behalf—Ps. cxix. 94.

On this account also he is *bound to* them

God has pledged himself that "he will not forsake his people"—

He has assured them, that no weapon formed against them shall prosper—

He never will break the covenant he has entered into—Ps. lxxxix. 34, 35.

This affords a sure ground of hope to his people—

The church of old urged it as a reason for his return to them—Is. lxiii. 15—19. *This is remarkable strong.*

And every believer may adopt the patriarch's plea—Gen. xxxii. 12.

Infer,

1. Of what importance is it to know that we are interested in Christ!

We cannot claim God for our God unless we have believed in Christ—

If therefore we have not an evidence that we have indeed believed, we can derive no comfort from these promises—

Yea, rather, we have reason to fear that we shall be overwhelmed with God's wrath, and be made to "dwell with everlasting burnings"—

Let us then not leave this matter in doubt and suspense—

Let us "flee to Christ for refuge, as to the hope set before us"—

We may then assuredly expect these promises to be fulfilled to us—

2. What consolation does the gospel of Christ afford!

Every man must expect to "pass through fire and through water"—

It is our appointed way to the kingdom of heaven—Acts xiv. 22.

In the hour of death, if not before, we shall feel need of support—

But God has provided in the text abundant consolation—

We need not fear any thing whilst we can rest on this promise—

Let us then adopt the triumphant language of the Psalmist—Ps. xxiii. 1, 4.

GOD'S DARK DISPENSATIONS TO HIS SAINTS.

Gen. xlii. 36.—And Jacob their father said unto them, &c. (H.)

THESE are the words of Jacob, in great perplexity and distress; the occasion of which we are acquainted with in the foregoing verses of this chapter. He concluded Joseph to be dead, and looked upon Simeon as lost; in both which he was mistaken: and the thoughts of parting with Benjamin cut him to the heart, as if it were to send him to the grave; and therefore he cries out, "All these things are against me." But Joseph was safe in honor, Benjamin would be so too, and well received; Simeon would be set at liberty, all the family would be kindly entertained, and the father sent for, to be nourished by his beloved son: and thus all was making for his comfort and advantage, that appeared so black and dismal, and from whence he expected nothing but ruin. And, as Jacob's is not a singular case, I shall endeavor,

I. To show GOD'S DEALINGS WITH HIS PEOPLE, even when he is working their deliverance, and designs their good, are often dark and intricate.

1. This was the case with Jacob. God designed the preservation of him and his family in Egypt, by Joseph's advancement there; but how unlikely the means he made use of, in order to it, and yet how wonderfully was the end proposed, accomplished.

2. Thus it was with the deliverance of Israel from Egypt, four hundred and thirty years after. They were exceedingly oppressed by Pharaoh; see the complaints of the people to Moses and Aaron; Ex. v. 21; and the complaint of Moses before the Lord, on the same occasion; ver. 22, 23; and after they were brought a little on their way out of Egypt, their danger was increased, chap. xiv. 8, 9. The pursuing army was behind, the sea before, on either hand mountains, that forbade their flight or escape; to all appearance, every thing was working towards their destruction; and yet this was the way that God took to accomplish their deliverance, by opening the sea to give them passage, and drowning their enemies, who ventured to follow them. Ver. 26—28.

3. Thus it was with Daniel, and the three Hebrew worthies. God resolved to deliver and save them: but the way in which he chose to do it, was by suffering the first to be cast into the lions' den, and the others into the fiery furnace, and yet by keeping them unhurt, to the confusion of their enemies.

4. David was designed for a throne, and anointed to it: but, before he reached it, he was driven from place to place, as a partridge upon the mountains; and reduced to that distress, that he seemed to conclude his case desperate, and his destruction certain. 1 Sam. xxvii. 1.

5. Such also were God's dealings with Job: he resolves to bless Job's latter end more than his beginning, but how unlikely a way to this, to be stripped of all, and reduced to the deepest distress; to be plundered by his enemies, censured by his friends, Satan let loose in the sorest manner to afflict him, and God writing bitter things against him. Who could have thought, that saw him in his low condition, that the issue would have been so bright and blessed.

Thus God's dealings with his servants have often a sad aspect, as if he was set on their destruction; when he is consulting their truest advantage, and promoting their salvation. Verily he is a God that hideth himself, when he is at the same time the God of Israel, the Saviour. Wraps himself in clouds and darkness, before he shines through to their comfort. But this leads me to consider,

II. Whence it is that a CHILD OF GOD may be ready to conclude that to be against him, which is really for him.

1. This proceeds from their weakness of faith, as to God's wisdom and power, faithfulness and love. We are slow of heart to believe, that he is able to bring good out of evil, and light out of darkness; that he hath hidden designs to serve by all his dealings with his servants, which he knows how to bring about, and will not fail to do in the appointed way and time, which are always to be left to him, who is wonderful in counsel, and excellent in working.

2. By looking to Providence, and loosing sight of the promise. Rom. viii. 28.

3. Judging by sense. When afflicted and pained, we are apt to feel and complain, that "all these things are against us;" but faith speaks in a very different language. Ps. lxxiii. 1.

4. By looking down to the present world, and our interest in it. When this is chiefly regarded, that which tends to lessen our comforts in it may be thought to make against us; but that which is contrary to our temporal welfare, may promote our everlasting happiness.

5. Through rashness; viewing only a part of his work, and not waiting for the issue. Jacob, who cried out so passionately, "all these things are against me," in the end discovered his mistake.

6. Through not attending to the usual method of God's dealing with his people, and our own, and others' experience of the happy purposes he has served by it. He makes rich, by first making poor: he heals by wounding and making them sick: he quickens in the way to heaven, and better prepares them for it, by all the sufferings of the present life. 2 Cor. iv. 17.

III. The grounds upon which we may conclude that what the CHRISTIAN apprehends to be against him, shall in the end terminate in his favor.

1. From God's relation to him: God is his Father; Rom. viii. 15; and is particularly concerned for his good and happiness, even in affliction and distress. Heb. xii. 10.

2. From God's love to him. See his language to his people; Isa. xliii. 4; and this love will engage all his perfections for them.

3. From his express promises. Rom. viii. 28. Things shall have a better issue than they expected. He that dwelleth in the secret place of the Most High shall abide under the shadow of the Almighty, and there be safe from fear of evil. Isa. xl. 1, 2.

IV. Why is it that the LORD chooses this way to promote the best interests of his followers.

That he really does so, is clear from Jacob's case; and what we sometimes think to be a judgment, is a mercy. The fish that swallowed Jonah was a mean to bring him to shore. This way the Lord chooses,

1. For his own glory, as appears from the case of Lazarus. John xi. 4.

2. To discover their corruption, and to try their graces. Deut. viii. 2.

3. To quicken, and make them more earnest in prayer. The more dark his dispensations are, the more fervent and enlarged we should be in prayer.

4. To sweeten and endear the mercy he grants them, after all their fears and doubting to the contrary.

5. To heighten their thanksgiving for the mercy bestowed. How thankful must Jacob have been, after all his difficulties, to find his children all alive and well. How was the thanksgiving of Israel enlarged, upon their deliverance from danger at the Red Sea! It produced the song, Ex. xv.

Application.

1. Let us be anxiously careful to assure ourselves, as to our special **relation** to God, as his children in covenant with him, devoted to his service.

2. Let us be aware of judging God's purposes of grace by the external dispensations which make way to bring them into effect. The promise is often just about to be fulfilled, when, to an eye of sense, it seems at the greatest distance. In the evening-time, when least expected, it shall be light. Wherefore,

3. Beg that faith may not fail, when surrounding circumstances seem dark and dismal. In every place he can come to us, and in the deepest distress he can relieve us. Isa. xli. 10.

4. Beware of entertaining narrow thoughts of God in the deepest distress. Believe him always the same whatever changes you meet with.

Lastly, While you are apt to say on earth, " all these things are against me," press on with greater earnestness to heaven. There all your tears shall be wiped away; and there you shall have "fulness of joy, and pleasure for evermore."

THE LOVE OF GOD TO THE WORLD.

John iii. 16.—" God so loved the world," &c. (P.)

IN the former part of this chapter, we have an interesting conversation recorded between our Lord and Nicodemus, an eminent Jew. He instructs him respecting the nature of the new birth, his design in coming into the world, and the happiness of those who receive him.

Let us contemplate,

I. THE UNSPEAKABLE LOVE OF GOD. " God so loved the world."

Man, in consequence of his apostacy from God, had fallen into an abyss of misery, from which he could never have extricated himself; but " God so loved the world," &c. What world? The expression admits of different acceptations : sometimes it is applied to the universe, the heavens, the earth, the sea, the elements, angels, men, animals, &c. Sometimes it is used in scripture, when speaking of the Roman empire, as Matt. iv. 8 ; at other times the Jewish nation, Luke ii. 1; but here it means the world of his intelligent creatures, the human race, 1 John, ii. 2. " God so loved," &c. ; how much, the Apostle could not tell. " There is," (as an eminent commentator justly observes,) " an eternity of meaning in the word ' so,' which we must die to know." The expression is most vehement and forcible—" God *so* loved," &c., *so* richly, *so* freely, *so* inexpressibly, *so* infinitely.

His love to the world was,

1. Unmerited. There was nothing in man to attract it, much less to merit it. We were guilty, and rebellious against him ; but notwithstanding this, " God so loved," &c.

2. Universal.—"The world." It was designed and intended for the world. Hence our Lord's final commission to his disciples was, " Go ye in to all the world," &c. Mark xvi. 15.

3. Unsolicited—Though a blessing so rich and valuable, and so much needed by man, yet it was never implored by him. For we were not only enemies, but in a state of spiritual darkness, when we were reconciled to God by the gift of his Son. It was,

98

4 Unparalleled. No human being could have equalled this act of mercy.

"Love so amazing, so divine, demands," &c.

5. Incomprehensible.

"God only knows the love of God."

II. THE EVIDENCE OR MANIFESTATION OF THAT LOVE. "He gave his only," &c.

1. Intentionally. "He was the Lamb slain from the foundation of the world," Rev. xiii. 8. When man sinned, it was promised "the seed of the woman shall bruise the serpent's head," Gen. iii. 15. This promise was renewed to Abraham, Isaac and Jacob, as well as to most or all of the prophets—"And in thy seed shall all the nations of the earth be blessed." Gen. xxii. 18.

He gave his Son,

2. Typically. Under types, and shadows, and emblematical representations. Isaac, and Jacob, and Joseph, and Jonah, were all types of Christ, Matt. xii. 40. The rock, the manna, the brazen serpent, were each of them typical of him who "came into the world to save sinners." He gave his Son,

3. Prophetically. "A prophet shall the Lord your God raise unto you; him," &c. "Behold, a virgin shall conceive," &c., Isa. vii. 14. "His name shall be called, Wonderful," &c. Isa. ix. 6. "Behold I lay in Zion for a foundation," &c., Isa. xxviii. 16. "He is despised and rejected of men," &c., Isa. liii. 3. "Rejoice greatly, O daughter of Zion," &c., Zech. ix. 9.

4. Actually. "When the fullness of the time was come, God sent forth," &c., Gal. iv. 4. He was born in Bethlehem, fled to Egypt from the rage of Herod, returned back again to Nazereth, and continued there till he commenced his public ministry.

III. THE GRAND DESIGN INTENDED: "That whosoever believeth," &c. Thus faith is the key by which we unlock all the divine promises, and by which we become interested in all the blessings of the gospel. It implies,

1. The assent of the understanding. "Rabbi, thou art the Son of God," &c., John i. 49.

2. That we receive him in all his offices, as our teaching prophet, our atoning priest, and our ruling king. And, "as many as received him, to them," &c. John i. 12.

8. That we rely upon him for the pardon of our sins, the acceptance of our persons, and the sanctification of our natures. Such is the faith that is necessary to salvation; the object of which is Christ, and the end of which is full salvation.

1. "That we might not perish." The meaning of this emphatic expression is the same as "losing the soul," Matt. 16, 26. It means to be eternally lost—to be ruined—to be damned; for "he that believeth shall be saved; but he," &c. Mark, xvi. 16. It is to sink into everlasting darkness—to endure unquenchable fire—to bear inexpressible misery. It is

"To writhe, to pant, to toss beneath the load,
And bear the weight of an offended God."

It is banishment from the presence of the Lord, and from the glory of his power; for "the wicked shall be turned into hell,"

2. "That we might have everlasting life." He came, that he might PUR-

99

CHASE " everlasting life ;" and this life begins in the soul on earth ; for what is grace, but glory begun ; and glory but grace consumated and perfected ? He came to give a LEGAL TITLE to eternal life. " Eye hath not seen, nor ear heard, nor heart conceived, what God hath prepared for them that love him." He came that he might become an expiatory sacrifice for sin. None could accomplish this grand design but him. " He that spared not his own Son, but freely delivered," &c., Rom. viii. 32. He came that he might exalt us to glory. Hence, he is not only " the author, but the finisher of our salvation. He not only begins, but carries on the work, till the top stone is brought forth with shoutings of "Grace, grace unto it."

Improvement.

1. Address those who disregard and slight this love. The greatest blessing God bestowed upon the world, will be to you the greatest curse. O harden not your hearts against his love, but melt beneath its influence

" His offered benefits embrace,
And freely now be saved by grace."

Some may limit the mercy of the Holy One; but listen to his own word, and hear the rich encouragement he offers you himself—" Ho every one that thirsteth," &c.

2. Let those who enjoy the benefits of Christ's atonement, and who feel his love shed abroad in their hearts, " hold fast the beginning of their confidence, steadfast unto the end," Heb. iii. 14. And, finally, brethren, " be ye steadfast and unmoveable, always abounding in the work of the Lord; for as much as ye know that your labor shall not be in vain in the Lord," which may God of his infinite mercy grant, for his name's sake, Amen.

THE NAME OF THE LORD A STRONG TOWER.

Prov. xviii. 10.—The name of the Lord is a strong tower: the righteous runneth into it, and is safe. (H. H.)

IN the Proverbs of Solomon we must not expect to find long and accurate statements of Divine truth, nor elevated strains of devotion founded upon it : the scope of the book is rather by brief sentences to fix upon the mind truths already acknowledged, and to shew the excellency of them in their effects. The passage before us is very instructive in this view, namely, as illustrating the blessedness attendant on true piety. But it commends itself to us yet more forcibly, by exhibiting a contrast between the dispositions and habits which religion inspires, and those which are indulged by the whole ungodly world. The text informs us what " the righteous man" does : the verse following our text informs us what the worldling does : the one makes God his refuge ; the other trusts in his wealth, or some other idol equally vain : the one founds all his hopes on God, as made known to us in the Scriptures of Truth ; the other, on some vanity, that has no title to confidence but " in his own conceit."

It was to mark this contrast that the blessedness mentioned in our text was confined to " the righteous." Solomon did not mean to intimate, that an unrighteous man, if he would flee to this tower, should be shut out: for the most unrighteous man in the universe is invited to come to it; and, like the cities of refuge, its gates stand open day and night for the admission of all who desire to flee to it for refuge. But the truth is, that none but the righteous will run to it: none but they who are sensible of their guilt and danger, and are fleeing in earnest from the wrath to come, will enter in. All others deny the necessity of submitting to so humiliating a measure: they think they are safe enough without it. The believing penitent, on the contrary, is thankful for such a refuge, and is in the habit of running to it on every occasion: and therefore to him, and to him alone, is the security confined.

To elucidate the passage, we will endeavor to unfold,

I. THE CHARACTER OF GOD—

By " the name of the Lord" we are not to understand the mere *word*, Jehovah, as though that would afford us any security. This is a vain and foolish superstition, that has no foundation whatever in the Oracles of God. But, by " the name of the Lord" we must understand his character; as we learn from that expression of David, " They that know thy name," *i. e.* thy character, " will put their trust in thee." Ps. ix. 10. Consider then the character of Jehovah,

1. As described by himself—

God, in infinite condescension, was pleased to make known himself to Moses, and by an audible voice to " proclaim his name:" Exod. xxxiv. 5 ; " The Lord passed by and proclaimed, The Lord, the Lord God, merciful and gracious, long-suffering, and abundant in goodness and truth ; keeping mercy for thousands, forgiving iniquity, transgression and sin, and that will by no means clear the guilty." Exod. xxxiv. 6, 7. Now we would ask the trembling sinner, What character he would wish Jehovah to bear ? Would he wish God in no instance to testify his displeasure against sin, but to treat all men alike, putting no difference between " the guilty" who are going on in all manner of wickedness, and the penitent, who are turning from all iniquity ? No: there is not a penitent in the universe that would wish God to act in a way so unworthy of his divine majesty. But if he desire to be assured of mercy to returning penitents, it is not possible that any words he could devise could more richly portray this attribute, than those which God himself has used. Consider them distinctly and separately, — — —and see how constantly they have been verified towards you hitherto, and how abundantly they contain all that you can desire.

2. As revealed to us in Christ Jesus—

The Lord Jesus Christ is " Emmanuel, God with us ;" and he is particularly called, " The image of the invisible God," because in him the whole character of the Deity is made, as it were, visible to mortal men. He is " the brightness of his Father's glory, and the express image of his person ;" and his whole character is marked in the name given him before he was conceived in the womb. Matt. i. 21, 23. The name " Jesus" is the same with Joshua, or " Jehoshua," that is, Jah Osea, Divine Saviour. What a glorious and comprehensive name is this ! All that he has done and suffered for us, and all that he has promised to us, is contained in it; together with his perfect sufficiency for all that he has undertaken to effect. The trembling sinner finds in the very name of Jesus a pledge of all that he wants. Besides, whilst we contemplate him in the whole of his work and offices, we are expressly authorized to apply to ourselves the benefit of them all, and to call him, " The Lord our Righteousness." Jer. xxiii. 6. Follow this idea in all its bearings, and what unsearchable mysteries of love and mercy will it unfold to our view !

Such being the name and character of God, let us contemplate,

II. THE INTEREST WE HAVE IN IT—

It is indeed "a strong tower"—

Consider every perfection of the Deity: there is not one which is not "a chamber where we may hide ourselves till every calamity be overpast." Isa. xxvi. 20. The wisdom, the goodness, the love, the power, the faithfulness of Jehovah; who that is encompased by them does not feel himself in an impregnable fortress? Truly they are not merely a wall, but "a wall of fire" round about the righteous; of fire, which whilst it protects the fugitive, will devour the assailant.— — —What a tower too is the Lord Jesus Christ in the whole of his work and offices! Well is he said to be "a strength to the poor, a strength to the needy in his distress, a refuge from the storm, a shadow from the heat, when the blast of the terrible ones is as a storm against the wall." Isai. xxvi. 4. Yes, "the man" Christ Jesus, in his Mediatorial character, is such "a hiding-place," Isai. xxxii. 2; where no adversary shall "ever penetrate."

All who run to it shall "be safe"—

Who shall ever approach "to harm" those who are thus protected? 1 Pet. iii. 13; Surely "they shall be kept in perfect peace." They are "safe:" safe from the curses of the broken law; for "there is no condemnation to them that are *in Christ Jesus*" Rom. viii. 1;— — —They are safe too from the assaults of Satan; for "their lives are hid with Christ in God," where Satan can never come, Col. iii. 3, 4,— — —In a word, they are safe from every kind of evil; for God has said of those who make the Most High their habitation, that "no evil shall befall them" Ps. xci. 9, 10;— — The persecutor may touch their body, but cannot reach their soul: Luke xii. 4, 5; they shall sooner be fed with ravens, than be suffered to "want any manner of thing that is good." Ps. xxxiv. 9, 10. And if any thing occur that has the semblance of evil, they may be assured that it shall work for their present and eternal good. Rom. viii. 28. 2 Cor. iv. 17, 18. Like Elisha, they are surrounded with horses of fire and chariots of fire; 2 Kings vi. 14—17; and any assaults made upon them shall only terminate, as in Elijah's case, with the confusion and ruin of their enemies. 2 Kings i. 9—14.

Suffer now a word of EXHORTATION—

1. Study much the character of God—

"To know God, and Jesus Christ whom he hath sent, is, as our Lord informs us, "eternal life." All other knowledge is mere vanity in comparison of this. Without this we have nothing to warrant our hopes or to dissipate our fears— — —"Acquaint then yourselves with God, and be at peace"— — —

2. Maintain constant and intimate communion with him—

You know how a child runs to his parent on every occasion: do ye in like manner run unto your God. This is the very character of the true christian; "The righteous runneth unto God as his strong tower." Get to him under every fear, and every want, and every distress: and "cast your care on Him who careth for you"— — —

3. Assure yourselves of the safety which you are privileged to enjoy—

Well may you say, "If God be for me, who can be against me?" See how David exulted in his security! Ps. xviii. 1, 2, and xxvii. 1;— — — and learn like him to glory in your God: for it is God's desire that you should enjoy all possible consolation. Heb. vi. 18. Your Saviour has assured you, that "none shall pluck you out of his hands:" lie there then in peace and safety, "knowing in whom you have believed, and that he is able to keep that which you have committed to him"— — —When he has lost his power to save, then, and not till then, shall any enemy prevail against you.

GOD'S FAITHFULNESS TO HIS PROMISES.

Joshua xxiii. 14.—Behold, this day I am going the way of all the earth: and ye know in in all your hearts and in all your souls, that not one thing hath failed of all the good things which the Lord your God spake concerning you: all are come to pass unto you; and not one thing hath failed thereof. (H. H.)

It has been common in all ages to pay peculiar attention to the words of dying men: and the more eminent their characters were, the more regard has been shown to their last instructions or advice. The person speaking in the text, was, in some points of view, distinguished even above Moses himself: for though Moses was the appointed instrument of bringing the Israelites out of Egypt, he was forced to leave them to the care of Joshua, who alone was commissioned to settle them in Canaan: and who was therefore a more illustrious type of Jesus, whose name he bore,* and whose character he prefigured. The dying words of such a person, when speaking too, the dictates of inspiration, may well be considered as calling for more than ordinary attention; especially when the scope of them was to vindicate the honor of God, and they were delivered in a way of solemn appeal to the whole nation of the Jews. But they have yet a further claim to our regard, because, though primarily applicable to those to whom they were immediately addressed, they are equally applicable to the Lord's people, in every place, and every age.

To illustrate them in this view, we shall,

I. Notice some of those good things which the Lord our God has spoken concerning us—

In order to mark what we are principally to insist upon, the faithfulness of God in performing his promises, we will specify some that were made,

1. To the Church at large—

God promised to the Church the gift of his dear Son. Gen. iii. 15. Gen. xxii. 18. Deut. xviii. 18. Isa. vii. 14, and ix. 6, and liii. 6. Dan. ix. 24. Jer. xxiii. 6. — — — the abiding presence of his Spirit. Prov. i. 23. Isa. xxxii 15. Ezek. xxxvi. 25—27. John xv. 26. John xvi. 14. Ib. ver. 8. Zech. xii. 10. Rom. v. 5. 2 Cor. i. 22. — — — and a final triumph over all her enemies. Isa. xxvii. 2, and xxxiii, 20, and liv. 17. Jer xxxi. 35—37. Matt. xvi. 18.

To individual members in particular—

Though the names of individuals are not specified, their characters are delineated, and that too in such a way, that all who study the sacred oracles may read, as it were, their names in them. There are distinct promises made to the humble. Isa. lxvi. 2. Jam. iv. 6. Isa. lvii. 15. — — — the weak. Isa. xlii. 3, 4, and xl. 11, and xli. 14, 15, 17, 18. 2 Cor. xii. 9. Amos ix. 9. — — — the tempted. 1 Cor. x. 13. Heb. ii. 18. —·— — the backslidden. Jer. iii. 14, 22. Hos. xiv. 4. — — — and especially to them that trust in God. Isa. xxvi 3. Ps. cxxv. 1. Jer. xvii. 7. 8. — — — In that class is every rank and order of true Christians comprehended, "Verily it shall be well with the righteous." Isa. iii. 10.

These are "great," "exceeding great and precious promises:" 2 Pet. i. 4. and the persons who correspond with the different characters, are at full liberty to apply them to themselves.

Having taken a short view of the promises we may proceed to,

II. Show the faithfulness of God in fulfilling them—

* The names *Joshua* and *Jesus* are the same in Greek.

103

There is in the minds of all who have heard the Gospel, a general conviction of the truth and faithfulness of God—

It is seen that God has already fulfilled all that he has promised in reference to the Church at large. Besides what he did for the Jews, Josh. xxi. 43—45, he has sent his Son; he has poured out his Spirit; he has maintained his Church, notwithstanding all the efforts that have been used both by men and devils to destroy it. And from hence we feel a persuasion, that his word shall be fulfilled in other respects also. We do not indeed suffer our convictions to operate as they ought; yet we revolt at the idea that " God should lie. Numb. xxiii. 19, and we know that " he cannot deny himself." 2 Tim. ii. 13. — — —

All who have ever sought after God at all, have had proofs of his veracity to their own experience—

The Israelites " knew in all their hearts, and in all their souls," that God had fulfilled his promises to them. And are there any who have ever called upon him, or trusted in him, and not found him ready to hear their prayers, and to supply their wants? If we look back to seasons of peculiar trial, shall we not find some manifestations of his mercy, sufficient to shew, that, if we have not received more from him, it has been owing to our own backwardness to ask, rather than to any unwillingness in him to give — — —

Nor can the whole universe produce one single instance wherein his promises have failed—

We can make the same appeal to you, as Joshua, after sixty years' experience did to the Israelites. Bring forth every promise from the Bible; then search the annals of the world: and inquire of every creature in it, to find one single instance of God's violating or forgetting a promise; and if one instance can be *proved*, we will consent that his word shall henceforth be called in question. Tell us then, To whom has he " been a wilderness?" Jer. ii 31. What penitent, believing, and obedient soul hath he ever forsaken? Heb. xiii. 5. Isa xlix. 14, 15, and liv. 7—10. He himself bids you " testify against him." Mic. vi. 3. But we defy the whole world to impeach his veracity, or to contradict our assertion, when we say, that "*all* which he has promised us is come to pass; not one thing hath failed thereof" — — — God may have delayed the accomplishment of his promises, or fulfilled them in a way that was not expected: but not one of them has ever failed.

Address,

1. Those who have not considered the faithfulness of God—

In spite of the general conviction of God's truth that floats upon our minds, there is a proneness in us to indulge a thought, that his mercy will in some way or other interpose to prevent the execution of his threatenings. But the veracity of God is pledged as much for the accomplishment of his threatenings as of his promises: and of this he *labors in the most earnest manner* to persuade us. Ezek. xxiv. 13, 14. How many, alas! are now experiencing in hell what they would not believe when they were on earth! Let us learn to " tremble at God's word." Let us remember, that though the antediluvian scoffers said, as others now do, " Where is the promise of his coming?" 1 Pet. iii. 3—4, he did come at last, though he bore with them a hundred and twenty years. And in like manner he will overwhelm us also at last with the deluge of his wrath, if we enter not into the ark before the door be shut against us — — —" We are going the way of all the earth," whether we be old or young, rich or poor: and as death finds us, so shall we remain forever. Stay not then till death overtake you; but join your selves to the Lord, and to his people. "Come with us, and we will do you good; for *the Lord hath spoken good concerning Israel.*" Numb. x. 29.

2. Those who are tempted to doubt his faithfulness—

Let not delays lead you to harbor unbelieving fears. God sent not his Son till four thousand years after he had announced his purpose to the world: nor did he bring Israel out of Egypt till the time fixed in his promises was just expired. If a few more hours had elapsed, his promise to Abraham had been broken: but God remembered the very day; and then inclined the rebellious Pharaoh to submit: yea he disposed the Egyptians to "*thrust his people out*" from their land, on "*the self-same day*" that he had fixed 430 years before. Exod. xii. 51. Tarry then the Lord's leisure. Take the promises of God as your support, and "claim them as your heritage forever." Ps. cxix. 111. Be not hasty in concluding that God will not accomplish them. 1 Sam. xvii. 1. Ezek. xxxvii. 11. But take them with you to a throne of grace, and plead them as the saints of old were wont to do. Gen. xxxii. 12. Then you shall find them all to be "yea, and amen, in Christ." 2 Cor. i. 20. "If things be marvellous in your eyes, do not imagine that they must therefore be so in the eyes of God, Zech. viii. 6; for as " there is nothing too *hard* for him" *to do*, so there is nothing too *great*, or too *good*, for him to *give* to his believing people.

3. Those who are relying on his faithfulness—

It cannot but be a source of unspeakable comfort to observe, in how many passages the faithfulness of God is expressly pledged for the performance of his promises. Does he promise to forgive our sins, 1 John i. 9; to deliver us from temptation, 1 Cor. x. 13; to further in us the great work of sanctification, 1 Thess. v. 23, 24; and to preserve us to the end? 2 Thess. iii. 3. We are told in each, that he is "*faithful* to do it" for us. It is also delightful to reflect, that "his word is *tried*. 2 Sam. xxii. 31. Solomon's testimony was precisely that which is given in the text, 1 Kings viii. 56: and the more we trust in God, the more evidence shall we have that " he keepeth covenant and mercy to a thousand generations." Deut. vii. 9. But remember that his fidelity to you requires in you fidelity to him: it lays you under a tenfold obligation to " hold fast the profession of your faith without wavering." Heb. x. 23. See then that ye bear in mind the vows that are upon you, and that ye execute all that ye have undertaken in your baptismal covenant. Labor to be found "children that will not lie; so will He be" your faithful and almighty "Savior." Isa. lxiii. 8.

CONFIDENCE IN GOD A SOURCE OF CONSOLATION.

2 Tim. i. 12.—I know whom I have believed; and I am persuaded that he is able to keep that which I have committed unto him against that day. (H. H.)

MAN is born to trouble: and it is of the greatest importance to him that he should know where to turn his eyes in the day of adversity. The gospel directs us to a reconciled God in Christ Jesus, who has engaged to be our support and comfort under every distress. The christian has many trials peculiar to himself: but the gospel is fully adequate to his necessities. Its power to support him may be seen in the passage before us. St. Paul is exhorting Timothy to stedfastness in the cause of Christ: ver. 8; and, for his encouragement, he tells him what was the ground of his own consolations under the heavy afflictions which he was now enduring for the sake of Christ. He tells him, that, notwithstanding he was immured in a dungeon, and in daily expectation of a violent and cruel death, he was neither "ashamed" nor afraid: for that he had a firm persuasion of God's ability to keep him; and that persuasion afforded him ample support.

To illustrate the text, we may observe,

I. THE CHRISTIAN COMMITS HIS SOUL TO GOD—

The apostle doubtless committed unto God the concerns of the church: but it is rather of his soul that he is speaking in the words before us, because it was *that* which alone could be in danger at the day of judgment. In like manner,

Every christian commits his soul to God—

We know what it is to commit a large sum of money to the care of a Banker: and from thence we may attain a just notion of the christian's conduct. He has a soul which is of more value than the whole world: and he feels great anxiety that it should be preserved safely "against that day,' when God shall judge the world. But to whom shall he entrust it? He knows of none but God that can keep it; and therefore he goes to God, and solemnly commits it into his hands, intreating him to order all its concerns, and, in whatever way he shall see best, to fit it for glory.

To this he is prompted by manifold considerations—

He reflects on the fall of man in Paradise, and says, ' Did Adam, when perfect, and possessed of all that he could wish, become a prey to the Tempter, when the happiness of all his posterity, as well as his own, depended on his stedfastness; and can such a corrupt creature as I, surrounded as I am by innumerable temptations, hope to maintain my ground against my great adversary? O my God, let me not be for one moment left to myself; but take thou the charge of me; and let " my life be hid with Christ in God:" then, and then only, can I hope, that at the last coming of my Lord I shall appear with him in glory.' Col. iii. 3, 4.

He bears in mind also his own weakness and ignorance.—He is conscious that " he has not in himself a sufficiency even to think a good thought;" and that " it is not in him to direct his way aright." Hence he desires to avail himself of the wisdom and power of God; and cries, " Lead me in the right way, because of mine enemies:" " Hold thou me up, and I shall be safe."

But more especially he considers the gracious commands of God.—God has not only permitted, but enjoined, this surrender of our souls to him. 1 Pet. iv. 19, and Isa. xxvi. 20. O what a privilege does the christian account it to obey this divine injunction! How thankful is he that God will condescend to accept this deposit, and to take care of this charge! Hence he avails himself of this privilege, and says, " Hide me under the shadow of thy wings!" " O save me for thy mercy's sake !"

Whilst he acts in this manner,

II. HE IS PERSUADED OF GOD'S ABILITY TO KEEP HIM—

He does not merely presume upon God's sufficiency: he is well persuaded of it,

1. From the report of others—

He is informed by the Inspired Writers, *that God created the world out of nothing; and that he upholds and orders every thing in it;* insomuch that not a sparrow falls to the ground without his express permission. Hence then he argues; ' Did God create my soul, and can he not uphold it? Did he form my enemies also, and can he not restrain them ?* Has he numbered even the hairs of my head, and will he overlook the concerns of my soul

He is told *that God is ever seeking opportunities, not only to exert, but also magnify, his power in his people's cause.* 2 Chron. xvi. 9. This is meant by "shewing himself strong." Shall all that vigilance, then, be exercised in vain ? or shall any be able to prevail against him ?

He is assured also *that God never yet lost one whom he had undertaken to keep:* he never suffered "one of his little-ones to perish." Matt. xviii. 14. "None was ever plucked out of his hand ;" John x. 28. 29 ; not the smallest grain of wheat, however agitated in the sieve, was ever permitted to fall upon the earth." Am. ix. 9. "The gates of hell have never been able to prevail against his church." Then, says the christian, "I will trust, and not be afraid." My Saviour, in the days of his flesh, "lost none that had been given him :" John xviii. 9 ; "Whom he loved, he loved to the end ;" John xiii. 1 ; and therefore I am persuaded he will perfect that which concerneth me, Ps. cxxxviii. 8, and "complete in me the good work he has begun." Phil. i. 6.

2. From his own experience—

The christian well remembers what he was by nature ; and knows by daily experience what he should yet be, if Omnipotence were not exerted in his support. And hence he argues thus ; 'Has God created me anew, and by an invisible, but almighty, influence turned the tide of my affections, so that they now flow upward to the fountain from whence they sprang ; and can he not keep me from going back ? Has he kept me for many years, like the burning bush, encompassed, as it were, with the flame of my corruptions, yet not consumed by it; and "can any thing be too hard for him ?"———

These arguments are indeed of no weight for the conviction of others ; but to the christian himself they are a source of the strongest conviction, and of the richest consolation : yea, from these, more than from any others, he is enabled to say, "I *know* whom I have believed."

Moreover,

III. THIS PERSUASION IS A STRONG SUPPORT TO HIM UNDER ALL HIS TRIALS—

Many are the difficulties of the christian's warfare : but a persuasion of God's ability to keep him,

1. Encourages him to duty—

The path of duty is sometimes exceeding difficult : and too many have fainted in it, or been diverted from it. But we may see in the Hebrew youths what a persuasion of God's power will effect. They braved the furnace itself, from the consideration that God could deliver them from it, or support them in the midst of it. Dan. iii. 17, 18. And thus will every christian "encourage himself in God," and "be strong in the Lord and in the power of his might."

2. Strengthens him for conflict—

Under temptations of Satan, or the hidings of God's face, the most exalted christian would sink, if he were not supported by this hope : "I had fainted," says David, "unless I had believed verily to see the goodness of the Lord in the land of the living." But the thought that the grace of Christ is sufficient for him, will turn all his sorrows into joy : 2 Cor. xii. 9, and Rom.

*See this argument suggested by God himself, Isaiah liv. 15—17. *q. d.* "Your enemies are forming weapons; but I formed *them ;* and whatever skill they exercise, I will defeat their attempts."

vii. 24; he will chide his dejected spirit, Ps. xlii. 11, and return again to the charge, knowing that at last " he shall be more than conqueror through Him that loved him." Rom. viii. 37.

3. Enables him to endure sufferings—

Many and great were the sufferings of St. Paul; yet says he, " None of these things move me, neither count I my life dear unto myself." Thus every christian must " go through much tribulation in the way to the kingdom :" but he learns, not only to bear, but to "glory in tribulation," because it gives him a more enlarged experience of God's power and grace, and thereby confirms his hope, which shall never make him ashamed. Rom. v. 3—5.

4. Assures him of final victory—

Those who have not just views of God are left in painful suspense : but they who know whom they have believed, are as much assured of victory, as if all their enemies were lying dead at their feet. Compare Isa. l. 7—9, with Rom. viii. 33—39.

We shall further IMPROVE the subject,

1. For conviction—

All persons are ready to think that they are possessed of true and saving faith. But faith is not a mere assent to the truths of the gospel, or even an approbation of them. It includes three things ; *A committing of the soul to Christ ; a persuasion of his ability to save us ; and a determination to go forward in dependence upon him, doing and suffering whatever we are called to in the path of duty.*

Have we *this* faith ?— — —

2. For consolation—*

If there be any amongst us weak and dejected, let them turn their eyes to God as their almighty friend. Let them know that " He is able to make them stand :" Rom. xiv. 4 ; he is " able to make all grace abound towards them, that they, having always all-sufficiency in all things, may abound unto every good work." 2 Cor. ix. 8. It is God himself who suggests to the fainting soul these very considerations ; and he requires nothing, but that we wait on him in order that we may experience their truth and efficacy— — — Isai. xl. 27—31.

" Now unto Him that is able to keep us from falling, and to present us faultless before the presence of his glory with exceeding joy, to Him be glory and dominion for ever and ever, Amen." Jude, ver. 24, 25.

*If this were the subject of a FUNERAL SERMON, the excellencies ef *the deceased* might here be enumerated, and *the survivors* be comforted by the consideration that THEIR KEEPER lives for ever.

LOVE TO GOD, THE GREAT COMMANDMENT.

Mark xii. 28—30.—And one of the Scribes came, and having heard them reasoning together, and perceiving that he had answered them well, asked him, Which is the first commandment of all? And Jesus answered him, The first of all the commandments is, Hear, O Israel, The Lord our God is one Lord : and thou shalt love the Lord thy God with all thy heart, and with all thy soul, and with all thy mind, and with all thy strength : This is the first commandment. (H. H.)

IT is no uncommon thing for those who plainly declare the truth, to be beset by cavillers—

Our Lord who spake as never man spake, endured continually the contradiction of sinners against himself—

He had been captiously interrogated by Pharisees, Herodians, and Sadducees: and having silenced all of them, was again attacked by one of the Scribes, who either was, or thought himself, more subtle than the other Pharisees who had already been confounded. Verse 13, 18, 28., with Matthew xxii. 34, 35.

The answer of our Lord to him, will lead us to shew,

I. WHO IS THE CHRISTIANS' GOD—

Our Lord being questioned respecting the law, answered him out of the law.   Deut. vi. 4, 5.

His answer which is given more fully than in St. Matthew's Gospel, intimates,

1. That we must know God before we can love him—

Our love to God must be founded on what he is himself, and what he is, and will be, to us—

Without such a knowledge of God, all our pretences to love him must be vain—

2. That there is but one God—

The heathen in general worshipped a multitude of gods—

Some, who were better instructed, supposed that there were two powerful Beings; the one the author of all good, the other of all evil—

Our Lord declared, in opposition to all such erroneous notions, that there was but One self-existent Jehovah, who made and governed all things—

3. That that God exists in Three Persons—

Some of the Jews, before the time of Christ, thought there was a deep mystery contained in these words of their law, Bp. Patrick on Deut. vi. 4.

Many early Christians were persuaded, that in these words God had given to the Jews an intimation of his subsistence in Three Persons.   Bp. Patrick on Deut. vi. 4.

This is certainly the scriptural view of God, Matt. viii. xxviii. 19; and we may well take occasion from the text to speak of it; though it would not be prudent to found the doctrine altogether on the words before us—

Having called our attention to the One object that is worthy of our affections, he shews us,

II. OUR DUTY TOWARDS HIM—

We must not only love God, but our love to him must be,

1. Supreme—

Our esteem of God should be so exalted, our desire after him so intense, and our delight in him so exquisite, that no created good should rival him for one moment in our affections—

Our love to him should destroy all love to what is evil, and both limit and regulate all our lawful attachments.   Luke xiv. 26.

2. Abiding—

If we are to love him with *all* our heart, &c., there is no time when we are at liberty to offer him only a *divided* heart—

His excellencies never vary; and therefore our love to him should not change—

3. Operative—

Love to a fellow-creature is a mere pretence, if it do not approve itself to him in our actions—

Our love to God should make us exert all our powers for him,* and seek nis glory in all we do. 1 Cor. x. 31.

In further elucidating our Lord's answer, we shall endeavor to explain,

III. WHY THAT DUTY IS CALLED "THE FIRST AND GREAT COMMANDMENT"—

The Jews doubted whether the moral law, or the ceremonial rites of circumcision and sacrifices, were the greater—

Our Lord tells them that the duty of love to God was beyond comparison greater than any, or all others together—

1. It is the noblest exercise of our faculties—

Love, towards whomsoever it be exercised, whether friends or enemies, is a noble affection, and assimilates us to " God, who is Love"—

But the exercise of this affection towards God is suited to beings who are endowed with reason, and destined to immortality—

Such an employment is an anticipation of heaven itself—

2. It is the foundation of all our other duties—

Let the best services of a fellow creature be divested of this principle, and they are good for nothing even in our eyes—

How worthless then must all our actions be in the sight of God, if they do not originate in a regard for him, and in a zeal for his glory!—

Surely love to God, as our Creator, Redeemer, and Sanctifier, ought to be the one principle from which every thing else should flow—

Nor will any sacrifice go up with acceptance before God, unless it be inflamed with this heavenly fire—

INFER,

1. How dreadfully are we fallen!

Man originally fulfilled this command, just as they are now doing in heaven—

But how far are we from such a state—

What base and vile things have usurped the throne of God in our hearts—

Let us humble ourselves in dust and ashes—

2. How impossible is it that we should ever be justified by the works of the law!

If we would be justified by the law, we must *perfectly* fulfil this duty from the earliest to the latest period of our existence—

But who has fulfilled it *perfectly?* or does? or can?—

Let us then renounce all dependence on the law—

3. What reason have we to be thankful for the blood of Jesus!

The guilt we have contracted is more than words can express or imagination conceive—

Yet it may all be washed away in the fountain opened for sin—

O let us flee to Jesus, and bless God for such an all-sufficient Saviour—

4. How should we value " the glorious Gospel of the blessed God!"

The scope and intent of the Gospel is to restore us to our primitive state—

To bring us to love God with all our hearts is the end of of all its declarations and precepts, its promises and threatenings.

Let us then close with its offers, and shew forth its fruits—

* This is implied in the word *strength*.

GOD'S ADOPTING LOVE.

1 John iii. 1.—"Behold what manner of love the Father hath bestowed upon us, that we should be called the sons of God." (Sk.)

When the Danish missionaries, stationed in Malabar, set some of their converts to translate a catechism, in which it was asserted that christians become the sons of God, one of the translaters was startled, and said, " It is too much! Let me rather render it, ' they shall be permitted to kiss his feet.' " We cannot wonder at this, since even St. John appears quite overpowered by the same sentiment, and filled with rapturous amazement at the love of God therein exhibited.—" Behold," he exclaims, " what manner of love," how vast, unparalleled, and transcendent, " the Father hath bestowed upon us. that we should be called," and constituted—not dazzling geniuses, renowned philosophers, invincible heroes, imperial monarchs,—no, but " sons of God," the high, the omnipotent, the everlasting Jehovgh !—But this high title, together with the privileges of adoption, belong exclusively to believers in Christ. In John i. 12, 13, we see that men do not become the sons of God, by being naturally descended from this or that father, nor by having the title conferred on them by men like themselves, but by God's granting them that privilege through faith.

In order to enter into the apostle's views and feelings, let us consider,

I. The original state of those whom God adopts.—What were they ? They were " children of wrath even as others." As men, they were the creatures of God, but as sinners, they were,

1. *Criminals*, guilty both in principle and practice of rebellion against God. Traitors to the Majesty of heaven. Hating, spurning, and violating all the divine laws, they robbed their Maker and Benefactor of his just due, and exposed themselves to his righteous displeasure.

2. *Servants, slaves, and captives of sin.* " His servants ye are to whom ye yield yourselves to obey," &c. " Whoever committeth sin is the servant of sin." The word rendered servant signifies a *slave*, and justly denotes that bondage in which the unconverted are held, while enslaved by their own lusts, appetites, and passions.—Yea, they are represented as captives serving under their enemies, and wearing the chains of their oppressors.

3. *Children of Satan, and heirs of hell.* " Ye are of your father the devil," &c.—" Children of Belial."—" Children of wrath." " The wages of sin is death." They had no lot nor portion with the saints, but were liable to eternal misery, 1 Cor. vi. 9; Psa. ix. 17; Rev. xxi. 8.

4. *Spiritually dead.* Not only legally dead, as condemned to eternal death, but actually dead, as being destitute of all spiritual life and energy ; dead in trespasses and sins, rotting as it were in the grave of corruption, &c. Can such as these become sons of God? Yes, for such were all who can now call God, " Abba Father."—We now consider,

II. The method by which he brings them into his family. This method may justly increase our admiration. Three things were necessary in order to their adoption:—

1. *To provide a pardon for them.* As they were criminals, this was the first step towards their salvation, for while the curse hung over their heads, they could not participate the divine favor. Hence, to satisfy the claims of just.ce, honor the violated law, and open the door of mercy, Jesus is sent to die, the just for the unjust, to propitiate for their sins and take away the

curse, so that God may be just, and yet the justifier of those who believe
Behold! believe! adore!

2. *To subdue their hearts*, so that they may be disposed to receive the
mercy of God. To effect this, the Spirit of grace is sent to enlighten, soften,
humble, and afflict—to apply the word of truth—to strip them of all their
fancied worth and righteousness—then to lead them to the cross—to dispose
and enable them to lay hold on the atoning sacrifice by faith. By this act of
faith they obtain justification, and God, according to the gospel constitution,
receives them as his children. " Ye are all the children of God, by faith in
Christ Jesus."—" Whosoever believeth is born of God."

3. *To liberate them from the bondage of sin, and infuse a new principle
of life*. This is done at the same time that they obtain pardon through
Christ—they then are set free, they awake to righteousness, the love of God
is shed abroad in their hearts, and becomes thenceforth the vital, actuating,
governing principle of their souls.

Such is the method by which sinners are brought into the family of God.
Let us now regard,

III. THE DIGNITIES AND PRIVILEGES OF THEIR ADOPTION.

The sons of earthly grandees value themselves highly upon their birth and
parentage, although they neither inherit their ancestors' virtues, nor thereby
become wiser or more happy. But what is it to be a son of the greatest potentate, compared to being a son of God! The believer may boast a higher
descent than the proudest monarch that ever filled a throne. Nor is it an
empty boast; for all the sons of God,

1. *Inherit their Father's nature, and moral perfections;* i. e. they resemble him in all his imitable attributes. They are just, upright, true, merciful, generous, loving, compassionate, &c. They are renewed in the spirit
of their minds, in knowledge after the image of him by whom they are
created, and begotten anew. And, oh, how amiable, how noble, how sublime, is this heaven-born nature!

2. *They are united by the nearest and tenderest relations to Jesus Christ*
" He is the first-born among many brethren." " He is not ashamed to call
them brethren, saying," &c. This elder brother is their representative, their
husband, and their head. He dwells in their hearts by faith, and he ever
liveth in heaven to intercede for them.

3. *They have free access unto the Father on all occasions*, Eph. ii. 18;
Rom. v. 2.

4. *They enjoy their heavenly Father's approbation.* His Spirit bears
witness to their spirits, that they are his children, Rom. viii. 15, 16; Gal
iv. 6.

5. *They are heirs of God, and joint heirs with our Lord Jesus Christ*,
Rom. viii. 17. If each had been made heir of a world—a universe, it would
have been a trifle compared to this! " To be heirs of God," &c. What is
this but to be entitled to all that the Deity has, or is, or can do, to render
them happy? To be heirs of the God of the universe, and joint heirs with
Jesus his only Son, who inherits all; this is to reach the highest eminence
to which creatures can be elevated, and to be only less than God!

Hence the lofty titles given them. Priests, princes, kings. " Ye are a
chosen generation," &c. " Unto him who hath loved us, &c., and made us
kings and priests unto God and his Father," &c.

In life or death, time or eternity, height or depth, they are secure, blessed,
and inexpressibly happy.

View all these things in connexion—their original state—the astonishing method adopted towards them—and above all the transcendent privileges of their adoption, and you will exclaim, " Behold what manner," &c.

Our subject leads,

1. To correction of the false opinions formed by the world concerning the pious, whom it supposes miserable, low-spirited, unworthy. But " the world knoweth us not, because it knew him not."

2. To self-examination—are *we* the sons of God?

3. To excitement:—let the sons of God live suitably to their dignity.

GOD'S VISIT TO HIS PEOPLE.

Luke vii. 16.—God hath visited his people. (Sk.)

THE text is connected with an interesting narrative circumstantially detailed by the evangelist in the preceding verses. The Lord Jesus "went about doing good;" in the course of his travels he came to a city called Nain; many disciples and much people were with him. Some to gratify curiosity, others perhaps to entangle him in his talk, others to imbibe instruction. Near the gate of the city, they met a funeral procession, a young man cut down in the prime of life—a mother's only son, and she was a widow. A widow is a solitary character; the prop that once supported her is withdrawn; she has sometimes indeed the melancholy pleasure of beholding in her offspring the resemblance of him whose memory is ever dear to her; but in the widow before us, this slender consolation was denied her; she was following her only son to the grave. Jesus Christ compassionated her circumstances, and he drew near and said, " Young man, I say unto thee, Arise: and he that was dead sat up," &c. " And there came a fear on all, and they glorified God, saying, That a great prophet is risen up amongst us, and that God hath visited his people." We will state,

I. THE NATURE OF THIS VISIT.

1. *It was not an abrupt or unexpected visit, but a visit previously and variously intimated.*—God was accustomed to visit man in his primitive innocency; and the visits of Jehovah were sources of inexpressible joy to our first parents: but when man revolted from God, he no longer desired his presence. " I heard thy voice in the garden, and I was afraid." God however did not abandon man, but gave him a promise, Gen. iii. 15.

2. *It was a visit long and ardently expected.*—The words of Christ sufficiently prove this: "Verily I say unto you, that many prophets and righteous men have desired to see the things which ye see," Matt. xiii. 17.—"Your father Abraham rejoiced to see my day," &c. John viii. 56.

3. *It was a visit personally and punctually paid.*—Personally, as to the manner, " For in the fulness of time God sent forth his Son, made of a woman," &c. And punctually as the period. Daniel had referred to this, " Seventy weeks are determined upon thy people," &c. Dan. ix. 24.

4. *It was a visit generally known, and widely and extensively spread.*—John the Baptist did all that he could to give publicity to the character of Christ, and Christ himself " went about all Galilee teaching in their synagogues," &c. Matt. iv. 23. But,

5. *It was a visit almost generally disregarded.*—A few reverenced and adored the Savior, and exclaimed, "Never man spake like this man ;" but the great mass of the Jewish people rejected him. "He came unto his own, but his own received him not." View the insults they offered unto his person, and the contempt they cast upon his doctrines and miracles.

II. THE PURPOSES FOR WHICH THIS VISIT WAS PAID.

1. *To display the divine glory.* Every thing that God does in the kingdom of nature, providence, and grace, must in a certain sense refer to himself. "The heavens declare the glory of God," the glory of his natural perfections; but the visit which God in the person of Christ paid to his people, was to display the glory of the moral perfections of the Deity—wisdom, love, power, and mercy.

2. *To make an atonement for sin.*—God is the moral governor of the world.—When he made man he placed him under a law, a law whose penalty was death.—This law was violated—justice demanded punishment. No creature could make an expiation. God revealed himself in human nature. to make an atonement for sin. Hence "He was wounded for our transgressions," &c.—"He gave his life a ransom for many," &c.—"He was made sin for us," &c.

3. *To reveal a comprehensive and complete system of religious truth.*—Divine truth was sparingly and cautiously revealed under the Old Testament dispensation ; it was here a little and there a little ; and that which was revealed, was corrupted by the artifice or ignorance of men. But Christ declared, "To this end was I born, and for this cause came I into the world, that I should bear witness unto the truth," &c. John xviii. 37.

4. *To exhibit a perfect model of virtue.*—The Old Testament saints were patterns of piety—Joseph of chastity. Moses of meekness, Job of patience, Daniel of courage—but Christ was all perfection. See his submission to parental authority, his humility, his sympathetic feeling for the afflicted, his zeal for his Father's glory, his love, his patience, &c.

III. THE RETURNS WE SHOULD MAKE TO GOD FOR FAVORING US WITH SUCH A VISIT.

1. *We should admire and adore the condescension of the visitant.*—Never was there such a visit paid before ;—so voluntary ;—so little was there on the part of man to invite such a visitant ;—the treatment he was to meet with from the parties visited: all serve to excite our astonishment, and lead us to adore the condescension of our God and Saviour.

2. *We should form our lives upon the model of his.*—Let us study his character, let us imbibe his disposition, and let us copy his life, 1 John iv. 17.

3. *We should avail ourselves of all the advantages which God's visit to our world was designed to procure.*—He came to save sinners—to destroy the works of the devil—"that we might have life, and have it more abundantly." Let us seek salvation, &c.

4. *As God has visited us, let us visit him in return.*—He comes among us when we assemble in his name.—Let us meet him in his house—in our closets—at his table, and let us anticipate the time when we shall visit him in his kingdom. When he will send his flaming messengers to shout us welcome to the skies. "He is gone to prepare a place for us, and he will come again, and receive us unto himself." Amen. "Even so, come. Lord Jesus. '

THE GOD OF OUR SALVATION DAILY LOADETH US WITH BENEFITS.

Psalm lxviii. 19.—Blessed be the Lord, who daily loadeth us with benefits, even the God of our salvation." (Sk.)

"O Lord how manifold are thy works!" What a diversity prevails in all the walks of nature! How multiform are the operations of God in the church! What a variety of truths is displayed in the Bible! But were we to analyze the sacred volume, we should not find one sentiment of more frequent occurrence than that with which our text commences: "Blessed be the Lord!"—How proper then for our consideration! Nothing can be more calculated to inspire us with this sentiment, than the subject before us. Here we have,

I. What God is:—He is "the God of our salvation."
II. What God does:—He "daily loadeth us with benefits."
III. What we should do in return.—"Bless the Lord."

I. What God is.—"The God of our salvation;" salvation is deliverance from danger; the term is sometimes applied to deliverance from human enemies, then we call it a temporal salvation. It is generally however applied to the soul. Man is a sinner, and sin exposes him to danger; for "the wages of sin is death," and "the soul that sinneth it shall die." But there is deliverance from this danger; this is attributed to God.

1. *The scheme of salvation* originated in God. When man sinned, he could not restore himself to the forfeited favor and image of God. He had no desire for salvation—he could make no atonement for his sin—he could not extricate himself from the power of his enemies. But God pitied him in all his wretchedness; and "God sent not his Son into the world," &c. John iii. 17.

2. *The means of salvation are afforded us by God.* God sends us his gospel, containing good news of salvation; his ministers to declare the way of salvation. He gives us a day of salvation. He affords us Christian sabbaths, religious ordinances, and various means of grace in order to promote our salvation.

3. *The work of salvation is accomplished in the human soul by God's immediate agency.* "Behold God is become my salvation!" The Holy Ghost convinces of sin, and shows us the need of salvation; witnesseth with our spirits that we are saved; sanctifies the soul, and makes it his holy habitation; and seals it unto the day of redemption.

4. *The sole glory of our final salvation will endlessly redound to God.* In heaven we shall have clearer discoveries of the greatness, extent, and freeness of our salvation; we shall see the evils from which we have been delivered, and the hell we have escaped, and we shall feel how deeply we are indebted to God for our salvation, and sing "Salvation to our God," &c. Rev. vii. 10.

II. What God does for us;—He "daily loadeth us with benefits." Three things we notice here,

1. *The nature of God's gifts;*—they are "benefits;" a benefit is a kindness, a favor conferred, an act of love. God's gifts are benefits, not deserts; were God to deal with us according to our demerit, we should be loaded with punishments rather than benefits. Even our afflictions are benefits, as they "work for us," &c. 2 Cor. iv. 17; Heb. xii. 10.

> "Crosses from his sovereign hand,
> Are blessings in disguise."

2 *Their number.* We are loaded with benefits. Here we may enumerate the intellectual powers we possess—the health we enjoy—the age of the world in which we live—the country we inhabit—the civil and religious advantages with which we are favored, and especially the spiritual privileges which God has so graciously conferred upon us.

3. *The frequency of their communication.* He "*daily* loadeth us," &c. God's benefits come to us daily, they are new every morning; great is his faithfulness.

> "Each evening shows his tender love,
>   Each rising morn his plenteous grace;
> His waken'd wrath doth slowly move,
>   His willing mercy flies apace."

And these benefits flow to us *freely*, unsolicited, unemployed, unsought. *Seasonably*, exactly as we need them. Critics state, that instead of "daily loadeth us with benefits," it should be read, "who bears our burdens, or supports us every day." This is an interesting truth! In the wilderness God bare Israel as a man doth bear his son, Deut. i. 31. Or as an eagle bears her young on her wings, Deut. xxxii. 11. The promise is, "Even to hoary hairs will I carry you," Isa. xlvi. 4. We have our cares, and burdens, and anxieties, but God invites us to cast them upon him. Ps. lv. 22.

III. WHAT WE SHOULD DO IN RETURN.—"Blessed be the LORD." To bless, signifies to extol, exalt, or speak well of a person; and to bless the Lord is to speak good of his name.

1. *We should bless the Lord sincerely.*—Hypocrisy is hateful to God. What our lips express, our hearts should feel. In order to this, we should meditate on God's benefits, and on our unworthiness, sinfulness and great demerit.

2. *We should bless the Lord affectionately.*—Our gratitude should be the effusion of love. How pleasing is the exercise of praise when love tunes our hearts.

3. *We should bless the Lord constantly.* "I will bless the Lord at all times." The benefits of God are incessantly flowing to us, and our gratitude should be as constantly returned to him.

4. *We should bless the Lord practically.*—To say, "We praise thee, O God, we acknowledge thee to be the Lord;" while we practically violate his laws, must be abominable in his sight. Let us "praise him not only with our lips, but by our lives," &c. Conclusion,

1. *Is the Lord the God of our salvation?*—Are we saved from sin? from the dominion of sin? from our easily besetting sin? Salvation from sin is essential to our being saved from hell. God is the Saviour, and the only Saviour. He invites us to look to him, and be saved. O let us avail ourselves of his kind invitation! How desirable it is to be saved! May God be our Saviour, even the God of our salvation.

2. *Does he daily load us with his benefits?*—What a lesson for humility? What have we that we have not received? What an excitement for love to him who deals so bountifully with us! Does God bear our burdens! Let us learn to depend upon him. He will never suffer the righteous to be moved

3. *Are we saying "Blessed be the Lord."*—Are his statutes our songs in the house of our pilgrimage? Let us anticipate the period when we shall join the society of angels, and rival them in the chorus of praise.

> "Thee they sing with glory crown'd,
>   We extol the slaughter'd Lamb;
> Lower if our voices sound,
>   Our subject is the same."

ENCOURAGEMENT IN GOD.

1 Samuel xxx. 6.—But David encouraged himself in the Lord his God. (S. S.)

In seasons of prosperity the superior happiness of a christian is not visible to all—

But in adverse circumstances he has a manifest advantage over others—

The ungodly, when the cisterns from whence they draw their water are broken or emptied, have no comfort left—

But when every stream is dried up, the godly have still access to the fountain itself—

This was experienced by the church of old—Hab. iii. 17, 18.

And it is beautifully exemplified in the history before us—

David was in great trouble, being suspected by the Philistines—Plundered by the Amalekites—and threatened by his own soldiers—

But in the midst of all he encouraged himself in God—

We shall shew

I. What reason he had to do so.

Though reduced to the greatest extremities, he derived encouragement

1. From the perfections of God as revealed in the word.

He was no stranger to the character of God as it was revealed to Moses—Exod. xxxiv. 6, 7.

Or to the unnumbered illustrations of it which the history of his nation afforded him—

Consequently he knew that there was nothing too hard for God to effect, or too great for him to give—

2. From the experience which he himself had had of God.

The lion, the bear, the Philistine giant, and the murderous rage of Saul had given him abundant proofs of God's superintending providence—1 Sam. xvii. 37, xviii. 11, and xix. 10, 11.

These he called to mind in this season of trial and distress—Ps. xlii. 6, lxxvii. 10, 11.

And wisely judged that, with such a friend on his side, he had no cause for fear—2 Cor. i. 10.

3. From the covenant which God had made with him.

God had covenanted with him to give him the throne of Israel—

Hence he was assured that his life should be spared till this promise was accomplished—

It was in this view that he was enabled to call God his God—

And the thought of this relation to God added tenfold confidence to his soul—

While we admire the conduct of David in this particular, let us consider

II. What reason we have to do likewise.

Certainly the grounds of David's encouragement are equally calculated for our support.

God is still the same almighty and gracious Being as ever—

His arm is not shortened, nor is his ear heavy with respect to us—

We may also see much of his goodness *in our own experience*—

Wonderful have been the ways in which he has dealt with us for the awakening, preserving, and sanctifying of our souls—

He has *also covenanted with us* that " he will never leave us nor forsake us"—Heb. xiii. 5.

Nor shall one jot or title of his word ever fail—

Are not these then grounds of encouragement to us as well as to David?—
But we have far greater reason to encourage ourselves in God than David nad—
We have seen more stupendous displays of God's *power*.
David had read of the wonders wrought in Egypt and the wilderness—
But what were these wonders when compared with the victories gained over all the passions and prejudices of the world by the preaching of a few poor fishermen?—
We have beheld more astonishing exercises of his *love*.
The history of the Jews records many instances of God's love towards them—
But what were these when compared with the gift of his dear Son to die for us, and of his holy Spirit to renew us?—
These things are as much beyond any thing that David had ever seen, as the substance is beyond the shadow—
We have experienced more abundant proofs of his *faithfulness*.
How many promises, made to the church at large, have been accomplished by the mission of Christ, and the gift of the Holy Spirit!—
And all the members of the church, from its first establishment to the present moment, have found the promises of the gospel fulfilled to them in their season!—
In proportion therefore as God's faithfulness has been tried and ascertained, our confidence in him must be increased—
Application.
1. Let us endeavor to secure God as *our* God.
Unless God be ours, we can have but little reason to encourage ourselves in him—
Let us then look to Christ, that through him we may find acceptance with God—
So shall God be our friend, our father, and our "eternal great reward"—Gen. xv. 1; John i. 12; 2 Cor. vi. 18.
2. Let us encourage ourselves in God.
We must expect to meet with many difficulties and troubles—
Nor can we find any grounds of encouragement in ourselves—
But in God there is all that we can either need or desire—
Are we then discouraged by outward difficulties or inward corruptions? let us direct our eyes to him, as our compassionate, almighty, and ever faithful friend—
Let us, like David, chide our unbelief, Ps. xliii. 5; and henceforth say with him, "In the day of my trouble I will call upon God"—Ps. lxxxvi. 7

GOD AND THE REDEEMER MUTUALLY GLORIFIED.

John xvii. 1.—Father, the hour is come: glorify thy Son, that thy Son also may glorify thee. (Pr.)

WE here find our Lord Jesus in a most solemn and affecting situation. He had often said that his hour was not yet come; but now it is fully arrived. Having comforted his disciples by an inimitable farewell address, he here concludes it by a prayer, which was offered in their hearing.

118

It does not seem that our Lord had in these words an immediate respect to nis sufferings: he appears rather to look through them, to the joy that was set before him. We have other instances of this, especially in John xii. 23, 24, 31.

The prayer presented in our text is intended to intimate, that the honor conferred on the Redeemer, in the establishment of his kingdom, would redound to the glory of God the Father.

I. Enquire in what respects GOD HAS GLORIFIED, and does still glorify his Son.

Whatever tends to raise him in the esteem of intelligent beings, or to exhibit the excellence of his character, is the means of glorifying him.

God is said to have 'magnified' his servant Joshua, when he wrought by nim before the face of all Israel. Josh. iii. 7. So Christ was glorified from his first coming into the world: angels worshipped him: witness was borne to him at his baptism, also on the mount of transfiguration, and by the miracles which he wrought.— — —But the principal part was to follow upon his sufferings and triumphs on the cross, as David was honored when he had killed the uncircumcised Philistine: then they sung his praises in their song

More particularly—

1. God has glorified his Son *in granting him the desire of his heart.*

It was an honor to Esther to be asked what was her petition, and what was her request; when she asked her own life, and the life of her people. — — —This honor was conferred on Christ; and he asked the life of his enemies, that he might be made a covenant for the people: their salvation was all that he desired. Isai. xlix. 8; liii. 11; Psa. ii. 8; xxi. 1, 2.

2. In bestowing mercy upon sinners *only in his name, and for his sake.* — — —It was an honor conferred on Joseph that he should have all things in his hand, and that all Egypt should be dependent upon him. It was also a great honor conferred on Job that he should be made a mediator, and that God should accept his three friends for his sake: this was more than enough to do away his reproach. Job xl. 8.— — —But to Jesus is given superior honor: God hears no prayer but in his name, gives no blessing but for his sake: and through his name the greatest sinners are pardoned, justified, and eternally saved.

3. God has glorified his Son in pouring forth *a richer effusion of grace* at the time of his ascension, than at any former period.— — —The mercy was to begin at Jerusalem, but to go on to the ends of the earth. Luke xxiv. 47.— — —It was at his coronation, that the captives among the Gentiles were set free: God reserved that honor to grace his triumph.— — —All the blessings that have since been given to the church, are given with a view of honoring him, and in consequence of his intercession.

4. In investing him with *the government of the world,* in subservience to the great ends of his mediation: ver. 2.— — —All that is going on in the earth is only making way for his kingdom, and the accomplishment of his designs. Ephes. i. 20—23.

II. In what respects the GLORY OF CHRIST redounds to the glory of the Father.

Wherein the Son is glorified, the Father is glorified also, and that by the same means. It is the office of the Holy Spirit to glorify Christ, and his work is to glorify the Father.— — —The honor of the Son does not disagree with that of the Father: there is no jealousy here, though some have affected to be very jealous for the Father's honor. John v. 23.-- — -Tne interests of the Lawgiver do not suffer by those of the Saviour: they are inseparably blended together, and cannot exist apart.

1. The gospel provides for *the honor of God*, in such a way as nothing else could have done. The moral law glorifies him in asserting his authority: the sacrifices under the ceremonial law glorified him, as containing a virtual acknowledgment that sinners deserved to die for their offences.— — But the Son of God magnifies the law by his obedience, and makes it honorable; satisfies divine justice by his atonement, and glorifies the name of the Lord.

2. The mediation of Christ exhibits *the divine character* as infinitely glorious.— — —All other mediums afforded only a partial view of his perfections; but his entire glory is seen in the face of Jesus Christ. The light of nature was insufficient to show the path of life, and it effected no moral change in the state of the world.— — —But wherever the doctrine of the cross is made known, idolatry and iniquity fall before it, God is glorified in the highest; on earth there is peace, and good will towards men.

3. Wherever Christ is believed in, the name of the Lord *is loved and feared*.— — —The Lawgiver is adored wherever the Mediator is embraced. All the christian graces do honor to God: repentance bears respect to his authority, faith implicitly obeys the dictates of his word, hope lifts up its eyes to his mercy seat, love cleaves to him as our portion, and his law is our delight.— — —The believer is of the same mind as Christ, making the divine glory the ultimate end of all.

We learn from hence—

1. What encouragement there is for sinners to *come to Christ*. The glory of God was the great hinderance in the way of acceptance: now it admits of a free salvation, and God is more abundantly glorified than he would have been in our condemnation. He can now pardon the greatest sins: look to him therefore, and be saved.

2. The motives that should urge us to pray for *the success of the gospel*. It is Christ's own prayer, and we may unite with him in it: "Father, glorify thy Son!"— — —Let us lay hold of this plea: it has always been successful, and always will. If we love God and the Redeemer, we shall pray and labor to promote their mutual glory in the world.

CHAPTER IV.

CHRIST.

CHRIST ONE WITH THE FATHER.

John x. 30.—I and my Father are one. (H. H.)

It might well be expected, that, if God should reveal his will to man, there would be many things disclosed by him, which exceed the narrow limits of human reason. This might more particularly be expected in whatsoever related to his own person and character: for, as we can know nothing of him any farther than he is pleased to reveal himself to us; and as we cannot even comprehend our own nature, or discover how the soul is united to the body;

it would be strange indeed if we could comprehend the mode of God's existence, and explain how there should be an union of Three Persons in the Godhead. In relation to such a mysterious subject, our wisdom is to ascertain what God has revealed concerning himself, and to receive it on the testimony of his word. This is the office of reason, as well as of faith: for reason requires, that we submit our understandings to the dictates of His wisdom, no less than our wills to the influence of His authority. That a Trinity of Persons in the Godhead is revealed, cannot reasonably be doubted, as long as the baptismal rite shall continue to be administered "in the name of the Father, and of the Son, and of the Holy Ghost:" for to imagine, that a creature is here associated with Almighty God in the highest possible act of Divine worship, were the height of absurdity, and impiety. The subject before us relates only to the union subsisting between Christ and his Father: to that therefore we shall confine our attention. We begin with,

I. THE ASSERTION OF CHRIST—

Our Lord says, "I and my Father are one." Now it must be remembered, that the same expressions are used, as in human compositions. so also in the holy scriptures, sometimes in a metaphorical and figurative sense, and sometimes in a plain and literal sense; and their true import must always be judged of by the context. This is particularly the case with respect to the expression before us; which is elsewhere used in reference to the saints, to mark the exalted state to which they are raised by their connexion with Christ, and the mutual interest which they should feel in each other's concerns: "I pray for them, that they all may be one; as thou, Father, art in me, and I in thee, that they also may be one in us; that the world may believe that thou hast sent me. And the glory which thou gavest me, I have given them; that they may be one, even as we are one: I in them, and thou in me, that they may be made perfect in one." John xvii. 20—23. Here the sense is obvious: no one could conceive for a moment that the union here spoken of is *personal*, as though the saints could be one *person* with God, or one *person* in their collective capacity: it simply means, that the saints are to enjoy an union with God and with each other, as nearly resembling that which subsists between Christ and his Father, as their situation and circumstances will admit of, namely, an union of sentiment, of affection, of will, and of operation. But, in the passage under our consideration, more is evidently intended: in that is implied, not merely a figurative, but a *real* and *personal* union, an union of nature and of essence. In proof of this, we must refer you to,

1. The whole scope of the passage—

Our Lord is speaking of the security which his sheep enjoyed; that "He gives unto them eternal life, and that they shall never perish, nor shall any one ever pluck them out of his hand." But, because he was speedily to be taken from them, and might therefore be supposed incapable of fulfilling this promise, he says, that "his Father was confessedly greater than all" created powers, yea, greater than he himself was in his human or Mediatorial capacity; and that "none should ever be able to pluck them out of his Father's hand." Yet, that they might know that he would not on account of his removal from them remit his care of them, he added, "I and my Father are one;"—'we are one, as in will, so in power; as in operation, so in nature and in essence: and consequently my sheep have a double pledge of their security.'

This is the plain meaning of the passage; and that it is so, may be clearly seen from.

2. The construction which the Jews put upon his words—

They took up stones immediately, to stone him: and when he inquired, for which of all his good works they were about to stone him, they replied, that it was "not for any good work, but for blasphemy; because that He, who was only a man like themselves, made himself God." Verses 32, 33. Now this shews incontestably what meaning *they* affixed to his words: it was not an ignorant individual, or persons ill acquainted with the received import of the words, that so interpreted them; but the whole audience, who perfectly understood what meaning his expressions were suited to convey.

The Jews were taught by God himself to be particularly jealous on the subject of idolatry; and to put to death any person who should, whether openly or in secret, attempt to seduce them to it. When therefore they heard our Lord arrogate to himself divine honors, they resented it, as they had done repeatedly before, by taking up stones to stone him as a blasphemer. John v. 17, 18, and viii. 58, 59. We do not say, that they were right in expressing their abhorrence of idolatry in this way; because they should have had the matter examined before a magistrate, and have acted according to evidence, and not according to the impulse of their blind passions: but we do say, that Jesus was justly accused of blasphemy, if he was not God; and that there was just cause for the indignation which his audience expressed.

But perhaps they were mistaken in their construction of his words: in which case we may be assured that Jesus would carefully rectify their error. But do we find that he did disclaim the assertion which they called blasphemy? No;

In his answers to them we find only,

II. His confirmation of it—

They had just complained that he kept them in suspense; and had desired that he would tell them plainly, who, and what, he was. He, in reply, declares that he had told them, and that they would not believe. Ver. 25. Had he told them that he was a mere man like themselves, they would readily enough have believed *that:* but when he tells them again that he was "one with his Father," they go about to stone him for blasphemy. Nevertheless, instead of revoking his word, he vindicates his claim; and establishes the justice of it,

1. By an appeal to the Sacred Writings—

Magistrates, he tells them, were in the Inspired Volume frequently dignified with the name of gods: Exod. vii. 1, and xxii. 28; and he refers them to one passage in particular well known to them all, "I have said, Ye are gods." Ps. lxxxii. 6. Now these were called gods on two accounts; first, because they were Jehovah's Representatives and Vice-gerents upon earth; and next, because *they were types of the Messiah, who was to be really and truly God*, even "Emmanuel, God with us." Isai. vii. 14. Matt. i. 23. 'Now,' says our Lord, ' if these persons, *in order to prepare you for the reception of your incarnate God*, were honored with the name and title of gods, and you readily acquiesced in it, with what reason can you, when your incarnate God appears, accuse him of blasphemy, because he assumes that title, or calls himself by a name which you justly consider as equivalent to it? You are looking for your Messiah; and that Messiah is expressly foretold under the character of "Jehovah's fellow," Zech. xiii. 7, who is "David's Lord as well as David's Son:" Ps. cx. 1, with Matt. xxii. 42—45; such therefore the Messiah *must* be; for "*the Scriptures cannot be broken:*" why then do you not acknowledge the justice of my claim? If indeed I do not give evidence enough that I am the Messiah, you may justly dispute my title to be regarded as God; but if I do, then you are the blasphemers, who rob me of my proper honor. Know ye then, that I am the Person, "whom the Father hath sanctified" and set apart from all eternity to the office, "and now hath sent into the world" to execute it: know also, that, instead of retracting any thing I have said, I repeat my assertions, and demand your acknowledgment of me in my true character.'

Thus our Lord confirms his assertion by an appeal to scripture. He next proceeds to confirm it,

2. By an appeal to his own works—

'I do not desire to be credited in such an assertion upon my bare unsupported word, without any corroborating evidence;' says our Lord: '"If I do not the works of my Father, believe me not: but, if I do, though ye believe not me, believe the works; that ye may know and believe, that the Father is in me, and I in him." Ver. 37, 38. Consider my works, both *the matter*, and the *manner* of them, and see if they do not justify every assertion I have made. Did ever *man* perform such miracles as I have done, so many, so great, so benevolent, so demonstrative of a divine agency? Moses indeed and the prophets wrought some few miracles: but *how?* they wrought them uniformly by application to Jehovah for the intervention of of his power: but look at my miracles: on some occasions indeed, I also, acting in my Mediatorial capacity, have acknowledged my dependence on him, and have acted "in his name," as his servant; Luke xi. 41—43; (for as Mediator, I *am* his servant:) but, as being *One* with the Father, I have wrought in instances without number by that power and authority which I possess in common with the Father. Whence had I the power to still the elements, as I have done; Mark iv. 39; or to expel Satan, Mark ix. 25, or to raise the dead? Mark v. 41; Luke vii. 14. When the leper justly acknowledged my power to effect whatsoever I *would*; to whom was I indebted for power to heal him, when I said, "I *will*, Be thou clean?"' Matt. viii. 3.

Such an appeal as this was sufficient to convince the most incredulous: and it receives much additional light from the manner in which the apostles wrought their miracles: they wrought them invariably *in the name of Jesus*; Acts ix. 34, and xvi. 18; and disclaimed all idea of any inherent power in themselves, or even of any goodness on account of which God had wrought by them; so fearful were they, lest by any means they should rob the Lord Jesus of the honor due unto his name. Acts iii. 6, 12, 16, with iv. 9, 10, 12.

Shall it be said that our Lord did not mean in this appeal to assert his true and proper Godhead? Then see both his words, and the sense in which his enraged adversaries continued to understand them: "Though ye believe not me, believe the works; *that ye may know and believe*, that the Father is in me, and I in him.—*Therefore they sought again to take him.*" Here are two things demonstrated; first, that his enemies understood him to affec equality with God: and next, that He, knowing that they did so understand him, renewed and confirmed the assertions which they had so interpreted. A clearer explanation of what he affirmed, or a stronger proof of WHAT HE IS, we cannot reasonably desire.

We are the more earnest in establishing the divinity of our blessed Lord, because it is intimately connected with every fundamental truth of our holy religion. LEARN then from it.

1. The dignity of his person—

Because God condescended to take our nature upon him, we require his love by denying him to be God. But know that Jesus Christ is indeed "the true God," 1 John v. 20, "the mighty God," Isai. ix. 6, "the great God and our Saviour," Tit. ii. 13, "God over all blessed for evermore." Rom ix. 5. He is "the brightness of his Father's glory, and the express image of his person;" Heb. i. 3; yea, in him dwelleth all the fulness of the God head bodily." Col. ii. 9. Hear what he himself saith unto Philip: Philip, having heard him speaking of the Father, as actually known to his disciples, and already seen by them, saith, "Lord, shew us the Father, and it sufficeth us." To this Jesus replies, " Have *I* been so long with you, and hast thou not known *me*, Philip? He that hath seen *me*, hath seen *the father;* and how sayest thou then, Shew us the Father? Believest thou not that I am in the Father, and the Father in me? Believe me, that I *am* in the Father, and the Father in me; or else believe me for the very works' sake." John xiv. 7—11. Now, I ask, if Jesus had not been really "one with the Father, would he have dared to use such language as this? And, if his disciples were guilty of idolatry in worshipping him, was not the fault altogether *his?* Were not his words and his arguments expressly calculated to mislead and deceive them? But there is no room for doubt on this head. We never can entertain too high thoughts of him; nor can we ever honor him as we ought, unless we "*honor him, even as we honor the Father.*" John v. 23.

2. The virtue of his sacrifice—

On the dignity of his person depends the whole value of his atonement. The apostle justly observes, that "it is not possible for the blood of bulls and of goats to take away sin:" and the same observation may with justice be applied to every creature, however exalted. But when we are assured that it was " *God* who was manifest in the flesh," 1 Tim. iii. 16, that it was "*the Lord of Glory* that was crucified," 1 Cor. ii. 8, and that it was "*God* who purchased the church with his own blood," Acts xx. 28, we no longer hesitate to declare that his death was "a full, perfect, and sufficient sacrifice, oblation, and satisfaction for the sins of the whole world." The Communion Service; and 1 John ii. 2. He was, it is true, "in the form of a servant; but he was also in the form of God, and thought it not robbery to be equal with God;" Phil. ii. 6—8; and therefore we may be assured that "his blood will cleanse us from all sin." 1 John i. 7. The ransom he has paid for us, is fully equal to the redemption of a ruined world: and the righteousness which he has wrought out for us by his obedience unto death, is all that is wanted for the justification of those who trust in it. The very name given him by the prophet declares this; for we are taught to "call him, JEHOVAH OUR RIGHTEOUSNESS." Jer. xxxiii. 16. Here then " the weary and heavy-laden may find rest unto their souls."

3. The sufficiency of his grace—

If Jesus were only a creature, those who trust in him might be addressed like the worshippers of Baal, "Cry aloud, for he is a god: either he is talking, or he is pursuing, or he is on a journey; or peradventure he sleepeth, and must be awaked." 1 Kings xviii. 27. He could not attend to the concerns of the whole universe at once; and therefore could not be a suitable object of our trust and confidence. But he is infinitely above all creatures, being "King of kings, and Lord of lords." Rev. xix. 16. He could truly say to Paul, and to every suppliant in the universe, "My grace is sufficient for thee." Let not any one then despond, as though his corruptions were irremediable, or his enemies invincible; for "God hath laid help for us upon

One that is mighty ;" Ps. lxxxix. 19 ; and the weakest of the human race that relies on him, may confidently say, "In the Lord have I righteousness and strength :" Isai. xlv. 24 ; "The Lord Jehovah is my strength and my song ; he also is become my salvation :" Isai. xii. 2 ; "The Lord is my shepherd ; therefore can I lack nothing." Ps. xxiii. 1.

4. The excellency of his salvation—

If we consider the price that has been paid, we may judge of the value of that redemption which has been purchased for us. Even in relation to the present life, we are told that " eye hath not seen, nor ear heard, nor hath it entered into the heart of man to conceive, the things which God hath prepared for them that love him." Isai. lxiv. 4 ; 1 Cor. ii. 9, 10. Under whatever figure they are spoken of, they are represented as exceeding all human apprehension : " the gift of them is unspeakable :" 2 Cor. ix. 15 ; " the riches of them unsearchable :" Eph. iii. 8 ; " the peace that is enjoyed by means of them, passeth understanding;" Phil. iv. 7 ; and " the joy which they produce, is unspeakable and glorified :" Eph. iii. 18 ; the love that bestowed them has " a height and depth, and length and breadth" that can never be explored. Eph. iii. 18. Respecting the future life, we are still further from being able to appreciate the glories of it. The description of heaven, as a city paved with gold, and enriched with every thing magnificent or good, affords but a faint idea of that blessed place ; Rev. xxi. 10—23 ; as the songs and music of its inhabitants very inadequately represent their blessedness and joy. Rev. v. 8—14, and xiv. 1—3. But this we know, that, both on earth and in heaven, the felicity of the saints shall be worthy of the sacrifice that was made to obtain it. Let not any one then seek it in a listless and lukewarm manner, as though it were of little value ; for it is a " great salvation," Heb. ii. 3, which the tongues of men and angels can never worthily describe, nor can the ages of eternity suffice to enumerate its blessings.

THE FIRST PROMISE.

Genesis iii. 15.—And I will put enmity between thee and the woman, and between thy seed and her seed : it shall bruise thy head, and thou shalt bruise his heel. (Sk.)

THE former part of this chapter is truly awful ! It contains a melancholy account of the introduction of evil into our world, and of man's apostacy from the Lord his God ; but here we find the first promise : and when that was made, the gospel day began to dawn. From that time to the present, all men have been placed in the hands of a Mediator: for Jesus was then appointed to redeem man, to avenge his wrongs, and to save him from the sad effects of sin. Our first parents understood this promise in *part;* but we understand it *fully.* They knew that a deliverer would come to bruise the head of their envious and malicious foe ; but we know by subsequent events, the character of this deliverer, and the means which he used to accomplish his plans of grace and mercy. The words of our text may be divided into two parts :—first, the Lord put enmity between the serpent and the woman, and between his seed and her seed;—and, secondly, the seed of the woman was to bruise the serpent's head, and the serpent was to bruise his heel.

125

I. The Lord put enmity between the serpent and the woman, and between his seed and her seed.

1. *The serpent is addressed, but the devil is intended.* He is called, "the dragon, that old serpent, the devil," Rev. xx. 2. Three reasons may be assigned why he is called a serpent;—first, he assumed that form when he tempted "the mother of all living," ver. 1.—Secondly, he is crafty, subtle, and cunning, 2 Cor. xi. 3.—And, thirdly, his influence on man resembles the deadly bite of a serpent, Gen. xlix. 17.

2. *The woman is named.* She was made "a help-meet for man," chap. ii. 18 : but she yielded to temptation, and drew her husband into sin. "Adam was not deceived, but the woman being deceived, was in the transgression." This is an *humbling* reflection to the female sex ; but let it be remembered, to their *honor*, that the Saviour is the seed of the woman.

3. *Wicked men are the seed of the serpent.* The devil is their father, and they are his children, by wicked works. This may be proved by what our Lord said to the Jews : "Ye are of your father the devil, and the lusts of your father ye will do," John viii. 44. The old serpent is an enemy of God, and this may be affirmed of all his children, without exception, Rom. viii. 7.

4. *The seed of the woman is Christ Jesus our Lord.* He was born of a pure virgin, without the concurrence of man, Matt. i. 23 ; and was made of a woman ; for, "when the fulness of time was come, God sent forth his Son, made of a woman, made under the law," Gal. iv. 4. But he who was made of a woman, was "Immanuel, which being interpreted, is, God with us," Matt. i. 23 ; and when the devil contended with him, he contended with God incarnate, 1. Tim. iii. 16.

5. *God put enmity between these parties; and they can never be reconciled.* This will not be doubted, when we consider their opposite characters :—the devil is *polluted* and *defiled*, but Christ is *pure* and *holy ;*—the devil is a *destroyer*, Christ is Saviour ;—the devil is a *merciless tyrant*, but Christ is a *mild pacific Prince*. A war was about to commence between them, in which the one was to conquer, and the other to be destroyed, Heb. ii. 14. For,

II. The seed of the woman was to bruise the serpent's head, and the serpent was to bruise his heel.

1. *By the head of the serpent, we are to understand the mischievous power of the devil;* and the figure is very appropriate, because the life and power of the serpent lie in his head. His bite leaves a poisonous liquor in the wound, which quickly mixes with the blood, and produces speedy death.

2. *To bruise his head, is to crush his power.* All his power has been employed in doing mischief ; and among his other works, we may reckon error, unbelief, sin, misery, and death: and therefore we rejoice in hope of that day, when his power shall be wholly destroyed, and when his deadly influence shall cease, Rev. xx. 10.

3. *Jesus came into the world, to bruise his head.* The first conflict between these parties, of which we have any account was in the wilderness of Judea ; and there our Lord was more than conqueror, Matt. iv. 1—11 : afterwards the almighty power of Jesus appeared, on many occasions, in casting devils out of the bodies of men; so that they trembled before him, and asked if he were come to torment them before their time, Matt. viii. 29.

4. *The head of the serpent was bruised by the death and resurrection of Jesus.* Under the influence of the devil, his impure seed, the wicked Jews, "killed the Prince of Life," Acts iii. 15 ; but in death, he made atonement

for sin, redeemed man, and gave a death blow to the serpent: and in his resurrection, he conquered death and the grave, and "became the first fruits of them that slept," 1 Cor. xv. 20.

5. *And he is now bruising the serpent's head, in the exercise of his grace and mercy.* After his resurrection he appointed a gospel ministry, Mark xvi. 15; ascended into heaven, till his enemies should be wholly subdued, Heb. ix. 12, 13; sent down his Holy Spirit, Acts ii. 1—4; and by the ministry of his word, and the agency of his Spirit, he bruises the head of the serpent in the hearts of all true believers.

6. That the serpent still exercises considerable power, is a fact which we cannot deny; but we may safely affirm, that *he has received incurable wounds*, and that his destruction is certain. Our Glorious Redeemer reigns and "must reign, till he hath put all enemies under his feet," 1 Cor. xv. 25; and then glorious times will follow to his church, and to the world, Isa· xi. 5—9.

7. *But the heel of Jesus was bruised by the serpent.* He suffered greatly in his human nature, while he tabernacled on earth, and his holy seed have suffered much from their adversary the devil; but it has only been a bruising of the heel, which is not a vital part. When Satan obtained leave to attack Job, the Lord said unto him, "Behold he is in thine hand: but save his life," Job ii. 6; and it is a pleasing thought, that this wicked and malignant spirit could never touch the life of our great Deliverer. It is true his body died, but that was only the heel or inferior part of his nature.

Inferences.

1. The influence of this serpent has been vast and extensive, the mischief which he has done is incalculably great; and even now, "he worketh in the hearts of the children of disobedience," Eph. ii. 2.

2. But it is matter of rejoicing, that we have a Saviour, and a GREAT ONE, who is both able and willing to deliver all who put their trust in him; and if we commit ourselves to his care, he will keep us safely against that day, when the serpent and all his seed shall be cast into hell, 2 Tim. i. 12.

2. That we may be *safe* and *happy*, we should "renounce the devil and all his works:" embrace the offers of the gospel; and place ourselves under the government and protection of the WOMAN'S CONQUERING SEED.

4. Placed under the banner of our Redeemer, let us not fear the *wicked one*, but constantly and courageously resist him, under an assurance that he will flee from us, James iv. 7. Soon we shall be out of his reach, and all the sad effects of his malice will be done away for ever. Amen.

ABRAHAM'S PROMISED SEED.

Gen. xxii. 18.—In thy seed shall all the nations of the earth be blessed. (S. S.)

THERE is nothing in man which can merit the divine favor: the promises of God to us are altogether free, resulting wholly from his sovereign grace: yet does God frequently *manifest* his love towards us in consequence of something done by us. Abraham, it should seem, was an idolater, when God first made himself known to him in his native land: and *then* did the Almighty promise, that in him should all the families of the earth be blessed. But, in the passage before us, Abraham is recorded to have performed the most extraordinary act of obedience that ever was known from the foundation of the world: and God takes occasion from that to renew his promise and, for his more abundant consolation, to confirm it with an oath. To ascertain the full import of this glorious prophecy, it will be proper to inquire

I. Who is the seed here spoken of.

It is not to all the natural descendants, or to that part of them that composed the Jewish nation, or even to the spiritual seed of Abraham, that these words refer: they speak of one particular individual, the Lord Jesus Christ.

1. To him all the types direct our attention.

The temple with all its utensils, the priests with all their habits and services, the sacrifices and oblations of every kind, all shadowed forth his work and offices. The principal events in the Jewish history, together with the great persons engaged in them, their lawgiver, their commanders, judges, kings, and prophets, prefigured him in different points of view, and, as so many lines, meet in him as their common centre. On this account we have reason to think that the prophecy before us relates to him.

2. In him all the prophecies receive their accomplishment.

However some of the prophecies might be partially fulfilled in Solomon or others, it is certain that all of them together were never accomplished in any one but Jesus. They were intended to designate HIM, that, when he should arrive, there might be no doubt of his being the very person foreordained of God to be the Saviour of the world. The minute description of the promised Messiah, together with the marvellous combination of circumstances that marked Jesus as the person foretold, lead us further to believe that the text had particular respect to him.

3. To him *exclusively* the text is applied by God himself.

St. Paul tells us that *the blessing of Abraham* was to come on the Gentiles through Jesus Christ; Gal. iii. 14; and that the words of the text related, not to others, but to Christ alone. Ib. 16.

This point being ascertained, let us inquire

II. In what respect all nations are blessed in him.

The full accomplishment of the text will not take place till that glorious period when the knowledge of the Lord shall cover the earth, as the waters cover the sea. Yet, in a limited sense, all nations have experienced the truth of this prophecy already.

1. They are reconciled to God through him.

Christ died not for one nation only; he was a propitiation for the sins of the whole world. Many of all nations have already believed in his name, and rejoiced in his salvation: and in every place they who believe in him shall find acceptance with their God. Col. i. 20—22.

2. They are united in one body in him.

He has broken down the middle wall of partition that divided the Jewish and Gentile world, and, having reconciled both unto God in one body by the cross, he has slain the enmity thereby. Eph. ii. 14—16. All mankind are now brought into one family, and are taught to regard each other as brethren: and in proportion as the religion of Jesus gains the ascendant over our hearts, we are united in love to every member of his mystical body.

3. They are blessed with all spiritual blessings.

There is not any thing that can conduce to our present or future happiness which Jesus will not bestow on his believing people. Adoption into his family, peace in our consciences, holiness in our hearts, and an eternity of glory in the Father's presence, are the certain portion of all his faithful followers. There is no difference between Jew and Gentile; all are admitted to the same privileges, and all shall participate the enjoyments.

INFER,

1. The antiquity of the gospel.

The sum and substance of the gospel is, that Christ is the only source of all spiritual and eternal blessings. Wherever this truth is strongly urged, men are ready to cry out against it as a *new* doctrine. But we can trace it, not only to the reformers of our church, but to the apostles, yea to Abraham also: for St. Paul declares, that when God spake the words to Abraham, he "*preached the gospel to him*," even that very gospel, whereby he and all the nations of the earth must be saved. Gal. iii. 8. Let this truth then no longer be reviled as novel, but be received as the one ground of all our hopes.

2. The importance of faith.

Abraham's faith in this gospel was imputed to him for righteousness: Gal. iii. 6, and by believing the same divine record we also must be justified. Ib. 7, 9. No doctrine whatever is more explicitly declared in scripture than this. Let us then acknowledge the necessity of faith, and look to the Lord Jesus Christ as that promised seed, through whom alone the blessings of Abraham can flow down upon us.

3. The connection between faith and works.

Faith was that principle which produced in Abraham such exemplary obedience: Heb. xi. 17, and the same root will bear similar fruits wheresoever it exists. Acts xv. 9. Indeed the pardon of past sins would be utterly insufficient to make us happy, if it were not accompanied with the renovation of our natures. To this effect St. Peter expounded, as it were, the very words of the text, declaring to the Jews, that conversion from sin was one of the first blessings which the Lord Jesus was sent to bestow. Acts iii. 25, 26 Let us then not consider faith and works as opposed to each other, but as possessing distinct offices, the one to justify our souls, the other to honor God, and to manifest the sincerity of our faith.

ISAIAH'S VISION OF CHRIST.

Isaiah vi. 5—7.—Then said I, Wo is me! for I am undone; because I am a man of unclean lips, and I dwell in the midst of a people of unclean lips: for mine eyes have seen the King, the Lord of hosts," &c. (Sk.)

THIS prophet was peculiarly favored by the Lord, and has ever been distinguished as the most eminent of the Jewish seers. He was singularly honored with clear and comprehensive views of the person and character of the Messiah; and minutely predicted the circumstances of his incarnation, and the triumphs of his kingdom. In this chapter, he was highly privileged, by having a distinct and glorious vision of the Son of God. It took place when he was in the temple, where "he saw the Lord sitting upon a throne, high and lifted up," attended by numerous seraphims, who were perpetually employed in rendering him their profoundest homage, and devoutly adoring his holy name, ver. 2, 3. The effects which these things produced on his mind, and what occurred on this interesting occasion, he informs us in the language of the text; from which we may learn, that this vision was,—glorious in its object,—instructive in its design,—and gracious in its influence.

I. THE PROPHET'S VISION WAS GLORIOUS IN ITS OBJECT:—"Mine eyes have seen *the King, the Lord of hosts.*" The dignified person whom he saw was the promised Messiah. This is evident from the testimony of St. John, who when referring to this chapter, expressly declares, "These things said Esaias, when he saw his glory, and spake of him." It is certain that "no man hath seen God," or the divine *essence* at any time, but his "only begotten Son hath declared him." When the prophet saw him "in the bosom of the Father;" he appeared in the two-fold character of *essential God* and an *Almighty Sovereign.* Hence he justly specifies,

1. *The divinity of his person*:—"The Lord of hosts," or according to Lowth, "*Jehovah* God of hosts." This language is certainly a legitimate and powerful argument, in proof of the deity of the Lord Jesus Christ. To deny this would be equally opposed to just reasoning and sound criticism. The prophet actually *saw* his *personal glory*, even the glory of the "only begotten of the Father;" and boldly asserts his essential divinity, as the second person of the triune Godhead. And this character of the Saviour perfectly accords with the descriptions given of him throughout the sacred writings. The eternity of his existence fully proves that he is absolutely God, and equal with the Father, John viii. 58, xvii. 5 ; Heb. xiii. 8. He is therefore justly called "both Lord and Christ,—the Lord of glory,—the Lord of all,—the Lord of hosts," Phil. ii. 11.

2. *The sovereignty of his character*:—"Mine eyes have seen *the King.*" Christ's kingly office is clearly revealed in the Scriptures, and is highly encouraging to his people, Ps. cxlix, 2. He is *a supreme king ;* even "the King of kings and the Lord of lords," Prov. viii. 15. *A universal king;* whose kingdom ruleth over all things, both visible and invisible, Col. i. 15—18 ; Rev. i. 18. *A spiritual king;* whom God has set upon his holy hill of Zion, to be the head and governor of his church, and reign in the hearts of his people, Ps. ii. 6 ; Luke xvii. 21 : Col, i. 13. *An everlasting king ;* who shall continue to reign and prosper when all other kings and their dominions shall be destroyed , "but of his kingdom there shall be no end," Dan. vii. 14 ; Heb. i. 8. How glorious is the Redeemer's character! Let us adore his name and gladly bow to his sceptre. Observe,

II. THE PROPHET'S VISION WAS INSTRUCTIVE IN ITS DESIGN ;—"Then flew one of the seraphims," &c. As no scripture is of private interpretation, this vision was, no doubt, intended not only for the personal benefit of the prophet, but also for the general instruction of mankind. It evidently illustrates,

1. *The nature of salvation;*—"Thine iniquity is *taken away*, and thy sin *purged.*" We are not only actually guilty, but morally polluted. When God therefore saves sinners, he takes away their guilt by his mercy, and purifies their hearts by his grace. Both pardon and purity are equally necessary for our present and final happiness. They are freely promised in the gospel, and are happily enjoyed by all the righteous, 1 Cor. vi. 11. This was certainly the blessed experience of the prophet, and such is still the salvation of all true believers.

2. *The medium of salvation;*—"Then flew one of the seraphims unto me," &c. Here God employed one of his angels as a messenger of his grace to the prophet. He came flying with a live coal in his hand, which was taken from off the altar. This was most probably the altar of burnt offering, which had always coals of fire burning upon it, Lev. vi. 12, 13. This manifestly typified the Lord Jesus Christ, as the atoning sacrifice for our sins, and the high-priest over the house of God for ever, Heb. ix. 14, xiii. 10 : 1 John iv. 10. The seraphs laying the live coal upon the prophet's mouth, might represent the necessity of a personal application of Christ's

atonement as the only medium of pardon, purity, and every spiritual blessing, Heb. xii. 24. It might also point out the sanctifying influence of the Holy Ghost, as a "spirit of burning and refining fire;" and is in the whole, an instructive and emblematical representation of the divine method of saving sinners to the end of time, Matt. iii. 11; John xiv. 6; Heb. iv. 14—16.

3. *The assurance of salvation.* This was unquestionably the privilege of the prophet. He was assured of it by the declaration of the seraph, and the sign which he received, verse 7. This, without doubt, was highly consola tory to his mind, and greatly encouraged him in his work. And though we cannot expect to receive it in the same way, it is still a possible privilege, and is enjoyed by many, who can declare, like David, what God has done for their souls. The Lord communicates it by his word and Spirit, and gives his people "the knowledge of salvation by the remission of their sins," Rom. viii. 15, 16; 1 Thess. i. 5. This will lead us to consider,

III The prophet's vision was gracious in its influence;—"Then said I, Wo is me! for I am undone," &c. All spiritual intercourse with God is profitable to the soul. This was manifestly the case in the instance before us. The prophet was both powerfully affected, and greatly profited by this heavenly vision.

1. *It was deeply humbling;*—"Wo is me! for I am undone," &c. I am struck dumb, "because I am a man of unclean lips," &c. He had such a discovery of the infinite splendor and purity of the Lord of hosts, that he was more than ever convinced of his own personal pollution, and of the sinfulness of the people among whom he dwelt. These things deeply humbled him before God, and filled him with unfeigned repentance and self-abasement. The manifestation of God to the soul is always productive of genuine humility and contrition of heart; and leads the penitent believer to exclaim, "Wo is me! I abhor myself, and repent in dust and ashes," Job xlii. 5, 6.

2. *It was personally sanctifying.* Whilst the prophet was abashed and humbled, on account of his uncleanness, he received a comfortable assurance of his pardon and acceptance with God. His sin was also purged, and he was made "a vessel unto honor," more deeply and fully "sanctified and meet for the master's use." By communion with God we feel his transforming power, and are changed into the same image, 2 Cor. iii. 18. A believing discovery of his glory and purity is always assimilating and hallowing in its influence, Ps. lxiii. 2, 3; 2 Cor iv. 6.

3. *It was highly encouraging.* The prophet was called to the painful task of addressing the Jews, who were "a disobedient and gainsaying people." He deeply felt the importance of his office, and the difficulty of his work; and humbled under a sense of his own inability to discharge the duties of his high commission. But by this divine vision his fears were instantly removed, and he was greatly encouraged to engage in the work which God appointed him to do, with great delight. When the Lord said, "Whom shall I send, and who will go for us?" the prophet immediately said, "Here am I, send me." Nothing is deemed hard or unreasonable by the believer, that appears to be the will of God, Phil. iv. 11—13.

To conclude,

1. Let us carefully search the Scriptures which testify of Christ, and reveal the way of salvation.

2. Let us diligently improve the privileges we enjoy, till we obtain the perfect vision of the "King eternal," 1 John iii. 2.

THE JOYFUL PROCLAMATION.

Isaiah lxii. 11.—Behold the Lord hath proclaimed unto the end of the world, Say ye to the daughter of Zion, Behold, thy salvation cometh; behold, his reward is with him, and his work before him. (Sk.)

FROM the very nature of prophecy, it must generally involve a degree of obscurity, which can only be fully removed by its accomplishment. But it is evident, that all the prophetic testimonies are not *equally* mysterious and difficult to comprehend. Some of them are *comparatively* plain and intelligible to the weakest capacity, and leave no reasonable doubt of their precise import and application. This is particularly observable in many of Isaiah's predictions of the promised Messiah, and the inestimable blessings of his kingdom. And though he frequently employs the most beautiful imagery, and describes with inimitable sublimity of language, the most glorious and important events, yet his writings in general are more distinct and perspicuous than the other prophets.—This chapter *primarily* predicts the deliverance of the Jews from the Babylonish captivity; and very probably refers to their *final restoration* as the people of God. But it also manifestly announces the propagation and triumphs of the gospel; and contains the most encouraging promises of the universal diffusion of divine knowledge, and the future prosperity of the christian church.—The text may therefore be regarded as the Lord's general commission to the prophet, and to all his faithful ministers, to proclaim the glad tidings of salvation throughout the world, both to Jews and Gentiles, " Behold the Lord hath proclaimed it." &c. Let us observe,

I. THIS PROCLAMATION EXHIBITS A GLORIOUS OBJECT.

" Behold thy *salvation* cometh." Such is the distinguished character of the Messiah. He is a *Saviour*. He *saves his* people from their sins, and is therefore called *their salvation*. For this purpose he came into the world —was delivered for our offences—and now ever liveth to make intercession for us. His saving character is perfectly such as our necessities require.

1. *He is the appointed Saviour.* When we had destroyed ourselves, in God was found help. He loved the world and sent his only begotten Son, that we might live through him. As the mediator of the new covenant, Jesus is frequently called God's *servant*, because he assumed humanity, that he might accomplish his *will*, and finish the *work* which he had given him to do, Isa. liii. 11; Heb. x. 5—7; John iv. 34. " The Lord laid on him the iniquity of us all," and exalted him with his right hand, to be a prince and a *Saviour*. It thus " pleased the Father, that in him should all fulness dwell," for the salvation of perishing sinners.

2. *He is the all-sufficient Saviour.* He is both divinely authorized, and infinitely qualified, to execute his saving office. He is "the propitiation for our sins," and hath obtained eternal redemption for mankind." In him, there is an inexhaustible plenitude of grace and truth. Millions have put their trust in him, and have proved the virtue of his name, Rev. vii. 13, 14: —and he is " the same yesterday, to-day, and for ever." He can save the vilest sinners, and will cast out none that come unto him. However *multiplied* our crimes—however *aggravated* our guilt—and however *deep* the *stains* of our depravity may be, Jesus is *able* and *willing* to redeem us from all iniquity, and save us to the uttermost, Psa. cxxx. 7, 8; Matt. xi. 28; Heb. vii. 25.

3. *He is the only possible Saviour.* There is no other way to the Father; nor any other mediator between God and man; ' For other foundation can no other man lay than that is laid, which is Jesus Christ." He alone has bought with a price, and can save us from wrath to come. He has been the *only Saviour* of his people in every age, Isa. xlv. 21, 22. Salvation is not the scheme of angelic wisdom, nor the production of human energy; but the special purchase of Christ's infinite merit, and the sovereign achievement of his omnipotent power, Titus iii. 4—7. No other Saviour is *necessary*, nor can any other be *found*; for " there is none other name under heaven given among men whereby we must be saved." *Behold thy salvation!*

II. THIS PROCLAMATION CONTAINS A GRACIOUS MESSAGE.

" Say ye to the daughter of Zion, Behold," &c. Whatever reference these words might have to Cyrus, who proclaimed liberty to the captive Jews, they more eminently describe the *office* and *work* of Christ, as the Redeemer and Saviour of sinners. Observe,

1. *His mysterious advent;*—" Behold he cometh." He had long been promised as the seed of Abraham, in whom all nations should be blessed. To him gave all the prophets witness, and greatly rejoiced in the anticipation of his manifestation in the flesh, 1 Pet. i. 10. 11.—Behold, now he *is come!* " The Word was made flesh, and dwelt among us." He is Immanuel, God with us.—' God with God, is man with men.' Glorious mystery! Infallible truth! Matchless love! 1 Tim. iii. 16; 2 Cor. viii. 9.

2. *His important mission;*—" *His work* before him." What an infinite work did he engage to accomplish! It includes all that he has *done* and *suffered* to redeem and save the world. His human incarnation—perfect righteousness—atoning sacrifice—triumphant resurrection—glorious ascension—and prevailing intercession, Rom. viii. 3, 34.—The work of *redemption* he gloriously *finished* in the days of his flesh, Heb. ix. 4.—But the work of *salvation* is still *before him*, in which he is *perpetually engaged*, and will not cease to carry it on, till he has *fully* accomplished all the designs of his mediatorial engagements, 1 Cor. xv. 24—28.

3. *His glorious recompence;*—" *His reward* is with him." In him are hid all the treasures of wisdom and knowledge, and all the unsearchable riches of salvation. From his infinite fulness, he freely and abundantly communicates the richest blessings to his believing people ;—he enlightens their minds—justifies their persons—liberates their souls—purifies their hearts—and inspires them with " joy unspeakable and full of glory ;"—he graciously bestows an inestimable treasure of *grace* here, and an ineffable reward of *glory* hereafter, 1 John iii. 2. This message must be published in all nations ;—" The Lord hath proclaimed," &c.

III. THIS PROCLAMATION DEMANDS SPECIAL ATTENTION.

The threefold repetition of the term *behold*, in the text, intimates the vast *importance* of the subject introduced, and the absolute *necessity* of attentively regarding the Saviour as proclaimed by the prophet. We should behold him,

1. *With devout admiration.* He is the most *glorious* and *interesting* object. He is altogether lovely in his person, character, works, and offices How great is his beauty, and how infinite his goodness! Behold his astonishing love, his attractive dignity, and his captivating grace! Embrace his truth—bow to his sceptre—and imitate his example ;—supremely adore his exalted name—and affectionately **exclaim**, " This is my *beloved*, and this is my *friend* "

2. *With believing application.* The Saviour is not an object of *sight*, but of *faith.* Beholding him, therefore, is an *act* of the *mind*, under the influence of his Spirit. By faith we *look* to him—*come* to him—*receive* him—and *trust* in him, as "the Lamb of God, which taketh away the sin of the world," John i. 12 ; Eph. i. 13. *Such* a beholding Christ, is always accompanied with a personal interest in his merits, and a participation of present salvation.

3. *With joyful anticipation.* "Faith is the substance of things hoped for, and the evidence of things not seen."—It looks to the unseen Saviour, and joyfully expects his *second appearing*, without sin unto salvation. The believer looks through all sufferings and discouragements, and greatly rejoices in hope of the glory of God—having a "desire to depart and be with Christ which is far better," Phil. iii. 20, 21 ; Col. iii. 3, 4. May all mankind speedily hear the joyful proclamation of the gospel—behold the ineffable glories of the Redeemer—and participate the exceeding riches of his grace!

CHRIST'S NATIVITY.

Luke ii. 8--11.—And there were in the same country shepherds abiding in the field, keeping watch over their flock by night. And lo, the angel of the Lord came upon them, and the glory of the Lord shone around about them; and they were sore afraid. And the angel said unto them, Fear not: for, behold, I bring you good tidings of great joy, which shall be to all people. For unto you is born this day, in the city of David, a Saviour, which is Christ the Lord. (Pr.)

In the circumstances attending the birth of Christ, we see much of the hand of God. The decree of Cæsar Augustus, which directed the Virgin mother to Bethlehem, is employed for the accomplishment of ancient prophecy : ver. 1—3. Mic. v. 2.— — —The low and humble state in which the Saviour was born, ver. 7, serves as a specimen of the treatment he should meet with from the world in general, while the ministry of attendant angels indicated the honor which God would put upon him notwithstanding. John i. 10, 11.

Let us notice some of the particulars of the history, before we enter on the immediate subject of the text—

1. Observe the interest which the *angels* felt on the occasion.— — —The minds of men were wholly occupied with the 'taxing,' and the decree of the emperor ; but *their* thoughts are full of Christ.— — —The rulers and principal inhabitants of Jerusalem overlooked what had happened at Bethlehem, as scarcely deserving of regard, while the humble shepherds in the field are visited by an angel from heaven.

2, Not only did an angel appear to them, but "the glory of the Lord shone round about them."— — —Angels sometimes made their appearance in human form, as in the instance of Abraham and Lot ; and then they excited no particular fear or dread. But on this occasion, so great and interesting, they appear in all their native dignity and glory, that it might be seen they brought a message immediately from God.

3. The effect it had upon the shepherds : "they were sore afraid," but were afterwards cheered by the heavenly messenger.— — —Mary Magdalene also was greatly alarmed at the appearance of the angel at the sepulchre

and as both these visions took place amidst the darkness of the night, it must have added a terrific grandeur to the scene.— — —Yet in this awful manifestation of the divine glory, there is a mixture of tender mercy; and the shepherds are filled with fear and hope, a presentiment of the feelings which the gospel should inspire.

4. The object proclaimed is the "Saviour."— — —When an angel turns preacher he does not speak of himself, nor draw the attention to that quarter, but to Christ, as the supreme object of regard. What an example to all who engage in the sacred ministry!

5. The good news was common to "all people," and not to one nation only.— — —The highest and best source of consolation is that which is common to all christians, and consists in the common blessings of salvation; and not that which distinguishes one people or one christian from another. David's principal desire, and also Paul's is equally the desire of all that truly believe. Ps. xxvii. 3; Phil. iii. 8.

6. The good news, though common to all people, was more immediately addressed to the shepherds, who like many others were waiting for the con solation of Israel. "To you" is born a Saviour, which is Christ the Lord — — —The gospel also is as much addressed to individuals, as if they only were the objects of it.

7. In this heavenly message particular attention is paid to time, place, and other circumstances, to show their agreement with ancient prophecy: ver. 11. Not an angel from heaven must be permitted to speak any thing contrary to what is written in the scriptures of truth. Gal. i. 8.

I. CONSIDER THE SUBJECT OF THE ANGELIC MESSAGE, AND SEE WHAT "GOOD TIDINGS" ARE CONTAINED IN IT.

1. The *birth of Jesus Christ* was itself good news.— — —This was the great object of prophecy from the beginning of the world, and the hope of the church in all ages. Zion was bid to rejoice in it, Zech. ix. 9; and the whole creation to be glad, Ps. xcvi.— — —God was now manifest in the flesh, even Immanuel, God with us. The Word was made flesh, and dwelt amongst us, the only-begotten of the Father, full of grace and truth.

2. The *gracious design* of his incarnation imported good tidings to a guilty and ruined world.— — —He came to do the will of God, to die as a ransom for us, to rise from the dead, to ascend into heaven, and make intercession for us.— — —The Son of God was manifested to destroy the works of the devil, to bring glory to God in the highest, on earth peace, and good will to men.

3. The *way of salvation*, which was effected by the coming of Christ, forms an essential part of the good tidings brought to us by the angel. To us is born "a Saviour," which is Christ the Lord.— — —Repentance and remission of sins are now preached among all nations; a free, full, and eternal salvation. These in effect are the tidings announced by the celestial messenger.

II. THESE TIDINGS ARE MATTER OF JOY, "OF GREAT JOY TO ALL PEOPLE."

The term here employed is strong, and never used but on great occasions; for the joy of harvest, or an important victory; but is fully applicable to the subject under consideration.

1. The coming of Christ was the joy of *the old-testament church*, while they lived only in the hope of this great event. Isai. xxv. 9; John viii. 56. How much more when it is fully realised.

2. All the joy of believers, *during the lifetime of our Saviour*, centred entirely in him.— — —Mary and Elizabeth, Simeon and Anna, and all that looked for redemption in Jerusalem, rejoiced and triumphed in 'he incarnation, when they saw the mercy promised to the fathers, and the performance of the holy covenant. Christ was the joy of his immediate disciples and followers, and his presence the only happiness they knew on earth.

3. All the joy *in the times of the apostles*, had an immediate reference to Christ and his salvation.— — —Jerusalem, which had been the scene of his deepest abasement, was afterwards filled with peace, and joy, and gladness, and resounded with the triumphs of the ascended Saviour. There was great joy also in the city of Samaria, but it was through the doctrine of the cross. The apostles triumphed in every place, but it was because the savour of his name was spread abroad. Whom having not seen, says Peter, ye love: in whom, though now ye see him not, yet believing, ye rejoice with joy unspeakable and full of glory.

4. Christ and his salvation made all their *troubles and sorrows light and momentary;* yea they counted not their lives dear for his sake. The history of the primitive church is a history of sufferings in the cause of Christ, and of joy and rejoicing in his holy name. This also is the way for us to bear up under all the sorrows of the present life.

III. Enquire what is necessary to render these good tidings a matter of real joy to us.

It is an undoubted fact, that they do not produce joy in all. They did not then, and they do not now.— — —Many think the tidings of the gospel not worth hearing.— — —Many who hear, neglect them, or feel no interest in them.— — —Some who seem to rejoice for a time become indifferent; and afterwards wither away.

To become the subject of real joy, these tidings require to be believed as true, and to be received with the utmost cordiality.— — —Christ was in the world, and the world knew him not; he came unto his own, and his own received him not. Those who did receive him were such as believed on his name, being born again.

In particular, it includes a deep conviction of our guilty, lost, and ruined state, which is pre-supposed by the gospel; and which must be felt and realized, before it can convey to us tidings of great joy.

Also a cordial reception of the gospel itself, as revealing the only way of salvation; obeying it from the heart, and receiving the truth in love.

OF THE INCARNATION OF CHRIST.

1 Timothy, iii. 16.—God manifested in the flesh. (H.)

The incarnation of Christ is a most extraordinary and amazing affair; it is wonderful indeed, that the eternal Son of God should become man; that he should be born of a pure virgin, without any concern of man in it; that this should be brought about by the power of the Holy Ghost, in a way unseen, imperceptible, and unknown, signified by his overshadowing; and all this in order to effect the most wonderful work that ever was done in the world, the redemption and salvation of men: it is a most mysterious thing, incomprehensible by men, and not to be accounted for upon the principles of natural reason; and is only to be believed and embraced upon the credit of Divine revelation, to which it solely belongs.

I. THE SUBJECT OF THE INCARNATION, OR THE DIVINE PERSON THAT BECAME INCARNATE.

The evangelist John says it was the Word, the essential Word of God; " The Word was made flesh, and dwelt among us," John i. 14; and he is said to be the " Word with God;" that is, with God the Father; and therefore must be distinct from him, Rev. xix. 13; Acts xx. 32; John i. 1. Wherever we read of any visible appearance of a Divine person in the Old Testament, it is always to be understood, not of the first, but of the second person. The Father prepared a body, a human nature in his purpose, council, and covenant, and not for himself, even for his Son, as he acknowledges; " A body hast thou prepared me." Heb. x. 5. That Divine person who came in the flesh, or became incarnate, is always distinguished from the Father, as being sent by him; " God sending his own Son," Rom. viii. 3. "God sent forth his Son," Gal. iv. 4, that is, God the Father, in both passages; as appears from the relation of the person to him, sent in the flesh, his Son. If the Father had been incarnate, he must have suffered and died; for that is the end of the incarnation, that the person incarnate might obey, suffer, and die, in the room of sinners; so Christ suffered in the flesh, and was put to death in the flesh. Nor is it the Holy Spirit that became incarnate, for the same reasons that the Father cannot be thought to be so; and besides, he had a peculiar hand, and a special agency, in the formation of the human nature, and in its conception and birth: when Joseph and Mary were espoused, before they came together, " she was found with child of the Holy Ghost:" and Joseph was told, in order to encourage him to take her to wife, that what was " conceived in her was of the Holy Ghost;" and therefore he himself was not incarnate. See Luke i. 35; Matt. i. 18—20. It remains that it is the second person, the Son of God, who is meant by " the Word that was made flesh," or became incarnate; and indeed, it is explained of him in the same passage; for it follows, " And we beheld his glory, the glory, as of the only-begotten of the Father." When this mystery of the incarnation is expressed by the phrase, " God manifest in the flesh:" not God the Father, nor the Holy Ghost, but God the Son is meant, as it is explained; 1 John iii. 8; for "this purpose the Son of God was manifested."

II. TO OBSERVE IN WHAT SENSE THE WORD, OR SON OF GOD WAS MADE FLESH.

John i. 14; Heb. ii. 14; 1 John iv. 2, 3; 1 Tim. iii. 16; signify, that he who is truly God, really became man, or assumed the whole human nature, as will be seen presently, in union with his Divine person.

1. What is meant by *flesh*, in the phrases and passages referred to, is a whole individual of human nature, consisting of soul and body, as when it is said, " There shall no flesh living be justified in his sight;" and again, "That no flesh shall glory in his presence," Rom. iii. 20; 1 Cor. i. 29, with many other passages; see Gen. vi. 12; Luke iii. 6; for such acts as being justified and glorying, can never be said of the flesh nor body, abstractedly considered; but of the whole man, or of individuals of human nature, consisting of soul and body; and in this sense are we to understand it, when it is used, of the incarnation of the Son of God, who took upon him the whole nature of man.

He took a true body, not a mere phantom, spectre or apparition, the appearance of a body, and not a real one. It is certain that Christ partook of the same flesh and blood as his children: and therefore if theirs be real, his must be so. Likewise, his body is called the body of his flesh, his fleshly body, Col. i. 22, to distinguish it from the token of his body in the supper; and from his myst.cal and spiritual body, the church; all his actions, and what is said of him, from his birth to his death, and in it, and after it, show it was a true body that he assumed. The very infirmities that attended him, though sinless, were proofs of his body being a true and real one; such as his fatigue and weariness in travelling, John iv. 6, his tears at the grave of Lazarus, and over Jerusalem, and his sweat in the garden, John xi. 35; Luke xix. 41, xx. 44. In short, it was through weakness of the flesh that he was crucified; which was not in appearance, but in reality.

2. Christ assumed a reasonable soul, with his true body, which made up the nature he took upon him, and are included in the flesh he was made. Christ asserts that he had a soul, and which, he says was exceeding sorrowful; and which was an immaterial and immortal spirit; and which, when his body died, and was separated from it, he commended into the hands of his Divine Father, Matt. xxvi. 38; Luke xxiii. 46.

2. In what sense the Word, or Son of God, was made flesh, and so became incarnate.

The Word could not be made at all, that is, created, since he is the maker and creator of all things; and therefore, he himself could not be made, nor created. But as other scriptures explain it, God the Word, or Son, was made and became "manifest in the flesh;" the Son that was in the bosom of the Father, the Word of life, that was with him from all eternity, was manifested in the flesh in time to the sons of men; and that in order to take away sin, and to destroy the works of the devil. 1 John i. 2, and iii. 5, 8.

III. THE CAUSES OF THE INCARNATION.

1. The efficient causes of it, God, Father, Son, and Spirit. The Father prepared a body for the Son in his purpose, and proposed it to him in council and covenant to assume it; and he sent him forth in the fulness of time. Heb. x. 5; Gal. iv. 4; Rom. viii. 3. The Son having agreed to it, being sent, came in the flesh, by the assumption of it; "he took unto him the form of a servant." Heb. ii. 14, 16; Phil. ii. 7, 8. The Holy Ghost had a very great concern in this affair; for that which was conceived in the virgin, was of the Holy Ghost. Matt. i. 20. Now, though all the three persons in the Deity had a hand in the wondrous incarnation, yet only one of them became incarnate; only the Son assumed the human nature. Some have illustrated this by three virgins concerned in working a garment, when only one of them puts it on and wears it.

2. The moving cause of the incarnation of Christ is the love of the Father, and of the Son, to mankind. "God so loved the world; herein is love, that God sent." John iii. 16; 1 John iv. 9, 10; And such was the love and condescending grace of the Son, that though he were in the form of God, of the same nature with him. Col. ii. 6—9; 2 Cor. viii. 9.

3. The final cause, or for whose sake, and for what the Son of God became incarnate. It was for the sake of lost sinners: "To us," or for us, for our sakes "a child is born, a Son is given." See Isa ix. 6; Luke ii. 10, 11; Matt. i. 21.

IV. THE PARTS OF THE INCARNATION ARE NEXT TO BE CONSIDERED, CONCEPTION AND NATIVITY.

1. Conception. This is a most wonderful, abs'ruse, and mysterious affair, and which to speak of is very difficult.

1. This conception was by a virgin; "Behold, a virgin !" this was a new thing, unheard of, and astonishing, which God created in the earth, in the lower parts of the earth, in the virgin's womb: a woman compassed or conceived, a man, without the knowledge of man. Isa. vii. 14; Jer. xxxi. 22. This was not natural, but supernatural.

2. This conception was through the power and influence of the Holy Ghost overshadowing the virgin.

3. It was a nature, not a person, that Christ assumed so early as at its conception; it is called the "Holy Thing," and not a person. The seed of Abraham; the form and fashion of a man, that is, the nature of man; as the form of God, in the same passage, signifies the nature of God. See Luke i. 35; Heb. ii. 16; Phil. ii. 6—8.

2. Nativity,

1. Of whom born,

1. Of a virgin: "a virgin shall conceive and bear a Son." See Matt. i. 18—23.

2. Christ was born of a virgin of the house of David, as in Luke i. 27. For the phrase, " of the house of David," is equally true of the virgin, as of Joseph, and may be connected with her. Acts xiii. 23; Rev. xxii. 16.

3. He was born of a virgin of the tribe of Judah; as she must be, since she was of the house of David, which was of that tribe. Gen. xxx. 10 Heb. vii. 14.

2. The place of his birth was Bethlehem, according to the prophecy in Micah, v. 2. See Matt. ii. 4—6; John vii. 42.

3. The time of his birth was as it was fixed in prophecy; before the sceptre, or civil government, departed from Judah. Herod was king in Judea when he was born, before the second temple was destroyed; for he often went into it, and taught in it: and it was at the time pointed at in Daniel's weeks. See Gen. xlix. 10: Mal. iii. 1; Hag. ii. 6, 7, 9; Dan. ix. 24. &c.

V. THE ENDS OF CHRIST'S INCARNATION ARE MANY; THERE IS A CLUSTER OF THEM IN THE SONG OF THE ANGELS. Luke ii. 14.

1. One end of Christ's incarnation was, to show forth the glory of God in it. The glory of his grace, kindness, and goodness to men, in the mission of his Son in this way; the glory of his faithfulness in fulfilling his promise of it: the glory of his power, in the miraculous production of Christ's human nature; and the glory of his wisdom, in bringing it into the world in such a manner as to be free from sin, and so fit for the purpose for which it was designed.

2. To make peace with God for men on earth; to make reconciliation for sin, was the work appointed him in covenant; and to do this was the reason of his being made, in all things, like unto his brethren; and make peace by the blood of his cross.

3. That man might receive the fruit of God's good will and favor towards them; even all the blessings of grace.

4. Particularly, Christ became man that he might be our God, our near kinsman, and might appear to have a right to redeem us; and he was, in the fulness of time, made of a woman, to redeem men from the law, its curse, and condemnation, &c.

5. Christ became man, that he might be a Mediator between God and men; and, the better to perform several parts of his office as such, he took upon him the nature of man, that he might have something to offer, as a priest, to be a sacrifice for sin, and make a satisfaction for it in that nature that sinned; and be a prophet like unto Moses.

THE JOY OF ANGELS AT THE INCARNATION.

Luke ii. 13, 14 —And suddenly there was with the angel a multitude of the heavenly host, praising God, and saying, glory to God in the highest, and on earth peace, good will toward men. (P.)

In this divine Anthem we are taught,

I. THAT THE INCARNATION OF THE SAVIOUR WAS A BRIGHT EXHIBITION OF THE GLORY OF GOD.

For thousands of years angels had beheld the unveiled glory of the DEITY; but they never saw the divine glory with any thing like the clearness with which they saw and felt the subject now. They had seen the glory of the divine *justice* in the punishment of their compeers; and something like *mercy* in the suspension of the sentence pronounced on guilty man. But O, when they saw Christ, the coequal and coeternal Son of God, take upon him a body that he might suffer and die to atone for the sins of men, and redeem them from the curse of the law, when they could not be redeemed by silver and gold—by human blood, by angelic interference, or by any thing short of the inestimably precious blood of the Son of God; here they saw JUSTICE shining in all its awful brightness, tremendous glory, and affecting majesty, in a way they had never seen it before. And when they saw that the love of God was ready to make such a sacrifice, that he spared not his own Son, but began to give him up for all; here was a display of MERCY indeed; here mercy appeared to be his darling attribute; here mercy flowed in a deeper, wider, more majestic channel, than they had ever before formed any just conception of. From this anthem we learn

II. THAT THE INCARNATION OF JESUS CHRIST WAS THE MEANS OF BRINGING PEACE UPON EARTH.

Sin had created on earth a most horrible WAR; a threefold war, dreadful and interminable, to which Jesus came to put an end.

1. *It had created war in every man's own bosom.* The passions were tumultuous: the mind of man was the erena of perpetual discord: he was ever at variance with himself. Now Christ came to put an end to this war, by procuring pardon for sin, peace for the conscience, tranquility for the passions, subordination for the appetites; reconciling reason to the conscience, and conscience to the law of God. Man, before, was constrained to cry out, if he felt his situation, "O wretched man that I am! who shall deliver me!" But redeemed man, man under a proper, believing view of the christian scheme as exemplified in our incarnate God, can say, "I thank God through Jesus Christ our Lord."

2. *Sin had created a horrible war between man and man.* It armed every man against his brother, strife, envy, jealousy, oppression, ambition, had caused a thousand interferences, jars, discords, and hostilities, and had made man a wild beast to his brother. But Christ came to put an end to this war; he came to preach the doctrine of universal charity; he came to exemplify universal charity. He came to proclaim that peace with God in the conscience, and that work of the mighty Spirit on the heart of man, that should tear from every breast, and extirpate from the very soil, all that was there of enmity, and sweetly constrain him to love his neighbor as himself.

3. *Sin had caused war between man and his* MAKER. Man was in rebellion with his Maker, and the Maker with man. But when Ch ist appeared in our nature, "God was in him, reconciling the world to himself, not imputing their trespasses unto them;" mercifully pardoning them on a plan

ε·nsistent with the strictest claims of his justice, and affording them grace to help in every time of need. And so amazing, so transforming is a proper view of his love, that they are brought to love him with a love like his own.

Well then, was Jesus designated "*the* PRINCE of PEACE!" Whatever of strife may be discovered in his kingdom, "an enemy hath done this." He does all to suppress it; and when his kingdom shall be fully established upon earth, wars shall terminate.

III. THAT THE INCARNATION OF THE DIVINE REDEEMER WAS A MARVELLOUS DISPLAY OF THE GOOD-WILL OF GOD TO MAN.

Good-will, in the abstract, nothing but good-will; love for love's sake. The angels had seen much of God's goodness to man *in the creation;* and *in providential dispensations.* They had seen that God had "not left himself without witness" of his benignant dispositions, continually giving them "rain from heaven, and fruitful seasons, filling their hearts with food and gladness;"—pouring from heaven, blessings, year after year, on the evil and on the good. But there were characters in this exhibition of God's good-will; there was a height, a length, a depth, a breadth, in this manifestation, which angel minds had never seen before.

In this was *most astonishing condescension.* That he was in "the form of God, and thought it no robbery to be equal with God, should be found in fashion as a man, and take upon himself the form of a servant;" that the "Ancient of Days," should become an infant;—that he who fills immensity, should be contracted, in appearance, to a span; that he, whom "the heaven of heavens cannot contain," should be born a babe in a manger; is an instance of condescension that proclaims this act of good-will to man, to be most unparalleled.

It was *altogether unmerited.* He shewed good-will to man; what for? Was there any thing in man to deserve it? No! He became incarnate for a race of rebels in arms against him; a rebel universe! then on the very core of whose heart was engraven, the deepest, deadliest animosity to that being, who left his own glory that he might wrap it around them

The most unparalleled love. The loftiest idea man can ever form of love, is, that a man lay down his life for his friend. But, in this instance, God lays down his life for us! God, the great law-giver, lays down his life for the most inveterate enemies, and for the foulest transgressors of that law which is "holy, just, and good."

Finally, it is "*good-will to men;*" that is, to human nature, to our fallen nature. There is a character of *universality* in it. Shew me the greatest sinner out of hell, and if he be *a man*, he is interested in this event. "He spared not his own Son, but delivered him up *for us all*. He took our common nature: "he gave himself, by the good-will of God, a ransom for all." The best cannot go to heaven any other way than through the Mediator; and, thank God, the worst, on repentance, may go to heaven by that way. We learn,

FINALLY. From the persons who sang this anthem, and the manner in which this event was celebrated, WHAT OUGHT TO BE OUR VIEWS, AND FEELINGS, AND CONDUCT.

1. *It should be laudatory.* We should tune up our feelings to the highest pitch, to celebrate a display of love, an act of mercy, which has no parallel in the universe. Angels had but little interest in it compared with us; had Jesus never become incarnate, they had been angels still. But if he had not come to take our nature, and to undertake our cause, we should have been ruined, lost, damned. Shall *they* celebrate in strains like these, this

141

glorious event, and shall *our* lips be sealed up in silence, or opened only in Bacchanalian sports! Shall *they* be so rapt, and *we* so dead and dull?—God forbid! Let us celebrate it in psalms, and hymns, and spiritual songs. If we be silent—if we mourn and complain, and think we have nothing to thank God for on all other days; let our hearts be touched, our lips opened; let us muse over the glorious scene, till our hearts burn within us, and all we have and all we are, becomes sacred to the praise of God! We are taught,

2. From the example of the angels, *that we should proclaim the* SAVIOUR *to others*. They were not contented to enjoy this themselves, but wished the whole creation to be vocal, and every thing that hath breath to praise the name of the Lord; and especially every sinner, every fallen man, every one in danger of sinking into hell-fire, but now about to be raised to the means of obtaining heaven. They wished by every means in their power, to excite men to unite with them in praising and celebrating the great God of love. Go, you, and do likewise. Proclaim the Saviour to Christless, prayerless, sensual, debauched, wicked sinners. And O, invite, entreat, persuade, with prayers, with tears, if it were possible, if it were needful, *with tears of blood*, to unite with you—to taste and see for themselves that God is love —that religion is happiness—that religious people have *two* heavens : one here, and another hereafter. Angels deemed it no disparagement to be thus employed, and it will be an honor to *you ;* and your tongues will never be a greater glory to you, than when you plead for Christ with success. But it will not be in vain; should you fail to kindle up the slumbering embers of love in the lukewarm—should you fail to swell the praises of the church to a more rapturous height;—yet, in watering others, you shall be watered *yourselves*. Angels never felt so much of heaven on earth, as when they thus sang; and you will never feel so much of the joy of angels, as when you are thus piously acting. You will then, indeed, have *a joyful* CHRISTMAS and *a happy* NEW YEAR. WHICH MAY GOD GRANT YOU ALL, FOR HIS MERCIES SAKE. AMEN.

THE IMPORT OF THE NAMES GIVEN TO CHRIST.

Matt. i. 21—23.—Thou shalt call his name Jesus : for He shall save his people from their sins. (Now all this was done that it might be fulfilled which was spoken of the Lord by the prophet, saying, Behold, a virgin shall be with child, and shall bring forth a son, and they shall call his name Emmanuel, which being interpreted is, God with us.) (S. S.)

THE dispensations of Providence are extremely dark and intricate—
The things which appear most afflictive often prove to be the richest mercies that could have been vouchsafed to us—
This was remarkably verified in the history before us—
Joseph was espoused to a virgin of consummate piety—
But, before their nuptials, she proved to be in a state which gave him reason to suspect her fidelity—
Desiring to exercise all the lenity which the case would admit of, he determined to put her away privily—
How distressing must such a state have been to this holy man!—

But **God** sent an angel to unfold to him the mystery, to declare the ends for which the child should be born, and to impose on the infant a name, that should mark his office in the world.

I. THE APPOINTMENT OF THE NAME.

God had often condescended to assign names to men—

Sometimes he had made an alteration in their names;* and sometimes totally changed them—†

Sometimes he had assigned a name before the child was conceived—John, Luke i. 13.

In these things he always acted with unerring wisdom—

When men have attempted to give significant appellations, they have only manifested how ignorant they were of futurity—‡

But God sees all things from the beginning to the end—

And his designation of Christ's name was a prognostic of his character—

The appellation given to the virgin's son was peculiarly suitable—

"Jesus" simply means a *Saviour;* Acts xiii. 23; and was a common name among the Jews—

It was sometimes assigned to those who were great deliverers—Neh. ix. 27.

It had been given in a peculiar manner to the son of Nun—Num. xiii. 16. Which name is precisely the same with "Jesus," and is so translated Acts vii. 45, and Heb. iv. 8.

He was eminently a Saviour, as leading the Israelites into the promised land, which Moses was not permitted to do—Deut. i. 37, 38.

But Christ, whom he typified, is a far greater deliverer—

He "does that for us which the law could not do"—Rom. viii. 3; Acts xiii. 39.

He leads the true Israel of God into their heavenly Canaan—

So remarkable an event may justly lead us to enquire into

II. THE REASON OF THAT APPOINTMENT.

Waving all other reasons, we notice two before us

1. To fulfil a prophecy.

Isaiah had foretold that the Messiah should be called Emmanuel—Isaiah vii. 14.

From the event it appears, that God did not intend this prophecy to have a *literal* accomplishment—

We may expect however that *the spirit of it* should be accomplished—

Now the name "Jesus" was in fact equivalent to Emmanuel—

"Jesus" means "divine Saviour;" and Emmanuel, God with us—See Bp. Pearson on the Creed, p. 70, 71.

And the evangelist himself tells us, that the imposition of *that* name was in order to the fulfilment of *this* prophecy—Matt. i. 22, 23.

2. To declare the infant's office and character.

The virgin's child was to be the Saviour of the world—

He was to save his people *by price,* and *by power*—

They were under sentence of eternal condemnation—

His life was the ransom to be paid for their souls—Matt. xx. 28.

*Abram and Sarai to Abraham and Sarah. †Jacob to Israel.

‡Eve named her first child, "Cain," which signifies, *getting;* thinking perhaps that she had now gotten the promised seed: having probably soon discovered her mistake, she called her second son "Abel," which signifies, *vanity.* But how misnamed were both! *This* proved a martyr for his God; and *that,* a murderer of his own brother.

Hence they are called his purchased possession—Eph. i. 14. See also 1 Cor. vi. 20, and 1 Pet. i. 18, 19.

They were also in bondage to sin and Satan—Luke xi. 21. 2 Tim. ii. 26. •

And he was to make them a peculiar people, zealous of good works—Tit. ii. 14.

Yea, he was ultimately to place them beyond the reach of all the penalties and pollutions of sin—

It was of importance that this great work should be represented in his very name—

And the text informs us that the name was given him for this very purpose—

Infer,

1. How precious aught the name of Jesus to be to all his followers!

What benefit can be bestowed like salvation from sin?—

A deliverance from its dominion is an unspeakable blessing—

The godly desire it no less than deliverance from hell itself—

And how delightful is pardon *to a burdened conscience!*—

How sweet is a sense of God's favor *in a dying hour!*—

What joy must the glorified soul possess *in the day of judgment!*—

Yet Jesus has bought it all with his own most precious blood—

He has bestowed it freely on all his faithful followers—

He will impart it liberally to all who will believe on him—

Is there not reason then for that divine anathema?—1 Cor. xvi. 22.

Will not the very stones cry out against those who refuse to praise him?—

Let Jesus then be precious to us all—

Let us adopt the grateful strains of that sweet Psalmist of Israel—Ps. ciii. 1—4.

2. How vain is it to expect salvation in the ways of sin!

Sinners seem to entertain but little fear about their souls—

They even encourage one another to commit iniquity with greediness—

But they cannot possibly be saved in such a state—

If they could, the angel should have assigned a very different reason for the appointment of Jesus' name—*

In that case, Christ would have been a minister of sin—

But who must not, with the apostle, express his abhorrence of such a thought?—Gal. ii. 17.

Our Lord has plainly told us what shall ere long be his address to self-deceiving sinners—Matt. vii. 23.

Let us then " flee for refuge to the hope set before us"—

And tremble lest we provoke *the Saviour* to become our *destroyer*—

*He should rather have said. " He shall save his people in their sins."

144

A SKETCH OF CHRIST'S NATIVITY.

Isaiah ix. 6.—For unto us a child is born, unto us a son is given; and the government shall be upon his shoulder: and his name shall be called Wonderful, Counsellor, the Mighty God, the everlasting Father, the Prince of peace. (Sk.)

OUR text is an ancient prediction of Christ's nativity, and a comprehensive outline of his glorious character, both in his humanity and in his divinity. After the lapse of many years, this prophecy was accomplished at Bethlehem in Judea. There the Messiah appeared as a child, and as the mighty God; for while he was laid in a manger, angels came down from heaven to adore him, Heb. i. 6. Let us join the Christian church in a cheerful and pious commemoration of that astonishing event; let us, on this glad day, call to mind the condescension of our blessed Saviour, and examine, with modesty and humility, his character and designs. This fine passage of Scripture will furnish our thoughts with rich materials: let us consider it in the order it stands before us.

I. UNTO US A CHILD IS BORN.

1. The prophet had an eye to the child Jesus, whose birth, in many points of view, *was an exact accomplishment of ancient prophecy*. It had been foretold that he should be born of a virgin, and he was born of the virgin Mary, Isa. vii. 14; Matt i. 22, 23—that he should come forth out of Bethlehem, the place where he was born, Mic. v. 2; Matt. ii. 1:—and that he should appear in low and mean circumstances, or " as a root out of dry ground," and he was born in a stable, because there was no room for Joseph and Mary in the inn, Isa. liii. 2; Luke ii. 7,

2. *Remarkable circumstances attended his birth.* He was made known, by an angel, to poor shepherds, who were watching their flocks by night, Luke ii. 11;—his birth was celebrated by a song of angels, chap. ii. 13, 14; —and the world, when the Prince of Peace came into it, was in a peaceful. tranquil state.

3. But the most important consideration is, *he was born unto us*, and for our salvation; for though this was spoken by a Jewish prophet, to the Jewish nation, yet we are assured, that in him all the families of the earth should be blessed, Gen. xii. 3. " He took not on him the nature of angls, but the seed of Abraham," Heb. ii. 16. Good angels did not need his mediation, and bad ones were not to share the benefits of his redeeming love; but he became man, that he might redeem and save sinners of the human race, 1 Tim. i. 15.

II. UNTO US A SON IS GIVEN.

1. *Our blessed Saviour is the Son of God.* He is called the Son of God in reference to his miraculous conception in the womb of Mary, Luke i. 35; he was the son of God by commission, being sent of God, John x. 36; he was declared to be the Son of God, by his resurrection from the dead, Rom. i. 4;—and he is the only begotten Son of God in his divine nature. John iii. 16; Heb. i.—3.

2. *Unto us this Son was given:* and he was the greatest gift that heaven could bestow on man, Rom. viii. 32. He was given to enlighten the world, John viii. 12;—to be a propitiation for sin, 1 John ii. 2;—to make reconciliation for iniquity, Dan. ix. 24;—to save the world, John iii. 17;— and to bring many sons unto glory, Heb. ii. 10.

III. THE GOVERNMENT SHALL BE UPON HIS SHOULDER.

1. This does not refer to the *political government* of the Jews. **In their** depraved state, they expected such a Messiah, and in their pride and vanity, they desired a great temporal king; but the kingdom of Jesus, which had been foretold by the prophets, was not of this world, John xviii. 36.

2. The *spiritual government* of the church, in all its vast and weighty concerns, was laid upon his shoulder: he is the head of the church, Eph 'v 15; Col. i. 18; and his faithful followers dare not acknowledge any otner Lord or master, Matt. xxiii. 8.

3. He is *able to bear the weight of government*, having all power both in heaven and in earth, Matt. xxviii. 18;—he is sufficiently wise to manage and direct all the affairs of this spiritual kingdom, as in him are " all the treasures of wisdom and knowledge," Col. ii. 3;—and he now rules, and ever will rule in righteousness, Heb. i. 8.

IV. AND HIS NAME SHALL BE CALLED WONDERFUL.

1. *He shall be what his name imports.* The Hebrews gave names which expressed the qualities of things, and the characters and offices of persons. Thus Jesus,was callled " Emmanual, which being interpreted, is, God with us ;" and for this plain reason, he was God with men, Matt. i. 21.

2. He was *wonderful* in his *person:* a child born, and yet the mighty God; the offspring of David as a man, and the root of David as God, Rev. xxii. 16; the son of David in his human nature, but his Lord in the divine nature, Matt. xxii. 45. He was wonderful in his love, 1 John iii. 16; and wonderful in all his undertakings. Who can comprehend his nature? Who can fully understand his great and merciful designs? Why do we ask after his name, and attempt to pry into inconceivable mysteries? Gen xxxii. 9; Judges xiii. 18. Oh let us stand, and wonder, and adore!

V. COUNSELLOR.

1. *A revealer of secrets.* He revealed the gospel, which is called the counsel of God, Acts xx. 27; the hidden wisdom, 1 Cor. ii. 7; but is now made manifest to all nations for the obedience of faith, Rom. xvi. 21; "even the mystery" which hath been hid from ages and generations, but now is made manifest to his saints, Col. i. 26. He is called the WORD OF GOD, because God speaks by him to the sons of men, Heb. i. 1.

2. *One who gives counsel*, Rev. iii. 18. Jesus gave counsel to men in the days of his flesh; and he now gives counsel by his Holy Spirit, by his written word, and by his faithful ministers. His counsel is *safe*, may be had on *easy terms*, James i. 5; and, if followed, will guide us to glory, Ps. lxxiii. 24.

VI. THE MIGHTY GOD.

1. The *titles* of God are given to Jesus. He is called God, John i. 1;— the great God, Tit. ii. 13;—the true God, 1 John v. 20;—and Lord, or Jehovah, Isa. xl. 3.

2. The *attributes* of God are ascribed to him. Eternity, Mic. v. 2;— omnipotence, Rev. i. 8;—omnipresence, Matt. xviii. 20;—and immortality, Heb. xiii. 8.

3. He *created* all things. The visible world, John i. 3;—the invisible world, including thrones, dominions, principalities and poweis, Col. i. 16.

4. Divine *worship* has been paid to him; by angels at his birth, Heb. i. 6;—by Stephen, the first martyr, Acts vii. 59;—by all who baptize in his name, Matt. xxviii. 19;—and by heavenly hosts, Rev. v. 13.

VII. THE EVERLASTING FATHER.

1. This clause, in the *Septuagint*, is, *the Father of the age, or world to come;* and in allusion to this, the gospel dispensation, under the reign of the Messiah, is called *the world to come.* Heb. ii. 5.

2. Jesus is *a Father to his people.* As a father, he *loves* them, *protects* them, and supplies their wants. He is the author of salvation to all who obey him, Heb. v. 9;—he was the founder of the new and eternal age; he is the father of a new race, the head of a new family which will never be extinct; and all believers are his seed, or children, Isa. liii. 10 : for by his obedience to the law, the atonement which he made, and the influences of his Holy Spirit, they are brought into life, and into a new state, Gal. ii. 20.

3. And he will be the *everlasting* Father of his people. Earthly fathers die; but Jesus says, " I am alive for evermore," Rev. i. 18; and he will be as a Father to them, and they will be as sons and daughters to him in the eternal world, Rev. xxi. 7.

VIII. THE PRINCE OF PEACE.

1. Our Lord is a PRINCE. He is the Prince of the kings of the earth, surpassing them in all that is great and excellent, Rev. 1. 5: and by him " kings reign, and princes decree justice," Prov. viii. 15. He is the Prince of life, or the author of all life, whether temporal, spiritual, or eternal, Acts iii. 15; for he created us at first, is the author of our new creation, and conducts us safely to eternal life, Eph. iii. 9, ii. 10; John x. 27, 28.

2. But here he is called the "PRINCE of *Peace.*" By him, all who believe have peace with God, Isa. xii. 1; Rom. v. 1;—he plants peaceable dispositions in the hearts of his subjects, James iii. 17;—his government promotes peace in the world, Heb. xii. 14;—and when the nations of the earth bow down to him, and acknowledge him as their Sovereign, they shall learn war no more, Isa. ii. 4.

Inferences.

1. Admire and adore the Saviour of the world; and instead of prying into the profound mysteries of his nature, bow the knee to him, and pay him homage, Ps. ii. 12; Phil. ii. 10.

2. Trust in him with an unshaken confidence for pardon, peace, holiness, and heaven, Matt. xii. 21.

3. Look to him in all difficulties and dangers for counsel and support; and ever give him the glory that is due to his holy name, Isa. xliii. 2, 3; John v. 23

4. Honor him, especially, on this festival, by temperance and sobriety, by praise and thanksgiving, and by acts of charity to his suffering saints, Gal. vi. 10.

5. And lastly, commit to his care your bodies and souls, your families and friends, and all your affairs; that he may have you and yours in his holy keeping against that day, when he will " judge the world with righteousness, and the people with equity," Ps. xcviii. 9.

CHRIST THE LIGHT AND SALVATION OF THE GENTILES.

Isaiah xlix. 6.—And he said, It is a light thing that thou shouldest be my servant to raise up the tribes of Jacob, and to restore the preserved of Israel : I will also give thee for a light to the Gentiles, that thou mayest be my salvation unto the end of the earth. (S. S.)

THAT the Gentiles were to be received into the church of God, was a truth which the Jews were backward to admit—.

Several years after the gospel had been preached to the Jews, Peter declined visiting the Gentiles, and was afterwards called to an account by the apostles themselves for going to them—Acts xi. 1, 2. This was six or seven years after Christ's ascension.

Nor could any thing but repeated miracles in their favor overcome the prejudices which he entertained respecting them—

Not but that the conversion of the Gentiles had been very frequently and plainly foretold—

The very passage before us, if there had been no other, was quite sufficient to raise an expectation of that event—

In the context there is a conversation between Jehovah and his Son—

The Messiah announces to the Gentiles his qualifications for the work to which he was called—Ver. 1—3.

But at the same time complains that his labors among the Jews were almost in vain—Ver. 4.

Nevertheless He declares his unshaken confidence that Jehovah would not leave him without ultimate success—Ib.

Jehovah then, in answer to his Son, assures him, that however he may be treated by the Jews, he shall be upheld and accepted in his work—Ver. 5.

And that his failure among the Jewish nation shall be far overbalanced by his success among the Gentiles—

To elucidate this prophecy we shall consider

I. The characters here given to Christ.

There can be no doubt but that the words of the text relate to Christ

They are far too strong to be applied to Isaiah himself—

Nor could they with propriety be spoken of any but the Messiah—

The expressions here used are similar to those which the prophet elsewhere uses in reference to him—Isa. xlii. 1, 6, and lx. 3.

They were evidently alluded to by the patriarch when he took up the infant Jesus in his arms—Luke ii. 30—32.

And are expressly quoted by St. Paul as having received their accomplishment in Christ—Acts xiii. 46, 47.

To him the characters, there specified, most eminently belong—

He is "the Restorer of Israel," having reconciled "many myriads" of them to serve God—

He is also the "Light of the Gentiles"—

Another prophet describes him as "the sun of righteousness"—Mal. iv. 2.

In the New Testament also he is repeatedly called "the Light of the world"—John i. 4, 9.

Others have enlightened the world by revealing the will of God—

But He alone reveals it by his Spirit to the souls of men—

He only, who opened Lydia's heart. can have access to ours—Acts xvi. 14.

He only, who opened the understanding of his disciples, can illumine our benighted minds—Luke xxiv. 45.

And this he does for them that lie in darkness and the shadow of death—

While his once favored people the Jews are blinded, he takes the veil from our hearts, and guides us into all truth—

Thus does he abundantly fulfil to us his gracious promise—John viii. 12.

He is moreover "the salvation of men even to the ends of the world."

Many of the judges and kings of Israel were Saviours in a temporal view—

But Jesus imparts to his followers a far more glorious salvation—

By his own blood he has "obtained an eternal redemption" for them—
And by his meritorious obedience he renders them completely righteous—
He is not merely a Saviour to them, but "salvation" itself—
As he procured, so he imparts, maintains, and perfects the salvation of those who trust in him—
There are none so remote but he extends to them the benefits of his death—
"He came to save the lost," in whatever quarter of the globe they be—
For this very end was he sent into the world by his heavenly Father—
And, as being expressly appointed to this office, he is called *God's* salvation—

In fulfilling these characters he displays

II. THE EXCELLENCE OF THE DISPENSATION COMMITTED TO HIM.

The dispensation of the law to the Jews was glorious.

There was much of the gospel communicated in and with the law—
The ceremonial rights were altogether "shadows of the good things which were afterwards to be more fully revealed—
The moral law itself, while it condemned the Jews, was intended to promote their salvation—
And many, in different ages, were guided to heaven by the light which was then afforded them—
The Mosaic law therefore was a rich blessing to that nation—
And the salvation of a remnant from among them clearly manifested the efficacy of the great sacrifice—

But the dispensation of the gospel to the whole world is incomparably more glorious—

It brings far greater good to men.

We must not disparage the salvation of one single soul—
Much less should we undervalue the mercy shewn to so many of the Jews—
But still, the Jews were a small body when compared with the Gentile world—
And it was but a little remnant, even of them, that obtained mercy—
But the publication of the gospel to the Gentiles has been the means of saving unnumbered myriads—
There are persons in every quarter of the globe who experience the efficacy of the Redeemer's blood—
Yea, every day and hour are multitudes ascending from the darkest corners of the earth to swell the chorus in heaven—
How much more glorious then is the dispensation which diffuses its blessings so extensively, than that which confined them to such a narrow sphere!—
Surely it would have been "a light thing to save the Jews" in comparison of such a multitude—
We may well therefore apply to this subject those words of the apostle—
2 Cor. iii. 9—11.

It brings also far greater glory to the Saviour himself.

Had none but Jews been saved by him, he might have appeared partial in his regards—
Or it might be thought that his sacrifice was but of a limited value—
But the extension of mercy to the Gentiles displays "the exceeding riches of his grace"—
And shews that his death is a sufficient "propitiation for the sins of the whole world"—

How transcendent is the Redeemer's glory in this view!—

And how glorious will he appear, when all that he has redeemed from every nation of the earth shall unite in ascribing salvation to him!—

The saving of a few from one nation only would not have been a suitable recompence for his work—

He might well have complained that he had "spent his strength for nought"—

But he will be fully "satisfied with the travail of his soul," because "the birth of his womb will be as the dew of the morning"—Ps. cx. 3.

We shall conclude with a word or two of ADVICE :—

1. Welcome the Saviour under the characters which are here given him—

We all need him as the light of our minds, and the Saviour of our souls—

Let none then boast of the light of reason, or "lean to their own understanding"—

Nor let us trust in our own goodness to merit, or strength to work out salvation—

Let us rather look to Jesus for the teaching of his word and Spirit—

And unite our acknowledgments with those of the saints of old—Isaiah xlv. 24.

Let us rejoice exceedingly that "help is laid upon One so mighty"—Ps. lxxxix. 19.

And let us receive him for all the ends for which he is offered to us—1 Cor. i. 30.

Let none say, I am so far off, I can never hope for salvation by him—

His exhortation recorded by the prophet yet sounds in our ears—Isaiah xlv. 22.

Nor shall any be ashamed who put their trust in him—

2. Do not attempt to separate his characters, but unite them—

In vain shall we hope to be saved by Christ, if he have not enlightened our understandings—

Though he gives not to all his people the same degree of knowledge, he invariably instructs them in the most important truths—

And if we have no views of the evil of sin, the deceitfulness of the heart, the beauty of holiness, and the suitableness of his salvation, we are still in a lost and perishing condition—

The text itself informs us that Christ becomes our salvation by being our light—

On the other hand, let us not rest in a speculative knowledge of these things—

We must manifest the practical and sanctifying effects of what we know—

We must be delivered from the love and practice both of open and secret sin—

Without this, the clearest perception of divine truths will be of no avail—

Let us unite in our experience what is thus united in Christ—

And seek to grow as well in gracious affections, as in the knowledge of our Lord and Saviour—2 Pet. iii. 18.

"THE CHILDREN OF ZION SHALL BE JOYFUL IN THEIR KING."

Psalm cxlix. 2.—Let the children of Zion be joyful in their King.   (Sk.)

THE first and purest form of government which the world ever knew, was a theocracy.   But in proportion as the minds of men became degraded and sensualized, this got into disrepute; and the *beau ideal* of polity was human monarchy.   To have the source of legislation in one of their own species appeared desirable to the thinking part of the community; places of emolument and exaltation presented themselves to the minds of the avaricious and aspiring; while the multitude were allured by a prospect of unbounded license, and by the hope of pomp and show.   Thus were the minds of all prepared to second the designs of any daring adventurer, who might aim at the usurpation of sovereign power.   The consequence was, that divine government was soon postponed to human; and from that time to the present, this example has been almost universally followed.   Theocracy is no more. There is however a freedom, and volatility about the human mind, which human laws cannot destroy, or even suppress, and hence the great desideratum in jurisprudence is, what can perhaps never be known, and certainly never reduced to practice, except by Him who first breathed into man a living soul.   Of his power in spiritual government, believers are illustrious monuments, as a consideration of our text will serve to prove.   The first thesis with which this passage furnishes us is,

I. BELIEVERS ARE " THE CHILDREN OF ZION."

1. *Zion is often used as an emblem of the church of God*.   Psa. ii. 6; Isa. xxviii. 16; Rom. ix. 33; 1 Pet. ii. 6.   It was stable, Psa. cxxv. 1; so is the church, Matt. xvi. 18.   It was secure, Psa. xlviii. 3, 11, 12; so is the church, Eph. v. 29.   The situation of Zion was exceeding beautiful, Psa. xlviii. 2; so is that of the church.   It is elevated above the din of the world, and " breathes the spirit of a purer air," Matt. v. 14.   Zion was a holy mountain; because on mount Moriah, which joined it on the north-east, the temple of God was built, 2 Chron. iii. 1; Psa. xlviii. 1; the church is holy also, Eph. v. 27.   Mount Zion was peculiarly loved by God, Psa. lxxxviii. 2; so is the church, Eph. v. 25.

2. *Believers are children of Zion by birth.* Naturally we are all " aliens from the commonwealth of Israel, and strangers to the covenants of promise," Eph. ii. 11, 12. We can obtain no entrance into spiritual Zion except by spiritual birth, John iii. 5, 6.   This birth is effected through faith in Christ, by the influence of the Holy Ghost, John x. 9; Rom. v. 1, 2; Eph. ii. 13; Tit. iii. 5, 6.   It is frequently preceded by deep anguish, and distressing solicitude, Jer. i. 4, 5; Acts ii. 37, ix. 6, xvi. 29, 30.

3. *Believers can continue children of Zion no longer than while they retain faith*, Heb. x. 38. By the retention of that faith which first introduced them into Zion, they still continue members of Christ's mystical body. Hence the exhortation of the apostle Paul, Col. iii. 6, 7. They therefore dwell in Zion, knowing that destruction attends their leaving it, John xv. 6. And from the public treasury of Zion they receive their support, they are fed and clothed, Luke xv. 22; John vi. 35, 51, 53—58.

4. *Zion is often emblematic of heaven*, Heb. xii. 22: Rev. xiv. 1.   If the church below be so secure, though still militant, and encompassed by enemies; so lovely, though surrounded by the clouds of sense; and so sacred, though environed by the unclean and polluted; who can describe or even imagine the security, the beauty, and the sanctity of the church of the

first-born in heaven; around which no night ever closes, on which no cloud ever rests, over which no wind ever blows, and towards which no sin ever approaches! 1 Cor. ii. 9; Rev. xxii. 4, 10—27.

5. *Believers are children of Zion by a title to heaven,* Acts xxvi. 18; Eph. i. 18; Col. i. 12; 1 Pet. i. 3, 4. The title to earthly inheritances is often very obscure and uncertain, and consequently not unfrequently the subject of protracted litigation; the title of believers to heaven is clear, and indisputable, Eph. i. 13, 14. The title to an earthly estate may be cut off. The title of believers to heaven is indefeasible. It is founded upon the promise, nay, upon the oath of God, Heb. vi. 17, 18; and though the grass may wither, and the flower may fade, yet the word of the Lord remaineth for ever. The second thesis presented by our text is,

II. Believers have a "King."

1. *Royalty is the centre of supremacy.* A king is a supreme governor. God in this sense is the king of believers. The pope is the head of the Romish church. Civil governors are the heads of national churches, but God is the head of his own, the true church; and consequently, all authority in that church is communicated from Him. Its officers and laborers are of his appointment. To some he grants the commission, "Go ye into all the world," &c., Mark xvi. 15; and to others, a more circumscribed commission. How great then is the impiety of those, who assume the garments of God's priesthood; professing the call of the Holy Ghost, without being even the subjects of God's spiritual kingdom!

2. *Royalty is the source of legislation.* God is the legislator of his people. His code is more pure than any ever conceived by the human mind, for the perfection of human jurisprudence, Rom. vii. 12. It does not result contingently from any thing like an arbitrary constitution of the divine will, but necessarily from the purity and wisdom of the divine mind. It does not merely refer to outward conduct, but extends itself to a cognizance of the thoughts and intents of the heart, Psa. cxix. 96. The revelation of it is clear, nor is an extraordinary extent of intellect necessary for its comprehension, Isa. xxxv. 8; for even those parts of it which defy unaided human research, are made known to man by the teachings of the Spirit, John xiv. 26; 1 Cor. ii. 13. For its requirements see Matt. xxii. 37—39.

3. *Royalty is the fountain of protection.* Probably, the ostensible reason for the appointment of a supreme governor, has been almost universally founded upon this principle. Thus the children of Israel, 1 Sam. viii. 19, 20. Their first reason for demanding a king, was, "that our king may judge us," *i. e.* protect us from the wrongs which may be inflicted by those who live under the same government; their second, "that he may go out before us, and fight our battles," *i. e.* protect us from the ambitious and unjust designs of surrounding nations. In the first of these senses, the protection of God over his subjects is not required, because the kingdom of God is "peace;" but in the second he exercises his royal power, far more completely and effectively than consists with the ability of any human monarch, Job i. 10; Psa. v. 12, xxvii. 1, xxxvii. 17, 39, lv. 22, cxviii. 8—12, cxlvi. 3—6. The third thesis, which our text presents us, is,

III. Believers should be "joyful in their King."

1. *Because he is the most glorious and dignified of all beings.* Consider his nature. He is the independent Jehovah, who was, Psa. xc. 2, xciii 2; who is, Exod. iii. 14; who shall be, Deut. xxxii. 40; Rev. xlv. 6. He is immutable, Psa. cii. 25—27; Mal. iii. 6; Heb. xii 8; James i. 17. He is omnipresent, and omniscient, 1 Kings viii. 27; 2 Chron. ii. 6, vi. 18 ·

Psa. cxxxix. 1—12; Jer. xxxiii. 23, 24. He is almighty, Gen. xviii. 1, xxxv 11; Rev. iv. 8. Consider his moral attributes, his benevolence, Exod. xxxiv. 6; Psa. lxxxvi. 5, cxlv. 8, 9; 1 Tim. ii. 3, 4; James v. 11; 1 John iv. 8. His justice, Deut. xxxii. 4; Psa. lxxxix. 4; Rev. xv. 3. His wisdom, Psa. civ. 24, cxxxvi. 5; Prov. iii. 19; Rom. xi. 33; Col. ii. 3; 1 Tim. i. 17. His truth, Psa. xxv. 10, lxxxvi. 15, c. 5, cxvii. 2, cxlvi. 6; Rev. xix. 11. Consider his works, and kingdom of nature, Gen. i. 1, xiv. 19, 22; Deut. x. 14; Psa. cxv. 16; Isa. xxxvii. 16; John i. 3; Acts xvii. 24. Consider his retinue, Psa. lxviii. 17, civ. 4; Heb. i. 6, 14. How closely the honor and joy of a nation are connected with the dignity of their monarch, will be evident without any attempt at illustration.

2. *Because by his charter they enjoy great privileges and immunities.* Whether any human monarch should be absolute, is a question which does not demand much discussion, as most men are agreed to decide it in the negative; for on the one hand a monarch is not always solicitous for the advantage of his subjects; and on the other, if he were, his capacities would not be equal to his wishes. But, the absolute sovereignty of God is justified by his independence, his benevolence, and his wisdom. He gains no advantage from his subjects; he is benevolently disposed towards them, and he knows how to put his designs into execution most advantageously for them; hence he communicates to them through his Spirit an evidence of their acceptance, Rom. viii. 16; and through his word exceeding great and precious promises, 2 Pet. i. 4. They possess peace and joy, Rom. xiv. 17, xv. 13. They have the privilege of rejoicing even in affliction, Rom. v. 3; 2 Cor. vi. 10. They enjoy a freedom from condemnation, John iii. 18, v. 24; Rom. viii. 1; and a well grounded hope of everlasting enjoyment, Rom. v. 2; Col. i. 5, 27; Tit. ii. 13, iii. 17; Heb. vi. 19. Nor is there any possibility for their charter to be revoked or taken away.

3. *Because the monuments of their great men are protected.* The Bible is a record of the saints. In it are contained monuments of their patience, meekness, courage, faith, and heavenly mindedness. Here we are taught to admire their virtues, and excited to follow their example, Heb. xi. and vi. 12.

4. *Because their enemies are totally inefficient to disturb his government,* Deut. xxxiii. 26—29; Psa. xciii. 1.

5. *Because his kingdom will ultimately be universal. and all opposing powers will be destroyed,* Psa. lxxii. 17, cx. 1; Isa. ii. 4, ix. 6, 7, xi. 9, xlv. 23; Jer. xxiii. 5; Hab. ii. 14; Mic. iv. 1—3; 1 Cor. xv. 25; Rev. xi. 15. Human enemies shall either be subdued by the influences of his grace, or destroyed by the power of his anger; and diabolical enemies shall be bound in chains of darkness, Rev. xx. 1—3.

> ' Come, then, and, added to thy many crowns,
> Receive yet one as radiant as the rest;
> Due to thy last, and most effectual work,
> Thy word fulfilled, the conquest of a world.'

REMARKS.

1. How great and glorious is the moral elevation of a believer, and how insignificant does the honor of this world appear contrasted with the dignity of a Christian!

2. How great should be our solicitude to become subjects of the spiritual kingdom of Jehovah.

3. How indefatigable should we be in spreading the knowledge of **God**, by personal instruction,—by example,—and by the dedication of property, talents, and influence!

CHRIST'S LOVE A PATTERN FOR OURS.

Eph. v. 2.—*Walk in love, as Christ also hath loved us, and hath given himself for us, an offering and a sacrifice to God for a sweet-smelling savour.* (H. H.)

To restore us to the divine image is one great end of all that the Lord Jesus Christ has done and suffered for us. There are indeed perfections in the deity which are incommunicable to any creature: but his moral perfections admit of imitation and resemblance: and therefore we are exhorted to "be followers, or imitators, of God, as dear children." Ver. 1. But in the person of our blessed Lord and Saviour, Jehovah is brought nearer to us, so that we may trace his very steps, and learn to follow him in every disposition of the mind, and every action of the life. Hence in the passage before us, whilst we are particularly informed of the manner in which he has displayed his love to man, we are exhorted to "walk in love, as he has loved us."

In our further elucidation of these words, we shall be led to speak of the Lord Jesus Christ in a two-fold view;

I. As a sacrifice to God—

It was not merely as a martyr that Jesus died, but as a sacrifice for sin. This appears,

1. From all the sacrifices of the Mosaic law—

For what end were these instituted, but to prefigure him? These beyond a doubt were offerings for sin, the victims dying in the place of the offerer and making an atonement for him by their blood: and if the Lord Jesus Christ did not correspond with them in this particular, and actually fulfil what those prefigured, they were all instituted in vain, and were shadows without any substance at all.

2. From the declarations of the prophets—

The prophet thus plainly speaks of Christ as dying for the sins of men, "He made his soul an offering for sin:" "He bare the sins of many:" "On him were laid the iniquity of us all." Isa. liii. 6, 10, 12. What is the import of these testimonies, if Christ did not offer himself a sacrifice for sin?

3. From the testimony of John the Baptist—

It was in reference to the lambs that were offered every morning and evening for the sins of all Israel, that the Baptist spake, when he pointed out the Lord Jesus as "the Lamb of God that taketh away the sins of the world." If Christ were not a sacrifice for sin, this testimony was not founded in truth.

4. From the declarations of Christ himself—

He constantly affirmed, that "he came to give his life a ransom for many:" that his blood should be shed for the remission of sins; and that by being "lifted up upon the cross, he would draw all men unto him."

5. From the united testimony of all the apostles—

All with one voice represent him as redeeming us to God by his blood, and offering himself as "a propitiation, not for our sins only, but also for the sins of the whole world." In a word, the whole tenor of the Sacred Writings proves, that " he bare our sins in his own body on the tree," and " died, the just for the unjust, that he might bring us to God."

But in all this he was further designed,

II. As an example to us—

In the circumstance before noticed, we cannot resemble him ; for " no man can redeem his brother, or give to God a ransom for him." Nevertheless in the love which instigated him to this we may resemble him. Our love, like his, should be,

1. Disinterested—

It is not possible for us to add any thing to him : we cannot make him more happy or more glorious by any thing that we can do : " our goodness extendeth not to him ;" " nor can we by any means profit him :" yet did he in this astonishing manner display his love to us. Thus in the exercise of our love we should not· consider whether the objects of it will ever be able to make us any suitable return : we should shew love in every possible way, without so much as desiring any return from man, or even desiring that our exercise of it should be known ; yea, even though we knew that it would only be requited with evil. We should love our very enemies ; and, " instead of being overcome of evil, should strive incessantly to overcome their evil with good."

2. Generous—

What unsearchable riches has he purchased even for his bitterest enemies ! He would not that any one of them should fall short of all the glory of heaven. True it is, that we cannot thus enrich the objects of our love : yet we should do all we can towards it, by providing for them not only the things needful for the body, but, above all, the things that may promote the welfare of the soul. Here the poor may be on a par with those who are able to give out of their abundance : for if they are constrained to say, "Silver and gold have I none," they may add, " but such as I have, give I unto thee ;" and then may proceed to speak to them of the Saviour, through whom they may obtain all the blessings of salvation. Thus, " though poor, we may make many rich."

3. Self-denying—

Our blessed Lord " emptied himself of all the glory of heaven," and endured all the wrath of an offended God ; and became a curse himself, in order to deliver us from the curse which our iniquities had deserved. And shall we decline exercising our love, because it may be attended with some pain or difficulty on our part ? No : we should not hesitate even to lay down life itself, if by so doing we may promote the eternal welfare of our brethren. 1 John iii. 16.

4. Constant—

" Whom our Lord loved, he loved to the end." There were many occasions whereon his immediate disciples displeased him : but he did not therefore " withdraw his mercy from them, or shut up his loving-kindness in displeasure." There are occasions also whereon we shall be called to exercise forbearance and forgiveness one towards another ; and we ought to meet those occasions with love proportioned to them. We should strive with all our might to " follow peace with all men," and to " keep the unity of the Spirit in the bond of peace."

Address—

1. Be thankful to Christ for all the wonders of his love—

Think how unworthy you were of all his love : for, it was " when you were yet enemies, that he died for you." Think too what must have been your state to all eternity, if he had not so " undertaken for you:" his sufferings under the hidings of his Father's face, and under the strokes of divine justice, shew what miseries awaited you in hell for ever, if he had not become your substitute and surety to discharge your debt. Oh! never for a moment lose sight of the obligations you owe to him for that " love of his, which passeth knowledge."

2. Present yourselves as living sacrifices to him—

This *may* be done; and it is the very end for which such astonishing mercies have been vouchsafed to you. Rom. xii. 1. Consider all that you are, and all that you have, as his; and let it all be devoted henceforth to the glory of his name.

3. Endeavor to resemble him more and more—

Whatever attainments you may have made, you must still be aspiring after higher degrees of love. 1 Thess. iv. 9, 10. Look at him then, not only as the ground of your hopes, but as the pattern for your imitation. Trace him in all the labors of his love: trace him from heaven to earth, and from earth to heaven: trace him in all that he either did or suffered: and study to resemble him in the whole of his spirit and deportment. In all his labors " God smelled a sweet savour;" even as he had done in those offerings and sacrifices by which Christ had been shadowed forth: Gen. viii. 21; Lev. i. 9; and though your labors of love can never resemble his, as making an atonement for sin, they shall, like his, come up for a memorial before God, and be accepted as well-pleasing in his sight. Heb. vi. 10, and xiii. 16.

CHRIST THE DAY-SPRING.

Luke i. 78, 79.—Through the tender mercy of our God; whereby the day-spring from on high hath visited us, to give light to them that sit in darkness and in the shadow of death, to guide our feet into the way of peace. (Pr.)

THESE words contain an animated but highly figurative description, of our Lord Jesus Christ. He is, indeed, the bright and glorious day-spring from on high which hath visited us. The word here translated " day-spring," occurs also in the Old Testament, where it is considered " the branch;" but the most literal interpretation of the Greek word is "the East," or the place whence the light comes. This expression may intimate the pre-existence of our Lord Jesus Christ: as we well know, that the sun exists before he arises upon us, so Christ also existed, before he appeared upon our earth in the form of sinful man; and it may also refer to the high and exalted station of the Redeemer of mankind. Our text contains,

I. A VERY MOVING OR AFFECTING VIEW OF THE STATE OF MANKIND, WITHOUT THE LORD JESUS CHRIST:—"They are sitting in darkness and the shadow of death."

II. A VERY INTERESTING DESCRIPTION OF OUR LORD JESUS CHRIST,—he is, "The day-spring from on high,"

III. A VERY ENCOURAGING REPRESENTATION OF THE DESIGN OF OUR SAVIOUR'S MISSION INTO OUR WORLD, "to give light" and "to guide our feet," &c.

I. A VERY MOVING OR AFFECTING VIEW OF THE STATE OF MANKIND WITHOUT THE LORD JESUS CHRIST.

In Scripture, *darkness* sometimes means the judgments of God—sometimes the afflictions of God's people—sometimes sin, (as, for instance, men love *darkness* rather than light, that is, they love sin rather than holiness,)—sometimes it means the grave—sometimes hell itself; but it is frequently used in Scripture with regard to the moral state and condition of mankind by nature, which is darkness indeed; and then, (as in the text,) it means the absence of that knowledge of Christ which is essential to impart comfort to the human mind, or bring to a saving acquaintance with him as the only way of salvation. This absence of the knowledge of Christ leaves us in darkness—as to *the moral character of God*—as to *the purity of his law*—as to *the evil nature and dreadful consequences of sin*—as to *the genuine source of happiness to the human mind*—and, finally, as to *a future state.*

But without the knowledge of the Lord Jesus Christ, mankind are not only sitting in darkness, but in the *shadow of death.* The Scriptures contemplate death as spiritual, temporal and eternal. If you ask me, whether there is such a thing as spiritual death in this world, I answer, yes, there is, and it consists in that separation of the best affections of the soul from God, which is so evident in every unregenerate mind. When man transgressed the commands of his Creator, his desires after his God became paralysed, and death—a spiritual death—passed upon all his affections, and upon all those enjoyments he had hitherto experienced in communion with him.

Notice three particulars in the phraseology of this part of our text,

I. A shadow always supposes the existence of the substance. And do we not behold every day on our right hand and on our left the ravages of death? and are not the mourners which go about our streets continually, sufficient to satisfy us that he is abroad in the world, and busily engaged on every side?

2. The object which creates a shadow in which we are sitting must be very near. And who can tell how near death may be to each one of us, or how soon we may have to pass through the dark valley. But,

3. A shadow even of the most terrible object, is a very inoffensive thing. A lion. with his savage aspect, his ferocious countenance, his glaring eyes, his erect mane, apparently ready to pounce upon you for his prey, is certainly a formidable object; but the *shadow* of a lion, thus savage and ferocious, is as harmless as the shadow of a lamb. Thus death, however formidable he may really be to the wicked, is stripped of all his terrors, and becomes only a *shadow* to the believer in Jesus.

II. OUR TEXT CONTAINS A VERY INTERESTING DESCRIPTION OF THE LORD JESUS CHRIST.—He is *the day-spring*, &c. This we shall attempt to illustrate and to justify.

1. The day-spring, or the sun is *the great source of light;* so is the Lord Jesus Christ: he is the great source of *natural* light, for he first formed and still commands the rising and the setting sun—of *intellectual* light, for it is he who forms our mind as well as our bodies—of *rational* light—of *spiritual* light—and of all those beams of light which, shooting their radiance over our present path, afford us also some bright glimpses of the glory of a future state.

2. The day-spring is *gradual and progressive.* And how gradually has spiritual light dawned upon our world, if we take a review of the history of our species from the morning of time to the present moment! The light which the patriarchs posesssed may be compared to the grey shadows of twilight, or as the morning spread upon the mountains. When we say that the light of the gospel has increased since the days of the apostles, we mean not

that the gospel, as preached by them, was incomplete or ineffectual; but, that holy men, by more copious effusions, and fuller manifestations of the Holy Spirit, and by events and circumstances which are continually transpiring, are enabled more thoroughly to understand and consequently more clearly to preach and to explain the grand truths it contains. But the increase of spiritual light in the mind of man is also gradual. Conviction of sin is the first dawning of this light; and as he proceeds in the divine life, he becomes more and more enlightened, and is continually making new discoveries, and increasing in knowledge, holiness, and the fear of the Lord; " for the path of the just is as the shining light, increasing more and more unto the perfect day."

3. The day spring is *certain and irresistible.* When the proper time arrives, what can prevent the rising of the sun? The darkest, densest clouds, storms or tempests, or the most violent agitations of the atmosphere, cannot prevent or hinder him from arising in his majesty, and shedding his beams through the heavens; and the incarnation of Christ, or the rising of the spiritual day-spring was certain, and had been long predicted; but what clouds of opposition strove against its rising, and endeavored at once to extinguish its glorious, its delightful beams!

4. The day-spring or the light of the sun, is *free and common to all;* so it is with Christ and his gospel; by this, we mean to say that the atonement of Christ is sufficient for all; that there is efficacy enough in his righteousness for all; that there is an abundant sufficiency of the influences of his spirit for all; that the invitations of the gospel are freely addressed to all; and that the blessings of the gospel are offered to all. At the same time, it must be admitted, that they only can be benefitted who *accept* these blessings thus freely offered; and that those who receive not, must bear upon their own heads the guilt and punishment which must inevitably follow their rejection of them.

III. Our text contains a very encouraging representation of the design of our Saviour's mission into our world. The Lord Jesus Christ is the sum and substance of all that is contained either in the Old or the New Testament. Take him away, and we may fairly ask, what is there left? there may, indeed, be the shadow, but the substance is gone; there may be the breathless corpse, but the animating spirit is fled, and no real life remains. This head divides itself into the two following particulars. He came,

1. To give *light.* But before Christ could be known and acknowledged as the light which was to enlighten the world, it was necessary that he should show himself amongst us in the same way as the natural sun must arise and shine upon the world before he can impart light to the world; and in order, therefore, that Jesus might appear as this spiritual light, he has shown himself in the dignity of his *person,* in the perfection of his *atonement,* in the fulness of his *grace,* in the *willingness* he has manifested to save unto the uttermost all that come unto God by him, and in the *discovery* he has made of the way in which moral pollution may be purged from the heart of man. Repentance and faith are not in any way meritorious in themselves; and yet they are inseparably connected with every sinner's salvation. Thus we see how Christ has become a light unto the world, and what discoveries he has made to us of things which belong unto our eternal salvation; but of which, without him, we should have remained in total darkness.

2. He came to *guide our feet into the way of peace.* He is himself the very Prince of Peace. By nature we are enemies to God by wicked works, consequently far from every source of peace. But the design of his mis-

sion into our world was to guide our feet again into the way of peace, by effecting our reconciliation with his Father, through the shedding of his most precious blood, and hereby making peace. Thus the apostle declares, "For he is our peace;" and again, "We have peace with God, through our Lord Jesus Christ."

But peace in Scripture is also frequently to be understood in a very extended sense. It was a common form of salutation, and intends "all good." Thus it was used by Boaz to his reapers, and by Christ himself to his disciples. And Christ came to guide our feet into the ways of all good, which, without him, would have continued in the ways of all evil.

There are four things we shall notice by way of improvement to the whole :—

1st. The infinite condescension of Jehovah in interposing in our behalf. Eternity will be quite short enough to unravel this mysterious and delightful theme, if we consider from what misery it raises, and to what glories it exalts us.—2ndly. The Christian's duty and privilege. It is his duty to trust in the word of the Lord in the times of darkness. There are times when the natural sun does not shine upon the world ; and it is the believer's privilege sometimes to walk in the light of God's countenance.—3rdly. Notice the miserable state of those who hear the sound of the gospel, and yet remain at a distance from this light ; and, lastly, If the pleasures of religion be so great upon earth, what must be the enjoyment of believers in the upper world?

CHRIST A GREAT SAVIOUR.

Isaiah xix. 20.—They shall cry unto the Lord because of the oppressors, and He shall send them a Saviour, and a great One, and he shall deliver them. (S. S.)

God usually vouchsafes his mercies when we are reduced to the greatest straits—

This is manifest in his most remarkable dispensations of providence and of grace—

In the greatest extremity God promised to send a deliverer to Egypt—*

But there is a further reference to Christ as the Saviour to the Gentile world—†

And it is in seasons of heavy dejection that He reveals himself to them—

To him therefore we must look as the Saviour foretold in the text—

I. In what respects He is "a great Saviour."

It is justly said by the Psalmist that "his greatness is unsearchable"—Ps. cxlv. 3.

Nevertheless we may, not unprofitably, endeavor to illustrate it.

*In this view it seems applicable to the angel who slew 185,000 of Sennacherib's army : for, though that deliverance was more immediately vouchsafed to the Jews under Hezekiah, yet in its consequences it extended to Egypt. Sennacherib had before conquered and ravaged Egypt ; and it was most probable that if he had taken Jerusalem he would have again proceeded thither with his victorious army, and reduced that already desolated kingdom to the lowest ebb of misery. But perhaps there may be a further reference to some other deliverers.

†This appears from the whole context, ver. 18—25.

He is great when considered *in his own person.*

He has a name above every name either on earth or in heaven—

He is exalted to be a prince that can give repentance and remission of, sins—Acts v. 31.

The voice of inspiration calls him, "the great God and our Saviour"—Tit. ii. 13.

He speaks of himself in terms of similar import—Isa. xlv. 22.

Nor can any thing be more glorious than the description given of him by the prophet—Isa. ix. 6.

He is also great in respect of the *salvation he has wrought out for us.*

Who can count the number of the sins from which he has delivered us?—

Or estimate the misery from which he has redeemed us?—

Through our whole lives we have been heaping up treasures of wrath—Rom. ii. 5.

Yet there is no condemnation to us if we be interested in him—Romans viii. 1.

Besides, he has purchased for us an eternal inheritance in heaven—

We must know all the glories of heaven and the horrors of hell, before we can fully appreciate the greatness of his salvation—

But before we speak peace to ourselves it becomes us to inquire

II. FOR WHOSE DELIVERANCE HE IS SENT.

Great as his mercy is, it will not indiscriminately extend to all—

They, for whose relief he comes, are " oppressed" with the burthen of sin—

The generality, alas! are well contented with their bondage—

If he should offer to deliver them they would thrust him from them—Acts vii. 37, 39.

But there are some who mourn like the saints of old—Isa. vi. 5. Rom. vii. 24.

They desire nothing so much as to be delivered from their corruptions—

For these Jesus came down from heaven, and died upon the cross—

Nor, though they be lawful captives, will he leave them in the hand of their enemies—Isa. xlix. 24, 25.

They at the same time " cry earnestly to the Lord" for deliverance.

There are some, it must be confessed, who are uneasy in their sins, yet do not with fervor and constancy implore his mercy—

Such therefore, notwithstanding their uneasiness, obtain no help from him—

His mercy is promised to those alone who seek it with importunity—Matt. vii. 7; Ezek. xxxvi. 37.

But humble and believing suppliants shall never be rejected by him—

They shall find him a great, compassionate, and all-sufficient Saviour—

APPLICATION :—

Let *those who are unconcerned about their sins* reflect on their state—

Would God have sent them *such* a Saviour if their condition had not required it?—

Or, will they take occasion from this grace to live more securely in their sins?—

Let them consider that their cries, however available now, will soon be of no effect—Luke xvi. 24, 25

Let *those who are conflicting with sin and satan* lift up their heads with joy—

However desperate their state may seem, their redemption draweth **nigh**—
Nor shall all the powers of darkness rescue them from their Redeemer's
hands—John x. 28.
Let *those who have experienced deliverance* adore their Lord—
Let them still go on, "strong in the grace that is in Christ Jesus"—
And soon they shall join in eternal Hallelujahs to God and to the Lamb.

WHAT WE OUGHT TO THINK OF CHRIST.

Matt. xxii. 42.—What think ye of Christ? (Sk.)

1. It is certain that the most correct views of Christ may be obtained
from the Holy Scriptures, for these testify of him, John v. 39. The Old
Testament testifies of Christ, in a great variety of promises, types, and prophecies. Luke xxiv. 44; Acts x. 43. The New Testament testifies of
Christ, by recording the history of his life; by inculcating his doctrines;
and by exhibiting the blessings of his kingdom. Christ is therefore the sum
and substance of the inspired writings.

2. The testimony thus given is most highly creditable; for it is the testimony of *infinite knowledge*, which cannot mistake, Acts xv. 18, and the testimony of *unbounded goodness*, which will not deceive, Deut. xxxii. 4.
Under the guidance of these divine oracles, let us observe,

I. WHAT WE OUGHT TO THINK OF CHRIST. That we may entertain distinct ideas of this interesting subject, let us consider,

First, What we ought to think of Christ's *person.*

1. We ought to think that *he is truly man*, possessed of a human body,
and a human soul, by which that body is animated. He is repeatedly *denominated* man. Thus he is called by Peter, in his sermon on the day of
Pentecost, Acts ii. 22, and by Paul in his epistles, see 1 Cor. xv. 21—47;
1 Tim. ii. 5. And he is *described* as man, in his birth. "When the fulness," &c., Gal. v. 4, 5. In his *growth;* "and Jesus increased," &c.,
Luke ii. 52. And in the common *infirmities;* through bodily exercise, he
felt weary. That he might be prepared for renewed labors of piety, and benevolence, he took rest in sleep. His mind was the subject both of grief and
joy; and his body, of pain and death. It behoved him in all things to be
made like unto his brethren, Heb. ii. 17.

2. We ought to think that *he is also truly God.* This appears,—From
his *names*, he is called "The mighty God," Isa. ix. 6. He is also called,
Immanuel. God with us," Isa. vii. 15; Matt. i. 23. "The Lord our Righteousness," Jer. xxiii. 6. "God," John i. 1; Acts xx. 28. "God over all,"
Rom. ix. 6. "The great God and our Saviour," Tit. ii. 13. "The true
God, and eternal life," 1 John v. 20.—From his *works;* he is "the Creator of the universe," John i. 3; Col. i. 16; Heb. ii. 8—10. And the preserver of it, in its existence, and in its order, Col. i. 17; Heb. i. 3.—From
his *perfections;* he is eternal, without beginning, Mic. v. 2. He is omnipresent, John iii. 13; Matt. xviii. 20; omniscient, John xxi. 17; Heb. iv.
12; omnipotent, Psa. xlv. 3; Rev. i. 8, and immutable, Heb. ii. 12, and
xiii. 8.—From his *pre-existent glory*, which he enjoyed from eternity, John
xvii. 5. This glory was seen by Isaiah, chap. vi. 1—3 and is ascribed to

our Lord, see John xii. 41.—From the *worship* paid him by God's approved servants; by Christians on earth, 1 Cor. i. 2; by angels, Heb. i. 6, and by glorified saints, Rev. vii. 9, 10.—And from the *gifts* conferred by him; as forgiveness of sins, Acts v. 31; adoption into God's family, John i. 12; the gift of the Holy Ghost, Acts ii. 33, and eternal life. This he engages to give his followers, John x. 28; Rev. ii. 10, and this they expect from him, 2 Tim. iv. 3.

3. We ought to think that *Christ is God and man united in one person*, John i. 14; 1 Tim. iii. 16. This thought of Christ, renders all assertions respecting him perfectly consistent and harmonious. Thus we perceive how truly he is both the child born, and the mighty God. The Son, and the Lord of David, Matt. xxii. 45. The Root and the offspring of David, Rev. xxii. 16. Having considered what we ought to think of his person, let us consider,

Secondly, What we ought to think of his *name;* "Christ."

1. *This name is usually connected with that of Jesus.* Under this conjunct name of Jesus Christ, he is represented as coming into the world to save us, 1 Tim. i. 15.—Under this name he is preached to us, by his servants, 2 Cor. iv. 5; 1 John i. 2.—And under this name we must, as Christians, believe on him, Acts xvi. 31.

2. We should think, *how this name, thus connected, is expressive of his great work, and the various offices by which he effects it.* The name Jesus, signifies a Divine Saviour; and is expressive of his *great work.* This is to save mankind, Matt. i. 21; John iii. 17. To save them, by redeeming them from all sin, Psa. cxxx. 8. By restoring them to all the blessings forfeited by sin, 1 Pet. iii. 18. And by preserving them unto eternal life, Jude 24, 25.—The name of Christ, signifies *anointed*, and is expressive of those *various offices* which he sustains in effecting his work of human redemption. Of his *prophetic* office; as anointed to teach us, Isa. lxi. 1; Acts iii. 22.—Of his *kingly* office; as anointed to govern, protect, and reward us, Psa. ii. 6. Of his *priestly* office; as anointed to atone for our sins; to make intercession for us; and to bless us, Heb. iii. 1, and ix. 26, and vii, 25, 26, and ix. 28.—Those who desire to become interested in him as their Saviour, are required to receive him in all his offices, as the Lord's anointed, John i. 11, 12.—And all who thus receive him, are blessed by him, Psa. ii. 12. Hence let us consider,

Thirdly, What we ought to think of the *privileges* enjoyed by his subjects.

1. *These are various;* they include illumination, John viii. 12,—liberty, John viii. 32,—rest, Matt. xi. 28,—purity, John xiii. 8; 1 John i. 7,—protection, Isa. xl. 11; 1 Pet. i. 5,—provision, Matt. vi. 33. And eternal glory, John xii. 26.

2. *They are exactly adapted to our natural state and exigencies.* We are ignorant, and want illumination; enslaved, and want liberty; burdened, and want rest; defiled, and want purity; defenceless, and want protection; needy and immortal, and want eternal enjoyments.

3. *They are amply sufficient* to fulfil all our desires, Col. i. 19; Psa. cxlv. 19.

4. *And they are certain*, to all who obey him, Heb. v. 9. Let us consider,

Fourthly, What we ought to think of his *demands.*

1. *These are most graciously proposed by himself*, Matt. xi. 28, 29.

2. *They are highly reasonable.* We should learn of him; for he is an infinitely wise and kind teacher, Isa. xlviii. 17. We should obey him; for he is our rightful sovereign, having redeemed us by the price of his blood, 1 Cor. vi. 19, 20, and by the power of his grace, Psa. cxvi. 16. We should confide in him, for he is an all-sufficient, and never-failing friend, Isa. xxviii. 16, and xii. 2.

3. *They are truly pleasant to those who are endued with his grace.* For his grace enables us to do his will, Phil. ii. 12. And it inspires us with love, which makes our duty our pleasure, 1 John iv. 4; Matt. xi. 30. Thus we ought to think of Christ. And let us now observe,

II. WHY WE SHOULD THUS THINK OF CHRIST. We should thus think of him,

1. *Because those views of Christ are true and correct.* They are those views which we know God has of him. And these views must be adopted by us, if we would choose the way of truth, Psa. cxix. 30.

2. *Because we must think aright concerning Christ, that we may act aright towards him;* for ignorance of Christ must ever prevent a due acknowledgment of him.—If we do not think aright concerning his *offices;* we shall never learn of him as our Prophet; we shall never obey him as our King; nor trust in him as our High Priest, John i. 10, 11. If we do not think aright concerning his *divinity;* we shall not duly honor him, John v. 23. The Samaritan woman, not knowing him, omitted prayer to him, John iv. 10. The princes of this world not knowing him, put him to death 1 Cor. ii. 8.

3. *Because we must act aright towards Christ, or we cannot be saved by him.* Those who will not hear him will be destroyed, Acts iii. 23; Heb. xii. 25. Those who will not obey him, must be executed as his avowed enemies, Luke xix. 27; Rom. ii. 8, 9; 2 Thess. i. 7—9. Those who do not trust in him, remain under God's curse, Jer. xvii. 5. And those who deny his divinity and atonement, destroy themselves, 2 Pet. ii. 1. Having thus considered what we should think of Christ, and why we should thus think of him, let us

III. APPLY THE QUESTION. "What think ye of Christ?"

1. *Do you think him an imposter*—one who deceives the people? John vii. 12.—Then consider the *prophecies* which have been fulfilled in him, 2 Pet. i. 19.—Consider the *predictions* spoken by him, Matt. xvii. 22, 23; Luke xxi. 12, and xix. 41—44.—Consider the *miracles* wrought by him; consider, and believe, John xiv. 11; 2 Chron. xx. 20.

2. *Do you think him a mere man, and not God?* If so,—Consider, his names, works, attributes; his former glory, honors, and donations.—Consider these proofs of his divinity, and submit to his authority; by engaging in his service, and confiding in his mediation, Psa. ii. 12.

3. *Do you think little or nothing concerning him?* Is he not in all your thoughts? Psa. x. 4. If thus forgetful of him,—Consider his gracious remembrance of you, Psa. cxxxvi. 23; Luke i. 78, 79; Psa. viii. 4.—Consider this, and lament your ingratitude, Isa. liii. 4; Zech. xii. 10.

4. *Do you now think less of Christ than you formerly did?* Jer. ii. 32. If so—consider your fall; and return to him as at first, Rev. ii. 5; Hos. xiv 1, 2.—Consider his unwearied kindness, and hope in his mercy, 1 John ii. 1; Psa. cxxx. 7.

5. *Do you think Christ desirable,* and long to find him? Job xxiii. 2, 3. If so, then now open your hearts to receive him, Rev. iii. 20,—and now you will find salvation ready for you, Luke xiv. 17.

6. Do you think and find Christ an inestimable treasure? 1 Pet. ii. 7 Then carefully abide in him, 1 John ii. 28,—steadily walk in him, Col. ii 6.—and hope for his beatific presence, John xiv. 2, 3 ; 1 John iii. 2.

THE FOUNTAIN OPENED.

Zech. xiii. 1.—In that day there shall be a fountain opened to the house of David and to the inhabitants of Jerusalem for sin and for uncleanness. (Sk.)

An inspired apostle assures us, that to Christ, " give all the prophets witness ;" and their various testimonies concerning him, are highly descriptive of his character and work, as the Redeemer and Saviour of his people. He is distinctly represented by a rich variety of metaphors and figures, which strikingly illustrate the nature of his offices, and the operations of his grace. He is the *Sun of Righteousness*, to enlighten our minds—an *infallible physician*, to heal the maladies of our souls—a *spiritual refiner*, to purify our hearts—and an *inexhaustible fountain*, to supply all our hearts, by " the exceeding riches of his grace." He possesses an infinite plenitude of blessings, which he is ever ready to communicate to perishing sinners. In the text, the prophet evidently " testified beforehand the sufferings of Christ, and the glory that should follow ;" prophetically anticipating the personal manifestation of the Messiah, and the unspeakable benefits resulting to mankind from his atoning sacrifice, he exclaims with holy joy and gratitude, " In that day," &c. Let us pray that we may comprehend the import, and realize the truth of these words, while we consider,

I. The fountain that is opened. The term *fountain* is a metaphor, and is used in the text to represent the mediatorial character of Christ, as the *source* and *medium* of salvation to the human race. The figure is highly appropriate and instructive. " A fountain opened," implies,

1. *The plenitude of Divine grace.* It is not a *wasting stream*, that soon exhausts its store ; but a *never-failing fountain*, ever flowing in plenteous supplies for every demand. The Lord Jehovah is emphatically styled, " The fountain of living waters, and the God of all grace." The saving influences of the Holy Ghost are figuratively called *water ;—water of life ;*—and the *washing of regeneration*, John iv. 14 ; 1 Cor. vi. 11. And the Lord Jesus Christ as the Author of salvation, graciously exclaims to a perishing world, " If any man thirst, let him come unto me, and drink." In him there is an unlimited fulness of " grace and truth," Col. i. 19 ; John i. 16. Millions have been refreshed by this fountain, and still it is undiminished. There is " enough for all, and enough for evermore."

2. *The freeness of Divine grace.* It is not a fountain *sealed up*, and *forbidden ;* but freely *opened* and *accessible* to all. None are excluded from participating its richest blessings, Rev. xxii. 17. No personal merit, or moral worthiness, is required in its willing recipients. All are invited, and are welcome, to drink the living streams of bliss, " without money, and without price." The Saviour will not cast out any that come unto him. He opened a fountain of *life* by his *death*, and in infinite compassion, declares, "I will give unto him that is athirst, of the water of life freely.—Blessed are they which do hunger and thirst after righteousness, for they shall be filled." Observe,

II. The period when it was opened. "In that day," &c. When this expression occurs in the prophetic writings, it generally refers to the *actual appearing*, or *spiritual reign* of the Messiah In this sense we understand it in the text, as referring to Christ's assumption of our nature, and sacrifice for our sins. But we ought to notice respecting this fountain, that,

1. *It was virtually opened in the original scheme of redemption.* According to God's gracious promise to mankind, Christ is called, "The Lamb slain from the foundation of the world." When the counsel of peace was between them both; the covenant of redemption was made in Jesus Christ, as the Mediator between God and man, Rom. iii. 24—26. This scheme of reconciliation was, in due time, announced to the world; and the fountain of grace *gradually revealed* and *opened* in the various promises of the Redeemer to the patriarchs, the emblematic shadows of the Mosaic dispensation, and the inspired predictions of the holy prophets, John viii. 56; Rom. iii. 21, 22.

2. *It was actually opened in the mediatorial work of the Redeemer.*—When the fulness of time was come, Christ was manifested in the flesh, to accomplish the will of God, and procure the salvation of sinners. He then *fully opened* this fountain, by fulfilling all righteousness in his own person —becoming the propitiation for our sins—rising again for our justification— ascending to heaven to be our Advocate with the Father—and diffusing an enlarged dispensation of the Holy Ghost; it was ministerially opened in the labors and writings of the apostles, as "ambassadors for Christ," 1 Cor. i. 23, 24, 30. And it still continues *open*, issuing in copious streams through all the doctrines, promises, and ordinances, of the Gospel, to satisfy the thirsty souls of them that repent and believe, John vii. 38. Consider,

III. The people to whom it is opened. "The house of David, and the inhabitants of Jerusalem." It is very evident,

1. *This fountain was primarily opened to the Jews.* This is the express declaration of the text. To the *Jews* Christ was promised, and to them he came as his own people, according to the flesh. His personal ministry was generally confined to them; and though they crucified him as an impostor, his blood was shed for their sins; and he commanded his apostles to open their commission at Jerusalem, and preach the gospel *first* to the "lost sheep of the house of Israel," Luke xxiv. 46, 47, &c.

2. *This fountain is now graciously opened to the Gentiles.* The blessings of the Messiah were not to be confined to the Jewish church.—He was sent "to be a light of the *Gentiles*, and for salvation to the *ends of the earth.*" "By the grace of God he tasted death for every man;" and his "unsearchable riches" are to be preached in "every nation, and to every creature." Jews and Gentiles are equally welcome, for there is now no difference, Rom. x. 12, 13; Eph. ii. 14—18. Unnumbered millions of Gentiles have proved the cleansing power of this *fountain*, which is *rapidly opening* and *extending* its healing virtues to "every kindred, tongue, and people." Our text also specifies,

IV. The purpose for which it is opened. It is "for sin and for uncleanness." This implies,

1. *A fountain is opened for the expiation of sin.* The death of Christ was a *perfect sacrifice*, by which an *atonement* was made for the sins of mankind. The Divine perfections *harmonized*, and a new and living way of salvation opened to fallen sinners, Psa. lxxxv. 10 Heb. x. 18—22. *Such an expiation* was absolutely necessary—was typified by the Jewish sacrifices

—was announced by the prophets—and was ultimately accomplished, **when** Christ was " wounded for our transgressions, and his soul was made an offer ing for sin," John i. 29; 1 John iv. 10.

2. *A fountain is opened for the destruction of sin.* It must not only be *sacrificially expiated*, but *personally destroyed*; and " for this purpose the Son of God was manifested, that he might *destroy* the works of the devil." He effects this *destruction* by the merit of his death, and the operation of his grace, Tit. ii. 14. All sin is *moral uncleanness*, and spreads its infectious disease through every power, both of body and soul. The ceremonial purifications under the law were *emblematic* of the *efficacy* of *this fountain*, Heb. ix. 13, 14. The blood of Christ cleanseth from all sin, 1 John i. 8, 9. Have we come to this living fountain? It is *open* and *free* for all " Believe, and be saved." " Come drink, aud thirst no more."

NOAH'S ARK A TYPE OF CHRIST.

1 Peter iii. 21.—The like figure whereunto, even baptism, doth now save us. (S. S.)

God has marked the necessity of holiness no less by the dispensations of his Providence than by the declarations of his grace. His destroying of the whole world for their iniquity, evinced, as strongly as any thing could, that sin should never go unpunished, and that the righteous only should be saved. In this view St. Peter introduces the mention of that well attested fact, and declares that the salvation, experienced by Noah in the ark, was typical of that which we experience by Christ, and into which we are brought by our baptism. The text is by no means free from difficulties: to render it as intelligible as we can, we shall consider

I. THE TYPICAL SALVATION HERE REFERRED TO.

God had determined to overwhelm the world with a deluge.

Though there had been so few generations upon earth, that Noah's own father (Lamech) had been contemporary with Adam for sixty years, and lived till within five years of the flood, so that Noah, and the people of that generation, had, for no less than six hundred years together, received instruction only at second hand from Adam himself, yet had " all flesh corrupted their way," insomuch that " God repented that he had made man," and resolved to destroy him from off the face of the earth.

But for the preservation of the righteous he instructed Noah to make an ark.

This vessel was not constructed according to man's device, but by the special direction of God himself. To the eyes of man it doubtless seemed an absurd attempt: but " the foolishness of God is wiser than man ;" and the event justified the hopes and expectations of Noah.

In the mean time he called the people to repentance by the ministry of Noah.

God exercised forbearance towards them 120 years. But they " received his grace in vain." And the means used **for** their salvation only ripened them for destruction.

When the appointed time **was** come, he ordered Noah and his family to **go** into the ark.

The symptoms of the flood did not yet appear, but these favorites of heaven were to condemn the world, not in word only, but in deed. By manifesting their faith, their fear, and their obedience, they were practically to condemn the world's unbelief, security, and disobedience. Heb. xi. 7. And, upon their entrance into the ark, " God shut them in" with his own hand, that the door might be secure against the violence of the wind and waves.

Then the waters, that destroyed all the world besides, bore them up in perfect safety.

Every other refuge now proved vain. The unbelievers found to their cost the truth of God's threatenings. Their numbers did not screen them from his judgments. Nor was the fewness of the elect any bar to their acceptance and salvation. They rose, while others sank in the mighty waters. Nor, if any cleaved to the ark, did that avail them. The very builders of the ark perished. They, and they only, who were in the ark, were made the monuments of saving mercy.

This history being altogether typical, we shall consider.

II. THE CORRESPONDENT SALVATION WHICH WE ENJOY.

Baptism is spoken of in the text as the *antitype*,* of which Noah's flood was the type. But we apprehend the apostle's meaning to be, that Noah's salvation in the ark was typical of our salvation under the christian dispensation.† This subject will be best understood, not by drawing the parallel between the flood and baptism, or between the ark and Christ, but by exhibiting *the fact* of our salvation as corresponding with that of Noah.

God has determined to punish the world with an everlasting destruction.

His word bears frequent and most undeniable testimony to this solemn truth———Matt. xxiv. 37—39. 2 Peter ii. 5, 9. Psalm xi. 6 and 9, 17.

But he has prepared a Saviour for those who repent and turn unto him.

Human sagacity never could have devised a way of saving sinners consistently with the honor of God's perfections. But God has sent and qualified his only begotten Son, that, through him, all who believe might be justified from all things. And though salvation through the death of Christ be " to the Jews a stumbling-block, and to the Greeks foolishness," yet to them that are called to partake of it, it has invariably proved the power of God and the wisdom of God. 1 Cor. i. 23, 24.

Ever since the method of salvation has been announced to the world, God has been inviting sinners to embrace it.

The first plank of this ark was laid, if we may so speak, when God promised to Adam a " Seed, who should bruise the serpent's head,"—From that day, it has been erecting visibly in the world, in order that, while men were warned of their danger, they might see their remedy: and now, for nearly six thousand years, has God exercised forbearance towards an impenitent and unbelieving world.

By " baptism" we embark, as it were, on board this divinely constructed vessel.

When we are baptized into the faith of Christ, we profess our persuasion that " there is salvation in no other," and our desire " to be found in him,"

---

* Ἀντίτυπον. †The relative ᾧ cannot agree with κιβωτῇ, which is feminine, but must agree with ὕδατος, or rather perhaps with the whole sentence; this last construction renders the sense of the passage incomparably more clear; on which account it is here preferred.

not having our own righteousness, but that which is of God by faith in him Acts iv. 12; Phil. iii. 9. Thus we come to be *in him,* as a branch in the vine, as a man-slayer in a city of refuge, as Noah in the Ark. Not that this benefit is annexed to the mere outward form of baptism, but to that baptism which is accompanied with " the answer of a good conscience towards God."*

Being then *in* Christ, we are saved " by his resurrection."†

It should seem, that Noah's inclosure in the ark for so long a period was a kind of sepulture; and his elevation on the waters, till he afterwards came forth from the ark, was a kind of resurrection, when he took possession of a new world. Thus, according to St. Paul, " we are buried with Christ by baptism into death, that like as Christ was raised up from the dead by the glory of the Father, even so we also should walk in newness of life: for if we have been planted in the likeness of his death, we shall be also in the likeness of his resurrection." Rom. vi. 4, 5. This appears to be *intended* by St. Peter in the text, and to be, on the whole, the most natural, as well as most beautiful, construction of it: as Noah entered into the ark, and was saved by its elevation above the water-floods, so we, by baptism, enter into Christ, and are, by his resurrection, saved from sin and Satan, death and hell; yea, like Noah too, we are brought safely to the possession of a new and heavenly world.‡

INFER,

1. How deeply should we reverence the ordinances of God!

What is said of baptism is true, in a measure, of every other ordinance: yet how shamefully is both that, and every other ordinance, profaned amongst us! Let us remember, that all the institutions of God are intended to help forward our salvation: but, if trifled with, they will fearfully aggravate our condemnation.

2. How careful should we be to obtain " the answer of a good conscience !"

In the apostles days, as well as in ours, they, who applied for baptism, were *interrogated* with respect to their faith and practice: nor could the mere ablution of the body profit them, if they had not a correspondent purity of soul. Thus it is with us: we shall in vain receive the rite of baptism, or partake of the Lord's Supper, if we cannot *declare, as in the presence of God*, that it is our desire and endeavor to be holy as God is holy. Let us then not lay an undue stress upon outward observances of any kind; but rather seek a conformity to the divine image; for it will surely be found true at the last, that " the pure in heart shall see God," but that " *without holiness no man shall see the Lord.*"

---

*See the words following the text.　　　　　　　　†Ib.

‡If the opposition between διεσώθησαν δι' ὕδατος and σωζει δι' ἀναστάσεως be marked the sense of this difficult passage will be more apparent.

ISAAC A TYPE OF CHRIST.

Gen. xxii. 6—10. And Abraham took the wood of the burnt-offering, and laid it upon Isaac his son: and he took the fire in his hand and a knife: and they went both of them together. And Isaac spake unto Abraham his father, and said, My father: and he said, Here am I, my son. And he said, Behold the fire and the wood: but where is the lamb for a burnt-offering? And Abraham said, My son, God will provide himself a lamb for a burnt-offering. So they went both of them together. And they came to the place which God had told him of, and Abraham built an altar there, and laid the wood in order, and bound Isaac his son, and laid him on the altar upon the wood. And Abraham stretched forth his hand, and took the knife to slay his son. (S. S.)

Many and wonderful are the instances of faith and obedience recorded in the scriptures. But no action whatever (those only of our Lord himself excepted) has at any time surpassed or equalled that related in the text. It justly obtained for him who performed it, the honorable title of The Father of the Faithful, and, The Friend of God. Jam. x. 21, 23. We shall find it profitable to consider,

I. The history itself.

Abraham had often enjoyed intimate and immediate communion with the Deity. But now he heard the command which was of a most singular and afflictive nature.

God in some way clearly intimated to Abraham his will: nor left him to doubt one moment, whether it were his voice or not. He commanded Abraham to take his only, his beloved son Isaac, and to offer him up as a burnt-offering in a place that should afterwards be pointed out. How strange the order! How difficult to be complied with! How well might Abraham have said, "Would to God I might die for thee, O Isaac, my son, my son!"

Instantly, however, and without reluctance, he arose to execute the will of God.

Had he presumed to reason with God, what specious arguments might he have adduced for declining the way of duty! The certainty of his being reproached by Sarah, "A bloody husband art thou to me:" Exod. iv. 25, 26, the offence that would be taken by all the neighboring nations against him, his religion, and his God: the counteracting and defeating of all the promises which had been made by God himself, and which were to be accomplished solely in and through his son Isaac: Gen. xvii. 19: all this, with much more, might have been offered in excuse for his backwardness, if indeed he had been backward, to accomplish the will of God. But he conferred not with flesh and blood. Gal. i. 16.

Nor was he diverted from his purpose during the whole of his journey.

Having prepared the wood, he proceeded instantly, with Isaac and his servants, towards the place, that God had pointed out. Nor did he open his intentions to Sarah, lest she should labor to dissuade him from his purpose But what must have been his thoughts every time that he looked on Isaac? Yet never for one moment did he relax his determination to execute the divine command. Having come in sight of the mountain, he ordered his servants to abide in their place, lest they should officiously interpose to prevent the intended offering. He put the wood on his son, and carried the fire and the knife in his own hands. Affecting as these preparations must have been to a father's heart, how must their poignancy have been heightened by that pertinent question, which was put to him by his son! Ver. 7. His answer, like many other prophetical expressions, conveyed more than he himself probably was aware at the moment. Without giving a premature disclosure of his intention, he declares the advent of Jesus, that Lamb of God, who in due time should come to take away the sin of the world. Ver. 8. John i. 29. Thus for three successive days did he maintain his resolution firm and unshaken.

Having arrived at the spot determined by God, he with much firmness and composure proceeded to execute his purpose.

He built the altar, and laid the wood upon it in due order. Then with inexpressible tenderness announced to Isaac the command of God. Doubtless he would remind his son of his preternatural birth ; and declare to him God's right to take away, in any manner he pleased, the gift he bestowed. Job i. 21. He would exhort him to confide in God as a faithful and unchangeable God; and to rest assured, that he should, in some way or other, be restored, after he was reduced to ashes, and have every promise fulfilled to him. Having thus gained the consent of his son, he binds him hand and foot, and lays him on the altar ; and, with a confidence unshaken, and obedience unparalleled, holds up the knife to slay the victim. Whether shall we more admire the resolution of the father, or the submission of the son ? O that there were in all of us a similar determination to sacrifice our dearest interests for God ; and a similar readiness to yield up our very lives in obedience to his will !

Nothing but the interposition of God himself prevented the completion of this extraordinary sacrifice.

God had sufficiently tried the faith of his servant. He therefore, by a voice from heaven, stopped him from giving the fatal blow ; ordered him to substitute a ram in the place of Isaac ; renewed to him with an oath his former promises ; rendered him a pattern to all succeeding generations ; and, no doubt, is at this instant rewarding him with a weight of glory, proportioned to his exalted piety.

Almost every circumstance in this narrative deserves to be considered in,

II. Its typical reference.

Waving many less important points, we may observe that Isaac was a type of Christ.

1. In his appointment to be a sacrifice.

Isaac was a child of promise, born in a preternatural way, of a disposition eminently pious ; yet him did God require for a burnt-offering : it must not be Abraham's cattle, or his son Ishmael, but his beloved Isaac. Thus was Jesus also the promised seed, named, like Isaac, before he was conceived in the womb : He was born, not after the manner of other men, but of a pure virgin : He was that only, that beloved son, in whom the Father was well pleased : yet him did God appoint to be a sacrifice. A body was given him for this very purpose. Heb. x. 4. 5. He was ordained from eternity to be a propitiation for sin : Rom. iii. 25 : nor did the Father recede from his purpose for 4,000 years. Having set apart his son for this end, he changed not : and Jesus, at the appointed time, became obedient unto death, even the death of the cross. Phil. ii. 8.

2. In the manner of being offered.

Isaac bore the wood on which he was afterwards to be lifted up ; and voluntarily yielded up his body to be bound. and his life to be destroyed in God's appointed way. Thus did Jesus bear his cross to the place of his crucifixion ; and, having been bound was lifted up upon it. On the very spot where Isaac had been laid upon the altar, was Jesus (most probably) offered in sacrifice to God.* And by whose hand was Isaac to bleed, but by that of his own Father? By whom too did Jesus suffer, but by Jehovah's sword? Zech. xiii. 7; Isa. liii. 10. It was not *man* who made him so to agonize in the garden; nor was it man that caused that bitter complaint upon the cross. Luke xxii. 44; Mark xv. 34. Nevertheless it was with the perfect concurrence of his own will that he died upon the cross; "He *gave himself* an offering and a sacrifice to God of a sweet smelling savor." Eph. v. 2.

There is one point however, wherein the resemblance does not appear.

For Isaac was found a substitute; for Jesus none. Neither the cattle on a thousand hills, nor all the angels in heaven, could have stood in his place. None but Jesus could have made a full atonement for our sins. He therefore saved not himself, because He was determined to save us.

INFER,

1. How marvellous is the love of God to man!

We admire the obedience of Abraham: but God had a right to demand it: and Abraham knew, that he was about to give his son to his best and dearest friend. But what claim had we on God? Yet did he give up his Son for us sinners, rebels, enemies; nor merely to a common death, but to the agonies of crucifixion, and to endure the wrath due to our iniquities. Isa. liii. 6. What stupendous love! Shall any soul be affected with a pathetic story, and remain insensible of the love of God? Let every heart praise him, trust him, serve him: and rest assured that He who delivered up his Son for us, will never deny us any other thing that we can ask. Rom. viii 32.

2. What an admirable grace is faith.

The faith of Abraham certainly had respect to Christ, the promised seed. Heb. xi. 17—19. And, behold how it operated! So will it operate in all who have it. It will keep us from staggering at any promise, however dark or improbable; and will lead us to obey every precept, however difficult or self-denying. Let us seek his faith: and while we are justified by it from the guilt of sin, let us manifest its excellence by a life of holiness.

JOSHUA A TYPE OF CHRIST.

Deut. iii. 28.—Charge Joshua, and encourage him, and strengthen him; for he shall go over before this people, and he shall cause them to inherit the land which thou shalt see. (S. S.)

JOSHUA was a very eminent type of Christ. The text naturally leads us to shew this: and we shall trace the resemblance of Joshua to Christ.

I. IN HIS NAME.

The name of *Joshua* was intended to designate his work and office.

His name originally was Osea, but was altered by Moses to Joshua. Num xiii. 16. This, doubtless, was of God's appointment, that he might be there-

---

*Mount Calvary was one of the mountains in that small tract of country called the land of Moriah: and from verse 2, it can scarcely be doubted, but that it was the very spot pointed out by God. It could not possibly be far from the spot; and therefore, when the place for the sacrifice of Isaac was so accurately marked, it can scarcely be thought to be any other, than the very place where Jesus was offered 2,000 years afterwards.

by rendered a more remarkable type of Jesus. This name imported, that he should be *a divine Saviour;** and though, in the strictest and fullest sense, it could not properly belong to him; yet, as he was to be such a distinguished representative of Jesus, it was very properly given to him.

The name of *Jesus* still more fitly characterized the work that was to be performed by *him.*

This name is precisely the same with Joshua in the Greek language; and repeatedly do we, in the New Testament, translate it, "Jesus," when it ought rather to have been translated, "Joshua." Acts vii. 45; Heb. iv. 8. It was given to our Lord by the angel, before he was conceived in the womb: Matt. i. 21; and the express reason of it was assigned, namely, that "he should *save* his people from their sins." To him it is applicable in the fullest extent, because he is "God manifest in the flesh," "Emmanuel, God with us;" and because he is the author, not of a typical and temporary, but of a real and eternal salvation, to all his followers. Heb. v. 9.

This striking coincidence, with respect to the name, may prepare us for fuller discoveries of a resemblance.

II. In his office.

Joshua was appointed to lead the Israelites into the promised land.

Moses was certainly intended to represent the law, which was admirably calculated to lead men through the wilderness, but could never bring them into the land of Canaan: one offence against it destroyed all hope of salvation by it: Gal. iii. 10; it made no provision for mercy: its terms were simply, Do this and live: Rom. x. 5; and, for an example of its inexorable rigor, Moses himself was, for one unadvised word, excluded from the land of promise. The office of saving men must belong to another; and, for this reason, it was transferred to Joshua, who had been both appointed to it, and thoroughly qualified by God for the discharge of it. Deut. xxiv. 9.

Jesus also was commissioned to bring his followers into the Canaan that is above.

He, probably in reference to Joshua, is styled the Captain of our salvation: Heb. ii. 10; and he appeared to Joshua himself in this very character, proclaiming himself to be the Captain of the Lord's host. Josh. v. 13—15. "What the law could not do, in that it was weak through the flesh," the Lord Jesus Christ came to effect. Rom. viii. 3. He has been divinely qualified for the work; and, like Joshua, was "encouraged to it, and strengthened in it," by an assurance of God's continual presence, and support. Isaiah xlii. 1, 4, 6. He leads his people on from grace to grace, from strength to strength, from victory to victory. Ps. lxxxiv. 7; 2 Cor. iii. 18; Rev. vi. 2. Nor will he ever desist from his work, till he shall have subdued his enemies, and established his people in their promised inheritance.

Happily for us the resemblance may be likewise traced.

III. In his success.

Nothing could oppose any effectual bar to Joshua's progress.

Though Jordan had overflowed its banks, its waters were divided, to open him a path on dry land. Joshua iii. 17. The impregnable walls of Jericho, merely at the sound of rams' horns, were made to fall. Josh. vi. 20. Confederate kings fled before him. Josh. x. 16. City after city, kingdom after kingdom, were subjected to his all-conquering arms: and almost the whole accursed race of Canaanites were extirpated, and destroyed. Joshua xii. 7, 24. The promised land was divided by him amongst his followers: Joshua

*Jah, which was prefixed to his name, is the name of God.

xi. 23, and xviii. 10; and he appealed to them with his dying breath, that not so much as one, of all the promises that God had given them, had ever failed. Josh. xxiii. 14.

And shall less be said respecting our adorable Emmanuel?

He "triumphed over all the principalities and powers" of hell; and causes his followers to trample on the necks of their mightiest foes. Rom. xvi. 20, with Josh. x. 24. He leads them safely through the swellings of Jordan, when they come to the border of the promised land; Isa. xliii. 2; and, having given them the victory, he divides among them the heavenly inheritance. Matt. xxv. 34. When he comes to number them at last, even though they may have sustained the sorest conflicts, it will be found, that not so much as one of them is lost: Numb. xxxi. 49, with John xvii. 12; and he will be able to appeal to the whole assembled universe, that not so much as one jot or title of God's word hath failed of its accomplishment. Thus will all of them be put into possession of "that rest, which remained for them," in the hope and expectation of which, they endured the labors of travel, and the fatigues of war. Heb. iv. 1, 9, 11.

INFER,

1. How earnestly, and how humbly, should all submit themselves to Jesus!

Notwithstanding Joshua's commission was, utterly to destroy the inhabitants of that sinful land, yet he both spared the Gibeonites, and made a league with them, when they humbled themselves before him; Josh. ix. 15; he, moreover, gave a special charge respecting the preservation of the harlot Rahab, who, in faith, had concealed his spies. Josh. vi. 22, 25. But resistance to him was vain: there were none that could stand before him. Thus must all thine enemies, O Lord, perish, if they do not prostrate themselves before thee in humility and faith. Shall we not then believingly receive his messengers, and, *in the use of his appointed means*, expect his mercy? Shall we not go and make a covenant with him, and yield up ourselves, with unreserved submission, to his commands? Yes: and if this conduct provoke the world to combine against us, we will call him in to our aid, and despise the assaults of earth and hell. Josh. x. 4.

2. How confidently may the very weakest christians go forth to their future conflicts!

Though Canaan was promised to the Israelites, yet they were all to fight for it: so neither is heaven to be gained without many severe conflicts. But what have we to fear, when we have such a Captain? "If he be for us, who can be against us?" Did he ever yet suffer one of his faithful followers to perish? If they have been wounded, has he not healed their wounds? If they have fainted, has he not renewed their strength? Has he not made them conquerors, yea, "more than conquerors?" Rom. viii. 37. What then, though we have mighty Anakims to contend with, and their fortresses be walled up to heaven? Let us "be strong and very courageous;" and we shall find that "the weapons of prayer and faith, though weak and contemptible to a carnal eye, are mighty through God to the casting down of strong holds, and every high thing that exalts itself against the knowledge of God." 2 Cor. x. 4, 5. Let us then "be strong in the Lord, and in the power of his might." Let us "put on the whole armor of God." Eph. vi. 10, 11 And let us look forward with confidence to the joyful period, when we shall receive our portion in the promised land, "the land that floweth with milk and honey"

CHRIST THE FOUNDATION.

1 Cor. iii. 11.—For other foundation can no man lay, than that is laid, which is Jesus Christ. (P.) •

IT is not here alone, but in many other scriptures, both in the Old and New Testament, that our Lord Jesus Christ is held forth under the notion of a foundation. We shall,

I. SHOW THE PROPERTIES OF CHRIST AS A FOUNDATION; what kind of a foundation he is; and, 1st. He is a *laid* foundation—"Behold I lay in Zion for a foundation a stone" Isa. xxviii. 16. "Behold I," *i. e.* God the Father; one that knew well enough how to do it; a God of infinite wisdom and power. The Lord Jesus Christ did not take upon himself this honor of being a mediator; no, he was called to it, appointed of God for such a purpose; and this is our comfort and joy. He that could best tell what would best serve to satisfy his offended justice, pitched upon his own Son for that purpose: this was the ransom he found for man. Job xxxiii. 24. "I have laid help upon one that is mighty; I have exalted one chosen out of the people." Ps. lxxxix. 19. 2nd. A *low* foundation—low laid; foundations are wont to be laid low; the lower the surer. So the Lord Jesus Christ, as a foundation, was laid very low, that he might be a meet foundation for us. He was "in the form of God, and thought it not robbery to be equal with God: but he made himself of no reputation, and took upon him the form of a servant, and was made in the likeness of man," &c. Phil. ii. 6—9. There were several steps of his humiliation. 1. Into the human nature. He condescended to be made a man; this was a long step downward. That the WORD should become flesh was more than if a star should turn into a cloud. 2. Into subjection under the laws. "When the fulness of time was come, God sent forth his Son, made of a woman;" made *under the law*—the moral law; nay, the ceremonial law. He was to be circumcised— presented in the temple—redeemed and ransomed with two turtles—bound to go up to all the feasts. 3. Into poverty and persecution, contempt and contradiction; to be spurned and trampled on. 4. To death itself: "he became obedient unto death, even the death of the cross," a most painful, shameful, and ignominious death. This is called *a lifting up*, John xii. 32, but it was *humiliation.* 5. To the grave. When he was buried, he was, as other foundations, laid under ground; and there was a necessity for all this; without it, there could have been no atonement, no reconciliation. 3rd. Christ is a foundation of *stone.* Isaiah xxviii. 16. A stone is the fittest thing of all others to make foundations of, because it is hard and firm, and yet easily hewn. Now Jesus Christ is a stone—a foundation—a rock. 1 Cor. x. 4. Observe again, 4th. He is a foundation *out of sight.* All foundations are so; we see the building, but we do not see the foundation: such a foundation is the Lord Jesus Christ. He is out of sight. Not below, as he once was, under the earth, but above, in glory. His *person* is out of sight, yet we love him. 1 Peter i. 8. His *presence* is invisible. He is with us every where, especially in his ordinances, but it is in an invisible way: we feel it, but we do not see it. Matthew xviii. 20, and xxviii. 20. His *proceedings* are invisible. The proceedings of his grace within—the proceedings of his providence without; Psalm lxxvii. ult. 5th. He is a *precious* foundation; Isaiah xxviii. 16. Though all stones in their places be useful, yet they are not all precious stones. Few buildings are built upon precious stones, but the church of Christ is precious *in himself;* he is of great worth and value.

"The chief among ten thousand, and altogether lovely." He is precious *in the account and esteem of his disciples.* To others he is a stone of stumbling, and a rock of offence; but unto them which believe, he is precious. 1 Peter ii. 7. Moreover, 6th. He is a *permanent* foundation; Isaiah xxvi. 4. He is the rock of ages, from everlasting to everlasting. The saints have been building on him from the beginning, and will build on him to the end of time. He is "the same yesterday, to-day, and for ever." His righteousness is everlasting; his promises are unchangeable. 7th. He is an *elect,* or *chosen* foundation, Isaiah xxviii. 16, chosen of God, and precious—"Behold my servant, whom I have chosen, mine elect, in whom my soul is well pleased," Isaiah xlii. 1. Once more, 8th. He is an *experienced* or *tried* foundation. He was tried by *God,* who laid upon him the iniquities of us all. He was tried by *men* and *devils,* who did their best against him, but all to no purpose. He has been tried by the *saints,* who have had occasion to make use of him, and he has never failed them.

II. WHAT IS OUR DUTY IN REFERENCE TO THIS FOUNDATION? It is our duty, 1st. To *believe all this concerning him.* That God hath laid him purposely for a foundation; anointed and appointed him to be a Prince and a Saviour, and given him to the world, that "whosoever believeth in him, might not perish, but have everlasting life." 2nd. To *behold and see our need of him.* There is no rearing a building without a foundation. We have each of us a building to rear, and what foundation have we? None in ourselves—no righteousness of our own to commend us to God—no strength or ability to any thing that is good. 3rd. To *renounce all other foundations.* They are but sand; and he that builds on the sand, his building will fall; Matthew vii. 24, *ad finem.* 4th. To *repair* to him. In the way of faithful and fervent prayer tell him you are sensible of your need of him, and that you are undone without him. 5th. To *build* upon him: in the great business of *justification;* to rest our souls by faith upon his meritorious righteousness. None but Christ! None but Christ! In all our *perils* and *dangers,* personal or public, we should fly to him, trust in him, rely upon him: "Faithful is he that hath promised," Psalm xlvi. 1, and lxii. 1, 2; and it is our duty, 6th. To *beware what we build* upon this foundation, in *opinion* and in *practice,* 1 Cor. iii. 12, 13, 14, 15. If we build loose, careless walking, our hopes built, will be accordingly wood, hay, stubble, &c.

CHRIST'S DILIGENCE IN SERVING GOD.

John iv. 34. Jesus saith unto them, My meat is to do the will of him that sent me, and to finish his work. (S. S.)

OUR blessed Lord throughout his whole life, was the most illustrious pattern of condescension to man and of fidelity to God. Both these dispositions were eminently displayed in the history before us. Notwithstanding he was already exhausted with a long and fatiguing journey, he had been laboring for the salvation of a most abandoned adultress: and when urged to intermit his exertions for a little while in order to recruit his strength by some necessary refreshment, he declared, that food was not so delightful to a famished body, as the prosecuting of the great ends of his ministry was to his soul.

From his words we shall take occasion to,

I. CONSIDER OUR LORD'S EXAMPLE.

Jesus in his human and mediatorial capacity, was the Father's servant. And the work assigned him was, to reveal in a more perfect manner the will of God, and to save mankind by his own obedience unto death.

In this work he engaged,

1. With fervent affection.

Nothing could exceed the delight with which he *undertook* this arduous task; Ps. xl. 7, 8; nothing the zeal with which he *accomplished* it. Luke xii. 50. Whether we view his private addresses to God, Heb. v. 7, or his public ministrations among men,* we shall see that in him was that prophecy accomplished, "The zeal of thine house hath eaten me up." John ii. 17.

2. With indefatigable diligence.

From the commencement of his ministry to the end of it not a day was unemployed. Frequently, after having labored all the day, he spent the night in prayer, and resumed his labors with the returning light. Like the sun in the firmament, he proceeded in one steady course through all the cities, towns, and villages; nor ever ceased from his work, till he could say. "It is finished."

3. With undaunted resolution.

What "continual opposition" did he endure! He was truly "a sign spoken against," or a butt of contradiction. Luke ii. 34. There was not any thing however perverse. scandalous, or contemptuous, but his ears were assailed with it from day to day. From the very first discourse he uttered till the hour of his crucifixion, his enemies never ceased to seek his life. John xi. 8. Yet did he persevere in the face of every danger, and at last complete his obedience, by surrendering up his life on the cross.

That we may profit from this great example, we will,

II. Propose it for your imitation.

We also have a work to do for God.

Our work is great; but O! how different from that which was committed to our Lord! We have not to satisfy the demands of justice, or to endure the wrath due to sin: blessed be God! *that* was the Redeemer's work; and it has been finished by him on our behalf. The work which we have to do, is to believe in Christ, John vi. 29, and, from a sense of his love to us, to devote ourselves unreservedly to his service. Rom. xii. 1.

Let us then engage in it,

1. Heartily.

"Whatever our hand findeth to do, we should do it with all our might." Eccl. ix. 10. A lukewarm service is unacceptable, yea, hateful, to God. Rev. iii. 15, 16. Let us then first labor to know the will of God, and then endeavor to do it with our whole hearts. Let us be "fervent in spirit, while we serve the Lord." Rom. xii. 11.

2. Uniformly.

It is not an occasional act of zeal that will please God, but a steady, conscientious, uniform discharge of our duty. Our spirit, alas! is often faint; and even when "the spirit is willing, our flesh is weak." But we must counteract our sloth, and "give all diligence to make our calling and election sure." 2 Pet. i. 10.

3. Courageously.

---

*He was filled with joy at the least prospect of success, verse 35, and grieved and wept when he could not succeed. Mark iii. 5; Luke xix. 41.

We shall surely meet with reproach and persecution, if we set ourselves in earnest to serve the Lord. 2 Tim. iii. 12. But let us "remember him who endured such contradiction of sinners against himself. Heb. xii. 3. Woe be to us, if we draw back through the fear of man. Heb. x. 38. We must hate, not only father and mother, but even our own life also, if we would be Christ's disciples. Luke xiv. 26. Let us then "take up our cross daily" after Christ's example, and "suffer with him, in order that we may be also glorified together." Rom. viii. 17.

ADDRESS,

1. Those who are unconcerned about the work of God.

Has not God appointed you a work to do; and ought you not to have begun it long ago? Is it expedient to leave it to a dying hour? What if you should die before it is finished? O begin instantly; for the "night cometh, wherein no man can work."

2. Those who do his work deceitfully.

God has pronounced such persons accursed, no less than if they did nothing for him. Jer. xlviii. 10. His service must be your "meat" and drink; the joy of your souls, and the business of your lives. See then that ye "approve yourselves to God as servants that need not to be ashamed." 2 Tim. ii. 15.

3. Those who are in a measure conformed to their Saviour's image.

Bless your God, who has thus far enabled you to serve him. But O! think how much you fall short of your heavenly pattern! Forget then what is behind, and press forward for that which is before you; Phil. iii. 13—15; so shall you in due season "rest from your labors," and be welcomed as good and faithful servants to the joy of your Lord. Matt. xxv. 21

CHRIST, HE THAT SHOULD COME.

Luke vii. 19.—Art thou he that should come? or, look we for another? (Sk.)

THESE words were addressed to our Lord by two disciples of John the baptist, who sent them to Jesus, and instructed them to make these inquiries for the confirmation of their faith.

1. The question could not be proposed on John's account, for he was fully convinced that Christ was the true Messiah. Of this he was assured by divine revelation, and the testimony of God the Father at our Lord's baptism, John i. 32; Matt. iii. 17. And that Jesus was the Messiah John uniformly testified, by speaking of him as the Son of God, as incomparably superior to himself, as the Lamb of God, and as come to baptize with the Holy Ghost.

2. But though John believed in Jesus, and thus bore witness to him, yet it seems these disciples and their brethren were led to doubt even the testimony of their master. It is probable they thus doubted, because they did not find Jesus setting up a splendid earthly kingdom, such as they expected the Messiah would establish; because our Lord was not so rigidly abstemious as their master was; and because no miracle was wrought to deliver John out of prison; which they concluded the Messiah would certainly be both inclined and able to work, on such an occasion.

177

3. For the kind purpose of removing their doubts, and satisfying their minds, John therefore prudently sent them to hear, and see, and judge for themselves; and with this view he taught them to make the inquiries now before us, " Art thou," &c. The purport of these questions may be expressed thus, 'Sacred prophecy leads us to expect that the Messiah, the Lord's anointed, will appear in this land about this time. We entreat thee therefore to inform us whether thou art this great expected personage or not; that we may respect thee according to thy proper character.' To these inquiries our Lord wisely answers by actions, rather than words, verse 21. Then he requires the messengers to go and inform John what they had seen and heard, ver. 22, 23. Hereby Jesus evidently referred to sacred prophecy for an answer to these important questions. And as we are no less interested in this answer than John's disciples, let us consider,

I. THE TESTIMONY OF SACRED PROPHECY CONCERNING THE MESSIAH.

1. *Respecting the Person who should come under this character.* He is spoken of and described as David's *Son*, and *Lord*, Psa. lxxxix., 29, and cx. 1; as Immanuel, Isa. vii. 14; the Child born, and the Mighty God, Isa. ix. 6.

2. *Respecting the time when he should come.* This was to be before the sceptre departed from the tribe of Judah, Gen. xlix. 10; within the seventy weeks of Daniel, or 490 years after the Persian decree which was passed for rebuilding Jerusalem, Dan. ix. 24—26; and during the continuance of the second temple, Hag. ii. 7, 9.

3. *Respecting the purposes of his coming.* These were to guide as a Prophet, Deut. xviii. 18; to govern as a King, Psa. ii. 5; to save us as our Redeemer, Isa. xxxv. 4; to feed us as a Shepherd, Isa. xl. 11; and to reward us as our Judge, Isa. xl. 10, and xxxiii. 22.

4. *Respecting some remarkable circumstances which would attend his coming.* As the performance of various benevolent miracles, Isa. xxix. 18, and xxxv. 5, 6; silent modesty in working these miracles, Isa. xlii. 2, 3; a gracious reception of the poor by him, Isa. xxix. 19, and lxi. 1; and the reception of him by the Jewish nation, Isa. viii. 14, and liii. 1. This is the testimony of prophecy, which St. Peter informs us is sure in its accomplishment, and should engage our attention, 2 Pet. i. 19. Let us therefore notice,

II. THE FULFILMENT OF PROPHECY IN THE PERSON OF CHRIST. Here observe,

1. *These prophecies must be fulfilled in some person;* as the time specified for their accomplishment has long been past. For the sceptre departed from the tribe of Judah, and the second temple was destroyed, about seventeen hundred and fifty years since; and Daniel's seventy weeks expired about forty years before these events took place. In other words, our Jesus, the Messiah, was cut off by death just when those weeks were expiring; and about forty years before the destruction of the temple. Observe,

2. *These prophecies have been exactly fulfilled in Jesus Christ.* Witness his *two natures*, human and divine, Rom. ix. 5; hence he was David's Lord; and Immanuel; the Child born, and the Mighty God. The *time of his coming;*—he came when the sceptre was about to depart from the tribe of Judah: as a proof of which, just at the time of his birth a decree for taxing the land of Judea was passed by Augustus, the Roman emperor, Luke ii. 1, 2, 5. He came just exactly at the end of Daniel's seventy weeks, or four hundred and ninety years after the commandment or decree given to Ezra to rebuild Jerusalem. And he came while the second temple stood:

and cleansed it, and taught in it. His *various offices:*—he is our Prophet, John vi. 14, and viii. 12; our King. Luke i. 33; Acts v. 31; our Saviour, Matt. i. 21; 1 Tim. i. 15; our Shepherd, John x. 11, 27, 28; and our Judge, Acts xvii. 30, 31. And *the circumstances attending his coming.* Was the Messiah to work benevolent miracles? Christ wrought such, as here in the presence of John's disciples. Was the Messiah to be Modest in performing them? so was our Lord, Matt. xii. 16—21. Was the Messiah to teach the poor? so did Jesus, Luke iv. 18, 21. Was the Messiah to be rejected by the Jews? so was Jesus, John i. 11. As all these prophecies have been fulfilled in our Lord, so we observe,

3. *They have been fulfilled in no other.* This is evident from the appeal of Christ's friends, the advocates of Christianity, who challenge the world to produce any person besides our Lord, in whom these predictions have been accomplished. And from the concessions of Christ's enemies, the Jews; who can produce no person besides our Jesus, whom they reject, and still perversely look for another. Hence let us consider,

III. THE CONCLUSION WE SHOULD DRAW FROM THIS ACCOMPLISHMENT OF PROPHECY IN THE PERSON OF OUR LORD. We should conclude,

1. *That our Jesus is certainly the true Messiah.* For infinite wisdom could not mistake in its prophetic descriptions; and infinite truth cannot mislead us, Deut. xxxii. 4.

2. *That we should look for no other Saviour.* To look for another would be *impious,* by discrediting God himself, 1 John v. 10; it would be *ungrateful,* by slighting the richest love, John iii. 16; it would be *unreasonable,* opposed to the clearest evidence, 2 Thess. iii. 2; it would be *unnecessary,* for Christ is all sufficient to save, Heb. vii. 25; it would be *vain,* for no other Saviour will come, Heb. x. 26; it must be *destructive,* Christ being our only remedy, Prov. xxix. 1.

3. *That we should see experimental proofs of Christ's divine authority.* The proofs arising from the fulfilment of prophecy are *rational* ones, and of no small importance; but those most satisfactory to us are experimental ones, resembling our Lord's miracles; including spiritual life, sight, strength, purity, health, and comfort. Seek these as of the first importance, Prov. iv. 7; Matt. vi. 33; seek them with confidence, for Christ is come for the purpose of bestowing these blessings on mankind, Isa. lx. 1, 2, 3; John iii. 17.

4. *That Christ's coming should engage Christians in the practice of holy duties.* As, compassion for lost sinners, Luke xix. 10; Phil. ii. 5; as evidence of this, pray and labor for their conversion, James v. 16, 19, 20; beneficence to the poor, 2 Cor. viii. 9; hope of perfect purity, 1 John iii. 8; and grateful adoration, Luke i. 68.

~~~~~~~~~~~~~~~

THE GLORY OF CHRIST.

Zech. ix. 17 —How great is his goodness, and how great is his beauty? (S. S.)

THE glory of Christ is manifested throughout all the holy scriptures— This is attested both by the apostles and by our Lord himself, Acts x. 43, Luke xxiv. 27, John v. 39.

179

In the New Testament he shines like the sun in an unclouded atmosphere—

In the Old, though generally veiled, he often bursts forth as from behind a cloud with astonishing beauty and splendor—

Such a view of him is exhibited in the chapter now before us*—

Nor could the Prophet himself forbear exclaiming with wonder and admiration, "How great is his goodness!" &c.

We cannot have our minds more delightfully occupied than in contemplating,

I. THE GOODNESS OF OUR LORD.

In the context he is set forth as the God of providence and of grace—

And in order to behold his goodness we must view him in both respects,

1. As the God of providence.

As all things were created, so are they upheld and governed by him—

To him we owe the preservation of our corporeal and intellectual powers.

We are continually fed by his bounty, and protected by his arm—

The meanest creature in the universe has abundant reason to adore him—

His own people in particular may discern unnumbered instances of his goodness in his dispensations towards them—

His most afflictive as well as his more pleasing dispensations afford them much occasion for gratitude and thanksgiving, Ps. cxix. 75.

2. As a God of grace.

Jesus is the one fountain of spiritual blessings to his church, Eph. i. 22.

Neither prophets nor apostles had any grace but from him, John i. 16.

To him must we ascribe every good disposition that is in our hearts, Phil ii. 13, Heb. xii. 2.

What reason then have his faithful followers to bless his name ! —

How thankful should they be that he called *them* by his grace !—

That he so distinguished them, not only from the fallen angels, but from multitudes of the human race !—

With what gratitude should they acknowledge his continued kindness !—

Though they have often turned back from him, he has not cast them off—

Yea rather, he has "healed their backslidings and loved them freely"—

Surely, every blessing they receive, and every victory they gain, should fill them with admiring thoughts of his goodness, 2 Cor. ii. 14.

Let every soul then comply with that injunction of the Psalmist, Psa cxlv. 7.

And, like him, repeat the wish, which a sense of his mercies must inspire, Ps. cvii. 8, 15, 21, 31.

If we have just conceptions of his goodness we shall be more able to behold,

II. HIS BEAUTY.

The world behold "no beauty nor comeliness in" the face of Jesus—

But the saints of "old saw his glory as the glory of the only-begotten of the Father"—

This we also may see, if we survey him,

1. In this divine character,

"We cannot by searching find out the Almighty to perfection"— .

* After foretelling the preservation of the Jews amidst the destruction of surrounding nations, the prophet called their attention to Christ, as their lowly but triumphant king (ver. 9,) who should redeem them by his blood, (ver. 11,) be a strong hold to all who should turn unto him, (ver. 12,) and save then with an everlasting salvation, (ver. 16.)

Little do we know of the greatness of his *majesty*, or the thunder of his power, Job. xxvi. 14.

We cannot comprehend his unsearchable *wisdom*, his unspotted *holiness*, his inviolable *truth* and *faithfulness*—

We can scarcely form any idea of the inflexibility of his *justice*, the extent of his *mercy*, or the heights and depths of his *love*, Eph. iii. 19.

We know that Jesus is the brightness of his Father's glory, and the express image of his person, Heb. i. 3.

But when we attempt to delineate that image, we only "darken counsel by words without knowledge," Job. xxxviii. 2

His glory is more than the feeble language of mortality can express—

2. In his human character.

Here we look at him, as the Jews at Moses when his face was veiled—

And can cantemplate him more easily, because he shines with a less radiant lustre—

Doubtless while he lay in the manger the virtues of his mind beamed forth in his countenance—

Nor is it to be wondered at that the Jewish doctors were so filled with admiration at him while he was yet a child, Luke ii. 46, 47.

But principally must we view him during the course of his ministry—

What marvellous *compassion* did he manifest to the souls and bodies of *men!*—

Not one applied to him for bodily or spiritual health without obtaining his request—

And when many were hardened in their sins he wept over them, Luke xix. 41.

Yea, he even pleaded the cause of those who mocked and reviled him on the cross, Luke xxiii. 34.

His *zeal for God* was ardent and unremitted—

It was "his meat and drink to do the will of his heavenly Father"—

Nor could any thing for one moment divert or deter him from the prosecution of his work—

His *meekness, patience, fortitude* were altogether invincible—

Whatever was amiable and excellent in man abounded in him, Ps. xlv. 2.

He was not merely virtuous, but virtue itself incarnate—

Nor, though continually tried in the hottest furnace, was there found in him the smallest imperfection or alloy, John xiv. 30.

3. In his mediatorial character.

With what readiness did he become a surety for sinful man, Ps. xl. 7, 8.

What astonishing condescension did he manifest in uniting himself to our nature!—

How cheerfully did he go forth to meet the sufferings that were appointed for him—

In the garden and on the cross, when to the eye of sense "his visage was marred more than any man's," his beauty was most conspicuous to the eye of faith—

His obedience unto death was the fruit of his love, and the price of our redemption—

How beautiful is he *now* in the eyes of those who behold his glory!—

And how will he "be admired and glorified by all" in the last day!—

Satan must have blinded us indeed if we be yet insensible to his charms, 2 Cor. iv. 4.

If we be true believers, he cannot but be precious to our souls, 1 Pet. ii. 7

APPLICATION.

1. To those who have never yet beheld the goodness and beauty of the Lord :—

We speak not *now* to those who seek his face, and long to enjoy him—

For though their sorrow endure for a night, joy will come to them in the morning—

But they, who pant not after him, are miserably ignorant of his excellency—

Their views of Christ are different from those of the most competent judges*—

And different from what they will shortly be in the eternal world—

Let such persons diligently consider the Saviour's character—

And cry to God for that Spirit whose office it is to reveal Christ unto us—

Then shall they both see the King in his beauty, and be changed into his image, Isa. xxxiii. 17, 2 Cor. iii. 18.

2. To those whose eyes have been opened to behold him,

Let your meditations of him be more sweet and frequent—

However much you know of him, there are unsearchable depths unfathomed—

Let your determination therefore accord with that of David, Ps. xxvii. 4.

View him as appointing your trials, and dispensing your mercies—

Consider him as the fountain from whence you are to have supplies of grace—

Look to him as the example which you are continually to follow—

Above all, rely on him as expiating your guilt, and interceding for you—

Thus will you glory in him as your "friend and your beloved"—

And at last will see him as he is and be like him forever.

~~~~~~~~~~

CHRIST THE LIGHT OF THE WORLD.

John xii. 46.—I am come a light unto the world, that whosoever believeth on me should not abide in darkness. (Sk.)

THERE is no subject more interesting to the Christian, than the character of Jesus Christ. He is not only infinitely glorious in his person, but exceedingly precious to his believing people. He sustains every character, and fills every office, that can possibly endear him unto them, and render him the supreme object of their attachment and delight. In him, therefore, they glory, and count all things but loss for the excellency of his knowledge. Through him they receive every blessing, and trust in his name for complete and eternal salvation. He reigns in their hearts by his grace, as their sovereign; and is the High Priest of their profession, by whom they draw near to God, and are cleansed from all unrighteousness. He is also their *infallible* teacher, imparting heavenly instruction to their minds, and delivering them from the fatal delusions of sin and Satan. This is the *specific*

* To the Father he is " chosen and precious," 1 Pet. ii. 4 ; to the angels, the subject of their praise, Rev. v. 11, 12; to saints of old, an object of great desire, Hag. ii. 7, John viii. 56 ; to all pious men at this time, their supreme good, Phil. iii. 7, 8.

character he assumes in the text, in which he declares to the Jews, " I am come a light into the world," &c. In these words the Saviour distinctly represents,

I. The design of his mission. " I am come a light," &c. He is *perfect* and *essential light* in his own essence ; and like the sun of nature, he sheds his enlightening beams to disperse the condensed darkness that envelopes mankind. He is the *source* and *medium* of all divine knowledge, and came a " light into the world " by his office—by his gospel—and by his Spirit.

1. *By his office.* He had long been announced in the vision of prophecy, as a divine prophet, "the sun of righteousness," and " a light to lighten the Gentiles," &c. And when he assumed human nature, he was recognised as a " teacher come from God ;" and " never man spake like this man," was the encomium bestowed on his teaching. He taught the most *sublime* and *important* doctrines ; explained the law and the prophets ; more clearly revealed the perfections and will of God—the redemption of the world—the way of salvation—the certainty of a future state, &c., John i. 18, iii. 16 ; Mark i. 15 ; Matt. vii. 13, 14 ; verse 28, 29. Such was the *prophetic office* and work of Christ, when he came " to give light to them that sat in darkness and in the shadow of death."

2. *By his gospel.* It is therefore emphatically called, " *the light* of the glorious gospel of Christ." The Mosaic dispensation was *comparatively* dark and obscure ; it was only the general *outline* and *shadow* of the more glorious revelation of "grace and truth, by Jesus Christ." *Now,* " life and immortality are " *fully* " brought to light by the *Gospel.*" It clearly unfolds the *whole system* of Divine truth, in its connection with the salvation of mankind ; it discovers the nature, blessings, and privileges of the covenant of grace ; and infallibly teaches the only way to happiness and heaven, 1 Cor. i. 21 ; Rom. i. 16. Wherever, therefore, the Gospel is disseminated, either in its *written* or *ministerial revelation,* it is graciously designed to " turn men from darkness to light, and make them wise unto salvation."

3. *By his Spirit.* A *measure* of the Holy Ghost has been given to mankind in all ages, Gen. vi. 3 ; Job xxxii. 8. But the most *enlarged diffusion* of his influence, is the distinguishing glory and promise of the Christian dispensation. When Jesus therefore was " glorified," he, according to his word, poured out of his Spirit more abundantly " on all flesh," to convince the world of sin, and guide his people into all truth, John vii. 39. As a Spirit of " wisdom and understanding," he dissipates darkness and error, and communicates all spiritual knowledge and holiness to them that believe, 1 Cor. ii. 10—15 ; 2 Cor. iii. 18. Thus Christ is the *true light of the moral world,* which, he assures us in the text, was *one important design* of his manifestation in the flesh. We shall now consider,

II. The principle of salvation. " That whosoever believeth on me." It must be acknowledged that faith, as an *abstract principle,* is difficult to define ; but when it is considered in connection with its *object* and *effects,* it is comparatively easy to comprehend, and hence, it is *thus* represented throughout the Scriptures. In the passage before us,

1. *The object of faith is specified.* " Whosoever believeth on *me.*' Christ is not the *exclusive,* but the *concentrating object* of Christian faith. We must believe in the triune God, and all revealed truth. But saving faith *principally* regards Jesus Christ as the Redeemer of the world, and the Saviour of sinners. We should believe in the divinity of his person—the au-

thority of his mission—the efficacy of his sacrifice—the dignity of his offices—and the sufficiency of his grace, &c.

2. *The nature of faith is implied.* " Whosoever *believeth*," &c. The personal exercise of faith is a *complex act* of the mind, by which we *fully credit* the record which God has given of his Son—*cordially approve* the appointed method of salvation—and *actually embrace* Jesus Christ as our all-sufficient Saviour. The different acts and operations of faith are *metaphorically* represented by *looking* and *coming to, receiving from,* and *trusting in* Christ, for every promised blessing of the gospel, &c., Isa. xlv. 22 ; Matt. xi. 28 ; John i. 12 ; Eph. i. 12, 13.

3. *The necessity of faith is suggested.* It is here made the condition of participating an interest in Christ. He *only* who believes in him as the light of the world, shall be delivered from darkness. He that *believeth not* is condemned already, and abides in the gross darkness of sin and death. But living faith receives all the personal benefits of redemption, and is the *only instrument* by which we can possibly obtain salvation and eternal life, Mark xvi. 16; John iii. 36. As closely connected with this principle, we may regard,

III. THE PRIVILEGE OF BELIEVERS. " They *shall not abide in darkness.*" The christian's privileges are exceeding great and glorious. That which is mentioned in the text is highly desirable, and is graciously promised to all the subjects of saving faith.

1. *They shall not abide in mental darkness.* They are naturally " alienated from the life of God through the *ignorance* that is in them." But by divine grace the eyes of their understanding are enlightened, and they receive correct and comprehensive views of the whole science of godliness. Being made " light in the Lord," they have new conceptions of every subject. Their former darkness is passed away, and " the light of the knowledge of the glory of God shines into their hearts through Jesus Christ," Isa. lx. 1 ; 1 Peter ii. 9.

2. *They shall not abide in spiritual darkness.* Sin and misery are justly represented by a state of *darkness*, Col. i. 13. But the Saviour delivers his people from guilt and condemnation, purifies their hearts, and fills them with joy and peace through believing, Eph. iv. 14. As God is light, they receive the impress of his moral image, which is " righteousness and true holiness." The light of grace both *illuminates* the mind, and *sanctifies* the soul, Psalm xcvii. 11.

3. *They shall not abide in practical darkness.* They shall no longer wander in the forbidden paths of sin and error, under the galling yoke of the prince of darkness. Being saved from the broad road of destruction, " they walk in the light as God is in the light," and their path shineth more and more unto the perfect day of ineffable bliss, ch. viii. 12 ; Col. i. 12. Let us then adore the Saviour's character, believe in his holy name, and " walk as children of light."

THE BENEVOLENT CONDUCT OF JESUS.

Acts x. 38.—Who went about doing good. (Sk.)

The Lord Jesus Christ, our adorable Saviour, had glory with the Father before the world was; but he laid aside that glory, and came into our world on an errand of love, John xvii. 5. But how did he spend his time on earth? Very little is kn)wn of his early life. The whole of what is recorded on that subject may be summed up in a few particulars; he was strong in spirit; he was filled with wisdom; the grace of God was upon him; when he was twelve years old, he sat in the temple with the Jewish doctors, and asked questions which astonished all who heard him; he was obedient to his parents; and he grew in wisdom and stature, and in favor with God and man, Luke ii. 40—52. But after he entered on his public ministry, to which he had been anointed by the Holy Ghost, he went about doing good, Matt. iii. 16, 17. Let us consider his conduct in the walks of life,—and endeavor to imitate him.

I. The conduct of Jesus. He "went about doing good."

1. Jesus did good to the *bodies* of men. He opened the eyes of the blind; he gave hearing to the deaf; and he raised the dead, Matt. xi. 5. Those miracles were truly benevolent; they promoted human comfort; and, perhaps, may be considered as emblems of those spiritual blessings which are bestowed on all true believers: whether they are designed to be viewed in this light or not, certain it is, that they point out the saving power of our glorious Redeemer.

2. He did good to the *souls* of men. The ignorant were instructed by him, in the essential doctrines and duties of religion, Matt. v. 1, 2; Luke xix. 47; John viii. 2. He reproved the guilty and warned the careless, that they might amend their ways and turn to God by true repentance, Matt. xxiii. 13—31. He preached good tidings unto the meek; he bound up the broken hearted; he proclaimed liberty to the captives; and the opening of the prison to them who were bound, Isa. lxi. 1. He strengthened the weak and wavering, and comforted mourning penitents, Matt. v. 4, xi. 28.

3. Our Lord *went about* doing good. He was an itinerant preacher. When persons in want applied to him for special blessings, he granted their requests, and sent them away rejoicing. But he did not wait for such applications. He went forth, with the finest feelings of pure benevolence and love, to seek and to save that which was lost, Luke xix. 10. And to accomplish his merciful designs, he frequently visited large and populous places, and places of public resort.

4. The motives of our Lord, in doing good, were *pure and perfect.* He was moved by the transcendent goodness of his nature to acts of kindness; the pressing wants and painful sufferings of men excited his pity and tender compassion; and all his works were directed to the glory of his Father, John xiii. 4. How widely different are the motives of many, in the exercise of charity, from those of our blessed Saviour! they seek the praise of men; he sought the honor of God: and they aim at their own glory; but he at his creatures good: they are partial to a few; but he was good to all.

5. Jesus *persevered* in doing good. It was his constant employment, and he was never weary of it. Even when he hung upon the cross, he prayed for his murderers, and saved the penitent thief, Luke xxiii. 34—43. And his death on the accursed tree, where he suffered as a sacrifice for sin, was an act of sublime and unparalleled love.

6. In all the works, and in all the ways of our Saviour, *his lovely temper and amiable conduct shone with resplendent glory.* How unlike the renowned conquerors and tyrants of the world, whose glory has been acquired by blood and slaughter! Nothing exalts the human character more than acts of disinterested benevolence; but Jesus was more than human. He was God and man; and yet it is the temper of the man Christ Jesus which we now contemplate.

II. WE SHOULD ENDEAVOR TO IMITATE THE CONDUCT OF JESUS.

1. *That we may do so, let us study the character and conduct of our great Exemplar.* To this end we should carefully read his public and private discourses, examine his temper, and weigh his conduct. There are three infallible sources of information on this subject: the ancient prophecies; the holy gospels; and the apostolical epistles. The prophets foretold his character; the evangelists have recorded it with artless simplicity; and the apostles, who knew him well, have confirmed the whole. By this course of study, we shall gain a clear, correct, and complete knowledge of the temper and conduct of our Lord.

2. *But those who copy after his blessed example, must have the mind which was in him,* Phil. ii. 5. Without this, there can be no successful imitation of his conduct; for the source of outward action is in the inner man. To have his mind, we must be born again of the Spirit of God, John iii. 3. All who are born from above, receive those principles of grace, which produce every thing that is excellent in the conduct of man. They are new creatures in Christ Jesus, and grace reigns in their hearts: they are influenced in all things by real goodness; by soft pity and tender compassion to the wretched; and by an ardent desire to promote the honor and glory of God.

3. *Having acquired the mind of Jesus, let us endeavor to imitate his conduct.* We cannot imitate his miracles; the attempt would be presumption; but we should endeavor to copy his benevolent actions. Particularly, let us go about, as far as opportunity may serve, to seek the sons and daughters of affliction; when we find them in their wretched abodes, let us pity them; and there let our pity be shown in acts of kindness. Feed the hungry; clothe the naked; instruct the ignorant; comfort the mourners; visit the sick, the prisoner, the fatherless, and the widow. Jesus will reward these works as if they were done to himself, Matt. xxv. 40.

4. *Let us proceed in these works of love, as the Lord may enable us.* More than this is not required; and less than this will not be accepted. The means of some are limited; but they must do what they can. Others abound in means: let these proceed on a liberal plan. It is recorded of the woman who anointed the head of Jesus, "She hath done what she could," Mark xiv. 8. No person will perish who does what he can. It was the opinion of pious Matthew Henry, that 'there is not a damned sinner in hell, but if he had done well, as he might have done, had been a glorified saint in heaven.' Note on Gen. iv. 7.

5. *This conduct will please the Lord, who is good to all, and whose tender mercies are over all his works,* Psa. cxlv. 9. He blesses us that we may be a blessing, Gen. xii. 2. This conduct accords with the spirit of the gospel, which breathes pure benevolence, and introduces "peace on earth, and good will towards men," Luke ii. 14. It resembles the employment of angels, who come down from heaven, on errands of love to the heirs of salvation, Heb. i. 14. And has been practised by the greatest and best of men in all ages.

186

1. In the world, and in the visible church, we have many bad examples; but we must not follow a multitude to do evil, Exod. xxiii. 2.

2. There are a few in the church who may be followed in some things; but whatever their excellencies are, we cannot safely follow them in all their ways.

3. But we have a perfect example in the conduct of our Saviour; and we are bound by the most sacred ties to walk in his steps, 1 Pet. ii. 21. May the Lord enable us to do so, for his name and mercies' sake!

THE COMPASSION OF CHRIST TOWARDS THE WEAK.

Matt. xii. 18—21.--Behold, my servant whom I have chosen; my beloved in whom my soul is well pleased: I will put my Spirit upon him, and he shall shew judgment to the Gentiles. He shall not strive nor cry; neither shall any man hear his voice in the streets. A bruised reed shall he not break, and smoking flax shall he not quench, till he send forth judgment unto victory. And in him shall the Gentiles trust. (S. S.)

ONE might gather almost as complete a character of Christ from the prophecies as from the gospels themselves—

Not only the great incidents relating to his life and death were foretold, but his spirit and conduct were most minutely delineated—

He had just withdrawn himself from the Pharisees who sought to destroy him—

And had strongly enjoined his attendants not to make known his miracles—

This conduct appeared strange to those, who were expecting him to erect a temporal kingdom—

But the Evangelist declares that these very things had been made the subject of prophecy many hundred years before—

The passage quoted by him from Isaiah is recorded, not with literal exactness, but according to its true import—It declares,

I. THE COMMISSION GIVEN TO CHRIST.

Christ was the Father's ambassador to our ruined world.

However, in his divine nature, Christ was equal to the Father, yet, in his mediatorial capacity, he was the Father's servant—

The office assigned him was to shew judgment, that is, the way of righteousness and salvation both to Jews and Gentiles—

And for this he was qualified by an immeasurable communication of the Spirit to him, John iii. 34, Isa. xi. 2, 3.

In this view the Father exceedingly delighted in him.

The Father doubtless regarded him as his beloved *for his own sake*—

But was peculiarly pleased with him as having undertaken the work of man's redemption—

In him he saw, as it were, all his own perfections glorified, and the thrones of apostate angels occupied by sinners of the human race—

Hence in triumphant exultation he declares his acquiesence in him, and calls every human being to "behold" him—

The prophet further specifies,

II. THE MANNER IN WHICH HE SHOULD EXECUTE IT.

He was to accomplish his work.

1. Silently.

There was to be nothing in him ostentatious, contentious, or clamorous—
Together with firmness and fidelity, he exercised continued gentleness and meekness*—

Would to God that many who bear a similar commission would learn of him to execute it in a similar way !—

2. Tenderly.

The terms here used seem to be proverbial—

The former metaphor is taken from reeds, which were used as musical instruments by shepherds, and which, when bruised, could no longer emit any melodious sound—

The smoking flax alludes to the wick of a lamp which, when the flame is extinct, produces an offensive smell—

Both these metaphors fitly represent the state of a soul bruised under a sense of sin, and lamenting that its grace is nearly extinguished while whole clouds of corruption are arising from it—

But Jesus, instead of despising its low estate, will rather fan the spark into a flame, and cause the worthless reed to send forth melody that shall delight the ears of God himself—

3. Successfully.

However gentle his exertions, he shall never ultimately fail—

As his forbearance towards his enemies gave them a momentary appearance of triumph, so he sometimes delays his aid even to his most favored people—

But he will at last prevail, and make his grace victorious in their souls—

To this description of the Saviour the prophet naturally subjoins,

III. Our duty towards him.

Blessed be God, our duty is our highest privilege—

We are commanded to trust in him,

1. For instruction.

Jesus is both qualified and commissioned to enlighten the Gentiles, Luke i. 78, 79, and ii. 32.

Nor are there any so weak and ignorant but that he can make them wise unto salvation, Matt. xi. 25.

Let us then, " not lean to our own understanding," but seek to be " taught of him," Eph. iv. 20, 21.

2. For acceptance.

It is not merely in his individual capacity, but as the head of the elect world, that he is so pleasing to his heavenly Father—

We therefore, if we believe on him, may be certain of acceptance through him, Eph. i. 6, 10.

Yea, God will not behold a spot in the most polluted soul, if it be only washed in his blood, and clothed in his righteousness, Eph. v. 27, Jude 24.

3. For victory.

None have need to despond on account of their own weakness and corruptions—

The " grace of Christ is sufficient," and shall prove so to all who trust in him—

" Wherever he has begun the good work he will carry it on unto the end," Phil. i. 6, Rom. viii. 37.

Application.

* His conduct, as related in the context, strongly illustrates this

1. The text is addressed to *all the sinners of the Gentiles.*

How gracious is God in thus inviting sinners to "behold" his Son —

And *how powerful the recommendation that is thus enforced by the example of God himself!*—

But can any thing be a stronger reproof to those, who, instead of choosing Christ, and being well pleased with him, have uniformly despised and rejected him?—

Say then, ye ungrateful world, whom will ye condemn; yourselves, or God?—

Still however, the invitation is addressed to you, "Behold my Son"—

O that ye may behold him now to your joy, and not hereafter to your confusion!—

2. But the words are more eminently suited to *the weak and desponding.*

More consolatory declarations could not have been desired by man, or given by God—

The lowest possible state of grace is here described in most appropriate terms—

And an assurance given that it shall prove victorious in the issue—

Let the desponding soul then learn to "trust" in Jesus—

And even in the midst of conflicts sing, "Thanks be to God, who giveth us the victory through our Lord Jesus Christ."

CHRIST AND THE BRAZEN SERPENT COMPARED.

John iii. 14.—As Moses lifted up the serpent in the wilderness, even so must the Son of Man be lifted up. (P.)

THE great object of revelation. is to display the work and character of Christ. He is exhibited by symbolical representations, in all the characters, places, sacrifices, and events, described in the Old Testament.

This is particularly the case, in reference to the brazen serpent, the lifting up of which, in a remarkable manner typified the death of the Son of God.

We now propose to point out the resemblance between the type and the anti-type.

I. They correspond with each other, in THE OCCASION OF THEIR INSTITUTION. The Israelites in the wilderness, murmured for want of water, and loathed the manna which came down from heaven.

For this, God sent fiery serpents among them, and many of the people died.

Nor was there any remedy for those who had been wounded—they, therefore cried unto GOD, and intreated Moses to intercede for them, and in answer to their prayer, the serpent was ordered to be erected. We are wounded by the more deadly sting of sin, its poison has pervaded all our faculties, and is bringing a speedy and everlasting destruction on our souls; but GOD in his own mercy, appointed his Son to suffer in our stead.

II. There is an agreement between them in THEIR QUALITIES. 1. The serpent was made of brass. This is an inferior metal, and of little value, and in this respect, it represented the human nature of Christ, for he was as a root from the dry ground, without form or comeliness. 2. There was only one brazen serpent for the whole of the Jewish camp; the camp was no doubt large, and extended for many miles, yet this sufficed for all; there is only one mediator between God and man, Jesus Christ the righteous; there is only one way to the Father, and that is by him; there is only one remedy for sin, and that is the precious blood of Jesus. 3. This serpent was appointed by God: if Moses had devised it himself, the wounded Israelites would have looked in vain for a cure.

Christ has not taken the office of a Saviour upon himself without authority; he has been appointed by the father, and qualified for it, by the outpouring of the Holy Spirit. All attempts therefore to look to any thing short of Christ, instead of healing our wounds, will aggravate our disorder. 4. When the brazen serpent was prepared, it was publicly lifted up. Moses would have acted most criminally, if he had kept it within his own tent: by so doing, the death of all the Israelites might have been laid to his charge.

The ministers of the gospel are to exhibit Christ to a sick and dying world, and " *woe, woe* be to them," if they are not "instant in season and out of season," in pointing sinners to the "lamb of God that taketh away the sins of the world," and the blood of those they warn not, will be upon their heads. It is fully the design of Christ, and the will of the Father, that even the ends of the earth, should look to him and be saved.

III. There is a resemblance in the MANNER IN WHICH BENEFIT IS DE-RIVED, both from the type, and the anti-type. 1. The Israelites were commanded *to look to it*. It was not sufficient that they heard about this remedy, that they understood its nature, or that they sent others to look to it; they were required to have a personal view of it, or they died miserably in the wilderness.

Religion with us is a *personal* thing; if we do not feel the wounds of sin, and if we have not a personal view of Christ as our Saviour, all the external means which we possess will be of no avail. 2. The Israelites were required to look to the brazen serpent *instantly ;* procrastination would have been immediately fatal in their case, and not less fatal will it be to us, if we delay looking to the adorable Jesus. "Now is the accepted time, now is the day of salvation." 3. They were required to look *steadily* and *constantly* upon the serpent. A mere glance would not suffice, their disease was too deeply imbedded to be removed in an instant—our eyes should always be directed to calvary, and while looking upon him, who is hanging upon the accursed tree, we may expect, that the power of sin will be destroyed within us, and that our souls will be purified by that healing power which proceeds from the cross. 4. If any in the Jewish camp disbelieved in the efficacy of the remedy provided, alas, there was no other means to procure a restoration to health; and there is reason to suppose that many did refuse to participate in this remedy, for it is added, "and many of the people died." So it is at the present day; there is *balm in Gilead, and a physician there;* but they will not come to him, that they may have life.

IV. There is a further agreement in THE EFFECTS THEY PRODUCE. 1. The brazen serpent effected a complete cure in every stage of disease; it mattered not whether they were just bitten, whether they were suffering great pain from the power of the disorder, or whether they were in the agonies of death; if they looked to the brazen serpent they lived.

All those who look to Christ shall be saved, notwithstanding the vileness of their moral characters, or the number of years they have lived in sin. The same blood which cleansed a cruel Manassah, a persecuting Saul, and a dying thief, is quite sufficient to remove every stain from our souls. 2. The number of those who were healed by looking to the brazen serpent was great; the princes and the people, children and their parents, came crowding to that part of the camp, where this wonderful remedy was found.

Neither is the number *small* who look to Christ; they already exceed the number of the stars; and the day will arrive, when those who are "ready to perish shall come from Assyria, and the outcasts from the land of Egypt, and shall worship the Lord in his holy mount at Jerusalem." 3. Moreover, the lifting up of the brazen serpent, in the end recovered the whole of the camp, so that a diseased person was not found; and by this circumstance, we are reminded of that period, when all nations, and kindreds, and tongues, and people, shall bow down and worship at the feet of the Messiah. From this subject learn, 1. How plain and simple is the way of salvation;—we simply look by faith to a crucified Saviour, and are healed. 2. How injurious to our welfare, is unbelief;—if we despise this ordinance of God, we perish.

CHRIST THE AUTHOR OF OUR SANCTIFICATION.

Rom. viii. 3, 4.—What the law could not do, in that it was weak through the flesh, God, sending his own Son in the likeness of sinful flesh, and for sin, condemned sin in the flesh; that the righteousness of the law might be fulfilled in us, who walk not after the flesh, but after the Spirit. (H. H.)

The necessity of holiness is allowed by all: the means of attaining it are known by few. Christ is regarded as the meritorious cause of our justification before God; but he is not sufficiently viewed as the instrumental cause of our deliverance from sin. He is represented in the scriptures as "our sanctification," no less than "our wisdom and our righteousness:" 1 Cor. i. 30, and we should do well to direct our attention to him more in that view. In the preceding context he is spoken of as delivering his peop from condemnation, and many judicious commentators understand the text as referring to the same point: yet, on the whole, it appears more agreeable both to the words of the text, and to the scope of the passage, to understand it in reference to the work of sanctification.* St. Paul had just said that "the law of the Spirit of life in Christ Jesus," that is the gospel, "had made him free from the law of sin, as well as of death." He then adds, that on account of the insufficiency of the law to condemn and destroy sin, God had sent his own Son to effect it; and that through his incarnation and death its power should be effectually broken.

From this view of the text, we are led to consider,

I. The end and design of Christ's Mission.

God's desire and purpose was to restore his people to true holiness—

Sin was the object of his utter abhorrence: it had marred the whole creation: it had entered into heaven itself, and defiled the mansions of the Most High: it had desolated the earth also, and all that dwelt upon it. To remedy the miseries introduced by it, and to root it out from his people's hearts, was a design worthy of the Deity; since, if once they could be brought to "fulfill the righteousness of the law," by walking, in their habitual course

---

* See Doddridge on the place.

of life, no longer after the flesh, but after the Spirit, eternal honor would accrue to him, and everlasting happiness to them.

The law was not sufficient to effect this—

The law was indeed perfectly sufficient to direct man, while he remained in innocence; and it was well adapted to reclaim him when he had fallen; because it denounced the wrath of God against every transgression of its precepts, and set forth a perfect rule of duty. But "it was weak through the flesh:" man was deaf, and could not hear its threatenings; dead, and could not execute its commands. Hence, as to any practical effects, it spake in vain.

God therefore, in order that his purpose might not fail, sent his only dear Son—

He sent his co-equal, co-eternal Son, "in the likeness of sinful flesh," and to be a sacrifice "for sin;"* that through his obedience into death, he might "deliver those who had been, and must for ever have continued, subject to bondage." How this expedient was to succeed, will come under our consideration presently; we therefore only observe at present, that it was a plan which nothing but infinite wisdom could have devised. It could no have entered into the mind of any finite Being, to subject God's only dear Son to such humiliation; to make him a partaker of our nature, with all its sinless infirmities; to substitute him in our place, and, by his vicarious sacrifice, to restore us to the image and favor of God; this does, and must for ever, surpass all finite comprehension.

But though we cannot fathom all the depths of this mystery, we may shew,

II. IN WHAT WAY IT IS EFFECTUAL FOR THE END PROPOSED.

We speak not of the way in which the death of Christ obtains our justification, but of the way in which it is instrumental to our sanctification. In reference to this, we say,

1. It displays the evil and malignity of sin—

The evil of sin had been seen in a measure by the miseries which it had introduced, and by the punishment denounced against it in the eternal world. But in what light did it appear, when nothing less than the incarnation and death of Christ was able to expiate its guilt or destroy its power! Let any person behold the agonies of Christ in the garden, or his dereliction and death upon the cross, and then go and think lightly of sin if he can. Surely if men were more habituated to look at sin in this view, they would be filled with indignation against it, and seek incessantly its utter destruction.

2. It obtains for us power to subdue sin—

Though man is in himself so weak that he cannot, of himself, even think a good thought, yet through the influence of the Holy Spirit he can "fulfil the righteousness of the law," not perfectly indeed, but so as to walk altogether in newness of life.† Now, by the death of Christ the promise of the Spirit is obtained for us; and all who seek his gracious influences, shall obtain them. Thus the axe is laid to the root of sin. "The weak is enabled to say, I am strong:" and he, who just before was in bondage to his lusts, now casts off the yoke, and "runs the way of God's commandments with an enlarged heart."

---

* This is the meaning of περὶ ἁμαρτίας. See Heb. x. 6, and 2 Cor. v. 21.

† There is a two-fold fulfilling of the law mentioned in the Scriptures; the one legal, the ther evangelical. Compare Matt. v. 17, with Rom. xiii. 8, and Gal. v. 14.

3. It suggests motives sufficient to call forth our utmost exertions—

The hope of heaven and the fear of hell are certainly very powerful motives; yet, of themselves, they never operate with sufficient force to produce a willing and unreserved obedience. While the mind is wrought upon by *merely* selfish principles, it will always grudge the price which it pays for future happiness. But let the soul be warmed with the love of Christ, and it will no longer measure out obedience with a parsimonious hand: it will be anxious to display its gratitude by every effort within its reach. "The love of Christ will constrain it" to put forth all its powers; to "crucify the flesh with its affections and lusts," and to "perfect holiness in the fear of God."

Infer,

1. How vain is it to expect salvation while we live in sin!

If we could have been saved *in* our sins, can it be conceived that God would ever have sent his own Son into the world to deliver us from them; or that, having sent his Son to accomplish this end, he would himself defeat it, by saving us in our iniquities? Let careless sinners well consider this; and let the professors of religion too, especially those in whom sin of any kind lives and reigns, lay it to heart: for if sin be not "condemned in our flesh," our bodies, and souls too, shall be condemned for ever.

2. How foolish is it to attack sin in our own strength!

A bowl, with whatever force it be sent, and however long it may proceed in a right direction, will follow at last the inclination of its bias, and deviate from the line in which it was first impelled. Thus it will be with us under the influence of legal principles: we shall certainly decline from the path of duty, when our corrupt propensities begin to exert their force. Our resolutions can never hold out against them. We must have a new bias; "a new heart must be given us, and a new spirit be put within us," if we would persevere unto the end. Let us not then expect to prevail by legal considerations, or legal endeavors. Let us indeed condemn sin in the purpose of our minds, and sentence it to death: but let us look to Christ for strength, and maintain the conflict in dependence on his power and grace. Then, though unable to do any thing of ourselves, we shall be enabled to "do all things."

3. How are we indebted to God for sending his only Son into the world!

If Christ had never come, we had remained for ever the bond-slaves of sin and Satan. We had still continued, like the fallen angels, without either inclination or ability to renew ourselves: whereas, through him, many of us can say, that we are "made free from the law of sin and death." Let us then trace our deliverance to its proper source; to the Father's love, the Saviour's merit, and the Spirit's influence. And let us with unfeigned gratitude adore that God, who "sent his Son to bless us, in turning away every one of us from our iniquities." Acts iii. 26.

UNION WITH CHRIST.

Eph. v. 30 —We are members of his body, of his flesh, and of his bones. (H. H.)

THAT the eternal Son of God assumed our nature, and lived and died for the salvation of men, is doubtless the fundamental truth on which we are to build our hopes. But we shall have a very partial view of that truth, if we consider it merely in reference to our acceptance with God. The apostles state it as the strongest of all motives to obedience, and as the pattern which, as far as circumstances will admit of it, we are bound to imitate. To go no further than the context; St. Paul is stating the duties of husbands and wives : and, having observed that wives are to be as obedient to their husbands, in all lawful things, as the church is to Christ, he shews, that husbands are not, however, at liberty to act the tyrant; but that they should at all times be influenced by love, and consult the good and happiness of their wives, as much as Christ himself does of the church, to whom he stands in a similar relation. Ver. 22—30.

The words before us are, in this view, deserving of the deepest attention; since they not only unfold a most mysterious and important truth, but tend in the highest degree to meliorate our tempers, and to diffuse universal happiness. Let us consider then,

I. THE UNION WHICH SUBSISTS BETWEEN CHRIST AND HIS CHURCH—

There is a *personal* union which Christ has with our nature, by means of his incarnation, John i. 14, and which was necessary for the executing of the great work which he had undertaken. Heb. ii. 11, 14, 16. But in this the whole human race participate, without any distinction. The union which Christ has with the church is distinct from that, and is,

1. Legal—

There is, among men, an union between a debtor and his surety ; insomuch, that if a debt be not discharged, the surety is as much answerable for it as if he had contracted it himself: and if, on the contrary, it be discharged by the surety, the creditor has no further claim on him that contracted it. Thus it is with respect to Christ and his church. He is the surety of the new covenant: Heb. vii. 22 ; having undertaken for us, he was charged with our debt ; " it was exacted of him, and he was made answerable." Isa. liii. 7. Bp. Lowth's version. Having paid the debt, his payment is put to our account; " By his obedience we are made righteous." Rom. v. 19. In a word, " He who knew no sin, was made sin for us, that we (who had no righteousness) might be made the righteousness of God in him." 2 Cor. v. 21.

2. Spiritual—

Very much is spoken in scripture respecting the spiritual union which subsists between Christ and his people. To mark that they stand by him alone, it is compared to a foundation and the superstructure. Eph. ii. 20—22. To shew that he is the one source of vital influence to them all, it is illustrated by a root and the branches. John xv. 5. To intimate that one spirit pervades both him and them, 1 Cor. vi. 17, it is set forth under the image of a body ; he being the Head, and they the members. Eph. iv. 15, 16. To convey some idea of the tender endearments with which it is accompanied, it is shadowed forth by a marriage union. This is the representation given in the text. He is our husband; Isa. liv. 5 ; and we are his bride: Rev. xxi. 9 ; and, as Adam said of Eve when she was brought to him, " She is flesh of my flesh, and bone of my bones," Gen. ii. 23, so may we say respecting the Lord Jesus Christ, "We are members of his body, of his flesh, and of his bones."

Whatever beauty there is in all the other figures, methinks there is a peculiar propriety in that which is now under our consideration, because it marks that volition, yea, and those means also whereby the union is effected. The Lord Jesus Christ displays before our eyes his excellency and glory, his suitableness and sufficiency ; and, by the constraining influence of his love inclines us to leave all that has hitherto been esteemed by us, in order to connect ourselves with him, and enjoy his presence. Ps. xlv. 10, 11. Mark x. 29, 30. We accept that gracious proposal, "Thou shalt not be for another man ; so will I also be for thee :" Hos. iii. 3 ; and being thus engaged by a solemn covenant, we surrender up ourselves to him, whether it be for better or for worse in this world, determining through grace to " be faithful unto him, even until death."

We prosecute the idea of a marriage union no further at present, because it will be more fully opened, while we shew,

II. THE BLESSINGS RESULTING FROM IT—

It is needless to expatiate upon the comforts and benefits of that relation among men : but we cannot be too minute in specifying the blessings that result from an union with Christ. The chief of them will come under our review, while we observe, that,

1. He has communion with us in all our trials—

One who understands the duties of a husband, and labors faithfully to discharge them, is ever ready to sympathize with his partner in her afflictions of whatever kind, and solicitous to the utmost to relieve them. What is done to her, whether it be good or evil, he considers it as done to himself. Thus it is with our blessed Lord. Are we tempted ?— — —a consciousness of his relation to us calls forth his sympathy, and engages his utmost exertions on our behalf, Heb. ii. 17, 18, and iv. 15,— — —Are we persecuted? He feels in his inmost soul the dagger that pierces us, Zech. ii. 8, Acts ix. 4. — — —Do we labor under distresses of any kind? "In all our afflictions he is afflicted ;" Isa. lxiii. 9 ; and every attempt made to mitigate our trouble, he accepts, as if he himself were personally relieved— — —Matt. xxv 35—40.

2. We have communion with him in all his benefits—

A woman, from whatever rank she be taken, is no sooner united in the marriage-bond, than she is exalted to a participation of all the honors and possessions of her husband. Thus it is with the church when united unto Christ. Is he possessed of a perfect righteousness, commensurate with the highest demands of law and justice ? They who are joined to him by faith, are partakers of it all, and may boldly call him, " The Lord our Righteousness." Jer. xxiii. 6. However sinful they may have been in former times, "in him shall they be justified, and in him may they glory"— — —Isai. xlv. 24, 25. Has he within himself an inexhaustible fountain of grace ? Col. i. 19. They may receive it out of his fulness: John i. 16; and having had a measure of it communicated to them, they may go to him for more : Jam. iv. 6 ; yea, whatever supplies they may need, they shall have sufficient for them ; 2 Cor. xii. 9 ; sufficient to mortify every sin, Rom. vi. 14, to fulfil every duty, Phil. iv. 13, to triumph over every enemy— — —Rom. viii. 37. Is he enthroned on high, the heir, and Lord of all things ? Heb. i. 2. Let not his people think that even these things are too great for them: for they shall have a throne like unto his throne, Rev. iii. 21, a kingdom like unto his kingdom, Luke xxii. 29, a glory like unto his glory— — —John xvii. 22.

ADDRESS,

1. Those who have reason to believe that they are "married to Christ"— Jer. iii. 14; Isa. lxii. 5.

If we congratulate our friends when they are settled in life with a fair prospect of happiness, shall we not much more congratulate you; you, who by your connection with Christ are become children of the living God? John i. 12. What earthly advancement can be compared with this? Who among the children of men is so wise to discern, so tender to regard, so able to relieve, your every want? We hope that you know your union with him. It is certainly your privilege to know it, and to rejoice in it. John xiv. 20. "Rejoice then in the Lord alway, and again I say. Rejoice"— — —Phil. iv. 4. But together with your privileges, remember also the duties which this high relation bringeth with it. Would you be unfaithful to him, or grieve him in any thing? God forbid. Remember the fervent attachment, Tit. ii. 4, the humble reverence, Eph. v. 33, the unreserved submission, ib. ver. 22, 24; 1 Pet. iii. 1, 5, 6, which a dutiful wife feels towards her husband: and let these feelings be transferred in the highest possible degree to your august "Head," Eph. v. 23; 1 Cor. xi. 3, and be exercised towards him without any intermission or alloy— — —*

2. Those who have no evidence that such an union has been formed—

They who have felt no need of an union with Christ, will be ready to say, like Ezekiel's hearers, "Ah! Lord God, doth he not speak parables?" Ezek. xx. 49. But indeed "we speak forth the words of truth and soberness." Acts xxvi. 25. You hope to bring forth fruit to God in some other way than by an union with Christ: but you may as well expect a branch to be fruitful, when separated from the vine. John xv. 4, 5. The image in the text is applied by St. Paul in reference to this very thing: he tells us, that "we must be married unto Christ, that we may bring forth fruit unto God." Rom. vii. 4. Moreover, if you be not united to Christ in this world, you will in vain hope for an union with him in the world to come. This is the time wherein you are to be betrothed to him. Seek then to know him: seek to become an object of his regard: seek to be united to him as intimately as he is to his Heavenly Father. John xvii. 21, and vi. 56, 57. Be not contented with *seeking*, but *strive;* strive to obtain an interest in his favor; nor cease from your labor till you can say, "My Beloved is mine, and I am his." Cant. ii. 16. Then shall you have the most delightful fellowship with him: 1 John i. 3; you shall have such manifestations of his regard, as the world can neither know nor receive: John xiv. 21, 22; ib. ver. 17; and, when all earthly connexions shall cease, your happiness shall be consummated in the everlasting fruition of his love. 1 Thess. iv. 17.

---

*If this were preached on the occasion of *a Marriage*, it would be proper to shew to the parties present, that their cheerful performance of their relative duties is indispensable, as an evidence of their union to Christ.

JESUS CHRIST, THE MOST EXCELLENT OF ALL TEACHERS.

John vii. 46.--Never man spake like this man. (H.)

So said the officers, whom the Pharisees and chief priests had sent to take Jesus Christ into custody, assigning this as a reason why they had not executed their commission.

When these officers went to take Jesus Christ, he was standing in the temple, and speaking boldly of the Spirit, which they that believe on him should receive, when the Holy Ghost should be given, after he was glorified: very likely our Lord was expounding some of the prophecies, for he said, "if any man thirst, let him come unto me and drink: he that believeth on me, as the Scripture hath said, out of his heart shall flow rivers of living water."

It must have been very delightful to hear Jesus Christ explain the prophecies, and particularly such as are contained in the 35th and 44th of Isaiah, the 2d chapter of Joel, and other places, where the Holy Spirit is spoken of under the similitude of a well, or a spring in the minds and hearts of inspired men; the mouth of a righteous man is a well of life, and Christian knowledge is a well of water springing up into everlasting life.

Many of the people when they heard this discourse, were persuaded that the speaker was an extraordinary person, and others thought he was the promised Messiah; many said, Of a truth, this is the Prophet, i. e. the Prophet spoken of by Moses. Others said, This is the Christ; the officers ventured to say, in general, Never man spake like this man. We unite these opinions, and affirm, Jesus is the Prophet like Moses, he is the Christ, he is the man who spoke as no man ever did speak, Jesus Christ is the most excellent of all teachers. They who were so happy as to attend his ministry, as it is written in the prophets, were all taught of God, and they who are so happy as to hear his doctrine now, though not honored to hear it from his own lips, may truly say, " Master, we know thou teachest the way of God in truth." Blessed is the man, O Lord, whom thou teachest out of thy law, though not out of thine own mouth!

I. WITH REFERENCE TO WHAT HE TAUGHT.
Jesus Christ had a full and perfect knowledge of what he taught.

1. He understood the subject of religion; herein he differed from those, 1 Tim. i. 4, 6, 7; Acts xvii. 23; Matt. xi. 27.

2. Understood the whole of religion perfectly; his understanding of religion was clear, complete, full, and without any defect; and there is not, in all his instructions, one line of guess-work; he hath built the whole of the Christian religion on certain principles, beyond all conjecture and peradventure. Hence the Scriptures are called lively oracles, the first principles of which were committed to the Jews, and perfected by the apostles. Acts vii. 38; Heb. v. 12; Rom. iii. 2; Heb. vi. 1; 1 Peter iv. 10.

3. He knew the perfections of God, the nature of man, the laws of Providence, which govern this world, and all the distributions of happiness and misery which shall take place in the next. Wisdom, in him, was natural, perfect, eternal, and out of his fulness all receive. If we ask, from whence the followers of Christ have their knowledge, the Jews, even Priests, Captains, and Sadducees, can tell us. Acts iv. 13; 1 Cor. xv. 10; Gal. ii. 20; 2 Cor. xii. 11.

II. As to the choice of his subjects.

Our heavenly Teacher, out of the rich abundance of his knowledge, made a judicious choice of the subjects of his ministry. He was governed in this by the condition of his disciples. (John xvi. 12.) As if he had said, I perfectly understand every thing; but I love you, I know the infancy of your faith, the strength of your temptations, &c. I therefore will adapt my instructions to your present condition. Our Lord hath discovered eminent prudence in the choice of his subjects.

1. The subjects taught by Jesus Christ are strictly and wholly true, he was opposed to those mentioned. Hab. ii. 18; Isa. ix. 15, 17. He taught the perfections, government, and worship of the true God, without mixing the traditions of men.

2. Important; there is nothing trifling, every thing is of the utmost consequence; how important to devotion is the knowledge of God, to the exercise of repentance; the knowledge of ourselves, for our faith; the knowledge of the true and real character of Christ; in all these articles Jesus Christ hath instructed us; our Lord did not waste his time, or the attention of his disciples, about articles of no consequence. John xvi. 21, 22.

3. Propriety; every thing he taught was proper for him to teach, and suitable for his disciples to learn; were they in danger, he gave them friendly warning; did they sin, he gave them reproof; were they inquisitive on proper subjects, he poured forth instructions; and when idle curiosity put them on asking questions, he turned their attention; when they were in trouble, he comforted them; and when attacked by their enemies, he showed them how to defend themselves. And, though he was always humble, yet he was never mean; always zealous, never frantic; always kind, never fond; always firm, never sour; always various, yet always the same, as to the choice of his subjects. "Never man spake like this man."

III. The manner.

1. Plainness and simplicity. There are none of what the apostle calls "great swelling words of vanity;" no fine terms, taken from the court of Herod. Matt. xi. 4, 5; Psa. lxxii. 1, 4, 6; Matt. xxi. 16. A plainness that could not but be understood by people the most likely to misunderstand it: " Never man spake like this man."

The subject he taught was stated simply, without mixture, or being rendered abstruse, by needless arguments. Prov. viii. 9. All the words of the law were written plainly. Deut. xxvii. 8; Hab. ii. 2. The apostles used plainness of speech. 2 Cor. iii. 12. But for this excellency Jesus Christ exceeded all, " and never man spake so plainly as this man."

1. The affecting manner in which he proposeth all his instructions to us. For example, in the parable of the prodigal son, we have the almighty, who is represented Nah. i. 3, 5, 6; Ps. lxxvii. 18, 19, pictured in one word, *Father*. A Father, patient and silent during all the provocations of a son; a Father seeing, when he was a great way off, melting with compassion for him, running, falling on his neck, &c.

2. What a picture of sin and wretchedness doth the life of the prodigal afford! A son, a son of such a Father, a younger son, going from home, with all his fortune, into a far country, wasting his substance, &c.

3. Repentance described in a very pathetic manner. " The son came to himself," &c.

4. The joy there is in heaven and in the church, at the repentance of a sinner, is set forth by the pleasure of the servants. All this is not only

clear and cold, like a sharp, frosty night, but clear and affecting: "Never man spake like this man."

IV. Consider one excellency more; THEY WERE ALL CONFIRMED BY HIS OWN EXAMPLE.

Many describe the road to heaven, but tread the way to hell; but he never did any thing to render his religion suspected. John i. 14; viii. 46. Hence it is said, " He began to do and to teach." Acts i. 1

Sum up all these together. A perfect knowledge of all truth: a wise choice of such truths; a clear manner of stating them, to carry conviction to the mind, to obtain assent and belief, and affecting the emotions of the heart with piety towards God and love to all men, together with example. Surely then we may say, Jesus Christ is the first and most excellent of all teachers, " Never man spake like this man."

CHRIST'S PERSONAL MINISTRY, MIRACLES, AND PROPHETIC OFFICE.

John i. 18.—He hath declared him. (H.)

THE verse, of which these words are the close, is part of John the Baptist's testimony concerning our Lord; it contains three propositions. " No man hath seen God at any time." Neither Moses, nor any other of the prophets, hath ever seen God as he is. " The only begotten Son is in the bosom of his Father." He, as the eternal, only begotten Son of the Father, is, and ever was, intimately present with him; he knows him as he is. " He hath declared him." He, as the prophet of the church, has made such discoveries of God, as never were made before, and has given us a plain and complete revelation of his mind and will in all things necessary to salvation.

I. CONSIDER CHRIST'S MINISTRY.

1. The contents of his ministry.

The principal subject of it was, that he, the promised Messiah, was come to set up his kingdom in the world. " He came preaching the gospel of the kingdom of God." Mark i. 14, 15.

In pursuit of this design, he set himself against human traditions, hypocrisy, and superstition; explained and vindicated the moral law. He introduced the everlasting gospel, as the last dispensation. " The Spirit of the Lord," said he, " is upon me." Luke iv. 18, 20, 21.

He declared God's nature and perfections, authority and government; opened the eternal counsels of his will for the salvation of lost sinners; displayed the riches of his free and sovereign grace, and proclaimed the wonders of his love. He intimated the saving design of his incarnation, life, obedience, sufferings, and death; cleared up the spiritual nature of his kingdom; insisted on the necessity of regeneration and repentance, &c.

He instructed his disciples in the great doctrines of mortification to this world, and heavenly-mindedness; of self-denial, humility, and Christian contentment; of brotherly love, meekness, patience, &c.

He delivered various prophecies of things to come, concerning his own death, resurrection, ascension to heaven, intercession, and exaltation: the effusion of his Spirit; the publication and success of his gospel among the

Gentiles; the infidelity and rejection of the Jews; the destruction of Jerusalem; his coming to raise the dead, to judge the world. To all this he added the doctrine of the sacraments, baptism, and the Lord's supper, as the ordinances of his kingdom, the seals of God's covenant, and the visible badges of discipleship to him.

2. The manner of Christ's fulfilling his ministry.

"Never man spake like this man;" the officers themselves being judges, who came to apprehend him; and the common people could not but observe, that he "taught like one having authority," and could not but "wonder at the gracious words." He spake with the majesty and authority of a God; not like the prophets of old, with a "Thus saith the Lord," but with a "Verily, verily, I say unto you:" and yet he did not seek his own glory, nor aim at ostentation and applause.

Zeal for the glory of God, detestation of all iniquity, and good will to men, breathed through all its holy ministrations. With what strength and evidence did he support his Father's honor, and confute the cavils of his adversaries! With what undaunted courage did he reprove the vices and errors of the age, never fearing the faces of men! With what admirable skill did he point or soften his reproofs, as the occasion of things required! With what compassion, condescension, and meekness, did he mourn over his obstinate hearers, and "grieve at the hardness of their hearts!" Matt. xxiii. 37; Mark iii. 5.

How tenderly did he expostulate with sinners of all ranks and degrees! How graciously did he invite and encourage the weary and heavy laden! "The bruised reed he did not break." Matt. xii. 20. "He gathered the lambs with his arms." Isa. xl. 11. And he had "the tongue of the learned." Isa. l. 4

"The words he spake were spirit and life." John vi. 63. He could add a quickening virtue and commanding energy to them; hence, when he said to one and another, "Follow me," immediately they left all and followed him. And as soon as he spoke to Nathaniel, the woman of Samaria, and Zaccheus; the first said, "Rabbi, thou art the Son of God." John i. 49. The second said, "Come see a man, which told me all things that ever I did." Chap, iv. 29. And the third "made haste, and came down." Luke xix. 5, 6.

3. The credentials of Christ's ministry.

Among these we might reckon the exact accomplishment of many remarkable types and ancient prophecies in him; his miraculous birth subsequent to that of John the Baptist, his forerunner; the extraordinary star, that appeared to the wise men of the east; the glory of the Lord, that shone round about the shepherds in the field, and the attestation of the heavenly host concerning him; the visible descent of the Holy Ghost upon him, at his baptism; and his Father's public testimony to him, "This is my beloved Son." Matt. iii. 16, 17.

1. His ministry appeared to be Divine by the miracles he wrought, whilst he was employed in it.

These were innumerable, and of various kinds, and not done in a corner; but before the learned, friends, and enemies. "He healed all manner of diseases, opened the eyes of the blind, unstopped the ears of the deaf, loosed the tongues of the dumb, cured cripples, cast out devils, and raised the dead."

2. At the close, &c. by miracles.

Surprising signs and wonders were seen at his death; all nature seemed to be flung into confusion. Luke xxiii. 45. "The sun was darkened at noon-day; the veil of the temple was rent in twain." Matt. xxvii. 45—51. And he rose again from the dead on the third day, according to his own prediction. John ii. 20, 21. This great event was attended with the " resurrection of many bodies of saints," Matt. xxvii. 52, 53, and with the testimony of angels, saying, " He is not here." Luke xxiv. 6. And when he had " shown himself alive to his disciples," Acts i. 3—11, he ascended up to heaven in their sight, and ten days afterwards shed down his Spirit abundantly upon them, according to his promise, Acts ii. 1—4.

II. TAKE A MORE COMPREHENSIVE VIEW OF CHRIST'S PROPHETIC OFFICE.

1. Christ teaches by the ministry of inspired men.

During the time of his personal ministry, he spake the word to his auditors, as they were able to bear it. Mark iv. 33. And he said to his own disciples, " I have yet many things to say unto you." John xvi. 12, He promised that, upon his departure, he would send his Spirit: " When he, the Spirit of truth, is come." John xvi. 13, 14.

And by this Spirit " he brought all things to their remembrance." John xiv. 26. He also revealed new doctrines to them, and " showed them things to come." Acts xxvii. 11, 16, 17. " He gave them the Spirit of power." 2 Tim. i. 7. It was likewise under his inspiration and influence, that they committed so much of the gospel revelation to writing. They therein " declared the testimony of God." 1 Cor. ii. 1—13.

2. He teaches by the ministry of others, who are not inspired.

As, " When he ascended up on high, he gave apostles, prophets, and evangelists," which were extraordinary officers, endued with miraculous gifts; so he gave pastors and teachers, to be standing officers in the church, for the " perfecting of the saints." Eph. iv. 1, 11—13. And his promise, to be with his servants always, Matt. xxviii. 20, looks forward to the ministers of the gospel till time shall be no more.

3. He teaches by an internal illumination, by means of all these external teachings.

By his external teachings he takes off the veil from our hearts, or removes their natural depravity and prejudices. This internal illumination teaches us to profit, there is something efficacious in it, for every man. John vi. 45. But without this internal work upon the heart, all external revelations would be ineffectual, as to any saving purpose: " Who hath believed our report?" Isa. liii. 1; 1 Cor. ii. 12, 14.

Our Lord Jesus, in the discharge of his prophetic office, undertakes the work of opening the heart, as he did the heart of Lydia. Acts. xvi. 14. He, by his Spirit, " convinces the world of sin." John xvi. 8. Hence the apostle John says, " The Son of God is come." 1 John v. 20. And, " Ye have an unction from the Holy One." 1 John ii. 20.

To conclude.

1. This shows the excellence and necessity of Christ's teachings.

With what light and authority, condescension, grace, and efficacy, does he teach us the way to pardon, peace, &c.

O, how thankful should we be for this great Prophet of the church!— " Blessed be the Lord God of Israel." Luke i. 68, 77—79.

2. The danger of refusing to hearken to this Divine teacher.

" For him," says God, " shall ye hear in all things." Acts iii. 22, 23. O, solemn injunction! and, O, dreadful ruin, to such as turn a deaf ear to him! " How shall we escape?" Heb. ii. 3. " See, then, that ye refuse not him that speaketh." chap. xii. 25

THE CHARACTER AND WORK OF JESUS CHRIST.

Matt. xxi. 10.—And when he was come into Jerusalem, all the city was moved, saying Who is this? (H.)

WHEN any person of a singular character, and who is represented as having done some remarkable works, makes his appearance in any age or country, he usually engages the attention of mankind. If he has achieved some great thing for the good of the human race, or of his country, he readily becomes an object of admiration, and receives the applause of the multitude; many of whom perhaps will afterward, from various considerations, commence his enemies, and persecute him with a hatred and rancour, equal, if not superior, to their former admiration and applause: so variable are the tempers of men, and of so little importance are their professed admiration and regard. This was evidently the character and behaviour of that multitude, who followed our Saviour in his progress to Jerusalem. And when he was come into Jerusalem, &c. It is intended by divine assistance,

I. To suggest several ANSWERS TO THIS QUESTION, put by the people of Jerusalem, concerning Jesus Christ.

1. Who is this? He is the glorious Personage who was typified and promised to the church as the true Messiah, and the Saviour of sinners. He is the great antitype of all the typical persons, places, and things, appointed to prefigure him, under the Old Testament. He was promised as the woman's seed. Gen. iii. 15. As Abraham's. Gen. xii. 3. In the character of Shiloh. Gen. xlix. 10. In his prophetical character he was foretold by Moses. Deut. xviii. 15. He was to be of the family of David. Jer. xxiii. 5. He was to be born of a virgin. Isa. vii. 15. Bethlehem was foretold as the place of his birth. Micah v. 2. It was foretold that he was to perform wonderful works. Isa. xlii. 7; xxxv. 5, 6. Had the Jewish nation paid proper attention to these things, they would not have rejected Christ, but hailed him as the true Messiah.

2. Who is this? He is a person of infinite dignity, the only begotten and eternal Son of God. John i. 14—18; iii. 16. He is the Son of God, as begotten by the Spirit of God. Luke i. 35. As being raised immediately from the dead by God. Acts xiii. 33. It is so said of others, much more so of Christ. Luke xx. 36. In his resurrection he was declared to be such: and as being made heir of all things in his Father's house. Heb. i. 4, 5. But more especially, he is the only begotten Son of God by nature, of the same essence with his Father, the eternal Son of God, who, when he became incarnate, came forth from the Father; John xvi. 27, 28; who was before Abraham. John viii. 58. Who preached to the antediluvians. 1 Peter iii. 18—20. Who made the world. John i. 3; Col. i. 14—18. And is God. Heb. iii. 4. God manifest in the flesh. 1 Tim. iii. 16. Possessing all the perfections of God, is the brightness of his glory, and the express image of his person.

3. Who is this? He is the only mediator between God and man. 1 Tim. ii. 5. Man in his primitive innocence, required no mediator; but when man sinned, a mediator was essentially necessary, to interpose between an offended God, and offending sinners. No angel was equal to the arduous undertaking; the Son of God, alone, was found equal to the work; hence the Father, in his infinite wisdom and love, appointed him to the service. Ps. lxxxix. 19.

4. Who is this? He is Head of the church by the Father's appointment. Ps. ii. 6; Luke i. 32, 33; Eph. i. 22, 23. He is her head, as it respects representation, being the second Adam, the first being the figure of him who was to come. Of government, as her King and Lawgiver, the scriptures being the great standing statute-book of his kingdom; which none must add to or diminish, at the peril of his salvation. Of saving influence, and the fountain of spiritual life to all her members. And of example, 1 Pet. ii. 21.

5. Who is this? He is that glorious Personage to whom the whole administrations of divine providence are committed. He is the Governor of the world. The Father has put all things under his care and management. He moves and directs the whole frame of nature, he directs the motions and propensities of his creatures, so as to render them subservient to his will. He appoints and conducts all the changes and revolutions of empires, raises some, and depresses others. He sits invisible at the helm of the great providential dispensations, and tremendous scenes of Providence which appear in our own day, and will bring glory to his name, good to his church, and destruction to his enemies out of them all. We may exclaim here, with Paul, on another occasion, "O! the depth," &c. Rom. xi. 33.

6. Who is this? He is the dignified and glorious Person, who is appointed by Jehovah the Father, to be the Judge of the world, and to pass the decisive and unalterable sentence, which will fix the conditions of all mankind through eternity. John v. 22; Acts xvii. 31; Rom. xiv. 10; Rev. xx. 12. Jesus will then appear in circumstances of awful and tremendous majesty. The whole race of mankind will be assembled at his tribunal, from hoary Adam to his youngest son. He will possess a perfect knowledge of all the characters and causes which will come before him, whether good or bad, and the final sentence will proceed accordingly. O! what a dreadful day will that be to the wicked, and how terrible their sentence! Matt. xxv. 41. But what an auspicious and joyful day to the righteous! They will lift up their hands with joy, to hear their gracious welcome to the Lord. Matt. xxv. 34.

7. Who is this? It is he who is appointed to be the blessed medium through which the happiness of the redeemed will come into their possession to eternity. In the state of primitive innocence, all blessings flowed immediately from God, in the channel of absolute love and goodness; but this channel of communication was shut up by sin; and after the introduction of moral evil, Jehovah could hold no gracious intercourse with man, but through a mediator. It is in this way, and in this only, that all the blessings of grace and glory can be obtained by them who believe. Of this David says, this is all my salvation, and all my desire. And Paul says to believers, ye are complete in him; for, in him all fulness dwells; and, my God shall supply all your wants, according to his riches in glory by Jesus Christ. And the burden of the song of the redeemed will be, unto him that loved us, &c. Rev. i. 5, 6.

The improvement.

1. How great and wonderful are the love and wisdom of God displayed in the scheme of redemption! Hence it is called, "the wisdom of God in a mystery; and the manifold wisdom of God."

2. How inexcusable are all those who reject the Redeemer, and despise the great salvation set before them in the word of God, and the preaching of the glorious gospel! Such, particularly, are all infidels, who reject the gospel revelation; all worldly professors, who love their farms and merchandise above God, and the word of truth. Matt. vii. 21.

3. Let christians daily implore the Redeemer by faith in his mediatorial character and offices. Believe on him, trust in him, depend upon him, as made of God unto them wisdom, &c. 1 Cor. i. 30.

4. Dwell much on the glorious excellency of Christ, and on the work he has performed, and will still perform, for you, and for his whole church. In your serious contemplations, often put the question to yourselves, "Who is this?" and study to consult suitable answers, according to the information already given. This is he, "who is the eternal Son of God, who hath loved me, and given himself for me," &c. &c.

5. Amidst the present convulsions of the nations, console your minds with the reflection, that Jesus is the Governor of the nations: and that he will order all things for the good of his church; and he, himself, "will be a wall of fire round about her, and the glory in the midst."

6. In an age like the present, when error, infidelity, and every vice abound, let me direct you, O believer, to stand fast in the faith and holiness of the gospel. "Contend for the faith once delivered to the saints." Live down all reproaches and aspersions cast upon your character, or religion, by the most exemplary purity and godliness; "For this is the will of God your Saviour, that by well-doing you may put to silence the ignorance of foolish men. Be steadfast and unmoveable, always abounding in the work of the Lord, forasmuch as ye know that your labor shall not be in vain in the Lord."

JESUS CHRIST IS THE WAY, THE TRUTH, AND THE LIFE.

John xiv. 6.—Jesus saith unto him, I am the way, the truth, and the life; no man cometh unto the Father, but by me. (Sk.)

THE prospect of our Lord's departure out of the world, filled the hearts of his disciples with trouble, because they had long enjoyed his gracious presence, and had indulged a hope that he was about to "restore again the kingdom to Israel;" but he comforted them with an assurance that "he was going to his Father's house to prepare a place for them, and that he would come again, and receive them to himself," ver. 1—3. When he had stated this, he added, "Whither I go ye know, and the way ye know," ver. 4. Bu Thomas, who was slow of apprehension, and apt to doubt, saith unto him, "Lord, we know not whither thou goest, and how can we know the way?" ver. 4. Then Jesus said, "I am the way, and the truth, and the life: no man cometh unto the Father but by me."

I. "I AM THE WAY."

1. As a way, or road, leads to a certain place, and as means lead to certain ends, so our Lord Jesus Christ is the way to all the blessings of grace on earth, and to all the glories of the upper and better world. Particularly,

2. He is the way to *pardon*. Through him our sins are remitted, when we believe in his name, Acts x. 43; and through him, the ministers of his word preach the forgiveness of sins, Acts xiii. 38.

3. Jesus is the way to *peace*. Wicked men are at war with God; but he is the medium of reconciliation, 2 Cor. v. 19; and all true believers have peace with God, through our Lord Jesus Christ, Rom. v. 1.

4. Christ is the way to *holiness*. "His blood cleanseth from all sin," 1 John i. 7; his Spirit sanctifies the soul by an application of that blood, 2

Thess. ii. 13 ; and he " gave himself for us, that he might redeem us from all iniquity, and purify unto himself a peculiar people, zealous of good works," Tit. ii. 14.

5. And our blessed Lord is the way to *heaven*. His merit gives us a title to it; his grace works in us a fitness for it; his Holy Spirit leads us to that happy world, Rom. viii. 14; and by his blood we shall enter with boldness into the holiest place, Heb. x. 19.

II. "AND THE TRUTH."

1. Jesus is the *fountain* of truth. All truth is known to him, John xxi. 17; all the treasures of wisdom are hid in him, Col. ii. 3 ; and all the divine truth that is known in the world has flowed from him.

2. He is the *revealer* of truth : he revealed truth, in former times, by his holy prophets ; he revealed truth himself, in the days of his flesh, John viii. 12; and he sent his apostles to reveal the truth to a dark and erring world, Acts xxvi. 18.

3. He is the constant *patron* of truth. The friends of truth are his friends ; and the enemies of truth are his enemies. His cause is the cause of truth ; he contends for it; and his truth must finally triumph : for " he shall bring forth judgment unto truth," or " victory," Isa. xlii. 3 ; Matt. xii. 20.

4. And he is the truth of all those promises, prophecies, and types of the Messiah which are recorded in the Old Testament; for they also had their accomplishment in him, John i. 17.

III. "AND THE LIFE."

1. Our blessed Lord has life in *himself*, John i. 4 ; and he is the author of life to all created beings, both in heaven and on earth, visible and invisible, John i. 3 ; Col. i. 16, 17.

2. He is the *spiritual life* of believers. They were quickened by him, Eph. ii. 1 ; they live by faith in him, Gal. ii. 20 ; and the constant supplies of their life are derived from him, as those of the branch are derived from the vine, John xv. 5.

3. Our Saviour is the life of the *body*, which " is dead because of sin," Rom. viii. 10 ; but he will raise it from the dead at the last day ; for he is " the resurrection and the life," John xi. 24, 25; his resurrection is a pledge of ours, and because he lives we shall live also, ver. 19.

4. And he may be called the life, as he gives *eternal life* to all who hear his voice and follow him, John x. 27, 28. Through him, " the gift of God is eternal life," Rom. vi. 23 ; and " he that believeth on the Son, hath everlasting life," John iii. 36 ; he hath an undeniable claim to it, and a sweet foretaste of it in his heart.

IV. "NO MAN COMETH UNTO THE FATHER BUT BY ME."

1. Men have no intercourse with the Father, in *this world*, but by Jesus Christ; but through him both Jews and Gentiles have free access, by one Spirit, Eph. ii. 18. In his name they offer up prayer and praise, and through him the choicest blessings are sent down from the *throne of grace*, Heb. iv. 16.

2. No man when he departs this life, can go to the Father in *the heavenly* world, but by Jesus Christ. He is gone before to prepare the place for us ; he will receive us to himself; and in that world, he will make us kings and priests unto God and his Father for ever, Rev. i. 6.

3. Jesus as *our Mediator, stands between us and the Father*, 1 Tim. ii. 5. He brings the offender and the offended together; and is the instrument of restoring us to the divine favor by the death of the cross, Eph. ii. 16.

4. This proves that the mediatorial plan is the only way of salvation to a sinful world ; and no man ever was saved, and no man ever will be saved, on any other plan, 1 Cor. iii. 11. The law cannot save us, and therefore salvation must be by grace ; and if by grace, then by Jesus Christ, Eph. ii. 13

INFERENCES.

1. We should be thankful for Christ, and gratefully bless God, for the unspeakable gift of his Son, 2 Cor. ix. 15.

2. It is our duty, and our privilege, to receive Christ, in all his sacred offices and characters, John i. 11.

3. Having received him, we should abide in him, John xv. 4; and we should walk in him, in holiness and righteousness all the days of our life Col. ii. 5.

4. Then we shall live with him, and reign with him, when time shall be no more ; and, with all the redeemed of the Lord, sing "blessing, and glory, and wisdom, and thanksgiving, and honor, and power, and might, be unto our God for ever and ever. Amen," Rev. vii. 12.

CHRIST IN HIS ORDINANCES.

Matthew xviii 20.—For where two or three are gathered together in my name, there am I in the midst of them. (Sk.)

THE Saviour delivered these words for the instruction and encouragement of his people, in every succeeding age of the church. In the preceding context he supposes the case of personal offence among his followers, and gives special direction for the amicable adjustment of such offences. The offended brother is directed to endeavor to convince, and reclaim the offender, by first going to him alone, and telling him of his fault: but if he will not hear him, he must take with him two or three witnesses ; and if he refuse to hear them and the church, he must be expelled their communion as an incorrigible transgressor, ver. 15–17. And to encourage their exertions in the exercise of Christian discipline, the Redeemer informs them, that all their faithful reproofs and decisions, in conformity to his instructions, would be highly approved and ratified in heaven. ver. 18. He also assures them, that their united prayers for the divine blessing in this and every case, would certainly be heard and answered ; assigning as a reason, his own omnipresence, which extends to all the assemblies of his saints ;—" For where two or three," &c. In this interesting declaration we shall notice—the duty it prescribes—the instruction it suggests—and encouragement it affords.

I. THE DUTY THE TEXT PRESCRIBES ;—It is to "gather" ourselves "together in Christ's *name*." This is evidently an important obligation ; and implies that we should meet,

1. *For the purposes of his worship*. When we worship the holy Trinity, in the unity of the Godhead, it should be with profound reverence, and godly fear, Psa. lxxxix. 7. We should not carelessly rush into his sacred presence ; but diligently seek a necessary preparation of heart, for the hallowed solemnities of devotion, Prov. xvi. 1 ; Eccl. v. 1, 2. As professing Christians we should faithfully attend the instituted ordinances of Christianity, to

confess our sins ;—to acknowledge the divine goodness ;—to call upon his holy name ;—to hear the instructions of his word ;—to commemorate the dying love of the Redeemer ;—and to receive the communications of his grace, Psa. xxvii. 4, and lxiii. 2–5.

2. *On the ground of his mediation.* We cannot approach the Almighty in our own names, because we are sinners, and enemies to him in our minds, and by wicked works, Rom. viii. 7, 8. Nor is there any name either in heaven or on earth, by which we can come to God, or be saved, but the all-prevailing name of Jesus Christ, Acts iv. 12. Through his atonement and intercession, " a new and living way is consecrated for us," to the " Father of mercies," John xiv. 6 ; Heb. x. 19–22. Whenever therefore we meet together in his name, we must have special reference to his character and office ; and entirely trust in his merits and mediation, for acceptance with God, and the attainment of every blessing, John xvi. 23, 24 ; Eph. ii. 12.

3. *Under the influences of his Spirit.* No worship can be acceptable to God, but that which is sincere and spiritual. " God is a Spirit, and they that worship him, must worship him in spirit and in truth." We must not only draw near to him with our spirits, in the sincerity of our hearts, but we must also worship him under the enlightening, enriching, and hallowing influence and power of the Holy Ghost, Jude 20. And hence he is given to help our infirmities,—to teach us how to pray,—and to make intercession for us ; that we may " worship God in the spirit, rejoice in Christ Jesus, and have no confidence in the flesh," Rom. viii. 26, 27 ; Eph. ii. 18. Such is our duty ; let us therefore consider,

II. THE INSTRUCTIONS THE TEXT SUGGESTS ;—These are various and important ; but the following points are clearly implied, and consequently claim our particular attention. We learn,

1. *The essential Godhead of Jesus Christ.* His human nature is necessarily *local* in its situation, and therefore can only be in *one place* at the *same period* of time. But the Saviour promises to be in the midst of all his assemblies, however numerous, and in any and every part of the world at the *same moment ;* which evidently proves that he must refer to his character as *God,* for in this sense only can his promise be true. As an infinite Spirit, his presence "fills both heaven and earth," Matt. xxviii. 20. And if he were not essential God, why should we meet in his name ? But because " in him dwelleth all the fulness of the Godhead bodily," we must worship and " honor the Son, even as we honor the Father," John v. 23.

2. *The divine origin of religious ordinances.* This appears from the institution and design of the Sabbath, Gen. ii. 3.—The positive injunctions of the moral law, Exod. xx. 8–11.—The Mosaic dispensation of ceremonies, Deut. xvi. 16. The example of Christ in the days of his flesh, Luke iv. 16.—The united testimonies and examples of the holy patriarchs, prophets, apostles, and primitive Christians, Psa. lxxxiv. 2—4 ; Mal. iii. 16 ; Luke xxiv. 53. Our moral obligations to God,—the general voice of Scripture,—the sacred character of religion,—and the instructive language of the text, in which the Saviour directs and encourages his people to " gather" themselves " together in his name."

3. *The comparative indifference of outward modes of worship.* Under the law, the Lord particularly appointed the various ceremonies to be used by the Jews in his worship ; but that dispensation is abolished by the coming of Jesus Christ. And though the Saviour taught the necessity and spirituality of the worship of God as a pure spirit, he did not enjoin any *external rites,* as essential to the acceptance of true devotion, Luke xviii. 1 ;

John iv. 23.—In the text, he does not fix the *time when*, or *place where* **we** should assemble in his name. Nor does he limit the *number*, or prescribe the particular *ceremonies* or *forms*, to be adopted by his worshippers. These things are *comparatively indifferent*, though many attach great importance to them, John iv. 20. But the Lord looks at the heart, and *whenever, wherever*, and *however* his people " worship him, in the beauty of holiness," he is in the midst of them, and will show them his salvation. This will lead us to observe,

III. THE ENCOURAGEMENT THE TEXT AFFORDS. It is the compassionate language of the Saviour, in which he assures his followers of his presence in all their religious assemblies. And according to this gracious promise, we are still encouraged,

1. *By the infinity of his presence.* His omnipresence is a doctrine highly consolatory to his people. By his *general* or *universal presence*, he fills all space, and exists in all duration, Heb. xiii. 8.—But in the text he means his *special* and *gracious presence*, which ever accompanies the saints, and inspires them with joy and gladness in his ways, Exod. xxxiii. 14,15; Luke xxiv. 32. He particularly manifests himself unto them in his worship, and is perfectly acquainted with the respective characters, motives, desires, and necessities of them that wait upon him, John xx. 19–22.

2. *By the certainty of his presence.* His promise is infallible. It was not limited to the apostolic age, but has been happily realized in every succeeding period of the church. He is never absent from his ordinances, for nothing can prevent his being present with his devout worshippers. And how encouraging is the reflection, that he is with them on every occasion, and in every place, whether they may be *many* or *few !* He does not despise the day of small things. Where even " *two* or *three* are gathered together in his name," whether they be rich or poor, learned or illiterate, he is certainly " in the midst of them."

3. *By the efficacy of his presence.* Without the presence of Christ, the assemblies of his followers would ever be barren and unprofitable. But according to his word, he is always with them, and that to do them good. He assists their devotions—answers their prayers—and fulfils their desires. He possesses an infinite plenitude of grace, and in his ordinances he communicates his blessings to them that unite in his worship. He enlightens the ignorant—pardons the penitent—strengthens the weak—succors the tempted—comforts the sorrowful—establishes the wavering—and renders to all a portion of grace in due season, which frequently induces them to exclaim, " Lord, it is good for us to be here."

We may infer from this subject,

1. The public means of grace are inestimable privileges, Psa. lxxxiv. 1.

2. The sin and folly of neglecting the worship of God, Heb. x. 25. And,

3. The duty and blessedness of meeting in Christ's name, Isa. xl. 31.

CHRIST'S TRANSFIGURATION.

Matthew xvii. 1, 2.—And after six days, &c.   (H.)

JESUS CHRIST appeared in this world in the form of a servant; yet sometimes the rays of his divine glory shone forth with peculiar splendor, and declared him to be the Prince of Life and the Lord of Glory. This was the case at his transfiguration on the mount, in the presence of Peter, James, and John. "His face shone as the sun, and his raiment as white as the light."

Let us consider,

I. Some important facts which are established by the TRANSFIGURATION OF CHRIST.

1. That he is the Son of God, and a Mediator between God and sinners.

At his transfiguration, a voice was heard out of the cloud, saying, This is my beloved Son, &c.; Matt. xvii. 5; a plain intimation that Christ is a divine person, and the Saviour of sinners.

There are three Persons that have communion in the same Divine Nature, and are one God; and the distinction between the first and second Persons of the Trinity is set forth in scripture by the relation of Father and Son. The Son is of the same substance with the Father, and has communion with him in all his infinite perfections: he is his only begotten Son; John i. 14; and the Jews attempted to kill him, because he called God his Father, &c. John v. 18.

God here calls him "his beloved Son," and he takes the highest complacency and pleasure in him; he was with him from eternity, and daily his delight. Prov. viii. 23, 30, 31. He loveth him, &c. John iii. 35.

He is well pleased with him in the accomplishment of our salvation: it is in Christ that God reveals his justice, wisdom, and love, in the highest perfection: he has obeyed the law in precepts and penalties, and made full satisfaction to God for the sins of mankind. It pleased the Lord to bruise him, &c. Isaiah liii. 10. How divine and able a Saviour is Christ! He is Emanuel, &c. Heb. i. 3.

He is the messenger of his Father's love; we are to "hear him." He has revealed to us the Father's intentions to save mankind by the merit of the cross; John iii. 16; he has declared that the greatest sinners may be pardoned and saved; he has promised the Holy Ghost to assist us in the work of salvation; John xvi. 7, 8; he has told his followers that they shall have his presence with them upon earth; that after death they shall be advanced to the kingdom of heaven; that their bodies shall be raised from the grave, and clothed with the robes of immortality and glory; and that they shall be for ever with the Lord. John xiv. 3.

The great God is well pleased with all those who fly to Christ for salvation. John vi. 40.

2. His transfiguration is an evidence that he will come from heaven at the .ast day, with great power and majesty. 2 Peter i. 16, 17, 18. Though Christ is man, yet the fulness of the Godhead bodily dwells in him: and if the Godhead diffused such a lustre over his body at his transfiguration, what superior brightness will it spread over his humanity when he comes to judge the world!

When Christ was transfigured, Moses, the giver of the Jewish law, and Elias, the restorer of it from many gross corruptions, appeared with him in glory, to teach us that the gospel is a more excellent institution than the law;

and that Christ will be attended with millions of angels and saints when he comes to judge the world. Luke ix. 30, 31.

Though Christ lived in low circumstances while he was upon earth, accompanied by poor fishermen, yet the glorified saints and angels will attend him at the last great day. Matt. xxv. 31 ; Jude, verse 14. Then he will raise the bodies of the saints, publicly own them for his people, and put them in possession of eternal life. Matt. xxv. 34.

He will judge the wicked, and condemn them to eternal torments. Matt. xxv. 41.

O what a joyful and terrible day will this be ! How will the awful solemnities of it turn to the honor of Christ our Redeemer! 2 Thess. i. 10.

3. His transfiguration is a pledge and emblem of the future glorification of the saints; he is their pattern and example, both in their sanctification and glorification.

Though their bodies turn to dust, they shall be raised, and richly endowed with divine and heavenly qualities; he himself is the first fruits from the dead. 1 Cor. xv. 20.

What divine beauty and lustre shall the bodies of the saints be clothed with, when they shall resemble the body of Christ, the Lord of glory ! Phil. iii. 21. They shall be so refined from all gross qualities, as to resemble a spirit in their nature : they shall be strong, lively, and active, and no hinderance to the soul in its holy desires and operations.

They shall see Christ in his glory. Col. iii. 4. They now see him by faith, and in the ordinances of the gospel: but then, face to face. 1 Cor. xiii. 12.

II. Make some observations upon the event, and the circumstances attending it.

1. God is sometimes pleased to grant unto his children very blessed manifestations of his presence and love, before he brings them into a state of peculiar suffering. God here owns Christ for his Son, before he suffers and dies.

2. The sight of Christ's glory is delightful to the saints. All the perfections of God shine with the brightest lustre in the person of Christ. Col. i. 15. The disciples were delighted with the views of his glory, and said, It is good for us to be here ; and wished to make three tabernacles, and there to abide. Verse 4.

3. When the Lord reveals the divine glory to his saints, their minds are impressed with a holy awe of his greatness and majesty.

When God revealed himself in a vision to Jacob, " he was afraid," &c. Gen. xxviii. 17.

At such seasons the saints behold his all-sufficiency, and sink into their own nothingness : his majesty and greatness, which fills them with humility and self-abasement ; his perfect purity, filling them with a sense of their own vileness.

When the disciples saw the cloud which overshadowed them, and heard God's voice, they fell on their face, and were sore afraid. Verse 5, 6.

4. The Saviour delights in comforting his people upon earth, as well as to save and bring them to heaven.

When the disciples were terrified at the displays of divine majesty upon the mount, Jesus came to them, and said unto them, Arise, be not afraid. Verse 6, 7.

The heart of Christ is full of tenderness towards his children, and he delights in speaking peace to them. Be of good cheer, said he. Matt. xiv.

27. Fear not, little flock. Luke xii. 32. Let not your heart be troubled. John xiv. 1. And, Peace I leave with you, &c. John xiv. 27.

Though Christ is now absent from his saints, as to his bodily presence, yet he often comforts them in the ordinances of the gospel, and revives them with the sweet promises of his grace; he speaks to them by his Spirit, and conveys peace and comfort to their hearts.

After these things, Jesus and his disciples came down from the mountain: the vision was at an end, and the glorious scene was finished. Matt. xvii. 9.

5. The presence of Christ with his saints here is but of short duration, and subject to many interruptions.

Having enjoyed the presence of Christ for a season in his ordinances, they come down from the mount of vision, into the valley of the world, and are employed about the concerns of life.

This glimpse of the Redeemer's glory, is an emblem of that immediate, full, and everlasting vision of his glory, with which the saints shall be blessed in the kingdom of God. For,

6. Their enjoyment of his presence there will be everlasting: it will never be interrupted by sin. They shall be so filled with a sense of his love to them, that they will always love and serve him with the greatest vigor; and their hearts will never wander from him. They shall be for ever with him. 1 Thess. iv. 17.

III. APPLY WHAT HAS BEEN DELIVERED.

1. If Christ is the Son of God, and the Saviour of sinners, we may infer the happiness of those who trust in him by faith. As God and man, in one person, he is a glorious Saviour, suited to the wants and necessities of guilty sinners.

As their Priest, he has satisfied divine justice for their sins: they are united to Christ, and their sins are pardoned.

As their Prophet, he teaches them divine things; yea, the whole will of God. And,

As their King, he guards them in all dangers, and enables him to overcome sin, Satan, and the world.

They have peace with God, through the atonement of Christ.

They are the sons of God, through faith in his blood.

And in virtue of that blood, they shall have admission into the beatific presence of God in heaven, where there are fulness of joy, and pleasures for evermore.

2. If the transfiguration of Christ is a pledge of the saint's future glory, the consideration of it should raise them superior to the sorrows of the present state.

How happy are they who are one with Christ, and are the heirs of salvation! They shall be enriched with the same glory which Christ now possesses in heaven.

Their number upon earth appears to be but few; but in heaven there will not only be Moses and Elias, a few humble worshippers, but the "general assembly," and whole "church of the first born," even an "innumerable company," saying, Salvation to our God, who sitteth upon the throne, and unto the Lamb for ever. Rev. vii. 9, 10.

CHRIST THE ONLY SOURCE OF LIFE AND BLESSEDNESS.

John xi. 25.—Jesus said unto her, I am the resurrection and the life. (Pr.)

FEW families, even among the godly, have been so eminently distinguished as was the family at Bethany. There it was that Lazarus and his sisters lived, whom Jesus loved, and where he spent many a happy hour.

In this beloved family, the brother was sick, and tidings were sent to Jesus. The disciples did not wish to visit Bethany for fear of the Jews; but Jesus went: and the text relates a part of his conversation with Martha, as he approached the village.

There is a great depth in many of the sayings of our Lord, which renders them difficult to be understood; and it seems by Martha's answer, that she did not wholly comprehend his meaning on the present occasion, verse 27.

I. ENDEAVOR TO EXPLAIN THE SUBJECT.

The general design of our Lord was to fix the faith of Martha on himself, as the fountain of life, of all life, both natural and spiritual.

More particularly—

1. The words were designed to *correct an error* in Martha's judgment; for she spoke as if his power was limited to *time.*— — —It was his intention to raise Lazarus, and he desired to do it in answer to faith; but her expectations seemed to be very low.— — —" If thou hadst been here, my brother had not died: but I know that even now, whatsoever thou wilt ask of God, God will give it thee:" ver. 21, 22.— — —This was saying little more of Jesus, than might have been said of another prophet: he therefore leads her to consider himself not merely as the medium, but the fountain of life, and the author of eternal salvation.— — —She believed that he would raise him up at the last day; but our Lord intimates that he could at any time raise him up; and she was required to believe this.

2. His calling himself *the resurrection*, was designed to correct another error which she seemed to entertain, as if his power could only have *prevented* the death of her brother Lazarus.— — —This Mary dwelt upon, as well as Martha, and the Jews likewise with unbelief: ver. 32—37.— — — But his calling himself " the resurrection," was like saying, My power is not limited merely to prevention; I come not so much to prevent as to restore.— — —Christ did not interpose to prevent the fall, but to restore us from its ruins; to seek and to save the lost.— — —He does not prevent our dying; but he brings us back from death and the grave. Hos. xiii. 14.

3. In calling himself *the life*, he intended to carry the idea still farther. The first means restoring to life, but the last the perpetuity of that life.— — —Christ not only raises his people from the dead, but he is their life when raised. He is not only the way to heaven, but the very life of heaven itself. John xiv. 6, Col. iii. 4.

4. The *resurrection and the life* of which he speaks, represents more than the simple fact of raising Lazarus.— — —The life which he received on his resurrection was only corporeal, and he was still liable to die again: but that of which our Lord speaks is common to all believers as the two following sentences explain it.— — —" He that believeth in me, though he were dead, yet shall he live; and whosoever liveth, and believeth in me, shall never die." It therefore means a resurrection to immortal life.

II. CONTEMPLATE THE LEADING TRUTH IN THE TEXT; NAMELY, THAT CHRIST IS THE ONLY SOURCE OF LIFE TO FALLEN CREATURES.

God is the fountain of life to creatures, considered merely as such; but where that life is forfeited and lost, Christ is the only restorer of it.— — — He is described as that life which is the light of men, ch. i. 4. He quickeneth whom he will, v. 21: and those who live, must live by faith in him. Gal. ii. 20.

The world since the fall is like the valley of vision, or a field of slaughter, some years after a battle, covered with the slain. Ezek. xxxvii. Angels might ask, can these dry bones live? If they can, it must not be by any human power, oh Lord God thou knowest!— — —Prophets, angels, ministers would despair; but Jesus is the resurrection and the life.

In various senses we may be said to be dead: more particularly—

1. We are *spiritually* dead, as the Prodigal was when lost to his father. "This my son," said he, "was dead, and is alive again; was lost, and is found."— — —By nature we are like dead bodies, without any soul for what is good and heavenly; we have no desire after God, or spiritual objects. Ephes. ii. 1.

But Christ's death brings life to the soul; through his atoning sacrifice, the Spirit of life in Christ Jesus breathes upon the dry bones, and they live; and there was no other consistent way in which this life could be imparted. — — —God would not have given his Holy Spirit, but for Christ's sake: if I go not away, said he, the Comforter will not come. Hence the great effusion on the day of pentecost. Acts i. 4, 8.

2. We are dead *legally*, as well as spiritually, dead in law as well as in fact.— — —As sinners we were under the sentence of death and condemnation, to be banished forever under the curse, and all the threatnings of God's righteous law stood against us. Gal. iii. 10.

But through the mediation of Christ, those who believe in him shall not come into condemnation, but are passed from death unto life. John v. 24.— — —They come out of their graves, like Lazarus; and their being forgiven all trespasses, is equivalent to the command, "Loose him and let him go." — — —Christ was treated for our sake as if he had been a sinner, and that we for his sake might be treated as righteous. 2 Cor. v. 21.

3. We are all subject to *corporeal* death; and though we should have been raised, whether Christ had died or not, yet not to life, but to endure the second death; to be carried from prison to judgment, and there to receive our everlasting doom. John v. 29.

But believing in Christ, and receiving the atonement, we are made one with him, and shall rise with him, and sit with him in heavenly places. Ephes. ii. 6.— — —Our resurrection to eternal life is a part of his mediatorial undertaking, and is secured by the promises which he has made to them that love him. John v. 27—29, vi. 39.

4. Through the mediation of Christ, each of these kinds of life becomes *perpetual.*— — —Our being delivered from the *curse* will be perpetual: "There is no condemnation to them that are in Christ Jesus—they shall never come into condemnation."— — —Being *quickened* also from a death in sin, we shall die no more: "because I live, ye shall live also."— — —Being *raised* up at the last day, we shall live for ever. There is "no more death," no sorrow or pain, but all tears shall be wiped away. Rev. xxi. 4.

If we wish to die and be lost, therefore, we shall turn away from Christ, and make light of him; shall prefer the things of the present world to his gospel and salvation, and depend on our own righteousness, to the rejection of his righteousness.

If we desire to live, we must believe in Jesus, come to him, and make him our all in all. John iii. 36.

CHRIST'S FAREWELL TO HIS DISCIPLES.

John xvi 16.--A little while and ye shall not see me: and again, a little while and ye shall
see me, because I go to the Father. (Pr.)

THIS is part of the last tender discourse of our Lord to his disciples,
which was omitted by the other Evangelists, but is given us by John. His
design throughout the whole of his address is to reconcile their minds to his
departure, and to arm them against future troubles. Such also is the kind
intention in the words of our text.

Our Lord's meaning, however, was not plain to the disciples; for they did
not fully understand him. He therefore took occasion to explain himself;
and the explanation extends to ver. 27.

I. ENDEAVOR TO ILLUSTRATE THE SUBJECT—
In general, it has a double aspect, a dark side, and a bright one—

1. Notice *the dark part* of the subject. Our Lord's first sentence seems
plainly to refer to his death: " ye shall not see me." In the course of five
or six days at most he would be taken from them, and they would be left
alone.— — —His farther explanation of this is given in ver. 20: they should
" weep and lament." This indeed they did, not only as having lost him
whom their souls loved, but as being nonplused as to all their future hopes
and prospects.— — —Their feelings must have been what ours would be,
if something were to transpire which would seem to prove that there was
nothing true in religion.— — —They walked about, not knowing what to
do with themselves: they communed, and were sad. Luke xxiv. 21.— — —
While this was the case, the world triumphed, the enemy rejoiced, and were
ready to say, See now what is become of your Messiah—where now is your
God!

2. Let us view *the bright part* of the subject.— — —Though the situation of the disciples was very painful, it should not be of long continuance:
" a little while and ye shall see me."— — —Does he mean at his resurrection? It would seem so but for the last clause, and the context—"because
I go to the Father."— — —If it be understood of their seeing him with
their bodily eyes after his resurrection, his going to the Father would rather
be a reason of the reverse, as in ver. 10. It is not therefore with their bodily eyes that they were to behold him, though that was true for a little time,
but with the eyes of their mind which from that time should be greatly irra-
diated: on his departure a flood of light should be poured upon them. In
confirmation of this sense of the passage, the enjoyment promised was to
remain with them; "no man shall take it from you."— — —The whole
context agrees with this construction: when the eyes of their understanding
were opened, this promise was fulfilled,

3. Observe *the similitude* by which the whole subject is illustrated, verse
21, 22.— — —The joy that should follow on Christ's going to the Father
should be so great, that it should make them forget as it were their sorrow.
— — —The little church of Christ was then like a woman in travail; it
was also the hour of Christ's travail, and they must be in travail with him.
— — —But when they come to see the fruits of all, they remember no
more the anguish. Their natural attachments to him after the flesh, were
henceforth swallowed up in spiritual and holy joy. 2 Cor. v. 16.

4. The *advantages* arising from Christ's going to the Father, are also exhibited for the purpose of reconciling the disciples to his departure, ver. 23

—27.— — —There are three things in particular respecting our Lord's departure, that are worthy of notice—

1. Our being allowed and directed henceforward to *make use of his name* in our approaches to the Father.— — —While he was upon earth, the disciples presented all their requests to him; or if to the Father, no special mention was made of the name of Jesus.— — —But now, after his soul had been made an offering for sin, his name shall be the plea: and thus we are furnished with a plea the most powerful and efficacious.

2. *A flood of light* was from hence poured upon the church.— — —A fulfilment of the prophecies would elucidate the various important events that had taken place, and the Holy Spirit was also given them in great abundance.

3. *Christ's intercession* on our behalf is also promised as one of the benefits consequent on his departure, ver. 26, 27; and hence the comfort it was intended to impart.

II. APPLY THE SUBJECT TO OURSELVES.

1. We may expect, in common with the disciples of Jesus, to have *a portion of tribulation*, or a time to weep and lament.— — —There are also special times for this, and when the world rejoice: times when the cause of Christ seems to be run down and going to ruin, through persecutions from without, or contentions from within.— — —The whole of the christian life is in some degree a time of weeping and mourning, while the men of the world appear to be cheerful and happy.

2. We may take comfort in this, it is *but for a little time*. At most it cannot be long, and God shortens many of our sorrows even here.— — — The disciples did not leave the world, till they had their sorrow turned into joy; and we may also live to see many of our troubles end. Psa. xl. 1.

3. It is our duty and happiness to *believe the promise*, without knowing how it shall be accomplished.— — —The disciples knew not how, but they were told that their sorrow should be turned into joy, and it was so.— — — We know not the ways of this world, nor the ways of God, and less still of the world to come: yet we are required to believe.

4. All the advantages arising from Christ's going to the Father, *apply to us* as well as to the primitive disciples; and it is our duty and interest to avail ourselves of them.— — —To make use of Christ's name, in praying for our own souls, or for his cause; to walk by the light which is now shed abroad, to pray for large measures of the Holy Spirit; and to take encouragement from his intercession to pray for spiritual blessings, assured that him the Father heareth always.

What an awful reverse to all this, is the state of the unbelieving sinner. John xii. 35.

OUR LORD'S DESIRE TO BE GLORIFIED IN HEAVEN.

John xvii. 4, 5.—I have glorified thee on the earth: I have finished the work which thou gavest me to do. And now, O Father, glorify thou me with thine own self, with the glory which I had with thee before the world was. (S. S.)

THE promises of God do not supersede the use of prayer—
They are rather encouragements to it, as being a guide to our desires, and the ground of our hopes—

It is necessary on our part in order to obtain the performance of them—
Ezek. xxxvi. 37.

The necessity was laid upon our Lord himself—Ps. ii. 7.

Hence, in his last moments, he prays for his promised reward—

I. OUR LORD'S APPEAL.

Christ acted in the capacity of a servant—

He considers now his work as completed, and speaks of it in that view—

He appeals to the Father.

1. That he had "glorified him on earth"—This he did.

In his life.

The whole of his life was conformed to the divine will—

Not the smallest blemish could be found in it—

In his doctrine.

He declared the Father to the world—

He directed persons to himself only as *the way* to the Father—

In his miracles.

These, though wrought by his own power, were ascribed to the Father—
John xiv. 10.

Hence the Father was particularly glorified by them—Matt. ix. 8.

In his death.

In this he most eminently glorified the Father—John xiii. 31, 32.

Even Peter in his death is said to glorify God—John xxi. 19.

Much more did Jesus both in the manner and end of it—

2. That he had "finished the work which had been given him to do."

He had fulfilled the law.

This was part of his commission—

It was necessary that he should fulfil it, both that the law might be honor
ed, and that a righteousness should be wrought out for us—

He did fulfil it in every point—

He had satisfied the demands of justice.

He had undertaken to expiate sin by the sacrifice of himself—

It was necessary he should do so as our surety—

He did it by bearing our sins in his own body on the tree—

He paid our debt to the uttermost farthing—

He had introduced a new dispensation.

He had fulfilled and abrogated the Mosaic ritual—

He had set up the kingdom of God among men—

He had commissioned and qualified men to carry it on—

This appeal afforded him just ground for the petition he proceeded to offer.

II. THE PETITION HE GROUNDS UPON IT.

He had before prayed to be glorified on earth, ver. 1.—

He now prays to be glorified in heaven—

He had a glory with the Father before the world was.

He was from eternity with God—John i. 1.

As God he had equal glory with the Father—

This glory he had laid aside.

He veiled his godhead in human flesh—

Being in the form of God he took on him the form of a servant—

Hence he is said to have "made himself of no reputation"—

He now desired to resume it.

The ends for which he had laid it aside were accomplished—

It was therefore expedient that he should resume it—

He prayed that his human nature might be exalted to a participation of i

This had been promised to him—Ps. xvi. 10, 11.

And it was now about to be conferred upon him—Phil. ii. 9.

This petition was highly reasonable as grounded on the foregoing appeal.

He had left heaven to promote the Father's glory—

He ought therefore to return to it for his own glory—

It was right that his body, which had been the instrument whereby the Father was glorified, should itself be glorified with the Father—

INFER,

1. How easy is it to see who are real christians!

Every true christian follows Christ, and walks as he walked—

But the end and aim of Christ's life was to glorify the Father—

Here then is a plain line of distinction whereby we may judge—

May we all dread the doom of the unprofitable servant!—

May we begin the work assigned us in good earnest!—

May we on our death-bed be able to make the same appeal, and offer a similar petition to that in the text!—

2. What ground of consolation is there for true penitents!

The work assigned to Christ was to redeem a lost world—

He perfected that work, so that nothing need or can be added to it—

Let penitents then confide in him, and rejoice in his salvation—

3. How blessed is the end of the christian's labors!

He here labors much and suffers much for God's glory—

But soon he shall be glorified with God himself—

He shall continue to enjoy that glory when the world shall be no more—

Let christians then look forward to the end with joy.

DEITY AND ATONEMENT OF CHRIST.

Heb. i. 3.—Who being the brightness of his glory, and the express image of his person, and upholding all things by the word of his power, when he had by himself purged our sins, sat down on the right hand of the Majesty on high. (Pr.)

Some of the earliest corruptions of christianity consisted in entertaining low thoughts of the person and work of Christ: had it been otherwise, much that is found in this epistle would have been irrelevant. We have cause however to be thankful for what rose out of these corruptions, both in this epistle and the gospel of John.

The text contains a divinely magnificent account of the person and work of Christ, partly in relation to his antecedent character, or what he was originally; partly to his taking on him the office of a priest, to purge away our sins; and partly also to his consequent exaltation at the right hand of God. Let us briefly review each of these great and important subjects.

I. Consider what is said of the person of Christ, PREVIOUS TO HIS BE COMING OUR SAVIOUR.

He is "the brightness of the Father's glory, the express image of his person, and he upholds all things by the word of his power"—

If this be not descriptive of his being *truly God*, it is not in the power of language to convey such an idea. There is a great resemblance between this passage and that in Phil. ii. 6, where he is represented as being originally "in the form of God, and thinking it no robbery to be equal with God:"

and as that passage was intended to show the deep humiliation of Christ, in taking on him "the form of a servant," so the description in the text is designed to show what it is that gives value to his sacrifice, and dignity and importance to the whole of the christian revelation.

The antecedent *glory of Christ* is a subject on which the Scriptures delight to dwell, as may be seen in various passages. Mic. v. 2 ; John i. 1—3; 1 John i. 1,2. It is on this principle that all the reasoning in this epistle rests, for this it is that places him infinitely above angels, i. 6—8; above Moses the lawgiver, iii. 4—6; and above Aaron the high priest, v. 4—6. The pre-existence of Christ was necessary to his assumption of our nature, and his pre-existent and essential glory rendered that assumption an act of infinite condescension. Heb. ii. 14—16; 2 Cor. viii. 9.

Let us attend to the meaning of the terms employed in the text, as far as we can comprehend them, for the subject is great and overwhelming.

1. Christ is here called *the brightness of the Father's glory.* The description is metaphorical, for it is not in the power of language to express what God really is, or to give a literal account of the divine nature. The allusion here is to the sun, sending forth its beams throughout the wide creation; and Christ is the emanation or effulgence of the divine glory. This perhaps is as just an idea as can be conveyed to us, of the union and distinction between the Father and the Son. He is in the Father, and the Father in him. God never was without a Son, any more than the sun in the heavens can exist without its beams; yet they are not so one as to admit of no proper or personal distinction. Christ is not the Father, yet there is such an equality, that he is emphatically "the brightness of his glory."— — —It is also through him that the glory of the divine nature is revealed and made manifest. God made the world by him, and by him he saved it: the Lord Jesus is therefore the shining forth of all this glory.

2. He is *the express image of his person,* the image of the invisible God. Col. i. 15. This also is figurative, alluding to the likeness of a son to a father, only this likeness is perfect. There is not an attribute or a feature in the character of the Father but what is also in the Son. Here is likewise a personal distinction consisting with a oneness of nature, and without any other subordination than that which is relative, as between a Father and a Son.

3. Christ *upholdeth all things by the word of his power.* Nothing can be more expressive of his godhead, for this is claimed as the special prerogative of God alone. Psa. lxxv. 3. Such then is the character of him with whom we have to do, as the apostle and high priest of our profession.

II. Observe what is said of his work in undertaking the office of a priest. " HE BY HIMSELF PURGED OUR SINS"—

This is expressive of the great object of his incarnation and coming into the world; and there are two things which demand attention—

1. *The efficacy of his sacrifice:* "he purged our sins." The term alludes to the ceremonial cleansings under the law, which were effected by sacrificial blood: ch. ix. 22. Hence David prayed, " Purge me with hyssop, and I shall be clean." Psa. li. 7. Our being cleansed by the blood of Christ is the substance of all these typical purifications. 1 John i. 7, 9. By his death he removed the penal effects of sin, and through the application of it by faith, the conscience is purified. The gospel therefore connects repentance and the remission of sins, and proclaims forgiveness amongst all nations. Luke xxiv. 47.

2. The ground or *reason of this efficacy:* "He by Himself purged our sins." When the Scriptures speak of Christ's miracles, they usually ascribe them to the power and authority of the Father, rather than the divinity of the Son. So also in his sufferings he was succored by the ministry of angels, and upheld by the power of God, seeing he had taken upon him the form of a servant, which required that he should act in subordination to him that sent him. Isa. xlii. 1; xlix. 8. But the scriptures as uniformly ascribe the efficacy of his sacrifice to the divinity of his person, as giving value and virtue to his sufferings. It is the blood of Jesus Christ, as he is the Son of God, that cleanseth us from all sin. 1 John i. 7. He hath purged our sins by the sacrifice of "himself," and hence we see the necessity of Christ's divinity in order to the atonement.

III. The exaltation which followed upon his offering himself as a sacrifice for us. "HE SAT DOWN ON THE RIGHT HAND OF THE MAJESTY ON HIGH."

1. By "right hand of God" is meant the *first place in his favor.* None are so high in the esteem of the Father, either in heaven or earth, as Christ; none have such honors conferred upon them, or such favors granted at their intercession. In all things he is to have the pre-eminence, for he is before all things, and by him all things consist. Col. i. 17, 18.

2. This is mentioned as *an honor which became him.* Conscious that he had done the will 'of God, and finished the work which he had given him to do, the Lord Jesus went and took the place which belonged to him. He sat down on the right hand of God, angels and authorities and powers being made subject unto him. 1 Peter iii. 22. While all in heaven cry, Thou art worthy to receive power, and riches, and wisdom, and strength, and honor, and glory, and blessing. Rev. v. 12.

IMPROVEMENT.

1. Seeing that God hath provided for us an all-sufficient Saviour, let us learn to trust him, and to call upon his holy name, remembering that there is salvation in no other. John iii. 35; Acts ii. 21; iv. 12.

2. We see the way in which our sins are to be expiated and removed; not by tears or sufferings of our own, but by the precious blood of Christ, and that alone. Nevertheless sin must be lamented and confessed, or it cannot be forgiven. 1 John i. 9.

3. The exaltation of Christ, as the reward of his humiliation, is to us a source of great encouragement. He is exalted as a Prince and a Saviour, to give repentance and the remission of sins; and is able to save all that come unto God by him.

4. The conduct of Christ in doing and suffering the will of God, and then entering into his glory, is given as an example for our imitation. Heb. xii. 2.

NECESSITY OF THE ATONEMENT.

Luke xxiv. 46, 47.—Thus it is written, and thus it behoved Christ to suffer, and to rise from the dead the third day: and that repentance, and remission of sins should be preached in his name, among all nations, beginning at Jerusalem. (Pr.)

It is remarkable how low the disciples were sunk, before the resurrection of Christ. That event was like a resurrection to them, and by it they were begotten again to a lively hope. 1 Pet. i. 3.

1. Observe, the words of our Lord, addressed to his disciples, were intended to *set their hearts at rest;* by showing them that nothing had taken place but what was foretold in the scriptures, and predetermined of God. — — —His plan was going on, whatever were the designs of men. This was like setting their feet on a rock when they were sinking: this truth they also remembered, and afterwards employed to an important purpose. Acts ii. 23; iv. 28.

2. The words were also designed to *explain to them* so much as they immediately needed, and no more.— — —There were other things that it behoved Christ to do, as well as to suffer: it behoved him to ascend to heaven, to reign, to intercede, to come again. But this was not their present concern, and therefore his death and resurrection only are mentioned.

I. Notice the GREAT AND INTERESTING FACTS which had lately transpired, and had filled the minds of the disciples with so much distress.

It was a fact then, that Christ had suffered—had risen again—and furnished them with a message of salvation.

1. *Christ had suffered,* had expired on the cross. This was an event on which all our salvation depended.

How did he suffer, and in what capacity? As a *martyr?* This is true, though not the whole truth. He did suffer indeed that he might bear witness to the truth, and for this cause came he into the world. John xviii. 37.

But this was not the principal cause of his sufferings and death: he suffered and died as a *substitute* in our stead. He was made sin for us, who himself knew no sin: he died for us, and bore our sins in his own body on the tree. 1 Cor. xv. 3; 2 Cor. v. 21; 1 Peter ii. 24.

As a martyr only, he suffered from the hands of wicked men; but as a substitute, he suffered from the hands of God.— — —"It pleased the Lord to bruise him, and put his soul to grief:" he bore the divine displeasure due to us.— — —He complained not of the former, but "endured the cross, despising the shame:" but in the latter case he felt and expressed himself in the strongest language. Matt. xxvi. 38, 39.— — —Job complained that his grief was heavier than the sand; and the church in captivity exclaimed, What meaneth the heat of this great anger. But all this was as nothing, compared with what Christ suffered, for he was made a curse for us. Deut. xxix. 23, 24; Lam. iii. 1; Gal. iii. 13.

2. *He had risen again.* This was another fact which had taken place: he had obtained a victory over the grave, and was loosed from the bands of death.— — —God had raised him up, according to the working of his mighty power, and this in token of his approbation, and acceptance of his sacrifice.— — —Yes, he is risen indeed, and hath appeared unto Simon This was the source of a lively hope, and an example of our own resurrection.

3. He had furnished his apostles with a *message of salvation*. This is called "preaching repentance, and remission of sins, among all nations." This was another important fact, which should soon be realised.

1. Observe, *repentance* was not itself followed by *remission*, as a necessary consequence: sin was too heinous to be thus atoned for.— — —Repentance is the duty of all mankind, as being a branch of the moral law and required by it, antecedently to all consideration of the coming of the gospel. But through the mediation of Christ, repentance and remission are now joined together.— — —Now, if we confess our sins, he is faithful and just to forgive us our sins: but this connection is all of grace.

2. The remission of sins is joined with repentance, for the honor of God's righteousness: yet it is not for the sake of repentance, but through the name of Jesus, that remission of sins is granted, and there is none in any other way. 1 John i. 7, 9.

3. This message of mercy is sent to *all nations*, "beginning at Jerusalem. This was now the worst city in all the world, for there they had crucified the Lord of life and glory.— — —Yet there the mercy was to begin, though it was not to end there. Such was the fulness of Christ's sacrifice, that its blessings should be extended to all nations: all men are now commanded every where to repent, because now mercy may be extended to all.

II. CONSIDER THE NECESSITY THERE WAS FOR THESE THINGS TAKING PLACE.

It was necessary, in particular, that Christ should suffer, and rise again from the dead, and that on two accounts—

1. It was necessary *from the scriptures of truth:* "thus it is written." — — —Moses and the prophets had all foretold that he should suffer and rise again, ver. 44. —— The seed of the woman, Gen. iii. 16 ; Abraham's lamb for sacrifice, the prophecies of David in Psa. xxii. lxix., and those of Isaiah liii. all predicted this event. —— So also his resurrection had been foretold, Psa. xvi. He should see his seed, prolong his days, and the pleasure of the Lord should prosper in his hands.

2. It was also necessary *from the nature of things.* "It behoved him to suffer;" it was not possible that the cup should pass from him. Matt. xxiv. 39 ; Luke xxiv. 26 ; Heb. ii. 17, x. 4. —— Yet it may be asked, in what sense did it behove him to suffer? Certainly he was not originally obliged to it: no, it behoved us as sinners to suffer, and not him. We should have suffered justly, had we been consigned to punishment: but this cannot be said of our Surety. It is only in consideration of two things, that it behoved him to suffer—

1. His own voluntary *engagements*. There was a necessity for his going through with the work which he had begun: he had sworn as it were to his own hurt, but repentance must be hid from his eyes.

2. Our *salvation* made it necessary. If we be saved, the cup must not pass from him ; otherwise God would have spared his own Son.— — —He must bear the curse, or it must fall upon us : he must drink the cup, or we cannot be exempt.

It was also fit that he should *rise again:* for if not risen, we are yet in our sins. —— His sacrifice would not have availed, had he not risen to carry it into effect: hence it is said that he died for our sins, and was raised again for our justification: and hence it is that he is able also to save to the uttermost. Rom. iv. 25, v. 10 ; Heb. vii. 25.

There was likewise a propriety in *repentance being preached in his name.* It was fit that pardon should then be proclaimed : the jubilee followed on the great day of atonement. Lev. xxv. 9. ———— It was not for the sake of repentance, but for his name's sake: yet without repentance there is no remission.

IMPROVEMENT.

1. We learn from hence the *way of salvation:* "repent and believe the gospel." This is the way for all men and for all nations to the end of time, and no other way will do.

2. We see the *allsufficiency* of salvation for the chief of sinners. The gospel might first have been sent to other nations, and last of all to the Jews: but to display its fulness it was to "begin" at Jerusalem.

3. The deplorable condition of those who perish in *unbelief*, and from under the sound of mercy. Matt. xxiii. 37.

~~~~~~~~~~~~~~~~~

CHRIST'S AGONY IN THE GARDEN.

Matt. xxvi. 38.—My soul is exceeding sorrowful, even unto death.   (Pı.)

The sufferings of Christ contain one of the great mysteries of godliness. It is a subject of which we know but little, and cannot fully comprehend; but it would be happy for us if we were better acquainted with it. It was Paul's prayer, that he might know the fellowship of his sufferings, and be made conformable unto his death.

The manner in which our Lord spent the last night, the night before his suffering, is highly impressive. He went with his diciples to the house of a friend in Jerusalem; and when evening was come, they entered an upper room to eat the passover; after which the supper of the Lord was instituted. Judas left the room, and had an interview with the Jews, according to a previous appointment. When he was gone, Jesus delivered his farewell discourse to his disciples, which is given in the 14th to the 17th chapter of John. At the close of this affecting address, Jesus offered up his intercessory prayer, in the hearing of his disciples. Taking with him his confidential friends, Peter, James, and John, he entered into the garden of Gethsemane; and here he began to be "very heavy, and sore amazed." The disciples who were with him beheld his agony, and heard the distressing words recorded in our text. Let us,

I. Attentively consider the fact: "His soul was exceeding sorrowful."

It was so indeed, and to such a degree as exceeded all his former sufferings. Christ's own testimony is sufficient to prove this: he never affected grief, nor magnified his sufferings. Men are apt indeed to represent their afflictions as greater than they are, and to complain too much; but it was not so with our blessed Lord. Great sorrows generally prevent loud complaints, and are like deep waters, which run the stillest. It was thus with Job, and also with Jesus.— — —He made no great complaint: a few words to his friends, and a few to his heavenly Father, are all that dropped from his lips. Isa. liii. 7; 1 Pet ii. 23.

Nearly all the evangelists have given an account of his sufferings in the garden, which they describe in various affecting forms of speech. Mark tells us that he begins to be "sore amazed:" ch. xiv. 33.— — —Luke that he was "in an agony, sweating as it were great drops of blood, falling to the ground."— — —Matthew tells us that he was "exceeding sorrowful even unto death."— — —What a scene was this?

Sorrow is the fruit of sin ; but here was no sin, though he was treated as if he had been the chief of sinners, yea the only sinner in the world ; as if divine vengeance had forgotten to run in its usual channels, it concentrated all in him. Blessed Saviour! Why art thou cast down, and why is thy soul disquieted within thee?— — —Considering the infinite dignity of his person, and how much he was the object of the Father's delight ; the scene is full of awful grandeur, and such as was never before exhibited.

II. Endeavor to account for it.

If Christ died merely as a martyr, as some have pretended, the overwhelming nature of his sufferings could not be accounted for. On this scheme, he would appear very inferior to many of his followers, who have suffered death for his sake with heroic fortitude. ——— Some indeed who deny the deity and atonement of Christ, have endeavored to remove the difficulty, by allowing that Christ is not only a mere man, but a very imperfect one, and bring this transaction in the garden as an instance of his timidity and want of resolution! Thus has the Saviour of the world been degraded by his followers, and betrayed by his professed friends. ——— Our blessed Lord challenged the Jews, saying, "which of you convinceth me of sin?" But it seems as if some of his pretended followers would accept the challenge, which even his enemies declined. Let us dread dishonoring the Saviour, by attempting to account for his agony in such a way as this.

In general, we may observe, it was now that the Father *withdrew himself* from his beloved Son : and what that would be to him, who can tell? "My God! My God! why hast thou forsaken me!"

It was now also that he poured out *his wrath* to the uttermost upon him ——— —As he had become the sinner's Surety, he must feel the weight of that curse which the sinner had deserved : and who knoweth the power of thine anger! ——— Who can estimate the tremendous evil and demerit of sin? Even Jesus himself was "sore amazed."

Now it was that the *prince of this world* came to make his last desperate attack upon him : this was the hour and the power of darkness. ——— The enemy had before tried what he could do by temptation ; and now he will try what the most awful terrors may accomplish. John xiv. 30. All these things meeting together, his soul became "exceeding sorrowful, even unto death."

More particularly—

1. The *greatness of his mind* rendered him more susceptible of grief than we can possibly experience or imagine. ——— As man, his intimate union with the divine nature, gave an enlargement to his powers beyond our highest conceptions. ——— It was no small part of Job's affliction that he was to be set at nought by persons so inferior to himself, and towards whom it would have been an act of condescension to have noticed them in any other circumstances.

2. His *infinite purity* freed him from all partiality. He therefore saw things as they were, and had a full view of the infinite evil of sin, as it affected the righteous government of God ; and this would render him susceptible of the greatness of his displeasure against it. ——— It is this which gives an edge to punishment : if God's displeasure against sin had been arbitrary, or severe beyond measure, even hell itself would be tolerable, and Christ would not have felt what he did. ——— We can bear con

tempt or suffering much better when we know they are undeserved, than when it is otherwise. ———— All that Christ felt, he knew to be the just desert of sin ; and this it was that gave poignancy to his sufferings.

3. His *love to the Father* was such that it must necessarily have affected him in an unknown degree, to be forsaken and put to grief by him. Isa. liii. 10. ———— The frowns of any one may be endured, excepting those of a friend : oh why hast "*thou* forsaken me !"

4. The love he bore *to the souls of men*, made their conduct towards him exceeding grievous. Had it been an enemy that should crucify and put him to open shame, he could have borne it : but he was wounded in the house of his friends, he was put to death by those whose life he came to seek. ———— When Satan came against him, it did not grieve him, but raised his abhorrence : but the prospect of suffering by the hands of men, filled him with bitterness of soul. Heb. v. 7.

III. IMPROVEMENT.

1. What a motive is here for *gratitude*, when we consider the results of this dismal hour. From hence it is that the curse is removed, and that the sorrows of the believer have nothing penal in them. Since he has drunk the bitter cup, there is nothing left for us : the means is now prepared for turning our sorrows into endless joys, and our tears into rivers of delight. John xvi. 20 ; 2 Cor. iv. 17.

2. What a motive for *repentance*, to think of the sorrows which he endured- ———— What has sin done : how evil in its nature and how bitter in its consequences.

3. Let the example of the suffering Saviour teach us *sympathy* towards the afflicted. ———— He bore our sorrows, and carried our griefs : in all our afflictions he himself was afflicted. Let us learn to bear each other's burdens, and so fulfil the law of Christ. Isa. lxiii. 9; liii. 4 ; Gal. vi. 2.

4. Let us also learn *patience* from his example, and consider him who endured the cross for us, lest we be weary and faint in our minds. Heb. xii. 2, 3 ; 1 Pet. ii. 21—23.

5. From his sufferings we may learn what will be the portion of the finally *impenitent*, who reject his salvation. Their sorrows will be insupportable, and unavailing. Matt, xiii. 42.

CHRIST'S INTERCESSION ON THE CROSS.

Luke xxiii. 34.—Then said Jesus, Father, forgive them; for they know not what they do. (Pr.)

WHAT a surprising contrast, between the treatment which the blessed Saviour received from his enemies, and that which they received from him in return, ver. 33.

We here see the wisdom of God overruling the enmity of wicked men. They crucify Jesus, to render his name infamous ; and place him between two malefactors, to cover him with reproach. But by this lingering, painful, and shameful death, an opportunity was given for the Saviour more fully to express his love. While suspended on the cross he uttered many things and all of them highly interesting and important. Here also he made inter cession for the transgressors.

I. Observe the petition itself: "Father, forgive them."

How well this agrees with the language of prophecy. Isa. liii. 12.

1. Notice *the magnitude of the blessing* prayed for, even "forgiveness."— — This includes all other blessings, and an interest in eternal life. Sin is the great mountain that stands between God and us, and prevents the man ifestation of his favor: if that be removed, all is removed. It is forgiveness that extracts the sting of death, and calms the terrors of a future judgment; for if God forgives, who is he that shall condemn. Forgiveness takes away the curse of the law, and the bitterness of all affliction in this life. In the present instance especially, it is a blessing greater than could be asked or thought, by any other than the blessed Redeemer himself.

2. Consider *the extreme unworthiness of the objects.*— — —Surely, if such be pardoned, it must indeed be according to the riches of his grace. They were not common sinners, nor had they committed any common of fence: they had killed the Prince of life, and crucified the Lord of glory. They had put him to open shame whom God had made heir of all things, and by whom also he made the worlds.— — —To pray for such sinners was love operating against hatred, and doing good against evil in the highest sense possible. He had met with enough from their hands to turn his heart against them; but his was love that many waters could not quench, neither could the floods drown it.— — —Such is his love to us also; for when we were enemies he died for us, and it is wholly owing to his intercession that we are spared and pardoned Rom. v. 10.

3. The *heinous nature of their offence:* "they know not what they do."— — —This very plea implies that it was an awful sin they were commit ting, though they were blinded to it; it was one on which the heavens frown ed with preternatural darkness, and the earth trembled while they perpetra ted the dreadful deed. It was such as might have awaked the vengeance of God, to send out evil spirits and destroy them. For offering insult to an angel in human form, the inhabitants of Sodom were smitten with blindness; but the guilt of the inhabitants of Jerusalem is not to be described.

4. The *efficacy of the petition*, in securing the blessing prayed for.— — — A good man might say of his murderers as Stephen did, Lord, lay not this sin to their charge; but it would not follow that they would certainly be for given. But the intercession of Christ is for ever prevalent, for him the Fa ther heareth always. The blood which then flowed from the cross gave effi cacy to his prayer; the plea itself was the cry of blood, even of that which speaketh better things than the blood of Abel.— — —The plea of the suf fering Saviour had an immediate reference to his death, the very design of which was to procure the forgiveness of sin. In this instance therefore he showed what was the object of his sacrifice, and how it would be carried into effect by his intercession. Luke xxiv. 46, 47.

II. The plea by which the petition is enforced: "they know not what they do."

1. It is such as would *have not been found by any other advocate.*— — — Who indeed could have devised any plea whatever for such an offence, and for such sinners; or who dared so much as to think of a plea in such a case! Yet the blessed Saviour finds one, and the only one that could avail. 1 Tim. i. 13.

2. It is a plea which shows *that sin has different degrees of guilt*, ac cording to the circumstances under which it is committed.— — —Sins com-

mitted through ignorance and unbelief, though great are not so aggravated as those committed against light and knowledge : hence it was that Paul obtained mercy, while apostates find none. 1 Tim. i. 13, Heb. x. 26—29. Heathens, though, guilty, are not so fearfully involved as those who have the gospel and reject it. Heb. ii. 3, xii. 25.

3. It is a plea which teaches us, that *for some there was no mercy*, though there might be for those on whose behalf it was offered.— — —There is a sin unto death, which has no forgiveness in this world, nor in that which is to come. Matt. xii. 32. And there were some among the Jews for whom there was no mercy for what they had done in this matter, though the populace in general, and many of the rulers, knew not what they did ; and hence it was that Peter afterwards exhorted them to repentance, in the hope of their being forgiven. Acts iii. 17—19.

4. Though their ignorance afforded a plea for mercy, *they were not to be pardoned without repentance.*— — —Christ never prayed that sinners should be forgiven only in this way, nor that they should be pardoned before they repent, for this would be incompatible with the whole design of his mediation. His intercession for their pardon therefore includes repentance, and hence it was that such multitudes of the Jews were afterwards pricked to the heart under Peter's sermon. Acts ii. 37. Sinners must know what they have done, before they can expect mercy. Jer, ii. 19.

IMPROVEMENT.

1. We see there is that in the nature of sin which *surpasses all our conceptions*. When sinners offend against God, oppose the gospel, and reject the Saviour, "they know not what they do." Would any one if he knew it, offend his best friend, serve his worst enemy, and plunge himself into endless ruin ? Or having brought himself into danger, would he reject the way of escape ! Yet such is the case with every unbeliever.

2. Still we learn that notwithstanding the evil nature of sin, *there is no reason for despair*, not even for the chief of sinners. If Jerusalem sinners can be pardoned, there is hope for all : and it was amongst these unparalleled offenders that the mercy was to begin, as an example to all nations. Luke xxiv. 47.

3. The conduct of our blessed Lord is set before us in this instance *as an example*, teaching us what must be our spirit towards our enemies and persecutors. Stephen followed this example, and we must learn to do the same. Acts vii. 60, Matt. v. 44, 45.

THE CRUCIFIXION.

Luke xxiii. 33.—And when they were come to the place called Calvary, there they crucified him, and the malefactors ; one on the right hand, and the other on the left. (Pr.)

How striking is the contrast between the conduct of Jesus, and that of his enemies. When they were come to Calvary, there they crucified him ; and while they crucified him, he prayed for his murderers, saying, Father, forgive them. for they know not what they do, ver. 34.

In offering a few remarks upon the text, there are three things particularly worthy of notice—the place where our Lord suffered—the nature of his sufferings—and the company in which he suffered.

I. Observe the place where our Lord suffered.

This is called Calvary, or Golgotha, a small eminence, about half a mile distant from Jerusalem. This was the common place of execution, where the vilest offenders were put to death.

Two things may be observed concerning this, one relating to the intention of the murderers, and the other effecting the intention of the writer—

1. The place where Jesus suffered, marks *the malignant design of his enemies.— — —*It was not without some reason on their part that they fixed on Calvary; it was to render his name and character infamous, to express the greatest abhorrence of both, to sink and ruin his cause by affixing an indelible disgrace. Hence it was that the cross of Christ became a stumbling block to the Jews, and to the Greeks foolishness. But in this they were ultimately disappointed.

2. The place as mentioned by the evangelist, *marks his strong affection.* — — —The sacred writer employs but few words, his narration is slow and solemn, and expressive of the deepest feelings of the heart. He points to the spot with peculiar emphasis, as Jacob did to the field of Machpelah, saying, "*There* they buried Abraham and Sarah his wife; there they buried Isaac and Rebekah his wife; and there I buried Leah." Gen. xlix. 31. Another instance of this form of speech occurs in the address of Ruth to Naomi: "Where thou diest, will I die, and *there* will I be buried." Ruth. i. 17. — — —Thus the evangelist points to Calvary, and with deep emotion says, *There* they crucified him.

3. We may also add that this directs us to *the place where we must look for mercy.*— — —There they crucified him, and thence our salvation comes. There the great sacrifice was offered up, the ransom price paid, and the great atonement made.

"There hangs all human hope: that nail supports the falling universe."

II. The nature of Christ's sufferings: "they crucified him."

The sin of which the Jews pretended to accuse our Lord, was that of blasphemy, because that "he being a man, made himself God; and calling God his Father, he made himself equal with God." By the Jewish law a blasphemer was to be stoned to death, and therefore they took up stones to cast at him; but being at that time under the Roman government, they had no power to put any one to death. They therefore brought him before Pilate, demanding that he should be crucified. The Roman law inflicted capital punishment by various other means, chiefly by decapitation; but crucifixion was fixed upon to gratify the malignity of the Jews, and the unrighteous judge yielded to their wishes. —— In all this however the hand of God may be traced, and his wisdom seen in overruling these events for the accomplishment of his own purposes.

1. The death of the cross, though selected by Jewish malignity, would be *the fulfilment of prophecy,* —— The disciples were blind to these things when they happened, but afterwards they saw plainly that thus it was written, and that thus it behoved Christ to suffer. Prophecy had foretold that they should pierce his hands and his feet, Psa. xxii. 16; and also his side, Zech. xii. 10; John xix. 34, 37. —— Our Lord also had himself foretold, in numerous instances, that he should be betrayed into the hands of sinners, and be crucified. John iii. 14, viii. 28, xii. 32, 33. He had also

rendered the idea familiar t y calling a profession of his name, with all the difficulties attending it, a bearing of the cross, in allusion to his carrying the cross to Calvary. Matt. xvi. 24, Mark x. 21, Luke ix. 23. ———— Hence also the doctrine of Christ crucified, as the only medium of our salvation, formed the very essence of the gospel itself. 1 Cor. ii. 2, Gal. iii. 1, vi. 14.

2. In our Lord's suffering the death of the cross, there was something *analogous to what we as sinners had deserved;* and probably it was with a view to represent this, that the Jews were suffered to crucify him—

1. It was a *lingering death*, and the Romans appear to have invented this mode of punishment on purpose to render death as dreadful as possible. In the case of our blessed Lord it was six hours, from the commencement to the end of the crucifixion, when, having power to lay down his life, he voluntarily gave up the ghost; but the malefactors had not then expired, and would probably have survived many hours longer. Mark xv. 44, John xix. 33. ———— All this time the sufferer would experience the most insatiate thirst, from the extreme anguish so long endured. Psa. xxii. 15, lxix. 21, John xix. 28. And in this lengthened pain and anguish there was something that represented the endless punishment of the wicked, the worm that dieth not, and the fire that is not quenched.

2. It was a most *painful death*, more so perhaps than any other that human malignity could devise. The wounds were all inflicted on the tenderest parts of the human body, but not so as to effect the seat of life. In the act of fixing the cross in the ground, with the sufferer suspended on it, his joints would be dislocated by the shock; and thus another prophecy would be fulfilled. Psa. xxii. 14. ———— These exquisite sufferings would shadow forth those torments of hell, in which the sinner shall thirst in vain for water to cool his tongue, and where the everburning sulphur is unconsumed.

3. The death of the cross was attended with *reproach and infamy;* none so painful, so ignominious as this. He was made a spectacle to angels and to men, and they that passed by wagged the head in derision and contempt. Yet he endured the cross, and despised the shame. ———— In this also there was a prefiguration of that public disgrace and overwhelming shame, which the righteous judge has awarded as the punishment of sin. Dan. xii. 2, Isa. lxvi. 24.

4. The death of the cross was an *accursed death*, both in the esteem of God and man. Gal. iii. 13. And the sentence to which sinners are doomed is, that they are to die the death, to die under the curse. Hence Jesus would come under the law, and into our place and stead, and so was made a curse for us.

III. The company in which he suffered: they crucified with him "two malefactors, one one the right hand, and the other on the left."

1. On the part of his enemies this was designed to render his death still *more ignominious and shameful,* and was no doubt contrived between Pilate and the chief priests. ———— Our blessed Lord was holy, harmless and undefiled, and separate from sinners; but now to overwhelm him with shame and public disgrace, they associate him with "malefactors." ———— Not content with this, they place him in the midst, to insinuate that he was the worst of the three. Here every circumstance tells, for every thing was intended to heighten the disgrace. ———— This arrangement might also be contrived for the purpose of discomposing his mind, during his last moments, by filling his ear with the blasphemies and reproaches of the dying malefac-

tors. When we come to die, the least comfort we hope for is a peaceful pillow, and the presence of a sympathizing friend. But here is the blessed Saviour, surrounded by an enraged populace, and expiring on the cross, amidst the execrations of his enemies, and the groans of dying malefactors

2. But on the part of God we may see something of *the wisdom of this appointment.* ———— Prophecy was hereby fulfilled, which said that he should be numbered with transgressors. Isa. liii. 11, Mark xv. 27, 28. ———— —By this means also the virtue of his sacrifice was made more fully to appear. Had two of his disciples been crucified with him, instead of two malefactors, it might have been imagined that they had contributed something to the efficacy of his sufferings : but as it is, it would appear that his own arm brought salvation, and his righteousness it sustained him. He trode the winepress alone, and of the people there was none with him. Isa. lxiii. 3. ———— Also by suffering in such society, an opportunity was given for the fuller display of his power and grace, in saving one of the malefactors in his last moments, and taking him from the cross to the paradise of God. ———— Moreover, the publicity of his crucifixion, rendered the evidence of his death more certain and indisputable ; so that his enemies could not pretend that there was any collusion ; and that which established the reality of his death, established also the reality of his subsequent resurrection, on which all the hopes of his followers depend.

THE EFFECTS OF CHRIST'S DEATH.

John xii. 31, 32.—Now is the judgment of this world : now shall the prince of this world be cast out. And I, if I be lifted up from the earth, will draw all men unto me. (H. H.)

INCONCEIVABLY arduous was the work which Christ had undertaken : yet amidst his heaviest trials his confidence never for a moment forsook him. He had just complained of the insupportable weight of his mental agonies ; yet not so complained, but that he had desired his heavenly Father to glorify his own name, whatever sufferings he might have to endure for that end. For the satisfaction of those who would otherwise have drawn wrong conclusions from those sufferings, the Father answered him by a voice like thunder, "I have both glorified it, and will glorify it again :" and immediately Jesus, with his wonted calmness, resumed his discourse respecting the nature and necessity of his approaching death, and confidently predicted,

I. THE ISSUE OF HIS CONFLICTS—

The world and Satan were his great adversaries : and though by his death they would appear victorious over him, yet he declared that by his death,

1. The world would be judged—

What we are to understand by "the judgment of this world," we cannot absolutely determine : but we apprehend the import of that expression to be, that his death would be the means of exhibiting in the clearest view, first, *the wickedness*, and next, *the desert* of the ungodly world.

Who would have conceived *the wickedness* of the world to be so great as it really is ? Who would have conceived, that, if God himself should become incarnate, and sojourn in a familiar manner upon earth, and cause the light of his perfections to shine around him, and diffuse innumerable blessings by the unbounded exercise of omnipotence and love, his creatures sh Alld rise up against him, and put him to death? Who would conceive too, that this should be done, not by ignorant savages, but by the people who had enjoyed the light of revelation, heard his gracious instructions, beheld his bright example, and received the benefit of his miraculous exertions: yea, that it should be done too, not by the inconsiderate vulgar, but by the rulers themselves, and by the priests and ministers of God's sanctuary? This shews what human nature itself is, even under the greatest possible advantages: and humiliating is the picture which it exhibits to us.

But *the desert* also of the world is manifested to us in the death of Christ: for Christ suffered the penalty due to sin: "to redeem us from the curse of the law, he became a curse:" and all the misery that he endured both in body and soul as our surety and substitute, was our deserved portion. He indeed, by reason of his office, could endure it but for a time: but the soul that perishes in sin, must endure it to all eternity. Death, which to him was the period of his release, will be to the condemned soul the commencement of its sorrows, of sorrows that shall endure to all eternity. The hidings of God's face and the sense of his wrath will be co-existent with the soul itself.

2. The prince thereof would be cast out—

Satan is called the prince, and the god, of this world, because he exercises an universal government over men who are his willing subjects. Eph. ii. 2; 2 Cor. iv. 4; 2 Tim. ii. 26. That which has given him this power, is *sin:* on account of *sin*, God has delivered men into his hands as their jailor and their executioner. But Jesus Christ has "finished transgression and made an end of sin, and brought in everlasting righteousness;" and has thus rescued from the hands of Satan a countless multitude, who shall be eternal monuments of his electing love and his redeeming power. Whilst yet he hanged on the cross, the Lord Jesus "bruised the serpent's head;" Gen. iii. 15; yea, "he spoiled principalities and powers, triumphing over them openly upon the cross." Col. ii. 15. At that moment did "Satan fall from heaven as lightning:" and though he still retains a sway over the children of disobedience, yet is he forced continually to give up his vassals to the Lord Jesus, and is made to flee from those, Jam. iv. 7, whom he lately "led captive at his will." Moreover, the time is shortly coming, (yea, in the divine purpose it was, as it were, then present,) when he shall be bound in chains of everlasting darkness, and be cast into that "lake of fire" which has from the beginning been "prepared for him and for his angels."

Next, our Lord predicts,

II. THE TRIUMPHS OF HIS GRACE—

By being "lifted up from the earth" was meant, his crucifixion. The expression refers to the lifting up the brazen serpent in the wilderness, which was a type and emblem of the death of Christ. Compare Numb. xxi. 8, 9, with John iii. 14, 15. The Evangelist himself tells us, that our Lord intended to intimate the peculiar kind of death which he was to suffer: and the people themselves understood him as speaking of his removal from them by death. Ver. 33, 34. Nor did his words convey the idea of uncertainty, which seems intimated in our translation: the event was fixed in the divine counsels from all eternity; and he spoke of it as certainly to be accomplished.*

Here then are two things to be noted;

* ίαν should be "*when*," and not "*if.*"

1. The event predicted—

Christ will "draw all men to himself:" He is that "Shiloh, to whom the gathering of the people should be ;" and we see on the day of Pentecost the commencement of this great and glorious work. Would we understand precisely the import of the expression, there we behold it exemplified in the clearest view ———— We must not indeed imagine that every individual of mankind will be drawn to Christ; for in every age many have rejected him: but some of all nations, professions, and characters, shall be drawn to him ; and at last shall be found a multitude that no man can number ———— Dan. vii. 13, 14.

2. The manner in which it shall be accomplished—

Men are not drawn to him like stocks and stones, but in a way consistent with the perfect exercise of their own free will. The power indeed is Christ's; and it is exerted with effect: but it is made effectual,—

First, *by shewing men their need of him.*—The eyes of all the wounded Israelites were drawn to the brazen serpent in the wilderness : they felt that they were dying of their wounds ; they knew that no human efforts could heal them ; and they were assured that a sight of that brazen serpent would effect their cure. This attraction was sufficient: they looked and were healed. Thus the jailor saw his own perishing condition, and asked, "What shall I do to be saved?" and was glad to embrace the Saviour proposed to him. Acts xvi. 30, 31. This is universally the first operation of Christ's victorious grace.

Next, he draws men *by the attractive influences of his grace.*—Because men know not how the Holy Spirit works upon the souls of men, they are ready to doubt, or even deny, his operations. But who doubts the agency of the wind? yet no man knows whence it comes, or whither it goes. It is visible in its effects ; and therefore its operation is acknowledged, notwithstanding it is involved in the deepest mystery. Why then should the operation of the Holy Spirit be doubted, merely because *the mode* of his agency is not understood? John iii. 8. Were it possible to question the evidence of our senses, we should deny the virtue of the loadstone, and represent any one as weak or wicked who should profess to believe it. But we behold its effects ; and our incredulity is vanquished. So then must we confess the agency of the Holy Spirit upon the souls of men, though we cannot comprehend every thing respecting it. Our Lord has told us, that "no man can come unto him, except the Father draw him :" **John vi. 44**; and the Psalmist affirms, that God makes us "willing in the **day of** his power." Ps. cx. 3. It is sufficient for us to know, that he draws us rationally, "with the cords of a man, and with the bands of love."

Lastly, he draws men *by discovering to them the wonders of his love.* Let but a glimpse of his incomprehensible love be seen, and every thing in the whole creation will be darkened : just as a view of the meridian sun renders every other object invisible. Paul tells us, that "the love of Christ constrained him :" it carried him away like a mighty torrent: nor will the soul of any man who feels it be either able or desirous to withstand its influence. As well might the angels in heaven be averse to serve their God, as the man that has tasted of redeeming love.

In this way then does the grace of Christ prevail; and in this way shall it triumph to the ends of the earth.

APPLICATION:

1. Seek to experience the attractions of his grace—

Nothing unde heaven is so desirable as this ———— Say then, with the church of old, "Draw me, and I will run after thee" ————Cant. i. 4.

2. Fear not the counteracting influence of men or devils—

Men may oppose you, and vaunt themselves against you: but they are already "judged" by the word of God; and, if they repent not, they shall be judged by the same at the tribunal of their God. If they do not themselves become such despised creatures as they esteem you to be, they will ere long "awake to shame and everlasting contempt."

Satan too may harass you: but he is a vanquished enemy: yea, he too "is judged:" John xvi. 11; and though, "as a roaring lion, he seeketh to devour you," you are provided with armor, whereby you may withstand him; Eph. vi. 11–13; and you have the promise of God, that "he shall be shortly bruised under your feet" ———— Rom. xvi. 20.

THE PROPITIATION.

1 John iv. 10.—Herein is love, not that we loved God, but that he loved us, and sent his Son to be the propitiation for our sins. (Sk.)

THE interesting and all-important inquiry, "What must I do to be saved?" could never have been answered by the light of nature. How guilty, polluted, and condemned creatures may be restored to the forfeited approbation of their God, is a mystery which human reason could never penetrate, as is evident from the numerous futile schemes which have been invented to regain the Divine favor.

The supposed intrinsic merit and excellence of human works—bloody sacrifices—grievous austerities, &c.,—the senseless dream of purgatory—vague and undefinable notions of Divine mercy. All these, and various other systems equally irrational and unsatisfactory, show the imperious necessity of a plan of salvation, revealed by God himself. This glorious plan is presented to our view in the words of the text. "Herein is love," &c.

The word rendered *propitiation*, signifies the *victim* or *atoning sacrifice* by which sin is expiated, and for the sake of which God can be propitious to a fallen creature—the *vicarious offering* presented in the sinner's stead. Our text therefore leads us to observe,

I. THAT THE STATE OF MAN REQUIRED A PROPITIATION. Viewing man as a moral and an accountable agent, who has offended his Maker, the need of a propitiation provided for him, will be very obvious if we reflect,

1. *On the perfection and excellence of the law which he has broken.* It is characterized as "*Holy, just, and good.*" Our Lord has comprised it in two essential points, viz. love to God, and love to our neighbor, Matt. xxii. 37—39. This law is—Divine in its *origin*—immutable in its *nature* —reasonable in its *requirements*—benevolent in its *tendency*—indispensable in its *obligations*. Such a law therefore is essentially good, and ought to be obeyed. The principle which refuses obedience is essentially evil—consequently the person who indulges it, must justly deserve punishment, even the penalty which the law denounces, viz. *death eternal.* It follows, that if man who has violated the law be saved from its malediction, while yet the law is perfectly honored, it must be through a propitiation, an atonement—a substitute offered, and suffering in his stead.

2. *On the inability of man to expiate his offences.* All his doings, sufferings, and sacrifices, can never atone for one of his sins, nor heal a single breach of the divine commands. Even repentance, though indispensable as a *means* of salvation, is in no way an expiation of guilt. It cannot undo what is already done. Its effect is rather prospective, than retrospective. It is no requisition of the law—consequently no satisfaction of its claims ; for the law demands innocence and obedience, not repentance. Hence it appears, that some other must provide the propitiation, through which guilty man can be honorably released from the direful penalty of the law.

3. *On the inflexible nature of Divine justice,* which supports the honor of the law, and enforces its claims. Justice is essential to God. Now if man justly merits punishment, justice must inflict that punishment, either on him, or on a proper and an adequate victim that may be justly substituted in its stead. Otherwise justice must relinquish its claims, and thus be proved not essential to God—or else it must be set aside by Divine mercy, and so exhibit its own weakness, and a discord among the Divine perfections. But as we cannot admit either of these blasphemous suppositions, it follows, that no way is left for the exercise of mercy in the salvation of man, but through the medium of a vicarious sacrifice, atonement, or propitiation. We will now show,

II. That Jesus Christ is the propitiation required.
Three arguments will establish this proposition :

1. *No creature could or would become a propitiation for man.* No creature can lay God under any obligation. No creature can, strictly speaking, merit any thing from God. Hence no creature can perform works of supererogation. Much less could any mere creature bear, in a limited time and capacity, the inflictions of infinite justice. And certainly no creature ever *would* (even if it were possible) make atonement for man. See this finely represented in Paradise Lost, book 3.

2. *Jesus Christ is every way adapted to become our propitiation.* "God was manifested in the flesh", &c. His obedience unto death was infinitely meritorious, as he united in himself the Divine and human natures ; by the one he was qualified to suffer—by the other infinite value and efficacy were conveyed into his sufferings ; so that the law was magnified and made honorable, and every claim of justice satisfied.

3. *The Scriptures every where testify that Jesus Christ is our propitiation.* Here we might produce the numerous *types* of the Old Testament Isa. liii. 5, 6, 7, 10; Matt. xx. 28; Rom. iii. 24, 25, iv. 25; 2 Cor. v. 21; Gal. iii. 13; Col. i. 20; 1 Tim. i. 15; Heb. ix. 22—26; 1 John ii. 2. The Father gave the Son, John iii. 16. The Son gave himself, Gal. i. 4. He offered himself through the Eternal Spirit, Heb. ix. 14. The sacred Three combine. Hence we observe,

III. That this propitiation is a glorious display of the love of God. "Herein is love," &c.
The whole Trinity concurred in the work of man's redemption, but the Father is here represented as the first mover. *He* sent his only-begotten Son. Some have exhibited Him as burning with implacable rage against mankind, till Christ died to make him merciful. How unscriptural as well horrid the idea ! Christ died because God *was* merciful—not to *render* him *so* ; but to prepare a channel for his mercy to flow in a stream of salvation to men. "Herein is love," &c. This love is,

1. *Unparalled in its nature.* Remark that it was wholly undeserved—entirely unsolicited—perfectly disinterested—contrary to man's own seeking

—-never invited by anything good, by any moral excellence in man. "Not that we loved God."

2. *Intense in its ardours.* Here let us regard—the dignity of the Sufferer—the depth of his degradation—the extremity of his sufferings.

3. *Immense in its extent.* It reaches to every age and every clime—to every character and every condition, even to the lowest and most abominable of the human race. It embraces all, John iii. 16.

4. *Glorious in its purpose and final issue.* It not only procured pardon for sin and present holiness—but designed nothing less than everlasting glory for all believers. Here "grace reigns through righteousness unto everlasting life by Christ Jesus our Lord."

Inferences:—

1. How pernicious is the doctrine of Socinianism, which completely destroys this only hope of a penitent, *redemption by Christ!* On the Divinity of Christ depends the atonement,—to renounce one is to renounce both. The atonement gone; either man must be absurdly made a meritorious creature, or the perfections of God must be set at variance, and one attribute must vanquish another.

2. How dangerous is the delusion of the self-righteous! They practically renounce, what Socinians professedly deny. No one can receive the atonement, who does not feel his need of it, and if it be not applied, it can be of no avail to any individual.

3. What abundant consolation does this subject afford penitent sinners. Only let them believe, and they shall see the glory of God.

4. In this love of God we are furnished with a rule and a motive for love to each other—"Beloved, if God so loved us, we out also to love one another."

THE SUFFERINGS OF CHRIST.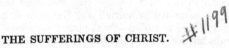

Isaiah liii. 10, 11.—Yet it pleased the Lord to bruise him, &c. (Sk.)

Of all the prophetic writings, none contain more clear and correct predictions of Christ, than those of Isaiah; and of all Isaiah's writings, none describe the Messiah more accurately, both in his suffering and exalted state, than this chapter. That the prophet here speaks of our Lord Jesus Christ, is evident from the words of the Holy Ghost in the New Testament. He applies verse the 4th to our Lord, Matt. viii. 16, 17; he "healed all who were sick, that it might be fulfilled which was spoken by Esaias the prophet, saying, Himself took our infirmities, and bare our sicknesses." He applies verse the 5th to him, 1 Pet. ii. 24, "Who his own self bare our sins in his own body on the tree, that we being dead unto sin, should live unto righteousness; by whose stripes ye were healed." He applies verses the 7th and 8th to him, Acts viii. 32—35, "The place of the Scripture which he read, was this, He was led as a sheep to the slaughter; and like a lamb dumb before his shearers, so opened he not his mouth. In his humiliation his judgment was taken away; and who shall declare his generation? For his life is taken from the earth. And the eunuch answered Philip. and said, I pray thee of whom speaketh the prophet this; of himself, or of some other man? Then Philip opened his mouth, and began at the same Scripture, and preached unto him Jesus." This example teaches us, that we also may, and indeed should, preach Jesus from the words now before us. For here we find a most interesting description of his character, his sufferings, and the happy effects of his sufferings. We are led to observe,

I. HIS CHARACTER. He was God's righteous servant, of whom God had before spoken by this prophet; chap. xlii. 1, "Behold," &c.

1. *He was God's servant;* who glorified God by obeying him, John xvii. 4. He served God *fully:*—his obedience was complete, Phil. ii. 8. "Being," &c. He served God *cheerfully;* with delight, Psa. xl. 7, 8; John iv. 34. He served God *constantly;* without intermission, John viii. 29. He served God *unweariedly;* till the work assigned him was done. He labored on and ceased not, till he was enabled to say, "I have glorified thee on earth, I have finished the work thou gavest me to do."

2. *He was God's righteous servant:* being unblamable in all his deportment, and never justly chargeable with sin. This appears—From the testimony of his *friends;* of Paul, 2 Cor. 21, "Who made," &c.; of Peter, 1 Pet. ii. 22, "Who did," &c.; and of John, 1 John iii. 5. "In him was no sin."—And from the testimony of his *enemies.* This was given by Judas, who betrayed him, Matt. xxvii. 3, 4, "Then Judas," &c.; by Pilate, who condemned him to death, Matt. xxvii. 24, "When Pilate saw," &c.; and by the centurion, whose soldiers crucified Christ; "Certainly," says he, "This was a righteous man; truly this man was the Son of God," Luke xxii. 47; Mark xv. 39.

3. As God's righteous servant, *he became a perfect example*, and an *acceptable mediator.* A *perfect example* to all his followers, of piety towards God; love to mankind; and personal purity, Phil. ii. 5; 1 John ii. 6. And an *acceptable mediator.* For it was requisite that our High priest should be harmless, Heb. vii. 26, "Such a highpriest," &c. And that our Advocate should be righteous, 1 John ii. 1, "We," &c. This was requisite, that God's righteousness might be declared in our salvation, Rom. iii. 25, 26, "Whom God," &c. Hence let us observe,

II. HIS SUFFERINGS. "It pleased the Lord to bruise him," &c. Here we learn,

1. *The extent of his sufferings.* He suffered,

In his *body.* He was bruised by cruel blows, Matt. xxvii. 30, "And they spit," &c.; he was wounded by the thorns, nails, and spear, ver. 5; he endured stripes by scourging, ver. 5; compare John xix. 1, "Then Pilate took Jesus and scourged him."

In his *soul.* He was put to grief by *the sins of mankind;*—the cruelty of his avowed enemies; see Psa. xxii. 14—16; and the treachery of his professing friends; of Judas, who betrayed him; of Peter, who denied him; and the other disciples who forsook him, Matt. xxvi. 56; Zech. xiii. 6. He was also put to grief *by diabolical suggestions*, Luke xxii. 53; Heb. ii. 18; and *by the suspension of divine comfort*, Matt. xxxvi. 38, and xxxvii. 46 We here learn,

2. *The singularity of his sufferings.* These being unlike those of others, he might properly adopt Jeremiah's language in another case, Lam. i. 12, for his sufferings were *unmerited.* He was perfectly righteous; and the only one who ever suffered without being sinful in nature or practice. His sufferings were *inflicted by God;* not merely by wicked men. God laid them on him, ver. 6. God bruised him; put him to grief; and made his soul an offering for sin. Wicked men indeed were the instruments of his sufferings; but God gave him up to death. Acts ii. 23; Rom. viii. 12. His suf-

ferings were *pleasing to God.* It pleased God to bruise him. He did **not** afflict Christ reluctantly, as he does his other children, Lam. iii. 22, 23. And yet our Lord *concurred* in his sufferings. His soul was made an offering for sin, readily, without hesitation; he poured out his soul unto death, as his own voluntary act and deed, ver. 12; he laid down his life freely, not by compulsion, John x. 15, 18; Mark x. 45. Hence let us observe,

3. *The general nature of his sufferings.* They were evidently vicarious; or sufferings endured by him as a substitute for others.

He became an *offering* for the *sin* of others, in their stead, 2 Cor. v. 21; 1 Pet. iii. 18. He bore the iniquities of *others.* "He shall bear their iniquities," or the punishment due to their iniquities, by just desert; as the loss of divine comfort, the curse and death. Gal. iii. 13, 14, "Christ hath," &c. His sufferings were a *"travail;"* this implies that they were pains endured by him, for the benefit of others:—to make them heirs of glory, Heb. ii. 10; to heal them, Isa. liii. 5; and bring them to God, 1 Pet. iii. 18. This leads us to consider,

III. THE HAPPY EFFECTS OF HIS SUFFERINGS. In consequence thereof,

1. *He shall prolong his days.* By rising from death to immortal life, Rev. i. 18. This was effected by himself; according to his own declarations, John ii. 19, and x. 18.—And it was the reward of his obedience unto death, Isa. liii. 12; Phil. ii. 8—11.

2. *He shall justify many by his knowledge.* "By his knowledge," &c. This implies, that through or by the knowledge of him, many will obtain justification.—By justification is meant the forgiveness of sins. Compare Acts xiii. 33 and 39. The knowledge of Christ includes a just view of him as the only acceptable mediator betwixt God and men, John xiv. 6; 1 Tim. ii. 5; a cordial approbation of him, 1 Cor. ii. 2; and affiance in him, Ps. ix. 10. All who thus know him, are justified through and by him, Rom. v. 1; Acts xiii. 39.

3. *He shall see his seed:* or his posterity, the fruit of his travail. This shall be a *numerous* seed, Heb. ii. 10; Psa. ii. 8, and cx. 3. And a *hopeful* seed; a general blessing, Matt. v. 13, 14; and finally happy, Isa. xxxv. 10. He shall *see* his seed: see them *flocking to him* for salvation, Isa. lx. 8; see them *saved by him* on earth, Isa. viii. 18; and *glorified with him* in heaven, Rev. iii. 21, and xvii. 14.

4. *The pleasure of the Lord shall prosper in his hand.*—The pleasure of the Lord is his Church; the object of his delight, Isa. lxii. 4; Psa. cxlvii. 11.—This is in Christ's hand; under his government and care, Deut. xxxiii. 3; John x. 27, 28.—It shall prosper there; be kept uninjured, Matt. xvi. 18, and extend universally, Dan. ii. 44.

5. *He shall see of the travail of his soul, and shall be satisfied.* He shall witness the blessings enjoyed by his redeemed servants: their interest in God's favor; their spiritual life, comfort, and honor, Rev. vii. 15—17. And seeing this he will be well pleased that he has endured the curse, death, grief, and shame for them, Psa. xxxv. 27; Zeph. iii. 17. From Christ's sufferings,

1. *Learn your obligations to cultivate a spirit of contrition,* or godly sorrow, on account of sin. Because your sins occasioned his sufferings at first, Zech. xii. 10. And they have since crucified him afresh, Heb. vi. 6; Psa. xxxviii. 18.

2. *Your encouragement, if penitent, to hope for salvation.* For Christ was *given* for your benefit, Rom. viii. 32, and is *exalted* for your benefit, Psa. lxviii. 18.

3. *God's claims on you as the subjects of redeeming grace.* On your services, 1 Cor. vi. 19, 20; Rom. xii. 1; Psa. cxvi. 1, 2; Rev. i. 5, 6. "Unto him that loved us," &c.

A SKETCH FOR GOOD FRIDAY.

John i. 29.—Behold the Lamb of God, which taketh away the sin of the world. (Sk.)

THE death of our Lord Jesus Christ, considered as the only saving remedy for a perishing world, demands our serious attention every day in the year; but on that particular day which is set apart by the christian church for the commemoration of his last sufferings, we should examine the subject with deep seriousness and awful reverence. The results of our examinations will amply repay our careful and diligent inquiries; for thereby we shall gain clear views of a subject, which of all others, is the most important to man; we shall feel ourselves deeply humbled before God, under a sense of those sins which nailed our Saviour to the tree; and our drooping spirits will be revived and cheered with a hope of salvation, by him who suffered on the cross. Our text points out Christ as the Lamb of God; affirms that he taketh away the sin of the world; and exhorts sinful men to behold him.

I. JESUS CHRIST IS THE LAMB OF GOD.

1. *The paschal Lamb was a type of Christ.* A parallel might be drawn in many important particulars; but we shall only mention one: by the death of that lamb, and the sprinkling of its blood upon the door posts, all the first-born of Israel were saved from death, Exod. xii. 6, 7; and we are assured by an inspired writer, that "even Christ our passover is sacrificed for us," 1 Cor. v. 7; and by his death, and the sprinkling of his blood, we are saved from wrath, Rom. v. 9.

2. *But Jesus is called the Lamb of God, especially in reference to the daily sacrifice,* which was offered up every morning and evening continually, and was a standing type of him, Exod. xxix. 38, 39. The lambs which were offered in the daily sacrifice, were to be without blemish, and our Saviour was without sin, 1 Peter i. 19; they made a *typical* atonement, but he made a *real* atonement, 1 John ii. 2; they were offered frequently, being imperfect; but our Lord was but once offered, being an *all-perfect* offering and sacrifice, Heb. ix. 25, 26.

3. *The prophet Isaiah foretold the Jewish nation, that the Messiah would be brought as a lamb to the slaughter,* and that "as a sheep before her shearers is dumb, so he would not open his mouth," chapter liii. 7. In this prediction, two things are clearly stated, first, the death of Jesus as a slaughtered lamb; and, secondly, his patience in that awful scene. He was manifested in the flesh to destroy the works of the devil, 1 John iii. 8; and to accomplish that great object, "it behoved him to suffer, and to rise from the dead," Luke xxiv. 46.

4. *Jesus now appears, as a lamb slain, in the heavenly world,* Rev. v. 6. That appearance, in all probability, is intended to remind glorified human spirits of their salvation by his atonement; and hence, while this great truth is denied by some on earth, it is celebrated with songs of praise, by the redeemed of the Lord, verse 8; and they ascribe to the Lamb who redeemed them, power and riches, strength and honor, and glory and blessing, ver. 12.

5. *Other things are affirmed of Jesus, as an atoning Lamb, which prove the propriety of this appellation.* The sanctification of the saints in heaven is ascribed to his blood, where it is said, they "have washed their robes and made them white in the blood of the Lamb," Rev. vii. 14; they overcame the accuser of the brethren, by the blood of the Lamb, chap. xii. 11; and they are made kings and priests unto God, by his blood, chap. i. 5.

II. He taketh away the sin of the world.

1. *The sin of Adam in the garden of Eden, affected the whole world of mankind*, Rom. v. 17-21 ; 1 Cor. xv. 21 ; but it is so far taken away by the Lamb of God, that all men will rise from the dead, and no man will suffer in the eternal world for what he did, 1 Cor. xv. 22 ; Ezek. xviii. 20.

2. *But by the sin of the world is meant, all the sins of men, whether Jews or Gentiles;* including every kind of sin, unless we may except that against the Holy Ghost, Matt. xii. 32 ; and every degree of sin ; so that a remedy is provided for all who go astray, Isa. liii. 6.

3. *Jesus taketh away sin, by the sacrifice of himself once offered,* Heb. x. 12 ; 1 Peter iii. 18 ; and all the sin which is taken away, is through his precious blood, Heb. ix. 32 ; for no man can remove his own sin from his conscience, nor can any man take away the sin of his brother, or give a ransom for him, Psa. xlix. 7 ; neither is there salvation in any other name than that of Jesus, Acts iv. 12.

4. *When men repent and believe the gospel, the guilt of their sin is taken away, by the Lamb of God;* and they are justified, accepted, and adopted into the family of God, Mark i. 15 ; Rom. v. 1 ; Eph. i. 6 ; Rom. viii. 16.

5. *By faith, the pollution of sin is taken away.* It is expressly affirmed, that we are sanctified by faith in Christ Jesus, Acts xxv. 18 ;—that our hearts are purified by faith, Acts xv. 9 ;—and that " the blood of Jesus Christ cleanseth us from all sin," 1 John i. 7.

6. *Through Jesus the Lamb of God, the practice of sin is taken away:* hence his followers excel in all holy conversation and godliness, 2 Peter iii. 11 ;—for he saves them from their sins, Matt. i. 21. Being saved by grace, they deny " ungodliness and worldly lusts," and " live soberly, righteously, and godly in this present world," Titus ii. 12.

7. *The tormenting fears which accompany sin, are taken away by the Lamb of God, from all who are perfected in love,* 1 John iv. 18 ;—so that they are no longer tormented, like other men, with frightful fears of death and hell, but rejoice in hope of the glory of God, Rom. v. 2.

8. *The sad effects of sin in a future state, will be taken away by the Lamb of God, from all who die in the Lord,* Rev. xiv. 13.—They will have a blessed and glorious resurrection, 1 Cor. xv. 51, 52 ;—they will appear with boldness in the day of judgment, 1 John iv. 17 ;—and they will " be for ever with the Lord," 1 Thess. iv. 18.

9. *All the sin which was taken away before Christ suffered for men, was taken away by him.* He was to be the Saviour, and when the first promise was made, the gospel day began to dawn, Gen. iii. 15. From that day to this, men have been placed in his hands, as the only Mediator; and through his gracious undertakings, the channels of mercy were opened immediately after the fall of our first parents.

10. *And if sin be taken away in the heathen world, it is by the Lamb of God;* for, through his blood, they may come " from the east and from the west, and from the north and from the south, and sit down in the kingdom of God," Luke ix. 29. Thus, " in every nation, he that feareth God and worketh righteousness, is accepted," through him who died for all, Acts x. 35.

III. Sinful men ard exhorted to behold him.

1. *The persons to whom these words were addressed by John the Baptist, beheld the Saviour with eyes of flesh;* for he was present among them, in his human body. In this sense we cannot see him, because he has left our world, and is gone to the Father, John xvi. 28.

2. *But we behold him by the eye of faith,* which enables us to look at things which are not seen, by the eye of the body, 2 Cor. iv. 18 ;—but all the internal views of the mind must be directed by that which is revealed in the written word, or we shall fall into foolish imaginations, 2 Cor. x. 5.

3. *To behold him as a religious duty, is to believe in him, and to trust in him for salvation,* Isa. xlv. 22 ;—and this is not merely one act of the mind, at some certain period of our lives, but a continued act, expressed by *looking* to Jesus, Heb. xii. 2.

4. Behold him in his *birth* at Bethlehem, in his *holy life* among the wicked Jews, in his *death* on Mount Calvary, in his *resurrection* from the dead, and in his *ascension* to heaven, where " he ever liveth to make intercession," Heb. vii. 25. Place these wonderful events, as they are recorded in the *Book*, before the eye of contemplation.

5. *Carefully behold him in his sacred offices.*—He was a prophet to guide us into all truth, Acts iii. 22, 23 ;—a Priest to atone and intercede, Heb. iv. 14 ;—and a King to govern and protect us, Rev. xvii. 14, xix. 16. Proper views of these offices will cheer your hearts, strengthen your hands, and inspire you with a blessed hope.

6. *As christian believers, behold him in his person.* He " is over all, God blessed for ever," Rom. ix. 5 ; he is man, in the proper sense of the word, having a reasonable soul, and a body which died and rose again, Luke ii. 52 ;—and he is God-man, and Mediator between God and men, 1 Tim. ii. 5.

7. *It becomes us to behold him with profound humility.*—He had no sin of his own, either original or actual, Heb. vii. 26 ;—but he suffered for our sins, and was " wounded for our transgressions," Isa. liii. 5 ; a thought which should lay us in the dust, and keep us there all the days of our lives.

8. *But behold him with grateful feelings.*—We love him because he is lovely ; but, especially, because he first loved us, 1 John iv. 19. Had he not undertaken our cause, we should have been lost, and what but love could have moved him to die for us ? Rom. v. 8.

9. *Hence we may behold him with entire confidence.*—His love is a proof that he is willing to save us ; and we know " he is able to save to the uttermost," Heb. vii. 25.—He offers salvation, Acts xiii. 26 ; he invites us to go to him, Matt. xi. 28 ; and he knocks at the door of our hearts, Rev. iii. 20.

10. *While we view him as our Saviour, let us also behold him as our exemplar.*—There are good examples among men, but they are all imperfect ; the example of Jesus should be placed before our eyes in all states and circumstances of life ; and we should endeavor to imitate him, as far as may be proper, in all our works, and in all our ways. To attempt an imitation of him in all things would be rash presumption ; but while we follow his hospitality, meekness, patience, zeal, love, and obedience, we shall be both safe and happy, 1 Peter ii. 21.

We conclude by observing, that all who thus behold the Lamb of God, shall see him at the end of the world with great joy ; that they shall meet him in the air, and that they shall remain with him as their bridegroom, in a blessed and glorious state of immortality, Rev. xxi. 2–9. Amen.

IT IS FINISHED.

John xix. 30.—It is finished.   (P.)

THESE words may be considered as including the following particulars :—
I. THE HUMILIATION AND SUFFERINGS OF THE SAVIOUR WERE FINISHED.

1. His humiliation was profound : He condescended to take humanity—was distinguished by poverty—had not where to lay his head.

2. His sufferings were intense : He was arrayed in mock royalty for the sport of a wanton crowd—suffered the excruciating death of the cross—endured the thunderbolts of divine vengeance.

3. But the sufferings and humiliation of Christ were now terminated.

II. THE PROPHECIES OF THE OLD TESTAMENT WERE NOW FULLY ACCOMPLISHED.

1. The prophets had predicted all the remarkable events in the Saviour's life : He was to be born of a virgin, at Bethlehem—to be despised and rejected by his countrymen—to bear his sufferings with meekness and resignation—to be numbered with transgressors—not a bone to be broken—to be cut off, but not for himself.

2. These prophecies receive their full accomplishment, as appears from the Evangelical history.

III. THE MOSAICAL DISPENSATION WAS NOW FOR EVER ABOLISHED.

1. This dispensation was only a typical institution.

2. It was now abolished—oblation and sacrifice were to cease—the veil of the temple was rent, as an indication of divine authority for its abolition.

3. The Jews were no longer the exclusive objects of the divine favor—the gospel was to be preached to the Gentiles also.

IV. THE REDEMPTION OF THE GUILTY WAS NOW COMPLETELY ACCOMPLISHED.

1. Man was in a state which required redemption.

2. The justice and veracity of the divine character demanded a satisfaction for sin.

3. This satisfaction was rendered by the Saviour—in the nature which had offended, and to the extent that the law required.

V. THE EMPIRE OF SATAN WAS FOR EVER DESTROYED.

1. The world was in bondage to the prince of darkness—led captive by the devil at his will.

2. This enemy was conquered by the Saviour—at his temptation in the wilderness, when he expelled him from those he possessed, and triumphed over him on his cross.

CONCLUSION.—Be grateful for the dispensation under which you live.

THE BENEFIT ARISING TO CHRIST FROM HIS OWN SUFFERINGS.

Heb. v. 7—9.—Who in the days of his flesh, when he had offered up prayers and supplications, with strong crying and tears, unto him that was able to save him from death, and was heard in that he feared, though he were a son, yet learned he obedience by the things which he suffered ; and being made perfect, he became the author of eternal salvation unto all them that obey him.   (S. S.)

THE priestly office, as marked out by God, belonged exclusively to the tribe of Levi—Yet our Lord, though he was not of that tribe to which the priesthood appertained, was truly and properly ¿ High Priest—He was constituted a priest of a different order from that of Aaron—And executed the duties of the priesthood in a far different manner than it was possible for any other person to perform them—He offered not the blood of bulls and of goats, but his own body, for the sins of the world—The apostle describing the manner in which he ministered, sets before us,

I. His conduct under his sufferings.

Never were the sufferings of any creature comparable with those of Christ.

His bodily sufferings perhaps were less than many of his followers have been called to endure*—But those of his soul were infinitely beyond our conceptions, Ps. xxii. 14, 15, with Matt. xxvi. 38—The assaults of Satan, and the wrath of God, combined to produce that bloody sweat in the garden of Gethsemane—Luke xxii. 44.

Under them he poured out his heart in prayer unto his heavenly Father.

He never lost sight of God as his Father, but addressed him with the greater earnestness under that endearing title, Mark xiv. 36—He knew that his Father was "able to save him from death"—He therefore repeatedly besought him to remove the bitter cup, and urged his petitions "with strong cries and floods of tears"—Not that he repented of the work he had undertaken; but only desired such a mitigation of his sufferings as might consist with his Father's glory, and the salvation of men—†

Nor did he desist from prayer till he had obtained his request.

Him the Father always heard—Nor was an answer now denied him—He was delivered from that which he chiefly deprecated‡—Though the cup was not removed, he was not suffered to faint in drinking it—He was strengthened by an angel in answer to his prayer, Luke xxii. 43—And clearly shewed what an answer he had received. by the dignified composure with which he immediately resigned himself into the hands of his enemies—John xviii. 4—8, 11.

His sufferings indeed could not be dispensed with; but they were amply recompensed by,

II. The benefit he derived from them.

The benefits accruing to our Lord from his own sufferings were.

1. Personal.

It was necessary for him as our high Priest to experience every thing which his people are called to endure in their conflicts with sin and Satan, Heb. ii. 17—Now the difficulty of abiding faithful to God in arduous circumstances is exceeding great—This is a trial which all his people are called to sustain—And under it they more particularly need his almighty succour—This therefore he submitted to learn—Though as the Son of God he knew all things in a speculative manner, yet he could not know this *experimentally*, but by being reduced to a suffering condition—This therefore was one benefit which he derived from his sufferings—He learned by them more tenderly to sympathize with his afflicted people, and more speedily to succour them when imploring his help with strong crying and tears—Ib. ver. 18.

*It is possible indeed that the perfect temperature of his body might give a more exquisite sensibility to the organs: but this is no where affirmed in scripture.

†John xii. 27, 28.—As a *man*, he could not but feel, and as a *good* man, he could not but deprecate the wrath of God: but he desired nothing that was inconsistent with the divine will, Matt. xxvi. 39.

‡The learned differ about the sense of ἀπὸ τῆς εὐλαβίας: some translate it *pro reverentia* others *ex metu*. See Beza on Heb. v. 7.

2. Official.

As the priests were *consecrated* to their office by the blood of their **sacrifices**, so was Jesus by his own blood*—From that time he had a right to impart salvation—From that time also he exercised that right—The persons indeed to whom alone he is "the author of eternal salvation," are, "those who obey him"—Not that they possess this qualification *before* he vouchsafes his mercy to them—But he invariably transforms his people into his own image—And makes them, like himself, obedient unto death—Phil. ii. 8.

We may LEARN from hence.

1. What we should do under sufferings, or a dread of God's displeasure.

We should not hastily conclude that we are not his children—Heb. xii. 6, We should rather go with humble boldness to God as our Father, Luke xv. 17, 18—We should plead his gracious promises, Ps. l. 15—Nor can we possibly be too earnest, provided we be content that his will should be done—(Alas! that there should be so little resemblance between our prayers and those of Christ!)—We should however consider *that* as the best answer to prayer, which most enables us to glorify God—

2. Whither to go for salvation.

The Father was "able to save his Son from death"—And doubtless he can save *us* also—But he has exalted his Son to be a Prince and a Saviour, Acts v. 31—To Christ therefore we are to go, and *to the Father through Christ*, Eph. ii. 18—In this way we shall find him to be the author of eternal salvation to us—Heb. vii. 25.

3. What is to be our conduct when he has saved us.

Jesus died "to purchase to himself a peculiar people zealous of good works"—We must therefore *obey* him, and that too as willingly in seasons of severe trial as in times of peace—We must be content to be conformed to the likeness of our Lord and Master—Let us be faithful unto death, and he will give us a crown of life—Rev. ii. 10.

CERTAIN SUCCESS OF CHRIST'S UNDERTAKING.

Isaiah liii. 10.—And the pleasure of the Lord shall prosper in his hand. (Pr.)

IN no part of the prophetic writings are the humiliation and sufferings of Christ detailed with such affecting minuteness as in this chapter, and inveterate indeed must have been the blindness and unbelief of the Jews, not to perceive and admit the force of such overwhelming evidence. The same prophecy however foretold that the report would not be believed, and that when the Saviour should appear he would be rejected and despised of men. Nevertheless he shall see his seed, he shall prolong his days, and the pleasure of the Lord shall prosper in his hand.

I. OFFER A FEW EXPLANATORY REMARKS ON THE TERMS OF THE TEXT.

1. By "the pleasure of the Lord" we are to understand, *his purposes concerning the cause of Christ*.— — —It was an important part of his good pleasure, that sinners should be redeemed by the blood of Christ, and this he delighted to accomplish. Psa. xl. 6—8. But this part of the will of God

---

*Τελειωθεὶς sometimes means "*consecrated;*" see Heb. vii. 28.

is supposed in the text to be already effected, and that another part is immediately to follow, relating to the progress of Christ's kingdom.

2. The success of Christ's undertaking, in the universal spread of the gospel, is called *the pleasure of the Lord*, because it is an object of his eternal purpose, and the end he had in view in the creation of the world. Col. i. 16.— — —It is true indeed, the accomplishment of God's design is said to be his pleasure, even when it relates to the punishment of his enemies; for " he will do his pleasure on Babylon, and his arm shall be on the Chaldeans;" but that in which he takes peculiar delight is the enlargement of Christ's kingdom. God takes pleasure in all his works, but more in the work of redemption than any ●ther, and more still in rewarding the obedience and sufferings of his well-beloved Son, than in putting him to grief. John x. 17; Phil. ii. 9.

3. The great work of subduing the world is here placed *in the hand of Christ.*— — —The work of redeeming sinners was committed to him, and he succeeded in that; and now the work of subduing the nations to the obedience of faith, is put into his hand. He is head over all things to the church, and all shall be made subservient to his will. All power in heaven and earth is given unto him, and he is sending forth his armies, that he may rule in the midst of his enemies, and triumph over all the earth. Psa. xlv. 3, 4, cx. 1—3.

4. It is here foretold that the work of Christ *shall certainly succeed*, and the pleasure of the Lord " shall prosper in his hand."— — —If placed in other hands it would have failed, but with him it must prosper. Adam was constituted the federal head of his posterity, but he failed in the undertaking, and all were ruined. Moses was charged with the redemption of Israel, but he failed of bringing them into the promised land; and as to the eternal salvation of any of them, it was effected only by the death of Christ, and not by the law of Moses. All others have failed and been discouraged, but he shall set judgment in the earth, and the isles shall wait for his law. Thousands among the Jews, and tens of thousands among the Gentiles, have submitted to his authority; and he shall still go on and prosper, till the whole earth be filled with his glory.

II. Consider the reasons why the pleasure of the Lord should prosper in the hand of Christ.

Two things are generally necessary to the success of any great undertaking; one is, personal fitness or qualification, and the other, the means of accomplishing the design.

1. Christ possesses, in an eminent degree, *the qualifications* necessary to the work he has undertaken.— — —Great and unconquerable zeal is required, where the work is arduous and attended with great difficulty, and nothing can be done without it. If a man, from mere worldly motives, engages in the work of the ministry, he will not be likely to succeed; his efforts and his zeal are totally inadequate to so important an undertaking. But Christ's heart was wholly set upon what he undertook, and his zeal shall bring it to pass. Isa. lxiii. 4.— — —Wisdom also is required. A good intention, accompanied with ardent exertions, is not sufficient; wisdom and understanding are necessary to conduct things to a proper issue; and these qualifications are possessed in an eminent degree by the blessed Saviour. Isa. iii. 13.— — —Faithfulness also to his engagements was eminently verified in him. Isa. xi. 5; Heb. iii. 2.

2. Christ possesses *all the necessary means* for carrying on his own cause in the world.— — —In consequence of his death the Holy Spirit is given,

243

to convince the world of sin, and to give success to a preached gospel.—— Christ is able also to save to the uttermost them that come unto God by him, and that in consequence of his intercession before the throne. He can keep us from falling, and present us faultless before the presence of his glory with exceeding joy.— — —All the arrangements of providence are in his hands; the fate of kingdoms and of empires, and whatever is necessary to the prosperity of his own most righteous cause, are entirely at his command.

Let us reflect, 1. That as God has entrusted his own glory in the hands of Christ, it becomes us to commit our all to him, that he may save us in the great day. 2. That those who labor with Christ in his cause have reason to take encouragement, for it is in his hands, and must finally prevail.

THE RESURRECTION OF CHRIST, GLAD TIDINGS.

Acts xiii. 32, 33. We declare unto you glad tidings,, how that the promise which was made unto the fathers, God hath fulfilled the same unto us their children, in that he hath raised up Jesus again; as it is written in the second Psalm, Thou art my Son, this day have I begotten thee. (S. S.)

THE resurrection of Christ was the foundation, whereon the whole edifice of our religion was built. To that Jesus himself directed his diciples to look forward as the evidence of his Messiahship; and, after he had risen, he appeared to them repeatedly for the space of forty days, that they might be enabled to testify of it with the fullest assurance. A select number were chosen by him for the very purpose of bearing witness to this wonderful event: and because St. Paul had not enjoyed the same advantage as the other apostles, he was favored with a vision of his Lord long after his removal from the sight of all other mortals, in order that he, as well as the others, might be able to testify of it from ocular demonstration.

In the words before us he speaks of Christ's resurrection.

1. AS AN ACCOMPLISHMENT OF PROPHECY.

The passage quoted by the apostle is very properly applied to this subject.

The Psalms were in the apostle's days arranged in the same order as they now are. And the scope of the second Psalm is to declare the triumph of Jesus over all his enemies by means of his resurrection from the grave, and of his consequent exaltation to the right hand of God. And he might well be said to be "begotten" in the day of his resurrection, because he was then formed anew, as it were, from the earth.

It is confirmed also by many other passages that predict the same truth.

As it was foreordained by God, so it was foretold in a variety of ways. Sometimes it was exhibited in types,* and sometimes in prophecies.† In one scripture, not quoted indeed in this place, but cited no less than six times in the New Testament, this marvellous event was predicted in terms so plain

*Isaac being put to death, as it were, by his own father, was received again from the dead in a figure, Heb. xi. 19. Jonah was raised again on the third day from the belly of a fish, Matt. xii. 39, 40. The living bird that was let loose after having been dipped in the blood of the bird that had been slain, represented Jesus as ascending to heaven with his own blood, Lev. xiv. 51, 53, with Heb ix. 12.

†Ver. 34, 35, with Isa. lv. 3, which certainly must include the resurrection of him that was to be "the leader and commander," and Ps. xvi. 10, which is so largely commented upon by St. Peter, Acts ii, 26--31.

that none could misunderstand it, who did not obstinately shut their eyes against the truth. Ps. cxviii. 22, with Luke xx. 17.

We must not however suppose this to be an uninteresting fact: for the apostle further speaks of it.

II. As GLAD TIDINGS TO THE SOUL.

To the disconsolate disciples the tidings of Christ's resurrection were doubtless exceeding joyful. But they ought to be no less so to us, since that event ascertains.

1. The virtue of his sacrifice.

Had he not risen, his death had been in vain. 1 Cor. xv. 14, 17, 18. We could have had no evidence that our debt was discharged, if our surety had not been liberated from the prison of the grave. But his resurrection clearly proved that he had satisfied the demands of law and justice, and it thereby affords us a ground of assured hope, and triumphant exultation. Rom. iv, 25, and viii. 34.

2. His sufficiency for our help.

If he were still dead, it would be in vain to look to him for help. But, when he had raised up himself, John x. 17, 18, and spoiled all the principalities and powers of hell, Col. ii. 15, and been exalted on purpose that he might be a Prince and a Saviour to give repentance to Israel and remission of sins, Acts v. 31, what may we not expect at his hands? Surely he is declared thereby to be the Son of God with power, Rom. i. 4, and to be able to save us to the uttermost. Heb. vii. 25. Let us only seek to know him in the power of his resurrection; Phil. iii. 10; and nothing shall be impossible unto us. Mark ix. 23.

3. The certainty of our own resurrection.

Our resurrection depended altogether upon his: if he had not risen, neither should we have risen: but because he rose, we shall rise also. Christ is the first-fruits, which, while it sanctified, assured also the whole harvest. 1 Cor. xv. 20. He is our forerunner, who is gone to heaven to prepare places for us, and will come again to raise us to the possession of them. Heb. vi. 20, John xiv. 2, 3. We therefore may consider death and the grave as vanquished for us, and look forth to the complete triumph which we ourselves shall have over them in the last day. 1 Cor. xv. 53—55. Because he liveth, we may be sure that we shall live also. John xiv. 19.

As a further IMPROVEMENT of this passage, permit me to observe,

1. How deeply are we interested in the writings of the Old Testament!

In them are promises of which we receive the accomplishment. The word of God is not of private interpretation, 2 Pet. i. 20, as though it belonged only to this or that individual. Many parts doubtless had a *peculiar* reference to those to whom they were spoken; but none have an *exclusive* reference. Let us then embrace the promises as spoken to ourselves, compare Josh. i. 5, with Heb. xiii. 5, 6, and expect the fulfilment of them to our own souls.

2. What enemies are they to themselves who despise the ministry of the gospel!

Many, when the gospel is preached to them, are ready to say, like the devils, We beseech thee torment us not. Matt. viii. 29, and Luke viii. 28. Yes, they look on faithful ministers as the troublers of Israel. 1 Kings xviii. 17. But the scope of our ministry is to " *declare glad tidings*," even to proclaim a crucified, and an exalted Saviour. Let any one contemplate the foregoing subject, and see whether it do not afford matter for rejoicing. Let men only forsake their sins, and we have not a word to utter which will not administer to them an occasion of joy.

245

3. What a near relation subsists between believers in all ages!

They are our fathers, and we their children. We are all of one family, all united to one head, Eph. i. 10, Heb. xii. 23, and all heirs of the same glory. Let us enjoy this thought, and look forward to the time when we shall sit down with all the patriarchs and prophets in the kingdom of our God. Matt. viii. 11, Luke xiii. 28.

THE MANIFESTATION OF CHRIST TO HIS DISCIPLES AFTER HIS RESURRECTION.

John xx. 19, 20.—Then the same day at evening, being the first day of the week, when the doors were shut where the disciples were assembled for fear of the Jews, came Jesus, and stood in the midst, and said unto them, Peace be unto you, &c. (Sk.)

When Paul preached before king Agrippa, concerning the sufferings of Christ and his resurrection from the dead, he made his appeal for the verity of the facts, to the publicity with which they were attended : " For the king knoweth of these things. before whom also I speak freely : for I am persuaded that none of these things are hidden from him ; for this thing was not done in a corner." Jesus Christ was a public character; what he did was for the benefit of the world.; and so far was he from concealing his designs, that he adopted the most successful methods to give notoriety to his acts, and extension to his plans. Multitudes heard his sermons, saw his miracles, witnessed his sufferings, and beheld his death : " And he showed himself alive after his passion, by many infallible proofs ; being seen of his disciples forty days, and speaking of the things pertaining to the kingdom of God." The text furnishes us with one of these proofs, and suggests several profitable topics for discussion. In it we have,

I. The appearance of Christ to his disciples. "The same day," &c. " where the disciples were assembled, came Jesus and stood in the midst." Here notice,

1. *The disciples were assembled.* Christ's disciples are accustomed to meet together ;—*love* leads them to do this; they love one another with pure hearts fervently :—*duty* binds them to come together, " Not forsaking the assembling," &c., Heb. x. 25 ;—*mutual benefit* excites them to associate with each other; Christ comes among them, Matt. xviii. 20. The world has its assemblies,— pleasure its assemblies,—commerce its assemblies,—and Christ's disciples their assemblies.

2. *This was a select assembly.* Promiscuous companies for the purpose of public and devotional exercises, such as singing, prayer, and preaching, have been sanctioned by the practice of all ages ; but these are not meant to set aside the use of select meetings, assemblies of disciples.

3. *It was private.* "The doors were shut." The peal of slander has long been rung against private meetings, and the vilest scenes have been associated with them ; but while we have such an example as this before our eyes, we may bid defiance to the revilings of men : fear of the Jews induced them to shut the doors: they had seen the storm of persecution that fell upon Christ, and fear suggested that a similar fate awaited them. Faith in God is the best antidote to the fear of man, Psa. lvi. 3 ;—" What time I am afraid." &c.

4. *It was in the evening.* Evenings are favorable for religious assemblies; multitudes are then at leisure, the business of the day is closed, and what can be more proper than to spend an hour, ere we retire to rest, in the worship of God?

5. *It was immediately after our Lord's resurrection.* How solicitous he was to cheer the minds of his disconsolate disciples; five distinct times he appeared to them the same day—a memorable day!—the first day of the week; what St. John calls the Lord's day;—a day which has been kept by christians to commemorate that extraordinary event, the resurrection of Christ. Though the doors were shut, yet Jesus entered: it is possible he might have done that in the ordinary way, without their observing it; or his entrance might have been miraculous,—" With God all things are possible."

II. THE BENEDICTION HE PRONOUNCED UPON THEM. He " said unto them, Peace be unto you:" this was his usual salutation. His disciples were charged to use a similar address, Luke x. 5;—Jesus Christ is the Prince of peace,—his kingdom is the kingdom of peace,—and his benediction is the blessing of peace. This benediction was designed,

1. *To dissipate their fears.* When Christ once appeared to them in a storm, they were afraid, and thought they saw a Spirit; hs then said, " Be of good cheer," &c., Matt. xiv. 27. Similar feelings were most probably excited now, but Jesus said, " Peace be unto you."

2. *To calm their troubled consciences.* The recollection of their cowardly conduct, in deserting their Master in his great extremity, must have been a source of deep anguish to them; and when they saw Christ standing personally before them, it would be natural enough to imagine thar he came with a design to upbraid them with their cowardice and crime: but he said, " Peace be unto you."

3. *As the medium of communicating good.* When Christ speaks peace, he communicates peace. When men use terms of commendation, however expressive they may be of their kindness towards us, they are mere words; but the words of Christ are the medium of communicating divine peace to us; " The words that I speak," &c., John vi. 63.

4. *As a prelude to their future success.* Peace among the Hebrews was a term of comprehensive import, including all blessings, temporal and spiritual. When Christ said " Peace be unto you," it was in effect saying—prosperity shall attend you.

III. THE SIGHT HE EXHIBITED TO THEM. " He showed unto them his hands and his side." This served to convince the disciples,

1. *That what they saw was real and not illusive.* The body which they beheld was that identical body which was laid in the sepulchre; and Christ showed unto them his hands and his side, to remove all their doubts. " Behold my hands and my feet, that it is I myself; handle me," &c., Luke xxiv. 37—40.

2. *To remind them of the love that he bore them, and the sufferings which he had endured for their sakes.* What could be more effecting? He showed unto them his hands—hands that had been transfixed to the cross—hands that still exhibited the prints of the nails; and he showed unto them his side, which had been pierced by the soldier's spear. Who can contemplate this tender and affecting scene, without exclaiming—behold how he loved them! Does the broken soldier exhibit his scars, and the marks of his wounds, to show that he has bled for his country?—so Christ showed his hands and side, to remind his disciples that he had bled for them. With the same body he now appears in the presence God for us. St. John saw in the

midst of the throne a lamb as it had been slain, &c. ;—and when Christ **shall** come enthroned in judgment, " every eye shall see him, and they also which pierced him," &c., Rev. i. 7.

IV. THE SENSATION THEY FELT ON BEHOLDING HIM. "Then were the disciples glad," &c. This gladness was,

1. *Founded in knowledge.* They knew that it was the Lord who had thus made himself visible to them ;—that it was he who had borne their griefs, and carried their sorrows They *saw* the Lord, they *heard* his voice, —and were favored with his benediction :—they knew that they were not deceived; they had the demonstration of their senses. The joy which God puts into the hearts of his people now, is of a similar kind ; not arising indeed from the perceptions of sense, but from the evidence of faith,—faith supplies the place of sense, Heb. xi. 1 ;—" Whom having not seen ye love," &c., 1 Pet. i. 8.

2. *Produced by love.* That the disciples had loved the Lord Jesus, none can doubt,—they had left all to follow him,—they had submitted to his instruction,—and continued with him in his temptation : it is true they had been scattered in a cloudy and dark day ; but they were now assembled to converse of him to whom their hearts clung with the fondest attachment ; and Jesus came and stood in the midst. Can we be surprised that the disciples were "glad when they saw the Lord ?" Gladness is opposed to grief ; they had seen the saddest sight that was ever exhibited in the world ; —a sight that made the sun to blush, and hide his head beneath the sable mantle of midnight ;—a sight that wrung their hearts with unutterable anguish ;—but the cause of their grief was removed ;—their Lord, who had been torn from them by the cruel hands of a lawless rabble, was now restored to them ;— he had been dead, but he was now alive again :—and " they saw the Lord."

3. *Associated with confidence.* The disciples entertained the most exalted ideas of their Master's character, but they had considerable doubts as to the result of his undertaking ; and when they saw him expire on the cross, they were almost ready to abandon hope, and sink into despair. He had indeed suggested that he should rise again from the dead, but they did not know what this rising from the dead could mean. But now " they saw the Lord," and their confidence was established ; as it would be natural for them to infer, that he who could burst the barriers of the tomb—reanimate his mortal frame—and terrify and disperse the Roman soldiery, *could do* whatsoever he pleased ; and that he *would* fulfil all his engagements, and accomplish all his promises.

From the text we have something,

1. *To confirm our faith.* The resurrection of Christ is attested by the most incontrovertible witnesses, who *could not* be deceived themselves, and *would not* deceive others.

2. *To guide our conduct.* Christ met his disciples when assembled ; therefore let us frequent the assemblies of the saints.

3. *To excite our expectations.* Christ comes to bless his people ; he said " Peace be unto you ; and he showed unto them," &c. Let us expect his blessing. Have we been ungrateful, fearful, or unbelieving ? So had the disciples, yet Christ blessed them ;—he is the same yesterday, to-day, and for ever ;—and he will bless his people with peace.

CHRIST THE RESURRECTION AND THE LIFE.

John xi. 25, 26.—Jesus said unto her, I am the resurrection and the. life: he that believeth in me, though he were dead, yet shall he live: and whosoever liveth and believeth in me, shall never die. (S. S.)

In great and long continued afflictions, we are apt to entertain hard thoughts of God. But, whatever be his intention with respect to the ungodly, we are sure that he designs nothing but good to his own peculiar people, even when he appears most regardless of their supplications. There are two ends which he invariably proposes to himself in his dispensations towards them; namely, the brighter revelation of his own glory, and the fuller manifestation of it to their souls.

In the history before us we have an account of a heavy affliction that had befallen a family, through the death of one, to whom Jesus had shewn a very peculiar attachment. He had been solicited to come and help them; but he had delayed his visit till the sick person had been dead four days. This however, though liable to misconstruction, he had done intentionally, in order that he might manifest more fully to the disconsolate sisters his own power and glory. Accordingly, when they intimated their persuasion, that, if he would pray to God for the restoration of their brother to life, God would grant his request, he told them that he needed not beseech God to effect it; for that he himself was the resurrection and the life: and was able to impart either bodily or spiritual life to whomsoever he would.

In considering this most remarkable declaration, we shall notice,

I. That part which relates to himself.

Martha having, in conformity with the prevailing opinion of the Jews, expressed her expectation of a general resurrection at the last day, Jesus says to her

"I am the resurrection."

Our Lord, in his divine nature, possessed omnipotence necessarily, and of himself. In his mediatorial capacity he was invested with it by his Father, agreeably to the plan concerted in the divine counsels. To him who had undertaken to procure salvation for a fallen world, was delegated all power requisite for the full discharge of that office. The restoring of his people to a new and heavenly life after death, was essential to their complete salvation: this therefore was committed to him; John v. 21, 25—29; and he both declared he would execute this great work, John vi. 39, 40, and gave an earnest of its accomplishment in raising himself from the dead. John x. 18; 1 Cor. xv. 20.

"I am the life."

In this term our Lord proceeds further than in the former, and asserts, that as he is the author and first-fruits of the resurrection, so is he the very principle of life whereby his people live. This might indeed be collected from many figurative expressions of scripture, which represent him as the fountain of life to all his people: John xv 1; Eph. iv, 15, 16; but we are not left to gather such an important truth from mere parables; it is asserted frequently in the plainest terms: he is a quickening spirit, 1 Cor. xv. 45, that liveth in us, John xiv. 6. and vi. 57, and Gal. ii. 20, and is our very life. Col. iii. 4. He is to the soul, what the soul is to the body; he prevades, animates, and invigorates all our spiritual faculties: by his secret energy our understanding is enabled to apprehend divine truth, and our will inclined to

249

obey it: and, without him, the soul would be as dead as the body **without** the soul.

.Let us now prosecute our enquiries into,

II. THAT WHICH RESPECTS HIS PEOPLE.

There is a remarkable correspondence between the two latter, and the two former clauses of the text; the latter declaring the operation of the powers expressed in the former.

1. As being "the resurrection," he will raise the bodies of his people.

Judging of things according to our weak reason, we are ready to think that the restoration of bodies, which may have undergone so many changes, is impossible. But cannot he who formed the universe out of nothing, collect the atoms that constitute our identity, and reunite them to their kindred souls? he can, and will; yea, that very Jesus, who died upon the cross, has the keys of death and of hell, Rev. i. 18, and will effect this by his own almighty power. Phil. iii. 21.

This clause might further intimate, that by the first act of faith in him our souls should be made partakers of spiritual life. And this would accord with other passages of scripture, John vi. 33, 35, and vii. 38, and x. 10, and prepare us for the next clause, which, raising in a climax, declares the benefits that shall result from a continued life of faith upon him.

2. As being "the life," he will preserve the souls of his people unto everlasting life.

The bodies of the saints must undergo the sentence denounced against sin; Rom. viii. 10; (though death to *them* is scarcely worthy the name of death: it is rather a sleep, from which they shall be awakened at the morning of the resurrection,) ver. 11, Acts vii. 60, 1 Thess. iv. 14, but their souls shall never die: none shall prevail against them; Isa. liv. 17; none shall pluck them out of Christ's hands; John x. 28; their life is hid in him beyond the reach of men or devils; Col. iii. 3; the vital principle within them is an ever-living seed, 1 Pet. i. 23, an over-flowing fountain: John iv. 14; as long as Christ liveth, they shall live also. John xiv. 19. The separation that will take place between their souls and bodies will only introduce them to a higher state of existence. which they shall enjoy until the day that their bodies shall be awakened from their slumbers, to participate and enhance their bliss.

We must not however fail to notice the description given of those to whom these promises are made.

Twice, in these few words, are these blessings limited to believers: not because our Lord disregards good works, or because they shall not be rewarded; but because we cannot do any good work unless we first receive strength from Christ by faith; John xv. 5; and because, if we obtained life by working, we should have whereof to glory before God: and God has decreed that no flesh shall glory in his presence, and that we shall glory only in the Lord. Rom. iii. 27; Eph. ii. 8, 9; 1 Cor. i. 29—31. It must never be forgotten that God has caused all fulness to dwell in his Son, Jesus Christ; Col. i. 19; and that we must, by a continued exercise of faith, receive out of that fulness grace for grace. John i. 16. It is by faith that we live, Gal. iii. 11, we stand, 2 Cor. i. 24, we walk, 2 Cor. v. 7, we are saved: Gal. ii. 16; in a word, " God has given us eternal life; but this life is *in his Son:* he therefore that hath the Son, hath life; and he that hath not the Son of God, hath not life." 1 John v. 11, 12.

The pointed interrogation with which our Lord closed this address to Martha directs us how to IMPROVE this subject: it suggests to us,

1. That all persons, however eminent in their profession, or decided in their character, ought to " examine themselves whether they be in the faith."

It was to one whom he knew to be an humble and faithful disciple, that Jesus put this question: well therefore may we who are of more doubtful character, consider it as addressed to *us ; " *Believest thou this ?" Believest thou that Christ is the only fountain of life ; and that there is no way of receiving life from him but by faith ? And dost thou believe these things, not in a mere speculative manner (for *that* many do whose souls are dead before God) but in such a way as to reduce them to practice ? The believing of this record forms the one line of distinction between those that shall be saved, and those that shall perish. If we truly receive it, we have already passed from death unto life : John v. 24 ; if we do not receive it, we are yet dead in trespasses and sins : we have not life now ; we cannot have life hereafter. A resurrection indeed we shall partake of ; but it is a resurrection to damnation, and not a resurrection to life : Ib. 29 ; we shall live ; but it will be a life justly denominated death, the second death. Rev. xx. 14. Let us not then defer our enquiries into a subject which is of such infinite importance.

2. That the believing of this record is the most effectual antidote against the troubles of life, or the fears of death.

If Martha had felt the full influence of these truths, she would have moderated her sorrows, under the persuasion that her loss was her brother's gain ; and that, if her brother were not restored to life, she should soon meet him in a better world. Thus in every state the consideration of these truths will afford to us also unspeakable consolation : for, if we believe in Christ, and have through him the possession of spiritual, and the prospect of eternal life, what cause can we have to complain ; what cause to fear ? The world will be divested of its allurements, and death of its terrors. Satisfied that all events are under the control of our best friend, we shall commit them cheerfully to his wise disposal : and looking forward to the day in which he will call us from our graves, we shall expect his summons with composure at least, if not also with a holy impatience. Let us then live by faith on our divine Saviour, assured that he will keep us unto eternal life, and exalt us, both in body and soul, unto the everlasting enjoyment of his presence and glory.

A SKETCH FOR EASTER SUNDAY.

Collossians iii. 1.—"If ye then be risen with Christ, seek those things which are above, where Christ sitteth at the right hand of God." (Sk.)

The festival of our Lord's resurrection is called Easter, from the *goddess Eoster,* whose festival was held by her idolatrous worshippers, in the month of April. The Greekes call it κασχα, and the Latins *pascha,* from *Pasah* a Hebrew word which is applied to the Jewish passover. The Asiatic churches kept this festival on the very day that the Jews observed their passover ; others the first Sunday after the first full moon following the vernal equinox ; and this, after a sharp controversy, which cost many lives, was settled by the Council of Nice. But though the christian churches differed about the *time* of keeping this festival ; yet they all agreed in showing particular respect and honor to the *feast;* and surely it is a day of joy and gladness, of holy triumph and of blessed hope. Our Lord is risen from the dead; and those who are risen with him, should seek those things which are above.

1. OUR LORD IS RISEN FROM THE DEAD.

1. The *death* of Jesus is affirmed by all the Evangelists. This is important; for if he did not really die, it would be trifling to argue on his resurrection. *Matthew* informs us that "he cried with a loud voice and yielded up the ghost," chap. xxvii, 50; *Mark* says, "Jesus cried with a loud voice, and gave up the ghost," chap. xv. 37; *Luke* states, that, "when Jesus had cried with a loud voice, he said. Father, into thy hands I commend my spirit. And having said thus he gave up the ghost," chap. xxiii. 46; and *John* affirms, that "he bowed the head, and gave up the ghost," chap. xix. 30. And as a proof of his death, it is observed, that "one of the soldiers with a spear pierced his side, and forthwith came there out blood and water." John xix. 34.

2. The body of Jesus was *laid in a sepulchre, and means were used by his enemies to keep it there.* The Jews recollected "that he said, while he was yet alive, After three days I will rise again," Matt. xxvii. 36; therefore they requested a *watch* to guard the body lest it should be stolen away, ver. 64; and Pilate gave orders to make it as sure as they could, ver. 65; "so they went and made the sepulchre sure, sealing the stone, and setting a watch," ver. 66.

3. Every attempt of his enemies, *to prevent his resurrection, was baffled and confounded.* There was a great earthquake, Matt. xxviii. 2; "the angel of the Lord descended from heaven, and rolled back the stone from the door and sat upon it; his countenance was like lightning. and his raiment white as snow; and for fear of him the keepers did shake, and became as dead men," ver. 4.

4. After his passion, he showed himself alive by many *infallible proofs.* He was seen of his disciples forty days, speaking of the things pertaining to the kingdom of God, Acts, iii. 4. He showed himself to Mary, Mark xvi. 9; to other women, Matt. xxviii. 9; to two disciples going to Emmaus, Mark xvi. 12; to Peter Luke xxiv. 34; to all the disciples, John xx. 19; to them again, chap. xx. 26; to the disciples at the sea of Tiberias, chap. xxi. 1; to the disciples in Galilee, Matt. xxviii. 16, 17; to James. 1 Cor. xv. 7; to the eleven, Mark xvi. 14; and to above five hundred brethren at once, 1 Cor. xv. 6.

5. The disciples *could not be deceived in those appearances.* They knew his person, his voice, and his usual manner of address. They were not credulous; hence they rejected the story of the women concerning his being risen, Luke xxiv. 11; and one of them would not believe without the most substantial proofs of his resurrection, John xx. 25. They saw him *often;* they heard him *speak;* they handled his body, ver. 27; they ate and drank with him: and they saw him ascend to heaven, Acts i. 9–11.

6. In relating the resurrection of Jesus, *the disciples had no design to deceive others.* They were plain honest men; they told a plain and unvarnished tale; they were all of one mind; by their testimony of Jesus, they exposed themselves to dangers, toils, and death; the whole world, whether Jews or Gentiles, were opposed to them; of themselves they were weak and feeble, and yet they never deviated from the truth, but many of them sealed it with their blood. Thus the resurrection of our Lord, on which the whole of Christianity stands, is supported by such proofs, that the man who denies it must be pronounced either insane or abominably wicked.

7. In the resurrection of Jesus, *prophesies were fulfilled.* It was foretold

that he should not see corruption, Psa. xvi. 10 ; and our Lord himself, who was a true prophet, predicted his resurrection on the third day, Matt. xii. 40; John ii. 19. Had he risen sooner, his death might have deen doubted by some ; and had he remained longer in the grave, he would have seen corruption. It is true he was not three whole days and nights in the sepulchre, but he rose on the third day, for having been buried on Friday, he rose on the Sunday, or the first day of the week.

8. The resurrection of our Saviour is ascribed to the FATHER, Acts ii. 32; and to HIMSELF, John x. 18 ; a proof that he and the Father are ONE, in a higher sense than some professing christians are willing to allow, John x. 30.

9. *He rose on the first day of the week:* hence that has been called the Lord's day, Rev. i. 10 ; and has been observed as the christian sabbath, Acts xx. 7 ; and this is highly proper, because his resurrection was the commencement of the new creation, Col. i. 18.

10. His resurrection proves, beyond a doubt, that *all his undertakings for man were accepted.* Had he been what the Jews called him, a *deceiver,* he would never have risen from the dead. Omnipotent power could not have been exerted to restore the life of an imposter, after it had been justly taken away. In that case, his disciples would have been finally scattered, and christianity would have been unknown ; but the seal of divine approbation was put upon him when he rose again, so that all he had said was confirmed, and all he had done was approved.

11. Death was *conquered* by his resurrection. There had been instances before of persons rising from the dead ; but they only rose to a state of mortality. Jesus was the first who rose from the dead to die no more ; and is on this account, " the first fruits of them that slept," 1 Cor. xv. 20. Death, the last enemy, has been forced to deliver up his prey ; the grave, his prison house, has been thrown open; and this foe has yielded to the mighty conqueror.

12. Finally, *The resurrection of our Lord is a proof that we shall rise from the dead;* "but every man in his own order: Christ the first fruits ; afterwards they that are Christ's at his coming," 1 Cor. xv. 23. The resurrection will be general, " for as in Adam all die, even so in Christ shall all be made alive," ver. 22. Had not our Lord risen from the dead, we might have thought that event *incredible;* but fact has put this subject out of doubt, Acts xxvi. 8.

II. THOSE WHO ARE RISEN WITH CHRIST, SHOULD SEEK THE THINGS WHICH ARE ABOVE.

1. While we remain in a state of nature, *we are spiritually dead.* We have no union with God, Eph. ii. 12 ; we have no relish for divine things, Rom. viii. 5 ; we are at enmity against God, ver. 7 ; and of course, we are dead in trespasses and sins, Ephesians ii. 1.

2. When we hear the voice of the Son of God, and obey it, *we are brought into spiritual life,* John v. 25. We are called to repent and believe the gospel ; Mark i. 15 ; and when we do so, by that power which accompanies the call, we rise into life, John iii. 36 ; 1 John v. 12.

3. This blessed change implies a *quickening,* Col. ii. 13 ; a *new birth,* John iii. 3 ; a new *creation,* 2 Cor. v. 17 ; and in our text, a *resurrection* with Christ: and it is as much the work of God, though in concurrence with the will of man, as the creation of the world, or the resurrection of the dead.

4. When we feel this saving change, we are " begotten again to a *lively hope,* by the resurrection of Jesus Christ from the dead," 1 Pet. i. 3 ; and this blessed hope has for its object a glorious immortality, and " an inheritance incorruptible, undefiled, and that fadeth not away."

5. We cannot be at a loss to know what is meant by *the things which are above;* because they are said to be in that world where Christ sitteth at the right hand of God. Those things include all the light, all the glory, and all the felicity of the heavenly state. There we shall be completely happy; our companions will be saints and angels; our employment will be praise; and we shall have "fulness of joy," and pleasures for evermore, Psa. xvi. 11.

6. Much is implied in *seeking* those things : particularly a *knowledge* of them; a *love* for them; and an *ardent desire* to be put in the possession of those ineffable glories. With these dispositions, we should use all the appointed means; for those things must be sought with diligence, in the way of christian duty.

7. But let us seek in a *right way:* first, in the name of Jesus, John xiv. 6; secondly, by faith in him, Rom. ix. 32 ; thirdly, with earnestness or holy strivings, Luke xiii. 24 ; and, lastly, with steady perseverence to the end, 1 Cor. xv. 58.

8. On this plan, we shall soon find *a better world,* and be for ever with the Lord, 1 Thess. iv. 17. The crown will be given to us, Rev. ii. 10. White raiment will be put upon us, Rev. vii. 13. Palms of victory will be put into our hands, ver. 9; and "God shall wipe away all tears from our eyes," ver. 17.

INFERENCES.

1. The resurrection of Jesus is a subject of *vast importance* to us and to all mankind. If true christianity stands on a rock which cannot be shaken, and all the hopes of christians will be realized; but "if Christ be not risen," preaching is vain, and the faith of christians is also vain, 1 Cor. xv. 14.

2. But *of his resurrection there can be no doubt,* in the mind of any one who examines the subject with candour. To such a one, the proofs are *irresistible* and certain; unless we could admit that the apostles were *ignorant* of what they *knew;* that they *told lies for the sake of reproach and suffering;* and that they *united* to maintain, and died to confirm a most shameful ʼalsehood. Surely it requires more faith to be an infidel than a christian.

3. Those who believe in his resurrection and session at the right hand of God, should rise above the world; keep heaven in their view : and urge their way forward to the celestial city. There they will overtake the Saviour; behold him in his glory; and enjoy him for ever and ever. Amen.

THE ASCENSION OF CHRIST.

Mark xvi. 9.—So then after the Lord had spoken to them, he was received up into heaven, and sat on the right hand of God. (Sk.)

THE life of Christ was the most extraordinary and eventful life, that was ever led upon earth : a life anticipated by saints—poutrayed by prophets—prefigured by types, and in the fulness of time exhibited to the world. Every circumstance, therefore, that was disclosed in a life which was eminently designed to be the pattern and the price of ours, excites a peculiarity of interest, which admits of no comparison; and if any event in such a life merits more than usual attention, it is unquestionably that which closed the impressive scene, and terminated the Saviour's mortal pilgrimage. We cannot contemplate the characters of men who have benefitted the world by the splendor of their talents, or the lustre of their lives, without feeling a spirit of inquisitive solicitude, to know how they finished their course, parted with their friends, and made their exit. We labor to catch the last glance of departing worth; and sigh to think that an impenetrable veil is thrown over that world of spirits to which we are rapidly tending. The text directs our thoughts to the ascension of our Saviour, a scene which cannot fail to excite our attention; we have here,

I. The period when Christ ascended—"After the Lord had spoken." &c.

II. The manner—"He was received up into heaven."

III. His subsequent situation—"And sat on the right hand of God."

I. The period when Christ ascended—"After the Lord had spoken to them." The substance of this speech is related in the preceding verses: Christ had *reproved, directed*, and *comforted* his disciples.

1. *He upbraided them with their unbelief and hardness of heart.* Unbelief involves us in moral blame, and merits the reprehension of him who judgeth righteously It supposes facts that deserve credit,—evidences to support them,—and disregard to those evidences. The fact here was the resurrection of Christ; a fact of the highest importance, "For if Christ be not risen, preaching is vain, and faith is vain, and the apostles were false witnesses of God," 1 Cor. xv. 14, 15. *This fact was supported by evidence.* Christ had previously intimated it, Mark ix. 9; John ii. 19—22. Mary Magdalene had seen him, Mark xvi. 9—11. He had also appeared unto two of his disciples, who had told it unto the residue, v. 13. *These witnesses deserved credit*, as they were competent to judge of what they had seen and heard; and it was not probable that they would seek to deceive others by a false testimony.—*But this fact was discredited.* Here we may see the na ture of unbelief generally. Truths of the most important character are presented to us,—evidences of the most indisputable kind are afforded, but unbelief refuses to admit these evidences. Christ also upbraided his disciples *with hardness of heart;* this not unfrequently gives birth to unbelief. Faith refers as much to the disposition of the heart, as to the assent of the understanding; and where the heart is hard and unfeeling, the importance of divine truth will be unperceived, and its evidences unexamined.

2. *He said unto them,* " *Go ye into all the world*," &c. *This was the direction which he gave his disciples.* The work assigned them was, " Preach the gospel;" not false doctrines, not human opinions, nor Jewish ceremonies. The sphere of their operation was, " all the world;" and their commission was " to every creature." Hence we infer, that the gospel is suited to the circumstances of all—designed for the benefit of all—and that the ministers of truth should aim at preaching it to all.

3. *Christ also comforted his disciples, by the promise of a miraculous influence, with which they should be invested.* " These signs shall follow," &c. " In my name shall they cast out devils." Devils had previously been subject to them, Luke x. 17; and according to the primitive fathers, the power of casting out devils was continued in the church for many years.— " They shall speak with new tongues:" this promise was remarkably fulfilled on the day of Pentecost, Acts ii. 4—12.—" They shall take up ser pents," Acts xxviii. 5;—" If they drink any deadly thing," either by acci dent or compulsion, "it shall not hurt them." " They shall lay hands on the sick," &c., James v. 14, 15. Such was the *reproof, direction*, and *encour*

agement which Christ administered to his disciples, previously to his **ascension**; let us notice,

II. THE MANNER. "He was received," &c.

1. *The ascension of Christ was accomplished by his own eternal power.* "Thou hast ascended on high," &c., Psa. lxviii. 18;—" When he ascended up on high," &c., Eph. iv. 8;—" They looked steadfastly toward heaven as he went up," &c., Acts i. 10. The acts of redemption were Christ's personal acts;—at his death he laid down his life for us, no man took it from him;—his resurrection was effected by his own infinite energy;—" Christ died, and rose again," &c., Rom. xiv. 9;—and at his ascension, "he went up to heaven," not in appearance only, but really and locally.

2. *The ascension of Christ was publicly witnessed by his disciples.* "While he blessed them, he was parted from them, and carried up into heaven," &c., Luke xxiv. 51;—" While they beheld he was taken up," &c. Acts i. 9;—he had previously told them, "It is expedient for you that I go away," &c., John xvi. 7. And during the forty days that he continued with them after his resurrection, when he was seen of five hundred brethren at once, and when he spake of the things pertaining to the kingdom of God, it is highly probable that he had prepared their minds for the solemn scene which they were about to witness; for they were so far from being disappointed, or even sorrowful, at his removal from them, that they "returned to Jerusalem with great joy," Luke xxiv. 52.

3. *The ascension of Christ was hailed with transport by ministering angels.* That David spoke of the ascension of Christ in Psa. lxviii. 17, 18, is clearly proved by comparing it with Eph. iv. 8;—and there the Psalmist declares, " the chariots of God are twenty thousand, even thousands of angels : the LORD is among them," &c. Does not the whole passage refer to a military triumph, where the conqueror returns victoriously from the field of battle, amid the shouts and plaudits of the inhabitants, who come forth to hail him welcome to his native place? Psa. xxiv. 7, 8, xlvii. 5, 6. That angels felt a deep interest in what Christ did upon earth, is most incontestably proved from Luke ii. 13; Matt. iv. 11 ; Luke xxii. 43; Matt. xxviii. 2; Acts i. 10. And having announced the birth of Christ,—ministered to him in the wilderness,—strengthened him in his agony,—attended him at his resurrection,—did not,

> " Cherubic legions guard him home,
> And shout him welcome to the skies?"

" He was received up into heaven." Who received him? Did not angels, principalities, and powers? Did not the spirits of just men made perfect receive him into that exalted state of felicity? St. Luke declares "a cloud received him ;"—but who can tell what amazing scenes were unfolded beyond that cloud?

III. HIS SUBSEQUENT SITUATION. "He sat on the right hand of God." This is a figurative phrase ; and by it we understand,

1. *The honor and dignity to which our Saviour is exalted.* When monarchs elevate their favorites to sit at their right hand, it is considered as the highest point of distinction, 1 Kings ii. 19; Psa. xlv. 9. The dignity to which Christ's human nature is raised is inconceivably glorious, especially when contrasted with that state of shame and degradation to which he voluntarily submitted ;—how admirably is this illustrated by the apostle ; Phil. ii. 6—11.

2. *The rule and government with which he is invested.* Thus St. Paul declares, God hath " set him at his own right hand," &c. " And hath put all things under his feet, and gave him to be head over all things to the church," Eph. i. 20—22 ;—" The Father loveth the Son, and hath given all things into his hand, John iii. 35, v. 27. The government of the world and the church is in the hands of Christ; and he is set at the right hand of God, to carry on his mediatorial work,—" There he makes intercession for us," Rom. viii. 34 ;—" There he dispenses his favors," Eph. iv. 8, 11, 12 ;— " There he receives our prayers," Rev. v. 8.

3. *The tranquility and happiness of which he is possessed.* He had been a man of sorrows ; he had been stricken, smitten of God, and afflicted; his soul had been put to grief, and wrung with unutterable anguish. For the joy that was set before him, " He had endured the cross," &c.;—but he is now set down at the right hand of God;—this is a situation of exquisite pleasure, Psa. xvi. 11 ;—there he sees of the travail of his soul and is satisfied ;—and there are ascribed to him, " Blessing, and glory, and wisdom," &c., Rev. vii. 12. From this subject we learn,

1. *Christ finished the work which he came upon earth to accomplish.* He made an atonement for sin,—left us an example,—raised up apostles, gave them ample instruction,—established a new dispensation,—promised the gift of the Holy Ghost, &c.

2. *Christ has highly honored human nature.* That body which was wounded, bruised and scourged upon earth, is now seated at the right hand of God.

3. *Christ is exalted for our sake.* " To appear in the presence of God," &c., Heb. ix. 24 ;—this should give us confidence in our prayers,—excite our emulation,—and, above all, inspire our hopes. Our forerunner is already entered, the first fruits are gathered in,—and " to him that overcometh will I grant to sit with me in my throne," &c., Rev. iii. 21.

THE INTERCESSION OF CHRIST, A DEMONSTRATION OF HIS CAPACITY TO SAVE.

Heb. vii. 25.—Wherefore, he is able to save to the uttermost, &c. (H.)

St. Paul had always expressed a constant, tender, and zealous affection for his brethren, his kinsmen according to the flesh. This epistle is a remarkable monument of it. It is directed to the believing Hebrews, and its most evident design is, to animate them to adhere resolutely to the Christian faith. The mind of this excellent man was very capacious, and continually filled with a variety of schemes for the advancement of the gospel. As it was highly probable this, rather than any of his other epistles, would fall into the hands of many as yet unconverted Jews, he not only concealeth his name, against which they were strongly prejudiced, but in a very wise and happy manner, maketh use of such sentiments and such language as might be very proper to awaken and convince the unconverted, as well as assist the faith and joy of those who had believed in Christ.

In pursuit of these great and harmonious designs, the sacred writer insists largely on the dignity of the person and offices of our great Redeemer. He represented him as far superior to the most exalted angels. Heb. i. 4. To

Moses. Heb iii. 2, 6. To Abraham. Heb. vii. 4, 7. And to Aaron. Heb. vii. 11, 24. From hence he draweth the important inference in the text, "Wherefore, he is able," &c.

Consider,

I. WHAT ARE WE TO UNDERSTAND BY CHRIST'S BEING "ABLE TO SAVE TO THE UTTERMOST."

1. It implieth the danger and calamity of those to whom he is proposed as a Saviour. All were, without him, in a state of death, 2 Cor. v. 14 ; in a state of ruin, Rom. v. 12 ; but "in due time, Christ died for us." Rom. v. 6. "Who of God is made unto us wisdom," &c. 1 Cor. i. 30. Most men are soothed into an insensibility of their danger, hence they hear not the thunder of God's law, Gal. iii. 10, nor see the flaming sword of his vengeance. They sleep on the brink of a precipice ; what need of the alarm. Ephes. v. 14.

2. A power of working out complete deliverance for his people.

1. He is able to deliver them from the " curse of the law." Isa. xlii. 21 ; Gal. iii. 13 ; Acts xiii. 39.

2. From the pollution of sin. Rom. viii. 2. If he but speak, the work is done. Matt. viii. 3 ; 1 John i. 9.

3. From all the artifice and power of the prince of darkness. Col. i. 13. He knoweth how to deceive the deceiver, to detect every labored stratagem ; and, from the most dangerous snares, to teach such useful lessons of holy prudence, as shall tend to our constant safety. Ps. lxxiii. 24 ; John x. 21. " We shall be more than conquerers," &c. Rom. viii. 37.

4. To support his people in death, and receive their spirits to a world of glory. Ps. lxxiii. 26 ; 2 Tim. i. 12 ; Ps. xxiii. 4.

5. To raise their bodies from the dissolution of the grave, and conduct their complete persons to the regions of eternal felicity. John xi. 25 ; and verses 28, 29 ; Phil. iii. 21.

3. That the efficacy of his saving grace continueth the same throughout all succeeding ages. His energy wrought from the date of the first promise. Gen. iii. 15. By faith in him the elders obtained a good report. Heb. xi. 2. His victorious energy still continueth the same. Heb. xiii. 8.

II. WHAT EVIDENCE WE HAVE THAT HE IS REALLY SO.

1. He was commissioned by the Father for this great work. 1 John v. 11. He is the foundation-stone of our salvation. Isa. xxviii. 16. His name is Jesus. Matt. i. 21. God declared him to be his Son, at his entrance on his public ministry. Matt. iii. 17.

2. He appeareth in his person and character eminently fitted for the work. The mysterious union of the divine and human nature in the person of our blessed Redeemer, is that which renders him the secure confidence of our souls. Heb. vi. 19. He assumed a mortal immaculate body, that he might have somewhat to offer as a sacrifice. Heb. viii. 3 ; Eph. v. 2 ; John iii. 14. He was not only an excellent and holy man, but he was God. Rom. ix. 5 ; Heb. i. 3 ; Phil. ii. 6. Therefore, " able to save to the uttermost."

3. He has done and borne all that we can imagine necessary to effect it. 2 Cor. viii. 9 ; Phil. ii. 7, 8. Now he appeareth in the presence of God for us. Heb. ix. 24.

4. He hath been approved by the Father, as having completely answered this glorious design. His power to save, as Mediator, is founded on the efficacy of his atonement. Rom. i. 4 ; Matt. xxviii. 18--20.

5. He hath made such gracious promises of salvation as imply a full pow-

er of accomplishing it. Extent of grace implieth a correspondent extent of power. Titus ii. 11; 1 Tim. i. 15, 16; and iv. 10; Rom. v. 18.

6. He hath already begun, and carried on the salvation of a multitude of souls. Facts are stubborn things. There is a cloud of witnesses of all ages, nations, and tongues, who have been "washed, justified, and sancti fied." 1 Cor. vi. 11; Rev. vii. 13, 14. This is farther confirmed by the experience of thousands in the present day.

III. THE PARTICULAR ARGUMENTS FOR IT: "HIS EVER LIVING TO MAKE INTERCESSION FOR THEM."

The intercession which Christ ever liveth to make, is a proof of his being able to save to the uttermost; especially if we consider,

1. The foundation of it, his atonement. Heb. ix. 12. Had not Christ's atonement been satisfactory, his intercession would be vain. Indeed, God could not consistently have permitted him to enter heaven, much less to take up his residence there, under the character of an Intercessor.

2. The extent of it. The intercession of Christ is not merely his appearance before God, in the body in which he suffered, but it is attended with a constant and ardent desire that his death may be effectual to the purposes designed, in bringing many sons and daughters to God.

3. The perpetuity of it: "He ever liveth." Even at this moment Christ appeareth in heaven for us. Isa. xl. 28.

IV. THE CHARACTER OF THE PERSONS WHO ARE ENCOURAGED TO EXPECT SALVATION IN HIM: SUCH AS "COME UNTO GOD BY HIM."

A sinner must come to God through Christ. His coming to God implieth,

1. A firm persuasion of his being and attributes. Heb. xi. 6.

2. An earnest desire to secure his favor. Job. x. 12; Ps. iv. 6; xxx. 5.

3. A readiness to forsake whatever cometh in competition with him. Isa. xxvi. 13.

4. A willing subjection to his service. Luke x. 27; Rom. vi. 13; Psa. cxix. 16—127.

5. A keeping up a constant correspondence with him. Ps. lxxiii. 23; 1 John i. 3.

His coming to God through Christ implieth,

1. A deep sense of his need of a Mediator, in order to a comfortable intercourse with God; christianity is the religion of sinners; self must be humbled, that Christ may be exalted. 1 Pet. v. 6. Christ is our Day's man.

2. A full persuasion of his saving power. Mark ix. 24; Matt. viii. 2.

3. A cheerful confidence in the grace of Christ. John vi. 37; vii. 37; Matt. ix. 13; xii. 20.

4. A cordial approbation of the method in which he bestows salvation. Acts xx. 21; Rom. i. 17.

5. A constant care to maintain proper regards to Christ, in the whole course of our walking with God. Eph. ii. 18; Gal. ii. 20; 1 Pet. ii. 5.

Reflections.

1. How great is that salvation which the Lord Jesus Christ hath wrought out for us. Heb. ii. 3; Isa. xliii. 11.

2. How important is it that we all seriously inquire after this great salvation.

3. How great s the danger and misery of those who reject and affront such an Almighty Saviour. Rev. vi. 15—17.

4. How admirable and amiable doth the blessed Jesus appear, when considered as the great Intercessor of his people! Cant. v. 16.

5. With what holy boldness may the sinner draw near to God, in dependence on such an Intercessor. Heb. iv. 14—16; x. 19—22.

6. Let us adore the divine goodness, that such a salvation is offered us, in so reasonable, so easy, and so gracious a way. Rom. x. 3; Luke xix. 40.

7. Let us seriously examine whether we come to God by Christ. Acts xiii. 26.

8. Let those who have come in this manner, be thankful and courageous; let them go on till the God of peace bruise Satan under their feet; give them victory over death; and finally crown them with eternal life.

REDEMPTION BY THE BLOOD OF CHRIST.

Rev. i 5, 6.—Unto him that loveth us, and washed us from our sins in his own blood, and hath made us kings and priests unto God and his Father; to him be glory and dominion for ever and ever. Amen. (Pr.)

CHRIST is the object of praise and adoration as a divine person, being himself the Son of God; and there is also a glory attributed to him as Mediator, having redeemed us unto God by his blood. It is in the latter sense that glory and dominion are here ascribed to him, and let it be so ascribed for ever and ever. Amen.

I. We are led to consider what is implied in the text, namely, OUR POLLUTED AND DEFILED CONDITION AS SINNERS.

As coming out of the hands of our Creator, man was pure and holy, made after the image of God; but by sin we are become polluted. Yet men in general think nothing of sin, in any other way than as it affects the interests of society; and if free from outward offence, they then appear pure in their own eyes. But the defilement lies deep within, and out of the heart proceed all the evils of the life. Matt. xv. 19.

In particular, all the *springs of action* are defiled, all our thoughts, motives, and desires; so defiled as to pollute all our services and duties in religion. Even our righteousnesses are as filthy rags, and we are become abominable in the sight of God. Job xv. 16. Hence all the threatenings and curses are against us.

The corruption of our nature is such, that we are totally unfit for the society of holy beings; and while unrenewed we cannot enter into the kingdom of God. Like the leprous person we are thrust out of the camp, and cannot be admitted till the moral malady is healed.

Yet sinners think but little of their condition, and feel quite easy and contented as they are. But if God shine into the heart, we shall soon begin to see and feel our vileness, and mourn over it. All that are taught of God, are made to know the plague of their own heart. We see in what a manner David loathed himself when brought to repentance, and he is only an example of what every other penitent is made to feel. Psa. li.

II. Consider what Christ has done for us: "HE LOVED US, AND WASHED US FROM OUR SINS IN HIS OWN BLOOD."

He loved us——Love is the first moving cause of all, and therefore it is first mentioned: all that follows is the proper effect and expression of this love.

260

Love is the most estimable of all affections, and we generally value gifts and services done for us accordingly. If a person does ever so much for us, and not from love, it is but little regarded. Christ also values our services by the same rule, and thinks nothing of what we do, except it be from love to him. In the same way we are taught to value all that he has done for us, and to conceive of it as in the highest degree interesting, because it is the effect of love.

There are two things worthy of notice in the love of Christ, and which render what he has done for us so precious and inestimable——1. Its *freeness*. The love of Christ was fixed on us while we were yet sinners, while in our sins and in our blood, and antecedently to our being washed, which therefore could not be the ground or motive of his love. Ephes. v. 25, 26; Titus iii. 5.——2. Its *strength* or fulness. The love of Christ was such, that he gave himself for us; and greater love hath no man than this, that he lay down his life for his friend. 1 John iii. 16.

Again: He hath *washed us from our sins in his own blood*——The expression is figurative, but very strong: he hath purified us at the expense of blood. By this is meant his laying down his life for us as an atoning sacrifice, and it implies that nothing short of this would take away sin.— — — All ceremonial washings, all our prayers and tears, are utterly in vain; and nothing but the gospel can teach us how we are to be purified and made holy. Had it not been for the sacrifice of Christ, he that is holy, as angels are, should have been holy still; and he that is filthy, as men and devils are, must have been filthy still.

1. But why is our cleansing from sin *ascribed to the blood of Christ?* — — —Not because of any physical or natural efficacy, but because it is the life, and it is the blood that maketh atonement. Lev. xvii. 11. The life of the sinner is forfeited, and the life of the surety must become the sacrifice. Without shedding of blood there is no remission. Heb. ix. 22. It was not the sufferings of Christ merely, but his death, that made the atonement; and it was necessary also in his death, that there should be the shedding of his most precious blood. 1 Peter i. 19. Hence the evangelist is so careful to record the identical fact, that blood flowed from the Saviour's side while hanging on the cross. John xix. 34, 35. Hence also it is that our redemption is so repeatedly and emphatically ascribed to the blood of the cross. Ephes. i. 7; Col. i. 20; 1 John i. 7; Rev. v. 9.

2. What is there especially *in the blood of Christ that tends to cleanse from sin?*— — —The blood of bulls and of goats could not take away sin; it was not therefore by blood merely as such; nor would the blood of any mere creature suffice, however exalted in the scale of being. It was the *deity* of Christ that gave it this cleansing power. 1 John i. 7. He by the sacrifice of *himself* purged our sins, who is the brightness of the Father's glory, and the express image of his person. Heb. i. 3.

3. *In what manner does the blood of Christ cleanse us?*— — —We need a double purification; the removal of the curse due to sin, and the removal of its pollution. It is for the sake of the blood of Christ that we are pardoned and accepted; and it is in virtue of this also that the Holy Spirit is given to renew and sanctify the mind, and to cleanse us from all unrighteousness. The doctrine of the cross which gives peace to the mind, imparts also a spirit of purity.

4. *What then is needful to our being actually cleansed and pardoned?* — — —Only that we believe in Jesus, and repair to the fountain open for sin and uncleanness. He is able to save all that come unto God by him, but

261

none else. The annual atonement made for all Israel became effectual to those only who confessed their sins, and laid their hands upon the sacrifice: and none but the comers thereunto were benefitted by it. Those who reject the sacrifice of Christ must for ever remain unsanctified, and unforgiven, for there remaineth no more sacrifice for sin.

Having loved us, and washed us from our sins in his own blood, Christ hath *made us kings and priests unto God and his Father*——This denotes not merely what we shall be, but what we now are, a royal priesthood; and to this end he has washed us in his own blood, even as the priests of old were purified in the sacred laver, previous to their entering upon the sacerdotal office. Exod. xxix. 4. All believers are thus consecrated to the Lord, to draw near unto him, and to offer up spiritual sacrifices, acceptable by Jesus Christ. 1 Pet. ii. 5. They are the only true worshippers in the spiritual temple, and it is theirs to minister before the altar, and before the throne.

Finally: For all this love and mercy we are taught to ascribe glory and dominion to Christ. To him belong the honor and the glory of our salvation, and all that we receive from him must be cast at his feet. Nothing is more congenial to the heart of a real christian, than that the Saviour should be supremely loved and adored; and in no ascription could he acquiesce with greater cordiality than this which is here given. "To him be glory and dominion for ever and ever. Amen."

CHRIST THE ONLY SOURCE OF RIGHTEOUSNESS.

Rom. x. 4.—Christ is the end of the law for righteousness to every one that believeth. (B.)

THE Apostle having insinuated, ch. iii. 3, that God would cast off the Jews for their unbelief; and, ch. ix., shown that the rejection of the unbelieving Jews from being the church of God, and the reception of the believing Gentiles, to be his people, in their stead, was not contrary to the word of God, ver. 30—33, he proceeds, in this chapter, to point out the cause of these events, in the unwillingness of the Jews to accept that method of obtaining righteousness and salvation appointed by God,—Inquire we,

I. WHAT THAT RIGHTEOUSNESS IS, SPOKEN OF IN THE TEXT.

The righeousness here spoken of is evidently that which is necessary in order to eternal life, and which infallibly leads to it. Ch. v. 17, 21. It is termed "The righteousness of God," ver. 3; ch. i. 17, and said to be by faith. Ch. iii. 21, 22; Phil. iii. 9. It implies justification; ch. iii. 24; Tit. iii. 7; without which, as guilty, condemned sinners, we can have no title to eternal life, it being the only means of cancelling our guilt, and freeing us from condemnation, and which is followed by eternal salvation.—It implies regeneration or sanctification; see Phil. iii. 9, spoken of Eph. iv. 17—24; Tit. iii. 5, 6; John iii. 5, 6; without which we are not in Christ, 2 Cor. v. 17; Gal. vi. 15, and have no fitness for heaven.—It implies practical obedience; consequent on regeneration, Eph. ii. 10, and being the grand evidence that we are righteous. Luke i. 6; 1 John iii. 7. As to the necessity of this, see ch. ii. 6, 7; Rev. xxii. 14; and especially Matt. vii. 20. 21.

II. WHERE AND HOW THIS RIGHTEOUSNESS IS TO BE FOUND.

Not in, or by, the law; but in, and through, faith.—This righteousness considered in these three branches of it, is not attainable in, or by, the law moral or ceremonial. Not in, or by, the former. Ch. viii. 3. It requires perfect, constant, and persevering obedience; this we have not paid in time past, do not at present, and cannot in future, pay. Hence it finds us guilty of violating its spiritual and holy precepts, and has no pardon to give us; it finds us depraved, and has no new nature for us; it finds us weak and helpless, and has no supernatural aid to impart.—But may we not have the help we need from the ceremonial law? cannot the sacrifices of it remove our guilt? No. " It is not possible the blood of bulls and goats should take away sin." Heb. ix. 23; x. 4. Cannot the various washings, or purifications of it, renew and cleanse our souls? No: they can only impart a ceremonial cleanness, or remove " the filth of the flesh." Heb. ix. 13; 1 Pet. iii. 21. Cannot the various institutions respecting meats and drinks, and the observance of days and months, assist us to attain, at least, a practical righteousness or obedience? No: as they do not make the tree good, of course the fruit cannot be good; as they do not purify the fountain, the streams issuing thence cannot be pure. Matt. vii. 16—19. But wherefore then serve the law? why was it instituted? in order to Christ, who is " the end" of it. The end of it, here, means the *final cause.* Christ was the end for which the law was instituted; the moral law being chiefly intended to convince men of sin, ch. iii. 19, 20; vii. 7, 8, *viz.* of their guilt, depravity, and weakness, and thus to be a " schoolmaster to bring them to Christ," Gal. iii. 19—24, and the ceremonial law to shadow forth and exhibit his sacrifice and grace: —The end, may mean, *the scope;* the law continually points to Christ; the moral law directs the sinner to have recourse to him who fulfilled it, and removed the curse of it, for that justification which itself cannot give; and the ceremonial law directs him to look from its sacrifices and purifications, to the atonement and Spirit of Christ,—The end, sometimes means, the *perfection* or *completion.* Thus love is " the end," that is, the fulfilling " of the commandment;" 1 Tim. i. 5; Christ fulfilled the moral law in fully explaining its spiritual and extensive meaning, and freeing it from the corrupt glosses of the scribes; in obeying it perfectly in his holy life, in suffering its penalty, and in providing that it may be written in our hearts; he also answered in his person, all the types and shadows of the ceremonial law:—The end, means, the *period*, or *termination.* Ch. vi. 21. Thus the law, and the whole Mosaic dispensation, gives way to the gospel, ceases, and is abolished, 2 Cor. iii. 11, and the ceremonies of it are taken out of the way by Christ. Col. ii. 14.—" Christ is the end of the law for righteousness." For justification, or righteousness imputed, is only to be found in his obedience unto death. Rom. iii. 24; 1 Cor. i. 30; 2 Cor. v. 21. Regeneration, a new creation, and entire sanctification, are only to be found in Christ, by his Spirit and grace, who is made of God to us sanctification. John i. 14, 16; 2 Cor. v. 17; 1 Cor. i. 30. Practical righteousness is likewise to be had in him; his doctrine, the law of Christ, directs us how to walk; his promises and threatenings enforce his laws; his example allures us; and his grace enables us to walk in his ways. 2 Cor. xii. 9; Heb. iv. 14—16.

III. By whom this righteousness is to be found.

By "every one that believeth."

The nature of faith is described ver. 5—10; its object is, that God hath raised Christ from the dead. This demonstrated him to be the Son of God, ch. i. 3, 4, and, therefore, the Christ, the only Saviour, able and willing to save to the uttermost. Of this faith is persuaded, and, therefore, comes to him and trusts in him for salvation.—The resurrection of Christ was the broad seal of Heaven set to his doctrine, and establishes its absolute truth and deep importance beyond all doubt; of which faith is so thoroughly per suaded, as to lay it to heart, and wa.к according to it.—He was raised for our justification, to show that the atonement he had made for sin was sufficient, and accepted; of this faith is also persuaded, and, therefore, relies solely on the propitiation in his blood for justification. Ch. iii. 23, &c.; Gal. ii. 16—20. He was raised that he might ascend, and intercede, and receive for us "the Promise of the Father," for which faith thirsts and comes to him. John vii. 37, 38,—He rose and ascended as our forerunner This faith believes, and, consequently, anticipates immortality and glory.— He rose to give evidence that he will judge all mankind. Acts xvii. 31. Faith is persuaded of this, and prepares to meet him, desiring to be "found of him in peace, Our faith, in these respects, must be such as will enable us to "make confession with our mouth," even if that should expose us, as in the early ages, to imprisonment and martyrdom. Therefore, it must be "with the heart man believeth unto righteousness;" ver. 10; Christ must be endeared to us more than riches, honors, liberty, or even life itself, which, if we be called to it, must be parted with for his sake. As to the faith that does not part with sin, and give up every thing that stands in competition with Christ for our hearts, it is dead. James ii. 20—26 As to the origin of this faith. See ver. 11—17. It arises from the Word and Spirit of God. "The Lord opened the heart of Lydia, that she attended to the things spoken" by the Apostle. Acts xvi. 14; Eph. ii. 8, 9; Col. ii. 12. Therefore, hearing, reading, meditation, and prayer, are the important means which we must employ, with a becoming humility, seriousness, desire. and confidence of success.—And in the exercise of that measure of faith we have received, however small, it will be increased.

THE FULNESS OF CHRIST.

John i. 16.—And of his fulness have all we received, and grace for ₅ ᵤce. (Pr.)

The other evangelists give an account of Christ's human parentage, with the circumstances of his birth : but John gives a description of his glory as the Son of God, and of what he was before the world began. He is here spoken of as the Creator of all things, and as the light and life of men. His incarnation is next described, and with this is connected the passage before us. He dwelt amongst men, full of grace and truth; and of the fulness have we all received.

I. ILLUSTRATE AND EXPLAIN THE SUBJECT.

Three things require to be noticed—what is meant by the fulness of Christ —in what way is this fulness communicated—and in what respect may we be said to receive grace for grace?

1. What is intended by the "fulness" of Christ.— — —Not that which is essential to him as a divine person, for that is incommunicable : but that which belongs to him as Mediator, and which is communicated to all them that believe. Col. i. 19.— — —The meaning is, that the Word being made flesh, all the riches of grace designed for man were deposited in him, were given to him, and through him to us : as when Joseph was made lord of Egypt, and all were directed to go to him for the supply of their wants. Gen. xlii. 55—57. John vi. 27.

1. Christ was the covenant head of all his people, and it is out of regard to his worthiness that all his blessings are bestowed.— — —God made a

covenant with Noah, and had respect to that, in all he did for his posterity. Gen. vi. 18. Also with Abraham, Gen. xvii. 4 : with David, Psal. lxxxix. 28.— — —Thus in the counsels of divine grace, God hath blessed us in Christ Jesus, Ephes. i. 3. 2 Tim. i. 9.

2. All that is given to us freely, is to him a matter of just reward. He had power to lay down his life, and to take it up again. John x. 18 : power to quicken whom he will, John v. 25 : power to forgive sin even on earth, Matt. ix. 6 : power to give eternal life, John x. 28.— — —These things constitute the gospel, and which are denominated " the unsearchable riches of Christ." Thus it is, that through his poverty we are made rich. 2 Cor. viii. 9.

3. Though the riches of Christ are unsearchable, yet we may form some idea of their fulness by the freeness of the invitations and promises. "If any thirst, let him come unto me and drink ; he that cometh unto me, I will in no wise cast out : he is able to save unto the uttermost all them that come unto God by him : able to do exceeding abundantly above all we ask or think." — — —We may also judge of this fulness by what has actually been received from it.— — —We all derive from him, but he derives nothing from us. All that his servants have ever possessed, of gifts or of grace, and all that they have done, is from him ; and this, without his riches being either exhausted or diminished.— — —Had there ever been a time when the fulness of Christ should be exhausted, it was when through weakness he was dying on the cross. But lo ! even then it overflowed : " Father, forgive them—This day shalt thou be with me in paradise."

2. In what way is this fulness communicated ? By first receiving Christ: ver. 12.— — —The generality of mankind are like persons living near a fountain, but have nothing to draw with : they believe not in him, and so they receive nothing from him.— — —But there are some who receive him as he is revealed in the gospel, renouncing whatever stands in competition with him ; and by receiving him, they receive every supply of grace from him. — — —It is also through his dwelling in our hearts by faith, that we continue to receive : and by counting all things but loss for his sake, we are made to possess all things in him. Ephes. iii. 19.

3. How is it that we may be said to " receive grace for grace ?"— — — Some understand by it, a succession of blessings one after another, an abundance; others think it means grace received by us, corresponding with that which is in Christ, as a likeness is made to resemble the original. Christ was anointed, like Aron the high priest ; and as the sacred unction ran down to the skirts of his garments, so the anointing which was upon the Saviour was poured down upon all the members of his mystical body. We receive as it were the overflowings of that holy unction, and every portion of grace in our measure agreeing with the grace that is in him.

II. IMPROVE THE SUBJECT.

1. We learn from hence our condition as sinners : poor and needy, destitute of all good. All the self-sufficiency of sinners is only imaginary. The Laodiceans thought themselves rich, and increased with goods, and had need of nothing : but they were poor, and wretched, miserable, blind, and naked. He who thinks he knoweth any thing, knoweth nothing as he ought to know.

2. The way in which a poor lost sinner must be saved.— — —It is by receiving Christ, and deriving from his fulness : living upon his bounty, we are not only supplied, but made rich.

3. We see whence it was that those who have been the most eminent for grace have received all their supplies ; by receiving Christ and beholding his glory.- - — —This is our example, and our encouragement.

THE PRE-EMINENCE DUE TO CHRIST.

John iii. 35.—The Father loveth the Son, and hath given all things into his hand. (Pr.)

This is part of the testimony which John the Baptist bore to Christ, in answer to an insinuation suggested by the Jews, for the purpose of exciting his jealousy and suspicion, verse 26. John feels much on this occasion, that they should attempt to place him in competition with his Lord, and rejects the idea with great force of language.

1. He tells them that he could accept of no honors but such as God had given him, the principal of which consisted in his being the messenger of the Lord, to prepare the way before him, and to bear testimony of him ; and they knew that he never professed himself to be the Messiah: verse 27, 28.

2. John makes it out that all men *coming to Christ* as they had represented, was a proof of his being the Messiah, verse 29. He is the bridegroom, and the church is his bride. John is the bridegroom's friend, acting in subserviency, and doing his will; and this was honor enough for him. Now all things are in their proper place.

3. He gives them to expect that things *would go on* in this direction, and that Christ would be more and more glorified, though he himself should not, verse 30.

4. John then illustrates the subject more fully, and *preaches Christ* to his followers, as the only way of life and salvation, verse 31—36.

We here see how much of the evangelical ministry was possessed by John the Baptist, much more indeed than by Christ's immediate disciples, previous to the day of pentecost; and those who wish to throw him back ; as though he belonged to the Jewish rather than to the christian dispensation, do him great injustice. He was more than a prophet, an evangelist, and the immediate forerunner of Christ.

In the text John speaks *as an example* to his followers, that they might learn to be of God's mind, and to honor the Saviour as he had done, without being over-solicitous of the honor that might be due to himself.

I. Observe the love of the Father to Christ.

This is a subject on which the New Testament delights to dwell, and the love here mentioned relates both to the person and the work of Christ.

1. The Father loveth him *as the Son of God.*— — —Hence those terms of endearment and filiation so often applied to Christ, as God's "own Son," his "only-begotten Son," his "dear Son," and "the Son of his love."— — It is the love the Father bears to him that makes the gift of Christ for us so unspeakable, verse 16 ; especially the giving of him as a sacrifice for us. Rom. viii. 32 ; Zech. xiii. 7. Hence also the testimony given on the banks of the Jordan. Matt. iii. 17 ; and on mount Tabor, xvii. 5.

2. He loveth him for the sake of *his obedience unto death*, and because he gave himself for us. John x. 17.— — —Hence also he hath highly exalted him, Phil. ii. 9 ; and commanded that all men should honor the Son, even as they honor the Father. John v. 23.— — —So highly does he love the Son, that he will hear no petition but in his name, and pardon no sinner but for his sake. John xiv. 6.

3. The special proof of this love is, *that he hath given all things into his hand.*— — —Such universal terms are difficult to interpret, on account of their extent. We who understand so few things, cannot enumerate them all, but we may mention some. The general idea is, that the Father hath delegated to him all the great concerns of his moral empire. It is for him to

restore it to order, and the heavens must retain him unto the restitution of all things, Acts iii. 21: and when he shall have subdued all things, and put down all authority and power, he shall deliver up the kingdom to the Father, that God may be all in all, 1 Cor. xv. 24, 28.

More particularly—

1. All the dispensations of mercy are in the hands of Christ: it is for him to save or to destroy. John v. 21; xvii. 2. It pleased the Father that in him should all fulness dwell, and out of his fulness we all receive, Col. i. 19; John i. 16.

2. God has entrusted him with his honor and glory. He is the Mediator betwixt God and man, and he is to act the part of a merciful and faithful high-priest. His work was to secure the honor of the Lawgiver, while he exercised mercy as a Saviour; and he hath done it, John xvii. 1, 4.

3. The Father hath committed to him the salvation of his people, their redemption from the curse, and from the grave. John vi. 39, 40.

4. The control of the universe is in his hands, and he is Lord of all; angels, principalities, and powers being made subject unto him, Col. i. 16; ii. 10; Ephes. i. 22.

5. The government of the church is committed to him, and he is the only lawgiver in Zion. His will is the ground of all obedience, and even the moral law is under his authority, Matt. xxviii. 18—20; 1 Cor. ix. 21.

6. The administration of the final judgment. The Father judgeth no man, but hath committed all judgment unto the Son, John v. 22; 2 Cor. v. 10.

II. Consider the consequences arising out of this doctrine.

1. Whatever is given to Christ *is given to communicate*, like treasure committed to an almoner; and even the authority with which he is invested is for the good of his church and people. He hath received gifts for men, even the rebellious, that the Lord God might dwell among them, Psalm lxviii. 18.

2. If we desire mercy we must *come to Christ for it*. Go to Joseph, said Pharaoh to the poor of the land; and so the Lord says to us, Go to Jesus.

3. As the Father loveth the Son, and hath committed all things into his hands, so *we must follow his example*, and commit our all into his hands for time and eternity, 2 Tim. i. 12. Sure we cannot refuse to treat him with similar confidence; if we do, we are not of God. Jews and deists, under pretence of honoring the Father, reject the Son; but they will be found in the wrong at last, 1 John ii. 23.

4. At all events we must become *subject to Christ*, in one way or another; for to him every knee shall bow, and every tongue shall confess. He must **reign** till he hath put all his enemies under his feet, 1 Cor. xv. 25.

~~~~~~~~~~~~

CHRIST, ALL IN ALL.

Col. iii. 11.--Christ is all and in all. (H.)

How different is the language in which the sacred writers speak of Jesus Christ, from that adopted by many modern preachers and divines! Some will hardly condescend to name him: and, if they do, it is merely as a man a good man, a moral philosopher, or at most, a prophet, who taught maxims of wisdom, and confirmed them by a virtuous example. Whereas the primitive and apostolic writers always name him with an evident glow of affection and delight. In short, with them, "Christ was all and in all."

Let us endeavor to comprehend the phrase, "All in all; or, all in every thing." Implieth that the whole of christianity is full of Christ; and so it is. The sun is all in all to our system; he diffuseth light liberally to all the planets which revolve around him, and his heat penetrates the centre of the largest globes; on our earth he paints the flowers, embalms the fruits, ripens the grain, quickens all nature into life, and thus becometh all in all to us. Jesus Christ is the Sun of Righteousness; and whatever the sun is to the material world, that, and much more, is our Redeemer to the spiritual world; he is "all in all" in the system of christianity. Let us instance in a few particulars.

I. Christ is all in the scheme of salvation, as it respects God.

He is the covenant head, both of men and angels, and every gracious decree and purpose of the divine mind towards them hath an immediate respect to Christ; so, in the actual communications of the blessings, both of providence and grace, he is the only channel by which they are conveyed. He is the spiritual ladder which Jacob saw, whereby intercourse is opened between God and us.

II. Christ is all in all in the work of redemption, as it affects man.

He paid the price of our redemption, wrought out a perfect righteousness for our justification, and communicateth his Holy Spirit for our sanctification; he sitteth both our Prince and Advocate, at the right hand of his Father, where he will wait to intercede for us, until every son of God is brought to glory.

III. Christ is all in all in the sacred scriptures.

All divine truths connect and harmonize in him, like the rays of light collected in a focus; no considerable part of holy writ has a nearer or more distant reference to him. Abraham saw him afar off, and rejoiced in the sight; Moses pointed to him in all the services of the tabernacle; the Psalmist mingled the joys and sorrows of the Messiah with his own, or rather appeareth often to have forgot his own in meditating his: "To him give all the prophets witness." John showed him with his finger, "Behold the Lamb of God!" and all the apostolic writers delight even in the repetition of his name.

IV. Christ is all in all in the life of a believer.

His faith looks with a steady eye to the atonement; his repentance floweth from a believing sight of his sufferings and death, which also filleth his heart with gratitude and love: his hope is animated by a contemplation of his victories and glory; every grace receiveth its vigor from a believing view of Jesus. In all the troubles of life, and especially in the prospect of approaching death, this alone can comfort and satisfy the christian.

Is it not the want of looking more to Christ that maketh so many of the sons of God go lean from day to day? They look around them, the world is false, and friends are fickle; they look within them, all is dark and comfortless; let them look above, where Jesus sitteth at the right hand of God: there is strength, and righteousness, and peace, and glory.

V. Christ is all in all in the enjoyment of heaven.

"The Lamb that is in the midst of the throne shall feed them, and lead them to rivers of living waters:" so is he the all in all of the celestial authems. The Father delighteth to honor him, and beameth all his glory through his countenance; angels delight to honor him, and tune their golden harps to praise him; saints delight to honor him, and cast their starry crowns beneath his feet. Let us also delight to honor him.

THE LORD OUR RIGHTEOUSNESS.

Jeremiah xxiii. 6.—This is his name, whereby he shall be called, The Lord our Righteousness. (S. S.)

THE writings of the prophets no less than of the apostles testify of Christ: nor can we any where find a fuller exhibition of his character than in the words before us—As to *his origin*, he is "a branch from the root of David:" and, in *his character*, "a righteous" branch. *His office* is that of "a King;" and, as to *the manner in which he executes that office*, "he executes righteousness and judgment in the land." Look we for *the effects of his administration?* "In his days Judah shall be saved, and Israel shall dwell safely." Lastly, Would we know *in what light he is to be regarded?* "This is his name, whereby he shall be called, The Lord our Righteousness."

In these words the prophet sets forth,

I. THE DIGNITY OF CHRIST.

The inspired writers never seem afraid of speaking of Christ in too exalted terms—The prophet, in this very place, declares

1. His essential dignity.

There is frequent occasion to observe that, wherever the word LORD is printed in large characters, it is in the original, JEHOVAH. Now Jehovah denotes the self-existence of the Deity, and is a name incommunicable to any creature: yet is it here assigned to Christ—By comparing similar declarations in the Old Testament with the expositions given of them in the New, we know assuredly that this name belongs to Christ; and that therefore he is and must be "God over all blessed for ever,"—Isa. vi. 5, with John xii. 41, or Isa. xlv. 22, 23, with Rom. xiv. 10, 11, or Joel ii. 32, with Rom. x. 13, 14, or Mal. iii. 1, with Luke i. 76.

2. His official dignity.

The title of Jehovah belongs equally to the Father, to the Son, and to the Holy Spirit; but the additional title of "*Our Righteousness*" is peculiar to Christ alone—It imports that Christ has by his own obedience unto death wrought out a righteousness for guilty man; and that "this righteousness shall be unto all and upon all them that believe in him"—It is in this sense that St. Paul speaks of him as "made unto us righteousness,"—1 Cor i. 30.

The connexion between the different parts of this comprehensive name deserves particular notice: for, if He were not Jehovah, he could not be our Righteousness; seeing that as a creature, he could *merit* nothing; because he would *owe* to God all that he could do; and, "after he had done all, he would be only an unprofitable servant:" but as he is God, all which he does is voluntary; and his divinity stamps an infinite value upon his work; so that it may well merit, not for himself only, but for a ruined world—

Such is the dignity of our blessed Lord: He is Jehovah, one with the Father, in glory equal, in majesty co-eternal: nor is there one ransomed soul in heaven, who does not ascribe his salvation to the blood and righteousness of this our incarnate God—

While the prophet thus expatiates on the glory of Christ, he intimates also,

II. THE DUTY OF MAN.

Our duty as sinners, and as redeemed sinners, has especial respect to Christ: and it is summarily comprehended in the ascribing to Christ the honor due unto his name—But this must be done,

1. In faith.

To compliment Christ with any titles which we do not believe due to him, would be to insult him, like those who arrayed him in mock majesty, and cried, Hail, King of the Jews—We must fully believe him to be God: we must be persuaded that we neither have nor can have any righteousness of our own: and we must be assured that " He is the end of the law for righteousness to every one that believeth," Rom. x. 4.—If we entertain any idea of meriting any thing at God's hands by our own obedience, or of adding any thing of our own to his perfect righteousness, we dishonor and degrade him ; and, instead of performing our duty towards him, we violate it in the most flagrant manner : and, though we may be actuated by a blind zeal for the Father's honor, or for the interest of morality, we are indeed rebels against God, since he has commanded that " all men should honor the Son as they honor the Father," and that they should call him in faith, *The Lord our Righteousness*—

2. In sincerity.

As, to give him a title which we do not believe due to him would be mockery, so, to give it without a correspondent regard to him would be hypocrisy—Do we believe him to be Jehovah ? we must regard him with reverential awe, and yield ourselves up to him in unreserved obedience—Do we believe him to be the only Righteousness of the redeemed ? we must renounce entirely our own righteousness, and depend on him with our whole hearts—Do we view him in his complex character as Jehovah our Righteousness ? We must rejoice in having such an almighty friend, such a sure foundation—We must glory in him as "all our salvation, and all our desire"—A less regard to him than this, not only falls below our duty, but it is absolutely inconsistent with any scriptural hope, any prospect of salvation—

From this subject we may LEARN,

1. The way of salvation.

There are but *three* ways in which we can conceive it possible for any man to be saved : namely, by works, by faith *and* works, or by faith *without* works ; and the subject before us plainly declares which is the true one—Are we to be saved by our works ? No : for God would never have sent his Son to be our Righteousness, if we ever could have wrought out a sufficient righteousness of our own—Besides, our own works would then have been our righteousness, and the name here ascribed to Christ would not have belonged to him—Moreover, even in heaven itself, instead of ascribing " Salvation to God and to the Lamb," we must ascribe it to God and to ourselves—

Are we then to be saved by faith *and* works ? We still answer, No: for in whatever degree we trust in our own works, in that degree do we rob Christ of his official dignity ; and assume to ourselves the honor due to him alone--As far as our own merits are united with his as a joint ground of our acceptance with God, so far shall we have to all eternity a ground of glorying in ourselves ; yea, so far salvation will cease to be of grace ; whereas "it is of faith that it may be by grace, and that boasting may be for ever excluded"—Rom. iv. 16; Eph. ii. 8, 9.

Salvation must then be by faith *without* works; we must not endeavor either in whole or in part to "establish a righteousness of our own," but seek to be clothed in the unspotted robe of Christ's righteousness—This is the declaration of God himself; Rom. iv. 5; nor did the apostles themselves know any other way of salvation, Gal. ii. 16,—We must all therefore desire, with St. Paul, to be found in Christ, not having our own righteousness but his—Phil. iii. 9.

2. The excellency of that way.

What can be conceived more *comfortable to man* than to hear of such a salvation as this? Were we told that we must work out a righteousness of our own that should be commensurate with the demands of God's law, who could entertain a hope of ever affecting it?—If we were required to do something that should be worthy to be joined with the Saviour's merits in order to render them more effectual for our acceptance, where should we find one single work of ours that we could present to God as perfect, and as deserving of so great a reward?—The best man on earth must either sit down in despair, or live in continual suspense respecting his eternal welfare—But the righteousness of Jehovah appears at once, not only adequate to our wants, but to the wants of all mankind; and, by trusting in that, we find rest unto our souls—Nor can we devise any other method of acceptance so *honorable to God ;* since it refers all the glory to him; and necessitates all the hosts of the redeemed to ascribe the honor of their salvation to him alone—In spite of all the objections too that are urged against it, we can affirm that it is eminently *conducive* to the practice of *holiness*—Can we think of God becoming man in order to work out a righteousness for us, and not feel a desire to serve and honor him? "Can we continue in sin that grace may abound? God forbid"—An inspired writer assures us that "the grace of God which bringeth salvation teaches us to deny ungodliness and worldly lusts, and to live righteously, soberly, and godly in this present world"—

Let us then seek our righteousness in Christ alone; but let us shew by our lives, that this doctrine of faith is indeed "a doctrine according to godliness."

CHRIST THE HEAD OF THE CHURCH.

Colossians i. 18.—And he is the head of the body the church. (Sk.)

The Colossians had been converted to christianity, chiefly through the instrumentality of Epaphras, who was a minister of Christ, and a fellow helper with St. Paul. But they were in danger of being seduced from the simplicity of the gospel by designing or ignorant men. False teachers had crept in among them, who inculcated the worship of angels, abstinence from animal food, the observance of Jewish festivals, the mortification of the body by long continued fasting, and the conformity to external ceremonies, as necessary to salvation.—To all these things the apostle refers in different parts of this epistle. In the preceding verses to the text, he asserts the doctrine of the essential Godhead of Christ; a doctrine which he never overlooks in any of his epistles. Here he states the relation in which Christ stands to his church. " He is the head of the body," &c. Let us,

I. DESCRIBE THE CHURCH. This may at first view seem a needless task What need of description on a subject so plain? Who does not know what a church is? Have we not one in every parish? But it is with the scriptural, and not the common and corrupted application of the term, that we have to do. The term church in the New Testament uniformly refers to persons, and never to places. See Acts xx. 28; Rom. xvi. 5; Gal. i. 22. But by what marks were the members of the primitive churches desig nated?

1. *They were a people separated from the world.* The church and the world form two distinct societies. ' Ye are not of the world," said Chris to his disciples. Hence believers were charged, " Be not conformed to this world;" and to " have no communion with the unfruitful works of darkness;" and Christianity is the same through all the revolutions of time.

2. *They were a people scorned and greviously persecuted by the world.* Saul made havoc of the church. " Herod stretched forth his hand to vex certain of the church." At that time there was a great persecution against the church at Jerusalem. And the members of the church of Christ are still scorned and contemned by the ungodly part of mankind.

3. *They were a people who gave themselves up to the practice of prayer and supplication for themselves and their neighbors.* Christ encouraged his disciples to pray, by telling them that whatsoever they asked in his name, it should be done for them: at Jerusalem they prayed so fervently, that the whole house was shaken where they were assembled. See Acts xii. 5, xvi. 25. And the members of Christ's church still live, and always will live, in in the practice of prayer.

4. *They were a people who adorned their high profession by a consistent conduct.* We do not affirm that there were none among them who scandalized their profession, no brother who walked disorderly, no busy body in other men's matters. Alas! they were plagued with such people, but when detected they were cast out of the church. O how holy were the members of the church of Christ required to be!

II. SHOW WHY CALLED A BODY.

1. *To illustrate the beauty of its moral form.* The human body is the most beautiful structure in the world. Nothing is so much admired. How exquisitely beautiful is the church of Christ. Every member of it has put on Christ, and is invested with his moral image. "The King's daughter is all glorious within," &c., Psa. xlv. 13; Isa. liv. 11—13; Eph. v. 26, 27.

2. *To describe the variety of members of which it is composed.* " We have many members in the same body, but all members have not the same office." The eyes see for the body, the hands handle for the body, the feet walk for the body, the palate tastes for the body, and the nerves feel for the body. In the church there are various members. " God gave, some apostles; and some prophets; and some evangelists;" &c., Eph. iv. 11—14. In the church now, there are many members, who hold distinct offices. Some write books, some preach sermons, some serve tables, some visit the sick, &c. Every member is useful; but every member should know his place, and keep it.

3. *To display the harmony and union of all its members.* Who that contemplates his own body, can help be astonished at the union, which subsists between all the members of which it is composed! And the church, though composed of many members, is one body, one building, one temple

one flock, one family. There is not a union of circumstances, nor of sentiment; but a union of faith, of affection, and of effort. Disunion in the church the apostles deprecated, and for union they prayed, Eph. iv. 16.

III. ILLUSTRATE THE OFFICE OF CHRIST AS THE HEAD OF THE BODY.

1. *The head is the seat of dignity to the body.* It is above the body in point of local situation, and it is superior to the body in dignity and authority. And Christ is above all.

2. *The head is the seat of government for the body.* There can be no government where there is no head. Christ has the sole government in his church. The laws by which our conduct is regulated are his laws. The influence by which our sins are subdued is his influence. The account we shall have to give of our conduct is to him, and the retribution we shall receive is from his hand.

3. *The head is the seat of wisdom for the body.* The head thinks for the body, and directs all its movements. And Christ is made unto us wisdom. Without the direction and influence of Christ, we should be no more capable of guiding our steps aright, than a body without a head. Alas! where did we wander before Christ took us under his direction!

4. *The head is the seat of glory to the body.* Do we not honor the head peculiarly? And Christ is the glory of his church. We honor Christ by praying to him, praising him, loving him and trusting him with our all.

5. *The head is the seat of union to the body.* The origin of all sensation and motion, is in the nerves, and these proceed from the head, and unite all the parts of the body together. And Jesus Christ unites the members of his mystical body, and makes them all one in himself.

APPLICATION.

1. *Is the church a body?* Let me then inquire, Have I union with the body? Am I united to any christian society? Why not? If there were no christian societies, there would soon be no christian ministers, no fellowship of saints, and no religion in the land. Why do I not join some christian society? Am I holier than the members of which christian churches are composed? then they ought to share my counsels and prayers. Am I worse than they? then self-interest should bind me to cast in my lot among them.

2. *Is the church a body?* Then what a horrid thing is schism in the body. No man ever hated his own flesh. To see the members of a body bite and devour one another, how unnatural! O let us never permit the demon of discord to creep in amongst us!

3. *Is the church the body of Christ?* Then by helping christians we help Christ's members. Were Christ again upon earth, and to go about naked and destitute, we should rejoice to render him assistance. But he has his members, many of whom are poor, and afflicted, and forlorn; and what we do for them, he considers as being done for himself. Is one member weak? let us help him. Is another ignorant? let us instruct him," &c.

4. *Is the church the body of Christ?* Then will he not terribly punish those who insult his body? Persecutors will have a horrid hell, Zech. ii. 8; Matt. xviii. 6.

5. *Is Christ the head of the body?* Then what may not christians expect from him! What an endearing relation subsists between Christ and believers! We are members of his body, of his flesh, and of his bones. May we grow up into him in all things! Amen.

273

CHRIST THE PHYSICIAN OF SOULS.

Matthew ix. 12.--"But when Jesus heard that, he said unto them, They that be **whole** need not a physician, but they that are sick." (Sk.)

THOUGH Jesus Christ came into the world as the friend and Saviour of sinners ; yet he was in general rejected as an imposter, and deceiver of the people. The Jews having expected that he would appear as a temporal and victorious conqueror, despised his humble manifestation in "the form of a servant," and sought to put him to death, because he claimed the character of the Messiah. They regarded his doctrines as blasphemy, attributed his miracles to diabolical agency, and were greatly offended at his familiarity with publicans and sinners. And hence we learn from the preceding context, that Jesus having called Matthew to follow him, he promptly obeyed the divine command, and gladly entertained the Saviour as a guest at his house. But having most probably invited some of his former associates in sin to partake of his feast, for the benefit of the Redeemer's discourse, the fastidious Pharisees were highly indignant, and " said to the disciples, Why eateth your Master with publicans and sinners ?" But when Jesus heard that, "he said unto them," by way of vindicating his own character and conduct, and for the reprehension and conviction of the censorious Pharisees, "They that be whole," &c. This is supposed to have been a well known proverb among the Jews, which the divine teacher *spiritually* applies with peculiar propriety, for the instruction of his hearers ; and according to this sacred application of the words, they strikingly suggest, the nature and influence of sin, the character and office of Christ,—and the subjects and attainments of grace. Observe,

I. THE NATURE AND INFLUENCE OF SIN. The scriptures describe the exceeding sinfulness of sin, by every figure calculated to excite our abhorrence, and alarm our fears. And as the effects of sin on the *soul* greatly resemble the effects of disease on the *body*, it is frequently represented under this significant emblem. This is certainly the case in the text, in which the diseased state of the soul is evidently intended, by "they that are sick." The nature of this disease is truly deplorable, and replete with imminent danger.

1. *Sin is a moral disease.* It deeply affects mankind as moral and responsible creatures. It has totally destroyed original purity and happiness ; filled the world with disorder, misery and death. It has spread its poisonous infection through every faculty of the soul, and passion of the mind. The understanding is blinded,—the will is perverted,—the conscience is defiled,—and the affections are alienated from God, Eph. iv. 13. Not only is our moral constitution fatally diseased, but utterly ruined ; And there is neither spiritual life nor health in us. " Wo unto us that we have sinned ! The whole head is sick, and the whole heart is faint."

2. *Sin is a univresal disease.* It has mortally wounded every power, both of body and soul; and disseminated its infectious influence through the whole mass of mankind. It is the natural state of every human being, Psa. li. 5. It equally affects all ranks of men, and every distinct class of character. It universally prevails in every nation, and successively extends through every period of the world. Its desolating effects reach through all gradations of society, from the greatest monarch to the meanest subject ; from the imperial palace to the plebeian cottage. There is no exception, for all have sinned ; and sin infects the soul with every species of spiritual malady, and baneful influence, Isa. i. 6.

274

3. *Sin is a mortal disease.* It brings death and all our wo. It brings temporal death to the body, and renders all men subject to pain and dissolution, Rom. v. 15.—It brings spiritual death to the soul, and separates between God and his creatures, Eph. ii. 1—3. It also brings eternal death both to body and soul, in " the lake that burneth with fire and brimstone, which is the second death," Rom. vi. 23. How dreadful then is the disease of sin! It is the *original cause* of all suffering and sorrow here, and utter ruin and endless misery hereafter. But though the moral plague of human nature is so malignant, pestilential, and destructive, it is not desperate and irremediable. A perfect cure is obtained through the Saviour of sinners, who "was wounded for our transgressions," and by "whose stripes we are healed." Let us then consider,

II. THE CHARACTER AND OFFICE OF CHRIST. He represented himself in the text as a divine *Physician.* And in this capacity, as well as in all others, he possesses every possible qualification, suited to all the diversified circumstances, and adequate to the innumerable necessities of mankind.

1. *He is an accessible Physician.* All are invited to come unto him, " without money, and without price." Other physicians are in many cases difficult of access ; but whether rich or poor, all are welcome to come to Christ. He will never repulse the sin-sick penitents, but receive them graciously and love them freely, John vi. 37. In the days of his flesh, he went about doing good, and healing all manner of diseases ; and he is still present with us by his *word* and *Spirit*, to heal the maladies of our souls, Matt. xviii. 20 ; Rom. x. 6—9.

2. *He is an infallible Physician.* His infinite wisdom cannot err, nor can his omnipotent power fail of success. The most skilful human physicians are imperfect and fallible, and though they frequently administer temporary relief, their wisdom is often baffled, nor can they possibly preserve from ultimate death. But the Sovereign Physician of souls possesses an unbounded plenitude of " grace and truth," and can heal the most inveterate diseases of mankind, and fully redeem his people from all their iniquities. He is a *perfect*, a *present*, and an *everlasting* Saviour, Col. i. 19 ; Heb. vii. 25. With Him no case is difficult, nor disease incurable. " Is any thing too hard for the Lord ?"

3. *He is an unchangeable Physician.* In all ages his name has been "like ointment poured forth," to the " weary and heavy laden." When he assumed humanity, he gave sight to the blind,—cleansed the lepers,—healed the sick,—raised the dead,—bound up the broken-hearted,—and comforted the distressed, Matt. xi. 5 ; Luke vi. 17—19. And though he ascended to heaven, he is still the gracious benefactor and Saviour of sinners.—All other physicians are mortal and perishing, but " Jesus is the same yesterday, to-day, and for ever." The healing virtue of his name is *undiminished*, and the cleansing efficacy of his blood is *immutable*.

4. *He is the only appointed Physician.* All other helps are insufficient, and other remedies ineffectual ; " for there is none other name under heaven given among men whereby we must be saved." Nor is any other Saviour necessary, for Jesus is all-sufficient, and his saving abilities are commensurate to the moral wants of the whole world. I thank God, "there is balm in Gilead, there is a Physician there," who can perfectly heal the most *protracted* and *obstinate* disorders of the soul. Unto whom then should we go, but unto Him who can save to the uttermost ? and to direct and encourage our application unto him, we shall proceed to notice,

III. THE SUBJECTS AND ATTAINMENTS OF GRACE. "They that be whole," &c. This is a self-evident position, and is intended to illustrate tne penitent's character, and method of coming to Christ for salvation. It evidently suggests,

1. *We must deeply feel our spiritual maladies.* Self-ignorance is a deadly and delusive disease of the mind. Under its pernicious influence, we form the most erroneous estimates of our real state and character; which generally operate as effectual barriers to the reception of Christ. We suppose that we are *comparatively* whole and good, and therefore " trust in ourselves that we are righteous ;" and consequently reject the only remedy of sovereign grace. Such was manifestly the deluded state of the ancient Pharisees, and the lukewarm Laodiceans ; and such is still the infatuated state of all impenitent sinners and nominal Christians, Luke xviii. 9; 2 Cor. iv. 3, 4 ; Rev. iii. 17.—But when the Holy Spirit convinceth us of our ignorance, guilt, depravity, and wretchedness, we become deeply conscious of the plague of our hearts, and anxiously inquire, what we shall do to be saved, Acts ii. 37, xvi 30, 31.

2. *We must sincerely renounce our sins.* The habits of impiety greatly aggravate and augment the contagious distempers of our moral nature. It is therefore absolutely necessary, not only to be convinced of our sinful state, but we must also unfeignedly repent, and utterly forsake all our iniquities, Isa. lv. 7 ; Acts iii. 19. And being truly sensible of our dangerously infected and perishing condition through sin, we shall earnestly desire and seek an immediate deliverance from the pestilence of moral evil, and a participation of pardoning mercy and regenerating grace, Luke xviii. 13. For this purpose, and in this contrite state of mind,

3. *We must personally apply to the Physician of souls.* This is a duty universally enjoined, and essentially connected with the attainment of salvation. As no advantage can possibly be derived from any remedy, however excellent, unless it be actually applied, neither can we obtain an interest in Christ's saving benefits, except by a personal application unto him, in the appointed means of grace, John v. 40. We should come to the heavenly Physician penitently—believingly—importunately—immediately—and perseveringly, Matt. xi. 28 ; Isa. xiv. 22 ; 2 Cor. vi. 2. In thus coming to the Saviour, he will heal our backslidings,—restore us to spiritual health,—grant us perfect soundness of mind, and ultimately crown us with immortality and eternal life. We may learn from this subject the need we have of Christ,—the reason why he is rejected,—the sufficiency of his grace, and the efficacy of his healing power. May we embrace this truth, and rejoice in his salvation.

THE EXALTATION OF CHRIST.

Phil. ii. 9—11.—Wherefore God also hath highly exalted him, and given him a name which is above every name, that at the name of Jesus every knee should bow, of things in heaven, and things in earth, and things under the earth : and that every tongue should confess that Jesus Christ is Lord, to the glory of God the Father. (H. H.)

WE are told by an inspired Apostle, that the great scope of the Prophecies related to " the sufferings of Christ, and the glory that should follow." To the same points our attention is continually turned in the New Testament.

Sometimes they are stated as an accomplishment of prophecy, and as proofs of Christ's Messiahship: sometimes as grounds of our hope before God: sometimes as motives to stimulate us to duty: sometimes as models, according to which God will work in us: and sometimes as examples, which we are bound to follow: and sometimes as encouragements to follow those examples. It is in this last view that we are to contemplate this stupendous mystery at this time. The Apostle had said, "Look not every man on his own things, but every man also on the things of others." To illustrate and enforce this exhortation, he shews how the Lord Jesus Christ had emptied himself of all his own glory, and endured death, even the accursed death of the cross, for the salvation of men: and that in consequence of it he had received such tokens of his Father's approbation as were commensurate with the sacrifice which he had made. In considering this testimony of his Father's love, let us mark,

I. THE HEIGHT TO WHICH HE WAS RAISED—

The Lord Jesus Christ, *as God*, was incapable of elevation: but, *as man*, he was raised from the lowest degradation to the highest degrees of glory.

Amidst the depths of his humiliation he was greatly exalted—

At his baptism he received an audible testimony from heaven, together with a visible communication of the Spirit of God, in attestation of his Messiahship. In all the miracles he wrought, a further testimony was borne to him by the Father. And in his last hours, when in appearance he was even deserted by his heavenly Father, universal nature bore witness to him; the sun going down, as it were, at noon-day; the earth rending and quaking to its very centre; and the most convincing evidence being given to all, that he whom they crucified was indeed the Son of God.

But it was not till after that period that the exaltation spoken of in the text commenced—

At his resurrection, he was declared to be the Son of God with power. — — —At his ascension he led captivity itself captive, and, surrounded with myriads of holy angels, went to take possession of his Father's throne. — — —Seated on that, he is elevated above all the works of God's hand's above men, so as to be " higher than the kings of the earth," even " King of kings and Lord of lords ;" Ps. lxxxix, 27 ; Rev. xix. 16 ; and above angels also, " all the principalities and powers of heaven being made subject unto him." 1 Pet. iii. 22 ; Heb. i. 5, 8, 9, 13.— — —

The text requires us particularly to notice,

II. THE REASON OF HIS EXALTATION—

It was in consequence of his previous humiliation: it was,

1. As a reward of his sufferings—

In this view it had been promised to him,— — —Isai. lii. 13—15 ; and liii. 10—12. In this view he himself looked forward to it with intense desire,— — —Heb. xii. 2 ; John xvii. 4, 5. And in this view it was actually conferred upon him,— — —Dan. vii. 13, 14 ; Heb. i. 3, 4.

2. As the means of completing the work he had undertaken—

He was to redeem us, both by price, and by power. On this account, after he had paid the price of our redemption, he was invested with " all power both in heaven and in earth ;" and " all things were given into his hands," that he might order every thing for the accomplishment of his own will, and the furtherance of the work which he had begun. In him was all fulness treasured up, that he might impart unto his people all needful supplies of grace ; Eph. i. 20—22 ; and to him was all authority committed, that he might put all enemies under his feet. 1 Cor. xv. 25 ; Ps. cx. 1, 2. Thus, by his elevation, are his triumphs and the triumphs of all his people, finally and eternally secured.

But we have further to notice his exaltation in reference to,

III. THE END OF IT—

It was that he might be the one object,

1. Of universal adoration—

Of this he is most worthy, as all the hosts of heaven testifiy.— — —Rev. v. 11—13. And it must be paid to him: for God hath sworn with an oath, that it shall be paid to him by all in heaven, earth, and hell; Rom. xiv. 11; with Isai. xlv. 23; or if we will not yield it to him as the voluntary expression of our love, we shall be constrained to acknowledge his right to it, whilst we are suffering under the stroke of his avenging rod. Ps. ii. 1—3, 6, 9—12.

2. Of unlimited affiance—

By confessing him to be both Lord and Christ, I understand such a confession as proceeds from unfeigned faith. Rom. x. 9—11. And to this full affiance is he entitled, both according to his essential nature as God, and in his Mediatorial capacity as the Saviour of the world. Isai. xlv. 22. In what way is it to be manifested, the Prophet tells us: " Surely shall one say, In the Lord have I righteousness and strength." Isai. xlv. 24. As " the Christ," who died for us, he is our righteousness; and as " the Lord," who is the Head and Governor of all, we receive out of his fulness all needful supplies of grace and strength.

Nor let it be thought that this direction of our regards to him will derogate at all from the honor of the Father: for, on the contrary, it will be " to the glory of God the Father," whose wisdom has devised, and whose love has executed, so wonderful a plan for the salvation of men. On this subject we can have no doubt; since our Lord himself had told us, That God's very design in the whole of this stupendous mystery was, " that all men should honor the Son even as they honor the Father; and That he who honoreth not the Son, honoreth not the Father who hath sent him." John v. 22, 23.

Behold then,

1. How awful is the state of those who submit not to him!

We are equally rebels against him, whether we oppose him as Lord, or as Christ; whether we refuse to submit to his righteousness, Rom. x. 3, or to his government. O reflect, ye who are going about to establish a righteousness of your own, What will ye answer to him, when he shall call you to an account for usurping his office, and making void all that he has done and suffered for you?— — —And you, who, whilst professing to trust in him as your Saviour, live in disobedience to his commands, where will you hide your heads, when he shall say, " Bring hither those mine enemies who would not that I should reign over them, and slay them before me?" Whatever ye may now think, ye cannot invalidate the oath of God: he has sworn that unto him every knee shall bow; and, if ye do it not willingly, ye shall do it against your will, to your everlasting sorrow.

2. How blessed is the state of his obedient people!

Shall Christ be exalted to the right hand of God in vain? or will he refuse to impart to you out of his fulness? Fear not: you are committed to his care; and he will not lose one of you; "not one shall ever be plucked out of his hands." Whatever you need it is treasured up in him; and " his grace shall be sufficient for you." It may be, that in his service you may be called to endure many things: but if now " he sees of the travail of his soul and is satisfied," be assured that ere long it shall be no grief to you that you were humbled for a season: for, " if you suffer with him, you shall also reign with him," and " be glorified together with him," 2 Tim. ii. 12; Rom. viii. 17; in his kingdom for evermore.

BENEFIT OF RECEIVING CHRIST.

John i. 10—12 —He was in the world, and the world was made by him, and the world knew him not. He came unto his own, and his own received him not: but as many as received him, to them gave he power to become the sons of God, even to them that believe on his name. (H. H.)

THE blessings which administer to our worldly interest or bodily comfort, are equally welcomed by persons of all ranks and conditions: but those which have relation only to our spiritual good, are despised by many, and desired by very few. The light of the sun is not less prized by one than by another: all are sensible of its benefits, and value it accordingly. But "the Sun of righteousness has arisen upon us," and the benighted world regards him not: " he shines in the darkness, and the darkness apprehends him not." Ver. 5. Some however there are, who rejoice in his advent: and as they only have learned to appreciate his worth, they only shall enjoy the full bene-fits he confers.

The words of the Evangelist will lead us to shew,

I. THE CONTEMPT POURED ON CHRIST BY THE UNBELIEVING WORLD—
What was said of him in that day is equally true in this:

1. His own *creatures* " do not know him"—

It was Christ who formed the universe: " the world was made by him; and without him was not any thing made that was made." Ver. 3, with the text. He has moreover " been in the world" from the very beginning, "up-holding it by his power," Heb. i. 3, and ordering every thing in it by his superintending providence. Yet, before his incarnation, he was not known; neither yet now is he known, as the Creator and Governor of the world. His name indeed is known; but he is considered only as a great prophet. The generality of those who *doctrinally* maintain his proper Deity, never *practically* realize the thought, that "by him all things subsist." Col i. 17.

2. His own *people* " do not receive him"—

The Jews were called " Christ's *own*," because he had separated them from all other people, brought them out of Egypt, led them through the wil-derness, and derived his human nature from the stock of Abraham, their father. Their very country was called "Emmanuel's land." Isa. viii. 8. But we are *his* in a still more appropriate sense; because he has bought us with his blood; and we have been baptized into his name; and profess our-selves his followers. Yet we "do not really receive him," any more than the Jews themselves did. We do not receive him *in the character which he bears in the holy scriptures*— — —We do not receive him *for the ends and purposes for which he came*†— — —

Alas! what contempt is this which we pour upon him! We can shudder at the indignities offered him by the Jews; but we ourselves are no less criminal than the people who crucified and slew him: they through ignor-ance apprehended and executed him as a malefactor: we, with our eyes open, cry, " Hail, Master," and betray him. Matt. xxvi. 49.

But that we may not continue to treat him thus, let us consider,

*He is a Prophet to teach us, a Priest to atone for us, a King to rule over us and in us. Do we receive him under these characters?

†He came to justify us by his blood, to sanctify us by his grace, and to save us with an everlasting salvation. Do we receive him for these ends?

II. The honor he confers on those who believe in him—

A " receiving of Christ," and a " believing in him," are represented in the text as of precisely the same import. It is superfluous therefore to add any thing more in explanation of the terms. The benefits accruing from faith are the objects which next demand our attention. Unspeakable is the honor of becoming a child of God: yet to every one that believes in him, our blessed Lord gives,

1. To bear this relation to God—

" To the Jews belonged the adoption," Rom. ix. 4, as far as related to the external privileges of it. But we, on believing, "are made partakers of the divine nature." 2 Pet. i. 4. We become the children of God as well by regeneration as adoption: yea, faith is at once the means, Gal. iii. 26, and the evidence, 1 John v. 1, of our sonship with God. There is no interval of time left for us to give proofs of our sincerity, before God will acknowledge us as his: but the instant we believe in Christ, we are " sons and daughters of the Lord almighty." 2 Cor. vi. 18.

2. To enjoy the privileges of this relation—

The children of a stranger are not noticed by us, while our own children are admitted freely into our presence, and are the objects of our tenderest solicitude, our unremitted attention. We feed them, we clothe them, we protect them, we provide every thing for them that is suited to our circumstances, and that will contribute to their welfare. In all these respects believers find God a Father to them. They can go into his presence, " crying Abba, Father;" Gal. iv. 6; and obtain from him whatever is necessary either for their support or comfort.

3. To possess an inheritance worthy of that relation—

Parents account it a duty to provide for the future maintenance of their children, and not merely for their present subsistence. With this view they lay up fortunes for them, which they are to inherit after the decease of their parents. Similar to this is the provision made for those who believe in Christ. They are " begotten again to an inheritance that is incorruptible and undefiled, and never-fading." 1 Pet. i. 3. " Being sons, they are heirs, heirs of God, and joint-heirs with Christ." Rom. viii. 17. Nor shall they merely divide their Father's inheritance among them; but every one of them shall enjoy the whole, and have his happiness enlarged, rather than diminished, by the communication of it to others.

Learn then from hence,

1. The folly of unbelievers—

One would suppose, that, in calling them to believe in Jesus Christ, we urged them to make the greatest sacrifices, and to resign every thing that could conduce to their happiness. But, on the contrary, we only invite them to " receive;" to receive " the greatest gift" which God himself is able to bestow: John iv. 10; to receive Him, in whom they will find all that they can possibly desire. We require them to surrender nothing but what will make them miserable; and to receive nothing which will not make them happy. How unreasonable does their conduct appear when viewed in this light! If we were to offer them bags of gold, we should find them willing enough to accept as many as we could bestow. But when we exhort them to accept *Him* who is of more value than ten thousand worlds, they turn a deaf ear to our most importunate intreaties. See, ye unbelievers, see your extreme folly! and remember, that the day is coming, when that rejection of Christ, in which you now glory, will become the ground of your bitterest lamentation.

2. The unspeakable benefit of faith—

There are many things which put a considerable difference between one man and another. The influence of wealth and dignity exalts some far above the level of their fellow-creatures. The acquisition of knowledge and wisdom has no less effect in elevating the characters and conditions of men. But all the distinctions in the universe do not avail to dignify a man so much as faith. Faith brings Christ into the soul, and puts the poorest of men into the possession of "unsearchable riches." Faith makes him, from a child of the devil, a child of God; from an heir of misery, an heir of glory. Faith elevates him from death to life, from infamy to honor, from hell to heaven. "Faith, even though it be small as a grain of mustard-seed," produces all these wonderful effects. Cultivate then, my brethren, this divine principle. Labor to have it in more continued exercise. Let Christ, the greatest object of faith, be more and more precious to your soul. Thus shall you be really the most distinguished characters on earth, and ere long "inherit the kingdom prepared for you by your heavenly Father."

~~~~~~~~~~

FAITH IN CHRIST AN ANTIDOTE TO ALL TROUBLE.

John xiv. 1.—Let not your heart be troubled: ye believe in God; believe also in me.
(II. H.)

As God is eminently distinguished by that character, "The comforter of all them that are cast down," so did Jesus evince his title to it during the whole time of his sojourning on earth: there was no distress which he did not remove from those who made their application to him; and not unfrequently did he anticipate the wants, which the unbelief or ignorance of his followers made them unable to express. He had now been revealing to his disciples the things which were speedily to be accomplished: and, perceiving that they were greatly dejected by the prospect before them, he encouraged them in the words which we have read; "Let not your hearts be troubled:" and then he prescribed an antidote, sufficient to dispel all their fears: "Ye believe in God; believe also in me."

In discoursing on these words, we shall show,

I. The troubles which he taught them to expect—

There were three in particular which seemed most to affect them;

1. Their bereavement of his presence—

This, if it had been only to a remote quarter of the globe, or after the manner of Elijah's departure, would have greatly depressed their minds; because of the love he had manifested towards them, and their entire dependence on him for instruction and support— — —but to have him withdrawn from them by cruel sufferings and an ignominious death, was distressing beyond measure; so that the very thought of it filled them with the deepest concern— — —

2. The disappointment of all their worldly hopes—

They had supposed he was about to establish an earthly kingdom, and that they should be exalted to situations of great dignity. But when they heard, that, instead of reigning over other nations, he was to be rejected by his own; and that, instead of elevating them to posts of honor, he himself was to die upon a cross; they knew not how to reconcile these things with his former

281

professions, or how to bear the shame which such a disappointment would unavoidably occasion— — —

3. The persecutions they were to meet with from an ungodly world—

Hitherto they had been screened from persecution, their Lord and Master having borne the brunt of it in his own person: but now they understood that they were to drink of his cup, and to endure all manner of sufferings, and death itself, after his example. This excited painful apprehensions in their minds, and caused them the most serious disquietude— — —

What means he used to dissipate their fears, will be found in,

II. THE REMEDY HE PROPOSED—

The verbs in our text may be taken either imperatively or indicatively; and many think it would be better to construe both of them alike: but the spirit of the passage seems best preserved in our translation; which acknowledges, that they *do* believe in God the Father, and exhorts them to place the same confidence in him as in the Father. They now thought they should lose him entirely and for ever. To rectify this error, he enjoins them, notwithstanding his removal from them, to believe in him,

1. As present with them in their trials—

Though he would not be present to the eye of sense, he would be really nigh to them on all occasions. Wherever they should be, there would be no bar to his admission to their souls: he would come and visit them, and dwell in them, and manifest himself to them, as he would not unto the world. This would be a far greater blessing to them than his bodily presence; so that they had no reason to regret his apparent withdrawment from them.

2. As interested in their welfare—

They had never found him indifferent about any thing that related to them: nor would he forget them after he should have been taken from them into heaven: on the contrary, he was going thither to prepare mansions for them; and he would still enter into all their concerns, sympathizing with them in their afflictions, and regarding every thing that should be done to them as done immediately to himself. If any should give them a cup of cold water only, he would acknowledge it as an obligation conferred on him; and, if any should presume to touch them in a way of injury, *he* would resent it as if they " touched the apple of *his* eye."

3. As sufficient for their support—

They had seen what wonders he had wrought during his continuance amongst them: and they must not imagine, that, because he offered up his soul a sacrifice for sin, he was therefore deprived of his power to perform them: for though he would, in appearance, be crucified through weakness, he did really posses all power in heaven and in earth. They might still look to him for the relief of every want, and support in every trial; and they should assuredly find his grace sufficient for them.

4. As coming again to recompense all that they might endure for his sake— .

He had told them, that he would come again, and *that* too in all the glory of his Father, with myriads of attendant angels, to judge the world. They need not therefore be anxious about any present trials, since he pledged himself to remember all that they should do or suffer for him, and richly compensate their fidelity to him.

These were subjects on which he had often conversed familiarly with them: and if only they would give him credit for the accomplishment of his promises, they might discard their fears, and be of good comfort.

It will be not unprofitable to consider more distinctly,

III. THE SUFFICIENCY OF THIS REMEDY TO DISPEL ALL ANXIETY FROM THEIR MINDS—

Faith in Christ is a perfect antidote against troubles of every kind. Faith has respect to him in all his glorious offices and characters:

1. As the Saviour of the soul—

What has that man to do with fear or trouble, who sees all his iniquities purged away by the blood of Jesus, and his soul accepted before God?— — If he forget these things, he may be cast down by earthly trials: but if he keep this steadily in view, the sufferings of time will be of no account in his eyes: he will feel that he has ground for nothing but unbounded and incessant joy— — —

2. As the governor of the universe—

Who that sees how perfectly every thing is under the control of Jesus, will give way to fear or grief? Not a sparrow falls, nor a hair of our head can be touched, without him: and, if he suffer any injury to be inflicted on us, he can overrule it so as to convert it into the greatest benefit. What then have we to do, but to let him work his own will, and to expect that all things shall work together for our good?— — —

3. As the head of his people—

He is to all his people the head of vital influence; and will he forget to communicate what is necessary for the welfare of his members? We are weak; and our enemies are mighty: but is that any ground for fear, whilst we remember whose members we are? Can we not do all things through Christ strengthening us?— — —

4. As the Judge of quick and dead—

The distribution of rewards and punishments is committed unto him; and he has told us what sentence he will pronounce on all his faithful people. And will not that word, " Come ye blessed," or that, " Well done good and faithful servant," richly repay all that we can do or suffer for him in this world? Can we survey the thrones of glory he has prepared for us, and be afraid of the trials that await us here?— — —

Behold then,

1. The happiness of believers—

They *may*, they *must*, have their trials; and whilst they possess the feelings of men, they will find some trials grievous to be borne: but they neither have, nor can have, any cause for anxious fear: whilst God is for them, none can be against them. Let them therefore " be careful for nothing," but " cast all their care on Him who careth for them."

2. The misery of unbelievers—

Where has God said to *them*, " Let not your hearts be troubled?" No such word can be found in all the sacred volume. They have need of continual fear and terror: for, what refuge have they, whilst they are not united unto Christ by faith? Whither can they go under the trials of this life? and what consolation can they have in the prospect of eternity? Better were it, if they die in such a state, that they had never been born. Hear then what Jesus says to you: Look unto ME, and be ye saved, all the ends of the earth; for I am God; and besides me there is none else. His address, in the text, is a proof of his Godhead, and consequently of his sufficiency to save all that come unto God by him.

CHRIST'S LOVE TO HIS PEOPLE.

Mark iii. 31--35.—There came then his brethren and his mother, and, standing without, sent unto him, calling him. And the multitude sat about him, and they said unto him, Behold, thy mother and thy brethren without seek for thee. And he answered them, saying, Who is my mother, or my brethren? And he looked round about on them which sat about him, and said, Behold my mother and my brethren! For whosoever shall do the will of God, the same is my brother, and my sister, and mother. (H. H.)

IT is common for persons to feel an undue degree of solicitude for the bodily welfare of their friends, whilst they have little anxiety for the spiritual and eternal welfare of mankind at large. Hence, if a minister be in danger of impairing his health by his exertions, they are ready to say to him, "Spare thyself:" but, if thousands be perishing all around them for lack of knowledge, they are not so ready to stir him to increased activity and diligence. The near relations of our Lord were under the influence of this partial regard, when "they went out to lay hold on Jesus, and said of him, "He is beside himself;" or, as it might rather be translated, "He is transported too far." Ver. 20, 21, ὅτι ἐξέϛη. It should seem that it was with that view that they called for him at this time: they were afraid that he would sink under the weight of his continued labors. But he felt, that both health, and life too, were well sacrificed in such a cause: and therefore he disregarded their message, and turned it into an occasion of expressing the greatness of his regard for his obedient followers.

From the declaration of our Lord, we shall be led to shew,

I. THE CHARACTER OF THOSE WHOM JESUS LOVES.

This is expressed in few, but comprehensive words; "They do the will of God." But what is this will? It includes two things:

1. They believe in Jesus Christ—

This is eminently the will of God: 1 John iii. 23, and till this be done, nothing is done to any good purpose: the persons remain, and ever must remain, objects of his wrath. John iii. 18—36. *This therefore they do in the first place*— — —And they do it humbly, renouncing utterly every other ground of hope— — —and thankfully adoring God from their inmost souls for *such* a refuge— — —

2. They seek after universal holiness—

This also is the will of God; 1 Thess. iv. 3, nor are the loudest professions of attachment to Christ of any avail without it. Matt. vii. 21. *And this also they do.* And they do it unreservedly, accounting "no commandment grievous," 1 John v. 3, and in a progressive manner, never thinking they have attained, while any thing remains to be attained. Phil. iii. 12—14.

We pass on to consider,

II. THE REGARD HE BEARS TOWARDS THEM.

Our Lord gives them the preference to his nearest relations, *as such;* and honors them with the most endearing appellations of brother, sister, mother. Now from this we must understand, that,

1. He bears the tenderest affection towards them—

We naturally expect the warmest affection to subsist between persons so closely allied to each other. But the love that is found amongst earthly relatives is but a faint image of that which both Christ and his Father feel towards all their obedient followers. John xvi. 21.

2. He will give them the most familiar access to him—

His mother and his brethren were all this time without, whilst Jesus and his attentive followers were within, the house: and, though solicited by his own mother, he would not go out to *her*, because it would deprive *them* of the instructions which they were anxious to receive. And who can tell, what gracious communications Jesus will vouchsafe to those who serve him in spirit and in truth? They shall never seek his face in vain: they shall never call for him, but he will answer them, Here I am. Compare John xiv. 24, with Isa. lviii. 9, and lxv. 24.

3. He will order every thing for their good—

Any man that is not devoid of principle will consult the good of his family, when the management of their affairs is committed to him. And will not Jesus, who is constituted "Head over all things for the express benefit of his church," Eph. i. 22, be attentive to the wants of his obedient people? Will he not supply all their wants, mitigate all their sorrows, and overrule all things for their eternal good? Rom. viii. 28.

4. He will own them as his, in the last day—

Suppose him in that day surrounded by the whole assembled universe; and many who were once related to him in the flesh, or who once professed themselves his followers, calling upon him, and saying, ' We want a nearer access to thee; " we have eaten and drunk in thy presence; we have cast out devils in thy name, and in thy name done many wonderful works;" we are your brethren, your sisters, your nearest and dearest relatives.' Methinks he will then renew the same gracious declaration that is contained in our text; "Who is my mother, or my brethren?" And then, "stretching out his hand towards his obedient followers, he will say, Behold my mother, and my brethren: for, whosoever did the will of God, the same is my brother, and sister, and mother."

INFER,

1. How reasonable are the terms on which Christ proposes to acknowledge uss a his disciples!

He requires that all who would be his disciples should *apparently* cast off all regard for their nearest friends and relatives. Luke xiv. 26. I say *apparently;* for nothing is *really* farther from his intentions, than to encourage, either by *this* declaration, or by that in the text, any disrespect to our parents: on the contrary, we are commanded to *honor* our parents; and are told by the Apostle, that "that is the first commandment with promise." But when our love or obedience to earthly parents stands in competition with our obedience to Christ, then we must resemble Levi; in commendation of whom it is said, "He said unto his father and to his mother, I have not seen him, neither did he acknowledge his brethren, nor knew his own children." Deut. xxxiii. 9, with Exod. xxxii. 26—28. And shall this appear harsh or unreasonable? See what Jesus has done for us: He knew not his mother and his brethren in comparison of his believing and obedient people: and shall we prefer our earthly relatives to him? If he has so loved us, who are altogether polluted, and deserve nothing but evil at his hands, how much more should we so love *him*, who is altogether lovely, and deserves infinitely more love at our hands than eternity will be sufficient to express!

2. What encouragement have we to comply with these terms!

In complying with the terms which Christ has proposed, and adhering to him in opposition to the will of earthly friends, we may possibly incur their displeasure, and feel to the uttermost of their power the effects of their resentment: they may frown upon us, disown us, disinherit us. But "when father and mother forsake us, the Lord will take us up." His express promise is, that for one father, mother, brother, sister, house, or estate we lose for his sake. we shall even in this life receive an hundred fathers, mothers.

brothers, sisters, houses, and estates. Mark x. 29, 30. Does any one ask, How shall this be accomplished? We might answer, that it is abundantly verified in the regard shewn to us by the Lord's people : but, independen of that, we say, the Lord Jesus will give himself to us, and be to us more than ten thousand relatives, or ten thousand worlds. Let any one say, whether the love of Christ, the grace of Christ, and the glory of Christ, do not compensate an hundred-fold for all the creature-love, and all the temporal advantages, that we can lose for him? Let the determination then of Joshua be ours ; that whatever course others may follow, and whatever obstacles they may lay in our way, " we, with God's help, will serve the Lord."

3. How unlike to Christ are they, to whom a compliance with these terms is odious!

None are so odious in the eyes of the ungodly world as the true, faithful, determined christian. The generality, instead of loving him in proportion to his advancement in piety, will despise him ; and will make his high attainments, not only *the occasion,* but *the measure,* of their contempt. They will be ashamed to acknowledge a pious character as a relation, or friend, or even as an acquaintance. They would rather be seen in public with an infidel or a debauchee, than with one who was eminent for his love to Christ. But how unlike to Christ are *they ;* when the very thing which endears them to him, renders them odious in *their* eyes. Surely it will be well for such persons to consider what Christ's views of *them* must be ? for if the godly are so precious to him *because* they are godly, surely the haters and despisers of godliness must for *that very reason* be most hateful in his eyes. Accordingly he has told us, how he will resent the contempt shewn to his people ; and that " it were better for a man to have a millstone hanged about his neck, and to be cast into the sea, than that he should offend one of his little ones." Matt. xviii. 6.

CHRIST'S CARE FOR HIS SHEEP.

Isa. xl. 11.—He shall feed his flock like a shepherd : he shall gather the lambs with his arm, and carry them in his bosom ; and shall gently lead those that are with young. (H. H.)

THE holy Psalmist, speaking of Jehovah's care of him, says, " The Lord is my Shepherd :" and then, from the union of the Godhead with the pastoral office, he infers, "Therefore I shall not want." Ps. xxiii. 1. The same incomprehensible union is mentioned by the prophet in the passage before us. The Heralds that proclaimed the advent of the Messiah were commanded to draw the attention of men to him in these words, " Behold your God !" The person thus announced, is further described in the words preceding our text; "Behold! the Lord God will come:" and then it is added, " HE shall feed his flock like a shepherd." Now when it is considered how prone the Israelites were to idolatry, it cannot be conecived that the prophet should speak of the Messiah in such exalted terms, if they did not properly belong to him. But the Prophets generally, and Isaiah in particular, are very full and explicit in declaring, that Jehovah was to become incarnate, and by the sacrifice of himself to redeem and save a ruined world. It is not however of his *person* that we now propose to speak, but of his *office ; that* being the particular point to which my text refers : yet it would be improper to pass over such a strong testimony to the divinity of our blessed Lord, because, in the judgment of all, but more especially of Jews, it must have the effect of silencing every doubt upon that important subject. And it adds no little interest to the description here given of him, when we know, that He who so condescends to minister as a Shepherd to the least and meanest of his flock, is the Most High God: according as it is written, "To us a child is born, to us a Son is given; and his name shall be called The Mighty God." Isai. ix. 6.

The words which form the ground-work of our discourse, will lead me to set before you,

I. A GENERAL VIEW OF OUR LORD AS A SHEPHERD—

The character of a shepherd is frequently assigned to our blessed Lord, in the Scriptures both of the Old and New Testament: Ezek. xxxvii. 24; Zech. xiii. 7; Heb. xiii. 20; 1 Pet. v. 4; and every duty pertaining to that office is executed by him :—

1. He gathers them to his fold—

They are "wandering upon the dark mountains, in a cloudy and dark day;" Ezek. xxxiv. 6; "every one going in *his own* way," Isai. liii. 6; and "after the imaginations of his own heart."— — —Jer. xxiii. 17. The paths of all, though differing from each other according as the age, the inclinations, and the diversified temptations of the different individuals may lead them, — — —all agree in this, that they are far distant from the ways of God's commandments. Rom. iii. 11, 12. But "he searches for them, and seeks them out:" he follows them by the preaching of his word, by the dispensations of his providence, by the mighty working of his Spirit; and having found them, "he apprehends them" by his pastoral crook, Phil. iii. 12; and "makes them willing" to return with him, Ps. cx. 3; and "carries them home upon his shoulders rejoicing."— — —Luke xv. 5, 6.

2. He provides for their wants—

Oh! how sweet are the pastures into which he leads them! Ezek. xxxiv. 14. Who can express the delight which a converted soul experiences in feeding upon the promises, "the exceeding great and precious promises" of his God? — — —In comparison of the food provided for the sheep of Christ, all else is but as "husks on which the swine subsist." Luke xv. 16. Isai. lv 2. This is set forth in Scripture under the image of a luxurious feast: Isai. xxiv. 6; and verily it is "a feast of fat things" to all the saints; a feast on which the even angels themselves might account it a privilege to partake.— — —Ps. lxxviii. 25.

3. He affords them his effectual protection—

Weak as they are, and beset with many enemies, they are preserved in perfect safety.— — —1 Pet. i. 5. He who laid down his life for them, will suffer "none to pluck them out of his hand."— — —John x. 11, 28. "They lie down beside the still waters," Ps. xxiii. 2; which are a just emblem of the tranquility of their own souls.— — —"They are kept in perfect peace, because they trust in him." Isai. xxvi. 3.

4. He administers to them according to their diversified necessities—

Amongst them there will be some who are sick, or diseased, or injured by some misfortune: but he knows all their particular cases, and imparts to them the relief which they severally need; "bringing back those which have been driven away, binding up that which has been broken, and strengthening that which is sick;— — —Ezek. xxxiv. 16; and never intermitting his care of them, till he has brought them to his fold above.— — —Ps xxiii. 5. 6.

But our text requires us to take,

II. A more particular view of him as ministering to the weak and needy—

Let us notice then in a more especial manner,

1. His tenderness to the weak—

The lambs which have been but recently brought forth, may be supposed incapable of proceeding with the flock to any distant pasture. But these " he will gather with his arms, and carry in his bosom." " He will not despise the day of small things." Zech. iv. 10. There is not one in all his flock so weak, but he will pay the most minute attention to its necessities. He who gave so particular a charge to Peter to " feed his lambs," and required this of him as a necessary proof of his love, John xxi. 15, will not himself neglect his lambs ; but rather will augment his tender assiduities in proportion as the weakness of the lamb calls for more peculiar care : he will even take it up, and " carry it in his bosom." In what an endearing view does this place the character of our blessed Lord !— — —How sweetly encouraging is this consideration to those who feel their weakness, and are ready to despond because of it !— — —Let us remember, that when his disciples would have kept persons from troubling him with their little children, he reproved them, and said, " Suffer little children to come unto me, and forbid them not; for of such is the kingdom of heaven." Mark x. 14. Whether therefore you be children in respect of your natural or spiritual birth, fail not to come to him, assured, that he will bear with your infirmities, and " perfect his own strength in your weakness."— — —2 Cor. xii. 9.

2. His compassion to the afflicted—

He will have respect to the state of his flock, even as Jacob had, who " would not overdrive them one day, lest they should all die." Gen. xxxiii. 13, 14. So our blessed Lord " will gently lead that which is with young." There are amongst his people many who are weary and heavy-laden with a sense of sin, and bowed down greatly by reason of the difficulties of their way. But to the former he sends a special invitation, with an assured promise of rest : Matt. xi. 28 ; and to the latter he authorizes us to declare, that " he will raise them up." Ps. cxlvi. 8. In truth, he is pre-eminently distinguished by this, that " he will not break the bruised reed, nor quench the smoking flax ; but will bring forth judgment unto victory." Matt. xii. 20. Consider what is implied in these metaphors : a bruised reed is, according to human appearance, incapable of even sending forth a melodious sound ; and smoking flax has, as it were, but a hidden spark of fire, whilst it is sending forth whole clouds of corruption : yet will Christ fan the expiring spark to a flame, and attune the reed to send forth the most heavenly strains. Let none then despond, however destitute they may be of any thing to encourge them from within ; but let them "be strong in the Lord, and in the power of his might." — — —Eph. vi. 10.

Let me now ADD a few words,

1. In commendation of this good Shepherd—

Whence is it that all do not put themselves under his care ? Is there any want of love, or tenderness, or power in him ? God frequently, by his prophets, called on his rebellious people to testify against him, and to say, Whether there had been any want of kindness or care in him : " O my people, what have I done unto thee ? and wherein have I wearied thee ? Testify against me." Mic. vi. 3 ; Jer. ii. 5, 31. " What could I have done more for my people than I have done ?" Isai. v. 4. So do I now, in the name of this good Shepherd, call upon you all this day, to bear, if you can, your testimony against him. Whom did he ever neglect or despise ? Whom that sought him, did he ever refuse to receive? Whom that trusted in him did he ever omit to supply according to his necessities?— — —If then no complaint ever was, or could be made against him from the world, let every heart appreciate his excellency, and every soul commit itself to his care.*

2. For the augmentation and encouragement of his flock—

You who have to this hour been going astray, and walking in the way of your own hearts, reflect upon your guilt and danger, and "return now without delay to the Shepherd and Bishop of your souls."— — —1 Pet. ii. 25. As employed by him, I come now to search you out, and to bring you home to his field.— — —Eph. iv. 11; Mark xvi. 15; Jer. xxiii. 4. O think, how delightful it will be to "hear his voice calling every one of you by name," John x. 3, and "going in and out with you" as long as you shall remain in this dreary wilderness, ib. ver. 9, and then performing the same office for you in the realms of bliss! Rev vii. 17. "O listen not to the voice of strangers"— — —but, follow him— — —that you may be one fold under one Shepherd for ever and ever. John x. 5, 9, 16.

SECURITY AND COMFORT IN CHRIST.

Isaiah xxxii. 2. –A man shall be as an hiding-place from the wind, and a covert from the tempest; as rivers of water in a dry place, as the shadow of a great rock in a weary land. (S. S.)

THERE is no greater blessing to a nation than a well-ordered government— The due administration of justice, together with the protection of our person and property, afford to any people a just ground of joy and thankfulness— Such a government did God promise to the Jews under Hezekiah—But a greater than Hezekiah is here—Under the figure of an earthly monarch, Christ is promised—And the text informs us,

I. WHAT BLESSINGS WE ENJOY IN AND THROUGH CHRIST.

The metaphors, though four in number, suggest but two ideas

1. Security.

We have very little conception of winds and tempests in this climate—But the wind that rent the mountains before Elijah, 1 Kings xix. 11, and the tempest that desolated the land of Egypt, Exod. ix. 23—25, may serve to shew us how welcome a secure place must be to one who is exposed to such formidable dangers—Yet no storms on earth can fully paint to us the dangers to which we are exposed by reason of sin, Ps. xi. 6.—But the Lord Jesus Christ affords us perfect security from them all—In him we have a Goshen where no hail can come, a mountain which the wind can never affect—The billows, which shall overwhelm the whole creation besides, shall not be able to destroy us—In Christ we have an ark that can never perish—

2. Comfort.

We, in this quarter of the globe, know as little of excessive drought and heat, as of overwhelming storms and tempests—But the state of the Israelites in the wilderness, Exod. xvii. 2, 3, and of Jonah at Nineveh (Jonah iv. 8,) may aid our conceptions—How delightful was the gourd to *him*, and how

*If this were a subject for an *Ordination* or *Visitation* Sermon, the Clergy should be urged to follow the example of this good Shepherd.

reviving to *them* were the streams that gushed from the rock !—And does no a soul oppressed with sin or persecution, or fainting with desire after righteousness, experience as much distress as they ?—Behold then the preciousness of Christ!—He will be not only as a shade or as water to the weary and thirsting soul, but as " rivers of water" that can never be exhausted, and a " shadow of a great rock" through which the beams of the sun can never penetrate—Many can attest his excellency in these respects—Nor shall any who seek refuge in him be ever diappointed of their hope—

But as these things are spoken of Christ as " a man," it will be proper to shew,

II. How we enjoy them in him as "a man."

Christ is truly and properly God—But he is God manifest in the flesh—And it is to him as incarnate that we stand indebted for these blessings.

1. As man, he died for our sins.

To his atonement we owe all our hopes of salvation—If he had not expiated our guilt we could never have obtained mercy—If he had not purchased for us the gift of the Holy Ghost, we never could have mortified our inward corruptions—But through his death we are freed from the apprehensions of wrath ; and through his Spirit we are filled with righteousness, and peace, and joy, Rom. xiv. 17,—Hence our song will ever be, To him who loved us and washed us from our sins in his own blood, be glory and honor—Rev. i. 5.

2. As man he intercedeth for us in heaven.

As our peace was effected by the death of Christ, so is it maintained by his intercession—Now it is as man that he appears in the presence of God for us ; and liveth on purpose to carry on this part of his priestly office—By virtue of this our persons and services find acceptance with God—Pardon is given us for our renewed transgressions, and strength is imparted to surmount our manifold temptations—Hence is our salvation justly ascribed, and *that* in a very peculiar manner, to his intercession for us—Heb. vii. 25.

3. As man he is our head and representative

Christ is the second Adam, the Lord from heaven, 1 Cor. xv. 45, 47,—Our life is now treasured up in *him*, that it may no longer be exposed to the assaults of our great adversary, Col. iii. 3,—It has pleased the Father that in *him* should all fulness dwell ; and that out of his fulness all should receive, who shall ever be partakers of his grace, or of his glory, John i. 16,—Whether we want wisdom to guide us, righteousness to justify us, or sanctification to make us holy, we must look for all of it in and through Christ—As in Adam, our first covenant-head, all died, so in Christ, our new covenant-head, shall all be made alive—1 Cor. xv. 22.

4. As man he shall judge the world in the last day.

All judgment is committed to him because he is the Son of man, John v. 27,—And what can tend more to our security and comfort than this ?—Will he, who shed his blood for us, give up what he has so dearly purchased?—Or he who both interceded for us, and supplied our wants, consign us over to perdition ?—Will he not rather bear testimony in opposition to our fierce accuser, and own the work he had both wrought for us and in us ?—Doubtless, if we should feel a degree of security and comfort in having a very dear friend for our judge on earth, much more may we rejoice in having for our judge in the last day, him, who bought us with his blood and renewed us by his Spirit—

We do not mean to exclude his Godhead from this great work of redemption—It is that which gives efficacy to all which he did and suffered as man—

But nevertheless it is as man. that is, as the God-man, that we feel our relation to him, and have access unto him as our sympathizing friend—

INFER,

1. What objects of pity are they who have no interest in Christ!

They are exposed to all the wrath of a sin-avenging God—And where, where will they flee for safety?—Where will they even procure a drop of water in that land of drought and misery, to which they shall be banished?—Alas! there is no protection but in this city of refuge; there is no water but in this fountain—O that men would consider what they shall do in the day of their visitation!—And flee for refuge to the hope that is now set before them—Heb. vi. 18.

2. How highly privileged are they who believe in Christ!

They are not exempt from occasional distress either of soul or body—But they have an almighty friend to whom they can carry their distress—They go to him when heavy laden; and find rest unto their souls—They feel themselves secure in their blood-sprinkled dwellings—But their privileges will not be fully seen till the last day—Then how happy in having a covert from the wrath that overwhelms the ungodly world!—Then to have their Saviour both for their witness and their judge!—Let us all cleave to him with full purpose of heart; and desire to know him more and more as our friend and our beloved."

CHRIST'S EXERCISE OF SUPREME POWER OVER THE INVISIBLE WORLD.

Rev. i. 17, 18 —Fear not; I am the first and the last: I am he that liveth, and was dead; and behold, I am alive for evermore, Amen; and have the keys of hell and of death. (S. S.)

MAN, while he continued in a state of innocence, communed freely with his Maker face to face: but from the time that sin entered into the world, he has dreaded the presence of the most High, and fled from it with fear and trembling. Whenever God has been pleased to appear to any of his people, the sight has uniformly filled them with terror; and in some instances, almost deprived them even of life. This was the effect produced by a vision vouchsafed to John. Our blessed Lord, in a habit somewhat resembling that of the high priest, revealed himself to his beloved disciple: and so august was his appearance, that John, unable to endure the sight, fell at his feet as dead. But our Lord, in condescension to his weakness, dispelled his fears by making known to him the perfections of his nature, and the offices which in his mediatorial capacity he sustained.

In discoursing on his words we shall consider

I. OUR LORD'S RECORD CONCERNING HIMSELF.

A more glorious description of Jesus is not to be found in all the sacred writings: he declares himself to be

1. The eternal God.

The terms, "the first and the last," are intended to express eternity: ver 8, 11, and Rev. xxii. 13, and, in this view, it is an incommunicable attribute of Jehovah. It is often used to describe God in places where he contrasts himself with the gods of the heathen: Isa. xliv. 6, and it always characterizes him as infinitely superior to all creatures. But Jesus here arrogates it to himself. Eternty had been ascrib 1 to him both by prophets and apostles: Prov. viii. 22—30, Mic. v. 2, Joh 1 i. 1, Heb. xiii. 8, but he here claims it himself as his own prerogative; i or, notwithstanding he was in the form of a servant, he thought it not rob ery to be equal with God. Phil. ii. 6. Hence then it is evident that Jesus s one with the Father, "in glory equal, in majesty co-eternal," God over ll, blessed for evermore.— Rom. ix. 5.

2. The living Saviour.

He, whose brightness now exceeded that of the meridian sun, once hung upon the cross. But, says he, "*though*, καὶ, was dead, yet I am the living One, ῾Ο ζῶν, possessed of life in myself, John v. 26, and the source of life to others; and immutably living, to carry on the work which I began on earth." "Behold" this with wonder, yet with a full assurance of its truth; for, I, the "Amen," "the true and faithful witness, declare it unto thee. Now as the former assertion shews us what he was in his divine nature, this informs us what he is in his mediatorial office "He died for our offences, and rose again for our justification;" and is, not only our advocate with the Father, Rom. viii. 34, but the head of vital influence to all that believe. Eph. i. 22, 23.

3. The universal Sovereign.

By "hell" we are to understand, not the habitation of the damned only, but the whole invisible world: and "death" is the door of introduction to it. Now to "have the keys" of these, is to have the power over them, together with the entire appointment of men's states in reference to them. Isa. xxii. 22. And this power does Jesus exercise. Whomsoever he will, and in whatever time or manner he sees fit, he consigns to death, and fixes instantly in heaven or hell: "He openeth and no man shutteth; he shutteth, and no man openeth." Rev. iii. 7. Hence it appears that every event in this world also, must be under his control; and consequently, that he is the universal sovereign.

From the encouraging address which accompanied this record, we are led to consider

II. Its TENDENCY TO COMFORT AND SUPPORT THE SOUL.

When a similar vision was vouchsafed to Daniel, its effects, which were also similar, were counteracted in the same manner. Dan. x. 5—12. Now this record of our Lord was well calculated to dissipate the fears of John; and may well also be a comfort to us

1. Under apprehensions of temporal calamities.

Impending dangers and distresses will often excite terror, and overwhelm the soul with anxious dread. But what ground of fear can he have, who has the eternal God for his refuge? What injury can arise to him, whose soul is in the Redeemer's hands, and for whose benefit all things are ordered both in heaven and earth? "Not a hair of his head can perish" but by special commission from his best friend. "Thousands may fall beside him, and ten thousand at his right hand;" but "no weapon that is formed against him, can prosper." If his eyes were opened to behold his real situation, he might see himself encompassed with horses of fire, and chariots of fire: 2 Kings vi. 17, and, standing as an impregnable fortress, he might defy the assaults of men or devils. If his God and Saviour be for him, none can be against him. Rom. viii. 31.

2. Under fears of eternal condemnation.

No man can reflect upon his own character without feeling that he deserves the wrath of God: and every one that is sensible of his own demerits, mus tremble lest the judgments he has deserved should be inflicted on him. Yet a just view of the Saviour may dispel his fears, and cause him to rejoice with joy unspeakable." Does his guilt appear too great to be forgiven? He that offered an atonement for it, is the eternal God. Acts xx. 28. Do doubts arise respecting his acceptance with the Father? Behold, that very Jesus who made atonement for him, ever liveth to plead it as his advocate, and to present it before the mercy seat. 1 John i. 1, 2. Do death and hell appal him with their terrors? they are altogether subject to the control of Jesus, whose power and faithfulness are pledged for the salvation of all his ransomed people. John x. 28, 29. To the weakest then we say in the name of this adorable Saviour, "Fear not:" though thou art "a worm, thou shalt thresh the mountains;" Isa. xli. 10, 14, 15, and though thou art the smallest grain that has been gathered from the field, thou shalt be treasured safely in the granary of thy heavenly Father. Amos ix. 9.

APPLICATION.

We cannot conclude the subject without applying it to those who are ignorant of Christ. Surely we must not say to you, "Fear not;" but rather, "Fear and tremble," for he whom ye have despised, is the eternal God; and ever liveth to put down his enemies, and to make them his footstool. He has only, as it were, to turn the key of the invisible world, and your souls will be locked up in the prison, from whence there is no redemption. O consider this, ye that live unmindful of this adorable Saviour; and prostrate yourselves at his feet, while his offers of mercy are yet extended to you

---

CHAPTER V.

THE HOLY SPIRIT.

CHRIST'S OFFER OF THE SPIRIT.

John vii. 37, 38.—In the last day, that great day of the feast, Jesus stood and cried, saying, If any man thirst, let him come unto me, and drink. He that believeth on me, as the scripture hath said, out of his belly shall flow rivers of living water. (S. S.)

OUR blessed Lord incessantly labored for the salvation of men—
Nor could their ungrateful returns at all divert him from his purpose—
His life was sought, and he knew that persons were sent to apprehend him—
Yet, instead of rejecting them with abhorrence, he sought to win them by love—
And importuned them to accept his richest blessings—
His address to them on this occasion contained,
I. AN INVITATION.
The time and manner of the invitation are worthy of notice.
This was a day of peculiar sanctity, and of uncommon festivity—*

* It was the eighth and last day of the feast of tabernacles, Lev. xxiii. 34, 36.

And it seems that some customs, not required in the original institutions of the law, obtained among the Jews at that time—*

Happy to improve the opportunity, Jesus stood in the most conspicuous place, and, with an exalted voice, claimed their attention—

And, despising equally the censures of the uncharitable, and the persecutions of the proud, he made them fresh overtures of mercy—

The invitation itself was beyond measure gracious and kind.

While they only panted for his blood, he longed for their salvation—

He pointed himself out to them as the only fountain of living waters—

And assured them of his readiness to impart whatsoever they stood in need of—

He excepted none from his offers, provided they did but "thirst" for his blessings—

What could have a more conciliatory effect on his blood-thirsty murderers?—

Lest, however, his invitations should be slighted, he enforced 't with,

II. A PROMISE.

He first explained what he meant by "coming to him."

It was not a mere outward, but an inward and spiritual application, that he wished them to make to him—

They were to "believe in *him*," as possessing all fulness in himself—Col. i. 19.

And as the person appointed of the Father to convey blessings to them—Ps. lxxii. 17.

In a full persuasion of this truth they were to come to him by faith—

And to "draw water with joy from this well of salvation"—

For their encouragement he promised them a rich effusion of his Spirit.

By "living water" our Lord meant the gift of his Spirit—Ver. 39.

That "rivers of this living water should flow out of his belly," imported, that the believer should have a constant spring of consolation within him, which should refresh all who came within the sphere of his influence—

Of this blessed truth the scriptures had abundantly testified—†

And our Lord now confirmed it to them by a most solemn promise—

He assured them, as he had before done the Samaritan woman, that his communications to them should prove a source of unutterable and endless joy—John iv. 10, 13, 14.

We shall further IMPROVE this subject by addressing,

1. Those who have no desire after spiritual blessings.

Alas! how many are there who are insatiable in their thirst after earthly things; but never once desire the blessings which Christ is exalted to bestow!

---

*It is said that on this day they went annually to the pool of Siloam, and drawing water from thence returned with it in procession to the temple, where they poured it out with all possible demonstrations of joy. At what time this custom arose, it is not easy to determine; but probably it commenced after the Babylonish captivity; and was adopted in reference to that prediction, Isaiah xii. 3. Nor is the design of it precisely known: but it seems most likely that they then commemorated the giving of water out of the rock in the wilderness; and called upon God for rain, which was so necessary to them at that season. Perhaps the more spiritual among them, might pray also for those spiritual blessings, which their promised Messiah was appointed to bestow. These circumstances serve as the foundation of our Lord's address, and reflect much light upon it.

†Some, because our Lord's words are not found in scripture, καθὼς εἶπεν ἡ γραφὴ with ὁ πιστεύων εἰς ἐμὲ: (translating εἶπεν, hath *required*) but there are many passages that speak to the same effect, though not in his express terms. See Isaiah xliv. 3.

Perhaps too they think that they contract no guilt by their neglect of him—

But it is with no small indignation that God speaks of their conduct—Jer. ii. 13.

Nor would their folly be hidden from themselves, if they only considered what "broken cisterns" the sources of their comfort have invariably proved—

O that they would drink of the living fountain before they experience the want of one "drop of water to cool their tongues!"—

2. Those who desire spiritual blessings, but know not where to go for them.

Many, like those whom our Lord addressed, look no further than to the outward duty—

But he directed their eyes to himself as the true Siloam, John ix. 7, the only fountain of good—

Thus must we also direct you to faith in Christ, as the one means of obtaining blessings from him—

Whatever delight you may take in duties, you must remember that ordinances are but the medium of communication between Christ and you—

And that the benefits you receive will be proportioned to the faith you exercise on him—

3. Those who desire spiritual blessings, but fear that Christ is unwilling to impart them.

Too many are discouraged because their prayers are not answered instantly—

They conclude themselves so unworthy as to have excited nothing but aversion in the heart of Christ towards them—

But are you unworthy? and were not they also to whom the text was addressed—

Have you waited long in vain? and is there not a special promise given for your encouragement?—Isa. xli. 17, 18.

Have you nothing to present to Christ in return? Then he bids you come without money and without price—Isa. lv. 1; Rev. xxii. 17.

Will it be an unparalleled act of mercy? Then is it that new thing which he has undertaken to perform—Isa. xliii. 19, 20.

Fear not then, but renew your application to him with increased fervor—

And your soul shall ere long "be as a watered garden, and like a spring of water, whose waters fail not"—Isa. lviii. 11.

THE ENDS FOR WHICH THE HOLY SPIRIT IS GIVEN TO US.

Ezek. xxxvi. 25—27.—Then will I sprinkle clean water upon you, and ye shall be clean: from all your filthiness, and from all your idols, will I cleanse you. A new heart also will I give you, and a new spirit will I put within you: and I will take away the stony heart out of your flesh, and I will give you an heart of flesh. And I will put my spirit within you, and cause you to walk in my statutes, and ye shall keep my judgments, and do them. (S. S.)

The promises of the Old Testament frequently refer to different and distant periods—

In these periods they receive different degrees of accomplishment—

The promise before us was partly fulfilled in the deliverance of the Jews from idolatry after their return from captivity in Babylon—

295

It had a further accomplishment on the day of Pentecost—
Its final completion will take place at the millenium—
This appears by its connection with the foregoing verse—
In the mean time it is daily fulfilled to the church of God—
It may lead us to consider the ends for which God gives us his Spirit—
He sends down his Spirit

I. To cleanse from sin.

The heart of man is full of " filthiness and of idols."

There is nothing so worthless, but it is idolized by us; nothing so filthy but it is harbored and indulged—

The idols indeed are not set up in our houses, but in our hearts, Ezek. xiv. 3.

And if the filthiness appear not in open enormities, yet are our flesh and our spirit contaminated with it throughout—

Hence God pronounces the whole race of man to be " filty and abominable"—

Nor indeed can any words sufficiently represent our deformity, Jer. xvii. 9.
To cleanse us from these God imparts his Holy Spirit.

The Spirit of God is here compared to " clean water"—

He is often spoken of in Scripture under this metaphor, John vii. 38, 39.

His sprinkling of this water on us is in allusion to the sprinklings of the ceremonial law—

It was by sprinkling, that holy persons and vessels were sanctified—

It is for the same end that God sends his Holy Spirit upon us—

The blood of Christ alone can cleanse from the guilt of sin, 1 John i. 7.

But the Spirit cleanses from the love and power of it—

Nor does the operation of the Spirit supercede the atonement—

It rather presupposes an affiance in the blood of Christ*—

Though the operation of Christ's blood and spirit are distinct, yet they are never divided, 1 John v. 6.

The one is as necessary in its place, and as effectual, as the other—

By his Spirit he cleanses the soul " from all its filthiness and all its idols."

The corruption of the heart is not indeed utterly extinguished—

But the love of sin is taken away, and its power is broken—

St. Paul ascribes this effect to the Spirit in the strongest terms, Eph. v. 25—27.

In order to effect this permanently, God sends his Spirit

II. To renew the heart.

A change must be radical, in order to be effectual, Matt. xii. 33.

The heart, by nature, is hard and insensible as a " stone"—

The soul is altogether " dead in trespasses and sins"—

The understanding is blind, the will obstinate, the conscience seared—

A dead body is insensible of its own corruption—

So is the soul insensible of its state, because it is spiritually dead—

God therefore takes away this " stony heart out of the flesh"—

He does not really alter the powers of the soul—

The faculties remain the same as they were before—

---

* The purifying of the Levites well illustrates this. They were cleansed by the sprinkling of water on them: yet not so cleansed but that they needed to offer an atonement. The atonement and the sprinkling *jointly* produced the *full* effect. See Numb. viii. 6, 7, 8, 12.

But a new direction is given to them—
They are also assisted by him in their respective functions—
Hence they appear to be altogether new—
He gives in exchange " an heart of flesh."
It is characteristic of the new heart that it is tender—
It is deeply affected with its own sin and misery—
It is melted with a sense of God's unbounded mercies—
Thus in fact the christian is made " a new creature"—
In this way God prevails by the Spirit
III To SANCTIFY THE LIFE.
What was before metaphorically, is here plainly expressed—
God, by renewing the soul, changes also the life.*
The unregenerate man accounts the commandments grievous—
The renewed person longs for a perfect conformity to them, Rom. vii. 22
He henceforth " walks as Christ himself walked"—
By the indwelling of his Spirit he "causes" his people to obey him
We cannot explain the mode of the Spirit's operations—
We are sure, however, that he does not act on men as mere machines—
He draws them in a rational manner as free agents—
He constrains them by enlightening their understanding and inclining their will—
He makes them delight in receiving and obeying his influences—
Their language is invariably like that of the church of old, Cant. i. 4.
In order to IMPROVE this promise, we would lead you to contemplate
1. Its freeness.
To whom is this promise made, but to those who are filthy and idolatrous, insensible and obdurate ?—
Let none put it away from them as not belonging to them—
But rather let all lay hold on it, and plead it before God—
2. Its suitableness.
What would any one, who knew his wants, ask of God ?—
Can any thing be conceived more suitable than the things here promised ?
Let those who feel their need of cleansing, and renovation, rejoice that God has promised them the desire of their hearts—
3. Its preciousness.
Well does the apostle say, that the " promises are precious"—
What can he want, that has this promise fulfilled to him ?—
Such an one may defy either men or devils to make him miserable—
In the purification and renewal of his soul he has all that man can desire

---

THE GIFT OF THE HOLY SPIRIT.

Luke xi. 13.—" If ye then, being evil, know how to give good gifts unto your children: how much more shall your heavenly Father give the Holy Spirit to them that ask him." (Sk.)

IN the important and instructive paragraph with which our text is connected, we find,

* The salt being cast into the fountain, the streams are henceforth salubrious. See 2 Kings ii. 21.

1. A pious request presented to our Lord by one of his disciples 1st. "Lord teach us how to pray," &c. From this request it is conjectured, that John the Baptist, according to the usual custom of the Jewish teachers, had given his disciples certain forms of prayer to guide and assist their devotion. A similar favor from our Lord appears therefore to be thus requested by his disciples.

2. Our Lord's compliance with this request. "He said unto them, When ye pray, say," &c., v. 2—4. Here we find those petitions used as a *form* of prayer, which had previously been recommended in the sermon on the mount as a *model* of prayer. Thus we have the highest authority to use this prayer as a form.

3. An exhortation is subjoined to seek the blessings of salvation by importunate prayer. This is urged by the example of a friend, prevailed on by importunity to grant a favor, v. 5—9;—by the success of all earnest persevering supplicants, v. 10;—by the natural kindness of earthly parents, who do not give their children stones for bread, serpents for fishes, nor scorpions for eggs, v. 11, 12.—And in our text, by the infinite goodness of God; "If ye then," &c. These words exhibit our privilege—prescribe our duty—and encourage our hope—as the followers of Christ.

1. These words EXHIBIT OUR PRIVILEGE as the followers of Christ. This is, to enjoy the gift of God's Holy Spirit. Here let us observe,

1. *What is meant by the Holy Spirit.* This we may learn by noticing some particulars respecting the Holy Spirit, which we find recorded in the oracles of God. These inform us—that the Holy Spirit may be grieved; for we are cautioned against grieving him, Eph. iv. 30; that he intercedes for us, Rom. viii. 26, 27; that he reproves the world, John xvi. 7, 8; that he guides, hears, speaks, and shows things to come, John xvi. 13. Now to grieve, to intercede, to reprove, to guide, hear, speak, and show things to come, are all personal acts; hence we are assured that the Holy Spirit is a person.

The Scriptures also inform us, that the Holy Spirit is a person against whom unpardonable sin may be committed, Matt. xii. 31, 32; and to lie to the Holy Ghost, implies lying unto God, Acts v. 3, 4; and that those in whom the Holy Ghost dwells are temples of God, 1 Cor. iii. 16. Hereby we are assured that the Holy Spirit is a *divine* person, and truly God.—And in this we are also confirmed by the divine ordinance of baptism, Matt. xxviii. 19; and by the apostolic benediction, 2 Cor. xiii. 14.

2. *That the Holy Ghost is enjoyed by all real Christians.* This is evident from the Apostle's solemn declaration, Rom. viii. 9: "If any man," &c. It therefore follows that none can be Christ's approved servants here, nor partakers of the glory hereafter, but those who have his Spirit; and that all who are truly his, enjoy this heavenly gift.—From our Lord's promise, John vii. 37—39. This assures us that all believers are invited to receive the Holy Spirit, and actually to enjoy his gracious influence. This is further evident from the description given us of gospel salvation, Tit. iii. 5, 6. Hence observe,

3. *For what purposes he is received by them.* They receive him—as a Spirit of *penitence* and *prayer;* showing them their sin and danger, Zech. xii. 10; and exciting in them desires of salvation, Matt. v. 6.—As a Spirit of *power;* strengthening them, and enabling them to renounce sin; lay hold on Christ; bear their trials; overcome their enemies; and persevere in the path of piety, Eph. iii. 16; Job xvii. 9.—As a Spirit of *comfort;* to inspire them with assurance and hope, Rom. viii. 16. 17.—As a Spirit of *purity;* to cleanse them from all sinful practices, 1 Cor. vi. 11; all sinful tempers, dis-

positions, and imaginations, Ezek. xxxvi. 25—29. As a Spirit of *wisdom;* to lead them in the way of righteousness, Rom. viii. 14.—And as a Spirit of *fruitfulness;* by which the glorify God, Gal. v. 22, 23; John xv. 8, That we may obtain this gift, the words of our text,

II. Prescribe our duty. This is, to ask as God requires.

1. *Ask sincerely;* in truth. The Lord is near to such as call upon him in truth, Psalm cxlv. 18. Call upon him, as this implies,—in the spirit of true repentance; considering, lamenting, confessing, and forsaking all sin. This God commands, Prov. i. 23; and encourages, Acts ii. 38, 39.—And in the spirit of holy fervour, with desires and cries, Psalm cxlv. 19.

2. *Ask evangelically;* according to the gospel method of approaching God; with entire dependence on the mediation of Jesus Christ, John xiv. 6. For gospel salvation is the gift of God through Christ, and should be sought as such, Rom. vi. 23; Col. iii. 17; John xiv. 14—16.

3. *Ask importunately;* with unceasing application; till you are filled with this heavenly gift as a Spirit of power, of purity and of comfort, Eph. v. 18. This importunity our Lord requires, Luke xi. 9; and it appears highly proper; for the gift of the Holy Spirit is an invaluable acquisition; it may be lost after having been enjoyed, Heb. vi. 4, 6; it will be lost, if not carefully guarded, Rev. iii. 12. And most probably, it would not be prized and guarded as it ought to be, if it had been given without our earnest importunity. Therefore, in requiring this, our Lord manifests the greatest kindness to us.

4. *Ask believingly:* in confident expectation of obtaining. To ask in doubt of success, when we ask as God requires, must dishonor him; by questioning his power, or goodness, or truth. Unbelief therefore renders prayers unavailing, James i. 5—7. To ask in faith, must consequently honor God, Rom. iv. 20, 21. Hence faith in prayer is required of us, Heb. x. 19—22. Thus also the words of the text,

III. Encourage our hope. "If ye then," &c. Here we are led to notice,

1. *That mankind are naturally evil.* They are ignorant, and know but little; they are poor, and possess but little; they are selfish, and inclined to keep what they have for their own enjoyment, Tit. iii. 3.

2. *Yet they know how to give good gifts unto their children.—Good* gifts; things suitable to their wants, and conducive to their welfare.—They *give* them: freely, however unmerited; readily without delay; unweariedly, though often repeated; cheerfully, with comfort to themselves.—They *know* how to give them: they have sufficient ability to confer them; sufficient love to bestow them; sufficient wisdom to adapt them.

3. *But God is certainly your Father, if you ask the Holy Spirit as he requires.* Your Father, by regeneration, adoption, and covenant, 2 Cor. vi. 17, 18.

4. *And God being your Father, you cannot fail of obtaining the gift of his Holy Spirit.* For he is your *heavenly* Father; all-sufficient to bestow this gift upon you, Gen. xiv. 22. He is your *covenant* Father; engaged to give it, Ezek. xxxvi 27. He is a *good* Father; inclined by love to bless you, Rom. viii. 32. A *wise* Father; who knows how to adapt its various influences to your wants, Eph. i. 7, 8. And a *gracious* Father; disposed to give it freely, Rev. xxii. 17. This gift therefore is as certain as God's power, his truth, his love, his wisdom, and grace.

APPLICATION.

1. *Recollect your privilege with suitable acts of piety.* Such as—*self-examination.* Do you enjoy this gift as a Spirit of penitence, &c., 2 Cor

xiii. 5.—*Humiliation:* on account of your enjoying no more of it, James iv. 2, 8–10. *Holy care:* to cherish and improve what divine influence you enjoy. By obeying Christ, Rev. iii. 2; and imitating St. Paul, Phil. iii. 13, 14.

2. *Recollect your duty with perseverence in it*, Col. iv. 2. Neither be discouraged by seeming delays, Heb. ii. 3; nor rest in present attainments, 2 Pet. i. 5–11, and iii. 14

2. *Recollect your encouragement with steadfast hope*—of receiving the Holy Spirit in all his influences; as a Spirit of prayer, penitence, power, &c., 1 Pet. v. 10, 11.

OFFICES OF THE HOLY SPIRIT.

John xvi. 8—11.—And when he is come, he will reprove the world of sin, and of righteousness, and of judgment: of sin, because they believe not on me; of righteousness, because I go to the Father, and ye see me no more: of judgment, because the prince of this world is judged. (H. H.)

In judging of the dispensations of God's providence or grace, we are extremely apt to err—

Hence we often mourn for things, which, if we knew the end of them, would afford us occasion for joy—

This was the case with the disciples, who were dejected on account of their Lord's approaching departure from them—

To relieve their minds, our Lord not only promised them another Comforter, but told them for what ends and purposes that Comforter should come—

I. To "convince the world of sin."

This office the Spirit executed among the Jews—

The sin of rejecting Christ was that which the Spirit was more particularly to reveal to the world—

And he discovered it fully by his *miraculous operations* on the disciples*— and wrought an irresistible conviction of it by his *gracious influences* on the hearts of thousands—

This office too he yet executes in the christian church—

The external testimony which he gave, remains the same in all ages—

The internal witness is given to those only whom " God has ordained to life"—

To them the Spirit shews the number, the greatness, the malignity of their sins—and particularly, the guilt, and danger of that unbelief, in which they have ignorantly lain—

This is the Spirit's work; nor is it wrought in any, but by his almighty power—Zech. iv. 6; 2 Cor. v. 5; 1 Cor. xii. 11.

If he proceeded no farther, he would not be a Comforter; but it is his office also,

II. To convince the world " of righteousness"—

This also was accomplished by him on his first descent from heaven—

---

*Christ had stated, as it were, the whole credit of his Messiahship on this one point: consequently, the visible descent of the Spirit, accompanied with the miraculous gift of tongues was such an attestation to Christ, as could not be doubted, and such a reproof to his murderers as could not be withstood.

Christ, though professing himself the Saviour of the world, had been **crucified** as a malefactor—

The Spirit therefore was to evince, both that Christ was a righteous person, and that through his righteousness others also might be saved—

Accordingly, by his descent, the Spirit proved these things beyond a doubt—

He shewed that Christ was accepted of the Father (which he would not have been, if he had been an impostor,) and had finished all that was necessary for our salvation; seeing that, if any thing had remained to have been done on earth, he must have returned hither in order to complete it—See the text.

He moreover inclined, and enabled multitudes to believe on HIM for righteousness, whom they had just before reprobated as worthy of universal execration—

And yet daily is he occupied in glorifying Christ among us—

Whomsoever the Spirit convinces thoroughly of sin, he leads also to discoveries of Christ—

He shews to the soul the suitableness and all-sufficiency of Christ's righteousness to all those who trust in it—Ver. 14.

And leads them, with holy glorying, to say, "In the Lord have I righteousness and strength"—Isa. xlv. 24.

He has yet further undertaken,

III. To CONVINCE THE WORLD OF JUDGMENT—

He shewed to the first christians that Satan was a vanquished foe—

By the descent of the Spirit it was manifest, that Christ had triumphed over sin and Satan, death and hell—Eph. iv. 8; Col. ii. 15

By his gracious influences also, he rescued myriads from their power—and inspired them with an holy confidence, that they should finally prevail over all their spiritual enemies—2 Tim. i. 12.

Thus at this day does he cause the weakest to exult over their fallen enemy—

However active and malicious Satan is, his head is bruised, Gen. iii. 15, his power is limited, Rev. ii. 10; 1 Peter v. 8, his doom is fixed—Rom xvi. 20.

Of this the Holy Spirit assures the weak and trembling believer—

And puts into his mouth, even in the midst of all his conflicts, that triumphant song—Rom. viii. 38, 39.

Uses,

1. Of conviction—

All true christians have received the Spirit for the ends and purposes for which he is here promised—

In vain then will be our orthodoxy in sentiment, if we have not this evidence of our conversion to God—ib. ver. 9.

Let us pray that the Spirit may be poured out upon us—

And let our views of our guilt and weakness lead us to glory in Christ alone—

2. Of consolation—

Are we bowed down with a *sense* of sin? we may be sure that Christ has sent his Spirit to work that conviction in us; and that, if we be instant in prayer, he will, by the same Spirit, lead us also to a view of his righteousness—

Are we ready to despond by reason of the *power* of sin? the resistance which the Holy Spirit has enabled us already to make to its dominion, is a pledge that "we shall be more than conquerors, through Him that loved us." Rom. viii. 37.

Let us only seek the Spirit as our Comforter, and we need regret no loss, no pain, no trouble, that may be the means of bringing him into our hearts.

THE POURING OUT OF GOD'S SPIRIT.

Acts ii. 17.--And it shall come to pass in the last days, saith God, I will pour out of my Spirit upon all flesh. (Sk.)

In this highly interesting chapter we find an account,

1. Of the divine *testimony* borne to the truth of the gospel, by the descent of the Holy Ghost on the day of Pentecost. Here it appears, that by inspiration, the apostles were enabled at once to speak various languages which they never before understood;--that what they were thus inspired to declare, were the wonderful works of God; or the operations of his mercy, power, and wisdom, displayed in our redemption by Christ;--and that all who were then at Jerusalem heard those wonderful works of God declared in their own respective languages. This intimated that the gospel was designed for the benefit of all the human race. In the succeeding verses, we have an account,

2. Of the different *effects* which this event produced on the different characters who witnessed it. In the devout, it excited amazement, which led them to make serious inquiry respecting what was occurring, ver. 5-12. In the careless, it excited contempt; which led them to oppose the gracious designs of God, and to treat the work of God with derision and blasphemy, ver. 13. But the wrath of man, in this, as in former cases, turned to the praise of God; for in the sequel we find an account,

3. Of Peter's *discourse* in reply to those aspersions thus cast on the works of God by his wicked opposers. In this discourse Peter repels the senseless charge of drunkenness, ver. 14, 15--and shows that this remarkable occurrence is in fact the fulfilment of prophecy, ver. 16, 17. "But this is that which was spoken by the prophet Joel, And it shall come to pass, in the last days, saith God, I will pour out of my Spirit upon all flesh." In improving these words it may be proper to make some observations on them—and some application of them. Let us make,

I. Some observations on them. Here we may notice,

1. *The blessing promised; God's Spirit.* "I will pour out of my Spirit, saith God." By the Spirit here promised is certainly meant both his miraculous and saving influence. *His miraculous influence.*—This was imparted to confirm the truth of the gospel, and to promote the spread of it in the world, Heb. ii. 3, 4; 1 Cor. xiv. 22. By means of this influence, the apostles, and many primitive christians, were endued with various gifts; as the gifts of wisdom, or knowledge, or faith, or healing, or miracles, or prophecy, or discerning of spirits, or divers kinds of tongues, or the interpretation of tongues: see 1 Cor. xii. 6-11. By the Spirit here promised is also meant,— *his saving influence;* this is enjoyed by all believers in Christ, John vii. 37, 39. The effects of this influence are intimated by the testimony of John the Baptist, Matt. iii. 11. These effects are farther intimated, by the fiery appearance which the Holy Ghost was pleased to assume on his descent, verse

3. For as fire enlightens, purifies, and warms; so believing souls are *enlightened* with knowledge, *purified* from sin, and *invigorated* with power, by the influences of God's Holy Spirit, 2 Tim. i. 7. Let us notice,

2. *The manner of its dispensation;* it will be poured out. This indicates—*the prerogative of God;* that the influences of his Spirit are at his disposal. He withholds 'those influences, or dispenses them, or withdraws them, as he pleases, Matt. xx. 15; Eph. i. 11; Phil. ii. 12, 13. The pouring out of God's Spirit also indicates—the *special properties* of the blessing promised. For instance, that it will be *gratuitous;* or given freely, like water from a fountain, John iv. 10; Rev. xxii. 17. That it will be *abundant;* given bountifully, without restraint, Eph. v. 18; Psa. lxxxi. 10 And that it will be *perpetual;* given in unfailing succession, Tit. iii. 5, 6. Let us notice,

3. *The extent of its influence* upon all flesh. By all flesh is meant the whole human race, however distinguished, by descent, by circumstances, or by sex. However distinguished by *descent;* whether of Jewish or Gentile extraction. This appears from the gift of Christ, Isa. xlix. 6; Luke ii. 30–32, and from the gospel ministry, Luke xxiv. 47. However distinguished by *circumstances,* whether bond or free. Both may obtain it, and both need it. The slave, with this, enjoys liberty, 2 Cor. iii. 17. The master, without this, is a slave, 2 Tim. ii. 26; Col. iii. 11. Or however distinguished by *sex;* whether male or female. For however the female sex may be enslaved by savages, oppressed by the heathens, or degraded by Mohammedans, yet christianity regards both sexes with equal favor: see Gal. iii. 26–29. This promise farther intimates, that the blessing thus free for the whole human race, shall become generally enjoyed by them, Psa. lxxii. 6, 8. Hence let us notice,

4. *The season of its communication*—The last days. By the last days are certainly meant the days in which we now live. These are called the last days, because they are the days of the gospel dispensation; which is the last dispensation of grace that God will ever establish with mankind, Heb. xii. 27, 28. And during these days this general out-pouring of God's Spirit may be expected from scripture prophecy. See Psalm ii. 8; Isa. ii. 1–10; Dan. ii. 44. As these prophecies suppose the pouring out of God's Spirit, let us notice,

5. *The certainty of its effusion.* It shall come to pass, saith God, in the last days, "I will pour out of my Spirit." This event is certain—for it is *predicted,* and it will be fulfilled. The word of prophecy is sure, 2 Pet. i. 19. It is *promised,* and will be performed. The word of promise is faithful, Psa. lxxxix. 33, 34. It is predicted and promised by *God:* whose power enables him, whose truth engages him, and whose honor binds him, to accomplish his word, Num. xxiii. 19; Psa. cxvii. 2.

Having made some observations on these words, let us now make,

II. Some application of them. In doing this, consider,

1. *The strong claims which this subject has on our attention.*

It claims attention *by the importance of the blessing which it exhibits.* The importance of this blessing appears from the *effects* ascribed to it. It is by God's Spirit that we are quickened when dead in sin, Ezek. xxxvii. 14. By this Spirit we understand our duty, as prescribed by God's word, Prov. i. 23. By this Spirit we are strengthened for all pious exercises, Eph. iii. 16. By this Spirit we are delivered from the oppression of sin, Rom. viii. 2. By this Spirit we are restored to the whole image of God, 2 Cor. iii. 18. By this Spirit we are comforted, with love, hope, and joy, Rom. v 5, and x

13, and xiv. 17. By this spirit our pious exertions are rendered successful, Ezek. xxxvii. 7–10; 1 Cor. iii. 6. Thus the influence of God's Spirit is highly important, as it is necessary to our salvation; for without it we cannot enjoy life, nor wisdom, nor liberty, nor strength, nor holiness. It is of importance, as it is necessary to our comfort; for without it we must be destitute of love, and hope, and joy. It is of importance, as it is necessary to our youthfulness; for without it we must labor in vain, Psa. cxxvii. 1. This subject claims attention, *by our interest in the season of its communication.* We live in the last days, when God's Spirit is expressly promised: when it may be confidently expected; and when it should be earnestly sought in the use of all proper means. This leads us to consider,

2. *The duties to which this subject urges us.* It particularly urges us— to *apply* for the saving influences of God's Spirit, as he requires us in his word. By repentance, Acts ii. 38, 39; by faith in Christ, John vii. 39; Gal. iii. 14; and by earnest importunate prayer, Luke xi. 13. It urges us— to employ all those *means* which the Spirit of God is known to bless, that we may be instrumental in saving those around us; as good conversation, good books, and a faithful gospel ministry, Eccles. xi. 6. To implore the *general* effusion of God's Spirit for the conversion of the whole human race. This should be done by us individually, in our secret retirements; like David, Psa. li. 18, and lxxii. 18, 19, and Isaiah lxii. 1. And it should be done by us collectively; in social worship, Psa. xc. 16, 17; Luke xi. 2. To cultivate deep *humility* of spirit; by self-diffidence in all our pious engagements, Jer. x. 23; Zech. iv. 6, and self-abasement, in our devout and grateful acknowledgments to God, 1 Cor. xv. 10, and liii. 7; Psa. cxv. 1. Let us consider,

3. *The hopes with which this subject inspires us.* On engaging in the duties to which our text urges us, it encourages us to hope—*for the saving influence of God's Spirit in our own souls:* from the equity of God as our judge, Luke xviii. 7; from the kindness of God as our friend, Luke xi. 9, 10, and from the love of God as our father, Luke xi. 11–13. Our text encourages us to hope also—*for the general effusion of God's Spirit on the human race.* This is certain; for God here promises it, " I will pour out my Spirit," &c. And this should be *expected now:* for it will be done in God's time, Isa. lx. 19. And God's time is these last days, Psa. cii. 13; Isa. xxxii. 1, 2, 15–17.

THE HOLY SPIRIT FIGURED BY LIVING WATER.

John iv. 10.—If thou knewest the gift of God, and who it is that saith to thee, Give me to drink; thou wouldest have asked of him, and he would have given thee living water. (B.'

THE circumstances under which these words were spoken are the following—

Consider,

I. What we are to understand by the gift here mentioned, and represented under the FIGURE OF LIVING WATER.

Jesus Christ, in an especial manner, is the " gift" of God. John iii. 16; Rom. viii. 32; 2 Cor. ix. 15. Though, on this occasion, suffering from natural thirst, he wished for a little water from the well of Samaria, yet he himself is " the fountain of living waters." He is the chief object of saving knowledge, both as the gift of God, and as the fountain of living water. An application to him for this water arises from a knowledge of him, in order to which we must receive " the Spirit of wisdom and revelation." Eph. i. 17. ——

But the Holy Spirit is rather intended, which is elsewhere represented under the emblem of fire; Matt. iii. 11; Isa. iv. 4; and of air, or wind; John iii. 8;—here, under that of water; and in John vii. 37, 38 ; because he washes and cleanses the soul from the guilt and pollution of sin; Ezek. xxxvi. 25; refreshes the thirsty; ver. 14, and chap. vii. 37; heals the sick. Rev. xxii. 1, 17. He is represented as " *living* water," as being the only source of life to the dead in sins; and, having quickened, he makes them fruitful in righteousness. Isa. xxxii. 15–18 ; xliv. 3, 4 ; li. 3 ; Eph. v. 9. ——

As to the necessity of this water. We are, in ourselves, filthy, and need to be cleansed;—unhappy, and need to be refreshed;—disordered, and need to be healed:—dead, and need to be made alive;—barren. and need to be made fruitful.

The excellency of this water is manifested from our Lord's words in the fourteenth verse,—" Whosoever drinketh of the water that I shall give him," will find it so reviving and satisfying to his soul, that he " will never thirst;" he will not want the means of refreshment, be dissatisfied or unhappy; that is, provided he continue to drink thereof. If ever his thirst, or his dissatisfaction and uneasiness, return, it will be the fault of the man, not of the water. But the water, the spirit of faith, love, hope, and joy, of holiness, and happiness, " shall be in him," an inward living principle, " a well;" *a fountain* " of water:" for a well is soon exhausted; "springing," (αλλομενν,) *bubbling up*, and flowing on " into everlasting life;" which is a confluence, or an ocean of streams, arising from this fountain. ——

II. WHERE THIS LIVING WATER IS TO BE HAD, BY WHOM, AND ON WHAT TERMS.

It is to be had in Christ.—Not only in the Deity, who is infinitely great, glorious, holy, and just, and, as such, far distant from us; but in " God, manifest in the flesh;" who is our friend, kinsman, and brother. It is procured for us by his death. John xvi. 7. It is received on our behalf, in consequence of his resurrection and ascension. Psa. lxviii. 18 ; Acts ii. 33. Hence he waits to bestow the cleansing, refreshing, life-giving water, on those who apply to him; John vii. 37; Rev. xxi. 6; and from this consideration, we have great encouragement to ask Christ for it. ——

This living water may be had by all that are poor, and need it; Isa. xli. 17; by all who thirst for it; John vii. 37; Rev. xxi. 6; xxii. 17; by all who come to Christ, " If *any man* thirst," said he, "let him come unto me;" and by all who ask, " Thou wouldest have *asked* of me." ——

Though it was purchased dear by Christ; he gave a great price that he might have a right to impart it to sinners, and that he might render them capable of receiving it, yet we may have it as a free gift, " without money, and without price." ——

III. THE REASON WHY MEN ARE INDIFFERENT ABOUT IT, AND EITHER APPLY NOT TO CHRIST FOR IT, OR APPLY WITHOUT SUCCESS.

They *know it not*; John xiv. 17; neither the nature of the blessing, nor the great value of it, nor the necessity of obtaining it.

They know not Christ in the dignity of his person,—in his great condescension and love,—in the sufferings he endured that we might have this water,—and as the fountain of it. ——

They do not apply at all; do not confess their need of, nor ask the communication of, spiritual influences. ——

Or, if they ask, they do not ask aright, sincerely, earnestly, importunately, perseveringly, believingly, consistently. ——

APPLY the subject: showing, that ignorance, arising from an aversion to saving knowledge, and the love of sin, is no excuse; Isa. v. 12, 13; Luke xix. 44;—the state and danger of those who remain destitute of the sacred influence of the Spirit;—the duty and advantage of immediate and fervent supplication for it. Prov. i. 22–28, 32.

THE WORK OF THE SPIRIT IN STRENGTHENING MEN FOR SUFFERING OR DUTY.

Rom. viii. 26.—Likewise the Spirit also helpeth our infirmities: for we know not what we should pray for as we ought : but the Spirit itself maketh intercession for us with groanings which cannot be uttered. (S. S.)

An hope of eternal happiness is as an anchor to the troubled soul—
It enables a person to bear up under the heaviest afflictions—
But the mind of a believer would soon faint, if it were not strengthened from above—
God therefore communicates his Spirit to his people under their trials—
By his Spirit he enables them to go forward in the way of duty—
St. Paul has been speaking of sufferings as the Christian's portion here, ver. 17, 18.
He has mentioned "hope" as a principal support to the soul under them, ver. 24.
He now specifies the Holy Spirit's agency as another mean of confirming and establishing the soul—
This agency of the Spirit we may consider
I. IN SEASONS OF SUFFERING.
Men are, in themselves, too weak to sustain many or severe trials.
There is much impatience in the heart of every man—
It too often discovers itself even in those who are, on the whole, pious—
Sometimes it is called forth by small and trifling occasions—
How passionately did Jonah resent the loss of his gourd! Jonah iv. 8, 9.
How bitterly would the disciples have revenged an act of unkindness! Luke ix. 54.
There is no trial so small but it would overcome us, if we were left to ourselves—
And they who have endured heavy trials, often faint under small ones—
But God sends his Spirit to help the infirmities of his people.
We cannot exactly discriminate between the Spirit's agency and theirs—
Indeed the Spirit acts in and by their endeavors—
He leads them to see the source and tendency of their trials—
He strengthens the natural vigor of their minds—
He suggests to them many consolatory thoughts—
Thus he fulfils to them his gracious declarations, Ps. cxlvii. 3.
These operations of the Spirit are yet more manifest

306

II. In seasons of prayer.

God's people " know not even what to pray for."

A great variety of passions may agitate their minds—

When this is the case, their petitions may be unbecoming and sinful—

Even a sense of guilt will often stop the mouth before God ; compare **Ps.** xxxii. 3, and 5.

Sometimes also trouble itself will utterly overwhelm the soul, and inca· pacitate it for prayer, Ps. lxxvii. 4.

Our Lord himself seems to have experienced such a purtu bation of mind, John xii. 27.

Nor are there any praying persons who have not often found themselves straitened in the exercise of prayer—

It yet oftener happens that they know not how to pray " as they ought."

We may easily utter good and suitable words before God—

But it is by no means easy to pray with fervent importunity—

An insurmountable languor or obduracy will sometimes come upon the soul—

Nor though we were ever so fervent can we always exercise faith—

Many have felt the same workings of mind with David, Ps. lxxvii. 7—10.

At such seasons they cannot pray as they ought—

But the Holy Spirit will " make intercession for them."

Christ is properly our advocate and intercessor, 1 John ii. 1.

But the Spirit also may be said to " intercede for us"—

The Spirit intercedes *in* us at the *throne of grace*, while Christ intercedes *for* us at the *throne of glory*—

He sometimes enables us to pour out our hearts with fluency—

This he does by discovering to us our wants, quickening our affections, and testifying to us God's willingness to answer prayer—

He does not, however, always operate in this way—

He will make intercession " with unutterable groans."

The joy of christians is represented as being sometimes inexpressible, 1 Pet. i. 8.

But frequently a sense of sin overwhelms them—

Then sighs and groans are the natural language of their hearts—

Nor are such inarticulate prayers unacceptable to God—

We have a remarkable instance of their success in the history of our Lord, John xi. 33, 38, 41.

Perhaps no prayers are more pleasing to God than these, Ps. li. 17.

Infer,

1. How many are there who live all their days without prayer !

Those in whom the Spirit intercedes are often made to feel their inability to pray aright—

Under a sense of their infirmities they are constrained to cry to God for the help of his Spirit—

But many pass all their days without any painful sense of their weakness—

They satisfy themselves with a formal performance of their duties—

Such persons never pray in an acceptable manner, John iv. 23.

Real prayer implies fervor and importunity, Isa. lxiv. 7.

And it is in vain to think that we have the spirit of grace, if we have not also the spirit of supplication, Zech. xii. 10.

May we therefore never be of those who fulfil that prophecy ! Matt. xv. 7, 8.

2. What comfort may this passage afford to praying people!

Many are discouraged by the difficulties which they experience in the duty of prayer—

If they feel not an enlargement of heart, they doubt whether their prayer will be accepted—

But God will notice the groaning of his people, Ps. xxxviii. 9.

Such inward desires may often be more pleasing to him than the most fluent petitions—

They are, in fact, the voice of God's Spirit within us—

Let not any then be dejected on account of occasional deadness—

Let every one rather follow the advice of the prophet, Hab. ii. 3.

God, in due time, will assuredly fulfil his promise, Ps. lxxxi. 10.

THE HOLY GHOST IS THE AUTHOR OF ALL SOLID HOPE.

Rom. xv. 13.—Now the God of hope fill you with all joy and peace in believing, that ye may abound in hope, through the power of the Holy Ghost. (S. S.)

CHRISTIANS, even in the purest ages of the church, have been too ready to indulge a spirit of bigotry and contention—

The Jewish and Gentile converts in every place were much addicted to it—

St. Paul, studious to counteract it in those at Rome, shews that Christ, though a minister of the circumcision, intended to incorporate the Gentiles into his church—

And prays for both parties, that, as the means of restoring union among themselves, they might be endued with more grace—

His words shew us,

I. THE PRIVILEGES OF TRUE CHRISTIANS.

The world forms a very false estimate of the christian's portion—

And christians themselves too often live below their privileges—

It is their privilege to be filled,

1. With lively joy.

No one in the world has so much cause for joy as they ———

Nor is their joy like that of sinners, which soon expires in spleen and melancholy—Eccl. vii. 6, and Prov. xiv. 13.

They may "rejoice evermore," and that too with "joy unspeakable"—

2. With abiding peace.

It would be thought by many that "peace" should have preceded "joy"—

But the experience of God's people accords exactly with the scriptures—Compare Isa. lv. 12, with the text.

Being freed from the torment of a guilty conscience, they have peace with God—Rom. v. 1.

Christ has both purchased for them, and bequeathed to them, his peace, which passeth all understanding—John xiv. 27, and Phil. iv. 7.

Their "peace may well be as a river, since their righteousness is as the waves of the sea"—Isa. xlviii. 18.

3. With assured hope.

This is the fruit. rather than the root, of peace and joy—

They have the promise and oath of God on their side—Heb. vi. 17, 18

And have already received in their souls an earnest of their inheritance—Eph. i. 14.

Well therefore may they enjoy a confident expectation of the promised land—

All indeed are not sufficiently studious to " walk thus in the light"—

But, what the apostle prayed for on the behalf of all, all may possess—

The apostle further directs us,

II. How WE MAY ATTAIN THE ENJOYMENT OF THEM.

In this short and comprehensive prayer we are taught to seek them.

1. From God as the fountain.

God in Christ is the " God of hope," and the source of all good—James i. 17.

In vain will be the use of other means, if we apply not to him in prayer—

But nothing is too great for God to give to the believing suppliant—

2. By faith as the means.

We can receive nothing but by the exercise of faith—James i. 6, 7.

But " in believing we shall be *filled* with joy and peace"—

It is faith that enables us to realize invisible things—

And, by experiencing the joy of faith, our hope will be confirmed—Rom. v. 5.

3. Through the Holy Ghost as the agent.

There is no power less than his that will produce these things—

The whole work of grace is, not by might or by power, but by God's Spirit—Zech. iv. 6.

He will afford us clear discoveries of the heavenly glory—

He will witness to us our adoption, and seal us with God's image—1 Cor. i. 22.

And thus while he forms us to a meetness for heaven, he gives us also a foretaste of it in our hearts—

INFER,

1. How much happier is the christian than others even in this world!

2. How happy will he be when he shall receive these communications from the Deity, not through the narrow and obstructed channel of faith, but immediately at the fountain head!

3. How deservedly will they be left destitute of this happiness hereafter, who now give the pleasures of sin their decided preference!

THE HOLY SPIRIT'S APPLICATON OF THE PROMISES OF SCRIPTURE.

Ephesians i. 13, 14.—In whom also after that ye believed, ye were sealed with that Holy Spirit of promise which is the earnest of our inheritance until the redemption of the purchased possession unto the praise of his glory. (P.)

It would be quite foreign to our present purpose to enter into a particular consideration of all the several expressions which this passage of scripture contains. It may be proper, however, to observe, that the *sealing* of the spirit of which the apostle here speaks, is evidently a distinct act from *faith :* and the sealing of the Holy Spirit appears to be a metaphorical expression to denote that the same divine agent who had implanted in their souls a principle of faith, and brought this principle into exercise, had likewise produced in their minds an assurance of their interest in the promises of the gospel, and in the blessings of salvation by a Redeemer.

PRELIMINARY OBSERVATIONS.

1st *Obs.*—That there is such a being as the *Holy Spirit* how else are we to understand the following passages, and others of a similar import, which are contained in the word of God: Gen. vi. 3; Prov. i. 23: Luke xi. 13; John vii. 37—40; Rom. viii. 16, 26; Eph. iv. 30.

2nd *Obs.*—That the Holy Spirit is a *divine* person, possessed of the names, titles, and attributes of Deity, the great author of divine and glorious works, and an object of divine adoration.

3rd *Obs.*—That this divine Spirit is the subject of many revealed and precious *promises.* And this may be one reason why he is called in the text the "Holy Spirit of promise."

4th *Obs.*—That a true and saving *faith* in Christ is the special gift of the divine Spirit a principle produced by his gracious operations on the heart, and ordinarily effected by means of a preached gospel. It was by this means the Ephesians were brought to trust or believe in Christ. Read the text.

5th *Obs.*—It is the peculiar office of the Holy Spirit, to carry on and complete the work of sanctification in those who believe, and to comfort their minds by a sweet und spiritual *application* of the promises of grace in Christ Jesus to their souls. Such was the comfort imparted to the Ephesians, who, after they believed, were sealed with the Holy Spirit of promise.

6th *Obs.*—That it is a matter of unspeakable importance to *know* and believe, on substantial evidence, that we are the subjects of the Spirit's sanctifying and comforting influences; or, in other words, that we are interested in the promises of scripture, by an application of them to our souls, through the agency of the Holy Spirit. By this remark we are led to inquire

How we may know when a promise of scripture is applied to the mind by the Holy Spirit?

This is an inquiry which is highly interesting, and of the greatest consequence; an inquiry on which many, it is to be feared, have too hastily decided. They have cried, "Peace, peace to themselves," when in reality they have had no peace. The *presumption* of some, and the *enthusiasm* of others, have led them to draw conclusions for which they have had no substantial evidences, to the dishonor of God, and to the injury of their own souls. That we may guard against those dangerous rocks on which thousands, alas! nave split, we shall do well to remember, that,

No attainments in religious *knowledge*, however extensive, which are merely speculative and natural, will warrant us to conclude, that any particular promise belongs to s.

No distinctions of *birth* or *station:* no moral virtues or moral qualifications, however amiable and praiseworthy in themselves, can authorize us to believe that this or the other promise of the gospel is ours.

No external *profession* of religion, however flaming that profession may be, is of itself sufficient to entitle us to what may be termed a personal and possessive interest in the promises of scripture.

No inward *suggestions* of the promises of scripture to the mind, however powerful; no pretended visions, or dreams, or revelations from heaven, however extraordinary, can lead us with safety to conclude on a spiritual application of the promises of scripture to our hearts. Even the devil may bring texts of scripture to the mind, and misapply them to deceive persons; and in dreams,

310

and visions, and revelations, there may be found some cheat or imposture of the devil; but the Spirit's witness to the heart, suitable to the revelations in scripture, cannot deceive us. In order, therefore, to know that a promise of scripture is applied to the heart by the Holy Spirit, it is necessary to ascertain,

1st. That our *characters* answer to the characters of those who have a right to claim an interest in the promises, viz. that we are believers in Christ —that we are real christians—that we are the disciples of Christ indeed. They only who are brought to believe or trust in Christ, are sealed with the " Holy Spirit of promise."

2nd. To know that a promise of script re is applied to the mind by the Holy Spirit, we must be led to *see our need of his assistance,* and to implore his gracious influences, to apply to our hearts those promises which may be suited to our particular circumstances. This, it appears, was the conduct of David when he had provoked the Holy Spirit to withdraw for a season his comforting influences. He humbly draws near to God in the exercise of prayer, and expresses his reliance on the Spirit of grace to visit him again with that holy joy and peace in believing which he had formerly experienced; [see Psalm li. 9—13.] And the apostle Paul, in praying for the Ephesians, declares his own sentiments, and at the same time directs them in what manner they should act, as the means of obtaining and enjoying this exalted privilege (Eph. i. 15, ad finem.)

3rd. The Holy Spirit, in applying the promise of scripture to the heart, enables us to discover a similarity between our *state* and the state of those for whom the promises are expressly designed. For example, the promises of divine forgiveness are made to the subjects of true evangelical repentance, and to excite us to repentance is the work of the Spirit; but if the Spirit has never led us to sorrow for sin after a godly sort, we can have no right to the promises of pardoning mercy. Those promises of scripture, likewise, which speak of the special favor, protection, and love of God, belong *exclusively* to those who are enabled to fear him, to make him their trust, and to set their hope in him and love him, (Psalm xxxi. 19; xxvii. 14; xviii. 30; xxxvii. 40; xxxii 10; cxii. 7.) But if God be not the object of our fear. and confidence, and love, these promises do not belong to us.

4th. In the application of a promise of scripture to the heart, the Holy Spirit impresses the mind with a *conviction that the promise is true,* and gives the soul a persuasion on scriptural grounds, that God is both able and willing to perform it. " I know," says the believer, in glancing at a promise of the divine word, " that this is the promise of God, my father and friend, with whom there is no variableness nor shadow of turning. To his people in general this promise belongs ; and having a good hope, through grace, to believe that I am one of his people, this gracious promise belongs to me."

5. We may know that a promise of scripture is applied to the mind by the Holy Spirit, when, upon a strict and impartial examination, we are directed to conclude, that we are possessed of those several *qualifications and graces of the christian life* which are inseparably connected with a right application of the promises to the heart. What these graces are the apostle particularly enumerates, Gal. v. 22, 23. These graces are not the *causes,* but the necessary *evidences* of an interest in the promises.

6th There is ground to believe that we are interested in the promises, when our *general conduct,* both personally and relatively, answers to the rules and obligations prescribed in the word of God. " Without *holiness,*" it is written, " no man shall see the Lord ;" and if no man without holiness

311

shall be permitted to see the Lord in heaven, no man without holiness can really enjoy the promises of God on earth.

Inferences.—Let us rejoice in the promises of revelation, and bless God for them. They all proceed from him, are made sacred by an oath, and ratified by the death of Christ.

It becomes us also to examine, with the strictest and closest attention, what is the foundation of our title to the promises? Do we judge of our interest in them by our *frames* and *feelings*, or by the evidences of a work of grace in our souls? O let us beware of a false application of the promises ! To misapply them is exceedingly dangerous.

To you who have reason to hope that the promises are yours, but whose minds respecting this matter are yet in a state of doubt and uncertainty, it may be said, because you are thus suffered to walk in darkness, and have no light, it is no proof that you are uninterested in the promises. Many good men are in a similar state. The servants of God do not all attain to an equal degree of assurance; but it is what you should seek after, and never be satisfied without it.

Finally—Let those who have felt and enjoyed the application of the promises to their souls, remember their obligations to sovereign Mercy ; and "having these promises, dearly beloved, cleanse yourselves from all filthiness of the flesh and spirit, perfecting holiness in the fear of God."

THE WITNESS OF THE SPIRIT.

Rom. viii. 16.—The Spirit itself beareth witness with our spirit, that we are the children of God. (S. S.)

THERE is a tribunal before which we must all appear at the last day—
But we need not wait till that time to ascertain our true character—
Every man has a tribunal erected in his own bosom—
The conscience, according to the light it has received, accuses or excuses, those who will listen to its voice—
This is common to heathens as well as christians—Rom. ii. 15.
But God's people are favored with the additional testimony of the Holy Spirit—
Of this the apostle speaks in the passage before us—
We shall endeavor to shew,

I. WHAT IS THE WITNESS HERE SPOKEN OF.
Witnesses imply a doubt of the thing which is to be confirmed—
The thing to be ascertained here is, " That we are the children of God"—
Respecting this, many are in suspense all their days—
But God has provided means for the removal of these doubts—
He has been pleased to give us the witness of his Spirit.
1. Through the medium of rational deduction.
We may judge of our state by comparing it with the declarations of scripture—
God has given many marks and characters of his own people—e. g. 1 John iii. 10.
We may examine by these how far our practice corresponds with our duty—
And know from the testimony of an enlightened conscience our real state

This is a scriptural way of judging—

St. Paul used it ;* and exhorts us to use it—2 Cor. xiii. 5.

St. Peter represents the attainment of this as a principal part of our baptismal engagement—1 Peter iii. 21.

St. John also assures us, that this is the way in which God would have us to know our state—†

2. In a way of immediate impression.

The Spirit, as a " Spirit of adoption," testifies to the believer's soul, that he belongs to God—

Not that this testimony is given without *any* reference to the scripture—

Yet it is imparted in a more instantaneous manner, and in a far higher degree, at some times than at others—

God by his Spirit sometimes " sheds abroads his love in the heart" in such a measure, and shines so clearly on the work he has already wrought there, as to convey immediately a full persuasion and assurance of an interest in his favor—

As by " the sealing of the Spirit" he stamps his own image on his children for the conviction of others, so by " the witness of the Spirit" he testifies of their adoption for the more immediate comfort of their own souls—

These manifestations are vouchsafed, for the most part, to prepare the soul for trials, to support it under them, or to comfort it after them—

But they cannot be explained for the satisfaction of others—

Yet may they be sufficiently proved from scripture to be the privilege and portion of true believers—‡

To guard the doctrine against every species of delusion, we shall shew,

II. How TO DISTINGUISH IT FROM ALL FALSE AND ENTHUSIASTIC PRETENTIONS.

Many, it must be confessed, have pretended to this witness on false grounds—‖

And Satan is ready enough to help forward such delusions—

But the witness of the Spirit may be distinguished from all enthusiastic pretentions to it, if we consider attentively—

1. What precedes it.

Conviction of our lost estate—faith in the Redeemer—and devotedness to God as our rightful Sovereign, must precede it—

If we have not these things, we cannot be God's children; and we may be sure the Spirit will never attest a falsehood—

2. What accompanies it.

Humility of mind—a jealous fear of ourselves—and a love to the weakest of God's people, attended these divine communications—

*He knew that God required real integrity of heart. Psa. li. 6. He therefore labored to attain it, Acts xxiv. 16. He had the testimony of his conscience that he had attained it, Heb. xiii. 18. And this testimony was a ground of joy before God, 2 Cor. i. 12.

†We cannot convey to any man a just idea of sensations which he has never felt; they must be experienced in order to be understood. The work of the Spirit in regeneration is not fully understood even by those who are the subjects of it, notwithstanding its effects are as visible as those of the wind, John iii. 8. We cannot expect, therefore, that this less visible operations should be more intelligible to those who have never experienced them at all. See Rev. ii. 17.

‡See Rom. viii. 15. 2 Cor. i. 21, 22; and Eph. iv. 30; which clearly shew, that the Holy Spirit does operate on the souls of God's people, and perform towards them the office both of a sanctifier and a comforter.

‖Some have fancied that the Spirit witnessed their adoption because they have had a singular dream, or a portion of scripture has been suddenly and strongly impressed upon their minds, or they have enjoyed peculiar comfort in their souls.

Whereas prid   and conceit, with a presumptuous confidence, and a contempt of others, are ever found in deluded enthusiasts—

3. What follows it.

Manifestations of God to the soul always produce zeal in his service—victory over sin—and a longing for the enjoyment of him in heaven—

But supineness, subjection to evil tempers, and a forgetfulness of the eternal world, generally characterize the self-deceiving professor—

Let every one therefore examine his pretentions by these marks ———

ADDRESS,

1. Those who know nothing of this testimony of the Spirit.

You probably do not understand the regenerating influences of the Spirit; and yet you see them manifested in the lives of many around you—

Do not then condemn the witness of the Spirit merely because you cannot comprehend it—

Rather pray to God that you yourselves may be his children—

In this way you may hope that the Spirit will testify of your adoption—

2. Those who profess to have received it.

A delusion in this is above all things to be guarded aga nst—

If your dispositions be habitually bad, your pretensions are all a delusion—

Where the witness of the Spirit is, there will the fruits also of the Spiri! be—

3. Those who long to receive it.

To have the full witness of the Spirit is desirable, but not necessary—

It is a great mercy if we enjoy his lower attestations in a good conscience—

Let us labor to serve God, and leave to him the time, manner, and degree, in which he shall reveal himself to us—

4. Those who now enjoy this witness.

The manifestations of God to the soul are a very heaven upon earth—

Let them therefore be duly esteemed and diligently improved—

But beware lest you " grieve the Spirit by whom you are sealed"—

Be looking forward with increasing earnestness to your inheritance—

And while you enjoy the inward witness that you are the children of God, let the world have an outward evidence of it in your lives.

THE SEALING OF THE SPIRIT.

Eph. i. 13, 14.—In whom also after that ye believed, ye were sealed with the Holy Spirit of promise, which is the earnest of our inheritance, until the redemption of the purchased possession, unto the praise of his glory.   (S. S.)

THE blessings which we receive through Christ are innumerable—

Many are mentioned in the preceding part of this chapter—

One of the last and greatest blessings which we receive in this life, is the sealing of the Holy Spirit—

This was vouchsafed to many of the saints at Ephesus—

We shall shew,

1. What the sealing of the Spirit is.

The metaphor of sealing conveys no inadequate idea of the Spirit's operations.

A seal stamps its own image on the wax that is impressed by it; and marks the thing sealed to be the property of him that sealed it—

And the Holy Spirit forms all the lineaments of the divine image on the soul that is sealed by him; and shews that it belongs to God—

But the text itself affords us the best explanation of this term.

The future inheritance of the saints consists in a perfect conformity to God's image, and a perfect enjoyment of his love—

The sealing of the Spirit is an "earnest of that inheritance," or, in other words, *a part* of that inheritance already vouchsafed to the soul, and *a pledge* that the remainder shall in due time be given to it—

This gift of the Spirit is to be continued to the church till the final consummation of all things—*

The experience of individuals may vary with respect to it; but there shall always be some in the church who possess and enjoy it—

We are also informed respecting,

II. THE MANNER IN WHICH IT IS EFFECTED.

The *agent* is none other than the Holy Ghost.

It is not in man's power to sanctify his own soul—

Nor can any one assure himself that he is the Lord's—

To impart these blessings is the prerogative of God alone—2 Cor. i. 21, 22.

The *subjects* of this work are true believers.

An unbeliever cannot possibly be sealed; because the Holy Spirit would never mark those as God's property, who do not really belong to him—

Nor are persons usually sealed on their first believing in Christ—

This higher state of sanctification and assurance is reserved for those, who, "after having believed," have maintained a close walk with God—

They must first be "in Christ," and then for Christ's sake this benefit shall be vouchsafed unto them—

The *means* by which it is effected, are the promises.

We do not presume to limit the Spirit's operations—

But his usual method of sealing is by applying the "promises" to the soul—1 Cor. ii. 4; 1 Thes. i. 5.

Of themselves, the promises can accomplish nothing; but, through his divine power, they have a comforting and transforming efficacy—2 Pet. i. 4.

The apostle further specifies,

III. ITS PROPER TENDENCY AND OPERATION.

The sealing of the Spirit will never elate a man with pride.

It may seem indeed that such distinguishing mercies would puff us up—

But their invariable effect is to humble those who receive them—

All the saints of old abased themselves in proportion as they were favored of God—Job xlii. 5, 6, and Isa. 6, 5.

Nor can there be any stronger evidence that a work is not of God, than its producing a contrary effect upon us—

It is intended solely to honor and glorify God.

Every work of grace should lead the mind to God as the author of it—

And the more exalted the mercy, the more powerful should this effect be—

Now this, above all, administers to us the greatest cause of thankfulness—

And will certainly incline us to love and serve him from whom it has been derived—

*The church is Christ's "purchased possession," Acts xx. 28. And its complete "redemption" from all the penal effects of sin will be at the day of judgment, Rom. viii. 23.

ADDRESS.

1. To those who are ignorant of this sublime subject.

To many, alas! the sealing of the Spirit is mere foolishness—

But those who account it so, "speak evil of things that they understand not"—

Let us seek to experience it ourselves, instead of censuring those who do—

2. To those who desire to be sealed.

God is willing to bestow this blessing on all who seek it—

If we possess it not, we should enquire what there is in us which has occasioned God to withhold it from us—

And live more on the promises, that by them it may be imparted to our souls—

3. To those who are sealed.

What a mercy is it, that you, who might long since have been sealed for condemnation, have, according to the good pleasure of God, been sealed for heaven!

Be thankful to God for this unspeakable gift—

Be careful too that you grieve not him by whom you have been sealed—Eph. iv. 30.

But improve the promises yet further for your progressive advancement in true holiness—2 Cor. vii. 1.

CHAPTER VI.

GOOD ANGELS.

THE NATURE AND MINISTRY OF ANGELS.

Psalm xxxiv. 7.—The angel of the Lord encampeth round about them that fear him, and delivereth them. (H.)

THIS psalm is supposed to have been penned by David when he changed his behavior before Achish, the king of Gath, called in the title of this psalm, Abimelech, this being a common name for all the kings of the Philistines; as Pharaoh was common to the kings of Egypt; and as Cæsar was common to the Roman emperors. The history of David's situation is recorded. 1 Sam. xxi. 10. The means of his deliverance is particularly noticed, in the text and context. He prayed to his God. Verse 4–6. His friends also prayed for him. Verse 5. And the angels of God encamped round about him. The angel, or angels of the Lord encampeth round about them that fear him, &c. Such is the love of God to his children, that he appoints many angels, on particular occasions, no less than a host, enough to form an encampment, to save his servants. I shall,

1. OFFER A FEW REMARKS RELATIVE TO THOSE BEINGS WHO TEND THE RIGHTEOUS, and,

1. They are real beings, not imaginary beings, or apparitions only. This was the error of the Sadducees. Acts xxiii. 8. But the scripture declares them to have a personal subsistence. Hence they are said to be sent forth. Heb. i. 14. They are spirits that speak. Acts x. 19. They are living

creatures; Ezek. i. 5; by which are meant angels, as they are called cherubim. Ezek. x. 16. And they are called authorities and powers. 1 Peter iii. 22. And as such possessing understanding and will; and they do such things as none but reasonable agents can do. They admire God's wisdom. Eph. iii. 10. They converse with each other; and excite each other to glorify God. Isa. vi. 3.

2. They are secondary beings. Some heathen philosophers supposed the angels to be co-eternal with God; but this cannot be. There cannot be but one first, one eternal Being. This is God's prerogative. Heb. i. 12. God created them. Col. i. 15. In one of the six days, during which all things were created. Exod. xx. 11. For before the seventh day, the heavens and all the hosts thereof, were created. Gen. ii. 1, 2. The stars are the hosts of that heaven which we behold; but the angels are the hosts of the third heaven, which to us on earth is invisible; they are so called. Neh. ix. 6. They were created before the earth; therefore before the third day of the week, for on that day the earth was created, when the sons of God shouted for joy. Job xxxviii. 7. In the Septuagint, it is all the angels. It is probable they were created, with the light, on the first day of the week, hence called morning stars, not only stars, in respect to their brightness and glory but morning stars, as being formed in the morning, the very beginning of creation.

3. They are most excellent and glorious creatures. Man is the most excellent creature upon earth; but inferior to angels even in his best estate. Ps. viii. 5. Solomon calls them higher than the greatest tyrants that oppress the earth. Eccl. v. 8. Of all creatures, they most resemble God. They resemble God in being spiritual beings, not clothed with flesh and blood as we are. They are immortal beings, and what they now are, they shall ever be. They are wise and knowing, as it respects nature and the affairs of the world. Dan. x. 13. And their natural knowledge is increased by the experience of near six thousand years. They also possess a great deal of revealed knowledge concerning the scriptures. Dan. x. 21. Also concerning individuals before they are born. Dan. xi. 6. Hence they are said to be full of eyes. Rev. iv. 6. Eyes behind, knowing what is past, and eyes before, knowing what is to come. They are holy beings, called holy ones. Dan. iv. 17. Holy angels. Matt. xxv. 31. Angels of light. 2 Cor. xi. 14. All these things show that the angels, of all other creatures, most resemble God.

4. They are very numerous. They are called a great company. Psa. lxviii. 11. There are thousands of them, ver. 17. The chariots of God are twenty thousand, even thousands of angels; nay, there are millions of them. Dan. vii. 5-10; Rev. v. 11. Nay, they are innumerable. Heb. xii. 22. Bildad asks, is there any number of his armies? Job xxv. 3. Christ tells Peter that he could call to his assistance twelve legions (a legion is 6,666) of angels, which was equal to the amount of the whole Roman army. God can spare multitudes of angels to the assistance of his servants.

5. They are very powerful. They excel in strength. Ps. ciii. 20. They are called mighty angels. 2 Thes. i. 7. One angel is able to destroy all the men in the world. Their great power is manifest by what they have done. Iron gates cannot stand before them. Acts xii. 10. An angel can make the earth shake; Matt. xxviii. 2; and occasion a most terrible destruction in a short time, as in the case of the first-born in Egypt: the army of Senacherib: Sodom and Gomorrah, &c.

6 They are orderly. Hence called an host, or an army. It is **certain** that some, in their employment and office, are superior to others. There **are** some who are captains and leaders of others, who follow them. The **text** says, the angel of the Lord encampeth, &c. One angel cannot make a camp, but many can, under the conduct of one, as doubtless was the case here. One particular angel announced the birth of Christ. Luke ii. 9. And **a** multitude under his conduct, praised God upon the occasion, ver. 13. The scriptures speak not only of angels, but also of archangels: these are styled chief princes. Dan. x. 13. We have the names of one or two. One is named Michael; Dan. xii. 1; Jude 9; 1 Thes. iv. 16; who seems to be the chief of all the angels and arch-angels of God, and who by a way of eminence is called the archangel, and the great prince. Dan. xii. 1. They are supposed to be seven in number, signified by the seven lamps in the temple, before the mercy seat. Zech. iv. 10. Hence John speaks of the seven spirits of God, &c. Rev. v. 6. Who are called seven angels. Rev. viii. 2. These seem to be the general inspectors of the whole world, and thence are said to be sent forth into all the earth.

7. They are all at God's disposal. Hence called the angels of the Lord, angels of God, and spirits of God: they are sometimes called the spirits of the Lord. 1 Kings xviii. 12; Acts viii. 39. He is their great head and leader, and is hence called, the Lord of Hosts. They stand in his presence. Luke i. 19. And do his pleasure. Ps. ciii. 20.

II. Consider who are the objects of their attention and care.

1. The world in general. Many great men have been wonderfully protected and delivered by the angels of God, out of respect to the church and people. This was the case with Darius, the Persian emperor; Dan. xi. 1; also Alexander the Great; and neither of them feared God; but they were God's instruments to accomplish his designs in the world, and as such, protected and delivered by angels.

Great mercies and judgments are dispersed by them. They are as a lamp to the righteous, to light and direct them; and as coals of fire to the wicked, to punish and consume them. David expected they would punish his enemies. Psa. xxxv. 5, 6. Sodom was destroyed by them. Gen. xix. 13. Seventy thousand Israelites fell by the plague, which was brought upon them by an angel. 2 Sam. xxiv. 16. When Jerusalem was to be destroyed, the angels forsook it, and a voice was heard saying, let us go hence. And Tacitus reports that in Jerusalem there was a voice heard, greater than human, saying the gods are departed from this place. The trumpets in the Revelation, signifying judgments on the Roman empire, were sounded by angels; and the vials, denoting judgments on the papal power, are poured out by an gels, because these things are effected by their ministry.

In times of war wonderful victories are obtained by their invisible agency. They occasioned the sound in the mulberry trees, through which David obtained the victory. 2 Sam. v. 24. See also, 2 Kings vii. 6. The angels fought against the king of Persia. Dan. xi. 20. No wonder that the inconsiderable number of Grecians routed and destroyed the Persian army, which consisted of several millions, when the angels fought against them.

The great revolutions which happen in the world are effected by their ministry; when the living creatures went, then the wheels went with them. The world moved as the angels of God moved. They deposed Nebuchadnezzar, and gave his crown to another. Dan. iv. 17. When Belshazzer was slain, Babylon taken, &c., it was by their agency. An angel wrote the hand-writing on the wall, intimating to the king and his nobles the fate which awaited them

When Darius got the empire, an angel assisted him to keep it. Dan. **xi. 1.** The great revolution which took place in the world at the conversion of Constantine the Great, was brought about by angels. Rev. xii. 7. Thus we see, that this visible world is by God's appointment governed by the invisible world.

2. The church of God. This might be signified by the cherubim on the cu tains belonging to the tabernacle. Exod. xxvi. 1. Also by the cherubim on the walls of the temple. They promote the salvation of the church. Heb. i. 14. An angel directed Peter to Cornelius and his family. Acts x 30. Paul and others were directed by an angel to preach in Macedonia. Acts xvi. 9. When Jerusalem was besieged by the Assyrians, it is said the angel of the Lord went out, and smote the camp of the Assyrians. 1 Kings xix. 35. From which it appears, that an angel did reside in, and preside over that city, where the temple was, who, upon this occasion went out of it. So then, as one observes, angels are the guard of the queen of heaven, the Lamb's wife.

3. Individuals who fear God ; such are the objects of their particular and special care. They preserve them from many evils, which otherwise would befal them. Ps. xci. 11, 12. They journey with them and protect them. Gen. xxviii. 12 ; xxxii. 1, 2. Paul experienced this. Acts xxvii. 23, 24. An angel appeared for Israel against Balaam. Numb. xxii. 32. And for Elisha against the king of Syria. 2 Kings vi. 17.

They convey positive blessings, by assisting God's servants in their undertakings ; as in the case of Darius already mentioned, although he did not fear God ; and in the case of Abraham's servant for the bood of his family. Gen. xxiv. 40. Also, by instructing them, as in the case of Dan. ix. 22 ; and Zech. i. 9. And the shepherds ; Luke ii. 10. And Mary ; John xx. 12. And Elijah ; 2 Kings i. 15. And Hagar ; Gen. xvi. 9. An angel smote Zechariah for his unbelief. Luke i. 20. And doubtless, they visit God's children with diseases, to correct them for some sin they have been guilty of.

They have a great influence upon the minds of men. Evil angels can suggest evil thoughts into the mind ; see the case of Judas. John xiii. 2. Also Ahab. 1 Kings xxii. 22. So also good angels influence the minds of good men : and although all good thoughts are originally from God, yet he makes use of the ministry of angels for this purpose.

They stood by good men in their afflictions, to strengthen and comfort them. It was so with our Lord, in his temptation ; Matt. iv. 11 ; and in his agony ; Luke xxii. 43 ; also, Isaiah vi. 7 ; and with many of the martyrs, in the days of popery ; the angels standing by them, and quenching the violence of the fire.

Angels appear in due time to deliver them. See the case of Lot and his family. Gen. xix. 16. Also, Daniel vi. 22. And Peter ; Acts xii. 11. And the apostles. Acts v. 19.

They do not forsake good men at death, but carry them to heaven : it was so with Elijah. 2 Kings ii. 11. And Lazarus. Luke xvi. 22. The souls of good men pass through the devil's territory, the air, but they are safe under the convoy of angels.

They will collect all the righteous together at the great day, in order to a happy meeting with their Lord. Matt. xxiv. 31 ; xiii. 41.

They will also associate, and join with the redeemed of the Lord, in celebrating the praises of God and the Lamb for ever and ever. Rev. vii. 9— 12.

III. What is necessary on our part that we may enjoy THE BENEFIT OF THEIR PROTECTION.

1. We must endeavor after an interest in Christ; for all the angels are at his command. It is through his mediation that we obtain the benefit of their ministry. John i. 51. If we are Christ's, all things are ours, even the angels of God.

2. We must be careful to walk in the fear of the Lord; for his angels encamp about such, says our text; this was Cornelius' character; and while he was praying, an angel came to him. Acts x. 2, 3. Also of Daniel, who was favored in the same way. Dan. ix. 20, 21. See how those who feared God were preserved. Ezek. ix. 4—6.

3. Let us imitate the angels in doing all the good we can, in every station or relation; both to the world and the church. We should strive to do the will of God on earth, as the angels do in heaven.

4. Let us remember that the eyes of angels are upon us; they witness all our actions. Eccl. v. 6. They are present at our assemblies. 1 Cor. xi. 10. Let us remember these things and act accordingly, and we shall soon associate with them in the walks of the paradise of God. Zech. iii. 7.

MINISTERING SPIRITS.

Heb. i. 14.—Are they not all ministering spirits, sent forth to minister for them who shall be heirs of salvation? (Sk.)

MAN is naturally an inquisitive creature; and under the influence of an intense thirst for the acquisition of knowledge, he is led to ask questions, read books, pursue studies, and use all the means that can augment his stock of information. On all the topics connected with our interests as citizens of the world, we gain ample information by perusing the works of men; but the Bible is the chief medium, through which information on religious subjects is freely and circumstantially communicated. Some of those subjects are frequently brought forward, largely discussed, and pointedly insisted on; others are only incidentally mentioned, as they do not form essential parts in the economy of human redemption. The text refers to one of those subjects; and though our salvation might have been secured, even if we had never known it, yet it cannot be uninteresting to men in general; and it is peculiarly calculated to administer comfort to every pious soul. We will therefore consider,

I. THE NATURE OF ANGELS;—they are *spirits*. Many of the ancient philosophers, and not a few of the christian fathers, believed that angels were clothed with some kind of bodies composed of the purest particles of matter, which they called *ætherial*; but the scriptures speak of them as spirits, Psa. civ. 4. As *spirits* they possess natural and moral perfections; of the former, they have 1st, *understandings, clear and comprehensive.* Their knowledge is vastly extended; the wisdom of an angel is proverbial. David was said to be as an angel of the Lord, to discern good and bad; and wise, according to the wisdom of an angel, 2 Sam. xiv. 17—20. The angels know much of God, they behold the displays of his glory, they are his ministers to do his pleasure; they are acquainted with his works, they sang together, and shouted for joy when the foundations of the earth were laid, Iob. **xxxviii. 7.** And they know much of what is doing in the world. **2.** *As spirits they possess great power;* David declares, "they excel in strength," Psa. ciii. **20.** We deem that man the strongest, who can put in motion the largest quantity of matter; what cannot an angel do? It is generally thought, that the immense slaughter of all the first-born of Egypt was accomplished by an angel. The hundred and eighty-five thousand, of the army of Sennacherib, that fell in one night, were slain by an angel, 2 Kings xix. 35. It was an angel that inflicted the pestilence upon Israel, when seventy thousand were cut off. 2 Sam. xxiv. 15. And Herod was smitten by an angel, when eaten up with worms, Acts xii. 23. **3.** *As spirits they possess great activity, or swiftness of motion.* They are represented as " being full of wings;" how easily and swiftly do they transport themselves from place to place: even the finer particles of matter are amazingly volatile, how inconceivable is the velocity of light! but how tardy compared to the speed of an angel! **4.** *As spirits, they are endowed with liberty.* This is essential to a moral agent; it is said of fallen angels, that they left their first estate; it was a personal act, and a matter of choice; " Freely they stood, who stood; and fell who fell; not free, what proof could they have given of true allegiance?" &c. And as spirits, they possess moral perfections; such as *purity of affections:* they are eminently termed *holy angels:—benevolence of disposition:* how ardent is their zeal for God. Some are termed seraphim, which signifies *burning.* How much they delight in our happiness. How glad to bear the tidings of peace on earth, and good will towards men.

II. THE CHARGE OF ANGELS. *Them who shall be heirs, &c.* Whether they minister to men promiscuously, I dare not say; the Bible is silent on the subject: and how far it is consistent with reason to suppose an angel ministering to a sot, or a debauchee, I leave you to judge. *The heirs of salvation* are the objects of their charge. Salvation here means that final and complete deliverance, which God will accomplish in behalf of his saints, and that ineffable glory, and inexpressible happiness, with which they will be invested. Salvation is an *inheritance*—glorious in its nature—satisfying in its enjoyment—eternal in its duration. Oh! how unlike earthly inheritances. *An heir* is a person who has a just right to a certain possession—who can make out a legal title to it—but who is in a state of minority, and not of age to possess it. All this applies to the saints; they are born of God, and " if children, then heirs, heirs of God"—this gives them a right to their heavenly inheritance—they have a legal title in the promise—but they are at present in a state of minority.

III. THE CHARACTER OF THEIR MINISTRATION. In considering the ministration of angels, we must be careful not to attribute to them any work that will interfere with the influence of the Holy Ghost upon the soul of man. Man is a totally depraved creature; and the whole of his salvation, from its commencement to its close, is accomplished by the Divine Spirit, without any intermediate agency. **1.** *Angels minister to our instruction, when we are liable to miss our providential way.* How dark and intricate in many instances is the path we have to tread: but how clear and extended the perceptions of angels. The following scriptures sufficiently prove that they direct the *heirs of salvation* in the time of difficulty, Gen. xvi. 9; Judg. xiii. 13, 14; Matt. i. 20,—ii. 13; Acts x. 3. **2.** *Angels minister to our deliverance in the times of danger,* 2 Kings vi. 17; Psa. xxxiv. 7,—xci. 11; Dan. vi. 22,—iii. 25; Acts xii. 7. **3.** *Angels minister to our comfort in the seasons of distress.* In our Saviour's deepest agony, there appeared unto him an angel strengthening him, Luke xxii. 43. And as the strength communicated unquestionably referred to some consolatory thoughts suggested to his mind, may not we also derive *comfort* from such a source? 4. *Angels minister to our release from the body, and our admittance into heaven.* Witness Lazarus, Luke xvi. 22.—See 2 Pet. i. 11.—The ministration of angels is, 1. *Divine in its authority:* they are sent. 2. *Active in its nature:* they are sent *forth.* 3. *Universal in its agency: all* ministering spirits. 4. *Benevolent in its results:* they minister to our salvation. INFER, 1st. The wonderful care of God over us in appointing us such ministers; how various their orders, how immense their numbers, Dan. vii. 10 2. What a motive to induce us to hate sin; the *holy* angels are with us, and how hateful must sin be in their sight. 3. From the office of angels, let us learn where true greatness lies, Matt. xx. 26. 4. From the activity and zeal of angels in doing good, let us emulate their example.

CHAPTER VII.

WICKED ANGELS.

OF EVIL ANGELS.

Eph. vi. 12.--We wrestle not against flesh and blood, but against principalities, against powers, against the rulers of the darkness of this world, against spiritual wickedness in high places.

DIVINE Revelation declares that all angels were originally created holy and happy, yet they did not all continue as they were created, some left their first estate. The text contains the whole scriptural doctrine concerning them. In prosecuting this important subject, I will endeavor to explain, 1. The nature and properties of evil angels; and 2. Their employment.

With regard to the first, we cannot doubt but all the angels of God were originally of the same nature.

Their original properties were, doubtless alike. There is no absurdity in supposing Satan, the chief of the wicked angels, to have been one of the first, if not the first arch-angel. Endowed with an understanding, wisdom and strength, incomprehensible to us.

We do not exactly know either what was the occasion of their apostacy, or what effect it immediately produced upon them. Some have, not improbably supposed pride, mentioned in Ps. ii. 6, 7. When they shook off their allegiance to God, they shook off all goodness, and contracted all these tempers which are most hateful to him and most opposed to his nature. Ever since, they are full of pride, envy, cruelty, and rage against the children of men.

In the prosecution of their infernal design, they are diligent in the highest degree.

One circumstance more we may learn from the scriptures concerning the evil angels; they do not wander at large, but are all united under one common head. It is Satan, that is styled by our blessed Lord, "The prince of this world;" yea, the apostle does not scruple to call him, "The god of this world." He is termed the devil by way of eminence:—Apollyon, or the destroyer;—the old serpent from his beguiling Eve under that form :—and the angel of the bottomless pit. We have reason to believe that, the other evil angels are under his command and do his pleasure.

II. THE EMPLOYMENT OF THE EVIL ANGELS.

They are as far, as God permits, governors of the world. Agreeable to which, is that expression of Satan, Matt. iv. 8, 9, when he showed our Lord all the kingdoms of the world and the glory of them : all these things will I give thee, if thou wilt fall down and worship me. It is a little more particularly expressed in Luke iv. 5, 6.—They are the rulers of the darkness of this age, of the present state of things, during which the whole world lieth in the wicked one. He is the author of all ignorance, error, folly and wickedness.

They are continually warring against the children of men. They are ever watching to see whose outward or inward circumstances, whose prosperity or adversity. whose health or sickness, whose friends or enemies, whose youth or age, whose knowledge or ignorance, whose blindness or idleness, whose joy or sorrow may lay them open to temptation. They are constantly walking about as a roaring lion, seeking whom they may devour. It is by these instruments that the foolish hearts of those that know not God are darkened ; yea, they frequently darken, in a measure, the hearts of them that do know God. The god of this world knows how to blind our hearts and to obscure the lights of those truths, which at other times, shine as bright as the noon-day sun. By these means, he assaults our faith—endeavors to weaken our hopes of immortality and destroy our confidence in God.

This enemy of all righteousness is equally diligent to hinder every good word and work.

He is continually laboring with all his skill and power to infuse evil thoughts into the hearts of men.

He likewise labors to awaken evil passions or tempers in our souls. He endeavors to excite those passions and tempers, which are directly opposite to the fruit of the Spirit. He is the author of all unbelief, atheism, ill will, hatred, malice, envy.

As no good is done or spoken by any man, without the assistance of God, working together in and with those that believe in him ; so there is no evil done, or spoken without the assistance of the devil, who worketh with energy, with strong, though secret power in the children of disobedience. Thus he entered into Judas, and confirmed him in the design of betraying his master ; thus he put into the heart of Ananias and Sapphira, to lie unto the Holy Ghost ; and, in like manner, he has a share in all the actions and words and designs of evil men. As the children of God are workers together with God in every good thought, or word, or action ; so the children of the devil are workers together with him, in every evil thought, or word, or work.

It remains only to draw a few plain inferences from the doctrine which has been delivered.

As a general preservative against all the rage, the power and subtlety of your great adversary, put on the panoply, the whole armor of God. So shall ye be able to withstand all the force and all the stratagems of the enemy ; so shall he be able to withstand in the evil day.

To his fiery darts and his evil suggestions, oppose the shield of faith.

If he inject doubts, whether you are a child of God: fears, lest you should not endure to the end ; take to you for a helmet the hope of salvation. Hold fast that glad word. Eph i. 3.

Whenever the roaring lion, walking about and seeking whom he may devour, assaults you with all his malice, and rage and strength, resist him steadfast in the faith.

Lastly, if he transform himself into an angel of light, then are you in the greatest danger of all. Then have you need to beware, lest you also fall, when many mightier have been slain—then have you the greater need to watch and pray that ye enter not into temptation.

THE RELAPSED DÆMONIAC.

Matt. xii. 43—45.—When the unclean spirit is gone out of a man, he walketh through dry places, seeking rest, and findeth none. Then he saith, I will return into my house from whence I came out; and when he is come, he findeth it empty, swept, and garnished. Then goeth he and taketh with himself seven other spirits, more wicked than himself, and they enter in and they dwell there: and the last state of that man is worse than the first. Even so shall it be also unto this wicked generation. (S. S.)

THOUGH the general scope of the parables is, for the most part, plain and obvious, it is often difficult to see the precise meaning of some circumstances contained in them—

This is the case with the parable before us; the minuter incidents of which may be considered perhaps rather as ornamental, than as essential parts of the parable itself*—

Its import, on the whole, suggests the following observations—

I. PERSONS, ONCE DELIVERED FROM SATAN, ARE AGAIN OPEN TO HIS ASSAULTS.

Satan certainly has power over the hearts of men.

There is much ascribed to his agency in the holy scriptures—

He is said to blind the eyes of unbelievers, 2 Cor. iv. 4, and to rule in their hearts, Eph. ii. 2.

Though he has not the same power over men's bodies as he once had, he evidently possesses their souls, and drives them to perdition, Mark ix. 22

But he often loses his dominion through the preaching of the gospel.

Paul was commissioned to turn men from the power of Satan unto God, Acts xxvi. 18.

And the gospel was the weapon whereby he rescued them from his dominion, 2 Cor. x. 4.

The same divine energy also attends it, when used by us, 2 Tim. ii. 25, 26.

Though conversions are more rare than in the apostle's days, they are not less real—

Yet they who have been delivered from him, are still open to his assaults

* Our Lord had cast out a devil; and this was by the Pharisees imputed to a confederacy with Beelzebub. After shewing the absurdity of such a notion, he contrasted their state with that of the Ninevites and the Queen of Sheba; and compared them to a relapsed demoniac, who would be in a worse state than if Satan had never gone out of him at all. If we proceed to explain all that is spoken respecting the unclean spirit, we must interpret it of Satan, ejected from the Jews, and going in *dry*, that is, unfrequented places, or places *not watered by the gospel*, to find rest among the Gentiles; and, upon being pursued thither by the preaching of the apostles, returning to take more full possession of the Jews than ever; since, however reformed some of them might be, they were, as a nation, perfectly prepared, through their inveterate lusts and prejudices, to receive them

How often did he repeat his attacks on Peter! Matt. xvi. 23, Luke xxii. 31.

With what envious malice did he buffet Paul! 2 Cor. xii. 7.

How did he renew his attempts even on Christ himself! Compare Luke iv. 13, John xiv. 30, Luke xxii. 53.

Thus he still watches for his opportunity to destroy *us*, 1 Pet. v. 8.

Nor shall we be wholly out of his reach, till we are finally discharged from our warfare, Eph. vi. 11, 12.

We had need therefore to watch against this subtle enemy ; for

II. If we be a second time subjected to Satan's dominion, our last state will be worse than the first.

It is certain that Satan can never finally prevail against the elect.

This is evidently implied in the character which is given of them, 1 John ii. 13, 14, and v. 18.

The promises of God also insure to them the victory over him, Rom. xvi. 20.

Hence they are taught to defy all the powers of darkness, Rom. viii. 38, 39.

They, into whom he may return, are described in the text.

The true children of God desire to be ever " filled with the Spirit"—

Nor will they suffer the things that please Satan to abide quietly in their hearts—

But self-deceivers are satisfied, like Herod, with a partial change, Mark vi. 20.

And continue with their old affections and lusts unmortified, Ps. lxxviii. 36, 37.

Judas, Ananias, Demas, no doubt, retained their love of this world—

Hence Satan found their hearts " swept" indeed, and " emptied" of gross sin, but still *furnished* for his reception—

And, wherever this is the case, he will surely, however expelled for a season, return ere long with increased power—

On his return to them their state will be worse than ever.

The Holy Spirit will be grieved, provoked, quenched, Eph. iv. 30, Isa. lxiii. 10, 1 Thes. v. 19.

Their consciences will be silenced, and made callous—1 Tim. iv. 2.

Their evil habits will return and gain an irresistible dominion—

They will live only to treasure up wrath against the day of wrath—

And the deliverance, which they have neglected to improve, will fearfully aggravate their final condemnation—2 Pet. ii. 20, 21.

Inquire,

1. Have we ever yet been delivered from Satan ?

Perhaps many doubt whether they have ever been possessed by Satan—

But this alone is sufficient to prove, that they are yet under his dominion.

That usurper reigns in all till he is vanquished and expelled by Jesus Christ—

And it is only in answer to fervent prayer, that the adorable Saviour puts forth his power to drive him out—

2. Are we yet daily maintaining a strict watch against him ?

If he has been cast out of us, he is seeking his opportunity to return—

Nor can he be kept away, but by constant prayer and watchfulness—

Let us then guard every avenue of our hearts—

Let us implore the aid of our divine inhabitant—

The exertion of our own power in dependence on the intercession and grace of Christ, will insure us a successful issue of the conflict, Jam. iv 7, with Luke xxii. 31, 32.

~~~~~~~~~~~~~~

THE MEANS OF DEFEATING SATAN'S MALICE.

1 Pet. v. 8, 9.—Be sober, be vigilant: because your adversary, the devil, as a roaring lion, walketh about, seeking whom he may devour: whom resist, stedfast in the faith. (S. S.)

THERE are many who deny the influences of the Holy Spirit—
No wonder therefore if the agency of Satan be called in question—
But there is abundant proof in the scriptures that Satan exercises a power over the minds of men—
St. Peter had learned this truth by bitter experience—
In this view the caution he gives us is worthy of particular attention.
I. THE MALICE OF SATAN.
Satan is the great adversary of mankind—
It was he who caused the fall of our first parents, Gen. iii. 1—5.
He has exerted a similar influence over all their descendants—
He still maintains his enmity against the seed of the woman, Gen. iii. 15.
He is justly compared to "a roaring lion"—
He is subtle.
The lion prowls with subtilty in search of prey—
This is noticed in David's description of wicked men, Ps. x. 9, 10.
Satan also uses many devices to destroy souls, Eph. vi. 11.
He suits his temptations to us with astonishing craft—
He draws us into his snare before we are aware of his designs, 2 Cor. ii. 11.
To be acquainted with his devices is a most eminent and useful part of christian knowledge, Ib.
He is active.
The lion ranges far and wide in search of his prey—
And Satan "walks to and fro throughout the earth" Job. i. 7, and the text.
He ceases not from his exertions day or night, Rev. xii. 10.
He is the more diligent as knowing that his time is limited, Rev. xii. 12.
He has legions of emissaries acting in concert with him, Mark v. 9.
If at any time he suspend his attacks, it is but for a season, that he may return afterwards with greater advantage, Compare Luke iv. 13, with Luke xxii. 53.
He is cruel.
(1) The lion little regards the agonies which he occasions—
Nor has Satan any compassion for the souls which he destroys—
(2) The savage animal kills to satisfy the calls of nature—
But our adversary reaps no benefit from the destruction of men—
(3) His exertions serve only to increase his own guilt and misery—
Yet is he insatiable in his thirst for our condemnation—
He is powerful.
Feeble is the resistance of a lamb against the voracious lion—
Still more impotent are men before "the god of this world"—

Satan has a limited power over the elements themselves*—

The ungodly are altogether subjected to his will, Eph. ii. 2, 2 Tim. ii. 26.

Nor would the saints have the smallest power to resist him, if God should deliver them into his hands†—

If we believe this representation of Satan's malice, we cannot but desire to know

II. THE MEANS OF DEFEATING IT.

Our adversary, though great, is not invincible—

There is one stronger than he, that can overcome him, Luke xi. 21, 22.

And God has prescribed means whereby *we* also may vanquish him.

Moderation

An undue attachment to the things of time and sense gives him a great advantage over us—

He will not fail to assault us on our weak side‡—

But a deadness to the world will in some measure disarm him—

He prevailed not against our Lord, because he found no irregular affection in him, John xiv. 30.

Nor could he so easily overcome us if we disregarded earthly things—

A contempt of life has been a principal mean whereby the saints and martyrs in all ages have triumphed over him, Rev. xii. 11.

Vigilance

Unwatchfulness, even in a victorious army, exposes it to defeat—

Much more must it subject us to the power of our subtle enemy—

St. Peter had experienced its baneful effects—

He had been warned of Satan's intention to assault him, Luke xxii. 31.

He had been commanded to pray lest he should fall by the temptation,—Luke xxii. 40.

But he slept when he should have been praying, Luke xxii. 45, 46.

He stands in this respect, like Lot's wife, Luke xvii. 32, a monument to future generations—

But vigilance on our part will counteract the designs of Satan—

The armed christian, watching unto prayer, must be victorious, Eph. vi. 18.

Fortitude

The timid christian falls into a thousand snares, Prov. xxix. 25.

The only way to obtain a victory is, to fight manfully—

And this is the duty of every follower of Christ, Eph. vi. 10, 13

We must never give way to Satan, Eph. iv. 27.

We are called to wrestle and contend with him, Eph. vi. 12.

Nor shall our resistance be in vain‖—

Faith

Unbelief is a powerful instrument in the hands of Satan—

He excites it in us that he may turn us from the faith—

We must therefore hold fast *the doctrines of faith*—

We should not suffer ourselves to be moved from the hope of the gospel—

This is our anchor whereby we must outride the storm, Heb. vi. 19.

---

* Job. i. 12. 19. He is called "the prince of the power of the air."

† Many who have appeared lights in the church have been swept away by the tail of this great dragon, Rev. xxii. 3, 4.

‡ It was he who instigated Judas to treachery, and Ananias to falsehood: but he wrought by means of their covetousness, John xiii. 2, Acts v. 3.

‖ James iv. 7. Satan is not only checked but *terrified*, and vanquished by the resistance of the weakest christian.

We must also stedfastly exercise *the grace of faith*—
This is the weapon whereby we evercome the world, 1 John v. **4.**
And by this shall we triumph over Satan himself, Eph. vi. 16
APPLICATION.
Let not the ungodly despise this adversary—
But let them seek deliverance from him through the gospel, Acts xxvi. **18.**
And let the godly be continually on their guard against him, 2 Cor. xi. **3.**
So shall they experience that promised blessing, Rom. xvi. 20.

THE MEANS OF SECURITY FROM SATAN'S MALICE.

Luke xxii. 31, 32. And the Lord sain, Simon, Simon, behold, Satan hath desired to have
you, that he may sift you as wheat: but I have prayed for thee, that thy faith fail
not. (S. S.)

THE agency, or even the existence, of evil spirits is scarcely credited
amongst us—
But there is nothing more certain than that they exist, and act in the
world—
To conflict with them constitutes a principal part of the Christians war
fare, Eph. vi. 12.
And to be aware of their devices is no inconsiderable attainment in Chris
tian knowledge, 2 Cor. ii. 11.
There is however a Being who is able to counteract their agency—
Of this we have a proof in the history before us—
Satan, the prince of the devils, meditated the destruction of Peter—
Our Lord with affection and earnestness warned Peter of his designs—
And, by his own intercession, secured him against his assaults.
I. THE MALICE OF SATAN.
Satan is the great adversary of mankind.
He was once as bright a morning star as any in heaven—But he rebelled
against the Most High, and incurred his displeasure, 2 Pet. ii. 4.
Full of hatred against God, he sought to efface his image from our first
parents—
Through subtilty he prevailed to the destruction of them and us, 2 Cor
xi. 3.
Nor does he cease to assault those who through grace are restored—
He desires to agitate and distress them.
This is evidently implied in the expression in the text—
He has various ways of effecting his purpose—
He may harass us with temptations and persecutions—
He may perplex us by artful insinuations and suggestions—
His efforts were exerted against all the apostles—*
But the more eminent any are, the more they are hated by him—
Peter was distinguished for his knowledge and intrepidity, Matt. xvi. **16**
Yea, he had had a peculiar honor conferred on him, Matt. xvi. 18.
On this account Satan's malice raged against him more especially—
But his ultimate end is to prove them hypocrites, or to make them apos-
tates.

*Ῥμας.

This was evidently his design in assaulting Job, Job i. 9, 11 ; and ii. 5. And in asking permission to try the disciples—†

Nor would he leave one faithful person upon earth—

" As a roaring lion he seeks to devour" all—

He can do nothing indeed but by divine permission—‡

But if suffered to fulfil all his will, he would destroy every soul—

His influence on the herd of swine shews what he would do to men, Matt. viii. 32.

Not one vassal of his would escape the fate of Judas, Compare Luke xxii. 3, with Matt. xxvii. 5.

But God has not left his people without means of resistance.

II. Our security.

God has both armed his people for the combat, and given them a great Deliverer—

Faith is the grace whereby he enables us to maintain our stand.

It was by faith that we were translated from Satan's kingdom into Christ's Gal. iii. 26.

It is by that also that our daily warfare is to be carried on, 2 Cor. i. 24.

Yea, through that are we to attain our full and final salvation, 1 Pet. i. 5

Faith is the shield whereby alone we can ward off the darts of Satan, Eph. vi. 16.

If that fail, we are exposed to the fiercest assaults of our enemy—

If we lose our hold of the promises, we shall be driven away as chaff—

We shall have no point around which to rally our scattered forces—

Whereas, if faith be strong, we shall hope even against hope, Rom. iv. 18, 20.

And, though wounded, we shall return with fresh vigor to the combat—

Nor shall our great adversary be able to prevail against us, Rom. x. 11

Hence that earnest caution against unbelief, Heb. iii. 12.

And that express direction respecting the mode of opposing Satan, 1 Pet. v 8, 9.

But the intercession of Christ is necessary to uphold our faith.

Peter's faith would have failed utterly if he had been left to himself—

But through the intercession of Christ he was preserved—

Thus we also should " make shipwreck of our faith"—

But our prevailing Advocate pleads for us also, John xvii. 20.

As our High-Priest he bears us on his breast-plate before the throne, Exod. xxviii. 29.

He obtains for us fresh supplies of the Spirit—

In this way he, who has been the author of our faith, will also be the finisher, Heb. xii. 2.

Hence the encouragement given us to rely on the intercession of Christ, Rom. viii. 34.

Hence the encouragement given us to regard it under every backsliding, 1 John ii. 1.

Hence the encouragement given us to rest assured of Christ's power to save, Heb. vii. 25.

Infer,

1. What need have we to be ever on our guard !

† 'Εξητησατο seems to imply a kind of challenge, as in the case of Job, wherein he under took to prove them to be but chaff, if God would suffer him to make the trial.

‡ He could not afflict Job more than God saw fit to suffer him : nor could he enter into the swine without our Saviour's permission, Matt. viii. 31.

Perhaps at this moment Satan may be desiring to sift *us*—
And what if God should give us up into his hands ?—
If suffered to exert his strength, he could soon dissipate whatever is good in us—
Nor should our past zeal in God's service remove our apprehensions—
That would rather provoke Satan to more activity against us—
Let us then " not be high-minded but fear"—
Let us follow the salutary advice which our Lord has given us, Matt. xxvi. 41.
Let us plead with fervor those important petitions, Matt. vi. 13.
At the same time let us " put on the whole armor of God"—
And prepare, as God has taught us, for the assaults of our enemy, Eph. vi. 13—18.
2. What a mercy is it to have an interest in Christ!
They who know not Chrtst are wholly under the poyer of Satan, 2 Tim ii. 26.
But they who are Christ's have a watchful and almighty guardian—
Our Lord provided for Peter's safety, before Peter even knew his danger—
Thus " will he keep the feet of all his saints"—
He will suffer none of them to be plucked out of his hand, John x. 28.
If he permit Satan to sift them, it shall be only for the removing of their chaff, Compare 2 Cor. xii. 7. with Heb. xii. 10, 11.
He has pledged his word for the security of the weakest of his people, Amos ix. 9.
Let us therefore commit ourselves entirely into his hands—
Let us beg him to remember our unworthy names in his intercessions—
And to deal with us as with Joshua of old, Zech. iii. 2—4.

CHAPTER VIII.

MAN.

CREATION OF MAN.

Gen. i. 26.—And God said, Let us make man in our image, after our likeness. (H. II.)

THOUGH men constantly trace their origin to their immediate parents, and frequently to their remoter ancestors, yet they rarely consider when, or how they first came into existence, or whether any change has taken place in their nature since they came out of their Creator's hands. That there was a period when no such creature as man existed, even reason itself would teach us; for every effect must proceed from some cause : and therefore the formation of man, however remotely we trace his origin, must, in the first instance, have been the product of some intelligent Being, who was eternally self-existent. But we are not left to the uncertain deductions of reason: God has been pleased to reveal unto us (what could not otherwise have been known) Heb. xi. 3, the time and manner of our creation, together with the state in which we were created. And these are the subjects which we would now propose for your consideration:

I. THE CIRCUMSTANCES OF OUR CREATION—

We may not unprofitably notice somewhat respecting *the time*—

Five days had been occupied in reducing to order the confused chaos, and in furnishing the world with whatever could enrich or adorn it. On the sixth, God formed man, whom he reserved to the last, as being the most excellent of his works; and whose formation he delayed, till every thing in this habitable globe was fitted for his accommodation. It is not for us to inquire why God chose this space of time for the completion of his work, when he could as easily have formed it all in an instant: but one instructive lession at least we may learn from the survey which he took of every day's work; it teaches his creatures to review their works from day to day, in order that, if they find them to have been good, they may be excited to gratitude; or, if they perceive them to have been evil, they may be led to repentance. At the close of every day, God pronounced his work to be "good:" but when man was formed, and the harmony of all the parts, together with the conduciveness of each to its proper end, and the subserviency of every part to the good of the whole, were fully manifest, then he pronounced the whole to be "*very good.*" From this also we learn, that it is not one work or two, however good-in themselves, that should fully satisfy our minds; but a comprehensive view of all our works, as harmonizing with each other, and corresponding with all the ends of our creation.

In *the manner* of our creation there is something worthy of very peculiar attention—

In the formation of all other things God merely exercised his own sovereign will, saying, "Let there be light," "Let such and such things take place." But in the creation of man we behold the language of consultation; "Let us make man." There is not the least reason to suppose that this was a mere form of speech, like that which obtains among monarchs at this day; for this is quite a modern refinement: nor can it be an address to angels; for they had nothing to do in the formation of man: it is an address to the Son, and to the Holy Ghost, both of whom co-operated in the formation of Him who was to be the master-piece of divine wisdom and power.* This appears from a still more striking expression, which occurs afterwards; where God says, "Now man is become like *one of us*, to know good and evil." Gen. iii. 22. And it is confirmed in a variety of other passages, where God, *under the character of our "Creator," or "Maker,"* is spoken of in the plural number.†

We must not however suppose that there are three Gods: there certainly is but One God; and His unity is as clear as his existence: and this is intentionally marked in the very verse following our text; where the expressions, "*us*" and "*our*" are turned into "*he*" and "*his:*"—"God created man in *his* own image; in the image of God created *he* him."

Here, then, we may see an early intimation of the *Trinity in Unity;* a doctrine which pervades the whole Bible, and is the very corner-stone of our holy religion. And it is deserving of particular notice, that, in our dedication to our Creator at our baptism, we are expressly required to acknowledge this mysterious doctrine, being "baptized in the name of the Father, and of the Son, and of the Holy Ghost." Matt. xxviii. 19.

*The work of Creation is ascribed to Jesus Christ, John i. 1—3, and to the Holy Ghost, Gen. i. 2; Job xxvi. 13; and xxxiii. 4.

†See Job xxxv. 10; Isaiah liv. 5; Eccl. xii. 1. These are all plural *in the original.*

The text informs us further respecting,

II. THE STATE IN WHICH WE WERE CREATED—

There was some "likeness" to God even in the nature of man. "God is a spirit," who thinks, and wills, and acts. Man also has a spirit, distinct from his body, or from the mere animal life: he has a thinking, willing substance, which acts upon matter by the mere exercises of its own volitions, except when the material substance on which it operates is bereft of its proper faculties, or impeded in the use of them. But the image of God in which man was formed, is, properly, two-fold:

1. Intellectual—

"God is a God of knowledge." He has a perfect discernment of every thing in the whole creation. Such, too, was Adam in his first formation. Before he had had any opportunity to make observations on the beasts of the field and the birds of the air, he gave names to every one of them, suited to their several natures, and distinctive of their proper characters. But it was not merely in things natural that Adam was so well instructed; he doubtless had just views of God, his nature and perfections: he had also a thorough knowledge of himself, of his duties, his interests, his happiness. There was no one thing which could conduce either to his felicity or usefulness, which was not made known to him, as far as he needed to be instructed in it. As "God is light without any mixture or shade of darkness," 1 John i. 5, so was Adam, in reference to all those things at least which he was at all concerned to know.

2. Moral—

Holiness is no less characteristic of the Deity than wisdom. He loves every thing that is good, and infinitely abhors every thing that is evil. Every one of His perfections is holy. In this respect, also, did man bear a resemblance to his Maker. "God made him upright." Eccl. vii. 29. As he had a view of the commandment in all its breadth, so had he a conformity to it in all his dispositions and actions. He felt no reluctance in obeying it: his will was in perfect unison with the will of his Maker. All the inferior appetites were in habitual subjection to his reason, which also was in subjection to the commands of God. We are told respecting the Lord Jesus Christ, that he was "the image of God," 2 Cor. iv. 4, "the image of the invisible God," Col. i. 15, "the express image of his person." Heb. i. 3. What the Lord Jesus Christ, therefore, was upon earth, *that* was man in Paradise—"holy, harmless, undefiled." Heb. vii. 26.

That man's resemblance to his Maker did indeed consist in these two things, is manifest; because our renewal after the divine image is expressly said to be in knowledge, Col. iii. 10, and in true holiness. Eph. iv. 24. Well, therefore, does the apostle say of man, that "he is the image and glory of God." 1 Cor. xi. 7.

INFER,

1. What an awful change has sin brought into the world!

Survey the character before drawn: and compare it with men in the present state: "How is the gold become dim, and the find gold changed!" Men are now enveloped in darkness, and immersed in sin. They "know nothing as they ought to know," and do nothing as they ought to do it. No words can adequately express the blindness of their minds, or the depravity of their hearts. —— Yet all this has resulted from that one sin which Adam committed in Paradise. He lost the divine image from his own soul; and "begat a son in his own fallen likeness:" and the streams that have been flowing for nearly six thousand years from that polluted fountain, are still as corrupt as ever. O that we habitually considered sin in this light, and re-garded it as the one source of all our miseries!

2. What a glorious change will the Holy Spirit effect in the hearts of all who seek Him!

In numberless passages, as well as in those before cited, See notes (m) and (n), the Holy Spirit is spoken of, as "renewing" our souls, and making us "new creatures." 2 Cor. v. 17. What Adam was in Paradise, *that* shall we be, "according to the measure of the gift of Christ." "Instead of the thorn shall come up the fir-tree, and instead of the brier shall grow up the myrtle-tree." Isa. lv. 13. He will "open the eyes of our understanding," and cause us to "know all things" that are needful for our salvation: 1 John ii. 20, 27; and at the same time that he "turns us from darkness unto light, he will turn us also from the power of Satan unto God:" "He will put the law in our *minds*, and write it in our *hearts*." Heb. viii. 10. Let not any imagine that their case is desperate; for He who created all things out of nothing, can easily create us anew in Christ Jesus: and He will do it, if we only direct our eyes to Christ: "We all beholding as in a glass the glory of the Lord, shall be changed into the same image from glory to glory, even as by the Spirit of the Lord." 2 Cor. iii. 18.

3. What obligations do we owe to the ever-blessed Trinity!

If we looked no further than to our first creation, we are infinitely indebt-ed to the sacred Three, for making us the subject of their consultation, and for co-operating to form us in the most perfect manner. But what shall we say to that other consultation, respecting the restoration of our souls? Hear, and be astonished at that gracious proposal, "Let us *restore* man *to* our im-age." "I," says the Father, "will pardon and accept them, if an adequate atonement can be found to satisfy the demands of justice. "Then on me be their guilt," says his only dear Son: "I will offer myself a sacrifice for them, if any one can be found to apply the virtue of it effectually to their souls, and to secure to me the purchase of my blood." "*That* shall be my charge," says the blessed Spirit: "I gladly undertake the office of enlight-ening, renewing, sanctifying their souls; and I will "preserve every one of them blameless unto thy heavenly kingdom." Thus, by their united efforts, is the work accomplished; and "a way of access is opened for every one of us through Christ, by that one Spirit, unto the Father." Eph. ii. 18. O let every soul rejoice in this Tri-une God! and may the Father's love, the grace of Christ, and the fellowship of the Holy Ghost, be with us all ever-more! Amen.

OF THE IMMORTALITY OF THE SOUL.

Gen. ii. 7.—And he became a living soul. (H.)

THOUGH the body die, and when it dies, the soul dies not; it survives the body, and not only lives after it, but lives for ever, it never dies: though the body without the soul be dead, yet the soul without the body is not dead. When the body returns to the earth and dust, from whence it sprung, the soul returns to God, its immediate author: the body may be killed by men, but not the soul: no man has any power over that, none but God that made it: the soul is immortal, it is not capable of death, that is, in a natural and proper sense.

When it is said the soul is immortal, it must be understood that it is so in its nature; and is not liable to death either from any thing within itself, or without it; but not that it has such an immortality as God himself has, "who only hath immortality;" he has it of himself. Angels, and the souls of men, have their immortality of him, who has made them immaterial and immortal spirits; his immortality is without beginning, and any prior cause of it; theirs has a beginning from God, the first cause of them: his is independent; theirs depends on him, "in whom they live, and move, and have their being." That the soul of man is immortal, may be proved,

I. From the consideration of the soul itself—its original, nature, powers, and faculties.

(1.) From the original of it. It is not of men: "What is born of the flesh is flesh;" and not only carnal and sinful, but frail and mortal. "All flesh is grass," withering, decaying, and corruptible; it is the very breath of God, and has a similarity to him, particularly in immortality; "God breathed into man the breath of life." Gen. ii. 7. Elihu says, Job xxxiii. 4, "The breath of the Almighty hath given me life;" a life that will never end. Hence God is described as he that "formeth the spirit of man within him." Zech. xii. 1, and as God is the former of the souls of men, so he is the supporter of them; he "upholds their souls in life." The most malicious and cruel persecutors can only kill the body, and after that they have no more that they can do; they cannot kill the soul. Luke xii. 4.

(2.) The immortality of the soul may be proved from its nature; which is,

1. Spiritual, of the same nature with angels, who are made spirits, spiritual substances. Heb. xii. 9—23. The souls of men are of the same nature with angels, and they die not. Ps. civ. 4; Luke xx. 36; 1 Cor. ii. 11.

2. The soul of man is simple, unmixed, and uncompounded; it is not composed of flesh and blood, &c. as the body; a spirit has none of these.

3. It is immaterial, it is not composed of matter and form; nor is it a material form, educed out of the power of matter. Matter is divisible, discerptible, may be cut to pieces: not so the soul: it is out of the reach of every slaughtering weapon; the sharp arrow cannot penetrate into it, nor the glittering spear pierce it, nor the two-edged sword divide it.

4. It has no contrary qualities which threaten with destruction; it is neither hot nor cold; neither moist nor dry.

5. The soul of man is made after the image, and in the likeness of God, which chiefly consists in that; it bears a resemblance to the Divine nature, being the breath of God, it is a likeness to him, and particularly in its immortality.

(3.) The immortality of the soul may be proved from its powers and faculties.

(4.) Its understanding. There is a spirit or soul, in man, as Elihu says. Job xxxii. 8. And the inspiration of the Almighty giveth him understanding; an intellective power and faculty of understanding things. Ps. xxxii. 9; Job xxxv. 11.

1. The understanding of man can take in, and has knowledge of, things spiritual and incorporeal, immaterial, incorruptible, and eternal; which it would not be capable of if it were not of the same nature itself: the images of these things would not be impressed on it, nor would it be susceptible of them.

2. The soul of man has knowledge of eternity itself: though it may be observed, there is great difference in its apprehension of an eternity past, and of that which is to come: when it considers the former, it is soon at a loss, and at a full stop, is obliged to return and cannot go on; it is like a bird that attempts to soar aloft, and take flights it is not used nor equal to, it flutters and hangs its wings, and is forced to descend. But when the soul fixes its thoughts on an eternity to come, how readily does it apprehend how that shall proceed without end! with what pleasure does it roll over millions of ages in it! The reason of this difference is, because the soul itself is not from eternity, but has a beginning; whereas, it will endure to eternity and have no end.

3. The knowledge which the mind and understanding of man has of things in the present state, is very imperfect, through the brevity of life; and therefore it may be reasonably concluded, that there is a future state, in which the soul will exist, and its knowledge of things be more perfect. Arts and sciences have been cultivating many thousands of years, and in some ages great improvements have been made, and especially in latter ends; and yet there is room·for farther improvements still: the knowledge of the best things, which good men have, as of God, of Christ, and of the mysteries of grace, is now very imperfect; those that know most, know but in part, and see through a glass darkly; but there is a state in which their souls will exist, when they shall see God face to face, see him as he is, and know as they are known.

4. The knowledge the mind of man has of things now, is not in proportion to the powers that he possesses. How many are there that die in infancy, and as soon as they are born, whose reasoning powers are never called forth into action and exercise; and how many die in childhood and youth, before these powers ripen, and are brought to any maturity? Now can it be thought these powers are bestowed upon them in vain? There must be then an after-state.

5. Let a man know ever so much in this present life, he is desirous of knowing more; let his acquisitions of knowledge be ever so large, after a life of studious search and inquiry, he is not satisfied, he still wants to know more; and what he has arrived unto is only to know this, that he knows but little. Now this desire of knowledge is not implanted in man, by the Author of nature, in vain; wherefore the soul must remain after death, when it will arrive to a more perfect knowledge of things.

2. The will of man is another faculty of the soul, the object and actings of which show it to be immortal.

1. The will has for its object universal good. It naturally desires complete happiness, which some place in one thing and some in another, but it is not perfectly enjoyed by any. Now there must be a future state, in which true happiness will be attained, at least by some, or else the actings of the will about it will be in vain.

2. God is the summum bonum, the chief good, the will of man rightly pitches upon, nor can it be satisfied with any thing less; good men choose him as their portion; but then he is not perfectly enjoyed as such in this life. wherefore in order to this the soul must remain after death, and be immortal.

3. The will has its desires. and which desires, even the best, are not satisfied in this life. "Whom have I in heaven but thee?"

4. The actions of the will are free, not forced by any creature; its acts are independent of the body, and can live without it.

335

5. The will is not weakened, nor indeed any of the powers and faculties of the soul impaired, by sickness and approaching death; though the outward man perish, the inward man is renewed day by day; yea, when the body is become speechless and near expiring, the faculties of the soul are in exercise; a man understands clearly what his friends about him say, and can by a sign, by the lifting up his hand, signify his faith, hope, joy, and comfort; all which show that the soul sickens not with the body, nor becomes languid, nor dies with it.

II. The immortality of the soul may be proved from the light of nature and reason.

1. From the consent of all nations. Cicero says, That as we know by nature that there is a God, so we judge by the consent of all nations, that souls remain after death and are immortal: and in every thing, he says, the consent of all nations is to be reckoned the law of nature: so Seneca calls it, a public persuasion or belief.

2. This may be concluded, from an extinction of man, soul and body, being abhorrent to man; the death of the body, though nature be reluctant to it; yet, in many instances there has been a voluntary and cheerful submission to it: many good men have not loved their lives unto death.

3. It may be argued, that the natural desire in men to be religious, in some way or other; this is so natural to men, that some have chose rather to define man a religious, than a rational animal. All nations have had their gods they worshipped.

4. There is a consciousness of sinning in men; guilt arises in their consciences, on account of sins; even in the very heathen there is a conscience bearing witness in their actions.

5. Not only from the stings of conscience, but from the horror and dread wicked men are sometimes siezed with, as Felix. These things not only show that there is a Divine Being to whom men are accountable for their actions; but that there is a future state after death, in which men exist, when they shall be either in happiness or in misery.

6. The belief of this may be farther argued, from the providence of God concerned in the distribution and disposal of things in this life, which is oftentimes very unequal: wicked men prosper, and good men are greatly afflicted. Ps. lxxiii. 2, 3, 12—14; Jer. xii. 1, 2. Good men if they have hope in this life only, they would be of all men the most miserable. Luke xvi. 25; 1 Cor. xv. 19. Wherefore,

7. The immortality of the soul may be concluded from the justice of God; who is the judge of all the earth; for righteous is the Lord, though his judgments are not so manifest in this life: it is a righteous thing with God to render tribulation to them that trouble his people, and to fulfil the promises he makes to his saints.

8. If the soul be not immortal, but dies with the body, the brutes, in many things, have the advantage of men; and their state and condition in this life is, in many respects, superior to ours; they are not so weak and helpless at first coming into the world; not subject to so many diseases; in some the senses are quicker, and they have more pleasure in the exercise of them.

III. The immortality of the soul may be proved from the sacred scriptures.

Eccl. xii. 7. The soul, or spirit, is said to return to God that gave it. Matt. x. 28. Fear not them which kill the body, &c. This is to be proved,

1. From scripture doctrines; as from the doctrine of God's love to his people, which is everlasting. Jer. xxxi. 3. But this would not be true, if

336

the souls of God's beloved died; hence it would follow, that death can, and does, separate from the love of God, contrary to the apostle's firm persuasion. Rom. viii. 38, 39. Also from the covenant of grace, which is said to be an everlasting covenant. 2 Sam. xxiii. 5. But it is well known, that in all covenants there are confederates, and if one of the parties covenanting die, the covenant is at an end. The argument used by Christ to prove the resurrection of the dead, from covenant interest, Matt. xii. 31, 32; Luke xx. 38, equally proves, or rather more clearly, the immortality of the soul. And particularly the immortality of the soul may be concluded from the grand promise of eternal life, in the covenant made before the world began. Tit. i. 2; 1 John ii. 25. But how can this promise be fulfilled, if the souls of those to whom it is made are not immortal? It may be argued from the doctrine of adoption, another blessing in the covenant; by virtue of which saints are heirs of an eternal inheritance. Likewise it may be argued from the doctrine of Christ respecting his work, the blessings of grace by him, and the services and benefits farther to be expected from him, as the redemption of the soul by the blood of Christ, which must be shed in vain: nor can it be called eternal redemption if the soul be not immortal. The doctrine of the judgment, whether particular or general, is a proof of the soul's immortality. Moreover, the doctrine of future rewards and punishments confirms this truth; for, if the soul be not immortal, a good man cannot be rewarded in a way of grace, nor enjoy happiness in consequence of his piety, since there will be no subject of it remaining; nor a wicked man punished for his sins for the same reason.

2. The immortality of the soul may be proved from scripture instances; as from the cases of Enoch and Elijah, who were translated, soul and body, that they should not see death; as not in their bodies, so not in their souls. Abraham, Isaac, and Jacob, who died, and yet after death were living, even in the times of Christ; also from the spirits in prison, in the times of the apostle Peter, who were disobedient to the warnings of Noah; and from the resurrection of some particular persons; who, after death, were raised and lived again, their souls, which die not, being returned to them; 1 Kings xvii. 21, 22, and from the souls under the altar, whose bodies were killed; Rev, vi. 9, 10, and from the instances of persons committing their spirits to God at death. Ps. xxxi. 5; Luke xxiii. 46; Acts vii. 59; 1 Pet. iv. 16, 19.— Lastly, all such scriptures which speak of the joys of heaven, and the torments of hell.

IV. ANSWER SOME OBJECTIONS.

1. From reason. As,

1. That which has a beginning has an end. But this is not always true; angels have a beginning, but not an end; they die not.

2. The powers of the soul are said to decay, as the body decays; but this is only true of the powers of the sensitive soul, or part of man: not of the rational soul; not of the faculties of the understanding and will.

3. When a man dies, nothing is seen to go out of him but his breath, which vanishes away: but it is no wonder the soul should not be seen at its departure, since being a spirit, incorporeal and immaterial, it is invisible.

4. Some will have it, that this is only a contrivance of men in power, a piece of state-policy to keep men in awe. But those men were either bad or good men: bad men would be unconcerned about ways and means to serve the cause of religion; and good men would never make use of a known lie, to serve such purposes.

2. From scripture As,

1. From such scriptures which threaten the soul with death in case of sin Gen. ii. 17 And it is expressly said, the soul that sins shall die. **Ezek.** xviii. 4. To which may be replied—That there are various sorts of death: there is a spiritual or moral death; it is a being dead in trespasses and sins; and lies, not in the substance of the soul, but in the qualities of it. And there is an eternal death, the destruction of both body and soul in hell; this lies not in the destruction of the being of either, but in the misery of both: and there is a natural death, such as of the body, which the soul is not capable of.

2. From what is said of man. Ps. lxxviii. 39, and cxlvi. 4. This is expressive of the brevity of the bodily life of man.

3. From such passages which speak of man's going at death from whence he shall not return. Job x. 21, and xiv. 10. But these are to be understood, of his returning to his house, and former manner of living and employment of life. Chap. xii, 10. And when it is asked, Where is he, when he dies? it is easily answered, He is returned to the dust; and his soul is gone to God, and is either in bliss or wo.

4. From those places which speak of the dead as NOT: Rachel was weeping for her children, because they were not. Jer. xxxi. 15. But this cannot be meant of non-existence, either of soul or body.

ORIGINAL SIN.

Genesis iii. 13.—The serpent beguiled me, and I did eat. (Sk.)

THE origin of things is frequently involved in darkness; and the more remote the period of their commencement, the greater mysteriousness envelops their origin. Things seen at a distance are usually seen indistinctly; and facts are often related without the pomp of circumstance. This is exemplified in the subject before us. The text is a brief narration of one of the most awfully portentous acts, which was ever perpetrated upon earth; to this source, we may trace back all the crimes in their endlessly diversified circumstances, which have inundated the world; and here we see the germination of a seed, which has taken deep root, and filled the earth with poisonous fruit. Had the fact recorded in the text been merely of a speculative character, it might even then have excited curiosity, and elicited inquiry; but as we have all reaped a harvest of ills, from the seed sown on that fatal occasion, it cannot be an unprofitable exercise, to spend a few moments in recalling to mind what we know of this transaction. Two things claim our attention,

I. THE ACT OF THE SERPENT. He "beguiled me."

II. THE ACT OF THE WOMAN. "I did eat."

But who, or what was the serpent? In the first verse of this chapter, the serpent is represented as a "beast of the field:" but to suppose that any beast of the field, would of his own accord, and at his own instigation, beguile the woman, and seduce her to sin, would be an absurdity too palpable to be admitted; as it would imply, that the serpent was superior to the woman in intellectual endowments; and that he meditated her ruin by carrying

338

into effect a most mischievous design. Bnt as God made every thing very good, and as all animals were inferior to the human pair, we must refer to some other cause for the existence of this act.

The most common opinion is, that the devil animated the body of the serpent, and spoke to Eve through his organs. In reference to this, he is called the "old serpent," Rev. xii. 9. And St. Paul said to the Corinthians, "I fear as the serpent beguiled Eve," &c., 2 Cor. xi. 3; but he could not fear that that "beast of the field," described by Moses, would corrupt the christians at Corinth. That the devil can so far possess human, or animal bodies, as to act upon them and speak through them, is most satisfactorily proved from the legion who possessed the poor demoniac, and said to Jesus, "What have we to do with thee?" &c., Matt. vii. 32. And then entering into the bodies of the swine, &c. And this enemy possessed every qualification for managing the deep-laid plot which he had so artfully devised. *He was endowed with extensive knowledge.* Angels possess amazing powers of intellect, and though fallen angels lost all moral excellency by their fall, yet they most probably retained much of their original vigor of understanding. Satan knew in what part of the universe to find the original pair; he knew their circumstances—the law they were under—the misery that would ensue on their violation of that law—and probably the mischievous results in reference to posterity. *He also possessed the most consummate wickedness.* He is called the "wicked one," and "an evil spirit." The devil is a being replete with wickedness: and this was the most wicked scheme that was ever devised. What wickedness to mar such beauty, and blight so much excellence, as creation presented when adorned in all its pristine glory! What wickedness to involve innocent and holy beings in guilt and misery! beings who deserved no such treatment, and merited no such conduct! Oh how many are there in the world who too successfully imitate this arch fiend! who are wise to do mischief; who employ their exalted powers of mind in imposing on the credulous, and ruining the innocent! But how did the serpent beguile the woman?

1. *By attacking her when alone.* I infer this, not only on the ground of a commonly received opinion, but from the narrative itself. Here we see the whole of the conversation carried on between the serpent and the woman; Adam had no share in it. The devil must have known that Adam was the superior, from the circumstance of his being first formed, and Eve being made a "helpmeet for him." Had Adam been present, they would most probably have taken sweet council together, on a subject of so much consequence. How wise it is in affairs of great moment to pause, and hesitate, and deliberate, and take advice of our superiors.

2. *By directing her attention to the prohibited object.* There was much in the garden of Eden to admire, and much to enjoy: one tree only was prohibited; to this object the serpent directed the attention of the woman, and induced her to look at it. talk of it, and desire it. We have many prohibited objects. These we should fly from; never trust our eyes to gaze on objects which are likely to excite desires of an unholy nature in our hearts. "Abstain from the appearance of evil." Oh had Eve done this, how effectually would she have broken the snare of the devil!

3. *By a prospect of advantage on eating the forbidden fruit.* Nothing weighs so much with a human being as profit. What will not a man sacrifice for the distant prospect of gain? Eve expected to be like the gods, that is, as the angels. Eve must have known, that there were such beings as angels. Who can doubt but that they made their appearance to our primitive

parents in paradise, as they appeared in after times to Abraham, Lot, &c.? And it is not improbable, but that they assumed a glorious appearance; the idea of being like them, produced a most fascinating effect on the mind of Eve. But this was all mere artifice with the tempter, who knew that instead of being as gods, they would be more like fiends, by partaking of the forbidden fruit. How many of the sons and daughters of Eve have been lured by the tempting bait of ambition, and who by aping their superiors have plunged themselves into an abyss of misery!

4. *By plausibly reasoning with her on the subject.* He knew that nothing could be done by open attack; that every thing must appear plausible and imposing; he therefore began by questioning Eve, " Hath God said, ye shall not eat of every tree of the garden?" Here was just enough to excite curiosity. Hath God said such a thing? Is this reasonable? What could such fair fruit be created for, but to be eaten? It is highly probable, that more conversation ensued than is here recorded. How forcibly does this teach us to resist the first temptations to evil, to hold no parley with the enemy.

5. *By confidently asserting, that it was a mistake under which Eve was laboring.* "Ye shall not surely die." He first tempted her to doubt, by an awful insinuating question; and then to disbelieve, by a bold, daring, mischievous lie,—the first lie that ever was uttered upon earth. This is the usual process by which he carries on his dark designs, exciting men to question the truth of established opinions, &c. Confident assertions have often great weight with innocent and unsuspecting minds. "Goodness thinks no ill, where no ill seems." Here was not only a bold contradiction to the truth of God, but an artful and base insinuation, that he had prohibited this fruit through some sinister design. "For God doth know," &c., ver. 5.

II. THE ACT OF THE WOMAN. "I did eat." This was the original transgression. Here sin entered into the world, and we learn,

1. *That the sin of Eve was a personal act.* "I did eat." Whatever blame might be imputed to the serpent, still the act of eating was all her own. The sin of the tempter was a totally distinct thing from her sin. Here was no force, no constraint, nor over-ruling power to impel her to eat; the concurrence of her will—the taking of the fruit—and the eating of it, were personal acts for which Eve only was accountable. Our sins also are personal. Temptations we all have, and innate tendencies to evil; but these are not imputed to us as sin, till we give them the concurrence of our wills, and sanction them by indulgence.

2. *The sin of Eve was a carnal act.* "I did *eat.*" Here was the sin, it was in *eating.* The temptation was presented to the senses; "The woman saw that the tree was good for food." It is difficult to say, how she could *see* this, unless we admit with Milton, that she had seen the serpent eat of it. What if it *were* good for food? she needed not food; there were trees in abundance all around her, laden with fruit as fair and good as that which she coveted. "And that it was pleasant to the eyes;" but must every thing be eaten that is pleasant to the eye? And "a tree to be desired to make one wise;" here "lust conceived, and brought forth sin." Most of our temptations come to us through the medium of our senses, and sin is chiefly gratifying as it affects the animal part of a man. Sinners are nominated carnal men, that is literally, fleshly men; men who are in the flesh, who live after the flesh, and who sow to the flesh: and though sin is deeply seated in the mind, yet the members of the body become its instruments.

3. *The sin of Eve was a prohibited act.* It was a direct violation of a plain, known, positive law. The law was as *plain* as language could make

it: it was *known;* for though God gave it to Adam, prior to the formation of Eve, yet God, or her husband, had revealed it to her; her whole conversation with the serpent, evinced that she knew it: and it was *positive,* "Thou shalt not eat of it." All our sins are of a similar character, as they are transgressions of laws, plain, known, and positive.

4. *The sin of Eve was a presumptuous act.* In eating of the fruit, she must have presumed that God was insincere in what he said; that his words were not the words of truth; that the death with which she was threatened would not be inflicted; that she would escape the punishment though she ventured on the sin. Such is the presumption of sinners generally: they do not dare to give the lie to God, by any verbal protestation, but they act as if they believed that God was insincere in what he has said, and many of them are given up to strong delusions to believe a lie.

5. *The sin of Eve was a ruinous act.* She no sooner became a sinner than she became a tempter; she gave unto her husband, and he did eat also; and thus ruin was entailed on their posterity. Whether Adam would have eaten without the seduction of Eve is uncertain. Adam was not deceived; he knew better: but such is the force of bad example, that Adam, intelligent and holy as he was, plunged himself into sin and misery, to follow the example of his wife. Sinners are not satisfied with standing alone; they press others into the snares by which they themselves are entangled.

From this subject we learn,

First, *The true character of original sin.* Man was created holy, but not immutable. How far immutability can be an attribute of any created being, I must leave. God gave our first parents a law, plain, positive, and easy to be kept. Could any thing be more reasonable? A being subject to no law is subject to no government, and accountable to no superior; and to suppose that God should make a being capable of obeying him, and yet give him no law as the test of his obedience, is absurd.

Secondly, *How much ought we to be on our guard against the attacks of enemies.* If Eve in Paradise met with an insidious foe, who beguiled her, how can we hope to escape temptations? "We should suspect some danger nigh, where we possess delight." "Watch and pray."

Thirdly, *That God will call us to an account for our conduct.* Eve little suspected, while feasting on the interdicted fruit, that God was near to judge her. Let us live with eternity in our view, and bring every thing to bear on the day of reckoning.

Fourthly. *To adore the mercy of God.* Man was spared, a Saviour was promised, and the designs of the devil were frustrated.

THE FIRST TRANSGRESSION CONDEMNED.

Gen. iii. 17, 18, 19. And unto Adam he said, Because thou hast hearkened unto the voice of thy wife, and hast eaten of the tree, of which I commanded thee, saying, Thou shalt not eat of it," &c. (Sk.)

In the first chapter of this book, we find the parents of our race created pure and upright, and placed on a state of trial. In the third, we are informed of their temptation and rebellion. And here we see their Maker and their Judge coming to call them to their account; to convict them of their crimes; and to pronounce their sentence. Our text more particularly records the crime proved, and the sentence pronounced.

I. THE CRIME PROVED.—Here we may remark, that the culprit does not dare to plead, "Not guilty." 'Tis true, he blames his temper, and indirectly blames God himself; yet he confesses the fact of his transgression, ver. 12. The judge condemns the criminal's conduct in several particulars. Instance,

1. *His listening and yielding to temptation;*—"Thou hast hearkened unto the voice of thy wife." From temptation none is exempt. Nor is there any sin in being tempted. See the difference between being tempted and yielding to temptation, in our Saviour's case, Matt. iv. 1—10. His resistance of *repeated* attempts was *prompt* and *firm*. By way of contrast, look at Eve, *parleying* with the tempter, and captivated by "the desire of the flesh, the desire of the eye, and the pride of life," ver. 1—6. Which of those examples should we follow? A proper answer must consist with the following observations.—*The relative situation of the tempter is no justification of our compliance.* Has he been our benefactor? Such was Adam's tempter. His "*help meet,*" chap. ii. 13,—his only human support. The Hebrew children were *under great obligations;* yet they refused to to sin, Dan. iii. 12. Or may the person who tempts us be our friend *in future?* All Adam's hopes and expectations from human kind centered in her who offered him the forbidden fruit. But this did not excuse him. Even Balaam says, "I cannot go beyond," &c., Num. xxii. 18. See also Dan. iii. 15; Heb. xi. 24.—*The relation in which the tempter stands to us is no justification.* Earthly ties can, in no other case, be so close as those which bound the parties in this transaction here condemned. She was not only *his wife,* but literally, part of himself, ver. 20—24. Here our Lord's remarks, Matt. x. 32—36.—*The affection we may bear the tempter is no justification.* As it is now the duty of husbands to love their wives, so, without question, Adam in his best estate was not deficient in this part of his duty. Milton, indeed, supposes that his affection for "her, his sole delight," was the only cause of his fall; that

> —————————"He took and ate,
> Against his better knowledge; not deceived:
> But fondly overcome of female charm."

This view of the case seems to be supported by 1 Tim. ii. 14, "*Thou hast hearkened to the voice of thy wife.*" But

> "Consciences and souls are made,
> To be the Lord's alone."

2. *His neglect of God's word;*—"Which I commanded thee." Here is reference to *supreme authority;* "*I* commanded," who am *thy author,* &c.;—reference to *almost unlimited indulgence;* thou hast eaten of THE tree—the *only* prohibited one; and this excepted only as a test of obedience, and a means of thy confirmation in holiness, and of rising to a higher felicity;—reference to *friendly caution;* he was forewarned of danger. Yet see,

3. *His open, positive transgression of a known law;*—"I commanded thee," personally and plainly; but "*thou hast eaten.*" If, in the *first* transgression, we find, on the part of Eve, vain curiosity, sensuality, and ambition; and on that of Adam, insubordination and idolatry, we may also mark the like principles and operation in sin in general, Gen. xxxiv. 1; Deut. xxxii. 15; Rom. i. 25; James i. 14, 15.

II. THE SENTENCE PRONOUNCED ;—" *Cursed is the ground*," &c. We notice here,

1. *Deprivation*—of all the *fruits and pleasures of Eden;* enjoyed while living in obedience. Man is driven forth from the garden, to procure "bread" —and "herbs" from a "*cursed*" land. Precisely the case of backsliders ; who, like the prodigal, feed on husks. Hence the candid acknowledgment and prudent resolution, Hos. ii. 7.

2 *Toil ;*—" In the sweat," &c. God, who made nothing in vain, intended that his creatures should exercise their powers. Holy angels are employed, Psa. ciii. 20 ; Heb. i. 14 ; so was innocent man, Gen. ii. 15. So is glorified man, Rev. vii. 15. But in sinful man, exercise degenerated into toil. So now, they who forsake God, *hew* cisterns, &c., Jer. ii. 13.

3. *Disappointment ;*—" Thorns and thistles," &c. These shall interrupt thy labors, and mock thy hopes. See the effects of sin described, Haggai i. 6. Mark the caution, Prov. xxiii. 31. Whence,

4. *Sorrow ;*—arising from vexatious disappointment,—from a recollection of loss,—from family feuds, chap. iv. 3,—from gloomy anticipations ; and this continually : "In sorrow—all the days," &c.

5. *Increasing infirmity;*—" Till thou return," &c. Adam was created in full vigor, but now he began to "*return* to the dust." His body became the subject of dissolution ; and he might look forward to the time when "the strong men should bow," &c., Eccl. xii. 2—5. "*Dying*, thou shalt die."

6. *Death itself;*—" Unto dust *shalt thou* return," &c. This the final proof of his folly. And this might be the consummation of his punishment. For,

7. *Justice is tempered with mercy.* The sentence is not immediately executed. The criminal has a *respite:* a *subsistence:* and an *opportunity of repentance.*

Let the subject teach us,

1. *A lesson of humility.* We are the degenerate children of such a parent.

2. *A lesson of caution.* Mark the *process* of falling. Satan presents some suitable object. We appear—desire—covet—throw off restraint—and transgress, in intention, and in fact. Mark the *danger* of falling. Our first parents fell from their paradisaical state, and by a small temptation. Wherefore, "watch," &c., Matt. xxvi. 41. For, mark the *consequences* of falling. All the evils we feel or fear.

3. *A lesson of encouragement.* Respited we may recover our Eden, by means of "the second Adam, the Lord from heaven." Contrast—the first involving himself and us in guilt, pollution, and misery—the second the reverse of this, Rom. v. 12—21.

THE EXTENT OF MAN'S DEPRAVITY.

Rom. iii. 10—20.—It is written, There is none righteous, no not one : there is none that understandeth, there is none that seeketh after God. They are all gone out of the way, they are together become unprofitable, there is none that doeth good, no not one. Their throat is an open sepulchre ; with their tongues they have used deceit ; the poison of asps is under their lips : whose mouth is full of cursing and bitterness. Their feet are swift to shed blood. Destruction and misery are in their ways : and the way of peace have they not known. There is no fear of God before their eyes. Now we know that what things soever the law saith, it saith to them who are under the law : that every mouth may be stopped, and all the world may become guilty before God. Therefore by the deeds of the law there shall no flesh be justified in his sight. (S. S)

THE scriptures are the only, and infallible source of divine knowledge—
To them the apostles continually refer in support of their doctrines—
No subject is capable of more ample proof from them than that before us—
St. Paul is shewing that all mankind are guilty and depraved—
In confirmation of this he cites many passages from the Old Testament—
See Ps. xiv. 1–3.   Prov. i. 16, 18.   Isa. lix. 7, 8.
From these, as stated and improved in the text, we are led to consider,
I. THE REPRESENTATION WHICH THE SCRIPTURE GIVES OF OUR STATE.
The testimonies here adduced, declare, that the most lamentable depravity pervades,
1. All ranks and orders of men.
" There is none righteous, no not one"—*
Righteousness is a conformity of heart and life to the law of God—
Where is the man on earth that possesses it by nature ?—
Where is the man whose deviations from this standard have not been innumerable ?—
" There is none that understandeth."
The natural man has no discernment of spiritual things—1 Cor. ii. 14.
His practical judgment is in favor of sin and the world—
" There is none that seeketh after God."
The things of time and sense are diligently pursued—
But whoever cultivates divine knowledge, or seriously enquires after God ? Job xxxv. 10.
" All are gone out of the way."
Men universally prefer the way of self-righteousness to that of faith in Christ—
And that of sin and self-indulgence to holiness and self-denial—
No one that sees them would imagine, that they really intended to tread in the steps of Christ and his apostles—
" They are together become unprofitable."
God has formed us for his own glory, and each others good—
But unregenerate men never attempt to answer these ends of their creation—†
Hence they are justly compared to things worthless and vile—Luke xiv 34, 35, and John xv. 6.
" There is none that doeth good, no not one."
Nothing is really good, which is not so in its principle, rule, and end—‡
But where is the action of any natural man that will stand this test ?—
2. All the faculties and powers of men.
Nothing is more offensive than an open sepulchre ; Matt. xxiii. 27 ; or more venomous than an asp—

*The apostle has so arranged his quotations as to form a beautiful climax, every subsequeat passage affirming more than that which precedes it.

†They may do good to the bodies of men ; but never shew any real solicitude about their souls.   Indeed, how should they, when they care not for their own souls?

‡ The fear and love of God are the *principle*, the scriptures the *rule*, and God's glory the end of Christian obedience, 1 Cor. x. 31.

Yet both the one and the other fitly represent the effusions of a carnal heart—

"Out of the abundance of the heart the mouth will speak"—

Deceit, calumny, invective, yea, in many instances, the most horrible oaths and execrations will proceed from it—*

Hence that awful description of the human tongue—James iii. 6.

From *words* we are ready also to proceed to *actions*, yea, even the most cruel and atrocious—

Who that sees with what readiness nations engage in war, will question the declaration in the text?—

Hazael revolted at the idea of murder, when warned of his propensity to commit it; yet notwithstanding his present feelings, how "*swift* were his feet to shed blood!"—2 Kings viii. 12, 13, with ib. ver. 15, and xiii. 7.

How many at this day are impelled by shame even to destroy their own offspring!—

How frequently do men engage in duels on account of the slightest injury or insult!

And in how many instances might we ourselves, when irritated and inflamed, have committed murder in an unguarded moment, exactly as others have done, who in a cooler moment would have shuddered at the thought!—

The instance of David, who, though "a man after God's own heart," murdered Uriah, and many others with him, to conceal his shame, is sufficient of itself to shew us, what the best of men might commit, if left to themselves—2 Sam. xi. 14—17.

Well we may apply to this subject that humiliating language of the prophet—Isa. i. 5, 6.

Thus, God himself being witness, instead of walking in "paths of peace" and safety, we all by nature prefer the "ways which bring destruction and misery" both on ourselves and all around us—Ps. xxxvi. 1.

The whole of our state is properly summed up in *this*, that "there is no fear of God before our eyes; so entirely are our understandings blinded, and our hearts alienated from him, by means of our innate depravity—†

This humiliating view of our state should lead us to consider,

II. The inferences to be deduced from it.

Those which the apostle suggests in the text will suffice for our attention at this time—

1. We are all "guilty before God"

It seems inconceivable to many, that they should really be obnoxious to everlasting misery in hell—

And they will plead their own cause with zeal and eloquence—

If they concede it with respect to some more heinous transgressors, they will deny it in reference to themselves—

But God has taken care that "*every* mouth should be stopped"—

It is not possible to express the universality of men's wickedness more strongly than it is expressed in the words before us—‡

---

*No less than four expressions, and those exceeding strong, are used to declare the evils of the tongue.

†Verse 16 and 17, relate primarily to the evil which men do to *others*, though they may include what they do to themselves. See Isaiah lix. 7, 8.

‡ "None, no not one;" "none; none; none, no not one;" "all; all together;" "every mouth;" even "al. the world." Can any, after this, fancy himself an exception?

All then must "become guilty before God," and acknowledge their desert of his wrath and indignation—

They must feel their desert of condemnation, as much as a man that has been condemned for parricide feels the justice of the sentence which is pronounced against him—

O that we might all be brought to such unfeigned contrition! we should "not then be far from the kingdom of God"—Ps. li. 17.

2. We can never be justified by any works of our own.

" We *know* that what the law saith, it saith unto them that are under the law"—

Now the law saith, " Do this and live : transgress it, and thou shalt die"— Rom. x. 5 ; Gal. iii. 10.

But it speaks not one word about mitigating its demand to the weak, or its penalties to the guilty—

How then can any man " be justified by the works of the law ?"—

Can a man be guilty, and not guilty ? or can he be condemned by the law and yet justified at the same time, and in the same respects ?—

Let all hope then, and all thought of justification by the law be put away from us for ever—

God has provided a better way for our justification, namely, through the blood and righteousness of his dear Son—Rom. iii. 21, 22.

And to lead us into that way was the intention of the apostle in citing the passages that have already been considered—

Let us improve this humiliating representation for this salutary end—

So shall we be " justified freely by grace, through the redemption that is in Christ Jesus"—Ib. ver. 24.

UNIVERSAL CORRUPTION OF MANKIND.

Psalm liii. 2, 3.--God looked down from heaven upon the children of men, to see if there were any that did understand, that did seek God. Every one of them is gone back, they are altogether become filthy, there is none that doeth good, no not one. (Pr.)

THIS is not merely a description of the state of mankind in David's time, but a description of human nature at all times, and is applied by an apostle to the state of the world many hundreds of years after the words were written. Rom. iii. 10—12.

I. SEEKING THE LORD IS HERE SUPPOSED TO BE THE CRITERION OF A GOOD UNDERSTANDING.

That it is so, will easily be made apparent; and these two things are with great propriety connected together. It is only " the fool that saith in his heart, there is no God ;" a true understanding sees it to be well for the universe that there is a God, and that it would be every one's interest to seek and obey him. Psa. xcvii. 1.

1. Seeking the Lord includes our *choosing the best good for our portion*, and supposes that we are seeking a happiness superior to what this world can afford. This is what the truest wisdom would dictate : but this blessedness is only to be found in God, whose lovingkindness is better than life Communion and intercourse with him is the sum of all enjoyment ; his ser

vice is its own reward, and those who have truly entered into it would never wish to go out free. Psa. xix. 10, 11, xxvii. 4.

2. Seeking the Lord includes *repentance for sin;* and this is what a good understanding would lead to, for it is altogether consonant with right reason. Job. v. 8. If nothing but our own interest were consulted, it would lead to this; and hence it is said of the prodigal when he repented, that he came to himself, an'¹ he that had been lost was found. Luke xv. 17.

3. It in ludes the sacrifice of every earthly good *for his sake*, and accounting his f? or to be better than life. This is what a good understanding would approve it being its proper province to form a just estimate of things. Who then acted the wiser part, Esau who sold his birthright, or Jabez who desired it that he might be blessed indeed? Who gave the best proof of a good understanding, Cain in leaving his native country because God was there; or Moses in forsaking Egypt because the Lord was not there? Was the rich man in the gospel, wise in setting his heart upon the good things of this life; or David, who desired not to have his portion with the men of this world. Psa. xvii. 5.

4. Seeking the Lord includes the resting all our hopes of salvation *upon the promises of his word;* and this is what a right understanding would approve. Hence he is called a wise man who built his house upon a rock; and he whose hope is in the promises of God, to the exclusion of every other ground of confidence, is equally wise and safe. There is no other door of hope, no other way of acceptance, but what is provided in the promises of the gospel.

II. ALL MEN BY NATURE ARE CORRUPT, AND UTTERLY DESTITUTE OF THIS UNDERSTANDING. "THERE IS NONE THAT DOETH GOOD, NO NOT ONE."

1. The loss of the divine favor is *the greatest of all evils*, and yet no one lays it to heart, or is careful to seek after it.— — —It might have been expected that men would have seen their folly in forsaking him, the fountain of living waters; would have had their eyes open to behold the tempter, who at first seduced them from God, and be anxious to return unto him from whom they have deeply revolted. Instead of this, there is none that understandeth, none that seeketh after God.— — —It is also the greatest of all evils that God has departed from us, and that he hides his face in anger. His favor is lost and gone; we are now without hope, without God in the world, and have no friend in time of need. We and all that we possess, are under the curse.— — —To be contented in such a state, and indifferent about the favor of God, is truly dreadful: yet such is the case with all men by nature.

2. God visits men with *such afflictions*, and brings them into such cir cumstances, as are directly adapted to make them feel their need of him: and yet God is not in all their thoughts. Job. xxxiii. 15.— — —Men either im agine that God does not see the evils with which they are visited, or that it is better to seek relief from any other quarter; like Ahaziah, who sent to the God of Ekron in a time of sickness, as if there were no God in Israel. 2 Kings i. 2, 3. It might be expected that sickness and death would lead men to seek after God; but no, there is none that understandeth, and the workers of iniquity have no knowledge.

3. By nature we have *no love to God*, and therefore do not seek him.— — —The object of our affection is necessarily an object of desire; nothing but enmity, or the most perfect indifference, can render us unmindful of the

friendship of God. And what an insult is offered to the Majesty of heaven, that we have lost his favor, and are indifferent about it.

4. Men are full of *pride and self-sufficiency*, and hence they do not seek after God. Psa. x. 4. Religion is too mean for their notice, and fit only for the attention of the vulgar. Many say in their hearts with Pharaoh, who is the Lord that I should obey his voice?— — —Great things are promised to them that seek the Lord; they shall be sure to find him, and obtain the remission of their sins; yet these promises are diregarded, and God is utterly forgotten.

III. The Lord keeps a strict eye upon the conduct of men towards him: "He looked down from heaven to see if there were any that did understand, that did seek God."

But though "every one of them is gone back, and they are altogether become filthy;" yet some are distinguished by grace, and there is a generation of them that seek thy face, oh God of Jacob. Psa. xxiv. 6. His eye is upon all such, and he will be found of them in truth; they shall never seek his face in vain. Isa. xlv. 9. He heard Ephraim when he was mourning alone, and solitary; and Jonah when he cried unto him out of the belly of hell. Jer. xxxi. 18. Those who repent and return to God, shall find him like the father of the prodigal, ready to forgive.

The Lord also notices those who do not seek him, and his eye is upon all their ways. He sees the wicked preferences of the heart, all their pride and contempt of him. Awful thought, to be under his inspection while utterly regardless of his presence, and sinning against heaven and before him.

How great is the loving kindness of God in promising salvation to them that seek him; and how inexcusable to neglect and forsake so much mercy. What bitterness will it add to the reflection, that all is lost through our own wilful neglect; and that God is for ever far from us, because we desired not the knowledge of his ways. Prov. i. 28—31.

SIN THE OFFSPRING OF OUR OWN HEARTS.

Jam. i. 13—15.—Let no man say, when he is tempted, I am tempted of God: for God cannot be tempted with evil, neither tempteth he any man: but every man is tempted, when he is drawn away of his own lust, and enticed. Then when lust hath conceived, it bringeth forth sin; and sin, when it is finished, bringeth forth death. (H. H.)

There are temptations necessarily connected with the christian life, and which often, through the weakness of our nature, become the *occasions* of sin: and there are other temptations which are the direct and immediate *cause* of sin. The former are external; the latter are within a man's own bosom. The former may be referred to God as their author, and be considered as a ground of joy: the latter must be traced to our own wicked hearts; and are proper grounds of the deepest humiliation. This distinction is made in the passage before us. In the foregoing verses the former are spoken of; ver. 2, 12, in the text, the latter.

In the words of our text, we notice the *origin*, the *growth*, and the *issue* of sin. We notice,

I. Its origin—

Many are ready to trace their sin to God himself—

This is done when we say, "I could not help it:" for then we reflect on our Make, as not enduing us with strength sufficient for our necessities. It is done also, though not quite so directly, when we ascribe our fall to those who were in some respect accessary to it: for then we blame the providence of God, as before we did his creative power. It was thus that Adam acted, when he imputed his transgression to the influence of his wife, and ultimately to God who gave her to him. Gen. iii. 12.

But God neither is, nor can be, the Author of sin—

He may, and does, try men, in order to exercise their graces, and to shew what he has done for their souls. Thus he tempted Abraham, and Job, and Joseph, and many others. But these very instances prove that he did not necessitate, or in any respect influence, them to sin; for they shone the brighter in proportion as they were tried. But he never did, nor ever will, lead any man into sin. And though he is said to have "hardened Pharaoh's heart," and to have "moved David to number the people," he did not either of these things in any other way than by leaving them to themselves. Exod. iv. 21, and 2 Sam. xxiv. 1, with 2 Chron. xxxii. 31.

All sin must be traced to the evil propensities of our own nature—

"A clean thing cannot be brought out of an unclean;" and therefore no descendant of Adam can be free from sin. We have within us a secret bias to sin; which, however good our direction appear to be, operates at last to turn us from God. That bias is called "lust," or desire, or concupiscence: and it works in all, though in a great variety of degrees and manner. All sin is fruit proceeding from this root, even from "the lust that wars in our members;" and in whatever channel our iniquity may run, it must be traced to that as its genuine and proper source.

This will appear more strongly, while we mark,

II. Its growth—

It first formation in the soul is often slow and gradual—

"Lust," or our inward propensity to sin, presents something to our imagination as likely to gratify us in a high degree. Whether it be profit, or pleasure, or honor, we survey it with a longing eye, and thereby our desire after it is inflamed. Conscience perhaps suggests that it is forbidden fruit which we are coveting; and that, as being prohibited, it will ultimately tend rather to produce misery than happiness. In opposition to this, our sinful principle intimates a doubt whether the gratification be forbidden; or at least whether, in our circumstances, the tasting of it be not very allowable: at all events, it suggests that our fellow-creatures will know nothing respecting it; that we may easily repent of the evil; and that God is very ready to forgive; and that many who have used far greater liberties are yet happy in heaven; and that consequently we may enjoy the object of our desire, without suffering any loss or inconvenience. In this manner the affections are kindled, and the will is bribed to give its consent:* then the bait is swallowed. the hook is fastened within us; and we are "dragged away"† from God, from duty, from happiness; yea, if God do not seasonably interpose, we are drawn to everlasting perdition.

Its progress to maturity is generally rapid—

The metaphor of a fetus formed in the womb, and brought afterwards to

* Isa. xliv. 20. See this whole process illustrated, Gen. iii. 1—6.
† These seems to be the precise ideas intended to be conveyed by δελεαζόμενος & ἐξελκόμενος.

the birth, is frequently used in scripture in reference to sin. Job xv. 35, **Ps.** vii. 14, with the text. When the will has consented to comply with the suggestions of the evil principle, then the embryo of sin is, if we may so speak, formed within us; and nothing remains but for time and opportunity to bring it forth. This of course must vary with the circumstances under which we are: our wishes may be accomplished, or may prove abortive: but whether our desire be fulfilled or not, sin is imputed to us, because it formally exists within us: or rather it is brought to the birth, though not altogether in the way we hoped and expected.

We proceed to notice,

III. Its issue—

Sin was never barren: its issue is numerous as the sands upon tne seashore: but in every instance the name of its first-born has been "death." Death is,

1. Its penalty—

Death is temporal, spiritual, and eternal, was threatened as the punishment of transgression while our first parents were yet in paradise. And on many occasions has the threatening been renewed, Ezek. xviii. 4, Rom. i. 18, and vi. 21, 23, Gal. iii. 10— — —So that sin and death are absolutely inseparable.

2. Its desert—

The fixing of death as the consequence of trangression was no arbitrary appointment. The penal evil of death is no more than the moral evil of sin. Consider the extreme malignity of sin: What rebellion against God! What a dethroning of God from our hearts! What a preferring of Satan himself, and his service, to God's light and easy yoke! View it as it is seen in the agonies and death of God's only Son: Can that be of small malignity which so oppressed and overwhelmed "Jehovah's fellow?" Of those who are now suffering the torments of the damned, not one would dare to arraign the justice of God, or to say that his punishment exceeded his offence: whatever we in our present state may think, our mouths will all be shut, when we have juster views, and an experimental sense, of the bitterness of sin. Matt. xxii. 12.

3. Its tendency—

We may see the proper effect of sin in the conduct of Adam, when he fled from God, whom he had been accustomed to meet with familiarity and joy. Gen. iii. 8. He felt a consciousness that his soul was bereft of innocence; and he was unable to endure the sight of Him whom he had so greatly offended. In the same manner sin affects our minds: it indisposes us for communion with God; it unfits us for holy exercises: and, if a person under the guilt and dominion of it were admitted into heaven, he would be unable to participate the blessedness of those around him; and would rather hide himself under rocks and mountains, than dwell in the immediate presence of an holy God. Annihilation would be to him the greatest favor that could be bestowed upon him; so truly does the Apostle say, that "the motions of sin do work in our members to bring forth fruit unto death." Rom. vii. 5.

ADVICE—

1. Do not palliate sin—

Though circumstances doubtless may either lesson or increase the guilt ot sin, nothing under heaven can render it light or venial. Our temptations may be great; but nothing can hurt us, if we do not ourselves concur with the tempter. That wicked fiend exercised all his malice against our adorable

Lord ; but could not prevail, because there was nothing in him to se ond or assist his efforts. So neither could he overcome us, if we did not voluntarily submit to his influence. All sin therefore must be traced to the evil dispositions of our own hearts; and consequently affords us a just occasion to humble ourselves before God in dust and ashes. If we presume to reflect on God as the author of our sin, we increase our guilt an hundred-fold: it is only in abasing ourselves that we can at all hope for mercy and forgiveness.

2. Do not trifle with temptation—

We carry about with us much inflammable matter, if we may so speak ; and temptation strikes the spark which produces an explosion. How readily are evil thoughts suggested by what we see or hear; and how strongly do they fix upon the mind. " Behold how great a matter a little fire kindleth!" Let us then stand at a distance from the places, the books, the company that may engender sin. And let us, in conformity with our Lord's advice, "watch and pray, that we enter not into temptation."

3. Do not for one moment neglect the Saviour—

There is none but Jesus that can stand between sin and death. Indeed even " he overcame death only by dying in our stead: and we can escape it only by believing in him. We deserve death: we have deserved it for every sin we have ever committed. Ten thousand deaths are our proper portion

Let us then look to Him who died for us. Let us look to him, not only for the sins committed long ago, but for those of daily incursion. Our best act would condemn us, if he did not " bear the iniquity of our holy things." He is our only deliverer from the wrath to come: to Him therefore let us flee continually, and " cleave unto him with full purpose of heart."

MEN'S HATRED OF THE LIGHT.

John iii. 19—21.—This is the condemnation, that light is come into the world, ana men loved darkness rather than light, because their deeds were evil. For every one that doeth evil, hateth the light, neither cometh to the light, lest his deeds should be reproved. But he that doeth truth cometh to the light, that his deeds may be made manifest, that they are wrought in God. (H. H.)

IT appears strange to many, that the everlasting happiness or misery of the soul should be made to depend on the exercise of faith. The declaration of our Lord, That " he that believeth shall be saved, and he that believeth not shall be damned," is regarded by them as " a hard saying:" they see no proportion between the work and the reward on the one hand, or between the offence and the punishment on the other. In the words before us we have a solution of the difficulty. We are taught that faith and unbelief are not mere operations of the mind, but exercises of the heart; the one proceeding from a love to what is good; the other from a radical attachment to evil. Our blessed Lord had repeatedly inculcated the necessity of believing in him, in order to a participation of his proffered benefits. He had also represented unbelievers as "already condemned," even like criminals reserved for execution. To obviate any objection which might arise in the mind of Nicodemus in relation to the apparent severity of this sentence, he proceeded to shew the true ground of it, namely, That, in their rejection of him, men are actuated by an invincible love of sin, and by a consequent hatred of the light which is sent to turn them from sin.

In opening the words of our text, we shall shew,

I. WHAT IS THAT LIGHT WHICH IS COME INTO THE WORLD—

Christ is called "The light of the world," "The true light," "The Day-star," and "The Sun of righteousness that arises with healing in his wings." But,

It is *the Gospel* which is here said to have "come into the world"—

The glad tidings of salvation were now published by Christ himself; and both the manner in which that salvation was to be effected, and the manner in which it was to be received, were clearly revealed. Our blessed Lord had in this very discourse with Nicodemus declared, that "the Son of Man was to be lifted up upon the cross, as the serpent had been in the wilderness," in order that all who were dying of the wounds of sin might look to him and be healed. He had repeated again and again this important truth, on which the salvation of our fallen race depends. This mystery had from eternity been hid in the bosom of the Father; but now it was made fully manifest. *This* "light was now come into the world."

The gospel, in this view of it, is fitly designated under the metaphor of "light"—

Light is that, without which no one thing can be discerned aright.— And how ignorant are we, till the light of the gospel shines in our hearts! We know nothing of ourselves, of God, of Christ, or of the way to heaven. We cannot even appreciate the value of the soul, the importance of time, the emptiness of earthly vanities. We may indeed give our assent to the statements which we hear made upon these subjects; but we cannot have an experimental and abiding sense, even of the most obvious truths, till our minds are enlightened by the gospel of Christ.

Light causes all other things to be seen in their true colors.—Thus does also the gospel: in setting forth the Son of God as dying for our sins, it shews us the malignity of sin; the justice of God which required such an atonement for it; and, above all, the wonderful love of God, in giving us his only dear Son, in order that we might have peace through the blood of his cross.

Light carries its own evidence along with it.—Thus does also that glorious gospel of which we are speaking: it is so peculiarly suited to the necessities of man, and at the same time so commensurate with his wants; it is so calculated to display and magnify all the perfections of the Deity, and is in every respect so worthy of its Divine Author; that it commends itself to us instantly as of heavenly origin, the very master-piece of Divine wisdom.

One would imagine that such light should be universally welcomed: but since this is not the case, we shall proceed to shew,

II. WHENCE IT IS THAT MEN REJECT IT—

It is but too evident, that, as in former ages, so now also, men reject the light. But whence does this arise?

It is not because they have any sufficient reason to reject it—

If there were any thing in the gospel that rendered it unworthy of men's regard, they would have some excuse for rejecting it. But,

They cannot say that it is *inapplicable in its nature.*—We will appeal to the world, and ask, What is there, that guilty and helpless sinners would desire? Would they wish for a Saviour? Would they be glad that the whole work of salvation should be committed into his hands? Would they be especially desirous that nothing should be required of them, but to receive with gratitude, and improve with diligence, what the Saviour offers them? In short, would they be glad of a free and full salvation? *This* is precisely such a salvation as is provided for them in the gospel.

They cannot say that it is *inadequate in its provisions.*—If the gospel brought salvation to those only who were possessed of some amiable qualities, or to those who had committed only a certain number of offences; if it made any limitation or exception whatever in its offers of mercy; if it provided pardon, but not strength, or grace to begin our course, but not grace to persevere; if, in short, it omitted any one thing which any sinner in the universe could need, then some persons might say, It is not commensurate with my necessities. But we defy the imagination of man to conceive any case which the gospel cannot reach, or any want which it cannot satisfy.

They cannot say that it is *unreasonable in its demands.*—It does indeed require an unreserved surrender of ourselves to God: and on this account it appears to many to be strict and severe. But let any one examine all its prohibitions and all its commands, and he will find them all amounting in fact to these two; "Do thyself no harm ;" and, "Seek to be as happy as thy heart can wish." If there be any thing in the gospel which bears a different aspect, it is owing entirely to our ignorance of its real import. The more thoroughly the gospel is understood, the more worthy of acceptation will it invariably appear.

The only true reason is, that they "hate the light"—

Till men are truly converted to God, "their deeds are universally evil ;" yea "every imagination of the thoughts of their hearts is evil, only evil, continually." Now the gospel is a light which shews their deeds in their proper colors.

It reproves their ways.—They have been "calling good evil, and evil good; and putting bitter for sweet, and sweet for bitter." In reference to these things, it undeceives them. It declares plainly, that they who do such things as they have done, and perhaps have accounted innocent, shall not inherit the kingdom of God.

It mortifies their pride.—It not only shews them that they are obnoxious to the wrath of God, but that they are incapable of averting his displeasure by any thing which they themselves can do. It brings down the proud Pharisee, and places him on a level with publicans and harlots. It requires every man to acknowledge himself a debtor to divine grace for every good thing that he either has or hopes for. All this is extremely humiliating to our proud nature.

It inculcates duties which they are unwilling to perform.—Humility and self-denial, renunciation of the world and devotedness to God, enduring of shame and glorying in the cross; these, and many other duties, it enjoins, which to our carnal and corrupt nature are hateful in the extreme; yet the gospel inculcates them with a strictness not to be lowered, a plainness not to be misinterpreted, and an authority not to be withstood.

These, these are the grounds on which the gospel is rejected. If it would admit of persons following their own ways, or of their accommodating its precepts to their own views or interests, they would give it a favorable reception. But as it requires all to be cast into the very mould which it has formed, and will tolerate not the smallest wilful deviation from its rules, it is, and must be, odious in the eyes of the ungodly; "they love darkness rather than it; nor will they come to it, lest their deeds should be reproved."

A just view of these things will prepare us for contemplating,

III. THEIR GUILT AND DANGER IN REJECTING IT—

Doubtless every kind of sin will be a ground of "condemnation." **But** men's hatred of the light is that which chiefly, and above all other things,

1. Aggravates their guilt—

The gospel is a most wonderful provision for the salvation of fallen man. It is the brightest display of divine wisdom, and the most stupendous effort of divine goodness. The rejection of this therefore, especially as proceeding from a hatred of it, argues such a state of mind as no words can adequately express. The malignity of such a disposition rises in proportion to the excellence of the gospel itself. We presume not to weigh the comparative guilt of men and devils, because the scriptures have not given us sufficient grounds whereon to institute such a comparison: but the guilt of those who reject the gospel far exceeds that of the heathen world: the wickedness of Tyre and Sidon, yea, of Sodom and Gomorrah, was not equal to that of the unbelieving Jews: nor was the guilt of those Jews, who rejected only the warnings of the prophets, comparable to that of those who despised the ministry of our Lord. In like manner, they who live under the meridian light of the gospel in this day will have still more, if possible, to answer for, than the hearers of Christ himself; because his work and offices are now more fully exhibited, and more generally acknowledged. And in the day of judgment the gospel will be as a millstone round the neck of those who rejected it: not having been a savor of life unto their salvation, it will be a savor of death unto their more aggravated condemnation.

2. Insures their punishment—

If men did not hate the gospel itself, there would be some hope that they might in due time embrace it, and be converted by it. If they would even come to the light in order that the true quality of their works might be made manifest, then we might hope that they would be convinced of their wickedness, and be constrained to flee from the wrath to come. But when they dispute against the truth, and rack their invention in order to find out objections against it; when they indulge all manner of prejudices against the gospel; when they withdraw themselves from the ministry of those who faithfully preach it, and say, as it were, to their minister, "Prophesy unto us smooth things, prophesy deceits;" what hope can there be of such persons? Their hearts are so hardened, that it is scarcely possible to make any impression upon them: if a ray of light do shine into their minds, they will endeavor to extinguish it as soon as possible; they will go to business, to pleasure, to company, yea, to intoxication itself, in order to stifle the voice of conscience, and to recover their former delusive peace. Alas! they are not only perishing of a fatal disorder, but they reject with disdain the only remedy that can do them good: they therefore must die, because they persist in drinking of the poisonous cup that is in their hands, and dash from their lips the only antidote and cure.

APPLICATION—

In so saying, thou reprovest us—

Behold! we declare unto you, that light, even the glorious light of the gospel of Christ, is now come into the world ——

Ye *lovers of darkness*, reject not this blessed gospel. Little can sin contribute to your happiness, even while you are most capable of tasting its pleasures: but what it can do for you in a dying hour, or in the day of judgment, it is needless for me to say. Let it not then keep you from coming to the light. Surely it is better that "your deeds should be reproved," while you have opportunity to amend them, than that you should continue in them till you experience their bitter consequences. You would not travel in the dark when you could enjoy the light of day, or refuse the assistance of a guide that would lead you into the path which you professed to seek. Only then act for your souls as you would do in your temporal concerns, and all shall yet be well. Believe in Christ, and you shall yet be saved by him ; as well from the commission of sin, as from the condemnation due to it.

Ye *who profess to love the light*, be careful to " walk as children of the light." Bring every thing to the touchstone of God's word. Try your spirit and temper, as well as your words and actions by this test. See whether you take the precepts of Christ as your rule, and his example as your pattern. For the sake of the world too, as well as for your own comfort, you should come continually to the light. If you would conciliate their regard for the gospel, or remove their prejudice from yourselves, you should "*make your works manifest* that they are wrought in God." You should let your light shine before men, that they, seeing your good works, may glorify your Father that is in heaven.

~~~~~~~~~~~~~~~~

VILENESS AND IMPOTENCY OF THE NATURAL MAN.

Rom. viii. 7, 8. The carnal mind is enmity against God; for it is not subject to the law of God, neither indeed can be. So then they that are in the flesh cannot please God. (H. H.)

To those who know not what is in the heart of man, it must appear strange that persons not very dissimilar in their outward conduct should be adjudged to widely different states in the eternal world. But in the most imperfect of the regenerate, there is a predominant principle of love to God ; whereas in the best of unregenerate men there is a rooted enmity against him : and this alone places their characters as far asunder as heaven and hell.

St. Paul has been speaking of the final issues to which a carnal and a spiritual mind will lead : and because it may seem unaccountable that the one should terminate in death, while the other is productive of eternal life and peace, he assigns the reason of it, and shews that the carnal mind is enmity against God, and that a person under its influence is incapable of rendering him any acceptable service.

In the Apostle's words there are three things to be considered,

I. His assertion—

The mind here spoken of, is that which actuates every unregenerate man—

" The carnal mind" does not necessarily imply a disposition grossly sensual ; it is (as it is explained in verse 5) a savoring of earthly and carnal thing in preference to things spiritual and heavenly. And this is the disposition that rules in the heart of every Child of man— — —

This " mind is enmity against God"—

There is not one of God's perfections, to which this disposition is not adverse. It deems his holiness too strict, his justice too severe, his truth too inflexible ; and even his mercy itself is hateful to them, on account of the humiliating way in which it is exercised. Even the very existence of God is so odious to them, that they say in their hearts, "I wish there were no God." Psa. xiv. 1. He did once put himself into their power; and they shewed what was the desire of their hearts by destroying his life; and, if they could have annihilated his very being, they would, no doubt, have gladly done it.

This mind is not merely inimical to God, for then it might be reconciled; but it is "enmity" itself against him, and must therefore be slain, before the soul can ever be brought to the service and enjoyment of God.

This assertion, though strong, will not be thought too strong, when we consider,

II. His PROOF—

The carnal mind "is not subject to the law of God"—

The law requires that we should love God supremely, and our neighbor as ourselves. But the carnal mind prefers the world before God, and self before his neighbor. There are different degrees indeed, in which a worldly and selfish spirit may prevail; but it has more or less the ascendant over every natural man; nor is there an unregenerate person in the universe who cordially and unreservedly submits to this law.

It not only is not subject to God's law, but "it cannot be"—

There is the same contrariety between the carnal mind and the law of God, as there is between darkness and light. It has been shewn before, that the carnal mind is enmity itself against God; and that the very first principle of obedience to the law is *love*. Now how is it possible that enmity should produce love? "We may sooner expect to gather grapes of thorns, or figs of thistles."

This incapacity to obey the law of God is justly adduced as a proof of our enmity against him: for if we loved him, we should love his will; and if we hate his will, whatever we may pretend, we in reality hate him.

A due consideration of the Apostle's argument will secure our assent to,

III. His INFERENCE—

We cannot please God but by obeying his law. All external compliances are worthless in his eyes, if not accompanied with the love and devotion of the soul. But such obedience cannot be rendered by the carnal mind; and consequently they who are in the flesh, that is, are under the influence of a carnal mind, "cannot please God:" they may be admired by their fellow-creatures; but whatever they do will be an abomination in the sight of God.

This is so plain, that it scarcely admits of any confirmation: yet it may be confirmed by the Articles of our Church, which plainly and unequivocally speak the same language. Art. 10th and 13th.

On the whole then we may LEARN, from this subject,

1. The grounds and reasons of the Gospel—

The principal doctrines of the Gospel have their foundation, not in any arbitrary appointment of the Deity, but in the nature and necessities of man. We must seek reconciliation with God through Christ, because we are " enemies to him in our minds by wicked works." We must seek the renewing influences of the Spirit, because our nature is altogether corrupt, and incapable of either serving or enjoying God. When therefore we hear of the indispensible necessity of being born again, and of the impossibility of being saved except by faith in Christ, let us remember that these are not the dogmas of a party, but doctrines consequent upon our fallen state, and therefore of universal and infinite importance: and that, if we were to be silent on these subjects, we should be unfaithful to our trust, and betray your souls to everlasting ruin.

2. The suitableness and excellence of its provisions—

If man were commanded to reconcile himself to God, or to renovate his own nature, he must sit down in despair. Darkness could as soon generate light, as fallen man could effect either of these things. But we are not left without hope: God has provided such a Saviour as we want, to mediate between him and us: and such an Agent as we want, to form us anew after the Divine image. Lt us then embrace this Gospel, and seek to experience its blessings. Let us, as guilty creatures, implore remission through the blood of Jesus; and, as corrupt creatures beg the Holy Spirit to work effectually in us, and to render us meet for a heavenly inheritance.

IMPERFECTION OF OUR BEST SERVICES.

Iasiah lxiv. 6.—We are all as an unclean thing; and all our righteousnesses are as filthy rags. (H. H.)

HUMILITY is that grace which is most suited to our condition as fallen creatures; and, that we may be assisted in the pursuit of it, God has graciously given us, not only promises for our encouragement, but patterns for our imitation, and models for our use. We cannot have any more instructive pattern that which is exhibited in the repenting Publican, or in the returning Prodigal. Of models, that which David has left us, in the fifty-first psalm, is perhaps the most distinguished, and of most general utility: but that which is contained in this, and part of the preceding chapter, excepting only some few expressions, is almost equally applicable to the christian world. The whole of it is a prayer drawn up by the prophet for the use of the Jews, when they should be in captivity in Babylon. We shall not enter into it at large, but shall confine our attention to the passage which we have just read, which most justly describes our state before God,

I. IN GENERAL TERMS—

There were many things considered as unclean under the Jewish dispensation: and whosoever touched them, was deemed unclean; and, till he had been purified according to the law, he was kept both from the house of God and from all his fellow-creatures, lest he should communicate to others the defilement which he had contracted. Hence, when the prophet says, "We are all as an unclean thing," he must be understood to say, that we are,

1. Unclean in ourselves—

Who can look inward for one moment, and not confess this melancholy truth?—

2. Defiling to others—

The whole of our intercourse with each other tends to foster some vile affection, some "earthly, sensual, or devilish" inclination— — —

3. In a state of separation from God and his people—

We have by nature no delight in God: we are averse to his service, his worship, his people; our "carnal minds are enmity against him," and against every thing that leads to him, or sets him before our eyes— — —We "say continually in our hearts, Depart from us; we desire not the knowledge of thy ways."

Wretched as our state appears from this representation, the prophet sets it forth in a far more humiliating view,

II. BY A PARTICULAR COMPARISON—

In the former clause of the text the prophet speaks of us as we are *on the whole:* but in the latter part he speaks of our *"righteousnesses" only:* and these he compares to a leprous garment, which by God's express command was to be consigned to the flames. The truth of this comparison appears, in that all our best deeds are,

1. Defective—

If we measure them by a standard of our own, we may discern no flaw in them : but the perfect law of God is that by which they must be tried: and where has there been one action of our lives that has fully come up to that standard ?— — —We are required to love God with all our heart, and all our mind, and all our soul, and all our strength ; and our neighbor as ourselves : but what duty that we ever performed to God or man will stand this test ?— — —Hence we must confess, that every thing we have done has been impure in the sight of God— — —

2. Mixed with sin—

Pride and self-righteousness cleave to us as long as we are in an unconverted state ; and the more exemplary our conduct is, the more it calls forth, and seems to justify, those hateful propensities. Let the most moral person look into his own heart, and see whether, instead of being filled with self-lothing and self-abhorrence on account of his defects, he do not find a self-preference and self-complacency arising in his heart, and prompting him to say, like the elated Pharisee, "I thank thee, O God, that I am not as other men." Now this is a fly, that would render the most precious ointment offensive. Eccl. x. 1. While such a disposition as this is harbored in our hearts, we, and all that we do, must be hateful in the sight of God, and render us fit only to be cast, as most abhorred objects, into the fire of hell.*

This subject may be IMPROVED for,

1. Our conviction—

We are very backward to acknowledge ourselves so depraved as we really are. But this declaration of God is sufficient to humble the proudest heart. It is not atrocious sinners only that are thus vile, but *" all,"* all without exception. Nor are our worst actions only thus defiled, but *all,* even our best; *" all* our righteousnesses are as filthy rags." Let all then, without exception, humble themselves as " unclean," Isa. vi. 5, and " vile," Job. xl. 4, and altogether destitute of any thing that is good. Rom. viii. 18.

2. Our direction—

Our own righteousness must be wholly renounced ; and all of us must enter into the kingdom of heaven on the very same footing as publicans and harlots. This is humiliating to our proud nature ; but it must be done : for, if it would be unseemly to introduce to an earthly monarch his bride clothed in " filty rags," much more would it be so to present our souls to the heavenly Bridegroom clad in such polluted garments as ours. St. Paul himself felt the necessity of a better righteousness than his own; Phil. iii. 9, and, if ever we would find acceptance with God, we must seek it altogether through the righteousness of Christ.

3· Our comfort—

We need not be dejected on account of the foregoing representation ; since

---

* See Lev. xiii. 47—58, but especially ver. 55, where it was appointed, that though the plague had not spread, or changed its color, yet if it had eaten off the knap from the cloth, the cloth was to be burned, because it was *"fret inward."* So, though the whole conversation of a man be not polluted, or even *visibly* bad in any part, yet if there be an inward disposition that is depraved, our great High Priest, when he shall inspect our hearts, will certainly pronounce us leprous, and execute the law upon us.

there is a righteousness offered to us in the gospel, even "the righteousness of Christ, which is unto all, and upon all them believe." Rom. iii. 22. This is commensurate with our wants: it is absolutely perfect; and it was wrought out by Him, Dan. ix. 24, in order that we might be clad in it, and "that the shame of our nakedness might not appear." Rev. iii. 18. Rejoice therefore all ye who are conscious of your own depravity, and pray to God that "Christ may be made righteousness unto you;" 1 Cor. i. 30, and that you, both in time and eternity, may glory in him as "the Lord your righteousness." Jer. xxiii. 6.

IGNORANCE DESTRUCTIVE.

Hos. iv. 6.—My people are destroyed for lack of knowledge. (H. H.)

IGNORANCE, as it respects the things of this world, is attended with many evils. It disqualifies a man for those situations in life that require the exercise of wisdom and discretion: it degrades him in society below the rank of those who would otherwise be deemed his equals or inferiors: and it not unfrequently leads to idleness, dissipation, and vice. But ignorance of religion is of infinitely worse consequence; because it insures the everlasting destruction of the soul. To this effect God speaks in the words before us; from which we shall be led to shew,

I. THE IGNORANCE OF THE CHRISTIAN WORLD—

The Jews, as well those of the ten tribes as those who worshipped at Jerusalem, were called "the people of God," because they had received the seal of his covenant in their infancy, and professed to acknowledge him as their God. In like manner *we*, having in our infancy been baptized into the faith of Christ, may, in a lax and general sense, be called his followers, and his people. But among nominal christians there is an awful lack of knowledge; an ignorance,

1. Of themselves—

How little do they know of their *blindness!* They suppose themselves as competent to judge of spiritual as they are of carnal things; though God tells them, that they cannot comprehend the things of the Spirit for want of a spiritual discernment. 1 Cor. ii. 11, 14.

How little do they know of their *guilt!* Do they really feel themselves deserving of God's eternal wrath and indignation? They cannot cordially acquiesce in that idea, notwithstanding they are expressly said to be under the curse and condemnation of the law. Gal. iii. 10.

How little do they know of their *depravity!* They will acknowledge, that they have this or that particular infirmity: but they have no just conception of the total depravity of their hearts; or of the truth of God's testimony respecting them, that "every imagination of the thoughts of their hearts is evil, only evil, continually." Ps. xiv. 2, 3; Gen. vi. 5.

How little do they know of their utter *helplessness!* They imagine that they can exercise repentance and faith just when they please, though they are declared by God himself to be incapable of themselves to do any thing, John xv. 5, even so much as to think a good thoug t. 2 Cor. iii. 5.

359

2. Of God—

They may have some general notions of his power and goodness: but what know they of his *holiness?* Do they suppose that sin is so hateful in his eyes as he represents it to be? Heb. i. 13.

What know they of his *justice?* Are they persuaded that, as the moral governor of the universe, he must enforce the sanctions of his own law; and that, however merciful he may be, he neither will nor can clear the guilty? Exod. xxxiv. 7.

What know they of his *truth?* They read many threatenings in his word; but they do not believe that he will execute them. Luke xvi. 17.

3. Of Christ—

They confess perhaps his Godhead, and acknowledge him as a Saviour. But what know they of him *as he is in himself?* Do they discern his beauty, his excellency, his glory? Is He in their eyes "chiefest among ten thousand, and altogether lovely?" Cant. v. 10, 16.

What know they of him *as he is to us?* Do they comprehend any thing of the breadth and length, the depth and height, of his unsearchable love? Eph. iii. 18, 19. Have they any adequate idea of his tender sympathy and compassion? Heb. ii. 18, and iv. 15. Have they been filled with an admiration of his fulness, his suitableness, his sufficiency? 1 Cor. i. 30.

If more were necessary to confirm this melancholy truth, we would appeal to God's own assertion respecting us, that our stupidity and ignorance are more than brutish. Isa. i. 2, 3.

Lest such ignorance should be thought venial, we proceed to notice,

II. The fatal consequences of it—

Doubtless the degrees of criminality attached to ignorance must vary according to the opportunities which men have enjoyed of obtaining knowledge. But in all men who have the light of the gospel set before them, a lack of spiritual knowledge,

1. *Tends to* their destruction—

Every sin is destructive, but more especially impenitence and unbelief. And what is the occasion of these? Must they not be traced to ignorance as their true and proper source? If men knew what ignorant, guilty, depraved, and helpless creatures they are, could they refrain from sorrow and contrition?— — —If they knew what a holy, just, and immutable God they have to do with, could they do otherwise than tremble before him?— — —If they knew what a merciful, loving, and adorable Saviour there is, whose bowels are yearning over them, who is ever following them with invitations and intreaties, and who longs for nothing so much as to save their souls, could they turn their backs upon him? Could they help crying to him for mercy, and desiring an interest in his salvation?— — —If a man, feeling himself in imminent danger of perishing in the sea, cannot but avail himself of the assistance offered him for the preservation of his life, so neither can a man who feels his danger of everlasting destruction neglect and despise the salvation offered him in the gospel.

2. *Will issue in* their destruction—

God himself best knows what he has ordained and decreed: and as the fates of men will be determined by him at last, to him, and to his word, we make our appeal.

We want to ascertain the states of those who are ignorant of the gospel: God tells us plainly, "They are lost." 2 Cor. iv. 3.

We want to be informed whether their ignorance will not be considered as a sufficient plea for their rejection of the gospel? God assures us, that instead of operating in that view, and to that extent, it shall itself be the ground of their condemnation. Isa. xxvii. 11.

We would fain hope that the Lord Jesus Christ will interpose for them at the last day, to avert or mitigate their sentence. But we are told, on the contrary, that he himself will come to judgment, for the express purpose of taking vengeance on them. 2 Thes. i. 7, 8.

Here we leave the matter. If ye will not believe such plain and positive declarations of God, we shall in vain hope to make any impression on your minds by any feeble arguments of our own.

INFER,

1. How carefully should we improve the means of grace!

The ordinances are appointed of God for our instruction in spiritual knowledge. Should we then absent ourselves from them on slight occasions? or should we be content with a formal attendance on them, while yet we derive no solid benefit to our souls? O let us remember that our *all* is at stake: and whether we hear, or read, or pray, let us do it as for eternity.

2. How earnestly should we pray for the teachings of God's Spirit!

Whether we be learned or unlearned, we can know nothing but as we are taught of God. In respect of spiritual knowledge, the rich have no advantage above the poor: yea, the poor have rather the advantage of the rich, inasmuch as they have more docility of mind; and God has promised to reveal to babes the things which are hid from the wise and prudent. James ii. 5; Matt. xi. 25. Let us then beg that our eyes may be opened, and that through the influences of the Spirit we may know the things which are freely given to us of God. 1 Cor. ii. 11; Eph. i. 18.

3. How thankful should we be for any measure of divine knowledge!

To be wise unto salvation is to be wise indeed. All other knowledge is as nothing in comparison of this. Blessed then are they who can say, "This I know, that, whereas I was blind, I now see." John ix. 25; Matt. xiii. 16. Yes, believers, "blessed are your eyes, which now see:" for if ignorance is destructive to the soul, knowledge, on the other hand, provided it be spiritual and practical, will surely save it. Isa. liii. 11; John xvii. 3, with 1 John ii. 3, 4.

MORAL PRAVITY THE ORIGIN OF INFIDELITY.

John iii. 19. And this is the condemnation. that light is come into the world, and men loved darkness rather than light, because their deeds were evil. (Sk.)

We cannot attentively review mankind in general, without being compelled to admit one of the following things—either that the Governor of the world is not a *holy* Being, or that it is not his will that the subjects of his moral government should resemble him;—or if it be his will that they should resemble him, he has not clearly revealed it; or if he has clearly revealed it, that the subjects of his moral government are deeply depraved and guilty of direct rebellion against God; for nothing can be more obvious than that the world lieth in the wicked one.

To which of these causes must we ascribe this wickedness? To the first —*that God is not a holy Being?* Impossible! for He is "the high and lofty One—whose name is Holy, and who dwelleth in the high and **holy** place,"—and who is " glorious in holiness. Shall we ascribe it to the second—*that it is not his will that the subjects of his moral government should resemble him?* Equally impossible! This would be to suppose that *infinite wisdom* could take pleasure in *folly ;*—*infinite purity*, in *pollution ;*—*infinite order*, in *anarchy ;*—and *infinite benevolence*, in *misery*. Shall we trace it to the third—*that he has not clearly revealed his will?* The sacred Scriptures of the Old and New Testament will render its ascription to this cause eternally impossible;—Moses and the Prophets, Jesus Christ and the Apostles, proclaim as with one voice, " Be ye holy, for the Lord your God is holy." Whence originates the wickedness which is in the world? Not in God, but in man ;—" *Men love darkness* rather than light, *because their deeds are evil.*"

Our text suggests a variety of observations.

I. THAT LIGHT IS COME INTO THE WORLD.

The preceding verses determine the application of this metaphor to Christ. It is frequently applied to him both in the Old and New Testament, Isa. xlix. 6 ; lx. 3 ; John i. 4, 5, 9. The propriety of its application is obvious from various considerations.

1. *Through Christ, the evil of sin is exhibited in its strongest light.* That *sin is an evil of great magnitude* is demonstrable from the *effects already produced.* The expulsion of our first parents from Paradise, Gen. iii. 24 ; iii. 16—19, the pains of conception and child-birth—the noxious productions, and comparative infertility of the earth—the convulsions of nature—war, with all its infernal concomitants—an innumerable train of diseases—and death. It is also demonstrable from the punishment which awaits it hereafter.—Its wages is death eternal, Rom. vi. x3. But in *neither*, nor in *all* these put together, does its turpitude appear in so strong a light as on the cross of Christ. It is an evil so great, that nothing can expiate it but the death of the Son of God. It is a disease so inveterate and malignant, that nothing can heal it but the blood of Immanuel. It is a ruin so complete, that nothing can restore it but an omnipotent Deliverer.

2. *Through Christ, the love of God is transcendantly manifested.* God's love manifested in creation, particularly in the creation of angels **and** men.—More strikingly in the redemption of the human race. *In the medium of that redemption ;* the incarnation, life, sufferings, death, resurrection, and intercession of Christ. *In the subjects of that redemption ;* the subjects of creating power had never offended—the subjects of redeeming love have, Rom. v. 8. The former never resisted the operations of their Creator, but were as clay in the hands of the potter—the latter frequently make strong and long-continued resistance. Yet his love, in spite of unworthiness and resistance, perseveres in its operations to save.

3. *Through Christ, a flood of light is shed on the doctrine of a future state.* This doctrine not *peculiar* to Christianity—vestiges of it in both ancient and modern Paganism—believed by Jews, Matt. xxii. 32 ; Acts xxiii. 8, 9 ; but enlightened by Christ, 2 Tim. i. 10. He teaches it, Matt. xxv. Exemplifies it in his own resurrection, 1 Cor. xv. 20—22, and shows the connection between our present character and our future state. It suggests,

II. THAT MEN GENERALLY REJECT LIGHT, AND LOVE DARKNESS.

Darkness when applied to moral subjects, denotes both ignorance and sin, Rom. xiii. 12. Our text, in each of these senses, has been, and continues to be, most awfully verified.

1. *It was verified in the conduct of the Jews, in rejecting Christ.* The

glory of God less eminently displayed in the law than in the gospel.— The law gives the knowledge of sin, Rom. vii. 7. The gospel reveals salva, on, Eph. i. 13. The sacrifices of the law were beasts, Heb. x. 4; of the gospel the Son of God, Heb. x. 10. The law, compared with former dispensations of mercy, was full of glory—compared with this its glory is obscured, 2 Cor. iii. 7—11.

2. *It is verified by all rejectors of divine revelation.* Every infidel dwells in a region of darkness and uncertainty : he abounds in speculations without truth, conjectures without certainty, and queries without solutions. With all his researches, he cannot answer one of the following questions :— Has man an immaterial spirit ? Will this survive the dissolution of the body? If so, will its future state be like its present, or will it be a state of retribution ?—And if so, " what must we do to be saved ?"—The Bible answers them all, but he rejects this.

3. *It is verified by all who place religion entirely in the performance of its outward duties.* These deny the power of godliness. All pretensions to assurance of salvation, they contemn as fanaticism. But the Scriptures teach such assurance, Rom. viii. 16, 17 ; 1 John iii. 14, 24 ; iv. 6, 13 ; and v. 2, 19. On any other supposition than the attainableness of such assurance, many passages are not only nugatory, but absurd, 2 Cor. xiii. 5.

III. THAT THE REASON WHY MEN REJECT LIGHT AND LOVE DARKNESS IS MORAL PRAVITY.

Bad systems are the offspring of bad hearts, while on the other hand, those systems *re-act* upon those hearts, and perpetuate and increase their depravity. It is not the deficiency of evidence, but the love of sin which,

1. *Produces atheism.* Wherever there is a creature, there is demonstration of the existence of a Creator, Psa. xix. 1 ; Rom. i. 20. The atheist knows that if there be a God, he must hate and punish sin. Being resolved to persist in sin, that he may proceed quietly, he persuades himself to reject his existence.

2. *Produces deism.* Deists in general have never read the Scriptures with attention ;—instance Hume : nor studied the Christian and Deistical controversy.—Their hostility arises from opposition to the holiness of its requisitions.

3. *Produces opposition to the doctrine of divine influence.* Divine influence consistent with reason. Taught by Scripture, John xvi. 8 ; Eph. ii. 1 ; Rom. viii. 16 ; 2 Cor. 1, 4. Confined not to the apostolic age, but extends to the end of time, Acts ii. 39 ; 2 Cor. iii. 11 ; Heb. xii. 28.

IV. THAT THE CONSEQUENCE OF REJECTING LIGHT AND LOVING DARKNESS IS CONDEMNATION.

Condemnation. Implying.

1. *In this life.*—Mental perturbation, Isa. lvii. 20, 21. God's curse accompanying the dispensations of his providence, Deut. xxviii. 15—20. A fearful looking for of judgment, Heb. x. 27.

2. *In the life to come.* The final sentence. The nature of future punishment. Its duration.

Conclude with three remarks.

1. No man will be finally condemned because he was once a sinner, but because he refused a Saviour.

2. No man can be saved who rejects Christ;

3. He who receives Christ shall enjoy the Divine favor here, and glory hereafter.

MAN'S ABUSE OF GOD'S PATIENCE.

Eccl. viii. 11.—Because sentence against an evil work is not executed speedily, therefore the heart of the sons of men is fully set in them to do evil. (S. S.)

Sin is in itself an evil of a crimson dye—
Nevertheless its malignity may be greatly increased by the aggravations with which it is attended—
One can scarcely conceive any thing that can enhance its guilt so much, as the committing of it in hopes that God's mercy will pardon it—
Yet this is the very ground on which the world indulge themselves in the commission of it—" Because," &c.

I. The extent of man's wickedness.
That sin exists in the world is visible to all—
But the degree in which it prevails is very little known—Men sin
1. Habitually
All are not equally vicious in their lives—
But all forget God and neglect their own souls
Successive years serve only to confirm this habit—
We may all adopt the confession of the church of old, Jer. iii. 25.
2. Deliberately
It were well if we never sinned, but through ignorance or inadvertance—
But what schemes have we formed for the accomplishment of sinful purposes!—
How often have we seen the sinfulness of our desires, and yet gratified them! Rom. i. 32.
The very bent and inclination of our souls has been towards wickedness— Job xv. 16.
3. Without restraint.
A regard to our reputation or interest may impose some restraint—
A fear of hell may also prevent the gratification of some desires—
But few are kept from evil like Joseph, by the fear of God, Gen. xxxix. 9.
That is the only restraint which proves uniformly effectual, Jam. ii. 11.
4. Without remorse
We must at times have felt some convictions of conscience—
But we, for the most part, stifle them by company, amusements, &c.—
Many attain to dreadful hardness of heart and impenitence, 1 Tim. iv. 2.
The prophets description may well be applied to each of us, Jer. viii. 5, 6.
Thus are " men's hearts fully set in them to do evil."
They walk after the imagination of their own hearts—
Neither mercies nor judgments can prevail with them to do otherwise—
If their sins were followed by a visible and immediate punishment, men would not dare to live in this manner—
But God defers the execution of his judgments
II. The occasion of it.
God is not an unconcerned spectator of sin.
He has appointed a day for the revelation of his righteous judgment—
At present he forbears to inflict vengeance—
This very forbearance emboldens men to sin—" because," " therefore.'
From the delay of punishment men think
1. That there is but little " evil" in sin.
God indeed calls sin " an evil work"—
But his forbearance towards sinners is thought to indicate indifference—

This however is a fatal delusion—

He has marked the evil of sin in many awful instances, 2 Pet. ii. 4—6

He will soon undeceive this blind infatuated world, Eph. v. 6.

2. That there is no "sentence" gone forth against it.

Men would gladly persuade themselves that they have no cause to fear—

The temptation whereby the serpent beguiled Eve, is cherished by them, Gen. iii. 4.

But the wrath of God is indeed denounced against sin, Rom. ii. 8, 9.

Every species and degree of sin renders us obnoxious to his displeasure, Rom. i. 18.

3. That the sentence (if there be any) will never be " executed"

Since God defers punishing, it seems possible that he may decline it altogether—

The apparent disproportion between the offence and the punishment seems to countenance this idea—

To confirm our hope we are apt to compare God with ourselves, Psa. l. 21. ·

But, however long God delay, he will surely strike at last, Eccl. viii. 12, 13.

Thus they take occasion from God's forbearance to persist in their evil ways.

David mentions this effect as arising from it in his day, Psa. lv. 19.

St. Peter foretells the prevalence of this iniquity in the last days, 2 Pet. iii. 3, 4.

Experience proves how universally it obtains at present—

INFER

1. How great the folly, as well as wickedness, of unregenerate men!

If there were a bare possibility of eternal punishment, how mad were it to continue in sin!—

But God has pledged himself that he will inflict it on the impenitent— Matt. xxv. 46.

Every moment's continuance in sin increases the condemnation, Rom. ii. 4, 5.

What extreme folly then is it so to abuse the forbearance of God!—

May we be ashamed of ourselves, and repent in dust and ashes—

2. What need have we to be cleansed by the blood and spirit of Christ!

What but the blood of Christ can ever expiate the guilt we have contracted?—

What but the spirit of Christ can ever deliver us from such habits?—

That we can never renew our own souls is certain, Jer. xiii. 23.

Let us therefore wash in the fountain opened for us, Zech. xiii. 1.

And let us apply to God for his almighty aid, Lam. v. 21.

3. How dreadful must be the state of those who continue impenitent!

There is a certain measure of iniquity which sinners are left to fill up— Gen. xv. 16

When this is full, nothing can avert the divine vengeance, 1 Thess. ii. 16.

Already are the arrows of divine justice pointed at them, Ps. vii. 11—13.

Eternity itself will be the duration of the punishment, Mark ix. 43—48

The time is coming when Jerusalem's state will be ours, Luke xix. 42.

Let us then tremble lest we exhaust the divine patience, Zeph. ii. 2, 3.

Let us diligently improve this day of salvation, 2 Cor. vi. 2.

THE DECEITFULNESS OF THE HEART.

Jeremiah xvii. 9.—The heart is deceitful above all things and desperately wicked: who can know it?

TRUE and faithful is the testimony of God. Men may amuse themselves and their fellow creatures with empty, high-sounding descriptions of the dignity of human nature and the all-sufficient powers of man, but every humble and truly enlightened person must at once perceive and acknowledge the truth of the text, that the heart, &c.

But by the blessing of God it may be useful to turn our attention to this important subject and point out some of the plainest and most decisive evidences of the deceitfulness of the human heart, which scriptural observation and experience afford. It is demonstrable and apparent, 1. From men's general ignorance of their own character. There is nothing in the history of mankind more unaccountable and at first view more surprising than that self-partiality which prevails amongst them. One would be apt to imagine that it should not be so difficult a matter to arrive at a just knowledge of our own character, possessing as we do every possible advantage for obtaining it. We have constant access to our own bosoms and are more interested in the discovery than in the acquisition of any other kind of knowledge. But we see that in point of fact, this knowledge is the rarest and most uncommon: nor is it difficult to account for the moral phenomenon, since the heart is, &c.

2. The deceitfulness of the heart appears from men's general disposition to justify their own conduct. This disposition our first parents discovered immediately upon their eating the forbidden fruit. When Jehovah appeared to Adam and charged him with guilt, he attempted to justify himself by laying the blame upon the woman, and in the same manner, the woman blamed the serpent.

3. The deceitfulness of the heart appears from the difficulty with which men are brought to acknowledge their faults even when conscious that they have done wrong. This necessarily follows from that disposition in human nature to which we have already adverted, viz. the disposition on all occasions to justify our own conduct. Hence men are in general so backward to acknowledge their faults, and so displeased with those, who are so faithful and friendly as to point them out. How few can bear to be told their faults. This is the sure and ready way to make most men your enemies.

4. The deceitfulness of the heart appears from the disposition which men discover to rest in the mere notion and forms of religion, while they are destitute of its power. In the present age of the church there have been too many of this character: men who from selfish and worldly motives have taken up a profession of religion without understanding its nature or feeling its power; having a name to live, but being spiritually dead.

Balaam was a remarkable instance of this. He was a man of extensive knowledge and superior gifts. He was not a stranger to religious impressions for in his calm reflecting moments, he desired to die the death of the righteous.

5th, and lastly. The deceitfulness of the heart appears in the highest degree when we overlook the real motives, and mistake the workings of their own corruptions for the fruits of the spirit of God. That there is such deceitfulness in the world none can doubt, who considers the dreadful enormities that have been committed under the sound name of religion.

On the whole as the ways in which men deceive themselves are so various, can we be too jealous over our own hearts? He that trusteth to his own heart is a fool, says Solomon, and the reason is obvious, for the heart is, &c. Let us give ourselves to self-examination instead of indulging in a censorious disposition or looking abroad to discover the faults of our neighbors. Let us descend into our own breasts and observe the plagues of our own hearts. Let us look not merely to our own actions but likewise to the principles and motives from which they proceed. Let us consider our conduct not in the light, in which self-partiality would present it to our view, but in the light in which an impartial spectator would view it—in the light in which God's word teaches us to consider it and in the light in which it will be judged at last, when God will bring to light the hidden things of darkness and make manifest the councils of all hearts. We are all more or less liable to self-deceit and they who think, they have the least of it, are in general the most of all under its dominion. Let us therefore distrust our own judgments, and sensible of our own ignorance and liableness to mistakes, let us pray for the teaching of his spirit and say with Elehu, that which I see not teach thou me.

THE ENMITY OF THE CARNAL MIND.

Romans viii. 7.—The carnal mind is enmity against God. (Sk.)

In the first four chapters of this epistle, our apostle *establishes the important doctrine of justification by faith.* This he does—by showing that all mankind have sinned, and need salvation, chap. iii. 23. That being transgressors, we cannot be saved by the merit of works, iii. 28. And that all God's approved servants have been saved by faith: for Abraham was thus saved, as a specimen of the uncircumcised, iv. 1, 3, 10, 11. And David, as a specimen of those saved in circumcision, iv. 5-7. In the succeeding chapters, our apostle *guards this doctrine* against all licentious abuse, to which it might be liable through human depravity. Here he shows, that gospel liberty is freedom from sin, chap. vi. 14, 17, 18, 22. That believers are enabled to walk in this liberty, viii. 2—4. That their continued salvation depends on their thus walking, viii. 1, 13. And that a contrary deportment would imply rebellion against God. For "the carnal mind," &c. Enmity is a confirmed dislike to an object, accompanied with a disposition to oppose it, and if possible, to injure it. In improving our text, let us consider the object, the subject, and the evidences of this enmity, here spoken of.

I. The object of this enmity. This is God, who may be justly considered as the kindest, the loveliest, and the greatest of beings.

1. *God is the kindest of beings.* This appears,

From his *creating goodness.* In making us creatures capable of enjoying him; of enjoying the assurance of his favor; of bearing his holy image; of sharing in his heavenly glory; and in creating us for this benevolent purpose, Rev. iv. 11; Psa. xxxv. 27, 28.

From his *sustaining care:* by which he consults our best interests; preserves us from all evil; and constantly provides for us, Psa. viii. 4; 1 Pet v. 7.

From his *redeeming mercy;* which devised the scheme of our redemption, Psa. cxxxvi. 23; Luke i. 78, 79; and confers its benefits, Mic. vii. 18, 19.

And from his patient *long-suffering:* which is designed to promote our repentance; by exciting us to it, Rom. ii. 4; and encouraging it, 2 Peter iii. 9.

2. *God is the loveliest of beings.* This he evidently is—

For his kindness is most *extensive,* and impartial. It embraces all his creatures without exception, Psa. cxlv. 9. It is most *disinterested,* aiming not at his own profit, but ours, Psa. cxvii. 1, 2, and xxxvi. 7. It is most *prompt* in its exercises. He waits to be gracious, Isa. xxx. 18. It is most *generous* in its displays, not accompanied with upbraidings, Jam. i. 5. And most *durable* in its continuance, it will never end, Psa. ciii. 17, 18.

3. *God is the greatest of beings.* He is infinite in *wisdom,* to discern and frustrate all the devices of his enemies, Prov. xxi. 30; infinite in *power,* to execute all his purposes, Jam. iv. 12: and infinite in *happiness;* enjoying felicity, which cannot be augmented; and security, which cannot be violated. Consequently, he is incapable of error through ignorance; of selfishness through want; or of cruelty through fear. "Great is the Lord, and greatly to be praised: and his greatness is unsearchable," Psa. cxlv. 3. But though he is the kindest, and loveliest, as well as the greatest of beings, yet all do not love him. "For the carnal mind is enmity," &c. Let us therefore consider,

II. THE SUBJECT OF THIS ENMITY. The carnal mind.

1. *The mind,* the immortal part of man: the most noble part of the most dignified creature on earth. This the human mind must be—because it is *rational;* capable of admitting true conceptions of things; capable of retaining those conceptions, of comparing them, and of deducing just conclusions from them, Job xxxv. 10, 11. And because it is *free* in all its acts. It is capable of choosing what reason requires, and of rejecting what it forbids. This is incontestable, from God's gracious influence, Phil. ii. 13; his proposals to mankind, Deut. xxx. 19, 20; and from the complaints brought against the impenitent, John v. 40; Matt. xxiii. 37.

2. *The carnal mind:* the natural mind of man; that mind which we bring with us into the world. The uninspired, unrenewed mind, which is not enlightened, purified, and governed, by God's Holy Spirit, Jude 19. The human mind, while it remains in this state, is called carnal,—because of its *descent.* Our minds are certainly transmitted with our bodies, by what is called natural traduction. This appears from scripture: for "on the seventh day God ended his work which he had made;" that is the work of creation, Gen. ii. 2. But this he could not have done, if he continues to create human souls. It is also said, "in the day that God created man, in the image of God made he him," Gen. v. 1, but of Seth, it is said, "And Adam begat a son in his own likeness, after his image," Gen. v: 3 Hence our Lord justly concludes, "That which is born of flesh, is flesh," John iii. 6. When the tree is corrupt, the fruit must be corrupt also, Matt. vii. 17. The soul's descent by natural traduction is also evident from facts; for children resemble their parents in mental dispositions, no less than in features. The mind is also called carnal or fleshly, because of its *affections* and *exercises.* With respect to its affections, it supremely desires and delights in the things of this world. Those things which gratify the desires of the flesh, the desires of the eye, and the pride of life, 1 John ii. 15, 16; Phil. iii. 18, 19. With respect to its exercises, all its purposes, its aims, and its contrivances are employed to obey its own will, in opposition to the will of God, Gen. vi. 5.

It must therefore follow, that those who act under the influence of the carnal mind, are enemies to God by wicked works. Which leads us to observe,

III. THE EVIDENCES OF THIS ENMITY. Enmity of mind must in itself be unseen, but may be perceived by its overt acts. For instance, when a subject is at enmity against his sovereign, he manifests it by aversion from all intercourse with him, wilful disobedience to his commands, hostile opposition to him, and hatred to his friends and servants. Thus also enmity against God is manifested,

1. *By aversion from communion with him.* To this God graciously calls us, Isa. lv. 6; 2 Chron. vii. 14. But this man naturally rejects, Job xxi. 14, 15; Isa. lxiv. 7.

2. *By wilful disobedience to God's known commands.* These he sets before us in his word, and by his servants; but man rebels against them, Dan. ix. 9, 10.

3. *By hostile opposition to him. Opposition to an amicable agreement with him,* Jer. vi. 16; ii. 25; to the gracious strivings of his Spirit, Acts vii. 51: and to the interests of his kingdom; by endeavoring to prevent its extension, Matt. xxiii. 13; and to seduce its subjects, Prov. i. 10; 1 Kings xiv. 16.

4. *And by hatred to his friends and followers.* This they manifest by reviling, slandering, and tormenting them, Matt. v. 11; John xv. 19; Heb. xi. 37.

This enmity of the carnal mind against God, teaches us,

1. *That all mankind are naturally in a degenerate state.* Man, when at first created, was made *upright;* he was then just and grateful towards his Maker, Eccl. vii. 29. He was *very good,* Gen. i. 31. And he was *crowned with glory* in himself, and with *honor* by the inferior creatures, Psa. viii. 5, 6. But man, as an enemy to God, is *unjust,* for he robs God by self-desecration, Rom. vi. 13. He is *ungrateful,* for he returns the greatest evil he is capable of repaying, for the greatest good he is capable of enjoying, Isa. i. 2. He is *injurious* to his dearest connexions, Prov. iii. 33; Deut. xxviii. 18. He is *debased* by captivity to his greatest enemy, 2 Tim. ii. 26; and by condemnation to everlasting infamy, 1 Sam. ii. 30; Dan. xii. 2. To this degeneracy all mankind are naturally subject, however amiable in tempers, or polished in manners, Psa. xiv. 2, 3. This teaches us,

2. *That an entire change of mind is necessary to our eternal salvation.* Are your minds at enmity against God? Are you averse, &c.? Then consider—your enmity exposes you to certain destruction, Thes. i. 7—9; Prov. xxix. 1. This destruction is certain; from God's knowledge of your sins, Job xxxiv. 21, 22; from his justice, Rom. ii. 6, 8, 9; and from his truth, Psa. lxviii. 21; Deut. xxxii. 40, 41. A change of mind is therefore indispensably requisite; every other change is insufficient; whether it be of sentiment, name, or outward conduct, Gal. vi. 15; John iii. 7.

3. *To obtain this change should engage our most serious concern.* Seek it in God's way; by repentance, Acts iii. 19; by prayer, Psa. li. 10; for Christ's sake, Eph. iv. 32. Seek it in God's time; now, without excuse or delay, Job xxii. 21; Psa. xcv. 7, 8. Seek it with confident expectation; from the success of others, Col. i. 21; from God's amicable disposition, 2 Cor. v. 19; his entreaty, 2 Cor. v. 20; and his promises, Isa. lv. 6, 7.

A CORRECT ESTIMATE OF HUMAN LIFE.

Psalm xc. 12.   So teach us to number our days, that we may apply our hearts unto wisdom. (Sk.)

Of all the blessings which the adorable author of our being has conferred upon man, there are few more important than that inestimable boon which we denominate *time ;* because it is that, on the continuance of which infinite wisdom has rendered every other good in some measure dependant. Yet, alas ! notwithstanding the vast importance of our fleeting moments, how few are there who attach to them a proper estimate, and improve them according to their value.   This lamentable abuse of time appears to have been commensurate with the existence of moral pravity ; for the apostle Paul, in two of his Epistles, reminds the churches of the importance of " redeeming the time," Eph. v. 16; Col. iv. 5.   And the devout author of the psalm before us, evidently conscious of the proneness of man to neglect and abuse time, raises his pious ejaculation to heaven, and prays, " *So teach us to number our days, that we may apply our hearts unto wisdom.*"   As the same disposition in the human heart is still in operation, let us endeavor to counteract its influence by considering,

I. The means of ascertaining a correct estimate of human life.

II. The particulars of which this estimate consists.

III. The important effect which it tends to produce.

I. The means of ascertaining a correct estimate of human life.

The pious psalmist was deeply sensible of his dependence upon God, and hence he " gave himself unto prayer."   Prayer was the means which he used ; and this powerful instrument is universally necessary, and universally applicable.   This will appear if we proceed to notice,

1. *The natural indisposition of man to improve the fleeting moments of life.*   This humbling and lamentable truth forces itself upon us, supported by all that weight of evidence which *personal experience* and *daily observation* regularly furnish.   Multitudes of our unhappy fellow creatures are devoting their passing hours to purposes decidedly hostile to those for which time was originally designed : whilst others, in some degree persuaded of the vast importance of time, are nevertheless deferring its proper occupation and use to some uncertain future period ; and thus year after year steals into eternity unimproved, charged with an awful report to the throne of the final Judge, Luke xii. 16—20 ; Acts xxiv. 25.   Even the Christian, acting in some measure under the influence of that estimate of life which the volume of inspiration furnishes, has reason to mourn over many blanks and vacancies which occur on the pages of his history.   Hence, all have need to pray, " So teach us to number our days," &c.

2. *The sovereignty of Jehovah over the human heart.*   That Omnipotent Being, who is the sole object of prayer, has the entire control of man ; for he reigneth in the armies above, and on the earth beneath.   He can instruct the most *ignorant mind ;* subdue the most *turbulent passions ;* and conquer the most *obdurate heart.*   By a thousand means, unknown to erring man, he can effectually impress a true estimate of time upon the human mind.   The boisterous winds—the tumultuous ocean—and the hearts of the children of men, are equally subject to his almighty dominion. 1 Chron. xxix. 11. 12, 17—19.

3. *The direct appointment of infinite wisdom.*   " The Father of lights," from whom proceedeth " every good gift," has in his infinitude of wisdom

appointed and sanctioned prayer as the medium between heaven and earth: and whatever blessings we may need at the hands of our beneficent Creator, we are taught to expect them only through the lively exercise of fervent prayer. This momentous truth is supported by the testimony of *the sacred Scriptures*, and by the *experience of the truly pious in every age of the church*, Ezek. xxxvi. 37; Matt. vii. 7, 8; Jam. i. 5, 6; iv. 2, 3.

4. *The tried efficacy of prayer.* If prayer were an untried experiment, then we might entertain some doubts respecting its influence, and should have a plausible reason for hesitancy in resorting to it; but doubt is precluded, and hesitation superseded, by that overpowering strength of evidence with which the efficacy of prayer is supported. Myriads of witnesses of its power encircle the throne of Jehovah in the regions of immortality; and myriads more, still on earth, are daily feasting on the bounty of their God, through this admirable medium of divine intercourse. But we need not ascend up to heaven for evidence in support of this truth; nor need we wander to distant parts of the earth to collect convincing proofs: our researches need not exceed the limits of the present congregation; here doubtless we have many witnesses that

> " Prayer ardent opens heaven, lets down a stream
> Of glory on the consecrated hour
> Of man in audience with the deity."

Exod. xxxiii. 18—23: xxxiv. 5—7; James v. 16—18.

II. THE PARTICULARS OF WHICH THIS ESTIMATE CONSISTS. By " numbering our days" we are not to understand the psalmist to mean that it is the duty of man to ascertain the period of his mortal existence; this is one of those " secret things which (exclusively) belong to the Lord." That estimate of human life referred to in our text, doubtless includes a correct idea of its importance, together with a conscientious improvement of its parts. In thus " numbering our days," it will be necessary to consider,

1. *The smallness of their number.* The life of man is circumscribed in its limit; and though we may mark its progress by certain periods, and thus divide it into small portions, yet, generally, threescore years and ten will terminate our mortal story, and consign the most athletic to the " house appointed for all living." This is a very narrow limit, compared with its *antediluvian extent*, and with *the important work which ought to be effected*, viz. the gloom of ignorance dispelled—the oppressive load of guilt removed —and the deep-fixed stain of moral pollution washed away, Psa. xxxix. 5. James iv. 14.

2. *The rapidity of their flight.* Human life is not only limited in its duration, but also fleeting in its progress. The several portions of which it is composed steal away in rapid succession; and all the boasted power and wisdom of man are insufficient either to impede their progress, or to recall them when they have passed away. The Holy Ghost has made choice of the most fleeting objects in nature, in order to impress the human mind with a correct idea of the rapid course of time, and excite the sons of Adam to the proper occupation and improvement of their fleeting moments, Job vii. 6: Job. ix. 25; Psa. xc. 10.

3. *The uncertainty of their continuance.* Although man is capable of understanding an extensive variety of interesting subjects, yet the termination of his mortal existence is a point which he can never expect to ascertain. This solemn period infinite wisdom has concealed from the most prying curiosity. This is one of those prerogatives which Jehovah has exclu-

sively reserved to himself. The mouldering, moss-grown annals of the dead in our grave yards, together with the daily occurrence of human mortality, sufficiently establish this humbling truth, Job xxi. 21, 23—25; Luke xii. 19, 20.

4. *Their influence on our eternal destiny.* The present state of man is probationary in its nature, and decisive in its influence upon his eternal condition. It is in time that the character is formed for eternity. Earth alone is the scene of operation for that mercy which is exercised through the amazing provisions of the gospel of Christ, and which is of essential importance, as a preparation for participating the felicities of the heavenly world. The unhappy being who, "driven away in his wickedness," quits the stage of life without this gospel meetness for the skies, has

> "No patron! intercessor none! Now past
> The sweet, the clement, mediatorial hour!
> For guilt no plea! to pain no pause! no bound!
> Inexorable all! and all extreme!"

Dan. xii. 2, 3. Matt. xxv. 31—46; 2 Thess. i. 7—10.

III. THE IMPORTANT EFFECT WHICH IT TENDS TO PRODUCE ;—"That we may apply our hearts unto wisdom." "Wisdom" is a term very frequently used, and variously applied in the sacred Scriptures; viz. to mechanical genius, Exod. xxxi. 2, 3;—general literature, Acts vii. 22 :—natural instinct, Job xxix. 17;—that prudence which enables a man to discern what is proper to be done, Eccles. x. 10 ;—and to true religion, Psalm cxi. 10; James iii. 17. To the last two ideas or senses alone our text seems to direct our attention. 1. The term "wisdom" sometimes describes that prudence which enables a man to discern and perform those actions which accord with the fitness of things. If the days of man be so few, so fleeting, so uncertain, and so momentous, it certainly is highly proper to seize the passing moments as they fly, and conscientiously devote them to those purposes which will produce the greatest possible benefit. Preserving them with a miser's care, from being associated with unprofitable, unnecessary, and (much less with) ungodly actions. It is the distinguished prerogative of man

> "To raise
> A royal tribute from the poorest hours ;
> Immense revenue! every moment pays."

Much time may be saved by guarding against *unnecessary sleep—useless commixion with ungodly men—unprofitable reading*—and, in short, every exercise and pursuit which cannot be engaged in to the "glory of God," 1 Cor. x. 31. The advice of an eminent divine of the last century on this point, is worthy of being engraven upon our hearts: "Never be unemployed a moment. Never be triflingly employed. Never while away time." 2. "Wisdom" is sometimes applied to true religion. The application of the heart to this, is the great end of life; and no man has his heart properly influenced with the shortness, uncertainty, and importance of time, who does not make this the grand business of his life. It is very possible to apply the *head* without having the *heart* influenced. The man who, under the influence of a proper estimate of time, is the subject of this important application, has experienced a general renovation of his moral nature; he is "renewed in the spirit of his mind;" he experiences a lively union with God through faith in Jesus Christ; and he is solicitous to "comprehend with all saints what is the breadth, and length, and depth, and height, and to know the love of Christ, and be filled with all the fulness of God." Influenced by a spiritual principle, he is the subject of a spiritual enjoyment, and gives proof of the whole by holiness of practice. Gal. v. 22—25.

This subject tends,

1. To detach our affections from earthly objects.

2. To excite us to diligence in our Christian calling.

3. To alarm the trifler, and awaken in him a lively sensibility of his awful condition.

THE FRAGILITY OF HUMAN LIFE.

Job xiv. 1, 2.—Man that is born of a woman is of few days, and full of trouble. He cometh forth like a flower, and is cut down: he fleeth also as a shadow, and continueth not. (Sk.)

DEATH is justly designated "the king of terrors:" before him the monarch trembles and the subject is afraid, and to his dread sceptre all must bow, since "it is appointed unto men once to die," Heb. ix. 27. The great duty of man, therefore, is to conduct himself as a candidate for eternity, by securing an interest in Him who conquered death in his dark domains, and is able to deliver them who through fear of death are subject to bondage, Heb. ii. 14, 15. If death plunged man into the gulf of annihilation, he might pass through life fearless of its close; but when we consider it connected with eternal results, it becomes the duty and wisdom of all to improve the present moment. With such an object in view, let us notice,

I. THE IMPORTANT IDEAS SUGGESTED IN OUR TEXT.

II. IMPROVE THEM BY PRACTICAL INFERENCES.

I. THE IMPORTANT IDEAS SUGGESTED. From our text we learn,

1. *That human life is flattering in its commencement:*—Man "cometh forth like a flower." Imagery more appropriate could not have been selected. Children are like flowers in the bud, unfolding their beauty as days and months increase; their innocent actions—their broken accents—the expansion of the mind, and the acquisition of new ideas, fascinate and involuntarily allure the affections of their fond parents, who watch over them with the tenderest anxiety. In one child they see a human form, which the maturity of age will render beautiful.—In another, a nerve that will riot in danger.—A third, displaying clearness of thought, and sobriety of judgment; and a fourth, manifesting a combination of qualities admirably adapted to the purposes of life. In the opening bud the father's eye discovers much to excite hope, and the mother sees with delight the child of promise; but alas!

> "Nipt by the wind's unkindly blast,
> Parch'd by the sun's directer ray,
> The momentary glories waste,
> The short-lived beauties die away."

The flower is cut down, Psa. ciii. 15, 16; Isa. xl. 6, 7; James i. 10, 11; 1 Pet. i. 24.

2. *Disastrous in its continuance:*—"Full of trouble." Misfortunes and calamities surround us on every hand, and proclaim nothing certain in this

uncertain world. To calculate on unruffled peace, or uninterrupted prosperity, in this mutable state, is presumptuous ; our stay on earth is connected with trials of various kinds, and no situation can exempt us from suffering. The word of God, experience, and observation, confirm the doctrine of our text, and testify that " man is born to trouble as the sparks fly upward," Job v. 7.

3. *Contracted in its span:*—" Few days." Life, in its longest period, is but a short journey from the cradle to the tomb. This made the pious and venerable patriarch to exclaim, " Few and evil have the days of the years of my life been," Gen. xlvii. 9. Various are the figures employed to illustrate the shortness of human life; it is compared to " a step," 1 Sam. xx. 3 ;— " a post," Job ix. 25 ;—" a tale that is told," Psa. xc. 9 ;—" a weaver's shuttle," Job vii. 6 ;—and " a vapor," James iv. 14.

4. *Incessant in its course:*—" Fleeth as a shadow." Human life is measured by seconds—hours—days—weeks—months—and years. These periodical revolutions roll on in rapid succession, and are strikingly illustrated by the image in our text, which is supposed to be taken from the shadow cast by the sun on the earth. Some suppose it the shadow of the sun dial: but whether we consider it as the shadow of the evening, which is lost when night comes on ; or the shadow on a dial plate, which is continually moving onward ; or the shadow of a bird flying, which stays not ;—the figure fully represents the life of man, which is passing away, whether we are loitering or active, careless or serious, killing or improving time.

5. *Eventful in its issue.* Death introduces us into the fixed state of eternity, and puts a final period to all earthly enjoyments and suffering : the soul dismissed from its clay tabernacle, is introduced into a world of spirits, from whence there is no return. The wicked, at death, exchange their supposed happiness for perpetual misery, and their imaginary light for thickest darkness, " where the worm dieth not," &c., Mark ix. 48. The righteous, at death, leave the wilderness, and enter the promised land ; exchange a state of suffering and conflict, for an eternity of peace and rest: so that death, though terrific in any form, is the harbinger of good to the christian ; proclaiming victory to the warrior, rest to the pilgrim, a crown for the conqueror, and repose for the weary.

II. IMPROVE THEM BY PRACTICAL INFERENCES. Such being the character of human life, it is the duty and wisdom of piety,

1. *To enrich the juvenile mind with religious instruction.* " Man cometh forth as a flower," therefore let instruction drop as the rain, and fall as the dew : no time must be lost; the bud is unfolding, and

" If good you plant not, vice will fill the mind."

Combine your efforts, and strengthen each other's hands, since

" Children, like tender osiers, take the bow,
And, as they first are fashioned, still will grow."

2 *Improve the dispensations of Providence.* If your few days are crowded with troubles of various kinds, look to the Disposer of events : " all things work together for good to them that love God," Rom. viii. 28. Are you the subjects of bodily affliction? remember here " we have no continuing city," Heb. xiii. 14. Are you bereft of friends, who died in the Lord? think of that which was a solace to David under his affliction, 1 Sam. xii

23. Are you in darkness as to the design or final issue **of your sufferings?** " trust in the name of the Lord," &c., Isa. l. 10.

3. *Be diligent.* Your days are few; the fugitive moment refuses to stay, and each second brings you nearer either to heaven or hell. Think, mortal man, of that part which dieth not, and live for eternity: for, " behold, now is the accepted time; behold, now is the day of salvation," 2 Cor. vi. 2. " Whatsoever thy hand findeth to do, do it with all thy might," Eccles. **ix. 10.** Pray with Moses, Psa. xc. 12.

4. *Maintain a noble detachment from the world.* We are strangers and pilgrims on earth, dwelling " in houses of clay, whose foundation is in the dust, which are crushed before the moth," Job iv. 19; tenants at will. Why then should we be so fond of earthly toys, when

> " Each pleasure hath its poison too,
> And every sweet a snare."

Our days flee away as·a shadow; it therefore " remaineth, that both they that have wives be as though they had none; and they that weep, as though they wept not: and they that buy, as though they possessed not," &c., 1 Cor. vii. 29, 30.

5. *Live in a constant readiness for your change.* The eventful hour is at hand; therefore " be ye also ready," Matt. xxiv. 48. Live as dying creatures in a dying world. Make religion the business of your lives, the controlling principle of every action. Frequently examine yourselves whether you have faith in, and love to, our Lord Jesus Christ; whether you are in possession of, or earnestly seeking, that " holiness, without which no man can see the Lord," Heb. xii. 14. " Be not deceived! God is not mocked!"

APPLICATION.

1. *To the young.* Your strength, beauty, and all other accomplishments, are only like flowers: boast not yourselves of to-morrow; rather to-day say to God, " My Father, thou shalt be the guide of my youth."

2. *To those who have escaped the dangers of infancy and inexperienced youth.* For what purpose have you been living? Has Christ had the pre-eminence, or have earthly things engrossed your affections? Forget not that you are dying creatures, and " prepare to meet your God," Amos iv. 12.

3. *To those of you whose days have dwindled to the longest span.* Your hoary locks, trembling limbs, and palsied heads, proclaim the number of your days. Are your souls ripe for the heavenly garner? If not, for once be serious; hasten to Jesus, the only shelter from the impending storm.

CHAPTER IX.

THE WAY OF SALVATION.

THE GOSPEL COVENANT.

Jeremiah xxxi. 33.--This shall be the covenant that I will make with the house of Israel: After those days, saith the Lord, I will put my law in their inward parts, and write it in their hearts, and will be their God, and they shall be my people. (Pr.

The glorious properties and holy effects of the gospel are here described and foretold, in contradistinction from the law of Moses. God had made a covenant with Israel, of which Moses was the mediator; but that did not secure the obedience of the people. He now therefore will make a new and better covenant, of which Christ is to be the mediator: and in this, the blessings of salvation are absolutely promised and made certain: ver. 31, 32.

1. The gospel is called a "covenant," a new covenant, in distinction from the ceremonial law, which was also called a covenant. It is so denominated, to intimate the certainty of the things promised, for covenants are confirmed by an oath: hence most of God's solemn promises to his people are so called.

2. It is a covenant made with "the house of Israel;" that is, the church of God, of which Israel was a type; yet not with the church immediately, but through the blood of the Mediator. The gospel is to us a matter of free promise: but in the hands of Christ it is a covenant with us, and on our behalf. He performs the conditions of it, and seals it with his blood. Making a covenant with any one is a sign of peace between the parties; and this new covenant is a sign of good will towards the house of Israel.

3. Making it "after those days," means after the abolition of the ceremonial law, and so rendering the former covenant void. The new covenant was introduced by the ministry of John; more fully by that of Jesus; and was finally confirmed by his death. The authority of the ceremonial law ceased immediately after this event, and both Jews and gentiles were considered as under a new dispensation. This subject is fully stated in the epistle to the Hebrews.

4. This new covenant implies that what the first could not secure this is intended to accomplish; and what that only shadowed forth this actually performs. The promise it contains was made after all other means failed, and when the house of Israel was gone into captivity. God had before written the law on tables of stone, and that did not succeed: now therefore he will write it on the heart, and the consequence is, that "he will be their God, and they shall be his people."

The import of these promises, and the grace discovered in them, will form the subject of our meditation—

I. Consider the import of the promises.

The leading promise in the text, and that which lays the foundation of all the rest is—"I will put my law in their inward parts, and write it in their hearts."

In general observe, this new inscription is not intended to render the written law useless. Some have imagined that the law written in the heart was to become the rule of duty, and that the other is thereby superseded: but the moral law is of eternal obligation, and can never be made void.— — —Writing it in the heart, denotes in general, an inward *conformity* to the divine

376

law, and therefore it is not the law itself.— — —The law in the heart is at best imperfect, and therefore cannot be the rule of duty.

More particularly—

1. The law written in the heart is *not any new law*, but the same as was at first impressed on the soul of man, and afterwards engraven on tables of stone. — — —Man was created after the likeness of God, in righteousness and true holiness : and was therefore perfectly conformed to the law in all its parts.

The law was defaced *by sin*, and another law introduced into our members, warring against the law of the mind ; so that man by nature is not subject to the law, neither indeed can be. Rom. viii. 7.— — —Regeneration therefore consists in new engraving that law, and re-impressing the divine image on the soul of man, which sin had defaced.

2. By writing the law in the heart is meant a giving an *inward knowledge and approbation of it*, as it is expressed in another passage. Isa. li. 7.— — — The heart is like the ark of the covenant, in which the tables of the law were kept ; it becomes the depository of this sacred trust.— — —Where the law is thus written, there is a knowledge of its purity, extent and spirituality ; an approbation of what God requires, and a devotedness to his service. Ps. xl. 8. Rom. vii. 22.

3. It includes a *supreme affection of the divine law*, and a delight in all its requirements.— — —That on which we have placed our affections is said to be in our hearts ; and there it is that God has fixed his law.— — — Before this work is begun, there is nothing but enmity to God and his government : afterwards it becomes our meat and drink to do his will.— — — The obedience rendered is not merely founded on the authority of the Lawgiver ; it is also excited by a view of the excellency and goodness of the law itself.— — —The law without commands, and the law within inclines to obedience ; so that such persons become as it were a law unto themselves.

4. It implies a *tenderness of conscience*, and a dread of sin ; a quick discernment of its evil nature, and carefulness to avoid it.— — —If the law be written in the heart, it will feel for God's honour ; and like Eli, it will tremble for the ark when it seems to be in danger.— — —This law is so deeply engraven that it shall never be obliterated ; but its characters shall become increasingly legible, and a conformity to the mind and will of God a matter of continual delight.

Another promise is, "I will be their God."—The sacred Lawgiver forbids our seeking any other god ; but we have all rejected him and sought another portion.— — —Now therefore he will himself become our portion, and will make the matter sure : we have been servants of sin, but he will make us servants of righteousness. Lev. xi. 4. Isa. xxvi. 13. Jer. vii. 23.

It is added, " They shall be my people."— — —Israel had often promised to be his people ; but they as often forsook him, and broke his covenant. Now they shall forsake him no more, nor will he forsake them forever. Heb. viii. 12. xiii. 5.

II. The grace discovered in these promises.

1. When God created man, he *made him upright;* nor could he make him otherwise.— — —Man is now corrupt and fallen : and seeing the divine law is obliterated from his heart, God might never have written it there any more. It is of free and unmerited mercy that it is otherwise.

2. Our losing the moral image of God was *a voluntary act;* if we are without it, it is what we naturally choose.— — —We love to be without God in the world, and desire not the knowledge of his ways. The carnal

mind is enmity with God, and is not subject to his law. Great therefore is the grace that could restore the divine image to such a fallen and sinful creature.

3. It is still more that he should promise to be *our God*, and ensure to us such an unspeakable inheritance— — — For God to be our friend, secures every thing; and all good is comprehendeded in it.

Inferences,

1. If ever we be saved, we see it must be by grace alone. We have nothing to glory in, for God is all in all.

2. We learn from hence, wherein true religion consists; not in being made free from the law, or treating it with indifference; but in cherishing the highest esteem for its authority.

3. The dreadful depravity of human nature, that should render an almighty work of grace necessary to restore us to a proper frame of mind, and that nothing short of our being new created should suffice.

4. Unless the divine law be written in our heart, we have no part in the covenant, and no interest in the Saviour.

SALVATION BY CHRIST ALONE.

Acts iv. 12.—Neither is there salvation in any other: for there is none other name under heaven given among men whereby we must be saved. (H. H.)

FROM the account given us of the miracles wrought by our blessed Lord, we should be led, not only to acknowledge him as the true Messiah, but to consider what we ourselves may expect at his hands. His apostles, Peter and John, had healed a man who had been lame from his birth. The spectators, filled with astonishment, were ready to ascribe the honor of this miracle to them: but they told them by whom it had been effected, even by Jesus, whom they had rejected; but who, notwithstanding their contempt of him, was, and by this miracle had proved himself to be, " the head stone of the corner." Ver. 11. They then directed the attention of their auditors to their own eternal interests, and assured them, that as Jesus alone restored the cripple to the use of his limbs, so Jesus alone could save them from everlasting perdition.*

In discoursing upon the words before us, it will be proper to notice,

I. WHAT IS IMPLIED—

Nothing can be more clearly implied than *that there is salvation for us in Christ.* It may be thought that it is unnecessary to insist upon so plain and obvious a truth, more especially among those who call themselves christians: but this truth is far from being universally known; and the grounds on which it stands are very little considered: and, if it were as well understood as we are apt to imagine, still there would be a necessity for dwelling frequently upon it, on account of its vast importance, and of " determining with St. Paul to know nothing among our people but Jesus Christ, and him crucified."

In confirmation of it, we shall appeal,

*It is evident that the text refers, not to bodily healing, but to a salvation which the apostles themselves, and all their hearers, stood in need of.

1. To the typical representations of Christ—

There were a great variety of sacrifices under the law, which typified the Lord Jesus Christ. The lamb that was offered every morning and evening, foreshewed " the Lamb of God that should take away the sin of the world:" and the scape-goat, which bore the iniquities of all Israel into an uninhabited wilderness, exhibited in yet more striking colors the removal of our guilt by a transfer of it to the head of Jesus. To dwell on all the ceremonies that were appointed on different occasions for the expiation of sin, is needless: suffice it to observe, that " the blood of bulls and of goats could not take away sin;" and that if those offerings had not respect to Christ, they were altogether unworthy, either to be prescribed to man, or to be accepted for him. But the efficacy of those sacrifices for the ends for which they were instituted, proves, beyond a doubt, the infinitely greater efficacy of that sacrifice which Christ in due time offered on the cross. Heb. ix. 13, 14.

2. To the positive declarations concerning him—

Nothing can be conceived more clear and strong than the scripture declarations of Christ's sufficiency to save. How forcibly has the prophet marked the extent, Isa. xlv. 22, the fulness, Isa. i. 18, and the freeness, Isa. lv. 1, 2, of his salvation! He invites " all the ends of the earth," even persons defiled " with crimson sins," to accept all the benefits of the gospel, " without money and without price." In the New Testament the same things are spoken with all the energy that language can afford. All, without exception, are exhorted to come to Christ, Matt. xi. 28; John vi. 37, with all assurance that he will cleanse them from all sin, 1 John i. 7; Acts xiii. 39, and bestow upon them freely all the blessings of grace and glory. John iv. 10, and vii. 37, 38. Is all this a mere mockery and delusion? It surely is so, if Christ be not " able to save to the uttermost all that come unto God by him." Heb. vii. 25.

3. To matter of fact—

We can draw aside the veil of heaven, and point to some before the throne of God, who are such monuments of grace, as leave no doubt respecting the sufficiency of Christ to save any others whatsoever. Behold that man, a murderer; a murderer of no common stamp: he was not satisfied with shedding the blood of a few of his fellow-creatures, or of those who were deserving of death; but he " made the very streets of Jerusalem to run down with blood, and that with the blood of innocents." Moreover, this was but a small part of the guilt he had contracted; so various and so enormous were his crimes. Yet is he, even Manasseh, a chosen vessel, in whom God is, and for ever will be, glorified. 2 Chron. xxxiii. 1—13.

Seest thou that woman also? We know not the particulars of her conduct; but she was so vile and notorious a sinner, that it was a disgrace to notice her, yea our Lord's condescending to notice her was made a ground of doubting his divine mission: nevertheless she also, though once possessed by seven devils, is now in glory. She received, while yet upon earth, an assured testimony, from our Lord himself, that her sins, numerous as they were, were all forgiven: Luke vii. 47, 48; and now is she singing the triumphs of redeeming love as loud as any in heaven.

We could easily refer to a multitude of others, whose enormities were beyond all measure great, who nevertheless were " washed, justified, and sanctified, in the name of the Lord Jesus, and by the Spirit of our God." 1 Cor. vi. 9—11. But enough has been said to put out of all question the blessed truth we are insisting on, namely, that Jesus is a Saviour, and a Great One, and able to deliver all who trust in him. Isa. xix. 20.

379

Let us now turn our attention to,

II. WHAT IS EXPRESSED—

What solemn asseverations are these in the text. One would have supposed that the former of them would have been quite sufficient: but the apostle thought no repetitions superfluous, nor any accumulation of words too strong, on such a subject as this. Indeed, it is of infinite importance to every one of us to know, that, as there is salvation for us in Christ, so *" there is no salvation in any other."*

1. There is not—

In whom else can we find the requisites of a Saviour? In whom can we find a sufficiency, either of merit to justify, or of power to renew, a sinner? If we should apply to the highest angel in heaven to give us of his merit, he would tell us that " he himself is only an unprofitable servant; for that he does no more than is his duty to do." Luke xvii. 10. If we should intreat him to change our hearts, he would confess his utter inability to effect so great a work. Shall we then look to ourselves? We are full of sin. Our merit is found—where? not in heaven truly, but in the lake that burneth with fire and brimstone. Rom. iii. 19. " Nor have we in ourselves a sufficiency even to think a good thought;" 2 Cor. iii. 5; much less to renew ourselves after the divine image. None but Jesus could atone for sin: none but Jesus could yield such an obedience to the law as should be capable of being imputed to others: none but Jesus can send down the Holy Spirit into the souls of men, or say to them, " My grace is sufficient for you :" 2 Cor. xii. 9; and therefore " there is no other name under heaven given among men whereby we can be saved."

If there were any other Saviour, the most eminent of God's servants would have had some intimation of it. Abraham, the friend of God, and the father of the faithful, would probably have heard of him: but he knew of none other; for he sought acceptance through Christ alone, and was justified solely through faith in him. Rom. iv. 3–5. David too, the man after God's own heart, who was inspired to write so much respecting Christ, would probably have been acquainted with such an important fact in order to his own salvation; but he sought refuge in none but Christ; " Purge me with hyssop," says he, " and I shall be clean; wash me, and I shall be whiter than snow." Ps. li. 7. We might hope at least that some information of this kind would have been given to the apostle Paul, who was more fully instructed in the mind and will of God than any other person: yet he knew of no other name but that of Jesus; he renounced all hope "in his own righteousness that he might be found in Christ;" Phil. iii. 9; and "he determined to insist on nothing, in all his ministrations, but Jesus Christ, and him crucified." 1 Cor. ii. 2.

Whether therefore we consider the insufficiency of all the creatures to stand in the place of a Saviour to us, or the utter ignorance of all the prophets and apostles respecting the appointment of any creature to sustain that office, we may be sure that there is none other than the person mentioned in the text, who is a man indeed, but is, at the same time, "God over all blessed for evermore."

2. There cannot be—

We presume not to be wise above what is written; or to say what God might have done if he had pleased : but we are fully warranted by the scriptures to say, that, consistently with his honor, as the Moral Governor of the Universe, man could not have been saved without a Mediator: nor could any Mediator besides **Jesus have** been found to execute all that was necessary for our salvation. It was necessary that the justice of God should be satisfied for the violations of his law; that his holiness should be displayed in a marked abhorrence of sin; that his truth should be kept inviolate by the execution of his threatenings; and that his law should be honored, as well by an obedience to its precepts, as by an enduring of its penalties. Now none but Jesus, who was God as well as man, could effect all these things, and therefore none but he could save us.

But there is yet another ground on which we may deny that any other could save us; namely, that if we were indebted to any other, either for righteousness or strength, we could not join in the songs of the redeemed in heaven, but must separate from the heavenly choir, Rev. vii. 9, 10, and ascribe to ourselves, or to some other, (inasmuch as we were indebted to ourselves or them,) the honor of our salvation. And how would this comport with the dignity of Jehovah, who has determined " that no flesh should glory in his presence?" It is in vain to say that the glory would ultimately accrue to him: for if we be saved by, or for, any thing of our own, we may, and must, so far take the glory to ourselves: Rom. iv. 2; and that would create discord in heaven, and be irreconcileable with the honor of the Divine Majesty.

ADDRESS,

1. The careless—

Wherefore are men so indifferent about their spiritual concerns? Is it that they are in no danger of perishing? If that were the case, why is so much said respecting salvation? and why are we cautioned so strongly against relying on any but Jesus Christ? Surely the very circumstance of Christ being sent down from heaven to die for us, is enough to alarm all our fears, and to convince us, that, if the salvation offered us could be procured by none but him, the danger of those who are not interested in him must be inexpressibly great. Let the careless then consider this; and flee for refuge to the hope that is set before them.

2. The self-righteous—

It is difficult to convince those who are looking to Christ *in part*, that they are really renouncing Christ *altogether*. But the scriptures are so plain on this point, that there cannot be the smallest doubt respecting it. Salvation is " of faith, on purpose that it may be by grace:" Rom. iv. 2; and if it be, whether in whole or in part, by our own works, it ceases to be of grace: it must be wholly of grace, or wholly of works: Rom. iv. 16; it must exclude boasting altogether, or else admit it. But boasting must be excluded wholly: Rom. xi. 6; and therefore all dependence whatsoever on our own works must be wholly and for ever renounced. Rom. iii. 27. If we will not accept salvation on these terms, " Christ shall profit us nothing." Ib. ver. 8.

3. The desponding—

The person healed by Peter and John was a very fit emblem of our state by nature and practice. " We are transgressors from the womb." But, desperate as in appearance our condition is, there is in Jesus a sufficiency of power and grace to make us whole: " his name, through faith in his name, shall give us a perfect soundness, in the presence" of God and man. Gal. v. 2, 4. Let none complain as though they were beyond the reach of mercy: for there is nothing impossible with Jesus: " with him there is mercy; with him is plenteous redemption; and he shall redeem Israel from all his sins." Acts iii. 16, and iv. 10.

THE WAY OF SALVATION.

Titus iii. 15. Not by works of righteousness which we have done, but according to his mercy he saved us, by the washing of regeneration, and renewing of the Holy Ghost. (Sk.)

IF human language present us with any word with which we should become familiar, any subject we should be concerned to understand, or any enjoyment we should be anxious to realize; that word, that subject, that enjoyment, is salvation. Salvation is the noblest science, the most invaluable acquisition, and the highest happiness. Without salvation, life is a maze of error, death a gulf of horror, and eternity a scene of punishment. Considering how important a part of a minister's duty it is to explain the nature of salvation, to correct the mistakes so common concerning salvation, and to urge upon his hearers the necessity of securing salvation, I cannot do better than recommend the text to your most serious attention. The doctrines contained in it are,

I. THAT SALVATION IS NOT EFFECTED BY HUMAN AGENCY. "Not by works of righteousness which we have done," &c. Does this position require evidence? Then consider,

1. *Where there is no salvation there are no works of righteousness.* Man is a totally depraved creature; "the imagination of the thoughts of his heart is only evil continually," Gen. vi. 5. Where then are his "works of righteousness?" Are works of righteousness the genuine effects of righteous principles? In the carnal mind these principles have no existence. For man "is very far gone from original righteousness, and of his own nature inclined to evil, so that the flesh lusteth always contrary to the spirit;" and the works of the flesh are, "adultery, fornication," &c., Gal. v. 19—21.

2. *Works of righteousness, even where they exist, possess no saving effect.* They are the evidences of salvation, and not the causes of it. They show that men are saved, but they do not operate in producing salvation. They accompany salvation, but they do not precede it. Works of righteousness possess no saving efficacy: they can never control one evil thought, conquer one evil habit, nor extirpate one evil temper; nor has God ever saved one sinner by works of righteousness.

3. *The Bible disclaims the merit of human agency in salvation,* Isa. lxiv. 6; Dan. ix. 7; Rom. iii. 20—28; xi. 5, 6; Gal. ii. 21; Eph. ii. 8, 9.

II. THAT SALVATION ORIGINATES IN THE DIVINE COMPASSION. "According to his mercy he saved us," &c. Mercy is a certain modification of love, and is that sensation of mind which inclines us to pity and relieve the subjects of misery. Love regards pleasing objects, mercy miserable objects. Adam, when he fell from God, plunged himself into misery.—His misery arose from the forfeiture of his original innocency—from the absence of his God—from his irregular and depraved passions—and from the "fearful looking for of judgment and punishment." His salvation could not originate in himself, as he could neither make an atonement for his offence, nor eradicate the principles of corruption which had taken deep root in his nature. Our salvation is according to God's mercy: it

1. *Accords with the tender sympathies attributed to that mercy.* Read the descriptions which are given of God, Psa. xxv. 6; li. 6; Isa. lxiii. 15; Luke i. 78; James v. 11. Had man been suffered to perish without an offer of salvation, his destruction might have accorded with the justice of God; but

there would have been no perceptible harmony between *his* punishment and God's *tender mercy*.

2. *It accords with the readiness ascribed to that mercy*, Neh. ix. 17. God is represented as being ready to pardon, Isa. xxx. 18. Waiting to be gracious, Micah vii. 18, delighting in mercy. Oh with what readiness did the mercy of God provide a Saviour for man, and with what willingness does the Father run to meet the returning prodigal.

3. *It accords with the descriptions given of the greatness, fullness, and extent of that mercy*, Num. xiv. 19; we read of "the greatness of God's mercy," Psa. v. 7; of "the multitude of his mercy," Neh. ix. 19; of "his manifold mercies," Psa. cxix. 64; the "earth being full of his mercy," Psa. cxlv. 8. "His tender mercies being over all his works." Our salvation accords with these descriptions, in the great and tremendous evils from which we are delivered—in the immensity of blessedness to which we are raised—in the extended and universal offers made of this salvation to mankind, and in its suitability to the unnumbered necessities of our nature.

4. *It accords with the perpetuity of that mercy.* Oh how often does that delightful sentence occur; "His mercy endureth for ever," Psa. cxviii. 1. Our salvation harmonizes with that mercy. Eternal salvation is obtained for us.

III. THAT SALVATION IS ATTENDED BY AN IMPORTANT CHANGE. "By the washing of regeneration." This term is very important and expressive; it is used to describe that inward and radical change which takes place in the human soul when it becomes the subject of salvation. This is variously represented, John iii. 3, by "born again;" Eph. ii. 10, "created in Christ Jesus;" iv. 24, "created in righteousness," &c.; ver. 23, "renewed in the spirit of your mind." But nothing can be more expressive than regeneration, which implies a reproduction or a *new regeneration*. The soul in its essence and faculties remains the same; but it has a new generation of perceptions, feelings, tendencies, and habits. This is called *washing*, perhaps in reference to baptism, which was an initiatory ordinance, to which all submitted who became proselytes to the christian religion; or to signify that regeneration purifies the soul from moral pollution, as washing does the body from the "filth of the flesh." We are saved "by the washing of regeneration," that is, delivered from sin and all its tremendous consequences in the other world.

1. Delivered from the *love* of sinful pleasures and carnal delights, by having the "love of God shed abroad in our hearts."

2. From the *guilt* of sinful practices, by having a knowledge of salvation by the remission of our sins.

3. From the *prevalence* of sinful habits, by the principles of holiness, and the power of the Divine Spirit.

4. From the *commission* of sinful acts, by the total regeneration of our natures, 1 John v. 18.

IV. THAT SALVATION IS ACCOMPLISHED BY A DIVINE INFLUENCE. "By the renewing of the Holy Ghost." All the influences of God upon the human soul, are effected by the agency of the Holy Ghost.

1. The light and information which we receive on divine subjects, are communicated by the Holy Ghost, John xiv. 26; 1 Cor. ii. 11, 12; 1 John ii. 20.

2. The conviction we have of our personal danger is derived from the same source, John xvi. 8.

3. The change which is produced in the minds of christian believers is attributed to the Holy Ghost, John iii. 5—8; 1 Cor. vi. 11; 2 Cor. iii. 18

4. The assurance of salvation is by the witness of the Holy Ghost. For this reason he is called the Comforter, John xiv. 16; Rom. viii. 16.

Inferences :—

1. How awful the delusion of those who depend on themselves or their works for salvation.

2. How deeply we are indebted to the divine mercy for salvation! Let us sing of the mercies of the Lord for ever.

3. How indispensible is regeneration! Salvation without it is impossible.

4. How deeply anxious should we be to secure the influences and agency of the Holy Ghost, Luke xi. 13.

NO REMISSION WITHOUT BLOOD.

Heb. ix. 22.—Without shedding of blood there is no remission. (S. S.)

THE external administration of religion has been extremely different in different ages of the world: but the method of acceptance with God has been invariably the same.   Before the Mosaic ritual was formed, pardon was dispensed through the blood of sacrifies: and since it was abolished, men obtain mercy through that blood, which the sacrifies both before and under the law were intended to prefigure.

To mark the correspondence between the sacrifices under the law, and that offered by Jesus on the cross, is the great scope of the Epistle to the Hebrews.   In the preceding context it is observed, that the tabernacle and all the vessels of the ministry were purged with blood; and then it is asserted as an universal truth, "that without shedding of blood there is no remission."

This assertion being of infinite importance, we shall

I. ESTABLISH IT.

The observances of the ceremonial law shew that men were saved by blood under the Mosaic dispensation

For every offence, sacrifices were to be offered according to the rank and quality of the offender: and whatever animals were sacrificed, whether bullocks, goats, lambs, or pigeons, they were to be slain, and their blood was to be sprinkled both on the altar, and on the offerer: and it was by the blood so sprinkled, that the offerer was cleansed from guilt.   If a person were so poor that he could not bring a pair of young pigeons, he was at liberty to offer a measure (about five pints) of fine flour: a portion of which, answerably to the destruction of the beasts, was to be burnt, in order to shew the offender what he merited at the hands of God. Lev. v. 6—13.

There were indeed other purifications, some by fire, and others by water: but these were for ceremonial only, and never for moral, defilement.

Thus, the law, with the one exception above mentioned, spake exactly the language of the text.

The same way of salvation still obtains under the gospel

The typical sacrifices are indeed superseded by the one sacrifice of Christ But it is through his sacrifice, and through it alone, that any man is saved

This is capable of *direct* proof from scripture.

The warning which Eli gave to his sons, when they poured contempt upon the sacrifices, and caused them to be abhorred by the people, not obscurely intimated, that acts of injustice towards men might be punished by the magistrate, and yet be forgiven through the great sacrifice: but that, if any person poured contempt upon the sacrifices, he rejected the only means of salvation, and must therefore inevitably perish. 1 Sam. ii. 17, 25.

There is yet a stronger assertion to this effect in the chapter following the text, where it is said in the most express terms, that they who reject this sacrifice have nothing to expect but wrath and fiery indignation; Heb. x. 26, 27, which could not be true if there were any other way of salvation provided for us.

It may be yet further proved by arguments, which, though of an *indirect* nature, are not the less satisfactory than the foregoing.

If salvation be not by blood *the whole Mosaic ritual was absurd.*

For what end could so many innocent beasts be slaughtered, and consumed by fire, if it were not to prefigure the great sacrifice? If they were intended to shadow forth the way of salvation through the sacrifice of Christ, there was abundant reason for such observances: and the lives of myriads of beasts were well bestowed in such a cause. But on any other supposition the legal sacrifices, having no typical reference, were unworthy of God to institute, or of man to offer.

If salvation be not by blood, *the prophets grossly misrepresented their Messiah.*

Christ was spoken of as "making his soul an offering for sin;" as having "our iniquities laid upon him;" as "wounded for our transgressions," that he might "heal us by his stripes:" Isa. liii. it was foretold that he should "be cut off: but not for himself;" that he should "finish transgression, make reconciliation for iniquity, make an end of sin, and bring in an everlasting righteousness:" Dan. ix. 24, 26. Yea, he was prophesied of as "a fountain that should be opened for sin and uncleanness:" Zech xiii. 1, and John, who was more than a prophet, pointed him out as that very Lamb of God, that should take away the sins of the world. John i. 29. Now what can be the meaning of these passages? how are they applicable to Christ, if they do not mark out his atonement? and what truth is there in such representations, if we are not to seek remission through his atoning blood?

If salvation be not by blood, *the declarations of the apostles, yea, and of Christ himself, are far more likely to mislead, than to instruct the world.*

Christ expressly told his disciples, that his "blood was shed for the remission of sins." Matt. xxvi. 28. And the apostles uniformly declare, that God purchased the church with his own blood; Acts xx. 28; that our reconciliation to God, Eph. ii. 16. Col. i. 20, and our justification before him, Rom. v. 9, together with our complete redemption, Eph. i. 7. Rev. v. 9, are by blood, even by the blood of Christ, that spotless Lamb. 1 Pet. i. 19. Is this the way to teach men that they shall be saved by their works? Must we not utterly despair of understanding any thing they have said, if we are not to expect salvation by the blood of Christ?

The apostle's assertion being thus fully established, we shall

II. Improve it.

The death of Christ has an aspect upon every thing that relates to our souls. But, not to enumerate many points, let us reflect on

1. The evil of sin

We are assured that not one sin could have been forgiven without shedding of blood. Nor was it the blood of bulls and of goats only that was necessary, but the blood of God's dear Son, even of Jehovah's Fellow ; what then must sin be, that required such a sacrifice ? We behold the evil of it in the miseries that are in the world ; and still more in the torments of the damned : but most of all do we see its malignity in the sufferings of the Son of God : without which not the smallest transgression could ever have been expiated Let us then view sin in this light, and we shall no more account it a small and venial evil.

2. The folly of self-righteousness.

Self-righteousness consists in substituting something of our own in the place of the atonement, or in blending something of our own with it. In either case we utterly make void the death of Christ. Gal. ii. 21. And what madness is this ! It is, in fact, to shut ourselves out from all hope of pardon, and to rivet our sins upon our souls for ever.

It may be thought indeed that Christ died to purchase us a right and power to save ourselves by our works. But if this was the case, why did St. Paul impute the rejection of his own nation to their going about to establish their own righteousness ? Rom. ix. 31, 32, and x. 3, and why did he desire to be found in Christ, *not having his own righteousness?* Phil. iii. 9. Why did he declare that if any man were circumcised with a view to obtain justification by the law, Christ should profit him nothing? Gal. v. 2, 4. Why did he contrast salvation by grace, and salvation by works, so as to shew that they could not be blended or consist together ? Rom. xi. 6. This alas ! is a refuge of lies, which, together will all who flee to it, with be swept away with the besom of destruction.

Let us not then dare to put ourselves in that way, wherein God declares there is no remission.

3. The encouragement which the gospel affords to sinners

When it is said that "without shedding of blood there is no remission," it is doubtless implied, that through shedding of blood there is remission. And what a glorious truth is this ? how refreshing to the weary soul ! Let it be contemplated with holy joy and wonder. There is no sin, however great, from which the blood of Christ will not cleanse the soul. 1 John i. 7. David, after contracting the foulest guilt, was yet able to say, Purge me with hyssop, and I shall be clean ; wash me and I shall be whiter than snow. Ps. li. 7. Let every one then go to the fountain opened for sin ; let him plunge, as it were, beneath that sacred flood ; and he shall instantly become pure and spotless in the sight of God. Eph. v. 25, 27.

4. The wonderful love of Christ

He knew that sin could not be forgiven, unless he would take upon him our nature, and make atonement for us by his own blood. And rather than leave us to perish as the fallen angels, he accepted the hard conditions. left the bosom of his Father, put himself in our place, and submitted to endure the penaly due to sin. O what transcendant love ! how inconceivable its heights, how unsearchable its depths ! Eph. iii. 18, 19, Let our minds dwell upon it continually ; that our hearts being warmed with this mysterious, incomprehensible love, we may be ever vying with the hosts of heaven in singing, To him who loved us and washed us from our sins in his own blood, be glory and dominion for ever and ever. Rev, i. 5, 6.

SINNERS BROUGHT NIGH BY THE BLOOD OF CHRIST.

Ephes. ii. 13.—But now in Christ Jesus, ye who sometimes were afar off, are made **nigh by** the blood of Christ. (Sk.)

THE Ephesian christians, previous to their conversion, were Gentiles, ver. 11; and thus were aliens from the commonwealth of Israel, and strangers from the covenants of promise, verse 12. The prophets had foretold that Jesus should be given "for a light to the Gentiles,"—for God's salvation to the ends of the earth, Isa. xlix. 6. Jesus came,—the Gentiles were enlightened:—the ends of the earth saw the salvation of God; and "in Christ Jesus those who had been far off, were made nigh by the blood of Christ."

The language of our text is as applicable to the state of the converted among *us* Gentiles, as it was to the case of the converts at Ephesus—for all such among us—"*Were far off,—are made nigh—in Christ Jesus,—by the blood of Christ.*"

I. WE WERE SOMETIMES FAR OFF. This intimates *distance*, and signifies that we were ignorant of God, chap. iv. 18. Destitute of his image, chap. v. 22—24. Under his displeasure, chap. ii. 1—3. Unconnected with his church, ver. 11, 12.

What a significant idea! How far were we from a true, an experimental knowledge, of God,—of the things of God: how far from any resemblance to his moral image; from any conduct, but such as merited his displeasure! And we were in disposition, in affection, equally distant from his church,— his people.

The apostle's words include another idea connected with this distance; namely, the time.

Ye were *sometimes* far off. It was with many of us a long time; with all a *miserable* time, and a *dangerous* time.

But thanks be to God! these times are passed away; our text says ye *were* far off.

Here let us pause, and think on what we *were*.

What the *peculiar nature* of our erroneous path, our remote situation, **was,** is comparatively of little consequence. Some of us were lost in the cares of the world. Some were deluded by the deceitfulness of riches. The lust of other things held some captive. While others were intoxicated by pleasure, or enchanted by worldly science, or drawn away by the meaner things which attract the attention of sordid souls. It is enough, more than enough, *that we were far from God.* Let us now turn our attention to our present situations.

II. Now ARE WE MADE NIGH. These words convey to the mind, ideas of *Relationship,—Friendship,—Union,*—and *Communion.*

Relationship. Real christians are children of God, 2 Cor. vi. 17, 18; Gal. iii. 26. They are brethren, Matt. xxiii. 8. And they are as properly related, in a religious or spiritual sense, both to God and to each other, as men are related to each other by natural ties, see John i. 12, 13; Gal. iii. 26.

Friendship. Among men of the world, all relatives are not friends; but christians are in a state of friendship with God, with Christ, and with each other, John xv. 14, 15; 1 John iii. 14.

Union. Jesus is the vine; christians are the branches, John xv. 5. **He** is the body; they are the members, chap. v. 30. They are the members, too, one of another, Rom. xii. 5; 1 Cor. xii. 12, 13. Again, they are represented as stones of the same building, Jesus being the chief corner stone, ver. 19—22.

387

Communion. They have intercourse with God, as a child with his parent, Rom. viii. 15; Gal. iv. 6, as a man with his friend. They have communion with each other, see 1 John i. 3, 6, 7; Col. iii. 16.

Thus we are made nigh; and our text leads us in the next place to consider how this blessed, this important change has been effected.

III. IN CHRIST JESUS,—BY THE BLOOD OF CHRIST.

In Christ Jesus. He is our Mediator; God with God; man with men, see 1 Tim. ii. 5; Heb. xii. 24.

It is here the distant parties meet. Here the Gentile meets the Jew, ver. 14. Here the returning sinner meets a gracious, a merciful, a forgiving God, chap. i. 6, 7, and ver. 18. Here persons that were distant, that were hostile, meet, cordially unite, and perfectly agree, see Gal. iii. 28, 29; Col. iii. 11; John x. 16. Here even Saul of Tarsus meets the followers of Jesus of Nazareth on amicable terms; and the same mouth, which before breathed out threatening and slaughter, now breathes nothing but friendship and love. Here all *real* christians of every sect and name meet: and *here* all men may know that they are disciples of Christ, because they love one another, John xiii. 35. Here, too, they all ascribe their salvation to Jesus; and glory in being "made nigh."

By the blood of Christ. Under the old dispensation, this blood was yearly typified by that of the paschal lamb, Exod. xii. 4, 5; 1 Cor. v. 7;—daily by that of the sacrificial lamb, Exod. xxix. 38, 39; John i. 29;—and frequently by that of other sacrifices, Heb. chap. ix. and x. Covenants were ratified by blood, Exod. xxiv. 8; Heb. ix. 18—20; "and without shedding of blood is no remission," Heb. ix. 22. "We enter into the holiest by the blood of Jesus," Heb. x. 19. Almost every important circumstance connected with our salvation has reference to the blood of Christ. We are *redeemed* by his blood, chap. i. 7; Col. i. 14; 1 Peter i. 19; Rev. v. 9. *Justified* by his blood, Rom. v. 9; *washed, cleansed* by his blood, 1 John i. 7; Rev. i. 5, and vii. 14; *we conquer* through his blood, Rev. xii. 11; *we are made nigh by his blood.*

The shedding of the blood of Christ was the last grand act, as a sacrifice for the sins of mankind; a sacrifice, without which we could have no hope; without which we must have perished, Acts iv. 10, 12. Well then, may such frequent mention be made of the *blood of Christ.* It is all in vain to talk of reconciliation with God—nearest to God—to the people of God, but by the *blood of Jesus.*

Let us close the subject by inquiring.

Where are *you?* Some, I fear, are still "*afar off.*" How awful is your situation! Here you assemble with the people of God; you stand, you sit near them; perhaps you dwell under the same roof with some of them; but alas! in a religious point of view, at what a vast distance are your souls from God and his people! Perhaps you stand this moment near the verge of hell! Oh, that my voice could reach and recal you! Rather, may the voice of that "blood which speaketh better things than the blood of Abel," reach you, and bring you nigh!

Ye who are made nigh! Remember where you were; remember your deliverance, and your deliverer. Think on your present situation, thus strikingly described, Heb. xii. 22—24. Let the caution, Heb. iii. 12—14, have its proper influence on your conduct; and you may with safety and propriety adopt the following triumphant language, Rom. viii. 35, 38, 39

REPENTANCE.

Mark vi 12.—And they went out and preached that men should repent.   (Sk.)

The prea:hers here mentioned were our Saviour's disciples; the time referred to, was that period of Christ's ministry, when he called unto him the twelve, and sent them forth by two and two.   But it is the *subject* of their preaching, which principally arrests our attention; they preached "that men should *repent.*"   This was exactly the manner in which the Lord Jesus, as a public teacher, began his work, ver. 14, 15, and Matt. iv. 17,—the way in which John the Baptist had commenced his, Matt. iii. 2; Mark i. 4; Luke iii. 3,—and the apostles, on the day of Pentecost, and afterwards, proceeded in the very same manner, Acts ii. 38, and iii. 19, and xxvi. 20.   We infer, that the doctrince of repentance is of primary importance; and that we should frequently make it the subject of our ministry.   Allow me to occupy the present time, in describing its *nature*, and enforcing its *necessity*.

I. The nature of repentance.   The term repentance, when religiously applied, signifies a change in the disposition of the mind from what is bad, towards that which is good, Ezek. xviii. 30; Jer. xxv. 5.   It must, indeed, be allowed that the word has a somewhat diffcrent meaning in certain passages of the Holy Scriptures; as when God is said to repent, &c.; but the former is its usual, plain, and obvious meaning; and that which I would endeavor to develop and illustrate by the following observations.

1. *Repentance begins* with a consciousness of the depravity, the guilt, and the danger connected with our fallen and unrenewed state, associated with a serious concern about the consequences, Ezek. xx. 43, and xxxvi. 31; Acts ii. 37, and xvi. 30.

2. *This view of ourselves*, if repentance be genuine, *is attended by considerable uneasiness and pain of mind*, mixed with a *godly sorrow* on account of our crimes and our danger; *sorrow*, arising as much from regret that we have offended the greatest and best of beings, as from the dread of that punishment which our sins deserve, 2 Cor. vii. 9, 10; Luke xviii. 13, 14, and xxii. 62.

3. *Another quality of true repentance* is a *hatred to sin*, shown to be real by fruits meet for repentance; such as aversion at the sight of wickedness—a constant endeavor to avoid all evil—and a sincere desire to do the will of God, Isa. lv. 7; Ezek. xviii. 21; Psa. li. 13; Acts ix. 6.   This hatred to sin is uniformly accompanied by,

4. *A desire to be delivered from sin;* from its guilt—its power—its pollation—and its consequences.   And this desire leads to a diligent and an earnest use of all the means calculated to secure such deliverance, Psa. li., *et passim.*

5. *Repentance is the gift of God,* Zech. xii. 10; Acts v. 31; and though in all its distinct operations, it may in various individuals, differ in degree, yet its nature is always the same; combining the above qualities, and constituting the only way to Christ, who casts out none that *thus* come to him for salvation.   Let us now consider,

II. The necessity of repentance.   This may be understood from the following particulars.

1. *God commands and requires it*, Acts xvii. 30.   The doctrine was delivered by the Saviour, and by the Baptist, in the form of a command: *Repent ye*, was their mode of address.

2. *All need repentance*, because all have sinned: those who have lived lives as regular as St. Paul lived previous to his conversion, as well as those whose lives have been irregular and immoral, must repent. If there be any difference, it is this, that we are not required to repent of *such* sins as we have not committed.

3. *There can be no pardon, no salvation without repentance.* So the word of God teaches, Luke xiii. 3,—so we infer from the very nature of things. Is it rational to ask for pardon, unless there be a consciousness of guilt? Would not the circumstance of offering pardon or salvation to one who felt no need of such a favor, be absurd? Would any one prize such an inestimable blessing, unless he had previously felt guilt and sorrow, and had feared the awful consequences of dying without the forgiveness of sin, and the favor of God?

From the whole of the subject,

1. *Let the mere moralist know*, that repentance is as necessary for him, as it was for the Pharisees, in the days when Christ addressed them, as in the following passages :—Matt. iii. 7, 8, and xxiii. 27, 33; Luke xviii. 9—14.

2. *Let the Antinomian know*, that he must personally repent or perish, Psa. xxxiv. 18, and cxlvii. 3, and Isa. lxvi. 2.

3. *Let every fallen professor be aware*, that he can never be restored without repentance, Rev. ii. 5.

4. *And let every sinner under heaven be assured*, that Christ is able to save unto the uttermost, them that *thus* repent and believe the gospel.

JUSTIFICATION BY FAITH.

Rom. iii. 28. We conclude that a man is justified by faith without the deeds of the law. (B.)

THESE words contain a conclusion drawn from the principles laid down in the preceding context, which we must examine, if we would understand and feel the force of the inference. Having expressed his readiness to preach the Gospel at Rome, St. Paul proceeded to show the need which all have of the Gospel, the "wrath of GOD being revealed against all unrighteousness and ungodliness of men," and to point out the wickedness and inexcusableness of the Gentiles, and also of the Jews, in evidence of which he alleges the testimony of their own inspired writers, David and Solomon, in the best ages of their church. Hence all being sinners, and involved in guilt and condemnation, and therefore incapable of being justified by the law, natural or revealed, GOD has appointed another way of justification; —we say a man is "justified by faith without the deeds of the law." It will now easily appear :—

I. WHAT IS MEANT BY JUSTIFICATION.

The justification here meant is not that which comes upon all men, even infants, through the righteousness of Christ. Ch. v. 14, 15 18. It is not that which shall take places at the day of judgment, spoken of, ch. ii. 13— 16, and by our Lord, Matt. xii. 37, which will be, not indeed by the merit, ch. vi. 23, but by the evidence of works. Rev. xx. 12; xxii. 12. It is the justification, which the true people of God experience, and possess on earth; 1 Cor. vi. 11; Tit. iii. 7; which is—not the being acquitted of all blame, or declared to be innocent, which is the meaning of the word "justified," in courts of law : Psa. cxliii. 2 ; ch. iii. 20 :—not the being made innocent, or holy, or righteous, which would confound it with regeneration or sanctification :—But the having righteousness accounted, or imputed, to us, sin not imputed, sin pardoned, or the sentence of condemnation gone out against us reversed, and our obligation to punishment cancelled, and this by a judicial act of God. This implies, and draws after it, acceptance and adoption, but differs from these things, as it does also from regeneration.

II. In what sense we are to be "justified by faith."

When the Apostle says, we are " justified by faith," he does not speak of the *moving cause* of justification, which is the divine love, mercy, or grace ; and hence we are said to be justified by grace ; ver. 24 ; Tit. iii. 4—7 : nor of the *meritorious cause*, which is the redemption of Christ ; ver. 24, 25 ; Isa. liii. 11 ; 2 Cor. v. *ult.;* and hence we are said to be "justified by Christ ; Gal. ii. 17 ;—nor of the *efficient cause*, either of the preparation necessary, as conviction and repentance for sin, or of a sense of this justification ; this is the Holy Spirit, and may be meant, Tit. iii. 7 :—nor of the *instrumental cause on the part of* God, which is his Word, viz. his declarations and promises respecting pardoning the penitent : of this our Lord speaks, John xv. 3 :—But of the *instrumental cause on our part*, which is faith—in Christ, as the Son of God, the Messiah, the Saviour, able and willing to save : John iii. 16—18 ; Gal. ii. 16 ; this implies that we come to him ; John vi. 37 ; vii. 37 ; Matt. xi. 28 ; that we trust in him, as " delivered for our offences," ch- iv. 25, trust in his blood, ch. iii. 25, and that we receive him, John i. 12,—in God, ch. iv. 24,—in his mercy and promises through Christ, ch. iv. 17—23. Those who have this faith are justified, and none without it. Thus, in different senses, we are justified, by grace, by Christ, by the spirit, by the word, by faith.

III. How this is " without the deeds of the law."

The law meant here, is chiefly the moral law, ch. ii. 17, 18, 21—23, 25. The sins mentioned in this chapter, ver 10, 18, are all breaches of the moral law ; it is this also which is meant, ch. vii.—The deeds of this law are the obedience required in it, viz. in the Ten Commandments, or in those two respecting love to God and our neighbor, which comprise all the rest. These deeds cannot merit our justification, because they cannot precede it, we neither do, nor can do them till we are justified ; then only do we begin to love and serve a pardoning God.—But how does this consist with St. James' doctrine ? ch. ii. 14—26. Abraham was justified years before Isaac was born, but his offering him up at God's command, showed the reality and power of his faith, that it wrought by love, a love to God greater than to Isaac. Thus it declared and evidenced his faith. So was Rahab's faith evidenced, and in this way our faith must be made manifest ; for the works of the law must follow our justification. Our faith must " work," Gal. v. 6 ; 1 Thess. i. 3 ; the law must be " established," ver. 31, and its " righteousness fulfilled in us," by love, ch. viii. 3, 4 ; xiii, 10 ; Gal. v. 14. We must make the law a rule of life, must view ourselves in it as in a glass, that we may see our great deficiency, and be kept in an humble disposition ; must consider it as holding out to our view that " holiness without which no man shall see the Lord."—But our obedience to the law can never merit our acceptance even after our justification ; we can claim this and eternal life solely on the ground of our justification through Christ's merits.

Inferences.

No one that is penitent need despair on account of his sins—no one should presume on account of his righteousness.—If we be justified by faith, we may be justified *now*.

NATURE OF REGENERATION.

John iii. 3.—Verily, verily, I say unto thee, Except a man be born again, he cannot see the kingdom of God. (Pr.)

In the conduct of Nicodemus, to whom these words were addressed, there are several things worthy of notice—

1. He had a *general conviction* of the truth of christianity, though ignorant of some of its leading principles. He knew that Christ was sent of God, and yet could not understand the doctrine of the new birth. This is a very common case; there are many who know that the gospel is true, who are yet unacquainted with its sanctifying and renovating influence.

2. Nicodemus being a great man, a ruler of the Jews, was in part ashamed to *own the truth,* and to be seen amongst its decided friends. He did not like to appear in the daytime, and therefore "came to Jesus by night;" but it would have been to his honor openly to have owned the cause of Christ.

3. He came to Jesus for *instruction,* but our Lord intimates that instruction was not all he needed; he must be "born again," and could not receive instruction to any saving purpose without it. Herein lies the fitness and propriety of our Lord's answer. The plainest truths are full of darkness to an unrenewed mind, because they can only be spiritually discerned. 1 Cor. ii. 14. Nicodemus however was at length brought to receive the truth in love, and he became a disciple of the Lord Jesus. John xix. 39.

I. Endeavor to explain the nature of the change mentioned in the text, or what it is to be "BORN AGAIN."

The expression is figurative, but denotes a real and important change. It is sometimes called a being "created anew" in Christ Jesus; being "quickened" from a death in sin: giving a "new heart," and putting a "right spirit" within us: being called out of "darkness," into his marvellous "light;" putting off the "old man," and putting on the "new man," and becoming "new creatures" in Christ Jesus. By these, and a variety of similar expressions, this great moral change is denoted.

1. From all these we may see, that it means something more than a bare *reformation of conduct.*— — —Such language as that in the text would not have been employed to express a mere outward change, for that may take place without any renovation of the heart.— — —Besides, Nicodemus need not have "marvelled," if this had been all; for every one would admit that some sort of morality attaches to the profession of religion.— — —Nor does it appear that Nicodemus himself needed such a change as this. He was a "pharisee," and therefore had to boast of his own righteousness; and like Paul, as touching the law he was blameless.— — —Neither was it needful for the Holy Spirit to produce such a change as this, for it might exist without his special influence, and has existed where that influence is denied.— — —The change insisted on by our Lord is effected by the agency of the Holy Spirit: it is therefore an internal change wrought upon the soul, a being "born of water, and of the Spirit."

2. Nor does it consist merely in having *the understanding enlightened,* for Nicodemus was possessed of some religious light, and yet he must be "born again."— — —There may be a great deal of light in the head, and yet the heart remain the same. Many are enlightened in hearing the word, and yet are far enough from being new creatures in Christ Jesus. They are still estranged from the life of God, and from the power of religion, notwith-

standing their superior means of information.— — —Wherein then does this change consist, and what is it to be born again?

3. To be born of the Spirit consists in *a change of heart* respecting God, and the things of God. It is a change in the disposition and temper of the mind, or the turning of the heart to God; a change in the judgment and affections, effected by the agency of the Holy Spirit. It is that change which produces repentance and faith, and from which every holy exercise of the mind proceeds, as streams from the fountain, and as branches from the root.

More particularly—

1. To be born again is to have *the image of God restored in the soul,* and to be created anew in righteousness and true holiness. As in our natural birth we are made to bear the image of the earthly, so in this the image of the heavenly.— — —Man was once in the image of his Maker; he was made upright, in the likeness of God created he him: but that image was defaced by sin, and totally lost by the fall.— — —Man in his original state was what he ought to be; his understanding was all light, without any darkness at all; his will was all rectitude, without any deviation from the standard of truth; his affections all purity, without the least defilement, and his heart was wholly on the side of God.— — —But now all is lost and gone, and we are by nature children of wrath. Regeneration is the re-impression of this image upon us, bearing a resemblance to the moral perfections of God, and being changed into the same image from glory to glory, as by the Spirit of the Lord

2. Regeneration is *the commencement of a new life in the soul,* the beginning of a new state of things. It is to become new creatures; old things are passed away, and behold all things become new, and we enter as it were into a new world.

1. It is accompanied with a new set of *thoughts and sentiments,* so that no one object of a moral kind now appears in the same light as before. All the views and prospects of the mind are changed, and we begin to know things after a different manner. We begin to have new thoughts of ourselves as sinners, and of Christ as the Saviour; new thoughts of God and his righteous government, of the law and of the gospel, of this world and that which is to come.— — —Or if our thoughts be not materially altered on these subjects generally, we are very differently affected with them, and feel a new interest in them, unknown to ourselves before.

2. It is accompanied with a new set of *affections and attachments.* We had hopes and fears, joys and griefs, pleasure and pain before; but now they are derived from a different source. We have now very different objects of desire and of dread, and sources of pleasure totally unknown before. It is all a new state, and a new world. The Lord hath led us by a way that we knew not, and in paths that we have not known. Isa. xlii. 16.

3. There is now a new set of *principles and motives.* If we attend to the same religious duties as formerly, yet it is in a very different manner. The same things which were before burdensome, are now delightful; and what was formerly done from a spirit of self-righteousness, is now done to the glory of God. Fear used to be the impelling motive, now it is love. Before, it was the hope of being delivered from misery; now it is delight in the thing itself, and the service of God is desired for its own sake.

4. There is also a new set of *companions and associates.* We had our friends and attachments, and so we have now; but they are of a different description. We are no longer strangers and foreigners, but fellow-citizens

with the saints and of the household of God. The righteous are **now the** excellent of the earth, in whom is all our delight.

These are some of the leading features of the change intended in the **text.** Let us now attempt,

II. AN IMPROVEMENT OF THE SUBJECT.

1. Let us *examine ourselves*, and what we know of this change in our own souls. Are we conscious that some such change has passed upon us? Some indeed may look back to the time when they were enemies to God at heart, and others to the time when they were in a state of indifference and un-concern; but in all real believers there is a change like that which we have briefly explained, though it may be more or less evident to those who are the subjects of it.

2. We learn from hence, what is *essential to true religion*, and to its very existence in the soul. It is in vain to think ourselves christians, unless we are born again. We know nothing as we ought to know without this, and our profession is a mere delusion.

3. We see to whom we are *indebted* for this great moral change, even to the Spirit of the living God, who quickeneth whom he will. Who made thee to differ; and what hast thou, that thou hast not received? All our sal-vation is of God, from the foundation to the top-stone thereof. Grace, grace unto it.

NECESSITY OF REGENERATION.

John iii. 3.—Verily, Verily, I say unto thee, Except a man be born again, he cannot see the kingdom of God. (Pr.)

HAVING explained the nature of the change intended; that it does not con-sist in a mere reformation of conduct, or in the understanding being merely enlightened, but in an inward change of heart, in which we are made to bear the moral image of God, and are created anew in Christ Jesus, that it is the commencement of a new life, accompanied with new sentiments and affec-tions, new principles and motives of conduct, and that this change is the im-mediate product of the Holy Spirit;—our business now will be to consider,

The necessity of this change, or why we must be born again, in order to our seeing the kingdom of God.

This necessity applies, not only to some, but to all without exception, ir-respective of our former state or character, for there is no respect of persons with God.

Here it will be proper to consider a few things which render this change of heart necessary.

The solemn asseveration of our Lord, ought indeed of itself to be suffi-cient to convince us of its absolute necessity. As a teacher come from God, his doctrine must be true, and the peculiarly solemn manner in which he speaks on this occasion, is deserving of special regard. "Verily, verily, I say unto thee, Except a man be born again, he cannot see the kingdom of God."

Other considerations however may be added, to show the necessity of this change: some of which are the following—

1. The *depravity of human nature* affords abundant evidence, that ex-

cept a man be born again, he cannot see the kingdom of God.— — —We should not need to be regenerated, if we had not first become degenerate; if not wholly ruined by sin, we should not need to be created anew and born again. The state of human nature is like the house infected with the leprosy; repairing will not do it, it must be re-constructed.— — —That which is born of the flesh is flesh : if we had any good thing in us, we need not be created anew to good works. If not dead in trespasses and sins, and beyond the hope of recovery, we need not be quickened according to the working of his mighty power, which he wrought in Christ, when he raised him from the dead.— — —But such is our state by nature, that we are wholly corrupt; there is none that doeth good, no not one; the heart is deceitful above all things, and desperately wicked; all the imaginations of the thoughts of the heart are evil, only evil, and that continually; tne carnal mind is enmity against God, not being subject to his law, neither indeed can be.— — — Such is our moral condition, and while it continues so, we connot see the kingdom of God.

2. The *nature of the heavenly world* renders this change necessary Flesh and blood in its present state, cannot inherit the kingdom of God, There must be a meetness, before we can be made partakers of the inheritance of the saints in light, and such a meetness as corresponds with the nature of that inheritance : all true enjoyment arises from congeniality, or an agreement in the disposition with the object to be enjoyed.

1. In order therefore to " see" the kingdom of God, there must be a *spiritual discernment.* All the objects of that kingdom are spiritual and holy, and cannot be known but by a spiritual and holy mind. The natural man receiveth not the things of the Spirit of God, for they are foolishness unto him; neither can he know them, because they are spiritually discerned. 1 Cor. ii. 14. Man is wholly blind to the equity of the law, and to the grace of the gospel; he sees no glory in the Lawgiver, and none in the Saviour. The eyes of his understanding must be enlightened, by the Spirit of wisdom and revelation, or he can have no perception of the moral beauty and excellency of heavenly things. Eph. i. 17, 18; Matt. xvi. 17.

2. To see the kingdom of God, we must have *a spiritual taste,* a holy relish for divine things, otherwise heaven could not be a place of enjoyment to us. The glory and happiness of the future state will eminently consist in a delightful and profound contemplation of God's perfections, in intimate nearness to him, and in having fellowship with the Father, Son, and Holy Spirit. But what fellowship hath righteousness with unrighteousness; and what communion hath light with darkness? 2 Cor. vi. 14. There is no entering into the kingdom, no enjoyment of its bliss, without an ardent relish for spiritual and holy things. 1 John i. 7.

3. The heavenly state requires a *disposition for holy activity,* a heart to love and serve the Lord. Though the redeemed shall cease from their present labors and sufferings, they shall not be unemployed, but shall serve God day and night in his temple. Heaven will be a place of unbounded activity; he maketh his angels spirits, and his ministers a flame of fire. There his servants shall serve him, with unwearied zeal and assiduity.— — —But how totally unfit for all this is man in his unregenerate state, having no heart for God, or for holy exercises; and to whom a Sabbath on earth is wearisome ! Either heaven must cease to be what it is, or the sinner's heart must be renewed.

4. There requires a thirsting and a *longing after holiness,* not only to be free from sin, but to desire it as the perfection of bliss, the very essence of

salvation.— — —But the holiness of that world would utterly confound the sinner. Isaiah, when he had only a vision of the Holy One, cried out, I am undone, I am a man of unclean lips! And when Peter had a display of the purity and glory of the Saviour, he exclaimed, Depart from me, oh Lord, for I am a sinful man.— — —What then would the sinner do? He might have some relish for a Mahometan paradise; but how could he endure the effulgence of bliss and purity which surrounds the throne of God?

In addition to the nature of the heavenly state, as rendering regeneration necessary, we might observe,

5. The *immutability of God* shows that such a change is indispensable. A change there must be somewhere, since so solemn an asseveration has been given; and if it cannot be in him, it must take place in us. If it were possible that the nature of things might alter, or that God should cease to hate evil and love holiness, a sinner might be saved without any change of heart: otherwise it is absolutely and for ever impossible. The irrevocable sentence of God is, "there shall in no wise enter into it any thing that defileth, or that worketh abomination:" but man is all uncleanness, and therefore cannot enter. If on earth two cannot walk together except they are agreed; it is impossible that a holy God and a polluted creature should dwell together in heaven.

How utterly vain then is every hope of salvation without regenerating grace: and how needful to enquire into our own state individually, and how we stand in the sight of God.

The reality of this change must be judged of by its effects, and their accordance with the Holy Scriptures. 1 Pet. ii. 1—3.

THE IMPORTANT REQUEST.

Psalm xxv. 11.—For thy names sake, O Lord, pardon mine iniquity; for it is great. (Sk.)

The absolute dependance of the creature on the Creator, renders prayer equally the duty and privilege of mankind. We are therefore taught both by reason and Scripture, " that men ought always to pray and not to faint." And though the omniscient Jehovah perfectly knows our necessities, and the blessings which we desire; " yet for all these things will he be inquired of to do them for us." And hence the righteous have in all ages, cultivated a spirit of genuine devotion, and lived in habits of gratitude and praise. Thus the royal Psalmist, as "a man after God's own heart," was deeply imbued with the "spirit of grace and supplication," and enjoyed intimate intercourse and communion with " the Father of mercies." Many of his prayers and thanksgivings are recorded in this book, which are greatly diversified in their character and tendency; and eminently suited to the various states and circumstances of the saints in every succeeding period of the church. In this psalm, David lifts up his soul to the Almighty, and boldly professes unshaken confidence in his name,—gratefully acknowledges the divine goodness,—and earnestly implores, in the text, his mercy and salvation; " For thy name's sake, O Lord, pardon," &c. This important prayer contains, an ingenuous confession of sin,—an appropriate request for pardon,—and an argumen urged to obtain success.

I. AN INGENUOUS CONFESSION OF SIN;—"Mine iniquity is great." Whether David here refers to his conduct in the matter of Uriah is very uncertain; but it is evident that he was deeply conscious of some defection from the Lord, which greatly distressed his mind, and led him to confess and bewail the greatness of his transgression. And as fallen and guilty sinners, we shall be induced to adopt a similar confession, if we seriously consider,

1. *Our sins are great in their number.* The scripture hath concluded all under sin, and the whole world is guilty before God. But all men do not run to the same excess in wickedness; yet the crimes of every sinner are *innumerable.* Sin is the transgression of the law, which is "holy, just, and good," and requires perfect, universal, and constant obedience. It is exceeding broad, extending to every thought, desire, purpose, word, and work of the moral creature. How often then do we all offend, and come short of the glory of God! How many have been the follies of our childhood,—the crimes of our youth,—and the backslidings of our riper age! How numerous are our sins of omission and commission; open and secret; in heart and life! Hence said Eliphaz to Job, "Is not thy wickedness great, and thine iniquities infinite?" And David declares, "Innumerable evils have compassed me about, mine iniquities are more than the hairs of mine head; therefore my heart faileth me."

2. *Our sins are great in their turpitude.* We are divinely assured, that "sin is an evil and bitter thing;" and the exceeding vileness and deformity of its nature, appear—*from the Being against whom it is committed,* who is infinitely great, good, and glorious, and delights in the happiness of his creatures, Psa. cxlv. 9; 1 Tim. ii. 4;—*from the dignity and circumstances of its subjects;* who are created, redeemed, and preserved for the glory of the Creator; and blessed with every privilege to facilitate their immortal interests, Rom. ii. 4;—*from the degrading characters which it sustains;* as ignorance, ingratitude, enmity, rebellion, bondage, folly, shame, disease, death, &c.,—and *from the awful effects which it produces;* in dishonoring the Almighty, rejecting the Saviour, destroying the sinner, filling the world with miseries, and hell with the vengeance of eternal fire! Behold then how horribly vile, malignant, and detestable is sin! Psa. v. 5; Jer. xliv. 4; Hab. i. 13.

3. *Our sins are great in their demerit.* The punishment due to sin must be in proportion to the majesty and glory of God, whose dignity it daringly insults, and whose law it impiously violates. Who then can calculate the wages of ungodliness, or the horrors of perdition! We may, however, partially discover the desert of sin, as exhibited in the doom of the fallen angels—the expulsion of man from paradise—the overthrow of Sodom and Gomorrah—the judgments inflicted on the wicked in every age—the evils and calamities which abound in the world—the sufferings and death of Christ for mankind—and the final destruction of the ungodly, "from the presence of the Lord, and from the glory of his power." But description fails; for language cannot express, nor the mind fully conceive, the just demerit and awful consequences of transgression. Tremble then, ye stout hearted sinners, and earnestly cry, "Save, Lord, or we perish!" And thank God, salvation is possible. Our text affords encouragement to the penitent, and contains,

II. AN APPROPRIATE REQUEST FOR PARDON;—"O Lord, pardon mine iniquity!" This ardent petition is highly impressive in its manner, and comprehensive in its import, and is strictly applicable to all who feel and lament the burden of sin; as,

1. *The language of genuine repentance.* The Psalmist was evidently conscious of the guilt and deformity of his iniquity, and was deeply humbled and contrite under a sense of his unfaithfulness. His backslidings reproved him, and he was penitently filled with his own ways, ver. 18. His unfeigned compunction of heart was accompanied with a penitential acknowledgment of sin, and earnest prayer for divine forgiveness, ver. 7. Repentance is absolutely necessary to obtain pardon, and is therefore sacredly enjoined as an imperious duty on all mankind, Acts xvii. 30. It is distinguished by deep conviction—sincere contrition—humble confession—gracious shame—practical fruits—and divine acceptance, Matt. iii. 8; Psa. li. 17.

2. *The language of devout solicitude.* David was well assured that God only could forgive his sin; and hence, in the text, he sincerely and fervently prays, "O Lord, pardon mine iniquity, for it is great." Faithful prayer is a sure evidence of true penitence, and is essentially connected with the attainment of mercy, and every spiritual blessing, Psa. li. 1; Ezek. xxxvi. 37. When Jesus Christ apprehended Saul of Tarsus, he assured Ananias of the *fact* of his repentance, by emphatically declaring, "Behold, he prayeth." And when the penitent publican went up to the temple to pray, he devoutly exclaimed, "God be merciful to me a sinner; and went down to his house justified." Penitential prayer is always characterized by sincerity of heart—humility of mind—agony of spirit—and fervency of manner.

3. *The language of humble confidence.* The royal suppliant was undoubtedly acquainted with the appointed method of salvation; and implicitly confided in the mercy and goodness of God, for the remission of his sins. He was therefore believingly induced to call on the name of the Lord, in full expectation of obtaining the blessing requested. Prayer always supposes a measure of confidence in the Being addressed, and an encouraging hope of succeeding in the object desired. Such a reverential boldness is highly necessary when we approach the throne of grace, to solicit mercy to pardon, "and find grace to help in time of need," Heb. x. 19—22. This appears to have been the devout state of the Psalmist's mind, when he presented the prayer in the text, which also includes,

III. AN ARGUMENT URGED TO OBTAIN SUCCESS;—"For thy *name's sake*, O Lord," &c. This plea is peculiarly appropriate and emphatic; and may be regarded as suggesting, that,

1. *The pardon of sin displays the glory of the divine perfections.* God's name signifies his nature; and this intimates that David expected forgiveness, solely on the ground of his infinite mercy and goodness. And if it be the glory of a man to pass over a transgression, it is surely much more to the glory and honor of God, to "pass by the transgression of the remnant of his heritage, because he delighteth in mercy." By the sovereign act of pardon, through the scheme of redemption, the glorious character of the Deity is eminently displayed, as a God of essential justice, holiness, goodness, faithfulness, and love, Rom. iii. 25, 26; 1 John i. 9. The perfections of Jehovah equally *co-operate* and perfectly *harmonize*, in redeeming and saving sinners, Psa. lxxxv. 10. "Who then is a God like unto thee, that pardoneth iniquity, and retaineth not his anger for ever?"

2. *The pardon of sin demonstrates the efficacy of Christ's atonement.* We are assured, that "without shedding of blood there is no remission." And hence the Jewish sacrifices were emblematic types and shadows of the sacrificial death of the "Lamb of God, which taketh away the sin of the world." Pardon therefore originates in divine love, and is procured by virtue of Christ's sufferings and mediation, Luke xxiv. 46, 47; 1 John ii. 1, 2

But a personal *apprehension* of his precious blood by faith, is necessary to obtain an experimental *realization* of his redeeming benefits, Gal. ii. 20 Believers thus individually *prove*, that " Christ our passover is sacrificed for us ; in whom we have redemption through his blood, even the forgiveness of our sins."

3. *The pardon of sin exemplifies the truth of the sacred scriptures.* The Lord, throughout his word, solemnly engages, *fully* to absolve the guilt of returning penitents, Exod. xxxiv. 6, 7; Isa. i. 18; Acts xiii. 38, 39. He is ever ready to forgive, and waits that he may be exalted, and glorified in our salvation. The truth of his promise is happily realized by all the subjects of pardoning mercy, who "believe with the heart unto righteousness." They faithfully credit his declarations, trust in his goodness, and, through the pardon of sin, actually experience that " all his promises are yea and amen in Christ Jesus."

In conclusion, we may warn the careless—encourage the penitent—and congratulate the saints, who have received " the knowledge of salvation, by the remission of their sins."

THE PENITENTIAL SACRIFICE.

Psalm li. 17.—The sacrifices of God are a broken spirit ; a broken and a contrite heart, of God, thou wilt not despise. (Pr.)

DAVID, deeply humbled for his sin, compares his present state of mind to a sacrificial victim, ready to be offered upon the altar. Such victims were separated from the flock or herd, and set apart for God. The penitent also separates himself from customary intercourse, and mourns apart. He no longer considers himself as his own, but the Lord's ; to whom he now dedicates himself, by a solemn and voluntary devotion. Psa. iv. 3. Rom. xii. 1.— — And as the typical sacrifices were put to death, in order to their being offered ; so the penitent becomes dead to the world, and dead to sin, and is crucified together with Christ.— — —The legal sacrifices were reiterated, year by year, and day by day, Heb. x. 11. So, though there may be special occasions for repentance as in the case of David; yet the sacrifice of a broken heart, and of a contrite spirit, must be the daily offering of every sinner who seeks acceptance with God.

I. ENQUIRE WHAT IS INCLUDED IN THIS SPIRITUAL SACRIFICE.

A broken and a contrite spirit is not merely one that is distressed, nor one that is distressed for sin. Rachel was distressed for her children, and Micah about his gods ; but it had nothing to do with true repentance. Cain and Judas sunk into despair, from a sense of guilt and wretchedness ; but in them it was that kind of sorrow which worketh death, and not that repentance which is unto life. 2 Cor. vii. 10.

1. A truly contrite spirit is deeply affected with *the evil of sin*, as it dishonors God, and is injurious to ourselves and others.— — —This is exemplified in the case of the Prodigal, Luke xv. 21 : in the case of the Publican, Luke xviii. 13 : and in that of David in the context, ver. 4.— — —The conviction of such a penitent is, that he has ruined himself, beyond the power of the whole creation to redeem ; that if God should utterly destroy him, the

sentence would be just; and if saved it must be of unbounded grace and love Ephes. ii. 4, 5.— — —A broken spirit is deeply contrite, and almost in danger of being swallowed up of grief. Psa. xxxviii. 3, 4; 2 Cor. ii. 7.

2. A contrite spirit groans under the burden of *inherent corruption*, as well as of sins actually committed: ver. 5, 6.— — —A true penitent is made to know the plague of his own heart, and to cry out for deliverance. Rom. vii. 23, 24. Hence some christians, after they have attained to a good hope through grace, and walked humbly with God for many years, complain more bitterly than ever of indwelling sin, and can find no relief but in the atoning blood. Those who seek justification from their own sanctification, invert the order of the gospel; and it is impossible that imperfect obedience should yield perfect peace.

3. A broken and contrite spirit trembles at the least indications of *divine displeasure.*— — —Not only judgments inflicted, but judgments threatened or only apprehended, fill it with dismay. Isa. lxvi. 2; Psa. cxix. 120.— — A true penitent trembles more at God's word than others do at his rod. 2 Chron. xxxiv. 18, 27; Job xxxi. 33.

4. A broken spirit patiently submits to the severest *chastisements*, and will bear the indignation of the Lord, from a conviction of having deserved it, and from the hope of future deliverance. Mic. vii. 9.— — —When God smites, the penitent also smites, and is at all times disposed to take part with God against himself. He giveth his cheek to him that smiteth him, and putteth his mouth in the dust. Lam. iii. 29, 30; Jer. xxxi. 18, 19.

II. God's gracious acceptance of such a sacrifice.

This is expressed negatively; "a broken and a contrite spirit, oh God, thou wilt not despise." It is so worthless in itself, consisting of nothing but the groans and tears of a broken-hearted penitent, that he might well despise it; but he will not. It is presented with so many imperfections, and in a manner so unworthy of his notice, that he might reject both the offerer and his sacrifice; but he will not—

1. Because he delights more in *showing mercy*, than in whole burnt offerings or sacrifices. If he accepted the sacrifices under the law, it was only as they pointed to the great atonement to be made in the end of the world, and as they were accompanied with the penitential confessions of the offerer. And now especially, as these outward sacrifices have ceased, he will accept that which is spiritual. 1 Pet. ii. 5.

2. The sacrifices of a broken heart, offered up *in the name of Jesus*, cannot fail to be accepted, because they are perfumed with his incense, and presented through his intercession. Ephes. i. 6; Rev. viii. 4.

3. God has made *many promises* to the humble and the contrite, and has testified his acceptance of them and of their offering. Psa. xxxi. 20, cxlvii. 3; Isa. lvii. 13. See the case of Ephraim, Jer. xxxi. 20; of the Publican, Luke xviii. 14; and of the woman that was a sinner, vii. 50.

Let then the trembling soul be comforted: God will not despise the day of small things, nor let us despise it. Matt. xii. 20.

INVITATION TO ENLARGED PRAYER.

Psalm lxxxi. 10.—Open thy mouth wide, and I will fill it. (Pr.)

It was a heathen practice to worship the sun and the moon; the former at the time of its rising, and the latter at the time of its change. Hence some have thought, that God appointed the time of the new moon for the worship of his courts, in order to counteract the species of idolatry.

This psalm seems to have been composed for the feast of the new moon, and perhaps for the first new moon in the year.— — —This expostulation in ver. 8, 9, is very tender: the consideration by which it is enforced is what God had done, and what he would still do for his people. If he were insufficient, they might seek after a "strange god:" otherwise they were without excuse.

The "opening of the mouth," may either allude to children who cry for food, or to one who asks a favor; and it teaches us that God is able to fulfil our most enlarged desires.

I. Explain the exhortation.

"Open thy mouth wide," that is, ask much, and God will give it: expect much from him, and you shall not be disappointed.

1. Be not content with temporal blessings, but ask for those which are spiritual and eternal. It is not unlawful to desire the good things of life, but they are not chiefly to be desired. Any one spiritual blessing is of far greater magnitude than the whole world; and if we would enjoy these, we must open our mouth wide.— — —To ask for these is to desire God for our portion: it is to ask for an interest in his heart, and not merely to the bounty of his hand, but for that which shall endure for ever.— — —For example, do not be content with a reprieve from punishment, but ask for pardon. Do not ask for what is not promised, for that you may never have; but for what is promised, that you may have abundantly.— — —Do not ask for such a kind of righteousness, and for so much religion as may pass before men; but for that in which you may stand before God.— — —Do not so much desire to be delivered out of trouble, as to get good by it.

2. Be not satisfied with a small degree of religion, but aspire after and pray for much; much of the power and much of the comfort of it. He that desires so much religion as may carry him to heaven, will never come there at all. The Lord taketh pleasure in them that fear him, in them that hope in his mercy.— — —Pray not only for that faith which is saving, but for that which is strong, giving glory to God. Not only for that love which is sincere, but for that which abounds in all knowledge, and in all judgment. Phil. i. 9. Desire to have not only peace with God, but holy freedom and intimate communion with him. 1 John i. 3.

3. Let us pray not only for those things which concern our own souls, but also for the good of the souls of others; for the good of the cause of Christ, and his kingdom at large.— — —Keep not silence, and give him no rest, until he establish and make Jerusalem a praise in the earth. Isa. lxii. 6, 7. Ask to be blessed in the blessedness of God's chosen, and to see the good of his nation. Seek the salvation of others, and you will find your own. Psa. cvi. 4, 5.

4. Ask all in faith. Faith in the divine promises is of great importance in enlarged prayer. Much of our coldness arises from unbelief: if we believe. we shall receive. John xv. 7.

401

II. ENFORCE THE EXHORTATION.

Consider what need there is for enlarged prayer, and why we should open our mouths wide in seeking God—

1. Our wants are very great and pressing. We are immortal, guilty, dying creatures. Think of what we are capable of suffering and enjoying. An eternity of bliss or woe is before us : we are candidates for the one, and if we miss it, we fall into the other.— — —How important and interesting is our situation : we are walking as it were on a narrow bridge, with an unfathomable gulf on either side. Crowns of glory are before us, and the pit of perdition is beneath us.

2. Great as our wants are, they are not too great for God to supply.— — His heart is large and he will give us according to his riches in glory. Phil. iv. 19. Open thy mouth wide, and he will fill it.

We may judge of the liberality of another, partly by his words, if he be faithful, and partly by his actions : and in this way we may know something of the divine beneficence.— — —His promises are a faithful index to his heart, and these are exceedingly great and precious. "I will be their God : their sins and iniquities will I remember no more : I will never leave them nor forsake them." Psa. xlviii. 14 ; Isa. xli. 10. We may also know what God will do for them that ask, by what he has done already. Consider what he did of old for the Patriarchs, and for Israel : how he pardoned, blessed, and saved them.— — —But more still since then, in the gift of his Son : and how shall he not with him also freely give us all things. Rom. viii. 32.

3. The redemption of Christ Jesus is also large. By it provision is made for all our wants, and a medium for the conveyance of every blessing. On this ground it was that our Lord encouraged his disciples to ask largely in his name. John xvi. 23, 24.— — —The love of God to sinners wanted a medium by which to express itself, like the soul of David towards Absalom ; and the sufferings of Christ as our substitute sufficiently proved, that God was the enemy of sin, while he was the sinner's friend. Rom. iii. 26.— — Divine love also wanted something worthy of being rewarded. God would have given us eternal life, but there was nothing to justify its bestowment. Man by sin became utterly unworthy : but in Jesus he is well pleased : let us therefore come boldly in his name. Ephes. iii. 12 ; Heb. iv. 16. If we receive and enjoy but little, it is because we ask but little, and do not ask in faith. James iv. 2, 3. 1 John v. 14.

THE GOOD OLD WAY.

Jeremiah vi. 16.—Thus saith the Lord, Stand ye in the ways, and see, and ask for the old paths, where is the good way, and walk therein, and ye shall find rest for your souls.

It is the Lord that speaks in our text, and when he speaks, it is both our duty and interest to obey his voice. It is our *duty;* for he is our rightful governor : "It is he that hath made us, and not we ourselves; we are his people, and the sheep of his pasture." His hands have made and fashioned us, and we should therefore pray for understanding that we may learn his commandments. It is our *interest* to obey the Lord ; because the way of holy obedience is the only way to escape eternal misery: "for unto them that are contentious, and obey not the truth, but obey unrighteousness, indig·

nation and wrath, tribulation and anguish" will be certainly rendered by the righteous Judge of all. To obey the Lord is also conducive to our happiness ; for he is the Lord our God, who teaches us to profit; and in consequence of hearkening to his commandments, our peace will flow as a river. The work of righteousness is peace ; and all the ways of wisdom are ways of pleasantness. This is confirmed by the declaration in our text, " Stand ye in the way, and see," &c. That we may seek and find the rest thus promised, let us consider,

I. THE WAY HERE RECOMMENDED. Here observe,

1. *The way itself;* called the good old way. This cannot be the way of the wicked ; for their way is not a good one, Ps. xxxvi. 4, Neither is it the way of peace and rest, Isa. lvii. 20, 21. It must be the way of *Scriptural piety;* that way prescribed by God in his word, Ps. cxix. 1, 165. This way, we find represented by St. Paul as comprising, "faith that worketh by love," Gal. v. 6. *Faith in Christ,* or *receiving* him in all his offices, as our Teacher, Sovereign, Redeemer, and Benefactor, Matt. xi. 28—30; John i. 12 ; and *walking* in him as we have received him, Col. ii. 6. *And love as the fruit and effect of this faith,* 1 Tim. i. 5. This charity includes love to God and all mankind, Matt. xxii. 36—39. And this love is the sum of all God's moral precepts, Rom. xiii. 10 ; Matt. xxii. 40.

2. *This course of faith and love is called a way.* It is so called, because it *leads* to the enjoyment of *eternal life,* Matt. vii. 14 ; Ps. xxxiv. 34. It is the *certain* way to eternal life, Rom. ii. 7 ; Ps. lxxxiv. 11.—And it is the *only* way to eternal life, Heb. xii. 14 ; Matt. vii. 21.

3. *It is called the old way.* This it certainly is with regard to us, because it is at least as old as the *reformation.* This is incontestable, when we appeal to the history and the writings of all our most renowned divines, through whose instrumentality the reformation was so happily effected.—It is as old as *Christianity.* This is evident from the doctrine of our Lord himself, John xiv. 1, and xv. 12, and of all his apostles. Witness Paul, in those passages above referred to ; Peter, 2 Pet. i. 5—7 ; and John, 1 John iii. 23. It is as old as the *Mosaic dispensation:* For Moses himself was actuated by faith, Heb. xi. 24—27. And he repeatedly taught the way of love, both towards God and man, Deut. vi. 45; Lev. xix. 18.—It is as old as the *patriarchial ages;* as the days of Noah, Heb. xi. 7; as the days of Enoch, Gen. v. 24 ; Heb. xi. 5; as the days of Adam, Heb. xi. 4. And it must have been as old even as the days of Adam, when in a state of innocence : for he was made upright, Eccles. vii. 29; and as such, he could not but believe in God and love him.

4. *It is called the good way:* and this it evidently is, because *those who walk in it are good,* James iii. 17 ; Eph. v. 8, 9.—Because *those who walk in it do good.* They prove general blessings to their *families,* Deut. v. 29; to their *country,* Proverbs xiv. 34 ; and to the *world* at large. Matt. v. 13, 14.—And because the *way itself is good.* It is good in its *origin,* being prescribed by infinite goodness, Ps. cxliii. 10 ; and it is good in its *tendency,* leading to the happiest results, Prov. xix. 23. That we may enjoy the benefits of this way, let us consider

II. GOD'S COMMANDS RESPECTING IT. " Stand ye in the ways," &c.

1. *Stand ye in the ways and see.* In this part of God's counsel, some facts are assumed, and some duties are enjoined.—*Some facts are evidently assumed :* as that though there is but *one good* way, yet there are *many evil* ways : for instance, there are the ways of open and secret sin, of irreligion, of self-confidence, formality, and apostacy.—That *all* mankind by nature are

walking in *some* evil ways, Isa. liii. 6.—That we are naturally *ignorant* of the good old way, Jer. x. 23.—And that in the use of proper means we are capable both of *discovering* it, and *walking* in it. Hence we find in this counsel.—*Some duties evidently enjoined.* "Stand ye in the ways and see." *Stand;* make an immediate *pause* for the purpose of *consideration*, Hag. i. 5.—And *see;* seriously *examine* in what way you are walking. Is it in the way of outward or secret sin? or irreligion? or self-confidence? or formality? or apostacy? "Let every man prove his own work," 2 Cor. xiii. 5. Observe well the *tendency* of every evil way. Look before you, and consider whither it leads; it ends in death, Rom. vi. 21.

2. *Ask for the old paths: where is the good way?*—Inquire—By *searching the scriptures*, John v. 39. This is the *map* that describes it.—*By asking direction of God;* who is ready to give it, James i. 5; Prov. ii. 3–5. By *associating with the pious;* who are walking in it, Prov. xiii; 20.

3. *And walk therein.* This command requires you—*To get into it.* Do not remain out of it by delay, Job xxii. 21; and xxxvi. 18. Do not stop short of it, by resting in deficient attainments: as merely talking of it, thinking aright concerning it, and desiring it. Get into it, by coming to Christ as he invites you, Matt. ii. 29; and by coming to God by him, John xiv. 6; Heb. vii. 25.—*To keep in it*, by steadfast resistance of temptation, 1 Pet. v. 8, 9: Luke xxi. 36.—And *to go forward in it,* by improving in piety, 2 Cor. vii. 1; 2 Pet. i. 5—11. Having considered God's command respecting this way, observe

III. THE PROMISE BY WHICH HE ENCOURAGES US TO OBEY HIM :—"And ye shall find rest for your souls." Here observe,

1. *The blessing promised;*—"Rest for your souls." *Rest*—*gracious rest in this world;*—from the anguish of guilt, Isa. xii. 5;—from the oppression of Satan, Matt xi. 28;—from tormenting fears, Ps. xxxiv. 4:—from inward defilement, John xv. 2; 1 John i. 9;—and rest in the pleasant service of a beloved master, Matt. xi. 30; 1 John v. 3.—*Glorious rest in heaven*, Heb iv. 9;—from all temptation, Job iii. 17: from all suffering, Rev. xxi. 4:—and from all danger, Matt. vi. 20.—Rest for your souls. Rest attended with *consciousness* of enjoyment in this life, Rom. viii. 1, 2; and after death, Rev. vii. 14, 17. Rest, such as your souls require, because it is *eternal*, Ps. xvi. 11.

2. *The certainty of our obtaining it;*—"Ye *shall* find rest for your souls." On your seeking it as God requires, it is certain,—from God's *allsufficiency:* he who promises it is the Lord, who has it to give, Gen. xiv. 22.—From his *kindness:* he calls you to enjoy it, Isa. xlv. 19;—and from his *truth:* he engages that you shall find it, 1 Thess. v. 24.

APPLICATION.

These words show us the falsehood of some common objections to a course of piety;

1. " *That this strict religion is a new way!*" No, it is the old way: sin is the new way, devised by Satan, for the purpose of leading men to hell.

2. *That it is an injurious way, unfavorable to the interests of mankind!*" No, it is the good way, and most highly beneficial, 1 Tim. iv. 8; Prov. xii. 36.

3. " *That it is a melancholy way!*" No, it is the way of peace and rest: peace through life, Luke i. 78, 79; peace in death, Ps. xxxv i; and rest for ever. Rev. xiv. 13.

THE VITAL EFFICACY OF FAITH.

James ii. 26.—For as the body without the spirit is dead, so faith without works is dead
also. (Sk.)

THE subject of discussion in this chapter, is the practical tendency of
genuine faith. It appears that many persons in the apostolic age perverted
the doctrines of the gospel. Though they professed to embrace Christianity,
their faith did not produce the fruits of a holy life and heavenly conversation.
The apostle, therefore, shows them the utter insufficiency of such an empty
profession; and the absolute necessity of that faith which invariably demonstrates the genuineness of its character by the efficacy of its influence. He
faithfully reproves them for their unjust partiality, and affectionately inculcates the practice of piety as the result of unfeigned faith. And to enforce
this impressive doctrine, he appeals to certain well known examples of faith
and obedience. He distinctly specifies Abraham and Rahab, who evinced
the reality of their faith by their works; the former, " when he offered Isaac
his son upon the altar;" and the latter, when at the peril of her life she concealed the Jewish spies. From these premises the apostle draws the interesting conclusion in the text;—"For as the body without the spirit," &c.
These words bring before us the subject of christian faith, and suggest to
our consideration the necessity of its possession,—the excellency of its character,—and the efficacy of its principle.

I. THE NECESSITY OF ITS POSSESSION. This the apostle assumes; nor does
he enter into any general description of its abstract nature. He simply represents it as an *essential* and *vital* principle of genuine piety, which displays the reality of its existence by the purity of its influence. And as the
spirit is necessary for the existence of the body, so faith is indispensable to
the possession of pure and undefiled religion. And hence,

1. *It is a duty divinely required.* It is the very foundation and principle
of vital godliness. The existence and perfections of the Deity, demand its
vigorous exercise: for without faith it is impossible to love or please God,
Heb. xi. 6. The written revelation, also, of his will, is the *ground* and
rule of living faith; and enjoins it as the indispensible duty of mankind, 2
Chron xx. 20; John vi. 28, 29 , xx. 31; 1 John iii. 23. And whatever is
commanded by God, is unquestionably the incumbent obligation and reasonable service of his intelligent creatures; for he requires nothing but what is
perfectly wise, " holy, just, and good."

2. *It is the only way of salvation.* We are condemned by the law as
transgressors; and we cannot escape its final penalties, by any thing that we
can *do* or *suffer*, Rom. iii. 19, 20. But Christ hath redeemed us from the
curse of the law, being made a curse for us." He is therefore the *way* to
the Father, and the only medium of salvation, John xiv. 6; 1 Cor. i. 30.
But it is only *by faith*, that we can realize an interest in him as *our* Saviour;
" He that believeth not is condemned already," Mark xvi. 16; John iii. 16
—18; Acts x. 43, xvi. 30, 31. Some, however, have thought that there is
a manifest opposition between St. Paul and St. James on this subject; but
this cannot exist in reality, because they both wrote by the inspiration of the
same spirit. But in describing the same doctrine under *different views* and
circumstances, they naturally adopted a different mode of expression, while
they maintained perfect unity of sentiment, Rom. iv. 3; James ii. 23.

3. *It is an essential property of religion.* It is the most distinguishing
principle of christianity, and the distinctive character of the righteous.

Without faith all external professions and ceremonies are vain, Gal. v. 6. It is necessary for the attainment of every spiritual blessing, and the perform ance of every christian duty, " for whatsoever is not of faith is sin " It is connected with every hallowed principle, disposition, enjoyment, and practice; and is the very *life, spirit* and *energy* of personal religion, which is significantly called, " the *work* and *profession* of faith." And as closely connected with the necessity of this gracious principle, we must consider,

II. THE EXCELLENCY OF ITS CHARACTER. This is evident from the scriptures in general, and especially from the testimonies of Jesus Christ and his apostles. It is emphatically called " precious faith," and exceeding great and glorious things are spoken of it in the inspired memorials of the saints. In this chapter, St. James admirably describes it as a principle of inestimable value, and the distinguishing excellence of our holy religion. And this will appear, if we observe,

1. *Faith is divine in its Author.* It is not the mere effort of reason; it is the special *gift* of God's grace, Eph. ii. 8; Col. ii. 12. He reveals the object—enjoins the duty—imparts the power—and inspires the grace of faith. But still it is a *personal act* of the mind, by which we credit divine truth— embrace the Saviour—and obtain salvation. No man can believe without supernatural aid; but by the ability which the Lord bestows, the obedient penitent " believes with the heart unto righteousness," and continues coming, trusting, and " looking unto Jesus, the author and finisher of faith," Heb. xii. 2.

2. *Faith is vigorous in its operations.* It is not an empty *notion*, but a living *principle*. This distinction is very important, and is clearly described by our apostle, ver. 18–20. It is possible to have many general *notions* and speculative *opinions* in religion, when we are utterly destitute of *living faith*. When faith is merely *notional*, it is fruitless; but when it is *genuine*, it produces the most gracious effects. As a principle of spiritual *life*, it quickens all the powers of the soul, and brings them into constant exertion, Gal. ii. 20. It grasps the Deity—lays hold on the Saviour—renders him precious to the soul—embraces the divine promises—resists evils and temptations—promotes stability and diligence—and endures tribulations, as " seeing him who is invisible," 2 Cor. v. 7; Heb. x. 38.

3. *Faith is consoling in its prospects.* It looks not at the things which are seen, but at those things which are not seen. It is accompanied with a consciousness of the divine favor, and an assurance that " all things will work together for our good." It affords consolation under every trial, and enables the christian to "glory in tribulations." It far exceeds the glimmering rays of reason, and mysteriously *penetrates* and *grasps* the invisible realities of immortal bliss, 2 Cor. v. 1; 1 Pet. i. 8, 9. Faith thus cheers the mind, en courages the hope, and animates the pursuit, of the believer, and supplies the place of present vision, by becoming " the *subsistence* of things hoped for, and the *demonstration* of things not seen." From this description of the excellency of faith we may easily discover,

III. THE EFFICACY OF ITS PRINCIPLE. This is distinctly asserted in the text. The comparison is peculiarly elegant and impressive. As there can be no living human body without a spirit, even so there can be no saving faith without good works;—" For as the body," &c. When faith is genuine, it always promotes,

1. *Works of purity and holiness.* It teaches its possessors to "come out from the wicked, and be separate, and touch not the unclean thing." They are deeply convinced of the exceeding sinfulness of sin, and abhor it as that

" abominable thing which the Lord hateth." They also discover the moral beauty of holiness, and practically " adorn the doctrine of their Saviour in all things," Tit. ii. 11—14. Their faith produces a hallowing influence, both on their minds and morals ; and as a tree is known by its fruits, so true faith is distinguished by its legitimate effects of " holiness and righteousness of life," Matt. vii. 17—20.

2. *Works of conquest and triumph.* The warfare of christians is called. " the good fight of faith." They are surrounded by numerous enemies, Eph. vi. 12. But *mighty faith* subdues sin—resists Satan—conquers the world —and triumphs over affliction, death, and the grave, 1 Cor. xv. 55–57; Heb. xi. 24, 25 ; 1 Pet. v. 8, 9 ; 1 John v. 4. Thus by faith the patriarchs, prophets, and apostles, were "more than conquerors through him that loved them," and obtained the crown of eternal life, Heb. xi. 32–39 ; 2 Cor. iv. 10–13.

3. *Works of love and benevolence.* When we believe in Christ, the love of God is shed abroad in our hearts ; for faith works by love to God and all mankind; even to our enemies, Matt. v. 44.

4. *Works of zeal and perseverance.* The true believer is always zealously affected in the cause of Christ. He greatly rejoices in the prosperity of Zion, and mourns when she declines. He prays for the extension of the Redeemer's kingdom, and endeavors to promote the cause of righteousness and peace, Hab. iii. 2 ; Rom. x. 1. Under the animating influence of faith, we shall never grow weary in well-doing but " always abound in the work of the Lord, till we receive the end of our faith, even the salvation of our soul.

We may learn from this subject,

1. The necessary union between faith and works.
2. The duty and importance of self-examination.
3. The peace and felicity of " holding fast faith and a good conscience.

GOD'S METHOD OF HEALING, OFFENSIVE TO THE PRIDE OF MAN.

2 Kings v. 12.—" Are not Abana and Pharpar, rivers of Damascus, better than all the waters of Israel? may I not wash in them, and be clean ?" (Sk.)

" ALL scripture," saith Paul, " is given by inspiration of God, and is profitable—for instruction in righteousness." *All* scripture, not particular parts or books only, but *all* and *every* part of it. Hence those who confine themselves to particular passages, and do not read the whole, deprive themselves of much important instruction. Not only may we derive profit from those facts which are immediately connected with the redemption of the soul,—or from the prominent doctrines of the gospel,—or from the precepts or promises of Christianity, but also from those parts which do not appear to have any connection with the gospel, or any particular bearing towards Christ. An attentive examination of many of these will show us how much we need Christ, and will lead us to prize his gospel. As there is no village in the kingdom from which a way may not be found to the Metropolis so there is no passage in the Bible which may not be connected with Christ.

Many of the historical parts of scripture, though they say nothing of Christ, abound in instruction. They exhibit many a beacon to admonish us of danger, and many a light to direct our course. In them we see men placed in a variety of situations, and under various aspects of providence, by which human character is developed, and the secret springs of moral actions are made manifest. Such histories instruct us in the knowledge of the human heart, a knowledge which in point of importance is second only to the knowledge of God. The history before us is of this character. Let us lift our hearts to the Father of lights, that we may be instructed. Our text suggests a variety of ideas, to which I shall call your attention in succession.

I. THAT GREAT MEN ARE NOT EXEMPTED FROM THE EVILS WHICH ATTACH TO OUR COMMON NATURE. Naaman was a great man, a commander-in-chief of the Syrian forces, a man honorable and valorous, but he was a leper. From one class of evils riches might exempt their possessors— the evils of poverty, perplexity, anxiety and embarrassment. But in many cases the opulent, through habits of vice. which are always expensive, or from a silly vanity to appear greater than they really are, participate as largely in these evils as the humblest tradesman. But from other ills they have no exemption.

1. *None from those which attach to the body.* None from *affliction* in its almost endless diversity, sometimes affecting the body, sometimes the mind- and sometimes both. None from *disappointment.* Man the is creature of hope, but his hopes are frequently not realized. His heart is fixed on a particular object, from which he expects to derive perpetual pleasure; but either it is removed out of his sight, or the supplies it sends forth are scanty, and but at intervals, or instead of being a never-failing spring of pleasure, it becomes a fountain of pain, and anguish, and misery. None from *death.* The sentence is pronounced upon all, " Dust thou art, and unto dust shalt thou return ;" which with equal promptness is executed in the palace, as in the cottage, upon the prince. as upon the peasant.

2. *None from those which attach to the soul.* Great men like others are involved in the effects of the original transgression : born in sin : in whose nature is sown a corrupt seed which vegitates without the counteraction of divine grace ; grows with their growth, and strengthens with their strength, till it becomes a great tree producing wild grapes. Their hearts contain a principle of rebellion, which ramifies itself through all the faculties of the soul, darkening the understanding,—perverting the will,—depraving the affections,—corrupting the memory,—and producing overt acts of rebellion in the life. *Great men*, like others, "are by nature children of wrath," and liable to eternal death. But it is pleasing to remark,

II. THAT THERE ARE NO EVILS ATTACHING EITHER TO BODY OR SOUL, WHICH GOD CANNOT REMOVE.

1. *He can heal the body.* This he can do either with or without means. Sometimes he heals miraculously,—such were many of the cures wrought by our Lord,—by his apostles,—such also was the resuscitation of the Shunamite's son by Elisha,—and of Lazarus, and the widow's son by Christ. But though he could have done every thing without means, he has chosen to do almost every thing with them both in nature, in providence, and in grace. He could have so constituted man as that food should not have been necessary to his sustenance; or he could have caused food to have been spontaneously produced without any labor on his part. But he has done neither. Man requires sustenance; and to obtain it he must plough, and sow, and reap He could have accomplished all the revolutions which have taken place in the world by his own fiat, without employing a single instrument; but instead of doing so, to accomplish the changes which have been effected, he has em-

ployed a Moses—a Cyrus—an Alexander—a Cæsar—a Titus—a Cromwell —a Bonaparte—and a Wellington. He could have irriadiated the minds of the whole human race, and perfectly instructed them in the knowledge of his character and will by the immediate inspiration of his own Spirit, without either Bibles or ministers; but he has not done so. On the contrary, in grace, as in nature and providence, he accomplishes the purposes of his will by a continual instrumentality. In conformity with his general plan, he appoints means in the case before us, verse 10.

2. *He can heal the soul.* By applying the sacred balm of pardoning mercy to the wounded conscience—by secretly, but powerfully operating upon the *will,* and giving it a new direction—by purifying and elevating the affections by strengthening *the moral powers* through the "law of the spirit of life in Christ Jesus, making us free from the law of sin and death,"—and by making the memory the depository of soul purifying truths. It is however deeply to be lamented,

III. THAT THE SIMPLICITY OF GOD'S REMEDIES ARE FREQUENTLY OFFENSIVE TO THE PRIDE OF MAN. Look at the case before us. What could be more easy than the remedy suggested? "Go, and wash in Jordon seven times." But its simplicity was that which rendered it objectionable with Naaman. Besides, he had previously arranged in his own mind how the cure was to be performed, verse 11. The patient dictated the plan of his own cure, and because the physician prescribed a different one, he was indignant. This spirit of proud dictation to God, directly opposed to that childlike docility with which we should always contemplate him, has frequently led to the rejection of his plans.

1. *It led the Jews to reject Christ.* They desired the Messiah, as Naaman desired a cure. But as Naaman had previously determined by what process the cure was to be effected, so they had formed in their minds what kind of Messiah he was to be. He was to be a great man, an illustrious prince, and a mighty warrior. He was to emancipate the Jews from vassalage, to conquer the Romans, and to extend his dominion from sea to sea, and from river to the ends of the earth. But because their carnal expectations were not realized, they put him to death.

2. *It leads many to reject the peculiar doctrines of the gospel.* The divinity of Christ,—the doctrine of the atonement,—and spiritual regeneration. Why is the divinity of Christ, for instance, rejected? Because the scriptures do not teach it? Impossible; for to him they ascribe the *name,* and *attributes,* and *works,* and *worship* of Jehovah. No, it is because men bring a previous creed to the Bible, instead of deriving their creed from it. They melt the Bible into the mould of their opinions, instead of melting their opinions into the mould of the Bible.

3. *It hinders many from closing in with God's method of justifying the ungodly.* He offers a free pardon to men as sinners, The pride of the human heart rejects this, and brings a price,—comparative innocence,—works of righteousness,—acts of charity,—or tears of penitence. The price is already paid and accepted, and the salvation already purchased can only be received by men as sinners who have nothing to pay. There is no royal road to the favor of God, any more than to learning; no, the rigid moralist and the profligate must be justified on the same terms. But,

IV. WHEN GOD'S REMEDIES ARE ADOPTED, THEY NEVER FAIL TO SUCCEED. Look at the case before us, verse 14. In the cures by the brazen serpent,—in the case of the man whose eyes were anointed with clay,—in the conversion of St. Paul,—of the Phillippian jailer,—of the great **cloud** of witnesses in every age, and especially of the present. Conclude,

1. *With an address to those who are insensible of their disease.* See how the moral leprosy has affected all your powers.

2. *Address those who desire to be healed.* The Jordan is flowing,—the fountain is open.—Come now, wash and be clean.

THE SINNER'S REFUGE.

Hebrews vi. 18.—That by two immutable things, in which it was impossible for God to lie, we might have a strong consolation, who have fled for refuge to lay hold upon the hope set before us. (Pr.)

THE apostle was greatly concerned for the perseverance of those who professed to believe in Jesus; when some of them seemed to turn back, he labored with all his might to reclaim them. In some parts of the epistle he appears to deal sharply with them, in the beginning of this chapter especially, he faithfully warns them of the danger of apostasy; yet towards the close, he holds up the greatest encouragement to a perseverance in faith and holiness.

J. The description given of a true believer: " HE HAS FLED FOR REFUGE."

The allusion is to the cities of refuge under the law, which were provided for the manslayer. Deut. xix. 1—6.

The words before us are full of meaning, and contain three things in particular worthy of notice—

1. *The sinner's dangerous condition* is fully implied.— — —He is exposed to some evil which threatens to overtake, and to overwhelm him with misery: this is common to all sinners.— — —Death, like the avenger of blood, is out after him, and will soon overtake him.— — —Wrath is in pursuit of him, and will finally come upon him, if he should not have reached the city in time.— — —The sinner has transgressed God's holy law, and is under condemnation. If death should overtake you, ere you reach the city of refuge, you perish forever. Do not trifle therefore, do not loiter; but flee for thy life.— — —Men would not be indifferent where life was in danger: and shall we, while our souls are in danger of the wrath to come !

2. Observe *the refuge provided.* This is called " the hope set before us." — — —There can be no doubt what this means: it might be doubtful to some under the Old Testament, but surely it is not so to us.— — —Christ crucified is the hope of the hopeless, and the only name given under heaven whereby we must be saved.— — —This is the Lamb which God has provided for a sin-offering: his death is the only source of our life: here is a full salvation, sufficient for the chief of sinners. John iii. 14.— — —If we confess our sins, he is faithful and just to forgive. 1 John i. 9. In him all the threatenings of God are turned away, and there is no more wrath; there is no objection from the nature, the number, or the aggravations of our offences. Isa. i. 18; Matt. xii. 31.

Hither it was that David fled, saying, Purge me with hyssop, and I shall be clean.— — —This is still the refuge of poor sinners, and here only can we find safety.

This hope is said to be *set before us.* God has set before us in his word, Christ and him crucified; and has called our attention to this as the only foundation of hope. Isa. xxviii. 16.

He is a refuge *near at hand*, or immediately " before us." No circuitous ways of preparation or amendment are prescribed : we are directed to look to him and be saved, to believe on him and receive eternal life.— — —Were it otherwise, what had been the condition of the dying thief. Behold, I bring near my righteousness, and my salvation shall not tarry. Isa. xlvi. 13.

The way also is *made plain*, that those who flee for refuge may not be hindered in their flight. Deut. xix. 3.— — —The sinner's refuge is set so fully in view by the gospel, that every faithful minister, every true believer can direct you to it.

3. The *state of mind necessary to our fleeing to it.*— — —Nothing indeed is nesessary as a qualification, nor as giving us a right warrant to come, but the free invitations of the gospel to the most unworthy.— — —Any sinner may come, but every sinner will not come; only those who believe in Jesus.

Fleeing to this refuge implies *a sense of our sinful and dangerous condition.*— — —This Paul had by means of the law : without this we are whole, and need not a physician. Those who flee for refuge are such as see themselves to be wholly sinful, and that God's displeasure against them is altogether just.

It implies also our understanding and *believing the gospel.* It is not merely being driven by fear, but drawn by love.— — —It is to have all our unwillingness removed, and to fall in with God's way of salvation with the whole heart.

II. The ground which God has given to such for " STRONG CONSOLATION."

Two things are mentioned, and they are both immutable; the promise, and the oath of God. Thus the Lord gave hope and comfort to Abraham, and thus he gives strong consolation to believers in Christ: ver. 13.

And why did he give the promise and the oath? He did so to *Abraham*, in order to meet all his unbelieving fears, arising from the difficulties he had to encounter, and because of the length of time he would have to wait for the performance of the promise.

To us also God has promised and sworn to give eternal life, if we believe in his dearly beloved Son.— — —Unbelief might suggest, "I am too sinful and unworthy, or there are insuperable difficulties in the way, and I shall never obtain the prize." But the promise and the oath contain an answer to every objection, and afford ground to the strongest assurance.

1. We see what encouragement there is for us as sinners to come to Christ. We come not with uncertainty, but under the sanction of a promise.

2. The motive for perseverance. If we hold out to the end, it will issue in eternal life.

THE PENITENT MALEFACTOR.

Luke xxiii. 40—43.—But the other answering, rebuked him, saying, Dost not thou fear God, seeing thou art in the same condemnation? And we indeed justly; for we receive the due reward of our deeds: but this man hath done nothing amiss. And he said unto Jesus, Lord, remember me when thou comest into thy kingdom. And Jesus said unto him, Verily I say unto thee, to-day shalt thou be with me in paradise. (Pr.)

CHRIST is said to have triumphed over principalities and powers on his cross, and surely the conversion and salvation of this poor sinner affords a wonderful instance of it, and serves as a specimen of his mercy to future ages. Well may it be said, " this is a faithful saying, and worthy of all acceptation, that Christ Jesus came into the world to save sinners, even the chief."

This unhappy man and his fellow sufferer were " malefactors," common thieves or robbers. They had probably been partners in guilt, and both suffered for the same offence: but how great the difference between them in the final hour. The one dies in his impenitence, the other owns that he suffered justly, though at first they both railed on the dying Saviour. We may therefore well consider the penitent thief as a singular instance of the power and grace of God towards the very chief of sinners. While falling himself a sacrifice to the malice of Satan, Jesus snatches a lamb as it were out of the mouth of the lion, and takes with him to paradise, a sinner who was sinking into the pit of destruction.

I. NOTICE IN THE DYING THIEF THE OPERATIONS OF GENUINE REPENTANCE.

His situation allowed him no other opportunity of showing his grief and sorrow for sin, than by the few words which dropped from his lips while he was suspended on the cross; but these afford full proof of his sincerity. His hands and feet were nailed, but his heart was free; and his lips not being yet closed in death, he will do all he can to glorify the Saviour.

1. He begins to rebuke the reviling malefactor: "Dost not thou fear God?" —— There were none left to defend the Saviour's cause: the disciples had all forsook him and fled, and his friends were standing afar off: the multitude around him were full of derision, and John and the woman who stood near the cross were overwhelmed with grief. —— The dying malefactor will therefore plead for him, and boldly reproves the daring sinner at his side, whose mouth was full of cursing and bitterness. —— This was genuine repentance, and genuine love, which could not bear that Jesus should be dishonored by railing accusations, nor that scandals should be cast on him.

2. He *confesses his sin*, and acknowledges the equity of his sentence. " We indeed," says he, " suffer justly." —— His confession was public and open, in the presence of innumerable witnesses, and of innumerable enemies. —— It was also of the most disinterested kind: he had nothing to hope for from man, no prospect of deliverance; there was nothing to extort his confession but the deepest sense of guilt. —— Here could be no room for fear, for they had done their worst upon him: he was looking to Christ for salvation, but owns his condemnation to be just. —— This indeed is confessing and giving glory to God, and that in the first place, and in the highest sense; for this confession was made *before* any plea for mercy was offered, so that whether he was saved or not, he justifies and glorifies God; and this is the spirit of genuine repentance.

412

3. He *vindicates* the character of Christ, while he unequivocally condemns himself. "This man has done, nothing amiss." ———— Herein indeed he charged his country with the guilt of crucifying the Lord of glory; and while he himself pleads guilty, he pleads the innocence of Christ before the same tribunal. ———— This is an instance of magnanimity worthy of the character of the true penitent. "Do I not hate them, oh Lord, that hate thee; and am I not grieved with them that rise up against thee?" Psa. cxxxix. 21.

4. His repentance is accompanied with *faith in Christ:* he called him "Lord." ———— Multitudes were deriding him, his disciples had all forsaken him, and he appeared in circumstances of the deepest abasement, sinking under weakness and disgrace; yet this poor sinner owns him as the Lord, a name which implies every high idea of Christ, 1 Cor. xii. 3. ———— He also believes that Christ had a "kingdom," a kingdom not of this world, and that he was going to possess it. Though he now appeared as an outcast from heaven and earth, yet he considered him as the Lord of the invisible world.

———— He must likewise have believed that Christ, when he came to his kingdom, would there be the advocate of sinners, and would make intercession for transgressors; or had he fully known this, his prayer could not have been more appropriate.

This was great faith, especially if we consider how this poor sinner came by the knowledge of Christ. Probably he could not read, was unacquainted with the prophecies, had never seen Jesus before, nor heard any thing about him; his enemies triumphed, his friends were scattered. What he hears is only from the mouth of his accusers, and he had to collect his knowledge of Christ from the derision and scorn of the multitude; yet he realizes all that in him which they denied to him.

5. His repentance is accompanied with *earnest prayer:* "Lord, remember me." ———— This is very brief, but full and comprehensive, being the utterance of the heart. ———— He does not specify the object of his prayer, yet he selects the most appropriate terms in which to express himself, and leaves it with the Lord to give him what he needed. Lord, remember me, think of me in love, like Joseph to the butler. When it goes well with thee, remember me. ———— He might have said, Lord, pardon me, bless me, and save me; but this includes all. Let me but have a place in thy heart, and all the rest will follow. ———— The terms were also remarkably adapted to his present condition; for who would "remember" him, if Christ did not? His enemies would all forget him in a little time; and his friends, if he had any, would be glad to forget him as a reproach to them—an outcast of society, a thief and a malefactor. "*Lord,* remember me." ———— He might have thought his sin too great to be pardoned, but he does not, neither does he despair of an interest in the Saviour's love: Lord, remember *me.* ————
Self-righteous pride would have prevented his making such an application for mercy as utterly in vain, and such a spirit would have objected to prayer on account of his utter unworthiness: but he is not discouraged by the greatness of his guilt. ———— Oh what faith; what a conviction of the infine ability of the Saviour.

II. View the conduct of our Lord towards him: "VERILY I SAY UNTO THEE, TO-DAY SHALT THOU BE WITH ME IN PARADISE."

1. Though Christ would take no notice of a reviler, nor give any answer to the language of reproach, yet he would *attend to the plea of mercy;* and to the plea of one of the most unworthy, and the least likely to obtain it. ———— He would hear the prayer of a perishing sinner whose heart was contrite, even in the hour of death What condescension, and what love!

413

2. He answered him *without delay.* ———— He for a time deferred the request of one poor woman who sought him with great importunity, and suffered her to be repulsed ; and though he answered at last, yet he kept her in long suspense. Matt. xv. 22, 23. ———— But this was an urgent case : the sinner was dying, and there was no time for delay : it was well the word was nigh him, and the Saviour so near at hand.

3. As the petition had *implied much,* so did the answer. ————·To be with Jesus, to be with him in paradise, was more than he could ask or think. This would be all in all, not only including the forgiveness of sin, acceptance with God, and eternal life, but more than could enter into the heart of man to conceive. ———— The penitent had only asked of Jesus to remember him ; but Jesus tells him he should be with him. He asked to be remembered at some future time, he knew not when ; but Jesus tells him that " to-day" he should be blessed.

4. The promise is pronounced with a solemn *asseveration ;* " Verily, I say unto thee." ———— This bears the form of an oath, and gives the fullest assurance for the performance of the promise. Heb. vi. 18.

REFLECTIONS.

1. We may observe, that there is a great difference between the conduct of this dying malefactor, and that of many dying penitents who are supposed to be converted. They often speak confidently of their state, and of their going to heaven ; but this poor man did not, though Christ said so of him He prayed that he might be saved ; and after what Christ said, he might believe that he should ; but he himself said not a word of that. The strong language that was used was Christ's, and not his.

2. The mercy shown to the penitent thief, affords an encouraging example to perishing sinners. Christ is now in his kingdom, the Advocate is with the Father, making intercession for us ; let us therefore come boldly to a throne of grace. ———— He does not forget Joseph, as the butler did. Glory and honor do not render him unmindful of his people : he is the same yesterday, to-day, and for ever.

3. There is a request on Christ's part as well as on ours : he desires to be remembered by us. 1 Cor. xi. 24. ———— He does not need it as we do but love desires it, and wishes to live in the mind of its objects.

~~~~~~~~~~~ ~~~~~~~~~~~

ATTRACTIONS OF THE CROSS.

John xii. 32.—And I, if I be lifted up from the earth, will draw all men unto me. **(Pr.)**

JOHN delights to dwell on the dying love of Christ, and cannot feel an equal interest on any other subject. In the last ten chapters of his gospel he narrates the principal events of the last few days of our Saviour's life on earth. In this chapter he represents him as having a conflict with nature, ver. 27 ; and then as uttering the language of victory and triumph : ver. 31.

1. Observe, the whole of this passage relates to *the effects* of Christ's death, which is mentioned in the present tense by way of anticipation, as if it had already taken place ver. 31.

2. *The world* is here considered as Satan's kingdom, and he is called "**the prince**" of it. He it is that rules and governs, both among Jews and Gentiles. ——— But now by the gospel, his kingdom should be overturned. Now is the cause of rebellion crushed, and the grand usurper is confounded.

3. The *drawing of all men* to Christ, denotes the influence of the gospel upon men of all nations, who had hitherto been led captive by the devil at his will; but they shall now become attached to Christ, as it is expressed in chap. xi. 48.

I. Consider the description given of true conversion: it consists in our being "DRAWN TO CHRIST."

We are drawn or influenced by those principles which gain an ascendency over us, or by those objects which govern our feelings or our interest. Thus the riches of the world allure the hearts of the covetous, its pleasures the mind of the sensualist, and its honors that of the ambitious. ——— By these mankind are bound to Satan's interest, and held in a state of subjection. A crown of glory has no influence on the carnal mind, which looks only at the things that are seen. ——— But when a sinner is renewed by grace, and brought to believe in Jesus, the chains are broken, and his heart is smitten with the love of a dying Saviour.

1. Religion had before *no charms*, the world being all in all. ——— Now that the sinner is converted, the Bible becomes a new book, and every thing is viewed in a new light. The law is seen to be holy, just and good; the gospel is inestimable, and all its promises are found to be exceedingly great and precious. ——— Now the sinner begins to wonder that he did not see these things before, and is at a loss to account for his past stupidity.

2. The world has now lost *its attraction*, its dominion over the heart is subdued. ——— The believer is crucified to the world, and the world is crucified to him. It is now become subordinate to higher interests, and is used without abusing it, knowing that the fashion thereof passeth away. 1 Cor. vii. 31.

3. The sinner was once drawn away by *self righteousness*, and cleaved to it as containing all his salvation. ——— He thought much of his religious attainments, and highly of himself on account of them. Luke xviii. 11. ——— But now this fine gold is become dim, and he counts all things but loss for Christ. Phil. iii. 8.

4. Once he *cleaved to flesh and blood*, and could not think of parting with friends and relations, father and mother, for Christ's sake and the gospel. He could not forget his father's house, nor think of forsaking Egypt, to endure affliction with the people of God: but like Orpah he must return to his country and to his gods, notwithstanding all his convictions of the truth. But now his heart is so attracted by the Saviour, that the ties of nature themselves begin to loosen; and like Moses and Ruth, he can forsake all for Christ. Ps. xlv. 10; Ruth i. 15, 16; Heb. xi. 24—26.

5. *Religious duties* were once *a burden to him*, and like Doeg he was detained before the Lord. His language was, what a weariness is it, and when will the Sabbath be over. ——— But now, holy duties are his delight, and his prayer is like that of the church of old, Draw me, we will run after thee. Cant. i. 4. ——— His heart is so attracted that he can find no such happiness any where else: it is good now to draw near unto God. Psalm lxxiii. 28.

Those things which before formed *the greatest objections* to religion, now become matter of choice. ——— He could not bear the reproach, the loss, the shame attending a profession of the gospel. But now like Moses, he can forsake Egypt; and with Paul, count not his life dear unto him for the name of the Lord Jesus. Acts v. 41, xxi. 13.

7. His heart is so drawn to Christ, that the thoughts of *being with him* is now the sum of his desire. Luke viii. 38. ——— Like Paul, he is even willing to depart, that he may be with Jesus. Phil. i. 23.

II. NOTICE HOW THE CROSS OF CHRIST TENDS TO EFFECT THIS.

The Jews put Christ to death in order to prevent his influence, and to make an end of his kingdom and interest in the world. John xi. 48, xii. 19. But it operated in a very different way; ch. xii. 24. ——— His glory followed up his sufferings, and was to arise out of them; the extension of his kingdom would therefore be a necessary consequence of his death. 1 Pet. i. 11.

1. Christ's being "lifted up" upon the cross would afford *the greatest possible display of love;* and love, of all principles, is the most attractive. ——— It is a melting consideration, that while we were yet enemies, he died for us. Hereby perceive we the love of God; herein indeed is love. Rom. v. 8; 1 John iii. 16, iv. 10.

2. It is through the cross of Christ that we have the words of *pardon, peace, and eternal life;* and these tidings become the grand attraction to lost sinners. ——— See how the gospel allured the hearts of John's disciples, and also those of Jesus. John i. 36—39, vi. 66—69. ——— Hence also the multitude followed him withersoever he went: this it was that drew the woman who was a sinner, to weep at his feet, and to wash them with her tears. Luke vii. 47. ——— It is by his being lifted up that he becomes the object of faith; it is by his death that death itself is destroyed, and life and immortality are brought to light. John iii. 13.

3. It was in virtue of this that *the Holy Spirit was imparted*, and this was necessary to render the gospel effectual. ——— It followed it in order of time, that it might appear in the order of nature, or to be the proper effect of it. ——— Without this all the loveliness, and all the love of the Saviour would have no influence: nor would the gospel feast be regarded, but every one would make light of it. Isa. liii. 1; Matt. xxii. 5.

III. The reason we have to expect that this INFLUENCE SHALL BE EXTENDED OVER ALL THE EARTH.

Christ's being lifted up has not yet had its full effect: he will eventually " draw all men unto himself"—

1. This is a part of *the promise* made to him by the Father, and the uttermost parts of the earth are to be his possession. Psalm ii. 8. Isaiah liii. 12.

2. It agrees with the general tenor *of prophecy*, that to him shall the gathering of the people be. Gen. xlix. 10; Dan. ii. 35; vii. 27; Mic. iv. 8: Rev. xi. 15.

We may learn from hence——1. That the way of salvation is Christ and him crucified——2. That the great object of the christian ministry is to exhibit the doctrine of the cross, as the means of converting sinners unto God ——3. That were this doctrine is faithfully preached, there is encouragement to hope it shall never be in vain.

THE CHARACTERISTIC MARKS OF TRUE PENITENCE.

Hosea vi. 1.—Come and let us return unto the Lord : for he hath torn, and he will heal us,
ne hath smitten and he will bind us up. (S. S.)

THE spiritual dereliction which the people of God have at times experienced, has ever been considered as the most afflictive of all chastisements : but it has also been the most salutary and most effectual.   The benefits arising from it were strongly exemplified in the Israelites, who after having long withstood the united efforts of all the prophets, were on a sudden constrained by it to turn to God with unfeigned contrition.

The words before us are the expressions of that repentance which was excited in the Israelites by God's departure from them, and by his grace that accompanied the affliction : Hos. v. ult. and they suggest to us a proper occasion to consider

I. THE CHARACTERISTIC MARKS OF TRUE PENITENCE

It will always be attended with

1. A sense of our departure from God

Unregenerate men live " without God in the world," and yet the thought of their being at a distance from God never enters into their minds.   But as soon as the grace of repentance is given to them, they see that they "have been like sheep going astray, every one to his own way," and that they never can find happiness but in " returning to the shepherd and bishop of their souls."

2. An acknowledgement of affliction as a just chastisement for sin

The impenitent heart murmurs and rebels under the divine chastisements : the penitent " hears the rod and him that appointed it." He blesses God for the troubles that have brought him to reflection ; Ps. xvi. 7, and cxix. **67.** and while he smarts under the wounds that have been inflicted on him, he regards them as the merciful tokens of parental love. Ps. cxix; 75.

3. A determination to return to God

When a man is once thoroughly awakened to a sense of his lost condition, he can no longer be contented with a formal round of duties.   He reads, hears, prays in a very different way from that to which he was wont to do. " What shall I do to be saved ?" is the one thought that occupies his mind : and he is resolved through grace to sacrifice every thing that would obstruct the salvation of his soul. To hear of Christ, to seek him, to believe on him, and to receive out of his fulness, these are from henceforth his chief desire, his supreme delight. Song v. 6, 8.

4. A desire that others should return to him also

As all the other marks, so this especially was manifested by the repenting Israelites.   This is peculiarly insisted on as characteristic of the great work that shall be accomplished in the latter day. Isa. ii. 3.   This has distinguished the church of God in all ages !   The penitent knows how awful the state of all around him is, and how much he has contributed by his influence and example to destroy them ; and therefore, though he expects nothing but " hatred for his good-will," he feels it incumbent on him to labor for their salvation : and, if it were possible, he would instruct, convert, and save the whole world.

To promote an increase of such repentance amongst us, we shall proceed to state

II. THE GROUNDS ON WHICH A PENITENT MAY TAKE ENCOURAGEMENT OT RETURN TO GOD.

417

Whatever grounds of despondency we may feel within ourselves, we may take encouragement

1. From a general view of God's readiness to heal us

God has not left himself without witness even among the heathen world; but has shewn, by his goodness to the evil and unthankful, that he is ever ready to exercise mercy.   But to us who have his revealed will, he has left no possibility of doubt: for "if he spared not his own son, but delivered *him* up for us all how shall he not with him also freely give us all things." The invitations and promises with which his word is filled, are a further evidence to us, that he is willing to receive every returning prodigal, and that he will in no wise cast out any who come unto him.   On this ground the whole world may adopt the words of the text, and say, " Come, let us return unto the Lord."

2. From that particular discovery of it which we have in the wounds he has inflicted on us

The Israelites seemed to lay a peculiar stress on this, and to infer, from the very strokes of his rod, his willingness to " heal and bind them up." They even felt an assurance that his return to them would be both speedy and effectual. Ver. 2. Song i. 4. Zech. viii. 21. John i. 41, 45.   Thus as soon as any person is brought to acknowledge the hand of God in his afflictions, he will improve them in this very way.   Whether his troubles be of a temporal or spiritual nature, he will adore God for not leaving him in a secure and thoughtless state, and for awakening him by any means to a sense of his guilt and danger.   He will begin immediately to argue as Manoah's wife : " Would the Lord have shewn me this mercy, if he had intended to destroy me?" Judg. xiii. 23.   Does a father correct his child because he has *no* love to him ?   Are not the very expressions of his anger to be viewed as tokens of his love, Heb. xii. 6. and as *an earnest* of his returning favor as soon as the child shall have implored forgiveness.

Let those then who feel the burthen of their sins, remember, that it is God who has given them to see their iniquities ; and that, the heavier their burthen is, the more abundant encouragement they have to cast it on the Lord. Matt. xi. 28.

APPLICATION.—To those who have deserted God

Let us only reflect on the months and years that we have past without any affectionate remembrance of God, or any earnest application to Christ as our Mediator and Advocate ; and we shall not need many words to convince us, that we are included in this number.   But let us consider whom " we have forsaken ; even God, the fountain of living waters ;" and, with all our labor in pursuit of happiness, we have only " hewed out for ourselves cisterns, broken cisterns that can hold no water." Jer. ii. 13.   Let our past experience suffice to shew us the vanity and folly of our ways : and let us " return unto him from whom we have deeply revolted."   But let us beware lest we " heal our wounds slightly."   Christ is the brazen Serpent to which all must look :   He is the good Samaritan who alone can help us, and who has submitted to be himself " wounded for our transgressions," that he might " heal us by his stripes."

2. To those who are deserted by God.

God does find it necessary sometimes to withdraw the light of his countenance from his people.   But, whatever he may have done on some particular occasions, we are sure that in general he does not forsake us till after we have forsaken him.   Hence, when the Israelites were deserted by him they did not say, let us pray that he will return to us; but, let us return unto him:

for they were well assured that, as the alienation had begun on their part, so it would be terminated as soon as ever they should humble themselves in a becoming manner. Let those then who are under the hidings of God's face, inquire, what has occasioned his departure from them: and let them put away "the accursed thing," and turn to him with their whole hearts. Let them rest assured, that "there is balm in Gilead;" and that, if they come to him in the name of Christ, their "backslidings shall be healed," and their happiness restored." Hos. xiv. 4. Lam. iii. 31, 32. Ps. xcvii. 11, and cxlvii. 3.*

* If this were the subject of a *Fast Sermon*, the APPLICATION might be comprised in the following observations. 1. The calamities of the nation are manifest tokens of God's displeasure, and calls to repentance.—2. All the efforts of our rulers to heal our wounds will be in vain, if we do not repent.—3. A general turning unto God would bring us speedy and effectual relief.

THE USE OF COVENANTING WITH GOD.

Chronicles xxix. 10, 11.—Now it is in mine heart to make a covenant with the Lord God of Israel, that his fierce wrath may turn away from us. My sons, be not now negligent. (S. S.)

A TRULY pious man will not be satisfied with serving God in his closet—
He will exert his influence to bring others also to a sense of their duty—
The public exercise of the ministry indeed belongs to those only who are duly called to it. Heb. v. 4.—
But all who are possessed of authority (parents, masters, magistrates, and kings,) should use it for the promoting of virtue and religion—
Christians of every rank and description should exhort one another. Heb iii. 13.—
We have a noble example set before us in the conduct of Hezekiah—
As soon as he came to the throne, he set himself to restore the service of the temple—
And called upon all, both ministers and people, to make a solemn covenant with their God—
The royal proclamation for the observance of this day speaks in effect the language of the text—
I. SHEW WHEN WE HAVE REASON TO APPREHEND THAT GOD'S ANGER IS WAXED HOT AGAINST US.
We cannot in all cases determine how far a dispensation may be sent in anger or in love—
But in general we may say, that God is greatly incensed against us—
1. When our sins are multiplied against him.
Sin is invariably the object of God's abhorrence. Hab. i. 13. Ps. v. 5.—
This truth is so evident that it needs not any confirmation—
It needs only to be applied with power to our hearts and consciences—
What lamentable depravity pervades every part of the nation!—
There is no iniquity, however heinous, which is not practised without remorse—
If we look into our own bosoms, what reason for humiliation may we find!—

What ingratitude for mercies received, and impenitence for sins committed!—

What rebellion against God, what contempt of his Son, what resistance of his Spirit, have we not occasion to deplore!—

And shall not God be avenged of such a nation as this?—

Yea, have not *we* reason to fear that *we* shall be monuments of his wrath—

2. When his judgments are multiplied upon us.

God often sends *temporal* afflictions to his people in love? Heb. xii. 6.—

But *spiritual* judgments are a certain token of his wrath—

Blindness of mind, obduracy of heart, and obstinacy in sin are among his heaviest judgments. Isa. vi. 9, 10.—

And have none of us reason to fear that these are now inflicted on us?—

But it is by temporal judgments chiefly that he punishes nations—

It was from these that Hezekiah judged of God's anger against the Jews Ver. 8, 9.—

And are not these multiplied upon our land at this time?—

Surely the displeasure of God can scarcely ever be more strongly displayed, than it is in the calamities under which we now groan—

But that none may yield to desponding fears we shall,

II. POINT OUT THE BEST MEANS OF AVERTING HIS WRATH.

Repentance towards God and faith in Christ are the means prescribed by God—

But it is not a slight and superficial use of these means that will suffice—

We should solemnly devote ourselves to God in a perpetual covenant.

Not that we should attempt to renew the covenant of works—

That would make void the Gospel, and seal our eternal condemnation. Gal. iii. 10.—

Nor should we think to add any thing to the covenant of grace—

That was once made with Christ, and is ordered in all things and sure. Heb. viii. 6.

But we should patiently and deliberately renounce all our former ways—

We should seriously give up ourselves to God as his redeemed people—

And intreat him to perfect us in any way which he shall see fit—

Such covenants as these have often been made by the most eminent saints.

Under the old Testament dispensation they were judged acceptable to God—

Omitting many other instances, we may notice the solemn covenant of Asa. 2 Chron. xv. 12–15.

Nor was that less remarkable which was entered into by Josiah. 2 Kings xxiii. 3.—

Isaiah and Jeremiah speak of the making of such covenants as characteristic of the gospel times. Isa. xliv. 5. Jer. l. 4. 5.

St. Paul highly commends the conduct of the Macedonians on account of their having thus given themselves up to God. 2 Cor. viii. 5.—

And recommends a similar practice to all christians of every age and nation. Rom. xii. 1.—

Nor can we doubt of their acceptableness to God.

Hezekiah manifestly supposed that God would accept him in this duty. *The text.*—

It was recommended to Ezra in circumstances where there was but little hope remaining. Ezra x. 3.—

And God himself expressly enjoined it as the means of averting his displeasure. Jer. iv. 4.—

Not that we are to suppose that there is any thing meritorious in such an act—

But, it tends, of itself, to the humiliation and confirmation of our souls—

And will be both accepted and remembered by our covenant God and Father. Deut. xxix. 12, 13.—

These means being at once so scriptural and so important, we shall,

III. Urge upon you the adoption of them.

We admire the tender and affectionate address of Hezekiah to the priests—

And with similar concern would we now invite you to the performance of your duty—

1. There is no time for delay.

Many are "negligent" at present in expectation of a more convenient season—

But who can assure himself that he shall be alive on the morrow. James iv. 14.—

Or that, if he be, he shall have an inclination to that from which he is now averse?—

Or that God will grant him the aids of his Spirit which are now refused?—

The voice of God to every one is, Seek me to-day, while it is called to day. Heb. iii. 13, 15.—

With respect to the nation, who can tell how soon the cloud that hangs over us may burst, and overwhelm us utterly?—

Let us follow the example of the repenting Ninevites. Jonah iii. 5—9.-

If "it be in our hearts to make a covenant," let it instantly be done Ps. cxix. 60.—

And let every one, while we are yet speaking, implore help of God to do it with sincerity—

2. If we neglect this duty, we *cannot hope* to escape the wrath of God.

Sodom was destroyed, because they laughed at God's threatenings as idle tales—

And the strongest empires, in succession, have fallen a sacrifice to their sins—

Who then shall protect *us*, if we continue to provoke the Majesty of heaven?—

But, whatever be the fate of the nation, we must all appear at the judgment seat of Christ—

And there none will be acknowledged as his people, who had not voluntarily taken him for their Lord and Saviour—

If then ye have any regard for your eternal welfare, neglect him no longer—

But, in the penitent language of the prophet, devote yourselves to his service. Isa. xxvi. 13.—

3. If we heartily engage in this duty, we have *nothing to fear*.

Were such a covenant general through the nation, God would soon remove his judgments—

But whatever come upon the land, God's faithful people shall be objects of his favor—

Though they may be involved in the general calamities, they shall be comforted with the divine presence. Ps. xxxiv. 18, 19.—

They need not therefore be agitated with fear on account of God's displeasure in this world—

Nor have they any thing to dread in the eternal world. Mal. iii. 17.

Let us then enter into this matter with our whole hearts—
And pray day and night for grace to perform our vows—
Unfaithfulness to our engagements will incense God still more against us—
And provoke him to inflict yet heavier judgments upon us. Jer. xxxiv. 18–20.
It were even better never to have vowed, than to vow and not pay. Ecc.
v. 5. 2. Pet. ii. 21.

He however, who puts it into our heart to make, can enable us to keep,
our covenant. Jude 24.

Let us then engage simply in dependence on the divine strength—

But found all our hopes of acceptance on that better and unchangeable
covenant, which Christ has entered into on our behalf—

~~~~~~~~~~~~~~~~~~~~~

THE REQUISITES FOR ACCEPTABLE PRAYER.

1 Kings viii. 38, 39.—What prayer and supplications soever be made by any man, or by all
thy people Israel, which shall know every man the plague of his own heart, and spread
forth his hands towards this house: then hear thou in heaven thy dwelling-place, and
forgive, and do, and give to every man according to his ways whose heart thou knowest. (S. S.)

RELIGION is often thought to be an employment fit only for weak minds,
or for those who have nothing else to engage their attention—

But it is worthy the pursuit of the wisest and greatest men—

Never did Solomon appear more glorious than when uttering these
words—

At the head of all his subjects he dedicated his temple to God—

He set them a bright example of piety and devotion—

And interceded, not for them only, but for all succeding generations.

In this portion of his instructive prayer we may see,

L. THE REQUISITES FOR ACCEPTABLE PRAYER.

An humble, upright, fervent, believing, submissive, obediential frame of
mind is necessary when we approach the throne of grace—

But the most essential requisites for acceptable worship are comprised in,

I. A deep sense of our own depravity.

The " plague of one's own heart" is, one's indwelling corruption*—

" Every one" has some " sin that more easily besets him"—

Not that a mere acquaintance with this plague is sufficient—

We must know the depth and inveteracy of our disorder—

Our knowledge too must produce an unfeigned self-abhorrence—

And a full conviction of our utter helplessness—

Nor without this knowledge can we offer up acceptable prayer—

We cannot lament what we neither feel nor know—

Or seek for mercy, when we perceive not our need of it—

While ignorant of our depravity, we are not in a state to receive mercy—

We should not even be willing to accept of mercy on God's terms—

* Some understand " plague" as expressing some loathsome disorder ; and the rather because it is translated "sore" in the parallel passage 2 Chron. vi. 29. This is the true sense
of it when it relates to the body ; but *here* the heart is represented as the seat of this disorder, and therefore it must be understood of sin. This is confirmed by what is said in the
text of God's knowing the heart.

The very offers of salvation would rather excite our displeasure than our gratitude*—

②. A believing view of Christ.

The temple of Solomon was the more immediate residence of the Deity—

All were on this account directed to look towards it when they prayed—

That temple was typical of the Lord Jesus Christ†—

In him "dwells all the fulness of the Godhead bodily"—

To him our eyes are therefore to be directed. Isai. xlv. 22.

We are to offer all our petitions to him, or in his name. John xiv. 13, 14.

This regard to him is neeessary to the acceptance of our prayers—

It is through him alone that we gain access to the Deity. Eph. ii. 18.

We cannot approach the Father in any other way. John xiv. 6.

Nor is there any other channel whereby the divine blessings can flow down to us, John i. 16.

On these accounts we must "stretch out our hands towards" HIM—

We must view HIM as our only source of spiritual blessings—

They who truly seek after God will soon experience,

II. THE EFFICACY OF PRAYER WHEN ATTENDED WITH THOSE REQUISITES.

Carnal, cold, or unbelieving petitions will receive no answer, Jam. iv. 3; Matt. xv. 8, 9; Jam. i. 6, 7.

But humble and believing prayer will obtain the richest blessings.

① National.

The passage before us relates to the whole Jewish nation—

It supposes them to have incurred the heavy displeasure of God—

And teaches them how they are to avert his wrath—

Nor did God leave them in suspense about the issue of such humiliation—

He declared in vision to Solomon that his petitions were accepted, 2 Chron. vii. 12–14.

The Jewish history affords many striking instances of deliverance vouchsafed to a repenting people.‡

Nor can we doubt but that the same means would still be crowned with the like success.‖

②. Personal.

He who "knows our heart" will grant all that we can desire, 1 John v 14, 15.

Forgiveness of sin.

Who more infamous and abandoned than that woman? Luke vii. 37, 39.

Yet she, in humility and faith, applied to Jesus, Luke vii. 38.

And received an assurance that her iniquities were forgiven, Ib. 47, 48, 50

Peace of conscience.

How troubled, almost to distraction, were the murderers of our Lord! Acts ii. 37.

---

*A man, not sensible that he had subjected himself to capital punishment by breaking the laws of his country, would reject with indignation, an offer of deliverance from an ignominious death: but a self-condemned criminal on the eve of his execution would receive such an offer gladly.

†See John ii. 19, 21, and compare Exod. xxiii. 21, with the expression, " My name shall be there." 1 Kings viii. 29.

‡ Jehosapht praying according to the direction in the text, 2 Chron. xx. 5—13, expressly reminded God of his promise, ver. 9. And the success of his prayer far exceeded all reasonable expectation; see ver. 22—25.

‖If this were a *Fast Sermon*, it would be proper to enlarge a little on this idea in reference to the peculiar state of the nation at the time.

But, according to Peter's direction, they looked to Jesus, Ib. 38.

And were immediately filled with "peace and joy in believing," Ib. 46.

*Deliverance from temporal troubles.

We cannot conceive greater temporal affliction than that endured by Jonah, Jonah ii. 1—3.

Yet, when to appearance irrevocably lost, he prayed in this manner, Ib. 4, 7.

And experienced a most unparalled deliverance, Ib. 10.

*Victory over our spiritual enemies.

With what vehemence did Satan assault the apostle Paul! 2 Cor. xii. 7

The afflicted saint cried with earnestness to the Lord Jesus, ib. 8.

His troubles were immediately turned into triumphant exultations, Ib. 9.

Renewal after the divine image.

Nothing on earth does a believer desire so much as this—

Yet this shall be attained in the same way—

An humble an believing view of Christ shall effect it, iii. 18.

*A peaceful death.

Stephen died by the hands of cruel and bloodthirsty enemies, Acts vii. 54

But he offered an humble and believing prayer to Christ, Ib. 59.

And his death was to him as a serene and peaceful sleep, Ib. 60.

A glorious immortality.

He who died *justly* by the hands of the public executioner must have merited in a high degree the wrath of God, Luke xxiii. 41.

Nevertheless in his last hour he directed his eyes to Christ, Ib. 42.

And that very day was he admitted with Christ to Paradise, Ib. 43.

APPLICATION.

Let none despair on account of the greatness of their sins—

Or of the judgments of God which are already inflicted on them.

God will suffer none to " seek his face in vain"—

Let every one then bewail " the plague of his own heart"—

And offer up believing prayers " towards God's holy oracle."*

* This will suffice for two Sermons, the first head being the subject of one, and the second head of the other. If it form the ground of one Sermon only, those particulars which are marked with an asterisk * under the second head may be omitted.

THE PRAYER OF JABEZ.

1 Chron. iv. 10.—And Jabez called on the God of Israel, saying, Oh, that thou wouldest bless me indeed, and enlarge my coast, and that thine hand might be with me, and that thou wouldest keep me from evil, that it may not grieve me. And God granted him that which he requested. (S. S.)

REMARKABLE is the honor which God puts upon prayer—

And numberless are the instances which are recorded of its efficacy—

Jabez is here mentioned in a long catalogue of names—

But while the names only of others are recorded, he is particularly noticed—

He is even declared to have been more honorable than all his brethren—

This distinction indeed might be given him on account of his primogeniture—

But it was certainly still more due on account of his piety—

Like the patriarch Jacob, "wrestled with God and prevailed"—

I. THE IMPORT OF HIS PRAYER.

In its primary sense it evidently related to *temporal* blessings.

God had promised his people an inheritance in Canaan—

But they were not able of themselves to drive out the inhabitants—

Jabez therefore, sensible of his insufficiency, prayed to God for help—

He begged for the blessing of God upon his own endeavors—

He desired to be preserved from the dangers to which his military exploits would expose him—

And to have, through the divine interposition, an enlarged inheritance in the promised land—

These requests he urged with a significant and earnest plea—

But there is reason to think it had also a *spiritual* meaning.

The earthly Canaan was typical of the heavenly kingdom—

The enemies also that were to be driven out, were typical of the enemies with whom the christian has to contend—

Moreover, the assistance, which God rendered to his people, was intended to show us what aid we might expect from him—

And what evil will a child of God deprecate so much as sin ?—

Surely nothing is so "grievous" to him as the prevalence of corruption, Rom. vii. 24.

Well therefore may Jabez be considered as looking beyond this world—

And as imploring a secure possession of his heavenly inheritance—

In both these views the prayer is well worthy of our notice.

II. THE EXCELLENCE OF IT.

It is the sentiment, rather than the expression, that gives excellence to prayer—

But in both respects we may admire that before us—

It was,

Humble.

He felt his entire dependence upon the power and grace of God—

This is intimated not merely in the petitions offered, but in the very manner in which they were offered—"Oh, that," &c.

Such humility is absolutely necessary to render prayer acceptable—

The more we abase ourselves, the more will God exalt us—

Let this be remembered in all our addresses at the throne of grace—

Diffusive

Jabez did not content himself with a mere general petition—

He opened distinctly his several wants to God—

A similar conduct is proper for us also, Phil. iv. 6.

Not that God needs to be informed of our wants, or that he will hear us for our much speaking, Matt. vi. 7, 8.

But we need to recite our wants, in order to impress our own minds with a sense of our utter helplessness and unworthiness—

Importunate

He enforced his request with a very earnest plea—

Nor, in reference to sin, could any plea be more proper for *him*—

We indeed should urge the prevailing name of Jesus—

But we may also properly deprecate sin as "grievous" to our souls—

Yea, a disposition to do this is both an evidence of our sincerity, and a pledge of the divine acceptance—

And, in pleading thus, we may well adopt the words of Jacob—Gen. xxxii. 26.

Believing

The title, by which he addressed the Deity, argued his faith in God—
It expressed a confidence in God as the hearer of prayer, Ib. 28.
It is in this way that we also should approach the Deity, Heb. xi. 6.
Without such faith our petitions will have but little effect, Jam. i. 6, 7.
But with it, they shall never go forth in vain, Mark xi. 24.
Prayer possessing such qualities could not fail of success.
III. The success with which it was attended.
We have no detailed account of God's kindness towards him—
But we are informed that God granted him all that he requested.
If Jabez was not straitened in asking, much less was God in giving—
"The prayer of the upright is God's delight"—
We cannot possibly enlarge our requests too much—
We lose much by not using more of holy vehemence, 2 Kings xiii. 19.

The promises made to us exceed not our desires only, but our conceptions, Eph. iii. 20.

Petitions offered in faith, have, as it were, the force of commands, Isaiah xlv. 11.

The more we abound in them, the more we shall find that saying true, Ps. lxxxi. 10.

And often will God vouchsafe us an instantaneous answer, Ps. cxxxviii. 3.
Let us therefore take encouragement from this concise history.
Many and great are the blessings we need from God—
But the throne of his grace is always open to us—
Let us then spread all our sins, and wants before him—
Let us approach him as our God in Christ Jesus—
Let us view him as a gracious answerer of prayer, Ps. lxv. 2, and lvii. 2
And our success shall surely correspond with that of Jabez—
"God never did, or will, say to any, Seek ye my face in vain"—
Application.
Let all now call to mind their several wants and necessities—
Let nothing be thought too small, or too great, to ask—
Let our prayers, like that of Jabez, be daily recorded in heaven—
Let the pressure of our wants, and the richness of our prospects, stimulate us—

Let us expect the accomplishment of that glorious promise—John xiv. 13, 14.

And in due time our prayers shall be turned into everlasting praises.

HUMILIATION FOR THE SIN OF THE HEART.

2 Chron. xxxii. 26.—Hezekiah humbled himself for the pride of his heart. (S. S.)

The best of men are liable to fall through temptation—
But they will deeply bewail any sin into which they have been betrayed—
Hezekiah was a man of very distinguished piety, 2 Kings xx. 3.

But he was not sufficiently aware, that his integrity was the effect of divine grace, and not of human power—

God therefore left him for a moment to the influence of his own heart—
Ver. 31.

I1 consequei :e of this he soon gave a proof of his inherent depravity—
But, on disco 'ering his sin, he instantly humbled himself for it before God—
We shall,

I. Shew the nature and grounds of Hezekiah's humiliation.

The sin committed by him does not in human estimation appear great.

The princes of Babylon sent to congratulate him on his recovery—

He received them with all the kindness and courtesy that he could express—

And shewed them every thing in his dominions that could afford them entertainment—

But his conduct was exceeding sinful in the sight of God; for in it,

1. He sought his own glory

Hezekiah evidently thought of nothing else at that time—

He wished to shew how great a man he was, in order that his alliance
might be courted, and his power feared—

Now this would have been highly criminal in any man, Prov. xxv. 27.

But it was especially so in him, at that particular juncture—

He had just been at the border of the grave; and therefore should have
been more impressed with the vanity of earthly grandeur—

And should have seen the folly and wickedness of *priding himself* in
things so empty, so worthless, so transient—

2. He sought his own glory in preference to God's honor.

He had now a happy opportunity of magnifying the God of Israel—

He might have told the ambassadors, what God had done for his nation in
former times—

He might have recited the wonderful restoration which God had at this
time afforded to himself in particular, together with the stupendous miracle
with which the promise of that recovery had been confirmed, 2 Kings xx. 11.

He might have commended Jehovah as an answerer of prayer—Ib. ver.
4, 5.

And in this way have exalted him above all the gods of the heathen—

And surely the mercies that had been vouchsafed unto him, demanded such
a tribute—

But he was pitifully occupied about self—

And basely preferred *his own* honor before God's—

3. He sought his own glory before the good of his friends

The ambassadors were shewing great kindness to him—

He should therefore have recompensed them in the best way—

He should have instructed them in the knowledge of the God of Israel—

And have told them how willing he was to become their God—

Thus perhaps he might have converted and saved their souls—

And have spread the knowledge of the true God in Babylon—

Yea, eventually, he might have been instrumental to the salvation of
thousands—

But he utterly forgot the necessities of their souls—

And was offering incense to his own vanity, when he should have been
promoting their eternal welfare—

This was his sin; and God denounced a heavy judgment against him on
account of it.

His riches were all to be taken away by the Chaldeans—

His own children were to be made eunuchs in the king of Babylon's
palace—

And the whole nation to be led into a miserable captivity—

But, if his offence was great, his humiliation also was remarkable.

427

He heard with trembling the judgments which God threatened to execute—

Instead of palliating his sin, he acknowledged at once the justice of the Deity in inflicting such a punishment on account of it—

In concert with all his subjects, he implored forgiveness at God's hands—

And, having obtained a respite of the sentence, thankfully acquiesced in the determinations of heaven, Isa. xxxix. 8.

While we see in him much to shun, and much to imitate, let us,

II. ENQUIRE WHETHER WE ALSO HAVE NOT SIMILAR GROUNDS FOR HUMILIATION?

Pride is deeply rooted in the heart of fallen man—

We are prone to be lifted up on every occasion.

We are vain of any *natural endowments* of body or mind—

The strong displays his strength; the beautiful, her beauty—

A penetrating mind, or tenacious memory, are made grounds of self-admiration, and self-preference—

Any *acquired distinctions* also become food for our vanity—

The man of wealth, of honor, or of power, assumes a consequence from his elevation, and demands from others a homage as his due—

The proficient in any act or science courts applause, and delights to have his talents admired—

Even the *gifts of grace*, through the depravity of our nature, become occasions of pride—

Not only an ability to speak or pray with fluency, but even an insight into the corruption of the heart, is often exhibited more for the purpose of attracting admiration than of doing good—

Whatever we have that elevates us a little above our fellow-creatures, our proud hearts are fond of displaying it, and pleased with the flattering attentions which it procures for us—

We indulge the disposition too to the neglect of God's honor, and of the eternal welfare of those around us.

How many glorious opportunities have we of speaking for God!—

What grounds of praising him might we find in the sacred records!—

How many too might we find in our own experience!—

And what unspeakable benefit might arise to mankind, if we carefully improved these opportunities!—

But how rarely is our intercourse with each other made subservient to these ends—

We waste our time in flattering attentions and unprofitable civilities—

We are as intent on gratifying the vanity of ourselves or others, as if our social converse were capable of no better improvement—

How much then do we need to imitate Hezekiah's humiliation!

However innocent we may think such conduct, it is highly criminal in the sight of God—

It renders us justly obnoxious to God's heaviest judgments—Matt. xii. 36. 37.

Should we not then humble ourselves before him in dust and ashes?—

Should not the forbearance he has exercised call forth our devoutest acknowledgments?—

And should we not adore his goodness even if he only delay to execute his threatened vengeance?—

Let us not attempt to palliate this common, but vile, iniquity—

But rather unite in deprecating the wrath we have deserved—

INFER,

1. What dreadful evils arise from small beginnings!

Hezekiah at first probably intended only to shew civility to his friends—

But through inattention to the motions of his heart, he fell into grievous sin, and brought on the whole nation the heaviest judgments—

And what enormities have not the motions of pride, of lewdness, of covetousness, or revenge, produced amongst ourselves, when, if they had been checked at first, they might have been easily subdued?—

Let us learn then to mark the first risings of sin in our hearts—

Let us remember, that God notices and abhors sin in the heart, no less than when it is brought forth into open act—

Let us intreat him to sanctify our inward man, 1 Thess. v. 23.

And *never to leave us to ourselves for one single moment*—

2. How great is the efficacy of fervent prayer and intercession!

The judgment denounced against Hezekiah was to have been speedily inflicted—

But he and Judah sought the Lord by humble and fervent prayer—

And the Lord deferred the evil till the next generation—

Thus will he do also in answer to our prayers—

If we turned to him as a nation, he would *prolong our national* prosperity—

And would *blot out for ever* the *personal* guilt of every true penitent—

Let us then humble ourselves for our abominations both of heart and life—

So shall we find God as gracious unto us, as he was to his people of old.

THE WOMAN OF CANAAN.

Matthew xv. 25.—" Lord, help me." (Sk.)

JESUS came down from heaven to save a perishing world, and his merciful regards extended both to Jews and Gentiles; but his ministry and miracles were, generally, confined to the lost sheep of the house of Israel. Here, however, we have an exception. A poor woman of Canaan came unto him on behalf of her daughter, and after a painful trial of her faith, he mercifully granted unto her the blessing which she desired. The whole account is highly interesting, and will furnish us with many important and useful observations.

I. THE PERSON WHO APPLIED TO JESUS, WAS A "WOMAN OF CANAAN."

1. Her *ancestors were a wicked race*, Lev. xviii. 24, 25;—and were driven out of their native country, as a just punishment of their enormous crimes. Deut. iv. 38. The Israelites, under the command of Joshua, took possession of their land; and, by divine appointment, it became their inheritance, Josh. xiv. 1, 2.

2. But the character and conduct of this woman is a standing proof, that *the descendants of wicked nations may be reformed and saved:* this was the case with the Corinthians, of whom the apostle Paul said, alluding to the abominable wickedness of the heathen world, " Such were some of you; but ye are washed, but ye are sanctified " 1 Cor. vi. 11.

429

3 Her *faith in the Son of God put the Jewish people to shame* They despised and hated him ; but she honored and adored him : and there are persons in the heathen world, in the present day, whose general conduct puts to shame the merely nominal christians of our highly favored land.

II. She applied to our Lord for her daughter, who was " greviously vexed with a devil."

1. In many instances *devils have had the power over the bodies of men and women ;* and that power has been exercised in tormenting those who have been under their influence. But we never read of these apostate spirits doing any good, or attempting to make any person happy. They are wicked and mischievous, and it will be dreadful to be delivered into their hands, Matt. xviii. 34, 35.

2. But *Jesus had power to cast out devils*, and to deliver men from their hellish rage and malice. A word of his terrified those foul spirits, and put whole legions of them to flight, Mark v. 9—13. This poor women had heard the fame of Jesus, Matt. iv, 24 ; and sought his help with humble confidence.

2. And *has he not power over devils now ?* Do they not tremble at the sound of his precious name ? He holds the powers of hell in chains; he destroys their influence in our hearts, Eph. ii. 1—4 ; and bruises Satan under our feet, Rom. xvi. 20.

III. The woman used means which were proper, and which well became her situation.

1. She addressed Jesus as the *son of David*, and thereby acknowledged that he was the Christ which should come into the world ; for the Jews called their Messiah the son of David, because he was to descend from him, and to sit upon his throne, Isa. ix. 7.

2. And *she cried for mercy :* the case of her daughter required the interposition of mercy. It was wise in her to go to Jesus, for he was full of grace, John i. 14 ; and it will be wise in us to go to him for a complete deliverence from the power and tyranny of our adversary the devil, who " as a roaring lion, walking about seeking whom he may devour," 1 Pet. v. 8. She was not ashamed of earnest prayer, but cried aloud ; let us also cry aloud, like David, out of the depths of penitential sorrow, Psa. cxxx. 1, 2.

IV. Jesus, as if he did not hear her cry, remained silent, and " answered her not a word."

1. He seemed to treat her with *contempt ;* but was trying and proving her faith, How often does he proceed on a similar plan, in his dealings with humble penitents, so that they are ready to ask, " Is his mercy clean gone for ever?" Psa. lxxvii. 8.

2. But let them *patiently wait* for his salvation, Psa. xl. 1. He may be silent for a time ; but mercy is in his heart. Only remain at the throne of grace, and continue to cry for mercy, and he will give an answer of peace, Gen. xli. 16.

V. His disciples, weary of her noisy cry, besought him to send her away.

1. It is highly probable, from the answer of Jesus, that *they wished him to grant her request ;* for, otherwise, there would be no point in his saying, " I am not sent but unto the lost sheep of the house of Israel." But allowing this, there is *no proof that they pitied her case*, as they only wanted to get rid of her, on account of the multitude of people brought about them by her loud cries.

2. But *the ministers of Jesus should pity all who are in trouble ;* kindly

bear with the little improprieties of behaviour which they may fall into, in such circumstances; treat them with the utmost tenderness, weeping with them-that weep, Rom. xii. 15; and, especially intercede for them with their heavenly Lord and Master. A feeling heart is a fine trait in a christian minister, Rom. ix. 1—3.

VI. In reply to his disciples, Jesus stated his mission to the house of Israel.

1. He calls them *lost sheep*, because they had gone astray, and were exposed to imminent perils. No animal in the world is more exposed to danger than a wandering sheep; and when the foolish conduct of men is set forth by this figure in the Holy Scriptures, their danger is forcibly pointed out: and were not the Jews exposed, in their wanderings, to error, sin, and punishment?

2. Jesus was sent, as a holy prophet, to *seek the wandering sheep* of the house of Israel; to bring them back to the fold of God; and to place them in safe and happy circumstances. To this he alludes in another figure, where he says, "How often would I have gathered thy children together, even as a hen gathereth her chickens under her wings, and ye would not?" Matt. xxiii. 37.

3. But *he was not sent as a prophet to the Gentiles*, nor did he send his disciples to them in the days of his flesh, Matt. x. 5, 6; but after his resurrection, he commissioned them to go "into all the world," and to "preach the gospel to every creature." Mark xvi. 15. Thus we have known the joyful sound, and we may walk in the light of the Lord's countenance, Psalms lxxxix. 15.

VII. Now the woman drew near and worshipped Jesus, saying, "Lord, help me."

1. She *paid him honor as the son of David;* but we dare not affirm that she worshipped him as God; because we are not quite sure that she was acquainted with his divinity. Kings were worshipped with *civil respect.* Thus the congregation of Israel "bowed down their heads and worshipped the Lord and the king," 1 Chron. xxix. 20. But we, who know the Saviour, as *God over all*, are bound to worship him with divine honors, Rev. v. 13.

2. The cry of the woman was, *Lord help me:* she knew he *could* help her, because he had helped others in similar circumstances; and she hoped he *would* help her, because she had heard of his wonderful compassion. With this conviction let us approach his mercy seat, resting assured that he is both able and willing to help us, in our lowest and most abject state.

3. Many persons would have been *offended* at the silence of Jesus; but this poor woman, being strong in faith, took no offence. It ill becomes a suppliant to murmur and complain, especially one who applies for blessings on the ground of mercy: and what other ground have we? We are sinners and there is no salvation for us, but by grace, Eph. ii. 8.

VIII. But when this woman paid honor to our Lord, and asked his gracious help, he spake to her with apparent unkindness.

1. He called the house of Israel *children;* but they were rebellious children, Isa. i. 2. They treated him cruelly; but he expressed tender love to them. That love continued. when their malice had brought him to the cross. There he said, "Father, forgive them; for they know not what they do," Luke xxiii. 34. He was not willing, after all, to give them up to wrath and justice, Hos. xi. 8.

2. The blessings which he was bestowing on those rebellious children, he called *bread*. By that bread he meant his wise instructions, his healing

431

power, and his nourishing influences. He was the bread of life, and if his own nation had received him as the true Messiah, he would have fed them with the bread of life, as he had fed their fathers by manna in the wilderness, John vi. 31—35.

3. Though his own nation despised that bread, yet he said to this Cananite, it is not meet to take it from them, and to cast it to the dogs. He did not call her countrymen dogs; but reminded her that they were viewed with *contempt*, on account of their impurities and abominations. This was not said with a view to reproach any class of men; but to prove her faith.

IX. THE WOMAN, CONSCIOUS OF HER VILENESS, ACKNOWLEDGED THE TRUTH OF HIS OBSERVATION; BUT HUMBLY CRAVED THE CRUMBS WHICH MIGHT FALL FROM HIS TABLE.

1. Here we see a remarkable instance of *genuine humility;* the poor Canaanite did not say a word about the degrading title, only, " *Truth, Lord.*" It was as much as if she had said, " let us be called dogs, we deserve such treatment, and I will not attempt to prove that we have any just claims to thy benevolence."

2. But her remarks were *ingenious and inimitably beautiful;* and the reason assigned, why it was not meet to give her the children's bread, was made the ground of her pleading. " The Canaanites, who deserved to be called dogs, ought not to expect the bread of children; but remember, Lord, that dogs eat the crumbs which fall from their master's table; and I only ask thee for the crumbs which are given to those animals."

3, How strong was her *faith;* how *persevering* her application; how *earnest* her desire to obtain the blessing! An humbled spirit is willing to be accounted vile. Let us carefully study, and humbly own, our vileness; and while we humble ourslves before the Lord, and deem the smallest favour an undeserved boon, his mighty hand will lift us up, James iv. 10; 1 Pet. v. 6.

X. WHEN HER FAITH WAS PROVED, JESUS SAID, "BE IT UNTO THEE EVEN AS THOU WILT."

1. Her faith in the power and merciful kindness of Christ was *great.* When he was silent she was not discouraged, but waited for an answer; and when he hinted at her unworthiness to receive the children's bread, she said, "Truth, Lord." Hence we learn that a steady and strong faith in our adorable Saviour, produces persevering prayer; and the humble penitent says, " I will not let thee go, except thou bless me," Gen. xxxii. 26.

2. The poor woman was blessed; her faith and prayer were *successful;* and her daughter was made whole from that very hour. And we may boldly affirm, that all our lawful petitions, offered up in the name of Jesus, will be heared and answered; for he has said, " Ask and it shall be given you, seek and ye shall find, knock and it shall be opened unto you," Luke xi. 9.

INFERENCES.

1. The usurped dominion of the devil, and the miseries of his deluded children, demand particular notice. Let us study his devices, 2 Cor. xi. 11; and resist him that he may flee from us, James iv. 7.

2. It is a pleasing reflection, that the head of this old serpent has been bruised, agreeably to the first promise, Gen. iii. 15; and that the seed of the woman has power to bind him in chains, Rev. xx. 1–3.

3. We should go to Jesus in all our troubles; exercise ourselves in a devotional faith; expect deliverance from him alone : and when delivered, give him the glory which is due to his holy name.

4. Our griefs and sorrows will soon come to an end; we shall be removed far from our enemy, the devil; and spend a blessed eternity with God our Saviour. He is now touched with the feeling of our infirmities; he has a loving heart and a strong hand; and is mighty to save his chosen people, Isaiah lxiii. 1.

RELIGION NOT A VAIN THING.

Deuteronomy xxxii. 47.—For it is not a vain thing for you; because it is your life. (Sk.)

ONE of our poets has compared the exit of a good man to the sun, which seems "larger at his setting." And never was the remark more fully illustrated and confirmed, than in the character and circumstances of Moses when he delivered the text. He had been great and good through life; but now his greatness and goodness appeared in higher perfection, and shone with more than usual radiance. The closing scene drew near, his race of peril and glory was just run. He had voluntarily chosen in early life to suffer affliction with the people of God, and now he convenes them together, and delivers in their ears his solemn, his final charge; a charge which for genuine affection, deep seriousness, grand and elevated sentiment, stern fidelity, and awfully prophetic warnings, has never found a parrallel. He rehearses the righteous acts of the Lord—reminds Israel of their rebellions—warns them of their danger—instructs them in their duty, and closes the whole by saying, "Set your hearts unto all the words," &c. ver. 46, 47. We will notice,

I. THE OBJECT TO WHICH MOSES REFERRED;—"It is not a vain thing," &c.

II. THE AFFIRMATION WHICH HE MADE CONCERNING IT;—"It is your life.'

I. THE OBJECT TO WHICH MOSES REFERS. This is stated in ver. 46, "Set your hearts unto all the words," &c. Two things are included in these words, viz. *personal* and *family religion.* Israel were to set their hearts to do all the words of the law themselves, and then to command their children to do them. There were many laws, or commandments, which Moses received from God, and delivered unto Israel, with which we have nothing to do. Some were ceremonial, relating to the peculiar mode of Jewish worship. Others were judicial, referring to the administration of justice among them. But the moral law, which was amplified in the ten commandments, and epitomised in those well known precepts, "Thou shalt love the Lord," &c., Matt. xxii. 37—39, concerns us as much as it did Israel, and we remark concerning it, that—*It is imperative in its nature.* "Thou shalt love," &c. We are not lawless beings, left to live at random; nor has God given us a law, and left it optional with us to observe, or not observe it. But it is imperative upon us; we must do it, or inherit a curse for omitting to do it. *It is comprehensive in its requirements.* It binds us to love God with all our powers, passions, and affections. Our thoughts, words, and actions, are to be inspired, regulated, and ruled by love.—*It is universal in its extent.* It binds every man, in every clime, and in every station to love God, and to love his neighbor.—*It is perpetual and eternal in its obligation.* It knows no change by the revolutions of years, it never can be abrogated. Should any inquire how this law is to be kept, Moses will instruct them, "Set your

433

hearts to all the words," &c.—*Set your hearts to consider the nature of this law.* This will instruct you, how utterly impossible is it for you to comply with the requisitions of this law, without renewing grace. "By the law is the knowledge of sin." Know the law and you will know yourselves. Counterfeit coin is best detected by comparing it with that which is genuine—*Set your hearts to pray for that grace which will enable you to love the law of the Lord.* Carnal men hate the law, because it is so holy, it allows of no unhallowed pleasures, sanctions no criminal indulgence; but good men have the law of God in their hearts, meditate in that law day and night, and are ready individually to say, " O how I love thy law !"—*Set your hearts to expect the accomplishment of that promise,* " The Lord thy God will circumcise thine heart," Deut. xxx. 6.

Family religion is also enjoined ;—" Ye shall command your children to observe to do all the words of this law."—*Parental duty must be regulated by the law of God.* Have you children? Get them to read, to understand, and to do what the Bible enjoins.—*Parental duty is authorized by the command of God.* It is imperative upon parents to command their children, " Ye shall command," &c. Such is the object to which Moses referred. Let us consider,

II. THE AFFIRMATION WHICH HE MADE CONCERNING IT ;—" It is not a vain thing," &c. Here are two things to be noticed; what religion is not, and what it is.

1. *It is not an empty, airy, unsubstantial thing.* For such the word vain frequently signifies. Job calls the months of his affliction " months of vanity." Idols are called vanity, and idolaters vain men. Religion is not a vain thing, not a phantom of the brain, not a cunningly devised fable, but a substantial reality that may be felt, tasted, and enjoyed.

2. *It is not a false deceitful thing.* Vain words are false lying words. Taking the name of God in vain, is using it falsely, as well as unnecessarily. Religion is not a false thing. There are indeed false systems of religion, and lying vanities substituted for religion, but the religion of the Bible is inviolably true; it emanates from a God of truth ; and it leads to truth in principle and practice. Infidels *say* it is false, but Christians *know* it is true.

3. *It is not a foolish senseless thing.* " Vain man would be wise ;" and ignorant men think religion is folly; and count the lives of its professors madness. " The preaching of the cross is to them that perish foolishness," &c. But religion is the essence of true wisdom ; under its influence, we aim at the noblest objects, by the adoption of the most eligible means for securing those objects.

4. *It is not a fruitless, unproductive thing.* " Vain is the help of man.' " Except the Lord keep the city," &c., Psa. cxxvii. 1. Religion is universally profitable, Prov. iii. 13—18, 1 Tim. iv. 8, vi. 6.

But the principal reason why it is not a vain thing is, " It is your life." To the Jews especially this was applicable, because,

1. *It was the means of prolonging their life.* Long life was promised to them, as the reward of obedience to the law of God. " Through this thing ye shall prolong your days," &c., Exod. xx. 12; Prov. iii. 16, x. 27 ; Psa. xxxiv. 12, 13. And though it may be said, that these promises do not belong to us, yet religion in numberless instances prolongs life, as it saves us from practices which tend to the extinction of life.

2. *It added to the happiness of their life.* God's design in all the dispensations of his grace is the promotion of human happiness. What a miserable kind of existence is life without religion ; to live under the curse of

God, ens aved to the devil, under the dominion of guilt, tormented with fears of hell, and every day fitting for damnation. But what a happy, glorious life does that man possess who loves God, and knows that God loves him.

3. *It promoted the utility of their life.* He who lives without religion. lives uselessly. The life of a wicked man is a curse rather than a blessing : and nonenity is preferable to existence, unless the end for which it is given be answered. Religion teaches us to live to be useful. We pray for others —set them good examples—consider the poor, and minister to the necessities of the afflicted.

4. *It prepared them for eternal life.* Heaven is eternal life ; not only eternal existence, but endless enjoyment. Religion prepares for this life. He who loves God with all his heart, is a vessel of honor fit for the Master's use ; and God will ere long receive him into his kingdom to behold his glory.

INFERENCES.

1. *Religion consists in setting your hearts to know and to keep the commandments of God.* This will serve to reprove those who place it in frames and feelings, fanciful notions, modes of faith, dreams, visions, raptures, &c.

2. *Religion is not a vain thing.* How awfully do thousands deceive themselves. Some treat it with sovereign contempt. Others profess to know it ; but their conduct belies their profession. How vain does it appear in the eyes of multitudes !

3. *Religion is your life.* Then tremble at the thought of living without it. Without it you are dead even while you live. O seek to know, love, and serve God. Then you will be " happy while on earth you live, mightier joys ordained to know."

THE PRODIGAL SON.

Luke xv. 23, 24.—Bring hither the fatted calf, and kill it ; and let us eat and be merry. For this my son was dead, and is alive again ; he was lost, and is found. (S. S.)

THE willingness of God to receive sinners is abundantly declared in scripture—

But in no place is it so amply, or so beautifully described as in the parable before us—

The reference which the parable has to the Jews and Gentiles will be more properly noticed, when we come to consider the conduct of the elder brother—

At present we may view it as a lively representation of a sinner's return to God—

The text leads our attention to three points (which are also the three listinguishing parts of the parable) namely, the prodigal's departure from his father, his return to him, and his reception with him—

I. HIS DEPARTURE.

He went from his father's house, litt e thinking of the ruin he should bring upon himself.

A The *occasion* of his departure was, that he hated the restraint of his father's presence—

And longed for independence, that he might gratify his own inclinations—

Hence he desired his father to divide him his portion—

But little did he think to what *extent* his passions would carry him—

Scarcely had he received his portion before he left his father

And departed to a distant country, where his actions would pass unnoticed—

Having thus thrown the reins upon the neck of his appetites, he was carried on with irresistible impetuosity—

From one degree of sin to another he rushed forward without restraint—

Nor stopped till he had wasted his substance in riotous living—

At last he began to feel the *consequences* of his folly—

He was reduced to a state of extreme wretchedness—

Yet he determined to do any thing rather than return to his father—

Though a Jew, he submitted for hire to the ignominious employment of feeding swine—

His wages however, there being a grievous famine in the land, would not procure him even necessary subsistence—

In vain did he attempt to fill his belly with the husks intended for the swine—

In vain did he solicit assistance from those who had known him in his more prosperous days—

" No man," either from gratitude or compassion, " gave him" any relief—

Such is the departure of sinners from the presence of their God

They have experienced the restraints of education—

But have sighed for liberty and independence—

With their growing years, they increasingly abuse the mercies which God has bestowed upon them—

Their reason, their time, and other talents they employ in the service of sin—

Though they do not all run to the same excess of riot, they live equally at a distance from God—

At last perhaps they begin to feel the misery which their neglect of him has brought upon them—

His providence too concurs with his grace to make a deeper wound in their conscience—

But they try any carnal expedients rather than return to God—

Nor can ever be prevailed on to turn unto him, till they have fully proved the insufficiency of the creature to afford them help—

Whatever they may think of themselves in such a state, they are really " *dead*," and " *lost*"—

But the prodigal was not gone beyond recovery, as is evident from,

II. His RETURN.

During his departure he had been as a person destitute of reason—

At last however, " *coming to himself*," he thought of his father's house

The various steps of his return are worthy of notice.

He first reflected on the folly and madness of his former ways—

And on the incomparably happier state of those who lived under his father's roof, and whom perhaps he once despised for submitting to such restraints—

He then resolved that he would return to his father, and implore his forgiveness—

Having formed the purpose, he instantly arose to carry it into execution—

And set off, destitute as he was, to obtain, if possible, the lowest office among his father's domestics—

These exactly describe the steps of a sinner's return to God

He first begins to see how madly and wickedly he has acted—

He feels that he has reduced himself to a wretched and perishing condition—

He considers how happy are those once despised people, who enjoy the favor of his heavenly father—

And how happy he himself should be, if he might but obtain the meanest place in his family—

With these views he determines to abase himself as a vile, self-ruined creature—

There are no terms so humiliating, but he finds them suited to his case—

He is rather fearful of not humbling himself sufficiently than of aggravating his sin too much—

He resolves that he will go to a throne of grace and ask for mercy—

Nor will he wait for any more convenient season, lest he should perish before the hoped-for season arrive—

He is ashamed indeed to go in so mean and destitute a condition—

But he despairs of ever going in any other way—

He therefore breaks through all the engagements he has made with sin and Satan—

And goes, with all his guilt upon him, to his God and Saviour—

He now perhaps may be deemed *mad* by his former companions—

But he should rather be considered as now " *coming to himself*"—

The effect of the prodigal's repentance appears in,

III. HIS RECEPTION

His father, it seems, was wishfully looking out for him—

And, on his first appearance, ran to testify his good will towards him

The sight of the returning child caused the father's bowels to yearn over him —

Nor would he suffer an upbraiding word to escape his lips—

When the prodigal began his confession, the father interrupted him with kisses—

And not only would not hear the whole of his confession, but would not even hurt his feelings by saying that he pardoned him—

He ordered the best robe, with shoes and a ring, to be instantly put upon him—

And killed the fatted calf in order to celebrate the joyful occasion—

What a delightful representation does this give us of the reception which penitents find with God!

God longs for their salvation even while they are at a distance from him.

He notices with joy the first approaches of their souls towards him—

Instead of frowning on the prodigal he receives him with joy—

Instead of upbraiding him with his folly, he seals upon his soul a sense of pardon—

He arrays him in robes of righteousness and garments of salvation—

He adorns him in a manner suited to the relation into which he is brought—

He provides for his future comfortable and upright conversation—

He rejoices over him as recovered from the dead—

And makes it an occasion of festivity to all the angels in heaven—

Thus do even the vilest sinners find their hopes, not only realised, but far exceeded—

They come for pardon, and obtain joy; for deliverance from hell, and get a title to heaven—

Their utmost ambition is to be regarded as the meanest of God's servants: and they are exalted to all the honors and happiness of his beloved children—

APPLICATION

Who would not wish to resemble this prodigal in his reception with his father—

But, in order to it, we must resemble him in his penitence and contrition—

Let none think that, because they have been more moral than the prodigal, they do not need to repent like him—

All of us without exception have walked after the imagination of our own hearts, without any love to his presence or regard for his authority—

Let all of us then cry for mercy, as miserable sinners—

The more vile we are in our own eyes, the more acceptable shall we be to God—

Some perhaps may fear to return, because they have been so exceeding vile—

But let none imagine that they have gone beyond the reach of mercy—

The promise of acceptance extends to all without exception, John vii. 37.

" There is bread enough and to spare" for all that will go to God—

Let all then accept the Saviour's invitation, Matt. xi. 28.

Let us this day afford an occasion of joy to all the hosts of heaven—

Then shall we ourselves be soon made partakers of their joy—

And dwell, as dear children, in our Father's house for ever and ever.

THE BALM OF GILEAD, A CURE FOR DISEASED SOULS.

Jer. viii. 22.—Is there no balm in Gilead? &c.   (H.)

THESE words were originally spoken of God's ancient people the Jews, who, at this time, it appears, were in a dreadfully declining state. They had provoked the Lord to anger with their graven images and strange vanities. ver. 19. The prophet Jeremiah was exceedingly affected on their account; ver. 21, and exclaims in the language of the text, " Is there no balm," &c.

I shall take occasion from these words, to consider,

I. THAT MANKIND UNIVERSALLY ARE IN A DISEASED STATE.

The soul of man is here meant, and hence the diseases alluded to are diseases of the soul. That the distempers of the mind are compared to wounds, disease, and sickness, will appear from Ps. xxxviii. 5; ciii. 3; cxlvii. 3; Ezek. xxxiv. 4; Matt. ix. 12.

We may here point out some of those diseases.

1. Atheism, infidelity, or unbelief of divine truths. This is a deadly disease, as it hinders the success of the gospel, and the saving of souls. Bad as this disease is, it is not to be found in hell. James ii. 19.

2. Ignorance of God and of gospel truths, even among those who profess to know him. Hosea iv. 6. There are multitudes living in the midst of gospel light, who are yet in gross darkness. They may be cured. Rev. iii. 17, 18; Jer. xxiv. 7.

438

3. Hardness of heart: hence they sit under the word, and hear the **most** terrible threatenings and curses denounced against their sins, and are as much unmoved as the seats they sit on. This may be cured. Ezek. xxxvi. 26; Phil. i. 6.

4. Earthly mindedness. This clogs the soul, and unfits it for spiritual exercises. The thoughts of God and eternity are thereby shut out. Other plagues kill their thousands, this kills its tens of thousands. Pharaoh's words are true of them. Exod. xiv. 3. There is help for this also. Cant. iv. 8; Col. iii. 1, 2.

5. Aversion to spiritual duties. There are thousands who would rather toil their bodies a whole day, than spend a quarter of an hour upon their knees with God in secret. Of Sabbaths and sermons they say, What a weariness is it? when will the Sabbath be gone? Mal. i. 13. For this we obtain relief. Ps. cx. 3; Isa. xl. 31; Ezek. xxxvi. 27.

6. Hypocrisy and formality in God's service: drawing near to God with our lips only; how unpleasant to God is a voice without the heart and affections. He heavily complains of it. Isa. xxix. 13. This also may be healed. Jer. xxxi. 33; Prov. iv. 18; 2 Cor. iv. 16.

7. Trusting to our own righteousness: depending upon our duties and performances for salvation, instead of believing on Christ, with the heart unto righteousness. Rom. x. 10.

8. Indwelling corruption. Sometimes it rises like a flood, swells high, and carries all before it. Ps. lxv. 3; Isa. lxiv. 6. There is help for this also. Ps. lxv. 3; Mich. vii. 19; Rom. vii. 24, 25.

9. Backsliding from the Lord: losing our spirituality and liveliness in God's service; then every grace decays in the soul, and the service of God becomes a weariness to us. This is a spiritual consumption, but it may be cured. Deut. xxx. 6; Hos. xiv. 4—6; John xiv. 19.

There are several symptoms which seem to render our discases almost desperate and incurable.

1. When the body is *universally* affected; and with a complication of diseases, the case is truly alarming, and this is the state of the soul. Isa. i. 5, 6. Still we may be recovered. David was. Ps. ciii. 2, 3.

2. When diseases are of long continuance, and rooted in the habit. This is the case of the soul. Ps. li. 5; Deut. xxviii. 59. Yet the Lord can make their dry bones live. Ezck. xxxvii.

3. When all around consider their case as desperate. This is often the case with sinners. Ezek. xxxvii. 3. And they often say with Israel, Behold our bones are dried. Ezek. xxxvii. 11. But see the promise in this case. Jer. xxx. 17.

4. When its threatening symptoms are not observed, so as to provide timely remedies; "although the fire be kindled round about as, we lay it not to heart." Our case is not unlike that of Israel. Isa. lvii. 17. But desperate as this case may be, there is hope of deliverance. ver. 18.

When the patient loses his senses, and becomes lethargic that he cannot be awakened. And this is often the case with sinners. Isa. xxvi. 11; xxix. 40. Yet still there is hope. Jer. xxxiii. 6.

II. THAT THERE IS A PHYSICIAN WHO CAN CURE ALL OUR DISEASES.

God himself is our physician. Exod. xv. 26. Our cure is the work of the whole Trinity; but especially of Jesus Christ, God incarnate, who came into this world with a commission to heal souls. He opened this commission at the commencement of his ministry Luke iv. 18. And afterwards. Mal. ix. 12, 13.

In this office of healer, he was typified by the brazen serpent. **John iii.** **14.** By the Sun of Righteousness. Mat. iv. 2. By the tree of life. **Rev.** **xxii.** 2.

The Lord Jesus Christ, being God-man, is nobly qualified to be our soul's physician. For,

1. He is infinite in knowledge, and understands all diseases, with the proper remedies, so that he can never mistake in any case, nor make wrong applications for the cure.

2. He has sovereign authority, and almighty power, whereby he can command diseases to come and go at his pleasure.

3. He hath infinite pity, and readiness to help the distressed; as he hath in him the compassion of a God, so he hath also the bowels of a man : hence he is inclined frequently to go to the sick without being sent for, and to the poor, who have nothing to give. On this account he is represented by the good Samaritan.

4. He hath wonderful patience towards the distressed, he bears with their ingratitude, and goes on with his work, till he has accomplished a perfect cure.

III. THE REMEDY WIHCH HE APPLIES TO EFFECT THE CURE, WHICH IS HIS *own blood*.

This is the true balm of Gilead which cures the sick soul. Isa. liii. 5. And although the Scriptures speak of other means of healing, all these are used in subserviency to Christ's blood, the blessed meritorious means of our cure, the only balm that procures all other means of healing us. These are,

1. The Spirit of God, with his gracious operations upon the soul. Gal. iii. 13, 14.

2. The word and ordinances of Christ. These are the leaves of the tree of life, which are for the healing of the nations. Ps. cvii. 20.

3. Afflictions. He sends these to make us feel how bitter sin is, to cause us to search our wounds, to mourn over them, and apply for the remedy. Isa. xxvii. 9.

4, Faithful ministers. The great Physician sends them to dispense sound and wholesome doctrines for that end. 1 Tim. vi. 3 ; Titus ii. 1.

5. Pious christians, even the poorest of them, help in this blessed **work** by their prayers. James v. 15. May such praying souls abound in all **our** congregations !

As to the Physician's method of applying the remedy. He,

1. Makes sinners sensible that they are sick, before he makes them whole; by convincing them of sin and misery. that they may prize Christ and his healing balm ; such are said to be sick. Matt. ix. 12. Now this preparatory sickness implies a discovery of the dangerous nature of the disease, sin ; an anxious care to be delivered from it; a dissatisfaction with all earthly comforts ; grief and sorrow of heart; Ps. xxxviii. 6, 18, despair of healing ourselves. Hos. xiv. 3. The absolute need of an infinitely wise and powerful Physician : a willingness to submit to his prescriptions, saying with Paul, Acts ix. 6.

2. Works faith in the soul, by his Holy Spirit; that is to say, he powerfully persuades and enables him to embrace Christ as his Saviour, and apply the balm of his blood and merits to his wounded soul, to remove guilt, to obtain pardon, and reconcile him to God. When this is done, the danger is over. John v. 24. To several diseased souls, Jesus said, " Thy faith hath made thee whole "

3. Accomplishes and perfects the cure, by the sanctifying influences of the Spirit, rooting out the very seeds of the disease, and makes the soul perfect in holiness, and meet for entering into heaven, where constant and uninterrupted health shall be enjoyed to all eternity.

IV. THE REASONS WHY SO FEW ARE HEALED, NOTWITHSTANDING THERE IS A BALM IN GILEAD, AND A PHYSICIAN TO APPLY IT.

The cause is surely in us. For,

1. Many are ignorant of their disease, and wilfully so: they have no feeling, no care, no fear; they boast the goodness of their hearts, and thank God for it.

2. Many are in love with their disease, more than with their Physician. God may say to them, as in Ps. lii. 3.

3. Many neglect the season of healing: they slight Christ and his offers in the gospel in the days of youth and health, and never inquire after him till it is too late.

4. Many will not trust wholly to Christ for healing; but Christ must have the sole honor of the cure, or he will not be their Physician.

5. Many will not submit to the prescriptions of Christ for healing; they will not submit to self-examination, repentance, contrition, godly sorrow, mortification, or self-denial, and therefore they are unhealed.

To conclude.

1. Let those who are in a diseased state, see their danger, for it is great; and if they do not apply to this Physician, they cannot be healed. Awake, therefore, O secure your soul! consider thy case, and flee to the great Physician for help.

2. The balm of Gilead is freely offered to you in the gospel. Isa. xlv. 22; Ezek. xviii. 32.

3. Consider how long you have slighted this balm already. Now improve your day like the people of Capernaum. Luke iv. 40; 2 Cor. vi. 2

4. And those whom he has healed, manifest their gratitude by living to his glory.

THE IMPORTANT QUESTION.

John ix. 35.—Dost thou believe on the Son of God? (Sk.)

THE text contains an important question addressed by the Lord Jesus to a highly privileged individual, on a most memorable occasion. The question relates to the most essential article of the christian religion; faith in the Son of God. The individual was a man, who, though born blind, had recently received sight; and the occasion was, when the Jews had excommunicated him for attesting the truth. Whether we regard the *sentiments* which the disciples entertained concerning this blind beggar, v. 2, or the *means* used by the Redeemer to open his eyes, v. 6, 7, or the *combination* of the Jews against Christ, v. 22, or the cogent and rational argument used by the poor man in vindication of his character, v. 30–33, the whole history is remarkable, and worthy a most attentive perusal. But the text at present demands our regard, and we will consider,

I. THE NATURE OF THE QUESTION :—*Dost thou believe?* &c. *To believe the Son of God* implies, 1st. Implicitly to credit the record which the inspired writers bore concerning him, especially concerning the divinity of his person, the merit of his sacrifice, and the power of his grace; that he is God over all blessed for ever—that he made his soul a sacrifice for sin—and that he is able to save them to the uttermost, that come unto God by him.

2. *To believe in the Son of God*, is to trust in him, Eph. i. 12, 13. Faith is simple credence when it refers only to a single proposition, but when it relates to a promise made by a benefactor to a starving mendicant, or a judge to a condemned culprit, it amounts to trust, confidence, and dependance. Christ is our sovereign benefactor; the benefits which he bestows are dearly purchased,—highly valued,—freely offered,—and graciously promised: but promised only to the children of faith: we must trust in Christ for their reception, and according to our faith so will it be done unto us.

3 *To believe in the Son of God*, is to receive him, John i. 12. Jesus Christ, in Matt. xii. 29, compares the soul of man to a house, and in Luke xi. 21, to a palace, a palace once glorious as the residence of the Deity, but now possessed by other inmates, and controlled by other lords, Isa. xxvi. 13; Matt. xv. 19, 20. But at the door of this palace Christ knocks for entrance, and all believers receive him, and receive him by the act of faith which perceives his excellencies, admires the suitableness of his character, and expands the powers of the soul for his reception.

4. *To believe in the Son of God*, is to realize his gracious presence; faith in this sense supplies the place of vision, by it we behold the Lamb of God, John i. 29; 2 Cor. iii. 18; Heb. xi. 27. Such is the nature of the question: let us,

II. OFFER SOME HELPS, TO ASSIST YOU IN ANSWERING IT.

1. Faith is a *divine principle;* and if you *believe in the Son of God*, the power to do so was divinely bestowed, in answer to your earnest and importunate prayers. You were once without Christ; you knew him not; you reposed no confidence in him; but you was roused from your sinful slumber; your eyes were opened, you saw your dreadful danger; Christ was proposed to you in all the dignity of his person, and in all the efficacy of his sacrifice: for a while you doubted and disbelieved; but you prayed, and said, "Lord, help thou my unbelief;" and at last you were enabled to cry in the language of believing Thomas, "My Lord and my God."

2. Faith is *a self-evident principle;* and if you *believe in the Son of God*, you cannot but know it, 1 John v. 10. Is faith credence; and cannot you know whether you believe the attestation of a fact? Is faith reliance; and cannot you know whether you depend on the veracity of him who has pledged his word to you? That doctrine which teaches that a man may *believe in the Son of God*, and not know it, is as contrary to sound divinity as it is to sound sense, as the Bible uniformly attributes effects to faith; and if the effects be not produced, the cause is not in action.

3. Faith *is a victorious principle;* and if you *believe in the Son of God*, you will conquer every adverse power, and put to flight the armies of the aliens. The records in the 11th chapter of Hebrews sufficiently confirm this truth. Do the sophisms of infidelity seek to beguile you? faith will detect and dissipate them. Do the fiery darts of the devil assail you? faith will quench them. Does the world spread its allurements before your eyes? faith will vanquish them, Eph. vi. 16; 1 John v. 4.

4. Faith *is a practical principle;* and if you *believe in the Son of God*, you lives will evince the genuineness of your faith. Believe in Christ, and

442

you will love him, for faith worketh by love ;—you will keep his commandments, for faith without works is dead ;—you will endure to the end, for the end of your faith is the salvation of your souls. Believe in Christ, and his ineffable beauties will attract your desires—his spotless life will excite your emulation—his dying love will melt your hearts,—his precious blood will purge your consciences,—his meritorious death will expiate your crimes,—and his glorious resurrection will ensure your immortality.

III. STATE SOME REASONS WHY AN ANSWER SHOULD BE GIVEN.

1. The *question is important;* the person who propose it is thy Sovereign, thy Saviour, and thy Judge. He is head over all things, and therefore has an indisputable right to propose this question. It is not impertinent nor unnecessary ; it concerns thy *faith,* that faith which has wrought such wonders, obtained such victories, silenced such misgivings, and without which thou must die in thy sins, and suffer the damnation of hell, John viii. 24 ; Mark xvi. 16.

2. The *question is personal;* "Dost *thou* believe ?" &c. Do not shift it off; it is not whether thy neighbors believe, but whether *thou* believest ; not whether thou hast a profession, a name, an opinion, but whether thou hast faith.

3. The *question is simple;* not complex, involving results that require the exercise of genius to solve. Many questions are so enwrapped in mystery, and have such bearings on other subjects that we are obliged to pause, hesitate, and ponder, before we can produce an appropriate answer ; but the question in the text is so plain, that a child, under the influence of the Holy Ghost may answer it.

4. But *the question is doubtful:* all men have not faith, some glory in their infidelity ; examine yourselves whether ye be in the faith. Dost *thou believe in the Son of God?* then worship him, verse 38.—Pray for an increase of faith, and anticipate the period when faith shall be lost in sight, and hope in all fruition.

NOAH'S FAITH AND OBEDIENCE.

Hebrews xi. 7.—" By faith Noah, being warned of God of things not seen as yet, moved with fear, prepared an ark to the saving of his house ; by the which he condemned the world, and became heir of the righteousness which is by faith."

THE character selected for our present consideration is particularly worthy of our attention and imitation. Though Noah lived in an age exceedingly corrupt and ungodly, he was deeply pious, and " found grace in the eyes of the Lord." He witnessed the most desolating calamity ; and was placed in a situation extremely difficult and affecting :—yet, as a righteous man, he walked in holy fellowship with God ;—and his eminent faith and obedience are *immortalized* in the text, for the *instruction* of all succeeding generations ; " *By faith Noah,*" &c.. In this illustrious example of primitive piety, we may remark,

I. THE WARNING HE RECEIVED. "Noah being warned," &c. The apostle here refers to the well-known history of the destruction of the antediluvian world ;—it was indeed an awful catastrophe, which was brought on mankind by their extreme corruption and abounding wickedness ! But **Noah,** who was a faithful servant of God, was mercifully preserved from the overwhelming scourge. According to the text,

1. *He was warned of the approaching deluge.* It was an event which could not have been previously known had it not been revealed by God ;—it was not the effect of a *natural cause*, but a *special judgment* of God, inflicted on incorrigible sinners. Long before its accomplishment, the Lord made known his purpose concerning it to Noah, for the instruction of himself and family, and for the warning of impenitent contemporaries. A distinct account of this revelation is found in the book of Genesis, chap. vi. 5–13.—Though these "things were *unseen as yet*," they were *certain* in their *fulfilment :*— and, in due time, fully came to pass according to the word of the Lord, Gen. vii. 17—23, &c. God is ever "slow to anger," and always *warns* before he *punishes :*—and hence,

2. *We are also warned of the impending danger.* Though we are not admonished of the same event that Noah was ; yet we are warned of "unseen things," which are *equally certain*, and much more *important* to mankind. All have sinned, and all are justly liable to suffer everlasting destruction. We are, therefore, *warned* of the danger of living and dying in our sins,—and of "suffering the vengeance of eternal fire," Ezek. xviii. 30–32 ; 2 Thess. i. 8, 9. Though these awful calamities are "unseen as yet," they are important *realities*, of which the Lord duly *warns us* by his word,—by his ministers,—by his spirit,—and by his providence, Ezek. xxxiii. 7—9, &c. The divine warnings are faithful,—affectionate,—urgent,—and incessant ;— let us, then, *attentively receive and diligently obey* them. That such was the conduct of Noah, appears from,

II. The obedience he displayed. "By faith Noah, moved with fear," &c. This inspired testimony reflects great honor on the character of this excellent patriarch, and fully explains the nature of his obedience, which is here so highly commended.

1. *He exercised implicit faith in God :*—he not only believed in his existence and perfection, but also, in all the *revelations* of his *will* and the *promises* of the *Messiah ;*—by *this principle* he obtained the blessings of salvation,—and was influenced in his general conduct ;—and hence, his obedience is expressly attributed to the faith in the text. "By *faith* Noah," &c., ver. 6. Faith is both a *saving* and *influential* principle ;—its *genuineness* must be proved by its *practical effects ;*—it works by love,—purifies the heart,— regulates the life,—and grasps invisible realities. No obedience can be acceptable to God, but that which arises from unfeigned faith, Rom. xiv. 23 ; James ii. 17, 18, 26.

2. *He was influenced by the fear of God.* We cannot suppose he feared for the temporal safety of himself and family, for God has assured him of their preservation, Gen. vi. 18 ; and as a *just* and *righteous* character, he had no reason for *distressing fear* respecting his eternal welfare :— but as a man of piety, he no doubt felt greatly alarmed, by the sudden destruction of the human race. His faith produced a *reverential fear* of God ; —a *compassionate fear* for perishing sinners ;—and a *cautious fear* of personal vigilance and faithfulness. Genuine *faith* and holy *fear* characterize the people of God in all ages, Mal. iii. 16 ; Acts x. 35.

3. *He promptly obeyed the will of God.* He strictly performed the divine injunction, in "preparing an ark to the saving of his house." The Lord gave him *special directions* for this purpose, all of which he *fully* complied with, Gen. vi. 22 ;—he cordially believed the word of God, and his faith produced practical conformity to his will. Though we are not required

444

to " prepare an ark" for our safety, yet we are all commanded to seek an interest in Christ, the sinner's refuge, and " work out our salvation with fear
and trembling," &c. And to encourage our imitation of Noah's character
and obedience, we shall proceed to consider,

III. THE DELIVERANCE HE OBTAINED. He was greatly honored by God,
and spared as a *special monument* of divine mercy in the midst of wrath.

1. *He was preserved from the general ruin.* How dreadful is the thought;
—how appalling the sight!—A world deluged with sin! The earth groaning and sinking under the crimes of its guilty inhabitants! The heavens
opening and pouring down the long-suspended vengeance on the incorrigible!
" They were eating and drinking, marrying and giving in marriage, until the
day that Noah entered into the ark ; and the flood came and took them all
away." How unprepared for such an awful change! Behold their frantic
minds seized with unutterable horror and amazement! But where shall they
look? To whom shall they go? Refuge fails!—the earth disappears!—all
is gone? See them flocking around the ark—entreating, grasping, and wailing! But alas! It is all in vain; the door is shut, and the man of God,
whom they had despised and insulted, is now preserved, and all his house,
for his sake. " Verily there is a reward for the righteous."

2. *He condemned the impenitent world.* He did not *formally* condemn
them as their *judge*,—but *ministerially*, as a " preacher of righteousness,"
and *practically*, by his pious example. His *faith* condemned their *unbelief;*
his *obedience* condemed their *disobedience*, &c. Thus every good man condemns and bears witness against the follies and practices of the ungodly world,
by a pious life and coversation.

2.-*He obtained the righteousness of faith.* He was not saved by *works,*
but solely by *faith.* He was justified and accepted of God, through the in
fintte merit of the promised Redeemer, which was imputed to him through
believing. Such has ever been the only way of salvation for fallen sinners
From this instructive case we should learn to consider our danger—estimate
the sinner's refuge—and " believe to the saving of the soul."

THE MEANS OF GRACE.

THE ADMIRABLE NATURE OF THE DIVINE ORACLES.

Psalm cxix. 129.—Thy testimonies are wonderful; therefore doth my soul keep them. (Sk.)

The love of the marvellous is a very prevailing passion among mankind. To witness uncommon scenes, and to hear tales of wonder and amazement, generally afford them much delight. Hence artful and designing men have found it easy to impose upon the multitude the most improbable and incredible accounts of places, persons, and events. And even those who are aware of the imposture, are too frequently pleased with the enchantment of novel and romantic stories, and pursue the illusions of the imagination till they lose all relish for reality and truth. But would they read the Bible, in humble dependance upon its Author, they would there " behold wondrous things out of his law," infinitely surpassing all that the natural heart has ever conceived, even the marvellous purposes and acts of the Most High. And on every sentence of this book is impressed the seal of truth. Such was the Psalmist's view when he uttered the text; in which he expresses,

I. His profound admiration of the Divine Oracles.—" Thy testimonies are wonderful." Since David's time these testimonies have been augmented by more than two thirds of the Bible—but to the whole his emphatic declaration may with the greatest propriety be applied. They are wonderful.

1. *In their style and composition.* In this respect they are

——*Wonderfully simple and plain*—This is their general character, notwithstanding occasional obscurities—No *histories* were ever so plainly related as those of the Bible—No *precepts* were ever more clear, or *promises* less ambiguous.

——*Wonderfully grand and sublime.* wherever the matter requires it.—Witness many of the Psalms—the book of Job—the prophets—Isa. xl., and lxiii., and the Apocalypse.

——*Wonderfully concise and expressive.* The sacred writers never burden their subject with a load of words—They never need many strokes to produce the requisite effect—every word is a feature, and the moral portrait is soon complete.—Witness the Proverbs, 1 Cor. xiii., &c.

2. *In their contents.* Here are comprised,

——*The most interesting records of facts.* Creation—Fall—Flood—the Call of Abraham, &c. &c. &c. The Incarnation—Life—Death, &c. of Christ.

——*The most astonishing displays of truth.* Here the perfections, works, and will of God, are gloriously exhibited.—More especially the amazing scheme of human redemption by our Lord Jesus, and all the variety of collateral doctrines which depend upon, or are connected with this economy. Well might the discovery of these truths be called " *marvellous light.*"

446

——*The most admirable and perfect rules of life.* The moral law, **its** explication by our Lord in Matt. xxii. 37—39, and his admirable Sermon on the Mount.—The great precepts, "repent and believe,"—together with all the directions furnished by the Apostles, &c., compose a sacred code of laws —easy of comprehension—suited to our ability—harmonized with each other—happy in their tendency—and honorable to God, Psa. xix. 7—11.

——*The most animating promises,* relative to all conditions and circumstances of the people of God. Blessings temporal, spiritual, and eternal— in prosperity, adversity, temptation, death, and beyond the grave, are guaranteed to the just, Psa. lxxxiv. 11.

——*The most tremendous threatenings.*—These are addressed to the wicked, the slothful, the faithless, the backsliding, Rev. xxi. 8.

3. *Wonderful in their efficacy,* Heb. iv. 12; Jam. i. 18; 1 Pet. i. 23. This efficacy is displayed,

——In the *alarm* they spread through the sinner's conscience. The hardened and audacious rebel feels himself arraigned at the tribunal of his own conscience, where he stands accused, convicted, and condemned, by that living word which is sharper than a two-edge sword, Acts ii. 37, 38, &c.

——In the *consolation* they inspire into the mourner's bosom, Acts ii. 41—47: Matt. xi. 28, &c.

——In the *moral transformation* of the most degraded characters. Witness the murderous Jews who crucified the Saviour. When the gospel was preached to them on the day of Pentecost, it transformed them into new creatures. Witness the Corinthians, some of whom were among the vilest of men, 1 Cor. vi. 9, 10, 11.—And witness thousands in the present day, who from being worse than brutes, become eminent for every christian virtue, through the word of God.

——In the *support through life,* and the *conquest over death,* which they afford all real believers. View the christian, in labor, in temptation, difficulty, in severe affliction—the word of God affords him support, and peace, and comfort. View him in the agony of death—the divine promises are applied to his soul, and he obtains the victory.—Exulting he asks " Who shall separate," &c., Rom. viii. 35—39.

Thus then truly wonderful are the testimonies of Jehovah, and truly reasonable is the profound admiration which the Psalmist expresses.—Let us now view,

II. THEIR PRACTICAL INFLUENCE.—" Therefore doth my soul keep them." Because thy oracles are so admirable, so excellent, so worthy of thee, their adorable Author, therefore doth my soul, my rational and intellectual part, receive and keep them as an invaluable deposit. This implies,

1. *That he treasured them up in his memory.* Unlike those inattentive persons who read or hear the word of God, but are not solicitous to under stand it, or to preserve the conceptions and impressions which it conveys, (like leaky vessels, these carry nothing away,) David took care to understand and to preserve the truth.—He knew it was the noblest employment for his memory to become the depository of God's testimonies, and every one of these was too important to be forgotten.

2. *That he kept them in the exercises of faith.* He received them as *God's* testimonies, and relied upon them as an immovable foundation. By this faith they became spirit and life to him. Without this vital realizing faith, though a man could repeat the whole Bible, and had the most systematic view of its contents, all would be vain. We only feel interested in the

447

scriptures in proportion as we heartily believe them—and it is only in the same proportion that they become efficacious.

3. *That he held them in constant esteem, and embraced them with earnest affection.* This he often expresses in this Psalm: "How sweet are thy words unto my taste," &c.—"Thy word is pure, therefore doth thy servant love it," ver. 20, 72. This ardent love to the world results from a thorough belief of it—And is an infallible test by which we may try the genuineness of our faith.

4. *That he kept them in obedient practice.* This was undoubtedly what the Psalmist intended, as all the other particulars are necessarily pre-supposed in this. He thus kept them—*Sincerely*, ver. 80.—*Cheerfully*, ver. 47.—*Diligently*, ver. 69.—*Continually*, ver. 44.—and *Universally*, ver 6.

Infer, 1st. How wide a contrast between David's esteem for the scriptures, and that noisy empty admiration of them which so many profess, but which is so uninfluential on their hearts and lives—They make fine speeches in their praise, and even contribute towards their circulation, while they neither understand, nor believe, love, nor practise, their all-important contents.

2. How carefully should we read and hear the word of God! We should constantly drink at this sacred fountain—be always digging in this inexhaustible mine. "Search the scriptures," said our Lord. Let us then read them with *prayer*, *attention*, and *self-application*, and meditate on them like David, day and night.

3. How great are our obligations to God for sending us his word!

4. How heinous is the guilt of those who neglect and abuse it.

OF THE LAW OF GOD.

Rom. vii. 12,—Wherefore the law is holy, &c. (H.)

The word law is variously used, sometimes for a part of the scriptures only, the Pentateuch, or five books of Moses; as when it is mentioned in the division of the scriptures by Christ, Luke xxiv. 44, and along with the prophets, and as distinct from them; John i. 45; see also chap. viii. 5, sometimes for all the books of the Old Testament, which in general go by the name of law, as does the book of Psalms on that account, as the places quoted out of it, or referred to in it, show; John x. 34; xii. 34; xv. 25; sometimes it signifies the doctrine of the scriptures in general, Ps. xix. 7, and the doctrine of the gospel in particular, Is. ii. 3; xlii. 4, called in the New Testament the law or doctrine of faith; Rom. iii. 27, and sometimes it signifies the whole body of laws given from God by Moses to the children of Israel, as distinct from the gospel of the grace of God, John i. 17, and which may be distinguished into,

1. The ceremonial law, of which this law was a shadow of good things to come by Christ, of evangelical things, and indeed was no other than the gospel veiled in types and figures.

2. Judicial, which respects the political state, or civil government of the Jews, and consists of statutes and judgments; according to which the judges of Israel determined all causes brought before them. Deut. xvii. 8—11 The government of the Jews was a very particular form of government; it was a theocracy, a government immediately under God, though he be king

of the whole world, and governor among and over the nations of it, yet **he** was, in a special and peculiar manner, king over Israel.

3. Moral, which lies chiefly in the Decalogue, or Ten commandments, Ex. xx. 3—17, and which our Lord has reduced, even both tables of the law, **to** two capital ones, love to God, and love to our neighbor; Matt. xxii. 39—40, as the apostle has reduced the commands of the second table to one, that **is,** love, which he calls the fulfilment of the law. Rom. xiii. 9, 10. And this law, to love God and our neighbor, is binding on every man, and is eternal, and remains invariable and unalterable; and concerning which I shall **treat** more largely. And consider,

I. THE AUTHOR AND GIVER OF THIS LAW.

God was the author and maker of it, Moses the giver and minister of **it** from God. There was a law in being before the time of Moses; or otherwise there would have been no transgression, no imputation of sin, no charge of guilt, nor any punishment inflicted; whereas death, the just demerit of sin, reigned from Adam to Moses. Besides the law given to Adam, there was the law of nature, inscribed on his heart by his Maker, as the rule of obedience to him, Rom. i. 19, 20; ii. 14, and which is reinscribed in the hearts of God's people in regeneration, according to the tenor of the covenant of grace, Jer. xxxi. 33. Now the law of Moses, for matter and substance, is the same which the law of nature, though differing in the form of administration; and this was renewed in the times of Moses, that it might be confirmed, and that it might not be forgotten, and be wholly lost out of the minds of men.

II. THE EPITHETS, OR THE PRORERTIES OF IT.

1. That it is perfect. The law of the Lord is perfect, Ps. xix. 7, which is true of the moral law, by which men come to know what is that good, and acceptable, and perfect will of God; Rom. xii. 2, what it is his will should be done, and what not be done; it takes in the whole duty of men, both to God and man; for to fear God, and keep his commandments. When the apostle John speaks of a new commandment, he means the old commandment to love one another, as he himself explains it, 1 John ii. 7, 8, and which he calls new, because enforced by a new instance and example of Christ's love in dying for his people, and by new motives and arguments taken from the same.

2. It is spiritual. " We know that the law is spiritual," says the apostle, Rom. vii. 14, which is to be understood of the moral law; for as for the ceremonial law, that is called the law of a carnal commandment, and is said to stand in carnal ordinances. Heb. vii. 16; ix. 10. The law reaches to the thoughts and intents of the heart, and the affections of the mind, and forbids and checks all irregular and inordinate motions in it, and the lusts of it. The assistance of the Spirit of God is necessary to the observance of it; and God in covenant has promised his people, that he will put his Spirit within them, and cause them to walk in his statutes, and keep his judgments, and do them. Ezek. xxxvi. 27.

3. The law is holy, and the commandment holy; it comes from a holy God, from whom nothing unholy can proceed; for holiness is his nature, and the law is a transcript of his holy will; the matter of it, or what it requires, is holy; even sanctification of the heart and life: and it directs to live holily, soberly, &c.

4. It is also just. There are no laws so righteous as the laws of God: the judgments of the Lord are true and righteous altogether. Deut iv. 8: Ps. xix. 9. It is impartia. unto all, and requires the same of one as of another and renders to every man according to his works; it is just in condemning wicked men, and in justifying those that believe in Jesus.

449

5. The law is good; the Author of it is good only, essenti·lly, originally, good; from whom every good and perfect gift comes. The law is materially good, it is morally good, it is pleasantly good, to a regenerate man, who, as the apostle, delights in the law of God after the inner man, and loves it, as David did, and meditates on it, as every good man does. Rom. vii. 22; Ps. cxix. 97; i. 2. And it is profitably good; not to God, Luke xvii. 10, but to men, their fellow-creatures, and fellow-christians, to whom they are serviceable, by their good works, Tit. iii. 8, and also to themselves; for though not *for*, yet *in* keeping the commands there is great reward, as peace of conscience. Ps. xix. 11; cxix. 165. The law is good, if a man use it lawfully, 1 Tim. i. 8.

III. THE USES OF THE LAW BOTH TO SINNERS AND TO SAINTS.

1. To sinners.

1. To convince of sin. Sin is a transgression of the law, by which it is known that it is sin. By the law is the knowledge of sin; not only of gross, actual sins, but of the inward lust of the mind; "I had not known lust, except the law had said, Thou shalt not covet." Rom. iii. 20; vii. 7.

2. To restrain from sin. Of this use are the laws of men; hence civil magistrates are terrors to evil doers so the law, by it menaces, deters men from sin.

3. To condemn and punish for sin. For sinners it is made, and against them it lies, to their condemnation, unless justified in Christ. 1 Tim. i. 9, 10. It accuses of sin, charges with it, brings evidence of it; stops the sinner's mouth from pleading in his own cause, pronounces guilty before God, and curses and condemns; "it is the ministration of condemnation and death.

2. It is of use to saints and true believers in Christ.

—1. To point out the will of God unto them. What is to be done by them, and what to be avoided; to inform them of, and urge them to their duty, both towards God and man.

2. To be a rule of life and conversation to them. Not a rule to obtain life, but to live according to; to direct their steps. "The commandment is a lamp, and the law is light." Prov. vi. 23. "Thy word is a lamp unto my feet." Ps. cxix. 105.

3. It is as a glass, in which a believer, by the light of the Spirit of God, may see his own face, what manner of man he is; how far short of perfection he is in himself. "I have seen an end of all perfection," &c. Hence,

4. They are led to prize the righteousness of Christ, since that is perfectly agreeable to the holy law of God; wherefore, "they desire to be found in Christ, not having on their own righteousness."

IV. THE LAW OF GOD CONTINUES UNDER THE PRESENT DISPENSATION FOR THE SAID USES.

Christ came not to destroy it, and loosen men's obligations to it, but to fulfil it; nor is the law made null and void by faith.

1. It does not continue as a covenant of works: and, indeed, it was not delivered to the children of Israel as such strictly and properly speaking, only in a typical sense.

2. Nor does it continue as to the form of administration of it by Moses; it is now no longer in his hands, nor to be considered as such.

3. It continues not as a terrifying law to believers, "who are not come to Mount Sinai, but they are come to Mount Sion." Nor are they awed and urged by its curses to an observance of it; but are constrained by the love of Christ.

4. Nor is it a cursing and condemning law to the saints; for "Christ had redeemed them from the curse of the law."

5. Yet it continues as a rule of walk and conversation to them, and is to be regarded by them as in the hands of Christ, their king and lawgiver. Believers, though freed from the law, in the sense before declared, yet are " not without a law to God, but under the law to Christ." 1 Cor. ix. 21.

OF THE GOSPEL.

Acts xx. 24.—The gospel of the grace of God. (H.)

There was gospel in the former dispensation, though called the legal dispensation; it was preached to Adam, to Abraham, and by Isaiah, and other prophets. Yet there is a clearer revelation and ministration of it under the present dispensation; as the law was, by the ministration of Moses, grace and truth; the word of grace and truth, the gospel, came by Jesus Christ, in a clearer and fuller manner than it had been made known before. John i. 17. Concerning which, the following things may be noted:

1. The name and signification of it.

The Greek word used for it signifies a good message, good news, glad tidings; the gospel is a message of good news from heaven, the far country, to sinners here on earth: such was the gospel Christ was anointed to preach; Luke iv. 18, compared with Isa. lxi. 1, and which his ministers bring, " whose feet are beautiful upon the mountains." Isa. lii. 7; Acts xiii. 32, 33. The Hebrew word used for the gospel, and the preaching of it, signifies good tidings also; and it is observed, by some, to have the signification of flesh in it which has led them to think of the incarnation of Christ; which is, undoubtedly, good news to the children of men, and a considerable branch of the gospel of Christ: and what has given Isaiah the character of an evangelical prophet, as if then present in his time; " To us a child is born:" Isa. ix. 6; see chap. vii. 14, and when the angel proclaimed the birth of Christ to the shepherds, he is said, " to bring good things." Luke ii. 10, 11. And this is one principal part of the gospel, the great mystery of godliness, " God manifest in the flesh." 1 Tim. iii. 16. Our English word gospel is of Saxon derivation; in which language, *spel* signifies speech: and so gospel is either *good speech*, which carries in it the same idea with the Greek and Hebrew words, or God's speech, which he has spoken by his Son, by his prophets, and by his ministers.

The word is variously used; sometimes it is put for the history of Christ's birth, life, and actions; such are the gospels according to Matthew, Mark, &c. Mark begins his history thus, " The beginning of the gospel of Jesus;" Mark i. 1; and Luke calls his gospel, " The former treatise he had made, of all that Jesus began, both to do and to teach:" Acts i. 1; and hence these four writers are commonly called evangelists. Sometimes the gospel is to be taken in a large sense, as including the word and ordinances: Matt. xxviii. 19, 20; Mark xvi. 15, 16, and sometimes strictly, for the doctrine of peace, pardon, &c. by Christ; hence gospel ministers, who bring good tidings of good, are said to publish peace, salvation, &c; Isa. lii. 7, the sum of which is expressed by the apostle, when he says, " This is a faithful saying," &c., 1 Tim. i. 15. Hence,

1. The gospel is called, the gospel of salvation, the word of salvation and salvation itself, Eph. i. 13; Acts xiii. 26; xxviii. 28, because it gives

an account of Christ, the author of salvation; of his appointment to it; of his mission, and coming into the world to effect it; and of his actual performance of it; of his being the able, willing, and only Saviour: and of the salvation itself, as great and glorious, perfect and complete, spiritual and everlasting; and because it describes also the persons that share in it, sinners, sensible sinners, &c.; Mark. xvi. 16; Acts xvi. 30, 31, and because it is, not only the means of revealing, but of applying salvation; for it is, to them that believe, "the power of God unto salvation."

2. The gospel of the grace of God; Acts xx. 24, because the several doctrines of it are doctrines of grace, or which exhibit blessings as flowing from the grace of God; redemption, pardon, &c.

3. The gospel of peace, the word of reconciliation; Eph. vi. 15; 2 Cor. v. 18; Acts x. 36; because it relates the steps taken in council and covenant: to form the scheme of man's peace with God; to lay the foundation of it, and to bring it about; Zech. vi. 13; Isa. liv. 10, and also relates the actual making of it; by whom, and by what means. Eph. ii. 14; Isa. liii 5; Col. i. 20; Rom. v. 10.

4. The gospel of the kingdom; Matt. iv. 23, because it treats both of the kingdom of grace here, showing wherein it lies; and of the kingdom of glory hereafter, pointing out the proper meetness for it. John iii. 5; Matt. v. 20; Luke xii. 32.

II. THE AUTHOR AND ORIGIN OF THE GOSPEL.

1. It is not of man; a device and invention of men. "I neither received it of men." Gal. i. 11, 12. It is not discoverable by the light of reason. Matt. xvi. 16, 17. Hence the gospel is frequently called, "a mystery;" the "wisdom of God in a mystery; the hidden wisdom;" and the doctrines of it, "the mysteries of the kingdom." Matt. xiii. 11.

2. The gospel is from heaven. It is good news from a far country: the gospel is, with the Holy Ghost, sent down from heaven: and Christ that spoke it, is He that speaketh from heaven. The question put concering the baptism of John, "Whence was it? from heaven, or of men?" may be put concerning the gospel, and answered as that; that is, from heaven; and not of man. 1 Pet. i. 12; Heb. xii. 25; Matt. xxi. 25. It comes also from God the Father, and is therefore called "the gospel of God." Rom. i. 1— 3. It comes also from Christ, the Son of God, and is called, "the gospel of his Son, the gospel of Christ, the word of Christ, and the testimony of Christ, and the testimony of our Lord," Rom. i. 9—16; Col. iii. 16; 2 Tim. i. 8, of which Christ is the subject, sum, and substance, as well as the author. Hence the apostle says, he received it "by the revelation of Jesus Christ." Gal. i. 12. It may be said, likewise, to come from the Holy Spirit of God, the inditer of the scriptures, wherein it lies, "who searches the deep things of it, and reveals them to men."

III. THE EFFECT OF THE GOSPEL, WHEN ATTENDED WITH THE POWER AND SPIRIT OF GOD.

1. The regeneration of men; who are said, "to be born again by the word of God," and to be "begotten again with the word of truth." 1 Pet. i. 23; James i. 18. Hence ministers of the gospel are represented as spiritual fathers. 1 Cor. iv. 15.

2. As in regeneration, souls are quickened by the Spirit and grace of God, this is ascribed to the gospel as an instrument. Hence it is called, "the Spirit which giveth life, and said to be, "the savor of life unto life." 2 Cor ii. 16, and iii. 6.

2

3. It is frequently spoken of as a light, a great light, a glorious light; and so is, in the hands of the Spirit, a means of enlightening the dark minds of men into mysteries of grace. "The entrance of thy word giveth light." Ps. cxix. 130. It is a glass, in which the glory of Christ, and of the riches of his grace, may be seen.

4. By it faith in Christ comes, and is ingenerated in the heart by the Spirit of God attending it. Hence, among other reasons, it is called "the word of faith." Rom. x. 8, 17.

5. When faith is wrought in the soul, the righteousness of Christ is revealed unto it in the gospel, and not at first believing only; it is revealed therein "from faith to faith." Rom. i. 17. Hence it is called "the word of righteousness, and the ministration of righteousness." Heb. v. 13; 2 Cor. iii. 6, 9.

6. It affords spiritual food, and is the means of feeding and nourishing souls unto everlasting life. It has in it milk for babes, and meat for strong men; and when it is found by faith, it is eaten by it with pleasure, and fills with spiritual joy. 1 Tim. iv. 6; vi. 3; Heb. v. 13, 14; Jer. xv. 16. Hence,

7. Is another effect, it yields much spiritual peace, joy, &c. The doctrines of it are calculated for such a purpose; it is glad tidings of good things; as of peace, pardon. When Philip preached Christ and his gospel in Samaria, "there was great joy in that city." Acts viii. 5, 8. All this must be understood of the gospel, not as producing these effects of itself, but as it comes, "not in word only, but with power." 1 Thess. i. 5—8; Ps. cx. 2; Rom. i. 16.

IV. THE PROPERTIES OF THE GOSPEL.

1. It is but one; there is another, as the apostle says, Gal. i. 6, 7. The same gospel which was in the beginning, and will be to the end of the world; the same under the Old Testament as under the New; the subject of it, Christ and salvation by him; the doctrines of it, of justification, remission of sins, &c. the same, only now more clearly revealed. For it is true of the gospel, what is said of Christ, it is "the same yesterday." Heb. xiii. 8.

2. It is called, from the objects of it, the gospel of the circumcision, and the gospel of the uncircumcision. Gal. ii. 7. Not that the gospel of the one is different from that of the other; it is the same gospel, only dispensed to different persons; the circumcised Jews, and uncircumcised Gentiles.

3. It is a glorious gospel; so it is called, 2 Cor. iv. 4; 1 Tim. i. 11. It has a glory in it exceeding that of the law, and the dispensation of it, 2 Cor. iii. 11, for the clearness, fullness, suitableness of its doctrines to the state and condition of men; and in which the glory of the person of Christ, his offices, and of the blessings of grace that come by him, is held forth in great splendor and brightness.

4. It is an everlasting gospel; which is the epithet given it, Rev. xiv. 6. It was ordained in the council and covenant of God before the world was, of which it is a transcript, and so was from everlasting; 1 Pet. i. 25; but "the word of the Lord endureth for ever."

453

THE NATURE OF THE GOSPEL.

Isaiah lii. 7.—How beautiful upon the mountains are the feet of him that bringeth good tidings, that publisheth peace ; that bringeth good tidings of good, that publisheth salvation ; that saith unto Zion, Thy God reigneth ! (S. S.)

IN order to understand the prophetic writings we must always bear in mind that they have a spiritual or mystical sense, as well as a plain and literal one— The words before us, in their primary meaning, evidently refer to the joy, with which the proclamation of Cyrus, when he permitted the captive Jews to return from Babylon to their native country, would be received—But they certainly relate also to the deliverance announced to us under the gospel dispensation ; for it is in this view that they are quoted by the apostle Paul, Rom. x. 15—We shall take occasion from them to shew,

I. WHAT THE GOSPEL IS.

It is described with sufficient accuracy in the text: it is,

1. A proclamation of "peace and salvation" to man.

The gospel supposes men to have offended God, and to be obnoxious to his everlasting displeasure—It further supposes that they have no way of conciliating the divine favor, or of warding off the stroke of his indignation— Coming to men in this helpless, and hopeless state, it publisheth tidings of peace and salvation : it represents sin as expiated by the atoning blood of Jesus ; and God as reconciled to all who will trust in his meritorious and all-prevailing sacrifice—This is the view which St. Paul himself gives us of the gospel ; in preaching of which gospel ministers resemble the messengers sent to Babylon, who had nothing to do but to proclaim a full and free deliverance to the wretched captives, 2 Cor. v. 18–20.

2. A declaration of Christ's power and grace.

The Chaldeans, who so grievously oppressed their Jewish captives, may justly represent to us the bitter and tyrannical dominion of sin and satan ; and Cyrus, who, without fee or reward, liberated them from their bondage, may be considered as the agent and representative of the Deity—As therefore the messengers would not fail to remind the Jews that Cyrus, the one author of their happiness, would continue to them his protection and favor while they maintained their allegiance to him ; so, in preaching the gospel, we are to declare, that Christ, to whom we owe the beginnings of our liberty, will complete our deliverance, and continue to us all the tokens of his love, provided we yield him, as we are in duty bound, a willing and unreserved obedience—Thus did Christ himself preach the gospel, saying, Repent, for the kingdom of heaven is at hand. Comp. Mark i. 14, 15, with Matt. iv. 17.

If we view the gospel in this light, we shall see immediately,

II. THAT IT IS A GROUND OF JOY.

By a beautiful figure, the very steps of the messenger hastening over the distant mountains are represented as inspiring us with joy. That the gospel itself is a source of joy, appears in that,

1. It has been considered so from the first moment of its promulgation.

Abraham, two thousand years before its promulgation, rejoiced exceedingly in that distant prospect of it, John viii. 56,—At the birth of Jesus, our deliverer, an host of angels congratulated the world, saying, Behold, we bring you glad tidings of great joy, which shall be to all people: for unto you is born a Saviour, which is Christ the Lord, Luke ii. 10, 11,—As soon as ever the full effects of the gospel came to be experienced, the converts, filled with

454

every malignant temper just before, were filled with joy, and eat their bread with gladness and singleness of heart, blessing and praising God, Acts ii. 46, 47,—No sooner was the gospel preached in Samaria, than there was great joy in that city : and, the instant that the eunuch had embraced it, he went on his way rejoicing, Acts viii. 8, 39,—Thus it is at this day an healing balm and a reviving cordial to all who understand and receive it—

2. It is in itself well calculated to create joy in our hearts.

Let but its blessings be felt, and it will be impossible not to rejoice—Did the Jews exult at a deliverance from a cruel yoke, and a restoration to their native country ? How much more must a sinner rejoice at his deliverance from death and hell, and his restoration to the forfeited inheritance of heaven !—The transports of joy manifested by the cripple whom Peter and John had healed, were the natural effusions of a grateful heart : we should have wondered if he had not so expressed the feelings of his soul : Acts iii. 8; but he had received no benefit in comparison of that which the believer enjoys when he first embraces the gospel of Christ—Hence our prophet represents the gospel as invariably producing such sensations as the husbandman feels when bringing home the fruits of the field, or the soldier when dividing the spoils of victory, Isa. ix. 3, 6.

3. It is, and ever will be, the one subject of thanksgiving in the realms of glory.

The glorified saints never have their attention diverted from it for one single moment : day and night are they singing to him who loved them, and washed them from their sins in his own blood, Rev. i. 5, 6,—And though the angels are less interested in this subject, because they never needed redeeming grace, yet do they join the general chorus, ascribing honor and glory to him that sitteth on the throne, and to the Lamb for ever—Nor will they ever be weary of this subject, such an inexhaustible fund is it of light, and happiness, and glory—

Infer,

1. How strange is it that the gospel should be treated with indifference !

That it is so treated, needs no proof : but how amazing that it should ever be slighted by those to whom it is sent ! that condemned criminals should disregard the offers of pardon sent them by their Prince !—O that there might be no more occasion for that complaint, Who hath believed our report ?—Let the very feet of the messengers who bring the tidings be henceforth beautiful in our eyes—

2. Of what importance is it to distinguished between mere morality, and the gospel of Christ !

Lectures upon honesty would administer but little comfort to a person about to be executed for breaking the laws of his country : nor can mere discourses on morality administer much comfort to a self-condemning sinner : and, if he mistake such discourses for the gospel, he is fatally deceived—The gospel is a full and free offer of salvation through the blood of Christ : and this is glad tidings indeed ; like " rivers of water in a dry place, or a shadow of a great rock in a weary land"—O that all who are ambassadors of God may remember the great scope of their ministry, and testify the gospel of the grace of God !—And let all who hear the joyful sound, improv the day of their visitation : blessed are they if they receive the truth in the love thereof; but most aggravated will be their condemnation if they despise the mercy so freely offered them.

THE CHANGE WROUGHT BY THE GOSPEL.

Isaiah lv. 12, 13.—For ye shall go out with joy, and be led forth with peace: the mountains and the hills shall break forth before you into singing, and all the trees of the field shall clap their hands. Instead of the thorn shall come up the fir-tree, and instead of the brier shall come up the myrtle-tree: and it shall be to the Lord for a name, for an everlasting sign that shall not be cut off. (S. S.)

THE change wrought annually on the face of nature from desolation and barrenness to beauty and fruitfulness, is a lively representation of the change effected by the gospel of Christ. " The rain and the snow descending on the earth" nourished the whole vegetable creation, and cause every part of it to spring forth in its appointed season: and, in the same manner, " the word of God, dropping as the rain and distilling as the dew" upon the souls of men, infuses life into them, and renders them fruitful in every good word and work. This is the parallel drawn by the prophet himself, who, expatiating on the subject, predicts, under the image of the Jews' return from Babylon, the progress of the gospel in renovating the intellectual and spiritual world. His words will lead us to consider

I. THE EFFECTS OF THE PREACHED GOSPEL.

The civilizing of the world is a very small part of the work which the gospel is intended to accomplish. It is sent

1. To inspire new feelings.

Man in his natural state is an entire stranger to spiritual joy, or solid peace. The peace that flows from a want of foresight or reflection, and the joy that consists in mere animal gratifications, he may possess: but he is as destitute of spiritual enjoyments, as the brute creation are of intellectual pleasure. His state however is wonderfully changed when he receives the word of God in truth. At first indeed he feels trouble and anguish; but as soon as ever he has a sense of his acceptance with God, his tears are wiped away, and " the bones which were broken rejoice." It frequently happens, especially where the preceding sorrows have been deep, that the joy which succeeds them is rapturous and abundant. The surprise of Peter, on the eve of his expected execution, was not unlike that of a new convert: suddenly, a light shone in upon him, and his chains fell off, and the prison doors flew open, and an angel conducted him out, so that he could not persuade himself that he was awake, but thought he saw a vision: thus when the new convert is first brought forth into light and liberty, and finds the obstacles, which had seemed insurmountable, removed, he is ready to think it must be all a delusion: it is with him as with those of old, " when the Lord turned again the captivity of Zion, we were like them that dream: then was our mouth filled with laughter, and our tongue with singing;" yea, " the very hills break forth before him into singing, and all the trees of the field clap their hands." We must not however suppose, that all are equally elated; or that the joy which any feel will continue with them; it will rather subside into a peaceful tranquility of mind . they may *go out with joy;* but they will be *led forth with peace.* The Saviour's joy, which is to be fulfilled in us, consisted rather in peace than exultation; and such is the legacy that he has left to us. John xvii. 13, and xiv. 27. At first we are like a stream rippling and murmuring near the fountain head; but afterwards we resemble rather the deepened river flowing with silent majesty.

2. To infuse new dispositions.

A thorny bush is unproductive and worthless; as a brier is unseemly and injurious. The one is a just image of the more decent of mankind; the other, of the more profane. All are low and groveling in their nature, having no desires beyond this present world; and too many, by their influence as well as by their example, would impede the progress of those who are walking in the good way. The fir-tree on the other hand lifts its head on high; while the myrtle diffuses its fragrance all around; and both of them retain their verdure all the year: yet such shall the vilest of mankind become, when once they embrace the gospel of Christ. They shall soar to heaven with devout affections; they shall spread around them a sweet savor of the knowledge of Christ; they shall be unfading ornaments in the place where they grow; and instead of wounding, like the brier, all that come in contact with them, they shall, like the myrtle, emit the sweeter fragrance the more they are bruised, and perfume, as it were, the very hand that bruises them.

To impress our minds with a due esteem for the gospel, let us proceed to consider

II. The excellency of those effects.

There is an inherent excellence in holy dispositions, which, independent of the consequences flowing from them to ourselves or to society, must render them amiable in our eyes. But, as the text limits our views to the honor which accrues from them to God, we shall content ourselves with observing, that the change effected by the gospel is to the Lord

1. An occasion of praise.

None who are quickened and renewed by the word ever take the honor to themselves: all with one voice cry, "He that hath wrought us for the self-same thing is God; therefore, Not unto us, O Lord, not unto us, but unto thy name be the praise." The greater the change that is wrought in any person's heart, the less will he be disposed to arrogate any thing to himself on account of it: and most of all, "when the top-stone of the spiritual building shall be brought forth, will he shout, Grace, grace unto it." From his first acquaintance with divine truth will he begin to speak of God with love and gratitude. His own experience will furnish him with an inexhaustible fund of praise and thanksgiving. Nor will his acknowledgments any longer be a dull recital of an established creed, but the lively effusions of a grateful heart.

Now if that be deemed excellent, which causes the name of any human being to be held in estimation, and to be transmitted to posterity with honor, how much more must that be excellent, which makes the name of God to be reverenced and adored!

2. A monument of glory.

It is not in this world only that God is glorified by the dispensations of his grace: at the day of judgment every saint will "be to him for a name, and for a praise and for a glory." "Christ will come to be glorified in his saints, and admired in all that believe." How sovereign will the grace of God appear to every one amongst them, when each sees himself as a brand plucked out of the fire! When stupendous wisdom will be discovered in the plan, whereby he has effected their restoration to his favor! What marvellous patience will he appear to have exercised towards them under all their backslidings; and what unbounded mercy in pardoning their multiplied transgressions! Nor will his power be less an object of admiration, when it is seen how wonderfully it has been exerted in converting their souls, and in preserving them unto his heavenly kingdom. Yea, as long as there shall exist one glorified saint in heaven, so long shall the perfections of the Godhead be most eminently displayed in the salvation of sinful man.

How excellent then must that change be, which to all eternity shall be the brightest mouument of the divine perfections! The work of creation is excellent, though it is so soon to pass away: but that, glorious as it is, has no glory by reason of the glory that excelleth in the new creation.

INFER,

1. What encouragement have men to hear the gospel!

As a person who had never seen the face of nature but in the depth of winter, would scarcely conceive it possible that so great an alteration could take place in it as is annually made within the space of a few weeks, so are many ready to imagine, that their hard and barren hearts are incapable of experiencing such a change as God requires. But his word is as powerful as ever: it is still "like fire, or like a hammer that breaketh the rock in pieces:" and though "it runs not, nor is glorified" to the same extent as in former days, yet wherever it is preached in sincerity and truth there are some to attest its efficacy, and to prove that "it is the power of God to the salvation of men." Let none then despair: for though "the treasure be put into an earthen vessel, God will display the excellency of his power by means 'of it:" he will plant the fir-tree and the myrtle where nothing grew but thorns and briers; "he will make the wilderness like Eden, and the desert like the garden of the Lord."

2. What a sure criterion have we whereby to judge of our state!

An insensibility with respect to spiritual things characterizes the natural man; and a quickness of perception with respect to them marks the person in whom the word of God has taken due effect. Have we then surrendered up our false peace, and our carnal joy? and have we attained to a scriptural "joy and peace in believing?" Have the creatures all around us been led, as it were, to sympathize with us, and congratulate us on the change? Look then next to the tempers and dispositions of the soul: have the low groveling desires of the carnal mind been made to ascend to heaven; and the natural aversion to holy exercises been exchanged for an unfeigned delight in them? In short, is God now glorified in the whole of our deportment, so that, whosoever beholds our spirit and conduct is constrained to admire the grace of God in us? Doubtless, this change is not perfect in any; nor can we expect it to be so, while we carry about with us this body of sin and death; but is the change begun? and is it carrying on towards perfection? O that on considering these questions we might have the testimony of our consciences that things are so! But if there be no evidence of these things, let us beware, lest, instead of being eternal monuments of God's love, we be objects of his everlasting displeasure.

FAITH ESTABLISHES THE LAW.

Rom. iii. 31.—Do we then make void the law through faith? God forbid: yea, we establish the law. (S. S.)

A GENERAL prejudice obtains against the way of salvation by faith—
But it prevailed equally even in the apostolic age—
Paul himself saw that his statement of the gospel did not escape censure—
He perceived that it was deemed injurious to the interests of morality—
He therefore anticipated and obviated this objection—

I. Whence it is that people suppose we make void the law through faith.

The truth, however clearly stated, is often misapprehended—

In explaining salvation by faith we affirm two things concerning the law,

1. That it has no power either to condemn or to justify believers—

It cannot *condemn* them, because Christ has redeemed them from its curse, Gal. iii. 13.

It cannot *justify* them, because they have transgressed it, and its demands of perfect obedience are unalterably the same—

Faith in Christ delivers us from the penal sanctions of the law, but does not lower its demands—

2. That our obedience to it makes no part of our justifying righteousness—

Faith and works, *as grounds of justification*, are opposite to each other, Rom. xi. 6.

If our works had any share in our justification we should have a ground of boasting, which is utterly to be excluded, Rom. iii. 27.

The smallest reliance on these makes void all hope by the gospel, Gal. v. 2, 4.

All dependence therefore on the works of the law must be entirely renounced—

These affirmations evidently exclude morality from the office of justifying—

They are therefore supposed to discountenance all practical religion—

But this mistake originates in the ignorance of the objectors themselves

II. That the believer, so far from making void the law, establishes it.

The power of the law is twofold; to command obedience, and to condemn for disobedience

The believer establishes the law in each o. these respects—

1. In its commanding power

He owns its absolute authority over him as God's creature—

All his hope is in the perfect obedience which Christ paid to it for him—

He looks upon his obligations to obey it as increased, rather than diminished, by the death of Christ—

He actually desires to obey it as much as if he were to be justified by his obedience to it—

2. In its condemning power

He acknowledges himself justly condemned by it—

He founds his hope in Christ as having borne its curse for him—

His own conscience cannot be pacified but by that atonement which satisfied the demands of the law—

Bereft of an hope in the atonement, he would utterly despair—

He flees to Christ continually " to bear the iniquity of his holiest actions"—

Thus he magnifies the law while the objector himself makes it void

III. That the person, who objects to salvation by faith alone, does indeed make void the law—

Objections against the doctrine of faith are raised from a pretended regard for the law—

But the person who blends faith and works effectually undermines the whole authority of the law—

1 Its commanding power

He is striving to do something which may serve in part as a ground of his justification—

But he can do nothing which is not imperfect—

Therefore he shews that he considers the law as less rigorous in its demands than it really is—

Consequently he robs it in a measure of its commanding power—

2. Its condemning power

He never thoroughly feels himself a lost sinner—

He does not freely acknowledge that he might be justly cursed even for his most holy actions—

He even looks for justification on account of that which in itself deserves nothing but condemnation—

Thus the advocates for the law are, in fact, its greatest enemies—

Whereas the advocates for the gospel are the truest friends to the law also—

Infer,

1. How absurd is it for persons to decide on religion without ever having studied its doctrines !

In human sciences men forbear to lay down their dogmas without some previous knowledge of the points on which they decide—

But in theology all, however ignorant, think themselves competent to judge—

They indeed, who are taught of God, can judge—

But unenlightened reason does not qualify us to determine—

Let us beware of indulging prejudices against the truth—

Let us seek to be " guided into all truth by the Holy Spirit"—

2. How excellent is the salvation revealed to us in the gospel !

Salvation by faith is exactly suited to man's necessities—

It is also admirably calculated to advance the honor of God—

Every man that is saved magnifies the law, and consequently the law-giver—

The commanding and condemning power of the law are equally glorified by the sinner's dependence on the obedience and sufferings of Christ—

But in those who are condemned, *its sanctions only* are honored—

Thus is the law more honored in the salvation of one, than in the destruction of the whole human race—

Let all then admire and embrace this glorious salvation.

THE OFFICE AND OPERATION OF FAITH.

Gal. v. 6.—In Jesus Christ neither circumcision availeth any thing, nor uncircumcision, but faith, which worketh by love.   (S. S.)

The peculiar character of the gospel is, that it shews how a sinner may be justified before God—

Yet the generality of christians are far from entertaining just views of this most fundamental point—

They confound the different offices of faith and works—

But St. Paul distinguishes them with much accuracy and precision—

He invariably declares that our justification is by faith—

Yet, though he denies to works the office of justifying, he invariably insists on them as the fruits and evidences of our faith—

Nothing can be more decisive than the declaration before us—

We shall

I. EXPLAIN IT

Man is prone to trust in outward rites and ceremonies

The Jews confided in the ordinance of circumcision—

The Judaizing teachers also among the christians inculcated the observance of that rite as a ground of hope—

Amongst ourselves also, many think it sufficient that they have been baptized—

Or expect to find admission into heaven because they have attended regularly at the Lord's table—

But no outward observances can avail for our salvation

An external conformity with the rule of duty may proceed from the basest principles—

It may spring from a desire to obtain man's applause, or to establish a righteousness of our own—

And it may consist with the indulgence of evil tempers and vicious appetites—

It cannot therefore of itself characterize the true christian—

Nor can it " avail *any thing*" towards procuring the divine favor—

If indeed it proceed from faith and love, it will be rewarded—

But if it be made the ground of our hope, it will prevent, rather than procure, our acceptance with God, Gal. v. 2.

That which alone can avail for our acceptance with God, is "faith"

All the promises of God are made to faith, Mark xvi. 16; Acts x. 43.

It is by faith that all the saints of old obtained salvation, Rom. iv. 3, 6, 7

St. Paul and St. James do not *really* differ respecting this—*

Nor do any passages of scripture *really* contradicts it—†

If salvation be *of grace*, it must be *by faith*, Rom. iv. 16.

Yet this faith must be productive of good works

It is not a mere notional assent to certain doctrines—

Nor is it a confident assurance respecting the safety of our own state—

But it is a living operative principle in the heart—

It is, on *our* part, the bond of union between Christ and our souls—

And it cannot but discover itself by " works of love"—

If it produce not holy tempers, and an unfeigned regard for the bodies and souls of men, it is no better than the faith of devils, Jas. ii. 19.

The declaration in the text being explained, we shall,

II. IMPROVE IT

Every part of scripture, rightly understood, is profitable for the directing both of our faith and practice, 2 Tim. iii. 16.   See the Greek.

We will improve this before us,

1. " For doctrine," that is, for the establishment of true doctrine

The way of salvation is simply by faith in Christ—

---

* St. Paul (Rom. iv. 1—5,) speaks of Abraham as being justified before God : St. James (ii. 21—23,) speaks of Abraham as manifesting his faith before man, and as justifying his pretentions to the divine favor by a suitable conduct and conversation.

† There are many expressions both in the Old and New Testament which *seem* to assert salvation by works: but they are only declarative of the character of those that shall be finally saved, or of God's gracious determination to reward those works which flow from faith. If they were interpreted in any other way, they would invalidate the whole gospel.

And every kind of work, ceremonial or moral,* must be considered as of no avail with respect to justification before God—

However necessary, however valuable, our obedience may be if performed aright, it ceases to be valuable the moment we depend upon it—

This is clearly stated in the text and context, Gal. v. 2—6.

And St. Paul himself was practically persuaded of this doctrine—Phil. iii. 9.

Let us then renounce all confidence in our own works—

And rely wholly on the blood and righteousness of Christ—

2. "For reproof," that is, for the refuting of false doctrines

Some have argued from the text, that faith saves us *as an operative principle*—

Thus they affirm that we are justified by something *within ourselves*—

But faith, *as a principle*, is not of, more value than love, 1 Cor. xiii. 13.

And if we were justified by it *as an operative principle*, we should have room to boast, just as much as we should if we were justified by love or any other principle—

The reason of our being justified by faith is, that faith unites us unto Christ, which is a property not common to any other grace—

Our works do not *make* our faith to be good or saving, but only *prove* it to be so—†

If our faith be genuine we shall discover it *to God* by a simple dependence upon Christ, and *to man* by the practice of good works—

3. "For correction" of unrighteous conduct

It must be confessed that many profess faith in Christ while their lives are unworthy of the gospel—

But such persons stand condemned even by their own profession—

No faith is of any avail, but such as "works by love"—

Let professors then weigh themselves in the balance of the sanctuary—

Let them examine their tempers, dispositions and actions—

Let them acknowledge that a proud, envious, passionate, unforgiving, covetous or selfish christian is as much a contradiction in terms, as an adulterous or murderous christian—

Let them put away either their profession or their sins—

4. "For instruction in righteousness"

To point out all the offices of love would be tedious—

But we must observe that it should operate uniformly, and respect both the bodies and souls of men—

Let us then exercise love, and abound in it more and more.‡

---

* The apostle does not deny that circumcision is of any avail merely because it is *a ceremonial* work, but because it is *a work ;* and because dependence on it would rob Christ of his glory. His argument therefore excludes works of whatever kind they be. Compare Gal. ii. 16.

† Just as fruit does not *make* a tree good, but only *manifests* it to be so.

‡ If this were the subject of a CHARITY-SERMON, it would be proper to open *here* the nature, excellence, and importance of the particular institution which was to be benefited: and then to exhort the benevolent in general, and believers in particular, to give it their liberal support.

THE RICHES OF DIVINE GRACE DISPLAYED.

Eph. ii. 4—7.—But God, who is rich in mercy, for his great love wherewith he loved us, even when we were dead in sins, hath quickened us together with Christ . . . . . . and hath raised us up together, and made us sit together in heavenly places in Christ Jesus: that in the ages to come he might shew the exceeding riches of his grace, in his kindness towards us through Christ Jesus. (S. S.)

WHAT an accumulation of sublime ideas is here presented to our view!—

Well might the Psalmist say that the meditation of God was sweet to him—

We scarcely know whether to admire more the grace of the benefactor, or the felicity of those who participate his blessings—

But the text requires us to fix our attention on that most delightful of all subjects, the riches of divine grace—

The apostle has in the preceding verses described the state of the unregenerate world—

He now displays the grace of God towards the regenerate

I. IN ITS SOURCE.

God is "rich in mercy," and "abundant in love"

Mercy and love are, as it were, the favorite attributes of the Deity, Ex. xxxiv. 6, 7.

The exercise of these perfections is peculiarly grateful to him, Mic. vii. 18.

There is an inexhaustible fountain of them in the heart of God, Rom. x. 12.

They have flowed down upon the most unworthy of the human race—

They will flow undiminished to all eternity—

While he retains his nature he cannot but exercise these perfections, 1 John iv. 8.

These are the true sources of all the grace displayed towards fallen man

Man had nothing in him whereby he could merit the attention of his Maker—

He was fallen into the lowest state of guilt and misery—

But the bowels of his Creator yearned over him*—

God felt (if we may so speak) an irresistible impulse of compassion towards him†—

Hence was it that the Son of God was sent into the world, John iii. 16.

Hence also were so many offers of mercy made to man—

And to this alone is it owing that so much as one has ever found acceptance with God—

But, to judge how great the love was wherewith he loved us, we must trace it

II. IN ITS OPERATIONS

The grace of God has been displayed towards us in ten thousand ways—

But we must confine our attention to its operations, as they are set forth in the text—

God has "quickened us even when we were dead in sins"

What is meant by "dead in sins," appears from the preceding verses—

* In this view, God's solicitude to find Adam, and his affectionate (perhaps plaintive) inquiry after him, Gen. iii. 9, are very striking.

† We may conceive of God as expressing himself in the language of the prophet, Hos xi 8. 9.

We were walking according to the course of this world—
We were the willing servants of Satan—
We were indulging all kinds of " filthiness, both of flesh and spirit"—
We were demonstrating ourselves to be, " by nature" as well as practice, " children of wrath"—
And we were utterly destitute of all power to help and save ourselves, Rom. v. 6.

Yet *even then* did God look upon us in tender compassion *—
He quickened us by that same Spirit whereby he raised Christ from the dead, Compare 1 Pet. iii. 18, with Rom. viii. 11.
In so doing, he united us "together with Christ," and rendered us conformable to him as our head—
What an astonishing instance of divine grace was this!
He has also " raised us up, and enthroned us together with Christ in Heaven"
The apostle had before expatiated on what God had wrought for Christ, Eph. i. 19, 20.
He now draws a parallel between believers and Christ—
What was done for Christ our head and representative, may be considered as done for all the members of his mystical body—
In this view Christians may be considered *figuratively* as risen with Christ, and as already seated on his throne—
Their hearts, their conversation, their *rest*, is in Heaven, Col. iii. 1; 2 Phil. iii. 20.
How has he thus verified the declaration of Hannah! 1 Sam. ii. 8.
How has he thus discovered " the exceeding riches of his grace !"
How worthy of God such a stupendous display of grace is, we shall see if we consider it

III. IN ITS END
God is not only the author, but also the end of all things, Rom. xi. 36.
Nor would it become him to do any thing but with a view to his own glory—
The manifestation of his own glory was the express end for which he revealed his grace, Eph. i. 6.
And this end is already in some measure attained
All ages, to the end of time, must admire the grace of God towards both the Jewish and Gentile world—
Every one, who partakes of that grace, must of necessity admire it—
The " exceeding riches of it" are unsearchable—
God's "kindness" too is infinitely enhanced by flowing to us " through Christ Jesus"—
The price paid by Christ will to eternity endear to us the blessings purchased—
At present, however, the design of God in revealing his grace is not fully answered—
But it will be completely answered in the day of judgment
Then, how exceeding rich and glorious will this grace appear !
Then the depth of misery, into which we were fallen, will be more fully known—
The spring and source of that grace will be more clearly discovered—
And all the operations will be seen in one view—

* This may be illustrated by Ezek. xvi. 4—6.

Then Christ, the one channel in which it flows, will be more intimately revealed to us—

How will every eye then admire, and every tongue then adore!

Surely nothing but such an end could account for such operations of the divine grace—

Let every one therefore seek to experience these operations in his own soul—

Let those who have been favored with them glorify God with their whole hearts.

~~~~~~~~~~~~~

THE REMEDY FOR THOSE WHO HAVE LOST THEIR SEASONS OF GRACE.

Jer. viii. 20—22.—The harvest is past, the summer is ended, and we are not saved. For the hurt of the daughter of my people am I hurt; I am black; astonishment hath taken hold on me. Is there no balm in Gilead? Is there no physician there? Why then is not the health of the daughter of my people recovered? (S. S.)

EVERY one acknowledges that it is his duty to trust in God—

But we are prone to creature-confidence—

Hence we are often left to faint under difficulties from which we might easily have been extricated—

Thus the Jews increased their distress by relying on the Egyptians for succor, when, if they would have trusted in God, they might have been delivered—

The prophet therefore takes up this affectionate lamentation over them—

I. WHO ARE THEY OF WHOM IT MAY BE SAID "THEIR HARVEST IS PAST, THEIR SUMMER IS ENDED, AND THEY ARE NOT SAVED?"

In its primary sense this passage is applicable only to the Jews, when they were attacked by the Babylonians—

But it may be applied to those who have lost seasons of spiritual relief—

The "summer and harvest" may be considered as seasons afforded us by God for providing for the necessities of our souls—

Many of these we have suffered to pass unimproved and unnoticed—

They therefore may be said to have lost their summer, &c. who have neglected to improve the seasons afforded

1. By nature

Youth is well fitted by nature for the work of conversion—

The mind is then more flexible, the passions more governable, and the conscience more tender—

But many have lost that favorable season—

2. By Providence

Mercies are sent by God to invite, *judgments*, to alarm—

But many who should have been drawn by them to seek after God, have remained impenitent—

The Sabbath also was instituted by God for the promoting of man's spiritual welfare—

On that day more especially God calls and converts sinners to himself—

But many have let those seasons pass, without obtaining the knowledge of salvation—

3. By grace

There are times when all experience *the strivings of God's Spirit—*
If they improved those seasons, God would "give them more grace"
But many stifle their convictions, and "resist the Holy Ghost"—
They who are in this predicament would do well to reflect on

II. THE MISERY OF THEIR STATE

The distress of the prophet's mind on account of the calamities that were coming on the Jews is most pathetically expressed—

But a view of the miseries impending over those who have lost their seasons of grace might well excite yet more painful apprehensions—

Their seasons lost are irrecoverable

Present time is often wasted, as though it were of no value—

But many would be glad on a death-bed to recall the seasons in which they had heard the tidings of salvation, or felt the motions of God's Spirit—

Such wishes, however, are all in vain—

Their seasons lost may never be renewed

We are apt to promise ourselves days and years to come, Acts xxiv. 25.

But how often does death disappoint our expectations!

Every lost season has greatly aggravated their guilt

The means of grace are most important and valuable talents—

The neglecting to improve them will be severely punished, Matt. xxv. 26, 30.

Every season they have lost has hardened their hearts

The word that does not quicken and save will stupify and condemn, Matt. xiii. 14, 15, 2 Cor. ii. 16.

Every lost season has grieved the Holy Spirit more and more

God will not alway strive with those who resist his motions, Gen. vi. 3

If he cease to strive with us, our destruction is inevitable, Hos. ix. 12.

How should we compassionate those who are in such a state!

How should every one adopt the words following my text! Jer. ix. 1.

But their condition is not desperate

III. THE REMEDY THAT YET REMAINS FOR THEM

We might be ready to suppose that such persons were incurable—

But the animated interrogatories in the text shew the contrary

Christ is a "physician" *able* and *willing* to save those who come unto him— — —

His blood is a "balm" that heals the most deadly wounds, Isa. i. 18, 1 John i. 7.

The true reason that so many die in their sins is, that they will not come to Christ for salvation, John v. 40.

Let every one then acknowledge that it is his own fault if he be not saved.

THE SCOPE AND TENDENCY OF THE GOSPEL.

Isaiah xl. 1, 2.—Comfort ye, comfort ye my people, saith your God: speak ye comfortably to Jerusalem, and cry unto her, that her warfare is accomplished, that her iniquity is pardoned; for she hath received of the Lord's hand double for all her sins. (S. S.)

THE ministerial office is fitly compared to that of a steward, who divides to every one his proper portion. 2 Tim. ii. 15. Luke xii. 42. The execution of it calls for much wisdom and discretion, because there must be a diversity both in the matter and manner of our addresses corresponding with the different states of the people to whom we minister. To some we must of necessity proclaim the terrors of God's law, however painful such a discharge of our duty may be: but the great scope of our ministry is to comfort the Lord's people, and be "helpers of their joy." The commission here given to the servants of Jehovah leads us to observe, that

I. GOD EARNESTLY DESIRES THE COMFORT AND HAPPINESS OF HIS PEOPLE

There are a people, who are eminently the Lord's people. Deut. vii. 6. 1 Pet. ii. 9. And that God is peculiarly solicitous to promote their comfort, appears,

1. From the commission which he gave to his beloved Son.

He sent his Son into the world to execute his eternal counsels—And our Lord himself, in his first public address to the people, declared, that the comfort of mourners was a principal object of his mission—Isaiah lxi. 1—3. Luke iv. 17—19.

2. From the end for which he sends his Spirit into the hearts of men.

God sends his Spirit to testify of Christ, John xv. 26, to witness our adoption into his family, Rom. viii. 15, and to seal us into the day of redemption, Eph. i. 13, 14,—In performing these offices, he comforts our souls—And he is, on that very account, distinguished by the name of *"the Comforter,"* John xvi. 7.

3. From the titles which the Father himself assumes.

He calls himself "The God of consolation," Rom. xv. 5, and "the Comforter of all them that are cast down," 2 Cor. vii. 6,—He compares his concern to that of a Father pitying his child, Psa. ciii. 13, and to a mother comforting with tenderest assiduities her afflicted infant, Isa. lxvi. 13,—Yea, he assures us that his regards far exceed those of the most affectionate parent in the universe, Isa. xlix. 15.

4. From the solemn charge he gives to ministers

He sends his servants "to turn men from darkness unto light, and from the power of Satan unto God." Acts xxvi. 18. And he especially charges them to "strengthen the weak hands, to confirm the feeble knees, and to say to them that are of a fearful heart, Be strong, fear not; your God will come and save you." Isa. xxxv. 3, 4. *Thrice* is that injunction repeated in the text: and in the execution of this duty we are justly called, "The helpers of your joy." 2 Cor. i. 24.

5. From the dispensations both of his providence and grace

When he suffered his beloved Son to be tempted in all things like unto us, it was with a view to comfort us under our temptations. Heb. ii. 18. And when he comforted St. Paul under his multiplied afflictions, he still consulted the comfort of his church and people: 2 Cor. i. 3, 4; yea, however he diversified his dispensations, he had invariably the same gracious object in view. Ib. 6.

As a further proof of his regard for our comfort, we may observe that,

II. HE HAS MADE ABUNDANT PROVISION FOR IT IN HIS WORD

The message which we are commanded to deliver to his people, contains in it the richest sources of consolation. We proclaim to them, that

1. Their "warfare is accomplished."

This, as referring to the captives in Babylon, foretold their deliverance from captivity. But it chiefly relates to the deliverance of the church from the bondage and misery to which they were subject under the Mosaic dispensation. The burthensome yoke of ceremonies was to be abolished at the coming of Christ, Col. ii. 14, and to be succeeded by a "law of perfect liberty"

467

Jam. i. 25,—A similar deliverance every soul experiences, as soon as ever it believes in Christ: the chains of sin, wherewith it was bound, fall off; Rom. viii. 2; and, though there yet remain many conflicts to be endured, yet is Satan's power irrecoverably broken; and the once captive sinner is brought into the glorious liberty of God's children, John viii. 36,—What rich consolation must this of necessity administer to the weary, and heavy-laden!—Matt. xi. 28—30.

2. Their iniquity is pardoned.

The Lord's people, not excepting the least or meanest of them, have all their iniquities forgiven, Col. ii. 13. Ps. ciii. 12. Acts xiii. 39,—What consolation then can they want? Let their circumstances in other respects be ever so afflictive, they may " be of good cheer:" Matt. ix. 2; for we have the united testimony of prophets and apostles that they are truly blessed, Ps. xxxii. 1, 2; Rom. iv. 7, 8.

3. They have received mercies that far overbalance all their afflictions.

The prophet does not mean that the Lord's people are punished beyond their deserts (for this were contrary both to scripture and experience) Ezr. ix. 13, but that their mercies far exceed any judgments which may have been inflicted on them on account of sin. God will punish his people, (and it is necessary that he should) but their enjoying of his favor, and their prospect of his glory, are mercies, in comparison of which their troubles are not worth a thought—Indeed their very chastisements are mercies in disguise; Heb. xii. 10; and have been acknowledged as such by those who have endured them in an abundant measure. Ps. cxix. 67, 75.

Let us LEARN then from this subject,

1 The genuine tendency of the gospel.

The gospel is generally considered as a source of melancholy, and consequently, as inimical to men's happiness. But the very reverse of this is true. It calls men indeed to repentance, and, *in this view*, may be considered as an occasion of sorrow: but it is a salutary sorrow that will be followed by joy: nor can any one duly reflect on the expressions of the text, without acknowledging, that a reliance on God's promises and oath revealed in the gospel, is, as it was intended to be, a source of " strong consolation," to all the people of God. Heb. vi. 17, 18. Let this absurd prejudice then be put away, and the gospel be received by us with gratitude and joy.

2. The wonderful difference between those who embrace, and those who disregard the gospel.

Can *that* be said of carnal and worldly men, which is here spoken of the Lord's people? Are *their* chains broken? *their* sins forgiven? *their* comforts greater than any judgments that await them? No: they are yet in bondage to sin and Satan; their sins are all " sealed up in a bag" against the day of judgment; and the wrath of God is shortly coming upon them to the uttermost. Then it will appear how great a " difference there is between those who serve the Lord, and those who serve him not." Mal. iii. 18. Let not this distinction then be made a subject of profane ridicule, but a motive to seek the Lord, that we may be numbered with his people, and be made partakers of his benefits.

THE ABUNDANT GRACE OF GOD

Romans v. 20, 21.—Where sin abounded, grace did much more abound: that as sin hath reigned unto death, even so might grace reign through righteousness unto eternal life, by Jesus Christ our Lord. (S. S.)

From eternity God determined to glorify his grace—
For this end he permitted sin to enter into the world—
The publication of his law also promoted the same end—
It served to shew how awfully sin had abounded—
And consequently to magnify that grace which destroyed sin—
To this effect the apostle speaks in the text and the words preceding it—
We shall endeavor to shew,

I. How sin has abounded.

The transgression of Adam was of a very malignant nature.

In the whole preceding context *that* sin in particular is referred to—

And it may well be considered as of a crimson dye—

It argued a contempt of God's goodness, which had bestowed so much upon him, Gen. ii. 8, 9.

It argued a doubt of his veracity, which was engaged to inflict the penalty, Gen. iii. 4.

It argued a rejection of his authority, which forbad the eating of that fruit, Gen. ii. 17.

It argued an attempt to invade the peculiar prerogatives of God, Gen. iii. 5.

Surely in this single transgression sin greatly abounded—

But sin spread also over the whole world.

Adam begat sons "*in his own* fallen *likeness*"—

All his descendents inherited his corruption, Job xiv. 4.

And cast off the yoke which their Maker had imposed upon them—

There was not so much as one single exception to be found, Ps. xiv. 2, 3

On this very account God once destroyed all but one family—

It had moreover prevailed in every heart to an awful degree.

Every faculty of men's souls was debased by it—

The understanding was blinded, the will made obstinate, the conscience seared—

All the "members of their bodies also were made instruments of unrighteousness"—

There was not an imagination of their thoughts that was not evil, Gen. vi. 5.

It even took occasion from the holy law of God to rage the more

God gave his law to discover and repress sin.

But sin would not endure any restraint—

It rose like water against the dam that obstructs its progress, Rom. vii. 8.

And inflamed men both against the law, and against him who gave it—

Thus, in using so good a law to so vile a purpose, it displayed its own exceeding sinfulness, Rom. vii. 13.

But God did not altogether abandon our wretched world.

II. How grace much more abounded.

God determined that his grace should be victorious—

And that it should establish its throne on the ruins of the empire which sin had erected—

For this purpose he gave us his Son to be a second Adam, Rom v. 14. 1 Cor. xv. 22, 45.

He laid on him the curse due to our iniquities—

—enabled him to " bring in an everlasting righteousness"—
—accepted us in him as our new covenant-head—
—restore us through him to eternal life—

Thus the super-abundance of his grace is manifest

1. In the object attained.

The destruction of man for sin was certainly tremendous—
Yet was it no more than what was to be expected—
The fallen angels had already been banished from heaven—
No wonder then if man was made a partaker of their misery—
But how beyond all expectation was the recovery of man !—

How wonderful that he should be restored while a superior order of beings were left to perish !—

And be exalted to a throne of glory from whence they had been cast down !—

This was indeed a manifestation of most abundant grace—

2. In the method of attaining it.

Sin had reigned unto death by means of Adam—
And certainly the destruction of the whole world for one sin argued a dreadful malignity in sin—
Yet was there nothing in this unjust or unreasonable—
But who could have thought that God should send us *his own Son ?*—
That he should constitute HIM our new covenant-head and representative ?—
That he should remove the curse of sin by HIS death—
——————— accept sinners through HIS righteousness ?—
——————— remedy by a second Adam what had been brought upon us by the first ?—

This was a discovery of grace that infinitely transcends the comprehension of men or angels—

3. In the peculiar advantage with which it was attained.

If Adam had retained his innocence, we also should have stood in him as our representative—
We should however have possessed only a creature's righteousness—
But in Christ we possess the righteousness of God himself, 2 Cor. v. 21.

Our reward therefore may well be augmented in proportion to the excellence of that, for which we are accepted—
Besides, the glory of God is infinitely more displayed in Christ, than ever it would have been if Adam had not fallen—
Our happiness therefore, in beholding it, must be greatly increased—
Thus our restoration through Christ will bring us to the enjoyment of far greater happiness than ever we lost in Adam, Rom. v. 15. This point is insisted on from ver. 15 to 19.

What can more fully manifest the superabounding grace of God?—

IMPROVEMENT.

1. For caution.

This doctrine seems liable to the imputation of licentiousness—
St. Paul foresaw the objection, and answered it, Rom. vi. 1, 2.
His answer should satisfy every objector—
But the reign of grace consists in destroying *every* effect of sin—
Therefore to indulge sin would be to counteract, and not to promote, the grace of God—
Let the professors of religion however be careful to give no room for this objection—
Let them " put to silence the ignorance of foolish men by well-doing "

2. For encouragement.

How strange is it that any should despair of mercy!—

The infinite grace of God has been exhibited in many striking instances, Luke vii. 47. 1 Tim. i. 14, 16.

Let us seek to become monuments of this mercy—

Let us not indeed " sin, that grace may abound"—

But let us freely acknowledge how much sin has abounded in us—

And yet expect through Christ "abundance of grace and of the gift of righteousness."

THE ABUNDANCE OF DIVINE GOODNESS.

Luke xiv. 22.—And the servant said, Lord, it is done as thou hast commanded, and yet there is room. (H.)

THESE words are part of a parable, in which much of the mystery of the gospel is contained; and the manifest design of it is, to show that, however successful the gospel of Christ has been in time past, sinners may yet come, and be received by Christ, and be for ever saved. " Wisdom hath built her house," &c.; Prov. ix. 1; and, among the highly favored guests, who are partaking of this joyful feast, " yet there is room."

Consider,

I. WHERE THERE IS ROOM.

1. In the mercy of God. It is over all his works, and from everlasting. Psa. cxlv. 9. It belongeth unto God. Psa. ciii. 17; Exod. xx. 6; Isa. xxx. 18; Psa. cxlvii. 11.

2. In the merits of Christ. He is an all-sufficient Saviour. Heb. vii. 24, 25; 1 John i. 7. The merit of his death is unbounded, as it respects man. 1 John ii. 2.

3. As to the power and efficacy of the Spirit to renew and change the hardest heart. Such a change is necessary, we have destroyed ourselves; and if ever we are recovered, it must be by help from heaven. Hos. xiii. 9. The conversion of a sinner is the Spirit's work; Titus iii. 5, 6; which the Father hath promised; Luke xxiv. 49; engaged to pour out; Zech. xii. 10; Christ died to open a way for it. Gal. iii. 13, 14.

4. In the household of faith. More members may be added to Christ's mystical body; in order to this the gospel is preached; the ministers of Christ labor, encouraged by the extensive request of their master, Christ, a little before his death. John xvii. 20. There is yet plentiful provision in our Father's house. Hosea xiv. 5. Those who come into the vineyard at the third, sixth, or ninth hour, do not hinder others from being invited and received at the eleventh; Rev. ii. 3; and we are still to pray that his kingdom may come, which is capable of increase, both as to number and perfection.

5. In the mansions of glory. They are many; John xiv. 2, 3; and all who overcome here, shall be made pillars there. Rev. iii. 12. The city is prepared for them; Heb. xi. 16; for this Jesus died; Heb. ii. 10; for this he prays. John xvii. 24. He has declared so much; John xii. 26; and when he shall appear, they also shall appear with him, &c., Col. iii. 4.

471

II. FOR WHOM IS THERE ROOM.

In general, there is room for all sorts and conditions of men; those of one kingdom and country as well as another. The gospel is sent into all the world, and to be preached to every human creature capable of hearing. Mark xvi. 15.

But more particularly.

1. There is room for the meanest and most despicable in the world. God is no respecter of persons. 1 Sam. xvi. 7. The things of the kingdom are revealed to babes. Eph. vi. 9. Not many wise or noble are called; 1 Cor. i. 26—29; the poor are chosen. James ii. 5. Lazarus in Abraham's bosom was once a beggar. Luke xv. 20. Jesus himself was poor while on earth. Matt. viii. 20.

2. The rich men are under no necessity of perishing, there is room for them. Their situation is indeed critical; Matt. xix. 24; their salvation very difficult; Mark x. 25; Luke xviii. 23; they must be delivered from trusting in riches: and with God this is possible. Matt. xix. 26.

3. The afflicted must not be forgotten, there is room for them. The pains of the body are no proof that God will not have mercy on the soul. Some of the most eminent saints have been in the furnace of affliction, as David, Hezekiah, Job: God has caused many to pass under the rod, that he might bring them into the bond of the covenant. Ezek. xx. 37.

4. There is yet room for such as have long stood out, neglecting, and making light of the invitations of the gospel. 2 Cor. vi. 2. The compassionate Redeemer is still saying, "Behold," &c., Rev. iii. 20.

5. There is yet room for such as have backslidden; having fallen into sin, after the most promising beginnings. Jer. iii. 22.

Lastly, to add no more; There is yet room for the chief of sinners. Pardon and peace were first proclaimed to those who crucified our God; Luke xxiv. 47; see 1 Tim. i. 15; and all that labor, and are heavy laden, are promised rest. Matt. xi. 28.

Application.

1. How justly may the gospel be called a joyful sound.

2. What encouragement for gospel-ministers still to preach this gospel: "Yet there is room."

3. When Satan suggests, "it is too late to repent, and be saved;" he may be silenced by the text, "Yet there is room."

4. Let none take encouragement from the text, to make light of the invitations of the gospel, or put off their repentance. For although there is room in the kingdom of grace and glory, yet we should remember there is room in the grave and in hell too: and how many have sunk into both, while neglecting their salvation.

5. This may be a source of consolation to pious souls, respecting their unconverted friends and relatives. They may yet be saved, for "yet there is room."

6. Being called into the kingdom of grace, and finding there is room, let this confirm your faith and hope, as to your reception to glory.

472

THE NATURE AND PROPERTIES OF THE SERVICE OF GOD.

oshua xxiv. 15.—If it seem evil unto you to serve the Lord, choose you this day whom ye
will serve. (B.)

THESE words imply what is generally acknowledged,—That man is a
rational and free creature.

Let us inquire,

I. WHAT IT IS TO SERVE THE LORD; AND WHAT ARE THE NATURE AND
PROPERTIES OF THIS SERVICE.

The foundation of the true and proper service of God must be laid in the
knowledge of him, 1 Chron. xxviii. 9,—in reconciliation with him, Heb. ix.
14,—in deliverance from other masters. Matt. vi. 24. Rom. vi. 14. Luke
i. 74. — — —

We must enter into his service by yielding or giving ourselves up, freely
and fully to be his servants. Rom. vi. 16. This implies that we no longer
yield ourselves to the world, the flesh, the devil, or sin; but to the Lord,
with desire that he would accept us through his Son, and confidence that he
does so. Hereby we are joined to the Lord in order to serve him. Isa. lvi. 6.

As his servants, we must be subject to his authority, and obedient to the
divine will, Rom. vi. 16, including—*Holiness towards God*, which is a death
to sin and deliverance from it, the being dedicated to God, employed for him,
conformed to him:—And *righteousness towards our neighbors;* truth, justice, mercy, love, and its fruits.

This subjection and obedience must be constant and universal. 1 Cor. x.
31. Psa. cxix. 6.

In what sense such do, and in what sense they do not serve God, may be
seen by reference to Psa. xvi. 2. Job xxii. 2, 3; xxxv. 5—8.

As to the properties of this service,—It must be *sincere* and *upright;* Jos.
xxiv. 14. 1 Chron. xxviii. 9. John iv. 23, 24,—*Reverential;* Heb. xii.
28; from a sense of his presence; Luke i. 75; his glory, wisdom, power,
eternity, immensity, supremacy. "Lo! God is here!"—*Fiducial* or filial,
i. e. with confidence and hope. Luke i. 74; Rom. viii. 15; Psa. ii. 11.
The foundation of this must be the mediation of Christ; justification through
him; Rom. v. 1; and the testimony of our conscience. 1 John iii. 21,—
Humble, Acts xx. 19; Mic. vi. 8; implying a deep sense of the distance
between him and us, a consciousness that we are not worthy to be permitted
to serve him, and that our best services are not worthy of his acceptance.—
Resigned, patient, and *contented;* from a conviction that his providence is
over all, and that all his dispensations are just, and wise, and kind; that his
eye is on each of his servants, and that he sets each to the work which he
sees he is most fit for, and puts each in the most proper place.—*Loving*,
from love, Isaiah lvi. 6, a willing mind, 1 Chron. xxviii. 9, and an undivided
heart. John xiv. 15; Matt. vi. 24,—*Disinterested;* with a single eye to
his glory. Rom. xiv. 7—9; 1 Cor. x. 31; Col. iii. 17.

II. WHETHER IT BE EVIL TO SERVE THE LORD, OR THE REASONABLENESS
AND ADVANTAGES OF THIS SERVICE.

The word *evil* is taken here in a peculiar sense, and means *unjust, unreasonable, disadvantageous*, or *unnecessary*.

Is it UNJUST, or UNREASONABLE for him to demand, or for us to pay this
service? He is our Creator, Preserver, and Redeemer, and ought we not to
be devoted to his glory, and obedient to his will?—As to the properties of
this service, since he searches the heart, is it unreasonable to serve him with

473

sincerity? or would hypocrisy be more appropriate? He is most great and powerful; is it unreasonable to serve him with reverence and fear? Mal. i. 6. He is merciful and gracious, and the friend and father of penitent believing souls; is it unreasonable to serve him with confidence and hope? He is most just and holy; is it unreasonable to serve him with humility? He is infinite in love and goodness, and has given his only Son for our sins; 1 John iv. 8; is it unreasonable to serve him from love? He is the Lord of glory, and the centre and source of glory; is it not more reasonable we should have regard to his glory, than our own?

Is this service of God DISADVANTAGEOUS?—In *life?* Many will think so, even as many as have gained, or suppose they have gained, profit, or honor, or pleasure by sin. Sin must be renounced, and all the gains of it; our idols; our lusts, the right hand must be cut off; the right eye must be plucked out; but this is only like the being obliged not to drink poison, or stab ourselves, or parting with a gangrened member.

The service of God is sometimes attended with other consequences, as the loss of our character, our property, our liberty, our life, distress, torture; and is not this disadvantageous?

Christ makes up for these losses. Disgraced among men, we are honored before God. Deprived of the riches of this world, we are put into possession of the unsearchable riches of Christ. Denied in carnal pleasures, we enjoy spiritual. Losing a short, uncertain, vain, miserable life, we gain a durable, immortal, and most blessed life in heaven.—View also the gains of this service.

These are,—The pardon of sin,—The favor of the greatest and best Being in the universe, on whom all other beings are dependant, and to whom they are subservient,—Communion with Him,—His direction, protection, and help, with a supply of all wants,—A good conscience; the consolations of the Spirit, and the hope of eternal life.

These things are to be enjoyed in life. Is it disadvantageous then to serve God in this life? If not; surely it is not—in *death.* What can the things we are required to *give* up, when we become the servants of God, do for us in that awful moment? sin, the world, fleshly lusts?

Will it then be disadvantageous, when the world is torn from us, to have a God to fly to? When " the earthly house of this tabernacle is dissolved, to "have a building of God, a house not made with hands, eternal in the heavens?" To have no guilt, fear, or anguish but peace, hope, and joy in the Holy Ghost?

But how great the benefit arising from the service of God,—In *eternity;* the intermediate state; at the day of judgment, for ever and ever?— — —

Perhaps you say, " I own it will do a man no harm, but there is no need of it." Let us inquire therefore, is it UNNECESSARY?—Can these ends be attained without it?

Can we escape the miseries in which we are already involved, without it?—Can we shun farther, greater, and eternal miseries without it?—Can we otherwise attain the perfection and happiness of which our nature is capable, either here? or hereafter?

III. I SHALL REFER THE MATTER TO YOUR JUDGMENT AND CHOICE WHOM YOU WILL SERVE.

If you still see things in a different light, and " it seem evil unto you to serve the Lord, choose you this day whom you will serve." Will you serve the *world?* consider what is in the world: "the lust of the flesh, the lust of the eye, and the pride of life;" the emptiness, uncertainty, and short

duration of these things, since the world is passing from us, and we from **it.** Conceive the world on fire, as it will be in the great day ;—a burning **God!**

Will you serve the *flesh?* Your body and animal nature, infirm, afflicted, dead, corrupted,—a rotten god! Or your corrupt nature, "the flesh lusting against the Spirit," and "warring against the law of your mind, and leading you captive to the law of sin ;" the greatest evil in the universe, and the fruitful source of all other evils ?— — —

In serving the world and the flesh you serve *Satan.* How will he reward you ? What is his inclination ? Does he love and wish you well ? What is his power ? What has he for himself ?—now ?—for ever ? Has he wisdom, or honor, or riches, or happiness ? The poet represents him as saying, and saying truly,

> "Where'er I am is hell! myself am hell."

Judge from hence what he can give you.

Bring the matter to a point this day.—You are at years to judge. You have the use of your reason; of liberty. You have had the matter fairly stated to you. Choose, therefore ; find a better master, better work, and better wages if you can. If you can find a better master, Jehovah can find a servant without you. If you do not want him, he does not want you.— Why this delay ? "Choose you *this day* whom ye will serve." Let me caution you against the folly and danger of procrastination in deciding a point, in which you are so materially interested.

If, after all, you choose to serve these other lords, that have had dominion over you, you must not expect me to give you directions how to serve them. There is no need I should, as your own heart, and the lives of a great majority of your fellow-sinners will sufficiently direct you. But I shall endeavor,

IV. To GIVE SOME DIRECTIONS TO THOSE WHO CHOOSE TO SERVE THE LORD, WITH A VIEW TO ASSIST THEM IN THAT IMPORTANT UNDERTAKING.

Read what follows the text; " Ye cannot serve the Lord," ver. 19.—This is spoken, not of an absolute, but of a moral impossibility, or a very great difficulty, which Joshua alleges to make the people more considerate in obliging themselves, and more resolved to fulfil their obligations.—You cannot serve God, while unacquainted with him; 1 Chron. xxviii. 9 ;—while not reconciled to him; Heb. ix. 14 ;—while under the power of other masters ; Luke i. 74 ; Rom. vi. 14 ;—while unchanged ; Matt. vii. 17 ; xii. 33 ; Luke vi. 43—45 ;—while possessed only of the strength of nature. John xv. 4, 5.

Acquaint yourselves with God,—by considering his nature and attributes, and the relations in which he stands to you, as manifested by his works and word ;—by prayer for the illumination of his Spirit. "I will give them a heart to know me." Jer. xxiv. 7.

Be reconciled to him, through his Son, by repentance and faith. Heb. ix. 14.

Seek deliverance out of the hands of your enemies by his Spirit. John viii. 33—36 ; Rom. viii. 2 ; 2 Cor. iii. 17.

Be born again, and made new creatures ; and then, the tree being good, the fruit will be good.

Seek grace to help you in time of need. Heb. xii. 28.

In order to all these, use the means of grace in private and public, and do not rest in them ; but look through them to the end.

PERSONAL AND FAMILY RELIGION.

Joshua xxiv. 15.—As for me and my house, we will serve the Lord. (B.)

THIS noble resolution of Joshua, though it has been celebrated from age to age, in all countries, where the Scriptures of the Old Testament have been known, and imitated, as well as commended by many individuals, yet has not always been understood, even by those that have undertaken to explain it, and to enforce it upon others.

I shall now add something to what has been advanced; I mean *family religion;* a necessary and important branch indeed, but one seldom treated on in public, and sadly neglected in private. And that I may lay down a proper foundation for what I have to say concerning this point I shall consider,

I. THE NATURE OF JOSHUA'S RESOLUTION.

It is a resolution of an *enlightened, awakened, justified, renewed, devoted, consistent, experienced, believer.*

Of a BELIEVER. Faith has been, and is necessary under every dispensation, Patriarchal, Mosaic, or Christian; as the Epistle to the Hebrews, ch. xi. evidently shows; it was as necessary for Joshua as for us. For, " without faith it is impossible to please God." Heb. xi. 6. It is necessary to believe in God, in his revealed will, in his declarations, promises, and threatenings. Heb. iii. 19; iv. 3. For want of this the Israelites perished in the wilderness; and for this Joshua and Caleb are so justly famed.

Of an ENLIGHTENED believer. Having a clear and distinct knowledge of him, whom he worships, 1 Chron. xxviii. 9.—A knowledge of his law, its spirituality, its great extent, and obligation. This convinces of sin.—A knowledge of the service of God, as requiring us to worship him in spirit and in truth; Matt. iv. 10; John iv. 23; to obey him Rom. vi. 16, from love; to promote his glory. 1 Cor. vi. 20. 1 Pet. ii. 2. In fine,—A knowledge of our own insufficiency, and where help may be found.

Of an AWAKENED believer.— Awakened out of the sleep of nature, Eph. v. 14, *i. e.* his insensible, unconcerned, and indolent state, as to spiritual things. Hence arises a just apprehension and sense of the majesty, power, holiness, justice, and goodness of God, producing reverence, awe, dread, fear of offending him, Josh. xxiv. 14; Heb. xii. 28; and of death, judgment, eternity, producing a deep concern and great diligence. This Joshua experienced. See the following verses.

Of a JUSTIFIED believer.—Abraham was justified, Gen. xv. 6; Rom. iv. 3, and David, Psa. xxxii., and so, undoubtedly, was Joshua. This is the foundation of that confidence, and hope, love, peace, and joy, essential to the service of God. Heb. ix. 14; iii. 6, 14. For we are to serve as *sons,* and not merely as *servants.* Rom. viii. 15. Gal. iv. 5.

Of a RENEWED believer.—Joshua was born in sin, like the rest of mankind, but born again and renewed. This is necessary: for we must " serve in newness of spirit," which we cannot do without we obtain a new spirit and a new heart. Matt. vii. 17; xii. 33. Luke vi. 43, 45.

Of a DEVOTED believer.—Sensible of God's mercy and love to him, and loving God in return, without which there can be no religion, Deut. vi. 5; xxx. 6; 1 Tim. i. 5; 1 Cor. xiii. 1, and saying, " What shall I render unto the Lord for all his benefits ?"—dedicating all to him, and employing all for him.

Of a CONSISTENT believer. Walking in all God's ordinances, and worshipping him in spirit and in truth, keeping all his commandments from love, and with a single eye; endeavoring constantly to promote his glory; being "sober and righteous, as well as godly in this present world," Tit. ii. 12; serving God in righteousness towards our neighbor, as well as in holiness towards himself. Luke i. 75.

Of an EXPERIENCED believer, who has made trial of this service.—

Therefore he could resolve for himself, in dependence on the grace he had already received, and still expected. And, as to his house, he knew either that they were like-minded with himself; or he purposed to use his endeavors that they might be so, and trusted in God, he should succeed.

II. WHETHER IT WAS A RESOLUTION SO REASONABLE AND WISE, THAT IT WOULD BE WELL FOR US TO IMITATE IT.

It was reasonable and wise. because Joshua knew that he was the CREATURE of God, who had been formed, and had received all his faculties and powers for this very end. Acts xvii. 26, 27.— — —

He knew that he was a DEPENDENT creature—Living, moving and having his being in God, and that he was spared and preserved for this end; not to eat, drink, or sleep; to gratify his senses and passions, or to please himself in any way, but to serve God. Matt. iii. 10; Luke xiii. 6—9.

An OBLIGED creature.—Having received innumerable benefits and mercies for this end. Rom. xii. 1. If the ox knoweth and serveth his owner, surely Israel should know and serve God. He thought it reasonable that he should know and serve the kind hand that fed him, and the author of all his mercies.

A REDEEMED creature.—Joshua was redeemed out of Egypt, and we are redeemed from the wrath of God for this end. 2 Cor. v. 14, 15; 1 Cor. vi. 20; Tit. ii. 14, 15.

A HIGHLY PRIVILEGED creature.—A member of the visible church, and favored with the light of the revelation of Jesus Christ for this end. Eph. v. 8—10; 1 Pet. ii. 9.

An ACCOUNTABLE creature.—That must be judged, how he had answered the end of his creation, preservation, and redemption, and what use he had made of his talents.

A MORTAL creature?—Yet immortal, that must pass certainly, soon, perhaps to-morrow, from a state of trial, to a state of retribution.

He knew, therefore, that to serve God aright, was essential to his everlasting happiness; to his escaping hell and attaining heaven.

That it was essential to his present happiness; as he could not otherwise have peace of mind, a good conscience, a hope of immortality, the favor, protection, and care of God, his direction and aid, all things needful and useful, and all things working for his good.

That it was essential to his usefulness to others, and particularly to his own family, to whom, especially, God had called him to be useful.

That what was his duty and happiness was also *theirs*. Therefore, out of love, he resolves for them, that they should serve the Lord.

Nor can we doubt that it was pleasing to God that he should do his utmost to induce his family to serve God, and how certainly it was the way to the accomplishment of God's promises. Gen. xviii. 19.

Of all these accounts his resolution was reasonable and wise, therefore since we are not debarred, but at liberty so to do, we should imitate him.

III. HOW WE MAY BE ENABLED TO DO SO.

As to *ourselves*,

We must see that we lay a foundation for the service of God, in an acquaintance and reconciliation with him, adoption into his family, a new birth, in consequence of repentance and faith ; whereby we receive an interest in, and union with Christ, and find in him righteousness and strength, and " grace to help in time of need."

We must make ourselves acquainted with every branch of the service of God, and of our duty.

We must not allow ourselves in the neglect of any branch of it, and, therefore, we must deny ourselves, and take up our cross.

We must be found in the constant use of the means, that the edge of our minds, when blunted, may be sharpened, and grace may be continued to us, and increased in us.

As to our *families*,

We must be deeply concerned that they should serve him.

We must set them a good example, and show,—that we serve God ourselves, and are neither hypocrites, which they may be apt to suspect, nor formalists.

We must instruct them, Deut. vi. 6—9, converse with them, read to them, make them read,—(and here we may remark the importance of children, servants, and apprentices learning to read,)—we must bring them under the word preached, if possible, on every Lord's day, and at other times, and inquire what they can remember of what they have heard. We must catechise them. This is the doctrine of the Lord. Bring up your children " in the nurture and admonition," Ephes. vi. 4. Discipline must be used by us, as it was by Abraham, " I know that he will *command* his children." Gen. xviii. 19.

We must also encourage them, and excite them every way in our power. We must give them proof that we are actuated only by love to them.

We must pray for them ; for each child by name, and must pray with them, and put them upon praying for themselves.

We must persevere in this exercise, notwithstanding all discouragements.

As a motive to this labor, for the benefit of our children, it may be mentioned, that we have been instrumental in bringing them into the world ; and shall we not endeavor to save them from hell ?

MORAL INABILITY COMPATIBLE WITH GOSPEL EXHORTATIONS.

Philippians ii. 12, 13.—Work out your own salvation with fear and trembling : For it is God that worketh in you both to will and to do of his good pleasure. (Pr.)

It is a happy sign that our religious sentiments are correct, when we find a use for every part of Scripture, and perceive an agreement in the whole. Some things in this passage require to be explained ; and if the explanation be just, it will not be inconsistent with other parts of Scripture, which declares unequivocally that our salvation is all of grace.

" Salvation" then consists of two parts : in a deliverance from the curse of the law, and from the dominion of sin. The first was effected by the death of Christ, without us. The latter is wrought by the Holy Spirit within us, changing the dispositions of the heart. The one is by price, the

478

other by power. In the first we are wholly passive, in the latter we are active by being acted upon. Now it is of salvation in the *latter* sense that the text speaks, because it is that in which we are properly concerned. The Holy Spirit "worketh in us," but it is "to will and to do." It is we, and not the Holy Spirit that repent and believe the gospel; that mourn for sin and mortify the deeds of the body. The exhortation in the text therefore s very properly addressed to us.

To "work out" our salvation, is not meant of working in a way of merit or desert; for in this sense, salvation is not of works, but of grace. But it is to grow in grace, to perfect holiness in the fear of the Lord, to work out our way through all the difficulties that lie before us, and to endure to the end that we may be saved. We must set our feet on all our spiritual enemies, and go on mortifying the deeds of the body that we may live.

This is to be done "with fear and trembling," a disposition of mind that must accompany all our striving to enter into the kingdom of God. The work itself is great and large, and the time allowed is short, very short for so important a concern as this. While pressing into the kingdom, we have reason to fear and tremble, lest we should not finally enter in and be saved. We are like persons on a dangerous voyage, and have cause to fear lest after all we should be shipwrecked.

It is God that worketh in us "to will and to do:" he gives us a heart to seek him, he keeps up every holy resolution till it is put into actual execution. It is of God that we are at *first* made willing to submit to mercy, and to be saved in his way, by coming to Christ for life. *Now* also it is of God, who makes us willing to give up all our idols, to watch and pray against every temptation, to run in the way of his commands, and to hold out in our christian course.

If it be asked *how* the Lord worketh in us? The answer is, not by forcing us against our will, but by making us willing, and that in a way suitable to our rational nature; namely by conviction, and by the influence of motives. Hence we are led to judge of things in a measure as they are, and to act from the clearest conviction of the understanding. Only let the mind be in a proper state, and the eternal realities of religion will operate powerfully upon us, and give to the mind an impulse that is irresistible. Views of the evil nature, and awful consequences of sin will render us willing to attempt its mortification, and to submit to every species of self-denial. Proper views of the gift of God will make us thirst for that living water, and dispose us most cordially to embrace the Saviour. John iv. 10.

From the passage thus explained, we may infer,

1. That *exhortations to holy duties do not imply any self-sufficiency in us*, without the influence of the Holy Spirit. They show us what ought to be, and so are proper both to saints and sinners. But something more is necessary to make us what we ought to be, and incline us to do what God requires of us. Exhortations place before us the motives to action, but it is the Holy Spirit that prepares the mind to receive them, and to yield to their influence.

2. *That the work of the Holy Spirit does not release us from obligation*, but on the contrary, affords an additional motive for our compliance with the will of God. There is as much need for us to strive to enter in at the straight gate, as if God had never promised the aid of his Holy Spirit. It is the same in natural things as it is in spiritual things; we are as much dependent in one case as in the other; and yet that dependence does not supersede the use of ordinary means. It is "in God we live, and move

479

and have our being;" yet we employ means for the preservation and contin uance of life, and should have no reason to expect it in any other way.

More particularly—

I. CONSIDER THE EXHORTATION ITSELF : " WORK OUT YOUR OWN SAL* VATION WITH FEAR AND TREMBLING."

This of necessity implies that a great part of our salvation is still to come, and is not wrought out; that much needs still be done in order to wean us from the present world, and meeten us for heaven.

1. There is much *remaining ignorance* in us, which needs to be re moved. We have not yet learned to think of ourselves as we ought to think, nor of God and spiritual things as we ought. We know but in part, and see as through a glass darkly. We have made but little proficiency in divine knowledge; there are heights and depths which we have not ex plored.

2. Much *remaining depravity* in our hearts, many unmortified affections and lusts. There is in us a great deal of pride and vanity, love of the world, impatience and fretfulness under the dispensations of Providence, and a thousand evils which daily beset us. How important then that we watch, and pray, and strive; that we embrace every opportunity of serving the Lord, and do whatsoever our hands find to do with all our might. We are like the Israelites when they entered Canaan: we have innumerable difficul ties to overcome, a host of enemies to subdue, before we can possess the land; and it is by little and little that we shall drive them out.

3. There are numerous *temptations and snares* that still await us: many as we have already escaped, there are still more in reserve. Satan will be working against us, the world will still be opposing us, and providences will still be trying. We shall need therefore great exertions, great grace, and great patience, to bear all, to overcome all, and endure to the end.— Ephes. vi. 13.

II. THE ENCOURAGEMENT GIVEN US: " FOR IT IS GOD THAT WORKETH IN YOU BOTH TO WILL AND TO DO OF HIS GOOD PLEASURE."

1. Consider *the goodness of God* in "working in us." He might have left us to get through as well as we could, and given us up to our own vile ness.———If a nation were enslaved, and a prince sent a powerful army to their assistance, it would encourage them to renewed exertions to obtain their freedom. How much more the aid which God has promised in the spiritual warfare, which is sufficient to make us more than conquerers through him that loved us.

2. Consider *the power of God*, and of what importance it is to have such an efficient ally.———When we consider the strength of our enemies, and the power of indwelling sin, we are sometimes ready to despair of obtaining the victory : but the consideration that God is on our side, and working in us as well as for us, is sufficient to animate us in the conflict, and to give us the assurance of ultimate success. Joshua xxiii. 10, Hag. ii. 4.

3. The *faithfulness of God* is also encouraging. He will not forsake the work of his own hands, but will perfect that which concerneth us, for his mercy endureth forever. Psal. cxxxviii. 8. If he excite spiritual desires, it is that they may be fulfilled; if he gives repentance, it is that it may be fol lowed with pardon and eternal life. Psal. cxlv. 19.

4. The consideration that all is wrought in us *by the Holy Spirit*, sug gests a motive to fear and trembling, as well as of humble confidence and hope. This should keep us from presumption, from running into evil, or letting down our watch. If God depart from us, or withdraw the influence

of his grace, we shall perish like Samson in the midst of the Philistines. It is only by diligence and watchfulness, that we may expect God to work in us to will and to do of his good pleasure.

How lamentably deficient is that system of religion, which finds no place for the renewing influence of the Holy Ghost! It is like the earth on which neither rain nor dew descends, but is cursed with perpetual barrenness and desolation.

Let us be careful that we do not grieve the Holy Spirit by the indulgence of self-sufficiency, to the neglect of his inspiring and sanctifying grace: always remembering that he it is who worketh all our works in us. Isaiah xxvi. 12.

~~~~~~~~~~~~~~~~~~~~~~

YOUNG PEOPLE TO BE TAUGHT THE HOLY SCRIPTURES.

2 Tim. iii. 15.—From a child thou hast known the holy Scriptures, which are able to make thee wise unto salvation, through faith which is in Christ Jesus. [Sk.]

THE Bible has by some been represented to be a book so profoundly obscure and mysterious, that none except persons of extraordinary learning and talents, can understand it. But such a representation is a libel upon the wisdom of its Author, and is equal to saying that he has given a revelation in which to the great mass of mankind, nothing is revealed. That the Bible contains mysteries, we admit—mysteries of godliness, which angels desire to look into, but which they cannot explain; profound depths which have not yet been fathomed by any created intellect. But this is not its general character. It contains much that is easy to be understood. As in a great river, which has its deep places in which the elephant might swim, and its shallow ones in which the lamb might wade, so in the Bible, whilst there is much to employ intellects of the highest order, so also is there much on a level with minds of ordinary size, and which even a way-faring man, though a fool, may understand. The apostle, who was perfectly acquainted with the character of divine revelation, was of this judgment. Instead of telling the common people that they could not understand the Scriptures, he informs them that they may even understand his knowledge in the mystery of Christ, Eph. iii. 4. And in the text he teaches that even children may know the Scriptures. I am going to show,

I. THAT THE SCRIPTURES ARE HOLY. The *Scriptures* include all the canonical books of the Old and New Testaments. To the former of these our Lord refers, John v. 39. And to these our apostle also refers in the text, and verse following. Other books have been added to these, but they are *apocryphal*, and though some of them contain some important historical information, and a richness of moral sentiment, yet they are so mixed with puerilities and absurdities, as to demonstrate their origin not to have been divine. That the Scriptures are holy, appears,

1. *From the character of their writers.* These were not wicked men, for such God never employs to declare his statutes, Psa. l. 16. To suppose otherwise would be as absurd as to suppose that he would appoint a pure stream of water to flow through a pipe polluted with the most offensive filth. God never employs the wicked in honorable work—but as pioneers to drain

481

bogs—to build bridges—to remove obstructions—to inflict judgments **upon** the beast and the false prophet,—and to be the executioners in his moral government. To the honorable parts of his work, he appoints only his own faithful servants. And for this *most* honorable, of being the medium of communication from God to man, he chose *holy men.*

2. *From their origin.* The books of Scripture are not, strictly speaking, the production of the persons whose names they bear. They are not the fruit of their learning, or genius, or talents. They were the mere amanuenses of Jehovah; for " all Scripture is given by inspiration," 2 Tim. iii. 16. Hence they contain truth without mixture of error.

3. *From their nature and tendency.* Many bad books have been written;—books awfully demoralizing;—intended and eminently calculated to destroy every pious, and moral, and virtuously social principle; and to introduce speculative and practical atheism, comprehending every species of profligacy and licentiousness. But the Scriptures are perfectly opposite to all this. He whom they reveal is *the grand object of worship is holy,* Isa. vi. 3. *His precepts are holy,* Psa. xix. 7, 8. The *sanctions* by which they are *enforced,* whether rewards or punishments, are *all promotive of holiness. His people are holy*—separated from common or sinful purposes, and set apart for God, 1 Pet. ii. 9. And the heaven which they reveal, and to which the faithful shall at last be received, is a *holy place.*

II. THAT THE HOLY SCRIPTURES'MAY BE KNOWN BY YOUNG PEOPLE.— Timothy had known them from a child; but as there does not appear to have been any thing in the intellectual character of Timothy, which distinguished him from others, is it fair to conclude that what *he* knew may be known by persons *now* of the same age. But to know them, we must,

1. *Be able to read them.* I do not mean, *able to read them* in the original, for though such ability has its advantages, they are not so great as some would-be linguists pretend. Linguists who are modest, will not say, that " they can furnish a better translation than we already possess." Unless we can read our own language, even this Bible thus translated will be a sealed book. There have been times when the art of reading was the privilege only of a few. Now all may acquire it, both rich and poor. The latter, if they cannot acquire it any where else, may acquire it in a Sunday School. We must,

2. *Read them in order, with deep attention and prayer.* It has been said, that " few books are more read than the Bible, and few, if any, are so little understood." It is a melancholy fact, that many who read the Scriptures, are scandalously ignorant of their sacred import. This arises partly from the *absurd* and *irregular* manner in which they search them. Instead of reading any sacred book consecutively, as they would a human composition, they read a chapter *here,* and a chapter or part of a chapter *there,* without any kind of reference either to the preceding, or intermediate, or subsequent parts. To understand them, *they must be read in regular order.— They must be read with deep attention.—The several parts must be compared*—the law with the gospel—types with their antitypes—predictions with their fulfilment. *We must avail ourselves of such helps as are within our reach*—such as ministers—well informed christians—and the works of pious and learned commentators. Above all *we must read in the spirit of prayer* for divine illumination—a sound judgment—a teachable spirit—a tenacious memory—sanctified affections—and an obedient will. To expect to become profitably acquainted with the Scriptures in any other way is enthusiasm. We proceed to show,

482

III. THAT THE KNOWLEDGE OF THE HOLY SCRIPTURES IS INFINITELY IMPORTANT. Knowledge in some cases is hurtful—in others useless—or beneficial only in particular circumstances—or its benefits are only temporary. But *this* is saving—embraces all circumstances—and extends its benefits through the whole of our existence. *The Scriptures are able to make us wise unto salvation, through faith which is in Christ Jesus.*

1. *They reveal our want of salvation.* Man sinned, Gen. iii. Through sin he forfeited the divine favor, and lost the moral image of his Creator. The forfeiture extended to all his posterity.—Hence all are *born* in sin, Psa. li. 5. All are *prone* to sin, Gen. viii. 21; Psa. xiv. 1. And hence also the seeds of mortality are sown in all, which in due time ripen into death.

2. *They reveal a Saviour.* The descriptions which they give of this Saviour, show that in him are united the divine and human natures. Of him are sometimes predicted things which can alone belong to the divinity, John i. 1, 3; Rom. ix. 5; Col. ii. 8; Rev. i. 8. At other times, those which belong only to the humanity. Such are all those texts which relate to his birth, progress in knowledge—sufferings—death, &c.—admit the twofold nature, and these are easily harmonized; reject it, and to harmonize them will be for ever impossible. Such a Saviour being infinite in wisdom, power, and goodness, must be all-sufficient.

3. *They reveal the method of salvation.* 1. *Through the death of Christ* —Intimated in Gen. iii. 15.—*Typified* in the offering up of Isaac, Gen. xxii.—By the various sacrifices under the law, Heb. x.—*Clearly predicted,* Psa. xl. 6—8, compared with Heb. x. 5—10; Isa. liii. Dan. ix. 26, 27.— The original law required death in case of transgression.—Christ, in dying, complied with that requisition;—declared the righteousness of God;—and obtained the remission of sins for all who have faith in his blood, Rom. iii. 25. 2. *Through faith in Christ.* The passage just quoted clearly teaches this.—Faith is the grand condition of the gospel, Mark xvi. 16; Acts xiii. 39, xvi. 31; Rom. v. 1. Without reference to Christ, and faith in him, the Old Testament Scriptures, to which our text refers, not only cannot make us wise to salvation, but the *typical, ceremonial,* and *prophetical* parts cannot be understood.—*Without Christ* these are destitute of meaning;—*with him* they furnish *saving instruction.*

4. *They reveal the extent of salvation.* To all people, Gen. xxii. 18; Luke ii. 10. To all cases, Isa. i. 18.—*The complete salvation of the soul from sin*—its guilt, love, power, pollution;—and of the body from the grave, and the eternal glorification of both.

From hence learn,

1. The importance of a personal acquaintance with the Scriptures.
2. The duty of parents in reference to their children.
3. The great utility of Sunday Schools.

DAVID'S ATTENTION TO HIS HOUSEHOLD.

1 Chron. xvi. 43.—And David returned to bless his house. (H. H.)

IT is truly delightful to see the operation of religion on the soul of man; how it transforms him from a carnal and selfish creature, into a spiritual and heavenly Being, who, like the sun in the firmament, steadily pursues his course, and shines brighter and brighter unto the perfect day. Beautifully was it exemplified by David in the history before us; in illustration of which we shall notice,

1. The work in which he had been engaged—

This was, the bringing up of the ark from the house of Obed-edom to Jerusalem: and,

A glorious work it was—

In itself, it was a work of vast importance. For many years had the ark lain in obscurity at Kirjath-jearin, without any application being made to it for instruction from God. But, when brought up to Jerusalem, it would be accessible at all times; and, in all difficult emergencies, the will of Jehovah might be learned from it. Indeed, the whole account respecting it shews us clearly, in what light it was viewed by the nation at large — — —

As a typical act, its importance rises still higher in our estimation. It was undoubtedly typical of Christ's ascension into heaven; for in that view it is spoken of in a great variety of Psalms, Ps. xxiv. xlvii. lxviii. cxxxii., and in that view the Psalms relating to it are quoted in the New Testament. Compare Ps. lxviii. 18, with Eph. iv. 8. Let other Psalms, from the 96th to 99th, be read as referring to both these events, and they will fully illustrate the importance of the work which David had just completed— — —

And it had been performed in a manner most acceptable unto God—

In its commencement, it was begun by consulting all the great men in the nation, who were stirred up to concur in it, ch. xiii. 1—3,— — —In its progress, nothing was left to human invention, as before; but all was conducted with the strickest attention to God's revealed will. Nor did David commit the service altogether to others: no; he himself attended the procession, and played and sang with all his might; yea, and danced also before the ark with such holy ecstasies, as to subject himself to the scorn and censure of his own wife; who being a stranger to those divine raptures, imputed them, not to pious fervor, but to indecent wantonness. But his joyous exultation was such as the occasion required, and such as, though condemned by Michal, was most pleasing unto God.

Having seen the service to which he had gone forth, we proceed to notice,

II. THE WORK TO WHICH HE RETURNED—

Though he might be well supposed at the conclusion of his service to need repose, yet he went home only to protract his labors in another way He returned to bless his house; that is,

1. To obtain blessings for them by his prayers—

He would not confine his religious exercises to public occasions, but went home to stir up in his family those blessed emotions with which his own soul was filled. He was anxious that all his wives, his children, and his servants should be partakers of his joy: and therefore he would unite with them in fervent supplication to the God of all grace, that they might themselves "know the Lord from the least even to the greatest of them," and all experience the blessedness of his salvation.

Here we behold a bright example, which it behoves us all to follow. Family prayer is, alas! too often neglected, or at best but coldly performed, by many, who profess a high regard for public ordinances: but the true child of Abraham will "command his house and children after him to fear the Lord," Gen. xviii. 19, and will say with Joshua, "Whatsoever others may do, I and my house will serve the Lord." Josh. xxiv. 15. If we have family wants, and family mercies, we should unite our prayers and our praises with our families, that God may be acknowledged as the one source from whence all good either has issued, or can be hoped for: and though we can easily imagine circumstances wherein such domestic services are impracticable, yet we cannot imagine any real piety to exist where such duties are wilfully neglected.

2. To render himself a blessing to them by his conduct—

It was promised to Abraham that he should not only be blessed himself, but be a blessing also to others: and this promise is in fact made to all the believing seed of Abraham. To make others happy was no small part of David's ambition. Hence he went to his house determining to contribute as far as possible to the edification and comfort of all connected with him. He would instruct the ignorant; and teach, not by precept only, but by example also. His determination was to " walk before his house in a perfect way" Psa. ci. 2,— — —He would not be proud, or imperious, or passionate, or fretful; but would regulate all his tempers and dispositions by the golden rule, of doing as he would be done unto: and " the law of kindness would be ever in his lips."

How different is this from the conduct of many, who from the public ordinances, in which they profess to take delight, go down to their houses to make them wretched and miserable, rather than to bless them! O let the professors of religion look well to this: for, as a consistent christian is a blessing wherever he goes, so an inconsistent christian is a curse, and a stumbling-block to all around him.

Learn then from hence,

1. How highly we are privileged—

The ark, even the Lord Jesus Christ himself, is present in the midst of us. To him we may have access; and of him we may inquire continually: and every blessing which was typically derived from the symbol of his presence, shall be really and spiritually obtained by all who seek him. If then David and the whole kingdom of Israel felt such exalted joy in the possession of that which was a mere shadow, let us not be unmindful of our privilege in possessing the substance.

2. In what way we should improve our privileges—

Let us not only rejoice in them ourselves, but endeavor to communicate the benefit of them to others. Let all who see us, be the better for us; and all who stand in any relation to us be constrained to say, that " God is with us of a truth."

THE APOSTOLIC MINISTRY.

Colossians i. 28.—Whom we preach, warning every man, and teaching every man in all wisdom ; that we may present every man perfect in Christ Jesus. (Pr.)

IT is one of the peculiar characteristics of the Messiah's reign, that under it the poor should have the gospel preached to them. The truth was taught in various ways before, but from hence a multitude of heralds should be sent forth to proclaim the good news of salvation.

——— The model of this practice is to be looked for in the New Testament ; and in the text we see that there were three things especially pertaining to the Apostolic ministry.

I. THE LEADING THEME OF IT WAS CHRIST : " WHOM WE PREACH."

Preaching Christ, and the cross of Christ, is emphatically called " the gospel," 1 Cor. xv. 2—3 ; and " the record which God hath given of his Son." 1 John v. 11. ——— The hearers of this gospel wanted something else : " the Jews require a sign, and the Greeks seek after wisdom ; but we preach Christ crucified." 1 Cor. i. 22, 23.

In justification of this practice, let us consider some of the cases to which the subject will apply—

1. There may be some who have lately been brought to a sense of *their sin and danger*, and may be come with some such question as that which filled the heart of the Phillippian jailer. ——— We preach Christ as the only hope, the only refuge of the lost.

2. Another may feel unhappy because he cannot perceive *how God can forgive sin*, consistently with justice and faithfulness. ——— The cross of Christ is the only solution of this difficulty, the only place where God and the sinner can meet and be reconciled.

3. Another having long been under conviction, is now *reformed :* he reads, and hears, and prays ; but can find *no rest to his soul.* ——— Christ only is the way, and he only can give him rest. Jer. vi. 16. Matt. xi. 28.

4. Some are full of *doubts and fears*, and want to obtain an interest in the promise of eternal life. ——— We preach Christ : and if this be nothing to you, you will find nothing else to do you any real good. But if the way of salvation by him is welcome to your soul, you may dismiss your fears, for all is yours.

5. Another is bowed down under *the ills and burdens of life*, and is ready to despond and say, I shall never see good. ——— Look to Jesus, lest ye be weary and faint in your minds ; consider his sorrows, and forget you own. Heb. xii. 2, 3.

6. Another is *hungering for the bread of life*, and longing to be edified and comforted. ——— The same doctrine which at first relieved us, will afterwards do to live upon, and nothing but Christ and him crucified will do us any real good. John vi. 57, 58.

7. It may be that some are *thoughtless and careless* under the word, still in a state of impenitence and unbelief. ——— But whether they will hear, or whether they will forbear, we must still go on preaching Christ and him crucified. This only is the power of God unto salvation, and this it is that furnishes motives both for repentance and faith. Isai. xlvi. 12, 13. Acts iv. 12. Rom. i. 16.

8. Some are *righteous in their own eyes*, are full, and have need of nothing ; and know not that they are poor, and wretched, and blind, and naked.

—— And what can destroy these vain hopes, and lay the sinner in the dust, but the exhibition of an able and all-sufficient Saviour, and of mercy undeserved. Isai. lv. 1. Rev. iii. 17, 18.

II. The practical manner in which the apostles preached this important doctrine: "WARNING EVERY MAN, AND TEACHING EVERY MAN IN ALL WISDOM."

Warning and teaching is in some respect distinct from preaching the gospel, which properly speaking consists in proclaiming the good news of salvation; yet it is a necessary appendage to it, and essential to the christian ministry. Some men under a pretence of preaching the gospel, have neglected it, and some have denounced it as legal; but it ought to suffice for us that the apostles, in preaching Christ, "warned every man, and taught every man in all wisdom."

1. They *warned every man*. Warning is an expression of kind regard: "as my beloved sons," says Paul to the Galatians, "I warn you." Those for whom we have no regard, we generally let alone, and suffer them to have their own way. —— Now the Scriptures makes use of warning in many cases, and we are required to do the same.—1 Where persons are in *a wrong road*, love will apprise them of it, and warn them of the danger. Exek. xxxiii. 8.—2 Where they are in a condition which exposes them to *ruin*, love will warn them to make their escape and to flee from the wrath to come. Matt. iii. 7.—3 Where men enjoy privileges and advantages which they have no heart to improve, they ought to be warned of the consequences, and exhorted to immediate repentance. Acts xiii. 41. —— These warnings are no other than the dictates of common prudence and benevolence, and can never be excluded from any thing like a rational exercise of the christian ministry.

2. The apostles *taught every man* in all wisdom, instructing them in the first principles of the oracles of God, giving them right views of their own character and condition as sinners, and showing them the suitableness and ability of Christ as a Saviour. —— Such also must be our labor, both in the pulpit and out of it, showing unto men the way of salvation. They are to be taught the evils they are to shun, and the good they are to choose; and this in order to their being brought to Christ, as the last and only refuge of the miserable and undone.

III. The end which the apostles had in view in the exercise of their ministry, and that is the salvation of their hearers, or "THAT THEY MIGHT PRESENT EVERY MAN PERFECT IN CHRIST JESUS."

They did not content themselves with forming the manners of their hearers nor merely with warning and teaching them: if not brought savingly to believe in Christ, they reckoned nothing to be done to any purpose. Gal. iv. 19

But how was Paul to present "every man perfect in Christ Jesus?" Did he hope to save all that heard him? Viewing them *collectively* he did not, for he knew that only a remnant would be saved. Acts xv. 14. Rom. xi. 14. But considering them *individually* he hoped for every man, and labored for their salvation.

God is not obliged to do all he is able to do to save sinners, though we are; and not knowing his counsel or design, it is for us to do our utmost, and leave the event to him. John xx. 30, 31, Rom. ix. 1—3, xi. 14.

We learn from hence, that the employment of Christ's faithful servants is to win souls to him, and it shall be their honor in the last day to present to him the fruits of their ministry. 2 Cor. xi. 2.

If this end be not answered, nothing is effected, and we shall lose our reward. A barren ministry is one of the greatest evils to be dreaded upon earth, and its consequences will be tremendous in the world to come. Ezek. xxxiv. 10. Zech. xi. 17, Matt. xxv. 30.

IMPORTANCE OF PREACHING CHRIST CRUCIFIED.

Gal. iii. 1.—Before whose eyes Jesus Christ hath been evidently set forth, crucified among you. (Pr.)

UNDER any circumstances it is both sinful and unwise to turn away from the truth as it is in Jesus; it bespeaks us blind to our own interest, as well as regardless of the glory of God. But that which rendered such conduct inexcusable in the Galatians, was the degree of evidence with which the gospel was attended, and the abundance of evangelical preaching which they enjoyed. It had been the great object of the apostles' ministry to set forth Christ, and perhaps they had done this more especially to the Galatians; so that though they had never seen Christ in the flesh, yet with such advantages as they possessed, it was as if they had actually seen him.

I. ENDEAVOR TO ASCERTAIN THE IMPORT OF THE TERMS EMPLOYED IN THE TEXT.

By "setting forth Christ crucified," is not meant a setting forth merely his bodily sufferings, or giving a tragical description of his agony in the garden or on the cross, The evangelists never attempt any thing of this kind in their narrative: on the contrary they state the circumstances with great brevity and simplicity, without any coloring or reflections of their own.— The principal reason is, that however great the sufferings which our Lord endured, the virtue of atonement did not consist in the degree of suffering, but in the dignity of him that suffered. Such a representation may indeed affect the passions, but other views of the subject are more edifying and more useful.

1. Christ is set forth in the gospel as *the great propitiation, by which God's righteousness might appear in the remission of sins.* Rom. iii. 25. ————— It was evident that God had pardoned the sins of old testament believers, and taken them to heaven, long before the true sacrifice was offered up; the righteousness of God's conduct was therefore in some degree implicated, and it was needful that it should be thoroughly cleared up. The gospel, by setting forth the death of Christ as an atonement for sin, makes a public declaration of God's righteousness, and shows at once how he can be just, and yet the justifier of him that believeth in Jesus.

2. Christ is set forth as *the great expression of divine love to a sinful and perishing world.*—— ——Other proofs had been given of God's love and mercy, in his long-suffering and kindness towards men; but this is the greatest of all, and infinitely surpasses all the rest. John iii. 16. If God would give an expression of his love to sinners, it became him to do it in a manner suited to the unbounded goodness of his nature; and herein he hath commended his love towards us. Rom. v. 8, 1 John iv. 9, 10.

3. Christ is set forth in the gospel as affording *the strongest proof of God's displeasure against sin.*—— ——The wrath of God had been revealed from heaven in various forms, against the ungodliness and unrighteousness

488

of men; but the sufferings of Christ for us were the grand expression of God's infinite hatred of sin. In him sin was openly and publicly condemned, when he was made a curse for us. Rom. viii. 3, Gal. iii. 13.

4. Christ crucified is set forth as *the only foundation of a sinner's hope.* — — —It is the tenor and import of the whole gospel, that there is salvation in no other. As the brazen serpent was exhibited to the Israelites for their healing, even so is a crucified Saviour exhibited to us as the only medium of life and salvation. Here it is that sinners must look, and from hence alone derive their hope of acceptance with God. John i. 29, iii. 14, 15·

5. The terms in the text further denote, *the high degree of evidence which attended the ministry of the apostles,* especially among the Galatians.— — —Christ was "set forth" of old by promises, by types, and prophecies; but all this was dark and obscure. Sinners are now directed to behold the Lamb of God, and we all with open face behold, as in a glass, the glory of the Lord. There was a peculiar plainness in the preaching of the apostles, and Christ was "evidently" set forth. crucified among them. It was now shown that types and prophecies received their accomplishment in Jesus, and the fullest possible demonstration attended it. Hence those who hear the gospel are the more sinful and inexcusable, in not obeying the truth, and receiving it in love.

II. Consider the importance of setting forth Christ in the preaching of the gospel.

It was the substance of the apostolic ministry to exhibit a crucified Saviour. Paul would glory in nothing else, and determined to know nothing else; all their preaching was called, "a preaching of Christ to the people."— — — It is also a principal part of the work of the Holy Spirit to take of the things of Christ, and show them unto us; it should therefore be the great object of the christian ministry to co-operate with this design. Three important ends in particular are answered by it—

1. To exhibit Christ crucified *will tend to prove the hearts of men,* and make them manifest; and nothing besides has so direct a tendency to do it. — — —If we have any real love to God, any love to righteousness, to the souls of men, or to our own souls, the doctrine of the cross will make it evident. We shall immediately feel and discover a peculiar relish for it, it will be to us as a savor of life unto life, and the name of Jesus will be as ointment poured forth,— — —If destitute of love to God and man, and all virtuous affection, the doctrine of the cross will be to us a savor of death unto death. The preaching of Christ crucified was to the Jews a stumbling-block, and to the Greeks foolishness; but to them which are saved, Christ the wisdom of God, and the power of God, 1 Cor. i. 23, 24.

2. To set forth Christ crucified is *the only way of giving peace to souls in distress for sin.*— — —When a sinner is brought under the terrors of the law, made to see and realize his guilt and danger, and to feel his need of a Saviour, he is apt to look inward for some qualification to recommend him to Christ; but to set forth a crucified Saviour is to point him to the only refuge, and to show him at once his remedy.— — —The penitent is often led to examine himself for evidences of grace in order to obtain comfort, and is as often disappointed, while the cross of Christ is overlooked. Let the sinner then direct his eyes to Jesus, and look to Calvary, for all his help must come from thence.— — —Or if we desire a more spiritual and humble frame of mind, no means are so effectual to its production as the contemplation of a crucified Redeemer. If the doctrine of the cross will make us

happy, we have great reason to be so; if it will not, theie is no help for us in God.

3. To exhibit Christ crucified is the way to draw forth and *bring into ex-ercise all the christian g· ices.— — —*The doctrine of the cross furnishes fresh motives for repentance, gives a direct incentive to holy love, and lays again the foundation of our hope. If this doctrine were withheia, or only occasionally exhibited, it would becloud the whole of the christian system, and deprive it of the power of healing the broken in heart.

4. The preaching of Christ crucified is that which *leaves all unbelievers without excuse.— — —*It will be impossible for those to plead ignorance of the way of salvation, "before whose eyes" this truth has been evidently set forth. If such should eventually perish, it will not be for lack of know-ledge, but for want of a heart to attend to the things which belong to their everlasting peace.

EVANGELICAL PREACHING.

Acts ii. 37.—Now when they heard this they were pricked in their heart, and said unto Peter and to the rest of the Apostles, Men and brethren, what shall we do? (Sk.)

PREACHING has ever been the principal means used for diffusing a know-ledge of christianity.

It was the method adopted and enjoined by the great Author of our religion, Matt. iv. 17, and x. 7; Mark xvi. 15; and that by which his apostles suc-ceeded in making known the gospel to the very ends of the earth, Mark xvi. 20; Acts v. 42; Rom. x. 14—18.

When engaged in properly, as to its subject and manner it is ever success-ful in accomplishing the great end for which it was originally adopted, 1 Cor. i. 21.——A striking instance of its early success is recorded in the chapter before us; and we are led by our text to inquire into—*the nature of that preaching which was so successful; and into the effects which follow ed such preaching,*

I. THE NATURE OF THE PREACHING may be understood from the context.

The subject was CHRIST.——The preacher's aim evidently was, to prove that Jesus of Nazareth was the true Messiah.

To do this *he speaks of him,* verse 22, as one that had been "approved of God among them by signs and miracles;" see John iii. 2, and xiv. 10, 11, and Acts x. 38.——*He then declares,* verse 23, that this was the person delivered to death "by the determinate counsel and foreknowledge of God;" see Luke xxiv. 26, 27, and thus introduces Christ as the Saviour,—the Sac-rifice for sin, Isa. liii. 10. *He next dwells on* his resurrection, and conse quent exaltation; verses 24—36, and asserts that he is both *Lord* and *Christ.* These things *he confirms*—by *Scripture,* verses 25—28,—and by sound *argument,* verses 29—36.

The *subject* was of the highest importance;——it was perfectly suitable to the audience;——

And the manner of treating it was excellent. The *discussion* was plain—concise—clear.——The *mode of address* was evidently courageous and bold.—It was such, as being equally removed from impertinence and self-confidence on the one hand, and from the fear of man on the other, such as

490

becomes those whom God employs to speak in his name: see Prov. xxix 25; Jer. i. 17.

The *preacher* who *thus* conducted himself, demands our consideration. It was PETER, a late fisherman of Galilee, Matt. iv. 18—20, one of the lower class of society.————PETER, a poor man, who said, "Silver and gold have I none," chap. iii. 5.————PETER, whose mind had never been stored nor expanded by the knowledge of the schools.————But *Peter*, who had learned of the Lord Jesus, the Teacher who came from God, John iii. 2; he was well acquainted with the holy Scriptures ;—he knew the truth experimentally ;—his soul was filled with the Holy Ghost;—he had good natural sense ;—he was *divinely* called to preach the Gospel ;—and *thus* qualified, he preached ;—power from above attended the word.

II. AND THE EFFECTS WHICH FOLLOWED well deserve our attention.

" *They were pricked in their heart.*" Hearers treat the word preached with indifference ;—or feeling its force, they resist it ;—or happily, like those whose case is before us, they yield to its convincing influence. These were pricked in their heart; see Heb. iv. 12. The address was made to their understanding,—their judgment,—their conscience ; and being accompanied by the power of divine grace, they were rationally, Scripturally, and feelingly convinced of the error of their ways ;

" *And said to Peter and to the rest of the apostles, Men and brethren, what shall we do?*" We may consider this as

The language of religious concern. They now perceived the vileness of their hearts ; and the wickedness of their conduct; and the great crime of slighting, rejecting, and crucifying the Lord Jesus, particularly affected them. They saw the danger of their situation, and were alarmed about the consequences, see chap. ix. 6. Hence we cannot but view it too, as

The language of religious distress. In all cases where sinners are wrought to a state of proper concern about their souls, that concern is accompanied by distress, on account of their having offended God, neglected the blessed Saviour,—grieved the Holy Spirit,—and ruined themselves ; see Jer. xxxi. 18, 19; Zech. xii. 10. Such are anxious to know how they may "flee from the wrath to come ;" how they may obtain salvation from sin here, and from its consequences hereafter ; see Acts xvi. 30. We may therefore consider this, as

The language of humble inquiry. Such an inquiry, from such a people, is truly striking. Think on their former prejudices ;—the contempt in which they had held Jesus and his followers ; the probability that there were among those who thus exclaimed, some of the higher classes,—priests at least, chap. vi. 7 ; and it must be acknowledged, that on this occasion, the power of divine grace to convince and to humble was singularly astonishing. And we learn from the subsequent verses, that this grace was no less powerful and conspicuous, in raising there, thousands of broken-hearted penitents, from a state of godly sorrow to that of holy joy.

Such was the preaching, and such were the effects.

Our minds are farther led to the following improvement.

CHRIST CRUCIFIED *is, and ever should be, the grand subject of the Christian Ministry.* The Lord Jesus commanded his apostles to preach in *his* name; see ch. xxiv. 47. They *began* thus, as we have now seen. Thus they *continued;* see chap. iii. 12, and iv. 5—12, and v. 30, and viii. 5, 35, and ix. 20, and x. 34—43, and xi. 20, &c.—to chap. xxviii., *They preached thus* to Jews and Gentiles, 1 Cor. i. 23, 24.

There is salvation in no other,—there is no other name whereby we can be saved, chap. iv. 12. JESUS,—his Deity,—his Incarnation,—his spotless Life,—his sacrificial Death,—his Resurrection, and Intercession ; JESUS, who is the author and finisher of faith,—should be, with ministers, " the first and the last,"—" all, and in all." *Most* of our discourses should be of *him* and *his salvation ;*—and *none* of them should be without a voice to say, " Behold the Lamb of God !"

We are also taught to adapt our discourse to our audience ;—and boldly to declare the whole counsel of God ; fearing the face of no man ; see Jer. i 7, 8 ; Ezek. ii. 6, 7.

In religion, it is of the utmost importance that the heart be affected ; (" they were pricked in their hearts ;") see Gen. vi. 5 ; Jer. xvii. 7 ; Joel ii. 13 ; Mark vii. 21 ; Prov. iv. 23 ; Psa. li. 10, 17. Sin hath its seat in the heart ;—*there* the change should begin : to be effectual, it *must* begin there. ——A mere. change of sentiments,—of opinions,—of profession, will avail nothing ; see chap. viii. 9, 13, 18, 23.

Persons may be so affected on account of their sin and danger, that they cannot, in some cases, avoid strongly expressing what they feel. While, therefore, we cautiously guard against, and check every thing in religious profession which is unscriptural, and that would lead to disorder and confusion ; we should be fully aware that there may *still* be cases in which persons religiously affected cannot help saying, " Men and brethren, What shall we do ?"

The essential importance of divine influence to render the word preached successful is another idea suggested by the circumstances connected with the text. Could any argument, any eloquence of Peter's, unaccompanied by the power of divine grace, have prevailed to awaken the consciences,—to bear down the prejudices,—and to subdue the pride of those who heard him ? And can preachers in our day succeed without such influence ? see John xv. 5 ; 1 Cor. iii. 6. Though the miracle-working power of the Holy Ghost is no longer necessary to give sanction to the supernatural doctrine of salvation by faith in a *crucified Saviour,* because *such* sanction has long since been sufficient ; yet the power of the Holy Ghost to assist God's ministers in their great work, and to convert and save sinners, *is ever alike necessary,* and is promised even to the end of the world, Matt. xxviii. 20 ; John xiv. 16 ; Luke xi. 13.

In the discharge of their sacred duty, let the preachers of the Gospel always seek,—always expect divine aid ;—and ever look for some success. ——And though that success may not always be such as they desired, yet, doing God's work in a right disposition. they may safely console themselves with these words :—" Surely my judgment is with the Lord, and my work with my God," Isa. xlix. 4.

CHRISTIAN MINISTERS, AND THEIR WORK.

Acts xvi. 17.—These men are the servants of the most high God, which show unto us the way of salvation. (Sk.)

FROM the context we learn, that Paul and Silas were directed by a vision to go to Macedonia, ver. 6—12. Lydia, being converted to God at Philippi, received them into her house, ver. 13, 15; from whence they were followed by a female, possessed with a spirit of divination, who cried, saying, "These men," &c. This testimony, though true, had a tendency to lessen their authority, as the natural inference was, that they were in league with her. The apostle Paul, seeing it in all its bearings, expelled the demon; which occasioned violent persecution, ver. 16—24. The words of our text, however, are true, full, clear, and distinct; let us, therefore, notice,

I. THE IMPORTANT WORK OF CHRISTIAN MINISTERS; viz. to show unto mankind the way of salvation; in doing which, it is necessary that they should,

1. *Define the nature of this salvation.* It is spiritual, and imports, 1. A deliverance from *contracted guilt.* The design of the gospel is to give a knowledge of salvation by the remission of sins, Luke i. 77. Hence Peter and his coadjutors, when brought before the Sanhedrim at Jerusalem, asserted that "Jesus whom the Jews had crucified, God had exalted with his right hand to be a Prince, and a Saviour," &c., Acts v. 31; and Paul, preaching at Antioch, said, "Be it known unto you, therefore, men and brethren, that through this man is preached unto you the forgiveness of sin," &c., Acts xiii. 38, 39. 2. *The bondage of sin;* hence the gospel is the power of God to salvation, Rom. i. 16; delivering the believer from the dominion of sin, Rom. vi. 22; and empowering his feebleness to do "the good and acceptable, and perfect will of God," Rom. viii. 2, 3. 3. *Its moral pollution,* Tit. iii. 5: in which text the apostle shows that we are saved by the washing of regeneration, &c.; while John asserts, "If we walk in the light as he is in the light, we have fellowship one with another, and the blood of Jesus Christ his Son cleanseth us from all sin," 1 John i. 5. 4. *Its fatal consequences;* in the everlasting happiness of the soul. Believers are kept by the power of God through faith unto salvation," 1 Pet. i. 5; and to such Jesus will appear the second time without sin unto salvation, Heb. ix. 28. So that it imports, not only a deliverance from all moral evil and its consequences, but it secures the enjoyment of grace here, and glory hereafter, Rev. xii. 10.

2. *Develope its source;*—The pure, disinterested, unmerited, unparalleled, and unsolicited mercy of God, John iii. 16. In contemplating the scheme of redemption, which originated in the eternal mind, we may exclaim, in the language of John, "Behold *what manner* of love the Father hath bestowed upon us," 1 John iii. 1. Such love as this furnishes a subject for the everlasting contemplation of men and angels.

3. *Proclaim its Author;*—the Lord Jesus Christ: for so hath the Lord said, "I have set thee to be a light of the Gentiles, that thou shouldest be for salvation to the ends of the earth," Acts xiii. 47. "And being made perfect, he became the Author of eternal salvation unto all them that obey him," Heb. v. 9. "God hath appointed us to obtain salvation by our Lord Jesus Christ," 1 Thess. v. 9. "Neither is there salvation in any other," Acts v. 12.

4. *Point out its necessity;*—By showing the *nature* of sin, 1 John iii. 4;—its *source,* Mark vii.-21, 22;—its *universal dominion,* Rom. v. 12, iii. 10—19;—and the irrevocable decree of God, Luke xiii. 3; John iii. 3; Heb. ii. 3, xii. 14.

5. *Explain its appointed method;*—1. *Repentance,* Mark i. 15;—originating in conviction of sin, Rom. vii. 9;—accompanied by sorrow for sin, 2 Cor. vii. 10;—manifested by reformation from sin, Luke xix. 8;—and expressed in ardent prayer to God, Luke xviii. 13. 2. *Faith towards our Lord Jesus Christ,* Acts xx. 21;—faith in his person and offices, importing

a full reliance in his merits for pardon and acceptance, Rom. iii. 24, 25 :—living faith, which subjects the soul to Christ in the way of obedience, Gal. v. 6.

II. Their high designation ;—"Servants of the most high God:" which imports,

1. *That their commission is from God.* To them he has said, "Go ye into all the world, and preach the gospel to every creature," &c., Mark xvi. 18. And their reply to the church is the language of the apostle, Eph. iii. 8. They are servants, "having this treasure in earthen vessels, that the excellency of the power may be of God," 2 Cor. iv. 7. Hence they can say, "as we were allowed of God to be put in trust with the gospel, even so we speak; not as pleasing men, but God, which trieth our hearts," 1 Thess. ii. 4.

2. *Their supplies are divine.* Their Master hath said, "Lo, I am with you alway, even unto the end of the world," Matt. xxviii. 20. In seasons of discouragement he says, "My grace is sufficient for thee," 2 Cor. xii. 9 ;—"Go to all that I shall send thee, and whatsoever I command thee, thou shalt speak. Be not afraid of their faces; for I am with thee to deliver thee, saith the Lord," Jer. i. 8.

3. *Their success is from God.* A minister may be sound in his judgment, orthodox in his creed, logical in his definitions, correct in his enunciation, rhetorical in his discourses, pathetic in his appeals, powerful in his application, and yet unsuccessful in winning souls; "Paul may plant, and Apollos water, but God giveth the increase," 1 Cor. iii. 7. St. Paul, who was chief of the apostles, felt this, when he said, "Brethren, pray for us, that the word of the Lord may have free course, and be glorified," 2 Thess. iii. 1. Ministers are God's servants,—to their own Master they stand or fall; they devoutly acknowledge the good done on earth, the Lord alone does it; hence their appeals to God for the aid of the Holy Ghost, without whom "nothing is wise, or strong, or good." It remains for us, therefore, to notice,

III. The duty of those among whom Providence may direct their labors; which is,

1. *To receive their message.* "Whosoever," said Christ to his disciples, "shall not receive you nor hear your words, when ye depart out of that house or city, shake off the dust of your feet," &c., Matt. x. 14, 15. Need we wonder that our Lord should say, "Take heed how ye hear?" Luke viii. 18. Let no man trifle with God's message, however feeble the instrument who has delivered it.

2. *Support their characters.* "Against an elder receive not an accusation but before two or three witnesses," 1 Tim. v. 19 :—"Touch not mine anointed, and do my prophets no harm," 1 Chron. xvi. 22.

3. *Respect their office.* "And we beseech you, brethren, to know them which labor among you, and are over you in the Lord, and admonish you; and esteem them very highly in love, for their works' sake," 1 Thess. v 12, 13.

4. *Supply their wants.* "For if the Gentiles have been made partakers of their spiritual things, their duty is also to minister to them in carnal things," Rom. xv. 27; 1 Tim. v. 17; 1 Cor. ix. 1—10.

5. *Facilitate their labors.* This you should do by, 1. *Your prayers,* Eph. vi. 18, 19; 1 Thess. v. 25; 2. *Your influence,* in its weight and extent.

494

To you 's the word of this salvation sent. Have you received **the truth?** Do you enjoy the salvation of the gospel? If you have not obeyed the gospel, how awful your state! 1 Pet. iv. 17. "Repent ye, therefore, and be converted, that your sins may be blotted out, when the times of refreshing shall come from the presence of the Lord."

OFFICE AND RESPONSIBILITY OF MINISTERS.

Ezek. xxxiii. 8.—When I say unto the wicked, O wicked man, thou shalt surely die! if thou dost not speak to warn the wicked from his way, that wicked man shall die in his iniquity; but his blood will I require at thy hand. (H. II.)

THE office of a Minister is the most important and most difficult of any that we can be called to sustain. It is the most important, because the salvation of multitudes depends upon it: and it is the most difficult, because it requires such self-denying habits, and spiritual affections. The responsibility also that attaches to it is such, that no man would dare to take it upon himself, if he had not a promise of peculiar assistance in the discharge of it. Ministers are the messengers of God to men: to them they must faithfully declare his whole counsel: however painful the truths may be which they are to deliver, and however averse men may be to hear them, they must execute their commission at the peril of their souls. To this effect God speaks in the words before us: in which we may notice,

I. WHAT GOD SAITH TO THE WICKED—

It is scarcely possible to conceive a more solemn declaration than that before us: "I say unto the wicked, O wicked man, thou shalt surely die!" Consider,

1. Who are the people addressed—

These are all who do not unfeignedly turn from sin to God. It matters not whether they be rich or poor, old or young, learned or unlearned. In some sense, it matters not whether their sins have been more or less heinous: for though there certainly are degrees of guilt, and some are more wicked than others, yet all are wicked, who are not following after God in righteousness and true holiness; and consequently, all such persons, however their characters may vary in other respects, are addressed in the text.

2. The declaration of God unto them—

Death is here denounced as the judgment to be inflicted on all who turn not to their God: and to the same effect the Inspired Writers uniformly speak, Isa. iii. 11, Rom. vi. 23, Jam. i. 14, 15. Nor are we at a loss to determine what is meant by "death:" it is the wrath of God, Rom. i. 18, the misery of hell, Rev. xxi. 8. This is the judgment that will come upon every individual who shall be found in the state before described. God may be considered as addressing himself to every individual of the human race; "O *thou* wicked man!" Nor is this fatal result of wickedness expressed in doubtful terms: there is no peradventure; the decree is fixed; "Thou shalt *surely* die!" Who can reflect on these words as proceeding from a God of infinite power and of inviolable truth, and not tremble?

3. The condition implied in that declaration—

If there were no ondition implied in the declaration, it would have been to no purpose to make known the declaration itself; since it could have no other effect than to torment men before their time. But as in the message to Nineveh, "that in forty days Nineveh should be overthrown," there was an implied condition, that, if they repented, the threatened vengeance should be withheld; so, in this case, there is an implied assurance, that the wicked, if they will repent, shall not die. And this is expressly stated in the following context: ver. 14—16, so that, awful as this passage is, it is no less encouraging than it is awful; because it assures the contrite and believing sinner that he shall never perish.

Together with this warning, we see in the text,

II. THE NECESSITY IMPOSED ON MINISTERS TO PROCLAIM IT—

Ministers are described as watchman, or sentinels, placed at a distance from the camp to give notice of the enemy's approach. Now this very character marks both their duty and their responsibility. But the consequences of neglect in any Minister are declared in two respects:

1. The person whom he neglects to warn, will perish—

If through the sloth or treachery of the sentinels a camp be surprised at midnight, nothing but confusion and ruin can ensue. Thus, if a person appointed to warn the wicked, neglect to do so, the wicked will continue regardless of their impending doom, till it is too late to avert it. And when the hour of vengeance is come, it will be to no purpose to say, "I was not aware of my danger; my Minister has betrayed me." No; the wicked have means of information within their own reach, independent of their Ministers; and they have secret intimations in their own consciences that they ought to repent: and therefore they must take the conseqences of their own wickedness: "they must die in their iniquity." How awful is this effect of one Minister's supineness! Alas! that hundreds, and perhaps thousands, should perish eternally, when, if he had warned them faithfully, they might have been saved for ever!

2. He himself also will be dealt with as the author of that sinner's destruction—

As a sentinel who, by neglecting to give notice of the enemy's approach, occasioned the overthrow of the army to which he belonged, would be chargeable with all the consequences of his neglect, so will the blood of all that perish through the Minister's neglect "be required at his hand." When they shall all stand before God, he will ask of the Minister, Why didst thou not warn that man, and him, and him, and him? It will be to no purpose to say, "Lord, he was rich, and I was afraid of his displeasure;" or, "Lord, he was poor, and I overlooked him;" or, "Lord, I was so engaged in business or pleasure, that I never thought about the souls committed to my charge." No: he must answer for every soul that perishes through his means, and must sink ten-fold deeper into the bottomless abyss than the most guilty of the people whom he has neglected and betrayed.

APPLICATION—

After stating these reasons for Ministerial fidelity, we need make no apology for "warning the wicked from their way:" or rather, we need apologize for not using far greater plainness of speech than we have ever yet done.

Hear then, ye wicked, with solemn awe, the voice of God to you. "O thou wicked *drunkard*, thou shalt surely die!" "O thou wicked *whoremonger*, thou shalt surely die!" "O thou wicked *swearer*, or *Sabbathbreaker*, thou shalt surely die!" Is there any one hear that, though free from gross sins, *lives in a neglect of secret prayer;* " O thou wicked man, *thou* shalt surely die !" *— — —

But while we declare these things, we would not be unmindful of the compassion which is expressed in the very mode in which God has denounced his judgments; " O thou wicked man !" This seems to intimate, that God is grieved for the misery of the wicked, even while he declares the doom that awaits them. So would we be ; and the rather, because we ourselves are involved in the same condemnation, if we do not repent and turn to God.

O then, brethren, whether ye have committed gross sins or not, remember that ye all need to humble yourselves before God as condemned sinners : ye all need to wash in the fountain of the Redeemer's blood : ye all need to " turn from your transgressions, that so iniquity may not be your ruin." O that God may enable you to accept this warning with all thankfulness ! We have striven, as it became us, to " deliver our own souls :" the Lord grant that, in thus endeavoring to " save ourselves, we may be instrumental to save also those that hear us !" 1 Tim. iv. 16.

THE APOSTLES CHOSEN.

Luke vi. 12, 13.—And it came to pass in those days that he went out into a mountain to pray, and continued all night in prayer to God. And when it was day, he called unto him his disciples; and of them he close twelve, whom also he named apostles. (H. H.)

THE short period of our Lord's ministry on earth rendered it expedient for him to employ others as his co-adjutors in the work. Accordingly, in reference to the twelve Patriarchs, who might be considered as the fathers of the Jewish Church, he selected twelve of his disciples, who should be his instruments for planting and establishing his church. There were other seventy, whom at a later period he sent forth, two and two, for the purpose of preparing the minds of the people for his personal ministry among them; Luke x. 1 : but the apostles were to be his stated servants after that he should have left this world and returned to his heavenly Father. The circumstances of their appointment were peculiar, and deserve our most attentive consideration. The night previous to their appointment he spent in prayer to his heavenly Father :† which remarkable occurrence it will be proper to notice in a threefold view :

I. AS AN ACT FOR OUR BENEFIT—

The appointment of the apostles was a work of singular importance—

They were to be employed in the church as his messengers to declare his truth—his witnesses to attest it—as patterns also to illustrate—and martyrs to confirm it. But whence could a number of poor fishermen attain " a sufficiency for these things ?"— — —

Hence our blessed Lord continued the whole night in prayer for them—

---

* This may be easily extended to the *formalist,* the *hypocritical professor,* &c.

† If we suppose προσευχῆ to mean " in a place of prayer," we still can have no doubt what his occupation there was.

His heavenly Father was able to furnish them for this great work, and to give them success in it; and therefore our Lord importunately sought for them the grace which they stood in need of: nor would he cease from his exertions, till he had obtained all that their necessities required. The benefit of his prayer was fully manifested as soon as they were endued with power from on high: then nothing could withstand their wisdom, or subdue their courage: they were deaf to menaces, and regardless of death. Their success was rapid, extensive, permanent: and we at this day enjoy the fruits of their labors. Through that prayer the apostles were richly furnished unto every good work; and were enabled so to establish the kingdom of our Lord, that neither earth nor hell have ever been able to prevail against it.

II. As a lesson for our instruction—

The ordination of ministers is also a most important work—

On them, under God, depends the everlasting welfare of thousands. We need only compare the state of those congregations where the gospel is faithfully preached with those which are under the superintendence of careless ministers: in the one will be found little but ignorance and irreligion; in the other, there will be many whose minds are enlightened with divine truth, and whose souls are quickened to a new and heavenly life.

But where shall persons be found duly qualified for the work—where those who will be willing to undertake it? True; if the Ministry of the Word be made a source of temporal emolument, there will be multitudes ready to engage in it: but if the "signs of a minister," or accompaniments of the ministry, be like those in the apostle's days, "reproaches, necessities, and distresses for Christ's sake," 2 Cor. xii. 10, 12, and the only *pluralities* be "labors, stripes, prisons, deaths," 2 Cor. xi. 23; ib. 24—28, there will not be many candidates for the office, nor will the qualifications for it be thought so common as they are at present. How few are ready to go and preach to the heathen, where the labor and self-denial are great, and the earthly recompence is small! Large benefices, where little is to be done, or the work can be done by proxy, are caught up with avidity: but if nothing but a future reward be held forth, and God say, "Who will go for us?" there are few indeed that will answer with the prophet, "Here am I, send me." Isa. vi. 8.

This, therefore, should be the subject of our devoutest prayers—

God himself has commanded us to commit the matter to him in prayer: "The harvest truly is plenteous, and the laborers are few; pray ye therefore the Lord of the harvest, that he will send forth *(thrust out)* ἐκβάλῃ, Matt. ix. 37, 38, laborers into his harvest." And truly, all ranks and orders of men are concerned to "labor earnestly in prayer" concerning it.

How fervently should *they* pray, *to whom the office of ordaining others is committed!* for "if they lay hands suddenly on any man, they make themselves partakers of other men's sins." 1 Tim. v. 22. Nor should *they* be less earnest *who are to be ordained.* When we consider how arduous their work is, and how great their responsibility before God; when we reflect that their word will be "a savour of life to the life and salvation of many, or a savour of death to their death" and condemnation; 2 Cor. ii. 16; and that the blood of all that perish through their neglect will be required at their hands; methinks it is a wonder that any one can be found, who, for the sake of filthy lucre, will dare to undertake it. Were the weight of the office duly considered, no one would presume to enter upon it without much prayer to God to qualify him for the discharge of it, and to bless his labors to the edification of the people.

498

But *the people themselves also* are no less concerned to pray, that God would " send them pastors after his own heart;" for the welfare of their souls essentially depends on the kind of ministry which they attend : if Christ be not exhibited to them in his person and offices : if they be not encouraged to receive out of his fulness all the blessings of salvation ; if they be not led into discoveries of the evil of their own hearts, and instructed in the nature of that change which the Holy Spirit will effect within them ; if, in short, they have not " the whole counsel of God set before them," they will be left to rest in very low attainments, if not to " perish utterly through lack of knowledge."

This lesson then should be learned by all ; and so learned, as to be reduced to practice.

III. As a pattern for our imitation—

Prayer is both the duty and the privilege of all—

Our blessed Lord had doubtless more intimate communnion with his Father than we can possibly have ; yet are we also authorized to call God " our Father ;" yea, we are commanded to do it, and to " open our mouths wide, that he may fill them." It is not, indeed, required of us that we should spend whole nights in prayer to God ; for that would probably, unless in some very peculiar circumstances, render us unfit for prosecuting the duties of the ensuing day : but we are required to " continue in prayer, and to watch thereunto with thanksgiving :" Col. iv. 2 ; and the more nearly we can approach to the example of our blessed Lord in the frequency and urgency of our prayers, Psa. xxii. 2 ; Heb. v. 7, the more remarkable will be the answers that we shall receive, and the more abundant the communications of God to our souls. If we wrestled more like Jacob, we should certainly prevail to a much greater extent than in general we do. Gen. xxxii. 34—36.

We should therefore resort to it on every particular emergency—

Though the particular object of our Lord's continuance in prayer does not occur to us, yet we all have some occasions that call for more than ordinary direction and assistance from God. On these occasions, whatever they may be, whether they relate to the body or the soul, to time or to eternity, we should go and spread our wants before God. His own command to us is, " In *every* thing, by prayer and supplication, with thanksgiving, let your requests be made known unto God." " In *all* our ways we must acknowledge him, and he will direct our paths."

In this then must all of us resemble the Lord Jesus Christ. In this has " he set us an example, that we should follow his steps:" and " we must walk as he walked." By this must all his followers be distinguished ; for they are " a people near unto him." They are hypocrites of whom it is said, " They will not always call upon God :" all true christians can say, Truly our fellowship is with the Father, and with his Son Jesus Christ."

APPLICATION :

Learn hence the real state of your souls before God. Prayer has often been called the pulse of the soul : and truly it is so ; for by that you may discern the state of the soul, incomparably better than you can by the pulse the state of the body. If you are prayerless people, you are dead, altogether dead in trespasses and sins. If your prayers are habitually cold and formal, they are such as God will never accept. No prayer will enter into the ears of the Lord of Hosts, but that which is offered " in spirit and in truth." Let us then beg of God to give us a spirit of grace and of supplication ; and let us interest ourselves with God for the welfare of his church. Let us especially remember " those who are over us in the Lord," and " labor always

fervently for them in prayer," that they may be enabled to fulfil their ministry with diligence and success. Thus shall we both insure blessings to our
own souls, and be instrumental to the hastening on of that day, when "all
shall know the Lord, from the least to the greatest," and "all flesh shall see
the salvation of God."

THE GROUNDS OF A MINISTER'S REGARD TO HIS PEOPLE.

2 Cor. vii. 3.—You are in our hearts to die and live with you. (H. H.)

THERE is in every man a quick sensibility with respect to any thing that
may affect his character: even a slight insinuation, that seems to convey reproof, is keenly felt. On this account we ought to be extremely cautious,
not only when criminating others, but even when vindicating ourselves; because a necessary self-vindication may easily be construed as an oblique censure upon others. We cannot but admire the delicacy of the Apostle's mind,
when asserting the integrity of his conduct towards the church at Corinth.
There were some in that place who had traduced his character: for the sake
of others therefore it was necessary that he should declare his innocence
with respect to the things that were laid to his charge. But fearing that, in
doing this, he might appear to cast a reflection indiscriminately on the whole
body, he adds, with exquisite tenderness and affection, that, so far from in-
tending to condemn them all, he was willing, if his other duties would admit
of it, to live and die among them.

In order to promote in all, this amiable disposition, we shall consider,

I. THE GROUNDS OF THE APOSTLE'S LOVE—

St. Paul felt a love towards the whole human race: but he was filled with
a peculiar affection towards the Corinthians on account of.

1. Their relation to God—

The Apostle had reason to believe that the Corinthians, notwithstanding
some great evils which obtained among them, 1 Cor. i. 11, and iii. 1—4,
and v. 1, 2, and vi. 5—8, and viii. 9—12, and xi. 18—22, and xiv. 26, were
truly converted to God; and that the greater part of them were very eminent christians, 1 Cor. i. 5—7, and 2 Cor. viii. 7.

This was a just ground for loving them. Indeed, if he had not been pen-
etrated with an unfeigned regard for them, he would have no evidence of his
own love to God: for "he who loveth him that begat, must love those who
are begotten of him. 1 John v. 1.

2. Their relation to himself—

Having been, in God's hand, the instrument of their conversion, he stood
related to them as their spiritual father. 1 Cor. iv. 15, and 2 Cor. xii. 14,
with Acts xviii. 1—18. Now, as a peculiar affection subsists between those
who bear this relation according to the flesh, so it is reasonable that there
should be a mutual regard between those also who are thus united in the
bonds of the Spirit. Doubtless the apostle did not confine his regards to
these: Col. ii. 1, but, having "travailed in birth with them," he felt all the
anxieties and affections of a parent towards them.

The fervor of his love will appear from,

II. THE WAY IN WHICH HE MANIFESTED IT—

We may notice in the context,

1. His affectionate remembrance of them—

He boasted of them wherever he went: he held them up as peculiarly worthy of imitation: 2 Cor. vii. 14, and 2 Cor. viii. 24, and ix. 1, 2, and so great was the satisfaction which he felt in hearing of their welfare, that it far over-balanced all the sufferings he endured. What clearer proof could he give of his affection for them?

2. His faithful admonitions—

Though he loved them, he was not blind to their faults. When he saw them deviating from the path of duty, he performed the office of a Monitor and Guide. He changed his voice towards them, as he saw occasion: sometimes he spake with the authority of an Apostle, 1 Cor. iv. 18, 19, and sometimes with the tenderness of a friend or parent. 2 Cor. ii. 1—5, and 1 Cor. iv. 14. This was an eminent proof of his love, because it shewed that his concern for their souls swallowed up every other consideration. Lev. xix. 17 with ver. 12.

3. His devotion to their service—

He regarded not wealth, or ease, or honor; but would have been contented "to live and die with them" who had but ill requited all his past kindness: Yea, he declared, that "he would most gladly spend and be spent for them, though the more abundantly he loved them, the less he were loved." 2 Cor. xii. 15. Nothing short of laying down our life for any person could testify more love than this.

Application—

1. Let us improve our intercourse with each other in life—

It is the happiness of a minister and his people to have frequent and familiar intercourse with each other. We have through the mercy of our God enjoyed it: but alas! how little have we improved it! Let us look unto our God for his blessing upon us in future: 2 Cor. vi. 11—13, for without that "neither Paul can plant, nor Apollos water, to any good purpose." 1 Cor. iii. 5—7.

2. Let us prepare for our separation in death—

As "the Priests under the law could not continue by reason of death," so neither can we under the Gospel. We must go to give an account of our stewardship; and you to answer for the advantages you have enjoyed. Let us be looking forward to that solemn meeting which we shall have at the bar of judgment. Let us implore help from God, that we may discharge our duties towards each other aright; and meet again, not as witnesses against each other, but as fellow-heirs of his glory. And the Lord grant that we may then be your joy, and that you may be "our joy and crown of rejoicing" to all eternity! 1 Thess. ii. 19, 20, and 2 Cor. i. 14.

A MINISTER'S CHIEF JOY.

3 John 4.—I have no greater joy than to hear that my children walk in truth. (H. H.)

THERE subsists between a minister and his people a relation which may not unfitly be compared with that of a father and his children. The metaphorical expression of a father is more strictly applicable to those whom a minister "has begotten through the gospel;" 1 Cor. iv. 15; but it needs not to be restricted to this sense: it may be used with greater latitude in reference to those over whom a minister watches, and for whose benefit he labors with parental anxiety, especially where the person to whom the paternal relation is ascribed is somewhat advanced in years. It should seem that Gaius, to whom St. John wrote this Epistle, was converted to the faith by the ministry of Paul: 1 Cor. i. 14; yet St. John properly includes him amongst his children, because he felt the same regard for him as for those who were the more immediate seals of his own ministry; the whole body of his people being in his different epistles frequently designated by that favorite appellation. 1 John ii. 1, and iii. 18.

Respecting the state of Gaius' soul, the apostle had heard the most satisfactory account; so that he could not shew his anxiety for the bodily health of Gaius more strongly, than by wishing it to prosper *in every respect*, περὶ πάντων, ver. 2, "even as his soul prospered." Having declared the joy which this information had afforded him, he states, in general, that he had no greater joy than what arose from such tidings as these.

From hence we shall take occasion to shew,

I. WHAT IS THE GREAT OBJECT OF A MINISTER'S DESIRE IN BEHALF OF HIS PEOPLE—

To bring men to the acknowledgement of the truth is the first labor of a minister: and, till that has been effected, no other relation exists between him and them than that which he has by nature, or that which he has in common with all mankind. But when they have embraced the truth, and are become members of the family of Christ, then the minister seeks their advancement in the divine life—

Christianity, as experienced in the soul, is not a sentiment, but a habit: it not merely informs the mind, but regulates the life: and, whilst it introduces "men from darkness unto light, it turns them also from the power of Satan unto God." Having brought souls to an enjoyment of Christ, and to a conformity to his mind and will, the minister desires to see them walk in the truth.

1. Consistently—

He longs to behold in them a holy consistency; a high state of heavenly affections, and a careful attention to the duties of morality. Morality however will not satisfy him if detached from fellowship with God: nor will the most sublime intercourse with God in prayer and praise approve itself to him, if it be not accompanied with a conscientious discharge of every personal and relative duty— — —

2. Steadily—

In them he expects to find a steadiness that bids defiance to temptation, and cannot be diverted from its purpose, either by the allurements of sense or the terrors of persecution: he would have his converts to be "stedfast, immoveable, always abounding in the work of the Lord." 1 Cor. xv. 58. A fixedness of mind he regards as absolutely essential to the christian character: and he is never satisfied with the state of his people unless he find that, in the midst of the severest persecutions, they are enabled to say, "None of these things move me, neither count I my life dear unto me, so that I may but finish my course with joy"— — —

3. Progressively—

This is implied in the term "walking," which is a progressive motion necessary to the christian life. There is no possibility of standing still in religion. Our motion, if not progressive, must be retrograde. Now, as a parent wishes to see in his children a gradual advancement towards maturity both in their bodily and intellectual faculties, so does a minister long for his people's progress towards perfection. He hopes to see in them a more entire devotedness of heart unto their God and Saviour; evincing itself in a greater spirituality of mind, an increasing indifference to the things of time and sense, and a more laborious engagement in every good work— — —In a word, he wishes to see their progress like that of the sun in the firmament, "their path shining brighter and brighter unto the perfect day." Prov. iv. 18.

The emotions with which St. John beheld this conduct in Gaius were most sublime : and such they will be in every faithful minister ; as will appear, whilst we shew,

II. WHENCE IT IS THAT THE ATTAINMENT OF THAT OBJECT FILLS HIM WITH SUCH EXALTED JOY—

St. John was not inferior to any one of the apostles in holy joy. He had been pre-eminently favored by his Lord and Saviour, insomuch that he was known by the name of " the disciple whom Jesus loved." He had beheld his Lord transfigured on Mount Tabor, and shining forth in all the glory of the Godhead. He had laen in the bosom of his Lord, as on many other occasions, so especially on that evening when the commemorative ordinance of the Lord's Supper was instituted: yet even "he had no greater joy than to hear that his children walked in truth." Much more therefore may we expect that ministers, less favored than he, should have no joy more exalted than that which the sight or hearing of their people's prosperity affords them. This is their sublimest source of happiness ;

1. Because it is by this only that the ends of their ministry are answered—

If the minister impart to his children "the sincere milk of the word," it is, "that they may grow thereby :" or, if he set before them "the stronger meat" of the gospel, it is, that those who are able to receive it may be the more nourished and strengthened for their future labors. If he see no growth in them, "he stands in doubt" whether they have ever been truly and savingly converted to the faith of Christ; and "he travails, as it were, a second time in birth with them, until Christ be fully and visibly formed in them." Gal. iv. 19, 20. But when he beholds the plants, which he is daily watering, thriving, and diffusing all around the fragrancy of holy and devout affections, he sees of the travail of his soul and is satisfied: and what the angels enjoyed at the first symptoms of their conversion, he enjoys from day to day : his very life is bound up in their welfare ; and "he then lives, when they stand fast in the Lord." 1 Thess. iii. 8.

2. Because by this only can God be glorified—

Nothing brings more dishonor to God than an inconsistent conduct in those who profess godliness. The very name of God is often blasphemed through the misconduct of those who call themselves his peculiar people. The ungodly world are not content with condemning the offending individual; "they speak evil of the way of truth" itself, as though that countenanced and even produced the evils that have been committed. On the other hand, "the person who brings forth much fruit glorifies God," and " by his well-doing puts to silence the ignorance of foolish men." To a minister who loves the Lord Jesus Christ in sincerity, and is jealous for the honor of his name, nothing can be more delightful than to see truth triumphing over error, and the kingdom of Christ exalted on the ruins of Satan's empire. On every fresh report that is brought to his ears, he will exclaim, " Hallelujah ! for the Lord God omnipotent reigneth !"— — —

3. Because without this they can have no hope of ever meeting their people in the realms of bliss—

How joyful is the thought of that hour, when the minister shall **go with** his people into the presence of his God, saying, "Here am I, and the children thou hast given me!" And how glorious will be the recompence of his labors, when he shall "have them as his joy and crown of rejoicing" to all eternity! 1 Thess. ii. 19, 20. If an earthly parent hear of his children, that they are advancing visibly in every thing that is good, so that, though he have no hope of seeing them in this world, he feels assured that he shall meet them again at the right hand of God, and dwell with them for ever in his immediate presence; the thought of a temporary separation from them is swallowed up in the joy that the blessed prospect affords him. So it is with the spiritual Parent, when beholding or hearing of the prosperity of his children: for he knows that he shall "rejoice in the day of Christ, that he has not run in vain, or labored in vain." Phil. ii. 16.

Permit me now to address you,

1. In a way of retrospective inquiry—

What report must I hear of you? What report have you to give me of yourselves? Has your walk been consistent, uniform, progressive?— — — Be assured, I am prepared to rejoice in your welfare with a truly paternal joy— — —

2. In a way of prospective admonition—

Great and manifold are your dangers, whatever progress you may have made. That you may escape them, "take heed to God's word," and follow the steps of your blessed Lord: and look to him for all needful strength. "Be strong in him," and you shall "be more than conquerors through him"

THE DUTY OF THOSE WHO ARE CALLED.

1 Thess. ii. 11, 12.—You know how we exhorted, and comforted, and charged every one of you, as a father doth his children, that ye would walk worthy of God, who hath called ed you unto his kingdom and glory. (H. H.)

NEXT to the example of our blessed Lord, there is none so worthy of imitation as that of St. Paul. He appears to have been so entirely cast into the mould of the gospel, that he was a living image of all that it requires. In the ministerial office especially he was almost a perfect pattern. His intrepidity, his singleness of heart, his self-denial, his fervent zeal for God, and tender love to man, never were surpassed, nor ever equalled by any human being. Respecting the purity of his intentions, and the probity of his conduct, he could appeal to all among whom he had labored, yea to God also: *no less than eight times in eleven verses does he repeat this appeal;* so conscious was he that he had exerted himself to the utmost of his power to promote the welfare of his fellow-creatures, and the glory of his God.

In the appeal before us we may notice,

I. THE DUTY OF CHRISTIANS—

The first great duty of those to whom the Gospel comes, is to believe in Christ. 1 John iii. 23. and John vi. 28, 29. But yet even this is subservient to a higher end, even to the attainment of holiness, and the glorifying of God by a heavenly conversation. The christian is not to be satisfied with low attainments, but to walk worthy of his God; to walk worthy of him,

1. As his governor—

God has given us a law which is a perfect transcript of his mind and will. This law is to be the rule of our conduct. In obeying it therefore we must not select the easier parts, and overlook the precepts which are more difficult: we must not attempt to reduce the standard to our practice; but rather endeavour to raise our practice to the standard. We should not inquire, How little can I do, and yet escape punishment? but rather, What can I do to please and honour my Divine Master? How shall I commend to others his government? How shall I convince them that his service is perfect freedom. How shall I illustrate his perfections by my own conduct? How shall I make my light so to shine before them, that all who behold it shall be constrained to glorify my God, and to take upon them his light and easy yoke?

2. As his benefactor—

God has "called" his people, not by the word only, but also by "the effectual working of his power:" He has called them to be subjects of "his kingdom" on earth, and heirs of "his glory" in heaven. Eph. ii. 19. 2 Thess. ii. 13. This distinguishing grace calls for every possible expression of love and gratitude. Our one inquiry therefore should be, "What shall I render unto the Lord for all the benefits that he hath done unto me? How shall I walk worthy of such a benefactor? Shall not my soul overflow with love to him? Shall I not "delight myself in him;" and "present myself a living sacrifice to him;" and strive incessantly to "glorify his name?" Shall I think any thing too much to do or suffer, for his sake? Shall I not seek to be "pure as he is pure," and "perfect as he is perfect?" Surely, "as He who has called me is holy, so should I be holy in all manner of conversation." 1 Pet. i. 15.

This is the christian's duty; thus to argue, and thus to live.

In order to enforce this subject yet further, we will consider,

II. The duty of Ministers—

It is through the exertions of ministers that God carries on his work in the hearts of his people. Ministers are set apart on purpose to teach men their duty, and to urge them to the performance of it. They stand related to their people as a parent to his children: and in the exercise of their high office, they are to address them with parental tenderness, and parental authority.

"Suffer ye then the word of exhortation," while we endeavour to impress upon your minds a due regard for holiness: and permit me, however unworthy of the sacred office, to address you,

1. In a way of affectionate intreaty—

"God has called you unto holiness:" and "this also we wish, even your perfection." Consider then, I beseech you, how much is to be attained by your advancement in holiness.

Consider, how it will *contribute to your present happiness.*—Experience must long since have shewn you, that there is no comfort in religion, when we are living at a distance from God, or in indulgence of any besetting sin We hope too you have found how "pleasant and peaceful are the ways" of godliness, when we are steadfastly walking in them. Go on, and you will have continually increasing evidence, that "*in* keeping God's commandments there is great reward."

Consider also how your piety will *promote the good of others.*—We speak not of the benefit that will arise to society from the good offices you do them; but of the effects which your good example will produce. If your life be not "such as becometh the gospel of Christ," the world will despise religion as a worthless unproductive thing: and those who profess godliness will be apt to catch the infection, and to sink into lukewarmness. But if you "walk worthy of your vocation," you will "by your well-doing put to silence the ignorance of foolish men;" you will constrain them to confess, that the principles which operate so powerfully on your souls, must needs be good; and you will perhaps win many, who would never have been won by the word alone. 1 Pet. iii. 1.

Consider further how it will *advance your eternal happiness.*—What though there be no *merit* in your works, shall they not be rewarded? Shall not every one reap according to what he sows; Gal. vi. 7, 8. and that too, not occording to the quality only, but the quantity also, of his seed? Yes; "every man shall be rewarded according to his own labour:" 1 Cor. iii. 8. he shall "reap sparingly or bountifully, according as he sowed;" 2 Cor. ix. 6. and every talent that is improved shall have a correspondent recompence in the day of judgment. Matt. xxv. 28, 29.

What further inducement can you wish for? Only reflect on these things, and surely I shall not have "exhorted" you in vain.

2. In a way of authoritative injunction—

St. Paul, when least disposed to grieve his people, said to them, "As my beloved sons, I warn you." 1 Cor. iv. 14. And in the text he tells us, that he "charged" them in a most solemn manner, and *testified* ($\mu\alpha\rho\tau\upsilon\rho\omicron\mu\epsilon\nu\iota$) unto them. Behold then, we testify unto you that the holiness which we inculcate is of prime importance, and indispensable necessity.

Consider that *nothing less than this will prove you to be real christians.* —If you are "Israelites indeed, you must be without guile." If fire descend from heaven into the bosom to consume your lusts, it will burn till all the fuel be consumed. The contending principles of flesh and spirit will never cease from their warfare, till the flesh be brought into subjection. Gal. v. 17. 1 Cor. ix. 27. "If you are Christ's, you have crucified the flesh with its affections and lusts." Gal. v. 24. Deceive not yourselves; for, "whomsoever you obey, his servants you are." Rom. vi. 16. If you are born of God, you will not harbour any sin. 1 John iii. 9. or be satisfied with any attainment; Phil. iii. 12—14. but will seek to be "righteous, even as God is righteous." 1 John iii. 7.

Consider that *nothing less will suffice to comfort you in a dying hour.*— When you come to that solemn season, things will appear to you in a different light from what they now do. The truths, which have now gained your assent indeed, but float in your mind as though the were devoid of interest or importance, will then present themselves to your mind as the most awful realities. What will you then think of cold and lifeless services? What bitter regret will seize yon, and terrible forebodings too perhaps, when you look back upon a partial obedience, and an hypocritical profession? O that you may not fill your dying pillow with thorns! O that you may serve the Lord in such a manner now, that in that day you may "enjoy the testimony of a good conscience," and have an abundant entrance into the kingdom of your Lord and Saviour!" 2 Pet. i. 10, 11. with Psa. xxxvii. 37.

Consider lastly, that *nothing less will avail you at the bar of judgment.* We repeat it, that you will not be saved *for* your works: but we repeat also, that you will be dealt with *according to* your works. It will be to little purpose to have cr l 'Lord, Lord,' if you are not found to have done the things which he commanded. Matt. vii. 21—23. with Luke vi. 46. God has said, "Cursed be he that doeth the work of the Lord deceitfully;" Jer. xlviii. 10. nor will eitner of our self-commendations, or the applause of others, avail us, if the heart-searching God do not bear witness to our integrity. **2 Cor x. 18.**

Behold then, as in the sight of God, we testify these things; and charge you all, that if you would ever behold the face of God in peace, you make it the great object of your life to walk as becometh saints, and to "adorn the doctrine of God our Saviour in all things."

APPLICATION—

The Apostle contended not himself with *general* exhortations; but addressed himself to individuals; even, as far as he could, to "*every one*" of his people. Let me then apply my subject more *particularly* to you, dispensing to each his portion in due season.

Are there among you *those who make no profession of religion?*—Think not, that you are excused from that strictness which is required of the saints. As the creatures of God, you are bound to obey him; and as "bought with the inestimable price of his Son's blood, you are bound to glorify him with your bodies and your spirits, which are his." 1 Cor. vi. 20. Nor should it be any consolation to you that you make no profession of religion, for, if you have not been called to be subjects of God's kingdom, and heirs of his glory, you are vassals of Satan, and partakers of his condemnation.

Are there *any who, by reason of their unsteady walk, are ready to doubt whether they have ever been effectually called?* Let me both "*exhort* and *charge*" them not to leave this matter in suspense; but to obtain of God that "grace that shall be sufficient for them." Let me at the same time suggest some considerations proper to "*comfort*" and support their minds. They would ask perhaps, How shall I gain the object of my wishes? How shall I walk worthy of my God? I answer, "WALK IN CHRIST," Col. ii. 6; in a continual dependence on the merit of his blood, and the assistance of his good Spirit. By his blood ye shall be cleansed from guilt: "by his Spirit ye shall be strengthened in your inner man," and be enabled to do whatever he commands. Phil. iv. 13.

Finally, let *all*, whatever they may have attained, press forward for the prize of their high calling, and endeavor to abound more and more.

DIVINE WORSHIP.

Psalm lxxxiv. 1, 2.—" How amiable are thy tabernacles, O Lord of hosts! My soul longeth, yea, even fainteth for the courts of the Lord : my heart and my flesh crieth out for the living God." (Sk.)

WHILE the Israelites were in the wilderness, on their way to Canaan, dwelling in tents, God commanded Moses to erect a tent or tabernacle for religious uses.—A part of this tent was peculiarly sacred, and called *the holy of holies;* adjoining this was *the holy place*, separated from the former by a veil; and connected with the holy place was a court where sacrifices were offered; and into which the people were occasionally permitted to enter, See Exod. xxv. 8, and xxix. 38—46; chaps. xxxvi. to xl; and Heb. chap. ix. At this tabernacle, as well as in the temple afterwards built by Solomon, the hosts of Israel assembled to worship God: here divine worship was performed according to the Jewish ritual; and here the God of Israel manifested his presence.

To a pious Israelite all these circumstances were very interesting; and these evidently were the things which excited the admiration, and called forth the warm desires of the Psalmist, when he uttered the language of the text.

Let these words lead our attention to—*The amiableness of divine worship ;* and to—*The manner in which devont worshippers are drawn to its sacred exercises.*

I. THE AMIABLENESS OF DIVINE WORSHIP may be discerned, by adverting to—The persons assembled,—Their engagements,—And some interesting results, to which such engagements lead.

Behold the assembly!—It is composed of rational, immortal, accountable creatures ;—of persons whose ages, relative situations, and conditions are various. They are assembled in the name of God their Maker and Preserver,—of Christ their Redeemer; their business is one, and is of everlasting importance. To adore the infinite Jehovah ;—to obtain pardon, regeneration, and holiness are the purposes for which they assemble ; and the Lord of Hosts is with them, Jesus is in the midst of them ; and angels unperceived join their assembly.

Proceed with them in their devotions.—Psalms, hymns, divine songs,— accompanied by melodious and harmonious sounds, say, or seem to say,— " Praise waiteth for thee, O God, in Sion." And their very ears are gratified, and their spirits are exhilarated, by harmony and melody, employed in so sacred, so good a cause.

Prayer to God forms another part of their solemn exercises. They approach " the footstool of their God :" they worship, they bow down, they kneel before the Lord their Maker, Psa. xcv. 6, and speak to and commune with the Father of their spirits ; and Jesus being their Advocate, their Mediator,—the petitions offered up through him are regarded ; and " the fervent prayer availeth much."

The ministry of the sacred word is another interesting circumstance connected with public worship. Here the holy scriptures are read, illustrated, and suitably applied. And God opening the eyes of those present, to behold wondrous things out of his law, Ps. cxix. 18, they realize, or may realize, what is so beautifuliy described in the following language, Ps. xix. 7—11.

Such engagements as the above, are, with the truly devout, accompanied by dispositions, sensations, and enjoyments highly, important. " God is a spirit ;" and they " worship him in spirit and in truth." They have " fellowship one with another, and with the Father, and with his Son Jesus Christ." And such a situation connected with such circumstances, is to them, " the house of God, and the gate of heaven," Gen. xxviii. 17.

Besides all this, if we look more minutely, and listen more attentively, we shall *behold* tears of penitence, and *hear* the sighing of such as are sorrowful on account of their sins, and shall have evidence that there are in the assembly, broken and contrite spirits, whom God will not despise, Ps. li. 17. To render the scene still more interesting ;—see cheerful countenances, that bespeak hearts conscious of his approbation, in whose favor is life, Ps. xxx. 5, and hear the song of praise, Isa. xii. 1, 2, and the language of deliverance, Ps. xxvii. 6, and xli. 1—3, and say, are not God's tabernacles amiable ? And may not those who love his worship, express their desire after it in the following language ? " My soul longeth," &c. Let us examine these words, and we shall perceive,

II. THE MANNER IN WHICH DEVOUT WORSHIPPERS ARE DRAWN TO ITS SACRED EXERCISES. The Psalmist desired—The *courts of the Lord, and the living God. All his powers were drawn towards these objects ; and drawn towards them in a very intense manner.*

The expressions—"*courts of the Lord*," and "*living God*," include all that is desirable in divine worship.—Some desire only the "*courts of the Lord;*" the place, the company, the outward expressions of divine worship. Others almost despise these, while they profess to desire "*the living God.*" —With the *former*, any observations about the divine presence in the place of worship, are accounted enthusiastic ;—with the *latter*, public prayer,— praise, and teaching,—are almost things of nought. But mark this devout worshipper :—with him there was something very desirable in *the courts*. The social assembly,—the outward act,—the very *place* where he usually worshipped, had strong attractions ; and yet these were desirable to him, only as they led to the glorious object of devotion,—*the living God.* Without his presence, all worship is a lifeless form ;—but when his "power and glory are seen in the sanctuary," the place is holy ;—the exercises are delightful : and such as call into action *all the powers of the truly devout.*

Observe,—"My *soul* longeth, my *heart* and my *flesh* crieth out." Sure ly, *soul*,—*heart*,—*flesh*, are intended to signify all those faculties which man can exercise in the worship of God. The Psalmist's understanding, his judgment, his will, his affections, and his desires, concurred :— all within him was drawn to the holy exercise ; while his eyes were turned towards the place,—his feet were willing to convey him thither, his hands were ready to be lifted up,—and his tongue was free for prayer and praise.

Mark, too, how intensely he was drawn;—his "*soul longed*, even *faint-ed* for the courts of the Lord : his heart and his flesh *cried out* for the living God." We need not dwell on these expressions, they speak for themselves ; rather let us strive to feel as the sacred writer felt. "Come holy Dove from the heavenly hill, and warm our frozen hearts." Think, oh think on the great, the adorable object of worship ; on his power, his goodness, his mer-cy, his love in Christ Jesus !—and say,—Do not all these demand the *warmest* and the *strongest* exercise of all our rational, and—so far as it is necessary for the expression of our feelings and views—of all our bodily powers ? See Deut. vi. 5 ; Matt. xxii. 37 ; Ps. xlii. 1, 2.

Ye formalists,—ye enthusiasts ;—ye men of reason unaccompanied by af fection,—of feeling unaccompanied by reason ;—and ye who, despise ordi-nances, as well as ye who trust in them ;—read this sacred book of devotion, the book of Psalms ; and learn how to worship God in "the beauty of holiness,"—"in spirit and in truth !"

Let the following reflections conclude the subject.—1. Such exercises— such dispositions—and such enjoyments, as we have been considering, are congenial to the employments and the happiness of heaven, See Ps. xvi. 11 ; John vxii. 24 ; 1 Cor. xiii. 12 ; Rev. vii. 9—12, 15, and xxi. 3. To that state, probably, the mind of the Psalmist ascended, when he uttered the words of the text, See Ps. xxiii. 6, and xvi. 11 ; at least *we* may presume so far, Heb. viii. 5, and chap. ix. and think on that period, when we shall serve God day and night in his temple above; Rev. vii. 15.

2. Let the subject teach us more than ever to value divine worship ;—more than ever to engage in it ; and to engage in it *better* than ever.

3. Let us recollect that a meetness for heaven is as necessary as a title ; and that the means of grace, when properly engaged in, are well calculated to promote that meetness.

4. And let us never forget, that if we would be benefited in divine worship we must look through the vail of outward things, and *principally* desire the presence of the *living God.*

INSTITUTION OF PUBLIC WORSHIP.

Gen. iv. 26.—Then began men to call upon the name of the Lord. (H. H.)

Of the various institutions of religion, some were clearly founded on an express appointment from God himself: others *appear* to have arisen, in the first instance, from the suggestions of holy men, and to have been afterwards authorized and established by divine authority. It is manifest that baptism was practised by the Jews long before it was appointed by Christ as the rite whereby his followers were to be consecrated to his service: but when it was first introduced, or whether by any express command of God, we know not. The change of the Sabbath from the seventh day to the first was sanctioned by the practice of the apostles: but whether they received any particular direction respecting it, we are not informed. The presumption indeed is, that all the observances which God has sanctioned, originated from him; and that men began to practise them in consequence of some intimations from him: but as this is not declared in scripture, we must be contented to leave the matter undecided. We are not any where told that God commanded men to meet together for the purposes of public worship. If we take the text in the precise sense that it bears in our translation, it should seem that public assemblies of worship were rather the offspring of necessity; and that they arose out of an increase of population, and a growing neglect of personal and family religion.

The text indeed is, in the margin of our Bibles, rendered differently: "Then began men to *call themselves by* the name of the Lord:" Nor are Commentators agreed to which of the versions we should give the preference. We shall therefore include both; and take occasion from the words to shew,

I. In what manner we should confess God—

The descendants of Cain, who had become "a fugitive and a vagabond in the earth," soon cast off all regard for God, and addicted themselves to open and shameless impiety. Lamech broke through the restraints which the Creater had imposed in relation to marriage, and "took unto him two wives;" leaving thereby an example, which in process of time effaced the very remembrance of God's original institution. From these and other abominations arose an imperious necessity for the godly to separate themselves from the ungodly, and to maintain by an open and more visible profession the honor of God in the world. This they did: and in so doing they have taught us,

1. To separate ourselves from the ungodly—

There is a certain degree of intercourse which must subsist between us and the world. But it is by no means desirable to extend it beyond that which the duties of our calling absolutely require. Our Lord repeatedly declares that his faithful followers "are not of the world, even as He was not of the world:" John xvii. 16. The apostles also with one voice guard us against cultivating the friendship of the world; James iv. 4; and teach us to come out from among them, 2 Cor. vi. 14—18, and to live as a distinct "peculiar people," 1 Pet. ii. 9, "shining among them as lights in a dark place." Phil. ii. 15. We should go to them, indeed, when duty calls, as the physician enters the infected chambers of the sick: but we should never forget, that "evil communications corrupt good manners;" 1 Cor. xv. 33, and that an undue familiarity with them is far more likely to weaken the spirituality of our own minds, than to generate a holy disposition in theirs.

In us should be verified the prophecy of Balaam, "Israel shall dwell alone, and shall not be reckoned among the nations." Numb. xxiii. 9.

To make an open profession of our attachment to Christ—

The godly, in the ante-diluvian world, called themselves children of God, as distinct from those who were only children of men: and it was foretold that a similar distinction should obtain among the followers of Christ. Isa. xliv. 5. If in one instance Peter failed in acknowledging his Lord, on other occasions he witnessed a good confession, and manfully withstood the threatenings of his enemies. Acts iv. 8, 10, 19, 20. It may be thought perhaps, that, because christianity is the established religion of the land, there is no occasion for such boldness now: but the sons of Cain and of Ishmael are yet amongst us: Jude 11; Gal. iv. 23, 29; there are in every place those who deride all vital godliness : and it requires almost as much fortitude to withstand their sneers and contempt, as it does to brave more cruel persecutions. There is the same necessity for us to "take up our cross and follow Christ," as there was for the primitive christians : and the command given to them to "be faithful unto death," is equally to be regarded by us: for the same conduct will be observed by the Judge towards men of every age and nation ; "he will confess those before his Father who have confessed him in the world," and "deny before his Father those who have denied, or been ashamed of him." Matt. x. 32, 33 ; Mark viii. 38.

But the text instructs us also,

II. In what manner we should worship him—

We can not doubt but that Adam and his pious offspring maintained the worship of God both in their families and their closets : but till' the human race were considerably multiplied, there was no occasion for what may be called *public* worship. But when the families became so numerous that they were obliged to separate, then it was necessary to call them together at stated times and seasons, that, by forming different congregations, they might all receive instruction at once, and keep up in their minds an habitual reverence for God.

The necessity for public ordinances is obvious; and the benefit arising from them is incalculable.

1. They preserve the knowledge of God in the world—

There is reason to fear, that if there were no public ordinances of religion the very name of God would be soon forgotten. Notwithstanding the establishment of such institutions, the generality are "perishing for lack of knowledge :" darkness has overspread the land, even a darkness that may be seen and felt. Exod. x, 21, with Isaiah ix. 2. But there is some light shining in the world ; and *that* is diffused almost exclusively by the public ministry of the word. Occasionally, God is pleased to instruct men by his word and Spirit, without the intervention of human agents : but, as he has set apart an order of men for the express purpose of propagating his truth, so he delights to honor them as his instruments to convey his blessings to the world. Compare Zech. iv. 11—14, and 2 Cor. iv. 7, with Acts viii. 26—39, and x. 9—44. Doubtless he vouchsafes his blessing to those who read and pray in secret, provided they reverence, as far as their circumstances admit, his public institutions : but never did he, from the foundation of the world, impart his blessing to those who continued to live in an avowed contempt of his ordinances : No : "he loveth the gates of Zion more than all the dwellings of Jacob." Ps. lxxxvii. 2.

2. They are the means of perfecting his work in his people's hearts—

God has told us that this was a very principal end for his ordaining men to preach the gospel; Eph. iv. 11—15; but it is by means of the public ordinances chiefly that ministers can address the people: and consequently the ordinances themselves are the means by which God accomplishes his end. We have said before, that God will also reveal himself to his people in secret: and it sometimes happens that their communion with him in private is more sweet and intimate than in the public assembly: but may we not ask, on the other hand, whether, when the heart has been cold and formal in the closet, it has not often been warmed and animated in the church? And is not much of the enjoyment experienced in secret, the result of instructions administered in the public ordinances? In the one they gather the food; in the other they ruminate and chew the cud: but the pleasure and nourishment derived to their souls must be acknowledged, in part at least, as originating in their public duties. To these has God promised his peculiar blessing; Exod. xx. 24; Matt. xxviii. 20; and therefore we should "reverence his sanctuary," and join with one consent in a public surrender of ourselves to God. See Zeph. iii. 9. Zech. viii. 20—22.

ADDRESS,

1. Those who have others under their control—

Parents, and Masters, you are responsible to God for the exercise of your power and influence. Will you then, either by precept or example, encourage a conformity to the world, or a disregard of the worship of your God? O "destroy not their souls, for whom Christ died!" Employ your authority for God: and, whatever opposition you may meet with in the world, learn to say with Joshua, "As for me and my house, we will serve the Lord." Josh. xxiv. 15.

2. Those who are acting for themselves—

If you have "chosen the good part," be careful that it "be not taken away from you," either though the love of this world, or through the fear of man. Be steadfast, and "endure unto the end, that you may be saved at last." If you lose your life for Christ's sake, you shall find it unto life eternal. But if you are "walking in the broad road," think whither it leads: and begin to serve your God in this world, that you may be honored by him in the world to come. John xii. 26.

SERMON OUTLINES

BY

CHARLES SIMEON, and others

VOL. II

CHAPTER I.

THE MEANS OF GRACE.

CONTINUED FROM VOLUME FIRST.

NEED OF DIVINE ASSISTANCE IN PRAYER.

Romans viii. 29.—Likewise the Spirit also helpeth our infirmities: for we know not what we should pray for as we ought: but the Spirit itself maketh intercession for us with groanings which cannot be uttered. (Pr.)

PRAYER has been the distinguishing practice of the godly in all ages, and no real believer can live without it. Yet for this, as well as for all other spiritual duties, we are insufficient, and need the Holy Spirit to teach and help us. Yea, more than in any other duty, as it is of all others the most spiritual, and therefore the most difficult to be performed aright. There is no nearness to God in this exercise, without a considerable degree of spirituality, and abstraction from the present world.

I. CONSIDER OUR INSUFFICIENCY FOR THIS GREAT DUTY: "WE KNOW NOT WHAT WE SHOULD PRAY FOR AS WE OUGHT.

It is intimated that we are insufficient in two respects, both as to the matter and manner of prayer.

1. As to the *matter of prayer:* "we know not *what* to pray for."——— We know some things that we want, and should ask for; but on the whole we are exceedingly ignorant and uninformed.

Particularly, *we are apt to pray for many things which if granted would be for our hurt:* and "who knoweth what is good for man in this life?" We may think uninterrupted health and prosperity would be desirable: yet afflictions are often amongst our greatest blessings, and continued prosperity might have been our ruin. ——— We may think it good that the life of our children and friends should be spared; yet we know not what they would be to us, if our desire were granted. Paul had a thorn in the flesh which he wished to have removed, but the Lord saw it needful to be there. ———We may desire a station in the church, which we are not qualified to occupy; like the two disciples who wanted to sit, one on the right hand and the other on the left, in the kingdom of their Lord; but were told "they knew not what they asked." ——— In all such cases our feelings and wishes must be subordinated to the will of God, saying with our blessed Lord, Not my will, but thine be done. We may ask as he did, to have the bitter cup removed; but we must also submit as he did.

Again: *We omit praying for many things which are essential to our good.* It is well that God's giving is not measured by our asking, and that he gives exceeding abundantly above all that we ask or think, Ephes. iii. 20. ——— We know not the difficulties that lie before us, and therefore cannot ask specifically for what is necessary. David saw none of these when he was anointed king, nor what troubles would attend his reign. If Peter had been duly aware of the temptation that would befall him, he might have prayed against that fatal hour: but it was well that Christ foresaw it, and

3

prayed for him that his faith might not fail. ———— Every day of our lives we know not what to ask in particular, and can only commit our way unto the Lord, that our goings may be established.

2. As to *the manner of praying:* " we know not what we should pray for *as we ought.*" ———— Even in those things which we know we ought to pray for, we know not how to ask aright, or in a proper manner. There are some things which we know we need, as our daily bread, the forgiveness of our sins, and to be kept from temptation : yet we know not how to pray for them in such a manner as is required. ———— It is intimated in the text that there is something belonging to the manner of true prayer, which is neces, sary to render it acceptable in the sight of God ; and that those who draw near to him are required to pray " as they ought." This may include the following particulars—

1. That *our hearts be fixed,* and engaged with God in this sacred duty. It must be the prayer of faith, pleading the promises, and relying on their fulfilment. ———— But how difficult it is to have our hearts thus engaged, thus intently fixed on the great object of prayer : how prone to turn aside like a deceitful bow!

2. That we approach God *with humility and deep abasement.* The gospel has placed us on low ground, and there we must stand whenever we appear before God ; as sinners ready to perish, as utterly unworthy, crying out with the publican, God be merciful to me a sinner. The Pharisee prayed, but knew not how to pray as he ought, and it availed nothing. ———— See the case of the poor woman, who did pray as she ought. Matt. xv. 22—28. It is such importunate prayer that takes the kingdom of heaven by violence.

3. That *our expectations from God should be enlarged.* To pray " as we ought," we must desire much and hope for much. We must believe in God's truth and goodness, in Christ's alsufficiency and willingness to save. "Open thy mouth wide, and I will fill it." We must pray always, and not faint ; and then like Jacob we shall prevail. ———— This however is the manner of prayer for which we feel our insufficiency, and need the influence of the Holy Spirit. We find it difficult, as Job did, to order our speech aright before him, by reason of darkness ; but if we possess the spirit of faith, we shall prevail notwithstanding.

4. That we urge *those pleas which God delights to honor.* What these are we may see in some examples of successful prayer, and shall find that they were all derived from the honor and glory of God, his covenant faithfulness and truth, and the prevailing name of the Lord Jesus. ———— When Moses pleaded for Israel, he pleaded the name and the faithfulness of God. Exod. xxxii. 10—14. ———— When Solomon asked great things for Israel, and that God would forgive his people, his plea is the covenant promise which he had given. 1 Kings viii. 25, 30, 39. ———— Hezekiah did the same, and also the apostles of our Lord, Isa. xxxvii. 14 ; Acts iv. 30.

II. OBSERVE HOW MUCH WE ARE INDEBTED TO THE ASSISTANCE OF THE HOLY SPIRIT, IN THE PERFORMANCE OF THIS IMPORTANT DUTY.

He is said to " help our infirmities," and to " make intercession for us." Without his influence there is no true prayer : we must pray with the Spirit and with the understanding also. ———— Saul had been in the habit of prayer while a pharisee ; yet when he was converted it was said, " Behold he prayeth," for he had never truly prayed before. ———— The inhabitants of Jerusalem were no doubt accustomed to attend the worship of the sanctuary ; yet it was not till the Holy Spirit was poured out upon them that they began to pray in real earnest. Zech. xii. 10. ——— Nor do believers ever prevail in prayer and supplication, but by his assistance. Such are their "infirmities," their ignorance, weakness, and wanderings of heart.

The "intercession" of the Holy Spirit, is not like that of Christ's : the latter is for us, but this is in us. It is the Holy Spirit that inspires us with a spirit of prayer, and it is he that teaches us both how and what to pray for as we ought. ——— He never excites desires, but such as are according to the will of God. The Lord also is said to know the mind of the Spirit, or what is of his inditing; and knowing this, he will assuredly answer. ——— It is the Holy Spirit that endues the mind with sacred fervor and earnestness, and furnishes it with sweetness of expression in prayer. When the mind is overwhelmed with grief and anguish, and unable to give utterance to the heart, he interprets " the groans that cannot be uttered, and maketh intercession for us."

IMPROVEMENT.

1. We are taught to acknowledge our utter insufficiency for what is good, and that the whole of our salvation is of grace. We can do nothing as we ought, and therefore nothing to deserve mercy at the hands of God.

2. While we feel and own our insufficiency, let us not presume to deny our obligations; for we are not only at the same time to pray, but required to pray as we ought.

3. We are from hence furnished with a criterion by which to judge of our own religion; for it is here taken for granted that the Lord's people are a praying people, and that they account it good to draw near unto God.

4. We are here taught to cherish the influence of the Holy Spirit, to depend upon it in the performance of every spiritual exercise, and to admire the infinite compassion of God the Holy Spirit to our manifold infirmities.

PRAYER PROVED TO BE A PROFITABLE EXERCISE.

Job xxi, 15.—" What profit should we have, if we pray unto him." (Sk.)

"I am the man that hath seen affliction," said Jeremiah; and with equal propriety might Job have adopted similar language. What affliction did he see in his family; in his substance; and in his person! and how afflictive were the ill-natured and sarcastic reflections attached to his character by his mistaken friends! they were puzzled to understand, why God had thus dealt with Job. As his afflictions were so sudden, so complicated, and so overwhelming they thought that some secret thing, some hidden wickedness, had drawn down the heavy judgments of God upon him. But Job confutes their unfounded assertions, and vindicates his own character, by showing, that this world, though the theatre of crime, is not the scene of punishment. "Wherefore doth the wicked live?" &c. verse 7. Why does not God punish them? They are not afflicted—neither in their persons, " The rod of God," &c. verse 9. Nor in their families, "Their seed is established," &c. verse 8. Nor in their property, "Their bull gendereth," &c. verse 10. Nor have they any inward depression of spirits, " for they take the timbrel and harp," &c. verse 12. But this prosperity could not be the result of innocence on their part, or of approbation on the part of God For "they say unto God, Depart from us," &c. "What is the Almighty that we should serve him, and what profit?" &c. That is, there is nothing in God to excite our homage, nor is there any thing in prayer to promote our welfare. Thus the sentiment in the text is as false as it is impious. But let us try to profit by this passage, while we consider,

I. THE EXERCISE ASSUMED—"If we pray unto him."

II. THE INQUIRY INSTITUTED—"What profit should we have?"

I. THE EXERCISE ASSUMED—"If we pray," &c. Prayer implies four things :

1. *A consciousness of want.* Man is a needy creature. He wants every thing! nothing is absolutely his own. Destitution is his inheritance; if God abandon him, he has nothing, and is nothing. He wants earthly blessings to support his body, and heavenly blessings to sustain and satisfy his mind. But many never pray, because they know not their necessities : they are ignorant of themselves, of their poverty, guilt and wretchedness. They are best qualified to pray who know most of themselves.

2. *Prayer supposes an object capable of supplying our wants.* This Being must know our necessities, and possess sufficient benevolence and power to supply them. Such is the Almighty, who is considered in this verse as the object of prayer. He knows us altogether, and his benevolence is equal to his knowledge, and his name is sufficiently indicative of his power to do us good. Prayers to saints or angels are impious, as they transfer the homage from the creator to the creature; and absurd, as angels are as dependant as men.

3. *Prayer implies an approach towards the Almighty.* Man is an alien from God; far gone from original righteousness. God is not in all his thoughts. The lusts of the flesh, the lusts of the eye, and the pride of life, absorb his whole attention. But when he begins to pray, his mind turns towards God. Hence prayer is called feeling after God, looking to him, seeking his face, and pouring out the heart before him.

4. *Prayer includes an expression of our wants.* They who pray speak to God : "Behold now I have taken upon me to speak unto the Lord," &c. Gen. xviii. 27. "While I was speaking in prayer," &c. Hannah spake in her heart, when she prayed, but her voice was not heard, 1 Sam. i. 13. "When ye pray, *say,* Our Father," &c. "Take with you words, and turn unto the LORD," Hosea xiv. 2. Let us express our wants *fully ;* let us not dissemble nor cloak our sins before the face of Almighty God; but confess them in all their variety, their malignity, and demerit. Let us do it *humbly.* God is an awful being; we are not worthy of the least of his mercies. Pride is hateful to God; but "he shall save the humble person." Let us do it *importunately :* God suffers us to plead with him, Luke xi. 5—10. xvii, 1—7. Do it by *faith ;* and especially do it in *the name of Jesus,* John xiv. 13, 14.

II. THE INQUIRY INSTITUTED. "What profit should we have?" &c. Selfishness is universally prevalent in the world. Wicked men are invariably selfish men ; "All seek their own, not the things which are Jesus Christ's." Hence the inquiry concerning profit in the text; and because prayer is deemed unprofitable, therefore it is neglected. But there is no exercise under heaven attended with so much profit as prayer.

1. *Prayer contributes to the removal of evil. Of moral evil.* Jabez prayed that God would keep him from evil; and God granted him that which he requested. David said, "I will confess my transgressions unto the LORD,

6

and thou forgavest the iniquity of my sin. *Of natural evil.--Affliction.* "Is any among you afflicted? let him pray." "Then they cried unto the LORD in their trouble, and he delivered them," &c. Psa. cvii. 6. Hezekiah prayed, and wept in his affliction, and God said, "Behold I will heal thee." 1 Kings xx. 5.— *Sorrow.* "I found," said David, "trouble and sorrow: then called I upon the name of the LORD," &c. Psa. cxvi. 1—4. Christ "offered up prayers and supplications, with strong crying and tears, unto him that was able to save him from death, and was heard in that he feared." —*Oppression.* Look at Israel in Egypt, "I have heard their cry," saith God, "by reason of their task masters, and am come down to deliver them," Exod. iii. 7, 8. See Peter shut up in prison; but prayer was made for him, and God delivered him, Acts xii, 5—16, 25.

2. *Prayer is instrumental in procuring good.* All good, for body and soul, for time and eternity, is promised to prayer. *Is it profitable to possess wisdom?* Yes, "if thou be wise, thou shalt be wise for thyself." Wisdom procures happiness, Prov. iii. 13. Length of days,iii. 16. Pleasure, verse 17. Promotion, Prov. iv. 8. And glory, iii. 35, iv, 9. But he who never prays is devoid of wisdom. See 1 Kings iii. 9; Dan. ii. 18, 23; James i. 5; Acts x. 31. *Is it profitable to possess power?* Power to resist the devil, to conquer our corruptions, and to vanquish and put to flight the armies of the aliens? Prayer supplies this strength. "In the day when I cried, thou answeredst me, and strengthenedst me with strength in my soul," Psa. cxxxviii. 3. The spirit helpeth our infirmities, but they who pray most acceptably to God have the largest effusions of that spirit, Luke xi. 13. Prayer is a most important part of the christians armour. *Is it profitable to possess protection?* See Psa. xviii. 3, lvi. 9. To possess *peace?* Phil. iv. 6, 7. To have *an assurance of heaven?* See the penitent thief, Luke xxiii. 42, 43. And the profit of prayer infinitely outweighs all other profit.—It is *divine.* Worldly profit consists in flocks, herds, money, &c. This, in faith, grace, love, happiness, &c.—It is *mental.* Worldly profit is sensual, all for the outward man; but he who prays is enriched inwardly; all his intellectual powers are profited.—It is *comprehensive.* Worldly profit is circumscribed, and bounded by time; the profit of prayer illimitable. —It is *universal.* Worldly profit affects us partially; this, in body, and soul, and substance. And the profit arising from prayer is secured without *risk,* and retained without any fears of *deprivation.* In conclusion observe,

1. *The conduct of the wicked is impious.* They not only live without prayer, but live as if God had no right to exact this duty of them. "What profit should we have, if we pray?"—But is it optional with you whether to pray or not? Are duties matters of opinion? No, God has made prayer imperative upon you; it is his commandment, and it cannot be violated with impunity.

2. *The conduct of the wicked is erroneous.* They consider prayer a profitless exercise, and therefore neglect it. But this calculation is totally unfounded. Prayer avails much. How strange that men who reason so conclusively in matters of science, should suffer themselves to be so grievously deceived as to the duties of religion!

3. *The conduct of the wicked is ruinous.* Without prayer salvation is unattainable, Prov. i. 24—31.

7

THE APOSTLE'S PRAYER FOR AN INCREASE OF FAITH.

Luke xvii. 5.—And the apostles said unto the Lord, Increase our faith. (Sk.)

IN the verses preceding the text, our divine Redeemer instructs his dis ciples in the nature and importance of a most difficult duty, that of forgiving injuries; a duty totally unknown or utterly disregarded, till taught by his doctrines, and enforced by his example; as the wisest moralists of the most enlightened nations represented the desire of revenge as the mark of a noble mind, and thought it more magnanimous to revenge an injury, than forgive it. "If thy brother tresspass against thee," &c. ver. 3. "Offences will come :" our views are dissimilar, our passions discordant, and our interests diversified; some offend by their dispositions—others by their manners— others by their conduct; some by their ignorance, and others by their wickedness; but whatever motive may actuate the offending person, or however frequently he may repeat the offence, yet, if he repent, "thou shalt forgive him." The apostles seemed aware of the difficulty attendant on the practice of this duty, and therefore said unto the Lord, "Increase our faith." In the text there are four general ideas implied.

I. THAT THE DISCIPLES OF CHRIST POSSESS FAITH. There can be no *increase* where there is no possession. We may infer the truth of the above assertion,

1. *From the nature of faith.* Definitions of faith are abundant; genuine faith implies the entertaining Scriptural views of the person and offices of Christ, accompanied by an implicit dependence on him for salvation, and a cordial reception of him in the heart. And if this view of faith be correct, it can exist only among the disciples of Christ. Infidels deny his existence —Arians and Socinians reject his atonement—Pharisees trust in themselves that they are righteous, and are ignorant of Christ's righteousness—and practical sinners of all kinds refuse to admit him into their hearts.

2. *From the character of Christ's disciples.* As disciples they are all instructed by him. In what?—the doctrines of faith. What do they learn? —to believe in his name, to submit to his authority, and to depend upon his truth. As disciples they follow him; does not this suppose the exercise of faith? Acts xiii. 38, They rejoice in him, Luke xix. 37. But their joy is the joy of faith, 1 Pet. i. 8.

3. *From the testimonies of revelation.* Jesus said to one, "O woman, great is thy faith!" To another, "Thy faith hath saved thee." He prayed for Peter, that his "faith fail not." Stephen was "a man full of faith," &c.

II. THAT AN INCREASE OF FAITH IS POSSIBLE. This will appear,

1. *From the power and goodness of its Author.* Faith is not an earthborn virtue, begotten by the mere exercise of the human faculties, but a grace that owes its existence to the agency of Jesus Christ. He is "the author and finisher of our faith," &c. Heb. xii. 2; Eph. ii 8; Phil. i. 29. And cannot he who bestows the gift, increase that gift? He who opens the eye of the mind to behold the glories of eternity, can shine with clearer light, and beam with greater lustre. His power is infinite, and his goodness unlimited.

2. *From the progressive nature of religion.* Religion is all progression, and every christian grace admits of an increase; its first implantation in the heart resembles a seed, which when cast into the earth germinates, and, by progressive and gradual growth, becomes a great tree. Christians are regarded as walking, running, pressing forward, all of which expressions de-

8

note increase and advancement. Religion must not be considered in detached parts, but as a complete system of holy principles, and heavenly fruits, which have a necessary dependence upon each other; and our increase in one, necessarily ensures an increase in the whole.

3. *From the admonitions of the Bible.* Christians are exhorted to "grow in grace," &c. 2 Pet. iii. 18. Earnestly to contend for the faith, &c. Jude 3. To build yourselves up, &c. ver. 20. These with many other texts in the New Testament, prove that an increase of faith is possible.

4. *From the experience of the saints.* Faith increases by exercise: every act of faith tends to give permanency and stability to the principle which gives it birth. Christians depend upon God for providential, spiritual, and eternal benefits; and that dependence increases in proportion as they know more of God, Psa. ix. 10.

III. THAT AN INCREASE OF FAITH IS GREATLY TO BE DESIRED. We infer this,

1. *From its nature.* It is a divine gift, and its existence is attributed to the operation of God, Col. ii. 12. That which God works in us must be desirable: as he is an infinitely good being, his works must necessarily bear a resemblance to himself.

2. *From its effects.* These refer—*To our own personal salvation.* We are justified by faith—saved by faith—Christ dwells in our hearts by faith—we stand by faith—live by faith—walk by faith—and have boldness of access to God by faith. *To the victories we gain over our enemies.* By the shield of faith we quench the fiery darts, &c. Eph. vi. 16. We conquer the world by faith, 1 John v. 4. The ancient worthies by faith "subdued kingdoms," &c. Heb. xi. 33, 34.—*To the moral influence of our example.* True faith produceth good works; for "faith without works is dead;" and good works are profitable unto men, Matt. v. 16; Titus iii. 8. That on which such high encomiums are bestowed in the bible, by which such amazing effects have been produced, and the absence of which involves men in condemnation here and eternal damnation hereafter, must be desirable. And as the most certain way of retaining faith, is by increasing in it, we may infer the truth of the above position.

IV. THAT MEANS SHOULD BE USED TO SECURE AN INCREASE OF FAITH. To accomplish this object,

1. *Study the character of its author.* Meditate on the power, wisdom, and goodness of our Lord Jesus Christ. Reflect on what he has done for mankind; contemplate what he has promised to do. Think meanly of the Saviour, and you will have little confidence in him; but think greatly and highly of him, and you will trust in him heartily, and believe in him fully.

2. *Get a more extensive acquaintance with the promises of God.* Read them frequently; treasure them up in your memories; hide them in your hearts; meditate on their greatness, variety and immutability; and labor to realize them in your own personal experience.

3. *Be on your guard against every thing that will deaden or damp the ardour of your faith.* Carnal company, worldly cares, spiritual supineness, filthy and foolish conversation,—all tend to sap the foundation of your faith, and destroy your dependence upon God. Chiefly,

4. *Pray for an increase of faith.* "The apostles said unto the Lord, increase our faith;"—"Go thou, and do likewise." Say it *humbly,* from a deep conviction of thy unworthiness, and the infinite dignity and goodness of thy Saviour:—say it *fervently;* pour out strong cries and fervent supplications in behalf of this blessing;—say it *importunately;* recollect the im-

9

portunate widow, and the poor blind beggar ;—say it in thy closet ;—say it in the assemblies of the saints ;—say it as thou walkest by the way ;—say it for thy own sake, and for the sake of others.

In conclusion, we address a word,

1. *To those who have no faith.* Your case is awful, you are condemned already, and the wrath of God abideth on you. You need say unto the Lord, Give us faith, impart the heavenly gift to us, and let us believe to the saving of our souls.

2. *To those whose faith has declined.* "Remember from whence you are fallen, and repent, and do your first works."

3. *To those whose faith remains in full vigour.* "Hold fast whereto ye have already attained, and walk by the same rule," &c. Keep faith in lively exercise, and soon you will receive the end of your faith, even the salvation of your souls.

THE DEBTOR'S PRAYER.

Matthew vi. 10.—Forgive us our debts. (Sk.)

THIS petition is taken from that comprehensive and well known compendium of devotion, which we call, for the sake of distinction, the Lord's prayer. A prayer which Christ condescended to teach his disciples; and a prayer which is designed to be a model for all our prayers. Forms of prayer were common among the Jews, and every public teacher presented one to his disciples; these forms were sometimes drawn out to a considerable length, and from them abridgments were not unfrequently made. We have the satisfaction to learn from God himself what prayer is, and what language we should use in our addresses to the throne of grace; and when a sovereign dictates a petition which he allows condemned culprits to present to him, who can question his willingness to grant their request?—The text is of universal consequence, and suggests to us ;—that we have debts,—that these debts may be forgiven,—and that it is highly important and desirable for us to obtain forgiveness.

I. WHAT ARE OUR DEBTS? This term *debts*, is by St. Luke xi. 4, rendered *sins*. St. John defines sin as a transgression of the law; of that particular law which every man is under to God. Jesus Christ has seen fit to reduce the whole of the moral law, which in the Old Testament is amplified into various precepts, into two positive injunctions. "Thou shalt love the Lord thy God," &c., Matt. xxii. 37—39. God's law is *universally binding;* wherever there are rational creatures in any part of the creation, there they are obligated to love God according to the extent of their capacities.— *It can never be abrogated.* Human laws change, worldly maxims vary, and many of the Jewish precepts were designed only for a single people and to be in use for a certain period, but this law is unchangeable. *It allows of no deviation.* It requires perfect, uniform, and undeviating obedience; and every man, through all the periods of his being, with an unchangeable intensity of desire, is required to love God, &c. This law we have all violated in instances innumerable.—We have done it, by omitting to do what the law positively enjoins; and by doing what the law plainly prohibits.—These deviations, sins, or trespasses, are in the text termed *debts.*

1. *Debts suppose two parties, the one of which has received goods, valuables, or commodities from the other.* This is our case. From God we have received all we possess; we owe our being to him, Acts xvii. 25—28. Our bodies are his workmanship, Psa. cxxxix. 13—16. He is the father of our spirits, Heb. xii. 9. For our property we are indebted to his blessing, Deut. viii. 18. He fixeth the bounds of our habitation, Acts xvii. 27. Indeed to each of us it may be said, "What hast thou that thou didst not receive?"

2. *Debts imply, that the returns made have not been proportioned to the property received.* Here also we all stand impeached. How deeply are we in arrears! Unnumbered benefits we have received from God, but what returns have we made? It is said of Hezekiah, "that he rendered not again according to the benefit done unto him:" and his conduct we have all too successfully imitated. Our time has been wasted,—our talents prostituted,—our hearts set on idols.—The members of our bodies have been instruments of unrighteous unto sin; and the powers of our souls have been darkened and degraded: and God and his benefits forgotten.

3. *Debts place their subjects in circumstances of embarrassment and danger.* How wretched is the man who is deeply in debt! Wherever he turns, he is sure to meet a creditor. who harasses and torments him for sums which he is totally unable to discharge. He lives every day under the expectation of an arrest, and calculates upon nothing but confinement in a jail. How descriptive is this of the state of sinners who are deeply in debt to God! who have made no returns of gratitude, love, nor obedience to their Maker! who are tormented with fearful apprehensions! liable to an arrest from Divine Justice, and in danger of being cast into the prison of hell.

II. OUR DEBTS MAY BE FORGIVEN.

1. *When we ask forgiveness for our debts, it supposes that we have no hope of discharging them.* We cannot pay them off: the immense and incalculable value of the benefits received, leaves no possibility of our making adequate returns for them: if God had never done any thing for us, but that of giving his Son to die for our sins, this would have laid us under such a mighty debt of obligation, that an eternity of gratitude would have failed to discharge the amazing sum; but he has given us his Spirit, his gospel, his ordinances, and his ministers. "Oh to grace what mighty debtors!" We cannot pay off our debts; they have been so long standing, accumulating, and increasing. Most of all, we have nothing to pay, we are insolvent debtors.

2. *When we ask forgiveness, it implies that our future obedience can never atone for our past defects.* If we had contracted a debt, our payment for goods in future would not discharge the old debt: we can never go beyond the requirements of the law; "Therefore by the deeds of the law," &c., Rom. iii. 20. But our debts may be forgiven. We infer this,—*First, from the character of God as revealed by himself.* He proclaimed his name to Moses; "The LORD God, merciful and gracious, long-suffering, and abundant in goodness and truth; keeping mercy for thousands; forgiving iniquity," &c., Exod. xxxiv. 6, 7. "He is ready to pardon," Neh. ix. 7. "Ready to forgive," Psa. lxxxvi. 5. "To him belong mercies and forgivenesses," &c., Dan. ix. 9. "I, even I, am he that blotteth out," &c., Isa xliii. 25.—*Secondly, from the atoning sacrifice of Jesus Christ.* That the sufferings of the Redeemer were sufferings for our sins, is a fact which the inspired writers most clearly demonstrate. "He was wounded for our transgressions," &c., Isa. liii. 5. "He hath made him to be sin for us," &c., 2

Cor. v. 21. "Christ was once offered," &c., Heb. ix. 28. "Who his own self bare our sins," &c., 1 Peter ii. 24. And the atonement of Christ for sin is the foundation of our hope of pardon. Hence remission of sins is preached in his name, Luke xxiv. 47; Acts xiii. 38, 39. And "God forgives men for Christ's sake," Ephes. iv. 32.—*Thirdly, from the promises of the Bible* "Come now and let us reason together," &c., Isa. i. 18. "Let the wicked forsake his way," &c., lv. 7. "All manner of sin and blasphemy," &c., Matt. xii. 31.—*Fourthly, from the testimonies of the saints.* Moses said to God, "Thou hast forgiven this people from Egypt even until now," Num. xiv. 19. "He being full of compassion, forgave their iniquity," Psa. lxxviii. 38. David said, "Thou forgavest the iniquity of my sin," Psa. xxxii. 5. Hezekiah declared, "Thou hast cast all my sins behind thy back," Isa. xxxviii. 17. "We have redemption through his blood, even the forgiveness of sins," Colos. i. 14. And if any other evidence be deemed necessary, to prove that our debts may be forgiven, the prayer in the text is sufficient. Christ has taught us to ask forgiveness; and what we are directed to ask, we may confidently hope to receive. But to whom is this forgiveness administered? To penitent believers; "He," (God) "pardoneth and absolveth all them that truly repent and unfeignedly believe his holy gospel." Repentance prepares the mind for the reception of pardon; and induces the sinner humbly and importunately to plead for it, Acts viii. 22. Faith enables him to claim the promises of forgiveness as his own, Acts xiii. 39.

III. THAT IT IS HIGHLY IMPORTANT AND DESIRABLE FOR US TO OBTAIN FORGIVENESS. Two things will serve to confirm the truth of this observation.

1. *A state of forgiveness is a state of positive enjoyment: Enjoyment,* arising from a consciousness of having escaped punishment; an unpardoned sinner is in danger of perdition; he is a child of wrath; God is angry with him, and punishment is threatened him; but when God forgives him, that wrath which was revealed from heaven against him is removed; and he has the knowledge of salvation, &c., Luke i. 77. *Enjoyment,* flowing from the peace of God which passeth all understanding. "For being justified by faith," &c., Rom. v. 1. *Enjoyment,* springing from the testimony of a good conscience, 2 Cor. i. 12. And how highly desirable is that state, which gives birth to enjoyments so divine, so rational, so pure, and so permanent!

2. *A state of forgiveness is a state of absolute security.* What has that man to fear, against whom Heaven has no accusation? "If God be for us, who can be against us? Who shall lay any thing to the charge of God's elect? It is God that justifieth. Who is he that condemneth?" A man who has obtained forgiveness from his God, may look every enemy in the face.—With his conscience he is at peace;—God will bruise Satan under his feet;—death will be to him a vanquished foe;—and heaven is his by title and by promise, Rom. viii. 17; 1 John ii. 25. Contemplating such privileges,—who can help exclaiming, "Blessed are they whose iniquities are forgiven, and whose sins are covered."

INFERENCES.

1. *If sins are debts, we cannot fail to recollect how awfully we are in arrears.* Let us make up our accounts, and as far as we can, form an estimate, ascertain how much we owe to God. Some of us are old and gray neaded! Oh what a debt is ours! How much have we received, but how little paid?

2. *Oh how promptly and earnestly should we sue for pardon.* Forgiveness is now offered, but if we delay to accept the generous offer, our great Creditor will issue an arrest against us, and we shall be cast into prison, and be confined in chains of darkness to the judgment of the great day.

3. *Has God forgiven your debts?* Cease not to reflect on the returns which duty binds you to make.—*Be grateful,* "Bless the LORD, O my soul," &c., Psa. ciii. 2, 3. *Cultivate a spirit of forgiveness towards others,* Matt. xviii. 23—35. *Let your love to God bear some proportion to the greatness of the obligations you are under to him.* "There was a certain creditor which had two debtors," &c., "and when they had nothing to pay, he frankly forgave them both; which of them will love him most?" Luke vii. 42.

PROPER METHOD OF PRAYING TO GOD.

Ps. xxv. 11.—For thy name's sake, O Lord, pardon mine iniquity! for it is great. (H. H.)

GOD is a mighty Sovereign, "who doth according to his own will," "neither giveth account to us of any of his matters." We may indeed mark the traces of wisdom and goodness in every thing which he does; but "his ways and his thoughts are very different from ours, and far above them." In the dispensations of his providence he pays no regard to the moral characters of men, but "makes the sun to shine equally upon the evil and the good." In the dispensations of his grace too he is far from preferring those whom we should think he would select. He often inclines the hearts of "publicans and harlots to enter into his kingdom," while he leaves less abandoned Pharisees and Formalists to perish in their sins. This if it be an humiliating truth, is also replete with comfort. If it take away all grounds of boasting, it cuts off at the same time all occasion for despondency. If he "have a right to do what he will with his own," the vilest person in the universe may approach him with a comfortable hope of acceptance, and may address him in the language of the text.

In these words of the Psalmist we may notice,

I. HIS CONFESSION—

David was not ashamed to confess that his sins were exceeding great—

There is no reason to think that David in this psalm adverts to his transgression with Bathsheba. It is probable that the psalm was penned many years before that event. The Royal Penitent speaks rather of his in-dwelling corruptions. He had long been accustomed to observe the workings of his own heart, and had often besought God to search and try him to the uttermost. Ps. cxxxix. 23, 24. In this way he had marked both the defects of his duties, and the evil propensities of his nature; and, from a review of all his actions, words, and thoughts, was led to acknowledge that his sin was exceeding great. Nor was this confession peculiar to him. Holy Job, as soon as he beheld his true character, exclaimed, "Behold, I am vile!" Job xl. 4. And Paul no sooner became acquainted with the purity and extent of God's law, than he saw himself a condemned sinner, and confessed, that "in him dwelt no good thing." Rom. vii. 9, 18.

And does not a similar confession become *us* also?

Let us only review our past lives, and we shall find too much occasion for the deepest humiliation. Have not many of us been addicted to open, known iniquities? and do not the consciences of such persons testify against

13

them that their sin is great? Have not many also devoted all their time and attention to *secular* concerns? and will they account it a light thing thus to despise God, and idolize the world? Have not others satisfied themselves with a formal round of duties, in which their souls were never earnestly engaged? and can they suppose that God is pleased with a mere lip-service, when their hearts are far from him? Have not others professed Godliness indeed, but walked utterly unworthy of their profession, being as proud, and passionate, as worldly too, and covetous, as those who have made no such profession? and can *they* suppose their sin is not great, when sinners are hardened, and God is blasphemed through their means?————But why do we speak of the *profane* and *worldly*, or the *formal* and *hypocritical?* Must not even the *saints* themselves blush and be confounded, when they consider how miserably they have fallen short in every thing? Must they not exclaim with St. Paul, "O wretched man that I am!"? Surely we must know little indeed of ourselves, if we do not all see how much the confession in the text is suited to our state.

When, like David, we are duly humbled under a sense of our guilt, we shall readily adopt,

II. His petition—

David could not rest without imploring forgiveness at God's hands—

He found a sense of guilt to be an intolerable burthen to his soul; Ps. xxxviii. 4; and well knew that it would "eat as a canker," till he had obtained the pardon of his sin. Hence he humbled himself before his God, and cried for mercy.

Nor shall *we* restrain prayer before God, if we will but consider the state of an unpardoned soul—

No words can fully express the misery of one who has all the guilt of his sins upon him. He has *no peace with God*, seeing that "God is angry with him every day," and "the wrath of God abideth on him." He has *no peace in his own conscience;* for though he may drown reflection for a while in business or pleasure, he is like the troubled sea which cannot rest, but casts up mire and dirt. Isa. lvii. 20. He is also *destitute of* any well-founded *hope:* he may buoy up himself with blind·presumption; but he will feel many misgiving fears, and forebodings of evil. He has *no comfort in his afflictions;* for, not having God for his friend, he cannot go to him with confidence, or obtain those refreshing consolations which strengthen and uphold the godly. *In a dying hour* he is yet more *wretched:* if he be not insensible as a beast, how does he regret his mis-spent hours, and wish that God would prolong his state of probation! But *in the eternal world his misery is completed:* he comes to the tribunal of Justice without any Mediator to reconcile him to God, or any Advocate to plead his cause: yea, the very voice which just before importuned him to accept of mercy, now bids him "depart accursed:" and from that moment his doom is fixed in everlasting burnings. Now can any man reflect on this, and not see the need of crying earnestly for mercy? Can our petitions be too earnest, or too constant, when they are appointed, and the only means of escaping all this misery?

But in our application for mercy, we must be careful to use,

III. His Plea—

The Psalmist derived all his hope of mercy from God himself—

He pleaded not the smallness of his offences or the multitude of his services, the depth of his penitence, or the fervor of his petitions. He knew that name, which had long before been proclaimed to Moses, to which, as to "a strong tower, the righteous *runneth* and is safe;" and to *that* he fled for refuge; from *that* he derived his only hope, his only plea.

Nor can we present any other plea than the name, the sacred name of Jesus—

Under the Gospel we are taught more clearly to ask in the name of Jesus, and are assured that petitions so offered shall never fail of acceptance. John xiv. 13, 14. But it is no easy matter to offer that plea in sincerity. Perhaps there is not any thing in the world more difficult. *We naturally prefer any other plea that can be devised:* and, even when we find that we have not in ourselves any worthiness on which we can rely, we are still averse to rest on the name of Jesus. We either *deem it insufficient* to procure acceptance for our prayers, or *make our unworthiness a reason for declining to urge it as our plea* with any confidence before God. But, unless we renounce every other hope, and rest entirely on the mediation and intercession of Christ, our prayer will never enter into the ears of our heavenly Father—

Observations:

1. The vilest of sinners has no reason to despair—

The confession, petition, and plea, which David presented at the throne of Grace, are suited to the very chief of sinners: nor, as the subsequent experience of David proves, can there be any state in which they shall not prevail. Let none then despond. Be it so, Our iniquities are great: but are they greater than Christ's merits, or beyond the reach of God's mercy? If not, let us exalt our adorable Saviour, and determine, if we perish, to perish crying for mercy in the name of Jesus.

2. The most eminent saints have no ground to boast—

There never was a creature that had any righteousness of his own to plead. And if God has had mercy upon any, it was purely and entirely for his own name sake. Ezek. xxxvi. 22, 32. Could we ascend to heaven, and ask the glorified saints what had been the ground of their acceptance, they would all " cast down their crowns at the feet of Jesus," and shout, with one consent, "Salvation to God and to the Lamb!" Rev. iv. 10, and vii. 10.—Let the saints on earth then lie low before God, and say continually, "Not unto us, O Lord, not unto us, but unto thy *name* be the praise."

3. Persons of every description must guard diligently against pride and unbelief—

Sin, of whatever kind, is both evil in itself and dangerous to us. But the consequences of pride and unbelief are peculiarly fatal. There is not any other sin which may not be forgiven, provided we seek mercy with real penitence and faith. But if we be too proud to confess our sins, and to plead the name and merits of Jesus for the forgiveness of them, we insure and seal our own condemnation. Let us then guard against *all* sin; but especially against these, which rivet all our other sins upon us. So shall we obtain favor with God, and " be to him for a name and for a praise for evermore. Jer. xiii. 11.

THE BENEFIT OF PRAYER.

John xvi. 24.—Ask, and ye shall receive, that your joy may be full. (H. H.)

THIS world is justly characterized as a vale of tears. Even they who ex-perience the most happiness, find many interruptions of it: nor is there any way of securing permanent tranquility, but by waiting upon God in prayer.

The disciples were sorrowful on account of the approaching departure of their Lord, with whom they had hitherto enjoyed the most familiar fellow-ship. Our Lord tells them, that though they would no longer be able to *inquire*, ver. 23, ἐρωτήσετε, of him, yet, if they would *ask*, ib. αἰτήσητε, of the Father in his name, he would grant them whatsoever they should need; and that the answers which they should receive to their prayers would abundant-ly overbalance the loss of their present privileges, and fill them with unutter-able joy.

In the direction given them, we may notice,

I. OUR DUTY—

It is comprised in one word, "Ask." Now this is,

1. An easy duty—

We do not mean that it is always easy to pray, (for there is nothing more difficult when the heart is indisposed for that exercise;) but that is the easiest condition that could possibly be imposed— — —and that, when the heart is in a proper frame, prayer is as easy to the soul, as breathing is to the body: it is the first, and most natural, effort of a living soul: " Behold, he prayeth!" Acts ix. 11.

2. A reasonable duty—

Man is a dependent creature; and it is but reasonable that he should ac-knowledge that dependence at a throne of grace, and ask for those mercies which he stands in need of. The very heathens have felt the propriety of supplicating their deities, and have established ordinances whereby they might conciliate the favor of their gods. It is true, that God knows our necessities before we ask: yet is it highly proper that we should spread them before him, in order that we ourselves may be humbled under a sense of them, and that God's mercy in relieving them may be more clearly seen.

3. A necessary duty—

Though God cannot be prevailed upon by dint of importunity,* yet he has appointed prayer as the means of obtaining his blessings. He has said, " I will be inquired of to do it for them." Ezek. xxxvi. 37. There is no room therefore left for us to speculate upon the use of prayer: it is quite sufficient that God has required it as means to an end: and if we will not comply with his injunctions respecting it, it is utterly in vain for us to expect his blessings.

4. An acceptable duty—

Prayer offered to the Deity without any respect to the mediation of Christ, is not acceptable ; but when presented in an humble dependence on his atone-ment, and intercession, it comes up before God as incense, and prevails be-yond the utmost extent of our conceptions. It is to prayer *offered in this manner*, that the promise in the text is given. Ver. 23, 24. And this has been the qualification of all acceptable prayer from the beginning. Abel was heard on account of his sacrifice. Heb. xi. 4. The penitents under the law obtained mercy in no other way. Heb. ix. 22. The Jews, when unable

* The expressions, Luke xviii. 7, 8, must not lead us to think of God as though he were wrought upon as we are.

by reason of their captivity, to offer their accustomed sacrifices, were to look towards the temple, which was a type of our incarnate God. 1 Kings viii 47, 48; Dan. vi. 10. And to that same Jesus must we look, trusting in him as "our Advocate with the Father, and as the propitiation for our sins." 1 John ii. 1, 2. Nor did any one ever ask *in this manner* without obtaining a supply of all his wants.

To counteract the backwardness of our hearts to this duty, let us consider,

II. OUR ENCOURAGEMENT TO PERFORM IT—

The promise of acceptance is without any limit or exception—

There is no exception with respect to the persons who may apply to God. The vilest person in the universe, provided he ask *in the manner prescribed in the text*, shall be heard as readily as the very chief of the apostles. His past iniquities, of whatever kind they have been, shall not operate as any bar to his acceptance with God— — —

Nor is there any limit respecting the blessings we implore: provided they will really conduce to our good, and to God's glory, they shall be given. However "wide we open our mouths, God will fill them"— — —Ps. lxxxi. 10; John xiv. 13, 14. The frequent and solemn repetition of this truth by our Lord himself, must of necessity remove all doubt upon the subject. Matt. vii. 7, 8.

And instances of its accomplishment occur in almost every page of the sacred writings—

Whether Abel's prayer was answered by fire from heaven which consumed his sacrifice, or by some other token of the divine favor, the acceptance of it was equally manifest, and the fact is equally encouraging to us. To recount the various instances that occurred from that period to the times of Christ and his apostles, would be a pleasing task, but would occupy many hours. Suffice it to say, that whether men's prayer has been offered for themselves Jonah ii. 1, 7, or for others, Exod. xxxii. 11—14; Acts xii. 5—9, and whether it has been of a more stated and solemn kind, Ps. xviii. 6, or only in a sudden ejaculation, Neh. ii. 4—6, it has equally prevailed; it has prevailed speedily, 2 Kings xx. 2, 4, 5; Dan. ix. 20, 21, 23, and to a most incredible extent; Jam. v. 17, 18; and shall yet prevail, by whomsoever it may be offered, ib. ver. 16.

This encouragement to prayer is greatly heightened by what is added respecting,

III. THE CONSEQUENCE OF A DUE AND ACCEPTABLE PERFORMANCE OF IT—

God delights in the prosperity of his people; and desires that they should be happy here, as well as in the world to come. It is with this view that he has enjoined prayer as a duty; because, when performed aright, it is the means of filling the soul with the sublimest joy.

1. It tranquilizes the most perturbed mind—

Let a person under any sudden irritation, or calamity betake himself to prayer, and he will speedily find the tempest calmed, and his agitations quieted. No other thing will operate like this. It will enable him to educe good out of every evil: it will not only blunt the edge of all his trials, but will turn his sorrows into joy. Ps. xxx. 8—11, and xl. 1—3.

2. It brings God nigh unto the soul—

God in answer to prayer will take away the veil which intercepts our views of him, and "manifest himself to us, as he does not unto the world." What an exhibition of his glory was that which he vouchsafed to Moses! What a bright display of Christ's excellency was that which the three favored disciples were admitted to behold on Mount Tabor! We say not indeed

17

that any similar vision of the Father or the Son shall ever be presented to our bodily eyes: but God will certainly "shine into the hearts of those who call upon him, to give them the light of the knowledge of his glory in the face of Jesus Christ;" 2 Cor. iv. 6; and will enable them to say, "Truly our fellowship is with the Father, and with his Son Jesus Christ." 1 John i. 3. What ineffable delight must such manifestations bring with them!——

3. It gives us an earnest and foretaste of heaven itself—

The happiness of heaven consists in the vision and fruition of God: and this, as far as it can be enjoyed by faith, is enjoyed in prayer. There is not any one who has abounded in the performance of this duty, but has had frequent occasion, when in his closet, to exclaim with Jacob, "This is none other but the house of God, this is the gate of heaven!" Gen. xxviii. 17. In such seasons as these a man has no occasion to search out evidences of his acceptance with God, or of his title to heaven: for the very intercourse which he has with the deity is, if we may so speak, heaven brought down to earth; it is an actual anticipation of heaven, and a pledge of his complete possession of it in due season.

ADDRESS,

1. To those who ask without receiving—

Think not that God has violated his promise. The reason of your not receiving is, that "you ask amiss." Jam. iv. 3. Your petitions are cold, formal, hypocritical; and you have not a due respect to the name of Jesus in presenting them to God. Perform your duty as you ought, and you shall never complain of a want of acceptance in it.

2. To those who have received answers to prayer—

Let not your communion with God puff you up with pride, but rather abase you in the dust. If once you grow vain and secure, you will provoke God to hide his face from you, and to withhold the communications of his grace. Rejoice in the glorious privileges you possess; but "rejoice with trembling."

THE BREAD OF LIFE.

John vi. 34.—Lord, evermore give us this bread. (Sk.)

THERE is displayed in the gospel a most admirable and delightful combination of doctrines, precepts, and promises; and the performance of each christian duty entitles us to the enjoyment of some gracious promise. This sentiment is exemplified in no employment more than that of prayer: an engagement in which all good men have delighted, and the pleasure of which increases in proportion to the frequency of its repetition and the fervor of its exercise. Thank God none need be at a loss for words in his addresses to the Divine Being: for, in addition to that comprehensive form of prayer, significantly designated "the Lord's Prayer," sentiments of petition, supplication, and intercession are interspersed through the inspired volume, many of which were used by holy men, who were disciples of our Lord, who heard the gracious words that dropped from his lips, and who were favored by his immediate instruction; one of these is recorded in the text. Our Lord had been pointing out the amazing superiority which he and his dispensation

18

possessed over the dispensation of food which miraculously sustained **the** Israelites in the wilderness. The disciples heard with attention, and when he had ended his instructive observations, they unanimously cried out, "Lord, evermore give us this bread." Observe in this prayer,

I. A BLESSING REQUESTED;—"This bread;" that is, the true bread from heaven," for the bread of God is He that cometh down from heaven, and giveth life unto the world," ver. 33. Bread is here, by Jesus Christ, represented as a type of himself; and to show its propriety, remark,

1. *Bread is of a vivifying quality.* Metaphors, which are drawn from earthly objects to represent heavenly ones, must necessarily be defective in expressing their full meaning. Bread, though of a reviving nature, cannot restore animation, when life is extinct; but the bread of heaven finds us in a state of death, and its efficacy is manifested in communicating life to our souls, Eph. ii. 1, as well as in supporting that life in all circumstances, Psa. xxiii. 2, 5.

2. *Bread is congenial to all appetites.* All have *naturally* a disposition for bread; and in the same manner, Christ, the bread from heaven, is exactly suited to satisfy the spiritual appetites of mankind; and as some tastes are vitiated to such a degree, that they do not relish bread, so many sinners prefer feeding on ashes and husks rather than on Christ, Luke xv. 16; Isa. lv, 2, xliv. 20.

3. *Bread is the common gift of God to the world.* Only a few possess the luxuries of life; but bread is for all, it is the greatest blessing that God ever bestowed-for the support of animal life; and "God so loved the world, that he gave his only begotten Son, that whosoever believeth in him might not perish, but have everlasting life," &c., John iii. 16, 17; and this is the greatest blessing the Almighty ever bestowed for the benefit of our souls. John xv. 5.

4. *Bread can only be useful as we partake of it.* It may be in our hands, but unless we feed upon it, it will be of no benefit to us. We hear Christ preached, we attend on his ordinances; but in vain is all this, unless we stretch forth the hand, eat, and live for ever, John vi. 27; 1 Cor. xi. 24.

II. A PERSON ADDRESSED;—"Lord;" who is the proper object of prayer, because,

1. *Prayer is the language of need;* and of this humanity is full. No sun rises that does not cast his beams on our wants; and whither should we go, but to Him, in whom dwelleth all the fulness necessary to supply the wants of mankind, John vi. 68; Col. ii. 9.

2. *Prayer is the expression of a dependent to a superior.* And who gave us life? who has supported it to the present moment? That God on whom we and all other created beings depend, Gen. i. 26, 27; Acts xvii. 26, 28.

3. *Prayer is the result of hope;* and surely, if ever there was a foundation for hope, it is in God, Psa. xlii. 11. He has condescended to assume the most endearing and encouraging characters, in his relations to mankind, Psa. xlviii. 14; 2 Cor. vi. 18. He has deigned to promise the full supply of our wants, and abundance of both temporal and spiritual blessings, 1 Pet. i. 4; Psa. cxxx. 8, xxxvii. 25. He has been the God of our fathers, 2 Cor. i. 10. Hope in the Lord is therefore founded upon a sure and rational basis.

III. A MODE OF COMMUNICATION STATED;—"Give us this bread."

1. *Because we can no more maintain spiritual life without it, than our bodies can live without food.*

2. Because we cannot borrow it with any possibility of returning it, on account of our necessitous circumstances. Nor do we ever receive more of this bread than we can use, Rev. iii. 17.

3. Because we cannot purchase it ; having been plundered by sin of every valuable we possessed, Acts viii. 20, 21.

4. Because we cannot earn it ; we have been disabled, nor can we move till we receive this invaluable restorative; and if we receive it, it must be as a gift, Luke x. 30; Tit. iii. 5.

IV. A PERIOD FOR ITS CONTINUANCE SPECIFIED?—"evermore."

1. Because in this world we shall always need it. To whatever state of grace a man may attain, he is still liable to fall, as appears from a variety of petitions and cautions which the scriptures contain, Psa. li. 12; Prov. i. 24—32; Matt. xxiv. 13; Luke ix. 62; 1 Tim. i. 19, 20; Heb. x. 38. 39. Let the Almighty withdraw his support for one moment, and we must die, and die eternally, Psa. lx. 11; Lam. iv. 16, 17.

2. Because the stores of divine goodness cannot be exhausted. Gratitude to an earthly ben factor will often prevent us from being importunate in our requests, lest by giving to us, he should impoverish himself; but this cannot be the case with the bread that cometh down from heaven, for that is undiminishable, Eph. iii. 18, 19.

3. Because it always will retain its efficacy and virtue. Unalterable in quantity, it is also unchangeable in quality, Heb. xiii. 8.

4. Because it does not induce satiety. Earthly food is too gross to allow its uninterrupting use; but on the contrary, as we receive this divine bread, our capacities to make use of it are enlarged, and our appetite increased for its continued communication.

5. Because in the world to come it will constitute our joy and felicity. Christ will still be the only delight of his saints, and will be their exceeding great reward for ever and ever, Rev. vii. 9—17.

NOTICE,

1. This bread must be sought with penitence, Matt. v. 4.
2. This bread will be found by faith, John iii. 36.
3. This bread must be received with gratitude, Psa. xcii. 1.

Have my hearers ever received the blessing of which we have spoken? if not, let the language of your hearts be, " Lord, evermore give us this bread:" for " Blessed is he that shall eat this bread in the kingdom of God."

FEEDING ON CHRIST THE ONLY MEANS OF SPIRITUAL LIFE.

John vi. 53—58.—Verily, verily, I say unto you, Except ye eat the flesh of the Son of Man, and drink his blood, ye have no life in you. Whoso eateth my flesh, and drinketh my blood, hath eternal life; and I will raise him up at the last day. For my flesh is meat indeed, and my blood is drink indeed. He that eateth my flesh, and drinketh my blood, dwelleth in me, and I in him, As the living Father hath sent me, and I live by the Father; so he that eateth me, even he shall live by me. This is that bread which came down from heaven: not as your fathers did eat manna, and are dead: he that eateth of this bread shall live for ever. (B.)

THE circumstances under which these words were spoken, are the following.

Consider,

20

I. What we are to understand by "eating the flesh of the Son of Man, and drinking his blood."

Eating his flesh, and drinking his blood, literally and carnally, as the Jews supposed, ver. 52, is not here meant; and this notion Jesus refuted and repelled. Ver. 63.—

Nor is the eating his flesh under the form of bread, and drinking his blood under that of wine, intended here, as the Papists suppose; nor the partaking the signs of his flesh and blood, as the Protestants speak, in the holy Eucharist.—For the Lord's Supper was not then instituted, and however Jesus might have the design of that sacrament in his mind, and make use of terms applicable to it, it is certain his hearers could not understand him as speaking respecting it.—In the case of the converted thief, and all that died in the faith, before the institution of that ordinance, it was not necessary to salvation, but the eating and drinking Christ's flesh and blood, is here declared to be necessary. Ver. 53.—It may be observed, also, that a participation of the Lord's Supper does not necessarily and universally produce the effects which are ascribed to the feeding on Christ, which is treated of in this discourse. Ver. 54—58.

The eating of Christ's flesh and drinking his blood, spoken of in the text, is of a spiritual kind, and means a participation in his merits, or an interest in his sufferings and death, in his blood and righteousness, his atonement and mediation, for our justification, sanctification, and spiritual consolation.—This is done by the agency of the Holy Spirit.—And hence it implies that we partake of his Spirit; ver. 63; 1 Cor. xii. 13; John iv. 10; vii. 37, 38; as the fruit of his death and resurrection, viz. to quicken, renew, Tit. iii. 5—7, strengthen, and comfort us.— — His Word also is implied; ver. 63; confirmed by his death, being the means of feeding us with knowledge, of refreshing, supporting, and nourishing our minds. The doctrines of the Word are often represented under this metaphor. Prov. ix. 5; Isa. lv. 2; Eccles. xxiv. 21. Now we are thus to partake of Christ by faith; by which we are persuaded of the sufficiency of his merits, and rely thereon for justification; persuaded of the efficacy of his Spirit, and apply for it, in order to regeneration, and renewal in righteousness; convinced and assured of the truth and importance of his Word, and yield a due attention to it, maturely considering and inwardly digesting it.

II. The necessity of this, and the advantages that result from it.

Without feeding thus on Christ, we "have no life in us;" ver. 53; we may have natural and animal life, vital heat, and motion; we may breathe, and speak, and use our bodily senses; we may have rational life, may apprehend, reason, judge, choose, and so forth. But we have not spiritual life; the favor of God, Psa. xxx. 5, union with him, Eph. iv. 18, a spiritual mind, Rom. viii. 6, spiritual warmth, or zeal breathing in prayer and praise, spiritual senses, a discerning and understanding mind, a vigorous choice, just judgment, and lively affections towards God. We have not eternal life, no title to it, no meetness for it, nor earnest of it. 1 John v. 11, 12.

If we do eat Christ's flesh and drink his blood, we have eternal life; ver. 54; a title to it in our justification; a fitness for it in our progressive sanctification; an earnest, or the beginning of it, in communion with God.

This is proved by the following verses. His, "flesh is meat indeed;" or is truly meat, and the most excellent meat; and his "blood is drink indeed." Ver. 55. Hereby we are refreshed, as with meat and drink; strengthened for our spiritual warfare, duty, and suffering, and nourished up to eternal life.—Hereby we have union with Christ, and a continuance thereof; ver.

56, we have the present life of grace; ver. 57; and shall have the future life of glory. Ver. 58.

III. How we may thus eat the flesh and drink the blood of Christ, and the steps to be taken in order to it.

We must prefer this spiritual meat before the bodily "meat which perisheth," ver. 27, and all earthly things.—We must expect it from Christ, as a *free gift*, ver. 27, 31—34, and must have no reliance on our own merit.—We must "come to him" for it, ver. 34—37, by prayer, in faith, being persuaded he will give it, and depending entirely on his power, love, and faithfulness.—We must, therefore, be "taught of God," by his Word, Spirit, and Providence; ver. 45; receiving thereby illumination, conviction, discipline.—We must be "drawn" by the Father. Ver. 43, 44. An attention to the great principles of natural religion, and obedience to its dictates, is a preparation for christianity. "If any man will do his will, he shall know of the doctrine, whether it be of God." John vii. 17.— — The miracles of God, the promises of God, the dispensations of Providence, especially afflictive ones, the influences of the Spirit, are given, and free for all. Thus he draws, "first by the iron chains of legal convictions, and secondly by the silken cords of redeeming love."* Instances of the former method we have in the Jailor, Acts xvi. 30, in David, Psa. xxxii. 4, in the Jews, Acts ii. 37, in Saul, Acts ix. 5, in the Woman of Canaan, Matt. xv. 22—28; and of the latter in the Woman of Samaria, John iv. 7—26, in Zaccheus, Luke xix. 2—10, in the Disciples,—in Lydia. Acts xvi. 14. Without this drawing, no man can or will come to Christ, whether he be moral or immoral, Jew or nominal christian, learned or unlearned, young or old. For, naturally, he neither feels nor sees his need of coming to Jesus; he has neither power nor will to come, being chained down by ignorance, pride, and self-conceit, by sloth, by unbelief, and hardness of heart.—This is a true, but humbling doctrine: and that the Father is "not willing any should perish," but is ready to draw all to Christ, is most encouraging.

APPLICATION.

Have you eaten the flesh and drunk the blood of Jesus Christ? Examine yourselves particularly.— —If you have not, your state is wretched and dangerous; and you have need to come without delay; and, therefore, to be drawn by the Father.—Be willing, be desirous to be drawn, or to hear him say, "Depart, ye cursed;" pray that he would draw you; yield to his attraction, "hear and learn of the Father;" hear the voice of his works, his Providence, his Word, his promises, his threatenings; hear the still small voice of his Spirit, and follow his direction.—Are you mourning for him; hungering for the bread of life, that "you may eat thereof, and not die?" Ver. 50. Then, he is drawing you; be encouraged and thankful.—Have you come to him, and partaken of his flesh and blood? Then, again, be thankful, and continue to feed on him, and use the strength you have received to his glory

* Fletcher.

22

BAPTISM

Acts ii. 38—41.—Repent, and be baptized every one of you in the name of Jesus Christ, for the remission of sins, and ye shall receive the gift of the Holy Ghost: for the promise is unto you, and to your children, and to all that are afar off, even as many as the Lord our God shall call. And with many other words did he testify and exhort, saying, Save yourselves from this untoward generation. Then they that gladly received his word were baptized: and the same day there were added unto them about three thousand souls. (Pr.)

WE here see the apostles in a very interesting situation, making their first general attack on the kingdom of darkness; opening their commission which Jesus gave them at his ascension, and " beginning at Jerusalem."

There were several important circumstances which attended the commencement of the apostolic mission. ——— 1. It was preceded by prayer: ch. i. 12—14. ——— 2. By intimate union among themselves: ii. 1. ——— 3. By an extraordinary outpouring of the Holy Spirit: ii. 2, 3. ——— The people beholding these things, some doubted, and others were filled with reproach; and this gives occasion for Peter's address in the words of our text. ——— The effect is, the murderers of Christ are pricked to the heart, and are exhorted to be baptized.

I. OFFER SOME EXPLANATORY REMARKS UPON THE TEXT.

1. They are exhorted to *repent*, and this previous to their being baptized. ——— Repentance is not a mere *reformation* of conduct, for that would not have been connected with " the remission of sins." ——— Nor does it consist merely in being *alarmed* at the consequences, for they were already in a state of alarm. ——— But it denotes *a change of heart*, sorrow for having sinned, not in that instance only, but in every other, though conviction might begin with that. It was a spiritual and evangelical repentance which the apostle required, such as is connected with faith in Christ and the remission of sins, and such as John preached. Acts xix. 4.

This exhortation does not merely point out what was their immediate duty: it also contains an intimation of mercy. ——— The fallen angels were not so admonished when they had sinned, but were pronounced accursed: and if we also had been left under the curse, there would have been no place for repentance.

2. They are next exhorted to be *baptized*. ——— Baptism is a solemn institution of Christ, by which we profess his name, and acknowledge ourselves to be his. It was therefore exhorting them to become his disciples, and to make an open profession of their love to him, even as they had formerly avowed their enmity against him. ——— They were required to believe in him, to own him as their Lord, and to take his yoke upon them. ——— It was also an act of obedience, to prove their faith in Jesus, and their love to him. Our submission to this ordinance must also be performed in obedience to the same authority.

3. Be baptized *every one of you*, is the divine command. Every one that heard the gospel was exhorted to repent, and every one that repented was commanded to be baptized. ——— We here see that it is not left as a matter of discretion, much less of indifference; but baptism is binding on all those who are the subjects of repentance and of faith. ——— Some indeed admit it to be a duty to those who *see* it to be so: but they think that is all. ——— True indeed it is, that a blind obedience is not required; but that those who profess the gospel should read and understand and obey from the heart the precepts which it inculcates.

4. This obedience is to be performed *in the name of the Lord Jesus.* —————— This denotes not so much the form of administration, as the authority on which it rests, and at the same time points out the medium of salvation. —————— Christ is Lord of the church, and of the souls of men; and what is done in religion is to be to his glory, and from regard to his authority.

5. Baptism is to be attended to, for *the remission of sins.* —————— When Paul was converted, it was said to him, " Arise and be baptized, and wash away thy sins ;" not literally, as if it possessed such a virtue in itself; but in the same sense, as we are said to " eat the flesh and drink the blood of Christ," in the sacred supper. —————— Baptism was a sign of forgiveness, and an emblem of the fountain opened for sin and uncleanness. —————— The real and only ground of forgiveness is the atonement of Christ: and this is intimated in their being baptized in his name, as in chap. x. 43.

6. They shall receive *the gift of the Holy Spirit:* this was extraordinary. —————— They should receive that very blessing of which they doubted and wondered—the spirit of prophecy: ver. 16, 17.

7. The promise is *to you and your children.* This was the encouragement addressed to the primitive converts, and the same is addressed to us—

1. Observe, the *promise* refers not to that which was made to Abraham, which included all his spiritual seed; but to that mentioned by Joel, and which is referred to in ver. 16, 17; compared with Joel ii. 28.

2. The term *children* here does not mean infants, but adults, the " sons and daughters that should see visions, and prophesy ;" that is, the Jewish posterity ; as when we speak of the " children of Israel," we do not mean the infant offspring of Jacob, but all his descendants in the times of Moses.

3. That which rendered the promise so peculiarly seasonable now was, that it stood against *the curse* which they had so awfully imprecated : " his blood be on us and on our children." Being pricked to their hearts, they might now think that the curse was coming upon them.

4. While it encouraged the penitent Jews, it also excluded their national prejudices and vanity; for the promise was to them that were *afar off,* among the Gentiles, as well as to them that are nigh.

5. The whole, whether to Jews or Gentiles, is restricted to *as many as the Lord should call.* This promise therefore cannot apply to any who are not called.

8. With many other words did Peter exhort his hearers *to save themselves* from that generation. —————— Repentance for sin, faith in Christ, and being baptized in his name, is the way in which they were to " save themselves:" not as authors of their own salvation, yet as being active in fleeing for refuge, as Lot did out of Sodom, or as the manslayer from the avenger of blood.

9. It is added, " Then they that gladly received his word *were baptized,*" though probably not all who were pricked in their hearts : for there might be many left, and we still see various characters in whom convictions have not this issue. True faith is receiving the word with gladness; not merely having the truth forced upon the conscience, but the heart open to receive it, and that with cordial approbation and inward joy.

II. DRAW SOME CONCLUSIONS FROM THE SUBJECT.

1. Observe, that God's truth sometimes finds its way to *men's consciences,* and that only : but this is not conversion. —————— It is not enough to be pricked to the heart: we must repent and believe the gospel. —————— Many rest in their convictions, and too many preachers give encouragement to such, as if these were evidences of grace. But not so with Peter, nor Paul and Silas, when they addressed the convicted and trembling jailor. Acts xvi. 31.

2. If we truly repent and believe the gospel, we must prove *the sincerity* of our faith by taking the yoke of Christ upon us, and keeping his commands. ———— It is a sad way of reasoning, that because we believe, we need not therefore obey ; and that because baptism is not essential, we may therefore be saved without it.

3. The argument from the text, in favor of *infant baptism*, is utterly groundless; for " as many" as received the word were baptized, and such only.

4. We learn the satisfaction there is in following the example of *primitive christians*, in keeping the commands of our Saviour. This has the promise of his abiding presence. Matt. xxviii. 20.

THE DESIGN AND IMPORTANCE OF THE LORD'S SUPPER.

1 Cor. xi. 24, 26.—This do in remembrance of me . . . . for as often as ye eat this **bread,** and drink this cup, ye do shew the Lord's death till he come. (S. S.)

The Corinthians had shamefully profaned the Lord's Supper—
St. Paul reproves them, and rectifies their views of that ordinance—
I. The design of the Lord's Supper.
Our ungrateful hearts are prone to forget the richest mercies—
To keep up " the remembrance" of his death, Christ instituted his last supper—
When we celebrate that ordinance, we " shew forth" his death.
The passover was a memorial of the deliverance vouchsafed to the Jews from the sword of the destroying angel—
At every returning celebration of it the reason of that ordinance was declared—*
Christ in his death has effected a greater deliverance for us—
In partaking of the bread and wine we " shew forth" his death—
We shew forth *the manner of it* as excruciating and bloody—†
We shew forth *the end of it* as a sacrifice for our sins—‡
We shew forth *the sufficiency of it* for our full salvation^2—‖
We shew forth his death " till he come"
Christ will, in due season, come again to judge the world—
Then his people will no longer need such memorials as these—
They will incessantly enjoy the brightest vision of his person, and the richest fruits of his death—

* In reference to Exod. xii. 26, 27, a custom obtained among the Jews that a child should ask the meaning of the passover, and that the person who presided should then give an account of its intent and origin, that so the remembrance of God's mercy might be transmitted to their latest posterity : and this was called " the declaration" or " shewing forth." Dr. Gill on the text.

† The breaking of the bread and the pouring out of the wine seem well calculated to impress this idea.

‡ In this light it is represented by St. Paul, 1 Cor. v. 7, and by our Lord himself, Matt. xxvi. 28.

‖ We express our affiance in his blood as the Jews did in the blood of the Paschal Lamb, when they sprinkled their door-posts with it, and eat of the flesh that had been roast with fire.

But till then the remembrance of his dying love, and the expectation of his future advent, must be thus preserved—

Such was Christ's end in instituting, and such should be our end in observing it—

To enforce the observance of this ordinance, we will proceed to shew.

II. The necessity of attending it.

The duty of commemorating our Lord's death is much neglected.

But a neglect of it involves us in the deepest guilt—

It implies,

1. Rebellion against the highest authority

Christ, the supreme governor of heaven and earth, has said, " Do this"—

Yet the language of too many is, " I will not"—

But they who disregarded *the passover* did not go unpunished—*

Much less shall they who slight the invitations to *Christ's supper*—Luke xiv. 24.

Surely it is no less than madness to persist in this rebellion—

2. Ingratitude towards our greatest benefactor

Christ has even "given his own life a ransom for us"—

And shall we disregard his dying command?—

On the same night that he was betrayed, did he institute these memorials of his death—

Had he *at that season* such a concern for us, and can we refuse to do so small a thing in remembrance of him ?—

The Jews went thrice every year up to Jerusalem, from the extreme parts of Judea, to commemorate their deliverance—

And shall we turn our backs on the table when it is spread before us ?—

Shall not God visit for such ingratitude as this ?—†

3. Contempt of the richest mercies

To communicate, without discerning the Lord's body, can profit us nothing—

But to approach the table in humility and faith is a sure mean of obtaining all spiritual blessings—

Christ sometimes reveals himself in the breaking of bread, to those who had not so fully discovered him in the ministration of the word—Luke xxiv. 30, 31.

And do they not manifest a contempt of these mercies, who will not use the means of procuring them?—

How may the Saviour take up that lamentation over them !—Matt. xxiii 37.

4. A renunciation of our baptismal covenant

In baptism we covenanted to renounce the world, &c., and to serve God—

This covenant we ought to renew and confirm at the Lord's table—

But our refusing to confirm it is a tacit renunciation of it—

And can we hope that God will fulfil his part while we violate ours ?—

---

* If a man had contracted any ceremonial defilement, or were on a journey, he might omit eating the passover at the appointed time ; only he must eat it a month afterwards. But if he forbore to eat of it without any such impediment, God said concerning him, " that soul shall be cut off, *that man shall bear his sin.*" Numb. ix. 7—11.

† Let such conduct be expressed in words : " Thou didst indeed give thy body to be broken, &c., for me ; and only requirest me to eat bread, &c., in remembrance of thee ; but I account even that too much to do for thee :" Who could dare to utter such language ? Or who would endure it if spoken by his servant or his child ? Yet such is the language of our actions.

Will he be our God when we refuse to be his people?—
We shall CONCLUDE with answering some excuses.
"*I am not prepared*"—How then can you be prepared to die?—*
"*I am afraid of eating and drinking my own damnation*"—
Are you not afraid of damnation for neglecting your duty?—†
"*I am afraid of sinning afterwards, and thereby increasing my guilt*"—
If sins after receiving the Lord's Supper were unpardonable, none should receive it till the last moment of their lives—‡
"*The time of administering it interferes with other engagements*"—
To those who cannot deny themselves in any thing, we say with Paul—Rom. iii. 8, ad fin.
But where the difficulties are insurmountable, God will accept the will for the deed—Matt. xii. 7.
They however, who are at liberty, should attend "as often" as they can—
Only they must be careful to communicate with reverence, humility, faith, and gratitude.

ON THE PREPARATION REQUISITE BEFORE THE LORD'S SUPPER.

1 Cor. xi. 28.—Let a man examine himself, and so let him eat of that bread and drink of that cup. (S. S.)

GOD is an holy and jealous God, and greatly to be feared—
In all our approaches to him we should be filled with awe—
But a want of reverence prevails among the generality of mankind—
Even real christians manifest it sometimes, and that too even in the most sacred ordinances—
St. Paul, reproving the Corinthians for their conduct at the Lord's Supper, lays down an universal rule for communicants—"Let a man." &c.
I. THE DUTY OF SELF-EXAMINATION IN GENERAL—
This is an important but much neglected duty—
It is strongly recommended in the scriptures—
The apostle expressly enjoins it on all—2 Cor. xiii. 5.
This injunction is remarkably strong and energetic— — —
There is great reason for it—
We cannot ascertain the state of our souls without it
It is evident that the generality of men deceive themselves—
We also are liable to the same deception through pride and self-love—
Nor can we form a right conclusion without a strict investigation—
A mistake respecting our state would be fatal
There is no repentance in the grave—
As we die, so shall we continue for ever—
The benefits to be derived from it are exceeding great.

* Is not this acknowledgment the strongest reason for immediate repentance?

† In neglecting duty you insure condemnation; in practising it as well as you can (to say the least) you *may* avert it.

‡ If you really desire strength, where would you so soon obtain it? But if you determine to live in sin, your condemnation will be equally sure whether you come or not.

If our state be found good, we shall rejoice in the testimony of a good conscience—

If it be bad, we shall be stirred up to flee from the wrath to come—

We should therefore live in the habitual practice of this duty—Ps. lxxvii. **5.**

But self-examination is more especially needful on certain occasions—

II. THE NEED OF IT BEFORE THE LORD'S SUPPER IN PARTICULAR.

This is intimated in the text; "Let a man examine himself, and *so* let him come"—

And indeed there is peculiar reason for it at that time—

That ordinance is a season of remarkable solemnity

There we see Christ crucified, as it were, before our eyes—

There we contemplate the most stupendous mysteries—

There we commemorate the greatest of all mercies—

There we are admitted to most familiar fellowship with God—

And does it become us to engage lightly in such an ordinance ?—

It is a season that calls for the exercise of all our powers

The understanding should be occupied in devoutest meditations—

The affections should be engaged to the uttermost—

And can we thus command our faculties without any preparation ?—

The neglect of self-examination may rob us of all the benefit of the ordinance.

Who can estimate the benefits we might receive if we came prepared ?—

But who has not often communicated in vain ?—

And has not our neglect been the true cause of this ?—

We should therefore be peculiarly attentive to it at such a season

To assist in the discharge of this duty we shall shew,

III. THE SUBJECTS WHICH WE SHOULD THEN MORE ESPECIALLY ENQUIRE INTO.

We should examine ourselves respecting

Our knowledge of the ordinance itself.

To come without a proper discernment is dangerous—Ver. 27.

We should enquire what we know of the nature and ends of the ordinance—

On a distinct view of these our profiting much depends—

The state of our souls before God

At the Lord's table we receive " the children's bread"—

We should enquire therefore whether we be God's children ?—

The immediate frame of our souls

We ought to have all our graces in lively exercise—Cant. iv. **16.**

APPLICATION.

Begin this necessary work without delay— — —

Yet set not about it in a legal manner or for self-righteous ends—

Do not trust in your preparation, or expect acceptance on account of it—

But look to Christ as the only ground of your hope towards God—

Neither stay away from the table because you have not spent so much time in preparation as you could wish—

Whether you have used more or less diligence you must go as the publican—Luke xviii. 13.

Be assured however that your profiting will for the most part be proportioned to your preparation.

THE CELEBRATION OF THE LORD'S SUPPER A CHRISTIAN DUTY.

1 Cor. v. 7, 8.—Purge out therefore the old leaven, that ye may be a new lump, as ye are unleavened.—For even Christ our passover is sacrificed for us: therefore let us keep the feast, not with old leaven, neither with the leaven of malice and wickedness; but with the unleavened bread of sincerity and truth. (Fk.)

The age of the apostles has sometimes been styled the golden age of Christianity. On many accounts it stands entitled to this high character. Then men became Christians, not because Christianity was the religion of the state, or because their predecessors were Christians, but from a conviction of its divine origin, truth, and excellence. Then they placed religion not in mere morality, or in the external observance of the institutions of Christianity, but in the renewing of the Holy Ghost.—Then the preachers of the gospel were alike eminent for piety, zeal, and gifts, workmen needing not to be ashamed. But even that age was not all gold;—there was some dross. False teachers crept in privily, and brought with them damnable doctrines. One of these, during the absence of St. Paul, had found his way into the Corinthian church. He preached another gospel. The demoralizing influence of such preaching was soon visible in the licentiousness of one of the members. The apostle ordered his excommunication, reminding them that vice is contaminating; "a little leaven leaveneth the whole lump."—Here he alludes to the Jewish passover; *then* all leaven was to be removed from their houses; *here* all sin from our hearts. "Purge out therefore," &c.

Our text teaches us three things.

I. THAT CHRIST CRUCIFIED IS THE TRUE PASSOVER, OF WHICH THE JEWISH WAS A TYPE. For an account of the Jewish passover read Exodus chap. xii. Several things here demand attention.

1. *The passover was of divine appointment.* It did not originate with Moses or Aaron, or any of the elders or people of Israel. It was not the offspring of human policy, but of God, ver. 1. So its antitype originated neither with angels nor men, but with God. It was neither in the *power* nor *wisdom* of man to devise and execute a plan, by which the divine attributes could be harmonized, and the sinner saved. But that which man could not do, God *has* done.

2. *The passover was appointed for the deliverance of the Israelites from bondage and death.* They were slaves, oppressed with labor, tormented with cruelty, Exodus i. 11—16. The Lord heard their cry, and stretched out his hand to save: so Christ's death was intended to deliver mankind from the slavery, guilt, love, pollution, and punishment of sin;—to lead from spiritual Egypt to the heavenly Jerusalem.

3. *The passover would benefit none unless the blood were applied*, ver. 7, and 13. So also the death of Christ will profit us nothing, unless through faith we become the personal subjects of its mystical application—*to our consciences*, "in purging them from dead works," Heb. ix. 14,—*to our hearts*, in cleansing them from all sin, 1 John i. 7.

4. *The passover was not only to be slain, and its blood sprinkled, but it was also to be eaten;* see the eighth and following verses. So we must eat the flesh of the Son of God, John vi. 53.—Spiritual life is sustained by Christ—by furnishing the understanding with *instruction*, and *mo tives*—and by pouring grace into the heart to act upon the *will*—to raise th *affections*—to purify the *heart*—and to produce *power* to please God.— Christ is indeed our passover.

II. THAT AS THE FEAST OF THE PASSOVER WAS TO BE CELEBRATED BY THE JEWS, SO THE EUCHARIST OR LORD'S SUPPER IS TO BE CELEBRATED BY CHRISTIANS. The Jews were to celebrate it—all the Jews and proselytes, Exod. xii. 47, 48,—but none else, verse 43,—it was to be celebrated as long as their dispensation should continue, verse 24,—as a memorial of their deliverance from Egypt, verse 27.—So the Lord's Supper is to be celebrated by all Christians—all who receive Christ as their Lord and Master—who make his word the rule of their faith and practice—who propose his glory as the object of their desire—and who, deeply conscious of the deceitfulness and weakness of the human heart, rely continually and implicitly upon Christ for the promised aid of the Holy Spirit to enable them to *will* and to *do* of his good pleasure. Those who are not Christians have no right to it;—Christ appointed it for his disciples only, Luke xxii. 14, &c.,—its being celebrated as a political test to qualify for civil offices is an awful profanation of the ordinance, and ranks among our national sins. But *all* Christians ought to celebrate it.

1. *Because Christ has commanded it*, Luke xxii. 19. Whatever he has commanded must be implicitly obeyed. To refuse obedience in any case because we do not perceive the necessity of the things enjoined, is totally to reject the authority of him who commands, and to make our obedience depend upon our perception of the fitness of the thing commanded.

2. *Because it keeps alive the important doctrine of salvation through the death of Christ.* The death of Christ is not to be viewed as an *ordinary* event—nor as the death of a martyr; but as a *propitiation* for sin, Rom. iii. 25. Our Lord's words perfectly agree with this view, and explicitly teach this doctrine. So long as this rite is performed, so long will the doctrine of Christ's sacrificial death be received in the church.

3. *Because it eminently tends to excite holy affections.*—Godly sorrow, arising from a conviction that our sins, in common with those of others, occasioned the sufferings and death of Christ, *Ardent love to Christ.*—Love begets love; remember its greatness as manifested in his incarnation—preaching—labor—suffering—death—resurrection—intercession—gift of the Holy Ghost—and all the blessings of the Christian dispensation. *Grateful obedience.*—Love is a constraining principle, it delights in doing the *will*—and copying the *example* of him whom we love. As the passover was to be an ordinance to the Jews forever, so the Lord's Supper is to be perpetuated in the Christian church to the end of time, 1 Cor. xi. 26

III. THAT IN ORDER TO ITS ACCEPTABLE CELEBRATION SEVERAL THINGS DEMAND ATTENTION.

1. *We should have correct views of its nature.* A fondness for mystery has led the Romish and Greek churches to interpret literally, what can only be metaphorically understood. Hence the absurd doctrine of *transubstantiation.* Neither the body nor blood of Christ is any more in the Lord's Supper, than the body and blood of the paschal lamb slain in Egypt in the time of Moses, was in the passover celebrated by our Lord and his apostles in Jerusalem.—In both cases the ordinances are merely *commemorative rites.*

2. *We should not ascribe an efficacy to it which it does not possess.* Many substitute it in the place of regeneration.—Hence the vilest debauchee, when he thinks himself dying, sends for a minister to come and give him the sacrament—having received it, he concludes his peace is made with God, and in this horrible delusion expires. Ministers should never administer it

to any person without explaining its nature, and showing that it is *not a Saviour*, but, like prayer, and hearing the gospel, *a means of salvation*.

3. *We should celebrate it with suitable dispositions. Not with malice.* For here we commemorate not malice but love—love to the worthless—love to enemies—love, where wrath and indignation had been merited. *Not with wickedness.*—For here we read God's aversion to wickedness of every kind—his method of removing it,—and our obligation to universal holiness. *But with sincerity and truth*—with purity of intention—and with an agreement between our principles and outward profession.

Conclude by answering a few objections.

I dare not keep the feast, for it is a solemn ordinance.—For the same reason you should neither pray—read the Scriptures—sing God's praises—nor hear his gospel preached; for they are all solemn.

2. *I am not prepared to receive it.* If you have not made up your mind to forsake sin, dare not to approach the table; but if you are resolved to be the servant of Christ, draw near.

3. *I have kept the feast formerly, but since then I have relapsed into sin.* Let this humble you, but let it no more hinder you from coming to the table, than from approaching the throne of grace.

THE APOSTLES' COMMISSION.

Matt. xxxviii. 18—20.—And Jesus came, and spake unto them, saying, All power is given unto me in heaven and in earth, go ye therefore, and teach all nations, baptizing them in the name of the Father, and of the Son, and of the Holy Ghost; teaching them to observe all things whatsoever I have commanded you: and lo, I am with you alway, even unto the end of the world. Amen. (S. S.)

THE apostles spoke and wrote in a most authoritative manner—
They issued commands, promises and threats, in the name of God.
We therefore naturally enquire, by what authority they acted—
The passage before us gives a most satisfactory account—
In these words of our Lord we observe,
I. THE AUTHORITY HE CLAIMED.
Jesus, as God, possessed all power equally with the Father—
But, as Mediator, he received his power from the Father—
He received it, partly, that by means of it he might execute his mediatorial office. John xvii. 2.—
And, partly, as a reward for executing it. Phil. ii. 8—11.—
This power extended over heaven and earth.
Less than this would not have sufficed for the ends for which it was given—
But by this he is enabled to overrule every thing for the accomplishment of his own purpose—
Nor is it at all diminished by the lapse of ages.
It shall indeed cease to act at the last day. 1 Cor. xv. 28.—
There will not then be any occasion for the exercise of it.—
But till all the members of the church be glorified, Jesus will exert this power for their good—
And his authority will be the hope and consolation of them all—

It was upon this that he founded,

II. THE COMMISSION HE GAVE TO HIS APOSTLES.

He had formerly sent them to instruct the Jews—

He now extends their commission to the gentiles—

They were to *teach* all nations.

As they were to baptize men in the name of the sacred THREE, no doubt they were first to make known the persons and offices of the holy Trinity—

They were to declare " the Father," as our offended, but reconciled God and Father—

They were to make known " the Son," as the sinner's advocate and propitiation—

They were to set forth " the Holy Ghost," as the enlightener, comforter, and sanctifier of God's elect—

They were to *baptize* their converts in the name of the sacred Three.

Having proselyted men to the Christian faith, they were to initiate them into covenant with God by baptism—

But though they first taught adults, and then baptized them, they reversed this order with respect to infants—

They took care, however, that in all cases the doctrine they preached should be recorded in the baptismal rite—

And that every christian should either expressly or virtually acknowledge it—

They were also to *instruct* their hearers in *practical religion*.

It is evident they were not to be *merely* moral preachers—

They must of necessity insist much on the offices of the Father, Son, and Holy Ghost—

But they were also to inculcate every moral duty—

And to enforce every obligation whether toward God or man—

This commission was arduous—We proceed to notice,

III. THE PROMISE HE ADDED FOR THEIR ENCOURAGEMENT.

The Apostles might well have been discouraged from attempting to execute so difficult a service.

They were, in themselves, poor, mean, and illiterate—

They had to propagate principles new, strange, detested—

———————— to oppose the lusts and prejudices of mankind—

———————— to bring men from sin to a life of holiness and self-denial—

And this, not only without human aid, but in opposition to all the power and policy of the world—

They could not therefore but feel themselves unfit for such a task—

But our Lord gave them a most encouraging promise.

When Moses declined the service to which he was called, God promised to be with him,   Exod. iv. 15—

Thus Christ engaged to succor his disciples in their work—

He assured them of his presence to direct, assist, and uphold them

And to give effect to their labours—

To this promise he called their particular attention ; " lo"—

Nor will he fail to accomplish it to the end of the world—

Nor was the affirmation added to it without peculiar energy,

"Amen" may be considered as an affirmation or a petition—

In either view it should not be overlooked—

The promise it confirms was the solace of all the Apostles—

And has been the support of all succeeding pastors—

32

Let every one then add "Amen," as importing both his wish and affiance—

INFER

1. How clearly is the doctrine of the Trinity revealed!

The Father, Son, and Holy Ghost, are here distinctly mentioned—

They are all mentioned *in the same manner*, and *for the same end*—

Whatsoever is meant by "the name" of the Father, must be understood also in reference to the Son and Holy Ghost—

And the baptizing of persons in their name must be considered as the most solemn act of worship to them—

Let none then doubt the truth or importance of this doctrine—

Let every one rather be daily worshipping the sacred Three—

And looking to them to perform their respective offices—

2. How highly should we value the ordinances of religion!

Many excuse themselves from attending on public ordinances, by saying, that they are equally profited at home—

But the converting and edifying of souls is the appointed labor of Christ's ministers—

And Christ has promised his special presence with them—

It must therefore be the duty of all to attend on their ministrations—

Let us then reverence his institutes, and seek his blessing—

Thousands yet daily experience the truth of his promise—

The poor, the weak, the desponding, are enriched, strengthened, comforted—

Nor shall any that truly hunger be ever sent away empty.

CHAPTER II.

EXHORTATIONS.

AN INVITATION TO PARTAKE OF GOSPEL BLESSINGS.

Isaiah lv. 1, 2.—Ho, every one that thirsteth, come ye to the waters, and he that hath no money: come ye, buy and, eat; yea, come, buy wine and milk without money, and without price. Wherefore do ye spend money for that which is not bread? and your labor for that which satisfieth not? hearken diligently unto me, and eat ye that which is good, and let your soul delight itself in fatness. (B.)

In the text, we have a most encouraging invitation to us Gentiles. Consider we,

I. To WHOM THE INVITATION IS MADE.

"Ho every one that thirsteth,"—"and he that hath no money."—

Those who *thirst* are invited. Thirst implies want, and, therefore, the needy are invited; all who need happiness. We naturally seek it in present things, in carnal pleasure, or worldly honor and wealth; but these things neither do nor can afford it.

Thirsty persons are sensible, keenly sensible, of their wants. Hence, those are especially invited, who are sensible of their need of these things.—

Those who are thirsty feel a desire for refreshing draughts; a strong, constant and increasing desire. Such, therefore, are particularly welcome.—

The thirsty are uneasy, distressed, and restless till they drink, and can be satisfied with nothing else. So those who are uneasy, unhappy, and restless to obtain pardon, the divine favor, a birth from above, and the sanctifying influences of the Spirit, and will be satisfied with nothing else, that is, the " weary and heavy laden," are still more particularly called.

The thirsty are active, and will take pains to gain refreshment. These are most of all invited.

But suppose they be very guilty, and have lived in the neglect of all their duties to God and man, and the commission of all kinds of sins ?—still, they are welcome. Those, who have *no money*, no good works, no righteousness, if they only thirst, shall be welcome.

II. WHAT IT IMPLIES, OR THE NATURE OF THE INVITATION.

"Come to the waters." This may be interpreted, "Come to the keys, wharfs, and ports, on navigable rivers, where foreign commodities are imported.—"

Buy what you absolutely want. Buy what is of infinite value,—pardon, of your sins, acceptance with God, adoption, regeneration, &c. Buy what will do you infinite good, will remove all your miseries, and make you happy, truly, continually, and lastingly happy ; what will enrich you, elevate your nature in the highest degree, and make you most glorious. Buy an estate, an inheritance, a kingdom, a crown.

Come and buy for nothing, "without money and without price." The blessings offered to you are invaluable; no price can be set upon them .

> " Their value vast ungrasp'd by minds create."

We are indeed, poor, and have nothing, but the blessings are already bought and paid for.—We may have them gratis, as free undeserved gifts.— And yet they shall be as much our own, as if bought and paid for by us.

Buy very cheap. You must part with clay, thick clay, that defiles, burdens, and destroys—the world, and sin. You must part with poison, and buy food ; you must part with rags, and buy costly and splendid clothing; you must part with chains, and buy crowns ; you must part with disorders and death, and buy health and immortality. Again,

Come to the waters and wash. Come, ye filthy ; ye that are defiled with guilt, come to the "fountain opened for sin and uncleanness;" ye that are defiled with the power and pollution, the ulcers and leprosy of sin, come and receive the Spirit of God, the washing of regeneration.

Come to the waters and drink. Ye thirsty ; come, and be refreshed with peace with God ; peace of mind, and the consolations of God's Spirit; in " the times of refreshing from his presence." Come, ye weary, and " I will give you rest."

Come and be healed. These are medicinal waters. The blood of Christ, the Spirit of God, the word of God, the waters of the sanctuary, are intended for the cure of spiritual diseases.

Come and be quickened, and made immortal. These are *waters of life.* Drink of them, and live ; yea, live for ever.

Fear not lest you should drink the waters dry. They shall increase continually, and impart their salutary effects to all who use them. (See Ezek. xlvii. 1—12.

The waters when you shall drink of them, shall become "milk;" sweet, balmy, and nourishing. Such are the truths and promises of the Gospel ; such the grace and love of God in Jesus Christ.

34

The " milk" shall become "wine," cheering, invigorating, strengthening. Gospel truths and promises, God's grace and love shall be productive of hope, joy, and strong consolation.

It is not enough that we come and look at the blessings which are offered , we must partake of them. We must *buy* them; they must be ours. We must *eat* them: applying them, in their several particulars, for our own use and benefit. But how? By faith. We must hear: hearken diligently." Come, not only to the ordinances, but " unto me," by faith in prayer.

III. THE ARGUMENTS WHEREBY THE INVITATION IS ENFORCED.

" Wherefore do ye spend money for that which is not bread, and your labor for that which satisfieth not?"

The rich live by their money , and the poor by labor. Both are gone out of the way of truth and happiness. The things which men pursue, the riches, honors, and pleasures of this world are not *bread*, they are not the proper food of the soul, are not suited to its nature, are not calculated to fill its capacity, and supply its wants ; to refresh it, to restore its wasted strength, to preserve its health, to nourish and make it grow. They do not invigorate, strengthen, or improve it.—

Neither do these things *satisfy* us. They do not even at present; but if they did, we have no hold upon them; they are perfectly uncertain, and will certainly leave us, when we shall be in greatest need of consolation.

Wherefore, then, do ye follow after these things ? Is it reasonable ? Is it wise ? Is it for your honor ? Is it for your interest ? Is it your duty ? Quite the reverse. — — Is it necessary ? Cannot you do otherwise ? Yes ; the grace of God is sufficient for you, and free for you.

But, do you object, we have nothing better to pursue, and must be active. Not so. Come unto me, and your soul shall live ; shall be quickened, in the possession of the favor of God, a union with him, his image, his nature, fellowship with him, holiness inward and outward, happiness present and eternal, according to an everlasting covenant.

Wherefore, " Ho, every one that thirsteth," all of you in general, and every one in particular, " come ye to the waters," &c. — —

GOD IS DESIROUS OF SAVING MEN.

Jer. xiii. 27.—Woe unto thee, O Jerusalem ! Wilt thou not be made clean ? When shall it once be ? (H. H.)

THROUGHOUT all the sacred writings we behold the goodness and severity of God: sometimes the one attracts our notice, and sometimes the other ; and in many places, as in that before us, we are both struck with the union and combination of them both. Jerusalem was the city of the living God, the residence of his peculiar people; yet he denounces woe against them : but at the same time he declares, in very pathetic language, the ardent desires of his soul to exercise mercy towards them.

From these most affecting words we shall take occasion to shew,

I. THE WOES WHICH IMPENITENT SINNERS HAVE REASON TO EXPECT—
This is a painful, but necessary, subject of our inquiries—
The punishment that awaits sinners in most tremendous—

The loss of heaven is one part of it: and who shall declare how great a loss this is?— — —The miseries of hell (which is the other part) are equally beyond the powers of language to describe, or of imagination to conceive— — —

This, however, the impenitent have but too much reason to expect—

" Woe unto thee !" says my text: and this is the voice of reason*— — — of scripture†— — —of experience‡— — —of the compassionate Saviour himself||— — —What stronger evidence can any man wish for? and how blind must he be that is not convinced by it!

But however merited and awful these woes, are, we see from the text,

II. How UNWILLING GOD IS TO INFLICT THEM—

He complains of men's obstinacy in rejecting the overtures of his mercy—

It is their sin only that exposes them to his displeasure: were that once removed, he would " rejoice over them to do them good." And whence is it that they are not cleansed from it? Has not God provided such means for their cleansing, as should certainly be effectual, if only they were applied? Has he not opened a fountain to cleanse them from guilt? Zech. xiii. 1 ; 1 John i. 7,— — —Has he not promised to sprinkle them with water that should purify and renew their very inmost souls? Ezek. xxxvi. 25—27, — — —Yes: but they are averse to that purification: they hate the very means by which it is to be attained, and the regimen whereby it is to be preserved— — —God would gladly effect the work for them, if only they would submit to it; but they will not. Ezek. xxxiii. 11. Hence those complaints so often uttered by the prophets, Ps. lxxxi. 11–13 ; Jer. vii. 23–26, and by Christ himself— — —John v. 40 ; Matt. xxiii. 37.

He expresses also an impatient longing for an opportunity to bless their souls—

Long has he waited to no purpose: yet still " he waiteth to be gracious unto us :" " he stands at the door of our hearts, and knocks." His address to us is, " Turn ye, turn ye from your evil ways ; for why will ye die, O house of Israel ?" Every day appears to him an age: Hos. viii. 5 ; Jer. xv. 6. " I am weary with repenting ;" he is at a loss, as it were, what to do, whether to give us up, or to use any further means. Hos. vi. 4, and xi. 8 ; Jer. iii. 4, 19. The complaint in the text is scarcely less the language of despondency, than of compassion ; " When shall it once be ?" It is as though he said, " My patience is almost exhausted : your return to me is the most earnest desire of my soul : but I fear I shall be forced, in spite of all my efforts to save you, to abandon you at last, and to execute the judgments which you so obstinately provoke."

ADDRESS,

1. Those who imagine that they have no need of cleansing—

What child of man has not need to be cleansed from that taint which we inherit from our first parents? Job xiv. 4, and xv. 14, and xxv. 4. And who has not contracted much moral defilement by means of actual transgression?— — —Let none entertain such proud conceits. The best amongst

* There must be a difference between the righteous and the wicked.

† Against ten thousand passages to this effect, there is not one syllable that has an opposite aspect.

‡ The union of sin and misery is felt by all. Where is there a sinner that is truly happy? See Isaiah lvii. 20, 21.

|| See how often woe is denounced, Matt. xxiii. 13, 14, 15, 16, 23, 25, 27, 29, 33.

us, no less than the worst, need to be washed in the blood of Christ and be renewed by his Spirit; and without this cleansing, must inevitably perish.

2. Those who are unwilling to be cleansed—

Many are unwilling to part with even the grossest lusts. What then must we say to them? Must we speak peace to them, instead of denouncing woes? If we were to do so, God would not confirm our word: so that we should only delude them to their ruin. But indeed they themselves would not be deluded by any such assertions: for, with whatever confidence they utter them themselves, they would not endure to hear them if uttered from the pulpit.

But it is not gross sin only that must be put away: we must be "cleansed also from secret faults:" whatever stops short of this, is ineffectual. The right hand, the right eye, must be sacrificed; and the whole heart be turned unto God— — —

3. Those who desire the cleansing of their souls—

It is of infinite importance that you seek this blessing aright. It is not in floods of tears that you are to be cleansed; though floods of tears are proper and desirable: it is the blood of Christ alone that can cleanse from the guilt of sin; and the Spirit of Christ alone that can cleanse from the power and pollution of sin. To apply these effectually, we must embrace the promises, and rest upon them, trusting in God to accomplish them to our souls. We must not first cleanse ourselves, and then embrace God's promises of mercy; but first lay hold on the promises, and then, by virtue derived from them, proceed to "cleanse ourselves from all filthiness both of flesh and spirit." 2 Cor. vii. 1, with Acts xv. 9.

INVITATION TO COME TO CHRIST.

Rev. xxii. 17.—And the Spirit and the Bride say, Come: and let him that heareth say, Come: and let him that is athirst, come: and whosoever will, let him take of the water of life freely. (H. H.)

RICH beyond expression are the blessings held forth to us in the Word of Life: and as free as light are the invitations given us to partake of them. Not only in the epistles to the Seven Churches, and in the other parts of this prophetic book, but throughout the whole scriptures, is every possible encouragement afforded to the sinners of mankind, to repent of sin, and to "lay hold upon the hope that is set before them" in the gospel. And here, in the close of the inspired volume, are invitations to us reiterated from every quarter, that we may be prevailed upon to accept of mercy, ere the door of mercy be for ever closed.

Let us consider,

I. THE BLESSINGS TO WHICH WE ARE INVITED—

They are here designated by "the water of life." We will notice them,

1. Generally—

The source from whence this water flows, is no other than the Lord Jesus Christ, the Saviour of the world. In the very chapter before us, "the pure river of the water of life" is said to "proceed out of the throne of God and of the Lamb." Ver. 1. As in the wilderness, the water gushing from the rock that had been smitten supplied the necessities of all Israel; so the Lord

37

Jesus Christ, when smitten with the rod of the law, poured forth the waters of salvation for the benefit of the whole world. 1 Cor. x. 4. He is "the fountain of living waters;" Jer. ii. 13; and whosoever cometh to him, may drink and live for ever. In the chapter before our text, the Lord Jesus Christ declared this to the apostle John: "I am Alpha and Omega, the beginning and the end. I will give to him that is athirst of the fountain of the water of life freely." Ch. xxi. 6. In the days of his flesh, he spoke repeatedly to this effect. To the Samaritan woman, of whom he had asked a draught of water, he said, "If thou knewest the gift of God, and who it is that saith unto thee, Give me to drink, thou wouldest have asked of him, and he would have given thee living water." John iv. 10. On another occasion, when the people had, according to custom, drawn water from the pool of Siloam, he stood in the place of public concourse, and cried, "If any man thirst, let him come unto me and drink: and out of his belly shall flow rivers of living water." This latter expression is then explained by the Evangelist, who adds, "This spake He of the Spirit, which they that believe on him should receive." John vii. 37–39. Now here we have, *in a general view*, the import of the expression in my text. The Holy Spirit is that water of life which Christ is empowered to bestow: and wherever that blessed Spirit is imparted, there is within the person's own bosom a principle of life, seeking for vent in all suitable expressions of duty to God; or, as our Lord elsewhere expresses it, "there is within him a well of water springing up unto everlasting life;" John iv. 14; to which the Holy Spirit, in all his tendencies and operations, leads us to aspire.

2. More particularly—

Three blessings in particular I will specify, as granted by our Lord Jesus Christ unto all who come unto him; namely, *pardon*, and *holiness*, and *glory*.

The Lord Jesus will in the first place bestow the *pardon* of our sins. He is said by the prophet to be "the Fountain opened for sin and for uncleanness:" Zech. xiii. 1; and all who come to wash in that fountain are cleansed from all their sins. In it even "sins of a crimson dye" are made "white as snow:" Isa. i. 18; as it is said, "The blood of Jesus Christ cleanseth from all sin." 1 John i. 7.

For the purposes of *sanctification* also shall this gift be bestowed: for, by the prophet Ezekiel, he says, "I will sprinkle clean water upon you, and ye shall be clean: from all your filthiness and from all your idols will I cleanse you. And I will put my Spirit within you, and cause you to walk in my statutes, and to keep my judgments to do them." Ezek. xxxvi. 25–27.

Eternal *glory* also will he confer upon them: for, when they have "washed their robes, and made them white in the blood of the Lamb, he will lead them unto living fountains of waters," Rev. vii. 14, 16, and will cause them to "drink of the rivers of pleasure which are at God's right hand for evermore." Ps. xxxvi. 8, and xvi. 11.

Let us now turn our attention to,

II. THE INVITATION ITSELF—

Here we cannot but notice the very peculiar urgency and freeness of it—

1. The urgency, to overcome reluctance—

"The Spirit says, Come." The Holy Spirit of God has undertaken the office of revealing Christ to men, and of bringing sinners to Christ for the remission of their sins. John xvi. 8, 14. He descended visibly on the day of Pentecost for these ends; and by the ministry of the apostles, as also by his operation on the souls of men, wrought powerfully upon multitudes.

whom he "made willing in the day of his power," and effectually subdued to the obedience of faith. Thus at this time also is he carrying on the work that has been assigned him in the economy of Redemption. In the written word, he speaks to us: by the ministry of his servants, he pleads with us: by the convictions which he fastens on our mind and conscience, he strives with us individually; if by any means he may constrain us to accept the blessings offered to us in the gospel. His voice to us every day and hour is, "Come," come to Christ as the Saviour of your soul.

"The Bride also says, Come." The Bride is the church, "the Lamb's wife," who has experienced in her own person all the blessedness of that salvation which she is so desirous of imparting to all around her. The church of old addressed her Lord, saying, "Draw *me*, and we will run after thee:" Cant. i. 4; that is, "Draw *me*, and I will not come alone: I will surely labor to the utmost of my power to make known to others the wonders of thy love, that they also may be partakers of my felicity, and unite with me in honoring and adoring thee." Thus the church does in every age. She is "the pillar and ground of the truth," 1 Tim. iii. 15, supporting it firmly in the world, and exhibiting, as by public inscriptions that are visible to all, the glory and excellency of the gospel salvation. She then unites with the Spirit of God in saying to all around her, "Come:" Come to Jesus and see what a Saviour he is. See in *me* what he both can and will do for you also; however far off you may now be, you may draw nigh to him with a full assurance of acceptance with him; and though now "aliens from the commonwealth of Israel, and strangers from the covenants of promise, you may become fellow-citizens with the saints and of the household of God." Eph. ii. 19.

"Let him also that heareth, say, Come." Those to whom the foregoing invitations are announced, should unite their efforts to make them known, and to induce every creature under heaven to accept them. Think not, brethren, that you have performed your duty when you have heard these invitations from the lips of your minister; no, nor when you have yourselves complied with his advice. You are all to be preachers in your own circles; all to repeat to your friends and relatives, your families and dependents, the glad tidings which you hear of a free and full salvation; and, with one heart and one voice, should join in saying to all around you, "Come, come, come." This was the conduct of Andrew and of Philip, when they had found the Saviour; John i. 40, 41, 43, 45; and this must be the conduct of us all, in our respective spheres.

2. The freeness, to counteract despondency—

"We are all invited to "take of the water of life freely." If we are "athirst," we are the very persons whose names, if I may so speak, are especially written on the cards of invitation. Indeed, if our names had been expressly recorded in this passage, we should not have had a thousandth part of the assurance of God's willingness to accept us that we now have; for there might be other persons of our name: but no mourning penitent in the universe can err in tracing his name in the designation that is here given.

It may be, however, that some may say, "I am not sufficiently athirst to be able to appropriate to myself this character. I should be glad indeed to obtain mercy of the Lord; but I do not pant after it as the hart after the water-brooks, and therefore I have not in myself the qualification that is here required." To counteract such desponding fears, the Saviour says, "*Whosoever will*, let him take of the water of life freely." If you have not all the *thirst* that you can wish, have you the *inclination?* have you the *desire?*

Then you are the person invited : and you must not dream of staying till you can bring certain qualifications along with you, but come and take these blessings "*freely*, without money and without price." Isa. lv. 1.

To impress this subject the more deeply on your minds, let me ADDRESS a few words,

1. To the reluctant—

Many are the excuses which you urge for your declining the invitation sent you in the gospel : and to you they appear perhaps sufficient to justify your refusal. But your Lord and Saviour will not be deceived : he sees the radical indisposition of your mind to the blessings which he offers you ; and will say of you, as he did in reference to those of old, " They shall never taste of my supper." Luke xiv. 16–24. You may be offering a variety of pleas : but he will put the true construction on them all, " Ye *will* not come unto me that ye may have life." John v. 40. O think, how bitterly you will regret your present conduct, when you shall see unnumbered myriads, who were once as far off from him as you now are, sitting down at the marriage supper of the Lamb, and you yourselves be cast out into outer darkness ! What weeping, and wailing, and gnashing of teeth will you then experience to all eternity ! Matt. viii. 11, 12. How will those words sound in your ears at the last day, " Often would I have gathered thee, as a hen gathereth her chickens under her wings; but ye would not !" Matt. xxiii. 37. Do but reflect on this one moment,—" *I would ; and ye would not.*" Verily, that reflection will constitute the very summit of your misery in hell. I pray you, hold not out any longer against the urgent invitations which are now sent you ; but come unto the Saviour, and accept the rest which he has promised to all that are weary and heavy-laden.

2. To the desponding—

What can the Saviour add to convince you of his willingness to accept and bless you ? Perhaps you will say, " I have tried to come to him, and I cannot: and I have tried so long, that I think it in vain to entertain a hope of final success." Is this the case ? Then hear what the Saviour says to you by the prophet Isaiah : When the poor and needy seek water, and there is none, and their tongue faileth for thirst, I the Lord will hear them, I the God of Israel will not forsake them : I will open rivers in high places, and fountains in the midst of the valleys : I will make the wilderness a pool of water, and the dry land springs of water. Isa. xli. 17, 18. Now I cannot conceive a case more desperate than that which is here depicted : The person is in himself " poor and needy." (There you will easily recognize your own character.) He has " sought for water," even for the waters of salvation. (That represents what you also profess to have done.) He has " found none." (There is your unhappy lot painted with the utmost precision.) " His tongue faileth for thirst;" so that he is ready to sink in utter despair. (What can you add to that, to bring it home more fully to your own case ?) Yet this is *the very person for whom God has reserved his blessings, and to whom he engages to impart them.* " But I am in such a state, that it is almost impossible to deliver me : you might as well expect a river to be running over the highest mountains, as for the waters of salvation to reach me." Is that the case ? says the Saviour : then " *I will open rivers in high places ;* I will make the wilderness a pool of water, and the dry land springs of water." See here, my brethren, what wonderful condescension there is in your Lord and Saviour, that he will so describe your case, that it should not be possible for you to fail in recognizing your own character, or to doubt any longer his ability and willingness to save you. Take then this passage; **and rely upon it;** and plead it with him; and expect the **accom**-plishment of it to your own soul. Then shall "your light rise in obscurity, and your darkness be as the noon-day." Isa. lviii. 10. You shall find that the Saviour is not "a fountain sealed," Cant. iv. 12, but "a fountain open-ed;" Psa. xxxvi. 9; Joel iii. 18; and "out of that well of salvation you shall drink water with joy" for evermore. Isa. xii. 3.

EXHORTATION TO A HOLY WALK.

Isaiah ii. 5.—O house of Jacob, come ye, and let us walk in the light of the Lord. (H. H.)

MANY prophecies there are which are not yet accomplished, especially among those which are to be fulfilled "in the last days," The last days were understood even by the Jews themselves as relating to the days of the Messiah; and they comprehend all the time from his first advent in the flesh, to the period when his kingdom shall be fully established upon earth. Hence the prophecies relating to that period must have different degrees of accomplishment; being partly fulfilled in the first triumphs of the gospel, but having a further and more entire accomplishment when all the kingdoms of the world shall become the kingdom of our Lord and Saviour Jesus Christ. Thus it is that we are to understand the prophecy contained in the preceding context. "The mountain of the Lord's house," that is, the gos-pel church, was established on the top of the mountains in the apostolic age, when it triumphed over heathen idolatry and Jewish superstition; and myri-ads of converts encouraged one another to serve and glorify their God: but we have not yet seen the time when "swords have been beaten into plough-shares, and spears into pruning-hooks, and nations have ceased to learn and practice the art of war." That time however will come; and we should long, and labor to the utmost of our power, to hasten it forward. We should even now anticipate it; yea, we *will* anticipate it: "O house of Jacob, come ye, and let us walk in the light of the Lord!"

Let us walk in the light

I. OF HIS TRUTH—

His truth now shines in its meridian splendor—

"The darkness is indeed past; and the true light now shineth." 1 John ii. 8. "The day-star has arisen," 2 Pet. i. 19; "the day-spring from on high hath visited us," Luke i. 78, 79; "the Sun of righteousness," Mal. iv. 2; shineth forth in his brightness: and the way of salvation through a crucified Redeemer is now so plain, "that no wayfaring man though a fool can err therein." Isa. xxxv. 8. —— —— "On the face of Moses there was a veil, that they who received the law should not see its full import: but if the gospel be hid, it is from those only whom the god of this world hath blinded;" since "we may all with open (that is, *unveiled*) face behold as in a mirror the glory of the Lord." 2 Cor. iii. 13—18. —— ——

Let us then walk in it—

Having the light, we should "believe in the light, that we may be the children of light." John xii. 35. 36. We should embrace with all thank-fulness the way of salvation revealed in the gospel. We should "*come to Christ*" as the appointed Saviour of a ruined world: Matt. xi. 28; we

41

should "*look to him*," as dying upon the cross for us : Isa. xlv. 22 ; we should "*build upon him*, as our only foundation ;" 1 Cor. iii. 11 ; and " *cleave unto him* with full purpose of heart ;" Acts xi. 23 ; and " determine to know non but him ;" 1 Cor. ii. 2 ; and to " glory in nothing but the cross of Christ ;" Gal. vi. 14 ; —— —— "Arise then, and *be enlightened*, for the light is come ; and the glory of the Lord is risen upon you." Isa, lx. 1. *The marginal reading.*

Whilst confiding in God as reconciled to us by the blood of the cross, we should endeavor to walk in the light,

II. OF HIS COUNTENANCE—

This is the privilege of a true believer—

So it is declared to be, by one who experienced it richly in his own soul. Ps. lxxxix. 15. God presents himself to us in the gospel under the endearing relations of a father and a friend, to whom we may carry every want, every trial, every difficulty ; and from whom we may expect a supply according to our need. He will be not only "*our God.*" but " *a God unto us,*" 1 Chron. xvii. 24. Putting forth all his wisdom, all his love, and all his power, to make us truly blessed. He will engage in this work "with his whole heart and with his whole soul ;" Jer. xxxii. 41 ; so that it must be utterly our own fault if we be not as holy, and as happy, as our hearts can wish. ——

Let us then enjoy our privilege—

Let us "walk with God," as Enoch did ; and " glory in him as the God of our salvation." See what holy joy David found in communion with him, Ps. lxiii. 1—5, and cxlv. 1—12, and cl. —— —— and shall we who live under a so much nobler dispensation experience less ? Shall not *we*, who have so much clearer views of Christ, "rejoice in him with joy unspeakable and glorified ?" O let us " *delight ourselves in God*," and have even now, "in the secret of his presence" and the consolations of his Spirit, an earnest and a foretaste of our heavenly inheritance. Ps. xxxi. 20. Eph. i. 13, 14. ——

But we shall in vain hope to enjoy his presence, if we walk not also in the light,

III. OF HIS COMMANDMENTS—

These are given by him " as a light to our feet and a lantern to our paths."—

Without them we should not "know how to walk and to please God ;" but by them we are fully informed in all things that are needful for us to do. Prov. vi. 23. They do not indeed descend to every particular circumstance in which we can be placed ; but they afford principles which are universally applicable, and which are quite sufficient for our direction when duly applied. The duty " of doing to others as we would be done unto," is so comprehensive as to embrace every part of our social duty, whilst it is so simple that it may be comprehended and applied by every one who desires to please God.

Let us then make these the one rule of our conduct—

Let us not attempt to reduce them to the standard of the world, but endeavor rather to raise our conduct to the standard of God's revealed will. Let us treasure up in our minds the most exalted precepts, and " hide God's word in our hearts, that we may not sin against him :" for " then shall we not be ashamed, when we have respect unto all God's commandments ——

In ADDRESSING " the house of Jacob," we must speak to,

1. Those who are nominally so—

It is but too true, that " all are not Israel, who are of Israel :' and those who are only of the house of Jacob by name and profession, may know it by their walk and conversation. Consider, I pray you, in what light you have walked : Is it not manifest, that the generality who call themselves christians are influenced only by the things of time and sense ; and that their principles and pursuits are altogether earthly? Know then, ye lovers of this present evil world, that, if God's word may be depended on, you are deluding yourselves to eternal ruin. Isa. l. 11. You " sow the wind and you shall reap the whirlwind. Hos. viii. 7. When will you begin to see, that " one thing," and one thing only, " is needful?" When will you learn to say, " Whom have I in heaven but thee? and there is none upon earth that I desire in comparison of thee?" That you should seek present as well as eternal happiness, we grant: but you should seek it where David did ; " Who will shew us any good? Lord, lift thou up the light of thy countenance upon us ; and that will put more gladness in my heart than any in crease of corn, wine, and oil can ever do." Ps. iv. 6, 7.

2. Those who are really so—

You have found that God in Christ is " a fountain of life; and in his light you have seen light." Ps. xxxvi. 9. You therefore are " children of the light and of the day." But if you are so highly distinguished in your character, think how distinguished you should also be in your conduct. Eph. v. 8. 1 Thess. v. 5. 6. The eyes of all are upon you : they will look particularly to see whether religion is such a source of happiness, as you profess. O shew them that "you need neither the sun to lighten you by day, nor the moon by night, since the Lord has been a light unto you, and your God your glory." Isa. lx. 19. Shew them that even in the greatest troubles you have a fountain of consolation to go unto : and that " when you walk in darkness, the Lord is a light unto you." Job xxix. 3. Mic. vii. 8. And, as it is eminently characteristic of Gospel times to encourage one another in the ways of God, see that you do so, " speaking one with another in psalms and hymns and spiritual songs, singing and making melody in your hearts unto the Lord." Then, from enjoying God in his courts below, you shall be taken to serve him in his temple above, where your largest desires shall be satisfied, and your utmost capacities be filled Rev. xxi. 22, 23. Ps. xvi. 11.

DAVID'S ADVICE TO SOLOMON.

1 Chron. xxviii. 9. And thou, Solomon my son, know thou the God of thy father, and serve him with a perfect heart, and with a willing mind : for the Lord searcheth all hearts, and understandeth all the imaginations of the thoughts : if thou seek him, he will be found of thee ; but if thou forsake him, he will cast thee off forever. (H. H.)

WHATEVER may have been their own conduct through life, it is the wish of most men in a dying hour, that their children should walk in the ways of probity and honor. But men of piety have higher views : they wish their children not merely to pass through this world with credit, but to obtain happiness beyond the grave.—The advice of David in the words before us, is precisely such as every religious parent would wish to give to his surviving family. Let us observe,

I. The advice here given—

The occasion was most solemn. David had desired to build a temple for the Lord, but was forbidden; and was directed to devolve that office on his son Solomon. All the princes and great men of the nation were convened to assist at the solemnity: and in the presence of them all did David direct his son,

1. Whom to seek—

The terms here used have doubtless a peculiar force. David does not say to his son, "Know thou the God *of Israel;* but "Know thou the God of *thy father;*" by which expression he evidently called the attention of Solomon to the character of Jehovah as exemplified in all his dealings towards *him:* it is as though he had said, "Know thou that *sovereign* God, who chose me above all to rule his people Israel ———— Know that *almighty* God who, in all my dangers from Saul or other enemies, has preserved me to the present hour ———— Know that *merciful* God who forgave me all my great transgressions in the matter of Uriah ———— and that *faithful* God who has fulfilled to me all his great and precious promises, in raising up thee to sit on my throne, and to build a temple to the Lord" ————

"*Know*" this God: study his character as displayed in all his conduct towards me: acquaint thyself with him in the most intimate and endearing manner: and seek him as thy friend, thy portion, thine eternal great reward! But remember that it is in Christ only that this character of God can be fully seen ———— Seek then to know God as reconciled to you in the Son of his love; and let "this God be your God for ever and ever."

2. How to serve him—

Integrity of heart is indispensable in all who would serve their God aright. *Absolute* perfection is not to be expected by fallen man: but that measure of perfection which consists in a total freedom from all guile, not only may, but must, be attained. To be "Israelites indeed," we must be "without guile." There must be no lust, which we desire to retain; no duty, from which we draw back; no sacrifice which we are averse to make: the will of God, even his whole will, without any limitation or exception, must be that to which we aim to be conformed ———— And in our labors to fulfil our duty, we must not be constrained by slavish fear, but by filial love. We must feel the service of our God to be perfect freedom; and find all our delight in it, like the angels, who "do his will, hearkening to the voice of his word" ————— As we are to love our God, so also are we to serve him, "with all our heart, and mind, and soul, and strength."

The importance of this charge is strongly marked in,

II. The considerations with which it is enforced—

Two arguments are here used to impress the more deeply on Solomon's mind the foregoing exhortation. They are briefly these;

1. That God is privy to our inmost thoughts—

If God could judge only by the outward appearance, we might with less danger be inattentive to our hearts: but the heart of man is as visible to him as the sacrifices when flayed and divided asunder were to the priests of old. Heb. iv. 13, τετραχηλισμένα. Not the thoughts only, but "the imaginations of the thoughts," the very first risings of them before they are formed into a distinct apprehension of the mind, are all seen and marked by him, so as to ascertain with precision their nature and quality; and to make them infallible grounds of condemnation or acquittal in the day of judgment. Not actions only, but "the spirits of men are weighed by him," so as to discern how much there is of good or evil in every inclination, affection, appetite, and motion of the soul.

What a reason is this for attending to the frame of our minds in the service of our God! That, and that only which is according to his word, will be accepted by him: whatever there is of formality, or hypocrisy, or of any evil principle, will all be separated as chaff from the wheat, to be consumed in the fire, when the wheat is treasured up in his garner. Alas! how little that is truly good, will be found even in the best of men! Consider this, all ye who would find acceptance with God; and endeavor to approve your-selves to Him, "who searcheth the heart, and trieth the reins."

2. That he will deal with us according as we conduct ourselves towards him—

It is grievous that men should explain away the plainest declarations of God, in order to accommodate them to human systems. There is nothing clearer in all the inspired volume, than that "God will be found of them that seek him, and cast off those who forsake him." We appeal to the experi-ence of all who are in the slightest degree acquainted with vital godliness. "Did God ever say to any man, Seek my face in vain?" ———— On the other hand, Who ever turned back from him, without suffering loss in his soul? Who has not found that the Spirit of God may be grieved and pro-voked to withdraw his gracious communications? Most assuredly he will not always strive with man, but will give us up to our hearts' lusts, if we wilfully harbor those dispositions or affections which are hateful in his sight Moreover, in the eternal world, he will recompense every man exactly ac-cording to his works; adjudging to his diligent servants a reward propor-tioned to their diligence in improving their talents, and to the disobedient ser-vants a punishment proportioned to their guilt.

Who can reflect on this, and not feel the force of the advice given in our text? Our happiness both in time and in eternity depends on our present diligence and fidelity. Let us therefore implore help from God, that we may so devote ourselves to him now, as to be approved by him in the day of judg-ment.

ADDRESS—

1. To parents—

You see in David, what should be your chief desire in behalf of your children. We say not that you should be indifferent about their worldly ad vancement; for that also is important in its place: but your great concern should be to have them truly pious and devoted to God. Labor then, by every possible means, to attain this point. Call them to you. and address them each by name with all tenderness and fidelity; remembering that you yourselves must answer unto God for the influence with which he has invest-ed you for their good; and that, if they perish through your neglect, their blood will be required at your hands.

2. To those who are coming forth into life—

Such advice as that which is given in our text, you are ready to judge pre-mature, or at least to think you have good reason for delaying your attention to it. But are you young, and moving in an elevated sphere, and engaging in concerns of vast importance? So was Solomon: yet were these no reasons for David to withhold the advice, or with Solomon to reject it. Re-member, it is for eternity, and not for time only, that you should live; and, if you disregard the admonitions of your parents, they who now so long for your welfare, will be swift witnesses against you at the day of judgment.

3. To all who are here present—

It is not unbecoming a minister of Christ to regard his flock with parental solicitude, or to address them in the language of our text. Let me then address each of you, as it were, in the presence of the whole collective body, and urge you to seek after God with your whole hearts. Rest not in a formal routine of duties, or in a partial conformity to his revealed will: but see that your "hearts are right with him;" and never rest till you have "the witness of his Spirit," and "the testimony of your own conscience, that in simplicity and godly sincerity you have your conversation in the world." Such a state of mind is most desirable for every one of us; and it is the best preparative, no less for the duties of this life, than for the enjoyments of the life to come.

RELIGION IS NOT A SOURCE OF EVIL TO THOSE WHO EMBRACE IT.

Jer. xxv. 5, 6.—Turn ye now every one from his evil way, and from the evil of your doings, ... and I will do you no hurt.

SIN is the greatest of all evils; because it is the source from which all evils flow. Nor can the miseries which it has introduced be ever remedied, but by a thorough turning unto God. This, Jeremiah tells us, was the remedy prescribed by *all the prophets:* ver. 4, with the text: and certainly it is the only one that can ever prove effectual.

The passage from whence the text is taken, contains, in addition to the words which we have cited, a dehortation or dissuasion from idolatry; together with an intimation, that a continuance in that sin would accelerate their ruin, and insure their exclusion from the promised land: they would persist in it "*to their hurt.*" Ver. **7.** On the contrary, if they would return to God, he would forbear to inflict upon them his threatened judgments, and "*do them no hurt,*"

But we omit that which related to the temporal state of the Jews, in order that we may fix your attention more immediately upon that part of the subject which is applicable to all persons in all ages of the world.

The text consists of,

I. AN EXHORTATION—

As idolatry was at that time the national sin of the Jews, so every one has some evil way to which he is more particularly addicted. We cannot pretend to trace all the shades of difference that are found in different men: we will rather arrange the whole under three great and comprehensive classes: to one or other of which, all, except true christians belong. We therefore say, Turn.

1. From profaneness—

That this is a common sin amongst us, needs no proof; we cannot open our eyes or our ears but we must be speedily convinced of it. —— ——

Let then as many of you as have entertained licentious principles, or indulged in vicious practices, "turn from the evil of your doings," yea turn from it speedily, and with utter abhorrence.

2. From wordliness—

While the young and gay are rushing into vice, and pouring contempt upon every thing that is serious, a great part of mankind are immersed in

wordly cares, and as regardless of religion as their more dissipated bre-thren —— ——

True it is, that these persons have more specious grounds on which to vindicate their conduct, inasmuch as it seems nearly allied to prudence and diligence. Still, however, while we highly approve of those virtues, we cannot but condemn a worldly spirit as evil : since it is declared to be incompatible with the love of God : 1 John ii. 15—17 : and therefore we say to all, " Turn from it," lest you deceive yourselves to your utter ruin.

3. From formality.

There is a very considerable number of persons, whose strictness of prinple, and correctness of manners, screen them effectually against any charge of profaneness ; while their indifference to riches and aggrandizement shews that they are not open, in any great degree, to the imputation of worldliness. But their religion consists in a mere round of duties, in which they have no real enjoyment of God, but only a self-righteous, self-complacent approbation of their own minds —— ——

That this also is evil, we cannot doubt, if only we bear in mind that God requires our *hearts* : Prov. xxiii. 26; and that every service, in which the heart is not engaged, is declared to be vain and worthless in his sight. Matt. xv. 8, 9. Compare 2 Tim. iii. 5.

In exhorting such persons to turn from the evil of their doings, we would by no means be understood to discourage diligence in attending on divine ordinances, whether public or private ; but only to guard against a resting in the performance of duties, and a substituting of that in the place of Christ. In appreciating our religious observances, let us judge of them by their spirituality, and by our enjoyment of God in them : and, if they be ever so devout, still let us remember that they make no atonement for sin, nor do they confer any obligation whatever upon God ; yea, rather, the more devout they are, the more we are indebted to God for that grace whereby we are enabled so to worship him.

To confirm the exhortation, God has been pleased to add,

II. A PROMISE—

At first sight the promise appears to be unworthy of God, and incapable of affording any great encouragement to those to whom it is made. But, if taken altogether abstractedly, it surely is no light matter for those who deserve all the judgments that God can inflict, to be assured, that he will never do them any hurt : and if considered in connexion with our fears and apprehensions, it will be found to contain the richest consolation. *In this view*, we observe, God will do us no hurt in respect of,

1 Our intellect—

When we begin in earnest to be religious, our friends are ready to suppose that we are, or shall soon be, beside ourselves : see Mark iii. 21. Acts xxvi. 24. 2 Cor. v. 13: nor can we altogether wonder at their judgment, when we consider how great the change is, (like a river turning back to its source,) and how unable they are to account for it. But they may spare themselves their fears; for God gives his people, not a spirit of delusion, but " of a *sound mind*." 2 Tim. i. 7. The prodigal's return to his father's house was the first proof of sanity, not of insanity : nor has any person a spark of true wisdom in him, till he begin to fear the Lord. Ps. cxi. 10. In conversion a man is made to form a correct judgment respecting his most important concerns ; and not only to view things in the same light that God views them, but to act agreeably to those views. As well therefore might the man whose eyes Jesus had opened be said to have suffered injury in his organs of vision, as a person thus enlightened in his judgment be said to have suffered in his intellect.*

2. Our friends—

We are taught to expect, that, on our becoming decided followers of Christ, "our greatest foes will be those of our own household:" Matt. x. 35, 36; and experience accords with the declarations of scripture on this head. But are we therefore injured in this respect? Our Lord has told us, and experience accords with that also, that if we lose any friends for his sake, he will repay us in kind, as it were, an hundred-fold. Mark x. 29, 30. A merchant who should part with his goods to such advantage as this, would surely not be thought to have sustained any loss. But besides this recompense in the present world, God himself will be our friend, both now and for ever. And would not *this* amply repay the loss of all earthly friends?

3. Our reputation—

Though the whole of our conduct be visibly improved, yet shall we, on turning to God, be loaded with opprobrium and contempt; and though something may be gained by prudence, or conceded to us on account of our celebrity in learning, there is no religious person that occupies the same place in the estimation of the world that he would do if he were not religious. If our Lord himself was "despised and rejected of men," Isa. liii. 3, and the apostles were deemed " the off-scouring of all things," 1 Cor. iv. 13, it is in vain for us to expect honor from man. Matt. x. 24, 25, with John v. 44. But are we therefore without honor? No: our very disgrace, when so procured, is a very high honor, inasmuch as it assimilates us to Christ, 1 Peter iv. 13, and is a testimony to us of our fidelity. Luke xxi. 13. But suppose that ignominy had nothing to counterbalance it here, should we have any reason to regret it when Christ "confessed us before his Father, and his holy angels;" and when they who despised us, shall "awake to shame and everlasting contempt?" Dan. xii. 2.

4. Our interests—

The laws of the land certainly afford us very great protection. Nevertheless it is no uncommon thing at this day for children and servants to be called to make very great sacrifices for the gospel sake. But be it so: they are forced, like St. Paul, to serve the Lord "in cold and nakedness," and in a privation of all earthly comforts. But are they eventually "hurt?" What if their spiritual consolations be proportioned to their temporal afflictions: have they not made a good exchange? Is not peace in the bosom incomparably better than money in the purse? The riches of this world are easily appreciated: but those which Christ imparts, are "unsearchable." Their despisers would, at a future day, give all the world for a drop of water only to cool their tongue. How rich then must they be who are drinking living waters eternally at the fountain head!

5. Our happiness—

Doubtless the godly have grounds of mourning peculiar to themselves: but are they therefore losers in respect of happiness? No: their sorrows, if I may so speak, are sources of joy: they would on no account be without them: they rather regret that they cannot sorrow more: they mourn because they cannot mourn, and weep because they cannot weep: and if at any time they have been enabled to abase themselves before God in dust and ashes,

---

* That people who are insane, may fix their thoughts upon religion, or that a person may become distracted by *misapprehensions* of religion, is confessed: but if religion would drive a man mad, the more religious he was, the more likely to be mad. Who does not shudder at the consequences that would result from that opinion?

tney look back upon such seasons as the most precious in their whole lives. But if they have sorrows unknown to others, have they not "joys also, with which the stranger intermeddleth not?" Let a promise be applied with power to their souls, or " the love of God be shed abroad in their hearts," have they not a very foretaste of heaven upon earth? Compare their state with that of others, on a dying bed: follow them in the instant of their departure from the body: see them welcomed to the bosom of their Lord: contemplate their eternal state, in contrast with that of their despisers; and then say whether they have any reason to complain, that their fidelity to God occasioned on the whole a diminution of their happiness?

ADDRESS,

1. Those who are yet following their evil ways—

We inquire not, What are the ways you follow: if you do not turn from *every* evil way to God, and devote yourself unreservedly to your Lord and Saviour, the issue will be the same, whatever course you take. Your guilt may be more or less aggravated, and your misery be apportioned accordingly: but, without entering into the different degrees of punishment, let me ask, Will not *sin* " do you *hurt?*"— — —And would not God do you *good*, if you would return unto him?— — —"Turn then from all your transgressions; so iniquity shall not be your ruin." Ezek. xviii. 30.

2. Those who are turning from their evil ways—

Halt not between two opinions: strive not to reconcile the inconsistent services of God and Mammon. Matt. vi. 24. "If Baal be God, follow him: but if the Lord be God, then follow him." There is a certain kind of turning unto God, by which you will suffer hurt on every side, and receive no benefit whatever. If your " heart be not whole with God," no good can accrue to you, nor can any evil be averted from you. The world will not approve of you, because you are too precise for them: and God will not approve of you, because you are not upright before him. Be not then temporizing and hypocritical, but open, decided, and consistent characters. "Follow your Lord fully:" "follow him without the camp, bearing his reproach." Heb. xiii. 13. Thus, though " your life may be accounted madness, and your end to be without honor, yet shall you be numbered among the children of God, and have your lot among his saints." Wisd. v. 4, 5.

THE SOURCE AND REMEDY OF DESPONDING FEARS.

Job xxxv. 14.—Although thou sayest thou shalt not see him, yet judgment is before him. therefore trust thou in him. (H. H.)

IN controversy there is need of the utmost candor; nor without it can we ever hope for a favorable issue. The friends of Job were grievously defective in it; and therefore utterly failed, either to convince him, or to be convinced themselves. But Elihu, who was an attentive auditor of the dispute, and who, on account of his youth, judged it indecorous to offer his sentiments till he saw that his elders were silenced, took up the matter with incomparably better temper and judgment, and, instead of bringing railing and unfounded accusations as the others had done, called Job's attention to many expressions he had used, and endeavored to convince him out of his own mouth. This was wise, and well adapted to the end proposed: and it is observable, that when God reproved the manner in which the other three had conducted the controversy, he said nothing to the disparagement of Elihu, nor required any sacrifice on his account.

It is certain that Job, though far from being a hypocrite, as his friends had represented him, had not always spoken quite advisedly with his lips. His self-justification had been occasionally too strong, and his complaints of God's conduct towards him somewhat irreverent: he had yielded also too much to despondency. He had complained that he could not understand God's dealings with him, and that he had no hope or prospect of deliverance from his troubles. Ch. xxiii. 8, 9. This is noticed by Elihu in the words before us; and the proper remedy for such desponding fears is pointed out to him: "although thou sayest thou shalt not see God, yet judgment is before him; therefore trust thou in him;" that is, place in God that confidence he deserves; and all will yet be well.

From the words thus explained we shall be led to consider,

I. The source of desponding fears—

There is far more of despondency in men than is generally supposed: perhaps it is, as much as any other thing whatever, a ground of their continuing impenitent in their sins.

The *ostensible* ground of men's fears is usually a sense of the extreme difficulty of their case—

Thus it was with Israel at the Red Sea, at the waters of Marah, at the borders of Canaan also, when the spies represented the cities as impregnable, and the inhabitants as irresistible. Thus it was even with the pious Hezekiah, when his sickness appeared to be unto death: Isa. xxxviii. 10-13, and thus it is with multitudes amongst ourselves, who imagine that their circumstances are so calamitous, as to be beyond the reach of any remedy. More particularly is this the case with persons under spiritual trouble; they are apt to imagine, that their sins are unpardonable, and that their corruptions are too inveterate ever to be subdued— — —

The *real* ground is a low apprehension of the perfections of their God—

This is the interpretation which God himself puts on the unbelieving fears of his people. When Sarah laughed at the promise made to her, the answer was, "Is there any thing too hard for the Lord?" and the complaint of God against the unbelieving Israelites was, that "they limited the Holy One of Israel." In fact, a just view of God's perfections would silence all fears: for if his wisdom, his power, his love, his faithfulness be really infinite, we have nothing to do, but to repose our confidence in him, and we are safe— — —

But it is a small thing to know the source of desponding fears, unless we apply,

II. The remedy—

This is prescribed in the words of our text:

1. Contemplate God—

What we are to understand by that expression, "Judgment is before him," may be ascertained by consulting a similar passage in the prophet Isaiah. Isa. xxx. 18. He will do nothing but what is right and good; nor will he omit any thing which it becomes him to do.

Consider what he has done in a way of power and grace— — —and is he not the same God as ever?

Consider what he has engaged to do: is there any thing that we can need, which is not made over to us by an express promise? Has he not said, that 'his grace shall be sufficient for us;" that "we shall have no temptation without a way to escape;" that "as our day is, so shall our strength be;" that "he will give grace and glory, and withhold no good thing" from his believing people? "Hath he then said these things, and will he not do them? hath he spoken, and will he not make them good?"

Consider, above all, the gift of his only dear Son! What else will he, or can he, withhold from us? Rom. viii. 32. Surely he will be "a strength to the poor, a strength to the needy in his distress, a refuge from the storm, a shadow from the heat, when the blast of the terrible ones is as a storm against the wall." Isa. xxv. 4.

Did we but duly consider his glorious perfections as already exercised for his people, and as specially pledged to be exercised for us, we should never entertain a doubt of his constant and effectual care. "His name would be to us as a strong tower, to which we should run, and be safe."

2. Trust in him—

"They that know his name will trust in him:" and to trust in him is the certain way to dissipate all fear. See how a confidence in God operated in the case of David: Psa. xlvi. 1—3, and Psa. xi. 1—4; and the same effect will it produce in us: "if we commit our ways to him, our very thoughts," (which are by nature fluctuating as the wind,) "shall be established." This then is what we must do: we must "cast all our care on Him who careth for us." It is the very direction which God himself gives to "those who walk in darkness and have no light:" Isa. l. 10; and if we follow this direction, "God will keep us in perfect peace;" Isa. xxvi. 3; and we shall be as Mount Zion, which cannot be removed, but standeth fast for ever." Psa. cxxv. 1.

ADDRESS,

1. To those who overlook difficulties—

This is the habit of men in general: and hence it is that they are so much at their ease. But it is no easy matter to turn to God aright. To repent and to believe in Christ are works far beyond the ability of man; nor can any man do either the one or the other, but by the influence of the Holy Ghost. Acts v. 31; Phil. i. 29. O let this be duly weighed! Let us remember, that "we cannot even say that Jesus is the Lord," (we cannot feelingly and believingly say it,) "but by the Holy Ghost:" 1 Cor. xii. 3; and let us not delay one hour to seek his effectual aid.

2. To those who unduly magnify them—

We certainly magnify our difficulties too much, when we deem them insuperable: for "the things that are impossible with man are possible with God." See the state of Jonah in the whale's belly: could any be conceived more hopeless? Yet from thence did he cry, and his prayer entered into the ears of the Lord of Hosts. Jonah ii. 1—7. Thus let us "never stagger at the promises of God through unbelief, but be strong in faith, giving glory to God." Rom. iv. 20. The greater our difficulties, let our application to him be the most earnest, and our expectations of his gracious interposition be the more enlarged: "Be of good courage, and he shall strengthen your heart all ye that hope in the Lord." Ps. xxxi. 24.

SEEKING THE LORD EXPLAINED AND ENFORCED.

Isa. lv. 6, 7. Seek ye the Lord while he may be found, call ye upon him while he is near: Let the wicked forsake his way, and the unrighteous man his thoughts: and let him return unto the Lord, and he will have mercy upon him; and to our God, for he will abundantly pardon. (B.)

In the verses now before us, the Prophet earnestly exhorts the wicked of all nations to seek the knowledge and favor of God by repentance and prayer, adding the most gracious assurance of his readiness to show " mercy and abundantly pardon.''

But to enter into the meaning and force of the exhortation, let us consider,

I. What is implied in seeking the Lord.

It is to seek the knowledge of the Lord, lost by the fall.—We do not mean the knowledge of his being, that he is; or, of his nature, what he is, a *Spirit*. This, however, the heathen did not know, or they would not have " changed the glory of the incorruptible God into an image made like to corruptible man, and to birds, and four-footed beasts, and creeping things.'' Rom. i. 23. Nor could hypocrites, if they were sensible of his spiritual nature, hope to please him by ceremonies, or any mere external services.— Nor do we mean the knowledge of his attributes, such as his eternity, omnipotence, omniscience, his infinite wisdom, equity and goodness; nor of the relations in which he stands to his creatures in general, or to mankind in particular, as our Creator, Governor and Benefactor. The works of creation, and the dispensations of Providence, manifest God in these respects. Rom. i. 20.—But we mean that knowledge of him which is by supernatural revelation, and communicated through his word, especially " the Word made flesh,'' and his Spirit. John i. 18; Eph. i. 17; 2 Cor. iv. 6; 1 John v. 20; Matt. xi. 27.

This is that acquaintance with him,—in his glory and majesty, producing the fear of him, which we have not by nature; Rom. iii. 18; a fear of reverence, a fear of awfulness, a filial fear of offending him.—In his holiness and justice, which produces humility. Job. xlii. 6; xl. 4.—In his mercy and grace, Jer. xxxi. 34, which produces confidence. Ps. ix. 10.—In his love and goodness, which produces returns of love, not only esteem, and desire, but grateful, complacential love, attended with zeal for his glory, and obedience to his will.

It is to seek his favor, lost also by the fall, for "by nature we are the children of wrath ;" Eph. ii. 3; and to be " accepted," or taken into favor. Eph. i. 6.

It is to seek his image, in which man was created, Gen. i. 27, but which he has lost, being earthly, sensual, devilish. James iii. 15. We are to " put off concerning the former conversation, the old man," &c. Eph. iv. 22—24.

It is to seek communion with him. This we have not by nature, "being alienated from the life of God, through the ignorance that is in us :" Eph. iv. 18; Col. i. 21; but we may attain it. 2 Cor. vi. 16; John xiv. 23; Eph. ii. 21, 22; 1 John i. 3.

It is to seek the everlasting vision and enjoyment of him. Matt. v. 8; 1 John iii. 2; Rev. xxi. 3—7; xxii. 3 4.

II. How, or in what way, the Lord must be sought.

As a preparation for seeking him, we must be sensible of our entire, or great want of him in all these respects; of the knowledge of him; of his favor; of his image; of communion with him, and the enjoyment of him.

We must be sensible of the excellency of these blessings; of their attainableness; of the absolute necessity of attaining them, in order to our salvation present and eternal.

We must feel desires; earnest, increasing, restless desires after him. Thus David, Ps. xlii. 1; lxiii. 1; Isa. xxvi. 8, 9.

Conscious these blessings before mentioned are God's gifts, we must seek them in prayer: Matt. vii. 7; and not only in *mental* prayer, though this be important, but in *vocal*. We must "call upon him."—In private. Matt. vi. 6. We mean not the *saying* our prayers, but really presenting our requests to God, for blessings which we know we want, and must obtain, or perish. We must pray sincerely, earnestly, importunately, perseveringly, and in faith, nothing doubting.—In our families, also, we must join in prayer to God.—In social meetings.—And in the public congregation; and, therefore, we should take care to be present in time.

But in the use of these means we must be consistent. The "wicked" must "forsake his way;" his ungodly, unrighteous, intemperate way. Tit. ii. 11, 12. "The unrighteous man," *the man of iniquity:* of injustice, fraud, violence, oppression; "his thoughts," his deceitful imaginations, that these things are reconcileable with religion, or that he can finally prosper in such a way, or escape the Divine vengeance.—*The man of vanity;* who pursues things unattainable, unsatisfactory, uncertain, transitory; "his thoughts," his delusive schemes, and contrivances to obtain happiness in this way. Or, let him who vainly thinks to enlighten his own mind, expiate his own sins, change his own nature, or do the will of God of himself, in other words, who vainly "goes about to establish his own righteousness, not submitting himself to the righteousness of God," desist from such thoughts.— And let him turn to the Lord, and expect these things only from him, and seek his happiness only in him. We must turn to him in judgment,—in choice,—in intention,—resolution,—affection,—in faith, believing his truths, declarations, promises in Christ, and coming to God only through him.

III. When we must seek the Lord.

"While he may be found."

—In life, with which, when it closes, will terminate all opportunities of seeking the Lord.—In health, not "in the floods of great waters." Ps. xxxii. 6.—In youth, the period of life more favorable than any other for obtaining true religion, and wherein a special promise is given, for the encouragement of those that begin early to seek the Lord. Eccles. ix. 10.—At least, while our day of grace lasts, and "he is near," by his Word, and the ordinances he has instituted among his people, and by his Spirit, convincing, alarming, drawing, assisting us in our endeavors.

We should remember, we cannot tell how long our day of grace may continue. With many it has ended on this side the grave. It was so with the Israelites in the wilderness, Ps. xcv. 8, 9, 11, and those who rejected our Lord's ministry, to whom he said, "Ye shall die in your sins." John viii. 21. Thus we may be given over to hardness and impenitence of heart, if we neglect to improve our present means, and the grace given to us. Prov. i. 28, 29.

We shall notice,

IV. The gracious promise made to such as seek him in that way, and at that time.

"He will have mercy upon him." Hebrew, "He will have the bowels of a mother to a child." Although past sins may have been many, great, aggravated, long continued; although present corruption, temptation, and ha-

53

bits of sin be very strong; although hinderances and oppositions be many; and apparently insurmountable; he will "pardon" us freely and fully.—He will subdue our iniquities, and "renew" us in the spirit of our minds."—He will "strengthen us with might in our inner man," and, "strong in the grace that is in Christ Jesus," we shall more than overcome all that oppose. 2 Tim. ii. 1; Rom. viii. 37.

"He will *abundantly* pardon." Hebrew, "will multiply to pardon." When such as have been guilty of very great wickedness, come to have a serious sense of their sins, and of the holiness and justice of God, they are almost inconsolable, and are wont to think their guilt too aggravated to be forgiven; hence the Prophet makes use of strong terms, and to encourage them, and lead them to repentance, he assures them God will multiply pardons as their sins have been multiplied. Rom. v. 20.—He will also again forgive, if we fall off and return to him in repentance. "He will heal our backslidings."

To reason earnestly with a person on some impropriety of his conduct.

THE TENDER EXPOSTULATION OF HEAVEN.

Ezek. xviii. 31.—Why will ye die? (H.)

How can we, without a melting heart, see and hear those compassionate words of the good God, saying to us, "Why will ye die, O house of Israel?" The house of Israel was the church of God, the company of those who had the book of God, the covenant and ordinances of God among them, and yet God asks them, "Why will ye die," and be lost for ever? Supposing him asking us the same question, you professed christians, you that now belong to the Israel of God, "Why will ye die?" Why will ye sin on, and refuse mercy and peace, and run yourselves wilfully unto eternal death and damnation?

Consider, and meditate the extent and importance of this question. How many more are contained in the bowels of it, or may be drawn suitable thereto? Many serious and weighty questions we may ask ourselves upon every word of the question in the text. As,

I. "Why will ye die?"

1. Why will you continue spiritually dead—Dead in your guilt, ignorance, unbelief, hardness of heart; dead to God, to religion, the ways of God, to heaven? Is there no such thing as communion with God? A having the conversation in heaven? A better country? Why continue dead to all this?

2. Why will you refuse the Author of life? Why put him to complain? John v. 40.

3. Why do ye reject and refuse the way of life, the good way that will bring you to eternal life? John xiv. 6, and the path he hath made known?

4. Why will you imbitter your own death? What a terrible death will you die, if you die in your sins?

5. Why will you venture on eternal death? Rom. vi. 23.

II. "Why will you die?"

1. You, who are such noble, rational creatures; you who are the first-born of the creation, Job xxxv. 11; you who have immortality written on your minds and consciences.

54

2. You, who are put in the Redeemer's hand.

3. You, who have a Bible, the book of God, put into your hand.

4. You, who have life so freely and frankly offered. Isa. lv. 1, 2.

5. You, who have a Saviour standing and knocking at your doors. Rev. iii. 20.

6. You, who have the Spirit striving with you. 1 Thess. v. 19.

7. You, who have the ministers of God's word.

8. You, who have the Lord urging the case with you. "Why will you die?"

9. You, who live within the compass of the christian church. Heb. xi. 40.

III. "WHY WILL YOU DIE?"

1. Are you resolved that the blessed God shall have no more glory in your salvation? Luke xv. 32.

2. Are you resolved that the Redeemer shall have no honor or satisfaction in you, or praise for you? Rev. i. 5, 6; Isa. liii. 11.

3. That the holy angels shall have no joy or comfort in you? Luke xv. 10.

4. Do you design that the devil and damned spirits shall have your company for ever?

5. Is it not enough in your eyes, that angels have sinned and died, but you must die also? 2 Peter ii. 4.

6. Is it not enough that your first parents died, but you must die too?

7. Is it not enough that the old world died, but you must die too? Gen. vi. 11—13. That Sodom and Gomorrah died, &c., but you must die also? Gen. xix. 24; 2 Peter ii. 5, 6.

8. Is it not enough that the old house of Israel generally died, but you must also die? The prophets complained. Isa. liii. 1.

9. Are the numbers to be saved so great, that you will not be one of that number?

10. Is heaven and life so dreadful a state, that you are resolved you will not come thither? Is death and hell so happy a state, that none but that will serve you?

11. Is the misery of the heathen world so small, that you are resolved your's shall be greater? Matt. xi. 20—24.

12. Are you such enemies to yourselves, that you are resolved to die, whatever is the consequence? Is it not enough to die once, but you will die twice? Rev. xxi. 8.

13. Have you a mind to try by experience what this death is? and to defeat the Redeemer's design in going to prepare places above for such as you? John xiv. 3.

And, lastly, Are you resolved to glorify no other attribute of God but his wrath and vengeance? Is this life hastening to an end? Is death approaching apace? Is the Judge at the door? Must you, in a few days, be either in heaven or hell? among the blessed or the damned? And yet, will ye not think of these things? "Why will ye die?"

THE SALVATION OF SINNERS DESIRED BY GOD.

Ezekiel xxxiii. 11.—" As I live, saith the Lord God, I have no pleasure in the death of the wicked," &c. (Sk.)

It is evident from the uniform conduct of Ezekiel, that he well understood, and faithfully discharged his duty, as a watchman unto the house of Israel. To this office God had appointed him, verses 7—9; and, in the execution of it, he plainly set before his people both their sin and their danger. But the house of Israel, being hardened in transgression, hated reproof, and endeavored to evade the force of it, by casting the blame of their sin and misery upon God himself. This they did in effect, by the plea of necessity, verse 10. " If our transgressions and our sins be upon us, and we pine away in them, how then shall we live ?" As if they had said, "Our case is hopeless, for it appears that God has decreed our destruction; and if we sin and suffer by the decree of God, how then can we be blamed ? can we alter his purpose, and live when God has doomed us to die ?" This impious reflection on God he strongly resents, and fully proves the injustice of it, in the language now before us: " As I live saith the Lord God, I have no pleasure in the death of the wicked; but that the wicked turn from his way and live: turn ye, turn ye from your evil ways; for why will ye die, oh house of Israel ?" These words lead us to observe,

I. The state of mankind as sinners. Here we learn that it is,

1. *A state of moral evil.* They walk in evilways. By the term *"way"* is meant a course of moral conduct, including the habitual actions, words, and thoughts, of mankind, Isa. liii. 6. The plural term *" ways"* is here employed, to intimate that the courses pursued by sinners are *various* in their kinds. They are ways of *rebellion*, or opposition to God's authority : they are open and avowed, such as St. Paul describes, 1 Cor. vi. 9, 10; Gal. v. 19—21; or they are secret and concealed, such as our Lord describes, Mark vii. 21— 23. There are ways of *impenitence*, or contempt of God's mercy : in which God is forgotten, Jer. ii. 32; and not sought, Psa. x. 4, cvii. 10, 11. There are ways of *self-deception*, or vain delusive hope, Prov. xiv. 12; such is the way of self-righteousness, Jer. xvii. 5, 6; Isa. i. 11: and such also is the way of Antinomianism, Prov. xxx. 12; Matt. vii. 21; Heb. xii. 14. But all their ways are *evil* however diversified. They are evil—because they are *iniquitous :* contrary to the rule of rectitude, 1 John iii. 4.—Because they are *painful :* occasioning present misery, Prov. xv. 19; Jer. ii. 19.—Because they are *destructive :* leading to certain ruin, Ezek. xviii. 30; Rom. vi. 21. Hence our text assures us that the state of mankind as sinners, is

2. *A state of imminent danger :*—a state in which they are certainly exposed to *death*, even to eternal death, Rom. vi. 23. By eternal death is meant the punishment inflicted on sinners in a future state, Rev. xxi. 8. This punishment is called death—*not because it implies annihilation ;* for the wicked still live, when they leave this world. Their continued existence is evident from their state *before* judgment, Luke xvi. 23, 24 ; from their sentence *at* judgment, Matt. xxv. 41—46; and their torment *after* judgment, Rev. xiv. 10, 11.—But this punishment is called death, because *in it there is some resemblance to natural death.* To omit other circumstances, the subjects of natural death are separated from the society of the living, and become the prey either of worms or of fire. Are the subjects of natural death removed from the society of the living? so the subjects of eternal death are *banished* from the presence of God, and of those who live to him, 2 Thess. i. 7—9; Matt. xiii.

40—42. Are the subjects of natural death the common prey either of **worms** or of fire? This they are, according to the different customs of different countries; some being committed to the silent grave, and some being consumed on the funeral pile. Thus also the subjects of eternal death are represented as being preyed on both by the *worm* and the *fire*, Mark ix. 43, 44. Their worm is an *accusing conscience*, which condemns them as being the authors of their own misery, Jer. iv. 18. The worms of the grave indeed, though dreaded, are not *felt*, and soon *die;* but this worm *never dies*, and the torture it inflicts must be endless. The fire that consumes the bodies on the funeral pile is only a *material fire*, kindled by feeble *mortals*, and must soon become *extinct;* but the fire of hell, if not material, must be something much more dreadful: it is kindled by the wrath of *God*, Isa. xxx. 33: and will *never* be quenched, Matt. iii. 12. However, the state of sinners in this world, though alarming, is not yet hopeless. Let us therefore observe,

II. THEIR DUTY AND PRIVILEGE AS SINCERE PENITENTS.

1. *Their duty.* This is, to turn from their evil ways;—" Turn ye," &c Turn from your ways of *rebellion*, by entire *reformation*, Isa. lv. 7; Ezek. xviii. 27.—Turn from your ways of *impenitence*, by earnest *prayer*, Hos. xiv. 1, 2; Luke xviii. 13. Turn from your ways of *self-deception*, by coming to God, trusting in Christ's mediation. John xiv. 6; and by seeking a new creation, Gal. vi. 16; Psa. li. 10.—Turn *seasonably.*: without delay, Isa. lv. 6; Job xxii. 21.—Turn *perpetually*: without defection, Jer. 1. 5.—Turn *believingly*: in confident expectation of salvation, Heb. x. 19—22. That as gospel penitents your confidence may be strengthened, observe,

2. *Their privilege.* This is, to be *saved from death*, and *enjoy life.*—To *be saved from death*, Ezek. xviii. 28. All genuine believers in our Lord Jesus Christ are saved from death by being delivered from the dominion of spiritual, and the sentence of eternal death, John xi. 25, 26. By means of this salvation from death, they are brought also—*To enjoy life.* The life enjoyed by them is comprehensive; including an interest in God's manifested favor, Psa. xxx. 5, lxiii. 3;—actual devotedness to God's service, Rom. vi. 13:—and the eternal possession of heaven, Rom. ii. 6, 7. Observe,

3. *The attainment of this privilege is as certain as it is desirable.* It is certain, from God's earnest *command;* " Turn ye, turn ye from your evil ways." This interests you in God's sincerity, Isa. xlv. 19.—It is certain, from God's solemn *oath;* " As I live, saith the Lord," &c. This interests you in God's *veracity*, Heb. vi. 18.—It is certain from God's gracious *expostulation;* " Why will ye die, O house of Israel?" This interests you in God's most affectionate regard. Almost every word in this kind expostulation emphatically expresses the great concern of God for the salvation of mankind. These words, therefore, " Why will ye die?" most forcibly suggest the most direct and distinct APPLICATION of our text.

1. *Why will ye* DIE? By continuing in sin, you choose death, the worst of all evils; and eternal death, which is the worst of all deaths. Carelessly to squander away your earthly goods and possessions is bad; to impair and destroy your health is worse; to waste and murder your time is worse still: for ' Time destroyed, is suicide: where more than blood is spilt.'—But to plunge your immortal souls into death eternal, is the very worst of crimes; for this is murder, self-murder, and even self-murder of the blackest description: it is an exploit of *wickedness* which can never be forgiven, and for which no atonement has ever been made.

2. *Why will ye die?* By what arguments can you justify your conduct at the bar of your own conscience? Is not God a better master than the de-

vil? Is not holiness better employment than sin! Are not the treasures of grace and heaven better enjoyments than hell and damnation? Is not the pursuit of life more rational and more conducive to happiness than the pursuit of death?—If it be, then in choosing death instead of life, your *folly* is as great as your wickedness. Every sinner therefore may justly exclaim with Saul;—"I have played the fool, and have erred exceedingly," 1 Sam. xxvi. 21.

3. *Why will* YE *die?*—Ye men! concerning whom there is still hope of salvation. You are not devils, for whom a Redeemer was never provided; you are not lost souls in hell, who are out of the reach of divine mercy; Christ still seeks you, that he may save you, Rev. iii. 20.—Ye Americans! the peculiar favorites of heaven; who enjoy the clearest gospel light, the greatest religious liberty, and the highest advantages for piety, in the richest abundance, Psa. cxlvii. 20.—Ye professing *Christians!* who are called by the name of Christ, and are encouraged in his word to seek him, 2 Chron. vii. 14; who are baptized in the name of Christ, and bound by the most solemn vows to serve him alone, Eccl. v. 4.—Ye *Protestants!* who are delivered from, and protest against the pernicious errors which have crept into the visible church of Christ; if you continue in sin, your *inconsistency* will be as great as your wickedness and your folly: and when judged at the bar of God, you must be found without excuse, Matt. xxii. 12, 13.

4. *Why* WILL *ye die?* Remember, if thou die eternally, it must be because you *will* die; your death must be the result of your own deliberate choice; for God *wills your salvation.* This is evident, not only from his word and oath here recorded, but also from his *long-suffering,* 2 Pet. iii. 9; —from the *tears* of Christ over perishing sinners, Matt. xxiii. 37; Luke xix. 41, 42; —and from his being *given* to die in our stead, Rom. viii. 32. And *Divine grace renders you capable of seeking salvation,* with the utmost certainty of success, Phil. ii. 12, 13. Then *resolve* with the prodigal;—"I will arise," &c., Luke xv. 18, 19. Imitate David in resolute *promptitude.* Psa. cxix. 59, 60. And confidently *hope* with Micah, Mic. vii. 18, 19.

REST FOR THE WEARY AND HEAVY LADEN.

Matthew xi. 28.—Come unto me all ye that labor and are heavy laden, and I will give you rest. (Sk.)

THE numerous miracles which our blessed Lord performed, proved that his mission was divine; and the various sermons and parables which he delivered, constrained those who heard him to exclaim, "Never man spake like this man!" Grace was poured into his lips; and in him were accomplished the words of the prophet,—"The Lord God hath given me the tongue of the learned, that I should know how to speak a word in season to him that is weary." He warned the unruly, instructed the ignorant, comforted the distressed, and poured the balm of consolation into the wounded spirit. Many were the gracious words which proceeded out of his mouth; and a few of his discourses have been recorded for the instruction, encouragement, and edification of those upon whom the ends of the world are come. Our text, found in one of these discourses, has ever been salutary to those who have felt distressed on account of their sin; and if there were no

58

other passage of the same complexion in the Bible, this would be sufficient to inspire hope, and to banish despair. The subject connected with these words, comprehends,

I. The persons addressed are described as "laboring, and heavy laden."

1. *They labor.* This expression signifies, the act of doing something which requires strong exertion. Many of the Jews labored hard to recommend themselves to God, by observing various rites and ceremonies, Rom. x. 3. They were required by divine authority to offer a great number of costly sacrifices ;—to travel to Jerusalem three times a year to worship God, and to observe various ritual precepts. In the days of our Lord, their teachers bound heavy burdens, and grievous to be borne, and laid them on their shoulders ; and thus the Jewish yoke became intolerably oppressive ;—" A yoke," said St. Peter, " which neither our fathers nor we were able to bear."

The Jews are not the only persons who have labored to merit heaven, by the performance of what are called religious duties : many who name the name of Christ, and profess to believe the articles of the christian faith, are not less sanguine in their expectations of being saved by their own endeavors ;—they toil and labor to cancel the debt which they have contracted, to atone for the sins which they have committed ; and thus to obtain that heaven, which they are conscious they have forfeited. But Jesus Christ is the only way to the Father,—the only Mediator between God and man,—the only Physician of souls,—the only Saviour of sinners, John xiv. 6 ; Acts iv. 12 ; 1 Cor. iii. 11.

2. *They are heavy laden.* They feel the burden of sin, Psa. xxxviii. 4 ; Isa. xxxviii. 14,—the reproaches of a guilty conscience, Prov. xviii. 14 ; Acts ii. 37,—the wrath of God abiding on them, Psa. xxxii. 4. Such persons are prepared to receive the blessing of the gospel, Matt. v. 4,—they are the individuals to whom the promises of pardon and salvation are addressed, Isa. lv. 1,—the very characters which Christ came to save, 1 Tim. i. 15 ; Luke xix. 10. Hence,

II. The invitation given to them ;—" Come unto me ;" which signifies, that,

1. *We must address Christ in prayer.* Prayer is the desire of the soul expressed to God ; it is God's appointed means, in the use of which he hath engaged to give us whatever we need, Matt. vii. 7. Prayer may be as effectually expressed by the sighs and groans of a broken and contrite spirit, as by the most suitable words. This duty is not only easy to perform, but it is indispensably necessary ; without prayer we cannot be saved, Ezek. xxxvi. 37 ; Rom. x. 13. Let us not, however, suppose, that there is any thing meritorious in prayer ; our prayers cannot purchase the favor of God, or the remission of sin.

2. *We must come in the exercise of faith.* Unbelief pours contempt on the Saviour, and excludes us from any share in the blessings of salvation ; but faith honors God, and secures an interest in all that Jesus has done and suffered for sinners ; see 1 Tim. v. 10 ; Rom. iv. 5 ; Acts x. 43, and xiii 38, 39 ; Heb. xi. 16. *We must believe that Christ is a suitable Saviour* Are we ignorant of God, of our duty, and of our privileges ? Christ is our wisdom. Are we under guilt and condemnation ? Christ is our righteousness. Are we in a state of moral defilement; polluted with sin, and altogether filthy and abominable ? Christ is our sanctification, 1 John i. 7; 1 Cor. i. 30, 31. Our stubborn wills he can subdue—our defiled consciences he can purge—our wicked hearts he can cleanse. In coming to Christ, we

should keep this in mind; "He is able to save" me; though my sins are ever so numerous, or aggravated, he can pardon them; though my nature is ever so much depraved, he can renew me : see Heb. vii. 25. *We must believe that he is a willing Saviour.* Why should we question his willingness ? Did he not voluntarily take our nature—endure the contradiction of sinners—and submit to be condemned, and scourged, and crucified ? Every groan he heaved, every tear he shed, every drop of blood he poured out, tells us that his heart is made of tenderness, and that he is full of mercy and of grace. *The text embraces all kinds and degrees of sinners :*—" Come unto me *all* ye that labor and are heavy laden." Whatever you have been, or whatever you have done, if you only come to the Saviour with an humble, lowly, penitent, and believing heart, he will receive you graciously. *And to whom would you go?* The law condemns you, your own consciences condemn you; you are wretched, Rev. iii. 17. Your repentance, your tears, your prayers, cannot save you; you must come to Christ, or perish. Let me entreat you to make an *early* application to Christ, Heb. iii. 15 ; 2 Cor. vi. 2, and you shall realize,

III. THE BLESSING PROMISED TO THOSE WHO ACCEPT THE INVITATION. A guilty conscience is compared to a troubled sea, which cannot rest : there is no peace to the wicked; no peace with God—no peace in the mind. As long as we continue under the guilt of sin, and the curse of the law, and the wrath of God, how can we expect to be at rest ? That soul must be dreadfully oppressed, and grievously tormented, which has such a load to sustain; but if we accept the Saviour's invitation, he will deliver us from all our perplexing doubts, and from all our tormenting fears.

1. *The cause of misery and distress will be removed.* All the anguish of mind which we ever felt, was the effect of sin; nor is it possible for us to be happy while under the guilt and power of moral evil. Our iniquities must be forgiven—our persons must be justified—before we can have peace with God. When the laboring and heavy-laden sinner comes to Christ, be lieves in him, and receives him in all his saving offices, he obtains the remission of sins, receives the Spirit of adoption, and is accepted in the Beloved Rom. v. 1, 11 ; Heb. iv. 3. His conscience no longer accuses him, 2 Cor i. 12 ; the law no longer condemns him, Gal. iii. 13 ; Rom. viii. 1,—the wrath of God no longer oppresses him, Isa. xxxviii. 17, and xii. 1,—he is no longer the slave of sin, Rom. vi. 14, 22, or the captive of Satan, 2 Tim. ii. 26 ; Col. i. 13,—he is saved from the fear of death and the dread of eternity. *Another cause of misery is removed,* by the renewal of the mind—the regeneration of fallen nature ; in consequence of which, the evil tempers and dispositions no longer predominate, and distress the soul, see Gal. v. 17—24.

2. *The comforts of religion are communicated.* These are genuine, va rious, and extensive, Prov. iii. 13—18. Oh what a change is produced in the views and feelings of a person who is justified freely by divine grace ! He thinks on the horrible dungeon out of which he has been brought : he calls to mind the wormwood and the gall—the guilt and anguish under which he labored : and contrasting these with the privileges of his present state, and the glory of his future prospects, he says, or sings, with the Psalmist, Psa. cxvi. 7—12. " Return unto thy rest," &c.

3. But we shall never realize the full import of the Saviour's gracious promise, until we enter upon that rest which remaineth for the people of God Isa. lvii. 2 ; Rev. xiv. 13. and xxi. 3, 4.

Let the subject teach

i. The self-righteous Pharisee, who is laboring to meet heaven by his imaginary good works, that such an attempt is foolish, and dangerous, and destructive, Rom. iii. 19, 20; Matt. v. 20, and xxi. 31; Isa. l. 11.

z. The mourning penitent,—that Christ kindly invites, and is waiting to receive him, 2 Pet. i. 4; Isa. lv. 7—9; Micah vii. 18, 19.

3. *The soul happily pardoned,*—to be thankful, Psa. cxvi. 12, 13,—to be humble, Ezek. xvi. 63,—to be watchful, 1 Cor. x. 12,—and steadfast, Rev. ii. 10.

AN INVITATION TO PARTICIPATE IN THE GOODNESS OF THE LORD.

Ps. xxxiv. 8.   O taste and see that the Lord is good.   (Sk.)

IF there be any exercise upon earth that bears a resemblance to the employment of heaven, or any sensation that men feel in common with angels, it is that of gratitude to God; and among all the inspired writers, no man engaged more heartily in this delightful occupation than David, who was the author of this psalm. It is in a peculiar sense a psalm of praise. David begins it by declaring, "I will bless the Lord at all times," &c. There are certain exercises in the Christian life suited to peculiar seasons, but praise is never unsuitable; gratitude is never ill-timed; "My soul shall make her boast in the Lord." Some boast in their wealth, others in their personal accomplishments: David gloried in the Lord; and not satisfied with doing this alone, he invited others to engage in the same exercise—"O magnify the Lord," &c., ver. 3. He then assigns the reason why he magnified the Lord, ver. 4—6; and in the text, under the influence of the same spirit, he adds, "O taste and see that the Lord is good." We have in this passage,

I. SOMETHING ASSUMED:—That "the Lord is good." There are few expressions that occur more frequently in the Psalms than this, and there is no sentiment that should be more deeply or constantly impressed upon our minds.

1. *God is infinitely good.* His goodness knows no bounds, limits, nor dimensions; so that we may well exclaim, "How great is thy goodness!"

2. *God is independently good.* His goodness is all his own; there are good men and good angels, but these are dependently good: their goodness is not essential to their natures.

3. *God is absolutely good.* His goodness can never be extended, nor diminished; our goodness is capable of increase; it may be augmented, perhaps to all eternity; but God's goodness is always the same.

4. *God is unchangeably good.* There is no variableness in his goodness: our goodness is mutable; we are liable to change every day, but God changeth not.

5. *God is universally good.* He is good to all, and good every where: his goodness is the same in every part of the globe, and in heaven and earth the same.

6. *God is eternally good.* His goodness endureth for ever; he cannot cease to be good.

II. SOMETHING IMPLIED:—That the goodness of the Lord may be *seen* and *tasted.* There are various mediums through which the goodness of the Lord may be seen.

1. *The creation is a kind of glass or mirror, which reflects the good-ness of the Lord.* There was a period in eternity, in which God alone existed; he was not necessitated to form any creatures; but he was pleased to do it, not so much to exhibit his eternal power, as to communicate his infinite goodness; hence when God finished his works of creation, he "saw every thing that he had made, and behold it was very good."

2. *The goodness of the Lord may be seen in the provision made for all creatures.* "These all wait upon thee," &c., Psa. civ. 27. "The eyes of all wait upon thee," &c., Psa. cxlv. 15. "Consider the ravens, for they neither sow nor reap," &c., Luke xii. 24.

3. *The goodness of the Lord may be seen in the redemption of the world by Jesus Christ.* Man, by his personal transgression, forfeited all title to the divine favor, and exposed himself to eternal punishment; but oh! the riches of God's goodness induced him to deliver up his own Son to death for our ransom. What but goodness, unmerited and unparalleled goodness, would provide for us such a Saviour? so *suitable* to our necessities, so *powerful* to help us, and so *willing* to do us good.

4. *The goodness of the Lord may be seen in the means of grace with which we are favored.* Here is the gospel, containing glad tidings and good news, spread before us. Here are the ambassadors of peace crying, "Ho! every one that thirsteth," &c. Here is the Spirit of God ready to work in us all goodness, and righteousness, and truth. Here are friends saying, "Come thou with us, and we will do thee good" And here are many personal, social, and religious advantages, all of which serve to display the divine goodness.

5. *The goodness of the Lord may be seen in the rewards of heaven;* rewards beyond the power of human conception, gratuitously bestowed, and lasting as eternity. But the goodness of the Lord may not only be seen but tasted. The soul has its appetites as well as the body. *Tasting*, literally, is proving the quality of any thing by the mouth, or palate. David said, "How sweet are thy words unto my taste!" St. Paul mentions some who had "tasted of the heavenly gift." To taste that the Lord is good, is to enjoy his goodness: we do this, 1. *When we receive a knowledge of salvation by the remission of our sins.* A soul laboring under a sense of guilt tastes the bitter bread of misery, and drinks the cup of baleful grief: but when God gives the burdened conscience ease, and communicates a knowledge of his favor, then the man tastes that the Lord is good. 2. *When the love of God is shed abroad in the heart.* When we feel that we love him because he first loved us. 3. *When the promises are applied to our hearts by the power of the Holy Ghost.* In seasons of inward conflict or outward opposition.

III. SOMETHING ENJOINED. "O taste and see," &c. This invitation, request, or admonition is.

1. *Divine in its origin.* David wrote it, who was a warrior, a politician, a monarch, and a divine; but he wrote it under the influence of the Holy Ghost, and therefore it is God that speaks to us in the affectionate language of the text.

2. *Reasonable in its nature.* We are endowed with powers and faculties capable of this exercise; we can taste and see that the Lord is good; and what God has rendered us capable of doing, it is reasonable that we should do. The inferior orders of beings see nature smiling around them, but the Lord of nature they cannot see: they taste their rich pastures, but the goodness of God they cannot taste.

3. *Pleasurable in its exercise.* Sometimes we contemplate the divine character with trembling awe ; God comes out of his place to punish the inhabitants of the earth for their iniquity. He rides in the whirlwind, and directs the storm ; and we hear the voice of God, and are afraid : but to taste and see that the Lord is good, produces feelings of another description ; feelings of pleasure, which can never be exceeded on earth, and enjoyments which can only be paralleled in heaven.

4. *Profitable in its result.* This is the only method by which we can enjoy God. The more we taste and see of the goodness of God, the more contentment we shall possess in our stations, and the more resignation to the allotments of God's providence. By tasting and seeing the goodness of the Lord upon earth, we shall be prepared for these exercises in heaven, and we shall anticipate with exquisite delight the period, when we shall see as we are seen, and know as we are known.

INFER,

1. That there is something more in religion than the mere profession, or outward form : there is the exercise of mental powers : a tasting and seeing the Lord is good. This is personal, and known only to ourselves.

2. How wretched those are who forego these pleasures, and refuse to comply with the requisition in the text,—who know nothing but animal gratification and sensual pleasure.

3. Those who enjoy personal piety, are anxious for others to realize the same enjoyment, and are ready to say to their families, friends, and neighbors, " O taste and see that the Lord is good."

4. If the Lord is good, let us learn the design of that goodness. Rom. ii. 4.

PURITY NECESSARY TO SALVATION.

Jer. iv. 14.—Oh Jerusalem, wash thine heart from wickedness, that thou mayest be saved. How long shall thy vain thoughts lodge within thee? (Sk.)

WHEN Jeremiah was called to the prophetic office, the moral state of the Jews was awfully degenerate and deplorable. As a nation, they had forsaken "the fountain of living water," and abandoned themselves to idolatry and every species of wickedness. Their defection and disobedience greatly displeased the God of their fathers, and caused him to chastise them for their impiety, and permit them to be carried captives into Babylon, under the galling yoke of their enemies. But previous to that calamitous event, the Lord sent his servants the prophets, to give them timely warning, and exhort them to immediate repentance. Such was manifestly the import and design of Jeremiah's commission, which he faithfully executed, in the midst of opposition and extreme discouragement. In the text and context he earnestly entreats the inhabitants of Jerusalem and Judea to return unto the Lord their God as the only way to be preserved from the *tyranny* of their enemies, and cleansed from the *impurity* of their iniquities ;—" O Jerusalem, wash thine heart," &c. But these words will strictly apply to mankind universally, as fallen and polluted sinners ; and explicitly suggest and declare the natural depravity of the human heart— the spiritual purity which the Lord requires— and the absolute necessity of personal holiness. Let us observe.

I. THE NATURAL DEPRAVITY OF THE HUMAN HEART ;—" Wash thine *heart* from wickedness." By the *heart*, we may here understand all the faculties of the soul, and passions of the mind ; and by the "*wickedness* of the heart," the total corruption and moral defilement of human nature. But this doctrine is frequently misrepresented, and often denied, and must therefore be explained and proved ; as a position founded in *truth*, and confirmed by *evidence*.

1. *This doctrine requires definition.* When we maintain that man by nature is *wholly* depraved, and destitute of all spiritual goodness, we do not mean to deny that he may not be endued with some *comparative* and *moral* excellencies of natural disposition and mental attainments. It is evident, from a very partial acquaintance with mankind, that many in their natural state possess highly intelligent minds, liberal sentiments, amiable tempers, and benevolent hearts ; but no man by nature is *spiritually good*, or pleasing to God. All are deeply fallen, polluted, and prone to every evil thought, word, and work, Eph. ii. 3. This depravity of the heart includes *the entire absence of the divine image.* God made man originally in his own likeness, in knowledge, righteousness, and true holiness ; but through sin we have become ignorant, corrupt, and ungodly, both in heart and life, Rom. iii. 12–18 ; Eph. iv. 18.—*A natural aversion to God and godliness.* Hence there is in the unregenerate heart a deep rooted dislike and hatred to the purity of religion, and the sacred exercises of spiritual devotion, which fully proves that "the carnal mind is enmity against God ; for it is not subject to the law of God, neither indeed can be," Col. i. 21.—*A universal propensity or disposition to evil.* The mind, the will, the conscience, and the affections, are altogether alienated from God, and *naturally* inclined to resist his truth, and indulge in all the polluted habits of vice, and unhallowed pleasures of sin. Such is the *original* degeneracy and internal wickedness of every human being by nature, Job xv. 16 ; John iii. 6 ; Rom. i. 29—32. But,

2. *This doctrine demands evidence.* It is sometimes much easier to state a position, than to prove it ; but in the case before us, the latter is no more difficult than the former. It is so obvious a truth, that man is a fallen and sinful creature, that it cannot be denied without a manifest contempt of reason, violation of conscience, and rejection of scripture.—*It is divinely revealed.* It is explicitly taught by Moses and the prophets, and by Jesus Christ and his apostles. They are perfectly unanimous in their sentiments and representations of this humiliating subject. They assure us that " every imagination of the thoughts of the heart is only evil continually ;—the heart is deceitful above all things, and desperately wicked ;—from within, out of the heart of man, proceedeth all evil ;—that which is born of the flesh is flesh ;—the body of sin shall be destroyed, even the old man, which is corrupt according to the deceitful lusts," &c., Mark vii. 20—23. *It is practically exemplified.* In every age and nation, " the wickedness of man has been great in the earth." The heathen moralists acknowledged the fact, but could not account for its origin and prevalence. Revelation, however, explains the subject ; and the various afflictions and miseries to which human nature is incident, fully demonstrate that we are " children of wrath, shapen in iniquity, and conceived in sin."—*It is deeply lamented.* The pious sincerely mourn over " the flesh which lusteth against the spirit," and earnestly desire and pray for its utter destruction ; that they may be " redeemed from all iniquity, and purified unto the Lord a peculiar people," Psa. li. 2, 3, 7. As closely connected with the doctrine of moral depravity, we may consider,

II. **The spiritual purity which the Lord requires;**—"O Jerusalem! wash thine heart from wickedness,—how long shall thy vain thoughts lodge within thee?" This affectionate and impressive address is highly instructive, and evidently implies,

1. *The possibility of obtaining purity of heart.* If it were impossible, the exhortation would be superfluous and vain; but it certainly is attainable, and therefore ought to be earnestly desired, and diligently sought. This will appear *from the design of redemption;* which was to " open a fountain for sin and uncleanness, and to purge our consciences from dead works, to serve the living God," Heb. ix. 13, 14; 1 Pet. i. 18, 19.—*From the ability of the Saviour;* who, by the characters he sustains, and the offices which he executes, is infinitely qualified to " save unto the uttermost, and redeem his people from all their iniquities," John i. 16; 1 Cor. i. 30.—*From the promises of scripture,* in which the Lord engages freely and fully to save them that believe, " by the washing of regeneration, and the renewing of the Holy Ghost," Ezek. xxxvi. 26, 27; 1 Pet. i. 4.—And *from the experience of believers;* whose hearts are purified by faith, " as vessels unto honor," sanctified, and meet for the master's use, and " prepared unto every good work," Rom. vi. 22; 1 John i. 7.

2. *The important duty of seeking purity of heart.* " O Jerusalem! wash thine heart," &c. This exhortation or command does not imply that we can cleanse ourselves from the stains of iniquity, but simply inculcates an immediate and diligent use of the means of grace, as necessary to obtain salvation, Ezek. xviii. 31. That " our hearts may be washed from wickedness," *we must repent of our sins:* for without repentance there is no forgiveness, nor peace with God, Isa. lv. 7; Acts iii. 19.—*We must believe in Jesus Christ;* for it is only by faith that we can realize an interest in his redeeming benefits, and participate the cleansing efficacy of the blood of sprinkling, Acts xxvi. 18; Heb. xii. 24.—*We must give ourselves unto prayer;* for the Lord will be inquired of for every blessing; and hence we should humbly and fervently pray, that we may be " washed and sanctified in the name of the Lord Jesus, and by the Spirit of our God," Psa. lii. 10; 1 Thess. v. 23.—*We must also seek the Lord without delay;* for " how long," saith the Almighty, " shall thy vain," wicked, unbelieving, and impenitent " thoughts lodge within thee?"—O Jerusalem! O sinners! cleanse your hands and purify your hearts in the blood of the Lamb, for now is the day of salvation, Isa. lv. 6; 2 Cor. vi. 2. This duty is strongly enforced by,

III. **The absolute necessity of personal holiness;**—" That thou mayest *be saved.*" Purity and happiness are inseparable. We are saved by being *purified;* and hence said Christ to Peter, "If I wash thee not, thou hast no part with me."

1. *Personal holiness is a necessary property of religion.* It is very possible to assume the profession and form of godliness, whilst we are entire strangers to its vital energy and power. And it is to be feared that many rest in the *letter,* without the *spirit* of christianity; and have a name to live, while they are *spiritually* dead. But pure and undefiled religion does not consist in the barren speculations of the deluded enthusiast, nor in the external ceremonies of the formal professor, Gal. vi. 15; it principally resides in the *heart,* enlightening, enriching, and hallowing every power of the soul unto the Lord; and directing every desire, disposition, and pursuit, to the glory of his name, 1 Cor. vi. 19, 20; 1 Pet. i. 15, 16. Without this *inter-*

nal purity and spirituality of mind, the profession of religion is **an empty** parade, and can profit us nothing, Rom. xiv. 17.

2. *Personal holiness is a necessary meetness for heaven.* Reason teaches us that there must be a similarity and agreement between the *faculty* of enjoyment and the *object* enjoyed. Now God is essentially just and holy, and therefore can never be the *portion* of impenitent and unholy souls. The scriptures also assure us, that " without holiness no man can see the Lord ;" " for nothing that defileth, or maketh a lie, can in any wise enter into the kingdom of God," Matt. v. 8 ; 1 Cor. vi. 9, 10. Deliverance from the guilt, the power, and the pollution of sin, is a doctrine uniformly taught by divine revelation,—is personally confirmed in the experience of the saints,—and is absolutely necessary to obtain complete and eternal *salvation* in the world to come.

These reflections should excite deep humility and self-abasement as fallen sinners, and promote an earnest application to Jesus the Mediator of the new covenant, whose " blood cleanseth from all unrighteousness."

THE GOSPEL CALL.

Matthew xxi. 28—33.—But what think ye ? A certain man had two sons ; and he came to the first, and said, Son, go work to-day in my vineyard," &c. (Sk.)

In these verses our Saviour shows by the parable of two sons, that penitent publicans and harlots were in a far more eligible state or condition for receiving the gospel, than self-righteous persons. For understanding this parable, it is necessary to consider generally and briefly, that our Saviour, by the first of these sons, represents publicans, harlots, tax-gatherers, and sinners of all descriptions, who convinced of their awful state and danger, by the preaching of the word, proved far better than at first they promised, turning away from all their iniquities, and readily and heartily embracing the gospel ; and by the second son, he represents the learned scribes and the self-righteous pharisees, who promised fair, and performed nothing. This parable was designed for the reproof and correction of the scribes and pharisees ; and therefore our Saviour appeals to themselves, that out of their own mouth he might judge and condemn them.

I. An injunction ;—" Son, go work to-day in my vineyard." This *certain man*, who had two sons, is intended to represent God. He came to the first, and said, "Son, go work to-day in my vineyard." Here we have the Father's command, *Go work*—thou must not be idle. Go work in *my vineyard*, thou must be employed where I appoint thee. Go work *to-day*, thou must do it immediately. This command of God concerns all of us : we are enjoined to go and work to-day in his vineyard,—to make religion our present business. Here we may observe,

1 *That true religion is a work ;* and though hard and difficult, yet pleasant and profitable. " Strait is the gate, and narrow is the way which leadeth unto life," Matt. vii. 14. Yet the " ways of wisdom are ways of pleasantness, and all her paths are peace," Prov. iii. 17. God's " commandments are not grevious," 1 John v. 3 ; and " in keeping of them their is great reward," Ps. xix. 11.

66

2. *That the gospel or ministerial call to this work requires and demands present obedience.* "Go work *to-day.*" To-morrow may be too late. "To-day if ye will hear his voice harden not your hearts," Heb. iii. 15. We are called to "work while it is day;" for "the night cometh when no man can work," John ix. 4. The brevity of human life, and the important work of our salvation to be accomplished while it lasts, are considerations which should occupy the attention, and deeply impress the heart of every one.

3. *That this call is full both of authority and affection;* because it is the command of a *Father*, and it is directed to us as *children.* "Go, son, work to-day in my vineyard." He calls him *son*, to remind him of his own authority, to oblige and dispose of him as he pleases, to excite him to reverence, confidence, affection, and obedience; and to assure him, on his compliance, subjection, and faithfulness, and of all paternal regards, and an ample remuneration. What encouragement is here given to sinners, to devote themselves to God and his service!

II. THE ANSWER OF THE SON;—"He said, I will not: but afterwards he repented and went."

2. *This answer of the son is a very unfeeling and impertinent one.* He might have been more respectful; and if he had not a mind to go, might have excused himself in more modest language, and not given a direct refusal, saying, *I will not.* This is the voice of corrupt nature, the language of folly and madness; and shows us the entertainment which the gospel injunctions meet with from the majority of those persons who are thus addressed. We see here a picture of the state of fallen man, the prevalence of the carnal mind, and how unwelcome the salvation of Christ is to practical sinners. They even treat him with most censurable neglect, and insolent contempt.

2. *But afterwards he repented, and went.* Some persons will not go from their word, lest they should be deemed inconsistent. Afterwards the son repented;—better late wise, than never wise. He changed his mind, from a conviction that he had done wrong: the immediate effect is obedience, he *went* into his father's vineyard. The gospel call meets with peremptory refusals from multitudes of those who hear it; they refuse "him that speaketh from heaven," Heb. xii. 25; which conduct exposes them to the greatest peril, —"How shall we escape if we neglect so great salvation?" Heb. ii. 3. Obedience is the sure way of escaping danger, and the only evidence of a change of heart. Well it is when profligate sinners amend their ways, and turn to God. *He repented;* and as a proof of it, *went* into the vineyard.

3. *Though this change of mind in him involves in it a contradiction, yet his conduct in this instance can be justified on the soundest principles both of reason and revelation.* On what grounds can a life of sin and disobedience be vindicated? Not on any correct view of man's responsibility while in this world; nor on the doctrine of a suitable retribution beyond the grave. Sin brings disgrace on the character of man, and renders him the subject of guilt and misery.

III. THE FATHER CAME TO THE SECOND SON, AND SAID, "Go, work to-day in my vineyard."

1. *This son had the same kind of call given him that the other had.* The same call, as to the sense of it, is given to all who are favored with the gospel; but it is very different in its effects, for to some it is "the savor of death unto death," while to others it is "the savor of life unto life," 2 Cor. ii. 15, 16. He answered, "*I go, sir; and went not.*" This answer is very different from that of his brother. He called his father "sir," expressive of respect and complaisance, and promised ready obedience. He did

not say, I will go, but "I go," promptly, immediately, now. But he *went not;* he spake well, but did nothing : saying and doing are two things. His answer should be ours; we should say from the heart, *We go :* but then we should take care that we act according to our profession of obedience.

2. *The command of our heavenly Father should be received with great reverence ;* and men should express their gratitude for such a gracious call, by a ready compliance. But alas ! many who make a pompous profession of obedience are the most reluctant to fulfil their engagements. How many are there in the christian world, who profess that they know God according to the holy scriptures, but daily deny him in their spirit and temper, as well as their words and works. What a deception ! Their foundation is sand, which will give way, and the whole imaginary structure fall down. And what will they do, when God calls them to judgment ?

Hence we learn, that the religion of many persons consists only in good purposes and resolutions ; but this will not avail, for they only are blessed who " do his commandments," as an evidence of possessing saving grace. Let us therefore secure the inward principle of saving grace, that we may be assisted to glorify God in all our works.

ISRAEL EXHORTED TO RETURN TO THE LORD.

Hosea xiv. 1, 2.—O Israel, return unto the Lord thy God ; for thou hast fallen by thine iniquity. Take with you words, and turn unto the Lord : say unto him, Take away all iniquity, and receive us graciously : so will we render the calves of our lips. (Sk.)

THE conduct of God towards Israel, and Israel's conduct towards God, form the most interesting topics with which the Old Testament abounds. David declared that God had not dealt so with any nation ; and as a confirmation of this, we need only review the series of wonders and miracles which adorn their whole history. And yet their conduct towards God excites almost equal astonishment, in the serious and contemplative mind. Their repeated murmurings and abominable idolatries often provoked the Divine Being to pour out his indignation upon them, but in wrath he remembered mercy. He raised up prophets, and sent them forth as the ambassadors of peace, to warn the people of their danger, and to call them to repentance. Hosea was a man of this description, who lived in the days of Uzziah, Jotham, Ahaz, and Hezekiah, kings of Judah. An epitome of his general message we have in the text. " O Israel, return," &c. We notice here,

I. AN AWFUL FACT STATED ; " Thou hast fallen by thine iniquity." The term *fall* is used literally, when we speak of a body descending from a higher to a lower situation : thus we say, the fall of a leaf, or the fall of a stone. But when the fall of angels or of man is mentioned, we understand the term figuratively : so we apply it in the text, " Thou hast fallen by thine iniquity." To explain this, we observe, God is a being of infinite dignity, and is called the Most High ; not because he occupies the most exalted sphere in a local sense, but because he is above all in his natural and moral perfections. Holy angels and glorified spirits, being most like God in the purity of their natures, are considered as surrounding his throne, and standing in his presence ; while the devil and his angels, who are farthest removed from all moral rectitude, are most degraded, cast down to hell, into a bottomless pit of fire and brimstone. A state of sin is a low estate; and when a man turns from good to bad, he is considered as fallen. Thus Israel had,

1. *Fallen from their allegiance to God.* There was a period in their history, when the Lord was their King, and they were under his immediate government; "but they rejected him that he should not reign over them," 1 Sam. viii. 7. "They have set up kings, but not by me," &c., Hos. viii. 4.

2. *Fallen from his worship.* "They had their molten images of silver, and idols," &c., Hos. xiii. 2. "They sacrificed upon the tops of mountains," &c., iv. 12, 13. And they were "joined to idols," iv. 17.

3. *Fallen from the enjoyment of his favor.* The Lord had a controversy with them, and was fixed to punish them, &c., Hos. xii. 2. "They have sown the wind, and they shall reap the whirlwind," viii. 7. "I will meet them as a bear bereaved of her whelps," xiii. 8. "Fallen by *thine* iniquity," The iniquity by which they fell was *personal*. "O Israel thou hast destroyed *thyself*," xiii. 9. "Israel is an empty vine," &c., x. 1. It was *mental*. "Their heart was divided," x. 2. Whoredom and wine had taken away their heart, iv. 11. It was *practical*. They rejected knowledge, forgot the law of God, practised swearing, lying, killing, stealing, and committing adultery; they had troops of robbers among them; and there was no truth nor mercy, nor knowledge of God in the land, iv. 1, 2, 6.

II. AN AFFECTIONATE EXHORTATION URGED. "O Israel, return unto the Lord thy God." Here observe,

1. *The persons addressed;*—"*Israel.*" A people once highly favored, but now degraded. Had the prophet used language expressive of their moral character, he might have designated them by the most odious epithets; but he calls them "Israel," to remind them of what they once were, the import of their name, and the high honor which God had put upon them. What affectionate men were God's prophets! How faithful, and yet how kind!

2. *The nature of the address;*—"Return." This supposes previous wandering. The people of Israel had wandered like a treacherous wife, who had forsaken her husband, Hos. ii. 5; they had gone after other lovers, but disappointment had attended them, ver. 6. Now the prophet invites them to "return." Have we acted the part of Israel? Oh let us return—now—with all our hearts—in the spirit of faith and prayer.

3. *The object to whom they were to return;*—"Unto the Lord thy God." The Lord, who has the sole right to rule and govern thee; "thy God," who called himself thy God, Psa. l. 7;—who acted towards thee as a God, in defending thee in danger,—comforting thee in distress,—directing thee in difficulty,—and providing for thee in necessity. Gratitude, affection, justice, honor, safety, and comfort, should induce those who have wandered from God to return to him.

III. INSTRUCTIVE DIRECTION ADMINISTERED;—"Take with you words," &c. Prayer may be offered unto God without words, 1 Sam. i. 13. But Israel was here directed to take *words,*—not bullocks nor sacrifices; these we may not all have in possession, but *words* we have at will. *Words of sincerity* should be taken, when we approach to God, not speaking what we never mean; hypocrisy is hateful in his sight. *Appropriate words*, such as best accord with our feelings and desires. *Words of humble confession.* David, Daniel, and the prodigal, will furnish us with words of confession. *Words of petition.* These the prophet records; say unto him, "Take away all iniquity." Iniquity was the cause of their fall, and in returning to God they were to pray for its removal.

1. *Take it away from our affections, that we may no longer love it.* Sinners love sin; there is a bent and tendency towards it in the carnal mind. God alone can take away that desire after sin from our hearts.

2. *From our consciences, that we may no longer labor under the burden of it.* Sin induces guilt, and renders us liable to punishment; God threatens sinners with hell. Awakened sinners groan under the burden of sin, and say, " Take away all iniquity."

3. *From our lives, that it may not have dominion over us.* God has promised to redeem Israel from all his iniquities, Psa. cxxx. 8. " How shall we that are dead to sin live any longer therein?" Rom. vi. 2.

4. *From our hearts, that we may be dead to it.* This is the subject of the prayer;—" Take away *all* iniquity." God can do this, for he is almighty; and because he directs us to pray for it, we may infer his willingness to answer our prayer.

" Receive us graciously." This is another part of the prayer which Israel was directed to offer unto God.

1, *Receive our prayers graciously.* One of the heaviest judgments which God can inflict upon sinners in this world, is to reject their prayers. This he may justly do, and laugh at our calamity, &c. It is all of grace that he deigns to receive our prayers.

2. *Receive our persons graciously.* Receive us into thy *family.* Sin has rendered us aliens and enemies, and we are by our iniquities children of wrath; but receive *us,* and put us among thy children. Receive us into thy *favor.* Our iniquities have rendered us liable to thy heavy displeasure; but oh forgive us, heal our backslidings. Receive us into union with thyself. Our iniquities have separated between us and thee; but cast us not off from thy presence. In the margin this is read, " Take away all iniquity, and give good." God is good—all good; and he gives good; and " no good thing will he withhold from them that walk uprightly."

IV. RETURNS OF GRATITUDE EXPRESSED ;—" So will we render the calves of our lips." By this expression we understand the fruit of our lips, " giving thanks to his name," Heb. xiii. 15. When the Jews received signal favors from God, they were accustomed to offer animal sacrifices, such as calves and bullocks, as returns of gratitude, 1 Kings iii. 4, 15 ; but " we will render the calves of our lips." " Thou desirest not sacrifice," &c., Ps. li. 16.

1. *Gratitude is a debt which all owe to God.* All the benefits with which our being is crowned, flow from God, and flow freely, liberally and constantly. Gratitude is the expression of obligation; and as our obligations to God know no bounds, our gratitude should know no end.

2. *Gratitude is a debt which gracious souls are ready to pay.* Fully to discharge this debt is impossible; but, like the woman in the gospel, they do what they can. When God takes away our iniquity, and receives us graciously, our first feelings are those of praise, Isa. xxxviii. 18, 19. As a proof that we " render the calves of our lips," let us render the homage of our hearts, and the actions of our lives.

Learn, 1. *That neither our civil nor religious privileges will preclude the possibility of falling by iniquity.* Whoever rose higher by the former than Israel? or whoever sunk deeper by the latter?

2. *That those who have fallen by iniquity should be induced to return to the Lord their God.* God invites them to return—promises to receive them—and gives direction by the prophet in the text how they should return.

3. *Those whose iniquity is taken away should individually say,* " Bless the Lord, O my soul." Psa. ciii. 2, 3.

JESUS WEEPING OVER PERISHING SINNERS.

Luke xix. 41, 42. And when he was come near, he beheld the city, and wept over it, saying, If thou hadst known, even thou, at least in this thy day, the things which belong unto thy peace! but now they are hid from thine eyes. (Sk.)

1. WHEN we see a man weeping, of whom but little is known by us, it is natural for us to set our imagination in exercise, that we may be able to ascertain the probable cause or causes of his distress. We very readily suppose that he is a man *weak* in his *intellects*, and liable to be thus affected by every unpleasant occurrence, however trifling;—or he has committed some heinous *crime*, and his conscience is wrung by bitter remorse;—or he is now overwhelmed by the pressure of some recent *affliction* in his *circumstances ;*—or some great calamity has befallen his *friends*, and the tears we behold are tears of sympathy.

2. Our text exhibits to our view a man in tears. But be not hasty in your conclusions : these tears are not indicative of *mental imbecility*, for in him dwelt all the treasures of wisdom and knowledge.—These tears are not expressive of *remorse*, for in him was no sin, and in all his deportment he was holy, harmless, and undefiled.—These tears are not occasioned by *personal afflictions*, they have no reference to himself.—They are not occasioned by the calamities of his *friends*, for their case, even at the worst, is very hopeful.—Why then does he weep? The reason is, he sees his *enemies*, his open and avowed enemies, obstinately bent on their own destruction. It is this that fills his heart with sorrow, his eyes with tears, and his mouth with this affecting language. "When he came near," on his last visit to Jerusalem, "He beheld the city," that city, the inhabitants of which had despised, rejected, and reviled him, and were now forming designs against his life. Well knowing the dreadful judgments by which this city would soon be laid desolate, he most compassionately lamented "and wept over it, saying, If thou hadst known," or, "oh that thou hadst known, even thou, in this thy day, the things which belong unto thy peace! but now they are hid from thine eyes." This lamentation, it appears, was lost on the Jews in general, but it is recorded for our instruction ; and under the divine blessing it may prove highly beneficial to us, by teaching us,

I. THAT GOSPEL BLESSINGS ARE CONDUCIVE TO THE PEACE OF MANKIND. They are the things which belong unto our peace. Here let us more particularly observe,

1. *What those things are to which our Lord refers.* That they are those blessings which he had called "the lost sheep of the house of Israel" to enjoy, but which they had obstinately rejected, is evident from similar complaints, see Matt. xiii. 14, 15; xxiii. 37; John v. 40. They include the blessings of grace in this world; and the blessings of glory in the eternal state.—*The blessings of grace in this world.* Deliverance—from bondage, condemnation, and guilty fears, Psa. cxvi. 16: Isa. xii. 1; Psa. xxxiv. 4; and *holiness*—both of heart and life, Obadiah 17; Rom. vi. 22.—*The blessings of glory in the eternal state.* An eternal life of rest, felicity, honor, and security, Rom. ii. 6, 7. Let us also observe,

2. *How these things are conducive to our peace.* They belong unto our peace as they produce sweet tranquility of mind, Eccl. ii. 26. This arises from *peace with God*, Rom. v. 1 ; *peace of conscience*, 2 Cor. i. 12 ; a *peaceable disposition*, James iii. 18; the *joy of victory*, Rom. viii. 37; 1 Cor. xv. 57; and the joy of *hope*, Rom. v. 2 and xiv. 17. Our text teaches us,

71

II. THAT THESE BLESSINGS MUST BE KNOWN TO BE ENJOYED :—" Oh that thou hadst known," &c.   The knowledge thus necessary, must be,

1. *A speculative knowledge;* that is, we must have a correct view of them, as they are exhibited in God's word,—For we are naturally *without* them, Rom. iii. 16—18.—We must *seek* them to *obtain* them, Job xxii. 21 ; Isa. xxvii. 5.—And we must *understand* them in order that we may *seek* them aright : we must understand the nature of them ; the necessity of them ; and the way to obtain them, Prov. xix. 2.   The knowledge here required must also be,

2. *An experimental knowledge.*   This is evident—From the *testimony of inspired apostles,* 2 Cor. v. 1 ; xiii. 5 ; 1 John v. 19.—And from the *nature of gospel blessings ;* spiritual sight, liberty, and health, must be experienced to be enjoyed.   Our text teaches us,

III. THAT A SEASON IS AFFORDED US FOR ACQUIRING THE KNOWLEDGE OF THESE BLESSINGS.

1. This season is here called *our day,* because it is the time in which we are called to labor for the blessings of peace, John vi. 27 ; Phil. ii. 12, 13; 2 Pet. iii. 14.

2. This season is *favorable for seeking the things here recommended ;*— for they are set *before* us, Deut. xxx. 19, 29 ;—we have *strength* promised to seek them with, Isa. xl. 31 ;—and we have *light* to seek them in, John xii. 36.   Hence, we should also recollect,

3. *This season is limited ;* it is only a *day.*   It began with the exercise of our reason ; it may be terminated either by death, the general judgment, the loss of our mental powers, or the departure of God's Spirit, Jer. vi. 8 ; and while it remains, it should be promptly improved, John xii. 35 ; Matt. xxiv. 44.   Our text also teaches us, with respect to gospel blessings,

IV. THAT IT IS GOD'S WILL THEY SHOULD BE ENJOYED BY US.   This is certain,

1. *From the wish of Christ ;—*" O that thou hadst known," &c.   Such a wish we find often repeated by God in his word, and expressed in the kindest manner ; see Deut. v. 29, xxxii. 29 ; Isa. xlviii. 18.

2. *From the tears of Christ.*   These demonstrate the *sincerity* of his *wish,* Deut. xxxii. 4 ;—the great *importance* of *godliness,* 1 Tim. iv. 8 ;— and the *dreadful doom* of *impenitent sinners,* Rom. ii. 8, 9.

3. *And from the visitations of Christ ;* see ver. 44.   He visited us by his *incarnation,* Luke i. 78, 79 ;—and he still visits us by the strivings of his *Spirit—* the gifts of his *providence,* Acts xiv. 17—and the ministry of his *word,* 2 Cor. v. 20 ; Luke xix. 10.   Hence we learn,

V. THAT ALL WHO SEEK THESE BLESSINGS ARIGHT, WILL OBTAIN THEM.

1. *To seek them aright, is to seek them as God requires :*—with respect to *time,* now while our day of visitation lasts, Job xxii. 21 :—with respect to *manner*—by faith in Christ, John v. 28, 29 ;—by receiving Christ, John i. 12 ;—coming to God by him, Heb. vii. 25 ;—and abiding in him, 1 John ii. 28.

2. *All who thus seek them will certainly obtain them ;* for Christ *died* for the chief of sinners, Zech. xiii. 1.   He *calls* them to seek salvation, Isa. i. 16—18 ; and *engages* not to *reject* them, John vi. 37.   Only those shall perish who despise him, Acts xiii. 41 ; and all such must perish, because they obstinately reject the only remedy, Prov. xxix. 1 ; John iii. 17.   Hence our text finally teaches us,

VI. THAT THE REJECTION OF THESE BLESSINGS IS PUNISHED WITH DE-STRUCTION.

1. *This is evident from Scripture:*—for all mankind by nature are sinners, Rom. iii. 23. As sinners, they are exposed to destruction, Prov. x. 29; and by impenitence, the only means of salvation are neglected, Heb. x. 26, 27.

2. *And it is evident from facts.* These Jews, through impenitence, became the victims of divine vengeance; and so must all impenitent sinners, 2 Thess. i. 7—9.

APPLICATION.

1. *Examine yourselves.* Do you enjoy the things which belong unto your peace? Gal. vi. 4,

2. *If not, seek them*—on *God's terms,* Acts xx. 21;— with your *whole heart,* Jer. xxix. 13;—and *without delay,* Job. xxxvi. 18.

3. *If thus seeking, expect salvation*—from Christ's *all-sufficiency,* Heb. vii. 25; and from his *goodness.* Recollect he visits you—weeps over you —wishes your salvation—has bled for you—and now waits on you, Rev. iii. 20.

~~~~~~~~~~

PROMPTITUDE OF CHOICE RECOMMENDED.

Joshua xxiv. 15.—Choose you this day whom you will serve. ·(Sk.)

THE text contains a most important piece of advice, addressed to a highly privileged people, by a most distinguished character, on a very memorable occasion. The speaker was Joshua, the successor of Moses, who was invested with his miraculous powers, and high prerogative. The period at which the text was spoken, was when he contemplated the near approach of death; and the individuals to whom it was addressed, were the elders of Israel, their heads, their judges, and their officers. There are seasons when the force of truth acquires additional energy; when the time, the place, and the circumstances, combine their influence to give permanency to the impression produced in the mind; and the period before us was one of those occasions. Imagine a venerable old man, grown grey-headed in the service of his God, and in active benevolence for the good of his nation; a man high in repute for his personal prowess, for his uniform and consistent character, for the splendor of his talents, for his disinterested integrity, rehearsing in the ears of the heads of Israel, the wonderful conduct of God towards them, reminding them of their degraded origin, "Your fathers dwelt on the other side of the flood," &c., ver. 2. Of the plagues inflicted on Egypt for their sakes, ver. 6, 7. How God defeated the design of Balaam, who came to curse the people, but was constrained to bless them altogether, ver. 9, 10. And he also reminded them of what God had done for them since they inhabited the land of Canaan. "Now therefore," said he, "fear the Lord," &c., "and if it seem evil unto you to serve the Lord. choose you," &c. Three things we will notice, the *act,* the *period,* and the *motives* for choice.

I. LET US NOTICE THE ACT OF CHOICE.

1. *Our choice should be divine in its object.* We should choose the Lord for our God. Choose God for our *sovereign,* that he may govern us, and that we may submit to his authority, and dispensations. For our *guide, that*

he may direct us amidst all the intricate snares of this world. For our *husband*, that we may be married to him. For our *portion*, that we may be satisfied with his favor, and for our *pattern*, that we may imitate him. O how many choose other objects!

2. *Our choice should be rational in its character.* It should be the result of rational conviction; the religion of some people lies solely in their passions, their hearts have been affected, their passions touched, and without counting the cost, or calling in the aid of their intellectual faculties, they commence their religious course, and join some body of professing christians; but alas! when persecution comes, they are offended, and their profession vanishes as the morning cloud, and as the early dew. Let us wisely consider what we are doing, so that we may be able to give an answer to every man who asketh us a reason of the hope that is in us.

3. *Our choice should be decisive in its nature.* In reference to many things in human life, we are called upon to hesitate in making our choice; and after we have made it, we are left in doubt as to its result. "For who knoweth what is good for man in this life?" But this cannot be the case, in reference to the subject before us. We all know that if we do not choose God for our portion, we must be inevitably ruined; and under the influence of this conviction, we should be so decided in our choice, as not even to have a longing wish for the world, or a single thought of returning again to its vain pursuits in quest of happiness.

4. *Our choice should be practical in its operations;*—"Choose you this day whom ye will *serve*." Having chosen God, you must serve him—*totally*, with soul and body; *uniformly*, not merely on the Sabbath, or among the friends of piety, but always and every where; *consistently* evince that you serve him. "Let others *see* your good works."

II. LET US NOTICE THE PERIOD OF OUR CHOICE;—"Choose you *this day*," &c.

1. *We should make our choice this day, because of the criminal neglect of which we have been guilty.* As soon as reason dawned upon our minds, and we were capable of making a choice, we ought to have chosen God for our portion, and have been uniform in our attachment to him, from that time to the present. But the days of our youth passed away in the total neglect of God; we purposed when arrived at maturity, to choose the good part; but alas! here also many of us failed, and now some of us are old, and probably have never yet been decidedly pious. Oh what culpable neglect attaches to us!

2. *We should make our choice this day, from a view of the shortness and uncertainty of our time.* "Time is short," our days are as a handbreadth, swifter than a post. We may die to-day, our departure may be sudden. Death often gives no signal of his approach; but should we have a lingering affliction, that is not a proper time to choose whom we shall *serve*.

3. *We should make our choice this day, because the present is the only time when God has promised the aids of his Spirit.* The power of choice is from God; that power is the effect of his gracious operations in us. But his Spirit will not always strive with us. God may be provoked to give us up to a reprobate mind. "Now is the accepted time."

4. *We should make our choice this day, because the difficulty of choosing will increase in proportion to our neglect of it.* Sin is a disease; the longer that disease prevails, the more inveterate it becomes. Sin is slavery; the longer we continue in it, the faster our chains are riveted, and the more difficult it is to burst them asunder.

74

III. LET US NOTICE THE MOTIVES FOR CHOICE. Joshua gave this charge to Israel; it is given to us now.

1. *The capacity which we have for choice, is a reason for its exercise.* God gives nothing in vain. Had we ranked no higher than brutes, and possessed nothing superior to blind instinct, the power of choice would have been precluded; but we are men, endowed with rational faculties, and capable under the influence of the divine Spirit of choosing God, and serving him.

2. *The perilous state in which we are without this choice, is another motive.* How miserable is a man without God! He who has never chosen God for his portion, has no interest in him, no union with him, no salvation from him. God is to him no refuge, Christ no Saviour, the Holy Ghost no comforter: heaven is no inheritance of his; ruin must inevitably seize his soul, if he continues in a course of sin.

3. *The happiness that results from our choosing God, should prompt us to comply with the requisition in the text.* He who has chosen God is in a state of safety and tranquility. His guilt is pardoned, his soul is renewed, his hope is like an anchor, sure and steadfast, cast within the veil, whither the forerunner is for him entered. The Lord's portion is his people, and Jacob is the lot of his inheritance.

Conclude by inquiring, What choice have we made? Where are our affections placed? Whom do we serve? What is our chief good? Some worship mammon. Some serve the devil. Expostulate with such. Why make such a choice? The world cannot make you happy. With the devil you will be tormented if you die in sin. Exhort those who have chosen God to cleave to him. Amen.

OUR LORD'S CONDESCENSION TO SINNERS.

Rev. iii. 20. Behold, I stand at the door, and knock: if any man hear my voice, and open the door, I will come in to him, and sup with him, and he with me. (S. S.)

THE ways of man are often made a standard whereby to judge of God—
Hence many foolishly "think him to be such an one as themselves"
But "his thoughts and ways are infinitely above ours"
This is remarkably manifest in the passage before us—
It is usual for inferiors to wait on their superiors—
The greater their inferiority, the more patience is expected of them—
But here the God of heaven waits upon his sinful creatures—
The declaration is made even to the Lukewarm Laodiceans—
It unfolds to our view,

I. THE WONDERFUL CONDESCENSION OF CHRIST TO SINNERS.
He represents himself as coming to them to be their guest—
But we must understand his words in a spiritual sense—
The hearts of natural men are shut against Christ.
Mankind have their hearts full of vile lusts and passions—
They utterly exclude Christ from his rightful habitation—
They bar the door against him by prejudice and unbelief—
He however condescends to seek admittance into them.
He "knocks" in various ways "at the door" of their hearts—
He intreats, promises, threatens, and expostulates by his *word*—

He awakens attention by the secret energy of his *Spirit*—
He calls also by alarming dispensations of his *providence*—
But the generality disregard his voice.
They are asleep, and even "dead in trespasses and sins"—
If awakened, they endeavor to lull themselves asleep again—
If they cannot do this, they rest in frivolous excuses, Cant. v. 2, 3.
Thus do they studiously and determinately resist his will—
Nevertheless he "stands" patiently waiting their leisure.
He might well depart at their first refusal—
But he knows how dreadful their state would then be—
He therefore "waiteth to be gracious" unto them—
On many he has waited a long series of years, Acts xiii. 18.
Of most it may be said as of Israel of old, Rom. x. 21.
This is a fact worthy of our highest admiration.
Well might he call us to "behold" it with wonder—
How wonderful, that the Creator should so condescend to a creature!—
How wonderful, that the Judge should become suitor to the criminal!—
How wonderful, that the self-sufficient God should seek in such a way to bless those who are inexpressibly vile and helpless!—
This must excite our admiration to all eternity—
The adorable goodness expressed in it will appear further by considering,
II. THE MERCIES HE DESIRES TO IMPART TO THEM.
He requires nothing of sinners but what he will enable them to perform.
He looks for no worthiness or merit in them—
He only desires that they "hear his voice, and open to him"—
He will himself "unstop their ears," and "incline their hearts"—
If indeed they obstinately persist in rejecting him, they cut themselves off from any hope in his mercy—
Upon their yielding to his solicitations, he will bless them.
The metaphor of a guest is still kept up—
It is a common metaphor in scripture, John xiv. 23.
The "supping" implies the most familiar intercourse with the soul—
This our Lord will vouchsafe to those who open their hearts to him—-
He will delight himself in the exercise of their graces, Cant. iv. 16.
He will communicate to them his richest consolations—
He will cause them to exclaim with the prophet, Zech. ix. 17.
Nor will he withhold these mercies on account of their past conduct.
He will with equal readiness become the guest of all—
No unworthiness or past obduracy shall hinder him—
He has declared this in the most express terms, "If *any* man." See also Isa. lv. 1; Rev. xxii. 17.
He has proved it in the most remarkable instances, 2 Chron. xxxiii. 9, 12, 13; 1 Tim. i. 13, 16.
There is a cloud of living witnesses ready to attest it—
We shall conclude with an ADDRESS to
1. Those who are living in a careless state.
You are yet strangers to the heavenly guest—
But this arises only from your own negligence and supineness—
Christ has been long knocking at the door of your hearts—
Every vile lust has been admitted, whilst HE has stood without—
May you never have that threatening fulfilled to you! Prov. i. 24—31
Let every one obey the prophet's exhortation, Isa. lv. 6.
2. Those who are awakened from it.

What a mercy is it that you have heard the Saviour's voice!—
Let it be your daily endeavor to open your hearts to him—
Guard against unbelief, which above all bars the door against him—
Let the sins which are offensive to him be put away—
Then shall the fact which so offended the Jews be realized in you, Luke xix. 7.
Thus shall you enjoy the most endearing fellowship with Jesus—
And you shall ere long "sup with him" in a better place, Rev. xix. 9.

AN EXHORTATION TO HOLINESS.

1 Peter ii. 11, 12.—Dearly beloved, I beseech you, as strangers and pilgrims, abstain from fleshly lusts, which war against the soul; having your conversation honest among the Gentiles: that whereas they speak against you as evil doers, they may, by your good works which they shall behold, glorify God in the day of visitation. (S. S.)

THE privileges of a sincere christian are exceeding great—
And the possession of them is secured to him by God himself, 1 Pet. i. 5.
His security however does not supersede the need of watchfulness—
On the contrary he is called to a continual warfare—
He needs therefore to be frequently reminded of his duty—
Hence Peter, having set forth the honors and privileges of God's people, proceeds to press upon them the practice of holiness—
We propose to explain and enforce the apostle's exhortation.

I. EXPLAIN

The manner in which it is introduced is worthy of notice.
A concern for the souls of men is characteristic of a pious minister—
Paul and John were eminent patterns in this respect—1 Thess. iii. 8; 3 John 4.
Peter exemplifies it in the passage before us—
He unites the tenderness of a father with the fidelity of an apostle—
The first part of it respects their "abstinence from fleshly lusts."
Impurity, intemperance, sloth, &c., are fleshly lusts—
Nor can any abstain from them without much prayer and vigilance—
This is enforced by two very important considerations.
Christians are "strangers and pilgrims" in the world—Psa. xxxix. 12; Heb. xi. 13.
This consideration strongly enforces abstinence from sin—It shews the folly of the Epicurean system, 1 Cor. xv. 32.
Moreover fleshly lusts "war against the soul"—
They destroy its dignity, its peace, its liberty, its salvation—
This should make us extremely careful to abstain from them—
The latter part of the exhortation respects positive holiness.
The christians were scattered through the Gentile world—
Their conduct therefore would be watched with a jealous eye—
On this account the apostle cautions them with respect to the whole of their deportment—
He exhorts them to maintain an honorable conduct in all things—
A very powerful motive is suggested to confirm this also—
Christians were universally represented as the worst of men, 1 Cor. iv 13

An unbecoming conduct in them would have confirmed this prejudice—
But a blameless conversation might conciliate esteem—
It might even be the means of converting their persecutors—
It would do so if God at the same time should visit them with his mercy*—
In this case it would cause them to glorify God—
This consideration might well operate as a motive to holiness—
St. Peter elsewhere urges it in this very light, 1 Pet. iii. 1.
II. Enforce.
Christians, however advanced, have need of this exhortation—
We therefore would address it to you with all earnestness—
We would not however forget the affection and tenderness due to you—
First then we beseech you to abstain from fleshly lusts.
Who amongst you is free from their baneful influence?
Who does not see that abstinence from them is necessary?—
Guard then against their first risings in the heart—
Beg of God that you may have grace to mortify them all—
We intreat you to consider,
1. Your present state and condition in the world.
You are here only as "strangers and pilgrims"—
You profess to be seeking "a city that hath foundations"—
You do not take up your rest in an inn, when on a journey—
Do not then retard your progress heaven-wards by sensual gratifications—
2. The dreadful tendency of fleshly lusts.
Who has not experienced the misery they bring upon us?—
Who does not know the consequence of indulging them?—
Let this thought make you flee from them with abhorrence—
We further beseech you to maintain an honorable conversation.
A few holy actions or dispositions will not suffice—
Religion most operate uniformly and universally—
Let the whole of your conversation therefore be blameless, Phil. ii. 15.
Nor need you despair of walking thus if you depend on Christ Phil. iv. 13.
For consider,
The tendency of such a life to remove prejudice.
The world is as ready to speak evil of christians as ever—
Nor will they regard your conduct in the church or closet—
They will enquire how you fill up your relative duties—
The sight of your blameless conduct will silence them, 1 Pet. ii. 15, and iii. 16.
The possibility that others may be converted by means of it.
Certainly many would be hardened by misconduct on your part—
On the contrary, some may be won by your good conversation—
At all events God will be glorified by means of your good works—
Let this stimulate you to unwearied watchfulness and care.

* This seems to be meant by "the day of visitation:" See Luke i. 68, 78.

PAUL'S DISCOURSE BEFORE FELIX.

Acts xxiv. 25.—And as he reasoned of righteousness, temperance, and judgment to come Felix trembled, and answered, Go thy way for this time; when I have a convenient season, I will call for thee. (S. S.)

MEN usually persist in sin without duly reflecting on its consequences— Hence the peace which they enjoy, notwithstanding they are exposed to the displeasure of the Almighty—
Yet the voice of warning and reproof will sometimes alarm them—
Too often, however, the alarm is only of short duration—
This was the case of Felix, when awakened by the preaching of Paul,
I. THE SUBJECTS OF THE APOSTLES DISCOURSE.
He was sent for to explain the principles he professed—
But he was not satisfied with gratifying the curiosity of his hearers—
He endeavored to reach their consciences, and convince them of their sins—
On this occasion he spoke of "righteousness, temperance, and judgment to come."
These subjects were well adapted to his audience—
Felix and Drusilla were both of an abandoned character*—
They needed to be "persuaded by the terrors of the Lord"—
Nor was it probable they would regard the tidings of salvation, unless they were first made sensible that they were lost sinners, Matt. ix. 12, 13.
Hence the apostle endeavored to prepare their minds for the gospel—
On these subjects he "reasoned."
He shewed the nature and extent of the duties—
He shewed the evil and danger of transgressing them—
He shewed the certainty and strictness of the future judgment—
A suitable lesson for avarice, iniquity, and oppression!—
And suitable, too, to every child of man!—
What degree of success attended this effort will appear from,
II. THE EFFECTS IT PRODUCED.
We read not of Drusilla being at all affected with the word—
But we are told of Felix, that he "trembled."
What a wonderful sight! the judge trembling before his prisoner!—
He had sinned in unnumbered instances, and was obnoxious to God' wrath—
He now heard of the day of retribution, and of the sentence of condemnation under which he lay—
And now, though he feared no earthly tribunal, he was shaken with terror and with guilt—
And was there not cause for trembling?
He was not, however, faithful to his convictions.
One might have hoped that he would have cried out like those of old, Acts ii. 37.—
But he sought to efface the impression made upon his mind—
He put off his attention to his soul to a more "convenient season."
What madness was here, to depend on the morrow in a concern of such importance!—

* Felix had induced Drusilla to forsake her own husband, and to marry him. he was moreover exceedingly avaricious and oppressive.

What season could be so convenient as *that* he then enjoyed?—

His conscience was then affected, and the Spirit was striving with him—

Moreover, he had then a faithful and inspired instructor before him—

Was he more likely to repent when he had seared his conscience, quench-ed the Spirit, yielded to Satan, and confirmed his evil habits ?—

But his future interviews with the apostle was of no avail—

One of the last acts of his government was marked with oppression and avarice—

Nor did he spare the innocence which he confessed, and admired, Ver. 26, 27.—

A melancholy instance of judicial blindness !—

APPLICATION.

Let this history serve as a CAUTION to us,

All of us have known, in some measure, the motions of God's Spirit—

All of us have felt, at times, some general apprehensions respecting the account which we must give at the day of judgment—

But how many have silenced their convictions, in hopes of finding some more convenient season for attending to them !—

And how many have died before the hoped-for opportunity arrived !—

Let us beware of this device of Satan, whereby he upholds his kingdom in the world*—

Let us remember that the same temptations will recur, and the same mo-tives influence us at future periods—

Let us attend to that salutary advice of the apostle, Heb. iii. 13–15.

And let us seek, without delay, that godly sorrow which worketh repen-tance unto salvation, 2 Cor. vii. 10.

AN EXHORTATION TO CARELESS SINNERS.

Eph. v. 14.   Awake, thou that sleepest, and arise from the dead, and Christ shall give thee light.   (S. S.)

THERE is a harmony in the Scriptures which many overlook and destroy—

Detached passages are often wrested to establish a favorite system†—

But the various truths of God should be viewed as they stand connected with each other—

There would then be diversity indeed, but no contrariety between them‡—

This observation will throw light, as on many other parts of Scripture, so on that before us in particular ; in which we have—

I. A COMMAND.

The Scripture abounds with useful and instructive metaphors—

Our state is here represented under the images of sleep and death–

---

* He does not tempt any to resolve that they will never repent ; but takes the more plaus-ible method of insinuating that they will have a more convenient season for repenting.

† Calls to duty are supposed to imply the sufficiency of man to do the will of God ; while the confessions or petitions of the saints, and the promises of divine aid given to them, are brought to justify a negligence in the use of means.

‡ God gives a *command*, Ezek. xviii. 31.   David, knowing his duty, and feeling his ina-bility to perform it, had long before presented this to God in the form of a *petition*, Ps. li. 10.   And God, to encourage such applications to him, *promises* to work in us that which he requires of us, Ezek. xxxvi. 26

Sleep implies a state of *inactivity* and *security.*
Men are busily employed about their worldly concerns—
But a lamentable supineness prevails with respect to spiritual things—
The generality do not apprehend their souls to be in any danger—
Death, judgment, heaven, and hell, do not seem worthy their notice—
God's threatenings against them are denounced without effect—
They are like Jonah, sleeping in the midst of a storm—
Hence they are described as "at ease from their youth," Jer. xlviii. 11.
To the same effect is the testimony of him that searcheth the heart, Ps. x. 4, 5.
Death includes the ideas of *impotence* and *corruption.*
An inanimate body cannot perform any of the functions of life—
It has within itself the seeds and principles of corruption—
The soul also, till quickened from the dead, is in a state of impotence—
It is incapable of spiritual action or discernment, John xv. 5; 1 Cor. ii. 14.
Its powers and faculties are altogether vitiated, Rom. vii. 18.
Whatever is loathsome and offensive to God proceeds from it, Mark vii. 21, 22.
So true is that humiliating declaration! Job. xv. 14—16.
Yet, notwithstanding this state appears so desperate, we must address to every one that is under it, the command, "Awake," &c.
Your inactivity and security involve you in the deepest guilt—
Your corruption of heart and life provokes the majesty of God—
Nor is your impotence any excuse for your disobedience—
It is your love of sin that disables you for duty—
Nor is God deprived of his right to command, though you have lost your power to obey—
Let every one then strive to comply with this heavenly call—
They who exert their feeble powers may expect divine assistance*—
To convince us that none shall fail who use the appointed means, God enforces his command with
II. A PROMISE.
Sleep and death are states of intellectual *darkness*—
Hence *light* is promised to those who obey the divine mandate—
Light in Scripture imports knowledge, Isa. viii. 20; holiness, 1 John i. 7; comfort, Ps. xcvii. 11; and glory, Col. i. 12.
And all these blessings shall they receive from Christ, the fountain of light, Mal. iv. 2; John i. 9.
Knowledge.
Spiritual knowledge every natural man stands in need of—
Nor is it attainable by the teaching of men, or the efforts of genius, Matt. xi. 25.
We can receive it from none but Christ, Matt. xi. 27.
Hence Christ invites us to come to him for it, Matt. xi. 29.
Nor shall an application to him ever fail of success, Psa. xxv. 9; Prov. ii. 3—6.
Holiness.
A despair of attaining this deters many from seeking it—
They think their inveterate habits cannot be rooted out, Jer. ii. 25.
But Christ is our "sanctification" as well as our wisdom, 1 Cor. i. 30.

* See Matt. xii. 10, 13. The man with the withered hand was unable to stretch it forth; but in attempting to obey, he was endued with strength.

His very name encourages us to expect deliverance from him, Matt. i. 21.
And he will fulfil the promises which he has made to this effect. Mic. vii.
19; Isa. i. 25.

Comfort.

A sense of guilt shall yield to holy joy, Isa. xxix. 19 ; and lxi. 3.
Deplored weakness shall be succeded by a divine energy, Isa. xxxv. 5, 6.
Our delight in him shall be spiritual and exalted, Isa. li. 11, and lviii. 11
It shall far transcend all earthly pleasures, Psa. lxxxiv. 10, and iv. 6, 7.

Glory.

Our Lord will not confine his blessings to this world, Psa. lxxxiv. 11.
He will raise his people to thrones of glory, Rev. iii. 21.
He will cause them to participate his own inheritance, Rom. viii. 17.
He will be the ground and object of their joy for ever, Isa. lx. 19 20.

APPLICATION.

What greater encouragement can any one desire ?—
What richer promises can any one conceive ?—
How suited are they to our necessities !—
Let every one consider the command as addressed to himself; "Awake,
Thou"—
Let all our powers and faculties be called forth to action—
In exerting ourselves let us expect the promised aid—
Thus shall we be eternal monuments of Christ's power and grace—

CHRIST'S OFFER OF THE SPIRIT.

John vii. 37, 38.—In the last day, that great day of the feast, Jesus stood and cried, saying,
If any man thirst, let him come unto me, and drink. He that believeth on me, as the
scripture hath said, out of his belly shall flow rivers of living water. (S. S.)

OUR blessed Lord incessantly labored for the salvation of men—
Nor could their ungrateful returns at all divert him from his purpose—
His life was sought, and he knew that persons were sent to apprehend him.
Yet, instead of rejecting them with abhorrence, he sought to win them by
love—
And importuned them to accept his richest blessings—
His address to them on this occasion contained,

I. AN INVITATION.

The time and manner of the invitation are worthy of notice.
This was a day of peculiar sanctity, and of uncommon festivity*—
And it seems that some customs, not required in the original institutions
of the law, obtained among the Jews at that time†—

* It was the eighth and last day of the feast of tabernacles, Lev. xxiii. 34. 36.

† It is said that on this day they went annually to the pool of Siloam, and drawing water
from thence returned with it in procession to the temple, where they poured it out with all
possible demonstrations of joy. At what time this custom arose, it is not easy to determine; but probably it commenced after the Babylonish captivity; and was adopted in reference to that prediction, Isaiah xii. 3. Nor is the design of it precisely known: but it seems
most likely that they then commemorated the giving of water out of the rock in the wilder
ness · and called upon God for rain, which was so necessary to them at that season. Perhaps the more spiritual among them, might pray also for those spiritual blessings, which
their promised Messiah was appointed to bestow. These circumstances served as the foundation of our Lord's address, and reflect much light upon it.

Happy to improve the opportunity, Jesus stood in the most conspicuous place, and, with an exalted voice, claimed their attention—

And, despising equally the censures of the uncharitable, and the persecutions of the proud, he made them fresh overtures of mercy—

The invitation itself was beyond measure gracious and kind.

While they only panted for his blood, he longed for their salvation—

He pointed himself out to them as the only fountain of living waters—

And assured them of his readiness to impart whatsoever they stood in need of—

He excepted none from his offers, provided they did but "thirst" for his blessings—

What could have a more conciliatory effect on his blood-thirsty murderers?

Lest, however, his invitations should be slighted, he enforced it with,

II. A PROMISE.

He first explained what he meant by "coming to him."

It was not a mere outward, but an inward and spiritual application, that he wished them to make to him—

They were to "believe in *him*," as possessing all fulness in himself—Col. i. 19.

And as the person appointed of the Father to convey blessings to them—Psa. lxxii. 17.

In a full persuasion of this truth they were to come to him by faith—

And to "draw water with joy from this well of salvation"—

For their encouragement he promised them a rich effusion of his Spirit.

By "living water" our Lord meant the gift of his Spirit—Ver. 39.

That "rivers of this living water should flow out of his belly," imported, that the believer should have a constant spring of consolation within him which should refresh all who came within the sphere of his influence—

Of this blessed truth the scriptures had abundantly testified*—

And our Lord now confirmed it to them by a most solemn promise—

He assured them, as he had before done the Samaritan woman, that his communications to them should prove a source of unutterable and endless joy—John iv. 10, 13, 14.

We shall further IMPROVE this subject by addressing,

1. Those who have no desire after spiritual blessings.

Alas! how many are there who are insatiable in their thirst after earthly things; but never once desire the blessings which Christ is exalted to bestow!

Perhaps too they think that they contract no guilt by their neglect of him—

But it is with no small indignation that God speaks of their conduct, Jer. ii. 13.

Nor would their folly be hidden from themselves, if they only considered what "broken cisterns" the sources of their comfort have invariably proved—

O that they would drink of the living fountain before they experience the want of one "drop of water to cool their tongues!"—

2. Those who desire spiritual blessings, but know not where to go for them.

Many, like those whom our Lord addressed, look no further than to the outward duty—

But he directed their eyes to himself as the true Siloam, John ix. 7, the only fountain of good—

---

* Some, because our Lord's words are not found in scripture, καθὼς εἶπεν ἡ γραφὴ with ὁ πιστεύων εἰς ἐμὲ; (translating εἶπεν, hath *required*) but there are many passages that speak to the same effect, though not in his express terms. See Isaiah xliv. 3.

Thus must we also direct you to faith in Christ, as the one means of obtaining blessings from him—

Whatever delight you may take in duties, you must remember that ordinances are but the medium of communication between Christ and you—

And that the benefits you receive will be proportioned to the faith you exercise on him—

3. Those who desire spiritual blessings, but fear that Christ is unwilling to impart them.

Too many are discouraged because their prayers are not answered instantly—

They conclude themselves so unworthy as to have excited nothing but aversion in the heart of Christ towards them—

But are you unworthy? and were not they also to whom the text was addressed—

Have you waited long in vain? and is there not a special promise given for your encouragement?—Isa. xli. 17, 18.

Have you nothing to present to Christ in return? Then he bids you come without money and without price, Isa. lv. 1; Rev. xxii. 17.

Will it be an unparalleled act of mercy? Then is it that new thing which he has undertaken to perform, Isa. xliii. 19, 20.

Fear not then, but renew your application to him with increased fervor—

And your soul shall ere long " be as a watered garden, and like a spring of water, whose waters fail not"—Isa. lviii. 11.

THE WORK OF REDEMPTION A MOTIVE TO CONVERSION.

Isaiah xliv. 22.—Return unto me; for I have redeemed thee. (S. S.)

It is almost incredible that rational beings should ever be so stupid as to cut down a tree, and carve out of it the image of a man, and, after having roasted their food with a part of it, bow down to the residue as to a God—But it is yet more astonishing that Jehovah, having been thus insulted, should invite the offenders to mercy, and urge them to accept it—Yet it is in this connexion that the text stands ; and it may well be addressed to *us ;* since, however free we be from gross idolatry, we all have worshipped and served the creature more than the Creator—Let us then fix our attention upon,

I. The invitation.

Our defection from God is too manifest to need much proof—Shades of difference there may doubtless be between different individuals ; but all have turned aside from God, and gone astray like sheep that are lost—But we are here invited to return to him,

1. With penitence.

The example of the Prodigal is that which we ought to follow—The consideration of our departure from God should fill us with shame and sorrow, and our idolatrous attachment to the creature humble us in the dust—This is the direction which God himself has given us, Hos. xiv. 1, 2; and it is to such humiliation alone that his promises of acceptance are made, Job xxxiii. 27.

2. With faith.

84

We are not to come to God with a mind full of doubts and suspicions, but with a full persuasion of his readiness to receive us—To what purpose is it to put away our contempt of his authority, if we deny or question the riches of his grace? Our conviction of his love and mercy should be as strong as possible; Mark ix. 22, 23; and we should with the most confident assurance rely on the death of Christ as a full, perfect, and sufficient sacrifice for all our sins—

3. With love.

God delights in a willing people; he would not have us regard him as a severe Master, but as a loving Father: instead of accounting his commandments grievous, we should consider his services as perfect freedom—Our disposition should be like that of Jesus when first he undertook our cause, Ps. xl. 7, 8;—Nor indeed can any thing but an unreserved surrender of ourselves to his service prove the truth of our repentance and the sincerity of our faith—

The full import of this invitation will be seen by considering,

II. THE MOTIVE WITH WHICH IT IS ENFORCED.

It is the Lord Jesus Christ who addresses to us the word of the text, See verse 21;—Now if he had enforced his invitation with a threatening of everlasting punishment, it would have called for our most attentive regard: but the motive here urged has tenfold energy—It may be considered,

1. As a tie upon our gratitude.

The redemption of Israel from Egypt, though great, was not to be compared with that which is wrought for us by the blood of Christ—The obligations which we lie under exceed all computation—Well therefore may this stupendous mercy be urged as an inducement to return to God—Indeed, this motive duly considered, could not fail of producing the desired effect—Suppose a prodigal, having left his father's house, and squandered away his substance, had been seized by his creditors and sold for a slave: suppose his father full of compassion, had gone, at the risk of his own life, and given all that he possessed as the price of his son's redemption: suppose the son returning to his evil ways, and actually going to sell himself again to his former master; if his father should follow him, with the invitation in the text, could he fail of success? Must not his son have an heart of adamant, if he could withstand such a solicitation?—The application of this to our own case is easy; O that we may realize the idea for our good!—

2. As an encouragement under our fears.

Notwithstanding the numberless proofs which God has given us of his readiness to forgive sin, we are apt to think him hard and inexorable—But the argument here used may well dissipate our unbelieving fears—Let us conceive the Saviour, at the very instant of his resurrection, meeting one of his murderers, and importuning him, by the very wounds which he had made, to accept of mercy, and assuring him that, if he would believe, the blood that he had shed, should cleanse him from the guilt of shedding it: could that man entertain a doubt of the Saviour's willingness to shew mercy?—This very thing is done to us, whose sins were the real occasion of Jesus' death: he meets us in the word, and, with his wounds yet exhibited before our eyes, addresses us in the words of the text—Let all unworthy conceptions of him then be put away, and every soul return to him as able and willing to save us to the uttermost—

APPLICATION.

Careless sinners overlook, alas! all these considerations—But if they would consider the Saviour as addressing *them*, and as following them with these words into all their retirements, yea, into all their resorts of gaiety and dissipation, what a damp would such a reflection cast on all their vicious appetites and unhallowed enjoyments!—Methinks it would not be possible for them long to withstand the influence of such a thought-- — —To *backsliding professors* these words must be applied with tenfold emphasis—How pungent must such an invitation be to those, who, having once experienced the efficacy of the blood of Christ, have relapsed into a lukewarm Laodicean state!—How shocking must their ingratitude appear, and how great their folly!—Let all such, if such there be amongst us, attend to this gracious call, and return without delay, to their duties, their priviliges, their enjoyments

THE NEARNESS OF SALVATION A MOTIVE TO DILIGENCE.

Rom. xiii. 11.—Now it is high time to awake out of sleep: for now is our salvation nearer than when we believed. (S. S.)

THE nearness of eternity may well excite us to improve the present hour—
This is a consideration as proper for believers as for unbelievers—
By it the apostle stimulated to activity the christians at Rome—
We shall consider,

I. HIS EXHORTATION.
Persons, at their accustomed hour, arise from their beds, come forth to the light, and engage in the duties of their respective callings—
Now "it is high time" for us, (as the apostle tells us, and "we know,")
1. To shake off our stupor.
The wise virgins, no less than the foolish, slumbered and slept—Matt. xxv. 5.
And the most zealous christians at times are apt to grow remiss—Rev. ii. 2—4.
But it becomes us all to resist this propensity to the utmost—
And to redeem every moment of our time for God—
2. To take a view of our prospects.
What glorious prospects has God set before us in his word!—
Should we not then be surveying them with admiration and joy?—
Should we be sleeping, when Christ and heaven are open to our view?—Luke ix. 29, 32.
Surely we should be ever standing as on Pisgah's top—Deut. iii. 25, 27.
3. To prosecute our duties.
The christian's work demands the utmost energy of his soul—
Unless we engage with our whole hearts, we can never discharge the offices of love—*
And are not multitudes around us "perishing for lack of knowledge?"—
Are not many of the saints also in need of consolation and support?—
What time then is there for loitering when so much is to be done?—
That the exhortation may have due influence upon us, let us consider,
II. THE ARGUMENT WITH WHICH IT IS ENFORCED.
Every day, and every hour, the believer draws "nearer to"
1. The termination of his conflicts.

* These are particularly referred to. Compare ver. 8, 10, with the text.

The nearer a racer comes to the goal, the more he stretches forth for the prize—

And shall not the christian be animated by the thought, that all his temptations, trials, difficulties are nearly ended?—

Well may he endure with patience, or exert himself with vigor, when the moment of his eternal rest is nigh at hand—

2. The period of his probation.

God has fixed the precise time for our continuance in his service—

And when that is arrived, we must "give account of our stewardship"—

Should we not then improve our talents with all diligence?—

It is in this way alone that we can hope to "give up our account with joy"—

3. The consummation of his hopes.

What does the christian look for, but a perfect conformity to God's image, and a complete possession of his glory?—

And perhaps a few days, or hours, may bring him to the enjoyment of it all—

Blessed thought! who that entertains it, must not glow with ardent desire for the moment of his dissolution?—Phil. i. 23.

And redouble his exertions to finish the work assigned him?—2 Pet. iii. 11, 12.

APPLICATION.

It is high time also for *unbelievers* to awake; for "their damnation slumbereth not"—2 Pet. ii. 3.

If they sleep a little longer, where, oh! where will they awake?—Luke xvi. 23, 24.

With what propriety may we address you, as Joshua did the Jews!—Josh. xviii. 3.

~~~~~~~~~~

CHAPTER III.

THE WORK OF GRACE.

OF THE PARDON OF SIN.

Psalm cxxx. 4.—There is forgiveness with thee. (H.)

THE doctrine of pardon is of pure revelation; it is not to be known by the light of nature; "As many as have sinned without law." Rom. ii. 12. Nor is this a doctrine of the law, which gives not the least hint of pardon, nor any encouragement to expect it. As many as have sinned in the law shall be judged by the law, condemned without any hope of pardon. Rom. ii. 12. Every transgression and disobedience of the law, or word spoken by angels, received a just recompense of reward; that is, proper and righteous punishment. Heb. ii. 2. Nor does the law regard a man's repentance, nor admit of any. He that despised Moses's law, died without mercy! Heb. x. 28. But the doctrine of pardon is a pure doctrine of the gospel, which Christ gave commission to his disciples to preach. Luke xxiv. 47; Acts xxvi. 18. Concerning which may be observed,

I. The proof that may be given of it, that there is such a THING AS PARDON OF SIN.

This is asserted in the text, "There is forgiveness with thee;" and by Daniel, "To the Lord our God belong mercies and forgiveness, full and free pardon of sin." Dan. ix. 9. It is a blessing provided and promised in the covenant of grace; "I will be merciful to their unrighteousness, and their sins and their iniquities I will remember no more;" Heb. viii. 12; it is the gracious proclamation the Lord has made of his name; "The Lord, the Lord God, merciful and gracious." Ex. xxxiv. 7. Christ was set forth a propitiation, through faith in his blood, for the remission of sins. Rom. iii. 25; Matt. xxvi. 28; Eph. i. 7. And Christ is "exalted to be a prince and a Saviour, to give repentance;" Acts v. 31, and it is, by his orders, published in the gospel; to which may be added, the numerous instances of it; the Israelites, who, as they often sinned, God had compassion on them, and forgave their iniquities, Psa. lxxviii. 38; and xcix. 8, and of David, Manasseh, and others, and of Saul the blasphemer, the persecutor, and injurious person; and of other notorious sinners. Ps. xxxii. 5; 1 Tim. i. 13; Luke vii. 37, 47. It is in this way God would have his people comforted, when burdened and distressed with their guilt and sin, Isa. xl. 1, 2; Matt. ix. 2; and they are favored with a comfortable experience of it, and peace of soul from it; Psa. lxxxv. 1—3; Rom. v. 11; they are directed to pray for it, Psa. xxxii. 5; and li. 2, 7—9; Dan. ix. 19; Matt. vi. 12. Pardon of sin is a branch of redemption by the blood of Christ. Eph. i. 7.

II. The phrases by which the PARDON OF SIN is expressed, and which will serve to lead into the nature of it.

1. By lifting it up, and taking it away; "Blessed is he whose transgression is forgiven, is lifted up, taken off from him, and carried away." Psa. xxxii. 1. Sin lies upon the awakened sinner, as a burden too heavy for him to bear: which is taken away by the application of the blood of Christ.

2. By the covering of it: "Blessed is he whose sin is covered." Psa. xxxii. 1. "Thou hast forgiven the iniquity of thy people, thou hast covered all their sin." Psa. lxxxv. 2. Sin is something impure, nauseous, and abominable, in the sight of God, and provoking in the eyes of his glory, and must be covered out of sight; and this cannot be done by any thing of man's; not by his righteousness, which is but rags, a covering too narrow to be wrapped in, and can no more hide his nakedness, than Adam's fig-leaves could hide his; nay, it is no better than a spider's web; and of which it may be said, "Their webs shall not become garments." Isa. lix. 6. Sin is only covered by Christ, who is the antitype of the mercy-seat which was a lid or cover to the ark.

3. By a non-imputation of it; "Blessed is the man to whom the Lord imputeth not iniquity!" Psa. xxxii. 2, does not reckon it, nor place it to his account, nor bring any charge against him for it, nor punishes for it; but acquits him from it.

4. By a blotting of it out: in such language David prays for the forgiveness of sin; "Blot out my transgressions—and blot out all mine iniquities!" Psa. li. 1, 9, and in the same way God declares his will to forgive the sins of the people; "I, even I, am he, that blotteth out thy transgressions!" Isa. xliii. 25, which language is used either in allusion to the crossing of debt books, drawing a line over them; or to blotting out a man's hand-writing to a bond or note, obliging to payment of money; hence the phrase of "blotting out the hand-writing of ordinances that was against us.' Col. ii. 14. Sins are debts, and these are numerous, and sinners poor, and unable to pay;

God for Christ's sake freely forgives; "I have blotted out, as a thick cloud." Isa. xliv. 22. Sins may be compared to clouds, for their quantity, their number being many; for their quality being exhaled out of the earth and sea, mount up to heaven, cause darkness, and intercept light; sin rises out of the earthly minds of men, who mind earthly things, and who are like the troubled sea, which cannot rest: and the sins of some, like those of Babylon, reach up to heaven, and call for wrath and vengeance to come down from thence; sin causes the darkness of unregeneracy, and is often the reason of darkness to such who have been made light in the Lord; it intercepts the light of his countenance and of Christ, the Sun of Righteousness: now, as a cloud is dispersed and dissipated by the breaking forth of the sun, which, overcoming the cloud, scatters it, so as it is seen no more: in like manner, through the rising of the Sun of Righteousness, with healing in his wings.

5. By a non-remembrance of it: "And their iniquities will I remember no more!" Heb. viii. 12; Isa. xliii. 25. God forgives and forgets; having once forgiven them, he thinks of them no more.

6. By making sin, or rather sinners, white as snow; so David prays, "Wash me, and I shall be whiter than snow." Psa. li. 7. So the Lord promises, "Thy sins shall be as white as snow." Isa. i. 18. "Her Nazarites are purer than snow." Lam. iv. 7.

III. WHAT SINS ARE PARDONED? SINS BOTH WITH RESPECT TO QUALITY AND QUANTITY.

1. For quality; they are called trespasses. Sin is a walking on forbidden ground, for which a man must suffer, unless forgiven; and transgressions of the law of God; a passing over and going beyond the bounds and limits prescribed it: and iniquities, which are contrary to the rules of justice and equity; and sins, errors, aberrations, strayings from the rule of God's word: when God is said to forgive iniquity, transgression, and sin, it takes in every kind and sort of sin; sins are called abominations; not that they are so to sinners, for they delight in them; but to God, to whom they are so very disagreeable. Sin is defined, a transgression of the law, 1 John iii. 4, a breach, a violation of it; which accuses of it, pronounces guilty for it, and curses and condemns; and is only forgiven by the Lawgiver, who is able to save and destroy. Sins are sometimes represented as debts: because being committed, they oblige to the debt of punishment, which God remits; " Who forgiveth all thine iniquities." Psa. ciii. 3; Isa. xxxiii. 24; Mal. iv. 2.

2. For quantity; all trespasses, sins, and transgressions are forgiven. Col. ii. 13; Psa ciii. 3. Some are more secret, some more open, some less, others greater, more daring and presumptuous; some sins of commission, other sins of omission; but all are forgiven. See Isa. xliii. 22—25.

IV. THE EFFICIENT CAUSE IS GOD, AND NOT ANY CREATURE, ANGELS NOR MEN.

It is not in the power of men to forgive sin; one man may forgive another an offense, as committed against himself; but not as committed against God: saints ought to forgive one another's offenses that arise among them; as God, for Christ's sake, has forgiven them. Eph. iv. 32: Col. ii. 13.

2. There is nothing a man has, nor can do, by which he can procure the pardon of sin, either for himself, or for others:

1. No man, by his riches, and the multitude of his wealth, can give to God a ransom for himself, or his brother make atonement and satisfaction for sin, and obtain the pardon of it. Riches profit not in the day of wrath: bags of gold and silver will be of no avail.

2. Nor is pardon of sin to be obtained by works of righteousness: could it, it would not be of grace; for grace and works are opposed to each other; men would be saved by works, contrary to the scriptures, since pardon is included in salvation, and that is by grace, and not works.

3. Nor is pardon procured by repentance; they are both gifts of grace; and though given to the same persons, the one is not the cause of the other, at least, repentance is not the cause of remission; for true, evangelical repentance flows from, and in the exercise of it, is influenced by the discovery and application of pardoning grace. See Ezek. xvi. 63; Luke vii. 37, 47. Nor is pardon procured by faith, as the cause of it; faith does not obtain it by any virtue of its own, but receives it as obtained by the blood of Christ. Acts x. 43; xxvi. 18.

4. Nor is it procured by a submission to the ordinance of water baptism; baptism neither takes away original sin, nor actual sin, not as to the guilt thereof, as the case of Simon Magus shows; for though the three thousand are directed to be baptized in the name of Christ, for the remission of sins; and Saul was advised by Ananias to arise, and be baptized, and wash away his sins, Acts ii. 38; xxii. 16, yet the meaning is not, as if remission of sins were to be obtained by baptism; but that by means of this ordinance, they might be led to the sufferings, death, and bloodshed of Christ, represented in it.

3. God only can forgive sin; it is his sole prerogative; it belongs to him, and no other. Mark ii. 7; Isa. xliii. 25; Dan. ix. 9. And this appears from the nature of sin itself; it is committed against God; and none but he against whom it is committed can forgive it. Who is a God like unto him that pardoneth iniquity? Mic. vii. 18. Saints in all ages never made their application to any other. Psa. li. 1; Dan. ix. 19; Matt. vi. 9, 12; Acts viii. 22.

V. The effects of pardon, that is, when applied; for the effects of it are not sensibly perceived, unless applied; which are,

1. Peace of conscience; when sin is charged upon the conscience, and there is no sight and sense of pardon, there is no peace; but no sooner is there a view of interest in justification, by the righteousness of Christ, and pardon by his blood, but there is peace. Rom. v. 1.

2. Cheerfulness of spirit: when sin lies as a heavy burden, without a view of pardon, the mind is depressed; it is filled with gloominess, as in the case of Cain: a wounded spirit who can bear? But when the Lord says, "Son or daughter be of good cheer, thy sins are forgiven thee!" cheerfulness takes place; the spirits are raised; the head is lifted up. Psa. li. 8.

3. Comfort of soul: whilst a gracious soul, under a sense of sin, apprehends that God is angry with him, he has no comfort; but when he manifests his pardoning grace, then he concludes his anger is turned away, and he is comforted: "Speak ye comfortably to Jerusalem." Isa. xl. 1, 2.

4. Access to God with boldness and confidence; a soul, under the weight and pressure of the guilt of sin, moves heavily to the throne of grace; and when he comes there, cannot lift up his eyes; but, looking downward, and smiting on his breast, says, God be merciful to me a sinner; but when it has a view of the blood, righteousness, and sacrifice of Christ, it comes with liberty, boldness, and confidence. Rom. v. 1, 2.

5. Attendance on divine worship with pleasure and delight: this flows from a sense of forgiveness of sin, and is one end of it; "There is forgiveness with thee, that thou mayest be feared." Psa. cxxx. 5; Heb. xii. 28.

6. Love to God and Christ is raised, promoted, and increased, by an application of pardon. Luke vii. 47.

7. Evangelical repentance, and the exercise of it, are much influenced by pardon of sin being applied. Ezek. xvi. 63.

8. Thankfulness of soul for such a mercy; than which there cannot be a greater: if a man be truly impressed with the sense of it, he will call upon his soul, and all within him, to bless and praise the Lord for all his benefits; and particularly for this, who forgiveth all thy iniquities! Psa. ciii. 2, 3.

ON CONVERSION.

Acts iii. 19.—And be converted. (H.)

CONVERSION, though it may seem, in some respects, to fall in with regeneration, yet may be distinguished from it. Regeneration is the sole act of God; conversion consists both of God's act upon men, in turning them, and of acts done by men, under the influence of converting grace; they turn, being turned. Regeneration is the motion of God towards and upon the heart of a sinner; conversion is the motion of a sinner towards God, as one expresses it. In regeneration men are wholly passive, as they are also in the first moment of conversion; but by it become active; it is therefore sometimes expressed passively: Ye are returned or converted, 1 Pet. ii. 25; and sometimes actively; A great number believed, and turned to the Lord, Acts xi. 21, and when it, the body of the people of the Jews, shall turn to the Lord, which has respect to their conversion in the latter day. 2 Cor. iii. 16.

I. WHAT CONVERSION IS AND WHEREIN IT LIES: The conversion to be treated of is not,

1. An external one, or what lies only in an outward reformation of life and manners, such as that of the Ninevites, for this may be where internal conversion is not, as in the Scribes and Pharisees.

2. Nor is it a mere doctrinal one, nor a conversion from false notions before imbibed to a set of doctrines and truths which are according to the scriptures; so men of old were converted from Judaism and heathenism to christianity: but all that were so converted to a doctrinal sense were not true and real converts; some had "the form of godliness without the power, a name to live," &c.

3. Nor the restoration of the people of God from backsliding, when they are in a very affecting and importunate manner called upon to return to the Lord; Jer. iii. 12, 14, 22; Hos. xiv. 1—4; so Peter when he fell through temptation, and denied his Lord, and was recovered from it by a look from Christ, it is called his conversion, Luke xxii. 32. But,

4. The conversion under consideration, is a true, real, internal work of God upon the souls of men.

1. In the turn of the heart to God, of the thoughts of the heart; which are only evil, and that continually, and about evil things, not about God, and the things of God: God is not in all their thoughts, nor in any of the thoughts of wicked men; but when converted, their thoughts are about their state and condition by nature, about their souls, and their eternal welfare; it is a turn of the desires of the heart which before were after vain, sinful lusts and pleasures; but now after God and communion with him, after Christ

and salvation : of the affections of the heart, which before were inordinate, and ran in a wrong channel, towards God, their hearts being circumcised to love him ; and whom they love with their whole hearts and souls, because he first loved them. Conversion is a turn of the mind from carnal things to spiritual ones, and from earthly things to heavenly ones ; yea, it is a turn of the will, which before conversion is in a very bad state, is stubborn and inflexible, biassed to and bent upon that which is evil, and averse to all that is good ; but in conversion God works in men both to will and to do of his good pleasure.

2. Conversion lies in a man's being turned from darkness to light ; the apostle was sent to turn them from darkness to light, Acts xxvi. 18, that is, to be the instrument or means of their conversion, by preaching the gospel.

3. From the power of Satan unto God, as in the above place. Acts xxvi. 18. Satan has great power over men in an unconverted state, his seat is in their hearts, which are the palaces in which he rules ; he works effectually with great power and energy in the children of disobedience ; but now in conversion they are turned from his power, he is dispossessed of them, and his armour taken from him in which he trusted ; the prey is taken out of the hands of the mighty.

4. Conversion lies in turning men from idols, to serve the living God ; not merely from idols of silver and gold, of wood and stone, as formerly, but from the idols of a man's own heart, his lusts and corruptions ; with respect to which the language of a converted sinner is, what have I to do any more with idols ? this is a blessing bestowed in conversion. Unto you first, God having raised up his Son Jesus, sent him to bless you, in turning away every one of you from his iniquities.

5. Conversion lies in turning men from their own righteousness to the righteousness of Christ ; not from doing works of righteousness, for such converted persons are most fit for, and most capable of, and are under the greatest obligations to perform : but from depending upon them for justification before God, and acceptance with him.

6. Conversion lies in a man's turning to the Lord actively under the influence of divine grace : and by this phrase it is often expressed in scripture, as in Isa. x. 21 ; Acts xi. 21 ; 2 Cor. iii. 16 ; men being thoroughly convinced that there is salvation in no other but in Christ, that it is in vain to expect it elsewhere ; they turn to Christ as their Lord and lawgiver, and submit to his commands, renouncing all other lords, and their dominion over them ; and though in their natural state they are like sheep going astray, in conversion they are returned to Christ, as the great shepherd and bishop of souls.

II. THE CAUSES OF CONVERSION.

1. The efficient cause, which is not man, but God.

1. Not by the power of man ; what is said of the conversion, or turning of the Jews from their captivity, is true of the conversion of a sinner, that it is not by might, nor by power, that is, not of man, but by my Spirit, saith the Lord of Hosts. Zech. iv. 6. Men are dead in a moral sense whilst unconverted ; they are dead in trespasses and sins, which are the cause of their death ; and their very living in them is no other than a moral death : nor can they quicken themselves, and unless they are quickened, they cannot be converted. Conversion is such an alteration in a man as is not in his power to effect ; it is like that of an Ethiopian changing his skin, and a leopard his spots. Such things are never heard of, as a blackmoor becoming wnite, and a leopard becoming clear of his spots ; and as unlikely is it, that a man should

convert himself. Jer. xiii. 23. A tree must first be made good, so as to bring forth good fruit.

2. Nor is conversion owing to the will of men; the will of man, before conversion is in a bad state; it chooses its own ways, and delights in its abominations, it is in high pursuit after the desires of the flesh and of the mind. Conversion is denied to be of the will of men; as the whole of salvation is not of him that willeth, so this part of it in particular; regeneration, with which conversion, in the first moment of it, agrees, is not the will of the flesh, nor of the will of man, but of God. Rom. ix. 16; John i. 13.

3. God only is the author and efficient cause of conversion. He that made man's heart, and formed the spirit of man within him, he only can turn their hearts, and frame and mould their spirits, as he pleases; the heart of a king, and so of every other man, is in the hand of the Lord; he makes his people willing in the day of his power, to do what they had before no will nor inclination to do, and yet they act most freely; the man-slayer did not more willingly flee to a city of refuge to shelter him from the avenger of blood, than a sinner, sensible of his danger, flees to Christ for refuge, and lays hold on the hope set before him.

2. The moving or impulsive cause of conversion, is the love, grace, mercy, favor, and good will of God; and not the merits of men; for what is there in men before conversion, to move God to take such a step in their favor; see 1 Cor. vi. 9—11; Eph. ii. 2—4.

3. The instrumental cause, or means of conversion, is usually the ministry of the word; sometimes, indeed, it is wrought without the word, by some remarkable, awakening providence or another, and sometimes by reading the scriptures; but, for the most part, it is through the preaching of the word; hence, ministers are said to turn many to righteousness: and the apostle Paul says, he was sent by Christ unto the Gentile world, to turn men from darkness to light; and this is done both by the preaching of the law and the gospel. The law of the Lord is perfect, converting the soul, Ps. xix. 7, the preaching of the law is made use of by the Spirit of God, to convince of sin, for by the law is the knowledge of sin; though some take this to be rather preparatory to conversion, than conversion itself, which may be ascribed to the gospel. Received ye the Spirit by the works of the law? that is, by preaching the doctrine of obedience to it; or, by the hearing of faith? that is, by the doctrine of the gospel, preaching faith in Christ; which is therefore called the word of faith, and by which it comes; for faith comes by hearing, and hearing by the word of God; Gal. iii. 2; Rom. x. 8—17; but then, the preaching of the word of the gospel is not sufficient of itself to produce the work of conversion in the heart: men may hear it, and not be converted by it; for who is Paul, or who is Apollos, but ministers, or instruments, by whom ye believed? 1 Cor. iii. 5.

III. The subjects of conversion.

Lost sinners redeemed by Christ are the subjects—I will hiss for them, by the ministry of the word, and gather them, which is another phrase for conversion, because I have redeemed them. Zech. x. 8. Sinners shall be converted unto thee; Ps. li. 13; sinners by nature and by practice, and some of them the worst and chief of sinners; and therefore the wonderful grace of God is the more displayed in their conversion. 1 Cor. vi. 11; 1 Tim. i. 3, 14, 15.

REGENERATION CONSIDERED IN ITS CAUSES AND BENEFITS.

1 Pet. i. 3—5.—Blessed be the God, and Father of our Lord Jesus Christ, which according to his abundant mercy, hath begotten us again unto a lively hope, by the resurrection of Jesus Christ from the dead. To an inheritance incorruptible, and undefiled, and that fadeth not away, reserved in heaven for you, who are kept by the power of God, through faith, unto salvation, ready to be revealed in the last time. (S. S.)

THE ungodly may be patient, but are seldom joyful, in affliction—
Their happiness almost entirely depends on outward circumstances—
But the regenerate have sources of joy peculiar to themselves—
Nor can they be in any state wherein they have not abundant cause to bless God—
The persons to whom St. Peter wrote, were scattered abroad, and in a state of persecution—
Yet he begins his epistle to them, not in terms of pity and condolence, but of praise and thanksgiving.
I. THE CAUSES OF REGENERATION.
Regeneration is a spiritual and supernatural change of heart—
But the text requires us to consider it not so much in its nature, as in its causes—
The *efficient* cause of it is God.
God under the Old Testament dispensation, was the God of Abraham—
Under the gospel, he appears under the more endearing title, "the God and Father of our Lord Jesus Christ"—
He is our God and Father also in and through Christ Jesus—
In this relation he is considered as begetting us again—
And he certainly is the Father of our spirits, both in their first formation, and in their subsequent renovation, Compare Heb. xii. 9, with Eph. ii. 10.
The *final* cause or end is our present and eternal happiness.
God begets his people to "a lively hope" *here*—
Their hope is widely different from the cold and carnal hope of the unregenerate—
He has prepared for them also an "inheritance" *hereafter*—
And this inheritance is unspeakably glorious—
Not corruptible, as earthly "treasures, which moth and rust will corrupt"—
Not defiled, like the earthly Canaan, by wicked inhabitants—
Not fading, by use, age, or enjoyment, like the pleasures of sense—
The *instrumental* cause is the Lord Jesus Christ,
Christ is the medium of every blessing, whether of grace or glory—
Our blessings are generally represented as imparted through his death—
But here, as in many other places, they are ascribed to his resurrection—
His resurrection assured to us the acceptance of his sacrifice—
It is also a pledge and earnest of the resurrection of all his members—
Besides, it enables him both to intercede for us, and to send the Spirit to us—
His Word and Spirit are, indeed, the more immediate instruments which God uses—
Yet more remotely may the Resurrection of Christ be considered as the instrumental cause of our regeneration—
The *moving* cause of it is his mercy.
God has not respect to any goodness or merit in the creature—
He is actuated only by his own grace and "mercy"—

Of this the conversion of a soul is a marvelous display—

If the state of a converted person be compared with that of one unconverted, or of one that has perished, he will appear to have experienced "abundant mercy"—

They who have experienced this change are sure to possess at last the benefits connected with it.

II. THE SECURITY OF THE REGENERATE.

Some even of the regenerate are ready to doubt whether God will bestow on them the inheritance they hope for—

Others fear they shall fall short of it through their own frailty—

But God has secured to them the full and everlasting enjoyment of it—

The inheritance is "reserved for them."

Earthly inheritances may be taken away by fraud and violence—

Not even crowns or kingdoms can boast of any stability—

But the saints inheritance is in heaven—

There it is out of the reach of all enemies—

God himself keeps it for his people, as their unalienable right—

They also are kept for it.

They are weak and helpless in themselves—

They are surrounded also with hosts of enemies—

But they commit themselves to God "by faith"—

In so doing they interest the power of God on their behalf—

God keeps them according to his promise, Isa. xxvi. 3 ; Jer. xxxii. 40.

God keeps them as in an impregnable garrison*—

God keeps them unto their full and final salvation—

INFER,

1. How happy are God's people here !

The change they have experienced in regeneration is truly blessed—

The prospects they enjoy are bright and glorious—

Their security enhances these blessings—

What then need they regard in this world ?—

Surely they should rejoice, though in the midst of tribulations—

Let every one then, when encompassed with troubles of whatever kind say, "Blessed be God, who hath begotten me again"—

2. How happy will God's people soon be !

Their inheritance, though at a distance, is a consolation to them—

The very hope of it fills them with joy unspeakable—

It will do this, even under the heaviest afflictions—

What sensations then will the full enjoyment of this inheritance excite !—

What joy will that be when it is without any alloy of sin or sorrow !—

But let us remember, that " we must be born again" in order to have any title to this inheritance, John iii. 3.

If we continue unregenerate, we shall inherit a far different portion—

But if we have really experienced the new birth, we are heirs of glory—

And the salvation reserved for us is " ready to be revealed"—

Let us then labor to secure this glorious inheritance—

And look for it with holy ardour and eager expectation—

This seems to be the import of the word φρουρουμένους

CONVERSION A GROUND OF THANKFULNESS.

Rom. vi. 17. God be thanked, that ye were the servants of sin; but ye have obeyed from the heart that form of doctrine which was delivered you. (S. S.)

EXEMPTION from the punishment of sin is doubtless an inestimable blessing—

But deliverance from its power is equally precious—

The most advanced christians greatly delight in this part of salvation—

Hence St. Paul thanks God for bestowing this mercy on the church at Rome—

We shall consider from the text,

I. THE CHARACTER OF ALL WHILE IN AN UNCONVERTED STATE.

All are "servants of sin" till they receive converting grace.

All indeed are not slaves to the same sin—

Some are led captive by their lusts and passions—

Others are drawn away by the pleasures and vanities of the world—

Others are under the dominion of pride and self-righteousness—

But all without exception are alienated from the life of God, Eph. iv. 18.

All are full of unbelief and self-sufficiency—

This, however humiliating, is an indisputable truth.

The scriptures every where assert this respecting fallen man, John viii. 34; Rom vi. 16, with the text.

The most eminent saints confess it to have been their own case, Tit. iii. 3

Experience proves it with respect to ourselves—

The very excuse which men offer in extenuation of their sins, viz. "that they *cannot* live as God requires," establishes this truth—

But it does not remain so in regenerate persons; as appears from

II. THE CHANGE THEY EXPERIENCE IN CONVERSION.

God instructs them in "the form of sound doctrine."

They hear the declarations of God in his word—

They are enlightened by the Spirit to understand them—

They have the word applied with divine efficacy to their souls—

This form of doctrine they "obey from the heart."

They yet indeed feel a law of sin in their members—

But "they no more serve sin" willingly as before—

On the contrary, "they now delight in the law of God"—

They obey it, not in appearance only or by constraint, but willingly and without reserve—

They are now cast, as it were, into the mould of the gospel.

This is the force of the original; and is the marginal version—

This is also the case, wherever the gospel takes effect, Col. i. 6.

The wax has every lineament of the seal, and the coin of the die—

So do they resemble God, who are renewed by the gospel, 2 Cor. iii 18.

The blessedness of this change will appear if we consider,

III. HOW GREAT A CAUSE OF THANKFULNESS SUCH A CONVERSION IS.

The apostle thanks God that they were no longer slaves of sin.

Sin is at all times a ground of shame and sorrow, Rom. vi. 21.

Paul esteemed it so in his own particular case, 1 Tim. i. 13.

Every saint of God views it in the same light—

St. Paul therefore did not mean that their subjection to it was a ground of thankfulness—

But the subject of his thanksgiving is, that the Romans, who once were slaves of sin, were now entirely devoted to God—

This is a ground of unspeakable thankfulness on many accounts.

1. On account of *the moral change* in the persons themselves.

What can be more deplorable than to be a slave of sin!—

What can be more amiable than to have all our actions and affections corresponding with the the word of God?—

Surely this is a ground of thankfulness—

2. On account of *the effects* of this change *on society.*

How much better member of society must a child of God be than a slave of sin!—

How much happier would the world be, if such a change were general!—

On this account therefore it became the apostle to be thankful—

3. On account of *the eternal consequences* that must follow this change.

They who die slaves of sin must suffer its punishment—

They are now the children of the devil, and must soon be his companions in misery, John viii. 44.

But the regenerate are children and heirs of God—

Surely eternity will scarcely suffice to thank God for this—

We shall conclude with a suitable ADDRESS,

1. To the unregenerate.

All who have not been freed from sin are of this number—

Alas! the friends of such have little cause to thank God for them—

They have rather reason to weep and mourn, Jer. xiii. 17.

They may indeed bless God that the stroke of vengeance has been delayed—

O that all such persons might know the day of their visitation!—

Let all cry to God for his converting grace—

Nor let any rest in an external or partial change—

Nothing but a cordial compliance with the gospel, and a real conformity to it, will avail us in the day of judgment—

2. To the regenerate.

The foregoing marks have sufficiently characterized these persons—

Such persons will do well to reflect on the mercy they have received—

The recollection of their past guilt will serve to keep them *humble*—

A consciousness of their remaining infirmities will make them *watchful*—

A view of the change wrought in them will make them *thankful*—

Let the regenerate then adopt the words of the Psalmist, Ps. ciii. 1—3.

Let them beware of ever returning to their former ways, 2 Pet. ii. 20, 21.

Let them press forward for higher degrees of holiness and glory, Phil. iii 13, 14.

3. To those who doubt to which class they belong.

Many, from what has been wrought in them, have reason to hope—

Yet, from what still remains to be done, they find reason to fear—

Hence they are long in painful suspense—

But let such remember, that sin, if truly lamented and resisted, does not prove them unregenerate, Jam. iii. 2.

On the contrary, their hatred of it, and opposition to it, are hopeful signs that they are in part renewed—

Nevertheless, let them endeavor to put this matter beyond a doubt, 2 Pet. i. 10.

Let them look to Christ as their almighty deliverer, John viii. 36.

Let them pray for, and depend upon, his promised aid, 2 Cor. xii. 9,

THE IMPORTANCE OF SANCTIFICATION.

Col iii. 11.—Christ is all, and in all.* (H. H.)

In order to ascertain the true sense of any passage of scripture, two things are to be attended to: we should mark the scope of the context, and compare the terms or phrases with similar passages of Holy Writ. By separating these canons of interpretation, we shall often overlook the true meaning of God's word, and put upon it a forced construction; whereas, if we unite them, we shall almost always find its just import.

It is undeniable that the verses which precede and follow our text refer to sanctification; see ver. 1—14; nor is there any thing which properly relates to our justification: and therefore we have a strong presumptive ground for interpreting the words of our text in reference to the new nature, which is spoken of in the verse immediately before it: nor could any thing but the peculiarity of the expression lead one for a moment to look for any other sense. But it seems that to interpret the word " Christ," as meaning the image of Christ, or the New Man, is to take a great, and almost an unwarrantable, liberty with scripture. Nevertheless, if we compare some other passages with the text,† we shall find that we are fully authorized to put this construction upon it, and that there is no necessity to understand it in any other way than that which the context so evidently requires.

The meaning then of the words before us is simply this. We should be daily putting off our old and corrupt nature, and be putting on a new and holy nature; because nothing else will be at all regarded by God: whatever advantages we possess, we have nothing, if we be not holy: on the other hand, whatever disadvantages we labor under, we shall suffer no loss, if we be holy: for the image of "Christ" on the soul "is all, in all" persons, and under all circumstances: where that is, God will be pleased; and where that is not, he will be eternally displeased.

In order to confirm this momentous truth, we shall shew, that, in the eyes of God, *our restoration to the divine image "is all in all."* It is,

I. THE ONE SCOPE OF ALL HIS PLANS—

What did he design in the redemption of the world at large?

When first he determined to rescue man from perdition, he decreed that he would " create us anew in Christ Jesus *unto good works,* in which he ordained that we should walk." Eph. ii. 10.

The means which he used for the accomplishment of our salvation had especial respect to this end, not to save us *in* our sins, but *from* them. Matt. i. 21; Acts iii. 26.

* The author has formerly treated this text as Commentators in general have done, in reference to our justification before God. But he apprehends on further consideration, that it refers rather to our sanctification. In either sense, the position is true, that " Christ is all ;" but the latter interpretation seems more exactly to convey the mind of the Spirit in this passage. The reader, by comparing the two statements. will be enabled to judge for himself.

† See 2 Cor. xiii. 5, where " Christ in us" must be understood of his image, because it is that whereby we are to ascertain whether we be in the faith. See also Gal. iv. 19, where " Christ formed in us" cannot be understood of Christ *personally,* but of Christ *spiritually,* i. e. of his image. Above all, see Rom. xiii 14, where the very metaphor which occurs in our context, is used. " Put on the new man," says our context, " for Christ," i. e. the putting on of Christ, or of the new man, " is all." And, in the passage referred to, is the very expression, " Put ye on the Lord Jesus Christ."

He sent his only dear Son to take our nature, and in that nature to live, to die, to rise again. But in all this he aimed, not at our happiness merely, but our restoration to the image which we had lost. Gal. i. 4; 1 Pet. i. 18, 19, and ii. 24; Tit. ii. 14. This is specified in terms peculiarly strong and energetic, in order that we may not overlook this truth as if it were only of secondary importance. Eph. v. 25—27.

He gave his Holy Spirit also for the same end: he gave him to humble us, John xvi. 8—11, to renew us, Tit. iii. 5, 6, to mortify all our vile lusts and passions, Rom. viii. 13, to fashion us after the divine image,* and to perfect that image in our souls. 2 Cor. iii. 18.

What does he design in imparting that redemption to individuals?

Wherefore did he choose any of us from before the foundation of the world? It was "that we might be holy, and without blame before him in love." Eph. i. 4. Why has he revealed his grace in our hearts? It was to "teach us, that, denying ungodliness and worldly lusts, we should live righteously, soberly, and godly in this present world." Tit. ii. 11, 12. If he apply his promises to our souls, or hide his face from us, it is alike for our profit, that we may be partakers of his holiness." 2 Cor. vii. 1, with Heb. xii. 10. Whatever be his dispensations towards us, "this is his will, even our sanctification;" 1 Thess. iv. 3; and this is his ultimate design in all, even to "carry on the good work he has begun," Phil. i. 6, to "sanctify us wholly," 1 Thess. v. 23, and to "perfect that which concerneth us." Psa. cxxxviii. 8.

But holiness is also,

II. THE ONE OBJECT OF HIS REGARD—

Nothing but that is regarded by him in this world—

The external ordinances of religion are not only worthless, but even hateful, in his sight, if destitute of solid piety. Isa. i. 11—16. On the other hand, the smallest particle of genuine goodness is not overlooked by him. 1 Kings xiv. 13. Even the semblance of it has sometimes been rewarded by him, in order that he might shew to mankind how great a value he has for it, where it really exists. 1 Kings xxi. 29. One single disposition is declared by him to be of great price in his sight. 1 Pet. iii. 4. The purposes which have never been realized in act, are highly commended by him. 1 Kings viii. 18. And wherever he sees a person laboring to do his will, he invariably reveals to him his love in a more abundant measure, John xiv. 23, and communicates to him his richest blessings. Isa. lviii. 10, 11.

Nothing but that will be regarded by him in the world to come—

When we shall stand at the judgment-seat of Christ, the inquiry will be, not, what we have professed, but what we have done: Matt. vii. 21—23, and xxv. 31—46; and a Gentile who has served God according to the light that he enjoyed, will be preferred before the christian, who has not made a suitable improvement of his superior advantages. Rom. ii. 25—27. Apparently trivial occurrences will be noticed in that day; and rewards will be dispensed, not according to the greatness and splendor of our actions, but according to their intrinsic qualities, and to the principle evinced by them. Matt. x. 42. We must not indeed imagine that there is any *merit* in our poor services, for there is imperfection in them all; and, "if we had done all that is commanded us, we should be only unprofitable servants:" but God delights in holiness; and wherever he beholds it, he will, of his own

---

*Eph. iv. 23, 24, with 2 Cor. i. 22. A "seal" is an impress of the divine image; and an "earnest" is the commencement of heavenly purity and joy.

grace and mercy, bestow upon it a proportionate reward, exalting those to the highest thrones in glory, who have made the greatest improvement of the talents committed to them. Matt. xxv. 19—23.

There will be no distinction made, except what is grounded on the different degrees of conformity to the divine image which the different individuals have attained. God will not respect the circumcised more than the uncircumcised, or the rich and learned more than the poor and illiterate. In all persons equally the image of Christ will be sought for; and the possession, or want of it, will determine their eternal state: "Christ will then be, as he now is, all, and in all.

We conclude with INQUIRING, *Who amongst you is like-minded with God?*

1. Ye children of this world—

How far are ye from according with God! With him, *Christ* is all; with you, *the world.* If ye may but enjoy the pleasures, the honors, the riches of the world, ye care not about the image of Christ: to be rich in faith and good works is no' the object of your ambition: *that* you leave to the old, the sick, the enthusiasts. But ah! if Christ be *all*, as indeed he is, think what a vanity ye are pursuing: think how poor ye will be in the day of judgment; and how you will then execrate your present ways. Be persuaded to be wise in time: and beg without delay that "Christ may be made unto you wisdom, and righteousness, and sanctification, and redemption." 1 Cor. i. 30.

2. Ye self-deceiving professors—

How many are there in the church, who will talk about Christ, and speak of him as the ground of all their hopes, while yet they are shamefully destitute of his image! Yes, grievous it is to say, that there are "many vaintalkers and deceivers" now, as well as in the apostolic age; many that are proud and passionate; many that are earthly-minded and covetous; many that are unchaste and lewd; many that are deceitful in their words, and dishonest in their dealings; many in short, whose tempers, and dispositions, and conduct, are a disgrace to their profession. Know ye, if such there be here present, that ye are as unlike to God as Satan himself is; and that all your knowledge, all your experiences, and all your professions, will only aggravate your condemnation, if you die in your present state. Job xxxvi. 13. You do well to rely on Christ, and to make him your *all* in point of dependence; but know for a certainty, that, however you may pretend to trust in him, you never can be saved by him, unless you become new creatures: 2 Cor. 5, 17; for "without holiness no man shall see the Lord." Heb. xii. 14.

3. Ye true believers—

You can appeal to God that you are like-minded with him in this grand point; and that you desire as much to be saved from sin, as to be delivered from hell itself. This is a blessed evidence that ye are born of God. 1 John iii. 10. While ye are thus panting after holiness, ye have nothing to fear; your faith is sound, James ii. 22, your hope is scriptural, 1 John iii. 3, and saving. Rom. v. 5, and viii. 24. Go on then from grace to grace, from strength to strength. 2 Pet. iii. 18. Be daily putting off the old man with its lusts, ver. 8, 9, and putting on the new man with all its characteristic graces. Ver. 12, 13. Be "growing up thus into Christ in all things as your living Head," Eph. iv. 15, till you have arrived at "the full measure of the stature of Christ:" ib. ver. 13; and when you have attained a perfec' meetness for the enjoyment of your God, you shall be like him, and with him for ever. 1 John iii. 2.

THE EXCELLENCY AND EFFICACY OF THE GOSPEL.

2 Cor. iii. 18. But we all with open face beholding, as in a glass, the glory of the Lord, are changed into the same image, from glory to glory, even as by the Spirit of the Lord. (S. S.)

The Jews, when compared with the heathen world, were highly privileged—

But the dispensation under which they lived was in every respect inferior to that of the gospel—

The apostle, in vindicating his own character, incidentally mentions the blessings which the Corinthians had experienced by means of his ministry—

Hence he takes occasion to set forth the superior excellency of the gospel above the law—

In confirmation of this point we will consider,

I. THE EXCELLENCY OF THE GOSPEL.

In the context the law is spoken of as a ministration of condemnation—

Whereas the gospel is a ministration of the Spirit and of righteousness—

It is a revelation of the "glory of the Lord."

The law was in some degree a manifestation of the divine glory—

It displayed, however, chiefly the majesty and holiness of the Deity—

But the gospel displays the love and mercy of God—

It exhibits all the perfections of God harmonizing and glorified in the work of redemption—

Thus it is a revelation of the glory of God in the face of Jesus Christ, 2 Cor. iv. 6.

It manifests this glory to the soul.

Moses veiled the divine lustre which shined in his face—

This was an intimation to the Jews that they could not comprehend the full scope of the law which he published, ver. 13.

But this veil is taken away by Christ, ver. 14.

The gospel reflects Christ's glory as a mirror reflects the sun—

We behold that glory "with open, i. e. *unveiled* face"—

This is the common privilege of "all" who believe—

Nor is it more excellent in its discoveries than in its effects.

II. THE EFFICACY OF IT.

The apostle ascribes a wonderful efficacy to the gospel—

Experience attests the truth of his declarations—

It transforms the soul into the divine image.

A view of Jehovah's glory caused the face of Moses to shine—

So a view of Christ's glory in the gospel changes our hearts—

It renews us after the very image of our Lord and Savior—

It does this, notwithstanding we may have been hitherto most abandoned—

Every fresh discovery which it makes to us of Christ's glory increases that effect.

The first exercise of faith in Christ makes a great change—

But subsequent views of his glory advance the work of sanctification—

In this way is our progress in holiness carried on to perfection—

This power, however, it derives wholly from "the Spirit of the Lord."

The gospel has not that power in itself—

Were its power inherent, it would operate uniformly on all—

But its operation is dependent on the will of God, 1 Cor. xii. 11.

The word is called "the sword of the Spirit"—

It is the Spirit's instrument whereby he subdues souls to the obedience of faith—

Every fresh effect produced by it arises from the concurring operation of the Spirit—

Yet, as it is the great instrument whereby the Spirit works, the effects are properly ascribed to—

INFER,

1. How great a blessing it is to have the gospel preached to us
Nothing else will produce the effects here ascribed to the gospel—
The terrors of the law may alarm, but will not sanctify the heart—
But the mild accents of the gospel win the soul—
A manifestation of Christ's glory constrains us to obedience—
Let all rejoice therefore in hearing the glad tidings—
Let all endeavor to experience these glorious effects—
2. Whence it is that many make so small a proficiency in holiness.
Many truly desire to advance in holiness—
But they seek it in dependence on their own strength—
Hence they make a small proficiency in the divine life—
They should rather use the means prescribed in the text—
They should be often occupied in surveying the glory of Christ—
The discoveries of his glory would do more than all their legal exertions—
Let every eye therefore be fixed on him, till the effects appear both in our hearts and lives—
Our views of him ere long shall be incomparably brighter, 1 Cor. xiii. 12
Then the effects also shall be proportionably increased, 1 John iii. 2.

THE GOSPEL FREES MEN FROM SIN AND DEATH.

Rom. viii. 2.—The law of the Spirit of life in Christ Jesus hath made me free from the law of sin and death. (S. S.)

THE world in general account it liberty to live loose to their passions—

But such freedom is indeed the sorest bondage to sin and Satan, Rom. vi. 16.

None possess true liberty but those who are freed by Christ, John viii. 36.

The state of the demoniacs when healed by Christ resembled theirs, Luke viii. 35.

Paul was made a glorious example of it to all ages—

He was once under condemnation, both because he adhered to the covenant of works, and was governed by his own impetuous will—

He now rejoiced in a freedom from the sin that he had indulged, and from the curse to which he had subjected himself—" The law of," &c.

We shall first *explain*, and then *improve* the text.

I. EXPLAIN IT.

It is not needful to state the various interpretations given of the text—

We shall adopt that which seems most easy, and agreeable to the context—

We will begin with *explaining the terms*.

" The law of the Spirit of life in Christ Jesus" is the gospel covenant as confirmed to us in Christ, and revealed to us by the Spirit.

The "Spirit of life" is the Holy Ghost, who is the author and preserver of spiritual life, John iii. 5. Eph. iii. 16.

The "law" of the Spirit is the gospel as revealed and applied by him— It is called a law because it has all the essential properties of a law*—

It is often spoken of as a law both by prophets and apostles, Isaiah ii. 3 Rom. iii. 27.

It is said to be the law of the Spirit "in Christ Jesus," because the blessings of the gospel are treasured up in Christ, confirmed to us through Christ, and received by us from Christ, Col. i. 19; 2 Cor. i. 20; John i. 16.

"The law of sin and death" may be understood either of the covenant of works or of our indwelling corruption.

The covenant of works is a "law" to which all are by nature subject—

It is called the "law of sin and death," because both sin and death come by that law†

Our indwelling corruption also operates as "a law" within us, Rom. vii 23.

It invariably hurries us on to "sin and death," Rom. vii. 5.

We shall next *explain the proposition contained in the terms.*

The proposition is, that "the gospel frees us from the curse of the law, and from the dominion of sin."

When we embrace the gospel we cease to be under the covenant of works, Rom. vi. 14, latter part.

We then partake of all the blessings which Christ has purchased for us—

We are liberated from the condemnation due to sin, Rom. viii. 1.

We are freed, through the aid of the Spirit, from the power of sin, Rom. viii. 13; and vi. 14, former part.

This proposition is to be understood as extending to all believers.

It is not true with respect to the apostles only—

It was exemplified in all the first converts‡—

And is experienced still by every sincere christian—

The text thus explained is capable of most useful improvement.

II. IMPROVE IT.

It is replete with very important *instruction.*

It shews us the wretched state of every unregenerate man.

We are all in bondage to "the law of sin and death"—

We are justly subjected to the curses of the broken law, Gal. iii. 10.

We are also led captive by our own corrupt appetites—

Even St. Paul himself was in this very state, Rom. vii. 9.

Let us then humble ourselves under a conviction of this truth—

It declares to us the only method of deliverance from that state.

It was the gospel which freed the apostle—

The same will avail for every other person—

We must however "obey the gospel," and receive it as our "law of faith"—

---

* A law is a precept enforced with sanctions; and such is the gospel: it is a precept, 1 John iii. 23; and it is enforced with the most encouraging and awful sanctions, Mark xvi. 16.

† Without that law there had been no transgression, and consequently, no sin (which is the transgression of a law;) nor death (which is the penalty inflicted for transgression)— Compare 1 John iii. 4. Rom. v. 13. 1 Cor. xv. 56. Hence it is called "the ministration of death and condemnation." 2 Cor. iii. 7, 9.

‡ One hour they were full of guilt and wickedness; the next they were rejoicing in the pardon of their sins, and in the practice of all holy duties. Acts ii. 46, 47

We must look for its blessings from Christ through the Spirit—

In this way we may all adopt the language of the text in reference to our own happy existence—

It affords also abundant matter of *reproof*.

It reproves those who despond as though there were no hope for them.

Many think their guilt too great to be pardoned, and their lusts too strong to be subdued—

But Paul's case was intended to prevent such desponding fears, 1 Tim. i. 16.

Let none therefore any more complain like those of old, Ezek. xxxvii. 11.

Every one may find encouragement in the power and mercy of God, Isa. lvi. 1.

It reproves also those who speak against an assurance of faith.

It would indeed be presumptuous in some to profess an assurance of faith—

But God is desirous that all his people should enjoy it, 1 John v. 13.

Let not any one therefore reprobate it as presumption—

Let every one rather seek the assurance expressed in the text—

It may administer *comfort* also to many sincere christians. .

Many are yet fighting against their manifold corruptions—

And because they obtain not a perfect deliverance, they tremble under apprehensions of the divine wrath—

But Paul himself bewailed bitterly his indwelling corruption, Rom. vii. 24.

Yet that did not prevent him from rejoicing in the partial freedom he experienced—

Let upright souls take comfort from this reflection.

TRUE BELIEVERS THE CHILDREN OF GOD.

Gal. iii. 26.—For ye are all the children of God, &c. (H.)

In the context the apostle shows the superior excellency of the gospel dispensation to that of the law. Those who were under it, were "shut up," &c. Ver. 23. It was only as a schoolmaster, &c. Ver. 24. The blessings of heaven are no longer confined to one nation, but extend to all; ver. 28; and especially to all true believers—"For ye are all the children of God," &c. I shall,

I. CONSIDER THE SONSHIP OF BELIEVERS UNDER THE GOSPEL.

I need scarcely observe, that believers are not the sons of God in the same sense as our blessed Lord, whose generation is ineffable; being one in nature, perfections, and glory with the Father.—But,

1. In common with the other intelligent creatures of God. In this respect, they have all one Father. In a peculiar manner, he is the Father of Spirits. In the intellectual powers, moral endowments, and immortality of the soul, they resemble him, for these are his image. Hence angels are called his sons, and Adam, the son of God; nay, the whole human race is said to be his off-spring. Acts xvii. 29.

2. They are children of God by their external profession, and a peculiar relation to him. In this sense, Israel is called his first-born, and his son, Hos. xi. 1; Matt. ii. 15.

3 This sonship consists chiefly in their regeneration and adoption. By the last, there is a change in their state. Formerly they were the slaves of Satan, and rebels; but now the friends of God, as was Abraham. By regeneration there is a change in their principles, disposition, and practice. They are born again, 1 Peter i. 23, and are partakers of the divine nature. The resemblance is real, though greatly inferior to the original. Hence, God is not ashamed to be called their God, nor is Christ ashamed to call them brethren. Which leads me to observe,

4. That this sonship is not a mere title or mark of distinction, but has privileges the most excellent annexed to it: there is no condemnation to them: they are his temples; led by his Spirit; abide in their Father's house; yea, in his heart and love; but particularly,

They have a title to incorruption and immortality, or a blessed resurrection. The body must die, but it is redeemed as well as the soul; was his habitation, while here, through the Spirit, and an instrument in his service; and he will raise it again. Rom. viii. 23.

They are born to a great inheritance. Though children of wrath by nature, yet, in virtue of adoption, they are heirs of salvation with eternal glory. They are heirs of God himself, Rom. viii. 17, and have indeed a goodly heritage. Psa. xvi. 5.

5. This sonship is equally the privilege of every believer in Christ. "Ye are all the children of God," says the apostle. They may be distinguished from each other, as to external circumstances in life, spiritual gifts and graces, but their filial relation is the same.

6. It is a privilege of which they are conscious, and hence they enjoy the comfort of it: with holy confidence, they cry, Abba, Father; Gal. iv. 6; and delight in approaching to him, with a childlike holy boldness in prayer.

II. How it is that they attain to this privilege and dignity.— The text says, by faith in Christ Jesus. To illustrate this, it may be proper to recollect,

1. That in the state of primitive innocence, Adam was truly the son of God: he resembled God. Gen. i. 27. This resemblance was effaced by sin, his former relation to God as his son then ceased, and he was turned out of God's family and garden as a rebel, while he and his numerous progeny became children of disobedience and wrath.

2. It is by faith, or a supernatural revelation only, that we are informed how this high prerogative of sonship may be regained. This surpassed the capacity of the wisest philosopher, and even of angels themselves. It is brought to light by the gospel. Gal. iv. 4, 5.

What a marvellous climax, and cluster of divine prodigies are here! Recount them with admiration! The mission and incarnation of God's own Son—his abject condition as a servant, under the grievous yoke of the law—himself a ransom for the slaves of sin—these slaves taken into fellowship with himself—to whom he grants this divine filiation!

3. We become the children of God, when we cordially believe in Christ: we are thereby brought into union with Christ, and into a dear relation to God, as his Father and ours. We are then born of God, and have the principle or seed of the life of God in the soul; and, consequently, are his children, and in an adopted state; suitable to that relation. John i. 12. To conclude.

1. From what has been said, let me address the children of God in the words of the beloved apostle. 1 John iii. 1. Be astonished ye heavenly principalities and powers, to see such base-born slaves, and rebellious crea-

tures taken into the family of God; rank in dignity with you, and made **heirs** of the same inheritance. Unmeasurable love!

The immunities and glory of the adopted state are beyond description. It is an adoption procured at an infinite price, and elevates to high honor. "Is it a light thing," said David, "to be the king's son-in-law?" But what is this when compared to that of being the sons and daughters of the Almighty.

2. Forget not the love and duty, submission and service, that results from this relation. If I be a father, says God, where is mine honor?

Should not this filial relation reconcile you to the cross, though heavy? It is the lot assigned by Infinite Wisdom, and sent in great kindness. Heb. xii. 6.

Are you indeed of the same family and Father? What a mighty motive is this to love as brethren, to be pitiful, and courteous, and kindly affected one to another, forbearing and forgiving one another, &c.

While mingled here with the children of this world, be watchful least you imbibe their spirit, learn their ways and vices, stain your character, and be a scandal to your profession. Remember that you have in you the blood-royal of heaven, and being washed in the blood of Jesus from your sins, return not to wallow in the mire—That ye may be blameless. Phil. ii. 15.

3. How insipid, alas! are subjects of this kind to the generality even of gospel hearers! Show them how to acquire a fortune,&c., and they will be all attention; but publish the riches of God's gracious adoption, they relish it not. Blinded sinner, what a fatal choice dost thou make! What though thou hadst the wisdom of a Solomon, the wealth of a Crœsus, the beauty of an Absalom, and were as high in dignity and power as ever Haman was, if thou art not a child of God, thou shalt at last lie down in sorrow, and be brought out of the grave to the day, the dreadful day of the perdition of ungodly men.

THE INCREASE OF CHRIST'S KINGDOM.

John iii. 30.—He must increase. (H.)

THESE are the words of John the Baptist, in answer to a complaint which his disciples made concerning Christ, who, it appears, was baptising great multitudes; v. 26; afraid, perhaps, that he would eclips the glory of their Master. John tells them, that he had told them before that he was not the Messiah, but his forerunner; and that now he was come, his joy was fulfilled, v. 29. He, says he, must increase. I shall consider,

I. WHAT THE INCREASE OF CHRIST'S KINGDOM AND GLORY IS WHICH WE ARE TO EXPECT.

It is the increase of his mediatorial kingdom. and the manifestation of his glory in the world. This implies,

1. The spread of gospel light through the world. It is in this way the man of sin is to be destroyed, 2 Thess. ii. 8, and the earth filled with heavenly knowledge. Hab. ii. 14.

2. That many burning and shining lights will be employed for this purpose—men full of holy fire an zeal for God, willing to run all hazards, by sea and land, to spread the glo of Christ, Dan. xii. 4.

3. That the number of Christ's subjects shall be greatly increased; this will be to his honor, Prov. xiv. 28. His arrows will be sharp in the hearts of his enemies, and his converts numerous as the drops of dew. Ps. cx 2, 3.

4. That truth shall triumph over error: that infidelity, Deism, Arianism, Socinianism, and popery, with all its superstition, shall then give way before the blaze of the Sun of Righteousness.

5. The increase of true piety, when the followers of Christ shall be wholly devoted to him—manifesting holy tempers, holy conversation, and a holy life.

6. An increase of zeal and public spirit among Christians. They shall boldly confess Christ before men; use every resource, and exert all their powers, to promote the good of mankind.

II. THE TIMES AND SEASONS OF THIS GLORIOUS INCREASE.

1. The apostolic age was the most remarkable time that was ever known; when every sermon made new conquests and additions to the church, till every city and corner of the vast Roman empire was filled with christians. But,

2. We have promises of a more full and glorious increase of Christ's kingdom in the latter day, or towards the end of the world, Dan. ii. 28—44; vii. 27.

The image represents the four grand monarchies. The Babylonian, is the golden head; the Medo-Persian, the breast and arms of silver; the Macedonian, or Grecian, the belly and thighs of brass; and the Roman, the legs of iron, &c. which was to break and bruise all the rest; Dan. ii. 40; but, in its last stage, was itself to be divided into ten lesser kingdoms, represented by the ten toes; and in another vision, by ten horns. Chap. vii. and Rev. xvii.

Then follows the establishment of the Messiah's kingdom. This is the stone mentioned Dan. ii. 34, which is to become a great mountain, and fill the world, v. 35. A kingdom which will swallow up all others and be established forever. Ver. 44.

These ten toes, horns, or kings, shall oppose the Lamb in his grand designs; but he shall overcome them by the word of his power, and shall range themselves under his banner; shall hate the whore of Babylon, the church of Rome, and make her desolate. Rev. xvii. 12—16.

Then shall the kingdoms of the world become the kingdoms of Christ. Rev. xi. 15.

The great river Euphrates will be dried up, to prepare the way for the kings of the east. Rev. xvi. 12.

The blindness of the Jews will be removed, and the fulness of the Gentiles shall come in. Rom. xi. 1, 25, 26.

Jerusalem shall be rebuilt, and be holy. Isa. lx. 10, 12, 13, 21.

The Jews shall be gathered out of all countries where they are dispersed Ezek. xxxvi. 24, 28.

All nations shall be gathered together to see his glory. Isa. ii. 2.

There shall be no more war between nations. Isa. ii. 4.

When these prophecies are fulfilled, what a glorious increase will it be to the Mediator's kingdom and glory! Then shall be accomplished the overthrow of Babylon and Antichrist, the destruction of the Turkish empire, the bringing in of the Jews, with the fulness of the Gentiles!

Glorious period! and we have ground to expect that we are arrived at the eve of that eventful period. Hence the establishment of Bible and Missionary So ieties, and the lively interest which rich and poor, and even **crowned** heads, are taking in the spread of the gospel to the ends of the earth.. indeed, such a public spirit for doing good was never before, to the same extent, witnessed in the Christian world. This appears to be the dawn of a glorious day.

But previous to this glorious event, there will be

1. A very general defection in the churches of Christ; 2 Pet. ii. 1; which, in many instances, is awfully the case already.

2. There will be great numbers of infidels, and profane scoffers, deriding serious godliness, and contemning the promises. 2 Pet. iii. 3, 4.

3. Great troubles in the world, and great fear and distress in the church. Dan. xii. 1; also Matt. xxiv., and Luke xxi.

4. Great security among the enemies of Christ, and the Romish harlot is lifted up with pride. Rev. xvii. 7, 8.

5. A marvellous revolution in one of the ten horns, Rev. xi. 13; or one of the ten kingdoms: this is understood by many of the kingdom of France. Then shall Christ arise, and his enemies be scattered.

III. THE REASONS WHY CHRIST MUST INCREASE.

1. Because it is the purpose and promise of God. Promised to the church. Jer. xxiii. 5. To Christ himself. Ps. ii. 8; and cx. 1, 2 And he will not alter. Ps. lxxxix. 34,.34.

2. Because for this very purpose God made the world, and he hath committed to Christ the administration of Providence. Isa. ix. 6. To secure the accomplishment of the glorious promises. Matt. xxviii. 18; Eph. i. 22.

2. Because Christ is the beloved of the Father. Matt. iii. 17. He fulfilled his will in the redemption of the world. Phil. ii. 8. And has obtained a name above every name, &c. Phil. ii. 8—10. To conclude, I would observe.

1. Under these circumstances it is in vain for any one to attempt to stop this glorious work. He must increase. Ps. ii. 1—4.

2. What encouragement we have to pray, as our Lord directs, "Thy Kingdom come."

3. How encouraging is the prospect to the friends of Christ? The church will outlive all its enemies. Christ must overcome, he must triumph.

4. And let every one, in their different spheres of action, do all they can to increase the Redeemer's glory. Dreadful shall be the state of those who are unconcerned in this great work. Amos vi. 1, 6; Esther iv. 14

THE SINNER'S FAITH.

Luke vii. 50.—And he said to the woman, Thy faith hath saved thee; go in peace. (S. S)

To associate with the ungodly world is by no means expedient for those who have been redeemed out of the world. Yet there is a certain degree of intercourse with them which is both proper and desirable. There is a medium between an affecting of their society for our own gratification, and a contemptuous separation from them. Our blessed Lord has exhibited, as in every thing else, so in this also, a perfect pattern. When invited by a Pharisee to dinner, he accepted the invitation with a view to instruct him and Jo

him good: and when a woman who had been a notorious sinner came to him at the Pharisee's house, he did not refuse her admission to his presence, but received with kindness the expressions of her regard, and imparted to her both the blessings and the comforts of his salvation.

The particular notice which our Lord took of the woman's *"faith,"* and the reward he gave her on account of it, leads us naturally to consider,

I. THE MARKS AND EVIDENCES OF HER FAITH

The first thing that calls for our attention is,

1. Her zeal.

She had doubtless seen many of our Lord's miracles, and heard many of his discourses; and though she was not yet one of his avowed followers, yet, having received good to her soul, she was desirous of honoring him to the utmost of her power. For this purpose she sought him out in the Pharisee's house, and went to him with a full determination to shew him some signal mark of her regard.

Now this argued no little zeal. She was of the weaker sex, and therefore the more liable to be condemned as officious, impertinent, and obtrusive. She was of a notoriously vile character, and therefore still more obnoxious to insult and contempt. But unmindful of these things, she went uninvited, to the house of a proud Pharisee (where she was least of all likely to meet with any favor) and (indifferent to the construction that might be put upon her conduct by any censorious spectators, or even to the treatment she might receive from them) in the presence of the whole company expressed to him all that was in her heart.

And what was it that enabled her thus to "despise all shame," and to triumph over the fear of man? Doubtless it was her faith: for the apostle says, "This is the victory that overcometh the world, even our faith."

2. Her humility.

Though she was bent on executing her pious purpose, she was solicitous to do it in as private and modest a manner as she could. She therefore went behind him as he lay upon the couch,* and, having easy access to his feet, placed herself there, without attracting the notice of the company, or interfering with the conversation that might be passing at table.

This also was a strong mark and evidence of her faith. She knew his august character, and felt herself unworthy to enter into his presence; yea, she accounted it the very summit of her ambition to be permitted to kiss his feet. It was in this way that the faith of the centurion and others shewed itself: Luke vii. 6, 7; Mark v. 25—28; and though, through the remaining pride and ignorance of their hearts, young converts often, like Jehu, seek the notice and applause of men, humility will always be found to exist in the soul in exact proportion to our faith.

3. Her contrition.

No sooner had she placed herself near the Saviour, than all her sins presented themselves to her mind, and filled her with deep compunction. Instantly she burst into a flood of tears, with which she bathed, as it were, the feet of her Lord, while she embraced them, in hopes of finding mercy from the friend of sinners.

Now it is the property of faith to "look on him whom we have pierced, and mourn." Zech. xii. 10. Yea, the more lively faith any have possessed, the more abundant has been their self-loathing and self-abhorrence. Job

They did not sit at table as we do, but lay on couches.

xiii. 6; Isa. vi. 5; 1 Tim. i. 15. We cannot doubt therefore but that faith was the principle from whence her humiliation flowed.

4. Her love.

While she wept over the Saviour's feet, she wiped them with the hairs of her head, and kissed them, and anointed them with odoriferous ointment. It was not possible for her to manifest stronger tokens of her affection.

And was not this also an evidence of her faith? Had she been an unbeliever, she would have seen "no beauty or comeliness in Jesus" that deserved her admiration: Isa. liii. 2; but believing in him, she accounted him "fairer than ten thousand, and altogether lovely," Cant. v. 10, 16, according to that declaration of the apostle, To them that believe, he is precious. 1 Peter ii. 7.

5. Her confidence.

She would not have ventured to approach the Pharisee in this manner, because she knew that he would despise her in his heart, and dismiss her with scorn. But she felt no apprehension of such treatment from the Saviour. She well knew his condescension and compassion; and therefore without reserve, and without fear, she cast herself upon his mercy.

In this too she shewed the strength of her faith. Unbelief would have suggested many doubts; Will he receive me? Will he deign to look upon such an abandoned wretch? But faith enabled her to approach him under a full persuasion, that "whosoever came to him should in no wise be cast out."

It was not in vain that she thus approached the Saviour; as we shall see, while we consider,

II. The fruits and consequences of her faith.

Though despised and condemned by the Pharisee, she was well rewarded by her Lord. She obtained from him.

1. The pardon of her sins.

Numerous as her iniquities had been, they were all in one moment blotted from the book of God's remembrance. Jesus, who "had all power on earth to forgive sins," pardoned all her offences, and " cast them, as it were, behind him into the very depths of the sea." What a blessed fruit and consequence of her faith was this! Had she been subjected to all the evil treatment that could have been shewn her, she would have had no reason to regret that conduct by which she had obtained so inestimable a blessing.

And was this peculiar to her? Shall not we also have our iniquities forgiven, if we apply to him in humility and faith? Shall the greatness of our sins be any bar to our acceptance with him, if we repent and believe? Let the word of God be deemed worthy of any credit, and all such apprehensions will vanish in an instant— — —Acts xiii. 39; Isa. i. 18.

2. An assurance of her acceptance.

Twice did our Lord repeat to her the joyful tidings, that her sins were pardoned, and that her soul was saved; and to confirm it, he bade her depart in peace. What a cordial must this have been to her drooping spirit! How transported must she have been with the joyful sound! And what comfort must she enjoy through life in a sense of the divine favor, and in a prospect of the divine glory!

But neither was this peculiar to her. It is true, that many real christians never attain to this high privilege: but it is owing to the weakness of their faith: if their faith operated as hers did, if it shewed itself in such humility, such contrition, such love, such confidence, such zeal, they also should hear him say to them, "Be of good cheer; thy sins are forgiven thee." What though he should not utter it by an audible voice from heaven, can he not reveal it to the soul by his Spirit, and enable us to say, " My beloved is mine, and I am his?" Cant. ii. 16. Yes: let us only glorify him to the utmost of our power, and he will give us a peace that passeth all understanding, Phil. iv. 7, and a full assurance of hope unto the end." Heb. vi. 11. See also 2 Tim. i. 12, and iv. 8.

3. Everlasting happiness and glory.

In the declaration of Jesus she received both an earnest and a pledge of her eternal inheritance. Nor can we doubt but that after waiting her " appointed time upon earth," she was admitted to the enjoyment of her Lord in heaven, not any longer to weep at his feet, but to sit with him on his throne, and to participate his glory.

Thus also shall it be with all who truly believe: " they shall never perish, but shall have eternal life"— — —John iii. 16.

From this history we may LEARN,

1. The nature of faith.

We cannot too carefully enquire into the nature of faith; for there is nothing respecting which so many, and such fatal, mistakes are made. Faith is not a mere assent to any doctrines whatsoever; but it is a living principle in the soul, which evidences itself by precisely such a regard to Christ as this woman manifested on this occasion. Would we then ascertain whether our faith be genuine and saving? let us enquire whether it lead us to Christ, in spite of all obstacles from without or from within, with humility and contrition, with love and confidence? For in proportion as we abound in these graces, or are destitute of them, we either possess, or are destitute of, a living faith.

2. The excellence of faith.

Admirable were the graces which this woman exercised; yet not one of them was noticed by our Lord: he overlooked them all; and noticed that only *which was least apparent, and which every one else would have overlooked,* namely, her faith. He knew that this was the root or principle from whence all her other graces sprang. It was this that led her so to honor him; and therefore he determined to honor it. And must not that be excellent which he so highly regarded, so studiously searched out, and so eminently distinguished?

But what is it that he here assigns to her faith? it is nothing less than the saving of her soul: he passes by all her other graces as having no weight or influence whatever in her justification before God, and specifies her *"faith"* as that which "saved" her. Is it possible to bestow a higher commendation on it than this?

If it be asked, why faith is thus distinguished above all other graces? we answer, it is because faith unites us unto the Saviour, and interests us thereby in all that he has done and suffered for us: but this cannot be said of any other grace whatever; and therefore, though every other grace *adorns* the soul, no grace but faith will *save* it.

Let us all seek to attain right sentiments on this most important point, and pray with the apostles, " Lord, increase our faith."

3. The condescension of Christ to believing penitents.

If a person of an abandoned character, however changed in his conduct, should come to us when in the midst of company, and that company of a higher order and a pharisaic cast, and should express such affection for us, our pride would be apt to rise; and, while we blushed for the degradation we seemed to suffer, we should be ready to condemn him for his impertinent intrusion, or perhaps to suspect that he was deranged in his mind. But Jesus accounted himself honored by the testimonies of the woman's regard; and, though he could not but know what reflections would be cast upon his character on account of his kindness to her, he vindicated her conduct, and richly recompensed her kind attentions.

Thus will he do to every believing penitent. He will compensate the scoffs of an unbelieving world by manifest tokens of his approbation. He will not regard the quantity or quality of a man's past offenses; but will speak peace to his soul, and in due time " wipe away all tears from his eyes" for ever. O that we might all consider this, and experience it to our eternal joy !

THE NATURE, SOURCE, AND MEANS OF SPIRITUAL PEACE.

Haggai ii. 9.—In this place will I give peace, saith the Lord of Hosts.   (B.)

IF this might be said of the temple at Jerusalem, where the sacrifices of bulls and goats were offered which could not take away sin, the prayers of Old Testament saints were put up, and the Law of Moses was read and expounded; the words may with, at least, equal, if not greater propriety be used of every place under the New Testament dispensation,—a dispensation much more perfect,—where the sacrifice of Christ, which does put away sin, and procure peace with God, is offered, the gospel of peace is proclaimed, the prayers of the New Testament saints are put up and presented through our great Hight Priest, and the Spirit of peace and love is bestowed.— —
Inquire we,

I. INTO THE NATURE OF THE PEACE HERE SPOKEN OF.

To understand this promise, we must observe, that man is by nature at enmity with God.—All are sinners. Rom. iii. 23.—All are under wrath. Rom. i. 18 : Eph. ii. 1—3.—There is an enmity on the part of man towards God. Rom. viii. 5—7; Col. i. 21.—Hence, guilt is charged, and condemnation and wrath denounced upon him by God.

The peace here intended includes,

Peace with God; i. e. forgiveness, acceptance, reconciliation with him Rom. v. 1.—When this is witnessed to the soul, by the Spirit of God, the enmity is removed, or the will is subdued, and the affections are brought into captivity to the obedience of Christ; whence spring " love, joy, peace, long-suffering, gentleness, goodness, faith, meekness, temperance."— —

Peace of conscience ; arising from the pardon of past sin, and power over sin. Rom. viii. 1—3; 6, 12—15.— —

A *peaceful, serene,* and *tranquil* state of mind; the will and affections being subdued, and all the tempers changed, and sanctified.   Col. iii. 12—15; Phil. iv. 7.— —

Peace with all men ; injustice, oppression, guile, fraud, covetousness, pride, anger, and other causes of discord and strife, being removed.— —

How great the excellency of this peace, and the blessedness of those that possess it!— —

II. WHO IS THE AUTHOR OF THIS PEACE, AND THE WAY IN WHICH HE WILL GIVE IT.

It is not *ourselves.*—Our own works cannot purchase it, nor reconcile God to us. They are all of them imperfect, stained with sin, and instead of procuring favor, deserve divine wrath.—Our own strength and endeavors, and our abstinence and religious duties, of whatever kind, cannot remove the enmity on our part, and reconcile us to God.—Nothing that we have done or can do, can pacify or give peace to an awakened conscience; can produce a really peaceful state of mind; or destroy those evil dispositions, which are the grand hinderences of peace among men.

It is not *others;* not their absolutions, prayers, or advices.— —

It is the *gift of God.* He is its author.—It comes from him as a free gift.— — —His mercy passes by our past sins, and pardons them; thus wrath on his part is removed. His spirit removes our enmity to him witnesses the pardon of sin, and gives us power over it. Hence we have peace with God, peace of conscience, tranquility of mind, and peace with all men. —But it comes through Christ, the blood of his cross, and the pacification made thereby. Tit. iii. 4—6; Col. i. 20; Eph. ii. 13, 14.— —How inestimable the ransom by which we obtain this blessing!— —

III. WHO ARE THE SUBJECTS OF IT; OR, THE PERSONS TO WHOM HE WILL GIVE IT.

It is purchased by Christ for all, and offered to all. 2 Cor. v. 18, 19; Isa. lvii. 19.

But it cannot be possessed by the wicked. Isai. lvii. 20. " God is angry with the wicked every day." Psa. vii. 11. Hence, the necessity of repentance.*

It cannot be the portion of the unbeliever. John iii. 18—36. Hence the necessity of faith.†

Repentance and faith are both the gifts of God, and must be sought in the use of prescribed means, as hearing the word and prayer. We hence obtain the light concerning the method of justification and peace; the sufficiency and grace of Christ are revealed by the Spirit, and our hearts are drawn to him.

IV. THE PLACE WHERE HE WILL GIVE IT, AND THE TIME WHEN.

At all times and places may be considered as holy under the gospel. John iv. 21.

Nevertheless when and where the gospel is preached, and prayer offered to God, repentance and faith are usually given, and Christ in his word and Spirit is peculiarly present. Matt. xviii, 20; xxviii. 20.

THE LIFE AND WALK OF A CHRISTIAN.

Galatians v. 25.—If we live in the Spirit, let us also walk in the Spirit. (B.)

As true christianity is divided into two grand branches, and is partly experimental and partly practical; so, there are two particulars which are chiefly deserving of notice in the character of a real christian; his inward life and his outward conversation. With regard to both of them, he differs essentially, I do not say, merely from profane and immoral persons, but from all

* Describe the nature and fruits of repentance.

† Describe the nature of faith, and the change consequent upon it.

that are carnal and worldly, from all that are not true christians, possessed of the genuine religion of Christ. And no wonder, for the spring and rule of his life and conduct are essentially different in him from what they are in them. They are influenced and directed by the powers of nature, he by the principles of grace; they by the spirit of the world and the customs and habits of men, he by the Spirit of God and the example and laws of Christ. Hence the exhortation of the Apostle in Eph. iv. 17—23, and in the text.—Consider we,

I. THE INWARD LIFE OF A CHRISTIAN.

"If we live *in*," or rather *by*, "the Spirit." It is evident the Apostle does not here speak of the life common to all men ; for if he had, he needed not not have made a supposition, "*if*." He does not speak, therefore, of natural life, whether animal or rational, consisting in the union of soul and body, and supported by breathing, the circulation of the blood and other fluids, by the reception of food and use of exercise. Nevertheless this is, in a sense, in and by the Spirit of that God who at first "breathed into our nostrils the breath of life," and " in whom we live move and have our being;" Acts xvii. 28. But he speaks of spiritual and eternal life,—the life which man lost by the fall, Gen. ii. 17, and of which by nature we are all destitute. Eph. ii. 1—3 ; Col. ii. 13.—This life consists in the knowledge of God, John xvii. 3 ; his love ; 1 John iv. 16 ; his favor ; Psa. xxx. 5 ; his image ; Eph. iv. 24 ; his heavenly, spiritual, and divine nature.— —By this spiritual life we have a title to eternal life, a meetness for it, and a foretaste of it —As to the vast importance of this life, it is the end of Christ's incarnation, 1 John iv. 9 ; John x. 10, of his miracles, his doctrine, and of divine revelation, especially of the gospel, John xx. 31 ; of the gift of the Holy Spirit, John xiv. 16—19. Indeed—we live by the Spirit, termed a quickening Spirit, John vi. 63 ; "a Spirit of life." Rom. viii. 2 ; the living water, John iv. 10—14 ; vii. 37, 38 ; the water of life, Rev. xxi. 6 ; xxii. 17. Hereby we are awakened, convinced, humbled, converted, and made to experience repentance unto life ; living faith. Col. ii. 12, 13 ; in the living and true God, the gospel, the Lord Jesus, and the promises whereby " the just live;" Heb. x. 38; Gal. ii. 20 ; an interest in Christ and union with him, John xvii. 20, 21 ; John xiv. 20 ; 1 Cor. xii. 13 ; when we are brought into this union, and only then, we have life, 1 John v. 11, 12 ; justification unto life, Rom. v. 18 ; regeneration on our entrance into this spiritual life ; sanctification by the same Spirit, 1 Pet. i. 2, whereby this life is continued and perfected.—Those who attain this experience are said to pass from death unto life.—This life is maintained, as well as communicated by the Spirit. If he be grieved, quenched, and done despite unto, it is lost. It is maintained also by the use of means, as the animal life is supported by breathing, food, exercise.— —

Thus we "live in the Spirit," in union and intercourse with the Spirit, which lives and dwells in us, as our bodies live in the air or light of this world.

II. THE WALK OF A CHRISTIAN.

The walk of a christian includes his tempers, words, and works, or his whole deportment. And this walk is *by* the Spirit. See ver. 16—26.—By the guidance of the Spirit, including that of God's word and providence, Rom. viii. 14.—The support of the Spirit affords courage, fortitude, resolution, power. Eph. iii. 16. The influence and drawings of the Spirit are necessary to it. Christians walk " after the Spirit." Rom. viii. 1—4. " *In*

the Spirit;" in the graces and fruits of the Spirit, in love, joy, peace, long-suffering, gentleness, goodness, faith, meekness, temperance, ver. 22.—
APPLICATION TO THE HEARERS.

Let me inquire,—Do you live by and in the Spirit? Do you walk by and in the Spirit? If you do not *live* you do not *walk* in the Spirit: we cannot walk without life. If you do not *walk* you do not *live* in the Spirit, or your spiritual life is in a very feeble, dying state. How great the misery of those who do not both *live* and *walk* in the Spirit, and the happiness of those that do! in regard of their own comfort, the glory of God, and the edification of others!— —

It should here be shown how the blessing is attained and retained.

THE GOOD WORK OF GOD IN THE SOUL.

Philippians i. 6.—He which hath begun a good work in you will perform it until the day of Jesus Christ. (B.)

THE steadfast and consistent profession, which was made by the Philippian christians, "from the first day" of their conversion, until the time he now wrote to them, a period of about twelve years, without ever being turned aside, or dishonoring their holy calling, afforded St. Paul the most heartfelt satisfaction, and a confident expectation that God would carry on the work he had so favorably begun in them, till it should attain perfection, and issue, at the second coming of Christ, in their everlasting glory.— —

Inquire we,

I. WHAT IS THIS WORK?

It is wrought in us: not only in the church of Christ in general, but in each individual member of it in particular; in the mind and heart, Heb. xiii. 21; 2 Thess. i. 11. Thus it is distinguished from the works of God wrought for us, as those of creation, providence, redemption, justification.— This work wrought in us is performed in every faculty or power of our inward man. It is a work of illumination in the understanding, gradual and increasing; of conviction and awakening in the conscience; of quickening and animating the affections; producing humiliation, shame, sorrow for, and hatred to, sin; esteem, desire, hope, joy, in regard to holiness and the divine author of it;—of conversion, implying the subjection of the will; the mortification, restraint, and due regulation, of the appetites and passions; change in all the dispositions. It is a work, producing divine graces in us, as repentance, spoken of 2 Cor. vii. 10, 11: faith, John vi. 29; 1 Thess. i. 3; 2 Thess. i. 11; Col. ii. 12: hope, 1 Pet. i. 3: love, to God and man, Rom. v. 5; 1 Thess. iii. 12: humility, resignation, patience, contentment, meekness, gentleness, long-suffering, and purity of intention and affection, and universal holiness, or a renewal after the divine image, 2 Cor. iv. 16; Tit. iii. 5.—In general, this work is wounding and healing; killing and making alive; pulling down and building up; breaking up the ground and sowing; stripping and clothing. Acts xiii. 41.

II. HOW DOES IT APPEAR THAT THIS IS A GOOD WORK?

It is painful in its commencement; for a discovery of our sinfulness and guilt, conviction of sin, humiliation, shame, grief for it, are not pleasing to nature; but though not joyous, like affliction at first, it afterwards yields most pleasant fruit; producing, even on earth, peace hope, joy, love, and other happy affections, Ps. cxxvi. 5.—It is good, as to its author, God, from whom nothing but good can proceed.—It is good as it respects his motive for working it, love to us.—It is good as to the means and agents, by whom it is effected in us, Christ, the Spirit, the word. 1 Thess. ii. 13. The end is good, even eternal salvation.— —

III. What are the proofs that this work is begun?

Many of these are mentioned by the apostle in the context.—"Fellowship in, (or through) the gospel, till now :" ver. 5; a participation with others in the blessings of it, manifested in their hearing, reading, meditating, understanding, and receiving the word, and not departing from it, like the way-side and stony-ground hearers; also, uniting in fellowship with the people of God.—Believing in Christ, ver. 29. The work of faith being in a measure wrought in them, and of consequence the new birth, John i. 12; 1 John v. 1, love, 1 John iv. 7, victory over the world, 1 John v. 4, 5; ii. 15, purity. Acts xv. 9.—Suffering willingly for the gospel, like the apostle, and thus being "partakers of his grace," ver. 7, 29, not forsaking him in his bonds, and when he stood up in defence of the gospel, but sharing in the reproach and persecution he endured; the faith and patience they thus exercised, proving the reality of their grace.—Rejoicing in Christ, ver. 26.—"Shining as lights in the world" by their unblamable and useful life, chap. ii. 15.— —

IV. St. Paul's confidence that God would carry on his work in them.

If God had not been willing to carry it on, he would not have begun it.—It is true, God works by means; but they were willing to use, and did actually use, and resolved to continue to use, the means.—Their perseverance, however, was not infallible. See ch. ii. 12, 13; Gal. v. 4.— —

Application.

To sinners. Is this good work begun?—You answer, "I do so and so." But what hath God done? hath he wrought in you to will and to do? Is it a good work, to rail, to lie, to cheat, &c.; to be proud, self-willed, discontented, envious, &c.?—To mourners. "He will not break the bruised reed." Matt. xii. 20. He hath wrought in you repentance, he will work faith: he hath convinced, he will convert; he hath wounded, he will heal; Hos. vi. 1; he hath brought down, and given sorrow, he will exalt and cause joy.—To believers. The work is but begun: the foundation is laid, that the superstructure may be raised; the tree is planted, that it may bear fruit; the child of God is born of his Spirit, that he may grow up from a babe to a young man and a father; the laborer is hired into the vineyard, that he may work.

THE SUCCESS OF THE GOSPEL IN THE DAYS OF THE APOSTLES.

Acts xii. 24.—But the word grew and was multiplied. (Sk.)

When Christ appeared on earth, he was opposed to the wicked Jews; and, after his ascension into heaven, his holy apostles were opposed both by Jews and Gentiles. The heathen nations raged, and the professing people of God imagined a vain thing; but the Lord laughed them to scorn, and had

them in derision, Ps. ii. 1—4. Herod the king persecuted the church, be cause it pleased the Jews; but when he robbed God of his glory, by allowing the people to pay him divine honors, he was eaten up of worms, ver. 23. Let us consider the opposition which was made to the word in those days: its rapid success; and the principal means of its extensive promulgation.

I. THE WORD WAS OPPOSED.

1. *By the word we may understand the gospel of God our Saviour.* This was sent in the first instance to the Jews. Hence the apostle Paul said to the Jews at Antioch, " Men and brethren, children of the stock of Abraham, and whosoever among you feareth God, to you is the word of this salvation sent," chap. xiii. 26. It is fitly called a word of salvation, as it explains the cause of salvation; points out the terms of salvation; explains its nature and extent; and offers salvation to all who believe, Mark xv. 16.

2. *Jewish prejudices opposed the gospel.* The Jews were fond of pomp and parade; they admired the letter of the law; but they were proud, formal, and carnal. No wonder that they opposed that word which required humility, Luke xiv. 11. They could not endure the spirituality of the gospel, Rom. ii. 28, 29. And their prejudices were strong against regeneration: because they were ignorant of its nature, and were under the dominion of sin and death, John iii. 3; Rom. vii. 24.

3. *Heathenish superstitions were opposed to the word.* They had imaginary gods without number; they had priests whom they revered, and who kept them in darkness; and they had an impure worship to which they were superstitiously attached. Christianity took away their gods, exposed their priests, and threw down their idolatrous temples and altars. Can we wonder that they rose up in arms against the word? Their craft was in danger; for the preaching of the gospel turned the world upside down, Acts xvii. 6.

4. *Human learning was opposed to the word of God.* The Greeks and Romans excelled in learning; but that learning produced bad effects. They were self-confident, proud, and apt to boast. The gospel was plain, clear, and simple; and it rendered all their fine reasonings, and all their displays of oratory, completely useless. Hence they could not endure it. It appeared to them foolishness, and unworthy to be received by philosophers, who imagined they knew more than either the Jewish prophets or Christ and his apostles.

5. *The devil opposed the gospel, by his influence and agency on the hearts of men.* Thousands, who were ignorant of his devices, were led by him into error and sin. He stirred up all his servants, whether Jews or Gentiles, to oppose the word. We have an instance of this kind in *Elymas*, whom Paul called a child of the devil, because he perverted the right ways of the Lord, under the influence and agency of that wicked spirit, Acts xiii. 8—10.

6. *In spreading the word, the apostles had to endure many grievous afflictions, both from wicked men and evil spirits.* They were treated with scorn and contempt; they suffered bonds and imprisonment, hunger and nakedness, hardships and deaths, 1 Cor. iv. 11—13; 2 Cor. iv. 8—11. But they were strengthened and supported by the Lord; and their labors were crowned with success.

II. OPPOSITION DID NOT PREVENT THE RAPID SUCCESS OF THE GOSPEL; FOR THE WORD GREW AND WAS MULTIPLIED.

1. *The word is fitly compared to good seed.* Our Lord used this figure

in his parable of the sower, where he says, "The seed is the word of God, Luke viii. 11. And the apostle Paul says, in reference to a preached gospel, "We have sown unto you spiritual things," 1 Cor. ix. 11.

2. *This seed was sown by the apostles in prepared hearts;* and it cannot bring forth good fruit unless the heart be prepared. When men repent, and seek the Lord, the *fallow ground* of their hearts is broken up, Hos. x. 12. The sinner is then convinced of sin; mourns under a sense of sin; and inquires, "What must I do to be saved?" Acts xvi. 30.

3. *When the word sinks into the heart, and takes deep root, it produces holy tempers and holy actions;* and when we abound in these, the word grows in us, and our prayers go up to God with acceptance. "If ye abide in me, and my words abide in you, ye shall ask what ye will, and it shall be done unto you," John xv. 7. Then we see the grace of God in its wondrous effects. How it grows we know not; but we have sufficient proof of its growth, when we see the blade, the ear, and then the full corn in the ear, Mark x. 28.

4. *The word is multiplied when many are converted to God by the instrumentality of converts.* One grain may produce *fifty*, and another a *hundred*. In those days one convert was frequently the honored instrument of bringing many to Christ, so that the word spread in all directions. Every member of the church felt it his duty to do what he could for his Lord and Master; and when this is the case, the word multiplies, by the blessing of God, Acts viii. 4.

II. But what were the principal causes of the extensive promulgation of the gospel in the age of the apostles?

1. *The extraordinary gifts of the Spirit, conferred on the apostles, and on many in the church, promoted the success of the gospel.* They spake with tongues, and wrought miracles; a plain proof that God was with them, and that he was the Author of that religion which they taught and enforced, Acts vi. 7, 8.

2. Another cause of the rapid spread o' the gospel in those days, was *the burning zeal of the apostles and primitive Christians.* They were always zealously affected in a good cause, Gal. iv. 18. Under the influence of this principle, they were diligent in the use of means; they were courageous; and did all things heartily as to the Lord, Col. iii. 23.

3. *Divine power attended the word.* This was absolutely necessary; for without that power nothing could have been accomplished, 1 Cor. ii. 4. Paul planted, and Apollos watered; but God gave the increase, 1 Cor. iii. 6; 1 Thess. i. 5. And when the word was clothed with divine power, it was "sharper than any two-edged sword," Heb. iv. 12.

4. *The holy tempers, and the holy conduct of the apostles, and of the first believers, produced powerful effects on the hearts of the people.* They were patient in sufferings; meek under provocations: and ever ready to forgive injuries. They were diligent in business; just in their dealings; and faithful to their promises. And when men saw their "good works, they glorified God," Matt. v. 16.

5. *The unity of the church gave success to the word.* They were closely united in affection, and all aimed at the same things, namely, the glory of God and the salvation of men. Their love to one another was proverbial. When the world saw this, and considered it as the fruit of christianity, many believed, and turned from dumb idols to the *living God*, Heb. x. 24.

6. *Persecution promoted the cause of Christ, and gave success to the word.* It discovered the *vileness* of the persecutors, and the real *worth* of

the persecuted. The one was *abhorred*, and the other *admired*. Hence the word of those holy and injured persons took effect; and it was frequently said, "The blood of the martyrs is the seed of the church."

7. *Judgments poured out on wicked men, and on persecutors, gave success to the gospel.* When Ananias and Sapphira were struck dead, "Great fear came upon all the church, and as many as heard these things," Acts v. 11. When Herod died by the visitation of God, the word grew and was multiplied; and when Elymas was struck blind, Sergius Paulus believed the word, Acts xiii. 12.

8. *The united prayers of the church gave success to the word.* All were crying out day and night, "Thy kingdom come." All prayed for the prosperity of the word, 2 Thess. iii. 1. And much prayer must be offered up in one day, if we would see a revival of religion, and a rapid spread of christianity, Heb. iii. 2.

INFERENCES.

1. How widely different was the propagation of Christianity from that of Mohammedism! The one was by the force of truth, and holy example; but the other was by the sword, and acts of violence!

2. The effects of primitive times have reached us in these last days. We have the truth which was then taught; we have christian ordinances and christian ministers. Miracles have ceased; but grace still abounds, 1 Tim. i. 15.

3. We lay no claim to apostolical gifts; but God has opened a wide door, in our day, for the spread of his gospel. Let us imitate the piety and zeal of the first christians; and may we live to see the blessed days of the Son of man! Amen.

THE CENTURION'S SERVANT HEALED.

Luke vii. 6, 7.—Then Jesus went with them: and when he was not far from the house, the Centurion sent friends to him, saying unto him, Lord, trouble not thyself: for I am not worthy that thou shouldest enter under my roof; wherefore neither thought I myself worthy to come unto thee: but say in a word, and my servant shall be healed. (S. S.)

NOTHING makes a wider breach among men than a difference in political and religious opinion—

But mutual good offices would greatly counteract this evil—

Though we can never hope to soften the rancour of all, we may by persevering kindness conciliate the esteem of many—

We have before us a remarkable instance of the efficacy of such conduct—

The Centurion was an heathen, an officer of an hostile nation, stationed in Judea to keep the Jews in subjection—

But instead of oppressing the Jews he had shewed them much favor -

He, in his turn, needed their good offices on behalf of his servant—

And they gladly became his advocates and intercessors—

They even prevailed on Jesus to work a miracle on his behalf—

To elucidate this miracle we shall consider,

I. THE CENTURION'S CHARACTER.

Soldiers, for the most part, are unfavorably circumstanced with respect to religion—

But here was one, though an heathen, whose character may well put to shame the greater part of the christian world—we may observe,

1. His love to his fellow-creatures.

His servant was grievously afflicted with the palsy nigh unto death—Compare Matt. viii. 6, with Luke vii. 2.

In this disorder, persons can do nothing for others, or even for themselves—

And in such a state, even dear friends and relatives are ready to think the care of one an heavy burthen—

Yet this Centurion administered to his servant with the tenderest affection—

And interested all he could in the promotion of his welfare—*

What could the servant himself have done more for the kindest master?

2. His piety towards God.

He had not embraced either the doctrines or discipline of the Jewish church—

But he had learned to acknowledge the only true God—

And he was glad to promote the worship of God, even though he himself did not acquiesce in the peculiar mode in which he was worshipped—

He even built a synagogue for the Jews at his own expense, ver. 5.

What an admirable pattern of liberality and candor!—

How different from those who will not do any thing without the pale of their own church!—

Surely he never afterwards regretted that he had so applied his wealth—

3. His low thoughts of himself.

He did not arrogate any thing to himself on account of his rank and authority—

Nor did he value himself on his benevolence to man and zeal for God—

While others judged him worthy that a miracle should be wrought for him, he accounted himself unworthy of the smallest favor—

This was the reason of his forbearing to wait on our Lord in person—†

How lovely does such an one appear in the eyes of God and man!—

4. His exalted thoughts of Christ.

He judged our Lord to be too holy to admit of converse with an heathen

He believed also that Jesus could effect whatsoever he pleased, by a word, and at a distance, without the intervention of any means, ver. 7.

Nor did he doubt but that universal nature was subject to his will far more than the most obedient soldier could be to the commands of his officer, ver. 8.

Thus did he ascribe to Jesus a power proper to God alone, Deut. xxxii. 39.

Well might our Lord's address to the discreet Scribe have been applied to him, Mark xii. 34.

Such a character as this could never meet with a repulse from Jesus.

II. THE KINDNESS VOUCHSAFED TO HIM BY OUR LORD.

Instantly at the request of the elders Jesus set off to the Centurion's house—

He who, though repeatedly importuned, declined to visit a *Nobleman's son*, John iv. 46—50, went, at the very first summons, to attend upon a *Centurion's servant*—

* He applied to some of the Jewish elders to use their interest with Jesus on his behalf.

† On our Lord's near approach to the house, the same humility that had kept the Centurion from going to him, compelled him. as it were, to go, lest he should seem guilty of disrespect. Compare Matt. viii. 13, with the text

And no sooner met the Centurion, than he richly recompensed his assiduity.

1. He expressed his admiration of the Centurion's faith.

We never hear of Jesus admiring the things of this world—

He rather checked in his disciples such ill-judged veneration, Mark xiii. 1, 2.

But when he beheld the Centurion's faith, "he marvelled at it"—

Not that such exercise of grace was *really* unexpected by him—

Jesus both knew what was in the Centurion's heart, John ii. 25, and had planted there the very grace which he exercised, John i. 16.

But Jesus, as our exemplar, would teach *us* what to admire—

And shew us that the smallest portion of true faith cannot be estimated too highly, 2 Peter i. 1.

Our Lord declared in his very presence, that this faith had not been equalled by any even of the Israelites themselves, ver. 9.

Such approbation from *his* mouth could not fail of comforting the afflicted Centurion—

2. He wrought the desired miracle in confirmation of his faith.

By a simple act of his will he restored the servant to perfect health—

And told the Centurion that it should "be to him according to his faith"—

Thus he removed the distress of the family in an instant—

Thus too he confirmed the faith which had shone forth so nobly—

And shewed that we could never expect too much at his hands—

What advantage for *eternal* life did the Centurion derive from hence!—

With what lively hope might he apply to Jesus for the healing of his soul!—

We can never suppose that such love and piety, such humility and faith were left to perish—

No, verily—That declaration shall be found true to all eternity, 1 Sam. ii. 30.

3. He declared that many such persons should be saved, while many, with clearer light and higher privileges, should be cast out.

They who profess the true religion may be called "the children of the kingdom"—

But how many of them are destitute of the attainments this heathen had made!—

How many would have imitated that vile Amalekite rather than him!— 1 Sam. xxx. 13.

How many grudge the necessary *contributions* for *keeping up* the houses of God!—*

What a doubting of Christ's power and grace, yea, what a proud conceit too of their own worthiness, is to be found among professing christians!—

Surely what our Lord said respecting the unbelieving Jews shall be realized in christians of this character, Matt. viii. 12.

And the humbler heathens, who walked agreeably to the light that they enjoyed, shall be preferred before them—

Nor can we doubt but that the Centurion, in reference to whom these things were spoken, shall be among that blessed number—

APPLICATION.

Let us then learn to plead earnestly for ourselves— — —

---

* What a contrast to him who, *entirely at his own expense, erected* a synagogue *for people of another communion !*

Nor let a sense of unworthiness keep us from carrying our wants to Jesus— — —

Let us also sympathize with, and intercede for others—

Job, like the Centurion, found benefit from his own intercessions—Job xlii. 10.

Nor shall *our* supplications be in vain either for ourselves or others.

~~~~~~~~~~~~~~~~~

JAIRUS' DAUGHTER HEALED.

Luke viii. 50.—When Jesus heard it, he answered him, saying, Fear not: believe only, and she shall be made whole. (S. S.)

AFFLICTIONS may well be deprecated by us as painful to flesh and blood—

But they are often the means of humbling us before God—

Multitudes came as suppliants to our Lord who would never have regarded him if they had not felt the pressure of disease or trouble—

The rich in general were the most backward to acknowledge him—

But they found that in the hour of affliction none other could do them good—

Hence occasionally we see the opulent presenting their supplications before him—

Nor did he reject the suit of any, whether they were rich or poor—

The answer he gave to a ruler of the synagogue is recorded in the text—

And it will naturally lead us to notice the rulers's faith.

I. HOW IT WAS TRIED.

Jairus (such was his name) had much to try his faith.

He had an only child (twelve years of age) in dying circumstances—

Having heard much of our Lord's miracles, he applied to him on behalf of his daughter—

And earnestly requested him to come and restore her health—

But while he was returning with Jesus to his house, his servants brought tidings that the child was dead—

This was a dreadful shock to the parent's feelings—

And might have utterly destroyed all his hopes—

Thus it is that the faith of God's people is often tried.

They are enabled to make application to their God and Saviour—

But the storm in the meantime gathers thick around them—

Their difficulties so increase, that their hopes seem almost blasted—

They have cried for pardon, and find only an increasing sense of guilt—

They have prayed for deliverance from corruption or temptation, and experienced the assaults of Satan more violent than ever—

Thus they are almost ready to think that God has cast out their prayer, and shut up his tender mercies from them—

It was in this manner that holy Job was tried—

Yea, the experience of most, however diversified, is generally found to agree in this. Ps. cvii. 5, 6, 12, 13, 18, 19, 26, 27, 28.

But this accumulated trouble, was permitted for the further exercise of the uler's faith.

II. HOW IT OPERATED.

He was enabled humbly and confidently to depend on Jesus.

It was his faith that first led him to Jesus for help—

Nor, when his case seemed desperate, did he give up his hope—

It is probable that our Lord might perceive some rising apprehensions in his mind—

But he sustained him instantly with that encouraging word, " Fear not"—

Jairus expected now that his child should be raised as from a sleep—

The idea of sleep, however, only called forth the derision of the mourners—

Such was the fruit of their ignorance and unbelief—

But the ruler himself resembled the father of the faithful, Rom iv. 18, 20, 21.—

It is in this way that true faith will ever shew itself.

It will surely lead us to Jesus for relief—

It will make us humble and importunate in our supplications to him—

We shall not presently turn from him because our difficulties increase—

We shall rather adopt the expressions of holy Job, Job xiii. 15.

Unbelief may prompt us to deride what we do not understand—

But faith will make us acquiesce in God's declarations, though we cannot fully comprehend them—

And expect the accomplishment of his promises, however his providence may appear to contradict them—

Jesus did not fail to respect the faith that honored him.

III. How IT WAS REWARDED.

Jesus answered the ruler to the full extent of all his wishes.

Our Lord reproved the excessive lamentations of the people—

And encouraged them to expect the restoration of the child—

But he would not suffer those who had derided him to be spectators of the miracle—

He took with him, however, persons sufficient to attest it—

He favored the believing parents with admission to behold it—

And restored their daughter, as it had been from sleep, in their very presence—

The child arose instantly, and walked as in perfect health—

For their further conviction he ordered food to be given to the child—

By this also he intimated, that though she was restored by a miracle, she was to be kept alive by natural means—

What a rich reward was this to the believing suppliant—

Nor shall any one who asks in faith, be disappointed.

Our Lord has commanded us to ask in faith, Mark xi. 24.—

And has assured us that petitions, so offered, shall be answered by him Matt. xxi. 22.—

Things the most impossible to man, shall, if they will conduce to our good and to God's honor, be effected by the prayer of faith, Mark ix. 23.—

Crimes the most atrocious that ever were committed, shall be pardoned, Acts xiii. 39.

Lusts the most inveterate that ever enslaved a soul, shall be subdued. Isai. lxi. 19.   1 Cor. vi. 11.

The dead in trespasses and sins shall be raised, like Christ himself, to a new and heavenly life, Eph. i. 19, 20, with ii. 5, 6.

Nor shall they fail of attaining eternal happiness in heaven, John. iii. 15 Isaiah xlv. 17.

APPLICATION.

Every man must expect trouble in this vale of tears—

123

The dearest friends must look forward to a day of separation—
But let every trouble drive us to the compassionate Jesus—
And every want be spread before him in prayer, Phil. iv. 6.
We are not now indeed to expect *miraculous* interpositions—
Nor ought we to ask for *temporal* blessings in an unqualified manner-
We should commit the concerns of this life to his all-wise disposal—
But for *spiritual* blessings we cannot be too importunate—
Nor can our faith in his word be too strong—
What he said to Martha he still says to us, John xi. 40.—
The advice of Jehosaphat is the best direction we can follow, 2 Chron xx. 20.—
Let us not then limit his tender mercies—
If we resemble the Samaritan lord, we shall fare like him, 2 Kings vii. 2—17.
Let us not in renewed troubles be like the unbelieving Jews, Ps. lxxviii 20.—
But let us bear in mind that encouraging declaration, Eph. iii. 20.—
And determine henceforth to live like the apostle, Gal. ii. 20.

GROWING IN GRACE.

2 Peter iii. 18.—But grow in grace, and in the knowledge of our Lord and Saviour Jesus Christ. To him be glory, both now and for ever, Amen. (Sk.)

ONE of the most pleasing traits in the character of a genuine christian pastor, is his generous, disinterested concern for the present and everlasting welfare of those whom the chief Shepherd has committed to his care. And it is peculiarly delightful to find the same disposition operating with unabated vigor, amidst an almost endless variety of cares and troubles, and after many years of separation have elapsed. This heavenly temper is more or less observable in all the epistles of the New Testament. Hear Paul's declaration to the Thessalonians, "For now we live, if ye stand fast in the Lord." Hear also how he felt, and how he prayed for the Ephesians; see chap. iii. 13—19. In the same spirit, Peter, also, endeavors to guard his christian converts against the principles and practices of infidels and scoffers, by pressing on their attention the importance of activity and perseverance in the great business of the soul's salvation, " Wherefore the rather, brethren, give diligence," &c., chap. i. 10—13. And in conclusion he says, " But grow in grace," &c. This is a subject to be *explained, recommended,* and *practised.* We therefore inquire,

I. WHAT IS MEANT BY GROWING IN GRACE? The word grace means favor, kindness, friendly affection. Hence the phrase, so common in scripture, of finding grace in the eyes or sight of a person, Gen. xxxiv. 11; 2 Sam. xvi. 4; Esther ii. 17. And hence, as it respects God, we are said to be *"justified freely* by his *grace,"* Rom. iii. 24. But the word is also variously applied to the *operations* and *effects* of this free favor. We at present consider it in two senses. First, As it expresses that *state* or *condition* of adoption and reconciliation into which believers are brought, Rom. v. 1, 2.— And, secondly, As it denotes *divine assistance,* afforded "in time of need," 2 Cor. xii. 9, through which the believer is " *strengthened* with might by the Spirit in *the inner man*," Eph. iii. 16. Here we must be indulged in a few remarks.

1. This state of reconciliation, &c., is not that of mankind in general; but is contra-distinguished from a state of *nature*, in which evil principles produce works of wickedness, which, as well as the workers of them, "God's soul hateth," Psa. xi. 5. " By nature we are children of wrath," Eph ii. 3, "and God is *angry* with the wicked," &c., Psa. vii. 11; Isa. xii. 1—3.

2. Wherever there is that *relative* change, by which a penitent is adopted into the family of God, there is also a *real* change in the man's principles and practice ;—a change of *nature*, as well as of condition. Indeed, the real change, which begins in repentance, whereby we sorrow for, hate, and forsake sin, precedes that faith whereby we believe with the heart unto righteousness ;—and which farther purifies the heart, Matt. iv. 17; Acts xx. 21. Yet,

3. The change is not so complete as not to admit of improvement; therefore the text says, " *Grow* in grace." As grace means free favor, this may refer to an advancement in the favor of God. God loves, and must love holiness. It is his own nature; and the more of it any person has, with the greater complacency does God regard him. He calls Abraham his friend; and John was " the disciple whom Jesus (peculiarly) loved." But the principal idea intended to be conveyed, seems to be that of improvement. Illustrate by the example of " little children," &c., John i; Eph. i. 12—14. The growth here enjoined, may well include, and must consist with, 1. An improvement in knowledge ;—" the knowledge of our Lord and Saviour Jesus Christ," that ye may be freed from the mistakes, confusion, and imbecility of infancy; and that your views of his *person* and *work*, and of your christian privileges, may be more *correct*, Eph. iv. 13, 14,—more clear, chap. i. 17—19,—and more comprehensive, chap. iii. 14—19. This will be attended with, 2. A corresponding improvement in *strength ;* from childhood—to *youth*—to *maturity.* " The righteous shall be stronger and stronger," Job xvii. 9. And 3. An improvement in *usefulness*,—that, in uniting in yourselves the experience, firmness, prudence, &c., of mature age, with parental solicitude, ye may be *nursing fathers* to the church, and " mothers in Israel." With a view to recommend the subject, we inquire,

II. What are the advantages of growing in grace? The improvement is,

1. *A personal advantage.* The christian's life is, in a great measure, made up of *doing* and *suffering.* An increase of grace will enable him to *do* the will of God more *easily*, and more *effectually*, Col. i. 9, 10; and to *suffer* it more *patiently* and *cheerfully*, v. 11. It is,

2. A *social* advantage. Society will be so far preserved from the baleful effects of *error, inconsistency*, &c. And many *good* things will be *done*, and *well done*, in the world, the church, the family, &c., which would otherwise be left undone, Phil. i. 9—11. Hence it is,

3. An advantage to *the cause of religion.* There is a pathos in the address, and an energy in the pious actions of an *eminently holy and thriving* soul, that can hardly fail to take effect.

4. It will advance *the glory of God.* It is he, who, through Jesus Christ, bestows grace, whereby we serve him acceptably ;—and " serve our generation" according to his will ;—and *endure* as seeing the Invisible, Matt. v. 13—16. Wherefore to him, as the *Origin* of good, and according to the

apostle's wish, to "our Lord and Saviour Jesus Christ, *as Mediator, be* glory, both now and for ever." Amen.

But this is a subject to be reduced to practice. It remains, therefore, that we inqure,

III. WHAT ARE THE MEANS OF GROWING IN GRACE? On this subject we may avail ourselves of what experience teaches us concerning the means which conduce to bodily health and improvement; among which are, proper care—proper nutriment—and proper exercise.

1. Proper *care*. This is so necessary, that before your children are capable of taking care of themselves, you anxiously keep them out of the way of harm. Observe, here, Paul's solicitude; "As a nurse cherisheth her children," &c., "*warning* every man;"—" we *charged* every one of you," &c., 1 Thess. ii. 7—11; Col. i. 28. And when we reach the years of discretion, we still find it necessary to guard against pestilential effluvia, accidential injuries, destructive practices, &c. So should we, in spirituals, avoid the pestilential atmosphere of the wicked;—"take heed, lest we fall;"—" flee youthful lusts, which war against the soul," &c., 1 Cor. xv. 33; Prov. iv. 14, 15.

2. Proper *nutriment ;*—rejecting, of course, what is *useless ;* and, more especially, whatever is *deleterious*. Much of what is useless, and much of what is poisonous, is to be met with, both in *conversation* and in *print*. Reject it; and seek that which will afford nourishment:—in. 1. Hearing and reading *the word*, 1 Pet. ii. 2. 2. Biography of persons whose pious *life*, and happy *death*, have exemplified the truth of scripture. 3. *Christian conversation*. 4. *Prayer;* and, in fine, every appointed or prudential means of grace.

3. Proper *exercise*. Without this, the most robust *body* will sink rapidly into the hands of the physician; and through them, into the grave. So, " health of mind is exercise; not rest." By reason of *use*, our senses are exercised to discern both good and evil, Heb. v. 13, 14; see also Matt. xiii. 12; Luke xix. 20—26. Have you a measure of faith, love, humility, patience? &c. *Use* grace, and *have* grace.

Remind *the sinner* of the awfulness of his case. " The *wrath* of God is revealed," &c., and it *abideth* on *him*, Rom. i. 18; John iii. 36; 2 Thess. i. 8, 9.

Let *the feeble-minded* remember, that grace admits of growth. " Who hath despised the day of small things?" Isa. xl. 11; Heb. iv. 15, 16.

On *adult believers*, the necessity of a farther growth should be urged—to prevent *apostasy*, ch. i. 1—9, and iii. 17,—to prevent *perdition*, ch. ii. 20; John xv. 6. And they may be *encouraged*, by the hope of " an entrance, ministered unto them abundantly, into the everlasting kingdom of our Lord and Saviour Jesus Christ," ch. i. 10, 11.

SPIRITUAL HEALTH.

Isa. liii. 5.—With his stripes we are healed. (Sk.)

FOR the transcendant importance of its matter, and the minuteness and a curacy of its prophetical descriptions, this chapter occupies an unrivalled eminence amongst the writings of the Jewish seers Here we have the humility of the Redeemer specified, ver. 2 ;—the contemptuous ideas of men respecting him described, ver. 3 ;—the acuteness of his sufferings asserted, ver 8, 9 :—the patience with which he endured his peerless sorrows antici pated, ver. 7 ;—and the grand design of the whole announced, ver. 4, 5, 6. Yea, such is the luminous and evangelical glory which pours upon our astonished vision in this portion of Scripture, that we almost forget that its inspired author lived near seven hundred years before the important events which he predicted took place ; we are inadvertently rather inclined to associate him with the eye witnesses of the sorrows of the Son of God. Under the influence of these considerations, we do not wonder that even the licentious Rochester, when immured in the chamber of affliction, should, by a calm investigation of this chapter, have been fully convinced of the authenticity of those Scriptures which had before constituted the butt of his profane ridicule; and, through divine mercy, rendered capable of subscribing to the words of our text, " With his stripes we are healed." With fervent aspirations to God for his blessing, let us proceed to discuss this truly interesting passage, in which we have,

I. A LAMENTABLE DISEASE ASSUMED.

II. AN INFALLIBLE PHYSICIAN SPECIFIED.

III. HIS MODE OF OPERATION DESCRIBED.

IV. AN EXTRAORDINARY CURE ASSERTED.

1. As there can be no cure effected where no disease exists, the assumption of disease is inseparably connected with this passage. The sacred Scriptures abound with figurative modes of expression ; hence the diseases of the body have been used as a medium of representing the moral pravity of human nature, Isa. i. 5, 6 ; Jer. viii. 21, 22. In attending to the prophet's figure, we shall consider the spiritual disease of man, as,

1. *The baneful result of transgression.* When God had formed man of the dust, and breathed into him the breath of life, he pronounced him " very good," and doubtless this approving testimony had both a moral and a phy sical application ; but, alas ! how are the mighty fallen !—how unlike the production of a holy and omniscient Being !—Man unhappily violated the paradisiacal commandment—mingled his pristine glory in the abyss of ruin— and introduced a hideous train of ills, of every shape and size :—and among these, a fixed inveterate aptitude to evil, holds a very prominent place, Gen. iii. 1—8 ; Rom. v. 12.

2. *Universal in its prevalence.* Some diseases of the body affect particular parts ; others diffuse their influence through the whole system. This moral disease pervades the whole man ; every member of the body, and every faculty of the soul, is thoroughly infected and deranged, Gen. vi. 5, Job xviii. 4 ; Mark viii. 21, 22 ;—and these baneful effects of the fall are diffused through the whole human kind. As totally as the man is fallen and depraved, so is the whole of his species involved in ruin ; infancy—childhood—youth—and tottering age—present indisputable evidence in proof of this humbling fact, Isa. liii. 6 ; Rom. iii. 10, 11, 23.

3. *Hereditary in its descent.* Some diseases of the body are unhappily entailed on posterity, and are transmitted in regular succession from father to son :—of this nature is the moral malady assumed in our text :—it has descended in one unbroken line, from the first guilty pair in Eden's garden, down to your preacher and his present audience ;—hence no happy intervening age of paradisiacal innocence has adorned the page of history ;—hence the biographical details of ages have not broken the painful monotony of human guilt, by the exhibition of one happy individual in a state of unmixed.

127

underived, pristine purity. The lineaments of moral pravity in the father, have been strikingly manifest in the son, Gen. iv. 1—8, viii. 21.

4. *Incurable by human energy.* The diseases of the human body frequently baffle the utmost skill of the medical science. All the wisdom and power of man have been exercised to impede the progress of this spiritual malady, but to little or no purpose; the senators of Greece and Rome have enacted laws, and the philosophers of both countries have disseminated their ethics abroad; but the radical principle of evil in the human breast has defied all their efforts—nothing less than a Divine Physician can effect a cure, Job. xiv. 4; Jer. xiii. 23.

II. AN INFALLIBLE PHYSICIAN SPECIFIED. Man has not been abandoned to his spiritual self-induced malady, without hope or help;—mercy has interposed—a physician has been provided—and one possessing the most ample qualifications, John iii. 14—17. He is,

1. *Infinite in wisdom.* Wisdom is necessary in order both to understand the disease, and properly to apply the remedy. Jesus, our Divine Physician, is " the wisdom of God."—He comprehends our spiritual affliction in all its ramifications—he cannot be deceived by false appearances, for " he knoweth what is in man, and needeth not that any should tell him," Jer. xvii. 9, 10; John i. 1—5, 14.

2. *Impartial in his attendance.* Man, in every station in life, is susceptible of partial feeling; the medical profession cannot be expected to be free from its influences. The splendor of the palace, and the grandeur of nobility, are more attractive than the humble cottage of the peasant; but the physician before us, is equally attentive to high and low—rich and poor—learned and illiterate;—yea, and is able to attend to the necessities of all at the same moment, Ezek. xxxiii. 17—19; Mark x. 46—52; Luke vii. 1—10.

3. *Ever easy of access.* Medical practitioners of great celebrity, in order to secure leisure for the purposes of health and domestic duties, are obliged to render themselves inaccessible at certain periods; but Jesus, the infallible Physician of souls, is ever easy of approach. This appears evident from his kind invitations, Isa. i. 18; Matt. xi. 28, 29;—his solemn declarations, Ezek. xxxiii. 11, 12; Matt. xxii. 37;—and his gracious promises, John vi. 37; 1 John i. 9;—as also from the uniform testimony of experience, in all ages, Psa. xxxiv. 18; cxviii. 21; Rom. x. 12, 13.

4. *Gratuitous in his practice.* It is just and proper that the exercise of skill and attention should be reasonably remunerated. But such is the peculiar excellence of this spiritual Physician, that a cure can only be obtained on gratuitous terms. The salvation of the gospel is " without money and without price;" and this method of deliverance is exactly adapted to our ruined condition, Isa. lv. 1, 2; Rom. iii. 24; Eph. ii. 8—10.

III. HIS MODE OF OPERATION DESCRIBED;—" With his stripes." The stripes which were inflicted on the blessed Redeemer, were connected with that death to which he gave himself for the life of the world, when " he bore our sins in his own body on the tree." This atonement, and faith in this atonement, are the only means of a sinner's acceptance with God; the only method by which a cure can be obtained, John iii. 36. This method is,

1. *Divine in its appointment.* It is not the fruit of the human imagination; the production of councils, or synods, however learned, or important: but the offspring of Jehovah; it comes to us under the sanction of the Deity. Isa. xxviii. 16; John iii. 16, 17.

2. *Easy in its application.* Not animal oblations—tedious pilgrimages— a course of painful penance—nor any of the other inventions of human

error;—but "repent and believe." The power is given, and its exercise is required, Acts iii. 19; xvi. 31.

3. *Universal in its adaptation.* The gospel way of salvation is admirably suited to all the possible constitutions, situations, and conditions of men, of every "nation, kindred, people, and tongue," Rom. x. 4—13: Acts ii. 9—11; 37—42.

4. *Infallible in its efficacy.* No case is too intricate, none too desperate, to admit of a cure: no individual in any age of time, ever made a scriptural application and was disappointed. The antediluvian saints realized its efficacy by an anticipating faith; the evangelists and apostles by immediate application; and believers since, by a retrospective reference to the sacrifice of Christ, have proved that he is "able to save to the uttermost them that come to God by him."

IV. AN EXTRAORDINARY CURE ASSERTED;—"We are healed." Were mortal ears susceptible of celestial testimony, the loud hosannas of the blood-washed throng on high would amply support this assertion; and multitudes of terrestrial saints would echo back the sound! Can we from experience adopt the sentiment?—This cure may be considered, as,

1. *Radical in its nature.* The cure effected by this Physician is not the removal of external symptoms, while the principle is unrenovated; not breaking off a few gross evils, while the seat of depravity is untouched; but, the understanding is enlightened; the will divinely influenced; the affections properly directed; the imagination spiritualized; and the memory sanctified; in short, the heart entirely changed, Ezek. xxxvi. 26; 2 Cor. v. 17.

2. *Convincing in its evidence.* Whenever a cure is effected there are visible proofs of such restoration; so in the case before us, when a sin-sick soul has made application to Jesus Christ in a scriptural manner, and has realized his saving efficacy, the effect is manifest; the faculties have received a new tone, and this renovation appears in holy tempers, spiritual conversation, and an upright, conscientious, line of conduct, Gal. v. 22—24; 2 Pet. i. 5—7.

3. *Happy in its influence.* Of this there cannot be a doubt entertained for a moment. Personally, the peace of God is enjoyed; divine support under affliction experienced: succor in the hour of temptation realized; and the joys of heaven anticipated. In the family the sacred scriptures are read; prayer regularly offered; diligence and economy promoted; and the salvation of dependants sought. In reference to the world, intercession is offered up, exhortation and reproof are administered; and religion recommended by pious example, Rom. v. 1; Josh. xxiv. 15; 1 Thess. ii. 10.

This subject tends, 1. To promote humility. 2. To produce self-examination. 3. To excite to fervent gratitude. 4. To encourage the desponding penitent.

GROWING IN GRACE.

2 Thessalonians i. 3.—We are bound to thank God always for you, brethren, as it is meet. because that your faith groweth exceedingly, and the charity of every one of you all towards each other aboundeth. (Pr.)

PERHAPS there is no christian society now on earth to whom this language is fully applicable; and it may be, if Paul had been writing to us, or to other christians of the present day, he would have adopted a different mode of address. It is nevertheless true, that among the primitive churches, they were not all alike prosperous, spiritual, and happy; but that at Thessalonica was one of the most amiable, and deserving of commendation. ——— It is a mercy however if these blessed fruits are found amongst us in any degree, and it is profitable for us to take the best examples presented in the scriptures, that we may learn our own defects, and be led to imitate what is more excellent.

1. Observe, in giving "thanks to God" for their growth in faith and love, the apostle plainly intimates that it was by *the grace of God* they were what they were. Though all that is evil in us belongs to ourselves, yet all that is good in us is of God alone, even that which is commanded and required at our hands.

2. The growth of faith and love plainly supposes that sanctification *is progressive*. It is like the kingdom of heaven in the world, which is compared to a grain of mustard seed, and a little leaven that leaveneth the whole lump. But if we had no inherent sanctification, and none but what is in Christ, this could not be true. Some indeed have endeavored to comfort themselves, and to comfort others, while in a low declining state, by certain examples in scripture; but it is our safest and best way to take examples of the most exalted kind.

3. The growth of faith is here connected with that of *brotherly love*, as a cause is connected with its effect. Certainly, if we grow in faith, we shall also grow in love; because the same principle which attaches us to the truth, will attach us to one another for the truth's sake. Christ is the centre of union; all who love him are taught of God to love one another.

I. ATTEND TO SOME OF THE EVIDENCES OF THIS GROWTH IN GRACE, MENTIONED IN THE TEXT.

Growth in grace is here supposed to be *visible*, or the apostle could not have seen it. It becomes visible by the fruits of righteousness which it produces; and if this be true of us, others will perceive it. Acts iv. 13.

1. Growing in faith will be seen in our taking increasing pleasure *in the means of faith*, the word of God. ——— We shall find delight in reading and hearing it, and it will be to us the joy and rejoicing of our hearts. Psa. i. 2, 3; Prov. vi. 20—23. The word of Christ will dwell in us richly in all wisdom, and be received as the ingrafted word. Col. iii. 16. Seasons of public instruction will be attended with delight, and we shall not hear the word from custom, but from far higher motives. Isa. ii. 2.

2. It will appear in a growing attachment to *the doctrines of Christ*, who is himself the great object of faith. ——— If a man could speak with great eloquence, he might please a certain description of hearers; but if Christ be not his theme, he would fail to please those who believe in him, for to them he is precious. 1 Peter ii. 7. When therefore it is chiefly the manner, and not the subject of address that is regarded, it bespeaks a religion too much

like that of the Corinthians, and not that of the Thessalonians. 1 Cor. ii. 4, 5.

3. Growing in faith consists in an *increasing acquaintance* with the mind of God in his word, as the ground of faith. ——— We may be brought to believe the gospel in one day, but it is the work of a whole life to become rooted and grounded in the truth; to know not merely what we believe, but why; and to be able to say with Paul, "I know whom I have believed." We may believe what is true, from being told that it is so; but it will do us very little good, unless we perceive the authority on which it rests, and the principle by which it is supported in the scriptures of truth. Our faith must not stand in the wisdom of men, but in the power of God.

4. It will be evident by increasing *patience* and *submission*, under all the ills of life. ——— This was noticed in the Thessalonians, amidst the persecutions and tribulations which they endured, ver. 4. If we faint in the day of adversity our strength is small, and our faith is weak. Matt. xiv. 31.

5. By an increasing *weanedness from the present world.* ——— This is the victory that overcometh the world, even our faith, both in prosperity and adversity. John also speaks of those as being strong, who have overcome the wicked one, and have the word of God abiding in them. 1 John ii. 14, v. 4.

5. Growing in faith appeared in the *love they had one to another* for the truth's sake. ——— Christians may live together without discredit, and esteem each other as friends; but to love as brethren, and as christians, is quite another thing. They may also love one another from being of the same mind, and yet not love on account of their being of the mind of Christ. ——— Or if there be true christian love existing, it may not "abound," as it did among the Thessalonians; yet this is necessary to prove that our faith "groweth exceedingly."

II. CONSIDER THE IMPORTANCE OF THE SUBJECT.

1. Growing in faith and love brings *glory to God*, verse 12. Bearing much fruit honors him, and recommends the gospel to others. John xv. 8.

2. It has an influence upon the *ministry of the word*, which is highly desirable. ——— It is next to impossible to preach to some people, who instead of growing in faith have no faith at all, and Paul himself found it so. Heb. v. 11. ——— But oh how different, where the souls of the people may be seen as it were in their countenances, and glisten in their eyes. Rom. i. 11, 12; Acts xi. 23.

3. If we do not make some progress in religion, we shall be *declining* and going backward. ——— There is no standing still in this race, no intermission in this warfare. If we grow not in faith and love, the seeds of indifference and unbelief will spring up and grow in their stead; will choke the word, and render it unfruitful.

4. If we do not grow in grace, our religion will at best become *doubtful*, and we shall have cause to tremble for the issue. Heb. x. 38. ——— It is the character of all true believers that they are making advancement in the divine life, and growing up in the image and likeness of God. Prov. iv. 18: 1 Pet. ii. 2; 2 Pet. i. 10, 11.

If there be some who have neither faith nor love, and are utterly unconcerned about it; what must be said to such? We must go on preaching the gospel, warning them to flee from the wrath to come, and leave the consequences.

CHRISTIAN PERFECTION AN OBJECT OF PRAYER AND OF HOPE.

Heb. xiii. 20, 21.—Now the God of peace, that brought again from the dead our Lord Jesus, that great Shepherd of the sheep, through the blood of the everlasting covenant, make you perfect in every good work, to do his will; working in you that which is well-pleasing in his sight, through Jesus Christ. (Pr.)

The believing Hebrews were in a very unsettled state: many of them had gone back, and others were hesitating. Hence there were many practical disorders among them, and a general tendency to apostacy. Hence also the numerous warnings given them in various parts of this epistle: ch. ii. 3. iv. 1, 11. But after all this, the apostle closes his address with the prayer in the text, which is presented to God under the most endearing character.

This prayer is applicable to us as well as to them; for we also are the subjects of many defects, and need to offer up the same request.

I. CONSIDER THE BLESSINGS PRAYED FOR.

The apostle here gives us a picture of what christians should be, and should aspire after. Let us therefore pray—

1. That we may be "made perfect."——— The word means to set right, to restore and put in order, as in Gal. vi. 1: it therefore applies to the disorders among the Hebrews and other christians. ——— It does not so much express what we shall be hereafter, as what we may be in this world; and points out that lovely uniformity of character which accompanies great grace. If we examine ourselves, we shall find many things wanting, or so imperfect as to need much to be done for us, to make us what we should be. ——— Some appear to be pious and devout, but are deficient in benevolence; they abound in the duties of the first table of the law, but are deficient in the second. ——— Some have knowledge, but little zeal, and are cold hearted; while others abound in zeal, which is not according to knowledge. ——— Some are tender and affectionate, but wanting courage and fidelity. ——— To abound in all the fruits of the Spirit, so as to exhibit a lovely uniformity of character, is to be "made perfect;" and this is unspeakably desirable.

2. Perfect "in every good work." ——— If we be christians, we are engaged in many good works: such as preaching, praying, hearing, reading, acts of kindness towards men, and of charity to the poor. ——— But there is a manner of doing these things which gives a sort of perfection to the christian character: if our minds are set in order, they will all be done in the spirit of the gospel, and in a manner very different from what they would otherwise be. ——— There is such a thing as speaking the word " as we ought to speak;"and of praying "as we ought." Ephes. vi. 20. Rom. viii. 26; xii. 8.

3. Perfect in every good work " to do his will." ——— We may be much occupied in religious concerns, and yet not do the will of God in them. ——— Sometimes for want of taking his word as our rule: we may go a round of religious duties, because others do the same, without any reference to the will of God. ———.Sometimes the motive may be deficient: we may do many things from nothing but mere vanity, self-righteousness, or a desire to be seen of men. ——— But if we are "made perfect," we shall do the will of God from the heart.

4. We are taught to pray that the Holy Spirit may " work in us that which is well-pleasing in his sight." ——— It is not in our corrupt nature to attain these things, without the influence of the Holy Spirit: it is he that excites desire in prayer, resolution in labor, and that makes us perfect in every good

word and work. ——— It is he that works faith in us by the promises, patience by sanctified affliction, and hope by the prospect of eternal life.

5. That all may be accepted " through Jesus Christ." ——— None are accepted but as believing in him; and no works of ours, but for his sake.

III. THE ENCOURAGEMENT WE HAVE TO PRAY FOR THESE BLESSINGS.

In offering up this prayer for the believing Hebrews, the apostle directed them and us to pray in the same manner, and from the same motives.

1. Great encouragement is derived from *the pacific character of God*, as " the God of peace." This view of the divine character is essential to our drawing near to him; and through a Mediator, there is now peace on earth, and good will towards men. ——— It is now with the world as it was with mankind after the deluge, when God accepted the sacrifice of Noah. Gen. viii. 20, 21.

2. From *the proofs* of his being the God of peace; "having brought again from the dead our Lord Jesus." ——— This is a doctrine of unspeakable importance, and supported by the clearest evidence. ——— 1. The resurrection of Christ is represented in the Scriptures as an act of almighty power, or as one of the greatest efforts of omnipotence. Ephes. i. 20. ——— 2. It is represented as a judicial release or discharge. Rom. iv. 25. ——— Simeon was kept as a hostage, having been surety for his brethren; but when they returned to Egypt, he was brought forth from prison, which was a sign of peace. God's having raised up Jesus from the dead, was declaring himself satisfied; it was smelling a sweet savor, as in Noah's offering. ——— Hence he was "raised for our justification," after being "delivered for our offences."

3. *The character* in which *Christ was raised up;* as "the great Shepherd of the sheep." He that raised the Shepherd from the grave, can raise us also from death, and gather together the scattered sheep. Ephes. i. 18. ——— It implies also that Christ has a people given him of the Father, and that for their salvation he went through all his sufferings: as such he died and rose again. ——— Paul was a shepherd, and did all he could, and there were other shepherds also; but Christ is the "great Shepherd" of the sheep; and God having brought them forth, it was in love to the flock.

4. *The ground* of his resurrection is *the sacrifice* he offered on the cross. ——— God's having raised him from the dead, was a proof of his having accepted the sacrifice in our stead; and this affords a powerful plea in prayer. ——— It is this which the ascended Saviour presents as the ground of his own intercession; and all our supplications must be founded on the same plea.

5. The blood which he shed, being "the blood of the everlasting covenant," affords additional encouragement in prayer. ——— This language may apply to the covenant made with Christ, as it is expressed in another passage, Zech. ix. 11: or to the covenant made with us through him, and which stands opposed to the covenant of works made at Sinai. ——— Covenants with sinful creatures have been made through the medium of sacrifices, and the covenant of grace is founded in the blood of the Mediator; and through it, it is that we have the cup of blessing.

THE OBJECTS, DESIGN, AND REQUISITION OF GOSPEL GRACE.

Acts xxvi. 17, 18.—I send thee, to open their eyes, and to turn them from darkness to light ; and from the power of Satan unto God, that they may receive forgiveness of sins, and inheritance among them which are sanctified by faith that is in me. (Sk.)

1. THESE words occur in the relation given by the apostle Paul of his conversion to christianity ; an event which was often referred to by himself, and has since been often appealed to by others, as a check to infidelity. It appears that the apostle's conversion was effected by means of our Lord's *personal* appearance to him. This personal appearance of Jesus, some considerable time after his death, proves the certainty of his *resurrection ;* and his resurrection proves that he is the *Son of God*, the promised Saviour of the world, Rom. i. 4. Thus we have the fullest proof that christianity is of God, and that Paul was divinely commissioned to teach it.

2. The narrative of this remarkable conversion being so important, we cannot but feel weil pleased with that repetition of it which we find in this book : especially as each account of it contains some interesting particular, not mentioned in the others. When St. Luke records this event in the 9th chapter, he informs us what the Lord said to Ananias, ver. 10--16; when St. Paul relates it himself in the 22d chapter, he informs us what Ananias said to him, ver. 12—14, and when he repeats it in this chapter, he informs us what our Lord said to him, ver. 15—18, "I am Jesus," &c. "I send thee to open their eyes," &c. These words teach us,

1. THE OBJECTS OF GOSPEL BENEVOLENCE,—or the persons to whom the gospel is sent. This we learn from the words which immediately precede our text, and from the text itself: here we are informed both who they are, and what they are.

1. *Who they are ;*—They are the people, and the Gentiles. "Delivering thee," &c., ver. 17. By *the people* is meant the *Jewish nation*, who were God's chosen people, Deut. vii. 6 ;—a peculiarly favored people, Deut. xxxiii. 29 ;—and a sinful people, who became rebellious, ungrateful, and degenerated, Isa. i. 2—4. To this people the gospel was first preached by Christ's command, Luke xxiv. 47 ;—and to this people will the gospel yet be preached with the happiest success, Rom. xi. 25, 26. By the *Gentiles* are meant *those nations of the earth which are not of Jewish extraction.* To them also the Messiah was promised, Isa. xlix. 6 ; for their benefit he was manifested in the flesh, Luke ii. 10, 11, 32 ; to them also the gospel is sent by repeated injunctions, Luke xxiv. 47 ; Mark xvi. 15; Matt. xxviii. 19 ; on their receiving the gospel, Christ redeems them from sin, Acts x. 34, Rev. vii. 9, 10 ; and they are promised to Christ for his inheritance, Psa. ii. 8. The people and the Gentiles must therefore include *all mankind ;* and hereby we are assured that God wills the salvation of all the human race, Ezek. xxxiii. 11 ; 1 Tim. ii. 4. Having seen who they are to whom the gospel is sent, let us now observe,

2. *What they are,*—or in what state the gospel finds them. *They are in darkness ;* for the gospel is sent to open their eyes, &c. They are in the darkness of *ignorance*, respecting the nature, necessity, and way of salvation, Psa. cvii. 10, 11. They are in *darkness ;* for they have closed their eyes by a deliberate rejection of divine light, John iii. 19, 20 ; Matt xiii. 15 ; and they are blinded by Satan, 1 Cor. iv. 4. *They are subject to the power of Satan.* This they evidently are, being *inhabited* by him, Eph ii. 2 ;—*devoted* to his service, John viii. 44 ;—and *governed* by his will, &,

THE WORK OF GRACE.

Tim. ii. 26. *They are condemned criminals ;* under a sentence of eternal death, John. iii. 18 ; Ezek. xviii. 20. *They are a disinherited family ;* for they have justly forfeited their title to heaven, Rom. iii. 23 ; and they have no well-grounded hope of it, Eph. ii. 12. Thus our state, through sin, is alarming ; but God has remembered us in mercy, Psa. cxxxvi. 23. Of this our text also assures us, by teaching us,

II. THE DESIGN OF THE GOSPEL MISSION,—or the purposes for which it was sent.

1. *It is sent to open our eyes, and to turn us from darkness to light.*— *To open our eyes ;* by calling our attention to the care of our souls, as the most important business of our lives, Matt. vi. 33 ; 1 Tim. iv. 8 ; Matt. xvi. 26. *To turn us from darkness to light ;* by engaging us to come to Christ for illumination of mind, Eph. v. 14 ; Matt. xi. 29 ; John viii. 12.

2. *It is sent to turn us from the power of Satan unto God.* To *turn us from the power of Satan ;* from his *dominion,* by subduing our evil habits, 2 Cor. x. 4, 5 ; and from his *service,* by effecting an entire reformation in our conduct, Tit. ii. 12. To *turn us unto God ;* with humble *contrition,* Luke xv. 18 ; with earnest *cries* for mercy, Luke xviii. 13 ; with *affiance* in his compassion, Psa. xiii. 5, and lii. 8 ; and with due *subjection* to his authority, Rom. vi. 13.

3. *It is sent that we may receive forgiveness of sins.* Gospel forgiveness implies, *full* forgiveness of all our past sins, both secret and open, Acts xiii. 38, 39. *Affectionate* forgiveness ; such as exempts us from the punishment due to sin, and interests us in God's paternal favor, Psa. xxxii. 1, 2 ; Luke xv. 22—24. *Assured* forgiveness, which is attested by the Holy Spirit, Isa. xii. 1 ; Rom. viii. 16.

4. *It is sent that we may receive inheritance among them which are sanctified.* To be *sanctified,* is to be *separated from sin ;* and *devoted to God's service,* Rom. vi. 22. This sanctification the gospel *requires,* 1 Thess. v. 23, 24, and iv. 7 ; and what the gospel requires, it instrumentally *produces,* Obad. 17 ; John xvii. 17. The *inheritance* of those which are sanctified, is *two-fold ;* a gracious inheritance in this life, 1 Cor. iii. 21–23 ; and a glorious inheritance in heaven, 1 Peter i. 3—5. And *all who obey the gospel enjoy this inheritance,* Psa. lxxxiv. 11 ; Acts xx. 32. That we may ensure the enjoyment of this inheritance, our text teaches us,

III. THE DUTY OF GOSPEL SUBJECTS ;—or the means by which its blessings are appropriated. All its benefits are obtained by faith in Christ ; " By faith that is in me." Here observe,

1. *What faith in Christ implies.* It appears from God's word that it implies—*Coming* to Christ, for rest from sin and its consequences, Matt. xi. 28 ; John v. 35. *Receiving* Christ, as our Teacher, Sovereign, and Redeemer, John i. 12 ; Matt. xi. 29. *Trusting* in Christ, for full salvation, pardon, acceptance, holiness, and heaven, Isa. xxviii. 16 ; Eph. i. 13. *Abiding* in Christ, till he comes to glorify us, 1 John ii. 28 ; Heb. xii. 2. And *walking* in Christ, by seeking all he calls us to enjoy, Col. ii. 6 ; Phil. iii. 12.

2. *The propriety of requiring faith in Christ as the means of salvation.* This is evident, because faith in Christ tends to inspire its subjects with the most profound *reverence for God,* who will not be approached by us without a Mediator, Psa. lxxxix 7 ; Heb. xii. 28, 29 ; with *dread of sin,* which rendered Christ's sufferings necessary, that we might be saved consistently with God's rectitude, Heb. ii. 10 ; Rom. iii. 25, 26 ; with *confidence in God ;* who has graciously given us the earnest of salvation, in the gift of

135

his Son, Rom. viii. 32 ; with *gratitude* to God, for his redeeming goodness, 2 Cor. v. 14, 15 ; 1 Cor. vi. 19, 20 ; Rom. xii. 1 ; and with deep *humiliation*, through a consciousness that our salvation is ascribable only to divine grace, Eph. ii. 8, 9 ; Tit. iii. 5—7.

APPLICATION.

1. *From the duty of gospel subjects, learn the importance of faith in our Lord Jesus Christ.*—*It is important*, as none can be saved without it, John iii. 36 ; Mark xvi. 15, 16. Hence, *seek salvation in no other way* but that of faith in Christ: not on the ground of mere mercy without a Mediator ; for God will not admit sinners into his presence on these terms, John xiv. 6 ; not on account of your sufferings, for these being the effects of sin, can never remove their cause ; not on account of your good morals, for you cannot atone for past offences by the imperfect fulfilment of present duties, Psalm cxliii. 2. *Rest in nothing short of faith in Christ.* Not in partial reformation, nor in correct opinions, nor in the mere outward form of godliness. Now actually come to Christ, receive him, and trust in him, Acts xxii. 16. *Persevere in the exercise of faith;* its continuance is necessary, Heb. x. 37.

2. *From the design of the gospel mission, learn your privileges as believers in Christ.* *Consider the blessings* you are called to enjoy ; these are illumination, conversion, pardon, sanctification. *Examine yourselves;* are you thus turned from darkness to light ; from the power of Satan unto God? have you received forgiveness of sins? are you sanctified,—redeemed from sin, and devoted to God? have you heaven in prospect? can you say with the apostle, 2 Cor. v. 1 ; 1 Peter i. 3. *Expect* those blessings, if exercising faith in Christ ; they are purchased for you, promised to you, and are now ready to be imparted, John xi. 40 ; Luke xiv. 17.

3. *From the objects of gospel benevolence, learn your duty as the followers of Christ.* As his professing followers you are called to *imitate him,* Phil. ii. 5 ; 1 John ii. 6. Like him, have *compassion* on perishing sinners ; whether relatives, the rising generation, adult neighbors, or the heathen world. However distinguished, their case is truly pitiable ; for they are blind, enslaved, perishing, helpless, and hopeless, Job vi. 14. *Impart gospel truth to them,* that they may be healed of their diseases, and saved from their destructions, Psa. cvii. 20. *Your consistent christian zeal will be attended with the happiest results.* Hereby you will concur with God in fulfilling the Messiah's request, Psa. ii. 8 ; you will promote the glory of God, Isa. lxi. 1—3 ; and you ensure eternal honor to yourselves, Daniel xii. 3 ; 1 Peter v. 3.

THE NATURE AND EFFECTS OF TRUE RELIGION.

James iii. 17.—The wisdom that is from above, is first pure, then peaceable, gentle, and easy to be entreated, full of mercy and good fruits, without partiality, and without hypocrisy. (H. H.)

RELIGION, like a tree, must be judged of by its fruits—
That which savors of pride, earthliness, or sensuality, is not of God—
Its character is justly drawn in the words before us—It is,

I. Holy in its nature—

Religion, above all other things, is entitled to the name of "wisdom"—

It enlightens the mind, informs the judgment, regulates the life—

And he who lives under its influence, is wise in the estimation of God himself—

Being from above, it resembles its divine author—

Religion is a beam issuing from God the fountain of light—

And, as "in him is no darkness at all," so neither is there any thing impure in that which flows from him—

It may be mixed with sin, but in its own nature it is "pure"—

And, in proportion as it prevails, it will dissipate the clouds of ignorance and sin—

All "spiritual or fleshly filthiness" will surely vanish before it, Matt. v. 8 Acts xv. 9; 2 Cor vii. 1.

In consequence of this it is,

II. Useful in its tendency—It renders us,

1. Amiable in our spirit—

Though men differ widely in their natural tempers, yet the unregenerate are, on many occasions, quarrelsome, fierce, implacable—

But as soon as ever religion exerts its influence on our minds, we mortify these unhallowed tempers, and become "peaceable, gentle, and easy to be entreated"—

From thenceforth it is the delight of our souls to cultivate and promote peace, to maintain in ourselves a meek and quiet spirit, and to exercise, as occasion may require, forbearance and forgiveness to all around us—

2. Benevolent in our conduct—

Compassion and diligence are inseparable attributes of true religion—

The real christian is not, like the barren fig-tree, covered with the leaves of an outward profession, but destitute of fruit—

He labors to abound in every good word and work, and to benefit to the utmost the bodies and souls of his fellow creatures—

His heart is "full" of love, and out of the abundance of his heart he both speaks and acts—

It is within us a living principle, that is,

III. Uniform in its operations—It extends,

1. To duties without limitation—

The grace of God will not admit of "partiality" in our obedience—

It will stimulate us to difficult and self-denying duties, as well as to those which are more easy and pleasant, 1 Tim. v. 21.

And will make us as solicitous to do what is right towards strangers or enemies, as towards our own friends or partizans, 1 Tim. v. 21.

2. To desires without reserve—

Religion penetrates to the inmost soul, and regulates all our motives and principles of action—

The person whose *outward* conduct *only* is good, is in God's sight no other than a "whited sepulchre"—

The man whose heart is right with God, will watch against all selfish ends, and endeavor to act with a single eye to the glory of his God—

Infer,

1. How unjustly is religion condemned in the world!

Many consider religion as destructive of all personal and social happiness—

But what is there in this representation of religion that deserves such a character?—

137

Let the world call it *folly* if they will; but God accounts it "*wisdom*"—

2. What reason have the most godly to blush and be ashamed!

We must not estimate our religion by our opinions so much as by our practice—

Doubtless we must build on Christ as our only foundation; but we have no evidence of an union with him any further than we raise upon him this holy superstructure—

Alas! what poor builders have the very best of us been; and how little progress have we made when we judge by this test!—

3. What need have we to wait continually upon our God in prayer!

This wisdom is "from above," and can be derived from God alone—

And how can we obtain it of him, but in the exercise of prayer?—

Let us then ask it of him, who has promised to impart it "liberally, and without upbraiding," James i. 5.

STABILITY THE GIFT OF GOD.

Psa. lxvi. 8, 9.—O bless our God, ye people, and make the voice of his praise to be heard; which holdeth our soul in life, and suffereth not our feet to be moved. (H. H.)

THE blessings of Providence, when uninterruptedly continued, are scarcely noticed: it is only when the loss of them has been painfully apprehended, or actually sustained, that we consider how much we were indebted to God for them. What were the particular trials that had been endured by David or the Jewish nation, we cannot precisely determine: but it is evident, that the deliverance vouchsafed to them had made a lively impression on the Psalmist's mind. Compare ver. 1, 2, with ver. 10—12. The words of our text would furnish exceedingly profitable meditations, if we confined them to their primary import; since the preservation of our life and health, amidst the many seen and unseen dangers with which we are surrounded, demands our most grateful acknowledgments. But a subsequent part of the psalm shews clearly that the writer had respect also to spiritual blessings; ver. 16; and therefore we shall draw your attention more especially to them; and shew,

I. WHAT A MERCY IT IS TO BE UPHELD IN THE WAYS OF GOD.

We feel somewhat of the obligation conferred upon us in our first awakening and conversion; but are by no means duly sensible how much we owe to our God for our daily preservation. But we shall learn better to appreciate this mercy if we consider,

1. To how many snares and dangers we are exposed!

We have frequent occasion to advert to the temptations with which we are encompassed in the world; and to notice the still greater dangers we experience from the corruptions of our own hearts; and the additional conflicts which we have to sustain with all the powers of darkness. We dwell not therefore so particularly on those things at this time; but rather mention the danger to which we are exposed even from lawful things. It is not only allowable, but highly proper, to prosecute our worldly callings with diligence; and to cultivate the tenderest regard for our wife or children: yet both the one and the other may engross too much of our hearts, and become hinderences to us in our journey towards heaven. Our food, our sleep, our studies, our recreations, may become snares, if we be not continually on our guard. It is therefore an unspeakable mercy to be upheld in the midst of such manifold temptations.

2. How many in like circumstances with ourselves, have fallen—

We are living in the full enjoyment of divine ordinances, and of whatever can conduce to the welfare of our souls. But are we therefore secure? Look back to the apostolic age: see how many then were seduced by error, Tit. i. 11; 2 Tim. ii. 18; or disheartened by the fear of man, 2 Tim. i. 15, and iv. 16; Matt. xxvi. 73, 74; or turned aside by the love of this world, Matt. xiii. 22; 2 Tim. iv. 10; or overthrown by unbridled passions. 1 Tim. v. 11, 12; 2 Sam. xi. 4. What reason then have we to adore the grace that has preserved *us!*

3. What would be the probable consequence of our falling—

Some who have fallen have been restored speedily; John xxi. 15—17; and some after a lapse of time; 2 Sam. xii. 13; but thousands have fallen to rise no more. The progress of declension is for the most part rapid. The heart becomes averse to holy duties: from secret neglects proceeds a backwardness to social conference and public ordinances. The conscience is gradually weakened, till it ceases to perform its office, or speaks in so faint a voice, that it is scarcely heard. The besetting sin then gains an entire ascendant, and leads him captive; till at last, God, filled with indignation against the base apostate, "gives him up to a reprobate mind," Ps. lxxxi. 11, 12; and either cuts him off by a sudden stroke, Prov. xxix. i; Acts v. 5, 10, or leaves him to protract a miserable existence, merely that he may bear testimony against his own impieties, and proclaim to those around him the foretastes which he already feels of his eternal destiny. Eccl. v. 17; with Prov. xiv. 32.

Such examples we have seen*: what a mercy it is that we ourselves, instead of being warned by others, are not made a warning to others!

4. What occasion we have given to God to let us fall—

Let us call to mind our own backslidings; our secret neglects; our tampering with temptations; our indulgence of evil passions; our vain-confident presumption: is it not wonderful that God has not long since said respecting us, "Let him alone;" Hos. iv. 17; "My Spirit shall strive with him no longer." Gen. vi. 3: "He likes not to retain God in his knowledge; so I will give him up!" Rom. i. 28.

If we be convinced of these things, let us proceed to consider,

II. THE DUTY OF THOSE WHO EXPERIENCE THIS MERCY—

There can be no doubt on this subject. If our souls have been upheld in life, we should,

1. Acknowledge God in our steadfastness—

"Who is it that has made us to differ" from others? 1 Cor. iv. 7. Have we by nature any more strength than they? or have we of ourselves a more abundant measure of goodness? No: it is " by the grace of God we are what we are; 1 Cor. xv. 10; we have been as much indebted to his protecting hand, as a new-born infant is to its mother's care. We should then acknowledge, that " of him our fruit is found; Hos. xiv. 8; Isai. xxvi. 12; that " it is he that hath wrought us to the self-same thing;" 2 Cor. v. 5; and that to him belongs all the glory of our stability. Ps. lxii. 8; and xxvi. 12.

---

* This was preached on occasion of a person that had made a profession of religion, going back to drunkenness, and dying in a drunken fit. See other examples, 1 Cor. x 6—11.

2. Bless and adore him for his great goodness—

It is not by cold acknowledgments merely that we are to requite the Lord, but by fervent and devout thanksgivings. It is not possible for language adequately to express the obligations we owe to him: and therefore we should call upon " all that is within us to bless his holy name."

Nor should we be content with doing this ourselves: we should invite the whole creation, as it were, to join us. We should labor to stimulate all to love and serve him; and to make his name known to the very ends of the earth. Isai. xii. 4—6, or xlii. 10—12. See also *the text.*

It is in this way that we should endeavor at least, as much as in us lies, to " render unto the Lord according to the benefits" he has conferred upon us.

3. Walk humbly and carefully before him—

We must not presume upon the kindness of our God, or imagine that, because we have been upheld hitherto, we are in no danger of falling: if we had attained the stability of St. Paul himself, " we must keep our body under, and bring it into subjection, lest we become cast-aways ourselves." 1 Cor. ix. 27. To neglect this were to tempt God. God has warned us plainly, that " he will be with us no longer than we continue with him; that if we forsake him, he will forsake us." 2 Chron. xv. 2. We therefore must not be high-minded, but fear; 1 Cor. x. 12; and take heed lest we fall; Rom. xi. 20; and " watch and pray lest we enter into temptation." Matt. xxvi. 41. If we would have our God to keep us, we must be careful to " keep ourselves." Ver. 18, with Jude 20, 21. We must look at the fearful examples that are before our eyes; Luke xvii. 32; Heb. iv. 11; and tremble lest we ourselves become similar monuments of instability, and of God's deserved wrath.

4. Commit ourselves continually to him—

God has engaged to " keep the feet of his saints;" 1 Sam. ii. 9; and directed us to commit ourselves to him for that purpose; 1 Pet. iv. 19; and assured us, that, if we do so, " he will establish our goings." 2 Chron. xx. 20. We should commend ourselves therefore to his gracious care and protection. We should say with David, " Hold thou up my goings in thy paths, that my footsteps slip not: Ps. xvii. 5: " Hold thou me up, and I shall be safe." Ps. cxix. 117. To this we are encouraged by our past experience of his mercy: we may from the kindness already shewn us, safely infer the continuance of it to our souls. Ps. lvi. 13. If we can say, " He hath delivered," we may properly add, " In whom we trust that he will yet deliver us." 2 Cor. i. 10.

But here arise two important QUESTIONS, which it is of the utmost importance to resolve:

1. Are our souls really alive to God?

In vain shall we speak of having " our souls upheld in life," if they have never yet been quickened from the dead. Let us then seriously, and as in the presence of God, inquire, Whether we have been made partakers of a new and living principle, whereby we have been enabled to die unto sin, and to live unto God? Let us not mistake a mere approbation of religion for real regeneration: we must have become new creatures, having new views, new pursuits, new desires, and new prospects, if we have been truly born again: 2 Cor. v. 17; and if this change have not been wrought within us. we are yet in our natural and unconverted state; we may have " a name to live, but are really dead" before God: notwithstanding we may have been preserved from any flagrant violation of our duty, we are yet " dead in trespasses and sins.'

2. Supposing that we are on the whole alive to God, have "our feet really been kept from falling?"

We must ascertain this fact, before we can cordially thank God for it. And is it indeed true of all who profess religion amongst us, that they have been kept? Have none of us acted unworthy of our high calling? Has there been nothing in our tempers, nothing in our worldly transactions, inconsistent with our profession? Or, supposing our outward conduct to have been unimpeachable, have there been no secret sins, which we have reason to mourn over; nothing for which we ought to blush and be confounded before God? Perhaps, if we look inward, we shall find more occasion to bewail our falls, than to bless our God for having kept us from falling.

But, if conscience testify that we have indeed walked uprightly before God, then let us imitate the example in the text, and not only bless and magnify him ourselves, but endeavor also to "make the voice of his praise to be heard" throughout the world.

STEADFASTNESS IN GOD.

Phil. iv. 1.—My brethren, dearly beloved and longed for, my joy and crown, so stand fast in the Lord, my dearly beloved. (II. H.)

St. Paul was a man of feeling, a man of love. He felt for all: for those whom he saw perishing in sin, he would willingly have endured all that men or devils could inflict, if only it might be instrumental to their salvation. Rom. ix. 3. For those who belonged to Christ, even though they had never seen his face in the flesh, he had great conflicts, striving if by any means he might promote their eternal welfare. But towards those who had been converted by his ministry, he felt as a father towards his children: he could say, "God is my record how greatly I long after you all in the bowels of Jesus Christ." Phil. i. 8. To such is this epistle addressed; as indeed the words of our text clearly evince. Such an accumulation of tender expressions can scarcely be found in the same space in all the Book of God. But what is the drift of them all? Why does he so labor to convince the Philippians of his love, and to conciliate their regards to him? it was, that they might be stirred up to give the more earnest heed to his exhortations, and to "stand fast in the Lord."

To be "in the Lord" is the character of every believer: he is united unto Christ by faith, and is engrafted into him as a branch of the living vine. But our blessed Lord cautions us again and again to "abide in him," and warns us against the danger of separation from him. John xv. 1—6. In like manner we are frequently exhorted to "stand fast in the Lord;" and so to continue in the faith grounded and settled, that we may not be moved away from the hope of the gospel."

To you then we would now address the exhortation, and say, Stand fast in,

I. Your allegiance to him—

Many things will conspire to draw you away from Christ—

The world, with its vanities on the one hand, and its terrors on the other, will assault you continually— — —the flesh also will operate to bring you into subjection to all its basest lusts— — —Nor will Satan be idle : he, with all his confederate hosts, will strive, by innumerable wiles and temptations, either to subvert your principles, or to vitiate your practice— — —It is a warfare into which you are brought, when once you enlist under the banners of Christ; and you must expect all manner of conflicts to your dying hour.

But you must be steadfast in your adherence to him—

You must be "good soldiers of Jesus Christ," and never cease to fight till you have obtained the victory. Neither hopes nor fears, neither joys nor sorrows, must be suffered to alienate you from him, or to damp your zeal in his service. True it is that the Lord gives you many great and precious promises, that he will keep you, and that nothing shall ever separate you from his love. Rom. viii. 35—39. But this is not to encourage supineness : but rather to make you more earnest in your application to him for protection and support. With the example of Demas before you, you should never cease to fear, lest you also should "fall from your own stedfastness," 2 Pet. iii. 17, and "be corrupted from the simplicity that is in Christ." 2 Cor. xi. 3. Aware of your danger, you must "fight the good fight of faith," and "cleave unto the Lord with full purpose of heart." "You must be faithful unto death, if ever you would obtain the crown of life."

Stand fast also in,

II. YOUR DEPENDENCE ON HIM—

From this also you are in danger of being drawn—

There is in us a continual proneness to self-confidence and self-dependence We are ever ready to lean to our own understanding to guide us— — —our own righteousness to justify us— — —our own strength to preserve us — — —It is a great matter to have the soul brought to a simple reliance upon the Lord Jesus Christ for every thing.

But we must live altogether by faith on Christ—

He is "Head over all things to his church," and has all fulness of blessings treasured up in him for our use. Eph. i. 22, 23; Col. i. 19. "He is made of God unto us wisdom, and righteousness, and sanctification, and redemption;" and from him must we receive them all, John i. 16, that in, and by, and for all, His name may be glorified— — —Isa. xlv. 24, 25.

Nor must any thing be suffered to weaken,

III. YOUR EXPECTATION OF HIS FUTURE ADVENT—

To that day there is a particular reference in the preceding context—Ch iii. 20, 21.

We are apt to lose sight of that awful day—

This is evident, from the remissness and negligence with which the things of eternity are pursued. Could we be dull and slothful with that day before our eyes ?— — —Could the allurements or terrors of the world have any influence upon our hearts, if we knew and saw that the Judge was at the door ?— — —

But we must stand continually in a state of preparation for it—

To wait for Christ's second coming is the habit of mind to which every believer is brought: 1 Thess. i. 9, 10; and in proportion as it is formed in the mind, is the progress which we have made in the divine life. 1 Cor. i. 7. We should not give way to sloth, like the foolish Virgins ; but have "our loins girt, and our lamps trimmed, and ourselves as those who wait for the coming of their Lord." We should look forward with a holy longing for that day, as the termination of all our conflicts, and the consummation of all our joys, Tit. ii. 13; 2 Pet. iii. 12,—— ——and comfort ourselves with the assured expectation that then we shall be ever with the Lord. 1 Thess. iv. 17, 18. With that period before our eyes, we shall "be diligent to be found of him in peace, without spot and blameless." 2 Pet. iii. 14.

Permit me, in CONCLUSION, to urge this matter, after the example of the apostle in my text.

JOYFUL IMPORT OF THE GOSPEL.

Acts viii. 8.—And there was great joy in that city. (Pr.)

THE christian church has from its infancy been subject to great vicissitudes, and like the moon it has continually waxed and waned. When the disciples first found the Messiah they were full of joy; when he was crucified they were covered with a cloud of darkness; but when he arose from the dead their hopes and joys revived again. The work of grace at Jerusalem, in the conversion of so many thousands, makes them a little heaven upon earth; but soon a storm of persecution followed. See the blessed Stephen stoned to death, and Saul making havoc of the church, verse 2. Yet out of all this evil much good arises, and now there is another triumph to the cause of truth and righteousness. "Philip went down to Samaria and preached Christ unto them—and there was great joy in that city."

I. IT IS DESERVING OF REMARK, THAT THE SEAT OF THIS HOLY TRIUMPH WAS "THE CITY OF SAMARIA."

Well may it be said, "the wilderness and the solitary place shall be glad for them, and the desert shall rejoice, and blossom like the rose;" for such indeed was the city of Samaria.

1. Its inhabitants consisted partly of *heathens* and partly of *apostate Jews*, who had a sort of half heathenised religion among them. They had been a superstitious and degenerate people from the time of Salmanezer, and such they still continued. 2 Kings xvii. 33, 34. ——— They set up a temple on mount Gerizzim in opposition to that on mount Moriah, and carried on a kind of worship which Christ condemned. John iv. 22. ——— They had also manifested the greatest aversion to the Jews, and to Christ and his followers as being of that nation. Luke ix. 51—53. A hopeless and inveterate people!

2. Yet this very city is celebrated for its *reception of the gospel*, and was one of the first to surrender to the arms of truth. ——— On the report of the woman, after the interview at Jacob's well, the Samaritans showed a disposition to listen to the gospel, and they received the Saviour very courteously. John iv. 39—42. And now when Philip went down and preached Christ to them, "the people with one accord gave heed unto those things which Philip spake, hearing and seeing the miracles which he did," ver. 6.

——— Thus was fulfilled the prediction of our Lord to the woman of Samaria, and also to his disciples. John iv. 23, 35. Thus also the Lord builds up Jerusalem, and gathers together the outcasts of Israel. Psa. cxlvii. 2. Isa. lvi. 6—8.

II. THE JOY WHICH NOW PREVAILED IN THE CITY OF SAMARIA IS FULLY ACCOUNTED FOR BY THE CAUSE WHICH PRODUCED IT

Joy is never excited but on some great occasion, and the seasons of religious joy are distinguished by some interesting or extraordinary occurrence Such was the joy and gladness at the preparation for building the temple of Jerusalem, 1 Chron. xxix. 9: at Hezekiah's passover, 2 Chron. xxx. 25, 26: at the rebuilding and dedication of the city wall, Neh. xii. 43; at the birth of Christ, Luke ii. 10—14; at the appearance of the star to the eastern magi, Matt. ii. 13; and at the ascension of our blessed Saviour, Luke xxiv. 52. All these were great events, and furnished an abundant source of joy and rejoicing.

We may therefore expect something great and interesting in the present instance, to fill a whole city with joy ——— and what was it? Answer, the glad tidings of the gospel: that Christ was come, that he died for sinners, that he had risen again, that he had ascended above all heavens, and lived to make intercession for transgressors; that through faith in him there was now forgiveness and acceptance with God, and this news was proclaimed to all nations.

Some may say that these are common things, and they have been proclaimed in other cities as well as in Samaria, and we have all heard of them before. ——— Be it so: if you have cordially received them, there is enough to occasion great joy; and if they have not produced such an effect, it is because they have not been fully realized by faith.

Let us then recapitulate the leading facts of the gospel, and observe the glad tidings contained in them—

1. Is it not ground for joy that *the Lord is come into the world to save sinners?* ——— This is what the church was looking for, nearly four thousand years. This was the great theme of prophetic inspiration, from age to age; and what Israel was commanded to rejoice in, even from the days of old. Zech. ix. 9. The prospect of our Saviour's advent inspired not only the ancient church, but even the whole creation with joy and gladness. Psa. xcvi. 11—13. ——— If therefore Samaria had not exulted in this great event, there would have been no sympathy, no correspondence with the ancient believers, and of course no evidence of their belief in its existence or reality. ——— If we also profess to believe in the coming of Christ, and the great objects of his appearance, and are still indifferent and unaffected, it proves our faith to be utterly vain. Shall glory to God in the highest, peace on earth, and good will to men be nothing to us; and yet shall we be allowed to call ourselves christians!

2. Is it not ground for joy that *Christ has laid down his life for us,* and redeemed us unto God by his blood? ——— It is true his death caused sorrow to the disciples for a time; but when they understood the design of that great event, their sorrow was turned into joy. ——— Consider in what light this interesting truth is held up to us in the scriptures. " But now in the end of the world hath he appeared, to put away sin by the sacrifice of himself—When he had by himself purged our sins, he sat down on the right hand of the Majesty on high." Heb. ix. 26, i. 3. On this inestimable sacrifice is founded a new and everlasting covenant, promising forgiveness, and securing eternal life to all that believe. Heb. viii. 10—12; 2 Cor. v. 18, 19; John iii. 16. ——— This is the source of the first hope and joy to an awakened sinner, and it has turned the sorrow of many into gladness. We may afterwards derive comfort from a consciousness of believing in Christ, and being interested in him; but the first is from looking to him, looking out of ourselves, and beholding the Lamb of God that taketh away the sin of the world

3. Is it not a matter of great joy that *Christ is risen from the dead?*— This proves that he was t e true Messiah, that his sacrifice is accepted, and that justice is fully satisfied. "The God of peace brought again from the dead that great Shepherd of the sheep, through the blood of the everlasting covenant—and raised him up and gave him glory, that your faith and hope might be in God." Heb. xiii. 20; 1 Pet. i. 21. ——— The resurrection of Christ is also the pattern and the pledge of our own resurrection, and is therefore on this account a matter of joyful exultation. 1 Cor. xv. 20; Phil. iii. 21.

4. Is it not matter of joy too, that *Christ has ascended into glory:* and that he ever liveth to make intercession for us? ——— On this ground it is that he is able to save to the uttermost all that come unto God by him. Heb. vii. 25. If any man sin, we have an advocate with the Father. 1 John ii. 1. ——— Having entered into his glory, he is become heir of all things, and possesses the power of enriching his church, and of ruling in the midst of his enemies. Psa. lxviii. 18; cx. 1, 2; Ephes. i. 20—22.

5. That through faith in his name there is *forgiveness of sin, and acceptance with God?* ——— The import of the gospel is, Believe in Jesus, and ye shall be saved; submit to his righteousness, and ye shall be accepted, whatever be your past sins, or present unworthiness. Look off from all duties of your own, and plead that obedience with which God is well pleased. Come unto me, says Jesus, and ye shall find rest to your souls—and him that cometh I will in no wise cast out. John vi. 37. ——— If such tidings do not gladden the heart, it is only because we have neither part nor lot in the matter.

6. Is it not a source of joy that this gospel *is now sent to all nations?* ——— Salvation originated with the Jews; theirs were the covenants, and the giving of the law; and of whom, as concerning the flesh, Christ came. But the Gentiles were to be grafted in, and to partake of the root and fatness of the olive tree; and now there is a community of privileges and of blessedness.

7. Was it not a special matter of joy to the Samaritans, that *they themselves had believed the gospel?* ——— If Israel of old rejoiced that they were willing to build the house of the Lord, much more may we rejoice to see the spiritual temple edified and built up, especially if our hands also are in the work. ——— Philip the evangelist rejoiced in the success of his labor, the Samaritans rejoiced in the doctrines of the cross, and that the kingdom of God was come nigh unto them.

REFLECTIONS.

1. If then the gospel bring tidings of great joy, why is it reproached as tending to gloom and melancholy? Can any thing be more unreasonable or unjust.

2. Why do individuals despond, while there is such an exhibition of mercy? Because they do not hearken to the gospel, nor receive the record which God hath given of his Son.

3. Why do not christians possess more joy and peace in believing? Because we have not more religion, do not live more under the influence of the gospel. Lord increase our faith.

THE SUBJECTS OF DIVINE GRACE EXHORTED TO CLEAVE UNTO THE LORD.

Acts xi. 23. Who, when he came, and had seen the grace of God, was glad, and exhorted them all, that with purpose of heart they would cleave unto the Lord." (Sk.)

THESE words are evidently connected w th the preceding verses, and the whole paragraph from, ver. 19, claims oui serious attention;—" Now they which were scattered abroad," &c. In this relation we observe,

1. *A display of God's perfections in the extension of his kingdom*, ver. 19—21. Of his *truth*; in protecting his church amidst cruel persecution, Matt. xvi. 18 :—his *goodness*; in sending the gospel to both Jews and Gentiles, Psa. cvii. 20, 21 :—his *wisdom*; in promoting his own glory by the malice of his enemies, Psa. lxxv. 10 :—his *power*, in giving abundant success to the labors of his servants.

2. This account teaches us *the true nature of a christian church*, ver. 22.—The church is capable of *hearing* and *acting*; for the church heard that some of the Gentiles were converted to the faith of Christ, and sent Barnabas to visit them, and confirm them in the faith. Therefore the church cannot mean a building set apart for divine worship, as some suppose; but a company of professing Christians united to assist each other in seeking the power of godliness, Acts ix. 31, and xii. 5. As a missionary of the church, Barnabas came to Antioch; " Who when he came, and had seen the grace of God," &c. By what Barnabas thus saw, and felt, and did, we are instructed to observe,

I. THAT THE CONVERSION OF SINNERS TO GOD, IS JUSTLY ASCRIBABLE TO HIS GRACE. This is evident from the subjects, the benefits, and the causes of conversion.

1. *The subjects of conversion are sinners*—who have *rebelled* against God, Isa. i. 2, 3,—who have cherished and manifested *enmity* of heart against God, Rom. viii. 7; Col. i. 21; and who have justly *forfeited* every favor at God's hand, Lam. iii. 22.

2. *The benefits of conversion are various.* Conversion is a *turning* to God, and implies both a *deliverance* and a *translation*, Col. i. 13.—*A deliverance from Satan*; from his service and dominion, Rom. vi. 14, 22.— And *a translation into the kingdom of Christ*; by the enjoyment of pardon, which entitles them to the kingdom of heaven, Col. i. 14; Tit. iii. 6;— and of purity, which fits them for the kingdom of heaven, Col. i. 12.

3. *The causes of conversion are meritorious, efficient, and instrumental.*—The *meritorious* cause is *Christ's mediation*, through which we are pardoned, Eph. iv. 32.—The *efficient* cause is the *Holy Spirit*, 1 Cor. vi. 11, which is God's free gift, Luke xi. 13.—The *instrumental* cause is *faith*, Acts xxvi. 18, which ascribes all it receives to the grace or favor of God, Eph. ii. 8: Tit. iii. 4, 5; 1 Cor. xv. 10. Our text teaches us,

II. THAT WHERE THE GRACE OF GOD IS ENJOYED, IT WILL BE SEEN IN ITS EFFECTS ;—" When he came, he *saw* the grace of God." The grace of God may be, and is seen,

1. *In the tempers of its subjects, or the dispositions of their minds.* Where grace reigns, pride, and unkindness, and unmercifulness, will be subdued, Col. iii. 12—14.

2. *In the conversation of its subjects*; this is pure, and profitable, Eph. iv. 22: Col. iii. 16, 17.

3. *In the actions of its subjects*; these are godly, righteous, and temperate, Tit. ii. 12.

146

4. *All who profess to enjoy the grace of God, should be careful thus to show it.*—On principles of *prudence;* that their own eternal salvation may be secured, 2 Pet. i. 5—10.—On principles of *piety;* that God may hereby be glorified, Matt. v. 16; 1 Pet. xi. 11. 12.—On principles of *benevolence;* that their weak brethren may be strengthened, Heb. xiii. 13, and that their pastors may hereby be comforted, 1 Thess. iii. 8; 3 John, ver. 4.—As an excitement to holy diligence, on this generous principle, our text teaches us,

III. THAT WHEN THE GRACE OF GOD IS SEEN, IT AFFORDS PLEASURE TO WELL-DISPOSED MINDS;—" When he saw the grace of God, he was *glad;*" and his joy was both pious and pure.

1. *His joy on this occasion was pious.* It was the joy of a saint excited by seeing the grace of God manifested, and sinners saved. He was glad— As "*a good man,*" *or a lover of mankind;* because hereby many were benefitted; being raised to a state of safety, happiness, and honor, Rom. v. 1; Eph. ii. 1—6; and the welfare of the civil state was also promoted, Prov. xiv. 32. He was glad—As *a holy man;* for he was "*full of the Holy Ghost.*" Hence he was glad, because the felicity of angels was hereby augmented, Luke xv. 10. Christ was hereby most pleasingly satisfied, Isa. liii. 10, 11; and God was hereby glorified, Isa. lxi. 1—3. He was glad—As a *faithful man;* for he " was *full of faith.*" Hence, he confidently expected the fulfilment of God's word, Ps. ii. 8. He beheld in these converted Gentiles, the earnest of Christ's universal dominion; and could exclaim with David, Psa. lxxii. 19, 20.

2. *His joy on this occasion was pure.* He was glad—though the subjects of this grace were Gentile *strangers;* it was not the joy of *bigotry:* and though *he* was not the *instrument* of their conversion; it was not the joy of *self-complacency.*

3. *His joy on this occasion was exemplary;* worthy of our *imitation.* Wherever the grace of God is seen we should rejoice: without *bigotry*, this is *unchristian*, Eph. v. 24; and without *envy*, for this is *devilish*, James iii. 14—16. Our text teaches us,

IV. THAT CLEAVING UNTO THE LORD IS THE INDISPENSABLE DUTY OF ALL CHRISTIAN CONVERTS.

1. *By the Lord is meant our Lord Jesus Christ;* who is our *Guide,* Ps. xlviii. 14,—our *Sovereign,* Matt. xxiii. 8;—our *Strength,* Psa. xlvi. 1;—and our *Foundation,* Isa. xxviii. 16.

2. *It is the duty of Christian converts to cleave unto the Lord.* Cleave unto him—By habitual *attention,* Acts iii. 22, 23; —by persevering *obedience,* Heb. v. 9; Psa. cvi. 3; by importunate *prayer,* Heb. iv. 16;—and by entire *dependance,* 1 Pet. ii. 5, 6; Jude, ver. 21, 22.

3. *All christian converts should thus cleave unto him.—All,* of every *age;*—of every religious *attainment;*—and of every *station* in the church John, xv. 5; Heb. iii. 12.

4. We should thus cleave unto the Lord " *With purpose of heart.*" This should and must be the object of our deliberate *choice,* Deut. xxx. 19, 20;—of our steadfast *resolution,* Josh. xxiv. 15;—and of our incessant care, 1 John ii. 28; Phil. iii. 16. Our text teaches us,

V. THAT AFFECTIONATE EXHORTATION IS CONDUCIVE TO THE STEADFAST PERSEVERANCE OF BELIEVERS IN CHRIST;—" He *exhorted* them," &c Here we may observe,

1. *To whom this exhortation should be addressed.* As cleaving unto the Lord is a duty required of all christians, so we find *all* of every description, exhorted in the oracles of God. *Private* christians are urged to this,

John xv. 4; Col. ii. 6; and *public* characters are also thus stimulated to exertion, 1 Tim. iv. 16.

2. *By whom this exhortation should be employed.* It should be given—By all those to whom the *care* of souls is *committed*, 1 Cor. xiv. 3; Col. i. 28;—and by all *private* Christians, in their mutual communications, Heb. iii. 13, and x. 24, 25.

3. *How this exhortation should be enforced.* It should be urged, by the consideration—of *our* own total *insufficiency*, Jer. x. 23; 2 Cor. iii. 5;—of *Christ's all-sufficiency*, Heb. vii. 25;—of *Satan's malice*, who purposes and seeks to destroy us, 1 Pet. v. 8, 9;—of the dreadful *evils* to which *apostacy* would expose us, Heb. x. 38; Rev. iii. 11; 1 Chron. xxviii. 9;—and of the *blessings* with which God is engaged to crown *unfainting perseverance*, Gal. vi. 9; 2 Pet. i. 10, 11.

THE GREATNESS AND PRECIOUSNESS OF THE PROMISES.

Pet. i. 4.—Whereby are given unto us exceeding great and precious promises; that by these ye might be partakers of the divine nature, having escaped the corruption that is in the world through lust. (S. S.)

COMMENTATORS are not agreed with respect to the connexion of these words—*

Nor is it of any great importance for us to enter into the difficulties of it—

The words themselves, whatever the precise connexion of them may be, are replete with instruction and comfort—

We shall take occasion from them to consider,

I. THE EXCEEDING GREATNESS AND PRECIOUSNESS OF THE PROMISES.

God, in infinite mercy, has given us many "promises"

Fallen man could not claim any thing at God's hands, Psa. cxliii. 2.

We were deserving of nothing but his wrath and indignation, Psa. cxxx. 3

But he was pleased to send his own Son to die for us—

And for the sake of Christ has promised us many blessings—

These promises are "exceeding great"

They offer the pardon of all our sins, Isa. i. 18.

They warrant us to expect strength for the performance of all our duties, 2 Cor. xii. 9.

They call us to enjoy the most intimate fellowship with God, 2 Cor. vi. 16

They assure us of everlasting happiness and glory, John x. 28.

Neither are the wants of the body, or the conveniencies of life overlooked, Matt. vi. 33; 2 Pet. i. 3; 1 Tim. iv. 8.

No wonder then that they should be "precious"

We cannot ascertain their full value—

But every true christian can adopt the language of David, Psa. cxix. 111

But the preciousness of them will further appear, if we consider,

II. THE END FOR WHICH THEY ARE GIVEN.

God would have us to be partakers of the divine nature.

* Some connect δι᾿ ὧν with "glory and virtue" in the preceding verse, and understands it thus; "by which glorious energy of the gospel are given to us," &c. Others, understanding the third verse parenthetically, connect δι᾿ ὧν with "God and Christ" in verse 2, and translate the words "by *whom*," &c.

The divine nature does not import the divine essence—
Nor does it mean a personal union with God—
To partake of the divine nature in these respects was the peculiar honor of Jesus Christ—
But the divine nature has respect to the moral perfections of the Deity—Col. iii. 10.
Of these God would have us to partake abundantly—
It is for this end that he has given the promises.
He does not intend merely to save us from destruction—
He has laid a plan for our everlasting happiness—
But holiness is essential to happiness—
We could not enjoy his presence, if we did not bear his image—
He has therefore given us promises, in order to make us holy—
And the promises, if duly applied, always operate in this manner—
Their suitableness to this end will be manifest, while we contemplate.
III. The effects they invariably produce.
There is a dreadful " corruption in the world through lust"
The desires of men are altogether vitiated—
The indulgence of them produces much corruption in the world—
But God's people " escape" this corruption.
They are not free from all sin—
But they do not live under the allowed dominion of any—
They flee from temptation with fear and trembling—
This is the description given of the saints at Sardis, Rev. iii. 4.
And this is the universal operation of true religion, James i. 27.
They escape it through the operation of the promises.
They have not in themselves a power to keep themselves pure—
But God promises " grace sufficient"—
They therefore trust in his promises, and plead them in prayer—
In so doing, they experience their cleansing efficacy—
Hence St. Paul urges the promises not merely as a motive to holiness, but as the means of attaining it, 2 Cor. vii. 1.
Infer,
1. How foolish are they who neglect Christ !
Christ is the person in whom all the promises are ratified and confirmed. 2 Cor. i. 20.
Nor can we be interested in one promise, unless we be united to Christ—
What madness then is it to neglect that blessed Saviour !—
What unspeakable blessings do the thoughtless world despise !—
Let us " awake from our sleep, and arise from the dead"—
Let us seek Christ with our whole hearts—
All things are ours, if we be his, 1 Cor. iii. 22, 23.
2. How mistaken are they who seek for holiness merely in a way of mortification, or in the exercise of their own powers !
Many seek long after holiness without attaining it—
The reason of this is, that they do not seek it in God's appointed way—
God has given them promises by which they may be made holy—
But they are afraid to embrace them till they can see themselves holy—
Thus do they, in fact, reverse the appointment of God himself—
Let such, however, submit to God's method of imparting a divine nature—
Let them embrace the promises as sinners, that they may become saints—
3. How highly privileged are the people of God !
Whatever is needful for them, in time or eternity, is secured—

For their consolation God has confirmed his promises with an oath, **Heb. vi. 17, 18.**

And all of them can, like Solomon, attest his fidelity, 1 Kings viii. **56.**

Let them therefore treasure up his promises in their hearts—

Let them do this for advancement in holiness as well as comfort—**Psa.** cxix. 11.

Thus shall they be enabled to say with David, Psa. xvii. 4.

And in due season shall that most precious of all the promises be fulfilled, John xii. 26.

CHAPTER IV.

CHRISTIAN GRACES.

THE INESTIMABLE PRIVILEGES OF BELIEVERS.

1 John iii. 2.—Beloved, now are we the sons of God, and it doth not yet appear what we shall be: but we know that, when he shall appear, we shall be like him; for we shall see him as he is. (S. S.)

Our Lord was hated, reviled, and persecuted unto death—

But we see how glorious was his person, and how exalted his character—

In the same manner his followers are treated with contempt—

But God declares their state to be the most honorable upon earth—

To this effect St. John represents them as slighted by man and honored by God—

I. THE PRESENT STATE OF BELIEVERS.

The scripture speaks of believers in the most exalted terms—

They are not merely servants, but "sons of God"—2 Cor. vi. 18

This they are,

1. By adoption.

Every believer was once a child of wrath, Eph. ii. 3.

But God takes whom he will into his own family, Eph. ii. 19.

He adopts them as his sons, and makes them heirs of his glory, Rom. viii. 15, 17.

2. By regeneration.

Once they had only a carnal mind that is enmity against God, Rom. viii. 7.

But they have been born again of the Holy Spirit, John i. 13.

They are renewed after the image of their heavenly Father, Col. iii. 10.

They enjoy this state "*now*"

Rich and poor, learned and unlearned, partake alike of this honor—

Nor does God withhold it from any on account of their remaining infirmities—

Even now, while the world despises them, does God own his relation to them—

What an unspeakably blessed state is this!

How different is it from the state they were once in!—

How great the privileges which they enjoy by means of this relation!—

How sweet the sense of this relation often is to their souls!—

To what a glorious state does it lead them in a better world—
Well might the apostle break forth in wonder and admiration, 1 John iii. 1.
Yet, blessed as it is, it falls infinitely short of what it will be,

II. THEIR FUTURE STATE.

Very little is known respecting this.
We can form no idea of spiritual and glorified bodies—
We cannot imagine how extensive will be the capacities of the soul—
We have very faint conceptions of perfect holiness and perfect happiness—
Even one who had seen Christ transfigured, says, "It doth not appear,"
&c.—

Yet there are some things revealed to us.
We shall see Christ, not merely by faith, but with our bodily eyes, Job
xix. 25—27.
Not veiled as formerly, but in all his glory—
We shall resemble him in all his imitable perfections—
This resemblance will result from our sight of him—
Even " our bodies shall be fashioned like unto his glorious body"—
This shall be fully accomplished at the great day of his appearing—
These things we may be said to " know"
We have already experienced the earnest of them in our hearts—
When we believe in him we have views of him, which we had not before—
These transform the soul into his image, 2 Cor. iii. 18.
Our Lord has given us the fullest assurance of these things, John xvii. 24.
St. Paul also leaves us no room to doubt, 1 Cor. xv. 49; Col. iii. 4.

INFER,

1. How wonderfully different the lot of believers and unbelievers!
Believers are the children of God—
Unbelievers are the children of the wicked one, John viii. 38, 44.
Believers can form no adequate conception of the happiness that awaits
them—
Unbelievers have no idea of the misery to which they are hastening—
How different will be the appearance of each in that day!—
How different their sentiments on seeing Christ upon his judgment-seat!—
For what different ends will their capacities of soul and body be enlarged!
What a different state will they experience to all eternity!—
Let none defer calling upon God for mercy—
Let all seek his regenerating grace, and an admission into his family—
If we believe in Christ these blessings shall be ours, John i. 12.

2. How bright the prospects of the true christian!
The christian's warfare will soon be over—
Then will come a blessedness which he cannot now conceive—
Another day may bring him to the full possession of it—
Let these prospects animate every pious soul—
Let none suffer their minds to be drawn away by the things of time—
Let every one stand ready to take his flight, 2 Pet. iii. 12.
Let the beloved apostle be our example, Rev. xxii. 20.

THE LIGHT IN WHICH CHRIST REGARDS HIS FOLLOWERS.

John xv. 15.—Henceforth I call you not servants; for the servant knoweth not what his lord doeth; but I have called you friends; for all things that I have heard of my Father, I have made known unto you. (S. S.)

KNOWLEDGE of every kind is excellent and useful—

But that of religion far transcends all other—

Hence we are commanded to pay a peculiar respect to those who labor in the word and doctrine. 1 Thess. v. 12.

Hence also our Lord himself, having revealed to his disciples the whole will of God, adduces his fidelity in this respect as one of the strongest tokens of his affection for them.

I. IN WHAT LIGHT CHRIST REGARDS HIS FOLLOWERS.

The state of believers under the gospel differs widely from that of those under the Mosaic dispensation—

They were in the condition of servants, but *we* of friends—

Christ assures us that from "henceforth" his people should be regarded by him in that light—

He has taken away from us the yoke of the ceremonial law.

This was an exceedingly heavy burden, Acts xv. 10.

But Christ has delivered his people from it, Gal. v. 1.

He has imposed only two rites, and those easy and instructive—*

His service is perfect freedom, 1 John v. 3; Matt. xi. 30.

He has delivered us from a sense of guilt.

The offerings of a Jew afforded no assurance that God had accepted him, Heb. ix. 9.

They were rather so many remembrances of his sin, Heb. x. 1—3.

But Christ has freed *us* from the pains of a guilty conscience, Heb. x. 14.

He has set us at liberty also from a servile spirit.

The Jews could not enter into the most holy place—

None could go there but the high priest; and he only on one day in the year; and then not without blood, Heb. ix. 7.

But now all believers are priests, Rev. i. 6.

The vail which separated the most holy place was rent at the death of Christ—†

All therefore may enter thither without fear, Heb. x. 19—22.

He has put us into the state of adult sons.

Believers under the law were like minors, or children under age, Gal. iv. 1—3.

But *we* are brought to the full possession of our privileges, Gal. iv. 6, 7

Our Lord proceeds to prove his assertion.

II. WHAT EVIDENCE WE HAVE THAT HE DOES SO REGARD US.

He still carries on the comparison between servant and friends—

He points out one particular wherein he has eminently distinguished us, and exalted us above all the Jewish saints—

He has revealed to us the perfections of God.

These were but little known to the Jews—

But Christ has more clearly revealed them—

He has declared them to us in his discourses, John i. 18.

* Baptism and the Lord's Supper.

† It was rent in twain from the top to the bottom at the very time of the evening sacrifice, by means of which it was opened to the view of all the worshippers in the temple.

He has exhibited them in his life, Heb. i. 3.

He has shewn us the way of acceptance with him.

This was but obscurely shadowed under the law—

Many even rested in the ceremonies themselves—

But Christ has plainly declared himself to be the way to the Father, John xiv. 6.

He has expressly told us that we have acceptance through his blood, Matt xx. 28, and xxvi. 28.

He has unfolded to us the privileges of God's people.

The Jews were encouraged by temporal promises—

But "life and immortality are brought to light by the gospel"—

Christ has fully opened to us our present privileges, John xiv. 23, and our future prospects, John xvii. 24.

He has "made known all which he himself had heard of the Father"

At that time he had not absolutely revealed *all*, John xvi. 12.

But he had declared all which he had been commissioned to reveal, or was necessary for them to know—

And he completed his revelation soon afterwards—

This was a most undeniable evidence of his friendship.

Servants are not admitted to the secret views and designs of their masters—

But Christ has made known to us all the mysteries of his Father's counsels, Col. i. 26, 27.

What abundant evidence of his friendship does this afford!

INFER,

1. How should we esteem the holy scriptures!

It is by the scriptures that Christ declares to us the Father's will—

In them therefore we see the strongest testimony of his love—

The written memorials even of a creature's love are dear to us—

Of what inestimable value then should we account the word of Christ!—

Let us regard it with the same affection as David did, Psa. xix. 10.

Let it "dwell richly in us in all wisdom," Col. iii. 16.

2. What love and honor should we shew to Christ!

We should not consider him *merely* as a lord and master—

We should rather view him as our dearest friend—

Let us then delight ourselves in communion with him—

Let us open to him all our cares, wants, fears, &c.

Let us give him that best proof of our regard, a willing and unreserved obedience, John xv. 14.

CHRIST PRECIOUS TO BELIEVERS.

1 Pet. ii. 7.—Unto you therefore who believe, he is precious. (S. S.)

THERE is a great difference between the views of natural and spiritual men—

This exists even with respect to things temporal; much more in those which are spiritual and eternal—

It appears particularly with respect to Christ—

Hence St. Peter represents him as disallowed of some, but chosen by others—

This was designed of God, and agreeable to the prophecies—
And it justifies the inference drawn from it in the text—
We shall shew,

I. THAT CHRIST IS PRECIOUS TO BELIEVERS.

We might suppose he would be so to all men; but he is not—
Nevertheless he is so to all that truly believe—
The history of the Old Testament affords abundant proof of this—
Abraham rejoiced to see his day, though at a distance, John viii. 56.
Job delighted in death as the means of introducing him to his presence, Job. xix. 25—27.
Moses esteemed reproach for his sake, Heb. xi. 26.
David regarded nothing in earth or heaven in comparison of him, Ps. lxxiii. 25.
Isaiah exulted in the prospect of his incarnation, Isa. ix. 6.
The New Testament scriptures confirm it.
The virgin, while he was yet in her womb, sang his praises, Luke i. 47.
The angels congratulated the shepherds on his incarnation, Luke ii. 10.
The just and devout Simeon after seeing him, could depart in peace, Ib. ver. 29, 30.
John baptist, as the bridegroom's friend, rejoiced in his voice, John iii. 29.
How precious was he to that Mary who was a sinner! Luke vii. 38.
St. Paul counted all as dung for the knowledge of him, was willing to be bound, or to die for him, and knew no comfort like the expectation of being with him, Phil. iii. 8; Acts xxi. 13: 1 Thess. iv. 18.
The glorified saints and angels incessantly adore him, Rev. v. 12, 13.
The experience of living saints accords with that of those who have gone before—*
The world even wonders at them on account of their attachment to him—

II. WHY HE IS SO PRECIOUS TO THEM.

They have reason enough for their attachment—
They love him *for his own excellence.*
He is infinitely above all created beauty or goodness—
Shall they then regard these qualities in the creature, and not in him?—
Whosoever views him by faith cannot but admire and adore him—
They love him *for his suitableness to their necessities.*
There is in Christ all which believers can want—
Nor can they find any other capable of supplying their need—
Hence they delight in him as their " all in all"—
They love him *for the benefits they receive from him.*
They have received from him pardon, peace, strength, &c.
Can they do otherwise than account him precious?—
We may rather wonder why all do not feel the same attachment.

III. WHY HE IS NOT PRECIOUS TO OTHERS.

There certainly exists no reason on his part; he is good to all—
But unbelievers cannot love him.
1. Because they have no views of his excellency.
The god of this world has blinded them that they cannot see him, 2 Cor. iv 4.
How then should they esteem him, whose excellency they know not?—

---

* There are many to whom he is preciousness itself; who account him as the pearl of great price, desire to know more of him, grieve that they cannot love him more, think afflictions good when they lead to him, and despise all in comparison of him.

They must of necessity be indifferent to him, as men are to things of little value—

2. Because they feel no need of him.

Christ is valuable only as a remedy, Isa. xxxii. 2.

Nor can any man desire him as a physician, a fountain, a refuge, unless he feel some disease, some thirst, some danger—

APPLICATION.

All, who have any spiritual discernment, feel a love to Christ—

He is beloved of the Father, of angels, and of saints—

None but devils and unbelievers despise him—

And shall any, who do not account him precious, be objects of his regard?—

Surely his final decision will correspond with that declaration, 1 Sam. ii. 30.

Let all then believe in him, that he may become precious to them—

Nor let any be dejected because they cannot delight in him as they wish—

The more we love him, the more shall we lament the coldness of our love—

In a little time all the powers of our souls shall act without control—

Then shall we glory in him with unrestrained and unabated ardor.

THE FRUITS OF GOD'S FAVOUR.

Hos. xiv. 5—7.—I will be as the dew to Israel: he shall grow as the lily, and cast forth his roots as Lebanon. His branches shall spread, and his beauty shall be as the olive-tree, and his smell as Lebanon. They that dwell under his shadow shall return; they shall revive as the corn, and grow as the vine: the scent thereof shall be as the wine of Lebanon. (S. S.)

THERE are instances of beautiful imagery in the scriptures equal to any that can be found in the works of the most renowned authors—

They are enhanced too by the importance of the subjects they contain—

In both respects the passage before us deserves peculiar attention—

Imagination cannot conceive a richer display of divine blessings than God here vouchsafes to his church and people—

I. THE FAVOUR WHICH GOD WILL SHEW HIS PEOPLE.

The metaphor of "dew" is at once simple and sublime—

The benefits of the dew are but little known in this climate—

But in Judea the metaphor would appear very significant—*

For some time after the creation, dew supplied the place of rain, Gen. ii. 6.

And, after rain was given, it still remained of great use—

The scriptures speak of it as an important blessing—See Gen. xxvii. 28, 39, and Deut. xxxiii. 13.

They represent the withholding of it as a calamity and curse, 2 Sam. i. 21

The communications of God to his people are fitly compared to it.

It distils silently and almost imperceptibly on the ground—

Yet it insinuates itself into the plants on which it falls—

And thus maintains their vegetative powers—

* Where the rains are periodical, and the climate hot, the dews are more abundant.

In the same manner God's visits to his people are secret—*
But he gains access to their inmost souls, 2 Cor. vi. 16.
He cheers and revives their fainting spirits—
And thus he fulfils to them his own most gracious promises, Isa. lviii. 11.
Were his communications refreshing only, and not influential on the conduct, we might be afraid of enthusiasm—
But his favor invariably discovers itself by,
II. ITS FRUITS AND EFFECTS.
The effects of the dew are seen by the progress of vegetation—
The descent of God's Spirit on the soul produces
Growth.
The "lily" springs up speedily, but is of short duration—
The cedars of "Lebanon cast forth their roots" to a great extent—
Thus the soul that is refreshed with divine communications—
The quickness of its growth often excites admiration—
Its stability defies the assaults of earth and hell—
While it "spreads its branches," and displays its vigor in every good word and work—
Beauty.
There is peculiar grace and "beauty in the olive-tree"—
And such is there in the soul that communes much with God—
What a lustre was there on the face of Moses, when he came from the mount!—Exod. xxxiv. 30.
And how is the lively christian "beautified with salvation?"—
His outward conduct is rendered amiable in every part—
His inward dispositions of humility and love are ornaments which even God himself admires, 1 Pet. iii. 4.
He is transformed into the very image of his God, Eph. iv. 23, 24.
Nor shall his beauty be ever suffered to decay—†
Fragrancy.‡
Lebanon was no less famous for its odoriferous vines than for its lofty cedars—
And does not the christian diffuse a savor all around him?—2 Cor. ii. 14.
How animated his discourse when God is with him!—
How refreshing and delightful to those who enjoy his conversation!—‖
How pleasing is it also to his God and Saviour! Mal. iii. 16; Cant. iv. 16
In proportion as he lives near to God, he fulfils that duty, Col. iv. 6.
Fruitfulness.
The "corn and the vine" are just emblems of a christian's fruitfulness—
They often wear the most unpromising appearance—
Yet are thay "revived" by the genial influences of the sun and rain—
Thus the christian may be reduced to a drooping or desponding state—
But the renewed influences of God's Spirit will revive him—
They make him "fruitful in all the fruits of righteousness"

* He comes not in the wind, the earthquake, or the fire, but in the small still voice, 1 Kings xix. 11, 12.

† Psa. i. 3. The olive, as an evergreen, retains its beauty; and in this respect also is a fit emblem of the true christian.

‡ This is twice mentioned in the text, and therefore deserves peculiar notice.

‖ See him before the sun has exhaled the dew, or the world abated the fervor of his affections; and how does he verify that saying! Prov. xvi. 24.

They too, who " dwell under *his* shadow," and are most nearly connected with him, will participate his blessings—*

INFER,

1. How honorable and blessed is the christian's state!

Often is he favored with visits from above, John xiv. 23.

And glorious are the effects produced by God upon him—

The whole creation scarcely affords images whereby his blessedness may be adequately represented—

Who then is so honorable? who so happy?—

Let all endeavor to maintain a sense of their high privileges—

And to " walk worthy of the calling wherewith they are called"—

2. How hopeful is the state of those who wait on God!

The promises in the text were given as an answer to prayer—

And they are made to all, who, "like Israel," plead with God—

If the dew be withheld from others, it shall descend on them, Judges vi 37, 38.

Its descent shall accomplish the utmost wishes of their souls—

They shall soon experience the fulfilment of that word, Isa. xl. 31.

EVERY CHRISTIAN POSSESSES THE SPIRIT OF CHRIST.

Rom. viii. 9.—Now if any man have not the Spirit of Christ he is none of his.   (B.)

An important and alarming declaration, which the professors of christianity would do well to consider maturely, and lay to heart; and particularly those who content themselves with a form of godliness, while they are destitute of the power of it. The apostle had just observed, " ye are not in the flesh," in a natural and unregenerate state, under the government of your animal appetites and passions, or of your corrupt nature, " if so be that the Spirit of God dwell in you;" for wherever he dwells, he governs, having regenerated our corrupt nature, and imparted a principle of genuine and true holiness. Then he adds, " Now," or, *but* " if any man have not the Spirit of Christ," residing in him, and forming him to such a temper and behavior, as characterizes a disciple of Christ, whatever that man's profession may be, " he is none of his."—But let us inquire,

I. WHAT IS IMPLIED IN BEING CHRIST'S.

There is a sense in which all men are *his;* viz. by right of creation; John i. 3; Col. i. 16; of preservation; Col. i. 17; of redemption. 1 Cor. vi. 20. But the apostle is to be understood in another and further sense. His true followers belong to him, as subjects to a prince; Psa. ii. 8; Matt. xxii. 11; Phil. ii. 11; as servants to a master; ch. xiv. 7—9; 2 Cor. v. 14, 15; as friends; John xv. 13—15; as brethren and sisters; Heb. ii. 11, 12; as children to a father; Heb. ii. 13; as a spouse to a husband; ch. vii. 4; 2 Cor. xi. 2; Eph. v. 25—32; Rev. xix. 7; as branches to a tree; John xv. 1; or as members to the head of the body. 1 Cor. xii. 12, 27; Rom. xii. 5; Eph. i. 22, 23.

* If he be a master, a parent, and especially a minister, the benefit of *his* revivals will extend to many.

II. What is meant by the Spirit of Christ.

Not, as some think, merely the mind of Christ, but the Holy Ghost, the Spirit of God, is here intended. See context. This is called the Spirit of Christ, because he had it, and has it without measure; John iii. 34; Rev. iii. 1; he has purchased it for his followers by his death, the price of our redemption; he has received it for them; Psa. lxviii. 18; Acts ii. 33; he has promised it to them. As the Holy Spirit is the promise of the Father, emphatically, Acts i. 4, so also of the Son. Luke xxiv. 49; John xiv. xv. xvi. How great the consolation of this to those who are desiring and looking for these sacred influences, that they were purchased and received for us by our friend, kinsman, brother, husband, and are promised by the Amen, the faithful and true witness! He actually confers it. John iv. 10; vii. 38; Acts ii. 38, 39.— —

III. How it appears that we must have this Spirit in order to be Christ's.

We cannot be Christ's unless we know him; John x. 14, 27; but we cannot know him without the Spirit of Christ. Matt. xi. 27; Gal. i. 16; John xvi. 14.—We cannot be Christ's unless we love Christ; 1 Cor. xvi. 22; but we cannot love him without that Spirit, the fruit of which is love. Gal. v. 22; Rom. v. 5.—We cannot be Christ's unless we obey him; 2 Cor. v. 15; Rom. xiv. 7; John xv. 14, xiv. 21; Heb. v. 9; but we cannot obey him without the inspiration and aid of his Spirit. John xv. 5; 2 Cor. iii. 5.—We cannot be Christ's without we have an interest in him, and be able to say, " My Beloved is mine, and I am his;" but this interest in him we cannot have without his Spirit. 1 Cor. xii. 13;—We cannot be Christ's without union with him, such as branches have with a tree, or members with their head; but this we cannot have without his Spirit.—We cannot be Christ's unless we have his mind in us; but this we cannot have without his Spirit; meekness, long-suffering, goodness, &c., being fruits of the Spirit.—We cannot be Christ's without we be new creatures; 2 Cor. v. 17; Eph. iv. 21—24; and it is impossible we should be so without his Spirit. Tit. iii. 5.

In conclusion observe,

How important a matter for inquiry to each, whether he has received the Spirit of Christ, and is the subject of his enlightening, gracious, and sanctifying operations, in consequence of which he is brought to know, love, and serve the Lord Jesus, to have an interest in him, and union with him, and to be "created in him to good works."— —How needful and indispensable a duty to apply to Christ, to whom is entrusted the dispensation of the Spirit, that we may obtain, and having obtained, may receive more and more of his influence and grace. Perceiving the necessity and excellence of this gift we must ask for it, we must thirst, John vii. 37, we must believe. Gal iii. 13, 14.

WALKING WITH GOD.

Gen. v. 24.—And Enoch walked with God. (Sk.)

Of this excellent man, but little is recorded in the word of God; four verses in this chapter, one in the epistle to the Hebrews, and two in the epistle of Jude, contain all that we learn respecting him. These records inform us,

1. *That he was the seventh from Adam;* or his descendant of the seventh generation. So the apostle pronounces him, Jude 14.

Hence he must have been contemporary with Adam, and probably enjoyed familiar converse with him during more than two hundred years; for Enoch was born in the six hundred and twenty-second year of the world, and Adam did not die till the year nine hundred and thirty. And converse with one who could, and no doubt did, so fully inform him respecting the creation, fall, and redemption of man, must have been a great privilege.—He was also favored with the good examples of the Patriarchs; of Seth, Enos, Cainan, Mahalaleel, and Jared, his pious father, whose piety may be fairly presumed from the name he gave his son; for the name Enoch signifies to instruct, initiate, or dedicate; and intimates that Jared had dedicated him to God from his birth, and was concerned to train him up in the way he should go. Thus in Enoch God's word was exemplified, Prov. xxii. 6. But amidst these advantages, he also witnessed the prevalence of ungodliness in the earth; for he lived when men both acted and spoke wickedly against God: these he faithfully warned, "saying, Behold," &c., Jude 14 15. Hence we learn.

2. *That he was a prophet:* He "prophesied.' This he did

By predicting future events; particularly the general judgment.—And by teaching sacred truth—reproving sin—warning the rebellious—and encouraging God's "saints" to hope for glory with him.

3. We also learn *that he was the pious head of a family;* "And Enoch lived," &c., v. 21, 22. He walked with God both in his single and in his marriage state.—He did not shun society to become pious, nor forsake society to practise godliness; but amidst the business and cares of a numerous growing family, he still carefully and resolutely walked with God. This leads us to notice,

I. His GENERAL CHARACTER: He walked with God. Here let us consider,

1. *What walking with God supposes.* To discover this, we must observe,—All mankind are naturally fallen; In Adam, Rom. v. 18; and by their own personal transgressions, Psa. xiv. 2, 3.—Our degeneracy implies enmity of heart, and actual rebellion against God, Rom. viii. 7; Isa. i. 2.—Consequently, agreement with God must precede our walking with him, Amos iii. 3. This agreement must include the removal of our guilt by God's forgiving mercy, Mic. vii. 18; and the removal of our enmity by a gracious circumcision of heart, Deut. xxx. 6; Rom. viii. 16, and v. 1, 5; 1 John iv. 19.

2. *What walking with God implies.* It must imply,

Faith in God, Heb. xi. 5, 6. Faith in him as our proprietor, who has a just claim on our services, Psa. xcv. 3, 6, 7, 8; and faith in him as our Redeemer, all-sufficient to bless and keep us, Gen. xvii. 1, and xv. 1.

A conformity to God's way; That *way prescribed in his word,* Psalm cxix. 30. The way of communion with him through Christ, John xiv. 6; Heb. x. 19—22. And that way *suggested by his relations and perfections.* The way of grateful self-dedication, Rom. xii. 1, and of humble affiance, 1 Pet. v. 7.

The *habitual recollection of God's presence,* Psa. xvi. 8; Prov. iii. 6.

The *enjoyment of his manifested favor,* Heb. xi. 5; Psa. lxxxix. 15, 16. Hence observe,

3. *Some advantages which result from walking with God.* As

Guidance in difficulties, Prov. iii. 6. ' He shall direct," &c., Psa. xxxii. 8 —Preservation from falling, Psa. xvi. 8.—Assistance in weakness, Isa. xli. 10.—Comfort in afflictions, Psa. xlvi. 1, and xciv. 19.—And improvement in piety, Prov. iv. 18. Having observed what is implied in this good man's general character, let us, for our farther instruction, consider.

II. SOME PECULIAR CIRCUMSTANCES CONNECTED WITH IT ; Particularly,

1. *The period of its commencement, and the time of its continuance.*

It *commenced* in what may be considered his *early youth ;* when he had not lived the twelfth part of the then usual age of man. This shows us, that early piety is acceptable to God, Prov. viii. 17. Seek it, Eccl. xii. 1 ; for early habits are most easily formed, and most lasting, Lam. iii. 27.—It *continued at least three hundred years.* This teaches us—That the pleasures of religion never cloy, Psa lxiii. 3, 4 ; and that God's grace is sufficient for the longest pilgrimage, Job xvii. 11.

2. *The relations under which it was sustained.* The relation of—a *family governor.* Hence, we see the falsehood of three common suppositions. First, "That solitude is necessary to piety." This is an error of superstition ; as christians we are called to sociability, Matt. v. 14—16. Secondly, "That religion is injurious to social duties and comforts." This is an error of prejudice, which is confuted by many living characters, Prov. xii. 26. Thirdly, "That we serve God only when we engage in acts of devotion." This is an error of ignorance ; for we also serve God acceptably, when we serve mankind in obedience to him, Acts xiii. 36 ; Gal. v. 13, and vi. 2, 10. This character was also sustained by Enoch, under the relation of—a *public teacher.* From this example, we learn, that teachers of others should be careful to walk with God themselves ;—in domestic life, that they may engage their families in God's service, Josh. xxiv. 15 ;—in public life, that their labors may be blessed by God, Psa. li. 12, 13 ; Mal. ii. 6.

3. *The scenes amidst which it was preserved.* These were examples of prevailing ungodliness ; when piety was generally reproached. Thus, when iniquity is general, it is our duty to be singular, Exod. xxiii. 2, for we are called by God to be a peculiar people, Tit. ii. 14 ; Rom. xii. 2.—A resolute confession of God in the face of an opposing world, is highly pleasing to him, Heb. xi. 5. "He pleased God," Numb. xiv. 24; Matt. x. 23. Those who honor God are honored by him, 1 Sam. ii. 30. This appears from,

4. *The glorious event which succeeded this holy walk.* "God took him." He was translated body and soul to heaven, without seeing death.—This removal was *gainful to him ;* it perfected his felicity. So the death of all true believers is followed by the eternal consummation of all their happiness, Phil. i. 21, 23 ; Luke xxiii. 43.

It was *honorable to God.* To his wisdom, in discriminating characters ; to his goodness, in rewarding the faithful ; and to his truth, in fulfilling his promises. So is the death of all his saints, Psa. cxvi. 15, and lviii. 11.

It was *beneficial to mankind.* It teaches mankind in all ages, that *there is another and a better world reserved for the righteous:*—as the ascension of Elijah and our Lord did afterwards, Heb. xi. 16 ; 1 Pet. i. 3, 4, 5.

That *piety is extensively profitable ;* being evidently conducive to our eternal, as well as to our present welfare, 1 Tim. iv. 8.

That *the redemption of our bodies as well as our souls is certain.* For we see God able and faithful to fulfil his engagements, Hos. xiii. 14 ; Phil. iii. 2.

That *an early removal, is no loss to the righteous.* For what is taken from time. is added to a blissful eternity. Rev. vii. 14—17.

And that *a sudden removal, when God appoints it, is no cause of terror to those who die in him;* for to all such characters sudden death becomes sudden glory, Rev. xiv. 13; 2 Cor. v. 8; Isa. lvii. 1, 2.

This interesting example teaches us,

1. *That to walk with God, is the common privilege of mankind.*—For what Enoch did, God calls us to do in his word, Jer. vi. 16; Mic. vi. 8; and the grace enjoyed by him is also free for us, Rom. x. 12.

We have free access to God through Christ, Eph. ii. 18; 1 Pet. iii. 18. And strength to walk with God is promised by him, Zech. x. 12.

2. To *walk with God is the indispensable duty of mankind.* For none can dwell with God hereafter, but such as walk with him here, Psa. v. 4, 5.

3. To *walk with God is the highest interest of mankind.* It is the sure and only way to heaven, Psa. lxxxiv. 11. Like Enoch, set yourselves to walk with God:—desire it, Psa. cxix. 5;—and in God's strength resolve on it, Psa. cxvi. 9, 18.

PRACTICAL RELIGION ENFORCED.

John xiii. 17. If ye know these things, happy are ye if ye do them. (H. H.)

So little was the virtue of humility understood among the Heathen, that neither the Greeks nor Romans had a word whereby to express the idea. The lowliness of mind and poverty of spirit which we admire as the summit of christian excellence, they would have accounted meanness and pusillanimity. But our blessed Lord has instructed us in a far clearer manner than the philosophers of old could do, and has illustrated every one of his instructions by his own example. The act of condescension that is recorded in the chapter before us, very strongly exemplifies the virtue of which we are speaking: though Jesus was the Lord both of heaven and earth, and his disciples were no higher than poor fishermen, he made himself their servant, and performed for them the meanest office, even that of washing their feet: and then told them that such was the spirit which he would have them cultivate, and such the conduct he would have them pursue towards all their fellow-disciples. He declared, moreover, that such views of christian excellence, attended with a corresponding practice, would prove to them a source of the richest happiness.

We shall not however confine our views to this particular virtue; but shall take occasion from the words of our text to point out, in a more general manner, the connexion between "knowing and doing" the will of God. We shall shew,

I. THEIR WORTHLESSNESS WHEN SEPARATE—

As for doing, without knowing, the will of God, that is impossible; since knowledge is, and must be, the foundation of all practice. No act can be a religious act, unless it be done with a direct reference to the will of God ordering and directing it to be done. But knowledge may exist without practice: but when it does so, it is altogether worthless.

1. It has no intrinsic excellence—

The devils have knowledge in common with us, and probably to a far greater extent: but do they possess any thing that is truly good? *Virtue is* good, even though it reside only in the mind, and have no scope for exercise; but *knowledge*, when considered without reference to practice, is as empty and worthless as ignorance itself.

2. It is productive of no good—

The science of astronomy, and the knowledge of the magnet, are among the most useful of human attainments: but of what use would they be, if not applied to practical purposes? In the same manner, the knowledge of medicine would never benefit any one, if it were not improved for the healing or preventing of disorders. Thus it is also with respect to divine knowledge. We may be able to delineate all the perfections of God, to trace all the ways of his providence, and to open all the wonders of redemption; we may be able to descant upon virtue, in all its bearings and relations: yea, as the apostle says, we may "understand all mysteries and all knowledge;" and what are we the better for it all, or what good do we effect by it, if it float only upon the mind, and never operate upon our life and conversation? We are only "as sounding brass or as tinkling cymbals." If it be said, that, by communicating our knowledge, we may influence others; *this* only amounts to what we are insisting on, that knowledge is of use only in reference to practice; and, that it then only does good. when it stirs men up to a suitable improvement of it.

3. It only aggravates our condemnation—

We are assured, that, "to him that knoweth to do good, and doeth it not, to him it is sin." Jam. iv. 17. Exactly as much good therefore as "*sin*" does us, so much does unimproved knowledge. Knowledge is a talent, of which we are to give an account: and "to whom much is given, of him will the more be required." The man who knew his Lord's will, and did it not, was beaten with many stripes: while the ignorant offender was beaten with comparatively few. Luke xii. 47, 48. Thus shall we find it in the day of judgment. If on the one hand, unavoidable ignorance will be considered as an extenuation of our guilt, so, on the other hand, will unsanctified knowledge prove a fearful aggravation of it.

We would not, however, depreciate either knowledge or practice; but rather point out,

II. THEIR EXCELLENCE WHEN COMBINED—

When connected with each other as the root and the fruit, they have an efficacy,

1. To please God—

The fruits of righteousness that spring from an enlightened mind, are truly acceptable to God. Heb. xiii. 16; 1 Pet ii. 5. They answer the end for which he originally gave us to his Son, Eph. i. 4, and ii. 10, and for which his Son laid down his life. Tit. ii. 14. There is not any one act that can flow from just views of ourselves and of Christ, which God will not behold with complacency, and accept with joy. Matt. x. 42; Jer. ix. 24.

2. To bring comfort into the soul—

Works of piety are like the incense which, when offered by the priest, not only honored God, but also regaled the offerer. It is truly said, (though many who admire the expression have very inadequate notions of its import,) that religion's "ways are ways of pleasantness and peace," and that "in keeping God's commandments there is great reward." Who ever set himself to serve and honor God, without finding that "the work of righteousness was peace, and the effect of righteousness was quietness and assurance for ever?" It cannot fail but that those who abound in the exercise of virtue, must have the testimony of their own consciences respecting it; and wherever that is, there must be a never-failing source of joy and peace. **2 Cor. i. 12.**

3. To embolden us in reference to the day of judgment—

That there is no *merit* in our works is certain: and if we were to found our hopes of acceptance with God upon them as meritorius, we should delude ourselves to our eternal ruin. Nevertheless we are authorized to expect that God will deal with us *according to* our works: and, if we have the testimony of our own consciences that it is our endeavor to " walk worthy of God unto all pleasing," we may "assure our hearts before him," and "have confidence towards him" in reference to his future judgment. 1 John iii. 18—21, and iv. 17. Knowing in our own souls that we have fought a good fight and kept the faith, we may say without doubt or fear, " Henceforth there is laid up for me a crown of righteousness, which the Lord, the righteous Judge, shall give me." 2 Tim. iv. 7, 8.

4. To augment our everlasting happiness—

Who need be told, that men will be rewarded in proportion to their improvement of their talents? Luke viv. 14, and xix. 16, 17; 1 Cor. iii. 8. This is so plain a truth, that it cannot be denied; and so encouraging a truth, that it ought not to be concealed. A life of holiness is even now recompensed by the richest consolations; but its full value will be known only in heaven.

From this subject we shall take occasion to,

1. Condole with the ignorant—

We have before observed, that knowledge is the parent of all acceptable obedience. What then must be your state while you are ignorant of those great things which belong unto your peace? God himself has told you, that you will find " no favor" at his hands, Isa. xxvii. 11, but will inevitably and eternally perish. Hos. iv. 6. Do but reflect on the condition of a soul that finds " no favor" at the hands of an angry God: surely " better were it for that person that he had never been born."

2. Counsel the enlightened—

Value not yourselves upon your knowledge, if you have not a practice suitable to it: for, it is " not the hearer of the law that is just before God, but the doers of the law shall be justified." Rom. ii. 13. You may say, " Lord, Lord," and profess to have known and served him in many things; but you can never enter into the kingdom of heaven, if you have not cheerfully and unreservedly performed his will. Matt. vii. 21, 23. Take care therefore that you " be not hearers only of his word, deceiving your own selves; but be doers of it also; for then only shall ye be blessed in your deed." Jam. i. 22—25.

3. Congratulate the practical Christian—

" Happy are ye," God himself being witness. Every prominent feature of your character has been mentioned by our Lord as a distinct and certain ground of blessedness. Matt. v. 3—12. You are fitly " compared to a wise man who built his house upon a rock." Matt. vii. 24—27. Compare the difference between such a man, and a foolish man that builds his house upon the sand: and you will then see your own happiness in a just point of view. Hold on then in this good way; and " as you have learned how to walk and to please God, see that ye abound more and more." 1 Thess. iv. 1.

FRUITS OF RIGHTEOUSNESS.

Phil. i. 11.—Being filled with the fruits of righteousness, which are by Jesus Christ unto the glory and praise of God. (Sk.)

SUCH was the apostle's desire and prayer for the Philippian christians. He had previously preached among them the gospel of Christ; and witnessed the demonstration of its power in their personal salvation. But when he wrote this epistle, he was a "prisoner of Jesus Christ for the Gentiles." Through the malice of his enemies, he was not permitted either to engage in the public work of the ministry, or to visit the churches of the saints. But his devout and zealous spirit could not be confined in the contracted precincts of his degraded dungeon. While he was detained from his regular ministerial labors, he wrote some of his most excellent epistles, to establish and encourage the primitive believers, in the faith and hope of the gospel. And to his pastoral instructions, he added fervent prayers and intercession for the welfare of his christian brethren. The text constitutes a part of a comprehensive prayer, which he offered to "the God of all grace," for the Philippian church: the whole of which is appropriate and sublime, and well adapted for general utility. The words selected for our present consideration, regard the nature—the fruits—the author—and the results of righteousness.

I. THE NATURE OF RIGHTEOUSNESS. We may observe, First, *The term righteousness is diversified in its meaning.* To ascertain its precise signification, we should consider the different objects of its application. Sometimes it refers to the Divine Being, and signifies the purity of his nature, and the perfection of his works, Psa. cxlv. 17. It also applied to the Redeemer, both in his personal and mediatorial character, 2 Cor. v. 21. We also read of the righteousness of the law, which implies uniform obedience to all its precepts and ordinances, as a perfect rule of moral rectitude, Eph. i. 6. Righteousness is also possessed by a man as a believer, and it is *relative* in its character—*internal* in its principle—and *practical* in its influence. This is the evangelical righteousness of faith in Christ. Phil. iii. 9.

Secondly, *Righteousness in the text signifies personal holiness.* Sin has corrupted all our moral powers, and rendered our souls unholy. But when we believe in Christ, we are freely justified and "saved by the washing of regeneration, and the renewing of the Holy Ghost." The divine nature is imparted, which consists in "righteousness and true holiness," as a meetness for "the inheritance of the saints in light." Thus, the work of God in the souls of his people, is called, "the *work of righteousness,* and the *kingdom of righteousness,* and grace reigning *through righteousness* unto eternal life."

II. THE FRUITS OF RIGHTEOUSNESS. This part of our subject, suggests the following truths. First, *Christian righteousness is productive of gracious fruits.* These fruits are both *internal* in the heart, and *external* in the life. The apostle speaks of the former, the latter will follow as a natural consequence. The fruits of righteousness include the exercise of unfeigned faith—peace which passeth all understanding—the love of God shed abroad in the heart—the testimony of a good conscience—the humble, heavenly mind of Christ—the implantation of every spiritual grace—joy unspeakable, and fully of glory—the indwelling, and operations of the Spirit, producing holy principles and dispositions, which practically appear "in all holy conversation and godliness.

Secondly. *The fruits of righteousness are abundant and progressive.* Hence the apostle prays that the Philippians might be *filled* with those fruits, which implies an *increasing plenitude* of grace and holiness. Perhaps he had reference to a very fruitful tree, that has all its branches laden with rich fruit, in a high state of perfection. It is certain, all the righteous are *really*, though not *equally* fruitful. Some bring forth "thirty, some sixty, and some an hundred fold." To be *filled* with the fruits of righteousness, is to realize *exalted degrees* of piety—to grow in every christian attainment—to "comprehend the breadth, and length, and depth, and height, of the love of Christ; and be *filled* with all the fulness of God." There is a *fulness* of grace here, and of glory hereafter, which we should desire and pray to enjoy.

III. THE AUTHOR OF RIGHTEOUSNESS. It is "by Jesus Christ." We are naturally unrighteous, and therefore all our righteousness, as christians, is of the Lord, through the mediation of the Saviour. First, *Righteousness is purchased by Jesus Christ as our Redeemer.* For this purpose, he was manifested in the flesh—fulfilled the righteousness of the law—died a sacrifice for the sins of the world—"made reconciliation for iniquity—and brought in everlasting righteousness, which is unto, and upon all them that believe." Jesus Christ having thus opened a new and living way of pardon and salvation, is justly styled, "The Lord our righteousness;" because by his atonement, he has *merited* righteousness and eternal glory for perishing sinners, Rom. iii. 22—26.

Secondly, *Righteousness is derived from Jesus Christ as our Saviour.* It is only through *believing* we can be saved; and faith is counted for righteousness, by virtue of the precious blood of Christ, that ratified the everlasting covenant. In him there is a plenitude of grace for the salvation of sinners; and when we believe in his name, he is "made unto us wisdom, righteousness, sanctification, and redemption." We receive of his fulness every grace and blessing to constitute us *relatively, personally*, and *practically* righteous. And through union with him, and participation of the influences of his Spirit, we become fruitful in righteousness, "that we may be sincere, and without offence, till the day of Christ," John xv. 1—8.

IV. THE RESULTS OF RIGHTEOUSNESS. "Unto the glory and praise of God." The *essential glory* of the divine essence is infinite, and therefore unchangeable; but the *manifestation* of his *glorious perfections* is the original design of all his works. Consider, First, Righteousness is "to the glory and praise of God," *in the scheme of redemption.* In this, we behold the *glory* of the wisdom, power, love, mercy, justice, and holiness of God displayed; in creating, preserving, redeeming, and saving rebellious sinners. God is evidently *glorified* in the origin, author, work, design, and effects of our redemption. His glory is thus made manifest, both to angels and men. Psa. lxxxv. 10; Luke ii. 14; 2 Cor. iii. 18.

Secondly, Righteousness is "to the glory and praise of God," *in the subjects of salvation.* They are conscious that all their good comes from him; and therefore, they gratefully ascribe praise and adoration unto him for all his benefits, Psa. ciii. 1—5. And in all their designs and deportment they "show forth his praise, do all to his glory, and glorify him in their bodies and spirits, which are his." And in the kingdom of heaven they will ascribe salvation, glory, honor, and power, unto God and the Lamb, for ever and ever, Rev. i. 5, 6. Let these observations stimulate our desires—promote our devotion—and inspire us with praise.

JACOB'S DYING CONFIDENCE.

Genesis xlix. 18.—I have waited for thy salvation, O Lord. (Sk.)

THE history of the patriarch Jacob is well known, and forms a very important and interesting portion of sacred biography. It is replete with admonitory caution and consolatory encouragements, which are highly profitable for the instruction and comfort of the saints. In the early part of his life, he was favored with the religious tuition and example of his eminently pious father, whose distinguished character is stamped with immortal renown in the imperishable annals of revelation. But notwithstanding the many advantages which he enjoyed in his youth, he did not on some occasions maintain that strict integrity of conduct, which is according to godliness. Yet it is evident, from the general aspect of his deportment, that he was deeply imbued with the spirit of holiness, and piously devoted to the God of his fathers. He firmly believed in the promised Messiah, and was repeatedly privileged with special tokens of the divine mercy and approbation. This chapter records the closing scene of his protracted life and labors, and contains his dying requests and solemn charges to his children, intermixed with various predictions of the future events connected with the twelve tribes of his family. And in the midst of his departing advices and devotions, he exclaimed in the text, with holy confidence and joy, "I have waited for thy salvation, O Lord." Thus this venerable patriarch commended his soul into the hand of his covenant God, in sure and certain hope of a blissful immortality beyond the grave. In attempting an improvement of his dying appeal, we shall notice,

I. THE IMPORTANT OBJECT FOR WHICH THE PATRIARCH WAITED—"Thy salvation." Some suppose that Jacob refers merely to temporal deliverances, but it is much more probable that he desired the complete salvation of his soul, through the divine Shiloh: which includes all the blessings of grace here, and of glory hereafter. In this general and extended sense of the term, salvation may be considered as only commenced in a state of probation, and perfected in the world of retribution.

1. Salvation is present in its commencement. It is the work of grace already begun in them that believe. It is not only a future portion joyfully anticipated, but also a present privilege actually enjoyed. The Lord now personally saves his people from the guilt, the power, and the pollution of sin, Eph. i. 7; Rom. vi. 14; Titus iii. 5;—from the curse and condemnation of the law, Rom. viii. 16; Gal. iii. 13;—from the tyranny and kingdom of Satan, Acts xxvi. 18; Col. i. 13;—from all their malicious and powerful enemies, and under every affliction and calamity of human life. Isa. liv. 17; 2 Cor. xii. 9. This salvation is progressive in its character, and admits of continual increase in christian knowledge, purity, and happiness. But this glorious state of grace is only the beginning and pledge of its final perfection.

2. Salvation is future in its consummation. Though the righteous are now initially saved from moral evil, and participate "holiness, without which no man shall see the Lord," yet they are not actually delivered from natural evil while in a probationary state. In the present world they are always surrounded with enemies, exposed to dangers, and subject to complicated trials. Here we have no continuing city, but seek one to come. "There remaineth a rest to the people of God." He saved them through every

166

period of their mortal existence; in the dark valley of the shadow of death; and in the great day of his wrath, when he shall come "to make up his jewels," Heb. ix. 28; Col. iii. 3, 4. Their bodies also shall be changed and fashioned like unto Christ's glorious body, and with their immortal spirits shall be *fully* and *eternally* saved from sin and all its direful consequences, to the perfect and endless fruition of the Deity, in whose "presence there is fulness of joy, and pleasures for evermore," Rom ii. 7. Such was the comprehensive and dignified object of Jacob's pious anticipation; and the source from whence he expected to derive it will appear by considering,

II. THE GLORIOUS BEING IN WHOM THE PATRIARCH CONFIDED—' *Thy* salvation, O *Lord*." He did not trust in the virtues of his ancestors nor expect salvation on the ground of his descent from Abraham, "the father of the faithful." He exercised implicit confidence in the Lord Jehovah, as the origin and donor of every blessing. He knew that salvation was solely a divine achievement, and therefore emphatically called it, " *Thy* salvation, O *Lord*."

1. *Salvation is divinely devised and provided.* When we had destroyed ourselves, in God was found our help. He piteously beheld our perishing condition, as depraved and guilty sinners, and in infinite wisdom and mercy devised a glorious scheme of reconciliation through the intervention of a Divine Mediator, 1 Tim. ii. 5, 6. By the actual accomplishment of his scheme of redemption, the perfections of the Creator are glorified—the moral law is practically magnified—a perfect atonement is made for sin—and eternal salvation is amply provided in Jesus Christ, for "the world that lieth in wickedness," John iii. 16; Acts v. 31; 1 Tim. i. 15. "Glory to God in the highest, and on earth peace, good will towards men!"

2. *Salvation is divinely revealed and promised.* It was primarily announced to our original progenitors in paradise, and was subsequently made known to the patriarchs and prophets, but is now more fully brought to light by the superior dispensation of "grace and truth," Col. i. 26—28. And it is not only explicitly revealed for our instruction, but is also graciously promised for our encouragement. The Lord faithfully engages to bestow every blessing of the covenant of grace on them who "unfeignedly repent, and believe his holy gospel," Isa. lv. 6, 7; Matt. xi. 28, 29; Acts xvi. 31. And all the divine promises are exceeding great and precious in their nature and effects, and infallibly certain in their authority and fulfilment. God is not slack concerning his promise, for his word is true from the beginning, 2 Cor. i. 20.

3. *Salvation is divinely imparted and realized.* Omnipotence alone is adequate to save the soul from sin and ruin. All human efforts, however wise and salutary, are totally inefficient and hopeless, 2 Cor. iii. 5.—But the infinite Jehovah is both able and willing to redeem us from all our iniquities. He can enlighten the darkest mind—pardon the most aggravated guilt,—renovate the hardest heart—and save to the uttermost all them that believe in his name. He is the only *Author* and *Finisher* of the salvation of his people, and from him every good and perfect gift freely descends, Eph. ii. 8, 9. He begins and completes the work of righteousness; and it will ever remain an important and consoling truth, that "salvation belongeth unto the Lord." In him therefore, like Jacob, we should put our trust, and patiently expect his saving grace. And for our direction and encouragement, the text specifies,

III. THE SACRED EXERCISE IN WHICH THE PATRIARCH WAS OCCUPIED.— "*I have waited* for thy salvation," &c. This language expresses the gracious state of mind in which this excellent saint both lived and died. He long waited for salvation according to the will of God, and was not disappointed. Let us therefore follow his pious example.

1. *We must wait for salvation patiently.* We have all gone astray from God "like lost sheep;" and have incurred his righteous displeasure. We are condemned by his law, and obnoxious to his wrath: but if we return unto him with penitent and obedient hearts, he will have mercy upon us, and abundantly pardon our sins, Luke xv. 20—24. Thus Jacob humbled himself before his God, and devoutly acknowledged that he was "less than the least of all his mercies," chap. xxxii. 10.—Genuine repentance is invariably necessary to obtain salvation, and it is only by thus *seeking* and *waiting* for it, that we participate its personal benefits, Hosea xiv. 1, 2, 4.—"The Lord is nigh unto them that are of a broken heart, and saveth such as be of a contrite spirit."

2. *We must wait for salvation believingly.* This is the only way of obtaining an interest in the Redeemer.—Abraham "believed God, and it was counted to him for righteousness." Jacob's faith was strong and vigorous, by which he fully credited the divine declarations, and gladly embraced the promised Saviour. Genuine faith is unchangeably the same, and is essentially connected with the salvation of our souls, John iii. 18, 36. It is a principle of *credence, affiance,* and *appropriation.* It is not a mere *opinion* of uncertain speculation, but an *habitual* and *vital* exercise of the mind, by which we are enabled confidently to exclaim, "Lo, this is our God; we have waited for him, and he will save us; this is the Lord; we have waited for him, we will rejoice and be glad in his salvation."

3. *We must wait for salvation importunately.* This primitive patriarch was an eminently devout character. A remarkable instance of this appears when he wrestled with the Lord, and nobly declared, "I will not let thee go, except thou bless me;" and as a mighty prince "he had power with God and prevailed."—Prayer is still indispensably necessary, and uniformly attended with certain success, Psa. xci. 15, 16. It must be sincere, humble, spiritual, fervent, and faithful. By thus *waiting upon* and *for* the Lord, he will assuredly hear our cries, and save us from all our troubles, Psa. xl. 1–3, l. 15.

4. *We must wait for salvation perseveringly.* It must be a patient, continual, and confident expectation of divine mercy, in all the appointed means of grace, and under every vicissitude of human life.—Thus good old Israel, after waiting for the Lord through a long series of years, and having found him a never-failing refuge and portion, he was at last enabled to die triumphantly in the faith, by which he had previously lived, joyfully declaring, "I have waited for thy salvation, O Lord."—"Mark the perfect man, and behold the upright; for the end of that man is peace."

We may learn from this subject the necessity of seeking salvation—the excellency of genuine religion—and the blessedness of "dying in the Lord."

AN INTEREST IN GOD THE MOST EFFECTUAL ANTIDOTE TO FEAR.

Gen. xv. 1. Fear not, Abram, I *am* thy shield, *and* thy exceeding great reward. (Sk.)

"THE Lord loveth the righteous." How demonstrable is this consolatory truth! He designates them by the most endearing titles. He confers upon them the most invaluable privileges. He permits them to hold with himself the closest communion. He manifests the most affectionate solicitude, to convince them of the deep interest he takes in their most minute affairs. God's conduct towards Abram abundantly illustrates the verity of these remarks.—The preceding chapter presents the first record of martial contest that has been transmitted to posterity; in which Lot, the nephew of Abram, and all his goods, had fallen into the hands of an unprincipled and ferocious soldiery. The tidings were conveyed to Abram, who most promptly armed his servants, amounting to three hundred and eighteen, and pursued after the conquerors; and, by a most judicious attack, succeeded in defeating them; and what to him was more desirable, in rescuing Lot, and his family, from their hands, and recovering all the spoils. "After these things, the word of the Lord came unto Abram, &c., saying, Fear not, Abram," &c. It would be natural for Abram, thus circumstanced, to fear lest the enemies whom he had routed should rally their forces, and by superior numbers overpower him; the text was therefore to him peculiarly appropriate. We will, in reflecting on it, consider,

1. THE PERSON ADDRESSED. Abram—a character rendered memorable for Faith—Prayer—Hospitality—and Obedience.

1. *Abram was a man of genuine faith.* The faith of Abram was *divine* in its object, "he believed God," Rom. iv. 3. *Unshaken* in its exercise, his faith was tried, Heb. xi. 17; but he staggered not, Rom. iv. 20. *Operative* in its principle, Heb. xi. 18. *Realizing* in its prospect, "he looked for a city," Heb. xi. 16. He is termed "faithful Abram."

2. *Of importunate prayer.* Witness the intercessions which he urged on behalf of Sodom. In these we perceive *feelings of profound self-abasement of soul,* "I am but dust and ashes." Gen. xviii. 27. *Sympathies of deep commiseration.* He saw the terrible storm of indignation ready to burst on Sodom. *Appeals repeatedly urged on the Divine Being.* "I will speak yet but this once," Gen. xviii. 32. But *principles of perfect submission.* Not a murmer of discontent is heard.

3. *Of cordial hospitality.* See Gen. xviii. 2—7. Kindness to strangers is highly commendable. The accommodations now provided for travellers were in the days of Abram unknown: but even in the apostolic age hospitality was deemed a praiseworthy virtue, Rom. xii. 13; Heb. xiii. 2; 1 Pet. iv. 9.

4. *Of uniform obedience.* His personal piety secured to him the high encomium of a "Friend of God." In reference to his domestic arrangements, the Lord declared, "I know him that he will command his children," &c., Gen. xviii. 19. And as to his general character, by works was his faith made perfect, Jam. ii. 22.

II. THE ADMONITORY PROHIBITION URGED. "Fear not, Abram." This prohibition cannot be designed to suppress the passion of fear; a passion common to human nature, and in our present state as necessary as it is common. Nor was it intended to divest Abram of that cautionary mode of conduct, which provides for safety in the time of danger. Much less are we to imagine that the prohibition includes that holy, reverential awe of the Divine

Being, which should be deeply fixed in our minds, Prov. xxiii. 17, xxviii. 14. But the fear prohibited is the apprehension of evil, attended with that uneasiness, anxiety, and torment, which are its usual concomitants.

1. *There is a fear of persecution.* The revilings of men, and the fines, penalties, and punishments which have been inflicted upon the righteous in various ages, have produced in their minds feelings of deep anxiety. Our Lord sought to arm his disciples against this kind of fear, Luke xii. 4. God said to Abram, "Fear not."

2. *There is a fear of poverty.* The disciples of Christ are chiefly "the poor of this world," Jam. ii. 5. Want often stares them in the face, and their fears are frequently excited, lest they should be deprived of the bread that perisheth, see Luke xii. 22—30. How far Abram was subject to this fear it is impossible to determine. In the early periods of the world commerce was unknown—the luxuries of life were few—famines were frequent and want prevailed to an alarming degree. Abram sojourned in a strange land, and might have been deprived of the common necessaries of life.

3. *There is the fear of pain.* Suffering is man's inevitable lot. The human body in its tendency to dissolution necessarily suffers, and where is the individual that has not indulged a painful presentiment in reference to the pain of dying? God said to Abram, "Fear not," Rev. ii. 10.

III. THE ENCOURAGING ASSURANCE ANNEXED. "I am thy shield," &c. This was designed as an antidote to fear. The shield anciently was a piece of defensive armor, usually composed of wood covered with leather, sometimes overlaid with plates of gold or brass.—The use of the shield was to defend the body against the darts of the enemy. God was Abram's defence, and he has been the defence of his people in all ages.

1. *He defends their persons.* Their *bodies.*—See Daniel in the den of lions; the Hebrew children in the fiery furnace; Paul when suffering shipwreck. Their *souls* in temptation.—"There hath no temptation taken you," &c., 1 Cor. x. 13; 2 Pet. ii. 9. From the power of evil. "The Lord shall preserve thee from evil," Psa. cxxi. 7; John xvii. 15.

2. *He protects their substance.* "Hast thou not made a hedge about him?" &c., Job. i. 10; "There shall no evil befall thee," &c., Psa. xci. 10. If God be our shield, our defence is *certain;* "The Almighty shall be thy defence," &c., Job xxii. 25; "My defence is of God," Psa vii. 19, lix. 9. Our defence is *universal.*—The shields of the people defended one part of the body only. God defends his people as the hen doth her brood, Luke xiii. 34. "He shall cover thee with his feathers," Psa xci. 4. *Constant.*—The earthly warrior may be divested of his shield; God will never leave his people. "He that keepeth Israel," &c., Psa. cxxi. 4.

3. *God is the reward of his people.* The king of Sodom had offered Abram rewards for interposing in his behalf; these he had rejected, saying that he would not even take a thread, Gen. xiv. 23. But God promises Abram that *he* will be his reward; *He is the author of his people's reward.* Their reward is not wages for service performed; but recompense freely and graciously given; infinitely surpassing all their claims, on the ground of any supposed worthiness; *He is the giver of their reward*; "the rewarder of them," &c., Heb. xi. 6. He appoints their kingdom, gives them their crown, places them on their throne, &c., Luke xxii. 29; Rev. ii. 10, iii. 21. *He is the object of their reward.* It is not their wonderful escape from perdition, nor the splendor of heaven, nor the society of angels, that will constitute their reward; but it is the possession of God, the light of his countenance, the consciousness of his love, and the enjoyment of his nature:

hence God is their portion and their heritage, and they are heirs of God. He is their *exceeding* great reward; exceeding all earthly rewards in the dignity of its origin—the vastness of its nature—the certainty of its communication—the felicity of its possession—and the perpetuity of its existence.

From the subject we learn,

1. *The security and safety of God's people.* God is their shield: they live in a world of enemies, and are surrounded by dangers, seen and unseen; but "the name of the Lord is a strong tower, the righteous runneth into it, and is safe."

2. *Their tranquility and happiness.* God is their reward; perhaps they have little to expect in this world but painful exercises; but their all is treasured up in God; and from his bounty and benevolence they cannot expect too much.

3. *The fearless confidence with which they should be inspired.* What can they fear, while God is their *shield* and their *exceeding great reward?* shall they fear tribulation, or distress, or famine, or nakedness, or peril, or sword? "Nay, in all these things, *they* are more than conquerors through him that hath loved *them.*"

ON PATIENCE.

Tim. vi. 11.—Follow after patience. (H.)

Among all the graces that adorn the soul of a christian, like so many jewels of various colors and lustres, there is not one more brilliant than this of patience: not one that brings more glory to God, or contributes so much towards making and keeping peace on earth; not one which renders a christian more happy within himself, or more agreeable to all about him. Even they who themselves possess it not, are sure to commend it in others. They set their seal to the truth, though by so doing they condemn their own practice. Consider,

I. The nature of patience.

Patience is a holy behaviour in affliction: it is not an insensibleness of present evils, nor an indifference to future good—"no affliction for the present is joyous." Our Lord himself was sensible of his sufferings, nor should we be coldly affected to the blessings for which God has caused us to hope; that would be a reflection on the excellency of the blessings—would make us negligent in our endeavors to obtain them.

Christian patience is a disposition that keeps us calm and composed in our minds, and steady in the practice of our duty, under the sense of our afflictions, or the delay of our hopes. It is sometimes called long-suffering, or, a length of mind. It is directly opposite to hastiness of spirit.

1. Patience secures the possession of our souls in every circumstance that tends to discompose our minds. Patience is a soul enjoying itself in every condition, an even sea in all winds; a serene soul in all weathers; a thread even spun with every wheel of Providence. Our Lord exhorts his disciples, when he had foretold the sufferings and dangers to which they would be exposed, "In patience possess ye your souls." Smart trials, or the deferring of our hopes, are apt to make our hearts sick; patience guards the soul, and keeps it sedate and sober under every affliction.

2. Patience prevents hasty and rash conclusions, either from present trouble, or the suspension of desired good. We are prone to make hasty conclusions from present appearances, and to charge the Lord foolishly : to question the truth of his promises, if they are not accomplished in our way and time ; or to suspect his mercy and goodness, because afflictions are our present lot. Psa. lxxvii. 7—9. Patience disposeth us to rest in God; I reckon the sufferings—"He who hath delivered, and doth deliver, will yet deliver." The patient soul is neither without tears, nor without hope ; neither over sensible, nor under sensible ; affected with all, cast down with nothing: quiet when tossed, very quiet when extremely tossed ; expecting his salvation from God, when none can be had from man. "Though he slay me." Patience is a soul at rest in God; substance gone, Ziglag burnt, all mourning, many murmuring—stoning—David makes up all in God. 1 Sam. xxx. 1—6.

3. Patience will fortify against any unlawful methods for accomplishing our deliverance or desires : the impatient endeavor by any means to obtain their wishes.—When the Philistines were coming against Saul with a formidable army, and his own people were much discouraged, he would not wait for deliverance in God's time and way. 1 Sam. xiii. 5, 14. Patience restrains from unlawful expedients ; "He that believeth shall not make haste"—"The Lord will provide," is the language of patience under the greatest sufferings.

4. Patience disposes the soul to perseverance in the way of duty, whatever discouragements may arise from the pressure of afflictions, or the deferring of hopes. This is the most essential part of patience, to persevere in our christian course, whether afflictions attend us, or whatever it may cost us. The impatient are apt to "faint and weary in their minds," and grow remiss : "but the righteous shall hold on his way ;" hence we are exhorted to "run with patience the race that is set before us."

III. ENDEAVOR TO RECOMMEND THIS GRACE TO YOUR ESTEEM, AND EXCITE YOU TO THE ATTAINMENT OF IT.

1. Patience is a virtue common to us with God. Long-suffering is his darling attribute ; and what is dear in his sight, ought to be no less precious in ours. And how marvellous is his patience, who daily pours his blessings on those who as daily offend, affront, and dishonor him! " he makes his sun to rise on the evil and on the good ;" he does not exclude the worst of us from those blessings, to which the best of us have no title. For the benefit of the impious as well as the pious, the ungrateful as well as the grateful, the seasons take their rounds, the elements work together, the light and heat exert their friendly influence, the fountains send forth their salutary streams, and the pastures flourish. The gospel is still preached to those who slight it ; the cup of salvation is still held forth to those who have so often dashed it from them ; and although God be provoked every day, he holds his hand, and waiteth to be gracious—although he have the power in his own hands, and the weapons of his indignation are all ready, he defers to strike ; and while judgments sleep, mercy calls night and day to sinners, "Why will you die?" His truth is denied ; his Son crucified ; and his long-suffering is made an argument against his existence ; and he is still patient, "What is man, then, that he should complain?"

2. The patience which we so much admire in God, shone forth yet more amazingly in the person of his Son. Was ever patience like that patience, which descended from a throne of glory, bore a long imprisonment in the womb, to sanctify sinners ; and lay in a stable to bring them to a kingdom!

Behold the Master baptized by his servant; and, with his disciples, he lived not as their Lord, but as the servant of all. How tenderly did he bear with their ignorance and infirmities, leading them gently as they were able to follow him; how patiently did he bear the contradiction of sinners, how was he wounded, who heals every disease, how was he fed with gall and wormwood, who reaches out to his people the fruits of paradise and the cup of salvation; and, at his crucifixion, when the heavens were confounded, and the earth trembled, "He opened not his mouth;" he endured without murmuring all that earth and hell could inflict, till he had put the last stroke to the most finished picture of perfect patience, and prayed for his murderers.

3. The patience thus practised by Christ is enjoined by his gospel, being indeed the badge of that gospel and its professors; "Ye have heard," says our Lord. Matt. v. 43. "Follow after patience"—"In patience." 1 Pet. ii. 21—23.

4. We find all the saints of God, who have been eminent for their faith in Christ, to have been as eminent for their patience, without which their faith must have failed in the day of trial: it being not through faith alone, but "through faith and patience," that they "inherited the promises." Faith begat patience, which, like a dutiful child, proved the support of its parent. Patience preserved Noah's faith all the time the ark was building and while it floated on the waters; through patience Abraham endured the severest trial that ever faith was put to; through patience, Jacob, persecuted by his brother, left his father's house; through patience, Joseph endured and forgave the ill treatment of his brethren; through patience, Moses, so often abused and insulted by a stiff-necked people, still entreated the Lord for them; through patience, David would not slay his implacable enemy, Saul; through patience, Job endured the loss of all things. We are compassed about with a cloud of witnesses, who, through the patience of Jesus Christ, "wandered about in sheep-skins." Heb. xi. 37, 38.

5. The present state of man renders the practice of this virtue absolutely necessary, if we would enjoy any happiness here or hereafter. Could we live in the world without sufferings, then were there no need of patience. But thus runs the sentence, Gen. iii. 17, "Cursed is the ground." Every man, from him that sitteth on a throne, to the man that lieth in a dungeon, must have labor and sorrow; and tribulation admits of no remedy but patience. The christian has need of patience—for "he that endureth to the end shall be saved." Wo unto you that have lost patience; and what shall ye do when the Lord shall visit you! Patience is the only armor that is proof against all assaults, and he who has it well buckled on, needeth not to fear any adversary.

6. And lastly, let me set before you, in one view, the incomparable excellences and advantages of this lovely grace. Patience commends us to God, and keep us his; patience is the guardian of faith, the preserver of peace, the cherisher of love, the teacher of humility; patience governs the flesh, strengthens the spirit, sweetens the temper, stifles anger, extinguishes envy, subdues pride; she bridles the tongue, restrains the hand, tramples on temptation, endures persecutions; patience produces unity in churches, and harmony in families; she comforts the poor, and moderates the rich; she makes us humble in prosperity, and cheerful in adversity; she teaches us to forgive those who have injured us, and to be the first in asking forgiveness of those we may have injured.

If, therefore, to be like unto God; if to be conformed to the image of Christ; if to follow the precepts of the gospel; if to write after the copy of the saints; if to render our present state comfortable, and ensure our final salvation; if to enjoy the incomparable excellences and advantages of patience: if these things are desirable, let us from henceforth give ourselves to the pursuit of this virtue, let us " follow after patience." And for this purpose let us adore and emulate the long-suffering of our God; let us contemplate and transcribe into our practice the patience of Jesus Christ; let us study and fulfil the precepts of the gospel; let us look at and emulate the examples of the saints; let us consider and alleviate the sorrows of our pilgrimage; let us seek until we obtain the heavenly grace of patience, with all her benefits and blessings conferred on her by Jesus Christ; into whose patience the Lord direct our hearts, until she have her perfect work in the salvation of our souls through the same. Amen.

CHRISTIAN FORTITUDE.

2 Pet. i. 5.—Add to your faith virtue. (H.)

THE apostle supposes those to whom he wrote to have obtained like precious faith with him and the other apostles, ver. 1, i. e. to believe the gospel as well as they. He proceeds to exhort them to give all diligence in building a proper superstructure upon their belief of the gospel. That which he recommends consists of seven important articles. The first mentioned, and which he immediately connects with faith, is virtue. " Giving all diligence, add to your faith virtue."

Some would understand virtue in a general sense for a universal regularity of mind and manners, or a disposition to all virtuous actions.—I take the word virtue in a more limited sense here, to mean the particular disposition of christian fortitude. What could more naturally be pressed upon us after faith, or a belief of the gospel, than courage in the profession of it, and in a practice correspondent to it? And what could more aptly follow upon this, than that we should add to our virtue, or courage, knowledge? or a growing acquaintance with the doctrines and duties contained in the rule of our faith, that our courage and resolution may not be ill-placed?

I. EXPLAIN THE NATURE OF CHRISTIAN COURAGE, OR FORTITUDE.

Courage, in general, is a temper which disposes man to do brave and commendable actions, without being daunted at the appearance of dangers and difficulties in the way. The christian life being a warfare, gives the principal occasion and opportunity to show christian courage. It is nothing else but to behave as " good soldiers of Jesus Christ." 2 Tim. ii. 3.

To explain it more particularly, it will be proper to shew,

1. For what it is to be exercised. For the cause makes it a christian grace. It is courage in Christ's cause; that is in maintaining the profession of the christian faith, and adhering to the practice of our duty, as far as we are convinced of the mind of God. 1 Tim. i. 18, 19.

But it must necessarily be presupposed, that we are careful to inform ourselves well about the mind and will of God, relating both to faith and practice, that our courage may not be blind and rash, without a good foundation to support it.

And, indeed, without such diligent inquiries, we are hardly like to be courageous in an hour of trial, whatsoever resolutions we may seem to have, while difficulties are at a distance.

2. Against what christian courage is to be exercised. It supposes oppositions, trials, and dangers in our way : else there would be no occasion for it. It is a temper, for which there will be no room in heaven ; and the need of it now ariseth from our present condition, as in a state of conflict.

1st. The power, the subtilty, and activity of the powers of darkness, call for courage in a christian. Upon this the apostle founds an exhortation to be strong, or courageous. Eph. vi. 10, 12.

2dly. The oppositions from within ourselves require courage. Our own irregular inclinations and affections and passions are difficult to be overcome.

3dly. The several discouragements or dangers we may meet with from other men, in the way of our duty, and even for our duty, make courage necessary. Solomon tells us, "that the fear of man bringeth a snare." Prov. xxix. 25. Courage is to overcome this snare. Acts xx. 24.

3. Wherein, or in what acts and instances it should express itself.

Insensibleness of difficulties or dangers is not a proper expression of it. It is not expected of a christian that his apprehension of these things should be less quick than other people's, or that he should have no natural reluctancy to them. Without that, there would be no trial of his courage. Nor are we to expose ourselves unnecessarily to dangers. We should exercise courage in conjunction with christian prudence, though it ought not to be under the restraints of carnal policy. It would rather be imprudence than duty, to act, in time of persecution, as some primitive christians did, who ran uncalled to the heathen tribunals, and cried, "I am a christian," on purpose that they might obtain the honor and reward of martyrdom. It is delivered as an ordinary rule by Christ himself to his disciples, when he foretells the persecutions that would await them. Matt. x. 23. Though circumstances may sometimes vary the case, and make even this inconsistent with duty. Nehemiah was so situated. Neh. vi. 11. Christian courage is to exert itself in such ways as these :

1st. In deliberate and vigorous resolutions for God and our duty, upon counting the cost. This is all that can be done, when difficulties and dangers are not actually present; seriously to consider them, and, upon balancing matters, to determine for a firm adherence to our Master, whatever it may cost us. Luke xiv. 26—30. The same thing Barnabas inculcated upon the church of Antioch. Acts xi. 23. Such a noble ardour in Paul was a bright part of his character. Acts xxi. 13.

2dly. In the suppression of distracting fear of evils at a distance. The coward often fears where no fear is; and, as well as the slothful man, creates to himself many imaginary dangers. Prov. xxii. 13. The brave soldier of Christ does not anxiously take thought about the morrow, but leaves future events to God's ordering. Psa. cxii. 7, 8.

3dly. In a vigorous application to our christian work, notwithstanding the stated and constant difficulties and oppositions attending it. Though Satan would hinder, and the world ensnare, and a corrupt heart resist, a courageous christian goes on as one resolved to conquer or die; striving to enter in at the strait gate. Luke xiii. 24 ; Matt. xi. 12.

4thly. In readiness to undertake hard and difficult services, when God calls to them. Such as may be eminently for the honor of God or the advantage of our generation, though we may foresee few to help us. **Psa. xciv.**

16. Or when duty obliges us to go upon an ungrateful errand. **Isa. vi. 8.** And especially when visible dangers await us, not to decline a service of which we are capable. Heb. xi. 27.

5thly. In a uniform steadiness of conduct under all the trials we actually meet with. It is no great expression of courage in common life, to talk big when dangers are remote, though he should meet suffering with a trembling heart; yet, if he stands his ground in the hour of temptation, he has the truest courage. As it has been observed of some of the bravest soldiers, they have come with a trembling hand into the battle, but when once engaged have done wonders.

II. WHAT MAY BE INTENDED IN THE EXHORTATION TO ADD VIRTUE, OR COURAGE, TO OUR FAITH.

This may intimate the imperfection of our faith, without this superstructure upon it. It is necessary to be added to our faith, in order to our acceptance with God. Rom. x. 9. Faith is dead, if it produce not a correspondent profession and course of action.

But that which I principally apprehend to be designed is, to intimate the just reason which our faith gives for christian courage. Christian faith is most fit to inspire with christian fortitude. For instance,

1. Faith discovers divine Providence as engaged for us, and with us, in all our difficulties. God frequently animated his servants under the Old Testament in hard services, by an assurance of his presence: Gen. xxvi. 24; Isa. xli. 10; Dan. iii. 17; like the Jewish nurses in Egypt, these were not afraid of the king's commandment. Faith will support us in the greatest dangers by this reasoning, "If God be for us, who can be against us?" Heb. xiii. 5, 6; 1 John iv. 4.

2. Faith proposes the divine Spirit, as directly provided to help our infirmities. Particularly for this very purpose, to inspire us with needful courage Eph. iii. 16. Agreeable to that ancient promise. Psa. xxvii. 14.

3. Faith represents our main enemies as already vanquished, and as having their chief power broken. The Captain of our salvation hath personally overcome them, and as the head of his church too. Col. ii. 15; John xvi. 33. Hence the intention of God in sending his Son, is represented to be, 'that we should be saved from our enemies.' Luke i. 71, and ver. 74, 75.

4. Faith gives us particular assurance, that our trials shall not exceed our strength; either the strength we have, or that which shall be imparted. 1 Cor. x. 13.

5. Faith sets in view greater evils to be feared from our cowardice, than can be feared from our adherence to God. Christ elegantly sets these the one over against the other. Luke xii. 4, 5; Heb. x. 38, 39. And the fearful, who choose always to be in the rear in danger, stand in the front of those who "shall have their part in the second death." Rev. xxi. 8. One would think this necessity, and the impossibility of escaping without it, should make even a coward to fight.

6. Faith assures us of the certain and glorious success of our courage. That our endeavors against our powerful enemies shall issue in a full conquest. Rom. xvi. 20. And though now a saint, after all his struggles, may have frequent occasion to mourn over the body of death, he may be assured that God " will deliver him from it, through Jesus Christ our Lord." Rom. vii. 24, 25. "And death itself, the last enemy, shall be destroyed." 1 Cor. xv. 26. And unspeakable rewards shall be the prize of the conquerors. We strive for mastery, not as uncertain what we are to obtain by it, but for an incorruptible crown. 1 Cor. ix. 25, 26; xv. 58.

7. Faith represents to us the noblest examples of such holy fortitude upon the same principle : all the excellent of the earth, particularly that noble collection of worthies, whose brave exploits are recorded in Heb. xi. The glorious apostle Paul himself; and, above all, the Captain of our salvation, who was an illustrious pattern of invincible courage in his work : he feared the face of no man in the course of his ministry, but boldly reproved sin and sinners. His enemies could not help owning it. Matt. xxii. 16; John vii. 25, 26. Consider him, that endured such contradiction of sinners against himself, lest ye be wearied and faint in your minds. Heb. xii. 2, 3.

Upon the whole,

1. Consider this grace of fortitude as a matter of the utmost importance in the christian life. The variety of oppositions and difficulties in our way make it necessary. We shall never make any considerable progress in the divine life without it, nor ever do much for God or our generation. 2 Tim. i. 7.

2. Cultivate therefore your faith, in order to the forming of your minds to holy fortitude. Frequently contemplate the establishing motives of the gospel, which are so full and apposite; and by prayer and frequent reviews of the grounds of your faith, endeavor to confirm your hope in the gospel.

3. Use all farther additional means to fortify your minds. Be prepared for the worst, by counting frequently the cost. Make clear the goodness of your case, for which you may be called to exert your courage. Make sure of the goodness of your state, and carefully exercise a good conscience

---

THE PRESENCE OF CHRIST THE HAPPINESS OF THE SAINTS.

Psalm xvi. 11.—Thou wilt show me the path of life. In thy presence is fulness of joy, &c. (H.)

THESE words originally belong to Christ, being applied by David to him, in the spirit of prophecy, as will evidently appear from the connexion in which they stand. They are also applicable to the real Christian, and are expressive of the happiness and joy he expects in a future state. Joy is the soul's rest and satisfaction in the enjoyment of a suitable good. Such as the good and enjoyment are, such will be the joy. The most perfect enjoyment of the most perfect good, must, therefore, cause the most perfect joy. Such is the joy of the blessed in heaven. It consists in being in Christ's immediate presence, and partaking of that fulness of joy, and those pleasures which are at his right hand for evermore.

Consider,

I. THE CHARACTER OF THOSE WHO SHALL BE THUS BLESSED : they are such as,

1. Repent of their sins, and are converted : who cease to do evil and learn to do well. Upon these the times of refreshing shall come from the presence of the Lord. Acts iii. 19.

2. Believe in Christ, with a divine, practical, purifying faith. Rev. vii. 14, 15.

3. Upright in their profession and performance of commanded duties, both to God and man. Ps. cxx. 13.

4. His servants, who follow him as their Lord and Master, and his imitable life as their copy and pattern. John xii. 26.

5. To conclude this head, if any require, as the Psalmist did, who shall ascend into the hill of the Lord? I answer as he did; he that hath clean hands, &c. Ps. xxiv. 3, 4.

II. WHEREIN THEIR BLESSEDNESS CONSISTS; and according to the text, it is occasioned, by being in the presence of God; and by that fulness of joy and pleasure, which are at his right hand.

The presence of God here spoken of, is

1. The presence of his glory, the most conspicuous lustre of his excellencies, or his perfections shining in the highest excellency of their brightness. Jude 24.

2. The presence of his face, as it is in the original text; "In thy face, or being before thy face, is fulness of joy." The presence of his glory, which is hidden here, will be unveiled in heaven, and presented openly to view, without veil or shadow. 1 Pet. iv. 13. For we shall see him face to face, &c. 1 Cor. xiii. 12.

3. His immediate presence; no longer manifested through obscuring mediums; here we have his presence in creatures, in providences, and in ordinances; but in heaven we shall enjoy him immediately, and without the intervention of means. Rev. xxi. 22, 23; xxii. 5.

4. His countenancing presence, so the apostle explains the text. Acts ii. 28. It is his presence as a pleased friend, father, and husband. To these he gives the presence of his pleased face, without a frown, and the light of his countenance without an intervening cloud. As his anger kindleth hell, so his favor, the light and smiles of his countenance, make heaven, see Rev. xxi. 3, compared with Zeph. iii. 17.

5. His fixed and abiding presence: we shall be forever with him, and he shall dwell among us. Rev. vii. 17.

6. His influxive and efficacious presence: a glimpse of it made the face of Moses shine. As it is reflected in the glass of the gospel; it changeth them that behold it into the same image from glory to glory; much more will it change you, who shall stand before his face in heaven, into the most perfect likeness of him in holiness and happiness your natures are capable of. 1 John iii. 2.

Their happiness is also occasioned by those joys and pleasures which are at God's right hand. Heaven is a situation of joy and pleasure, very different from our present situation, which is a state of tribulation and distress. John xvi. 33. The joy and pleasures of the heavenly world are,

1. Spiritual and heavenly. Not carnal or earthly. Our bodies shall be spiritual, so far, as not to need any of these supports and refreshments they do now. There will be no need of sleep, of meat and drink, of marrying and giving in marriage; but we shall be as the angels of God in heaven. Matt. xii. 25; 1 Cor. vi. 13. The more noble senses of seeing and hearing, the pleasure of which is mixed with reason, shall subsist, be spiritualized, and eternally satisfied with glorified objects, the chief of which shall be the glorified body of the Son of God. It is the joy of the Lord the saints enter into, the same for kind, though not for degree.

2. Pure, without mixture. Here there is a mixture of good and evil Heaven and hell are the extremes. Hell is a place of animated torment, heaven of unmixed joy: no sin there: no temptation or occasion of sinning: no serpent hissing in that paradise; all sorrow and cause of sorrow shall be done away. Rev. vii. 16; xxi. 4.

3. A multitude without number. There is not only a removal of every evil, but the presence and enjoyment of every good. The blessedness of heaven is resembled by every real good known to us here, all the glory and honor of the kings of the earth shall be there. Rev. xxi. 24—26. God who is an infinite and universal good, will feast his saints with fresh discoveries and communications of delight and wonder. Isa. lx. 19.

4. Full without any want. There every one shall enjoy a whole heaven, with all the felicities of it, and are blessed in every part in soul and body! all our wants shall be supplied, and our desires satisfied. Ps. xvii. 15.

5. Constant without diminution or interruption. Here our best enjoyments are often changeable and interrupted : but the joys of heaven shall never fade away. 1 Pet. i. 3, 4. God who is the source of their happiness remains unchangeably the same. The saints are fixed in his presence, and their happiness shall not be diminished on account of their number ; as in nature, every man hath a sun to himself, the same as if there were but one man in the world. Nor will it be diminished on account of the length of the enjoyment; for the divine presence is an eternal spring of pleasure. Psalms xxxvi. 9.

6. Perpetual. They are pleasures for evermore ; all the felicities of heaven are everlasting; everlasting consolation, everlasting joy, everlasting habitations, everlasting life. It is this that maketh heaven to be heaven indeed ; all its pleasures would be imperfect without it. It is an exceeding and eternal weight of glory. 2 Cor. iv. 17.

Improvement.

1. Hence see the folly and madness of those who seek their portion in this life ; in carnal and sensual gratifications ; dreadful will be their state at last. Ps. xcvii. 3 ; Matt. xxv. 41.

2. Let such glorious views and expectations comfort the heirs of glory in the midst of all their tribulations. 2 Cor. iv. 17·

3. Let it excite all such to diligence and activity in the ways of God. This is the very use the apostle makes of this doctrine. 1 Cor. xv. 58 ; Heb. xii. 1, 2.

THE CHRISTIAN'S DESIRE TO SEE GOD'S GLORY.

Exod. xxxiii. 18.—And he said, I beseech thee show me thy glory. (H.)

THESE are the words of Moses, a man singularly favored of God, by the manifestation of himself he made to him ; and still desiring to be more so, here expresses that desire in prayer to him. Perhaps he might desire too much ; more than he in his present state could bear ; and so far his request was denied, ver. 22. The request that Moses here makes, as duly regulated, is graciously answered, ver. ⸢ By his goodness, is there meant his glory ; as the LXX render it, ' will pass before thee with my glory ;" thou shalt have a transient view of ٠t, but the full discovery is reserved for a future state : and how this matter was to be conducted, see in verses 21, &c. Doubtless, a great deal of God, and his goodness, is to be seen and known upon earth ; but far, very far short of what will be enjoyed in heaven ; and the more of his goodness we experience here, the more insatiable is our desire after more.

By divine assistance, I shall consider,

I. WHAT IS MEANT BY GOD'S GLORY, WHICH THE CHRISTIAN DESIRES TO SEE.

1. It is glory, in his gracious conduct to sinners, in and through his Son. Any other discovery of God would be dreadful and terrifying, and instead of desiring it he would deprecate it. "God is a consuming fire," and, as such, inaccessible without Christ. 1 Tim. vi. 16. But Jesus has revealed him in the most amiable and endearing manner; John i. 18. in this way his glorious goodness is abundant. Ex. xxxiv. 6. It is in his wounds that we are secured from flaming wrath. Through him it is, that the glory of God shines, not with a destroying. but reviving light; and only as standing within this rock, we are able with comfort to behold it.

2. It is his glory, as manifested to his soul in pardoning mercy and love. It is pleasing to the Christian, to see the glory of God's goodness, in reconciling the world to himself by the death of his Son; 2 Cor. v. 19. but much more satisfactory for him to see the glory of God, as revealed to his own soul, so as to be able to say with Paul, "In whom we have redemption," &c. Eph. i. 7. This is his abundant goodness, as expressed chap. xxiv. 7. It is called the secret of the Lord. Job xxix. 4; Prov. iii. 32.

3. It is his glory, as manifested to the soul, making him a partaker of the divine nature. 2 Pet. i. 4. Improving and increasing; 2 Cor. iii. 18. this is called the mind of Christ; Phil. ii. 5. and the Spirit of Christ. Rom. vii. 9. It is called the beauty of the saints; Ps. xlv. 11. and it is that salvation with which God beautifies the meek; Ps. cxlix. 4. and by which they are prepared to see his glory in heaven. Matt. v. 9.

II. WHERE DOES THE REAL CHRISTIAN WISH TO SEE THE GLORY OF GOD.

1. In all his ordinances in this world, especially in the assembly of his saints. There God has promised to be. Ex. xx. 24. There he gives the most glorious communications of himself; and after these the Psalmist expresses the most vehement desire. Ps. xlii. 1, 2. He there alludes to the assemblies of his people. as he explains it. Ps. xxvii. 4.; and again Ps. lxiii. 1, 2. How much of the glory of his perfections are seen in his sanctuary? particularly in prayer and praise, when the hearts of his saints are warmed, enlarged, and raised to himself, while he supplies them with fresh strength, life, and comfort. And when his word is read, opened, and applied, what impressions are made? what effects are produced? How much of his glory has been displayed in this way?

But the glory of God, in his perfections, eminently shines in the ordinance of the Lord's supper; where Jesus Christ is eminently set forth as crucified before our eyes, suffering, bleeding, and dying, in our room and stead.

2. Much of God's glory is here to be seen. The glory of his wisdom, in devising the wonderful scheme of man's redemption, so as the seeming contrary pleas of his attributes might be adjusted, sin punished, the law magnified and made honourable, and yet the rebel pardoned. And when none else could, God himself found a ransom, appointing his own Son, in our nature, by dying, to become our Saviour; "Wherein," &c. Eph. i, 8. And seeing this, in the commemoration of his death, believers have been made to cry out, "O! the depth," &c. Rom. ii. 33.

3. How glorious is the discovery here made of his justice and holiness, in the satisfaction made for sin by the voluntary death even of God's own beloved Son to make way for sinners being pardoned and saved. And, considering who he was, and what he bare, and how he was treated, that we might be spared· the ruin of the offending angels, the drowning of the old

world, the burning of Sodom, and the punishment of sinners in hell for ever, do not altogether show forth the justice and holiness of God, like the sufferings and death of Christ, on the account of lost sinners.

4. Here divine grace is to be seen in its brightest lustre. In its freeness, without our merit, and against the highest provocation. In its condescension, in resolving to save us, however unworthy. In its sovereignty, passing by angels, and providing a Saviour for man. In its riches, as extendng to all mankind. John iii. 16.

5. Here is displayed the glory of God's faithfulness to his promises; in his being present in his ordinances, giving his people fresh light, strength, and comfort; and thus, in a sensible way, renewing his covenant with them, and assuring them, that all the blessing of it are theirs.

6. The Christian desires to see the glory of God above. Phil. i. 23. 2 Cor. v. 1, 2. The glory of the Lord sometimes fills his house, and his ordinances here below, which believers are admitted to see to their comfort and joy; but this is only preparatory to the inconceivably greater displays that will be made in heaven, which they expect, and earnestly desire. 1 John iii. 2; 1 Cor. xiii. 12.

III. WHY DOES THE CHRISTIAN DESIRE TO SEE HIS GLORY?

He desires to see it in his ordinances here,

1. Because the glory of God is transforming. The more he sees God in the manner described, the more he shall be like him. Some rays, as it were, were left upon him; and the disciples were so much raised above themselves, that it was remarked, "they have been with Jesus." Acts iv. 13.

2. The glory of God, thus shown to the Christian, is most reviving. Not any thing in this world can give that comfort to the soul, which the manifestation of God can do. Ps. iv. 7.

And the Christian wishes to see this glory in heaven,

1. Because it will be most clear and full. The manifestations which God will make of himself above, if communicated here, would dissolve our present frame; we could not see his face and live. Here, "his loving kindness is better than life." What then will it be when manifested in heaven?

2. The glory to be revealed above will be most satisfying. It is called a fulness of joy, and pleasures for ever; Ps. xvi. 11. and this David speaks of, as what he desired above every other thing. Ps. xvii. 15.

3. The manifestations of this glory in heaven, will be permanent and everlasting. The glory of God will be eternally open, and the saints shall eternally behold it, and that with the highest delight, without interruption, and without end.

Lastly, let us pray for it. And thus express our desires after it, for desire is the very life and soul of prayer: and those desires should be expressed to God who alone can show us his glory. And those desires should be expressed, especially in the assemblies of the saints, and with uncommon vehemence of desire, saying, "O Lord, I beseech thee, show me thy glory." And thus we shall express the high value we put upon it, and may reasonably expect a favorable answer. And to our prayers for clear manifestations of his glory, let us add our praises for those which we have already received; and thus begin the work of heaven while we are upon earth, in the hope of dwelling with God in heaven, to behold his glory for ever.

HONOUR AND PRIVILEGE OF THE SAINTS.

Psalm. iv. 3.—But know that the Lord hath set apart him that is godly for himself. (Pr.)

David's greatest troubles were on account of his religion, though he was not without trouble in other respects.— — —He was persecuted for his piety ; and his elevation to the throne of Israel raised him up many enemies who were inclined to dispute his right.— — —But he intimates that he did not usurp the government : it was God that anointed him king over Israel, and who set him apart for that purpose.— — —In vindicating his own claims, he asserts the honour and the privilege of all the saints—that God hath set them apart for himself.

Let us notice the character here givin of the saints—and the privilege with which it is connected.

I. ILLUSTRATE THE CHARACTER IN THE TEXT, OR INQUIRE WHAT IT IS TO BE TRULY "GODLY."

Godliness is that which immediately relates to God : it has him for its object, and in it we are made partakers of a divine nature.

True religion is by the apostle distributed into three parts, corresponding with the precepts of the moral law, which requires us to love God, our neighbors, and ourselves. Tit. ii. 12. To live "soberly," concerns ourselves, and consists in the government of the passions.— — —To live "righteously," respects our conduct towards others, and consists in our doing to them as we should wish they would do unto us. To live "godly," refers to our conduct towards God, and consists in making him the object of our veneration.— — —The two former may exist without the latter, but the latter cannot be without the former.

More particularly,

1. To be godly is to be like God— — —to imitate his moral character, and to bear a resemblance to it— — —to think, and act, and feel, in some measure, as he does— — —to be of one mind with him, in the great principles of moral government.— — —God is necessarily the friend of holiness, and the enemy of sin; to be godly is to be the same, according to our measure, hating the evil and choosing the good.— — —God is infinitely kind and merciful ; he is good to all, and his tender mercies are over all his works : and it is essential to true godliness that we be pitiful, kind and courteous, full of compassion, and gracious. Psa. cxii. 4. Matt. v. 44, 45. James i. 27. — — —God also is ready to forgive, slow to anger, and abundant in goodness and in truth : to be godly is to be like him, and to possess the same spirit.

2. To be truly godly is to live in the fear of God— — —to walk as in his sight— — —to have a special regard to his presence— — —seeking his approbation in all things.— — —Not only to conduct ourselves wisely before men, but to walk before the Lord with a perfect heart. Hence that command to Abraham, Gen. xvii. 1, and this only is true religion.

2. Godliness consists in making the will of God the rule of our life, the reason and motive of our obedience.— — —It is not merely what we do in religion, but why we do it, that makes it acceptable in the sight of God. If we read, or hear, or pray, and do all this from custom, or the force of example only, it is not godliness.— — —We may abound in religious observances ; but if we have no regard to the will of God, it is no better than will-worship.— — —Hence that serious interrogation : "Did ye do it unto me, saith the Lord of Hosts." Zech. vii. 5.

4. It is to make the glory of God the end of all we do— — —there is no godliness without this.— — —If we repent of sin merely on account of its consequences, as affecting ourselves, it is not sorrowing after a godly sort. — — —Love to God is not genuine, unless it has the excellence of his character for its object.— — —True godliness feels for the glory of God, and is deeply interested in its advancement.

5. If we be godly, we shall seek communion with God— — —shall delight in secret duties, in drawing near to him, and displaying all our heart before him.— — —Much intercourse with heaven is essential to the life and power of true religion.

6. To be godly is to make the enjoyment of God our chief portion, our ultimate bliss— — —relinquishing every other object in comparison of this — — —making his friendship our all in all and desiring his loving-kindness as better than life. This only is true godliness.

II. CONSIDER THE PRIVILEGES OF THE GODLY: "THE LORD HATH SET HIM APART FOR HIMSELF."

1. They are "set apart," as the first-born of Israel, and their firstfruits, by being devoted to the Lord— — —as the whole nation of Israel, who were chosen to be a peculiar people; or as the tribe of Levi, who were to be the Lord's inheritance.

1st. This consecration is accomplished by effectual calling, "being chosen from the beginning, through sanctification of the Spirit, and belief of the truth."— — —All that are truly godly are chosen out of the world, separated from the world, and ordained that they should bring forth fruit. John xv. 16.

2dly. They are also set apart in a way of providence, and God has a special regard to them in all his dispensations.— — —Though he will make an end of his enemies, he will not make a full end of them.— — —When he destroyed the old world, he set apart Noah for himself; and when Sodom was consumed, he did the same by Lot.

2. It is not without design that the godly are thus distinguished.— — — The Lord hath set them apart "for himself."

1st. That he may be glorified— — —"This people have I formed for myself, that they may show forth my praise."— — —They are God's witness before the world, to testify of the goodness of his government, and the exceeding riches of his grace— — —to give evidence of his truth and faithfulness, and of the efficacy of the blood of Christ.

2dly. That they may be finally saved, and become his everlasting portion. They are his, and he will set them apart in the last day, from the rest of the ungodly world— — —then he will gather up his treasure, and burn up the wicked as stubble. Mal. iii. 17.

Let sinners "know" this, that however they may treat the godly in this life, God is their friend, and he will delight in them to do them good.

Let the godly themselves "know" it for their comfort, and be assured that they are placed under divine protection.

ASSURANCE OF FAITH.

Psalm xxxv. 3.—Say unto my soul, I am thy salvation. (Pr.)

David was now suffering persecution, both from the tongue and from the hand of his enemies: ver. 1, 11. The beginning of the psalm is a continued prayer for divine interposition, where, under the form of an imprecation on his enemies, he pleads for his own protection and safety. The words of the text, which form a part of his supplication, appear to be interjected, as referring to his spiritual salvation; and could he but be assured of this, it would inspire him with courage against his enemies, and with confidence in the divine interposition on his behalf. But whether so understood or not, the passage may afford us some profitable reflections—

I. ALL OUR SALVATION, FROM FIRST TO LAST, IS FROM THE LORD.

He alone is the salvation of his people, and it ought to be expected only from him. Jonah ii. 9. He is pre-eminently the God of salvation, and this is his memorial in all generations.— — —Temporal deliverances are from him. Ask Daniel, who restrained the fury of the lions? Ask the Hebrew children, who quenched the violence of fire? Ask Jonah, who brought him out of the whale's belly? They would all answer, it was the Lord's doings, and marvellous in our eyes. 2 Cor. i. 9.

That salvation especially which is spiritual and eternal, can belong only to the Lord: all others are excluded from having any hand in it. Isa. v. 16; Eph. ii. 8.— — —The way of salvation is of his contrivance; he alone hath found a ransom, and devised means, that his banished ones be not expelled from him: all is the effect of his infinite wisdom and mercy. Eph. ii. 4, 5.— — —All the blessings of salvation, from its commencement in our justification, to its consummation in glory, are of his providing. The foundation of this building, and the headstone, are brought forth by him, who is wonderful in counsel, and mighty in working.

II. A KNOWLEDGE OF INTEREST IN GOD'S SALVATION IS ATTAINABLE, OR DAVID WOULD NOT HAVE PRAYED FOR IT.

It is true, all good people do not attain this assurance; some of them live and even die without it; yet it is attainable.— — —Comparative ignorance and unbelief are the chief preventives. ——— Some have actually attained· I know, says Job, that my Redeemer liveth. I know, says Paul, in whom I have believed. Primitive believers knew that when their earthly house should be dissolved, they had a building of God, eternal in the heavens. 2 Cor. v. 1.— — —A knowledge of interest in this salvation, is one of the principal objects of Holy Scripture. Rom. xv. 4; 1 John v. 13. It brings us to a conviction of our need of Christ, to our knowledge of him as. the only Saviour, to an acceptance of him in that character, and to a happy persuasion of our interest in his great salvation.— — —Those who do not actually enjoy this assurance, possess, notwithstanding, the principle from which it proceeds—faith, hope, a conscience purified by the blood of Christ, and. unfeigned love to the brethren. 1 John iii. 14; iv. 12.— — --If the certainty of our salvation were not attainable, we should not be commanded or encouraged as we are to seek after it. Heb. vi 11; 2 Pet. i. 10.

III. AS AN ASSURANCE OF SALVATION IS POSSIBLE, SO IT IS ALSO HIGHLY DESIRABLE.

This appears from David's seeking so earnestly after it: "Say unto my soul, I am thy salvation." The thing speaks for itself, what a satisfaction it would afford to be assured that we are going to heaven. What an antidote against the corroding cares and perplexities of life; what a source of contentment in the midst of poverty and want, and of joy in every tribulation. Hab. iii. 17; 2 Cor. iv. 17, 18.— — —What confidence would it inspire, in all our approaches to the mercy seat. Psa. lxiii. 1; Heb. x. 22. Those who are assured of their interest in Christ, come to God as to their best and only friend, as children to their father. Eph. iii. 12.— — -—This assurance is friendly to persevering holiness : nothing tends more to promote obedience, and a universal conformity to the will of God. 2 Peter i. 10; Psalm xxvi. 3.

IV. THE WAY TO OBTAIN THIS ASSURANCE IS, PARTLY BY SPEAKING TO GOD, AND PARTLY BY HIS SPEAKING TO US.

1. By speaking to God, as David does in the language of text, Prayer, fervent and constant prayer, is the principal means of clearing up our evidence. It is this that makes our face to shine, like the countenance of Moses, when descending from the mount. If we would meet the King of kings, we must do as when we wish to meet a friend; we must wait upon him in his walks. Thus David says, My soul follows hard after thee; and it was not long before he obtained what he so ardently desired. Ps. lxiii. 8. For every spiritual blessing, God will be inquired of and he must be sadly mistaken who thinks he has obtained assurance in any other way. When Peter was praying upon the house top, the sheet was let down; and while Daniel was on his knees, the angel brought him good tidings. Dan. ix. 23. And as assurance can only be obtained in this way, so in this way only can it be preserved. God would not leave Jacob, so long as Jacob said, I will not let thee go.

2. By God's speaking to us: "Say unto my soul, I am thy salvation." So that in order to this assurance, God and the soul must meet and converse together.— — —The testimony that David wanted, was personal and particular: Say unto "my soul," I am thy salvation. Jer. xxxi. 3. How is it that thou wilt manifest thyself to us, and not unto the world: yet so it is. When the Lord Jesus spake to Saul, in the way to Damascus, the voice was so immediately directed to him, that though his companions heard the sound, they understood not the speech.— — —The testimony is internal and spiritual, the Spirit bearing witness with our spirit, that we are the children of God. Men speak to the outward ear, but God has access to the "soul," and in the hidden parts can make us to understand wisdom. Rom. viii. 16-— — —When God speaks, it is not only encouraging, but effectual. There is no vocation, no consolation, like that which reaches to the heart. When God speaks, we not only hear but feel. Luke xix. 5, 6; xxiv. 32.

1. See what it is that alone can satisfy the soul of a good man. God gives to Esau a lordship, to Saul a kingdom, to Judas an apostleship, and they are satisfied. David also had a kingdom, but was not content: "Say unto my soul, I am thy salvation."

2. This prayer includes all other blessings. If God be our salvation, we have enough; all our desires are fulfilled, all our wants supplied.

3. Let those who have this assurance be thankful, but let them remember that it can be maintained only by habitual intercourse with God, and that it will need to be frequently renewed.

ORIGIN, PROGRESS, AND END OF TRUE RELIGION.

Phillippians iii. 12.—Not as though I had already attained, either were already perfect; but I follow after, if that I may apprehend that for which also I am apprehended of Christ Jesus. (Pr.)

There is an intimate connection between justification by the righteousness of Christ, and sanctification by the Holy Spirit; for in the same breath in which the apostle prays for the one, he also prays for the other.— — —Some who are advocates for free justification, deny both the doctrine of sanctification and progressive holiness: but here they are united.

Three things are taught us in the text; namely—the origin—the progress —and the end of true religion.

I. The origin of true religion in the soul: this consists in our being " apprehended of Christ Jesus."

The word signifies *seizing*, or laying hold of one, or taking him as it were into custody. Thus it is used in Acts xii. 4. 2 Cor. xi. 32.

Here the term is used figuratively, and alludes to Paul's being met with in his way to Damascus. Acts ix. 4, 5.— — —Thus it is that the Lord meets with poor sinners: sometimes by trying events in providence, as in the case of Manasseh and Ephraim. Jer. xxxi. Sometimes by the word preached, as in the case of Peter's hearers. Acts ii. Some who have attended the word from motives of curiosity, have thus been taken, like Zaccheus, and unable to relinquish their convictions.— — —Sometimes they have been overtaken at the mouth of the grave, and are apprehended, like the Phillipian jailor. Acts xvi. 29, 30. Sometimes by bringing them into difficulties which call their sin to remembrance, as in the case of Joseph's brethren. Sometimes by what is seen in godly people, the heart is taken captive, and " won by their conversation." Sometimes by solitary reflection, and so gradually as scarcely to know when or how.

But by whatever means it is, if Christ " apprehends" us, we are taken captive and held fast, not against our will indeed, but are sweetly constrained to surrender up ourselves to him. Christ will not lose his prisoner when he has taken him.

In whatever way our conversion is effected, or by whatever means, God is the first moving cause: true religion does not begin with any act or exercise of ours. Like lost sheep, we do not seek him till he first seeks us.— We should never find the way to God of our own accord; his word indeed exhorts us to seek him, and it is both our interest and our duty to do so: yet every real christian must say with Paul, " By the grace of God I am what I am." He that first loves us, first moves us to himself. Phil. ii. 13. 1 John iv. 10—19.

II. The progress of true religion : " that I may apprehend that for which also I am apprehended of Christ Jesus."

Though we are passive in being " apprehended," yet we then become active, and are drawn forth to " apprehend." Hence Paul, when taken captive, cried out, Lord what wouldst thou have me to do?

1. Observe, every thing we feel or do in religion here *is imperfect.*—Repentance, faith, love, obedience, all is imperfect: we know not but in part, and we prophecy but in part. Every kind of holiness is the same, and it is a mercy to be assured that such are not rejected. Matt. xii. 20

2. True religion teaches us *to feel and own it,* instead of pretending to the contrary.— — —If Paul had " not attained," it is presumption in any of

us to think we have: all pretences to entire freedom from sin are contrary to the Scriptures, to truth, and to universal experience. They indicate great ignorance of God's holy law, and of our own hearts. We shall always have occasion for that prayer: " Forgive us our debts, as we forgive our debtors."

3. Though perfection is not attained, it is of the nature of true religion to oe *pursuing after it.*— — —Here are several phrases by which this idea is expressed—" I follow after"—" forgetting the things that are behind"— " reaching forth to those which are before"—" pressing towards the mark." All these allure to a race, and are expressive of the utmost desire to win the prize.

1. These terms imply that true religion is something positive; that it not merely consists in our being kept from evil, or remaining barren and unfruit-ful, but in something absolutely good.

2. That it is essential to true religion to be progressive, and to follow after perfection, though at a humble distance from the mark.— — —Wo to him that is at ease in Zion, and pleads for imputed sanctification, as well as for im-puted righteousness.

3. That it interests the soul, like one who is running in a race: " reaching forth."—These terms describe the earnest breathings of the soul, and its long-ing after more holiness, like what is expressed in ver. 10.

III. THE END OF TRUE RELIGION: to " apprehend that for which we are apprehended."

We are apprehended " for" this purpose, that we might win the prize, and lay hold of it. This prize is a holy state; it is heaven, and eternal life, which believers finally attain.

1. Observe the encouragement for perseverence. Eternal life is before us : think of this in times of temptation, of persecution, and of arduous duty : let that fortify and animate us.

2. The connexion there is between our being effectually called and finally saved, or between grace here and glory hereafter. We are apprehended for this very purpose; and whom he justifies, them he also glorifies. Psa. lxxxiv. 11. Rom. viii. 30. 2 Cor. v. 5.

CHRISTIAN EDIFICATION.

2 Peter i. 5—8.—Giving all diligence, add to your faith virtue, and to virtue knowledge, and to knowledge temperance, and to temperance patience, and to patience godliness, and to godliness brotherly kindness, and to brotherly kindness charity. For if these things be in you, and abound, they make you that ye shall neither be barren nor unfruitful in the knowledge of our Lord Jesus Christ. (Pr.)

GREAT things are here ascribed to the knowledge of God, and of Jesus our Lord, ver. 2 : " grace and peace are hereby multiplied." All things pertaining to life and godliness are derived from hence, ver. 3. By it we are interested in exceeding great and precious promises, ver. 4. Yet we must not rest in knowledge, but add to it what is recommended in our text.

I. OBSERVE WHAT IS HERE SUPPOSED TO BE THE FOUNDATION OF THE CHRISTIAN CHARACTER, EVEN " FAITH."

187

Peter had before spoken of faith, and ascribed to it two qualities; namely, "its preciousness," verse 1, as having relation to a precious Saviour; and its being the same in all good men, under whatever dispensation they have lived, and whether they be weak or strong in faith: it still is "like" precious faith "with us."

The term "add" to your faith, denotes that faith must be first, as the foundation of all the rest; and indeed it is this which forms the basis of the Christian character. Jude 20.

More particularly, observe—

1. Nothing but faith will support the building. What is the virtue of heathens, and unconverted men?— — —What is the virtue of Jews and deists in modern times; or of nominal Christians?— — —It is destitute of all the graces mentioned in our text: it has nothing of temperance, patience, godliness, kindness, or charity belonging to it.— — —All attempts to build up men in holiness without faith, are utterly vain: we may build, but it must come down again. Faith in the Son of God is the foundation of all.

2. Faith is sufficient for this purpose: it is the root from whence all the graces grow, and the spring which waters and makes them fruitful. ——— No sooner did the murderous Jews believe in him whom they had crucified, than all these graces began to appear. Acts ii.— — —The profligate heathens the same; and thus it is to this day. When a sinner ready to perish embraces the gospel, he is from thence a new creature, cast in a new mould. Let him cease to oppose the gospel, and begin to obey it from the heart, and he becomes the servant of God, and his fruit unto holiness. Rom. vi 17—22.

II. NOTICE WHAT IS TO BE BUILT ON THIS FOUNDATION, OR ADDED TO IT.

"Giving all diligence." We must not stop at faith, for faith without works is dead: it is inoperative, and has no influence on the life. Such however is the faith of multitudes of nominal Christians, and of many also who make an open profession of religion.

"Giving all diligence." This implies that we shall not grow in grace, without care and close attention. Sloth and carnal ease will reduce our souls to a state like that of the vineyard of the sluggard, which is overgrown with weeds.— — —It is in grace as in nature; though the utmost diligence will fail without the blessing of God, yet neither will he give his blessing without diligence: the diligent soul shall be made fat, and he that watereth shall also himself be watered. Prov. xi. 25. xiii. 4.— — —Grace will not grow spontaneously; but must be watched and watered, by prayer and holy carefulness. Isai. xxvii. 3.

More particularly—

1. The first stone to be laid on your holy faith is "virtue."— — —We use this word for moral excellence in general, as distinguished from vice, or what is unlovely; but seems here to have a more specific meaning.— — — It is a military term, and denotes courage, fortitude or resolution: if it were what is generally meant by virtue, it would include all that follow in the text, and so could not be distinguished from them.

Give all diligence, that he may not be feeble, but strong in the grace that is in Christ Jesus: not like the fearful and unbelieving, but like those who took joyfully the spoiling of their goods. Like Peter and John, who waxed bold to speak the word of the Lord, or like him who witnessed a good confession.

2. The next is "knowledge."— — —This is to regulate virtue or courage; energy and zeal without knowledge, would be dangerous. Even

188

love itself requires to be under its direction. Phil. i. 9. Courage in a soldier, without knowledge to guide it, would be misapplied: let all your zeal and energy therefore be under the regulation of God's word. As soldiers, know your dangers in order to avoid them ; your enemies and their devices, to be able to meet and overcome them ; your obligations, in order to fulfil them.— — —In times of trial, heaven "expects every man to do his duty."

3. "Temperance." This denotes the right government of the appetites and passions. Also in giving to others admonition and reproof, so as to be angry and sin not. Psal. cxli. 5. Our Lord himself affords a kind and gentle reproof, in his conduct towards his disciples ; and Paul in dealing with the Corinthians. Gal. vi. 1. 1 Cor. iv. 21. Ephes. iv. 31, 32.

4. To these must also be added "patience," which denotes the enduring of evil ; as afflictions, persecutions, and reproches ; and in this we have the example of Christ. 1 Pet. ii. 20—23. Also in waiting for the coming of the Lord. James v. 7. 1 Thes. i. 10.

5. "Godliness," or piety. This is to be like God, to bear his image, to be of his mind, to love him, fear him, and keep his glory in view. This runs through the whole of the Christian character.

6. "Brotherly kindnes." This is that sweet disposition which feels towards the poorest Christian as a brother, in sympathising, and in rejoicing with him. Col. iii. 12. James i. 9, 10.

7. "Charity," or that candid disposition which thinketh no evil ; which puts the best possible construction on the conduct and actions of others, and which envieth not— — —a spirit of meekness and love. 1 Cor. xiii.

III. THE NECESSITY OF THESE ADDITIONS, THAT WE MAY "NEITHER BE BARREN NOR UNFRUITFUL.

It is here supposed that we may possess some knowledge of our Lord and Saviour Jesus Christ, and yet be very barren withal : and if the building be not raised in the manner that is here expressed, we shall be so.

1. That we be "not barren." A person may be said to be barren when he bears no fruit, or when there is nothing positive in his religion ; a sort of negative character.— — —But nothing merely negative will do : he has apparently put off the old man, but not put on the new : he was once like a wilderness, full of briers and thorns ; and now is like a barren heath. Jer. xvii. 5, 6. Matt. xii. 44.

2. That we be "not unfruitful." A person is unfruitful when he bears little fruit, and barren when he bears none at all ; a field may have some fruit, and yet not be fruitful. — — — God requires not merely the existence of true religion in the heart, but that it should grow exceedingly : and that "these things should be in us, and abound." 2 Thess. i. 11. 2 Pet. iii. 18.

GLORYING IN THE CROSS.

Galatians vi. 14.—God forbid that I should glory, save in the cross of our Lord Jesus Christ, by whom the world is crucified unto me, and I unto the world. (Pr.)

IT is a mark of false religion, that it leads men to glory in something else, and not in the Lord. The Jews valued themselves on circumcision, and their being the children of Abraham. The false teachers in the churches of Galatia displayed a great deal of vain-glorying, desirous of making a fair show in the flesh: ver. 12. They wished to ingratiate themselves with the Galatians, and to supplant the apostles. But Paul wholly disclaimed every thing of this kind, and declares his great object to be to glory in nothing but the cross of Christ. The language he employs is very strong, and expressive of the holy ardour of his mind, as will appear in the following particulars.

1. He considers the cross of Christ *as an object of glorying*. Had he consulted the opinion of the world, he would have found that it was the great shame of christianity. " Christ crucified was to the Jews a stumbling block, and to the Greeks foolishness."— — —It was Satan's design, in effecting the crucifixion of our Lord, to overwhelm his cause with contempt. It might therefore have seemed enough for Paul to say, God forbid that I should ever be ashamed of my Lord, though he was crucified: but instead of this, he accounts it an object of exultation.

2. It is with him *the only object* of glorying. Many would have thought that Paul might have gloried in some other things: his descent from the tribe of Benjamin, his zeal, his literary acquirements, his office, labors, success and reputation as an apostle.— — —He was formed to take a leading part in whatever he undertook. When an enemy to the gospel, he breathed out his whole soul in threatenings and slaughter against the church of God. When he became a friend, he was equally ardent in his defence.— — —Yet in none of these things would he glory, but in the cross of Christ.

3. He bears the most emphatic protest *against glorying in any thing else:* " God forbid !" Far be it from me to think of any other object. This mode of speaking is not used lightly. It is of the nature of a solemn oath, and applied to things which he held in the greatest abhorrence: so that those things with which others were elated, and in which they gloried, he most solemnly abjured. It would have shocked him to have valued himself on such grounds, or to have had his heart divided between Christ and the world. His language is, " Be HE my ambition, my joy, my hope, my life, my all !"

Oh what christians should we be, if our eye were thus single: if the things which make a fair show in the flesh, were regarded by us as they were by Paul.— — —" The world is crucified unto me, and I unto the world." I am as a dead man, and the world is dead to me: it has lost all its charms in my view, and it ceases to have any influence over me.

I. ENQUIRE WHEREIN THIS CRUCIFIXIÓN TO THE WORLD CONSISTS, AND WHAT ARE THE CHARACTERS IN WHICH THIS SPIRIT IS EXEMPLIFIED.

1. Certainly not in those who are *eaten up of the love of the world*, and whose sole concern it is to increase their wealth.— — —Yet there are men of this description, and that under a profession of the gospel. Some make haste to be rich, regardless of the means: others who are poor, may be of the same disposition, fretting and murmuring against God, and thinking hard of their lot.

The man who is dead to the world is one who is content with his portion: more concerned to devote what he has to the glory of God, than to increase it.— — —It is not him who can find no time for God and religion: but he who in all his ways acknowledges him, and sets the Lord always before him.— — —It is not him who retires from the world, like a monk or a hermit; but he who while in the world, devotes his all to God, and walks as in his sight.

Let but all our concerns and undertakings in life be subordinate to the interests of religion, and they will rather aid than hinder our christian course

Such a one may say with Paul, " The world is crucified unto me, and I unto the world."

2. This spirit is certainly not found in men whose grand object it is to *secure the approbation of the world*, and to gain popular applause. The opinion of the world is to some men the oracle in which they trust : under its smiles they live, and under its frowns they die. Hence their principal concern is to secure the approbation of men by temporising principles, and by every means of servile conformity.

But not so Paul : with him it was a light matter to be judged of man's judgment, or to enjoy the smiles of the rich and the great.— — —The man who is crucified to the world, is he whose chief concern it is to be approved of God : he who can bear adversity without being unduly depressed, and prosperity without being elated by it.

3. It is not found in those who *mix something worldly with their religion*, in order to make it palatable, that the offence of the cross may cease. This has been a principal source of corruption, in doctrine and in worship : great pains have been taken by false teachers and false professors, to render the doctrine of the cross more grateful to the carnal heart. The judaising teachers did this, and may have done it since.

To be as Paul, is to lay aside all carnal reasoning and worldly policy, and as new-born babes desire the sincere milk of the word : to keep the ordinances as they were at first delivered, and to maintain the purity of gospel worship and discipline.

II. The medium through which this deadness to the world is accomplished : "by the cross of Christ."

We may indeed be dead to the world, through the failure of mere natural powers, the infirmities of age, or the progress of disease; or from chagrin and disappointment, we may take delight in nothing.— — —But this is not the spirit inculcated by the example of Paul. The crucifixion of which he speaks is like that of a lesser light obscured by a greater : a little joy swallowed up by that which is unspeakable and full of glory.

1. Our *first believing in Christ crucified* produces this effect.— — —The love of former sins is relinquished : the things that have charmed us, charm us now no more : the company we once sought is no more desired : the riches, the honors, the pleasures of the world are no longer what they used to be : we say of all these things, get ye hence !— — —A new set of objects is now set before us, a new set of feelings is now excited : we have better riches, more abiding honors, more enduring substance, more refined pleasures, and delights.

2. The more deeply we enter into *the doctrine of the cross*, the more dead shall we be to every thing but Christ.— — —Paul at the latest period of life " counted all things but loss, for the excellency of the knowledge of Christ," and that he might still go on to " know him."— — —The wonders of the cross have fixed the admiration of angels, and, and produced in them a comparative indifference to every other object. Eph. iii. 10. 1 Pet. i. 12.— — —Be this my study on earth : my theme in heaven !

CHARACTERISTICS OF TRUE RELIGION

Isa. xliv. 5 —One shall say, I am the Lord's : and another shall call himself by the name of Jacob : and another shall subscribe with his hand unto the Lord, and sirname himself by the name of Israel.

It is remarkable how God, in his dealings with his people, mixes judgment with mercy. It was but a little before, that the prophet had foretold the captivity of Israel ; and the godly amongst them must have been greatly dejected by the tidings ; for what would become of the cause of God? For their encouragement however, their return is afterwards predicted, ch. xl. 1 : and here, though the last chapter speaks of giving "Jacob to the curse, and Israel to reproach," yet many great and precious promises are intermixed : ver. 1.

1. The Lord calls them by endearing names : "Jacob my servant, and Israel whom I have chosen," ver. 1. He loved them notwithstanding all their provocations

2. He reminds them of his having "made and formed them ;" not merely as creatures and as men, but as a nation and people peculiar to the Lord. He formed them for himself, to show forth his praise.

3. He teaches them to draw inferences that he would "help them and bless them," and their posterity after them ; and still he would remember his holy covenant, ver. 3.

4. Instead of their being swallowed up by the heathen, the time would come when the Gentiles should be accounted the seed of the church, and should "spring up as among the grass," ver. 4 : and though not born of Abraham, they should say, "I am the Lord's." What promises are these! That which stumbled the carnal Jews, and even some of the primitive disciples, had been the support and comfort of the fathers of the church. Jer. xvi. 19.

Our text contains not only a promise of the conversion of the Gentiles to the God of Israel ; but this promise affords a lively description of the nature of conversion itself, and furnishes *several interesting characteristics of true religion—*

I. IT IS PERSONAL.

All that is here said is spoken of *individuals.* "One" and "another' shall say, "I" am the Lord's. Many things are mentioned in the context, and elsewhere, of God's having chosen Israel as a *people ;* but that did not avail to their salvation. There was even then a distinction between Israel after the flesh, and after the Spirit ; between Israelites "indeed," and such as were so in appearance only ; and the children of the promise were counted for the seed. Psa. lxxiii. 1 ; Johh i. 47 ; Gal. iv. 28 ; Phil. iii. 3.

God has also favored our *nation* with the gospel, and we are called christians ; but those only are such who have believed with the heart unto righteousness.— — —The Lord favors some *towns* more than others ; but religion is still a personal thing, and not national or parochial. Some *families* are also highly favored in succession, one generation after another ; yet religion is still personal, and there is no trusting to mere external privileges. Matt. iii. 9.

II. IT IS CORDIAL, or with the whole heart.

It includes the entire renunciation of every idol, and a full surrender of ourselves to the Lord.— — —It begins in the heart : there is such a thing as being called "by the name of Israel," and swearing by the God of Israel;

yet not in truth, nor in righteousness. Isa. xlviii. 1. The Lord always had a right to our hearts, though he possessed them not; true conversion will lead us to say, " I am the Lord's."

1. Some for example have been given up to *open abominations.* They have been the slaves of brutal passions, wallowing in sin, and devoted to every species of iniquity; like the Corinthians who were madly set upon their idols.— — —But grace reaches many of these; and now they are washed and sanctified, in the name of the Lord Jesus, and by the Spirit of our God. 1 Cor. vi. 11.— — —The consequence of this is, a voluntary surrender of themselves to be the Lord's.

2. Others have been wholly *devoted to the world.* The love of money was the ruling passion; all their hearts and all their time was swallowed up in the cares of the world, and they were worshippers of the unrighteous mammon.— — —Yet we have seen in some of these, the love of the world giving way to the love of God, and a willingness to count all things but loss for Christ. Luke xix. 8; Phil. iii. 8.

3. Some have been in the highest degree *self-willed* and perverse. If reproved, they could not bear it; and he that reproved the scorner only got to himself a blot. Their tongues were their own, and they loved all devouring words.— — —But when religion reached the heart, these have become as little children, and all their pride has been abased. Now they are willing to sit at the feet of Jesus, and be numbered with his humble followers.

4. Some have felt a sensible and *strong aversion to God,* and every thing that is serious. They hated to think of him, or to be where he is worshipped; family prayer was a burden to them, and they wished to be free from the yoke of domestic authority.— — —Yet such as these have been reconciled by the blood of the cross, and have given themselves up to God.

5. Others have been peculiarly prejudiced against those *doctrines and ordinances* that are the nearest to the truth, and have proclaimed war against their author— — —Yet we have seen some of these brought to submit, and embrace those very truths they once opposed. Thus the scribes and pharisees who believed, joined the sect that was every where spoken against.

6. Not a few have been remarkable for their *carelessness and negligence* about their souls and eternal things. They have been light-minded, poor thoughtless creatures. Nothing had any effect upon them: they were not grieved for the affliction of Joseph, but drank their wine in bowls, and chaunted to the sound of the viol. Amos vi. 6.— — —But we have seen their careless ones made to think, and lay their folly to heart, and eventually to say, We are the Lord's.

III. TRUE RELIGION IS DECIDED.

Here is no hesitation; the surrender is full and unreserved. The language is not, I will or may be, but " I am" the Lord's. ——— There are many cases of an opposite description, which we have frequent occasion to observe.

1. Some persons remain in *suspense,* between God and the world. They have had many convictions: the kingdom of heaven is near them, and they are not far off: and yet they have gone back to the world, to see whether they cannot make better of it.

2. Some still cleave to *their own righteousness,* and cannot wholly give it up. But true religion will constrain us to part with every thing, to be the Lord's.

3. Others take *no decided part* in religion. If God's cause prosper, they have no joy, no part in it. If it decline they do not mourn. These per-

sons do not consider God's cause as their own, nor do they feel when it is dishonored.

True religion is the opposite of all this; it is decidedly for Christ, and makes his cause our own. Its language is, Thine are we, David, and on thy side, thou son of Jesse. 1 Chron. xii. 18.

IV. IT IS SOCIAL.

They shall "call themselves by the name of Jacob, and sirname themselves by the name of Israel." Those who are joined to the Lord will naturally feel a union with them that love him. Jacob and Israel were then the people of God; and the language of these converts would be, "We will go with you, for we have heard that God is with you." Zech. viii. 21 —23. There is a cleaving to the people of God, like that of Ruth to Naomi. Ruth i. 16.

There have been times and places in which, for a person to " subscribe" himself an Israelite or a Christian, would require a considerable sacrifice, and would cost him his liberty or his life. Yet true religion will cause us to cleave to the people of God, even in the worst of time. Mal. iii. 16; Acts iv. 23, ix. 26; Heb. xi. 25.

V. IT IS INFLUENCED BY EXAMPLE.

"One" shall say, I am the Lord's, "and another" shall call himself by the name of Jacob: "and another shall subscribe with his hand unto the Lord."——— It is here implied, that one person resigning himself unto the Lord and his people, would be the means of exciting others to do the same. The conversion of one sinner is oftentimes the occasion of converting another, and the obedience of one is followed by that of others. Hence the importance of social and family religion. ——— We are greatly influenced by example; and it is frequently seen, that if those who sustain a religious character live in the neglect of gospel ordinances, others will plead their conduct in justification of themselves, and consider them as of no importance. So on the contrary, if faithful and diligent in following Christ, others will be induced to follow the example.

Let us remember—1. That we must either be the Lord's or Satan's. *Servants* we must be: choose ye therefore this day whom ye will serve.—2. If we become the Lord's, it must become voluntarily : it must be the surrender of the heart, and of all we have to him.

CHRISTIAN CONTENTMENT.

Philippians iv. 11.—I have learned, in whatever state I am, therewith to be content.

THIS was the declaration of a great man of God: and it will be happy for us to aspire after his example. The Philippians had been very kind to him, in ministering often to his necessities, and he took it well at their hands: yet he wished them to know that he made no great account of the good things of this life, but could do without them.

It is not the language of boasting, however, of his own strength; no, he was indebted to Christ for all: ver. 13.— — —This is a lesson which but few have learned, but which is of great importance for us to study daily.

I. **EXPLAIN THE NATURE OF CHRISTIAN CONTENTMENT, AND WHEREIN IT CONSISTS.**

It does not consist in insensibility or indifference, as to our situation in the present life. Paul himself felt the hardships to which he was subject, and prayed to be delivered from them. He was keenly sensible of "the thorn in the flesh," and besought the Lord that it might depart from him. He also felt the injuries of men towards him, and prayed to be delivered out of the hands of the wicked and unreasonable. But he considered his lot in life as the will of God; and deeming that alone to be sufficient, he was quite content.

More particularly—

1. To be content is to be *satisfied with our station in life*, without envying those who are above us, or in superior circumstances.— — —Men in general are seeking great things for themselves, and make it their leading object to ascend up into the higher stations of society: but christian contentment is satisfied with its lot.— — —The former description of persons are always looking at those above them, and feel envy; while the latter look at those below them, and feel thankful.— — —The former is a sort of ambition which no means can gratify.

2. It is to be satisfied *in all the vicissitudes which may attend us in our station.*— — —If prosperous, we shall be thankful: if adverse, we shall consider that the hand of the Lord is in it. There is much self-deception in supposing that we should be content in another situation, if wholly discontent in that which we already occupy; though nothing is more common than for persons to imagine, that if they were only in such and such circumstances, then they should be happy, but it is all delusion.

Paul says, "In whatsoever state I *am;*" and the exhortation is, Be content with such as "ye have;" not with what ye might be, or might have. —————— It may be that we are poor, afflicted, oppressed: and can these things be agreeable? No, not in themselves: but viewed as the cup which our Father has given us to drink, and considering the whole of our lot as of divine appointment, we may feel content, let it be whatever it may. —————— This spirit too will humble us under the calamities which may befal the nation or the world; knowing that there is no evil in a city, and the Lord hath not done it. Amos iii. 6. 1 Thess. iii. 3.

3. It is made up of *resignation, humility, and thankfulness.* —————— The language of true contentment is, "Thou Lord shalt choose our inheritance—I will bear the indignation of the Lord—If he say, I have no delight in thee, here I am—The Lord is my portion, saith my soul, therefore will I hope in him."

II. **NOTICE THE EMINENT EXAMPLE OF CONTENTMENT AFFORDED US IN THE LIFE OF PAUL.**

Much of the meaning and force of language depends on the character and situation of the speaker. —————— If Paul had been in high life, in a state of affluence and ease, his words would have no force. But he was not: and what is more, his poverty and affliction were the effect of his religion, and his love to Christ. —————— He might have been otherwise, but he counted all things but loss for him. —————— Many persons circumstanced, as Paul was would have felt more keenly than he did.

The situations through which he had to pass were of no ordinary description, as may be seen by the enumeration given us in 2 Cor. vi. 4—10, and xi. 23—27. —————— Are we poor? so was he. Are we destitute and hungry? so was he. Are we afflicted and oppressed? so was he. And yet his language is, "I have learned, in whatsoever state I am, therewith to be content"

III. THE WAY IN WHICH HE ATTAINED THIS DESIRABLE STATE OF MIND: "I HAVE LEARNED"

It was not natural to him; but he received it, he "learned" it. And where did he learn it? Not at the feet of Gamaliel, nor while a pharisee; but in the school of Christ, and at the foot of the cross.

1. He learned it from *the precepts of God's word.*——He understood that it was God's right to govern, and ours to obey: that every thought is to be brought into subjection to him. This lesson also David learned, and taught to others. Psalm xxxvii. 1—7.

2. He learned it from *the principles of the gospel,* and so learned it as to make it his own. He learned it especially from the doctrine of the cross, by which he was crucified to the world, and the world to him. Gal. vi. 14.

3. From *the example of Christ himself.* —— He who was rich, for our sakes became poor—The cup which my Father giveth me, shall I not drink it—He was meek and lowly in heart: a man of sorrows and acquainted with grief. —— This was Paul's pattern, and he copied after it.

1st. It glorifies God and the gospel, to trust all in his hands, and to rely on its faithfulness and truth. The contrary disposition tends to dishonour both.

2dly. How much does this spirit of contentment promote our own happiness, and the happiness of others. What a blessed world would this be, if such a spirit universally prevailed.

3dly. It has the promise of God's presence: "Be content with such things as ye have, for he hath said, I will never leave thee nor forsake thee." Heb xiii. 5,

ADVICE TO THE AFFLICTED.

Psalm lxi. 2.—From the end of the earth will I cry unto thee, when my heart is overwhelmed: lead me to the Rock that is higher than I. H. H.

IN whatever situation we be, we shall find both consolation in the promises, and direction in the examples that are recorded for our use in the Sacred Writings. But in seasons of affliction principally will the holy Oracles be found precious, because they exhibit to us God's dearest children in similar circumstances, and point out to us the means, which they, in their troubles, found effectual for their relief.

In recommending the example of David, we shall,

I. MENTION SOME SEASONS WHEREIN OUR HEARTS ARE APT TO BE OVERWHELMED—

This is a vale of tears to all : but to some more especially,

1. From temporal calamities—

Bodily pains, loss of friends, 2 Sam. xviii. 33.; embarrassed circumstances, will weigh down the spirits even of the best. And though, at times, religion will enable them to triumph in the midst of all their tribulations, yet its more common operation is, to moderate their grief, to produce resignation in heir souls, and to sanctify the affliction to their spiritual advancement.

2. From spiritual troubles—

The *first convictions* of penitents are often accompanied with the deepest anguish; insomuch that, if God did not support them by a hope of his mercy, they might, like Judas, destroy themselves in utter despair. Their *subsequent views also of their in-dwelling corruptions* are frequently attended with such dejection, as quite to enervate the body and overwhelm the soul. Isai. xxxv. 3. 4. Rom. vii. 24. If to these be added *the hidings of God's face*, the soul may have a foretaste even of hell itself in the miseries that it endures. Ps. lxxvii. 2—9.

3. From the near prospect of death—

To a person enjoying the Divine presence, death has no terrors, Phil. i 21, 23: it is a welcome messenger, that cannot come too soon. But to one in spiritual darkness and desertion, it is inexpressibly dreadful; and the whole world would appear but a small price to pay for the respite of a few days. The ungodly, it is true, too often die as insensible as the beast: but the godly, who know the terrors of the Lord, cannot pass through that dreary valley without extreme horror, unless they have an inward witness of their acceptance with God. Ps. lv. 4, 5, and perhaps Isai. xxxiii. 10—14.

The example in the text may serve as a model, while we endeavour to,

II. Shew how we should conduct ourselves in those seasons—

1. To speake *generally*, we should betake ourselves to prayer—

God is the only source of strength and consolation. If we apply to the creature in our distress, we shall invariably find him but a broken reed. Hos. v. 14; Isai. xxxi. 3. On the contrary, the pressure that is on our minds will, for the most part, increase: or, if the trouble be removed, the removal will prove a heavier judgment than its continuance. But if we apply with humility to a throne of Grace, the desired effect will almost instantly appear. Isai. lxv. 24. There is no trouble from which prayer has not extricated the sons of men: it prolonged the life of Hezekiah, 2 Kin. xx. 1—6.; brought Jonah from the bottom of the sea, Jonah ii. 1—7; and restored to peace the tempest-tossed soul of David. Ps. cxvi. 3—8. For us also, if it be fervent, it shall effectually prevail, Jam. v. 16: there is no disquietude which it shall not pacify, "no sorrow which it shall not turn into songs of joy. Ps. l. 15. Wherever we are therefore, even "at the very ends of the earth," and however circumstanced, we should make our requests known unto God, in order to the attainment of solid peace. Phil. iv. 6, 7.

2. More *particularly*, we should beg of God to lead us to the Saviour—

David, though a king, had no sufficiency in himself: he was forced to look to one higher than himself, even to Jesus, the Rock of his salvation. Ps. lxxxix. 19. But how should he come to Jesus, unless the Father should draw him? John vi. 44. Hence he prayed so fervently, that God would "lead" him to that Rock. Thither then must we also go; for there alone can we find stability. Does guilt appal us? nothing but the blood of Jesus can compose our mind. Acts xvi. 29—31. Do temptations harass us? nothing but his grace can enable us to withstand them. 2 Cor. xii. 9. Do accumulated troubles threaten to overwhelm us? we can both do and suffer all things, if he strengthen us, Rom. viii. 37; yea, we shall be more than conquerors through him that loved us, ib. Like a shipwrecked mariner standing on a rock, we may defy the waves that roar beneath our feet. Such was the experience of David himself, Ps. xl. 1—3; and such shall be ours also, if the storms that threaten us drive us for security to that place of safety. Let us then, in every affliction, look to Jesus as our help; and, with a deep impression of our inability to go to him aright, let us cry unto God, "Lead me to the Rock that is higher than I!"

ADDRESS,

1. Those who experience no overwhelming troubles—

However serene the sky at present be, no man knows how soon a storm may arise. But supposing our voyage through life be ever so favourable, it must come to an end : and what shall we do in the hour of death without an interest in Christ? Above all, what must become of us, if we be not fixed upon that Rock at the day of judgment? Let us then improve our tranquil hours in securing an establishment on Christ Jesus ; that, however suddenly calamities may come, or death may summon us into the presence of our God, we may be found standing immoveably on the Rock of ages. Then, like Noah, shall we rejoice in God's favour, when thoughtless myriads shall be overwhelmed in the deluge of his wrath.

2. Those who are bowed down under trouble—

You are but too apt to carry your complaints to men, instead of spreading them before God. What wonder then you find no deliverance? Has not David told you, that this was his very experience ; and that nothing but the use of this remedy afforded him relief? Ps. xxxii. 3—5. Chide then, and resist, your backwardness to prayer. Lay the blame, not on God, who is willing to impart help, but on yourselves, who are unwilling to implore it. Your troubles are sent on purpose to drive you to the Saviour, whom, in a time of prosperity, you are too prone to neglect: and if you suffer them to produce that effect, you shall soon number them among your richest blessings.

GODLINESS WITH CONTENTMENT.

1 Tim. vi. 6.—Godliness with contentment is great gain. (H. H.)

To the great dishonor of christianity, there are many professors, and even preachers of it, who are more intent on promoting their own temporal interests, or the interests of their party, than on advancing practical religion in the world. Of such persons St. Paul is speaking in the context : and he enjoins Timothy to withdraw himself from them, as from persons who disgraced the christian name, by giving reason to people to conclude, that " they supposed gain to be godliness." In opposition to such characters, the apostle reverses that which he had stated as their opinion ; and declares, that though gain was not godliness, godliness was gain, yea, "great gain," if it were joined " with contentment."

In vindication of this sentiment, we shall shew,

I. WHAT WE ARE TO UNDERSTAND BY " GODLINESS."

The frame of mind which we may conceive the angels to enjoy, would be by no means suited to our state : we are sinners, redeemed sinners ; and therefore " godliness" must include such a frame of mind as becomes persons in our condition. In this view, it implies,

1. An affiance in God through Christ—

This is the fountain of all true religion. Whatever a man may possess without this, he has not one particle of real godliness. If we could suppose him to be as just and honest, as kind and amiable, yea, as devout and fervent as ever man was, still, if he had not the heart of a sinner, of a sinner justly condemned, and delivered from condemnation solely by the blood of **Christ,** he would be utterly destitute of true religion.— — — -

2. A devotedness to God in Christ—

This must spring from the former: for though faith and practice differ from each other, as much as the root of a tree does from the fruit it bears, yet we must by no means separate them, since they are equally essential to real godliness. A reformation of the external conduct, or a partial surrender of the heart to God, will not suffice : if we would be approved by God, we mus have our whole selves, body, soul, and spirit, sanctified" to his service.— — —And as Christ is the only Mediator through whom we approach to God so must Christ, that is. God in Christ, be our only Lord and Governor.

When we have just views of the nature of godliness, we shall see,

II. Its connexion with contentment—

Such godliness as has been described must bring contentment with it, since all who possess it must feel,

1. A consciousness that they deserve the miseries of hell—

No person can have an entire affiance in God through Christ, till he have felt his desert of God's wrath and indignation. And can such a person be discontented with any lot that may be assigned him ? Must he not, even in the most afflicted situation, say, " Shall a living man complain, a man for the punishment of his sins ?" Will he not call every affliction light, yea, lightness itself, in comparison of the misery he deserves ? Will he not, under the presure of the heaviest calamities, thank God that he is not in hell ?

2. A sense of infinite obligation to God for mercies received—

One who has within him the constituents of real godliness, must see himself to be infinitely indebted to God for the gift of his dear Son, for the knowledge of salvation by him, and for the prospect of everlasting glory. His sense of these mercies cannot but be heightened also by the consideration, that they were never once offered to the fallen angels, nor accepted by the great majority of those to whom they have been offered. Can such an one repine that he has a less measure of health, or riches, or temporal conveniences than others, when he is so far exalted above them in things of infinitely greater moment ?

3. A willingness to be conformed to the image of Christ—

No true disciple of Christ expects or wishes to be in a state different from that which his Lord and Master experienced when on earth. But what was the condition of Jesus in the world ? Did he live in ease and affluence and honor ? No ; " he was despised and rejected of men, a man of sorrows and acquainted with grief." He subsisted oftentimes on the benevolence of his friends and followers ; and often had not as much as " a place where to lay his head." Who that reflects on this, will murmur at his lot, even though nothing but poverty and persecution should await him ? Will he not check the first risings of discontent with this obvious reflection, " The disciple cannot be above his Lord: it is sufficient for the disciple that he be as his Lord ?"

The connexion of godliness with contentment being thus plain, let us, consider,

III. The advantage of it as so connected—

St. Paul tells us, that " godliness is profitable unto all things, having the promise of the life that now is, and of that which is to come." Let us view it then,

1. In reference to this life—

Money has obtained the exculsive title of "gain:" but godliness has an incomparably greater right to that appellation. There are three principal ends for which money is considered as valuable; namely, to provide present gratifications, to secure against future troubles, and to benefit our children or dependents. But in these respects it cannot for one moment stand in competition with godliness,—that godliness I mean which is connected with contentment. Suppose money to afford ever such high gratifications, (though it is very much over-rated by the generality,) will not pardon of sin, peace of conscience, and the enjoyment of the divine presence, far outweigh them all? Suppose money to afford effectual relief in trouble, (though it cannot assuage our pain either of mind or body,) what consolations can it afford equal to those which result from godliness and contentment? The utmost that money can do, is to procure some outward relief; whereas the piety above described will convert every cross into a comfort, and every trouble into a fountain of joy. We are ready to acknowledge that money has its uses, and very important uses too, in reference to our children or dependents, (though it not unfrequently is a curse to them rather than a benefit,) yet even in this view it is far inferior to religion: for the godly and contented man will instruct his children and dependents in those principles which he has found so beneficial to himself: and who can duly estimate the benefit of such instructions, confirmed and enforced by such an example? Who can value sufficiently the intercessions of such a friend? Suppose a dying man to address his surviving relatives, "I have not wealth laid up for you in my coffers, but I have thousands of prayers treasured up for you in heaven, which, I trust, will come down in blessings on your heads, when I lie mouldering in the dust: I have engaged my God to be the husband of the widow, and the Father of the fatherless; yes, my dear wife and children, I have intreated *him* to take care of you; and I believe that my prayers have not gone forth in vain:" I say, such a legacy would be far better than thousands of silver and gold.

Thus in every view for which money is coveted, godliness with contentment is a richer portion.

2. In reference to the world to come—

The blindest worldling in the universe is not foolish enough to think that "riches will profit him in the day of wrath." In the words following the text this point is established beyond all contradiction; "For we brought nothing into this world, and it is certain that we can carry nothing out." Here therefore all competition ceases; and "gain" must be confessed to belong exclusively to the godly and contented mind.

ADDRESS,

1. Those who boast of contentment, while they are destitute of godliness—

That persons may feel contentment while enjoying all that they can wish, we readily acknowledge. But we have not real contentment, unless we could be contented with any change of circumstances which God might see fit to appoint. Nor indeed can this fruit spring from any thing but real godliness. Therefore the complacency which many take in their own fancied contentment, while they are uninfluenced by vital godliness, is a delusion, which, if not rectified in time, will issue in the most fearful disappointment and misery.

2. Those who profess godliness, but manifest a worldly or discontented spirit—

The tree must be judged by its fruits. In vain are the highest pretensions to christian experience, if we be not dead to the world, and resigned to the will of God. O brethren, how many professors of godliness have, "through *desire* to be rich, βελόμενοι πλωτεῖν, ver. 9—11, fallen into snares and temptations, and into foolish and hurtful lusts, which have drowned them in destruction and perdition!" Remember, that "the love of money is the root of all evil, which while some have coveted after, they have pierced themselves through with many sorrows." But thou man of God, flee these things, and seek rather to be "rich towards God."

3. Those who profess both godliness and contentment—

Know, that you have a richer portion than crowns or kingdoms. You never can have occasion to envy any man. Only seek to grow in these divine graces. Give yourselves up wholly to God; and "having food and raiment, be therewith content." Verse 8. Godliness is "durable riches;" and one grain of contentment is worth a talent of gold. Let it appear, Beloved, that you live under a full persuasion of these things; and that your ardor in pursuit of heaven is accompanied with a proportionable indifference about the things of time and sense.

THE FRUITS AND EFFECTS OF HOPE.

1 John iii. 3.—Every one that hath this hope in him, purifieth himself, even as he is pure. (H. H.)

THE people of God are but little known to an ungodly world: instead of being considered according to their true character, they are regarded as hypocrites, enthusiasts, and disturbers of their brethren's peace. But this is easily accounted for: the world know not God; and therefore it is no wonder that they know not his people. But the saints themselves have a very inadequate conception of the honor that is put on them, or of the glory that is reserved for them. They know indeed that they are sons of God; but they have very little idea of what is comprehended in that relation: and as to their eternal state, they can form no precise judgment respecting it; they only know, in the general, that they shall be like God, and be with him for ever. Yet, though so little known to the world and to themselves they have marks whereby they may be clearly distinguished; they may be known by their uniform endeavors after holiness. To this effect the apostle speaks in the words before us; from which we shall take occasion to consider,

I. THE CHRISTIAN'S HOPE—

Christ is the fountain and foundation of a sinner's hope: without Christ, all must have perished: nor has the most eminent saint any more hope than a fallen angel, except as he is interested in the merits of Christ. But through *him** the believer has a glorious hope;

1. That he is a child of God—

Christ, having purchased us with his own blood, has reconciled us to God, and made us his children. He teaches his followers to consider themselves as standing in this relation to God, not merely like the angels who are his sons by creation, but in a more exalted manner by regeneration and adoption: and he teaches them to expect from him throughout their whole lives the blessings suited to that high dignity.— — —Verse 1; John i. 12, 13; Matt. vi. 6, 8, 9, 31, 32, 33.

*The text does not say, ἐν ἑαυτῷ in himself, but ἐπ' αὐτῷ in *him*, that is, in Christ.

Now the true Christian hopes that he is brought into this happy state, and that he shall receive from God all those endearing tokens of affection which the relation of sonship emboldens him to expect. This hope of his is founded partly on the merits of his Saviour, and partly on the internal evidence which he has, that he is interested in the Saviour. The mere circumstance of Christ having laid down his life for him, would not be a sufficient ground for him to number himself among the family of God: but when he has the testimony of his own conscience that he has sought acceptance with God through the death of Christ, then he is enabled to indulge a hope that the privileges annexed to such a state belong to him.

2. That he shall be with God, and like him, for ever—

The blessings which the saints enjoy are not confined to this life: " Being sons of God, they are also heirs; heirs of God, and joint-heirs with Christ." Rom. viii. 15—17. " Though they know not yet what they shall be, they know that, when they shall see him, they shall be like him: for they shall see him as he is." Verse 2. The time is coming, when they shall all be introduced into his immediate presence, and be with him, and like him for ever. This also is an object of the Christian's hope.— — —He believes that this is the heritage of the saints; and that " what God hath promised, he is able, and willing, to fulfil."

That this is no barren hope, will appear from,

II. THE EFFECT IT PRODUCES IN HIM—

Every Christian will endeavor to purify himself to the uttermost—

The Christian cannot wilfully live in any known sin: he will search out his corruptions, in order to subdue them; and his duties, in order to fulfil them.— — —He will propose to himself the Lord Jesus Christ as his pattern; and though he can never hope to attain absolute perfection in this life, he will not rest satisfied with any thing short of that. He would gladly be " holy as God is holy, and perfect, even as his Father in heaven is perfect." He considers how the Lord Jesus acted in reference to his God: how in reference to man; and what tempers he manifested in the whole of his deportment;— — —then he labors to follow *his* example, and to " walk in all things as he walked."

To these endeavors he will be stimulated by his hope in Christ:

He cannot endure to think himself a child of God, and yet act like a child of the devil: he cannot please himself with a prospect of enjoying and resembling God in a future life, without seeking communion with him and a resemblance to him in the present world. He will feel himself impelled to holiness by *a sense of duty;* he knows he cannot be saved in any other way. Ps. xxiv. 3, 4; Matt. v. 8; Heb. xii. 14; Rev. xxi. 27: by *a sense of gratitude;* 1 Thess. ii. 12; 2 Cor. v. 14, 15; yea, moreover, by *a love of holiness itself.*— — —Ps. cxix. 128.

We must not however imagine that it is by any power of his own that he thus " purifies himself;" the duty and the exertion are his: James iv. 8: but the power, both to will and to do, proceeds from God alone. Phil. ii. 13.

We shall improve this subject,

1. For conviction—

All profess to have a hope in Christ: but before we conclude that to be well-founded, we must examine what fruits it produces: Are we seeking after universal holiness? Are we contented with no measure of holiness short of perfection itself? Are we setting the Lord Jesus before us, and taking him for our pattern in all our tempers, and in our conduct towards God and man? This is the criterion by which St. John himself teaches us to judge of our hope: ver 6—10: and St. James confirms it—by declaring, that, if in any one point (the not bridling of our tongue, for instance,) we allowedly deviate from this path, our religion is vain. Jam. i. 26. O consider this, lest your hope be only as the spider's web, that will be swept away with the besom of destruction!

2. For encouragement—

Though we must not think our hope well-founded, unless it produce in us the fruits of righteousness, yet we must not imagine that our righteousness is to be *the ground* of our hope, or even *our warrant* to hope in Christ. The only ground of our hope must be found in Christ, and in the promises which God has made to those who believe in him We must go to Christ *as sinners;* and then he will enable us to live *as saints.* This distinction is clearly marked in the text: our hope in Christ is to precede, not to follow, the purification of our hearts: and our holiness is to be the fruit, not the root, of our hope. The same distinction is made by St. Paul also, who, having spoken of our sonship with God, says, "Having therefore these promises, let us cleanse ourselves from all filthiness both of flesh and spirit, perfecting holiness in the fear of God." 2 Cor. vii. 1. See the same also by St. Peter, 2 Pet. i. 4. We must not wait till we are cleansed, and then embrace the promises: but first embrace the promises; and then make use of them for the cleansing of our souls.

What encouragement does this afford to those who feel the corruption of their hearts, and who, if their own purity were to be *the foundation* of their hope, would be in utter despair! Go then, how polluted soever ye are, and seek pardon and sanctification at the hands of Jesus; and you shall find him "faithful and just, to forgive you your sins. and to cleanse you from all unrighteousness." 1 John i. 9.

HAPPY ISSUE OF SANCTIFIED AFFLICTION.

Psa. xcvii. 11.—Light is sown for the righteous, and gladness for the upright in heart. (Pr.)

THE mode of expression used in this passage is common in Hebrew poetry, which consists of a double sentence, the latter part of which is illustrative of the former. "Light" is here put for gladness, and "righteous" for the "upright in heart."— — —The whole is designed to teach us, that the most upright of men must expect a portion of darkness and sorrow for the present; but that it shall sooner or later come to a happy issue. All our enjoyments arise from contrast: if there were no darkness and sorrow here, light and gladness would not be what it will be hereafter.

I. NOTICE A FEW OF THOSE SORROWS WHICH ATTEND THE GODLY IN THE PRESENT STATE, AND OBSERVE THEIR HAPPY ISSUE.

There is abundant reason to expect a portion of darkness and sorrow in this life, because—

1. If we now sustain the character of "the righteous and the upright in heart," yet this was *not always the case with us;* and much of our present darkness and sorrow may be the bitter fruit of former sins.— — —Though God may have forgiven us, yet he may also continue to take vengeance on our inventions: personal and relative troubles may be the consequence. Ps. xcix. 8.— — —Manasseh must walk in darkness and sorrow, and seeing the fruits of his sin all his days.

Yet if found "righteous" before God, we shall be forgiven, and all this darkness shall be turned into light. God may chasten us here, but it will only be for a time: he will hide his face, but it will only be for a little moment, and the indignation shall be overpast. He will wipe away all tears from the faces of his people, and sorrow and sighing shall be heard no more. Psa. xxx. 5. Isa. xii. 1; liv. 7, 8; lvii. 16—19. Rev. vii. 17; xxi. 4.

2. Though "upright" on the whole, yet there have been *deviations in our conduct* since we were made "righteous," and many backslidings from God: and our present darkness and sorrow may be the fruit of these.— — —David had much of this in his latter days: the sword departed not from his house · and it may be so with us. Many eminent characters have at different times been driven aside into temptation, or some unexpected evil, which has darkened their sky, and eclipsed both their evidences and their comforts— — —Some easily besetting sin indulged, or some created good idolized, will eat up all our religion, and bring sorrow and darkness with it.

But if we be truly "righteous," things will come to a happy issue at last

3. Irrespective of particular sins, it pleases God in the present state *to humble and try us* by various dark dispensations of providence. Israel were to have the good land, but they must go through the wilderness to possess it. This was a dark passage, but the Lord led them about, that he might try them, and know what was in their hearts. Deut. viii. 3.

God sometimes brings his people into *dark and trying circumstances*, into situations from whence they can see no way of escape.— — —This was the case with Job: yet the Lord lighted his lamp at last, even in this world. Job xlii. 12; James v. 11.— — —Thus also with Judah in her captivity, Lam. iii. 5—9: yet the cloud was dissipated at last: and there are many such seasons in our life, if we did but keep a register of God's mercies.

Sometimes the Lord brings upon us a load of *relative grief and trouble*, such as we cannot unbind or get rid of.— — —Unhappy connections, disobedient children, become a source of overwhelming distress. Thus Jacob's grey hairs were brought with sorrow to the grave: at least the latter part of his life was greatly embittered by this means.— — —Unhappy connections in religion, union without fellowship in the Spirit, attended with discord and evil surmisings, are likewise productive of similar effects.

But if we are truly "upright," all these things will end well at last.

4. A large portion of sorrow and darkness that a good man endures in this life, *arises from what he has within him*, and continually carries about with him; even a body of sin and death, which makes him truly wretched.— — —Hence we are often in the dark in secret duties, in reading, and hearing the word.

But if upright all this shall be removed. God shall bruise Satan under your feet shortly: faith shall be finally victorious: we must therefore hope to the end, for the grace that shall be brought to us at the revelation of Jesus Christ. 1 Pet. i. 13.

Much darkness and sorrow also attend *the church of God*, collectively, as well as individual believers.— — —Israel was long in Egypt, but the Lord brought them out at last with a high hand: in Babylon also, but the day of their redemption came.— — —The church has often been in persecution, but God has confounded all them that rose up against it. So now, Christ will one day gather out of his kingdom all things that offend. Matt. xiii. 41—43.

II. Consider the ground of our hope for such an issue.

"Light is *sown* for the righteous, and gladness for the upright in heart;" and therefore, sooner or latter, it shall spring up.

204

1. It is sown in the *gracious purposes* of heaven.— — - -God has "prepared" things which ye have not seen, for them that love him: goodness is "laid up" for them that fear him, and trust in him before the sons of men. Ps. xxxi. 19. Cor. ii. 9. Col. i. 5.

2. It is sown for us in *the mediation of Christ.* All his sorrows are the seeds of joy to us: this is the procuring cause of all our comforts, both here and hereafter. All that he has done and suffered on earth, and all that he is now doing in heaven, will issue in the joy of his people: and what a harvest of light and gladness will arise! Ps. lxxii. 16.

3. In *the promises of God.*— — —The seed is sown, the word is gone out of his lips, and shall not return— — —pardon, preservation, and eternal life. Isa. lv. 11, 12.

3. In *the tears of godly sorrow.*— — —Christ's sorrows were the seeds of merit, these of meetness; but each will have their fruit.— — —Godly sorrow generally issues in hope and joy, even in this world, and shall end in everlasting life. Ps. cxxvi. 5, 6. Gal. vi. 8.

5. The very *troubles and trials themselves*, under which the righteous groan, being burdened, are the seeds of future joy, and shall work for them a far more exceeding and eternal weight of glory. 2 Cor. iv. 17.

1. Let us then be reconciled to affliction, and patiently wait for the light and gladness that will soon arise. Ps. xxx. 5.

2. Under all our trials, let us be chiefly concerned to be "upright in heart," and all will issue well. Ps. xlix. 14.

3. Wo to the unbeliever: darkness and sorrow are sown for him, and he himself is continnally sowing the seeds of eternal misery! Prov. i. 30, 31

THE PLEASURES OF TRUE PIETY.

Prov. iii. 17.—Her ways are ways of pleasantness, and all her paths are peace. (Pr)

WHATEVER be our age or circumstances in life, pleasure is the object after which the heart of man inspires: but the greater part of earthly enjoyments are unaccompanied with peace. They are surrounded with innumerable snares, and there is death in the cup. The great concern therefore is to enquire after a species of enjoyment, in which these bitter ingredients are not found, and where pleasure and peace are both united. This is found in true religion, and in that only.

I. ILLUSTRATE AND CONFIRM THE TRUTH TAUGHT US IN THE TEXT.

Here we shall notice what are the ways of true religion, and how they are accompanied with pleasure and peace—

1. The first of these ways is *the fear of the Lord.*— — —This is the beginning of wisdom, and of all true religion in the heart.— — —This in now-testament language is the same thing as repentance towards God, and faith in our Lord Jesus Christ.— — —Whatever there may be of religion without this, is not walking in wisdom's ways. You may read, and hear the word, and attend on means of grace; but you are not in her ways, without repentance and faith; and whatever pleasure you may find in all this, it is altogether spurious.— — —Walking in wisdom's ways is the beginning of a new life, a setting out for heaven in the path that truth has set before us.

The sorrow of repentance may be bitter for a time, but it is a bitter **sweet.** The pleasure of weeping at the foot of the cross exceeds every other pleas ure.— — —The Philippian jailor, amidst all his distress, rejoiced, believing in God. The Eunuch no sooner found the truth, than he went on his way rejoicing. Acts viii. 39, xvi. 34. This pleasure is also mingled with solid peace. Rom. v. 1, xv. 13.

2. Another part of wisdom's ways consist in *searching into the mind of God*, or the glorious truths of the everlasting gospel.— — —There is a source of intellectual enjoyment in studying the works of creation: but what a difference in contemplating this subject with and without a God, and the world with and without a providence. But in the gospel we find a greater work than all these. The work of redemption is the richest of all subjects, and engages the attention of angels. Eph. iii. 17.

Here also peace is connected with pleasure: here is a christian feast, and no danger of excess.

3. Another part consists in *walking in Christian fellowship.*— — —And oh how good and how pleasant a thing it is for brethren to dwell together in unity. Ps. cxxxiii.— — —Friendship and affection are the source of true enjoyment amongst rational creatures; and happiness can be found only in proportion as they exist. But religion opens a new source, and presents us with new and additional motives for affection and esteem, and so of pleasure; and by this means it heightens and endears all our attachments. David and Jonathan would not have been so united in soul, but for the influence of religious principle.

Here also is peace. No fear of the union being dissolved by death, but peace and joy may reign for ever.

4. Devoting ourselves *to the interest of Christ*, and laboring by every means in our power to promote it, is another of the ways of true wisdom. — — —If thy heart be with his heart, his interest will be yours; and then you will find pleasure in it, like that of the returning captives. Ps. cii. 14. Or like the builders of Jerusalem, who had a mind to work. Neh. iv. 6.

In this path we shall find peace as well as pleasure: the satisfaction arising from the service of Christ exceeds every other satisfaction.

5. Wisdom leads us in the way of *doing good to mankind in general.* — — —It fills us with compassion for the poor, with sympathy towards the afflicted, and induces us to seek the good of all: and this is the way of true blessedness.— — —A man of an envious or malignant spirit, may find some pleasure in gratifying it, by tormenting others; but he can have no peace. The heart and conscience are at variance.

But to love mankind, and do good, is sweet.

6. *Taking God's will as our rule* in all the affairs of life, and leaving consequences, is another part of wisdom's ways.— — —To do right, and leave it: to say, Thou shalt guide me with thy counsel: in all our ways to acknowledge him. Herein true pleasure and peace are found. Beasts of prey may shift for themselves; but the sheep of his pasture must know the shepherd's voice, and follow him. Ps. xxiii. John x.

7. Submitting with *meekness and contentment* to all the appointments of providence.— — —Such was the example of our Saviour; and if we learn of him, we shall find rest to our souls. Half the misery that is in the world arises from discontent.— — —How true then are the words of our text.

II. INFERENCES FROM THE SUBJECT.

1. We may learn from hence, how to estimate the *carnal pleasures* of a wicked world.— — —In all their mirth and levity, in all their dissipation,

do they find pleasure?— — —They may : but have they inward peace? No : how little therefore does it deserve the name of happiness.

2. How unreasonable are the *objections made to true religion*, as if it were unfriendly to our interests or our happiness.— — —This is one of the deceptions which Satan passes on a deluded world.

3. What reason to *congratulate* those who are walking in wisdom's ways, and who are decided in their hearts for God.— — —The lines have fallen to them in pleasant places, and they have indeed a goodly heritage.— — — Yours also is true enjoyment: be your portion mine.— — —Yours also is only the beginning of pleasure, but the foretaste of what is still to come. Ps. xiv. 11.

4. Hear what the testimony of Wisdom is to all. "This is the way, walk ye in it." Nothing but destruction and misery will be found in any other. Rom. iii. 16—17.

LOVE TO THE NAME OF THE LORD.

Malachi iii. 16.—Then they that feared the Lord, spake often one to another, and the Lord hearkened and heard ; and a book of remembrance was written before him, for them that feared the Lord, and that thought upon his name. (Pr.)

WHEN religion is in a low state at any particular period, it is considered as an excuse for the want of holy activity.— — —Many seem to think there is but little hope of doing any thing to purpose ; and that if we can but just keep alive in such a Laodicean state of the church, it is all that can be ex-pected.— — —How different the lesson taught us in this passage? In a time of general corruption, when the priests themselves had depraved the law— — —were enemies to true religion— — —and the common people like them— — —there were a few of another spirit.

1. Observe their *character:* they were such as "feared the Lord."— — —While all around them were practical atheists, they felt the importance of true religion.

2. What they *did:* they "spake often one to another."— — —Not content with public opportunities, they sought each other out, stirred one another up, and delighted in each other's good.

3. How their *minds* were employed: "they thought upon his name."— — —Thinking is not opposed to speaking, but to forgetting.— — —The Lord's name was dear to them : they were concerned for its glory, and grieved for its dishonor.

4. What the Lord did *for them:* "he hearkened and heard."— — — They met together privately, as the sorrowful disciples did for fear of the Jews: but there was one that hearkened— — —heard— — —and approved.— — — What is more, it was "written before him"— — — according to the custom of eastern kings, who kept records of all that was done for their honor. Esther vi. 1.

Enquire what is included in our thinking on the name of the Lord— — and what advantages will arise from it.

I. EXPLAIN WHAT IS MEANT BY THINKING ON THE NAME OF THE LORD IN A WAY THAT HE APPROVES.

This expression is descriptive of the nature of true religion.— — —What is *repentance* towards God, but thinking on his name with grief for having dishonored it.— — —What is *faith* in Christ, but thinking on his name with delight, as revealed in the gospel.— — —What is *love* to God, but thinking on his name affectionately, and with the highest satisfaction.

More especially, it includes an earnest and habitual concern for God's *cause and interest in the world,* and for the spread of the gospel. ——— The name of the Lord is more deeply interested in this, than in all other things besides, and therefore it requires more of our thoughts. ——— When David thought of his name, his heart was set on the prosperity of the Messiah's kingdom. Ps. lxxii. ——— Here God is glorified in the highest ——— the gospel is the overflowing of his blessedness.

More particularly—

1. If we think on the name of the Lord in a way that he approves, *all we do in religion will be directed to his glory.* ——— We may be zealous in holy duties—praying, reading, hearing the word—with a view to our own name. ——— This is not religion, but mere vanity. ——— In the conduct of Mary, Zachariah, and Elizabeth, we see how dead they were to their own honor, and how alive to the glory of God. Their souls did magnify the Lord, and rejoice in God their Saviour. ——— John also was willing to decrease, that the Saviour might increase. This only is true religion.

2. If we think on the name of the Lord, *we shall reckon no sacrifice too great for it.* ——— He who has but little affection for his holy name, will think much of what he gives ——— much of what he does to promote its glory ——— and much of what he may suffer on account of it. ——— The opposite of all this is true religion. Acts xxi. 13.

3. It implies that *we seek our own spiritual advantage in subordination to it.* ——— Many are coming and going to the house of God, merely to get comfort and cannot find it. ——— Primitive christians sought first the kingdom of God, and his righteousness ——— cultivated a public spirit ——— laid themselves out for usefulness ——— and were filled with joy and peace in believing. ——— They thought of nothing but Christ, and his name. This was the substance of their doctrine ——— the life of their religion ——— the source of all their enjoyments. ——— Hence they had no distressing doubts and fears. If we take care of God's honor, he will take care of our peace.

II. Observe in what manner God remembers those who remember him, or think upon his name.

God is not unmindful of any of his creatures, nor does he need a book of remembrance; but he will think of those to do them good, who think of him.

1. The Lord generally employs those who *love his name* as instruments in *promoting its glory.* ——— All the great things that have been done in the church, have been done by characters of this description. ——— Those that honor me, I will honor: but wo to the idol shepherd. Zech. xi. 17.

2. In seeing his holy name glorified, they find *their own reward.* ——— The pleasure of the Lord shall prosper in their hand: what else is their hope or joy. 1 Thess. ii. 19, 20.

3. Their labors shall be *remembered for good* in this life, and even when they are gone to their grave. ——— They are of one heart with God: their zeal is united with his zeal, and their labors shall not be in vain in the Lord. ——— The seed sown shall spring up, and future generations shall bless their memory.

4. At *the last day* the Judge will bring forth the book that was written before him, and read it in the presence of an assembled world. Matt. xxv. 21 —23. Heb. vi. 10.

1. There is no true religion but where the name of the Lord is loved and adored.

2. No hope of being useful in the cause of God without a portion of this spirit.

BLESSEDNESS OF SPIRITUALITY.

Romans viii. 6.—But to be spiritually minded is life and peace. (Pr.)

EXPERIENCE teaches us, that our greatest happiness consists in drawing near to God; that the love of God is its own reward; yet how prone are we to live at a distance from him.

There are some, however, in whom this spirituality wholly prevails : as among the blessed above, where all is life and peace.— — —In this world it prevails only in part, even in the best of men. We have much carnality within us : all our powers, principles, and actions are infected by it.— — — Yet if we have any true religion, we are in some degree spiritually minded. We mind the things of the Spirit, and walk after the Spirit.— — —This is essential to denominate us christian.

Consider wherein this spirituality consists—and the blessedness connected with it.

I. EXPLAIN WHAT IT IS TO BE "SPIRITUALLY MINDED."

- This subject, like some others in religion, is better felt than described. experience here is the best teacher.

1. To be spiritually minded is to have a *discernment of the holy beauty and excellence of heavenly objects.*— — —Spiritual things are spiritually discerned. 1 Cor. ii. 14. 2 Cor. iv. 6.— — —While in a carnal state, the mind is blinded by pride, by prejudice, by the vanities of the world It can see no beauty in spiritual objects: the holy character of God possesses no interest. There is no form or comeliness in the Saviour, that we should desire him— — —nothing desirable in the blessings of salvation— — —nothing lovely in the holy law or glorious gospel— — —in the worship, or in the people of God— — —no congeniality between the state of the mind, and the moral excellence of these objects.— — —But a spiritual mind can discern and feel their beauty and their worth: and in proportion to our spirituality, such will be our relish,— — —Nothing contributes more to our understanding and enjoying the Scriptures, than this state of mind. Then it is that we can exclaim with David, as in Psalm cxix. 103. cxxxix. 17.

2. It is such a state of mind as to *live as it were on spiritual enjoyments.* These are its food, and its treasure.— — —The desires of a carnal mind are nourished by carnal and sensual objects : but a spiritual mind is taken up with heavenly delights. The truths of the gospel are the food on which it lives, and the mind is hereby weaned from earthly objects.— — —The affections are now set on things above. Self-denial becomes more easy, and the ills of life are borne with greater patience and fortitude.

3. Spirituality is a state of mind which *delights in spiritual exercises* — — —reading, hearing, meditation, and prayer.— — —The more spiritually minded we are, the more we shall delight in holy duties, especially in those which are most spiritual; in close dealing with God and our own souls.

4. A spiritual mind will be apt to *turn every thing to spiritual purposes.* — — —It is the property of a carnal mind to convert every thing into carnal purposes; it finds food in every thing to gratify a sensual taste.— — —A worldly minded man does the same; he possesses the unhappy ingenuity of rendering every thing subservient to his worldly interest, and never loses sight of that.— — —A spiritual mind will be similarly disposed towards spiritual things: it derives instruction from every event, finds a sweetness in a thousand objects overlooked by others, like the bee that sips the honey from every flower. —— It turns all the mercies of God into matter of praise, all his judgments into matter of humiliation, and even the depravity of mankind into pity, lamentation, and self-reflection. It takes food out of the eater, and sweetness out of the strong.

II. THE ADVANTAGES ARISING FROM THIS STATE OF MIND.

It is "life and peace;" in its own nature—in its immediate effects—producing the most heavenly feelings and enjoyments.

1. Spiritual mindedness is accompanied with much *peace with God.*— —It gives a holy and heartfelt satisfaction, a disposition to rejoice in God, in all his perfections, and in his universal dominion.

2. It is accompanied with much *peace of conscience.*— — —It reconciles us to ourselves, and diffuses a sweet and holy calm. Oh that peace which passeth all understanding: how does it keep the heart and mind through Christ Jesus.

3. It diffuses life and peace under the most *trying circumstances.*— — —It is this which makes our heaviest burdens light, and gives a sweetness to every bitter cup.— — —Patience, humility, and love will all perform their part.

4. It will give life and peace even in a *dying hour.* Then will its advantages more especially be felt.— — —With what sacred peace and calmness did this state of mind enable Jacob to take his leave of the world, Gen. xlix. 18, Zachariah, Luke ii. 29. Paul, 2 Tim. iv. 6.

How important to cultivate this state of mind; by reading, by prayer, by watchfulness, by hearing the word, by delighting in the return of sacred opportunities.

HAPPY STATE OF THE PRIMITIVE CHURCH.

Acts iv. 33.—Great grace was upon them all. (Pr.)

THE power and the glory of the gospel may be seen in looking back on the times of the apostles: and such and more abundantly will be its glory in the latter day. —— It is peculiarly interesting to behold such a number brought to repentance, by such weak instruments too, and after the cause of Christ had been loaded with reproach by the crucifixion. Oh what a change and what a scene.

It is difficult to give the precise meaning of the text, or to know by what words to express it. We may form some idea of it by what we have now and then seen in some very eminent christians, and perhaps it is better judged of by comparison than in any other way. If great grace be seen in a minister, it makes his face to shine like that of Moses; or if in a private christian it makes him appear lovely, like one adorned in all the beauties of holiness.

We shall now seek an illustration of the text, by enquiring wherein such eminent grace appeared in these primitive believers.

Oh that by looking back on their conduct, we may be led to mourn over our great deficiency, and see from whence we are fallen, and repent.

1. Great grace appeared in their *earnest and united supplications.* ——— They had much communion with God in prayer, and this holy exercise was with them habitual. Acts i. 14. ——— On any extraordinary occasion, if they were in trouble or suffered persecution, prayer was their first and last resort: ch. iv. 31. ——— When Peter was in prison, prayer was made for him by the whole church, ch. xii. 5: and when Paul and Silas were imprisoned at Philippi, they spent the night in prayer: ch. 25. ——— When these primitive christians parted from each other they prayed together, though it was on the sea shore: ch. xxi. 5. ——— They were also much devoted to private prayer, ch. x. 9: and great grace will lead to much intercourse with heaven.

2. It appeared in their *stedfast adherence to the apostle's doctrine.*——— Great grace will prepare our hearts to understand the word, for it is that unction which teacheth all things; that which forms and adapts the mind to every part of the gospel. ——— Indifference to divine truth is always a sign of little grace, or of the total want of it; and it becomes us seriously to enquire whether our hearts are prepared for all we meet with in the apostles' doctrine. ——— A stedfast continuance in the truth is also a trial of grace. Not a continuance, indeed, in our own belief, because it is our own; for that may be where there is no grace; but to enter into the spirit of the apostles' doctrine, and to abide in it from love.

3. In a constant adherence *to the worship and service of God.* Acts ii. 42, 46. ——— Real religion was the object of supreme regard, and serving the Lord was their proper element: ch. iv. 46. All hands found some employment. ——— Peter and Paul viewed the whole world as lying before them, and they longed to go forth in the warfare: and wherever they went they made the service of Christ their proper business, whether on shipboard or in prison. ——— The History or Acts of the Apostles is full of their labours and travels for Christ; and churches were planted by them in almost every place. Ch. xiii. xiv.

4. In their great *love one to another.* ——— They were all of one heart and one soul: ch. iv. 32. They had all things common, neither said any of them that ought of the things which he possessed was his own. ——— This practice, however, continued only for a short time, during a special season of necessity. There were afterwards both rich and poor among them, but still they were of one heart. ——— Previous to their receiving the gospel they were at enmity with each other, and divided into sects and parties; but now all this was forgotten. Oh how interesting to see what religion can do!

5. These primitive christians were *full of holy joy* and peace in believing, and they triumphed in every place: ch. ii. 46. ——— Now was that prophecy fulfilled: "Behold, I create Jerusalem a rejoicing, and her people a joy" Samaria also was made glad with the tidings of salvation: ch. viii 8.

—— They had found the Messiah, had obtained mercy, and now they rejoice in serving him.

6. Their *spirit and deportment* were such as recommended their religion to the word: ch. ii. 47. —— They abounded in those christian graces which are lovely even in the eyes of men in general. They were neither surly nor morose, but pitiful, kind and courteous; easy to be entreated, full of mercy and good fruits, without partiality, and without hypocricy. Their conversation was such as becometh the gospel, and they adorned the doctrine of God our Saviour in all things.

What reason have we to mourn, that we so little resemble these holy men —— Oh how far do we come short of their ardent zeal, their love to Christ and the souls of men —— Yet let us be thankful for a little of that spirit which appeared so eminently in them. —— Bless God for the gospel, for the way of salvation, for the ordinances of Christ, for brotherly love and christian fellowship. Lord, increase our faith.

CHRISTIAN COMPASSION.

Hebrews xi. 12, 13.—Wherefore lift up the hands which hang down, and the feeble knees; and make straight paths for your feet, lest that which is lame be turned out of the way; but let it rather be healed. (Pr.)

The defection among the believing Hebrews seems to have arisen in part from the persecutions they met with on account of the gospel. They had been greatly oppressed by their unbelieving countrymen, and though they had not been called to resist unto blood, yet they had suffered " the spoiling of their goods," in the beginning of their profession. This at first they nobly endured, but afterwards fainted. Like their forefathers in the wilderness, when trouble overtook them, some of them were for going back, and others were disheartened.

The words of the text are taken from Isa. xxxv. 3, 4, and are addressed to the believing Hebrews as an admonition to comfort and encourage one another. The disheartened among them are compared to such as had been running in a race, or sustaining a protracted conflict till their knees began to tremble, and their hands to hang down; and in this condition, those who are strong ought to bear the infirmities of the weak.

I. Notice the religious state of those who answer to the description given in the text.

Were we to compare christians in general of the present day with those of the first ages, it would appear that they are grown weak and faint. We have but little of the zeal and activity which characterised the primitive church. The duties of religion are but faintly regarded, our resistance of evil is irresolute and undecided, and our fortitude in trials and adversities bears but little comparison with theirs.

The description, however, is more particularly applicable to certain individual cases and characters amongst us, who need the compassion of their brethren, under their various difficulties and discouragements.

1. Some are ready to faint under difficulties and *troubles of a worldly nature.* —— With all their toil, and care, and industry, though they rise up early, and sit up late, and eat the bread of carefulness, they are scarcely

able to ge along: and not casting all their care upon him who careth for them, the oad becomes too heavy, and they sink beneath the burden.
———— Yι if we keep near to the Lord, such things may be endured. Some poor people are very happy amidst all their privations, while others are faint an J weary in their course.

2. Some are discouraged through distrust, and *groundless fears of future ills.* ———— In addition to the troubles they already feel, they anticipate future ones which may never come. Thus David, in the former part of life, was rendered perpetua.'y uneasy by the apprehension that he should one day perish by the hand of Saul. ———— But if we could leave the future with God we should be happy, and by encountering our difficulties only one at a time we should get through them all at last. Matt. vi. 34.

3. Others are distressed not only with the difficulties of life, but from being under *the chastening hand of God.* ———— They could bear injustice and oppression from the hands of men; but when providence seems to be against them, they are utterly dismayed, and their strength is dried up. Flesh and heart fail them; and not finding sufficient relief in the promises, they faint in the day of adversity. ———— These things may be borne, however if God be with us; but if left to ourselves, our hands will soon hang down, and our knees be feeble.

4. Some are disheartened by repeated opposition from *the enemies of religion* ———— Though the laws of our country do not now admit of open persecution, there is nevertheless a great deal of enmity, reproach and unkindness to be endured oftentimes from friends and near relations for the sake of truth and of a good conscience. ———— This also may be borne, if we live near to God, and duly estimate the importance of christian principles; otherwise we shall soon grow weary and faint in our minds. It was well with these Hebrews while they were warmly attached to the gospel; but when they began to give that up, their strength failed them.

5. Some are greatly discouraged by *inward conflicts,* arising from the evil propensities of their own hearts. ———— It is more difficult to sustain this warfare than all the troubles that assail us from without. David could meet his numerous enemies in the field, and was not afraid of ten thousands of his people who set themselves against him; but when compassed about with his own iniquities, his heart utterly failed him, and he was not able to look up. Psal. xl. 12. ———— Some easily besetting sin, arising from constitution or peculiar circumstances in life, is sufficient to destroy the comfort of a believer, and almost to annihilate his hope. Whether it consists in an inordinate love of the world, or the indulgence of some sordid appetite, it interrupts communion with God, cuts off supplies of grace from above, and so weakens and relaxes all the energies of vital religion. The hands hang down, and the knees are feeble.

6. A *departure from evangelical truth* has weakened the strength of some by the way, and left them shorn of their dignity and glory.———— The relinquishment of any of the leading doctrines of the gospel, or mixing them up with a portion of error, tends as certainly to enfeeble the christian graces, and to destroy the stimulus to holy activity, as the indulgence of sin itself. Gal. v. 7—9.————If we begin to think less of the evil of sin, if we feel less our need of a divine Redeemer, and cease to go to God by him as lost and perishing sinners; if in this case we are christians at all, we shall soon grow faint and feeble, and exhibit little more than the mere form of godliness.

7. The despondency of some good people arises no doubt from a natural

gloominess in their constitution, which disposes them to dwell on the dark side of every subject, rather than on the other.— — —They think of their own unworthiness, and forget the worthiness of the Saviour. They are overtaken by some temptation, fall into sin, and forget that there is an Advocate with the Father. John ii. 1.— — —Partial or contracted views of the gospel, which hide from us the allsufficiency of Christ, and fix our attention chiefly on ourselves, have a most discouraging tendency. Heb. vii. 25.

II. THE DUTY OF CHRISTIANS TOWARDS ONE ANOTHER UNDER THESE DIS-COURAGEMENTS. "LIFT UP THE HANDS WHICH HANG DOWN, AND THE FEEBLE KNEES."

Though this exhortation is chiefly applicable to ministers, whose office it is to strengthen the weak, and to comfort the feeble-minded, it also points out the duty of all christians towards one another.— — —How much soever it may be neglected, it is unquestionably one of the great ends of christian society and fellowship, that we should be helpers of each other's faith and joy in the Lord.

1. In order to perform this duty aright, it is necessary to exercise much *tenderness and forbearance* towards those who are labouring under great discouragements.— — —Let the strong bear the infirmities of the weak, remembering that they are a part of the mystical body of Christ. 1 Cor. xii. 21, 25. The compassionate tenderness of the great Shepherd of the flock, is left as a pattern for our imitation. Isai. xl. 11. Matt. xii. 20.

2 Another way in which our compassion may be exercised is to point out to one another *the directions and consolations of the gospel,* according as the case may require; and here the tongue of the learned is necessary, to speak a word in season to him that is weary.— — —Are any discouraged by outward difficulties? Let them cast all their care on him who careth for them; let them commit their way unto the Lord, and be careful for nothing; but in every thing by prayer and supplication make their request known unto God. He that taketh care for the greater, will take care of the less.— — —Is the hand of the Lord gone out against any of our brethren? Let us relieve their own despondency by pointing out the end to be answered by afflictions; let us remind them of the sufferings of Christ, and of the weight of glory that shall follow.— — —Are any grieved and oppressed by irreligious connections? Remind them of him who endured the contradiction of sinners against himself, lest they be weary and faint in their minds— — —Are any disheartened and cast down on account of inbred corruption? Tell them to be looking still to Jesus, and to maintain the conflict till death: the God of peace shall bruise Satan under their feet shortly.— — —Does the weakness and faintness of any arise from a partial relinquishment or misconception of the gospel truth? Endeavour to instruct and teach them in all wisdom, restoring them in a spirit of meekness and love.— — —Does discouragement arise from a proneness to view the dark side of things? Turn to them the other side also. God's thoughts are not as our thoughts, nor his ways as our ways.

3. Let us be concerned to *remove the stumbling-block out of the way,* and so to "make straight paths for their feet." It is here intimated that the defection and irregularities of some of these Hebrews, became a stumbling-block to the rest. They had departed in some measure from the simplicity, of the gospel, and so were the occasion of "turning the lame out of the way."— — —If those who have been of longer standing in the church, begin to turn aside, or grow weary in their course, it will discourage the weak, and become a snare to the unwary.— — —In order therefore to heal

and strengthen others, it is needful above all things that we ourselves are found walking humbly with God; a zealous and holy example cannot fail to revive and quicken those who come within its influence. Hos. xiv. 7.

1. Let us learn from hence, that all our difficulties and discouragements in the ways of God arise from ourselves, and from the evil that is in the world. They originate in a departure from God, or from the simplicity of the gospel: and if we keep near to him, nothing can hurt us. His ways are ways of pleasantness, and all his paths are peace.

2. How lovely and how interesting is christian society, whose object it is to strengthen and encourage each other in the way to heaven: and how wretchedly defective must it be, if it has not this tendency.

3. How essential to the christian character are brotherly kindness, charity, and a disinterested but affectionate concern for the spiritual and everlasting welfare of our fellow christians. If their comfort and success be not an object of the tenderest solicitude, we are strangers to the benevolent spirit of the gospel.

TRUE RELIGION THE SOURCE OF JUSTICE AND BENEVOLENCE.

Gen. xlii. 18.—This do and live: for I fear God.

The history of Joseph never fails to be interesting, as often as we read it. Here we have an account of his brethren, coming the first time into Egypt to buy corn. On this occasion he spoke roughly to them, and put them in prison, but afterwards released them. His conduct towards them may be seen in verse 14 to 17.

1. Observe, his design in saying to them, "I fear God," when he committed them to prison, was to convince them that he did not do it wantonly or in cruelty; but that his conduct in this instance was regulated by the purest motives, and that they had no reason to expect any injustice at his hands.

2. What an effect it must have had on them, to find that there was a man in Egypt who feared the God of their fathers; a man too in a high and honorable station, and who was lord over all the land.— — —They themselves had lived in a religious family, and did not fear him.

3. Notice the connexion there is between fearing God, and dealing justly and mercifully with men. This has been verified in all ages; true religion is the parent of humanity, and of genuine benevolence.

I. INQUIRE WHAT IS INCLUDED IN THE FEAR OF GOD.

This term is descriptive of the whole of true religion, which is thus frequently expressed in various parts of the Old Testament.— — —If Joseph had lived in gospel times, he would probably have said, " I believe in Christ;" and the meaning is much the same.

Religion however does not consist in slavish fear or dread of the Almighty, in trying to please him as a hard master, or in praying to avert his vengeance. These are the feelings of an idle unprofitable servant, and not of a true believer.

But true religion is called the fear of God, because

1. It chiefly consists in a sacred and solemn dread of the Supreme Being; deep and reverential regard for his holy name, his worship, and authority

— — —Its tendency is to fill the mind with mingled sentiments of love and awe: where this is wanting, there is no genuine religion.

2. True piety produces tenderness of conscience, as one of its principal fruits and evidences— — —a fear to neglect what God requires, or to trifle with his commands, as well as the dread of doing what he has forbidden. — — —It is therefore with infinite propriety that all true religion is called the fear of the Lord.

3. Though under the gospel, fear is not the predominant spirit of believ ers, but love and joy; yet even there it is necessary, and neither love nor joy, nor any other part of true religion can exist without it.— — —We are exhorted to perfect holiness " in the fear of God," and this must accompany our highest joys.— — —This is the great preservative, both against presumption and despair. Heb. xii. 28.

II. CONSIDER ITS INFLUENCE ON OUR CONDUCT TOWARDS MEN: "This do, and live; for I fear God."

It is a fact well known in former times, that where the fear of God was not, there was no security for justice and mercy towards men. Hence the conduct of Abraham, when he came to Abimelech at Gerar. Gen. xx. 11.

This also is true of magistrates, and public rulers in general.— — — Hence the conduct of the unjust judge, mentioned by our Lord, Luke xviii. 4.— — —Even David, when he had lost his tenderness of conscience towards God, became cruel to Uriah, and also to the Amorites. 2 Sam. xii. 31.

On the contrary, where the fear of God prevails, there we shall find justice and humanity towards men: the kings of Israel were on this account esteemed to be merciful men. 1 Kings xx. 31.

As masters, it will make us kind; as parents, tender: as friends, faithful; as members of society, peaceable and well-disposed.

And how is this to be accounted for?

1. True religion, or the fear of God, impresses the mind with a sense of its accountableness. Without this, a man considers only himself; with it, a king will feel that he has a King above him; and a master, that he also has a Master in heaven.— — —Under this conviction, those who have little to fear from others, will fear God; and their conduct in the highest stations will be regulated by it. Neh. v. 15.— — —The principle that makes us feel that we are stewards, and must shortly give an account, is above all others adapted to inspire us with the love of justice and benevolence.

2. The fear of God will render us sensible of our own faults and failings, and of our need of mercy.— — —Such will be quickly aware that they owe ten thousand talents, and cannot therefore think of taking a fellow servant by the throat, and saying, Pay me what thou owest. Genuine religion will impart to us a spirit of meekness and kindness, and make us ready to forgive. Thus also it wrought in Joseph.

3. The fear of God is mixed with holy love: such therefore who possess this principle, will feel benevolently towards all that bear the divine image — — —whether as creatures, who are formed after his natural likeness, or as those who bear a resemblance to his moral nature.

1. We may from hence learn in what way we may hope to see the general state and condition of the world ameliorated· 'each men truly to fear God, and all the rest will follow of course.

2. We are here furnished with a rule for self-examination: the criterion of all genuine piety is the fear of God, disposing us to the exercise of justice and mercy towards men.

3. Whether we fear God or not, we are in his hands: by him we must be judged, and he w l reward every man according to his works

APOSTLES' PRAYER.

Luke xvii. 5.--The apostles said unto the Lord, Increase our faith. (Pr.)

The occasion of this prayer seems in this place to be the exhortation previously delivered, and which required the performance of a difficult duty, ver. 4. In this view it is highly proper, as faith is the grand moving principle by which every holy duty is performed. But whatever were the immediate occasion, the prayer itself is adapted to every part of the christian life.

I. Consider the general import of the prayer: "Lord, increase our faith."

1. Faith has respect to *revealed truth*, as its immediate object; and in the New Testament it more especially relates to Christ, as the substance of all the promises.— — —He was the great object in whom they believed. Thus Peter's confession, " We believe and are sure that thou art that Christ, the Son of the living God."— — —Faith in the all-sufficiency of Christ is that to which the promise of miraculous healing was addressed: " Believest thou that I am able to do this? If thou canst believe, all things are possible."— — —It was this which failed the disciples in the hour of danger: " Oh ye of little faith." Matt. viii. 26.

2. In praying for an increase of this principle, the apostles acknowledged that *their faith was weak.*— — —So indeed it appeared in a time of trial; and so does ours too frequently, if the strength of faith, as well as its genuineness, is to be judged of by its fruits.

3. In praying for more faith, they also acknowledged *their own insufficiency* to produce it.— — —Faith is indeed our duty, and unbelief a sin; but like every thing else that is truly good, it is all of grace: and it is God that worketh all our works in us. Ephes. ii. 8. Phil. ii. 13.

4. In directing their prayer to Christ, they virtually *acknowledge his divinity.*— — —To give or to increase faith is more than any mere creature can accomplish. A minister may offer evidence for the truth to be believed: but he can neither impart faith, nor increase it.— — —Christ alone is the author and the finisher of faith. Heb. xii. 5.

5. This prayer might in some measure be answered at the time, but was more especially so after our Lord's ascension.— — —When he came to the crown, he blessed his followers: he gave gifts unto men, and an abundance of his Holy Spirit. Acts ii. 33.

II. The reasons which render this prayer suitable to all christians.

If we are truly the followers of Christ, yet our faith is weak at best, and needs to be increased, and that for various reasons—

1. On account of its influence in obtaining *other spiritual blessings ;* for they are bestowed according to the measure of faith.— — —In performing *miraculous cures*, our Lord always looked at this. Many looked at worldly distinctions, but he did not: his eye was on the faith of the party. Matt. ix. 2. Acts xiv. 9, 10.— — —When he hesitated, it was for unbelief. Mark ix. 23, 24.— — —It is so in the bestowment of *spiritual blessings :* they are given in answer to the prayer of faith. Psal. xxxi. 19. Mark xi. 24.— — —The answer to successful prayer will also be found to be of this description. Gen. xxxii. 26.

2. Its influences under *dark and trying providences.*— — —Nothing but faith can sustain us under them. Ps. xcvii. 2. What could Jacob have done

but for the influence of faith? "I will surely do thee good," the promise said; yet nothing but evil appeared. —— What could he have done afterwards, when his children seemed to be taken away, in whom the promises were to be fulfilled? —— What could the pious captives have done in Babylon, had they not been sustained by faith in the divine word. Hab. ii. 3. —— What could we do amidst dark and threatening providences, and when Zion is covered with a cloud, were it not for the support which faith derives from the promises?

3. Its influence on the *deep mysteries of divine truth*, which faith only can receive and apply. Truth is like a deep fountain, and faith is the only means of drawing from it: it lies far beyond the reach of the carnal mind, and even of the greater part of modern christians. —— The doctrine of Christ crucified, of God manifest in the flesh, and the wondrous extremes which meet in the person and work of Christ, are like an immense ocean. The powers of reason could do nothing here; and reason, if she attempted to fathom it, would soon be drowned.— — —But faith is like a little bark, borne along the mighty waves, and conducts us safely into harbour.— — — The only enquiry of a true believer is, hath God said it? Then I receive it: Lord, increase our faith!

4. Our *spiritual enjoyments*, as they are derived wholly from the promises, are proportioned to the degree of faith.— — —The consolations themselves are no less now than in primitive times. Christ is the same yesterday, to day and forever: the gospel is the same, our prospects are the same. If our enjoyments are not the same, it is owing to the want of faith— — — What christians might we be, had we but more of this! Instead of God's house being a house of mourning, it would be a house of joy: instead of dragging on heavily, we should run in the way of his commandments with enlargedness of heart: instead of fretting under the frowns of the world, we should rejoice in every tribulation. Rom. v. 2, 3.— — —The promises are full for this life, as well as for that which is to come. We only want faith to realize and enjoy what God has given us in his word.

4. The influence of faith *on our life and conduct*, renders this prayer peculiarly suitable and important.— — —Without faith it is impossible to please God: nothing is done right, nothing is acceptable. Where it is weak, and mixed with much unbelief, it will leave us lifeless and inactive.— — — This also is the case where any of the leading doctrines of the gospel are doubted or denied. The Galatians ceased to run well, when their minds had been corrupted from the simplicity that is in Christ. Gal. v. 7, 15, 16 — — —On the contrary, where faith is lively, all will be alive. Heb. xi. — — —The disciples in our Lord's life time believed a little, and did a little: but afterwards how great the difference!— — —As preachers and as hearers, in prosperity and in adversity, faith in God is the life of all activity, and of submission to his will.

6. Its importance *in the hour of death*, renders it unspeakably desirable. — — —We know nothing of hereafter but by faith: with much of this we shall be prepared to meet the last enemy, and shall even desire to be offered up. Lord increase our faith! 2 Tim. i. 2.

COMMUNION OF SAINTS.

Romans 12.—That I may be comforted together with you, by the mutual faith both of you and me. (Pr.)

THE communion of saints was esteemed of such importance amongst early christians, as to make it an article of faith ; and where the spirit of it is preserved it still forms a charming part of the christian religion.

Our text gives us a brief description of it. Paul longed to see the christians at Rome, having as yet only heard of them by report. When going up to Jerusalem, he observed, he went not knowing the things that should befal him there, save that in every place bonds and afflictions awaited him. He wished to go to Rome, but little thought of being sent thither as a prisoner. In this epistle written from Corinth, he proposed taking them in his way to Spain, and promised himself much satisfaction in the interview. His hope was, that their mutual faith would be a comfort to each other.

I. ENQUIRE WHAT THERE IS IN THE FAITH OF MINISTERS TO COMFORT PRIVATE CHRISTIANS.

When christians see their minister, they expect to hear something concerning " the faith ;" and Paul takes it for granted it would be so with these christians at Rome.

Now there are three things in the faith of the ministers of the gospel, which tend to comfort the minds of the godly—

1. Its being *scriptural and decided*. ——— If the faith which we preach were antiscriptural, it might comfort the sinner and the hypocrite, but not the real christian ; to him it would be matter of grief. ——— If we dwelt in speculations, it might amuse and interest an ingenious mind ; but there would be no solid food for the godly. ——— Now the apostles were decided : they spoke what they believed and were assured of, and had not followed cunningly-devised fables; and it is this in the ministry of the word now, which affords comfort. ——— To see a minister decided on scriptural grounds, speaking the things of which he himself has been fully assured, is to see a guide who is well acquainted with his way, or a pilot who is conversant with his chart. ——— The opposite of this is distressing. ——— To see a guide stumbling in the dark, not knowing truth from error, but who now tells you this is the way and then that, and is at a loss to know what he should believe, must excite fear and distrust, and not comfort. ——— But Paul's gospel was not yea and nay ; but yea and amen in Christ Jesus. 2 Cor. i. 17—20.

2. Its being given them not for themselves only, but *as a public trust to be imparted*, renders it a source of comfort to believers. ——— In this respect Paul considered himself as "a debtor," both to the wise and the unwise : ver. 14. ——— He was entrusted with the " unsearchable riches of Christ," not for his own use merely, but that he might proclaim them among the Gentiles as an almoner. Eph. iii. 8. ——— He himself was poor, yet making many rich : he was afflicted and persecuted, in order that he might comfort others 2 Cor. i. 6 ; vi. 10.

3. Its being a *living principle in their own souls ;* the truth on which they live, and have ventured their own eternal all. 1 Tim. iv. 6. ——— Without an experimental acquaintance with the truth, there would be very little to edify and comfort others, whatever might be our attainments and gifts in other respects. ——— Its coming from the heart makes it interesting to the hearts of others : hence it is that an experimental ministry yields comfort to real christians, and no other ministry can do it. 1 Thess. i. 5, 6.

II. NOTICE WHAT THERE IS IN THE FAITH OF PRIVATE CHRISTIANS TO COMFORT THE MINISTERS OF CHRIST.

It is necessary that they should receive comfort, as well as impart it: and the faith of christians tends to do this, and that for the following reasons—

1. It furnishes them with *sentiments and feelings* in their preaching, which nothing else could do. ——— A believing, spiritual, attentive, and affectionate auditory, whose souls are engaged, tend to inspire thought and feeling in the preacher, which no previous preparation could excite. ——— So on the contrary, when unbelief, carelessness, or conceit appears, it tends to chill the soul, which is like a vessel confined in port for want of a gale. Heb. v. 11.

2. In the faith of private christians also we see the *travail of our Redeemer's soul*, and this gives us comfort. ——— If we love him, we cannot but rejoice in the success of his gospel. Every other consideration is of very inferior importance compared with this, however agreeable our circumstances may be.

3. In it we see also the *fruit of our own labors;* an answer to many prayers, and to many endeavors for the good of others. ——— This is highly encouraging to a faithful minister; and without it he spends his strength in vain. Isa. xlix. 4. Gal. iv. 19. 1 Thess. ii. 19.

4. In it we see the *pledge of your salvation;* and in proportion as we love your souls, this must comfort us. ——— As fellow creatures, as friends, as the relatives of dear friends, we cannot but love you: to see therefore the evidence of your conversion and salvation, is our highest enjoyment and reward. 1 Thess. ii. 8. 3 John 4.

III. WHAT THERE IS IN THE COMMON FAITH OF BOTH TO COMFORT ONE ANOTHER.

Common blessings are the best of blessings; and those blessings which ministers possess, not as ministers, but as christians in common with the rest, are the best of all. ——— What Paul desired for his own soul, is common to the meanest christian. Phil. iii. 8.

Now there are three things in the common faith of both ministers and christians, which tend to their mutual comfort—

1. *Its unity.* ——— Those who have never seen each other's faces in the flesh, yet when they come to converse together, will soon find their hearts to be one. ——— Paul had often felt thus, even when at a distance from christian friends. Col. ii. 5. ——— But he would feel much more from a personal interview; and hence he longed to see these believing Romans. that he might be comforted by " the mutual faith" of one another.

2. The *interesting nature of the truth believed*, has this tendency. ——— " This is a faithful saying, that Christ Jesus came into the world to save sinners—God was manifest in the flesh—God so loved the world." – ——— It is from the belief of this gospel, that there is now no condemnation. Hence we become the sons of God, and hence the hope of eternal life. ——— These are things of the utmost importance ; and being such, like a company of strangers who find themselves all embarked in the same ship, and going together, the mutual belief of them affords mutual comfort.

2. The promised *presence of Christ*, which attends such meetings of the godly for communion with each other, furnishes another source of mutual enjoyment. ——— It is only where Christ meets with his people, that real happiness can be found.

REFLECTIONS.

1. Learn the necessity of *faith in Christ*, in order to christian communion Unbelievers, or mere nominal christians, possess no fitness for it :

there is neither any bond of union, nor any medium of receiving or imparting christian comfort.

2. The necessity of *communicating* faith, in order to enjoy the benefit of christian fellowship. ———— That kind of discourse which tends to explain and render truth interesting, is of importance in promoting both the union and comfort of the godly.

3. If the fellowship of saints on earth be so desirable, what will it be *in heaven;* where no darkness will be felt, no discords, no calamities, no painful separations shall take place any more!

THE BLESSEDNESS OF FOLLOWING CHRIST.

John viii. 12.—I am the light of the world : he that followeth me, shall not walk in darkness, but shall have the light of life. (Pr.)

THERE were many pretended lights in the world, as there are now, and many who followed those wandering stars: but Christ is the origin of all true intelligence, the fountain of light and life to all his people. Like the lesser planets, they borrow all their light from him ; while he alone is as the mid-day sun.

I. CONTEMPLATE THE CHARACTER WHICH OUR LORD ASSUMES: "I am the light of the world."

The Jews objected to it, and do still object, ver. 13; and if he were a mere prophet, as some have said, and only a man, though inspired, the assumption in the text would indeed be inadmissible.

Our Lord not only distinguished himself from all false lights, and false prophets, but from all the servants of God that ever came before him, as in John i. 7—9.— — —They only shone with borrowed rays: his light is original and underived.— — —Their light was confined to time and place: his is universal, "the light of the world." Jews and Gentiles, rich and poor, learned and ignorant, all derive their light from him : those under the Old Testament, and those under the New.

More particularly—

1. Christ's being the light of the world means *what he is to others, as revealed in the gospel.*— — —The divine nature is sometimes expressed by this term, as when it is said, "God is light, and in him is no darkness at all :" but here it denotes what Christ is to the world.— — —If the light had been confined to his personal appearance, the sun would have been set when he left the earth. Instead of this, the light shone still brighter after his ascension than before : and it shall continue to shine, still more and more, unto the perfect day.

2. Christ as revealed in the gospel, sheds a light on *the character and designs of God.*— — —But for him, we should have known but little of his moral attributes; it is the Son that has "declared him," and it is in his face that we behold the glory of the Lord. John i. 18, xvii. 26; 2 Cor. iv. 6.

By the law written on our hearts we might have known something of the justice of God, and seen the terror of his majesty, sufficient to inspire us with dread, at the thought of appearing before him : but this would have been all. Whereas now, we see him gracious and glorious, a just God and yet a Saviour: glorified in the highest, and sending peace on earth.

3. The revelation of Christ casts a light on *the former dispensations.* — — —How dark and inexplicable would have been the types and shadows of the law, the prophecies and providences attending the Jewish church, had they not been followed by the doctrine of the cross.— — —The disciples themselves were all in the dark, till Jesus opened their understandings, and expounded to them all things written in the law and the prophets concerning himself. Luke xxiv. 25—27.

4. The doctrine of Christ affords the clearest discovery of *the way of a sinner's salvation*, so that it is now traced as with a sunbeam.— — —That faithful saying of Paul's, "that Christ came into the world to save sinners," casts more light on this subject than all the labors of man could possibly have effected.— — —Philosophy did nothing towards it. Even old testament believers saw only as through a glass darkly: but in the gospel we behold it all with open face.— — —Now, how clearly is the way of life revealed. The word is nigh thee, in thy mouth: and in thy heart: believe on the Lord Jesus Christ, and thou shalt be saved.

II. CONSIDER THE BLESSEDNESS OF THOSE WHO FOLLOW HIM: "they shall not walk in darkness, but have the light of life."

1. "Walking" implies that *life is a journey.* We are not at home, but travelling to another world.— — —There are many ways that lead to death, and but one that leads to endless life: hence the great importance of having the true light to guide us.

2. The promise implies that *many walk in darkness*, even all that follow not this light.— — —They go on stumbling, not knowing the way, nor whither they are going: all is doubtfulness, and dreadful uncertainty.

3. Those who follow Christ shall have *the light of life*, even that which not only illuminates, but cheers and quickens them along the road.

"Following" Christ supposes our believing on him. It is to follow him as the Shepherd of the flock, as disciples follow their Master; or rather, as a traveller who sees the light and follows after it, like the children of Israel who were guided by the pillar of fire through the wilderness.

1. Compare their state with that of *the heathen world.* They know nothing of the way, nor whither they are going; but vainly imagine that when they leave the world, they shall transmigrate into other bodies. But Christians know the way. John xiv. 3, 4.

2. Compare their state with that of merely *nominal Christians*, who know not the way, nor whither they are going, notwithstanding the objective light with which they are surrounded.

3. In comparisen of such as *follow Christ partially*, and not wholly, they may be said not to walk in darkness.— — —Some are blown about with every wind of doctrine, and are always at sea, without a compass or a guide.

In order to follow this light, we must be convinced of our own ignorance aud need of a guide. Pride and unbelief have darkened the understanding, and those who think they see are made blind. John ix. 39—41.

PRIVILEGES OF CHRIST'S FLOCK.

John x. 9.—I am the door: by me if any man enter in, he shall be saved; and shall go in and out, and find pasture. (Pr.)

Were we to enquire which is the true church; who are the ministers of Christ, and which is the way of salvation; we may learn it from this chapter. —————— The Jews indeed pretended that they only were the people of God; that their priests were the only ministers, and that salvation was confined to them. —————— But our Lord shows that those only are the true church which are his sheep, and who enter in by him; that those only are true shepherds who believe in him, and lead sinners to him; and that this is the way of salvation.

I. THE CHARACTER OF THOSE WHO TRULY BELONG TO THE FLOCK OF CHRIST.

They are such as enter in by Christ, "the door" of the sheepfold; that is, by *faith* in him. Many have entered in by *birth*: they were born in a christian land, and so are called christians. Thus it was with the Jews, who rested on their being the children of Abraham. —————— Others have entered into the fold by a mere *profession* of christianity: but coming in by "the door" is essential to our being Christ's sheep. All professions of religion come to nothing where this is wanting. John xiv. 6.

What is it then to enter in by "the door?" In general, it is to embrace Christ; to receive the truth in love, and that in three respects—

1. It is to embrace Christ *exclusively*, to the rejection of every other way of salvation. The way of salvation by the cross of Christ, is the great offence to the world; but he is "the door," and there is no other way of entering into eternal life. —————— Other things may be dispensed with, but this is indispensable: we may differ in minor matters and may agree to differ: but "what think ye of Christ;" is a question of vital inportance.

This has been the way of salvation from the *beginning*. All the promises made to the fathers included Christ: the promise of the woman's Seed ——————— of the Seed to Abraham, and all nations being blessed in him —————— the blessings promised to David in the everlasting covenant, had an immediate reference to Christ, and he was the substance of them all.

There is no other way of admission but by *faith in him*, as an atoning Saviour. This was clearly taught by the distinction made in the offerings of Cain and Abel, and this difference was observed throughout the whole of the Mosaic economy. —————— There is no other way *now*: the concurren language of the new testament is, "He that hath the Son, hath life; and he that hath not the Son of God, hath not life." John iii. 36. 1 John v. 12

2. It is to embrace Christ *practically*, so as really to "enter in" by the door into the sheepfold. This is to be doers of the word, and not hearers only. —————— Many stand and lie about the door, who never enter in: they think of it, but do not like such a narrow way, or they put it off to some other time. —————— To such however he is still a door of hope, and a refuge to the lost.

3. It implies that we do it *socially*. In entering in by the door, we enter into the fold among the sheep, and become one with God's people.

II. THE PROMISE MADE TO SUCH: "THEY SHALL BE SAVED."

The great question with a fallen creature is, What shall I do to be saved? And this is the answer: Christ is the way, and you must embrace him as such: there is no other way.

223

Consider its importance—

1. *We are lost*, whether we be saved or not. ———— As a sheep upon the mountains is lost from the shepherd and the flock, so are we lost; and should never find the way to God, but should wander and perish for ever. Isai. liii. 6. Ezek. xxxiv. 11, 12

2. If we be not saved, *our loss will be incalculable*. Our sins are upon our head, and we must die in the pit. ———— Other losses may be estimated, but this cannot: what shall a man give in exchange for his soul.

3. *If we be saved*, the good will be inestimable. It is salvation with eternal glory. ———— It includes not only deliverance from all evil, but the enjoyment of all good. 1 Cor. ii. 9.

III. THE PRIVILEGES WHICH SUCH ENJOY IN THIS WORLD: "they go in AND OUT, AND FIND PASTURE."

1. Observe, those who have once entered in by the door into the sheep-fold, *will go in again and again.*— — —The same gospel that first quickened us, will quicken us afterwards: the same food that first fed us, will still be our meat and drink. John vi. 64, 68.

2. Those who are in Christ, have *rich pastures* provided for them: the word and ordinances of God's house, and the green pastures in which he leads them for his name's sake. Psal. xxiii 2. Cant. i. 7. Isai. xlix. 10.

3. They have *free and secure access* to them, under the care of the great Shepherd; who guards their souls from beasts of prey, and will cause them to lie down in safety. Ezek. xxxiv. 13—15.

1. Let us learn the great importance of coming to Christ, and taking his yoke upon us: let us beware we do not stop short of this.

2. See to it that our religion has a right beginning; that we enter in by "the door," and in no other way.

CHRISTIAN HOPE AND CONSOLATION.

2 Timothy i. 12.—I know whom I have believed, and I am persuaded that he is able to keep that which I have committed unto him against that day. (Pr.)

PAUL was at this time a prisoner at Rome, and in the immediate prospect of martyrdom. But he was not ashamed of the cause in which he suffered, nor afraid of death in its most terrific forms: ch. i. 8. iv. 6. Oh how enviable was his situation! Some men desire to die great, that their names may live; or rich, that their families may be distinguished. But after all, who would not join with Balaam here; "Let me die the death of the righteous, and let my last end be like his!"

The general import of the words before us is, that Paul well knew the ground on which he stood, and felt satisfied in it.—He does not speak of himself as an apostle, but as a christian; and therefore what he says is applicable to all who believe in Jesus.

1. VIEW THE GROUND OF THE CHRISTIAN'S HOPE AND CONSOLATION; "I know whom I have believed"—

Paul stood firm and happy here, and many others have done the same: let us see wherein this confidence consists—

1. It arises from *a consciousness* that we believe in Christ, and have committed our souls into his hands, as a sacred trust until that day.— — —Much

is made of faith in the Scriptures; and what is it? It is to give credit to, or to receive the testimony of another; and as the testimony of Jesus respects himself as the only way of salvation, we cannot credit him without confiding or trusting in him. The words of Paul therefore are the same as if he had said, "I know whom I have *trusted.*"— — —We may believe the testimony of Peter or Paul, but Christ alone is the object of our confidence: hence it is explained by " committing" a trust into his hands.

Can you remember *the time* when first convinced of your guilty and un-done condition, and of salvation being in no other; and when you first began to trust in him and commit all to him?— — —Or if not the time, you are conscious that you have *no other hope:* it is not once only, but often, that you have committed your soul into the hands of the Saviour.

2. This comfort arises from the persuasion that *Christ is all-sufficient* for the purposes for which you have reposed your trust in him.— — —The text does not so much relate to the act, as to the object of faith. Paul was not thinking so immediately of his believing, though of that he was conscious, as of him in whom he believed: and this is the principal source of conso-lation.

It greatly concerns us to know in whom we have put our trust: none but real christians enjoy this satisfaction.— — —Others do not know where their trust is : they trust in they know not what, and know not whom.— — — Some in their idols, some in departed saints, others in their own supposed goodness: but all this is trusting in they know not what, and know not whom.

Let us then consider Jesus, and his all-sufficiency, as the exclusive ground of the christian's hope—

1. It is that Saviour to whom *all the prophets* have borne witness : the seed of the woman, the seed of Abraham—the Son of David.— — —He of whom Isaiah wrote, whose glory he foresaw, and whose sufferings he fore told. John xii. 41. Acts x. 43. Rom. ix. 5. 1 Pet. i. 10, 11.

2. Jesus is that Saviour in whom *all the godly* in all ages have put their trust, and have looked to him alone for salvation. Acts iv. 12; Heb. xi. 13. All the martyrs, all the good men we have ever known, put their trust in this almighty Saviour; and it affords the highest satisfaction to feel ourselves on the same ground.

3. It is him who in the fulness of time came into the world, and lived and *died for us.* This is the foundation that God hath laid in Zion, and our hopes are founded on a rock. 1 Cor. iii. 11; 1 Pet. ii. 6.

4. A Saviour who may be depended on for *his all-sufficiency* to save. His proper divinity renders him the object of our highest confidence: " He is able to keep that which we commit to him."— — —He also has an acquired ability, and an official authority, to save unto the uttermost, all that come unto God by him. Heb. vii. 25.

5. He is one that may be depended on for *his veracity* and truth. You may safely trust him, for he is the Amen, the faithful and true witness.— —. —We know whom we have trusted : trust him, oh ye perishing sinners.

6. He is one *whose love* is equal to his power. What he can do he will do.— — —He speaks with great affection to those who have committed themselves to him. They are given to him of God, as well as by their own voluntary surrender: and of this sacred charge he says, " I will lose noth-ing, but will raise it up at the last day."— — —He will also present them faultless before the presence of his glory with exceeding joy. John vi. 39. Jude 24.

225

II. THE IMPORTANCE OF ENJOYING THIS CONSOLATION UNDER ALL THE TRIALS OF LIFE, AND MORE ESPECIALLY IN THE NEAR APPROACH OF DEATH.

Paul felt it in his imprisonment, and therefore he was "not ashamed;" and as one who was now ready to be offered up, he knew whom he had trusted.

1. If the gound we stand on be *not firm*, at death we must sink forever. It is dreadful to be at a loss then, not knowing in whom we have believed, or where we have placed our trust.

3. Death often comes *unawares*, or if not, that is not a time for thought. Our house requires to be set in order, but much more our souls to be committed into safe hands.

3. Where this is the case, death is disarmed of its terrors, and we may join in the song of victory. 1 Cor. xv. 55—57.

HUNGERING AND THIRSTING AFTER RIGHTEOUSNESS.

Matt. v. 6.—Blessed are they which do hunger and thirst after righteousness; for they shall be filled. (H. H.)

MEN naturally desire happiness: but they know not in what it is to be found. The philosophers of old wearied themselves in vain to find out what was man's chief good. But our blessed Lord has informed us wherein it consists: it is found in holiness alone; which, when embodied, as it were, and exercised in all its branches, renders us completely blessed. In this sense we understand the words of our text; wherein are set forth,

I. THE DISTINCTIVE CHARACTER OF A CHRISTIAN—

It is a gross perversion of Scripture to interpret this passage as relating to the righteousness of Christ: for though it is true that every Christian desires to be clothed in that righteousness, and shall, in consequence of that desire, obtain his wishes, yet it is not the truth contained in the words before us: they certainly relate to that inward righteousness which every Christian must possess, and to that "holiness, without which, no man shall see the Lord."

Now the character of every Christian is, that he desires holiness,

1. Supremely—

Other desires are not eradicated from the human breast: the natural appetites remain after our conversion the same as before, except as they are restrained and governed by a higher principle. In proportion, indeed, as religion gains an ascendant in the soul, those words will be verified, "He that eateth and drinketh of the water that Christ will give him, shall never thirst." John iv. 14. But from the very commencement of the Divine life, all earthly things sink in the Christian's estimation, and are accounted as dung and dross in comparison of the Divine image. In this sense "Christ is all" to him, Col. iii. 11.*: and he can say, "Whom have I in heaven but thee? And there is none upon earth that I desire in comparison of thee "

2. Constantly—

While other desires remain in the heart, they will of course occasionally rise in opposition to the better principle: but the prevailing desire of the soul is after holiness. "The flesh may lust against the spirit and seem for

* Christ here means the image of Christ.—

a moment to triumph over it: but "the spirit will lust and strive against the flesh," Gal. v. 17. till it has vanquished its rebellious motions. The needle may be driven by violence from its accustomed position: but its attractions are ever towards the pole; and it will never rest till it has resumed its wonted place. Its momentary diversion serves but to prove its fixed habitual inclination. In like manner, temptation itself, in rousing up the soul to action, calls forth its heavenly tendencies, and displays the holy energies with which it is endued.

3. Insatiably—

Every other desire may be satiated; but the more of spiritual nourishment we receive, the more will our hunger and thirst after it be increased. St. Paul himself could not sit down contented; but forgetting what he had attained, he reached forth for higher degrees of holiness. Phil. iii. 13. It is only "when we awake up after the perfect likeness of our God, that we shall be satisfied with it." Ps. xvii. 15.

Truly enviable will this state appear, if we consider,

II. THE BLESSEDNESS ANNEXED TO IT—

To be filled with good and nutritious food is the utmost that the bodily appetite can desire. It is in this sense that we are to understand the promise in the text. The person who hungers and thirsts after righteousness, shall be made,

1. Truly righteous—

There is a negative kind of holiness, which is neither pleasing to God nor profitable to man: it consists merely in an abstinence from open sin, and a discharge of external duties. But real holiness pervades the whole man: it comprehends the whole circle of divine graces: it reaches to the thoughts and desires of the heart; and assimilates us to God in all his communicable perfections. Now this is that with which the true Christian shall be filled: in all his dispositions towards God and man, he shall be changed: he shall not only be delivered from all that would injure his character among men, but shall be "transformed into the very image of his God in righteousness and true holiness."

2. Progressively righteous—

That degree of perfection to which Christians may attain, is not gained at once. All the members of the new man, as well as of the material body, do indeed exist at the moment of our birth: but they are then in a state of infantine weakness: and their arrival at a state of maturity is a gradual work. Now this work shall be advanced in the souls of those who earnestly desire it: "they shall hold on their way, growing stronger and stronger. Job xvii. 9; and like the risen sun, "shining brighter and brighter unto the perfect day." Prov. iv. 18. "The Lord will perfect that which concerneth them," Ps. cxxxviii. 8. and "carry on his work until the day of Christ." Phil. i. 6.

3. Perfectly righteous—

Though absolute perfection is not to be attained in this life, yet every righteous person may expect it, as the completion of his wishes, and the consummation of his bliss. The moment that his soul is released from this frail tabernacle, it shall bid an everlasting farewell to sin and sorrow. The hunger and thirst which characterize him in this world, will then cease for ever: there will remain to him no heights unattained, no wishes unaccomplished: his soul will be "*filled*" with the desired good, yea, filled to the utmost extent of its capacity.

APPLICATION—

Are there *those who, instead of hungering and thirsting after righteousness, despise it?* Tell me, will ye despise it in the day of judgement? will ye despise it, when ye shall see the difference that is put between the godly and the ungodly? And what is that which ye prefer to it? Can ye say of your pleasures, your riches, or your honours, what our Lord says of righteousness? shall ye certainly be filled with those things? or if ye were, would they ever render you truly blessed? Go, ask of Solomon, or ask of any who have made the experiment; and see whether, in their sober moments, they will not confess those things to be " vanity and vexation of spirit?" O "spend not your money any more for that which is not bread, nor labour for that which satisfieth not; but eat ye that which is good, and let your soul be satisfied with fatness." Isai. lv. 2, 3.

Are there *those who rest in a form of religion?* Know that it is not the form, but the power, of godliness that God requires. The Pharisees of old abounded in outward duties; but " except your righteousness exceed theirs, ye shall in no case enter into the kingdom of heaven." That which you must desire, that which you must attain, is an universal change both of heart and life: "you must become new creatures: old things must pass away, and all things become new."

Are there *any discouraged because of the small proficiency they have made in holiness?* Doubtless this is a matter of lamentation to the best of men. If indeed we are excusing ourselves, and pacifying our consciences from the idea that in this frail state we cannot but commit sin, we are deceiving our own souls; for " he that is born of God, sinneth not;" John iii. 9. that is, he *allows not* himself in any sin, whether of excess or defect; whether of commission or of omission. But if "our souls are really athirst for God, and we are panting after him, as the hart after the waterbrooks," we need not fear. God will ere long " fill the hungry with good things;" " he will satisfy the longing soul, and replenish every sorrowful soul." The very idea of hunger is a painful sensation of want; and if holiness be the object of that appetite, all *shall be* well, yea, and all *is* well: " that soul *is* blessed, and *shall be* filled."

CONSOLATION TO THE DISTRESSED.

Ps. xl. 17.—I am poor and needy; yet the Lord thinketh upon me. (H. H.)

THAT part of the Holy Scriptures which most fully opens the exercises of the heart is the book of Psalms. There we see a man of God unbosoming himself before his Maker, and declaring all his hopes and fears, his griefs and consolations. Sometimes he speaks in the person of the Messiah, and sometimes in his own person: sometimes his words are applicable both to the one and the other. These varieties often appear in the very same psalm: some parts of which exclusively relate to the type, or to the antitype; and other parts are common to both. It is thus in the psalm before us. That it refers to the Messiah, there can be no doubt; because it is applied to him by God himself.* Yet there are in it some expressions, which

* Compare ver. 6—8, with Heb. x. 5—7.

228

should rather be explained in reference to David only. The twelfth verse in particular must be understood in this way: and the circumstance of all the following verses being repeated in another place, and formed into a distinct psalm by themselves, Ps. lxx., is a strong reason for referring them also to him principally, or perhaps to him alone. In the words of our text we notice,

I. His complaint—

David on some occasions was reduced to great straits and difficulties with respect to his temporal concerns; but he was also much tried in his spirit: and the complaint before us seems to have arisen from,

1. A sense of his guilt—

In verse 12, he speaks of "his iniquities having taken such hold upon him, that he was not able to look up; that they were more than the hairs of his head, so that his heart failed him." It is very probable that he alluded in some measure to those dreadful enormities which he had committed in the matter of Uriah. But he would not consider those actions merely as insulated and detached, but rather as indications of the extreme depravity of his heart:* and in reference to *that* he might well say of himself, "I am poor and needy." Indeed, who that knows any thing of the spirituality of God's law, or of his own innumerable departures from it, can use any other language than that in the text? Was Adam poor when despoiled of the Divine image through the commission of one sin; and are not we, whose iniquities are more than the hairs of our head? Was he needy when banished from Paradise, and doomed to eternal death; and are not we, who from our very birth have been "treasuring up wrath against the day of wrath?" Though God has forgiven us, it does not become us to forget what we are in ourselves, but to go softly before him all our days, repenting in dust and ashes.

2. A sense of his weakness—

David had other enemies than those who opposed his regal authority. He complains in another psalm, "Iniquities prevail against me:" Ps. lxv. 3: and he found it exceeding difficult to subdue them. On this account also he used the expressions in the text. He felt himself poor and needy in reference to every thing that he accounted good. He lamented especially his want of wisdom, and strength, and righteousness. Hence he cried, " Open thou mine eyes;" " O give me understanding in the way of godliness!" " Hold thou me up!" " hold up my goings in thy ways, that my footsteps slip not!" " Enter not into judgment with thy servant, O Lord! for in thy sight shall no man living be justified." Similar to this is the experience of all the saints. All are insufficient of themselves for any thing that is good; and the man who was stripped, and wounded, and left half dead, Luke x. 30, was but a faint emblem of the man who, feeling in himself innumerable corruptions, is unable to mortify so much as one of them, except as he is aided from above, and strengthened by communications of the Spirit of Grace. St. Paul himself lamented his state in reference to this; yea, he even surpassed the Psalmist in his humiliating confessions and mournful complaints. Rom. vii. 24.

But in the midst of all this, we view with pleasure,

II. His consolation—

He considered that God's thoughts were exercised upon him—

God is not an inattentive observer of any of his creatures: but " his eyes are more especially upon the righteous." Ps. xxxiii. 18, 19, and xxxiv. 15. As " his eyes were upon the promised land from one end of the year even

*In this light he speaks of them ir Ps. li. 5.

229

to the other," Job. xxxvi. 7; Deut. xi. 12, so are they upon his own people in every place and in every age. He says, "I know the thoughts that
I think towards you, thoughts of good and not of evil, to give you an expected end." Jer. xxix. 11. He thinks of his people with *tender compassion*—with *anxious care*—with *joyful complacency.* How tenderly did he
listen to the effusions of Ephraim's sorrow! Jer. xxxi. 18—20, and Hos.
xiv. 8. With what anxiety does he sit, as a refiner, to watch the vessel
which he is purifying in the furnace, lest it should by any means suffer injury by the process that was intended only for its good! Mal. iii. 3.—
With what exultation too does he say, "To this man will I look, even unto
him that is poor, and of a contrite spirit;" as though not all the angels in
heaven could engage his attention in comparison of such a sight! David
was sensible, that in the midst of all his spiritual distress he was not forgotten of his God; but that he was, notwithstanding all his unworthiness, an
object of his paternal care.*

What comfort must such a consideration afford him!

Surely greater consolation could scarcely be conceived than that which
would arise from this source. What must it be to have *unsearchable wisdom* contriving for his good!— — —*almighty power* ready to execute whatever Divine wisdom should judge expedient!— — —*unbounded mercy*
pleading, that his sins and frailties may not provoke God to withdraw his
loving-kindness from him!— — —and, lastly, *unchanging faithfulness* demanding on his behalf the accomplishment of all the promises!— — —The
consideration of these things must of necessity check every desponding fear,
and constrain him to exclaim, "Why art thou cast down, O my soul, and
why art thou disquieted within me? Hope thou in God; for I shall yet
praise him, who is the health of my countenance, and my God." Ps. xlii.
11. And every one who can realize this one consideration, has within himself an antidote for every fear, and a balm for every wound.

ADDRESS,

1. Those who know little of David's experience—

The generality of those who are called Christians would be ready to despise any one who should express himself like the inspired Psalmist. They
would suppose that he was under the influence of a weak deluded mind
But let them not congratulate themselves on their fancied superiority; for
they only betray their own ignorance. Rev. iii. 17, with Mic. iv. 12. Let
them rather seek to know themselves, that, being made sensible of their destitute condition, they may be made rich in Christ Jesus. 1 Cor. i. 30.

2. Those whose feelings are like his—

While you are complaining of your poverty, God is saying, "But thou
art rich." Rev. ii. 9. The truth is, that the more we are sensible of our
guilt and helplessness, the more ready God is to help and deliver us: "The
hungry he filleth with good things; but the rich he sends empty away.'
Indeed he paints the most destitute condition that can be imagined, on purpose that he may administer consolation to us under it. Isa. xli. 17, 18.
If any then be cast down as though there were no hope, let them plead with
him as David did: Ps. cxlii. 1—7; and they shall soon find by happy
experience, that "God's thoughts and ways as far exceed ours, as the heavens are above the earth."† ‡

* He knew it from both his past and present experience, Ps. xxxi. 7, with verse 5.
† See Ps. lxxii. 12, 13, which may be illustrated by Jonah i. 6, 15, & ii. 1—10.
‡ If this were a subject for a *Charity Sermon,* the *Application* should be altered, and another substituted, recommending the audience to imitate God by thinking of the distresses
of their fellow creatures

DANIEL'S CONFESSION.

Dan. ix. 3—7.—And I set my face unto the Lord God, to seek by prayer, and supplications, with fasting and sackcloth and ashes: and I prayed unto the Lord my God, and made my confession, and said, O Lord, the great and dreadful God, keeping the covenant and mercy unto them that love him, and to them that keep his commandments; we have sinned and committed iniquity, and have done wickedly, and have rebelled, even by departing from thy precepts and from thy judgments; neither have we hearkened unto thy servants the prophets, which spake in thy name to our kings, our princes, and our fathers, and to all the people of the land. O Lord righteousness belongeth unto thee, but unto us confusio of faces, as at this day. (H. H.)

FROM the earliest period, even from the time that God first had a visible church in the world, there have been particular seasons set apart for humilia-tion, and fasting, and prayer. In the christian church, the appointment of of forty days at this part of the year (Lent) for that purpose is of great an-tiquity.* The two days with which this season commenced were observed with peculiar solemnity: the one (Shrove Tuesday) was spent in recollecting and confessing† their sins; the other (Ash Wednesday) in fasting and sup-plication. That these institutions were carried to a very foolish excess, and that they degenerated into very absurd superstitions, under the reign of Po-pery, is readily acknowledged: but they were good in their origin; and our church has wisely retained such a portion of them as might tend to the real edification of her members: and if we were more observant of them than we are, we should find substantial benefit to our souls. But alas! we have run into an opposite extreme, insomuch that not only the observances are laid aside, but the very intention of them is almost forgotten: and instead of com-plying with the design which is intimated in the names given to the days, we render them perfectly ridiculous, by substituting a trifling change in our food for the most solemn acts of devotion before God.‡

Hoping however that on *this* day we are disposed to humble ourselves be-fore God, we shall,

I. ILLUSTRATE THIS CONFESSION OF DANIEL—

The manner in which he made his supplications is deserving of particular attention—

He " set his face unto the Lord God:" he did not rush into the divine pre-sence without any previous meditation, but endeavored to have his mind im-pressed with reverence and godly fear, that he might " not offer to his God the sacrifice of fools."

He " sought God by prayer and supplications, with fasting, and sackcloth, and ashes." By mortifying the body, he endeavored to aid the labors of his soul. Both the one and the other had been defiled by sin; and therefore he strove to make them partners in humiliation before God. Nor can we doubt but that the fervor of his prayers was greatly assisted by the bodily priva-tions which God himself has so often prescribed for this very end.

Nor must we overlook *the remarkable representation which he gave of the divine character* on this occasion—

* The number of days for fasting was not always precisely the same as now: but the ap-pointment itself may be traced almost to the times of the apostles.

† The word " shrove" is from the old English word " shrive," which signifies *to confess.*

‡ This is evident from the customs of having salt fish on Ash Wednesday, and pancakes on Shrove Tuesday. The latter in all probability arose from the people being reminded, or perhaps summoned, by a bell, to confess all their sins, παν κακον. From hence it was called the παν κακον, or *pan-cake* bell. Alas! how widely have we deviated from the intention of those who first enjoined the observance of that day!

231

He mentions in very expressive terms both *the Majesty* and *the goodness* of God; the one for the abasing, the other for the encouraging, of his soul.

What words can more strongly paint *the Majesty* of God? In various other passages, God is called "the great and terrible God:" Neh. i. 5, and ix. 32, and Deut. vii. 21; and well may he be addressed in such terms; for "who knoweth the power of his anger?" Let us only call to mind the judgments he has executed on sinners; on the rebel angels: on the antediluvian world; on Sodom and Gomorrah; on the Egyptian first-born; on Pharaoh and his hosts; yea, on the Jews in Babylon, which was the point referred to in the text; and we shall confess that "God is very greatly to be feared."

Yet he was not unmindful of the divine *goodness*. Notwithstanding God is angry with the wicked, he has "made a covenant" with his Son, wherein he engages to "shew mercy unto all that love him and keep his commandments." Now this covenant he has never violated; this mercy he has never refused to one who by faith laid hold on that covenant, and showed forth his faith by his works. And Daniel mentions this, in his address to God, as the ground on which he presumed to approach him, and ventured to hope for acceptance with him.

His confession before him is also worthy of notice, as being expressive of the deepest humility and contrition—

So deeply did he bewail his own sins and the iniquities of his people, that he strove by the most diversified expressions to make known his hatred of them: "We have sinned, and have committed iniquity, and have done wickedly, and have rebelled, even by departing from thy precepts, and from thy judgments; neither have we hearkened to thy servants the prophets, which spake in thy name."

Here he distinctly acknowledges to God *their transgression of his commandments*, and *their contempt of his reproofs*. These were indeed a just ground for his humiliation; since to no other nation had such a revelation of God's will been given, or such messages of mercy sent. Happy was it for him, and happy for the nation, that the reason of their chastisements was thus discovered; and that, by knowing wherein they had erred, they had learned wherein they were to amend their conduct!

There is yet one thing more on which we must make our remarks, namely, *his justification of God in all his dealings with them*—

Nothing but equity is ascribed to God; nothing but shame is taken to themselves: "O Lord! righteousness belongeth unto thee; but unto us confusion of face." He does not utter one word in extenuation of their guilt, or one complaint against the divine judgments: he declares rather, that to whatever extremities God might proceed, he could not but be righteous; and that, whatever mercies they might experience at his hands, nothing but the deepest self-abasement could ever become them. Thus he gives the most decisive evidence of true repentance, and exhibits an admirable pattern for penitents in all ages.

Having briefly illustrated this confession on Daniel, we shall,

II. Found upon it some suitable and appropriate observations—

1. We have the same sins to confess—

Without entering into any distinctions founded on the different terms which are here accumulated, let us only take the general division before mentioned, and call to mind *our transgression of God's commandments*, and *our contempt of his reproofs*.

Which of the commandments have we not broken? We may perhaps imagine, that, though we may have violated some, we are guiltless respecting others. But alas! if we take our Saviour's exposition of them, and remember, that an angry word is murder, and an impure look adultery, we shall find reason to bemoan our transgression of them all.

Nor is it any small aggravation of our guilt that we have despised those warnings and invitations which he has sent us in the gospel. The ministers of Christ have testified against our ways from Sabbath to Sabbath, and from year to year: yet how few have "hearkened to their voice!" how few have turned from their evil ways! how few have heartily embraced his salvation, or devoted themselves unfeignedly to his service! Let us in particular enter into our own bosoms, and consider what improvement WE have made of the truths delivered to us.— — —If we do this in sincerity, we shall be at no loss for matter of humiliation before God.

2. We have the same God to go unto—

We do not like to think of God's *majesty;* but he is, as much as ever, "a great a terrible God:" the apostle justly observes, " Our God is a consuming fire." Let us not dream of a God *all* mercy: the Deity is just, as well as merciful; and it will be found "a fearful thing to fall into the hands of the living God."— — —

On the other hand, the *goodness* of God is unalterable. He is still merciful to all who lay hold on his covenant; and will assuredly fulfil to them all the promises of that covenant. Heaven and earth may fail; but not a jot or tittle of his word shall ever fail.— — —

Let us entertain just conceptions of the divine character; and we shall have a frame of mind suited to our condition; we shall be under the joint influence of hope and fear; of hope without presumption, and of fear without despondency.

3. We ought to approach him in the same manner—

We should carefully prepare our minds for communion with God. The neglect of this is the reason that we so seldom obtain real fellowship with him. We should not lay aside, as it is to be feared we do, the duty of fasting; we should set apart seasons for more than ordinary humiliation; and more especially improve those seasons which are set apart by public authority.

We should search out our iniquities with diligence: and, instead of leaning to the side of self-vindication, should learn to justify God and to condemn ourselves. Nor shall we ever have our hearts right with him, till we can say, " God will be righteous, though he should cast me into hell; and nothing but confusion of face will become me, even though I were as holy as Daniel himself."

Let us then begin the employment this day, under a full assurance, that "he who thus humbleth himself under the mighty hand of God, shall in due time be lifted up."

HUMAN WEAKNESS SUBSERVIENT TO THE POWER OF CHRIST.

2 Cor xii. 9.—Most gladly therefore will I rather glory in my infirmities, that the power of Christ may rest upon me. (Pr.)

THE false teachers, who had perverted the minds of the Corinthians, did all in their power to traduce the character and talents of the apostle Paul, alleging that his bodily presence was weak, and his speech contemptible. The apostle modestly admits, that he did not use "enticing vords of man's wisdom," nor "come to them with excellency of speech;" and as to his talents and general appearance, he would say nothing. But if he must imitate their boasting, he would glory in the very things for which he was despised.

1. Then observe *the object* of his glorying, even "his infirmities." By these he does not mean his moral weaknesses, or sinful infirmities, but those natural defects and outward disadvantages which attended him; his affliction, reproaches, and persecutions, as it is explained in ver. 10.

2. *The reason* why he would glory in his infirmities, "that the power of Christ might rest upon him." Not that they were in themselves desirable, but they furnished an occasion for God to impart his grace, and Christ his power. Hence the apostle could say, when I am weak then am I strong; even as the consolations of the gospel are more powerfully felt in a season of adversity. When in necessities, Christ makes it up with his presence, and causes every thing to turn to our spiritual advantage.

I. NOTICE A FEW INSTANCES in which our being humbled, and made to feel our own weakness, prepares us to receive in a larger degree, the power and the grace of Christ.

It is God's usual way to empty us of ourselves, before he fills us with his own fulness; to render us weak, before we are made strong; to kill, before he makes alive.

1. A sense of our own weakness and insufficiency precedes *our first participation of divine strength and consolation.*— — —While Paul was alive without the law he felt no need of Christ, but when he died to his former hopes he began to live. The reason why many find no rest to their souls is, they are not weaned from self-righteousness, and have not been emptied from vessel to vessel. They are not helpless in themselves, and God till then withholds his help. Till then there is no coming to Christ, for those only come who are ready to perish.

2. A sense of our own weakness and insufficiency, during our progress in the divine life, *constantly precedes the communication of grace and strength.*— — —If in seeking heavenly wisdom we are wise in our own eyes, we shall not find it. If in times of temptation we are self-confident, we shall be left to fall as Peter did: but if with Jehoshaphat we feel that we have no might against this great host, and our eyes are upon the Lord, we shall be strengthened from above. If in serving our generation by the will of God we are self-sufficient, and depend upon our own zealous exertions, we shall soon be exhausted: but if we have no might of our own, we shall wait upon the Lord, and renew our strength. Isa. xl. 29—31; 2 Chron. xx. 12.

3. When ministers are most deeply sensible of their own insufficiency, *that is the most likely time for God to bless their labors.*— — —If they imagine themselves well prepared for their engagements, it is most probable they will fail in their attempts; and when they have the greatest expectation of doing good by their exertions, that is seldom the time for God to work. If ever they are strong in the Lord, and in the power of his might, it is when self is utterly renounced and annihilated; and hence the Lord often blesses his servants when their hands are weak, and their hearts are faint.

4. When the servants of God collectively are reduced to a small number, and their strength seems to be dried up, *then it is often God's time to work.* — — —When Gideon's army was strong, that was not the time to defeat the Midianites; but when reduced to three hundred, the Lord gave them the victory. When great expectations have been raised from the number and

strength of those engaged in any religious undertaking, it has often been the same; to show that it is not by might, nor by power, but by my Spirit, saith the Lord of hosts. Zech. iv. 6.— — —When God would raise up the Jewish nation, he did not call a number of them at once; but he called Abraham alone, and blessed him. Isa. li. 2. When he would set up Christ's kingdom, he did not convert a great multitude, and send them forth to preach: he called twelve poor fishermen, and endowed them with power from on high. 2 Cor. iv. 7.

II. Observe how the infirmities and ills of life are hereby converted into good to us, and become an object of glorying.

Infirmities, reproaches, and distresses, if they do but humble us and wean us from the world, will turn to our advantage.

1. In this view primitive Christians had must reason to glory in *the sufferings* they endured for Christ's sake, for at no period was there such a display of the power and grace of Christ, or so rich an enjoyment of the divine presence and blessing.

2. In this view we also may glory in some of our *heaviest afflictions*, as they have been the means of laying us low, and bringing us near to God. Many have been purified in that furnace, and can look back to it as the best season in their whole lives.

3. We may also for the same reason rejoice in some of our most painful *losses and disappointments.* It was never better with the Jewish church, as to spiritual prosperity, than when in captivity in Babylon. In the loss of all created good, she could rejoice in the Lord as her portion, and quietly wait for his salvation.

4. In this view we may have to glory *in the prospect of death itself.* Here every human hope vanishes, and flesh and heart must fail. Man then appears in the lowest state of humiliation and nothingness, possessing no hope but in the Lord: and that is often the time when the power and grace of Christ rest most eminently upon his people. That is a time when many a weak and drooping christian has been made to triumph, and the feeblest of all have taken the prey. The last and most formidable enemy is made the messenger of greater good than all that have gone before. Most gladly therefore may we glory in our infirmities, that the power of Christ may rest upon us.

ENCOURAGEMENT TO PURSUE THE CHRISTIAN RACE.

Hebrews xii. 3.—For consider him that endured such contradiction of sinners against himself, lest ye be wearied and faint in your minds. (Pr.)

Knowing the difficulties which these Hebrew converts had to encounter, and the weakness of their faith, the apostle watches over them with the utmost solicitude, endeavoring to comfort and encourage them by the example of our blessed Lord, as he had done in a former instance: ch. iii. 1.

We may here observe—1. That such things may befal us in our christian course, as to render us weary and faint in our minds. The cause itself is good, but there are many adversaries.—2. To grow weary and faint in our minds, is a very dangerous symptom. It often leads to apostacy: many a one has first begun to tire, and then to turn back.—3. It becomes us to watch carefully against it, and to arm our minds by the example of Christ.

I. NOTICE A FEW INSTANCES IN WHICH WE ARE IN DANGER OF GROWING WEARY AND FAINT IN OUR CHRISTIAN COURSE.

1. In reference to *a close and humble walk with God*, we are prone to draw back and grow weary.— — —The happiest seasons in religion have not sufficient influence to keep us always near to God, and desirous of communion with him. After a diligent attention to the word, a more constant engagedness in holy duties, after some special instances of self-denial, a more affecting sense of our own depravity, and of the pardoning mercy of God, how prone we are to grow cold, to draw back, and to sink again into worldly-mindedness and carnality.

2. It is the same also with respect to *public duties.*— — —Those who preach the word are in great danger of sinking into discouragement, if they labor without any visible success. Isaiah complained that so few believed his report, and both Jeremiah and Elijah were on the point of giving up their work.— — —In hearing the word, if not edified and comforted, we are prone to grow weary and dull, and to think that our hearing is all in vain.— — —In prayer, if the blessings we desire appear to be withheld, we are soon discouraged, though we ought always to pray and not to faint.— — — So difficult is it to walk by faith, and live by faith : to believe the promises, and to stay ourselves upon the Lord.

3. When *persecution or reproach* overtake us in our race, we are much in danger of turning back.— — —It is easy to follow Christ when things go well, and the world is at peace with us : but if called to forego our temporal interest, to lose some of our friends, and those of our own house become our enemies, we shall be in danger of growing faint and weary in our course. When thus beset, some have been utterly discouraged, and have gone back again into the world.

4. When burdened and oppressed with *a weight of worldly cares*, and brought into unexpected difficulties, the same danger attends us.— — —In the early part of life, when free from burdens of this sort, we can go on our way rejoicing, and find the path without a thorn ; but when filled with perplexing cares at a subsequent period, it is not so easy. Injuries and disappointments corrode the heart, unkindness and unfaithfulness exhaust our energies, and we move on slowly and heavily in the ways of God, faint and weary in our minds.

5. When struggling with *various temptations*, it is the same.— — —If there were no enemy to annoy, if no lion in the way, no Canaanite in the land, and no snares laid for our feet, we could proceed with alacrity and delight. But when burdened with temptations from day to day, with a load of indwelling sin, and our opposition becomes feeble and inefficient, we are in great danger of growing weary, if not of turning back.

6. *Long continued affliction*, is likewise attended with great discouragement.———Those who enjoy uninterrupted health do not know what others feel, who are under God's afflicting hand, and scarcely know what it is to be free from trouble. These things are apt to produce great discouragement, and even Job felt that they destroyed the hope of man : ch. xiv. 19.

7. When laboring under *a painful sense of guilt*, the mind is covered with gloom and darkness, and the heart is faint.— — —While all is peace within and without, while the conscience is kept tender, and the heart is right with God, it is easy to go forward : but when burdened with a sense of our many backslidings, and great unprofitableness, we are in danger of growing faint and weary, and of slackening in our course.

II. CONSIDER THE EXAMPLE OF CHRIST AS EXHIBITED FOR OUR ENCOURAGEMENT.

1. *What he had to endure* in his race, even "the contradiction of sinners against himself."— — —He was not only contradicted in words, but in actions. The whole of his doctrine, work, and conduct met with continual opposition; he was tempted in all points, and tried every way. He was laughed at by Herod, tempted by the devil, reviled by the Jews, smitten by the rabble, scourged by Pilate, and put to death.— — —Whatever opposition or difficulty we may meet with, it is nothing when compared with his; he met with "such contradictions," as no one besides ever did.

2. Consider *who it was* that endured all this, and *from whom* he endured it.— — —He was not only good and kind, as men may be; he was "holy harmless, undefiled, separate from sinners, made higher than the heaven;" the Son of God, the brightness of the Father's glory, and the express image of his person.— — —It is no wonder if we who are sinful, and were sometime foolish, and disobedient, should meet with such treatment; but that he should be subject to obloquy and contempt, is wonderful indeed. Affecting is the thought, that one of such infinite dignity, wisdom, and purity should be contradicted, blasphemed, and persecuted; and all this by "sinners," by sinners whom he come to save!

3. *The manner* in which he bore all this: he "endured" it.— — —He was a man of sorrows, and acquainted with grief, he hid not his face from shame and spitting. He endeavoured to bring sinners to the knowledge of the truth, and amidst all their hard sayings he expostulated with the utmost forbearance. He never gave up his course of holy obedience and meek submission, till he had finished it with joy.

4. Consider *for whom he endured it.*— — —For our sakes, and for ours only; it was in love to our souls that he suffered himself to be reviled, and evilly entreated. What a motive to endure for his sake, whatever opposition we may meet with, and why we should not be weary nor faint in our minds.

Let us learn from hence the necessity of keeping Christ's example in view, and of studying his character, in order to our perseverance in the ways of God.

Let those who contradict and blaspheme beware of the consequences, for they will soon have to give an account of all the hard speeches, which they have spoken against him. Jude. 15.

THE BELIEVER'S INWARD WITNESS.

1 John v. 10.—He that believeth in the Son of God, hath the witness in himself. (S. S.)

THE testimonies which God has given to his Son are numerous and convincing. There are three in heaven, and a similar number on earth, who bear record, that Christ is the Saviour of the world, ver. 7, 8, 11. But the believer has a distinct witness within himself; a witness, which gives a clearer insight into divine truth than any other, and fixes it with deeper conviction upon the mind. What this witness is will best appear, by considering what that is, of which it testifies.

It testifies of Christ, not only that he is a Saviour in general, but, more particulary, that he is

I. A NEEDFUL SAVIOUR

The believer feels within himself such a load of guilt, such inability to remove it by any sufferings or obedience of his own, and such utter unsufficiency for any good thing, that he is sensible he must perish, if "help be not laid for him upon one that is mighty." Ps. lxxxix. 19. As for his attempting to satisfy divine justice, or to discharge the debt he has incurred, he sees that the very thought of it is folly and madness. Nor has he any hope of ever renewing his own corrupt nature: as well might he think to change the leopard's spots, or the Ethiopian's complexion. Jer. xiii. 23. Hence, when he hears of Jesus as a Saviour, he acknowledges from his inmost soul, that such an one was needed by him, and that, without such an one, he never could have entertained a hope of mercy.

II. A SUITABLE SAVIOUR

When the believer compares his own necessities with the scripture representations of Jesus Christ, he perceives a wonderful correspondence between them, insomuch that there is nothing in Christ either superfluous or defective. Is the believer blind and ignorant? Christ is his wisdom. Is he guilty? Christ is his righteousness. Is he polluted? Christ is sanctification unto him. Is he enslaved to sin and Satan? Christ is his complete redemption. 1 Cor. i. 30, Rev. iii. 17, 18. Is Christ represented as bread to the hungry, and drink to the thirsty; as a Physician to heal, a Fountain to cleanse, a Sun to enlighten, a Shepherd to keep, &c. &c.? the believer feels within his own bosom that, which renders Christ precious to him in each particular view. He can find nothing in Christ, which his own necessities do no call for; nor any want in himself which Christ is not exactly qualified to supply.

III. A WILLING SAVIOUR

In the whole circle of the Christian's experience there is not any thing which does not throw light upon this subject. If he ask himself, What did I, to induce Jesus to take upon him my nature, and to die in my stead? What was there in me either of merit or of strength, that I should be stopped in my career of sin; that I should be pardoned, sanctified, and saved through his meritorious death, and his almighty grace? Did I choose him before he chose me? John xv. 16. Do I not daily give him abundant reason to cast me off; and is it not of his own mere mercy that he still maintains my peace with God? Surely then mercy is his delight, and the exercise of it, his chief glory.

IV. AN ALL-SUFFICIENT SAVIOUR

The believer is a wonder to himself; a bush burning, and unconsumed; a spark kept alive in the midst of the ocean: nor do the works of creation appear to him a stronger evidence of the almighty power of God, than his own preservation in the ways of godliness does, of the all-sufficiency of Christ. He cannot reflect on his errors and corruptions, his temptations and enemies, his falls and recoveries, but he is constrained to admire the efficacy of that grace, which alone has kept him, or alone restored him. As the woman who touched his garment, felt instantly within herself a proof of his ability to heal, Mark v. 28, 29. so the believer daily and hourly feels within himself a most indubitable testimony of Christ's "ability to save him to the uttermost."

OBSERVE FROM HENCE

1. How wonderfully has God, in the constitution of his gospel, consulted the benefit of the poor!

Suppose erudition or strength of intellect ha. been necessary to the obtaining of divine knowledge, how melancholy had been the condition of the weak and illiterate! But the gospel is like the hidden manna, which is to be known only by its taste, or the name upon the white stone, which can be read only by those who have actually received it. Rev. ii. 17. The broken and contrite heart, with an humble faith in Christ, will give an insight into the gospel, infinitely beyond all that books can impart, or the learned of this world obtain. Matt. xi. 25, 26. Let the poor then know, and duly improve, this their high privilege, their inestimable benefit.

2. How easily may we determine whether we be believers or not!

We need only consult our own consciences, and enquire whether we have an inward witness of the gospel salvation? Let not any one, however, suppose, that we are speaking of an inward persuasion of our interest in Christ. In that, we may easily deceive ourselves: but, in the former, we cannot. The inward witness gathers strength in proportion to our proficiency, and will exist, yea, will be perfected, in heaven itself.

3. What comfort we may derive even from our own corruptions!

Doubtless there is no ground of comfort in our corruptions, simply considered. Nevertheless, as reflecting light upon the gospel salvation, and especially as illustrating the power and grace of Christ, they may afford us some consolation. When they rage, then we may rejoice that there is one able to pardon our transgressions, and to heal our backslidings: and when, through grace, they are mortified, then we may rejoice that we are living witnesses of Christ's faithfulness and all-sufficiency.

THE LIBERTY WHICH CHRIST GIVES HIS PEOPLE.

John viii. 36.—If the Son therefore shall make you free, ye shall be free indeed. (S. S.)

WE are exceedingly backward to acknowledge our true state and condition—
   In consequence of this we disregard the remedy provided for us—
   And deprive ourselves of all the blessings of salvation—
   Nevertheless our gracious Saviour endures us with much long-suffering—
   And repeats to us the overtures of love and mercy—
   Thus he acted towards those who denied their need of freedom—
   Thus also he addresses himself to us at this time—
   It will be profitable for us to consider,

I. IN WHAT RESPECTS WE ARE IN BONDAGE.

We of this nation may justly boast of our civil freedom—
But we are, like all the rest of our species, under spiritual bondage
1. Under the curse of the law.

The law of God requires perfect and perpetual obedience—
It denounces also a curse against us for every transgression—Gal. iii. 10

Its precepts have been violated by us in ten thousand instances—Rom iii. 19, 23.

We all therefore, without exception, are obnoxious to its curse—

This may well be considered as a state of wretched bondage—Gal. iii. 23

239

2. Under the power of sin.

Sin has infected all the members of our body, and the faculties of our soul—Ps. liii. 3.

What can be conceived to argue a state of slavery so much as this—John viii. 34.

This construction is so obvious, that no Christian can doubt respecting it—Rom. vi. 16.

The church of old confessed her iniquities to have been a sore bondage—Isai. xxvi. 13.

And St. Paul himself could find no better image wherby to express the evil and bitterness of his indwelling corruptions—Rom. vii. 14, 23.

3. Under the tyranny of Satan

The influence of Satan over us is often denied and ridiculed—

But the wickedness of men is ascribed in scripture to his agency—Eph. ii. 2.

And every impenitent sinner is expressly said to be in bonadge to him—2 Tim. ii. 26.

4. Under the fear of death.

Many will shew a contempt for death on a field of battle—

But all fear it in its more gradual approaches—

Hence even the bravest are averse to meditate on death and judgment—

This is declared to be a state of wretched bondage—Heb. ii. 15.

Surely the Egyptian or Chaldean yoke was light in comparison of this—

Yet all may obtain a release from this yoke

II. How we may be delivered from it.

Vain are all attempts to liberate ourselves by our own strength

We cannot make satisfiction for one single breath of the law—

To do this, were beyond the power of the highest archangel—

Nothing but the blood of Christ can ever atone for sin—Heb. x. 4, 11, 12, 14.

We cannot by any means renew and sanctify our own hearts—

There is not in us a sufficiency even to think a good thought—2 Cor. iii. 5.

Our inclination and ability to do good can come from God alone—Phil. ii. 13.

It is not in the power of fallen man to resist the assaults of Satan—

There is provided for us armour of an heavenly temper—

And in that alone can any man hope to obtain the victory—Eph. vi. 11, 13.

We are no less unable of ourselves to disarm death of its sting—

In spite of all our efforts its terrors will appal the stoutest heart—

But " the Son" of God is able and willing to deliver us

Christ, as " the Son," is heir and Lord of all things—Heb. i. 2.

The very intent for which he came into the world was to give us liberty—Isai. lxi. 1.

He has paid down his own life as *the price* of redemption—1 Peter i. 13, 19.

And therefore may claim us as his " purchased possession"—

He is also commissioned to liberate us *by* his *power*—Luke xi. 20—22

All fulness resides in him for this very purpose—Ps. lxviii. 18.

Nor will he withhold this blessing from any believing soul—John. 12.

Unspeakably blessed are they to whom this blessing is vouchsafed

III. WHAT GLORIOUS LIBERTY WE MAY OBTAIN.

The liberty which sinners enjoy is merely ideal—

But that which Christ will give, is real and substantial—ʹΟντως.

1. He will free us from all our bondage.

The law shall never be suffered to execute its curse upon us—Rom, viii. 1.

Christ gave himself up as our surety, on purpose to redeem us from it—Gal. iii. 13.

It shall have no more power over us than a dead man over the wife that survives him—Rom. vii. 1—4.

Sin also shall be cast down from the throne which it has erected within us—

Nor, though it may renew its assaults, shall it ever regain its dominion—Rom. vi. 6, 14.

Christ will never suffer this great end of his death to be frustrated—Tit. ii. 14.

Satan himself too shall yield to the all-conquering arm of Jesus—Rom. xvi. 20.

And flee from the face of the very meanest of his saints—Contrast 2 Tim. ii. 26. with James iv. 7.

Nor shall death appear any longer formidable as an enemy—1 Cor. xv. 55.

It shall be accounted our gain, and numbered among our treasures—Phil. i. 23. 1 Cor. iii. 22.

2. He will introduce us to a state of perfect freedom

There is "a glorious liberty into which God's children shall be brought"—Christ will pour into their hearts a spirit of adoption—Rom. iii. 15.

And admit them to the most intimate fellowship with himself—Rev. iii. 20.

The most difficult duties also he will render pleasant to their souls—Ps. cxix. 32.

Nor will he confine his blessings to this present life—

To all eternity shall his redeemed delight themselves in him—

Their capacity of enjoyment shall be inconceivably enlarged—

And every power be freely exercised in its proper functions—

INFERENCES.

1. How glorious a Saviour is Jesus Christ!

There is no bond-slave whom he will not liberate—

He offers too this liberty "without money, and without price

He even esteems himself glorified in conferring it upon us—

Let us all admire and adore his goodness—

And by faith apply to him for this perfect freedom—

2. How just will be the condemnation of those that perish!

None ever perish but through their own fault—

Their condemnation is the consequence of their obstinate attachment to the bonds in which they are held—John iii. 19.

O that men would reflect how they will one day condemn themselves!—

Let it be remembered that such offers of mercy will never be made to us in the eternal world—

This is a day of grace; but there will come a day of vengeance—Isai. xxi. 2.

Let every one then lay the blame where it is justly due—

And follow without delay the salutary advice of David—Ps. ii. 12.

~~~~~~~~~~~~~~~~~~~~

BELIEVERS ARE CHRIST'S PROPERTY.

1 Cor. iii. 23.—Ye are Christ's. (S. S.)

TRUE Christians, however poor in this world, are inded the richest people in the universe—There is not any thing of which they have not the best use and enjoyment—All things temporal, spiritual, and eternal, belong to them—Yet they are not so rich in the property they possess, as they are in being themselves the property of another—The Apostle is enumerating in a climax the privileges of Christians—And having said that all things are theirs, he adds, as a more exalted privilege, that they are Christ's—To elucidate this truth, we shall consider.

I. WHOSE WE WERE.

The whole creation properly belongs to God—But mankind have alienated themselves from him—Nor, what ever difference may have been made between us and others by the grace of God, is there any difference between us by nature—As long as we continue unregenerate we belong

1. To ourselves

The natural man disclaims God's authority over him—And thinks himself at liberty to live to himself—This was once the state even of the apostles themselves—Tit. iii. 3. Nor is there one amongst us who was not once a rebel like unto them—Our understanding, will, and affections, we used as altogether our own—The members of our bodies too we employed wholly in our own service—Even in our religious actions we regarded self rather than God—Zech. vii. 6. With respect to all our talents of time, money, influence, &c. we said, " They are our own, who is Lord over us?"—Ps. xii. 4.

2. To the world

The world has an entire ascendancy over us by nature—

We adopt its maxims, follow its fashions, and obey its dictates—The pleasures, riches, and honours of it are the idols which we worship—What more can be wanting to constitute us its vassals?—Rom. vi. 16. Our Lord himself declares, that all such persons are, not merely the friends, but the property, of the world. John. xv. 19.

3. To Satan

Satan rules in all the children of disobedience—Eph. ii. 2. He leads them captive at his will—2 Tim. ii. 26. Hence he is called the god of this world—2 Cor. iv 4. And who amongst us has not fulfilled *his* will?—This then manifests us to have been his children—1 John iii. 8, 10. And, if we be not converted by divine grace, it may still be said to us, as it was to the Jews of old, Ye are of your father, the devil. John viii. 44.

By conversion, however, we are brought back to our rightful owner.

II. WHOSE WE ARE.

Christ is the heir and sovereign Lord of all things—Both men and devils are subject to his controul—But believers are his in a more peculiar manner—They are his people, Tit. ii. 14. his bride, Rev. xxi. 9. his very member—Eph. v. 30.

1. By donation from the Father

The Father, from eternity, chose a people for himself—Eph. i. 4. These he gave to Christ to be redeemed by him—John xvii. 6. And secured them to him by an everlasting covenant—Ps. lxxxix. 34—36. To his eternal purpose we must trace the distinction made between them and others—2 Tim. i. 9. And ascribe all our salvation to him alone—1 Cor. xv. 10.

2. By his own purchase

Though salvation is freely given to us, it was purchased for us at a most invaluable price—Christ gave his own life a ransom for us—The price he paid was no less than his own blood—1 Pet. i. 19. This is the great subject of praise in heaven—Rev. v. 9. Nor should it ever be forgotten by us on earth—

3. By the drawings of the Holy Spirit

No man, of himself, would go to Christ for salvation—All who are his, are drawn to him by the Spirit—John vi. 44. It is the Spirit who quickens and renews our souls—To him alone must we ascribe the power and the glory—Zech. iv. 6.

4. By their own voluntary surrender

All Christ's people are made willing to be his—Ps. cx. 3. They willingly renew their baptismal covenant—And give themselves up to him at his holy table—This they consider as their reasonable service—Rom. xii. 1. Yea, they rejoice in it as their highest privilege—This is the peculiar character of all true Christians—Jer. i. 5.

LEARN HENCE

1. The Christian's character

How different from what he himself once was, and the generality still are !— — —

2. The Christian's privilege

The most eminent Christians were once in as miserable a state as any— But now, how altered their condition!—How *happy* are they in comparison of what they were !—How infinitely preferable is Christ's service to Satan's !—And how rich the recompense they will receive from Christ in comparison of any the world could have given !—How *secure* too are they in the hands of Christ!—None shall be able to pluck them from him—John x. 28, 29. They shall assuredly be kept by the Father's power—John xvii. 11. 1 Pet. i. 5. And shall finally participate the Saviour's glory— John xvii. 24. Let them all therefore rejoice, and adore their God—Nor let them regard the frowns of an ungodly world—If Christ owns them, it signifies little who disowns them—

3. The Christian's duty

If we belong to Christ, we ought to live as his people—We should devote to ourselves, and all that we have, without reserve—This was the manifest end for which he bought us—Tit. ii. 14. Let every one then remember whose he is, and whom he is bound to serve—Nor let any one presume to alienate the Saviour's property—All that we have and are, should be employed for him—Our duty is summed up in the apostle's exhortations— 1 Cor. vi. 20.

THE PRIVILEGES OF CHRIST'S FLOCK.

Luke xii. 32. Fear not, little flock ; for it is your Father's good pleasure to give you the king-dom. (S. S)

AMONG the many faculties which exalt man above the brute creation, that of being able to look into futurity is by no means the least.—But while this in many instances elevates him with hope, in many other instances it depresses him with fear.—Hence he is often filled with anxiety to secure the good he hopes for, and to avert the evil which he dreads.—To discountenance this solicitude, and to teach men to live dependent upon God, is the scope of our Lord's discourse before us.—And, in the text, he fortifies his own peculiar people against fear and anxiety, by reminding them of the distinguishing favor of God towards them, and the glorious provision he has made for them. To elucidate his words we shall enquire,

I. WHY THE LORD'S PEOPLE ARE CALLED "A LITTLE FLOCK."

The metaphor of sheep is often used to characterize the followers of Christ.—Ingenuity might easily suggest a variety of particulars wherein the parallel between them may be drawn.—But, to limit our views within the strictest bounds of propriety, we observe that

They are called "*a flock*" principally from the peculiar regard shewn them by the Lord.

All who love and fear God, once "went astray like sheep that are lost." But they have been brought home by Christ, the great and good shepherd. And have been united together by him in one fold.—They are kept inclosed, as it were, and distinct from the world.—They "hear their shepherd's voice and follow him."—He "leads them into pastures" which he himself has provided for them. He administers to all their wants, "strengthening the diseased, healing the sick, and binding up the broken hearted." Ezek. xxxiv. 16. The lambs he carries in his bosom, and gently leads them that are witn young." Isa. xl. 11. And, however they may feed in different pastures, he considers them all as under his peculiar care—

They are called "*a little* flock" because they are but few in number.

In every age and every place their numbers have been small.—They are "the few that find the narrow way."—When indeed they shall be all assembled at the last day they will be more than the stars of heaven or the sands upon the sea shore for multitude. Rev. vii. 9. But before that period they will receive an astonishing increase.—The whole earth shall be overspread with them ; and *that* too in successive generation for a thousand years. Rev xx. 4. Till that day of God's power they will be a little flock when compared with the herds of the ungodly.—At present they are only "like the gleanings of the olive-tree, two or three upon the topmost branch." Isa. xvii. 6.

Interested as we must be in what relates to them, let us enquire,

II WHAT THEY HAVE TO FEAR.

They are not exempt from the common calamities of life.—In some respects they are more exposed to them than other people.—They have reason therefore to fear

1. Wants

Though man may provide for to-morrow, he cannot secure what he has provided.—Hence all are so desirous of placing themselves as far as possible out of the reach of any disastrous contingencies.—In making such provision the true Christian labors under many disadvantages.— He cannot use

CHRISTIAN GRACES.

those means of acquiring wealth which the generality of the world employ without any scruple.—He cannot devote *all* his time, and *all* his attention to secular engagements.—He dares not neglect his soul, even if he could gain the whole world by it.—Moreover, he has many in the world who would be glad enough to ruin him; but few, very few, that will exert themselves much to help him forward.—On these accounts he may at times be tempted to indulge excessive care, and to harbor fears of want and embarrassment.

2. Sufferings.

The flock of Christ are not only subject to the trials incident to our present state, but are liable to many sufferings peculiar to themselves.—They are " as sheep in the midst of wolves."—Often among themselves are found some that are " wolves in sheep's clothing."—Above all there is " a roaring lion ever seeking to devour them."—Now Christians are not only weak when opposed to Satan, but also when opposed to the world.—They cannot contend with carnal weapons. 2 Cor. x. 4. " The servant of the Lord must not strive."—The rebuke given to Peter when fighting for his Master sufficiently ties their hands from standing in their own defence. Matt. xxvi. 52. Their only weapons are faith and patience.—They are to conquer indeed, but it is by suffering even unto death. Rev. xii. 11. Well therefore may they entertain fears respecting these things.—For if they be not well armed with the mind that was in Christ, 1 Pet. iv. 1, they will faint in the day of adversity.

But the exhortation in the text leads us to enquire further.

III. Why, notwithstanding their dangers, they should not fear. God has " provided for them a "kingdom."

God condescends to call himself their " Father."—And deals with them as his children.—He has " prepared for them a kingdom" that is infinitely superior to all the kingdoms of this world.—The glory of it cannot be expressed or conceived; nor will the duration of it ever end. Heb. xii 28. This he has given to them for their inheritance.—It is *his determination* to invest them with it, and *his delight* to preserve them for it.—His almighty power is ever exercised for this purpose. 1 Pet. i. 4, 5. Yea, his whole heart and soul are engaged in accomplishing his gracious intentions. Jer. xxxii. 41.

This is a very sufficient antidote to all their fears.

Why should they be afraid of *want*, who have God for their Father, and a kingdom for their inheritance?—Can it be supposed that he who provides for the evil and unthankful, and sustains the ravens that call upon him, will neglect his own children?—Will he, who *of his good pleasure* bestowed upon them all the glory of heaven, refuse them what is necessary for their present sustenance?—Why too should they be afraid of *sufferings*, since " not a hair of their head can perish," " nor can even a sparrow fall to the ground, without the permission of their Father?"—If he see fit to let loose the enemy for the trial of their faith, will he not support their courage, and make them " more than conquerors?"—Besides, will not their " light and momentary afflictions work out for them a far more exceeding and eternal weight of glory ?" "And will not a kingdom abundantly compensate all their trials?"—Surely then they should dispel all fears; and commit themselves into the hands of a faithful God. Pet. iv. 19.

Address,

1. The flock of Christ.

God would have you without carefulness. 1 Cor. viii. 32. He bids you cast all your care on him who careth for you. 1 Pet. v. 7. And shall God

245

be so concerned about relieving your fears, and you not be concerned to honor him?—O chide your unbelieving thoughts, and say, Why art thou disquieted, O my soul?—Jehovah is my shepherd, I shall not want; Jehovah is my Father, I will not fear. Ps. xxiii. 1, 4. Surely if you reflect on the promises he has made to you, it will be impossible for you ever to be cast down again.—"Ye, my flock," says he, "the flock of my pasture, are men; but I am your God, saith the Lord God." Ezek. xxxiv. 31. "When you pass through the waters, I will be with you, and through the fire, you shall not be burnt." Isa. xliii. 2. See also John x. 27, 28. Consider, "If God be for you, who can be against you?"—O be careful for nothing; but in every thing by prayer and supplication with thanksgiving, let your requests be made known unto God; and the peace of God which passeth all understanding shall keep your hearts and minds through Christ Jesus, Phil. iv. 6, 7.

2. The herds of this world.

Shall we address you in the language of the text, Fear not? Alas! not only the scriptures, but also your own consciences would condemn us.—You may possibly have no particular cause to dread either wants or sufferings in this world, (though you cannot tell what may befal you before you die) but may you not have to "dwell with everlasting burnings," and want even "a drop of water to cool your tongue" in that world to which you are hastening?—Know assuredly, that your numbers will not screen you from the vengeance of an angry God.—If you be not of those who have put themselves under the care of the good shepherd, you will be considered as goats, and be forever separated from the flock of Christ—"He will set the sheep on his right hand, and the goats on his left."—You will then find to your cost, that not God, but Satan was your Father; and that with Satan must be your portion. John viii. 42, 44. It is not without much regret that God *now* gives you up to that misery. Hos. xi. 8. But in the last day he will find as much satisfaction, and be as much glorified, in your destruction, as in the salvation of his elect.—He now complains, "Thou hast wearied me with thine iniquities;" but then he will say, "Ah! I will ease me of mine adversaries." Isa. i. 24. Seek then to become the sheep of Christ—Beg him to bring you home to his fold, and to feed you in his pleasant pastures.—Then shall we all become one fold under one shepherd, and feed beside the living fountains of water to all eternity.

A SENSE OF WEAKNESS CONDUCIVE TO STRENGTH.

2 Cor. xii. 10. When I am weak, then am I strong.—(S. S.)

THERE are many things in scripture which appear inconsistent and contrary to truth. Christ is represented as God, and yet a man; as the Lord of David, and yet his son; as a lion, and yet a lamb. And, as his persons is thus variously described, so is his work. He is said to heal us by his own stripes, and to give us life by his death. But, however strange such expressions may seem, they contain many important truths. In the same manner the apostle's words, which we have now read, may be thought to imply a contradiction: but they accord with the experience of all God's people, and justly deserve the most attentive consideration.

In discoursing on this paradoxical assertion, we shall *illustrate, confirm,* and *improve* it.

I. ILUSTRATE IT.

A part of David's history will help to elucidate the words before us

When the champion of the Philistines defied, and terified, the whole army of Israel, David, "a stripling," without armor, defensive or offensive, (except a sling and a stone,) went forth against him ; and, though unused to war himself, entered into combat with that experienced and mighty warrior. But the weaker he was in himself, the more confident was he in his God: and instead of being intimidated by the threatening aspect, and, boasting determinations of his adversary, he was as assured of victory, as if he had seen his enemy already under his feet. 1 Sam. xvii. 45—47.

But the context will give the best clue to the apostle's meaning.

St. Paul laboured under a heavy trial, which he calls a thorn in his flesh, ver. 7, 8. Apprehensive that this would counteract his usefulness in the world, he cried most earnestly to the Lord Jesus Christ to remove it from him. But his Lord, not judging it expedient to grant him his request, promised him (what was incomparably b tter) more abundant communications of grace, whereby he should obtain in a more advantageous manner the desire of his soul. Observe the effect—Paul remained as weak as ever; but being persuaded that Christ's power should be the more magnified through his weakness, he was satisfied ; yea, rather, he made *that* a matter of joy and triumph, which had just before been a source of the greatest trouble. He was well assured that, however unable he was in himself either to bear his trials, or to fulfil his duties, he could not but succeed, when his almighty friend was pledged to succour and support him.

The apostle's assertion being equally applicable to all believers, we shall

II. CONFIRM IT.

A sense of weakness necessarily tends to make us strong, inasmuch as it makes us

1. Watchful against temptations,

If we conceive ourselves to be strong, we shall be fearless of temptation; and by exposing ourselves to it, shall be in greater danger of falling: whereas, if we feel our utter weakness, we shall not only pray, "Lead us not into temptation," but shall carefully shun the places, the books, the company, that may ensnare us. Like Joseph, we shall not parly with the tempter, but flee in haste: or, if we cannot flee, we shall oppose our enemy at first; and thus vanquish that, which, if it had time to gather strength, would soon vanquish us.

2. Importunate in prayer,

It is the sick alone who calls for a physician ; they who are strong in their own conceit, will never pray in earnest; but he who feels his need of divine assistance will seek it at a throne of grace. Now if we do not pray for God's aid, we cannot receive it; and therefore in the hour of trial shall surely fail. But, if we pray with importunity and faith, we shall obtain the things we ask for; and consequently shall be upheld, while others fall. It was by this means that Paul obtained strength ; "he prayed to the Lord *thrice:*" the answer vouchsafed to his petition dissipated all his fears, and strengthened him with might in his inner man: and similar means will always be attended with similar success.

3. Dependent on Christ,

In proportion as we fancy ourselves strong, we must of necessity confide in our own strength; the consequence of which may be sufficiently seen in the

247

repeated falls of Peter. But, if we are conscious that we are wholly with-out strength, and can do nothing of ourselves, we shall be more simple and uniform in our dependence on Christ. Now Christ will never suffer those, who trust in him to be confounded. He would consider it as an impeach-ment of his own veracity, if he did not give them "grace sufficient for them:" consequently, we never are so truly strong, as when we are deeply convinced of our own utter impotence.

This truth enters deeply into the experience of all the Lord's people: we shall therefore endeavour to,

III. IMPROVE IT.

Among the various lessons which it teaches us, let us especially learn two,

1. Not to be too much elated on account of any manifestations of the divine favour.

Paul was caught up into the third heavens; but soon afterwards we behold him crying, with much anguish of mind, under a severe affliction. Thus it may soon be with us. Indeed the seasons most distinguished by God's favour to us, are often most distinguished also by Satan's malice. It was immediately after they had received peculiar tokens of God's love, that he assaulted Paul, ver. 4. and Peter, Matt. xvi. 17, 23. and Christ himself. Matt. iii. 17. and iv. 1. Let us then, when most highly favoured, "rejoice with trembling,"Ps. ii. 11. and not while harnessed, boast as if we had put off our armour. 1 Kings xx. 11.

2. Not to be too much dejected on account of our manifold infirmities.

Jacob was lamed by God himself, that he might know he had not pre-vailed by his own strength. Gen. xxxii. 25. And Paul had a thorn in the flesh given him, "lest he should be exalted above measure." Now our in-firmities are very painful: but they are necessary, in order to keep alive in our minds a remembrance of our own weakness and vileness; and if we do but carry them to God in fervent prayer, he will glorify himself by means of them, and "perfect his strength in our weakness." "Let the weak then say, I am strong; Joel iii. 10. let them "be strong in the Lord, and in the power of his might; Eph. vi. 10. and, doubtless, they shall receive that effectual succour, which believers, in all ages, have experienced, Heb. xi. 34. and shall invariably find their "strength according to their day" of trial. Deut. xxxiii. 25.

BENEFITS ARISING FROM GOD'S RETURN TO THE SOUL.

Isai. xxx. 26.—Moreover the light of the moon shall be as the light of the sun, and the light of the sun shall be sevenfold, as the light of seven days, in the day that the Lord bindeth up the breach of his people, and healeth the stroke of their wound. (S. S.)

THE dispensations of providence, if rightly improved, are calculated to promote our spiritual welfare.—The Jews derived many instructive lessons from the dealings of God with them in Egypt and the wilderness.—But God here promises that more abundant knowledge and joy by means of their deliverance from the Assyrian host.* The grandeur, however, of the words

* That this is the literal import of the passage appears from ver. 31. compared with ver 25, 26.

before us evidently shews, that the prophet had respect to blessings, which no temporal deliverance was able to convey.—We shall therefore endeavour to point out some other seasons when this promise receives its fuller accomplishment.

1. AT THE FIRST RECONCILIATION OF THE SOUL TO GOD.

The convictions of an awakened conscience are as deep wounds to the soul.

Sin, though it be honey in the mouth, becomes gall in the stomach—Peter, Judas, and David in particular, shew what "*wounds*" it will make in the soul—Ps. xxxii. 1—6. Nor can any one view it aright, without, having his heart broken with a sense of its malignity—

But reconciliation with God heals these wounds.

The blood of Christ is that "balm of Gilead," which never was applied in vain—Jer. viii. 22. It operates as the sight of the brazen serpent on the dying Israelites, to restore to life and vigour those, whose state seems altogether desperate—John iii. 14, 15. David, after the foulest transgressions declared his persuasion of its efficacy to cleanse even him—Ps. li. 7, 8. And all who are reconciled to God through Christ, experience its full effects—Luke iv. 18. 1 Pet. i. 8.

And this is a season, wherein the knowledge and joy of the soul are much enlarged.

Till this great event is accomplished, the views of the soul are very contracted; nor is it acquainted with any joy but what is carnal.—But no sooner has this taken place, than the light of the knowledge of the glory of God shines into the heart, and all his perfections are admired and adored.—Now also the excellency of the gospel salvation is discovered; and the reasonableness of a life devoted to God is deeply felt.—Now is a new and inexhaustible source of happiness opened to the soul; and its peace and joy flow down like a river.—And all the pleasures that it ever enjoyed in the ways of sin, are no more in comparison of its present consolations, than the faint "light of the moon" to the invigorating rays of the meridian "sun"—

But this promise has a further accomplishment.

II. AT ANY RETURN OF GOD TO THE SOUL AFTER A SEASON OF DARKNESS AND DESERTION.

God finds it necessary sometimes to hide his face from his people, and thus to wound their souls afresh.

How the loss of God's presence afflicts a pious soul, may be seen in the lamentations and complaints, which the most eminent saints have uttered on such occasions. Job tells us, that God's arrows stuck fast in him, and that the poison of them drank up his spirit. Job vi. 4. And David even "roared for the disquietness of his heart." Nor are there wanting at this day many, whose experience accords with the description which that eminent saint has given of his—Ps. xlii. 3, 4, 6, 7, 9.

But the return of God binds up this breach.

The deliverence from such a state is compared by our Lord to the joy that succeeds the pangs of childbirth—1 John xvi. 21. Nor can its effects upon the soul be more fitly represented than in the language of the Jews on their return from Babylon—Ps. cxxvi. 1—3.

And this also is another season of peculiar instruction and comfort.

By this the soul obtains much deeper discoveries of its own corruptions; Job xlii. 5, 6. and more encouraging views of God's power and faithfulness—Isai. xxv. 1, 4. The depths of Satan's device also are more clearly discerned.—And, if its joys are less ecstatic than before, they are more pure and refined—

The full accomplishment of the text will take place,

III. AT THE HOUR OF DISSOLUTION.

God never entirely withholds his chastening rod in this world.

The whole of this life is a state of discipline — — —

But at death there is an end of every thing that is penal, or painful.

Whatever wounds may have pained us here, death will heal them all Rev. xxi. 4.— — —

Then will this promise be fulfilled in its utmost extent.

What amazing discoveries will be made to the soul on its first dismission from the body! And with what inconceivable raptures will it be transported, as soon as ever it shall enter the gates of heaven! Whatever it may have heard of the blessedness of the saints, it will surely say, that not a thousandth part had been declared to it. Then shall those descriptions given by the prophets, all be realized—Isai. lx. 19. 20. Rev. xxi 23. and xxii. 5. As for the joys it experienced below, they shall appear as nothing in comparison of those it will then possess.—What they tasted here, was through the medium of ordinances, and mixed with frequent sorrows, and, at best, of short duration.—But what they possess in heaven, will be immediate, unmixed, and everlasting—

INFER,

1. They, who have never yet been wounded in their souls on account of sin, are yet strangers to all spiritual light and happiness.

They may be conversant with all the depths of philosophy, and all the pleasures of sense.—But the unhumbled and unbelieving soul is yet blinded by Satan, nor has even the glimmering light of the moon with respect to spiritual concerns—2 Cor. iv. 4. and 1 Cor. ii. 14. Let such then beg of God to open the eyes of their understanding ; and let them seek those convictions of sin, whereby they shall be disposed to admit, and to love, the truth—

2. They who feel a wounded spirit, should labour to improve their convictions to the uttermost.

Too many endeavour to silence the accusations of conscience, and to drown its voice in business or pleasure.—But if we knew how ready God is to heal the broken spirit, and what unspeakable benefits would ultimately flow from our convictions, surely we should cherish them with care, and improve them with diligence.—Let us then not " heal our wounds slightly," but go to the blood of Jesus?—Then, " though weeping may endure for a night, joy shall come to us in the morning," even that "joy which is unspeakable and full of glory."

ALL THINGS WORK FOR GOOD TO GOD'S PEOPLE.

Rom. viii. 28.—We know that all things work together for good to them that love God, to them who are the called according to his purpose. (S. S.)

TRUE believers have the greatest encouragement to draw nigh to God—

They have supernatural assistance when pouring out their hearts before him—

And are assured by God himself that their prayers shall be heard—

Yea, sometimes, like the Israelites in Egypt, the more they renew their requests, the more they find their burdens increased—Exod. v. 6—8.

Hence, like them, they are also sometimes ready to murmur and despond—Ib. ver. 20, 21.

But, by grace they are enabled to wait patiently the Lord's leisure—

And invariably, in the issue, the clouds which they so much dreaded, burst in blessings on their heads—

This St. Paul declares to be the experience of all true believers—

His words lead us to shew.

I. THE CHARACTER OF TRUE CHRISTIANS.

Christians are sometimes described in the scriptures by their regard for God, and sometimes by God's regard for them—

The text leads us to speak of them in both points of view,

1. Their regard to God.

The "loving of God" is a character peculiar to true Christians—

Others are represented rather as "haters of God" and enemies to him in their minds—Rom. i. 30. Col. i. 21.

But they, who are partakers of his grace, have their natural enmity removed—

They behold his excellency, and are sensible of their obligations to him—

Hence they love him, and strive to love him with their whole hearts—

2. God's regard for them.

Their regard for him sprang not from any good dispositions in themselves—

It resulted purely from the manifestations of God's love to them—

He formed "purposes" of love to them from all eternity—Jer. xxxi. 3.

In due time he "called" them by his grace, and made them his people—

And this distinguishing favour is the true source of their love to him—

To this effect both our Lord and his beloved apostle testify—John xv. 16. 1 John iv. 19.

To the eternal purposes of God therefore, and not to the inclinations of our carnal minds, all the good that is in us, be traced—

To persons of this description the apostle announces,

II. THEIR PRIVILEGE.

It is under sufferings that the superiority of the Christian's state is to be seen to the greatest advantage—

Of them the apostle speaks; and declares that, of whatever kind they be, they shall work for the good of them that love God.

The Christian may be called to bear the heaviest *afflictions*—

But they shall bring him to consideration, stir him up to prayer, wean him from the world, and lead him to seek his rest above— — —

He may be assaulted also with the most distressing *temptations*—

But these will shew him the evil of his heart, and the faithfulness of his God—

They will also teach him to sympathize with his tempted brethren—

Even *death* itself will be among the number of the things that shall prove beneficial to him—

This is the most formidable enemy to fallen man—

It cuts him off from all means and opportunities of salvation, and seals him up under endless and irremediable misery,—

But to a true Christian it is a most invaluable treasure—1 Cor. iii. 22.

251

It puts a period to all his sorrows and temptations, and introduces him to the immediate, everlasting enjoyment of his God—

Nor need we doubt of this blessed truth.

The apostle speaks of it not as a matter of conjecture, but of certainty—

As he knew it, so may " we know" it, from the declarations and promises of God—Ps. xxv. 10.

Both David and Paul have attested it also from their own experience—Ps. cxix. 71.   Phil. i. 19.

Nor is there any Christian in whom it has not been realized—

It is not however *singly* or *separately* that all things work for good, but as taken "*together*" in a collective view—

Separately considered, many things may have wrought for evil, by producing sinful tempers or actions—

But when viewed as connected with *all* their effects and consequences, the most untoward circumstances will be found to have wrought for good—

This subject naturally suggests,

1. A rule whereby to judge of our election of God—

Our election of God can be known only by its effects, 1 Thes. i. 4, 5.

To ascertain it, we must enquire whether we have been *called* by his grace.

And whether, in consequence of that call, we *love God* supremely?--

If we experience these effects, we may safely conclude, that God has entertained eternal purposes of love towards us.—

But if we trace not these effects, our pretensions to an interest in his electing love is a fatal delusion.—

Let them, in whom these evidences are found, rejoice; but rejoice with trembling.—

2. A ground of consolation for the afflicted.

Afflictions are not at the present joyous, but grievous—

And under them we are ready to say, "All these things are against me"—

But the scripture tells us, "the trial of our faith is precious"—1 Pet. 1. 7

Let the afflicted then consider what "good" may be accruing to them—

Their troubles may be working so as to discover, prevent, punish, or destroy *sin*— — —

Or they may be working to impart, exercise, strengthen, or perfect *grace*— — —

What reason, in either case, have the afflicted to take comfort!—

We think little of inconveniencies if they do but promote our *temporal* interest—

Should we then be averse to any trials that may tend to our *spiritual* advantage ?—

Let us wait to see " the end of the Lord," and be solicitous rather about our future benefit, than our present ease—

3. A strong incentive to love and serve God.

Things are never represented as working for the good of the wicked—

On the contrary, their temporal blessings are often cursed to them—

Yea, even spiritual blessings only aggravate their guilt and condemnation—2 Cor. ii. 16.

Christ himself proves, not a Saviour, but a stumbling-block to them—1 Pet. ii. 7, 8.

But for God's people, all things, sin excepted, work for good—

Should they not then love him for such distinguished mercy ?—

Can they ever do enough for him, who so marvellously overrules all events for them ?

A CONSCIENCE VOID OF OFFENCE.

Acts x .iv. 16.—And herein do I exercise myself, to have always a conscience void of offence, towards God and towards men. (Sk.)

THE Jews charged the apostle Paul with high crimes, and employed Tertullus, an orator, to bring accusations against him before Felix, the governor. Tertullus flattered Felix, and abused Paul; but produced no proof of guilt in the holy apostle. The answer of Paul was manly, correct, and convincing. He had nothing to fear. His conduct had been pious and circumspect; for he had exercised himself "to have always a conscience void of offence both towards God and men."—But what is implied in a conscience void of offence?—And how should we exercise ourselves to have such a conscience;

I. WHAT IS IMPLIED IN A CONSCIENCE VOID OF OFFENCE?

1. *Conscience is the secret testimony of the soul, whereby it approves things that are good, and condemns those that are evil.* A good conscience is purified by the blood of Christ, 1 Tim. i. 5; Heb. ix. 14. An evil conscience is loaded with guilt, Heb. x. 22. And a hardened conscience does not feel the evil of sin, 1 Tim. iv. 2. Conscience has a rule of action; it compares action with that rule, and draws inferences from the comparison.

2. *To have a conscience void of offence, three things are necessary:*—First, a good rule of conduct; secondly, an impartial comparison of our conduct with that rule; and thirdly, a conviction that there has been a conformity of conduct to our rule. In that case, conscience does not charge us with wilful crimes; but assures us of innocence and rectitude. Advocates for sin, whether professors or profane, will not allow that any man has a conscience void of offence, but surely the grace of God is sufficient to keep us from all sin, 1 Cor. xv. 34.

3. *That man who has a conscience void of offence towards God, is inwardly pious, and practises all the duties of piety.* He believes in God, Heb. xi. 6; he fears God, Ps. cxxviii. 1; he loves God, Matt. xxii. 37, 38; he prays to God, Phil. iv. 6; he trusts in God, Isa. xxvi. 4; he praises God, Isa. xii. 1; and he worships God in spirit and in truth, John iv. 24. These are the principal duties of piety; and when we engage in them with true sincerity, we have a conscience void of offence towards God.

4. *He who has a conscience void of offence towards men, carefully follows two rules:*—First, he injures no man, either in his person, in his property, or in his character; and, secondly, he does all the good which is in his power to every man with whom he is connected, both in word and deed. He loves all men, he prays for all, and he is ready to forgive injuries and insults. While he walks humbly with his God, he is careful to do justly to men, and is ever ready to exercise mercy, Mic. vi. 8.

II. HOW SHOULD WE EXERCISE OURSELVES TO HAVE A CONSCIENCE VOID OF OFFENCE?

1. Let us use those means by which we may *obtain an enlightened conscience*, that we may understand our duty both to God and men. To this end carefully examine the word of God, which is the only safe guide of human conduct. Without this blessed book, we fall into error and sin; we dishonor God and injure men: and vainly imagine that we are doing what is fit and right. Thus Saul thought it right to do many things against the church: but he did those things in ignorance and unbelief, Acts xxvi. 9; 1 Tim. i. 13.

2. It should be an invariable rule with us, *to do nothing at any time, or*

under any circumstances, contrary to the dictates of conscience. **When** we act contrary to our views of things, we are self-condemned. If the conscience be not sufficiently enlightened, we should not venture to act against its warnings. Every one should be persuaded in his own mind that what he does is right; for if this be not the case, he cannot be guiltless before the Judge of all the earth. Whatsoever men do, without a conviction of its lawfulness, is sin to them; for whatsoever is not of faith is of sin, Romans xiv. 22, 23.

3. In this holy exercise we should *abstain from the appearance of evil;* for if we yield to any thing which our own mind condemns, or to any thing which appears evil in the eyes of wise and good men, we shall soon fall into great and gross sins, 1 Thess. v. 22. For this reason we should steadily follow what we deem to be right, even in *little things;* and scrupulously avoid evil of every kind and degree. If this rule be constantly followed, we shall seldom deviate from the path of duty.

4. That we may keep a conscience void of offence, let us *be careful not to enter into temptation.* We may be tempted to evil without our own consent, and without sin; but if we enter into it, we become guilty before God. We should resist the first attack of an enemy. Temptation when first presented to the mind is generally weak, and we are strong; but its strength increases and ours diminishes, when we enter into it. For this reason we should not enter into it at all, lest we be overcome in an evil hour, Matt. xxvi. 41.

5. As a farther help in this important work, *let us be vigilant.* We are surrounded by enemies, who are ready to seize every favorable moment to draw us from our duty. Let us look out for them, that we may not be taken by surprise. Watch against all evil, whether inward or outward; watch for opportunities of doing good: and watch for the coming of Jesus to judge the world. The admonition of our Lord will never be out of season, "What I say unto you, I say unto all, Watch," Mark xiv. 37.

6. To watchfulness let us add *prayer.* Let us pray for wisdom to conduct us safely through difficult circumstances, James i. 5. Let us pray for courage and strength, that we may be able to overcome all evil; and for that comfort and consolation which may be necessary for us in our trials and temptations. He who is always in the spirit of prayer, cannot live in any known sin; and for this reason, let us "pray without ceasing," 1 Thess v. 17.

7. It is essentially necessary, in this blessed exercise, to *avoid secret sins.* These are fully known to God, Ps. xc. 8. He will bring them into judgment, Eccles. xii. 14. Secret sins lead to open wickedness; and he who sins in the dark will soon transgress in open day. No man who lives in secret sin, whatever his pretensions are, has a conscience void of offence And his sin, though artfully concealed from men, will be sure to find him out, Num. xxxii. 23.

8. While we *set God before us,* in his justice and purity, and in his awful majesty and glory, we shall be careful to keep a conscience void of offence. This is our duty, and our privilege, Gen. xvii. 1; Ps. xvi. 8. His eyes are constantly upon us, and he hates all evil. Our love to him produces a hatred of evil; and if our love be without dissimulation, we shall abhor and detest it, Ps. cxvii. 10; Rom. xii. 9.

9. Let us *be conversant with death and judgment.* These are solemn subjects; they should occupy our thoughts in the morning when we awake; throughout the day, when we are engaged in business; and in the evening,

when we retire to rest. While this is the case we shall be careful neither to offend God nor to injure man.

10. And lastly, *we should exercise ourselves daily in meditations on the happiness of heaven, and the torments of hell.* There is a heaven of light and glory for good men; and there is a hell of darkness and shame for the wicked, Rev. xxi 23; Ps. ix. 17. He who has a good conscience, is an heir of immortal blessedness; but he whose conscience is loaded with guilt, is an heir of death and hell, Rom. vi. 23. Serious reflections on these subjects will keep us from sin.

INFERENCES.

1. While we keep a conscience void of offence, *we enjoy the approbation of God,* and are happy in his love, Ps. xi. 7.

2. When this is the case, *our minds are at rest,* and we enjoy that peace which passeth all understanding, Phil. iv. 7.

3. This takes away the *fear of man.* which brings a snare to the soul, and enables us to look every one in the face without a blush of guilt.

4. And while the conscience is void of offence *we are holy, happy and useful,* and all things go well with us both for time and eternity, Isa. iii. 10. May we all enjoy this invaluable blessing, through Jesus Christ our Lord, Amen.

THE EXCELLENCY OF UNION.

Psalm cxxxiii. 1.—Behold, how good and how pleasant it is for brethren to dwell together in unity. (Sk.)

AMONGST the numerous excellencies which are connected with true religion, the delightful union of which it is productive holds a very distinguished place. Through the influence of religion, men whose condition in life, disposition of mind, mode of education, and regular habitudes, have been not only widely different, but also directly opposed to each other; have become so closely united, that even Heathenism, with all its inveterate opposition to revealed truth, has been constrained to attest, "See how these christians love!" And this interesting union has not been confined to the christian dispensation, but was manifestly a striking feature in the piety of rural and patriarchal times; and it also constituted a distinguished excellency in the Jewish church. David bears testimony to its existence in his day, exclaiming in the spirit of admiration, "Behold how good and how pleasant it is," &c. It is very probable that this psalm was composed on the termination of that civil war, which had so long prevailed between the two houses of Saul and David: yet this language may very properly be applied, in reference to the harmony of religious societies or christian churches. In thus using this portion of Scripture we shall,

I. DEFINE THE NATURE OF SCRIPTURAL UNION.

II. ASSERT ITS TRANSCENDENT EXCELLENCE. And,

III. SPECIFY THE MEANS OF ITS PROMOTION.

I. DEFINE THE NATURE OF SCRIPTURAL UNION. This union may be considered as including—*Sentiment—Affection—Design—and Operation.*

1. *A oneness of sentiment.* Whilst the different denominations of chris-tians, in consequence of their early associations and impressions having been widely different, entertain notions contrary to each other on various subjects of minor importance, yet on the grand essential truths of christi-anity they are one. The fall, and consequent depravity of man; the divin-ity and atonement of Christ, the necessity and reality of the operations of the Holy Ghost, and justification by faith alone, are doctrines which form a kind of central point, at which the christian tribes meet, and sing,

> " Let names, and sects, and parties fall
> And Jesus Christ be all in all."

This is manifest by their writings, their public ministrations, and their union of defence when these truths are assailed.

2. *A union in point of affection.* All those who are the "children of God by faith," maintaining the same common principles, influenced by the same powerful motives, participating the same spiritual enjoyments, and bear-ing the same divine image, are the subjects of a mutual and tender affection, which expresses itself by various acts of kindness; such as administering to each other's necessities, steadily watching over each other's interests, studi-ously labouring to promote each other's happiness, and patiently bearing with each other's infirmities, Rom. xii. 5—10; Heb. vi. 10; 1 Pet. i. 22; Gal. vi. 2; Heb. x. 32—34; 1 John iii. 16, 17.

3. *A sameness of principle, and a union of heart, are very naturally productive of a similarity of design.* And Christians generally, and with steady uniformity, purpose to secure their own final salvation—to endeavour instrumentally, to effect the salvation of their friends and neighbours—to extend the kingdom of the Redeemer in the earth, having for their ultimate object the glory of God, Acts xxiv, 16; Rom. x. 1, xiv. 7, 8; 1 Cor. x. 31.

4. *Operation.* In this distinguished age of light and glory, the followers of Christ generally agree to merge their little differences on minor points of faith, in a unity of effort, to accomplish the grand object of their mutual pur-pose. If we turn our attention to school institutions, to Bible societies, and to Missionary establishments, we shall delightfully behold christians of all denominations rallying round the common standard, and marching on to cer-tain conquest.

II. Assert its transcendent excellence. There are many things which are very good, but not pleasant; while other things, which, to the vitiated inclinations of a depraved heart, appear delightful, are in reality injurious and destructive; but scriptural union is both "good and pleasant." This will appear, if we consider,

1. *Its moral fitness.* The union of the christian church is in exact agree-ment with the nature and perfections of God, John iii. 16; 1 John iv 8—10. Correspondent with the great designs of mercy in the gospel of Christ, Eph. ii. 13; Col. i. 20—22. And strictly congruent with the harmony of the heavenly world, Rev. vii. 9—17.

2. *Its pleasing appearance.* Whilst discord and hostility offend the eye, and pain the heart of the thoughtful observer, union, of whatever descrip-tion, tends to excite the most pleasurable sensations in the breast: but this is more especially the case when tranquillity pervades a religious society. When materials originally so discordant are brought into a state of delightful harmony, the scene is highly pleasing, and produces admiration, excites lively joy, and elicits sentiments of gratitude. The Psalmist felt the influ-

ence of such a scene, and made use of the most odoriferous compound, as a figure by which to describe the effect which was produced upon his mind.

3. *Its beneficial influence.* Union ever tends to augment the happiness of its possessor,—to recommend divine truth to mankind,—to extend the kingdom of Christ in the earth,—and to give strength and stability to the christian course, Rom. xvi. 16, 19 ; 2 Cor. xiii. 11.

III. SPECIFY THE MEANS OF ITS PROMOTION. In promoting christian union there are,

1. *Some things to be avoided.* If we would have peace in our own bosoms, and live in peace with our christian brethren, we must steadily avoid a spirit of evil surmising: and guard against hard and uncharitable thoughts, in reference to our fellow professors, resolutely resisting every inclination to evil speaking and detraction. If we indulge thoughts which are inconsistent with that "charity" which "thinketh no evil," we shall involve ourselves in condemnation, and be in the way of speaking those words, and performing those actions, which will prove destructive to the union and happiness of the church, Eph. L 1, 2, iv, 26, 27, 31 ; James iii. 13—18, iv, 11. In order to preserve christian harmony.

2. *There are some things to be performed.* As we are regularly dependant upon God for strength and support, it is of the utmost importance that we maintain constant communion with him by fervent prayer ; also that we uniformly regulate our conduct and conversation by that infallible directory which infinite wisdom has furnished, making the sacred Scripture our constant guide at all times ; steadily and conscientiously using every means which has a tendency to unite us more closely to our christian brethren. Finally, above all, let us labour to " grow in grace, and in the knowledge and love of God," so shall we be preserved from every evil, and regularly demonstrate " how good and how pleasant it is for brethren to dwell together in unity." This subject,

1. Excites to close and serious self-examination.

2. Teaches us that discord in religious societies impedes the progress of the gospel.

3. Describes a line of conduct for us in the future part of life.

EARLY PIETY EXEMPLIFIED IN JOSIAH.

2 Chronicles xxxiv. 3.—While he was yet young, he began to seek after the God of David his father. (Sk.)

IT was the observation of an inspired apostle, that " not many wise men after the flesh, not many mighty, not many noble, are called." God's people have generally been an afflicted and a poor people " the poor have the gospel preached to them," and " God hath chosen the poor in this world, to be rich in faith and heirs of the kingdom which he hath promised unto them that love him." But the individual exhibited to our view in the text, was differently circumstanced. He was a king, and sat upon a throne, and reigned over a great people ; and though many acts of his life are inimitable by us, yet in the view in which the text represents him, he is eminently worthy the attention of the junior part of my congregation. We will therefore notice three things,

I. The object after whom Josiah sought;—"The God of David his father."

II. The manner how he sought after that object; which will be seen by referring to this chapter.

III. The period of life when he did it:—"While he was yet young," &c.

I. The object after whom Josiah sought. Josiah sought after the God of David his father. Josiah lived four hundred years subsequently to David, but being David's remote descendant he is considered as his son. Also, when one person imitates another, by a familiar mode of speech, he is represented as his son. Abraham was the father of the faithful. "Ye are of your father the devil, because his works ye do." Josiah imitated David, see ver. 2. God was David's God

1. *God was David's teacher.* David was a man of extensive information, his knowledge was various; he knew much of God and his works; much of men and things; but he was indebted to God for his instruction. "The Lord is my delight," &c. Ps. xxvii. 1. "Thou through thy commandments hast made me wiser than mine enemies." "I will thank thee, O Lord, who hast given me counsel." David's soul was dark and ignorant by nature, but God instructed and taught him great things out of his law.

2. *God was David's comfort.* He was involved at times in great trouble; he had tasted the wormwood and the gall; the waves and billows had gone over him; he had experienced personal, family, and national trouble. But he had applied unto God, and was enabled to say, "In the multitude of my thoughts within me, thy comforts delight my soul." "Bless the Lord, O my soul," &c. Psa. ciii. 1, 2.

3. *God was David's delight.* David seemed totally at a loss to express the ardency of his attachment unto God. "O God thou art my God," &c. Psa. lxiii. 1. "As the hart panteth after the water brooks," &c. Psa. xlii. 1, 2. When deprived of the public ordinances of religion, he appeared even to envy the sparrows who made their nests near unto the house of the Lord, Ps. lxxxiv. 3.

4. *God was David's defence.* David had many enemies; they who hated him, he said, "were more than the hairs of his head." "But the Lord," said he, "is my rock, and my fortress, and my deliverer," &c. "When I cry unto thee then shall mine enemies turn back,"&c. Thus, Jehovah was the God of David, and after him Josiah sought; but let us describe,

II. The manner how he sought after God. Information on this subject we collect by perusing his history.

1. *He sought God from a deep conviction that his conduct, and the conduct of Israel generally, was highly offensive to God, and that they were exposed to imminent peril.* For in his reign, while they were repairing the temple, they found a copy of the book of the law, and by reading that, and comparing their conduct with it, they saw the criminality of their lives; and that wrath was ready to come upon them. Let us read our Bibles, and compare ourselves with the records of revelation.

2. *He sought God in deep self-abasement of soul.* When he heard the book of the law read, he rent his clothes, and wept, see ver. 19, 27. Humility best becomes those who seek the Lord; a view of our sins, a consciousness of danger, a consideration of the majesty and glory of God, all should tend to humble us.

He sought God by destroying the idols out of the land. Manasseh the grandfather of Josiah had reared up altars for Balaam, made groves, and worshipped the hosts of heaven. And Amon his father, had worshipped the carved image which Manasseh had made; but Josiah purged the land from idols, ver. 3, 4. Here we cannot exactly imitate him, but we should purge our hearts from idols: every human being is addicted to idolatry, to love the creature rather than the Creator; but God will have no rival, he will not give his glory to another.

3. *He sought God by restoring his true worship, and frequenting it.* The house of God had been neglected and forsaken, but Josiah got workmen, and builders, and artificers in great numbers, and they repaired the temple; and Josiah restored the passover, and the people celebrated it, "so that there had been nothing like it since the days of Samuel, neither did any of the kings of Israel keep such a passover as Josiah kept." Here too our conduct must necessarily vary a little from that of Josiah's; but those who would seek God, should frequent his public ordinances. These we have in abundance.

4. *He sought God with all his heart:*—"For like him, there was no king before him that turned to the Lord with all his heart, and with all his soul," &c. 2 Kings xxiii. 25 Here we must fully imitate Josiah; God demands our hearts, our whole hearts, and we must turn to him heartily, and in the most unreserved and decided manner.

III. THE PERIOD OF LIFE WHEN HE DID IT:—"While he was yet young," &c. "He was eight years old when he began to reign; and he reigned eight years, and then he began to "seek," &c. We should seek God while we are yet young, because,

1. *God is the best object whom we can seek.* "All nations before him are as nothing; and they are counted to him less than nothing and vanity." To whom then will you liken God? Examine all the objects which men are accustomed to seek after, and say which of those objects can be compared with the Lord?

2. *Youth is the best time for seeking God.* It is the *most acceptable* time with God, "I love them that love me, and those that seek me early shall find me." It is the *most pleasant* time with us. The yoke of Christ is then peculiarly easy, and his burden more than ordinarily light. How hard and difficult it is for old sinners to seek God! It is the only certain time we can command. How few live to see old age. "Man that is born of woman is of few days and full of trouble:" thousands die daily,—life is but "vapour that appeareth for a little time and then vanisheth away." Let me then persuade you, young people, to imitate Josiah. Reflect on the advantages attendant on such a mode of conduct. *There are personal advantages;* seek God, and you will find him,—seek God, and you will live. *There are relative advantages;* Josia's conduct stimulated others to seek God, and perhaps thousands and tens of thousands were benefited by his example. We cannot promise ourselves such extensive usefulness, but we may all be useful in a greater or less degree. How many of you, young people would gladden your parents by seeking the Lord! How useful might you be to your juvenile companion! But many young persons perceive no necessity for seeking the Lord; but this necessity exists, whether you see it or not. Oh! how awfully are you deceived! Others attach a degree of meanness to this exercise. To such we say, look at Joseph, Samuel, Solomon, Abijah, Daniel, Timothy, &c. But some have suffered the morning of their lives to pass away without seeking God: to such we address a word of exhortation, reproof, and encouragement.

YOUTHFUL PIETY.

Jer. ii. 2, 3.—Go, and cry in the ears of Jerusalem, saying, Thus saith the Lord, I remember thee, the kindness of thy youth, the love of thine espousals, when thou wentest after me in the wilderness, in a land that was not sown. Israel was holiness to the Lord, and the first fruits of his increase. (P.)

Now, in order that we may have our minds duly affected with the subject, it will be necessary,

I. To CONSIDER THE RICH AND GLOWING DESCRIPTION OF YOUTHFUL PIETY WHICH IS HERE GIVEN.

It is figurative language; but the figure is formed from reality, and Israel devoted to the God of Abraham is what the prophet intended to describe. And what is it in reference to youthful piety which God remembers?

1. *Its ardent affection;* "I remember the kindness of thy youth;" the glow of strong feeling which characterized thee. Young people feel greatly that which occupies their attention: the religion of the young is seldom the cold philosophic speculation or experience of age.

2. That the deep interest which you felt in religion was apparent in *a union of the soul to Christ.* "I remember the love of thine espousals." The Redeemer won you by his love; you felt the bond, and devoted yourselves to the Saviour.

3. Character of youthful piety; *it is a going after God.* "When thou wentest after me," &c. Your religion was not an invention of your own; it was not some worldly plan. It was the religion of the Scripture; it was clothed with an authoritative, "Thus saith the Lord."

4. Acceptable youthful religion is *not discouraged by difficulties and troubles.* When was it that Israel went after the Lord? "In the wilderness, in a land that was not sown." When there were no corn fields to gladden the eyes, and no water to quench the thirst; when they had nothing to live upon but the word, and presence, and Spirit of God. True religion is not that of fashion and custom, but that which God requires.

5. *The religion of an accepted youth is a religion of holiness.* Holiness is the character which he adopts, the atmosphere in which he breathes. "Israel was holiness unto the Lord."

Such is a brief description of the early piety which God delights to view in young people who are called by his name. I hasten

II. To NOTICE THE ASPECT WHICH THE DIVINE REMEMBRANCE OF YOUTHFUL PIETY MAY HAVE ON DIFFERENT CIRCUMSTANCES OF LIFE.

You may forget it, but HE never does. Your book of remembrance may be reduced to ashes, but his book remains, and every character in it is indelible. Two views may be taken of this remembrance.

1. *A view of approbation.* What a delightful view of early religion is this, that it is remembered with approbation! "I remember thee!"—And when is it that almighty God remembers with approbation and pleasure these traces of early piety?

When you are successfully struggling with the temptations of the world. I know that youth are exposed to strong temptations; but when you are struggling hard to maintain that integrity of character of which the world aims to deprive you; when you cultivate tempers which make you a derision to those around you; when you renounce pleasure rather than displease God; when you hold fast the beginning of your confidence steadfast unto the end, however it may be assailed and shaken: then God is well pleased.

and he says, "I remember thee, the kindness of thy youth," &c. Your early religion was not in vain; the impressions made in youth accompany you in your course of duty, and you still walk humbly with your God.

When you act under their influence in promoting the cause of truth and holiness. A pious youth is seldom slothful. Let a plan of usefulness be proposed, and who shall engage in it?—the young. They may not have all the means and all the prudence of the more aged, but theirs is the activity.

When its possessors are sunk into deep affliction. When laid on beds of sickness, and the world seems to be receding, O what delightful support do they then derive from the kindness of their youth, and the love of their espousals! And when they meet with disappointments in life; when difficulties rise in their path, and they know not which way to turn, what a satisfaction to think on the way in which they have walked before God!

When young people come to be old people. This will be the case if God permit; and I earnestly wish it may be so with those whom I address. Then, the remembrance of youthful piety taken by the blessed God, sheds a richer and a calmer satisfaction over the mind of the aged disciple, than anything else in the world can possibly yield.—And, finally,

In a dying hour. I need not carry the thought beyond this point. And tell me, which will afford greatest pleasure to the mind; that the Father of spirits has been loved and honored, or that he has been forsaken? Then, oh then it is he says with tenderest compassion, "I remember thee, the kindness of thy youth, &c.; and I will put under thee the everlasting arms, and will become thy portion for ever."

But this is the favorable side of the subject; and I should be unjust to my subject, and to the consciences of my hearers, if I were to leave it here. For the remembrance of youthful piety taken by God, may be

2. *A remembrance of regret and displeasure.* We are allowed to speak of the great God after the manner of men. He may act as though this were the language of his heart. I am afraid it is not necessary to go into the land of imagination, or to go beyond mournful facts, to demonstrate that many young persons, who appeared to be decidedly religious, have awfully sunk away. Some have gone into immoralities of the most flagrant character: others have become the disciples of a flimsy infidelity; and others who have not gone such lengths, have yet sunk down from the heights of piety into worldly conformity. Surely, I need not stay to *prove* this! Many of you can think of circumstances which prove all these particulars: you can remember one and another of your friends, dear to you as brothers and sisters, who have gone astray from the right path. Now, the truth is, God remembers these as much as he remembers the others; and it was to those in such a state that the words of the text were intended to be addressed. God is displeased, whether we think of it or not. That young man may have hardened himself in forgetfulness and sin, but let him know that God has it written in his book, that that young man is gone astray from his first principles. God is displeased; and very few who admit the being of a God, could bear in a solitary moment, or on the bed of sickness, or on the borders of the grave, to think of God's being displeased with them, without the deepest awe!

Let it be observed that the *day of divine desertion is not come.* You may have left God, but he has not left you. He has devised many means to bring you back. Sometimes he chastens your bodies with pain on the bed of sickness; at another time he plants difficulties around you which you cannot get through; sometimes he drives you to read your bibles; sometimes he brings you to hear a plain address like the present, when you are led to imagine that the preacher knows you intimately, and is describing your individual case. But if warnings be slighted, if providences be overlooked, if all means employed are in vain, if the youth determinately goes on to perdition;—the end will be dreadful indeed!—Such an end as will lead him to "mourn at the last, and to say, How have I hated instruction, and my heart despised reproof!" And to say it when "the harvest is past, when the summer is ended, and you are not saved!"

Such is the subject;—it is part pleasing and part painful—You may set the one against the other.

And now, there are various characters present whom I must address. Some here may say "The preacher has told my story, he has described me." O cannot some of you say "Wisdom's ways are ways of pleasantness, and her paths are paths of peace?" If so, go on your way rejoicing.

And cannot others say, and does not conscience oblige you to say, "We began with as good prospects as any around us, but the world beguiled us, and led us to our ruin!"—No, not to your ruin, if now you are wise enough to perceive your mistake, and apply to the only remedy.

And are there not some *thoughtless* ones here who will not properly apply to themselves what has been said? But, why not? What! my young friends, are you living among the professors of religion, and have *you* not devoted yourselves to God? Is there no kindness of youth, no going out after him, no following him, through the wilderness, no consecrated holiness, no first fruits? O, let me urge you to seek the Lord; and to seek him *now*, or it may be too late. Death is at the door;—the Judge is at the door, and you may be removed to judgment! O, why will you not accept the blessings of the gospel, and apply to that Saviour who would not reject you!

And now, *religious* young persons, I *congratulate* you; but I must also *warn* you. If you think yourselves secure, you are in more danger than others. Study your way; study your own hearts; study the religion of scripture. Be warned,—be animated,—be encouraged,—be faithful unto death.

There are some here who are in the *very bloom of life*, who can scarcely have had such feelings as have been described. O be persuaded now to come to Christ. He loves little children; he says, "Suffer little children to come unto me, and forbid them not.', He "gathers the lambs in his arms, and carries them in his bosom;" and the sooner you devote yourselves to him, the more likely are you to escape temptations. None are too young to die :—none are too young to live to Him in whose hands are "the keys of death and hell."

Look forward to the judgment of the final day. The book of remembrance will then be opened, and each will be judged according to what is written in that book. He that is ready for death, is ready for judgement, which will follow death.

Finally, let me entreat young and old;—and let the impression sink deep into my own heart;—to "give all dilligence that we may be found of Him in peace, without spot and blameless." And to Him be praise and glory for ever and ever, *amen and amen!*

GENUINE RELIGION ILLUSTRATED.

2 Thessalonians i. 11, 12.—Wherefore also we pray always for you, that our God would count you worthy of this calling, and fulfil all the good pleasure of his goodness, and the work of faith with power: that the name of our Lord Jesus Christ may be glorified in you, and ye in him, according to the grace of our God and the Lord Jesus Christ. (Sk.)

THE passions are the chief springs of that activity which every where appears. Of these, hope and fear, as they awaken desire, or produce concern, and in either case create uneasiness, are among the principal causes which determine our various pursuits. But no subjects appear so calculated to excite those passions, as the joyful or awful prospects the gospel opens to our view. Do worldly enjoyments charm us? How much more inviting, " an inheritance incorruptible," &c; angelic company, "fulness of joy, and pleasures for evermore." Do earthly things alarm us? The day approaches when we shall see "A God in grandeur, and a world on fire." "For the Lord Jesus shall be revealed," &c, ver. 7—10. In reference to this revelation, and its important issues, the apostle says, "Wherefore also we pray," &c, in which he seems to direct our attention to pure religion, in its nature,—source,—producing and sustaining principle,—end,—and measure.

I. RELIGION IN ITS NATURE ;—a *worthiness.* "That our God would count you *worthy of this calling,*"—of the glorification mentioned, ver. 10. While we should carefully guard against self righteousness, we should be equally watchful against an opposite error, which, under the guise of humility, would lead us to abolish some of the most essential distinctions between the sinner and the saint; and should testify with the apostles, 2 Cor. v. 14—17; Eph. ii. 1. 10; 1 Thess. ii. 11, 12; 1 John iii. 9. Agreeably to these declarations is the character in ver. 10. *"His saints"* in whom he shall be glorified. This expresses,

1. *Their previous worthiness of condition.* They are in this life *sanctified ones :* that is, set apart from *common* uses, from worldliness as well as wickedness, to *sacred* service, 1 Peter ii. 9; Heb. xiii. 15; Rom. xii. 1; 1 Cor. x. 31. Nay they are children, heirs of God, &c, Gal. iv. 4—7. And having been thus honourably related, and so consistently employed, they are counted worthy to be approved and exalted, Matthew xxv. 23, 34—36, 40. And it expresses,

2. *Their previous worthiness of disposition;* their aptitude or meetness for glory. The word saint, (from *sanctus,*) means chaste, divine, heavenly, as well as sacred. Such the qualities of genuine christianity. 'Tis the circumcision *of the heart,* Rom. ii. 29; a transformation by the *renewing of the mind,* Rom. xii. 2; Eph. iv. 23; a participation of *the divine nature,* 2 Pet. i. 4. In *itself* pure and peaceable, James iii, 17; in *its operations* godly and benevolent, Phil. iii. 3; James i. 27. Contrast this with the *vileness* of sin, and with the inherent *worthlessness* of forms, creeds, &c.

II. RELIGION IN ITS SOURCE ; *the goodness of God;* his free, spontaneous favour. "That he would fulfil *all the good pleasure of his goodness.*"

1. Here is an intimation that all their present religious views and feelings were the effects of divine grace. Hence the apostle prays, that God would count, or make, them worthy (Whitby, Doddridge, and A. Clarke,) of his kingdom, ver. 5, by *fulfilling* what he had begun.

2. That all is of grace will appear, if we contemplate man, as existing only in *the intention of his Maker,* or as really existing in his *state of in-*

nocence. Neither innocent man, nor innocent angel can have any *rightful claim*, on even a continuance of being. But,

3. Still less, if possible, has *fallen*, *sinful* man any good thing as matter of right. 'Tis of mercy that we are not in hell: Yet,

4. 'Tis "our Father's good pleasure" that we should *get religion*, Prov. iv. 7; Isa. lv. 1—3; Matt. vii. 7—11;—that we should *keep religion*, 1 Thess. v. 21; 1 Tim. i. 19; Rev. ii. 25, iii. 11;—that we should *improve in religion*, 2 Pet. i. 5—8, iii. 18;—and that we should *continue to improve*, 2 Cor. iv. 18; Eph. iii. 18, 19. Thus is fulfilled, or completed his 'pleasure,"which is "good,"—in its *author, operation, end*, 2 Cor. iv. 17. This doctrine hides pride from man. "Salvation is of the Lord."

III. Religion in its principle;—*faith.* "The work *of faith* with power." By faith here, we may understand the grace of faith, Heb. xi. 1; exercised on the word of faith, Gal. i. 23. This is,

1. *The producing principle* of religious affections and practice, Heb. xi. 6. It is such credence given to God's declarations, as determines the judgment and heart; and leads the subject of it to fear what is threatened, Heb. xi. 7;—to do what is commanded, Heb. xi. 8. 17;—and to expect, seek, embrace, what is promised, Heb. xi. 13, 19; Eph. ii. 8.

2. *The sustaining principle* of religious affections, &c. It sustains under threats and sufferings, Heb. xi. 35—39. It sustains against the smiles and allurements of the world, Gen. xxxix. 9; Heb. xi. 24—26. It "worketh by *love*," Gal. v. 6; 1 John iv. 19;—by *peace* and *joy*, Rom. v. 1, 2;—by *patience, hope,* &c, Rom. v. 3—5. In short, it attaches the heart to Him who is the" author and finisher of faith;" and at times wafts the soul to the upper regions, were it breathes a purer air, dwells amidst brighter prospects, and hears the hallelujahs of the blessed: so that its return to earth is felt as a return to pilgrimage and banishment, which the same faith, nevertheless, enables it patiently to bear, Heb. x. 35—39.

IV. Religion in its end;—" That the name of our Lord Jesus Christ may be glorified in you and ye in (or by) him." The end is twofold:

1. *The glory of the Redeemer:*—"glorified *in you.*" *At present:* his *love* appears glorious in his interesting himself about you;—his *wisdom* in in instructing you;—his *holiness* in making you saints:—his *power* in preserving and protecting you;—his *faithfulness* in fulfilling all his engagements, &c. This also refers to *hereafter.* "when he shall come to be glorified in his saints," &c. verse 10. "He shall change our vile body, like unto his glorious body," &c. Phil. iii. 19, 20. The saints shall shine, *by reflecting* his radiance, and thus bring glory to his name.

2. *The glory of the redeemed:*—"and ye in him." This may apply to, 1. The glorified bodies they shall receive. 2. The glorious perfection of their minds; freed from all ignorance, error, and moral taint. 3. The glorious distinction with which they shall be favoured, Col. iii. 4. And, 4. The glorious company and mansions to which they shall be raised, Heb. xii. 22, 23; Rev. iii. 21. And it should be remarked, that the glory which they have through him, and that whereby he is glorified in them is glory derived from him, or resulting to him *in his character of Redeemer*, as the representative of the triune Deity. This the redeemed feel and acknowledge; hence their praises of both him that sitteth. upon the throne and the Lamb, Rev. iv. 8—11, v. 11—14. This is certainly very much for us poor, sinful, wretched, dying worms to expect. But consider,

V. Religion in its measure or rule of dispensation;—"according to the grace of our God, and the Lord Jesus Christ." This exactly and fully meets your case. For,

1. Are you *poor, insolvent, destitute of good?* It is "according to" the *freeness* of "the grace of God," &c. Luke vii, 42; Titus iii. 3—7.

2. Are you *guilty* and *vile?* It is "according to the" *riches* of "the grace," &c. Eph. i. 6, ii. 4—7. See "*the grace of our God,*" John iii. 16; "*the grace of the Lord Jesus Christ,*" 2 Cor. viii. 9; Eph. v. 2. Nothing farther could be given. God's thoughts are not as ours, &c. Rom. v. 6—12.

3. Are you *weak* and *ignorant?* It is "according to" the *tenderness,* the *sufficiency,* and *constancy* of "the grace," &c. Isa. xl. 11; 2 Cor. xii. 9; Heb iv. 15, 16.

4. Are you *still doubtful and distressed?* It is "according to" *the former operations* of the same rich "grace;" in the cases of David, Manasseh, Paul, and others, who "had *much* forgiven," and were greatly blessed.

Careless sinner,—how will you meet that awful revelation? verse 7—9.

Formalists,—remember that you have to do with him "who trieth the reins and the heart." Unless the heart be renewed, he will not "account you worthy" of his unsuffering spiritual kingdom.

Penitents,—press into the enjoyment of happy piety. Grace is given you, and "he giveth more grace."

Believers,—be thankful, and expect a farther and more powerful "work of faith;" till "*all the good pleasure*" of divine goodness be fulfilled in you. Jude 24, 25.

THE FAITH AND HOPE OF JOB IN HIS REDEEMER.

Job xix. 25—27.—For I know that my Redeemer liveth, and that he shall stand at the latter day upon the earth: and though after my skin worms destroy this body, yet in my flesh shall I see God: whom I shall see for myself, and mine eyes shall behold, and not another; though my reins be consumed within me. (Sk.)

THIS celebrated text has been variously interpreted. While some, without any solid proof, have considered it as an interpolation, others have limited its meaning to the return of temporal felicity to Job; but if we carefully examine the preceding chapters, it will appear that he had no hope of deliverance from his calamitous circumstances, in the present world. Yet, while he was weighed down by a heavy load of afflictions, and misrepresented by his mistaken friends, he looked forward to the coming of his Redeemer; and had a comfortable assurance that he would avenge his wrongs, raise him from the dead, and bless him with the beatific vision. First, Job had a living Redeemer; secondly, he thought his afflictions would terminate in death; but, thirdly, he had a joyful hope of a happy resurrection from the dead.

1. JOB HAD A LIVING REDEEMER.

1. *The work of a redeemer is great and highly important.* First, *he pays a price* for the lost possession of his brother: "If thy brother be waxen poor, and hath sold away some of his possessions, and if any of his kin come to redeem it, then shall he redeem that which his brother sold," Lev. xxv. 25. Secondly, he saves and delivers him: "He saved them from the hand of him that hated them, and redeemed them from the hand of the ene-

my," Psa. c/i. 10. Thirdly he vindicates and avenges his brother: "**The** revenger of blood himself shall slay the murderer," Num. xxxv. 19.

2. *Christ is the Redeemer of men.* He bought us with his blood. We " were not redeemed with corruptible things as silver and gold, but with the precious blood of Christ, as a Lamb without blemish and without spot," 1 Pet. i. 19. He saves and delivers his people from the guilt and power, and from the pollution and punishment of sin. He " gave himself for us, that he might redeem us from all iniquity, and purify unto himself a peculiar people, zealous of good works," Tit. ii. 14. And he will vindicate and avenge his church: in allusion to this he says, "The day of vengeance is in mine heart, and the year of my redeemed is come," Isa. lxiii. 4.

3. *The Son of God, our great Redeemer, was living in the days of Job;* and he had a saving interest in him, in the afflictions which he suffered, from the devil and from men. He says, " My Redeemer liveth." If our Lord had no existence prior to his incarnation, Job should have spoken in the future tense, saying, " I know that my Redeemer shall live ;" but he spake correctly, for his Redeemer was then living. He had glory with the Father " before the world was," John xvii. 5. He was rich in a prior state of existence, yet for our sakes " he became poor," 2 Cor. viii. 9. He was the only begotten Son of the Father, John iii. 16.

4. *But how does it appear that the Redeemer of Job was the Son of God?* From these words, " he shall stand at the latter day upon the earth." This could not be affirmed of any *goel,* or kinsman of Job, who was then living; but the prediction, if applied to Jesus, is exceedingly appropriate. It was in *part* fulfilled when he appeared in our nature; for " when the fulness of time was come, God sent forth his Son, made of a woman, made under the law,," Gal. iv. 4. But it will be *completely* fulfilled when he arises in judgment; for the words may be rendered, *" he shall arise"* from his seat, and stand upon his feet, as a judge, to give sentence or to execute judgment. This was the posture in which judges always delivered their sentence; and hence we frequently read, in the Scriptures, of God arising to judgment, Job xxxi. 14; Psa. lxxiv. 22, lxxxii. 8.

5. *Job knew his divine Redeemer.* But how did he attain that knowledge? It might be by tradition. God had promised a Saviour and deliverer, and that promise was handed down from one generation to another. Besides, the promise which was given to Abraham, " In thy seed shall all the nations of the earth be blessed," was probably well known to Job; but it is most probable he knew his Redeemer by immediate revelation. God might make a discovery of this great truth to him,—first, to support him in his unparalleled affliction ; and, secondly, to comfort and encourage the church in after ages

II. Pious Job thought his affliction would terminate in death.

1. *When he spake the words of the text, his skin was destroyed.* He fell into the hands of Satan by the permission of the Lord: and he smote him with sore boils, from the sole of his foot unto his crown, chap. ii. 6, 7. These were fiery eruptions, or ulcerous eating sores, which destroyed the skin. "And he took him a potsherd to scrape himself withal." For *scrape,* says a learned author, the Chaldee and Arabic use a word commonly applied to pulling leaves and bark off from the tree. How deplorable was the state of Job, when scraping himself with potsherds! Well might he say, " Have pity upon me, have pity upon me, oh ye my friends !" verse 21.

2. *After his skin, he expected his whole body to be destroyed.* The word *worms* is not in the original, but is supplied by the translators; they

seem to have conjectured that his skin was destroyed by worms, and that they would proceed to destroy the body. How far this opinion is correct, we know not; but Job certainly had an idea, that the destruction of the whole body would speedily follow the destruction of the skin. The word *body* is also supplied, and properly, because that was certainly intended.

3. *Death and the grave, with their solemn attendants, closes every earthly prospect of that deeply afflicted, but eminently holy man* He afterwards said, "I know thou wilt bring me to death, and to the house appointed for all living," Job xxx. 23. And we also must die; but when we know not. These bodies, however beautiful and strong, will perish in the grave. "The righteous perisheth, and no man layeth it to heart," Isa. lvii. 1. But, like Job, he hopes to rise again.

III. Job had a joyful hope of a resurrection from the dead.

1. He positively affirms, that, after the destruction of his body, he *should see God in his flesh.* But how can that be the case, either with him or others, if the dead rise not. Man was created with a body, and will live in an embodied state, to all eternity; but that cannot be without a resurrection; because his earthly and material frame returns to dust, as a sad punishment of his apostacy from God, Gen. iii. 19. How God will raise the dead is unknown; but the fact is certain. It was revealed to Job, and has been indubitably proved by the resurrection of Jesus. With these eyes of flesh we shall see God our Saviour. What a happy sight! Then the sorrows of life will be past, death will be destroyed, and a blessed eternity will follow!

2. I shall see for *myself*, he says, "and mine eyes shall behold, and not another." Good men wish well to all; but they claim the blessings of grace and glory as their own. Others, no doubt, will see and enjoy the Redeemer; but I shall see and enjoy him for myself. He will appear in my cause; he will deliver me from death and the grave; he will vindicate my character; and he will avenge me of my foes. And all this will take place, though my reins, or vitals, are consumed within me; for all things are possible with God; and he who made the world can raise the dead.

INFERENCES.

1. Jesus has been the hope of pious men in all ages. Abraham rejoiced to see his day, "and he saw it and was glad," John viii. 56. Moses and all the prophets foretold his coming; and gave witness, "that through his name whosoever believeth in him shall receive remission of sins," Acts x. 43.

2. He is our only Redeemer and Saviour. We are lost, but he came to seek and to save us; we have enemies, but he has conquered them; we are dead, but we may live by him for ever.

3. It is both our duty and our privilege to renounce our own righteousness; to trust in him only; to love and honor him; and to follow him in the regeneration, through evil report and good report. Amen.

THE POOR MAN'S ACCOUNT OF HIMSELF.

Ps. xxxiv. 6.—This poor man cried, and the Lord heard him and saved him out of all his troubles. (Sk.)

THERE is an important reality in religion, which is enjoyed by all true believers. They do not follow cunningly devised fables, but receive the truth as it is in Jesus. They are enlightened, quickened, pardoned, adopted, and " renewed in righteousness and true holiness." And having obtained mercy of the Lord, they highly extol the riches of his grace. They become zealous in his cause, and greatly rejoice in the prosperity of Zion. They recommend religion to all around them, and earnestly desire the universal extension of its influence. And hence David, as a subject of saving grace, breathes in this psalm a spirit of " burning charity" and fervent zeal. In the preceding context he invites all men to unite with him to magnify and praise the Lord for all his benefits ; and in the text he encourages them, by the consideration of his own successful application to the throne of grace :—" This poor man cried," &c. These words describe—a humble character—a gracious privilege—and a happy deliverance.

I. A HUMBLE CHARACTER ;—" This *poor man*." It is highly probable that David here speaks of himself. Notwithstanding the dignity of his station as *a king*, he was deeply humble before God as a *saint*. Though he was not *temporally poor* as a man, he was *spiritually poor* and destitute as a sinner ; and *consciously poor* and dependant as a believer. This language was therefore, a faithful description of his humble state and experience, as the man after God's own heart. It is also uniformly applicable to two distinct characters of mankind, and may be justly adopted,

1. *By the contrite penitent.* Such are thoroughly convinced of their depravity and sinfulness ; and that naturally in them " dwelleth no good thing." They are entirely destitute of all the spiritual riches of knowledge, purity, and happiness ; and are ignorant, guilty, polluted, and miserable, Rev. iii. 17. They are " without Christ, having no hope, and without God in the world." What an awful state of poverty and wretchedness is this ! And yet such is the deplorable condition of all mankind by nature !—And those who truly feel their sinful and perishing state, readily acknowledge their total destitution of spiritual good ; and their utter insufficiency to please God, or save themselves. And hence the true penitent frequently exclaims, " Wo is me ! for I am undone—God be merciful to me a sinner—Lord, save, or I perish," Ps. li. 17 ; Isa. lxvi. 2.

2. *By the humble believer.* Though such characters are partakers of the ' unsearchable riches of Christ," they are still needy and dependant. They have many wants to be supplied,—many evils to be removed,—many enemies to overcome,—many difficulties to encounter,—many blessings to secure,—many dangers to escape,—many duties to perform ;—and without Christ they can do nothing. Hence they deeply feel their helplessness and dependance on God, and have no confidence in the flesh. They are grateful for what they already enjoy ; but their present attainments are very deficient. They have not already attained, neither are already perfect. Though they are " poor and needy, yet the Lord thinketh upon them for good." They are poor in spirit, but rich in faith, and heirs of heaven. The text also specifies,

II. A GRACIOUS PRIVILEGE :—" This poor man *cried*, and the Lord *heard him*." David was a man of eminent devotion. In all his afflictions and trials, he had recourse to God, and gave himself unto prayer. Nor did he pray in vain. In the case before us he mentions,

1. *The object of his worship;*—"The *Lord.*" He was no profane idolater, but a devout worshipper of the God of Israel. He had *correct views of his character,* as the only object of religious adoration, and the Giver of every good and perfect gift, Ps. xviii. 1—3. He was *acquainted with his will;* and hence he knew that it was both his duty and interest to wait upon him, and worship him in the beauty of holiness, Ps. xcv. 6, 7. He also *trusted in his name,* and expected salvation from him, Ps. lxii. 1, 2. He therefore carefully cultivated a spirit of prayer, and lived in holy fellowship with the covenant God of his fathers.

2. *The nature of his devotion:*—He " *cried* to the Lord." This intimates *earnestness.* He did not merely ask, nor seek; but he *cried* and *agonized,* like a person deeply distressed, or earnestly engaged in an important pursuit, Gen. xxxii, 24—26.—It includes *confidence.* He believed that God both *could* and *would* help and deliver him. He had frequently found it good to draw near unto him, and was therefore encouraged to trust in him for every blessing, Ps. cxxxiii. 1, 2.—It also implies *perseverance.* His crying to the Lord was not a *single* or *occasional* act of devotion; but his *regular* and *daily* practice, Ps. cxix. 164. He felt the constant necessity of divine succor and protection, which induced him fervently, faithfully, and diligently, to cry unto the Lord for mercy, and grace to help in time of need.

3. *The success of his prayer;*—"And the Lord *heard* him.' He is never inattentive to the cries and tears of his people, Isa. lix. 1.—"His eyes are over the righteous, and his ears are open unto their prayers."—He sees all their desires,—understands their " groanings which cannot be uttered,"—and hears all their supplications and thanksgivings both in public and in private, Ps. xl. 1.—He *accepts* their prayers. They approach him in the way of his own appointment, and worship him in spirit and in truth, Prov. xv. 8.—He *answers* their prayers. This was the case with the Psalmist; he " cried to the Lord," and he saved him in the day of trouble. The answers of faithful prayer are always *certain, seasonable,* and *compassionate;* for " like as a father pitieth his children, so the Lord pitieth them that fear him," Psa. xci. 15, 16; Matt. vii. 11; 1 John v. 14, 15.—The text records,

III. A HAPPY DELIVERANCE;—"The Lord *saved him* out of all his troubles."—Whether David here refers to some particular season of calamity or not, is uncertain; but his declaration is highly consolatory, and suggests the following instructions for the encouragement of the saints.

1. *They are frequently subjects of troubles.* This requires no argument to prove it: the Scriptures assure us, that this has always been the case; and experience sufficiently corroborates the fact. Yea, "many are the afflictions of the righteous," in this vale of tears.—They are subject to the common trials of human life, and are often chastised by the Lord for their profit in holiness, Heb. xii. 6—11.—They are frequently exercised with personal, domestic, spiritual, and temporal troubles; all of which are designed to " work together for their good."

2. *They are supported under their troubles.* They are not left to bear them alone; the Lord is with them, and into his hands they commit the keeping of their souls. They approach him with confidence, and find him to be their " refuge and strength, a very present help in trouble," Isa. xliii. 2; and lxiii. 9.—In their most trying seasons, his grace is sufficient for them, and will encourage them to possess their souls in patience. Hence

they feel fully resigned to the will of God, trusting in his wisdom and goodness, and " cast all their care upon him, for he careth for them."

3. *They shall be delivered from their troubles.* Thus the Psalmist and all the primitive saints, were saved from their sins and enemies, and out of all their troubles and afflictions. And God still delivers his people from many of their troubles while here, which they gratefully acknowledge with David in the text, Ps. ciii. 1—4. But whilst they are in a world of tribulation, their deliverance is not complete. " There remaineth therefore a rest to the people of God ;" where they shall be perfectly safe from all their troubles, both of body and mind, and " God shall wipe away all tears from their eyes," Isa. xxxv. 10.

This subject suggests,

1. The awful state of the prayerless, Job xxi. 15.—Arise and call upon God, that you perish not.

2. The manner in which we should come unto God.—It must be humble, fervent, and incessant. And,

3. The consolation and encouragement of the righteous. " Lift up your heads, for your redemption draweth nigh."

THE FATHER HONORS THE SERVANTS OF HIS SON.

John xii. 26.—If any man serve me, him will my Father honor. (Sk.)

EARTHLY monarchs are the fountains of temporal honors; but God is the fountain of eternal honors. The God and Father of our Lord Jesus Christ honors all who serve his beloved Son; and the honor which he confers, is as much above what the world can give, as the heavens are above the earth. Nor is this all; for while the honors which men receive of one another, are lost in death, those which God bestows, run on for ever. The servants of Jesus are now despised, as insignificant and worthless persons ; but ere long they will shine as the brightness of the firmament Dan. xii. 3.

I. MAKE A FEW OBSERVATIONS ON THE SERVICE OF CHRIST.

1. *Jesus has high claims on our services.* He created us : for "all things were made by him; and without him was not any thing made that was made," John i. 3. And is it not right that our Creator should govern us? Surely the creature is bound to obey the Author of his being! But he has claims on our services as our Redeemer ; " For ye are bought with a price : therefore glorify God in your body, and in your spirit, which are God's;" 1 Cor. v. 20. It will not be denied, by any man of reflection, that we should serve him, who has bought us with his precious blood. 1 Pet. i. 18, 19.

2. *He is our only Master;* " One is your Master, even Christ," Matt. xxiii. 8. Now, as a master has a right to command, and as servants are bound to obey, those who refuse obedience to Jesus, cannot, consistently, call him Master. The church is a house or family, and Christ is the governor of the house. The family is placed under his guidance and government, and every one should do what he commands. If his authority be denied, and if his commands be disobeyed, the whole family will fall into disorder; and when a house is divided against itself, it cannot tand, Matt. xii. 25.

3. *Our Lord is a good Master.* His work is pleasant in itself, and easy to his servants. He says, "My yoke is easy, and my burden is light," Matt. x. 30. He affords plentiful support to his servants, so that they never hunger, nor do they ever thirst, John vi. 35. And he will give great rewards, Rev. xxii. 14. These are things which are most agreeable to servants. Hence, when we voluntarily enter into service, we inquire after the character of the master; the nature of his employments; the support which he affords; and the rewards which he offers. We are aware that every blessing bestowed by our Master is the effect of grace; but it is as much our own as if we had merited it, and yet we humbly own that we are but unprofitable servants, Luke xvii. 10.

4. *The servants of Christ should obey him in all things.* His work is various: but whatever he commands is absolutely necessary. One serves him in the ministry of the word, and is ready, at his command, to go into all the world to preach the everlasting gospel, Mark xvi. 15. Another is employed in defending his cause by sound argument, being set for the defence of the gospel, Phil. i. 17. And all are required to practice those evangelical duties which relate to themselves, to men in general, and to God in particular; or, as the apostle Paul says, to "live soberly, righteously, and godly, in this present world," Titus ii. 12. Thus all are *employed;* all are *well* employed; and all are *constantly* employed.

5. *We should serve Christ in a right way.* Faithfulness is expected in a servant: and we should be faithful in all things, 1 Cor. iv. 2. Cheerfulness is necessary; a gloomy temper shows dissatisfaction, and is a reflection on our Master. Constancy and perseverance are necessary; for "he that endureth to the end shall be saved," Matt. x. 22. What we do, should be done with a single eye; "The light of the body is the eye: if therefore thine eye be single, thy whole body shall be full of light," Matt. vi. 22.

6. *We should be ever ready to obey the Son of God.* Paul, the apostle, required Timothy to be "*instant in season, and out of season,*" 2 Tim. iv. 2. The ear should be constantly open to hear the commands of Christ; and the heart should be constantly disposed to obey him, whether it be convenient or inconvenient to ourselves. When eastern despots command their slaves, it is a common reply, "To hear is to obey." And shall not we be always ready to obey our Lord, the moment we hear his voice.

II. Consider the honors which the Father confers on the servants of his Son.

1. *The service of Christ will not procure the honors of the world;—* "If ye were of the world, the world would love his own; but because ye are not of the world, but I have chosen you out of the world, therefore the world hateth you," John xv. 19. Learning, conquest, and wealth, are honored by men of the world; but holy obedience to Jesus Christ, is despised and contemned by men in general. But the servants of Jesus sit loose to human honors; they desire the good opinion of the wise and holy, but the good opinion of others is no credit to any man.

2. *If any man serve Christ he is honored with the friendship of God.* He has fellowship with the Father and with the Son, 1 John i. 3. Abraham was called the friend of God; and "they which be of faith are blessed with faithful Abraham," James ii. 23: Gal. iii. 9. "The Lord spake to Moses face to face, as a man speaketh to his friend;" and he is a friend to the truly pious, who sticketh closer than a brother, Exodus xxxiii. 11; Prov. xviii. 24. The friendship of great men is deemed an honor; but what is that when compared with the friendship of God?

271

3. *Every servant of Christ is honored with the special presence of God.* "If a man love me, he will keep my words: and my Father will love him, and we will come unto him, and make our abode with him," John xiv. 23. God dwells with the servants of Jesus, to direct their path in life; to defend them in the hour of danger; and to comfort them in the hour of affliction. His presence is a high honor, of which no man is worthy; but true believers enjoy it as their privilege, through the merit of Christ. God is at their right hand, and therefore they cannot be moved, Ps. xvi. 8. And he is with them in the waters and fires of affliction, Isa. xliii. 2.

4. *The servant of Christ is honored with a new nature.* All the tempers and dispositions of the soul, which are accounted great and good, are planted in his heart. He is generous to all who are in want; brave in the Christian warfare; pure in all his motives and ends; faithful to God and man; and upright in all his dealings. He is a dear child of God, and as far as grace enables him, he is a follower of God, Eph. v. 1. And is there any honor equal to this?

5. *Lofty titles are conferred on the servants of Christ.* They are called *elect,* or chosen; and are *precious,* or valuable, 1 Pet. ii. 6. They are called *sons* of God, 1 John iii. 2. They are the *bride* of Christ, Rev. xxi. 9. All their titles are expressions of real worth; and not like the flattering titles which are given to men, Job xxxii. 21. They are men of God; "a chosen generation, a royal priesthood, a holy nation, and a peculiar people," 1 Pet. ii. 9.

6. *The servant of Christ will be honored by the Father in the hour of death.* In death, the honors of the world come to an end; but in that awful hour the good man is highly honored. God is with him; holy angels minister unto him; he is about to be advanced to high preferment; and he is holy and happy. He can say, "My flesh and my heart faileth, but God is the strength of my heart and my portion for ever," Psa. lxxiii. 26.

7. *Honor will be put upon the servants of Christ in the end of the world.* They will rise to glory, 1 Cor. xv. 43. They will stand approved in the day of judgment, 1 John iv. 17. They will be openly invited to inherit the kingdom of God, Matt. xxv. 34. They will be assessors with Christ in the judgment, 1 Cor. vi. 2. Yea, they will judge angels, ver. 3.

8. *And eternal honors will be conferred on them in the kingdom of God.* When time is swallowed up in the ocean of eternity, they will wear the crown of life, James i. 12. They will be honored with the presence of God and the Lamb; with the society of angels and saints; with great personal glory; with high employments; with exalted seats; and with immortality, Rev. xxi. 3. 4.

INFERENCES.

1. Christian honors infinitely surpass the honors of the world. They are real, substantial, great, and durable; but those of the world are imaginary, empty, trifling, and momentary.

2. Human honors are frequently obtained by war, bribes, flattery, wealth and power; but divine honors are obtained by repentance, faith, holiness, and the grace of God in Christ Jesus.

3. Proud men will be humbled; their greatness will perish with the world. Therefore, "Let not thine heart envy sinners: but be thou in the fear of the Lord all the day long," Prov. xxiii. 17.

4. We should set a great value on divine honors; and if human honors fall to our lot, we should be humble. And while we are honored, either by providence or grace, let us give the glory to God, 1 Tim. i. 17

THE PIOUS SUFFERER EXHORTED TO GLORIFY GOD.

1 Pet. iv. 16.—Yet if any man suffer as a Christian, let him not be ashamed; but let him glorify God on this behalf. (Sk.)

In the latter part of the first age, the rage of Jews and Gentiles was exceedingly stimulated by the prevalence of the gospel; the apostles, therefore, considered themselves as especially called to comfort and encourage their suffering brethren. With this view, Peter reminded the disciples of Christ of the obligations they were under to suffer for their religion, and suggested a variety of motives to persuade them to do it cheerfully. See context; also chap. iii. 14—18. We are not in similar circumstances with the first christians: hence, the danger of our religion being superficial; yet, if any man's piety and decision of character subject him to suffering, "let him not be ashamed." We may therefore state,

I. What is implied in suffering as a christian.
II. Why characters who thus suffer should not be ashamed.
III. Their duty under suffering circumstances.

1. What is implied, &c. The term christian, was given to the disciples of Christ first at Antioch, and is used in three places only in the New Testament, viz. here; in Acts xi. 26; and xxvi. 28. It imports nothing less than an experimental and practical believer in the Lord Jesus Christ. To suffer as a christian, is,

1. *To suffer in the character of a christian.* Where piety has its seat n the heart, it will appear in the life; hence believers are the salt of the earth, to spread a salutary influence; and save the world from moral putrefaction:—the light of the world; as such they are to shine brighter and brighter to the perfect day;—a city set on a hill, to be seen and identified by all, Matt. v. 13—16. It was never the design of the Head of the church that any of its members should seclude themselves from society, John xvii. 15. It is the duty of all who believe in Christ to confess him before men, Matt. x. 32, 33; and to conceal our religion is a tacit denial of Christ, and opposed to the doctrine of our text.

2. *To suffer for discharging the duties of a christian.* Christianity frees its possessors from the slavery of custom; they are governed by the high principles of religion. In the service of God, like Joshua, xxiv. 15, and Daniel vi. 10, they are undaunted. Whatever is the opinion of the world, the work of God is to them of paramount importance. In domestic life, they are faithful, conscientious, and obliging; as religious characters, they are fixed in their views, and bold in their profession; in the civil world, they are true and just in all their doings, embodying principle and conscience in each action; while, as subjects of the realm, they are peaceable and quiet. If, therefore, such a conduct subject them to suffering, "let them not be ashamed."

3. *To suffer in the spirit of a christian.* If human enemies rise against you, think it not strange, but "in patience possess ye your souls," Luke xxi. 19. Should their unkindness and sin lead to an unjust impeachment of your character, the injury of your person or circumstances, suffer not the spirit of revenge to betray you into sin "Recompense no man evil for evil," Rom. xii. 17; but, if it be possible, "live peaceably with all men," ver. 18; and "if thine enemy hunger, feed him," ver. 20, 21. Like your Lord, be ready to forgive, and show that you have added to your courage, patience, &c. 2 Pet. i. 5—7. Let not persecu

tion either in its mild or terrific forms, intimidate you; remember him, " who, when he was reviled, reviled not again." &c. 1 Pet. ii. 23 ; take also for your example the apostles of our Lord, who would say, " Being reviled, we bless," &c. 1 Cor. xii. 13. Let that mind be in you which was also in Christ Jesus, Phil. ii. 5. Let us therefore consider,

II. WHY CHARACTERS WHO THUS SUFFER SHOULD NOT BE ASHAMED.

1. *Because they suffer innocently.* "If any man suffer as a murderer, or as a thief, or as an evil doer, or as a busy body in other men's matters," he has cause to be ashamed ; but if innocent, his record is with God, and he partakes of that satisfaction which is the good man's inheritance, Prov. xiv. 14. Let the craft and subtlety of the devil and man be directed against you, the shield of innocence will repel every dart. " Blessed are ye when men shall revile you, and persecute you, and shall say all manner of evil against you falsely for my sake," &c. Matthew v. 10—12.

2. *They suffer in a good cause.* Not like the man whom justice has arrested for dishonesty—the law condemned for perjury, or sentenced to death for murder ; theirs is the cause of truth, justice, mercy, benevolence, and piety. Their business is to get good, and do good—to injure no one by word or deed ; and while their motto is " Holiness to the Lord," and in all things seek to glorify him who has bought them with his blood, they should not be ashamed.

3. *They suffer from the purest motive.* Their conscientious exactness is not the result of fostered peculiarity, or with a view to be singular. God is their witness, that with sincerity and simplicity they wish to walk before him. His will is their law—his glory their end; and they esteem the approbation of God more than any thing this world can afford.

4. *They suffer for a blessed Master.* He is a high Priest who is touched with a feeling of their infirmities, Heb. iv. 15 ; and what they suffer for him, though painful, will conduce to their good, Rom. viii. 28 ; 2 Cor. iv. 16—18. "Think it not strange concerning the fiery trial which is to try you," &c. ver. 12, 13 ; "for unto you it is given, in the behalf of Christ, not only to believe on him, but also to suffer for his sake," Phil. i. 29 ; "and if we suffer, we shall also reign with him," 2 Tim. ii. 12.

4. *They suffer in imitation of the brightest examples.* Look at the catalogue of patriarchs, kings, priests, and prophets, Heb. xi. whose intrepidity, faith, patience, and purity, they follow. They have a noble army of martyrs before their eyes ; and as their great example, a suffering Saviour, Heb. xii. 1—3. Let us therefore consider,

III. THEIR DUTY UNDER SUFFERING CIRCUMSTANCES ; viz. to " glorify God on this behalf." We are not, however, to suppose that man can add any thing to the essential glory of God ; but they are to glorify God by,

1. *Devoutly acknowledging Him and his gifts,* 1 Chronicles xxix. 11, 12 ; confessing him " worthy to receive honor, glory, might, and majesty,' Rev. iv. 11. The very circumstance of their suffering should prompt them to this.

2. *By firmness in the day of trial.* Let them consider Him who endured the contradiction of sinners against himself, and not be discouraged ; let nothing shake their firmness, 1 Cor. xv. 58 ; but imitate the example of the disciples, who continued with their Lord in his temptations, Luke xxii. 28, 29. When the service of God demands their attention, let not secondary considerations discourage them. He who, for fear of persecution, or for the sake of his temporal interest, abandons religion, shall lose his soul ; and he who, in the time of persecution, abjures the religion of

Christ, is not only in danger of losing his soul, but his life, Matt. **x. 39;** "He that findeth his life, shall lose it." That was literally fulfilled in Archbishop Cranmer, who, for confessing Christ against the devil and the pope, was ordered to be burnt: to save his life, he recanted, and was, notwithstanding, burnt. In the service of God we must persevere, fearless of consequences. Honor God, and God will honor you, 1 Sam. ii. 30.

3. *By a faithful and patient endurance of suffering.* Should conflicts increase, friends forsake, and enemies combine against you, "rejoice inasmuch as ye are partakers of Christ's sufferings,"&c. ver. 13. Think it not strange if an ungodly world should hate you, John xv. 18. "All that will live godly in Christ Jesus, shall suffer persecution," 2 Tim. iii. 12; therefore, "in your patience, possess your souls," Luke xxi. 19. "Let patience have her perfect work," James i. 4: and glorify God in the exercise of that grace which his own hand has planted, and which his providence has suffered to be exercised.

To this act of glorifying God, they are encouraged from

1. *The declarations and promises he has made.* These are many, great, and various, Isaiah xli. 10, xliii. 1, 2, liv. 17; Matt. x. 32; James i. 12; Rev. ii. 10, xxii. 7.

2. *The honor it will confer upon them.* Let the warrior wave his bloodstained laurel, boast of the immensity of his possessions, purchased by the gore of his fellow men, and spread his fame from pole to pole;—a nobler award awaits *them;* their names shall continue when the annals of history are destroyed—their inheritance will not fade away—their memorial will endure for ever, 1 Pet. i. 3—5; Ps. cxii. 6.

IMPROVEMENT.

1. *Let us examine our experience by this test.* Do I believe in, and love the Lord Jesus Christ? Am I modestly, yet boldly, confessing him before the world? Can I patiently and cheerfully suffer for his sake?

2. *Let us encourage ourselves in the Lord.* In such a cause, for such a Master, with such promises, and in the strength of grace, let us pursue our course. Victory, rest, and glory, are before us.

3. *Let us pray for our persecutors.* Their state is awful—it is dangerous. May the Lord our God grant them repentance unto life.

WALKING IN TRUTH.

3 John 4.—I have no greater joy than to hear that my children walk in truth. (Sk.)

MINISTERS of our Lord Jesus Christ are appointed to watch over the souls of men; and the great day is fast approaching, when they must give an account of the charge committed to their care, Heb. xiii. 7. The apostles of our Lord excelled in the discharge of this duty; and those who are called to the same work, should copy after their example; then, being influenced by the apostolic spirit, they will rejoice *greatly*, like the beloved John, when their children enjoy spiritual health, and walk in truth. The joys of the apostle, both as a Christian and a minister, were many and great; but he asserts, in our text, that he had no greater joy than to hear that his children walked in truth.

I. The children of the apostle John walked in truth. His children were real Christians, both in heart and life; and all such walk in truth. But, as Pilate said to Jesus, "What is truth?"

1. *Truth refers to our thoughts, words, and actions.* Our thoughts are true, when we think of things as they are; our words are true, when we speak as we think; and our actions are true, when they are conformable to the Holy Scriptures; for then we "obey the truth," Rom. ii. 8. That we may *think* correctly, let us examine things carefully, 1 Thess. v. 21; that we may *speak* exactly, let us keep the door of our lips, Ps. cxli. 3: and that we may *act* the truth, let us live as in the immediate presence of the Lord, Ps. xvi. 8.

2. *The word of God, including both the Old Testament and the New, is a revelation of the truth.* That blessed book is the only infallible rule of faith and practice: but the word *truth*, in our text, may particularly refer to the gospel of God our Saviour, which, as a system of truth, is the perfection of all previous revelations, Gal. iii. 1. "The New Testament," says Locke, "has God for its author; salvation for its end; and truth, without any mixture of error, for its matter."

3. *Jesus Christ, our Divine Teacher, is called the Truth.* In his humble birth, holy life, painful death, blessed resurrection, and glorious ascension, all the promises, prophecies, and types of the Old Testament, relating to the Messiah, were *fully verified;* and while he dwelt on earth, he taught the truth of God in all its beauty and fulness. We read Socrates, Plato, Seneca, Cicero, and other eminently learned men, with caution, because there is a mixture of truth and error in all their works; but when we read the discourses of our adorable Saviour, we feel confidence and assurance, because he knew all things, and taught the way of God in truth, Matt. xxii. 16.

4. *To walk in truth, implies a strict conformity to its sacred dictates, in our experience, and in all our works and ways.* Here it may be observed, that God has not revealed truth merely to amuse us, or to satisfy our curiosity, but with a view to practical purposes; that it is one thing to believe and profess truth, and another to walk in it, Rom. i. 18; that faith and practice, so often *separated*, should be constantly *united;* and, finally, that he walks in truth, in every point of view, who has an enlightened understanding, a renewed heart, an edifying conversation, and a holy conduct, Isa. ii. 5; Ps. ci. 2; Eph. iv. 29; Rom. vi. 4.

5. *Those who walk in truth should be careful to hold it fast.* Solomon says, "Buy the truth, and sell it not," Prov. xxiii. 23. Rather part with wealth, fame, and even life, than truth. Be valiant for it, Jer. ix. 3; let your loins be girt with truth, Eph. vi. 14; be established in the truth, 2 Pet. i. 12; do nothing against the truth, 2 Cor. xiii. 8. That you may hold it fast, carefully recollect that it makes you *free*, John viii. 32; and that you are sanctified and purified through the truth, John xvii. 17; 1 Pet. i. 22.

6. *We should examine ourselves daily, whether we be in the truth, and how it affects our life and conversation..* Our knowledge is limited, and ever will be so: but are our views, as far as they extend, agreeable to truth: Is our experience in unison with the revealed truth of the written word? Are we advancing in sound and true experience? Is our conduct, in all things, consistent with truth? These inquiries, by the blessing of God, will promote our *love* of truth, and lead us to *honor* and obey it in all its requirements.

II. John had no greater joy than to hear of his children walking in truth.

1 *Joy implies gladness and exultation either in the possession or prospect of something which we deem good and excellent.* It is a lovely passion in a pious person; it exhilarates the spirits, even in afflictive and trying circumstances, 1 Cor. vi. 10; and produces a flowing tide of the most pleasurable feelings. No matter what our external circumstances may be; for, if we have religious joy in our hearts, we are substantially happy, and like Paul and Silas, can praise God at midnight, in a prison, though loaded with chains, Acts xvi. 25.

2. *Men of the world, who mind only earthly things, feel joy and gladness in the things of time and sense.* They are joyful and glad when their corn and their wine are increased, Ps. iv. 7; they joy in their own labor, and in their carnal pleasures, Eccl. ii. 10; they joy even in their vile hypocrisy and artful deceptions, Job xx. 5; yea, "folly is joy to him that is destitute of wisdom," Prov. xv. 21. But this joy, like the crackling of thorns under a pot, is but a sudden blaze, which is soon extinguished, Eccles. vii. 6. The *unsanctified* joy of Hamon was of short duration; and that which made his heart glad, led him to a gallows, Esther v. 9; vii. 10.

3. *But pious men joy in spiritual and eternal blessings*, more than in *the good things of this life, which are passing away.* The blessed operations of the Holy Ghost in their hearts are abundant sources of pure joy, Rom. xiv. 17; they joy in the God of their salvation, Heb. iii. 18; they receive the word with joy, 1 Thess. i. 6; they count it all joy when they fall into divers temptations or trials, James i. 2, and their joy is unspeakable and full of glory, 1 Pet. i. 8. It is similar to the joys of the blessed in heaven, and a sweet anticipation of eternal bliss; it is intended to comfort and cheer the hearts of the pious in this world of sin and sorrow; and, being furnished with matter of joy in every state, they are commanded to rejoice evermore, and in every thing to give thanks, 1 Thess. v. 16.

4. *Ministers of the gospel joy in the followers of Jesus, and especially in those whom they have been instrumental in turning to the Lord.* The apostle Paul expresses his *feelings* on this subject in the following words; "Ye are our joy and glory," 1 Thess. ii. 20. Under the influence of human weakness, a minister may feel joy when the people praise his sermons and extol his gifts; but, in his best moments, nothing affords him so much joy as the success of his labors, in the conversion of sinners, and the edification of saints. He rejoices in the prosperity of believers, as a parent rejoices in the prosperity of his children; for they are his hope, his joy, his crown of rejoicing, 1 Thess. ii. 19.

5. *It is certain that the beloved John, whose piety far exceeded that of most men, had many pure and exalted joys.* Among these we may notice —his union with Christ—his high and holy calling, as an apostle of our Lord—his fellowship with the church—his spirituality and heavenly-mindedness—reflections on his personal acquaintance with Jesus, and the distinguishing marks of his Master's love to him—and his prospects of a happy and glorious immortality. Inspired with these joys, and allowing that he had no other, he was happier far than the most elevated of those mortals whose only portion was in the present world; and in such a frame of mind as those joys produced, might look down on all the mighty sons of earth with pity and compassion.

6. *But he had no greater joy than to hear that his children walked in truth.* He does not say he had no *equal* to that, but he had none which was *greater.* But why did he rejoice so greatly in the consistent character and conduct of his children? The following reasons may be assigned:—

God was *glorified* in their fruit, John xv. 8;—the *truth* was *exalted* and *acknowledged* before men, Tit. i. 1;—the *ministry* was *honored*, 2 Thess. iii. 1;—they were *happy* in a consistent conduct, Rev. xxii. 14;—they were *useful* in the world, Rom. ii. 10; and John had the pleasing prospect of their being his *confidence* at the coming of the Lord, 1 John ii. 28. Baxter observes that " true ministers rejoice more for the welfare of men's souls, than in their procuring wealth and worldly honors."

7. *The joyous feelings of the holy apostle would carry him forward in his great work with increasing ardour.* The world, the devil, and sin, oppose every faithful minister; but he fights the good fight, and gains the victory, 2 Tim. iv. 7. 8. Bonds and afflictions abide by him; but he is not moved; he rejoices in his work, and counts not his life dear unto him. that he may finish his course with joy, and the ministry which he has received of the Lord Jesus, Acts xx. 23, 24. Such was the experience of the apostle Paul, such was the experience of John the Divine, and may this be the happy experience of every christian minister.

8. *Happy are the people who are favoured with a minister, whose greatest joy is their prosperity in pure religion.* Their best interests lie near his heart; he carefully teaches them the truth; he constantly remembers them in his prayers; he visits them in their afflictions; he sets them a good example; and watches over them in the Lord with constant care. Such ministers are worthy of double honor, 1 Tim. v. 17; and whatever treatment they meet with among men, they will be highly honored in the day of judgment.

CHRISTIANS REQUIRED TO CONTEND FOR THE FAITH.

Jude 3.—Beloved, when I gave all diligence to write unto you of the common salvation, it was needful for me to write unto you, and exhort you, that ye should earnestly contend for the faith which was once delivered unto the saints. (Sk.)

This epistle was written by Jude, "a servant of Jesus Christ," in the gospel ministry, to them who were "sanctified," or separated from an idolatrous world, " by God the Father, and preserved in Jesus Christ," from dangerous errors and wicked practices; and who were "called" to embrace the doctrines, engage in the duties, and share the privileges of genuine Christianity; and he devoutly prays that mercy, peace, and love, might be multiplied unto them. They were beloved by him, as all true believers should be by Christian ministers; and under the influence of Divine inspiration, he gave all diligence to write unto them on that salvation which is common to all who believe, whether they be Jews or Gentiles; but found it particularly needful to exhort them to contend earnestly for the faith which was once delivered unto the saints; because many seducing teachers had crept in among them unawares.

I. WHAT IS THAT FAITH WHICH WAS ONCE DELIVERED UNTO THE SAINTS?

1. *It is not a set of mere notions and opinions, founded on human reason, and supported by powers of oratory.* The heathen philosophers were famous for speculative notions, but were strangers to the truth as it is in Jesus. They had vast stores of human learning, but were ignorant of the God who

gave them being: and all men, nowever learned, who are in a state of nature, are ignorant of their Maker: for " the natural man receiveth not the things of the Spirit of God: for they are foolishness unto him; neither can he know them," 1 Cor. ii. 14.

2. *The faith of a Christian implies, either that act of his mind, by which he gives credence to revealed' truth; or, by a usual metonymy, the objects of his faith, including all the doctrines of Christianity.* The credence which he gives is founded on satisfactory evidence. He has examined the *character* of Christ and his apostles, and finds they were worthy of credit; he has examined the *doctrines* which they taught, and finds them worthy of God; he has examined the miracles which they wrought in open day, and before multitudes of witnesses, as proofs of their mission from God, and finds them to be *real* and highly important facts; and he has examined the prophecies which they delivered, and finds them exact predictions of future events. On these and other important grounds, he gives full credit to all the truths which they taught. The principal doctrines which he believes may be summed up in a few articles: such as, the being and perfections of God, Matt. v. 48; the government of the world by divine providence, Matt. x. 29, 30; the original purity and happiness of man, Gen. i. 27; his awful apostacy from God, 1 John v. 19; the atonement of Jesus Christ, 1 John ii. 2; the influences of the Holy Spirit on the hearts of men, Gal. v. 22, 23; justification by faith, Rom. v. 1; the necessity of inward and outward holiness, 1 Thess. v. 23; a resurrection from the dead, John v. 28, 29; a day of judgment, Acts xvii. 31; and eternal rewards and punishments, Matt. xxv. 46.

3. *This faith was once delivered to the saints.* It was delivered in *part* by the Jewish prophets; but *fully* by Christ and his apostles, Heb. i. 1, ii. 3, 4. It was delivered to holy persons, no only to illuminate their own understandings, but that they might communicate it to others, and thereby enlighten the nations which were in darkness and in death, Matt v. 15.

4. *Besides this faith or belief of truth, there is a living and working faith, which has been delivered by Christ and his apostles, as a term or condition of salvation.* This faith implies a *knowledge* of Jesus in his mediatorial undertakings; an humble *dependence* on him as our atoning sacrifice; and a receiving of him in all his sacred offices and characters, Mark xvi. 15; John i. 12; Rom. x. 10. Faith in the *doctrines* of Christianity precedes *saving* faith; but he who believes the truth, without being influenced by it both in heart and life, has only a dead faith, James ii. 26; while he whose faith is active and operative, is brought into spiritual life and divine love, Gal. ii. 20, v. 6; and thus faith purifies the heart, Acts xv. 9.

II. How should the saints contend for faith?—

1. *The faith of a Christian is worth contending for, being of great value, and of vast importance to man.* It brings him out of darkness into light: teaches him the knowledge of himself and of God his Saviour: and opens to his view a blessed and glorious immortality, 2 Tim. i. 10. Without this faith we should be buried in gross ignorance, frightful superstitions, and destructive delusions.

2. *The Christian faith has many opposers, and we must prepare to meet them in the field of battle.* This faith is opposed by Jews, Infidels, Mohammedans, and Heathens. Let us defend it by sound arguments, drawn from the written word. This is our weapon, and when skilfully used, will either convince our enemies, or put them to flight. They will not easily yield to logic, metaphysics, or oratory; but the sword of the Spirit, which is the word of God, will carry all before it, Eph. vi 17

279

3. *Contend earnestly for the faith of the Lord Jesus Christ, which is placed in your hands as a sacred deposite, to be preserved in its purity.* Some who contend for the faith *ex officio*, neither seem to believe it themselves, nor to wish others to believe. To them the doctrines of the cross have no charms; they are lovers of filthy lucre, and would surrender the faith for wealth and honor. But when we consider that the present happiness of men, and their future prospects, depend on their receiving and holding fast the truth, we are awakened to a holy *zeal*, and contend for the faith with a sacred *ardor.*

4. *But though we contend with earnestness, let us carefully avoid carnal weapons and angry passions.* Mohammed contended for *his* faith with the sword; the Roman Catholics have contended for *their* faith by racks and tortures; but the real Christian, in a spirit of meekness, contends 'not with carnal weapons, but those which are mighty, 2 Cor. x. 4. He uses sound words and potent arguments, and is able "both to exhort and convince gainsayers," Tit. i. 9.

5. *Never contend merely for the sake of victory, but with a view to do good.* He who aims at nothing but victory, is proud and vain; and would undertake to defend either truth or error, for the sake of a triumph. The man of God has better motives and ends in all his contentions; he constantly aims at the good of men and the glory of God; and when these objects are not likely to be promoted, he retires and mourns in secret. The apostle Paul was set for the defence of the gospel, Phil. i. 17; and it is very observable, that when he was brought before kings and great men, his only object was to prove the truth, and win them over to the cause of Christ, Acts xxvi. 28, 29.

6. *Beware of little petty controversies about either nonessential things, or things beyond the reach of human intellect.* Many questions which have agitated the church in all ages, have been foolish and trifling; and others have been profoundly deep and unfathomable. When we contend for that which is important and within our reach, we keep in the line of duty; but when we engage in disputes on fanciful and deeply mysterious things, we miss our way, and injure the cause which we profess to support. Such were the vain janglings which the apostle Paul condemned, 1 Tim. i. 3—7.

To conclude:—

Let us be thankful to God for his holy word, which is an infallible rule both of *faith* and *practice ;* let us believe what he has revealed, though we cannot in every instance understand the mysteries of our faith; let us seek no new doctrine, but carefully study that which has been delivered to the saints; let us arm our minds with *plain* and *solid* arguments, to defend this faith against the subtle and malicious attacks of infidels and heretics; let us bend all our force in support of *vital* truths; let us transmit our faith, in its purity and simplicity, to the rising generation; and, above all, let us contend for that faith which unites the soul to Christ, and which is, "the *substance* of things hoped for, and the evidence of things not seen," Heb. xi. 1.

FAMILY RELIGION.

Gen xviii. 19.—I know him, that he will command his children and his household after him, and they shall keep the way of the Lord, to do justice and judgment; that the Lord may bring upon Abraham, that which he hath spoken of him. (B.)

In the context we have a lively picture of the hospitality, simplicity, benevolence, and liberality of the ancient patriarchs, ver. 1. This appearance of God to Abraham seems to have had in it more of freedom and familiarity, and less of grandeur and majesty, than those of which we have hitherto read, and, therefore, more resembled that great visit, which, in the fulness of time, the Son of God was to make to the world. God knew and approved his piety and integrity, and was assured he would employ his authority, as a father and a master, for the promotion of religion and justice, and would communicate the knowledge he acquired, for the benefit of those under his charge.

Let us consider,

I. THE LIGHT IN WHICH ABRAHAM APPEARS IN THIS PASSAGE ; and how he was qualified for the duty here ascribed to him.

He appears,—A man of *knowledge;* not, perhaps, in the jargon of language, the refinements of sciences, the niceties of history, or the subtilties of speculation ; but in matters of the greatest moment to his own present and everlasting salvation, and that of others, namely, in religion and morality, here termed the "way of the Lord," "justice and judgment."— — —

A man of *piety.* He not only understood the way of the Lord ; but he loved, experienced, and practised it. Hence his concern and endeavor to impress it upon others. Without personal religion in the heads of families, we cannot expect they will sincerely and perseveringly endeavor to promote it in their children or servants. — — —

A man of *virtue.* Justice and judgment were as dear to him, and as much practised by him, as the "way of the Lord." He did not make doing his duty to God, a reason for neglecting his duty to his neighbor ; nor, what God had joined together did he put asunder.— — —

A man of *authority.* "He will command his children and his household after him." Observe the respect and obedience he enforced, and his great influence over his family.

This was owing to his *station.* God had made him their head, and they had been taught to acknowledge and revere the appointment of God.

His *knowledge* and *wisdom.*— — —

His known and approved *piety.* They knew God was on his side, and that if they opposed him, God would resent it.

His consistent *virtue.*— — —

A man of *fidelity.* Whatever knowledge, piety, virtue, or authority he had, he faithfully employed for *his* glory, who entrusted him with them, and to the end intended,—the good of others, and especially of his own family.

A man of *diligence.* He appears evidently to have been laborious in this duty.

II. THE NATURE OF THIS DUTY ; or his endeavors for the good of his family.

He not only prayed *with* and *before* his family, but interceded for them as a *priest.* This the ancient patriarchs and holy men of old did. They were priests in their own houses. Job i. 5. So should every master of a christian family be. Indeed every private christian is a priest unto God, (Enlarge respecting praying with and for every member of our family.)

He was a *prophet* in his family. He instructed them: not in matters of mere speculation, nor doubtful disputation,—this were foolish and unprofitable,—but in matters of experimental and practical religion and virtue.

He taught them the " way of the Lord," *i. e.* God's way towards them, as a Creator, Preserver, Benefactor, and their way towards God, or piety, and godliness; the true knowledge, fear, love of God, obedience to his commands, patience under his dispensations, contentment in all estates, the time being short, deadness to the world and sin, and devotedness to God; and, in order to all this, repentance towards God, and faith in Christ. (Here show how the being and attributes of God may be demonstrated even to children from the works of creation, &c. the truth of the scriptures also, and of christianity, &c.)

He taught them *virtue*, "to do justice and judgment,—truth, justice, mercy, charity, flowing from the love of our neighbour, and the love of God. Children should be taught to consider all men as allied to each other, being creatures of one Creator, made of one blood, partaking of one nature, mortal, immortal, bought by the Redeemer, &c. Also, children should be early accustomed to sincerity, veracity, strict honesty, plain dealing, pity to those in distress, a forgiving spirit, a readiness to relieve those in want. In order to this, as well as to the health of their own bodies, and the peace of their own minds, they should be taught temperance, chastity, self-denial, &c.—

Abraham taught his family, lastly, not barely to know these things, but to do them.

Now upon whom must this be inculcated?—Upon *children*. Deut. iv. 9. If our children be the Lord's they must be educated for him. If they wear his livery, and be called by his name, they must do his work. Wha' hypocrisy is it to dedicate our children to God in baptism, and promise they shall " renounce the devil and all his works, the vain pomp and glory of the world, with all covetous desires of the same, and the carnal desires of the flesh, so that they shall not follow, nor be led by them," and afterwards to take no care that they may fulfil it!—Upon *servants*. Abraham had born in his house, three hundred and eighteen servants, Gen, xiv. 14, *trained*, or, as the Hebrew word means, *catechized*. Our servants are entrusted to our care, and should be taught and directed by us, while in our family.

But how must our children and servants be instructed? Deut. vi. 6. &c. By conversation, advice, exhortation, reading, hearing, catechizing, &c. and especially teaching them to "know the scriptures." 2 Tim. iii. 15. Further,

He was a *king* in his house, and used authority.—He not only recommended these things, and advised, and set before them the advantages on the one hand, and the miseries on the other, of the conduct which they might pursue, but he solemnly enjoined and insisted on these things, on pain of incurring his displeasure, as well as that of God. He not only used *doctrine*, but *discipline*, Eph. vi. 4. He not only informed the understanding of his children and domestics, as it might gradually open, by doctrine, and reminded and admonished them, but he persuaded, turned, and subdued the will to God and man, as far as possible, by discipline, rewards, punishments, or corrections, especially with regard to his children.

III. How PLEASING IT WAS TO GOD, and the blessed consequences thereof to Abraham and his family.

Observe—The reason why God would hide nothing from Abraham. "For I know him," &c. Abraham was communicative of his knowledge, and improved it to the good of those under his care, and therefore God resolved to make communications to him.

The way to the accomplishment of God's promises; "That the Lord may bring upon Abraham that which he hath spoken of him."

Family blessings arise from family religion;—Temperance, frugality, industry, discretion.

Peace, quietness, love, harmony.

The favour, protection, care of God, his direction and aid.

All necessaries. Psalm xxxvii. 25. Matt. vi. 33.

Prosperity, as far as will be for good for us and our families.

Our prayers are heard.

Afflictions are sanctified to us, and we are supported under them.

We make a comfortable progress together in the ways of God, and receive many spiritual blessings.

We shall meet in his presence and kingdom hereafter, and spend an eternity together.

The sad reverse when this course is not taken.

Hence arise family curses—Intemperance, prodigality, idleness, imprudence.

Strife, contention, hatred, disturbance.

The displeasure of God, &c. and his curse on all we do.

Not even necessaries, perhaps, but beggary and want

Nothing prospers.

Our prayers are rejected.

We are abandoned of God in our afflictions, and hardened by them.

We go forward miserably in the ways of the Devil.

We shall meet at the left hand of the Judge in the great day, and in hell, amidst everlasting strife and misery.

CONFESSING CHRIST BEFORE MEN.

Matt. x. 32.—Whosoever, therefore, shall confess me before men, him will I confess also before my Father which is in heaven. (Sk.)

"ALL that will live godly in Christ Jesus shall suffer persecution." This apostolic maxim has been illustrated and established by the records of the Christian history in all ages. The carnal mind being "enmity against God" is decidedly hostile to the holy constitution and renovating designs of the gospel. Hence the annals of the church have been stained with the blood of martyrs, who with pious magnanimity have preferred immolation on the altar of bigotry, rather than violate the sacred rights of conscience. Of this course of suffering and death, Jesus Christ most fully apprized his followers, when he planted Christianity in the earth, Matt. x. 16—22. At the same time furnishing them with the most ample encouragement, steadily to persevere in the path of duty which lay before them; by referring to his own reproach and suffering, ver. 24, 25:—to the circumscribed extent of their enemies' malevolent influence, ver. 28;—to the minute care of Divine providence, ver. 29—31;—to the awful consequence of timidity and cow. ardice, ver. 33, 39;—and to the honorable and highly advantageous result of Christian magnanimity. The last description of encouragement is contained in the passage before us, in discussing which, we shall have to consider,

I. THE NATURE OF THAT CONFESSION WHICH CHRISTIANITY REQUIRES.

II. THE HONORABLE DISTINCTION WITH WHICH A STEADY COURSE OF CHRISTIAN FORTITUDE WILL BE CROWNED.

I. THE NATURE OF THAT CONFESSION WHICH CHRISTIANITY REQUIRES. This interesting confession includes various considerations, viz.

1. *An open avowal of the person and Messiahship of Christ.* The sacred Scriptures represent Jesus Christ as that " Word" which " was in the beginning with God," and which " was God;" the " Alpha and Omega, the beginning and the end, the first and the last;" and yet was " made flesh," and dwelling among the inhabitants of the earth, for the purpose of human redemption. Therefore, those who scripturally " confess Christ before men," unequivocally acknowledge his " eternal power and Godhead," and yet gratefully consider the mysterious union of the Divine nature with the human, as a luminous display of the love of God to fallen man; and as the divinely appointed means of rescuing him from everlasting perdition. And this they are not ashamed publicly to avow and support; in opposition to the presuming pride of human reason, which absurdly affects to reject and deny that which it cannot comprehend, John i. 1—3, 14, x. 30, xiv. 11; Col. i. 16, 17; John iii. 16; Phil. ii. 5—8. But as devils have thus confessed Christ, saying, " We know thee who thou art, the Holy One of God," it is necessary to proceed farther, and notice.

2. *A conscientious adherence to the fundamental doctrines of Christianity.* In every theory which the human mind is capable of embracing, there are certain grand principles which are individually essential to the existence and consistency of the whole. So the Christian character, while it has for its ground-work, a conscientious avowal of the person and messiahship of Christ, includes in its superstructure, a sincere confession of the deep-rooted depravity of the human heart, and its consequent moral imbecility, Gen. iii. 8—19; Jer. xvii. 9, xiii. 23; 2 Cor. iii. 5;—of the atonement and mediation of Christ, as the only legitimate medium of access to God, Isa. liii. 4, 5; 1 Pet. ii. 24; Rom. v. 11; Heb. vii. 24, 25; Rom. v. 1, 2;—of the reality of the Holy Spirit's influence, as a principle of spiritual light, renovation, life, and holiness, Eph. i. 17, 18, ii. 1; Rom. xv. 13; Ezek. xxxvi. 25;—of the justification of the penitent sinner through faith in our Lord Jesus Christ, John iii. 16—18; Rom. iii. 24—27, iv. 2—8; Gal. ii. 16, iii. 6—12;—and of holiness of heart and life, as the evidence of faith, and a meetness for the felicities of the heavenly world, 1 Cor. vi. 11; 1 Pet. i. 13—16; 1 Thess. iii. 13; Heb. xii. 10, 14; Col. i. 12.

3. *A declaration of the benefits received.* The true believer in the Lord Jesus Christ, having been made the partaker of innumerable blessings at the hands of his Divine Master, gratefully acknowledges his obligations, and with pious solicitude inquires, " What shall I render unto the Lord for all his benefits?" And he evinces his gratitude to God, by *aspirations of praise;—by carefully guarding the good which he has received;—by emulating more exalted enjoyments;—and by publishing, for the good of others, what God has done for him.* Ps. xxxiv. 1, 2; 1 Cor. xv. 57; Phil. iii. 8—16; Ps. lxvi. 16; Rom. x. 10; Acts xxiv. xxvi.

4. *Zealously supporting the cause of Christian truth.* No man can properly " confess Christ before men," without feeling a lively concern for

the promotion of the gospel in the earth. This pious zeal manifests itself, by *owning, adhering to, and kindly aiding the followers of Christ*, John xiii. 35;—*by administering affectionate reproof to the ungodly*, Lev. xix. 17; Eph. v. 11;—*by exhibiting an example of Christian excellence to the world*, Matt. v. 13—16;—*by contributing pecuniary support*, Prov. iii. 9; Luke viii. 3;—*and by submitting to reproach and suffering*, when circumstances require it, Acts vii. 54—60, xx. 24, xxi. 13; 2 Cor. xii. 23—33.

II. THE HONORABLE DISTINCTION WITH WHICH A STEADY COURSE OF CHRISTIAN FORTITUDE WILL BE CROWNED. "Him will I confess also before my Father which is in heaven." Although man is by nature a rebel against the Majesty of heaven; yet the subject of vital godliness is owned, and highly distinguished by his God, even whilst journeying down the vale of life; by the ample supplies which are furnished; the invulnerable defence with which he is favored; the divine enjoyments of which he is the partaker; and the animating hope with which he is inspired. But the blessed Redeemer doubtless refers to that solemn period, when,

> " The Judge, descending, thunders from afar,
> And all mankind are summon'd to his bar;"

that tremendous "day when God shall judge the secrets of men by Jesus Christ," "who will render unto every man according to his deeds." At that awful period of final decision, the Redeemer "will confess" his followers before assembled worlds, by

1. *An act of separation.* In the present condition of man, the Christian has to maintain a frequent intercourse with that class of his fellow creatures, who are under the influence of sinful habits and immoral dispositions; and this necessary intermixture is sometimes productive of painful sensations, and moral danger. Even in the silent grave the dust of the righteous and the wicked, in an intermixed state, rests till the morning of the general judgment, "when the dead shall be raised," and an eternal separation take place between "those who serve God, and those who serve him not," Matt. xxv 31—33; Luke xvi. 26.

2. *By an approving plaudit.* The Lord Jesus Christ, in the character of Judge, will publicly *own the persons*, and *approve the conduct* of those, who have boldly asserted his right, and suffered in his cause. Before angels, devils, and men, he will bear testimony to their faithfulness, and introduce them to those regions of unalloyed delight, where the "wicked cease from troubling, and the weary be at rest," Matt. xxv. 23, 34—40.

3. *By making them partakers of his glory.* Such is the amazing condescension of the "Captain of our salvation," that although it is through strength divine, that the Christian overcomes his enemies; perseveres in the path of righteousness; and achieves a final conquest; yet he addresses him, and acts towards him, as though the whole were effected solely by unaided human energy. He does not remind him of his dependence, and his obligations; but makes him the partaker of his honors, his throne, and his felicity. And this glory is *inviolable, eternal*, and yet *progressive*, John xiv. 1 2, 3; Matt. xxv. 46; Rev. iii. 5, 21, v. 10.

From this subject we learn,

1. That the human heart is, by nature, decidedly hostile to the spirit of the gospel.

2. That an entire change is essential to a scriptural confession of Christ.

3. That the Christian cannot ultimately be a loser by suffering for righteousness' sake

CHRISTIAN HOPE.

Romans v. 5.—And hope maketh not ashamed ; because the love of God is shed abroad in your hearts by the Holy Ghost which is given unto us. (Sk.)

The uniformity of christian experience, and its harmony with the sacred scriptures, furnish the most powerful arguments in opposition to the subtle sophisms of infidelity. Though the conditions of men widely differ, yet all those who are under the influence of that "faith which worketh by love," bear the same divine "image and superscription;" and though the several denominations of christians cannot harmonize on some minor points of theory, modes of worship, and forms of church government; yet they all find a central point at which they can meet, in the union of that christian experience described by the apostle in the verses preceding the text. In the passage before us, and its interesting context, the true believer recognises the foundation of his experience, in the atonement and resurrection of Christ, chap. iv. 25 ; the means of its existence and progress in that faith which is " of the operation of God," chap. v. 1, 2 ; its interesting gradation, ver. 3, 4 ; and its pleasing influence. Let us proceed to consider,

I. The nature of christian hope.
II. The effect which it produces.
III. The reason which it assigns.

In giving a general idea of hope, we may consider it as implying the *approbation* of its object ; either on account of its real or imaginary excellence ;—the *possibility* of possessing that object ;—the *desire* of attainment ; and a *pleasurable sensation of mind*, commensurate with our estimate of the object, and our prospect of possessing it. In confining our attention to christian hope, it will be necessary to consider,

I. *The magnificence of its object.* The hope of the christian is an object infinitely superior to every thing of an earthly kind ; it quits terrestrial scenes ; it mounts on high ; approaches the throne of the Eternal ; and fixes on the " glory of God" as its object. The term "glory" is sometimes associated with *conquest*, and in this sense it is the distinguished object of the believer's hope. That adorable Being, whose perfections he emulates is the universal conqueror ; and through him the christian hopes to overcome all opposition, triumph over every enemy, and seize the victor's palm in the regions of immortality, Rom. viii. 73 ; 1 Cor. xv. 57. "Glory" is sometimes descriptive of *grandeur*, and such are the exalted expectations of the christian, that he hopes to participate in the grandeur of his triumphant Redeemer, and vie with the sun when beaming forth in all his noontide refulgence, Dan. xii. 2, 3 ; Matt. xiii. 43 ; Rev. iii. 21. But by " the glory of God," the believer more generally understands the participation of *celestial felicity ;* the eternal enjoyment of the unveiled glories of the Deity ; comprehending the entire exclusion of every species of evil, the perfections of society, and the consummation of happiness, Matt. xxv. 34 ; 46 ; 1 Pet. i. 3, 4. But as ungodly men sometimes profess to have hopes of heaven, it is of considerable importance that we attend to,

2. *The purity of its motive.* The hope of the righteous is influenced by a motive widely different from, and superior to, that which excites the feeble and groundless expectation of the sinner. Whilst the wicked hope to go to heaven merely that they may escape that punishment which is the just award of their rebellious conduct ; the righteous have the same object in view, and hope to attain it from principles of *love to God, attachment to his*

people, delight in holiness, and an ardent desire to enjoy the presence of Jehovah, 2 Cor. v. 1—4; Phil. i. 23.

3. *The solidity of its basis.* The hope of the christian is not founded on a supposed goodness of heart, nor on a comparative superiority of character, nor yet on the mercy of God simply considered, for he remembers the righteous claims of divine justice; and therefore the basis of his hope is, the atonement of Christ, and a lively interest in, and union with the " true vine," John xv. 4, 5; Rom. v. 1, 2, viii. 1—9; Gal. ii. 20.

II. THE EFFECT WHICH IT PRODUCES;—"maketh not ashamed." Although every true believer in the Lord Jesus Christ is ashamed of his former sinful practices, of his late ungodly associates, and of every thing inconsistent with the holy constitution of the gospel; yet he is " not ashamed,"

1. *Of Jesus Christ and his truth.* He humbly acknowledges his need of him as an all-sufficient and a present Saviour; with holy gratitude and pious exultation he confesses his interest in his dependence upon, and his obligation unto him. He is zealous for the extension of christian truth in earth, and in various ways labours to advance his Master's interests among men, Matt. x. 32; Rom. i. 16: Gal. vi. 14; 1 Tim. i. 15, 16.

2. *Of the reproach which is connected with christianity.* Suffering and reproach have been connected with the progress of christian truth in all ages, and the records of the christian church have been stained with the tears and blood of the magnanimous soldiers of the cross, who, fearless of all consequences, have steadily avowed their attachment to their divine Master. Yea, they have rejoiced in having been permitted to participate in the sufferings of their Lord, Acts vii. 54—60, xx. 24, xxi. 13; Heb. xi. 35—40.

3. *Of his christian brethren.* The genuine follower of the Lord Jesus Christ, considers all who bear the image of his Master, however poor and afflicted they may be, as members of his heavenly Father's family, fellow heirs of the same eternal inheritance, and partakers of like precious faith with himself. He acknowledges them by acts of social intercourse, by participating in their sorrows, and by administering to their necessities, John xiii. 34, 35; Rom. xv. 1, 2; 1 John iv. 11, 12, 20, 21.

4. *Of pious exertion in the cause of Christ.* This the christian considers to be a duty incumbent upon him, and for the purpose of aiding this cause, he prudently declares what God has done for him; administers affection, admonition, and reproof to his fellow creatures; and engages in the regular ordinances of christianity according to his ability; crowning the whole with incessant prayer to God for the prosperity of Zion, Psa. lxvi. 16, cxxii. 6; 1 Cor. ix. 19—22.

III. THE REASON WHICH IT ASSIGNS;—"Because the love of God is shed abroad in our hearts," &c. The religion of the gospel is a reasonable thing, and all its effects are strictly consistent with that divine source from which they proceed, and its highly honored subjects are " able to give a reason of the hope that is in them."

1. *The strength of its evidence.* The residence of the Holy Spirit in the breast of the christian, furnishes him with an indubitable evidence of the heavenly origin and divine reality of his religion. The skeptic may cavil, and the sneering infidel may object, but the

> " Christian dwells, like Uriel, in the sun
> Meridian evidence puts doubt to flight,
> And ardent hope anticipates the skies."

The Spirit of love dwelling in his heart, bears ample testimony to his presence there, Rom. viii. 14—17; 2 Cor. vi. 16; Gal iv. 6. And this internal conviction is accompanied by external operations of corresponding character, as *spirituality of temper and disposition; obedience to the divine commandments; resignation to the divine will;* and *zeal for the divine glory,* Gal. v. 22—24; 1 John iv. 13—21.

2. *The fulness of that enjoyment with which it is connected.* "The love of God" is pleasingly adapted to the intense cravings of an immortal spirit; and when this love " is shed abroad in the heart," it produces happiness the most pure, the most satisfactory, and the most permanent. The burden of native guilt is removed, peace is experienced, joy fills the heart, and the expanding soul has large anticipations of celestial felicity, "rejoicing in hope of the glory of God," Romans v 11, xiv, 17; 2 Tim. iv, 6—8.

This subject tends,

1. To promote inquiry respecting our interest in this hope.
2. To elicit sentiments of gratitude from those who possess it.
3. To stimulate to diligence those who are " without hope.'

WATCHFULNESS, A PREPARATION FOR THE COMING OF CHRIST.

Mark xiii. 35, 36.—Watch ye therefore : for ye know not when the master of the house cometh, at even, or at midnight, or at the cock crowing, or in the morning ; lest coming suddenly he find you sleeping. (B.)

I name these words as the subject of a discourse, at this time, because I think nothing happens by chance; that the superintending providence of God is over all things, especially over the death of mankind, and that in a signal manner, when any individuals are suddenly and unexpectedly removed from this world. I think, likewise, that such dispensations are peculiar calls and warnings to the living to " prepare to meet their God;" and that it is the duty of those who " watch for souls," to endeavor to improve such events, and thus, in a certain sense, to be "workers together with God."

The Author, (having here mentioned several instances of sudden death, which had recently occurred,) then proceeds to consider,

I. WHAT WE ARE TO UNDERSTAND BY THE COMING OF THE MASTER OF THE HOUSE.

By " the master of the house," here, is meant Christ, as it is also in Luke xiii. 25. The world in general, and the visible Church in particular, and especially the spiritual part of it, are his house. Eph. i. 20—25; Heb. iii. 3—6.

His coming is represented in Scripture in different lights, and for different purposes.

In this chapter of Mark, and in the 24th chapter of Matthew, and the 21st of St. Luke, he is represented as coming to judge and punish the Jewish nation, his visible church of old, or his house, for rejecting him. Deut. xviii. 19, comp. with Acts iii. 23; Heb. xii. 15.

In other places he is represented as coming to judge all mankind at the last day. Ver. 24, 26; 2 Pet. iii. 3—12.

He is said to come. when he visits in a peculiar way, whether in judgment or mercy, any nation, or church, or any particular member of it. Rev. ii. 5, 16; iii. 3.

He comes to each of us at death. Rev. i. 18; ii. 25; iii. 11.

It is this last coming of Christ to which I would especially call your attention. For it is of the greatest importance to us, since—It will separate us from all below, from our occupations, enjoyments, possessions, families, relations, and friends, and even from our own bodies.—It will finish our state of trial, and determine our condition for ever; for, you know, we are here on our trial for eternity.—It will bring us into the unseen and eternal world, a new, untried, unknown state.—It will place us in the presence of God, that we may receive his smile or frown, may enjoy the effects of his favor and friendship, and communications of bliss from him, or feel the effects of his wrath, and find him to be a consuming fire.—It will make a most astonishing change in our circumstances.—It often comes suddenly, and gives no warning.— —

II. What is that watchfulness which is recommended as a preparation for his coming.

It implies life, spiritual life, in opposition to that sleep of death which is mentioned, Eph. v. 14; which text compare with Eph. ii. 1.— —

It implies a lively sense of the reality and importance of spiritual and eternal things, such as persons awake have of temporal things, the seeing, feeling, tasting them, so to speak, in opposition to that insensibility about them, which is implied in spiritual sleep.

It implies a thoughtfulness, care, and concern about them, in opposition to that thoughtlessness and unconcern about them, which is natural to us.— —

It implies a sense of our danger from our enemies, visible and invisible; from the Devil, the world, persons and things, the flesh, our own hearts, and the standing on our guard, in opposition to security of mind, and foolish peace.— —

It implies activity, and the vigorous exercise of every grace and virtue, as repentance, faith, hope, love, patience, &c., in opposition to indolence and sloth.— —

III. The vast importance of this watchfulness, as a preparation for every dispensation of divine Providence, and especially for death.

The spiritual life, and lively sense of the things of God, which are comprehended in this watchfulness, form a preparation for every event of Providence, as for temporal losses or gains, honor or dishonor, sickness, or health, &c.—We are thus armed against every enemy and assault.—We are fitted for every duty to God, our neighbor, and ourselves.—We are also in this way prepared for death.—

Does death separate us from all below? We are prepared to be thus separated, being dead to the world, and our wills being resigned to the will of God. Does it terminate our state of trial? We are prepared to have it terminated. Does it bring us into the invisible world? We are ready for that world; our thoughts and affections have gone before us, and we have made provision, and laid up treasure there. Does it bring us into the presence of God? The watchful are prepared for his presence, having by grace, through faith, ensured his favor, his friendship, his image, an acquaintance and fellowship with him. Does it make an astonishing change in our circumstances? The watchful are prepared for that change, having acquired a meetness for, and an earnest of heaven in their hearts. Does it often come suddenly, and give no warning? The watchful are habitually expecting it, and therefore are not surprised by its arrival. — —

But very different is the case with the unwatchful.—Suppose them, first, *unconverted* persons. If awakened on the borders of the grave, they are thrown into the greatest confusion and dismay; they are carried away from all those sensual possessions and enjoyments on which they once doted; their state of trial is ended, and they can never afterwards be quickened to spiritual life and renewed in holiness; they awake into a life worse than dying.— —Suppose them *righteous.* By their improvident slumbering they darken their evidences, and render their state uncomfortable; they cannot expect any peculiar support or consolation at a dying hour, or in the time of affliction; they are often left to wrestle with sore temptation; they make dismal work for bitter repentance on a sick and death bed; they have the misery of reflecting that they have omitted many duties to God and man which now can never be performed, have not attained those degrees of holiness they might have attained, and although they do not finally perish, they have deprived themselves of the reward they might have enjoyed. As they bring little glory to God in life, so they do him no honor in their death, and leave little comfort to their friends concerning them. Perhaps they leave them in doubt whether they are saved or lost.

IV. HOW WE MAY BE ENABLED TO TAKE THIS ADVICE, AND TO "WATCH;" and what are the means leading to that end.

We must not presume on a long life, which is a most dangerous temptation, and an abundant source of unwatchfulness; but we must set before us, and have always in view, the shortness and uncertainty of the present life, and the certainty and nearness of death.—We must remember, that unless we were lords of our own lives, and could appoint the time of our death, we can never be exempt from the duty of a wakeful and active attention to our spiritual and eternal interests.—Those whose constitutions are peculiarly feeble, or whose circumstances or employments expose them to peculiar danger, or who are arrived at old age, should consider themselves as being under especial obligations to be watchful.—We must be particularly on our guard against our own nature, and every person and thing around us, which tends to lull us asleep, and against sensuality and worldly cares. Luke xxi. 34.— We must remember that thousands are found sleeping, even thousands of professors, at the coming of their Lord.—We must pray much; a duty frequently inculcated in connection with watchfulness. Ver. 33; Luke xxi. 36; Eph. vi. 18.— —

HOLY ARDOR.

Psalm lxiii. 8.—My soul followeth hard after thee. (Sk.)

To mankind in general this passage must be quite unintelligible. "God is not in all their thoughts, consequently they neither desire nor seek him. They might use the text with great propriety to express their attachment to the world, and its various objects—" Riches, honors, power, pleasures, our souls follow hard after *you.*" It is only the christian that can truly adopt this language as his own. But even among professing christians too many are strangers to such sacred fervours—many feel them but too seldom—and few, if any, appreciate them aright. It will therefore be proper.

I. To DESCRIBE THIS STATE OF EXPERIENCE. It implies,

1. *A renunciation of the world.* This results from a conviction of its vanity. No man can follow God and the world at once, Matt. vi. 24; Luke xvi. 13; 1 John ii. 15. But we never renounce the world till we feel its vanity, and sensibly apprehend the fallacy of its *pretensions*—the unsatisfying nature of its *enjoyments*—the uncertainty and shortness of its *tenure.* In renouncing the world, however, we do not neglect its lawful concerns—shun human society—or despise the blessings of Providence. But we withdraw all *dependence* upon it—all *improper detachment* to it—and all *anxious cares* concerning it.

2. *A deliberate choice of God*, as the only adequate good of the soul. The soul must have some supreme object—The creature renounced, it can only cleave to the Creator, whom it now views as the sovereign Good, *suitable* to its nature—*adequate* to its wants—*permanent and secure* in possession.

3. *A vehement and intense desire after him.* This is the sense of the text. Perhaps the Psalmist alludes to a thirsty hart seeking the cooling brook, ver. 1; Psa. xliii. 1. The soul longs ardently to *know* God in Christ more explicitly—to be more perfectly *conformed to his image*—to have more *intimate communion* with him, and finally to *enjoy him* in all his plenitude for ever.

4. *The exercise of faith and hope.* God can only be known by faith—and unless we believe he is to be found, we shall never seek after him, Heb. xi. 2. The soul *apprehends* him as its God in Christ, and fully *anticipates* all the enjoyments which it desires. And in this exercise of faith and hope there is *present delight.*—The soul divinely sustained ("thy right hand upholdeth me") cheerfully and eagerly follows after God in the path of duty—in prayer, hearing, and all his ordinances. We are now led,

II. To INVESTIGATE THE REASONS WHY IT IS SO RARE.

It is obvious few christians enjoy this experience; at least it is only *occasionally*, and not *generally*, that their hearts are in this state. The principal causes of their languor are,

1. *Inattention to the state of their own hearts.* They are not recollected;—they do not examine themselves closely. Hence they are ignorant of their real condition, and do not keenly feel their wants.—But unless we are deeply sensible of our need of God, we shall never follow hard after him.

2. *Permitting the objects of sense to make too deep impressions.* These naturally tend to blunt the edge of holy desire, and to divide and weaken the soul. Whatever convictions may have been received of the vanity of the world, it will again obtain the ascendency without much watchfulness and firm resistance.

3. *Neglect of the instituted means.* This indeed is often the *effect* of losing spiritual ardor. But it is more frequently the *cause.* When we imagine that the holy flame will burn without the aid of additional fuel, and without fanning it by frequent approaches to God, we fall into a dangerous, and too often fatal snare.

4. *The indulgence of wrong dispositions, &c.* Unbelief, pride, vain curiosity, levity, censoriousness, uncharitable or useless conversation, &c. all these, like water, tend to damp and weaken, if not wholly to extinguish the desire for God

These are the principal reasons why David's experience is now so rarely enjoyed. But surely if christians knew how to value this state aright, they would never permit these causes so frequently to deprive them of it. In order to induce them to resist these hinderances, and to cultivate this state of soul, let us proceed,

III. To REPRESENT IT AS THE MOST DESIRABLE EXPERIENCE. Innumerable are the advantages which result from it. We can only name a few

1. *It is the best security against the allurements and troubles of the world.* A heart earnestly pursuing God has no leisure to gaze on the seductive charms of temporal good, and no disposition to pierce itself with the thorns of worldly solicitude. Comparative indifference to all but God, disarms both pleasure and pain of their power to injure, while the soul, free and disentangled, rapidly moves on in her heavenly course.

2. *It renders every duty delightful.* In this state nothing is done through custom, formality, or any other inferior motive—but every duty is performed with the highest views. God in Christ is aimed at in all—and oh ! how sweet is prayer or praise, reading or hearing, meditation or christian conversation, or even the commonest affairs of life, when we thus do all " in the name of our Lord Jesus," &c. Col. iii. 17.

3. *It prepares us for the largest communication.* We always receive from God what we earnestly and faithfully seek from him, Luke ii. 9, 10. In proportion, therefore, as our souls are enlarged by holy desire, humble faith, and earnest expectations, will be the divine communications unto them By this holy fervor the soul throws itself open to receive all the fulness of God, the shoreless, fathomless ocean of good.

4. *It advances our sanctification, and consequently qualifies us for heaven.* Detaching us from the creature, fixing us upon the Creator, leading us to communion and fellowship with him, we naturally imbibe more and more of *his Spirit,* become more and more transformed into *his likeness*—All sin vanishes from his powerful presence—pure universal love occupies our whole hearts, and thus we become meet for our inheritance among the saints in light.

Let us conclude by addressing,

1. Those whose hearts are wholly set upon the world. You cleave to visible objects, and entirely neglect your Maker, Benefactor, and Redeemer —your Sovereign, Lawgiver, and Judge. Oh consider—*the excess of your folly*—you prefer shadows to realities, vexation of spirit to peace of mind —misery to bliss. *The baseness of your ingratitude*—you reject your only friend, and side with his enemies. *The enormity of your guilt*—you idolize the creature, and pour contempt upon the Creator. —*The imminence of your danger*—you are exposed to the fierceness of the divine displeasure, to all the torments of hell, Jer. xvii. 5; John iii. 31.

2. Lukewarm and unstable professors—you are if possible more culpable than the former—Consider how inconsistent your character is with you *obligations—your engagements—your profession—*and your *interest.*

3. Ardent spiritually-minded christians—go forward—fear not the imputation of enthusiasm—fear no disappointment. Believe the promise—cherish the most sanguine hopes—Delight yourselves in the Lord, and he shall give you the desires of your hearts, Matt. v. 6; Rev. xxi. 6.

THE POOR AND CONTRITE THE OBJECTS OF GOD'S FAVOR.

Isa). lxvi. 2.—To this man will I look, even to him that is poor and of a contrite spirit and trembleth at my word.   (S. S.)

It often happens that accidental distinctions serve men as grounds of confidence towards God—

Many found their hopes on no better basis than Micah did—Judg. xvii. 13.

The Jews in particular thought themselves assured of the divine favor because of God's residence in their temple*—

But God shews them the folly of their notions†—

And declares the character of those, who alone shall be considered by him with any favorable regard.

I. Who are the ojects oe the divine favor?

Men choose for their companions the rich and gay—

But those, whom God regards, are of a very different character—

1. They *feel themselves destitute of all good.*

It is not temporal, but spiritual poverty, that distinguishes God's people—

They have discovered their total want of spiritual *wisdom*—Prov. xxx. 2, 3.

They are constrained to acknowledge that they have no *righteousness* of their own—Isai. lxiv. 6.

And that they are "without *strength*" for obedience—Rom. v. 6.   2 Cor. iii. 5.

They unfeignedly adopt the language of St. Paul—Rom. vii. 18.

Nor do they hope for mercy but as the *free gift* of God‡—

2. They *bewail the many evils they have committed.*

They have been made to see that sin is hateful to God—

And they have felt the bitterness of it in their own consciences—

They know experimentally the sensations of David—Ps. xxxviii. 4, 6, 8.

They loathe themselves for all their abominations—Ezek. xxxvi. 31.

Nor are their convictions merely occasional or transient—

They are *habitually* of a tender and "contrite spirit"—

3. They *pay a reverential regard to every word of God.*

They dare not say like the idolatrous Jews—Jer. xliv. 16.

They rather resemble the man after God's own heart—Ps. cxix. 161.

If the word be preached, they "receive it as the word, not of man, but of God"—

They hear the *threatenings* like the meek Josiah—2 Chron. xxxiv. 19, 27.

They attend to the *promises* with an eager desire to embrace them—

To every *precept* they listen with an obedient ear.‖—

---

* Hence that common boast among them, Jer. vii. 4.

† Ver. 1, 2.   The import of which is, How can you think that I, an infinite Being, who myself created those things of which you boast, can be allured by an earthly structure to continue my presence among you, if you persist in your evil ways?

‡ They say not, like the servant, Matt. xviij. 26. but desire to experience the clemency shown to insolvent debtors, Luke vii. 42.

‖ Luke Cornelius, Acts x. 33. and Paul, Acts xxii. 10. yea, the angels in heaven, Ps xiii. 20.

These, though generally considered by the world as weak and super-stitious, are not overlooked by the Supreme Being.

II. THE PECULIAR REGARD WHICH GOD SHEWS THEM.

The " eyes of God are in every place beholding the evil and the good"—
But he "looks to" *these*, in a far different manner from *others*—
This distinguishing favor implies,

1. Approbation of them.

From the proud and self-sufficient, God turns his face—James iv. 6.
But he "despises not the broken and contrite in heart"—Ps. li. 17.
Though so exalted in himself, he will not disdain to notice them—
His approbation of such characters stands recorded for ever—Luke xviii. 13, 14.

His reception of the prodigal is an eternal monument of the regard he will shew to *every* repenting sinner—

2. Care over them.

Wherever they go, his eye is upon them for good—2 Chron. xvi. 9.
He watches them in order to deliver them from danger—Ps. xii. 5.
He watches them in order to comfort them in trouble—Ps. cxlvii. 3.
He watches them in order to relieve them in want—Isai. xli. 17, 18.
He watches them in order to exalt them to happiness and honor—1 Sam ii. 8.

3. Delight in them.

There are none on earth so pleasing to God as brokenhearted sinners—
Their sighs and groans are as music in his ears—Ps. cii. 19, 20.
Their tears he treasures up in his vial—Ps. lvi. 8.
He dwells with them as his dearest friends—Isai. lvii. 15.
He rejoices over them as a people in whom he greatly delights—Zeph. iii. 12, 17.
He saves them *here* by the unceasing exercise of his power—Ps. xxxiv. 15. 18.
And reserves for them *hereafter* an inheritance in heaven—Matt. v. 3.

Nor shall the fewness of such characters render them at all less the objects of God's regard.

It must be acknowledged that they are but few—
But if there were only *one* in the whole world, God would find him out*—
Not all the splendor of heaven, nor all the acclamations of angels, should for a moment divert God's attention from him—
Though he were despised by all the human race, yet should he be amiable in the eyes of his Maker—
Nor should he want any thing in time or eternity—
Never shall that declaration in any instance be falsified—Ps cxxxviii. 6.

INFER,

1. How should we admire the condescension of God!

If we view only the material world we may well stand astonished that God should regard such an insignificant creature as man—Ps. viii. 3, 4.

But, if we contemplate the majesty of God, we cannot but exclaim with Solomon—1 Kings viii. 27.

Let then the declaration in the text lead our thoughts up to God—.
Let us adore him for so clearly describing the objects of his favor.
And let us express our admiration in the words of David—Ps. cx. 5—8.

* " To this *man*, &c. even to *him*, &c."

294

2. How shou'd we desire to attain the character that is pleasing to God! The poor and contrite are *exclusively* beloved of God—
If he look on others, it is only as he did on the Egyptians, Exod. **xiv.** 24, 25.

And how dreadful must it be to have *such* an enemy!—

But how delightful to have an *almighty, omnipresent* guardian!—

Above all, how awful must it be to have *him turn his face from us* in the day of Judgment!—

Let us then endeavor to humble ourselves before God—Isai. ii. 11.

And rest assured that the promised mercy shall in due time be fulfilled to us—James iv. 10.

~~~~~~~~~~

THE REWARD OF CHRIST'S FOLLOWERS.

Matt. xix. 27.—Then answered Peter and said unto him, Behold, we have forsaken **all,** and followed thee ; what shall we have therefore ? (Sk.)

WHATEVER enterprize we engage in, it is equally rational and just duly to consider the general merits of its character and the probable results of its issue. This is more especially the case when we embark in any cause which is likely to involve the most interesting and important consequences. Now this is unquestionably the character of religion, which is the one thing needful to every human being. In making choice therefore of this momentous subject, we should "first count the cost," and then willingly renounce every thing which is incompatible with its possession, or it is impossible to realize its personal benefits. This is evidently the doctrine that is taught in the preceding context, and which gave rise to the language of the text. The Saviour having described the snares of affluence, and asserted the impossibility of those who trust in riches to enter into the kingdom of heaven, (as strikingly exemplified in the case of the young ruler, with whom he had been conversing,) Peter, with his usual zeal and boldness, "answered and said, Behold, we have forsaken all," &c. These words clearly unfold the true character of Christ's disciples, and distinctly suggest the evils they renounced—the example they follow—and the reward they anticipate.

I. THE EVILS THEY RENOUNCE ;—"Behold, we have *forsaken all*," said Peter. And though Christ does not require all his followers to forsake their secular occupations and become ministers of the gospel as the apostles did, yet there are many things which we must renounce for his sake, or we cannot be his disciples, Matt. xvi. 24.

1. *We must forsake all our sinful practices.* As impenitent sinners, **we** "live after the flesh according to the course of this world, fulfilling the desires of the flesh and of the mind," Eph. ii. 2, 3. But as the followers **of** Christ, we must mortify the deeds of the body, "cease to do evil, and learn to do well." Every vicious habit must be fully abandoned, however painful to human nature, Matt. v. 29, 30.—Whatever is offensive to God and injurious to the soul, must be freely sacrificed to our best interests on the altar of conscience and truth.—"Let the wicked forsake his way, and the unrighteous man his thoughts." All sin of every description must be faithfully renounced, as utterly inconsistent with Christian discipleship, Tit. ii. 11, 12.

2. *We must forsake all our ungodly associates.* While we are of **the**

world we are companions of the wicked, are actuated by the same carnal principles, and governed by the same worldly maxims. But when Divine grace apprehends and subdues sinners, and convinces them of the vanity and corruption of the world, they immediately "come out from among them, and are separate, and touch not the unclean thing," 2 Cor. vi. 17, 18. And though religion does not forbid every kind of intercourse with the wicked, yet it teaches its subjects the evil and danger of making them their constant associates and intimate friends, 2 Cor. vi. 14—16; James iv. 4. And hence, like David, they become companions of them that fear the Lord, and their delight is with the excellent of the earth.

3. *We must forsake all our unholy attachments.* Religion regards the heart as well as the life. We must not only be outwardly separated from sin and sinners, but also inwardly renewed in the spirit of our minds, Eph. iv. 22—24. An undue attachment to the world was evidently the ruin of the hopeful young man whose character and conduct are recorded in this chapter. He loved his possessions, and was unwilling to give up every thing for Christ, ver. 21, 22; Matt. x. 37, 38. But his faithful disciples "crucify the flesh with its affections and lusts," and gladly forsake sin in all its diversified forms and fascinating snares. The text also asserts,

II. THE EXAMPLE THEY FOLLOW ;—" We have forsaken all and *followed 'hee.*" The apostles followed Christ, both *literally* and *morally*, as his personal attendants and approved disciples. They gladly received his word, acknowledged his Messiahship, and obeyed his injunctions. In these respects we also ought to be "followers of God as dear children."

1. *We should follow Christ as our teacher, by embracing his gospel.* He is an infallible prophet, and teaches the way of God perfectly. "He spake as never man spake," Matt. vii. 28, 29.—His word is spirit and life, and able to save the soul. It must be received believingly, gratefully, experimentally, and practically "as the power of God unto salvation," John viii. 31, 32.—As willing and obedient disciples, we must affectionately imbibe, and duly improve, all the instructions of his word and Spirit, "Hear ye him."

2. *We should follow Christ as our Sovereign. by obeying his precepts.* He is the King of Zion, and sways his sceptre in his church.—As our Redeemer, Saviour, and Judge, he justly demands the obedience of mankind, 1 Cor. vi. 19, 20.—We must obey him decidedly, cheerfully, faithfully, and constantly.—In vain do we profess to be *taught* by him, and trust in him, if we do not *obey* him. Obedience is the genuine test of discipleship, Matt. vii. 20. "Ye are my friends if ye do whatsoever I command you."

3. *We should follow Christ as our pattern, by imitating his example.*— "He did no sin, neither was guile found in his mouth; for he fulfilled all righteousness."—His example is perfect, extensive, intelligible, and distinctly recorded by the evangelists for our instruction and encouragement.—As far as possible we should imbibe the spirit that he manifested, uniformly follow the example which he left for our imitation, John xiii. 15; 1 Pet. ii. 21. We shall thus "walk as he also walked," and rejoice with all his disciples tn,

III. THE REWARD THEY ANTICIPATE ;—"What shall we have therefore?" Whatever motive might prompt this important inquiry, the Saviour kindly gave a full and explicit answer in the following context, by which we are taught,

1. *Following Christ will secure our personal salvation.* They "shall inherit everlasting life," ver. 29.—Now it is impossible to obtain the inheritance of glory without a previous possession of saving grace, Heb. xii. 14.

Those who reject Christ, are condemned already; but such as embrace and follow him " are saved by grace through faith." They take his yoke upon them, and find rest unto their souls, Matt. xi. 28—40. Conformity to his image and will, constitutes both the purity and felicity of his followers.

2. *Following Christ will secure our temporal interests.*—He assured his disciples that whatever worldly advantages they might sacrifice for his sake, they would certainly "receive manifold more in the present life," ver. 29. Though he did not promise them riches, he engaged to supply all their necessities.—Religion always casts a friendly influence over all our temporal concerns, and makes " all things work together for our good." It insures every blessing, both for life and godliness, for this world and the next, Ps. lxxxiv. 11 ; Matt. vi. 33 ; 1 Tim. iv. 8.

3. *Following Christ will secure our eternal happiness.* He therefore distinctly promised this to the apostles, in his answer to Peter, ver. 28. This promise is certainly glorious in its import, and infallible in its accomplishment. It is the end that crowns the work. Christians have respect to the recompense of reward, and follow Christ from earth to heaven. He is now precious to their souls, and soon they will appear with him in glory everlasting, John xiv. 2. 3 ; 1 John iii. 2.

Are we the followers of Christ? Do we follow him fully, or at a distance? Let his enemies repent and believe, and escape the wrath to come. But let the saints rejoice, and " follow on to know the Lord."

THE BLESSEDNESS OF FEARING GOD.

Eccl. viii. 12 —Surely I know that it shall be well with them that fear God. (S. S.)

NOTHING certain can be determined respecting God's favor from the outward dispensations of his providence, Eccl. ix. 1.

The wicked seem on the whole to prosper more than others, Psa. lxxiii. 5, 12.

Nevertheless the godly are by far the happier persons, Ps. lxxiii. 15.

It is of them only that the assertion in the text can be made—

We propose to shew,

I. WHO THEY ARE THAT FEAR GOD.

This, we may suppose, would be a point easy to be determined—

But, through self-love and Satan's devices, many mistake respecting it—

The characters described in the text may be distinguished by the following marks :—

1. They stand in awe of God's judgments.

Once they disregarded the displeasure of the Almighty—Ps. x. 5.

They would not believe that his threatenings would be executed—

But now they have learned to tremble at his word—Isai. lxvi. 2.

Awakened by his Spirit, they exclaim with the prophet—Isai. xxxiii. 14

The scriptures uniformly represent them in this light—Acts xvi. 29. and Ps. cxix. 120.

2. They embrace the salvation offered them.

In their natural state they felt no need of a physician—Rev. iii. 17.

They saw no suitableness in the remedy which the gospel offered them— 1 Cor. i. 23.

Their pride would not suffer them to submit to its humiliating terms, **Rom x. 3.**

But now they gladly embrace Christ as their only Saviour—

They flee to him, as the murderers did to a city of refuge—

This is the description given of them in the inspired volume, Heb. vi. 18.

3. They endeavor to keep all the commandments.

If ever they obeyed God at all, they served him only to the extent the world would approve—

Where the lax habits of mankind forbade their compliance with the divine command, they were afraid to be singular—

But they dare not any longer halt between God and Baal—

They have determined, through grace, to follow the Lord fully—

The language of their hearts is like that of David, Ps. cxix. 5, 6.

This was the very ground on which God concluded that Abraham feared him, Gen. xxii. 12.

These marks clearly distinguish those who fear God from all others.

The *formal Pharisee* has never felt his desert of condemnation, Luke xviii. 11.

The *merely awakened sinner* has never truly embraced the gospel, Acts xxiv. 25, and xxvi. 23.

The *hypocritical professor* has never mortified his besetting sin, Acts viii. 23.

It is *the person* alone, *who fears God*, that unites in his experience a dread of God's wrath, an affiance in Christ, and a love to the commandments—

Such persons, notwithstanding appearances, are truly blessed.

II. In what respects it shall be well with them.

They are not exempt from the common afflictions of life—

They have in addition to them many trials peculiar to themselves—

Yet it goes well with them.

1. In respect of temporal good.

They have a peculiar enjoyment of *prosperity*—

The ungodly find an emptiness in all their possessions, Job. xx. 22.

But the godly have not such gall mixed with their comforts, Prov. **x. 22** 1 Tim. vi. 17.

They have also peculiar supports in a season of *adversity*—

The wicked are for the most part miserable in their affliction, Eccl. **v. 17**

If kept from murmuring, it is the summit of their attainments—

But the righteous are enabled to glory in tribulation, Rom. v. 3.

And cordially to approve of God's dispensations towards them, 2 Kings xx. 19.

2. In respect of spiritual good.

They possess a peace that passeth all understanding—

They are filled with a joy utterly unknown to others, Prov. xiv. 10.

The work of sanctification is gradually carried on within them, 2 Cor. iv. 16.

As they approach towards death they grow in a meetness for heaven—

And are serene and happy in the near prospect of eternity, Psa. xxxvii. 37.

3. In respect to eternal good.

Who can set forth their felicity in the eternal world?—

Who can even conceive the weight of glory preparing for them .—

How will their faith be lost in sight, and their hope in enjoyment !—

Then indeed will that truth be seen and felt by them, Ps. cxliv. 15.

These things are far from being " cunningly devised fables."

III. What assurance we have that it shall be thus well with them.

No truth whatever is capable of clearer demonstration—

The topics from whence it might be proved are innumerable—

We shall however confine ourselves to three.

1. The fitness of things requires it.

No man can seriously think that there is one portion to the righteous and the wicked—

There is no well ordered government on earth where this is the case—

Much less can we suppose it possible in the divine government—

To imagine such a thing, is to strip the Deity of all regard to his own honor—

We may be sure that there shall be a distinction made in favor of his servants, Mal. iii. 18.

2. The promises of God insure it.

All *temporal* good is expressly promised to those " who fear God," Psa. xxxiv. 9.

All *spiritual* good also is given them as their portion, Ps. xxv. 12, 13.

Yea, all *eternal* good is laid up for them as their unalienable inheritance, Ps. ciii. 17.

All the promises are made over to them in one word, 1 Tim. iv. 8.

Can any one doubt a truth so fully established?—

3. The experience of all that ever feared God attests it.

Who ever found it unprofitable to serve the Lord? Jer. ii. 31.

What truly devoted soul was ever forsaken by him? Isa. xlix. 15.

Who ever complained that the means, by which he was brought to fear God, were too severe?—

Or that any affliction, that increased and confirmed that fear, was too heavy?

David indeed did at one time question the position in the text—

But on recollection he condemned himself for his rashness and ignorance—

And acknowledged that his vile suspicions contradicted the experience of God's children in all ages, Ps. lxxiii. 12—15, 22.

On these grounds we " assuredly know" the truth declared in the text.

We do not *surmise it as a* thing *possible*—

We do not *hope it as* a thing *probable*—

We *absolutely know it as infallibly certain*—

We are not surer of our existence than we are of this truth—

Without hesitation therefore we deliver our message, Isa. iii. 10, 11

O that the word may sink deep into all our hearts !—

And that we might from experience unite our testimony to Solomon's, Prov. xxviii. 14.

We beg leave to ask, whether they who fear *not* God, have any such assurance in their favor?

We are aware that they will entertain presumptuous hopes—

And that, in opposition to God's word, they will expect happiness—

But does the boldest sinner dare affirm that he *knows* it shall be well with him ?—

His conscience would instantly revolt at such falsehood and blasphemy—

Let those then, that fear not God, stand self-condemned—

Let them flee unto their God and Saviour with penitence and faith—

Let them so live as to preserve the testimony of a good conscience—

And then, however enlarged their expectations of good may be, they shall never be disappointed, Isa. xlv. 17.

THE JOY OF THE LORD IS OUR STRENGTH.

Neh. viii. 10.—The joy of the Lord is your strength.   (S. S.)

THE preaching of God's word is a very ancient ordinance—
In the context we have a description of the manner in which Nehemiah conducted it—
These means of instruction were useful in that day—
Nor are they less necessary in every place and age—
People need, not only reproof for what is wrong, but direction in what is right—
The Jews wept bitterly at the hearing of the law—
But Nehemiah corrected their sorrow as ill-timed—
And exhorted them to rejoice in God, who had done so great things for them—

I. WHAT REASON WE HAVE TO REJOICE IN THE LORD.

God is often said to rejoice over his people—Zeph. iii. 17.
But the joy here spoken of must be understood rather of that which we feel in the recollection of God's goodness towards us.
The Jews at that season had special cause for joy in God.
They had been miraculously delivered from Babylon—
This temple had been rebuilt in twenty years, and the worship of God restored—
And now, after seventy years more, the wall of the city was finished—
They had been enabled to surmount innumerable difficulties—ch. iv. 27.
They had prospered, even to a miracle, in their endeavors—ch. vi. 16.
These were tokens of the divine favor, and pledges of its continuance—
They were therefore called upon to rejoice with gratitude and confidence—
Nor was their sorrow, however just, to exclude this joy—
Such reason also have all the Lord's people to rejoice in the Lord,
They have experienced a redemption from sorer captivity—
And been delivered by more stupendous means—
Every day's preservation too is, as it were, a miracle—
Yet the work of their souls is carried on in spite of enemies—
Yea, *is expedited through the means used to defeat it*—
Surely then they should say, like the church of old—Ps. cxxvi. 3.
Moreover, these mercies are pledges and earnests of yet richer blessings—
They may well confide in so good and gracious a God—
They have indeed still great cause for sorrow—
Yet is it their duty to " rejoice *always* in the Lord"—Phil. iv. 4.
To promote and encourage this, we proceed to show,

II. IN WHAT RESPECTS THIS JOY IS OUR STRENGTH.

We are as dependent on the frame of our minds as on the state of our bodies—
Joy in God produces very important effects.
1. It disposes for action.
Fear and sorrow depress and overwhelm the soul—Isai. lvii. 16.
They enervate and benumb all our faculties—
They keep us from attending to any encouraging considerations—Exod. vi. 9.
They disable us from extending relief to others—Job ii. 13.
They indispose us for the most necessary duties—Luke xxii. 45.

We cannot pray, or speak, or do any thing with pleasure—
On the contrary, a joyous frame exhilarates the soul—Prov. xvii. 22.
David well knew the effect it would produce—Ps. li. 12, 13.
And every one may safely adopt his resolution—Ps. cxix. 32
2. It qualifies for suffering.
When the spirit is oppressed, the smallest trial is a burthen—
In those seasons we are apt to fret and murmur both against God and man—
We consider our trials as the effects of divine *wrath*—
Or, overlooking God, we vent our indignation against the instruments he uses—
But when the soul is joyous, afflictions appear light—Heb. x. 34. & xii. 2.
How little did Paul and Silas regard their imprisonment!—Acts xvi. 25.
How willing was Paul to lay down his very life for Christ!—Acts xx. 24.
This accords with the experience of every true christian—Rom. v. 2, 3, and 2 Cor. vi. 10.

APPLICATION.

1. Let us not be always brooding over our corruptions.
Seasonable sorrows ought not to be discouraged—
But we should never lose sight of all that God has done for us—
It is our privilege to walk joyfully before the Lord—Ps. cxxxviii. 5. & cxlix. 5. & lxxxix. 15, 16.
If we abounded more in praise, we should more frequently be crowned with victory—2 Chron. xx. 21, 22.
2. Let us carefully guard against the incursions of sin.
It is sin that hides the Lord from our eyes—Isai. lix. 2.
Joy will not consist with indulged sin—Ps. lxvi. 18.
Let us then " mortify our earthly members" and our besetting sins—
Let us be girt with our armor while we work with our hands—Neh. iv. 17, 18.
Nor ever grieve the Spirit, lest we provoke him to depart from us—
3. Let us be daily going to God *through Christ.*
If ever we rejoice in God at all, it must be through the Lord Jesus Christ—Rom. v. 11.
It is through Christ alone that our past violations of the law can be forgiven—Col. i. 20.
It is through Christ alone that the good work can be perfected in our hearts—Heb. xii. 2.
And, since " all things are *through* him, and *from* him, let them be *to* him also"—Rom. xi. 36.

THE CHRISTIAN SOLDIER'S WARFARE.

Ephesians vi. 12.—For we wrestle not against flesh and blood, but against principalities, against powers, against the rulers of the darkness of this world, against spiritual wickedness in high places. (Sk.)

IN this epistle, St. Paul reminds the Ephesians of their great obligations to God, on account of the gracious favors in which they were interested:

and having strongly urged them to a holy deportment answerable to their principles, their profession, and their privileges, he in conclusion exhorts them to " be strong in the Lord, and in the power of his might," ver. 12.

The *reason* why we should be "strong in the Lord," he assigns in our text. In improving and applying which let us consider,

I. THE ENEMIES WITH WHOM, AS CHRISTIAN SOLDIERS, WE ARE CALLED TO CONTEND. The term "christian soldiers," is thus employed, because in this paragraph, our apostle represents our present state as a warfare. Here we are instructed to observe,

I. *Our enemies are spirits;* not composed of flesh and blood. We wrestle not with flesh and blood, but with spirits. This implies, that *they are not material and compound beings*, but simple and immaterial; and as such, are capable of unwearied exertion. *They are not objects of sight and sense*, but invisible and impalpable; able to assault us when unperceived by us. *They are not inert in their natures*, but active and restless in the execution of their mischievous devices, Job i. 7; Matt. xii. 43. *They are not, and cannot be, subject to dissolution;* but, as spirits, they must be immortal. Here we are taught to observe,

2 *Our enemies are wicked spirits. They are maliciously wicked;* bent on injuring us. This is evinced *by their names:* a fallen spirit is called the *devil*, or calumniator; because he slanders men to God; he slanders God to men; and slanders men to each other. This he does for the purpose of sowing discord between God and his creatures, 1 Pet. v. 8. He is called *satan*, an adversary; because he sets himself up to oppose us. He is called an *enemy;* because he is filled with enmity against us, Rev. xii. 12. He is called the *old serpent;* because in this form he tempted Eve, Rev. xii. 9. He is called *Abaddon*, and *Apollyon*, the destroyer; because he desires and seeks our destruction, Rev. ix. 11. Their malice is also evinced *by their employment.* They go about seeking to destroy us: they seek to destroy our comfort, by depriving us of peace and joy in believing, 1 Pet. i. 6. They seek to destroy our piety, by divesting us of faith, hope, love, and purity, Luke xxii. 31. They seek to destroy our *usefulness*, by drawing us into sin, and rendering us stumbling blocks to those around us, Heb. xii. 15. They seek to destroy our *souls*, by engaging us in their service here, and bringing us to their own hell, hereafter, Matt. xxv. 41. *They are daringly wicked;* they are wicked spirits in high places: they first rebelled against God even in heaven itself; there was war in heaven, Rev. xii. 7. And they still approach the most sacred places that they may injure us; they assault us amid the avocations of civil and domestic life; in our religious retirement; in God's house; and even at his table, John xiii. 27.

3. *Our enemies are formidable spirits*,—being possessed of such qualities as are calculated to inspire terror. They are formidable on account of their *number;* it is not one enemy only that we have to contend with; we wrestle, or struggle against principalities. That our enemies are numerous is evident from the case of the demoniac, Luke viii. 30, who was possessed by a whole legion of them.

" From thrones of glory driven, by flaming vengeance hurl'd,
They throng the air, and darken heaven, and rule this lower world."

And it appears that numerous as they are, all of them are united, employed, and instructed to seek the ruin of mankind. They are formidable on account of their *strength:*—they are justly called " powers." Their power or ability to effect mischief, is evident from the case of Job, i. 12, ii. 6.

They are formidable on account of their *weapons*, being armed with **fiery darts**; their injections are tipt with poison, and hurled with fury. They are formidable on account of their *extensive influence*,—being rulers of the darkness of this world. The ignorance and sinfulness of mankind are subject to them, and employed against us. They are formidable on account of their *wiles*, see ver. 11; for they are naturally sagacious; and must have acquired much skill by long experience. Having considered our enemies, let us observe,

II. IN WHAT MANNER WE ARE INSTRUCTED TO CONTEND WITH THEM. From what our apostle adds on this subject, our duty is evident.

1. *We must contend with them in the armor of God.* This armor must be *all put on*, ver. 11, 14, 17. The whole of it is absolutely necessary; if any part be wanting, whether it be the girdle,—the breast-plate,—the greaves,—the helmet,—the shield,—or the sword,—the consequence must be fatal to us. This armor we must *retain* till our warfare is past, 1 Tim. i. 18, 19. This armor we must *take* and use whenever assaulted, ver. 13.

2. *We must contend with them in the spirit of prayer and watchfulness*, ver. 18. Pray with *all prayer*, that you may be strong in the Lord; that you may be girded by his wisdom and assisted by his power in all temptations. And *watch* thereunto, with all perseverance; that you may not at any time fall into the snares of your enemies, Mark xiii. 37; 1 Thess. v. 6; Eph. v. 16.

3. *We must contend with them in the exercise of firm resistance.* You must wrestle with them; in doing this, *get* all the strength you can by prayer, and *use* it, by striving against sin. Let your resistance be *early;* never enter into any league, truce, or parley with the enemy: resist him at his first approach, 1 Thess. v. 22; let your resistance be *courageous;* expect certain victory, Psa. lxviii. 1, 2; 1 Cor. xvi. 13; and let your resistance be *unwearied*, till you conquer, Psa. xviii. 37, 38. That you may be animated to persevere in this warfare, consider,

III. THE REASONS BY WHICH WE SHOULD BE INDUCED THUS TO CONTEND. Thus contend,

1. *Because the most important objects depend on this contention.* Your *steadfastness* depends on it, for your enemies seek to cast you down, Psa. cxviii. 13: your *liberty* depends on it, for they contend with you for the mastery, 2 Tim. ii. 5; your *glory* depends on it, for they contend with you about heavenly places, Rev. iii. 11; your *eternal life* depends on it, for they aim at murdering your souls, John viii. 44; the best *interests* of your *connections* depend on it, for it is likely to be well or ill with them, as it proves with you, Deut. v. 29; Prov. iii. 33; and without *contention*, these objects cannot be secured, Matt. xi. 12.

2. *Because victory is certain to the faithful soldiers of Christ.* Victory over the *world*, 1 John v. 4; victory over *sin*, 1 John i. 7; victory over *satan*, Rom. xvi. 20; victory over *tribulation*, Rom. viii. 35—37; and victory over *death*, 1 Cor. xv. 55—57. Thus contend,

3. *Because victory will be attended with certain glory.* A glorious *rest* from all painful toil and contention, Rev. xiv. 13; *glorious exemptions* from all penal evil, Rev. ii. 11, and from all natural evil, Rev. xxi. 4: and *glorious honors*, comprising the public approval of Christ our judge, **Rev. iii. 5;** a glorious *throne*, Rev. iii. 21; a glorious *crown*. Rev. ii. 10; and a glorious *kingdom*, Luke xii. 32; Dan. vii. 18.

THE CHRISTIAN'S TRIUMPH.

1 Corinthians xv. 57.—-But thanks be to God, which giveth us the victory through our Lord Jesus Christ.—(Sk.)

In the preceding verses of this truly interesting chapter, our apostle has been meeting the sophisms and cavils which the infidels and skeptics of his day opposed to divine truth; and, with the ability of "a master in Israel," has illustrated and defended that important doctrine of revelation, the resurrection of the dead. And in the close of a luminous and cogent train of argumentation, he directs our attention to the powerful influence of the religion of Jesus Christ at those most solemn of all periods, the hour of death, and the morning of the final judgment: the passage immediately before us forming a kind of ejaculatory conclusion to the whole, expressive of the most lively sentiments of gratitude, for that transcendent victory which the believer, through the "Captain of (his) salvation," is enabled to achieve

These words present to our serious consideration,

I. The christian's glorious triumph.

II. The means by which it is achieved.

III. The motives to gratitude which it furnishes.

I. The christian's triumph naturally leads us to consider,—*the enemies encountered,—the conflict sustained,—*and *the success experienced.*

1. *The enemies encountered.* Victory supposes a state of warfare, and consequently assumes the existence of enemies. The christian proposes the attainment of the image of God, and the promotion of his glory: together with the enjoyment of a celestial inheritance beyond the grave; and whatever is opposed to the nature of his object, and impedes its accomplishment, may very properly be denominated his adversary. The world with its terrific frown, or its alluring and deceitful smile; the corruption and treachery of the human heart, and the mighty powers of hell, are united in close and potent combination against the christian, and the heavenly object of his pursuit. This enmity is inveterate in its nature, and perpetual in its operation. Jer. xvii. 9; John xv. 19; Rom. viii. 7; 1 Pet. v. 8.

2. *The conflict sustained.* The warfare in which the christian is engaged requires the most prompt and vigilant exertion. In order to maintain his ground, and ensure success, his resistance must be *firm ;* no compromise can be allowed; no pacific overtures can exist with safety; to hesitate and parley, is to give way to the enemy, and relinquish the palm of victory. It must be with *steady perseverance :* the conquering christian maintains a firm opposition; not for a few months or a few years only, but he goes on from conquest to conquest, till his captain calls him from the field, to his eternal reward. In the spirit of *humble dependence ;* though he puts forth all his energies,—gives all diligence,—firmly and perseveringly maintains his post,— yet his hope of success is founded in the wisdom, power, and faithfulness of his divine leader, 1 Pet. v. 9; 2 Pet. i. 5—10; and iii. 17; Rev. ii. 10; and xii. 11.

3. *The success experienced.* Sustaining this conflict with this constant steady reliance on his God, the christian's conquest is *certain ;*—the nature of the gospel economy, the omnipotence and truth of Jehovah: and the luminous testimony of every age of time, all unite to ensure this victory. It is *complete* and *perfect* in its nature ;—the believer triumphs over the world, and self, and sin ;—the sting of death is extracted, and the fear of it destroyed ;—he exults over the falling powers of darkness ;—quits terrestrial scenes ;

—ascends to the throne of the Deity ;—and receives the victor's crown at the hand of the captain of his salvation, 1 John iv. 4—18; 1 Cor. xv. 55, 56 ; 2 Tim. iv. 6—8; Rev. iii. 21.

II. THE MEANS BY WHICH THIS TRIUMPH IS ACHIEVED. It is through the operation of divine beneficence in the gospel of Jesus Christ. Hence this conquest may justly be considered.

1. *Divine in its origin.* Man in his natural state, has no disposition for this conflict; nor does he inherently possess that strength which is necessary for conquest;—yea, so far is this from being the case, that all his inclinations and energies are in unison with those of the enemies of God, and decidedly hostile to the cause of truth, Gal. v. 19—21 ; therefore, both the disposition for conflict, and the strength for conquest, are derived,— they flow from the exhaustless fountain of goodness, through the channel of gospel provision, Jer. xiii. 23 ; 1 Cor. iv. 7 ; Ephes. ii. 1—8.

2. *Free in its communication.* "The *gift* of God." Every blessing bestowed upon man by the author of good, is communicated freely ; because man is the subject of guilt and condemnation, and has nothing of a meritorious nature to recommend or entitle him to the notice of Jehovah;—nor can he, in any way, ever remunerate or benefit a Being who is self-existent, self-dependent, and eternal;—one who is in his own nature perfectly and independently happy, Isa. lv. 1 ; 2 Tim. i. 9.

3. *It proceeds through the medium of sacrifice.* "Through our Lord Jesus Christ." God is a being who is just as well as merciful : man, by transgression, has violated the rights of divine justice, and offered insult to this perfection of the Deity :—justice required satisfaction ; but poor insolvent, self-ruined man could render none. Jesus Christ became our "surety;" "he bore our sins in his own body on the tree." Justice is honored : yea—

> " Here the whole Deity is known ;
> Nor dares a creature guess,
> Which of the glories brightest shone,
> The *Justice* or the *Grace.*"

See Isa. liii. 4—6 ; John i. 29; Rom. v. 8; Tit. ii. 14 ; 1 Pet. ii. 24.

III. THE MOTIVES TO GRATITUDE WHICH IT FURNISHES. The most lively gratitude is ever due from man to God, for the manifold favors which he continually receives at his hands ; but the anticipation of this victory ought, above every other consideration, to excite the christian to sing, "Bless the Lord O my soul, and all that is within me praise his holy name;" because of

1. *Our entire unworthiness.* Man being in his natural state a rebel against God,—opposed to his government,—his holiness,—and his truth,—in short, decidedly hostile to all the perfections of his nature,—has nothing to expect, on the principles of justice, but the satisfaction of its claims, by an interminable perpetuity of suffering ; for a being thus circumstanced to be delivered from this just extremity of wo, and to be enabled to triumph over "the last enemy," and participate the felicities of heaven, ought to call forth bursts of grateful adoration, Ps. xxxiii. 1.

2. *The amazing love which is displayed in this triumph.* The value of a gift is materially augmented, and the obligations to gratitude increased, by the difficulties and sacrifices which may be connected with its communication. Though nothing is difficult to the "Lord God Omnipotent," yet there is a sacrifice connected with the process of human redemption, of the most unparalleled description;—the Father delivered up his Son to poverty,

ignominy, and death, in order to extricate rebellious man from the gulf of ruin, John iii. 16; Rom. v. 8—11; 1 John iii. 1.

3. *The glorious result of this victory.* The believer not only experiences a victory over the world and sin, and triumphs over the fears of death, but also enters the regions of immortality; mingles with seraphic bands;—participates the glory of the Redeemer;—beholds, with ceaseless rapturous gaze, the transporting perfections of Jehovah;—swells the song of salvation;—and drinks full draughts at that exhaustless stream of joy which issued from the throne of God, Matt. xxii. 30; 1 Pet. i. 4; Rev. iii. 21, and vii. 15, 16, 17. Surely a victory replete with such blissful consequences demands the highest strains of praise from those who have a lively anticipation of it.

This subject, 1. Suggests the institution of a minute inquiry respecting the part we are taking in this warfare. And,

2. Furnishes ample consolation to the conflicting, suffering soldier of Christ.

HOPE IN DEATH.

Proverbs xiv. 32.—The righteous hath hope in his death. (Sk.)

THE most part of this book of Proverbs consists of short independent sentences, spoken by Solomon, the wisest of men, and as the Jews tell us, in the middle age of his life, when his understanding was in its greatest vigor, and under the inspiration too of the Holy Spirit of truth. Coherency of the parts, and dependence of one thing upon another, is not to be expected in a book of aphorisms; for every sentence is to be taken by itself, and includes an entire sense. We come therefore immediately to the words of the text,—"The righteous hath hope in his death." We shall,

I. ATTEND TO THE CHARACTER OF THE PERSONS THAT HAVE HOPE IN THEIR DEATH.

II. SPEAK AS TO THE OBJECT OF THEIR HOPE, OR SHOW WHAT THINGS THEY HOPE FOR.

I. ATTEND TO THE CHARACTER OF THE PERSONS THAT HAVE HOPE IN THEIR DEATH:—"the righteous."

1. On the mention of this character, that passage of the apostle is apt to offer itself to our minds, "*There is none righteous, no not one,*" Rom. iii. 10. Where then are the righteous persons to be found, that have hope in their death? We must consider, that the apostle, in the place quoted, means the legally righteous; none such indeed are to be found on earth; but Solomon here speaks of those that are righteous in a gospel sense, and many such are to be found.

2. *All men are now in a fallen state.* God made the first man perfect, Eccl. vii. 29; after his own image, Gen. i. 27; in integrity or righteousness, which was his honor; but he did not abide in the state in which he was made. The law that was given him to observe, he soon transgressed, though furnished with full ability to keep it; and so lost his innocence, or legal righteousness, made himself sinful, and brought guilt and moral pollution upon all his natural offspring. So that there is none righteous so as to be innocent and sinless: not one; all are conceived and born in sin, Psa. il 5, and so are sinners by nature. And as to practice, "there is not a

just,' or righteous, " man on earth that doeth good, and sinneth not," in a legal sense, Eccl. vii. 20.

3. *Yet every true believer in Christ is righteous, according to the covenant of grace.* Every believer in Christ is in him, and has rigteousness imputed to him, 1 Cor. i. 30. It pleased God on the fall of the first Adam, to set up his Son as a second Adam, that " as by the offense of one judgment came upon all men to condemnation, even so by the righteousness of one the free gift came upon all men to justification of life:" that " by one man's disobedience many were made sinners, so by the obedience of one shall many be made righteous," Rom. v. 18, 19. God hath made Christ, who knew no sin, a sin offering for us, that we might be made the righteousness of God through him, 2 Cor. v. 21. This system was the contrivance of infinite wisdom, originated in the free grace of God, is a doctrine that could be only known by divine revelation, in which it is exhibited in the clearest light: "the righteousness of God, by the faith of Jesus Christ, to all and upon all that believe," Rom. iii. 22. Believers in Christ are justified before God; their guilt is taken away; they are constituted righteous, restored to the divine favor, enjoy inward peace, and possess a title to heaven.

4. *Believers in Christ have also an inherent righteousness wrought in them by the Holy Spirit.* They are renewed by the Holy Ghost, Tit. iii. 5; and made partakers of divine nature, 2 Pet. i. 4. Though free justification and entire sanctification are different degrees of a work of grace on the heart, yet the former is preparatory to the latter; and even the former blessing is inseparably connected with the reign of grace within. " Sin shall not have dominion over you, for ye are not under the law, but under grace," Rom. vi. 14. All that live in the favor of God are graciously fitted for a life of holiness. They are created in Christ to good works, Eph. ii. 10; and with their new nature they have the Spirit of God put within them, to cause them to walk in his statutes, Ezek. xxxvi. 27.

5. *Believers in Christ are not only habitually righteous by their regeneration, but they endeavor to be actually righteous in imitation of Christ.* Being united to him, and led by his Spirit, they endeavor to walk as he walked. And the apostle says, " He that doeth righteousness is righteous, even as he is righteous," 1 John iii. 7. Being born again, born from heaven, they are in the way of faith and holiness' tending thither. They delight in the law of God after the inward man, and endeavor a conformity to it in the whole course of their actions. What God requires they sincerely try to render to him, the superlative love of their heart, and the impartial and constant obedience of their lives. These now are the righteous persons who have hope in their death.

II. Show the object of their hope, or what things they hope for in their dying moments. Hope is an expectation of something future and good, which God has promised; and the expectation of it is attended with pleasure and delight, in proportion to their thoughts of its excellency, and to the assurance with which they expect to enjoy it. Accordingly, the christian's hope is called " the rejoicing of hope," Heb. iii. 6. We shall mention a few things the righteous hope for in their dying moments.

1. *They hope for the gracious presence of God with them in that solemn crisis.* And indeed they never more need his reviving, supporting, and protecting presence, than when called to walk through the valley of the shadow of death. Their hope of this necessary and important blessing

is founded on such promises as these: "I will never leave thee, nor forsake thee," Heb. xiii. 5; "This God is our God for ever and ever: he will be our guide even unto death," Psa. xlviii. 14. "My flesh and my heart faileth : but God is the strength of my heart, and my portion for ever," Psa. lxxiii. 26. It is the consciousness of this gracious presence of God with them in their latter end that fortifies them against desponding fears, and refreshes their souls with light and comfort, when all other things appear dark and gloomy about them. Hence, David says, "Yea, though I walk through the valley of the shadow of death, I will fear no evil; for thou art with me; thy rod and thy staff they comfort me," Psa. xxiii. 4. From this promised grace and powerful presence of God, they hope for safety in their passage from this to the future world.

2. *They hope for the immediate admission of their souls into heaven:* that having guided them with his counsel during life, He will at death receive their spirits into glory, Ps. lxxiii. 24, to dwell in his presence, where there is fulness of joy, and pleasures for evermore, Ps. xvi. 11; where all evil is excluded. and all good is present, to fill the largest extent of their desires and wishes. The hope of this is founded on several promises : "If I go and prepare a place for you, I will come again, and receive you unto myself; that where I am, there you may be also," John xiv. 3. Christ in his testament, which is of force and unalterable by his death, appoints to his saints a kingdom, into which being risen, he as forerunner, is for them entered, with a declared purpose to prepare for their coming, and to keep open the way by his intercession. Hereupon their death comes under his direction and ordering, as having the keys of death and the invisible world. And when he sends death for the souls of believers, they have the like privilege that Stephen had, of committing them into his hand, as ready to receive them, and present them with acceptance to the Father. And thus being "absent from the body they are present with the Lord," which is far better, 2 Cor. v. 8; Phil. 1. 23; added to the "spirits of just men made perfect," Heb. xii. 23; and so they enter into the joy of their Lord, Mat*. xxv. 21.

3. *The righteous, in death, hope for the resurrection of their bodies in the appointed season, to a glorious immortality.* The hope of this they found on that declaration, "This is the Father's will who hath sent me, that of all which he hath given me I should lose nothing, but should raise it up at the last day," John vi. 39. The apostle says, "I have hope towards God, that there shall be a resurrection of the dead, both of the just and unjust," Acts xxiv. 15. Though the believers go down to the grave, they do not lose their relation to Christ, but remain united to him. They sleep in Jesus, and under his eye as guardian of the dust, which, however scattered, is precious and sacred; and them that sleep in Jesus will God bring with him, 1 Thess. iv. 14. Christ's resurrection is the pattern and pledge of the resurrection of the bodies of the saints, and will infer it as desirable and blessed. Christ being risen from the dead is become the first fruits of them that sleep, 1 Cor. xv. 20; and as he rose in glory, they shall in this respect be conformed to him, Phil. iii. 21. All this the righteous die in the hope of, and therefore can freely deposit their flesh in the dark and silent grave, where it shall rest in hope; foreseeing that eventful time, when it shall be raised from thence with unspeakable advantage, every way suited to the noblest operations of the perfected soul, and to all the important uses of the resurrection state.

4. *The righteous in their dying moments have a hope of eternal life,*

and complete salvation of their entire nature, soul and body, reunited at the resurrection; of all the promised glories of the heavenly state. Eternal life is the great promise of the gospel. "This is the promise that he hath promised us, even eternal life," 1 John ii. 25 ; and, "in hope of eternal life," Tit. i. 2. All the hopes of christian believers look towards this, and centre in it. These are some of the chief things the righteous hope for in death.

APPLICATION,—

The use that we are to make of this subject is obvious. Let us labor to be righteous persons, in order to our having hope in our death ; to have our sins pardoned through faith in the sacrifice of Christ, our souls sanctified by the Holy Spirit, and then to be holy in all manner of conversation. To this end, let us beg of God, in the name of Christ, for the Holy Spirit to assist us in the exercise of faith, to renew our nature, and enable us to walk in newness of life. And being on impartial trial, that we are real christians, let us live and die "waiting for the hope of righteousness," as the apostle describes the believers in his day, Gal. v. 5.

THE CHRISTIAN PILGRIMAGE.

1 Chron. xxix. 15.—For we are strangers and sojourners, as were all our fathers. (O.)

IN the preceding part of the chapter, we find king David, after having by his own example and entreaty requested the princes and the people to offer liberally in behalf of the house of God, who is not confined to temples made with hands, but fills heaven and earth, and the temple of the universe itself with his presence.—Hence the doxology begins at the 10th verse—

In the sequel we shall attend,

I. TO THE CONDITION OF THE PEOPLE OF GOD IN THIS WORLD—they are strangers and sojourners.

II. THEIR AVOWAL OF IT—"we are strangers and sojourners."

I. The saints are strangers and sojourners on the earth, because they are born from above—born not of corruptible seed but of incorruptible, which is the word of God, by the resurrection of our Lord Jesus from the dead : begotten again unto a lively hope of the heavenly inheritance—

They are born from above, having the blood-royal of heaven running in their moral veins : and therefore with a loftiness of sentiment becoming their high descent, naturally aspire after their native land. Having discovered something more noble than any thing which this world can afford; they leave to others the vain and the inordinate pursuits of its riches, its pleasures and its honors—

The saints are strangers and sojourners upon the earth, because they are absent from their best friends. An individual going to a foreign country, has generally few if any friends in that country. So in like manner christians have many foes, but comparatively few friends in the present world: their nearest and dearest and best friends in heaven. There dwells God their Father—Jesus Christ—the Holy Spirit—the sons of light, angels and archangels—Abraham, Isaac and Jacob—the prophets—the twelve apostles—the noble host of martyrs—all our pious friends.

They may be called strangers and sojourners, because their inheritance is in heaven. Strangers have generally no landed property or possessions in the foreign countries through which they travel—

309

So in like manner, the people of God have no portion in this world—their inheritance is in heaven—

Convinced, therefore, of the unsatisfactory notion of all earthly enjoyments, they look out for something more substantial—

The well-founded and lively hope of soon entering upon the enjoyment of this glorious inheritance, sustains them in every trial, wipes the tear from the eye that is dim with sorrow and sustains and animates and cheers them amidst all the ills of life—

The saints are strangers and pilgrims on the earth, because they are surrounded by many enemies and exposed to many dangers—

They find, in the natives of the country through which they pass, inveterate enemies. They are different in their moral pedigree; the men of the world are the children of the wicked one, love and serve him.—But they are the children of the Most High and as such serve and worship him, submit to his authority and obey his laws. This causes the children of the world to persecute the saints of God.—But besides the seductions of a wicked world, they have likewise to encounter the fierce assaults and the fiery attacks of the wicked one from without: while powerful corruptions lodge within their own breasts, throwing numerous barriers in the way of their progress towards heaven—

The people of God may be styled strangers and sojourners on earth, because they are making progress on their way towards heaven. A traveller is always desirous to reach the place of his destination and for this purpose is bending his course towards it.

So in like manner, the spiritual sojourners notwithstanding the great opposition and the numerous enemies which they have to encounter, will always be making progress in their journey—

The saints are strangers and sojourners on the earth, because their continuance here is short and uncertain. As the stranger only turns aside for the night, and in the morning pursues his journey, so the continuance of the spiritual traveller in this world is short and uncertain, Job xiv. 18, 19.

Human life even when protracted to its utmost verge is but a hand-breadth and a span. It has now decreased in a ten-fold proportion to what it once was; but even when prolonged to its former period, it was but a point—it was nothing when compared with eternity—

The saints, like strangers and pilgrims, will forget all their sorrows, and reflect with pleasure on the dangers of their earthly pilgrimage, when they reach their eternal home. As a traveller forgets all the hardships, which he endured on his travels, when he arrives at his native country, and recounts with pleasure his adventures, his difficulties and dangers to his admiring friends and beloved family—as the tempest-tost mariner—as the warrior—

So shall the saints forget their sorrows, and recall with pleasure the dangers of their earthly pilgrimage when they arrive at their Father's house—

II. Their avowal of it.

They confess it by their words, as well as by their actions—Abraham confessed that he was a stranger and sojourner with the children of Heth. Jacob confessed it to Pharaoh—David—Moses—

They confess it likewise by their actions. It frequently happens that men say one thing and mean another, so that their actions belie their words. But christians by their garb and language, by their practice and profession, by their sorrows and joys, and the whole tenor of their conduct, plainly testify to the world that they are strangers and pilgrims on earth.

IMPROVEMENT.

If we regard this world as a strange country, through which we are passing to our native home, we should endeavor to sustain as little injury by the way as possible—

Let us abstain from fleshly lusts that war against the soul—

If we we are really strangers and pilgrims, we will strive to be suitably prepared for our journey and make ample provision for that better country to which we are travelling—

It becomes strangers and pilgrims to endure, with patience and fortitude, all the ills they meet with in their journey heavenward—

If we view this world only as a scene of our pilgrimage, and heaven as the place of our eternal abode, we should above all things be solicitous about the way that leads to it—

If we are strangers and pilgrims here, we ought to maintain a deportment like those who belong to a better country·—

If we are strangers and pilgrims here, we should love one another as brethren and assist one another by the way—

CHAPTER V.

CHRISTIAN DUTIES.

ON THE ACCEPTABLE SERVICE OF GOD.

Hebrews xii. 28.—We receive a kingdom which cannot be moved, let us have grace, whereby we may serve God acceptably, with reverence and godly fear. (B.)

THE Apostle having stated, in the foregoing verses, the pre-eminent privileges and prospects to which true believers in Christ are admitted, and having shown, by a reference to the prophecy of Haggai, ch. ii. 6, the stability and permanence of the New Testament dispensation, which is to remain to the end of time as the only form a Divine worship and religion acceptable to God, from which alone men can obtain a certain and bright prospect of everlasting glory, he adds the words of the text, as a practical inference from his argument. See ver. 18—27.— —Consider,

I. WHAT IS IMPLIED IN SERVING GOD, AND WHEN IT MAY BE SAID WE SERVE HIM ACCEPTABLY.

To serve God is to worship him. Matt. iv. 10; Luke iv. 8; 1 Sam. vii. 3. See particularly Heb. ix. 1. where ordinances of Divine worship are termed "ordinances of Divine service;" and ver. 9, where worshipping God is termed "doing service;" and Acts xxvi. 7, where the twelve tribes, worshipping God statedly, are said to "serve him night and day." But what is it to worship God? It is to do him homage *outwardly*, by attending his appointed ordinances, public and domestic; *inwardly*, acknowledging, and being sensible of our dependence on him for life, and breath, and all things, temporal and spiritual: of our obligations to him as our Creator, Preserver, &c.; for all we are, (our members, senses, faculties;) for all we have; (time, talents, blessings;) for all we hope for, in this world or the next; of his absolute power and authority over us, as our Lawgiver, Gov-

311

ernor, and Judge.—It is to venerate his matchless glories; to adore and praise him with seriousness and solemnity, awe, and self-abasement, with joy and delight.—It is to feel in ourselves, and manifest to others, affections and dispositions suited to his Divine attributes, and the blessed relations in which he stands to us. (Explain this, and show that this alone is worshipping in spirit, and therefore in truth. John iv. 23, 24; Phil. iii. 3.)—In prayer, it is to ask only for what we really need, and what his word authorizes us to ask, and to do so with sincerity, fervency, and perseverance, and in faith.—It is to give thanks with gratitude of heart:—to hear, read, and meditate on his word with sincere desire, concern, and resolution, through God's help:—to understand, believe, and experience the efficacy of it, and to practice what we hear:—to receive the Lord's supper with faith and devotion, so as to "feed on Christ in our hearts with thanksgiving." This, and only this, is to worship acceptably,— —

It is to be subject and obedient to him, as a servant to a master, Rom. vi. 16; xii. 1.—We must yield ourselves to him. Rom. vi. 19, intelligently, willingly, entirely, and irrevocably, to be his subjects, servants, sons, and daughters, to which relations we are invited. This implies, that we no longer yield ourselves to the world, the flesh, sin, Satan, but to the Lord, with desire that he would, and in confidence that he does, accept us through his Son. Hereby we are joined to the Lord to serve him. Isa. lvi. 6. As his servants, we must give evidence of our subjection and obedience to his will in all things universally; Ps. cxix. 6; constantly. 1 Cor. x. 30.—In holiness, Luke i. 74, towards God; dying to, and delivered from the power of sin, Rom. vi. 18, the world, Gal. vi. 14, our own wisdom, will, and carnal inclinations. Gal. ii. 20. This implies, to be dedicated to God, employed for him, conformed to him.—In righteousness towards our neighbor, including truth, justice, mercy, charity, and its fruits.— —

It is to serve his cause; that which he is carrying on in the world: advancing his glory, and the present and everlasting good of mankind, by promoting the progress of his gospel, or of his truth and grace among men. John xii. 26.— —

As to the properties of this service.—It must be in sincerity and truth; Josh. xxiv. 14; termed by David, "a perfect heart." 1 Chron. xxviii. 9.— With reverence and godly fear, (text,) from a sense of his presence, Luke i. 75, before him, his glory, wisdom, power, eternity, immensity, supremacy. To which should be added, a watchful fear of our enemies, Prov. xxviii. 14, and a jealous fear of ourselves. Heb. iv. 1.—In confidence, or without a slavish fear; Luke i. 74; Rom. viii. 15; 2 Tim. i. 7; and a confidence arising from the mediation of Christ, Justification through him, Rom. v. 1, and the testimony of our conscience. 1 John iii. 21.—In humility of mind, Acts xx. 19; Mic. vi. 8, arising from a deep sense of the distance between him and us, and a consciousness that we are unworthy to be permitted to serve him, and that our best services are unworthy of his acceptance.—In resignation under all his dispensations, persuaded that his providence is over all; that all his dispensations are wise, just, and gracious; that his eye is upon each of his servants; that he puts each of them in his proper place, and will make all things work for their good.—In meekness, gentleness, &c. towards all men, even enemies.—All our services are to flow chiefly from love as their principle, to be guided by the Divine will as their rule, and directed to the glory of God as their end. 1 Cor. x. 31. Thus they will be performed with a " willing mind," 1 Chron. xxviii. 9; Matt. vi. 24, and the service of God will be perfect freedom.— —

II. The reasonableness and importance of thus serving him.

Every part of this service is reasonable, Rom. xii. 1, being different from the unreasonable services of the heathen in the worship of their gods, their bloody, lewd, ridiculous, unmeaning rites; the expensive, burdensome, shadowy, and hardly intelligible sacrifices and ceremonies of the Jews.—The christian's service of faith, love, and obedience is highly reasonable. For faith has for its object, not lies, but truth; love has beauty, excellence, goodness; and obedience commands, which are wise, holy, good. Few ceremonies are enjoined, and those most significant, as the sabbath, baptism, and the Lord's supper. Thus it far exceeds the service of the tabernacle and temple, though of Divine institution.— —

It is reasonable we should perform this service.—In justice: for we are God's by right of creation, preservation, and redemption.—In gratitude; for his numberless and great benefits.—Its infinite importance appears in that it is *our great interest*, in time and eternity.— —

III. How we may be enabled to serve the Lord as above described.

We must "have grace."—*Enlightening* grace. In order to our serving God, we must "know" him 1 Chron. xxviii. 9, must be acquainted with him; must know ourselves, or we shall not be humble, resigned, meek, as we ought to be; must know the Mediator, through whom alone we can come to God; must know God's will, or we cannot do it; and must know the truths of the gospel in general, which have a connexion with, and influence on our serving God.—*Quickening* grace; awakening the mind to a sense of the certainty and importance of spiritual and eternal things; convincing, humbling, begetting repentance unto life, a living faith, union with Christ, a spiritual mind.—*Pardoning* grace. See Heb. ix. 15. Without this we cannot serve God with confidence, hope, love, joy, peace, &c.—*Renewing* grace; for a currupt tree cannot bring forth good fruit, nor an impure fountain send forth clear streams. The heart must be changed, that the life may be changed: and we must be "created in Christ Jesus unto good works," if we would walk in them. Eph. ii. 10.—*Strengthening* grace; inspiring fortitude, resolution, constancy, and power to resist the devil, overcome the world, crucify the flesh, conquer the power of sin, and the fear of death; and enabling us to do, and persevere in doing, the whole wil of God.— —*Comforting* grace; supporting us in the midst of reproaches, injuries, losses, afflictions, the death of relatives and friends, and the various trials and troubles which we shall certainly meet with, chiefly by immortal hopes, and an earnest of heaven in our hearts.— —

CHRISTIAN PROFESSORS SHOULD IMITATE CHRIST.

1 John ii. 6.—He that saith he abideth in him ought himself also so to walk, even as he walked. (B.)

MANKIND, even in these christian countries so called, seem to be but too generally comprehended in two classes,—one consisting of persons who make no serious profession of true religion at all; and the other of those who make an empty, or, at least, inconsistent profession of it. With persons of the former class I have nothing to do on the present occasion; indeed it is not easy for a preacher of the gospel to have to do with them at any time, for they will take care not to come within the sound of his voice. But to the latter, many of whom are commonly present from time to time in all places of Divine worship, and therefore are probably here, I will address myself, especially on one point, the vast importance of imitating and resembling him, in whom we profess to believe, and whose disciples we regard ourselves. I am the more inclined to speak on this subject, because I am apprehensive that it is one much overlooked among some professors; and that on this account true and vital religion is greatly on the decline with them. Indeed, if I know anything of the christian world, it is verging fast towards Antinomianism. Men are beginning, more and more, to content themselves with mere doctrinal christianity, and to rest satisfied with right notions of those things in their heads, which they ought to experience in their hearts, and practice in their lives. This anti-christianism was beginning to pervade the church even in the Apostle's days, and some of them, especially St. James and St. John, used their utmost efforts to check the encroaching evil. This is evident from the general tenor of their epistle. As to St. John, it appears from many passages of this his first epistle, and especially from the paragraph from whence I take my text.— —Inquire we,

I. WHAT IT IS TO "ABIDE IN HIM?" AND WHO MUST BE UNDERSTOOD AS SAYING THAT THEY ABIDE IN HIM?

To abide in Christ, is to continue—in those relations in which, as children of God, we stand to him, as his disciples, his subjects, his servants, his friends, his brethren, his spouse.—In an interest in him as a Teacher, a Mediator, and a Saviour, being enlightened, reconciled, and saved by him; as our wisdom, righteousness, sanctification, and redemption.—In union with him, as the foundation on which we are built, the true vine of which we are branches, the living head of which we are members.— —

The Apostle does not speak here merely of saying in word, but of professing, and even of saying in our heart, or thinking respecting ourselves that we "abide in him." Now those who profess to abide in faith, in Christ and the Gospel, or to continue to be believers, do in effect profess to abide in him, for all true believers are in him. Gal. ii. 20; Rom. xi. 20; Rom. i. 16; 1 John v. 13.—All who profess to abide in hope, viz., an hope of eternal life, profess to abide in him; for all hope of eternal life, that is well grounded and lively, flows from union with Christ. Col. i. 27, 28.— All who profess to abide in love, profess to abide in him. 1 John iv. 16. Love is the fruit of the Spirit of Christ dwelling in us, Gal. v. 22, and can only be where he is.—All who profess to be in a justified state, profess to abide in him; for those to whom " there is no condemnation," " walk not after the flesh, but after the spirit," and " the law of the Spirit of life in Christ Jesus hath made them free from the law of sin and death ." Rom. viii. 1, 2; 1 John v. 11, 12.—All who profess to be regenerated, or converted, or created anew, profess to abide in him; for only those that are " in Christ" are new creatures; 2 Cor. v. 17; and those that are created unto good works, are "created in Christ Jesus." Eph. ii. 10.— —

II. In what sense, and in what respects, such ought to " walk even as he walked."

To "walk," here is a figurative expression, intended as in numberless other passages, to signify our spirit and conduct, all our dispositions, words and actions—and that towards God, our neighbor, and ourselves. If we profess to abide in Christ, or think we abide in him, we ought to take care that we be conformed to his example, in our tempers, words, and works. John xii. 26; Phil. ii. 5; Col. ii. 6; 1 Pet. ii. 21; text.

In what respects?—In seriousness of mind; not gloominess, or sullenness, or moroseness, but habitual seriousness, solemnity and awe, knowing that we are always in the presence of God, and on the verge of death, of judgment, and eternity, and that we have no light matters, but matters of everlasting moment, to attend to and insure. Thus Christ walked, and thus we ought to walk. In watchfulness, as conscious of the various dangers and the enemies which surround us. In self-denial.—In a spirit of abstraction and separation from the world. Jam. iv. 4; Matt. vi. 24; John xvii. 14, 16.—In spiritual-mindedness.—In love to God; John xiv. 31; 1 John iv. 16, 19; to his people; Eph. v. 1, 2; John xv. 12, 13; 1 John iv. 7; to all men, even our enemies. Luke xxiii. 34.—In zeal. John ii. 17.—In humility before God and man. Matt. xi. 29.—In resignation and patience before God. Matt. xxvi. 39, 42, 44.—In meekness and gentleness towards man. 2 Cor. x. 1; 1 Pet. ii. 23.—In a long-suffering and forgiving spirit. Eph. iv. 31, 32.—In a merciful, compassionate, and sympathizing disposition. Matt. xiv. 14; John xi. 35; Heb. ii. 17; iv. 15.—In blamelessness. Heb. vii. 26.—In usefulness, employing every grace and gift, and all our time and talents, for the glory of God, and the good of our fellow creatures. Acts x. 38; John iv. 34.—In temperance and chastity. In purity and universal holiness. John viii. 46; Heb. vii. 26.— —

[Conclude, by showing how we may be conformed to his example, and walk as he walked.]— —

THE DUTY OF CASTING OUR CARE ON GOD.

1 Pet. v. 7.—Casting all your care upon him, for he careth for you. (S. S.)

Inexperienced christians are generally partial in their views of religion—

They often exalt one duty, to the neglect, if not the exclusion of another—

But a proficiency in the divine life will discover itself by the united exercise of the various, and apparently opposite, graces—

Faith will not exclude fear, nor meekness fortitude—

Every grace will be limited and tempered by some other—

The soul must be humbled before God in dust and ashes—

Yet should it rely on him with most implicit confidence—ver. 6, 7.

I. THE DUTY OF CHRISTIANS.

Christians have learned "not to seek great things for themselves"—
Hence they are free from the corroding cares of avarice and ambition—
But they still have many grounds of care.
They cannot but feel some concern respecting their bodily wants—
The casualties of life may also occasion some uneasiness—
But they have other cares far more weighty and important—
They see many dishonoring their holy profession—
They feel within themselves also "an evil heart of unbelief"—
Nor are they ignorant of satan's devices to overthrow them—
Moreover, they frequently anticipate future evils—
And tremble, lest in the day of adversity they should faint—
Thus do they torment themselves with anxious and desponding fears—
It is their duty, however, to "cast their care on God."
To cast their care upon any creature would be fruitless—
And it would involve them in the deepest guilt—Jer. xvii. 5.
God alone is able to sustain their burthen—
On him they are commanded to cast it—Ps. lv. 22.
They must do so in the exercise of faith and prayer—Phil. iv. 6, 7.
Nor are any cares whatever to be excepted, "Cast all,"&c.
None are so small but they shall be regarded, none so great but they shall
be alleviated—
There is a backwardness in many to comply with this duty.

II. THEIR ENCOURAGEMENT TO PERFORM IT.

God extends his care to the whole creation—
But in a more especial manner careth for his people—
He conducted the Jews through the wilderness—
He interposed for them in all their dangers—
He supplied their every want—Ps. cv. 39—41.
Thus, though less visibly, he still regards those who trust in him—
He watches over them for good—2 Chron. xvi. 9.
He limits and restrains all their adversaries—Ps. lxx. vi. 10.
He sympathizes with them in all their afflictions—Isa. lxiii. 9. Heb
v. 15.
He imparts to them all temporal and spiritual blessings—Ps. lxxxiv. 11.
He hears and answers all their supplications—John xv. 7.
He accounts them his most inestimable treasure—Mal. iii: 17.
He communes with them as his sons and daughters—2 Cor. vi. 18.
He takes upon him the management of all their concerns—Isa. xlvi. 4.
What encouragement does this afford us to trust in him!
Our guardian and protector is infinitely *wise*—Isa. xxviii. 29.
He knows what trials we stand in need of—
He can suit all the circumstances of them to our necessities—
He can overrule them for our eternal benefit—
He is possessed of *almighty* power, Job xl. 2.
There is no difficulty from which he cannot extricate—Isa. l. 2, and
xliii. 13.
Nor duty which he cannot enable us to discharge—
Should we, for whom such wisdom and power are exercised, be anxious?
—Isa. xl. 27, 28.
Moreover he is *good* and gracious.
What innumerable blessings has he already bestowed upon us!
He has even given his own Son to die for us—

316

What then can we have to fear, if we trust in him?—Rom. viii. 32.

Above all, he is a *faithful* God.

He has promised seasonable protection and strength—Isa. liv. 10. Deut. xxxiii 25. 1 Cor. x. 13.

And is not his word a sure ground of confidence?—2 Sam. xxii. 31. Heb. x 23.

Surely then we should be filled with consolation rather than with care—Heb. vi. 18.

INFER,—

1. How needful is it that all should acquaint themselves with God!

Gaiety and dissipation may bear up the spirit in prosperity—

But God alone can comfort us in adversity—Job xxxv. 10.

At the hour of death we shall all need divine support—

Let the careless then begin to reflect upon their state—

Let them provide a refuge against the day of trouble—

Let them follow that salutary advice—Job xxii. 21.

2. How happy would christians be if they rightly enjoyed their privileges!

It is their privilege to be " without carefulness"—1 Cor. vii. 32.

If they trusted in God as they ought, nothing could disturb them—Isa. xxvi. 3.

Hence that exhortation to joy in God—Ps. v. 11, 12.

Let the afflicted saints then commit themselves to him—Mic. v. 4.

Let them know that duty is theirs, but events are his—

Let them, in the face of all difficulties, adopt the words of Joshua—Numb. xiv. 9.

Let them, with Hezekiah, repose themselves on God—2 Chron. xxxii. 7, 8.

~~~~~~~~~~~~~~~

THE NECESSITY OF PRAYER

Ezek. xxxvi. 37.—Thus saith the Lord God : I will yet for this be inquired of by the house of Israel, to do it for them ; I will increase them with men like a flock. (Sk.)

THERE is a very striking analogy between the natural and the spiritual world ; between the productions of nature, and the operations of divine grace. In the former, a variety of means are necessary for the attainment of providential mercies ; and in the latter, the duties of religion are essentially connected with the enjoyment of its personal privileges. In both cases the ends are made to depend on the means, which by virtue of the divine appointment and influence, are rendered efficient and successful. This is particularly evident in the important duty of prayer. The Lord has graciously promised innumerable blessings to mankind in his word : but in order to obtain them, we must earnestly call upon his name, with penitent and believing hearts. This chapter contains various promises, both of temporal and spiritual blessings to the Jews, which are also generally applicable to the Gentiles ; but we are assured in the text, that they can only be realized by faithful prayer ;—"Thus saith the Lord God," &c. These words will lead us to consider,

I. THE BLESSINGS FOR WHICH WE SHOULD INQUIRE;—"I will yet *for this* be inquired of by the house of Israel." This language manifestly refers to the inestimable benefits promised in the preceding context. Whatever God promises we may humbly desire and pray for, both for our own salvation and the welfare of all mankind.

1. *We should pray for ourselves.* We are sinful, indigent, and dependent creatures. God only can supply our wants and satisfy our desires. To him we must come, and devoutly inquire for every blessing which our circumstances need, 2 Cor. ix. 8; Phil. iv. 19.—Such as pardoning mercy—adopting love—quickening power—sanctifying grace—the indwelling Spirit —the consolations of piety,—ver. 25—27;—Ps. li. 9—12.—for light in darkness—strength in weakness—succor in temptation—assistance in duty—guidance in difficulty—peace in trouble—victory over enemies—triumph in death—and a blissful immortality beyond the grave, Ps. lxxxi. 10; Phil. iv. 6; Heb. iv. 16. For these and all necessary and promised blessings, for body and soul, for time and eternity, we must incessantly seek, and inquire of "the God of all grace."

2. *We should pray for the church of God.* Good men regard all the subjects of piety as brethren, Eph. iv. 4—6.—They feel interested in each other's welfare, and desire the peace and prosperity of Zion, Psa. cxxii. 6-9. —They pray for the extension and stability of her borders—the increase of her converts—and the unity and progression of her members, Hab. iii. 2; Eph. iii. 14—21; Phil. i. 9—11. Many such prayers have been offered by the pious, for the church of Christ in all ages, Ps. cxviii. 25; Isa. lxii. 67; Rom. xiii. 15.

3. *We should pray for the world.* We are commanded to "love our neighbors as ourselves," and "pray for our enemies;" even for those who "despitefully use and persecute us," Matt. v. 44. The Lord assures us that he will "give his Son the heathen for his inheritance," &c.; and that "the earth shall be filled with the knowledge and glory of his name," Ps. ii. 8; Isa. xi. 9; Jer. xxxi. 34. Encouraged by such declarations, we should "pray for all men; for kings, and for all that are in authority;"— for the universal dissemination of divine truth—and the glorious triumphs of the Redeemer's kingdom, in every nation, kindred, tongue, and people, Ps. xliii. 3; Isa. lxii. 1; Matt. vi. 10; Rev. xi. 15. If such are the the blessings for which we should inquire, we may observe,

II. THE MANNER HOW WE SHOULD INQUIRE FOR THEM. This is highly necessary, both for our instruction and encouragement. And for the proper discharge of this important duty the Scriptures furnish every needful direction, by which we are explicitly taught to inquire of the Lord.

1. *In the method which he appoints.* We cannot approach unto him acceptably, but through Jesus Christ, who is the high priest over the house of God for ever, John xiv. 6; Heb. vii. 17. He has sprinkled the mercy seat with his own precious blood, and "now appears in the presence of God for us." Through his mediation, under the influence of the Holy Ghost, we have constant boldness of access to the throne of grace, Rom. viii. 26, 27; Eph. ii. 18. This is the new and living way, which is divinely consecrated for mankind, to the "Father of mercies," Heb. iv. 14—16, chap. x. 19—22.

2. *With devout dispositions of mind.* The Lord looks at the heart, and when we enter into holy converse with him, we should inquire for the blessings of salvation *sincerely*, without hypocrisy, Matt. xv. 8; *humbly*, with reverence and godly fear, Ps. lxxxix. 7; *fervently*, with holy ardor, Gen. xxvii. 26;—*affectionately*, with hearts filled with love to God, and good

will to all mankind, Matt. vi. 14, 15; and *believingly*, in the lively exercise of faith, Matt. xxi. 22; 1 John v. 14, 15.

3. *In every situation of human life.* Whatever stations we occupy, or however different the circumstances in which we are placed, prayer is indispensably necessary. In private retirement, Matt. vi. 6;—in our families, Joshua xxiv. 15;—in the public ordinances of the gospel, Ps xxvii. 4;—and in our daily occupations, we should " pray always, with all prayer, and every where, lifting up holy hands without wrath and doubting," Eph. vi. 18; 1 Tim ii. 8.

4. *With diligent perseverance unto death.* We are invariably dependent on God, and continually need his special direction and blessing, as sinful and helpless creatures. Without him we can do nothing; and though he has promised every needful benefit, yet for all these things he will be inquired of to do them for us. And hence, we ought to " pray without ceasing, and in every thing give thanks," Rom. xii. 12. And in this sacred exercise, we shall be greatly encouraged by considering,

III. THE REASONS WHY WE SHOULD INQUIRE OF THE LORD. These are various; but we select the following only:

1. *Prayer is an ordinance of divine authority.* If it should be said, Why inquire of the Lord who knows our wants, and is ever ready to do us good? the text affords an appropriate answer to all such vain objections;— " *Thus saith the Lord God*," &c. Every duty which is distinctly revealed and divinely enjoined, is unquestionable in its authority, and imperious in its claims. Now this is certainly the case in reference to prayer. The Lord commands us to pray, Ps. v. 14, 15; Jer. xxix. 12; Luke xviii. 1;—he promises to hear and answer prayer, Ps. xci. 15, 16;—and he directs us how to pray, Matt. vi. 9—13.—If therefore we restrain prayer before him, we impeach his wisdom, despise his authority, and reject his ordinance, Job xxi. 14, 15.

2. *Prayer evinces the dependence of the creature on the Creator.* It powerfully reminds us of our own insufficiency, and the all-sufficiency of the Almighty, 2 Cor. iii. 5.—We feel innumerable wants which we cannot supply but we are taught to " ask and receive, that our joy may be full." We thus at once discover our utter indigence and dependence as finite beings, and the absolute necessity of praying *to*, and " trusting *in* the Lord Jehovah, in whom is everlasting strength."

3. *Prayer demonstrates the connection between duty and interest.* As intellectual beings, we are capable of moral actions and spiritual enjoyments. The Lord is therefore pleased to suspend the blessings he promises, on the performance of the duties he enjoins; and it is only by complying with the latter, that we can realize the former, Ps. xxxiv. 17; Jer. xxxiii. 3. This inseparable connection admirably displays the wisdom and goodness of God in the salvation of his people.

We may conclude by warning the prayerless of their danger,—and encouraging the devout to " continue instant in prayer."

PERSEVERANCE AND WATCHFULNESS IN PRAYER.

Eph. vi. 18.—Praying always with all prayer, &c. (H.)

THE believing Ephesians are here taught by the apostle what they have to expect in this world ; nothing less than a constant warfare, and that too with no common enemy, as may be seen by the description given, verse 12. He would not have them, however, be discouraged by the view of either the multitude or the strength of their opposers, nor yet to trust in the least degree to their own wisdom and strength, verse 10, when christians can do this, in the exercise of a strong faith, they may despise all the efforts of their most potent and malignant foe, and exult in the beautiful language of the apostle, " If God be for us," &c.

To manage the arduous conflict with success, it is requisite we should put on " the whole armor," verse 13, which the apostle describes; and then he introduces the words of my text: " Praying always," &c. intimating, that it was not enough to be duly apprized of the nature and strength of the enemy, and to have on the armor of defence ready for the attack ; but even then there must be much and constant prayer to God for wisdom, courage, and ability, to persevere in the conflict; for having once entered the field under Jesus, the Captain of our salvation, we must never think of obtaining peace, or putting off our armor, till we have reached the blissful shores of our heavenly Canaan, and can join in that delightful triumph of the church, Rev. xii. 10, 11. In our text the apostle directs the Ephesians—

I. To PRAY WITH ALL PRAYER.—What is the import of this expression? It may be considered under two ideas.

There are divers kinds of prayer. They are all important ; none of them can be slighted with propriety by the real christian. They occupy distinct and separate stations in the good man's general sphere of action, and it should be his care to keep them from clashing one with the other. As in a well-constructed piece of mechanism every wheel and every pin has its proper station, and performs its office in a regular manner, all operating to the production of one grand effect; so it is in religion. 1 Cor. xiv. 33. We are not to be at home engaging in private prayer, when duty calls us to public prayer, &c. It is natural to infer, from the view we have been taking of prayer, what a burden religion must be to a worldly man. With the real christian it is exactly the reverse : he can say with truth, that the service of his God " is perfect freedom."

Prayer is composed of a variety of parts. Some arrange these under a smaller, and some under a larger number of particulars. From the examples of prayer which we have in the old testament, and also from the manner in which Christ taught his disciples to pray, I am led to divide the parts of prayer into—Adoration, Confession, Petition, and Thanksgiving.

1. When we approach God in prayer, it should be with sentiments of profound veneration : he is the infinitely great and eternal God, and we are creatures but of yesterday : he is the holy and righteous God, and we sinners by nature and by practice. If then we know who and what God is, when we come near to his throne we shall adore and worship him in the most humble manner. A view of his majesty and greatness will penetrate our souls with godly fear, and a sense of the riches of his mercy will inspire us with trust and confidence. Our souls will feel much of that temper which is manifested in the language of Nebuchadnezzar, Dan. iv. 34, 35.

2. Another part of prayer is *confession*. The deep depravity of our nature, Jer. xvii. 9, and the numberless sins which proceed from that corrupt source, furnish abundant matter for this part of prayer. The fifty-first Psalm, the language of the returning prodigal, and of the publican who went into the temple to pray, are among the finest examples of genuine confession—of that kind of confession which the scriptures connect with salvation, inasmuch as it is said, "If we confess our sins," &c. 1 John i. 9.

3. The next branch of true prayer is *petition*. Man is an indigent creature in every respect, and can never be addressed in a more suitable language than Rev. iii. 17. He is, therefore, in himself the most forlorn and dependent creature; but it is only the christian who sees and feels, and, consequently, acts in conformity to this humbling truth; he comes as a beggar to the door of mercy.

4. The last branch of prayer is *thanksgiving* and *praise*. This is mentioned in a very distinct manner by the apostle. Phil. iv. 6. This branch of the subject may be divided into two parts. In the first there is a particular and direct acknowledgment made to God for the mercies received. We may illustrate this point by the language of David, Ps. ciii. 2, 3. The other branch of thanksgiving is more general. We have examples of this in Matt. vi. 13; Jude 24, 25.

II. IN THIS TEXT THE APOSTLE RECOMMENDS "PRAYING ALWAYS;" every work of the good man's hand should be prefaced, accompanied with, and followed by prayer. Acts vi. 4: 1 Thess. iii. 10.

In this part of the subject I shall particularly urge upon you constancy and perseverance in prayer.

1. To you who have in past times bowed your knee to the God and Father of our Lord Jesus Christ, and now live prayerless, we say, "Ye did run well, who did hinder you." Gal. v. 7. Such persons may be thus addressed, "Thou castest off fear." Job xv. 4. The Jews were an awful instance of this, as appears by Ps. lxxviii. 34—37.

The temporary and short-lived nature of the disposition of some men to pray, may be seen in the case of affrighted mariners, whose distress and conduct, when in danger of shipwreck, is beautifully described, Ps. cvii. 23—30. But no sooner is the storm ended, and they find themselves in safety, than they utterly forget the God on whom they called.

Such also is the prayer of the man who is affrighted by the grand and awful representations which the Almighty is pleased sometimes to make of himself in earthquakes, inundations, yea, even in ordinary storms of thunder and lightning.

Again, The subject is illustrated by the prayers of the sick man, who, while his recovery is yet doubtful, is constant and devout in his supplications: but all his devotions evaporate on the first symptom of returning health; to such persons may be applied the words of our Lord, Matt. xii. 45.

We address this part of our subject to backsliders in general. You, in times past, sought God by prayer, not only in the public assembly of his saints, but also in your closet; but now you have lost all the good impressions you once had, though, like Felix, whilst the preacher reasoned of righteousness, &c. Acts xxiv. 25. Though, like Herod, you heard the word gladly, and did many things, Mark vi. 20, yet now you set truth and conscience at defiance. If this is your character, what are you better than an apostate? How awful is your state! How justly may the words of scripture be applied to you! 2 Pet. ii. 21, 22.

(2.) I come now to urge constancy and perseverance in prayer on those christians who are often tempted to leave it off. The scriptures would not have abounded with such exhortations as 1 Thess. v. 16; Rom. xii. 12, where it not that the soul is liable to be discouraged by difficulties and temptations.

Sometimes they are tempted to this by their want of liberty and enlargement in prayer:—others are discouraged in prayer, because they feel so many short comings and imperfections in their prayers. You forget, christian, too much and too often, that your prayers do pass through the hands of Jesus Christ, and are perfumed with the incense of his merit: Rev. viii. 3, 4, others are tempted to give up seeking the Lord by prayer, because he delays to answer them. These are often crying out, Lam. iii. 44; Hab. i. 2. Yet remember, Hab. ii. 3. We have also many striking instances, in which the Lord has kept his people long praying and waiting, before he has vouchsafed to say, " Be it unto thee even as thou wilt." David relates his own experience, Ps. xl. 1—3. And it is also related of Abraham, Heb. vi. 15.—See Rom. viii. 24, 25; and James v. 7, 8. Be not, then, christian, discouraged by not receiving an immediate answer to your petitions: go on praying; the Lord is not slack concerning his promises:—and you have abundant proof, that " praying breath is never spent in vain."

III. OUR TEXT RECOMMENDS WATCHING UNTO PRAYER; the nearness and importance of the connexion between prayer and watching is plain, by the frequency of those passages in which they are jointly recommended to the christian, Luke xxi. 36; Col. iv. 2; 1 Pet. iv. 7. This apostle knew, by fatal experience, the vast importance of what he here recommended. It has been exemplified in the experience and practice of the saints. Neh. iv. 9.

(1.) The christian should watch for opportunities to pray, or he will be seldom find them.

(2.) In prayer we should watch over our own hearts, which are so deceitful and unstable. Prov. iv. 23.

(3.) Watch against hinderances to stated seasons of prayer. We are in danger of this from many sources.

(4.) Watch against intruders which would disturb you while exercising in prayer. If it is your desire to " attend upon the Lord without distraction," you must be constant and diligent in this duty. Gen. xv. 11.

(5.) Watch against the great enemy of souls, who is ever going about either to destroy them, or to disturb them in their religious exercises, which instrumentally subserve their eternal salvation. Job i. 6; Zech. iii. 1.

(6.) Watch for an answer to prayer. Too many, when they have finished prayer, rise up and go their way, and think no more about the matter. Not so the good man; he, like David, will not only say, " Show us thy mercy, O Lord, and grant us thy salvation:" but he will add, "I will hear what God the Lord will speak." &c. (Compare 1 King xviii. 1. 41—46, with James v. 17, 18.) So let us be looking and watching for an answer to prayer.

IV. CHRISTIANS SHOULD PRAY IN OR WITH THE SPIRIT. Praying " in the Spirit," either means praying under the influence of the Holy Ghost, or with divine fervor.

In speaking of divine fervor in prayer, I notice,

(1.) That it is urged by a variety of scriptures in which prayer is spoken of, all of which imply an earnest and vigorous exercise of the mind. To pray is to " pour out" the heart, Ps. lxii. 8; to "wrestle with God," Gen. xxxii. 24; to "cry," Ps. ix. 12; to "sigh and groan," Ps. xii. 5; to "strive," Rom. xv. 30 ; to "give God no rest," Is. lxii. 7; and in the text, it is "supplication in the Spirit." In all these places we are taught that true prayer is very fervent and importunate.

2. Earnestness and fervor in prayer may be urged by the consideration of the value of the blessings for which we pray; nothing less than "grace and glory."

3. We may take an argument to be fervent in prayer from the arduous nature of the conflict in which we are engaged.

4. Fervency in prayer is recommended by examples recorded in the word of God. Gen. xxxii. 26. 28. We have also a striking example of fervent prayer in the woman who came to our Lord, Matt. xv. 22 ; Luke xxii. 44.

V. WHEN A CHRISTIAN MAINTAINS A LIFE OF PRAYER ACCORDING TO THE DIRECTIONS GIVEN IN THIS TEXT, it will produce a very advantageous influence upon his spiritual warfare, and assist him in the use of the armor which God hath provided.

1. By thus exercising ourselves in prayer we shall *stand* firm in the day of battle. He that is much with God in prayer, stands not only on even, but on elevated ground, and must ultimately have the advantage.

2. Praying always with all prayer has a tendency to inspire the soul with *courage* in this arduous conflict. Living near to God in prayer makes the soul as bold as a lion; hence Elisha, who was a man of much prayer, when his house was surrounded by a host, was enabled to say to his servant, "Fear not." 2 Kings vi. 6.

3. They who pray always, and with all prayer, will be *skilful* and *active* in the use of the christian armor.

4. Abounding in prayer has a tendency to keep our armor bright and fit for use ; yea, it gives the christian soldier a promptness for action. By the means of prayer, the girdle of truth and the breastplate of righteousness are girded on tight; the helmet of hope, and the shoes of peace, fit well, and become proof against the most furious assaults ; and the shield of faith, and the sword of the Spirit, are grasped with a firm hand, and are wielded with energy.

5. It is by fervent and persevering prayer that the believer finally obtains the victory in every conflict. Whilst we cleave to the Lord with purpose of heart, and watch in prayer, satan gains little or no advantage over us --. To conclude,

1. Are we engaged in this holy warfare, with the description of which our text is connected? we shall not "endure hardness, as good soldiers " 2 Tim. ii. 3, but as we pray always and with all prayer.

2. What an awful state is yours, who have been induced to commence a life of prayer, either through the pressure of adverse providences, or the temporary alarms of your consciences, and have fallen back into a state of total indifference and irreligion. Isa. xxvi. 16. Ah, thoughtless sinner! thou wilt be in trouble again, and then with what face wilt thou return to a throne of grace.

Our last reflection is for the comfort and encouragement of God's praying people : keep on in the holy exercise: exemplify that sentence, " faint, yet pursuing." Let thy soul be animated with the pleasing thought, that Christ prays for thee, and the Holy Spirit makes intercession within thee. Through all the changes of the christian life, be this thy constant practice, "Praying always with all prayer,' &c.

THE DUTY OF PERSEVERING IN PRAYER.

Luke xviii. 1.—Men ought always to pray, and not to faint. (S. S.)

THE efficacy of prayer is continually exhibited in the sacred writings—
And every incitement to it is afforded us—
Nevertheless we are prone to faint in the performance of it—
To encourage our perseverance in it our Lord delivered a parable—
Waving all notice of the parable itself, we shall consider,

I. OUR DUTY.

To be always in the act of prayer would interfere with other duties—
That which is here inculcated, implies that we pray —
Statedly.
Regular seasons for prayer should be fixed—
Except in cases of absolute necessity, Matt. ix. 13, they should be adhered to—
We should constantly acknowledge God *in the public assembly*, Heb. x. 25.
We should maintain his worship also *in our families**
Nor should we on any account omit it *in our closets*†.—
Occasionally.
There are many particular occasions which require us to pray—
Prosperity, that God may counteract its evil tendency, Prov. xxx. 9.
Adversity, that we may be supported under it, James v. 13.
Times of *public distress or danger*, to avert the calamity, 2 Chron. vii. 14.
Habitually.
We should maintain a spiritual frame of mind—
We may have a disposition for prayer in the midst of business—
Nor will secret ejaculations prevail less than solemn devotions‡—
To pray thus is our duty; " We ought," &c.
It is a duty we owe *to God*.
He, our Creator, Preserver, and Redeemer, has commanded it—
Nor can anything absolve us from our obligation to obey—
We owe it also *to our neighbor*.
The edification of Christ's mystical body depends, not only on the union of every part with the head, but on the whole being fitly framed together, and on every joint supplying its proper nourishment, Eph. iv. 16; Col. ii. 19.
But if we be remiss in prayer, we shall be incapable of administering that benefit, which other members have a right to expect from us‖—
We owe it *to ourselves*.
A "spirit of supplication" is as necessary to the soul, as food to the body—

---

*Abraham and Joshua were noted for their attention to family religion: Gen. xviii. 19: Josh. xxiv. 15, and our Lord's example is worthy of imitation; he not only expounded his parables to his disciples in private, but prayed with them. See Luke ix. 18, which means, "he was at a distance from the multitude, and praying with his disciples."

†How frequent the stated seasons shall be, must be left to our own discretion. David's example is good, Ps. lv. 17. But as the morning and evening sacrifices were called the *continual* burnt-offering, so they may be said to pray *always* who pray at those returning seasons.

‡Compare 2 Sam. xv. 31, with 2 Sam. xvii. 14, 23. See also Neh. ii. 4, 6.

‖Samuel had a deep conviction of this truth; 1 Sam xii. 23.

Nor can we feel any regard for our souls, if we do not cultivate it—
It is, however, by no means easy to fulfil this duty.

II. THE DIFFICULTIES THAT ATTEND IT.

When we set ourselves to the performance of it, we shall find difficulties—
Before we begin to pray.
Worldly business may indispose our minds for this employment—
Family cares may distract and dissipate our thoughts—
Lassitude of body may unfit us for the necessary exertions—
We may be disabled by an invincible *hardness of heart*—
A *want of utterance* may also operate as a heavy discouragement—
By these means many are tempted to defer their religious exercises—
But to yield to the temptation is to increase the difficulty—
While we are engaged in prayer.
The *world* is never more troublesome than at such seasons—
Something seen or heard, lost or gained, done or to be done, will generally obtrude itself upon us when we are at the throne of grace—
The *flesh* also, with its vilest imaginations, will solicit our attention—
Nor will *satan* be backward to interrupt our devotions*—
After we have concluded prayer.
When we have prayed, we should expect an answer—
But *worldliness* may again induce a forgetfulness of God—
Impatience to receive the desired blessings may deject us—
Ignorance of the method in which God answers prayer may cause us to disquiet ourselves with many ungrounded apprehensions—
Unbelief may rob us of the benefits we might have received, James i. 6, 7.
Whatever obstructs God's answers to prayer, disqualifies us for the future discharge of that duty—

APPLICATION.

Let us not expect victory without many conflicts—
Let us remember the effect of perseverance in the case of Moses, Exodus xvii. 11—13.
Above all let us attend to the parable spoken for this end, Luke xvii. 2—8.
So shall we be kept from fainting under our discouragements—
And God will fulfil to us his own promise, Gal. vi. 9.

---

* He has various devices whereby he strives to accomplish his purpose. He will suggest "it is needless to pray:" or, "It is presumption for so great a sinner to ask any thing of God:" or, "it is hypocrisy to ask, when the heart is so little engaged." Sometimes he will inject into the christian's mind the most blasphemous and horrid thoughts; and at other times tempt him to admire his own fluency and enlargement in prayer. Such are the " fiery darts" with which he often assails the soul, Eph. vi. 16.

LOOKING TO CHRIST INSEPARABLY CONNECTED WITH SALVATION.

Isa. xlv. 22.—Look unto me, and be ye saved, &c. (H.)

By grace ye are saved. Eph. ii. 8. Now that faith, which is the instrumental cause of our salvation, is spoken of, in the sacred scriptures, by various metaphorical expressions: sometimes it is borrowed from earthly things, and particularly from the actions of the body. Matt. xi. 28; Isa. lv 1; Rev. xxii. 17. Or, as the manslayer, being closely pursued, &c. Heb. vi. 18.—Sometimes from the conduct of a dutiful and loyal people towards their royal sovereign, upon his entering among them, in his own territories. John i. 11, 12.—Sometimes the metaphor is taken from the ear; and faith is expressed by hearing his voice, as an impoverished, dying wretch, would hear of plenty and life. Isa. lv. 3. And sometimes the metaphor is taken from the eye, as in the text, and faith is represented as looking to Christ.

I. EXPLAIN THE DUTY HERE EXPRESSED BY THE METAPHOR OF LOOKING.

We are to observe, in general, that a man's looks often indicate his condition and frame of mind. By virtue of that strange union between the soul and the body, the dispositions of the one are often discovered by the emotion and appearance of the other. The eye, in particular, is a mirror, in which we may see the various passions of the mind; and is a kind of silent, yet significant language, that conveys to others those inward exercises which the tongue does not, or perhaps cannot express: hence we can understand a look of sorrow and compassion, a look of joy, and the look of a perishing supplicant. If an agonizing patient casts an eager look upon his physician, he understands it to be a silent petition for relief. When a dying husband fixes a wishful, tender look, upon his surviving half, and those other selves, his children, they know the melting language, and feel its resistless energy. And when a drowning man casts a wild and eager look towards a boat coming to his relief, we understand it to be the language of earnest importunity for speedy help.

Hence it follows, that looking to Christ implies those suitable dispositions and exercises of heart towards him, which are expressed by the earnest and significant looks of persons in a distressed condition towards their deliverer.

And, in such a case, it is natural to conceive a person expressing, by his looks, a particular and distinct knowledge, of his deliverer—an importunate cry for his assistance—a wishful expectation of it—an humble dependence on him for it—a universal submission to him—a hearty love and approbation of him—a joy and gratitude for his deliverance.

And these dispositions and exercises of mind towards Christ, I presume, are intended in the text by looking to him.

1. Looking to Christ implies a particular notice and distinct knowledge of him. John xvii. 3; Isa. liii. 11; xxvii. 11; Hosea iv. 6; 2 Cor. iii. 18

2. Looking to Christ implies an importunate eagerness for relief from him. Ps. xxv. 15. As a child falling into the hands of a murderer, on the sight of a parent coming to its help, so are we desired to look to Christ: this implies a sense of our need of him. Ps. cxxi. 1; Jonah ii. 4; John ii. 14, 15.

3. Looking to Christ implies a wishful expectation of deliverance from him. Isa. xvii. 7; Ps. cxxx. 6; Acts iii. 4, 5; Matt. xv. 22. 28.

4. Looking to Christ implies an humble dependence upon him for salva-

tion. This supposes a deep sense of our own utter inability; then **we see no** ground for self-confidence, when we shall place our trust in Christ alone: 2 Chron. xx. 12; Micah vii. 7. John xiii. 15.

5. Looking to Christ means a universal, cheerful submission to his authority. Ps. cxxiii. 1, 2.

6. Looking to Christ implies our hearty approbation of him as a Saviour. Love is often expressed by a look. 2 Sam. xxiii. 5.

7. Looking to Christ implies joy and gratitude. Ps. ciii. 1, 2.

II. Urge the duty by several weighty considerations.

It is the duty of saints and sinners, in all ages and places, to the end of the world; and the arguments to enforce it can never be exhausted; those in this copious text are sufficient.

1. It is salvation that is offered. "Look and be saved."

2. This salvation may be obtained upon low terms; it may be obtained by a look. "Look and be saved."

3. It is Immanuel, our incarnate God, that invites and commands us to look to him and be saved. We may trifle with the commands of a usurper, and reject the treacherous invitations of an enemy; but dare we trifle with the injunctions, dare we refuse the gracious invitations of our supreme Lord and heavenly King? Rom. xiv. 9. 11; Phil. ii. 9. 11.

4. It is Immanuel we are to look unto. "Look unto me." He is the glorious, attractive object we are called to behold. Ps. lxix. 20; cxlii. 4. And looking will not be in vain; for,

5. He is able to save us, upon our looking to him. "Look unto me and be saved, for I am God." And who can give us greater security of salvation? "If God be for us, who can be against us?"

6. Look unto him, for he is God, and there is none else. This implies that there is salvation in no other. Job. v. 1.

And lastly, We must look unto him, or drop into hell. Look to him! For we are particularly invited, being especially meant by the "ends of the earth." Therefore, "Look unto him and be saved all ye ends of the earth;" more especially backsliders, sensible sinners, &c

---

NOAH'S OBEDIENCE.

Genesis vi. 22.—Thus did Noah; according to all that God commanded him so did he. (Sk.)

Biographical researches are peculiarly interesting.—They teach us to form a proper estimate of mankind, and the various features in the human character; they convey correct ideas of the strong and capacious powers of the soul, and are eminently calculated to inspire us with a noble ambition to follow the most worthy and renowned of our species. There are some men, however, whose characters excite a more than common interest in our minds, especially those who have lived in a remarkable era of the world—who have accomplished some mighty achievement—and whose designs have met with the peculiar sanction of heaven: such was the subject of our text, Noah:—a man who witnessed the most desolating scourge which ever visited the world—who brought to perfection one of the most stupendous pieces of mechanism that was ever reared by human hands—and whose life was preserved as a reward for his obedience.

The text contains a high commendation of his character.—"Thus did Noah," &c. We will consider,

I. THE RULE OF NOAH'S OBEDIENCE, "All that God commanded." Mankind need a rule for their conduct. This rule should possess the following characteristics:—

1. *It should come forth from God, and have the Divine sanction.* No man can be a rule to himself; as he did not produce himself, is not dependent on himself, nor solely accountable to himself. No man can be an absolute rule for another; for all men are defectible, and subject to mutation: but a rule for human manners and conduct, should be perfect and immutable. The commandments found in the Bible, are God's commandments. The men who wrote them received them from God: some orally, others by inspiration; "God said to Noah," verse 13. The prophets prefaced their messages, by declaring, "Thus saith the Lord."

2. *It should be practical in its requirements.* A rule whose demands are impossible to be observed, is a contradiction. God's commandments are all practicable. He is not a hard Master: "His yoke is easy, and his burden is light." "His commandments are not grievous." But we must not judge of their practicability by the infirmities of our flesh; or the weakness of our reason; but by the power of God—the energies of grace—and the attainments of the saints. God charged Noah to build the ark; had human reason been consulted he would never have made the attempt.

3. *It should be plain and circumstantial in its phraseology.*—No man can act according to a rule which he does not understand. God's commandments are easily comprehended. The Bible may present mysterious things, and things inexplicable; but there is no precept mysterious, no commandment abstruse. Read the charge to Noah in the preceding verses, examine the commandments of God generally, plainness and perspicuity are their uniform characteristics.

4. *It should be beneficial in its results.* Human nature revolts at the idea of living by a rule which does not bear upon our personal interest. God never has laid, nor ever will lay, an injunction upon a human being which militates against his own happiness. God's commandments are the emanations of his love, and the welfare of mankind is their ultimate object; the precepts given to Noah serve to illustrate this. See Psalm xix. 11; Rev. xxii. 14.

II. THE NATURE OF NOAH'S OBEDIENCE. "According to all that God commanded him, so did he."

1. *Noah's obedience was pious in its principle.* Actions are the result of principles. The tree must be made good, before the fruit can be good. To suppose that a man will obey God, whose heart is not right before him, is a palpable absurdity. "Noah found grace in the eyes of the Lord." "Noah was a just man, and perfect in his generations. and Noah walked with God." Oh, how vain are all attempts to obey God without loving him!

2. *Noah's obedience was prompt and decided in its acts.* No sooner does the inspired writer close the account of the Divine admonition to Noah, than he immediately adds, "Thus did Noah;" Heb. xi. 7. It is said, he was "moved by fear;" and fear is always prompt in its acts. There is too commonly a culpable reluctance in our obedience, especially when the cros

res in the way; but, like David, we should make haste, and delay not to keep God's commandments, Psalm cxix. 60.

3. *Noah's obedience was laborious in its exercise.* To build an ark, not less than five hundred and twelve feet long, eighty-seven wide, and fifty-two high, and the interial capacity of which, according to Calmet, was 357,600 cubical cubits, was a prodigious undertaking, and required immense labor; the labor of the head to contrive, and the hands to accomplish. And does not our obedience to God require labor? Read Matt. xi. 12; John vi. 27; Heb. iv. 11. Is there no labor required in making the sacrifices which God demands;—in exercising the graces which he approves;—and in performing the duties that he requires? Here must be the exercise of the understanding, to know the commandments of God; of the will to submit to their authority; and of the faculties of the mind, and members of the body, to practise them.

4. *Noah's obedience was universal in its extent.* He did " according to *all* that God commanded him." A failure of the most trivial kind would have defeated his whole design; and endangered his own life, and the lives of all who were with him in the ark. His obedience was therefore exact, and he was attentive to do *all* that God commanded him. Oh, what a pattern for us to follow! Our obedience should be as broad as the commandment, James ii. 10.

5. *Noah's obedience was persevering in its course.* Impediments were most certainly thrown in his way. Were there no doubts that assailed his mind as to the possibility of the scheme? Were there no insults heaped upon him? Were there no temptations to relinquish the undertaking, during the long period of a hundred and twenty years? But Noah, not only began and continued, but finished his undertaking. We also shall have obstacles to meet with, in the course of our obedience; but we must persevere, hold on, and finish our course with joy, Matt. xxiv. 13.

6. *Noah's obedience was successful in its object.* The end crowned the action. His life was preserved as the reward of his toils and labors, and persevering efforts. See him shut up in the ark, secure in Divine protection, a world of water around him, millions of dead floating on its surface, the dwellings of men for ever demolished, and nature all in ruins.

Learn from the subject,

1. What terrible desolations sin makes in the world, and how the severity of God was displayed in making the very elements conspire to the destruction of those who had slighted the Divine counsels.

2. How tenderly God cares for his servants, and how easily he can provide means for their safety.

3. How much human security depends upon human exertion. The way of duty is the way of safety. Had Noah dared to disobey God, he would have perished in the flood. " Blessed are they that do his commandments '

SOBRIETY.

1 Thess. v. 6.—Let us be sober. (Sk.)

In the context the apostle exhorts the converts at Thessalonica to a variety of Christian duties, personal and relative, suitable to their state and privileges as Christians in general, and to their belief and expectation of Christ's second coming to judgment in particular. One of these personal duties we have in the text—*sobriety;* and as the apostle deemed it requisite to urge this on the attention and practice of one of the primitive churches, it is no less applicable to Christian ministers and people in the present day. In speaking of this duty, we shall describe,

I. THE VIRTUE OF SOBRIETY.

1. *This virtue has a principal regard to a man's self, and is equally adapted to persons of all ranks, characters, ages and sexes.* Speaking generally, it consists in observing those rules, and walking according to those methods, whereby they may secure and preserve their own health, ease, and reputation: it is to keep within those bounds which God has fixed for the right government of ourselves, our appetites, and passions, avoiding all inordinary excesses.

2. *Sobriety relates to the whole man, body and mind.* As to the mind, it bounds and moderates our thoughts of ourselves, and enjoins us to take the measure of our own worth from what we have received from God, and not from any opinion that others may entertain or express of us. It requires that we have a low and modest opinion of ourselves, and guards us against pride, self-conceit, haughtiness, vain glory, and ostentation. We are not to have an overweening conceit of our own abilities, not to contemn others, not to be insolent or imperious, not to stretch ourselves beyond our line. In this sense of the word *sobriety*, the apostle recommends to every man among the Christians at Rome, "not to think of himself more highly than he ought to think, but to think soberly, according as God hath dealt to every man the measure of faith," Rom xii. 3.

3. *As to the body, it consists in a regular and moderate desire, pursuit, and use of sensible enjoyments, such as are allowed for the promotion of its health and sustenance.* The correct notion of sobriety lies in neither denying the body what is useful and proper for it, as God is pleased to bless us with the necessaries and comforts of life; nor going beyond our necessities and stations, merely to gratify a sensual appetite, or, as the apostle expresses it, "using the world as not abusing it," 1 Cor. vii. 31.

4. *The apostle in the text considers the word in a more restrained sense, relating only to the use of meats and drinks, in opposition to gluttony and drunkenness.* I think it is evident from the context that this is his meaning; for immediately after the text, he adds, "They that sleep, sleep in the night; and they that be drunken, are drunken in the night: but let us, who are of the day, be sober." As if he should say, The heathen, with whom is the night or moral darkness, who want the cheering light of the gospel of Christ, indulge themselves in riot and excess: but let us Christians, who are of the day, enjoying the luminous rays of evangelical truth, be sober, for that is one of the rudiments it teaches, Tit. ii. 12.

5. *So that to be sober, in a limited point of view, is to use meats and drinks moderately, and for the purposes for which the almighty Donor bestows them.* The chief design of which is to render us capable of performing the duties of religion, as well as those of civil and domestic life, and do-

ing good to others according to our ability, means, and opportunity. We should, therefore, use the gifts of divine Providence, so as neither our reason nor health may be injured by them. To be sober, is to keep a strict and constant guard on our appetite, that we neither offend by a luxurious costliness in the quality, or excess in the quantity of those blessings granted for the nourishment and support of the earthly frame. To this purpose are the words of Solomon, when tempting dainties are set before us; "When thou sittest to eat with a ruler, consider diligently what is before thee: and put a knife to thy throat, if thou be a man given to appetite. Be not desirous of his dainties: for they are deceitful meat," Prov. xxiii. 1—3. Also he says, "Look thou not upon the wine when it is red, when it giveth his color in the cup, when it moveth itself aright. At the last it biteth like a serpent, and stingeth like an adder," ver. 31, 32.

II. Produce some reasons to enforce the practice of it.

1. *It is amiable and commendable.* A man governing himself by the rules of temperance, checking his sensual appetite restraining his inclination, especially when in the midst of plenty and affluence, is a character of peculiar interest. Such a person fills his station in life with credit to himself, and answers the design of God, in giving him reason to be the guide and director of his actions. How gratifying it is to behold a man whom providence has favored with the means of procuring whatever his heart may desire, habitually to deny himself, subdue wrong propensities, limit and restrain himself to what is consistent with and conducive to his health and support, without any excess. He that thus gains a conquest over himself, deserves a higher encomium than he that conquers a city or country. "He that ruleth his spirit, is better than he that taketh a city," Prov. xvi. 32. The conquest of ourselves is more glorious; for one gained by reason, is more noble to an intellectual creature than one gained by force.

2. *The contrary vices are odious and full of deformity.* In their progress they dethrone reason, and reduce the man to a level even with the brute. Reason is the glory of human nature, by which we are distinguished from animals, in the right use of which we are enabled to conduct ourselves with reputation and benefit; but to hurl this noble power from her legitimate seat, by giving heed to the demands of a low craving appetite, is the highest reproach.

Historians inform us, that the Lacedæmonians, in order to fortify their children against intemperate habits, exposed their slaves when in a state of intoxication, to their contempt and derision. And really, if a drunkard would but conceive the ridiculous figure he makes, either as staggering along the streets, or disgorging his nauseous load, or stunning the company with noise and impertinence, he would not be in charity with himself till he had cleared away this worse than brutal conduct by repentance and reformation.

These vices are a gross abuse of providential blessings, perverting them to purposes quite contrary to the intention of the Divine Author in bestowing such favors. They also occasion a serious abuse of precious time, which is dishonorable and disgraceful to a rational creature, who should know better how to value its worth. Life is vastly important, and the opportunities for performing its essential duties are fleeting and uncertain, and, when past, cannot be recalled. It becomes, therefore, a reasonable creature, rather to endeavor to recover lost time, by future attention and diligence, than squander away more, by associating with extravagant company, and indulging in riot and excess. See 1 Pet. iv. 3.

3. *Excess in meats and drinks, is an inlet to all manner of wickedness.*

He who loses the government of himself, and the proper exercise of his understanding, by gluttony and intoxication, what crimes is he not capable of committing, and under the influence of what restraints is he to prevent such conduct? Intemperance is the parent of impurity. "Be not drunk with wine, wherein is excess," Eph. v. 10, or, an unbridled dissolution of manners. It prompts men to injure others, excites to quarrels and contentions, and often leads to immediate destruction. "Who hath wo? who hath sorrow? who hath contentions? who hath babbling? who hath wounds without cause? who hath redness of eyes? They that tarry long at the wine; they that go to seek mixed wine," Prov. xxiii. 29, 30. It opens a way to the commission of the grossest crimes, and therefore Solomon adds, at the 33rd verse, "Thine eyes shall behold strange women, and thine heart shall utter perverse things." In a word, it is fraught with innumerable evils.

4. *A luxurious life produces fatal effects.* It causes the ruin of health and constitution,— human life is shortened by its pernicious influences. The consequences often are, violent inflammation of the blood, the bloated dropsy, the shaking palsy, consumption, fevers, &c., the forerunners of death. Whatever pleasure intemperate persons may pretend to enjoy in gratifying their passions, they will experience bitterness in the end, when the bones are full of the sin of their youth: "And thou mourn at the last, when thy flesh and thy body are consumed," Prov. v. 11. It also ruins the reputation of men, as well as their estate and family affairs. "The drunkard and glutton shall come to poverty," Prov. xxiii. 21. And then, last of all, it ruins the soul, without deep contrition and faith in Christ; for the apostle declares, such "shall not inherit the kingdom of God," 1 Cor. vi. 10. To avoid all this mischief, to which an intemperate indulgence of our sensual appetites exposes us, "let us not sleep, as do others; but let us watch and be sober."

III. Subjoin a few directions to that end.

1. *Let us consider ourselves as under the all-seeing eye of God.* As David did, set the Lord always before us, knowing that all things are naked and open to his eyes with whom we have to do, Heb. iv. 13; and that he sees through all the like artifices by which we would excuse or cover any irregularities. Did we daily consider this, it would be a happy expedient to prevent all excesses.

2. *Let us secure a saving interest in Christ and carefully keep in view his shining example.* He lived on plain provisions, and always maintained strict temperance both in eating and drinking: he never once exceeded in the least the bounds of regularity. He was sometimes at feasts, being invited, but even then he recommended by his example the doctrine he taught his disciples; "Take heed to yourselves, lest at any time your hearts be overcharged with surfeiting and drunkenness," Luke xxi. 24. Herein, as well as in many other things, he has left us an example, which we should aspire to follow.

3. *Let us avoid as much as possible the society of intemperate persons, and never in one instance choose them for our companions.* "Be not among winebibbers; among riotous eaters of flesh," Prov. xxiii. 20, lest you learn their ways, and insensibly fall into their sins. Bad company in this, as in all other cases, is most pernicious; for those who are contaminated with vice, will endeavor to corrupt others, and triumph in their success.

4. *We must use the greatest caution in those circumstances, where we are in the greatest danger.* One of which is, when we are entertained by our superiors. The honor we are then apt to think done us, and the temptation presented to gratify our appetite, is very likely to make us forget the

snare, and run into excess out of complaisance to the company. We ought, in such a case, to be particularly on our guard, since no pretence of civility to men, however highly distinguished, will justify our breach of the commands of God.

5. *Let us think frequently on the future judgment, and the strict account we must then give of our behaviour to the righteous Judge.* Intemperate persons must give a sad account of their abuse of providential blessings, which they should have received with thanksgiving, and used with moderation. In this particular then, " Let our moderation be known unto all men. The Lord is at hand," Phil. iv. 5.

THE DUTY OF GIVING THE HEART TO GOD.

Prov. xxiii. 26.—My son, give me thy heart. (H. H.)

This address, however it may be considered in some respect as delivered by Solomon to his son, must certainly be understood as proceeding from him who is wisdom in the abstract, wisdom personified, even from the Lord Jesus Christ, Prov. viii. 1, 22—32; and as directed generally to all the children of men, but especially to those who regard him as their sovereign Lord. And though the more immediate object of the address may seem scarcely suited to this view of it, (because those who are possessed even of incipient piety may seem less likely to fall into the snare which is there spoken of,) yet the caution is necessary for youth of all descriptions ; and, as a general lesson, it teaches us, that there is no snare whatever into which we may not fall, if our hearts be not given up to God ; and that the only sure way of being kept from sin of every kind, is, to give the heart to God.

Taking the words then as addressed by the Lord Jesus Christ to all who acknowledge his paternal authority, we will proceed to mark *the extent and reasonableness of this command.*

I. The extent of it—

To give our heart to God, implies that we give him,

1. The affections of the soul—

Those should all centre in him, and in him alone. Him we should desire as our supreme good, and in him should we delight as our chief joy— — — We should be able to say with David, " Whom have I in heaven but Thee ? and there is none upon earth that I desire besides thee." Ps. lxxiii. 25.

2. The confidence of the mind—

If there be any thing besides God in the whole universe, on which we rely, we do not really give our heart to him. To trust, though in ever so small a degree, in an arm of flesh, argues a departure of heart from God. Jer. xvii. 5. We should confide altogether in his wisdom to guide, and his power to uphold us, in his goodness to supply our wants, and his truth to fulfil to us the promises of his word. We should " trust in him with all our heart, and not lean either to our own understanding" or strength : we should consider him as alone able to help us, and as all-sufficient for our utmost necessities.

3. The service of the life—

Without this, all else is vain. Obedience is the certain fruit of love to

333

God, John xiv. 15, 21; yea, it is altogether identified with it: "This is the love of God, that ye keep his commandments." 1 John ii. 3—5, & v. 3. To the man that has given his heart to God, no commandment can be grievous. ib.

The extent of the command being ascertained, we proceed to shew,

II. THE REASONABLENESS OF IT—

To surrender up our whole selves to God, is called by St. Paul, "a reasonable service." Rom. xii. 1. And reasonable indeed it is ;

1. Because of his right over us, as our Creator—

God "made all things for himself: all that we are, and all that we have, was given us by him, to be improved for his glory. How then can we with propriety alienate any thing from him? A potter feels himself entitled to the use of the vessel which his own hands have made: and has not God a right to all the services that we can render him? Of all that have truly given their hearts to God, it may be said, "No man liveth to himself; and no man dieth unto himself: but whether we live, we live unto the Lord; and whether we die, we die unto the Lord: whether we live therefore or die, we are the Lord's." Rom. xiv. 7, 8.

2. Because of his mercies towards us, as our Redeemer—

The Lord Jesus Christ has "redeemed us to God by his own blood:" and by this has acquired a new right over us. To this effect the Apostle says, " Ye are not your own; ye are bought with a price: therefore glorify God with your bodies and your spirits, which are his." 1 Cor. vi. 19, 20. And in another place he gives this as the duty of every man according to the dictates of his most deliberate judgment: " The love of Christ constraineth us, because we thus judge, that, if one died for all, then were all dead; and that he died for all, that they who live should not henceforth live unto themselves, but unto him who died for them, and rose again." 2 Cor. v. 14, 15. Was he mistaken in his judgement? and are we at liberty to alienate from him what he has purchased at so great a price?

3. Because of his relation to us, as our Father—

If we profess to have been born again, and begotten to God by his word and Spirit, then are we yet further bound to him by the relation he sustains towards us: " What manner of love is this, wherewith the Father hath loved us, that we should be called the sons of God?" Can we have learned to cry, Abba, Father, and doubt whether the giving of our hearts to him be a reasonable service? The utmost then we can do to serve and honor him is no more than our bounden duty.

4. Because of the utter worthlessness of all his competitors—

What is there worthy to be compared with him? The whole creation is but as "a broken cistern that can hold no water." Shall we then, "for any thing that is in it, forsake the Fountain of living waters?" Survey the choicest blessings that the world affords; and they are all " vanity and vexation of spirit." Are these then to stand in competition with him who is the unfailing and only source of all blessedness? The more we see the vanity of all created good, the more we shall see the reasonableness of giving our hearts to God alone. We must not only not love our father or mother more than him, but must "*hate* every earthly relative, yea, and our own lives also, *in comparison* of him." Luke xiv. 26.

ADDRESS,

1. In a way of affectionate invitation—

In this view we may take the words of our text, even as an invitation to us from the Lord Jesus Christ to set our affections on him alone. And how

334

astonishing is it that he will accept such hearts as ours! If we of ourselves had presumed to offer them to him, how justly might he have rejected and despised the offering! Yet behold, he solicits it at our hands! And what can such an offering add to him? Does he need any thing from us? or can we add any thing to him? Oh then admire and adore this astonishing condescension; and let him not woo your souls in vain.

2. In a way of authoritative injunction—

This command of Almighty God is not to be trifled with. Let none presume to withstand it, or to delay his obedience to it: for if we obey it not, we never can behold his face in peace. 1 Cor. xvi. 22. Attend to it then; and see that ye obey it in truth. Give not to your God and Saviour a divided heart; for such an offering he will not accept: but give yourselves *wholly* to him; and so shall that promise be fulfilled to you; "I will be a Father unto you, and ye shall be my sons and daughters, saith the Lord Almighty."

THE DUTY OF WATCHFULNESS ENFORCED.

Mark xiii. 32—36.—But of that day and that hour knoweth no man, no, not the angels which are in heaven, neither the Son, but the Father. Take ye heed, watch and pray: for ye know not when the time is. For the Son of Man is as a man taking a far journey, who left his house, and gave authority to his servants, and to every man his work, and commanded the porter to watch. Watch ye therefore: for ye know not when the master of the house cometh, at even, or at midnight, or at the cock-crowing, or in the morning; lest coming suddenly he find you sleeping. (H. H.)

On different occasions, but especially at the close of his life, our Lord taught his disciples to look forward to a future period, when he would assuredly come again. He specified two objects for which he would come; the one was, to destroy Jerusalem; and the other, to judge the world: and, inasmuch as the former of these advents was typical of the other, he blended them both together, and thereby raised in them an expectation that they should take place at the same time. The truth is, that though the one was accomplished within forty years, and the other, notwithstanding more than eighteen hundred years have already past, remains yet to be accomplished at some distant and unknown period, they are both equally present in the mind of God, "with whom a thousand years are as one day, and one day as a thousand years:" And it is also true, that the day of death is to every man, *in effect*, as the day of judgment: so that the union of the two periods in their minds, notwithstanding their distance from each other, was strictly just, as it respected God, and highly salutary as it respected them. Not but that our Lord did make a clear distinction between the two periods: for in v. 30, he says, "This generation shall not pass till all *these things* (relative to the destruction of Jerusalem) be done; and then, in a way of contrast, he adds, "But of *that day* and *that hour*, namely, the day of judgment, knoweth no man." It is in reference to this latter period that he speaks in the words of our text; in discoursing on which we shall consider,

I. The duty inculcated—

Watchfulness and prayer are often united in the holy scriptures as duties of the first importance. In themselves they are different; but in their exercise they are inseparable: neither would be of any avail without the oth *r*: prayer without watchfulness would be hypocritical; and watchfulness without prayer, presumptuous. We shall therefore combine the duties, as though it had been said, *Watch in the exercise of prayer.* And that we may yet further simplify the subject, we shall not enter into a detail of particulars, but rather follow the general ideas of our text; and shew,

1. What we should watch and pray *against*—

Here we must include *every thing which has a tendency to lull us asleep.* We see how intent men are on all the things of time and sense: the lust of the eye, and the pride of life, so occupy them, that they find no time nor inclination for spiritual concerns— — —

Against these then we should "watch and pray:" we should watch, to prevent them from gaining an ascendant over our hearts; and cry mightily to God to keep us from yielding to their influence. Seeing how the whole world is led captive by them, we should tremble for ourselves; and day and night intreat God rather to leave us destitute of all earthly things, than to give us over to the love of them, or suffer them to deprive us of eternal happiness— — —

2. What we should watch and pray *for.*

To be found ready, at whatever moment our Lord shall call for us, should be the one object of our ambition. With this view, we should seek to be found in Christ, not having our own righteousness, but that which is of God through faith in Christ. Not content with a general hope of acceptance through Christ, we should wash our every sin, yea our every duty also, in the fountain of his blood, which must cleanse us from the "iniquity even of our holiest actions. We should seek also to " be renewed in the spirit of our minds," and to be transformed into " the image of our God in righteousness and true holiness." No attainments should ever satisfy us: if we were as holy as Paul himself, we should, like him, "forget the things that are behind, and reach forward towards that which is before." With a view to progressive holiness, we should carefully " abide in Christ," " living by faith on him," and receiving daily out of his fulness grace for grace: assured, that without him we can do nothing, but through him shall be enabled to do all things. In a word, we should seek to be ever ready to meet our God; yea to be "looking for, and hasting unto the coming of that day," when we shall be summoned to his tribunal, and receive our eternal doom— — —

For the attainment of this happy frame of mind, we should be watching our progress in the Divine life, and praying day and night *to God* to perfect in us the work that he has begun— — —

Let us next attend to,

II. THE CONSIDERATIONS WITH WHICH IT IS ENFORCED—

These may be comprehended in the two following:

1. The uncertainty of the time when our Lord shall call us—

The time of the general judgment is unknown to the holy angels: nor was it revealed even to the Messiah himself for the purpose of communicating it to us.* And there was good reason why it should be concealed; because if it had been represented as at a great distance of time, men might have become secure; whereas the idea of its speedy arrival tended to quicken all to holy exertion. In like manner the uncertainty of the time of our

---

* As God, one with the Father, he knew all things; but as the Mediator, he received his instructions from the Father, and delivered nothing but what he had before received. John xiv. 49. Rev. i. 1.

death has a very salutary effect; since it necessitates us to be always ready. The idea of a man going a long journey, and leaving his servants their appointed work, and ordering them to expect him every moment till they see him, justly illustrates this point. There is not a moment of our lives when we may sit down secure. The night was divided into four watches, which terminated at evening, at midnight, at the cock-crowing, and in the morning. Now at no one of these periods are we sure that we shall not be summoned into the presence of our God.

What a consideration is this to enforce the duty in our text! Who that reflects one moment on the possibility of his being called this night to the judgment-seat of Christ, must not desire to be found in the exercise of watchfulness and prayer?— — —

2. The awfulness of being found in a sleeping state—

In the parable of the ten virgins we are informed what we must assuredly expect, if we indulge in careless security; we shall be shut out from the marriage-supper of our Lord, and be "cast into outer darkness, where is weeping and gnashing of teeth." It will be to no purpose to plead, that we were not engaged in any wicked projects. We were "slothful servants," and therefore are justly regarded as "wicked:" we were unprepared, and therefore are justly cut off from all further opportunity to prepare for our great account; we treated heaven with contempt, and therefore we are consigned to the miseries of hell— — —

Who that contemplates these tremendous consequences, must not determine with God's help to watch and pray through the whole remainder of his days?— — —

Our Lord's concluding admonition, "What I say unto you I say unto all, Watch," will lead us to *address* some different descriptions of persons:

1. The old—

Is so much of your time gone, and will you not improve the remainder?— — —

2. The young—

What security have you against death, that you should delay so necessary a work?— — —

3. The afflicted—

God sends your afflictions on purpose to awaken you from your slumbers, and to stir you up to heavenly pursuits: What an aggravation will it be of your guilt, if these dispensations pass away unimproved!

4. The backslidden—

What an awful thing is it, that, instead of having advanced in the Divine life, you have lost in a good measure the life which you once had! Attend to God's admonition to the church of Sardis, lest he execute upon you the judgment that he threatened to inflict on them, Rev. iii. 2, 3.— — —

5. The more stedfast christian—

Experience proves that the exhortation to "watch" is not less necessary for you than for others. How many who are on the whole pious, grieve, by their unwatchfulness, their Divine Master! Be on your guard against such a slothful way of seeking him as his Bride was found guilty of, Cant. iii. 1; nor think to justify your sloth by such frivolous excuses as were urged by her. Cant. v. 2, 3. If you act like her, like her you will reap the bitter fruits in the hidings of his face. Cant. iii. 1—4. & v. 2—6. To you then no less than to others I would say, "Sleep not as do others, but watch and be sober." 1 Thess. v. 6—8.

WE SHOULD WATCH FOR OUR LORD'S SECOND COMING

Mark xiii. 37.—What I say unto you I say unto all, Watch. (H. H.)

GOD is pleased to speak to us, not only in his word, but by the dispensations of his providence. Calamities, whether foreign or domestic, whether public or personal, are sent by him to awaken our drowsy consciences, and to stir us up to a remembrance of our latter end. By all of them, whether menaced only, or actually inflicted, he addresses us, as Jesus did his disciples (whom he had forewarned of the evils coming upon Jerusalem, and hereafter also upon the whole world), "Watch therefore, for ye know not when the Master of the house cometh."

On a subject like this we should in vain attempt to speak any thing new. But though we may do no more than remind you of truths with which you are already well acquainted, it will not be unprofitable for me to suggest to your thoughts,

I. THE UNCERTAINTY OF THE TIME WHEN OUR LORD WILL COME TO JUDGMENT—

Our Lord, in illustrating what he had been speaking respecting the day of judgment, compares himself to a master leaving his house, and appointing his servants their work, and commanding his porter to watch, in order to admit him without delay at whatever moment he should return. He represents the precise time of his return to judgment as unknown to men, or angels, or even to himself; (so far at least, that the Holy Spirit, by which he was anointed to his prophetic office, had not communicated it to him as any part of the revelation which he was to make known to men;) and from thence inculcates the necessity of incessant watchfulness. Now, as the time of death is to us the commencement of our eternal state, and as it is equally unknown to us as the judgment itself, we shall direct our attention more particularly to that.

But what shall we say on such a subject as this? It needs neither proof nor elucidation: nor can any words make the uncertainty of life more evident, than the observation and experience of every man have already made it. We appeal to your observation of what takes place around you: Does not our Lord call men to death and judgment at every age, and often when his summons is least expected?— — —We appeal to your experience: Can you not recal to your minds many accidents which might have proved fatal? and do you not see, that you are yet liable every day and hour to be taken away by disease or accident?— — —

Instead of dwelling on so obvious a truth, we will endeavor to point out,

II. OUR DUTY ARISING FROM THIS CONSIDERATION—

Thrice in the space of a few verses does our Lord repeat the same injunction, "Watch," see ver. 33. To enforce this, we would say,

1. Expect the second coming of your Lord—

Put not from you, as you are too apt to do, the thoughts of death and judgment, but cherish them in your minds, and labor to get them impressed upon your hearts. Reflect upon their *uncertainty*, as to the precise period of their arrival, their *nearness*, their *awfulness;* and keep yourselves, as it were, in the daily and hourly expectation of them— — —

2. Prepare to meet him—

Two things are indispensable for all who would behold his face in peace, namely, "repentance towards God, and faith in our Lord Jesus Christ." These must be experienced by you— — —neither the one nor the other can

338

be dispensed with.— — —Get a deep repentance therefore, and a lively faith : and rest not in any state short of that which the scriptures require, and the primitive christians actually attained.

3. Guard against any measure of drowsiness which may interrupt or render doubtful your preparation for him—

It will be a fearful thing if the Master of the house "should find you sleeping." Yet who amongst us is not apt at times to be " weary in well-doing?" "The wise virgins, as well as the foolish, slumbered and slept :" yea, even the Apostles slept, when our Lord had bidden them watch. We should therefore " exhort one another daily, and so much the more as we see the day approaching :" and, instead of giving way to sloth, should use all possible means, to " strengthen the things which remain that are ready to die."

ADDRESS,

1. The careless—

How many continue such in spite of all the warnings which they have received from sickness in themselves, or the sudden deaths of others ! But what will they think of their conduct, when once they are taken hence ? If any one of us knew that a thief would certainly come this very night to break into his house, would he lay himself down to sleep as at other times ? Should we not watch, and use our utmost efforts to frustrate his designs ? Why then do we not act thus in reference to our souls ? Are our souls of less value than our property, or the concerns of time than those of eternity ? Are not the consequences of unwatchfulness sufficiently awful ? Matt. xxiv. 48—51. And is not our real danger increased, rather than diminished, in proportion to our security ? 1 Thess. v. 3. Prov. vi. 9—11. To every one then who is unconcerned about his eternal state, and unprepared to meet his God, we address the reproof which even heathen mariners gave to a prophet of the Lord : " What meanest thou, O sleeper? arise and call upon thy God, if so be that God will think upon thee, and thou perish not." Jonah i. 6.

2. The half-awakened—

Pardon the term : it is but too appropriate to the states of many, who, if good wishes would carry them to heaven, would not come short of it; but when God calls them to run, and strive, and wrestle, and fight, will not exert themselves in the way that requires. Nevertheless God's word is true ; " The kingdom of heaven suffereth violence, and the violent take it by force :" " Many shall *seek* to enter in, and shall not be able ;" none shall succeed but those who "*strive.*" Guard then against the fate of the foolish virgins, who were not aware of their want of Divine grace, till it was too late to obtain it. Matt. xxv.8—13. Let the Apostle's exhortation sink down into your ears, Rom. xiii. 11—14, and adopt instantly the resolution of the Prophet, " I will stand upon my watch-tower, and will watch to see what God will say to me, and what I shall answer when I am reproved " Hab. ii. 1.

3. The professing people of God—

Think not yourselves above the exhortation in our text : " What we say unto some, we must say unto *all*, Watch." See what a caution our blessed Lord addressed to his own Apostles, Luke xxi. 34—36 : and then say, whether *any* caution can be too strong for *you.* Many who have appeared to run well, have turned back again ; and not a few have died without ever returning to the good way from which they have departed. Be ye then on your guard, " lest, having known the way of righteousness, ye turn from the holy commandment delivered unto you." Beware of imitating the slothful conduct of the Spouse in Solomon's Song, lest, like her, you provoke your heavenly Friend to depart from you. Cant. iii. 1 & v. 2—6. Watch unto prayer with habitual persevering earnestness. Eph. vi. 18. You know the truths we have insisted on; act therefore agreeably to them, and to your holy profession. 1 Thess. v. 2, 4—8. "Have your loins continually girt, and your lamps trimmed, and yourselves as those who wait for the coming of their Lord."*

THE DUTY OF HOPING IN GOD.

Ps cxxx. 7, 8.—Let Israel hope in the Lord; for with the Lord there is mercy, and with him is plenteous redemption. And he shall redeem Israel from all his iniquities. (S. S.)

THAT advice which flows from experience is at all times most worthy of our attention. In this view the words of our text claim peculiar regard. David, in the Psalm before us, records a very signal deliverance which he had recently experienced, probably from an overwhelming sense of his own guilt and corruption; and, having informed us what methods he had used to obtain deliverance, and how effectual they had proved for his restoration to happiness, he recommends the adoption of them to all the people of God under all difficulties whatsoever; and assures them, that they shall not in any instance fail of success: "Let Israel," &c.

He sets before us,

I. OUR DUTY.

Hope in God, as men generally use the term, is nothing more than an unfounded expectation that God will save us, whatever be our state, and whatever be our conduct. But a scriptural hope implies a suitable regard to the things we hope for, and to him in whom our hope is placed. It implies,

1. That we pray to him with fervour.

This was united with the Psalmist's hope; ver. 1, 2; and it must also be with ours. Matt. vii. 7, 8. To pretend to hope in God while we neglect to spread our wants before him, is the grossest hypocrisy, and the most fatal delusion. Ezek. xxxvi. 37.

2. That we wait for him with patience.

It was in this manner that David exercised his hope. Ver. 5, 6. Nor can we act otherwise, if we be sincere in our profession. Rom. viii. 25. To be impatient, is an unequivocal mark of unbelief, and despondency. Isa. xxviii. 16; 1 Sam. xiii. 11, 12. But to wait patiently the Lord's leisure is the office and evidence of faith and hope. Hab. ii. 3.

3. That we depend on him with steadfastness.

The promises of God to those who seek him, must be the ground of our hope. Ver. 5. We are not to regard difficulties of any kind, as though they could prove any obstacle to God. However circumstances, both within and without, may seem to justify despair, we must "hope beyond and against hope," παρ' ἐλπίδα Rom. iv. 18; Job xiii. 15; Isa. i. 10, assured that, as nothing is impossible with God, so not one jot or tittle of his word shall ever fail

* Supposing this were a *funeral* Sermon for a truly pious person, some little mention of his character might be made here.

This duty being of infinite importance, and of universal obligation, let us consider,

II. OUR ENCOURAGEMENT TO PERFORM IT.

If we look inward, we shall find nothing but discouragement. But if, with David, we look to God, we may find abundant encouragement.

1. In his attributes.

While justice bears a frowning aspect, mercy smiles on the repenting sinner. God has opened a way for the exercise of his mercy in perfect consistency with the demands of justice; and to exercise it is his delight. Mic. vii. 18. This attribute is as essential to his nature as wisdom, or power, or any other. Exod. xxxiv. 6, 8. Nor needs he to have it excited by a view of our misery; (much less by any meritorious services of ours) it is ever "with him;" and is ready to manifest itself towards all those who call upon him. Rom. x. 12.

2. In his works.

"Redemption" is the crown of all his works: and this also is with him, that he may impart it to those who groan under their sore bondage. Yea, with him is "plenteous" redemption: he himself as our near kinsman, (bone of our bone, and flesh of our flesh, Eph. v. 30.) has the right of redemption vested in him: Lev. xxv. 25, 47, 48, 49; and having ability to pay the price, he will discharge our debt, and restore us, not only to liberty, but also to the inheritance which we have so basely alienated.

3. In his word.

The declaration of his determined purpose by an inspired writer, is equivalent to an express promise. And, if the extent and certainty of this promise be considered, what an encouragement will it afford us to hope in God! There is no limitation whatever to the promise, provided, like "Israel" of old, we wrestle with God for the performance of it. Gen. xxxii. 24—28. However numerous and inveterate our iniquities may be, they shall "all" be pardoned, and "all" subdued. Isaiah i. 18.

APPLICATION.

1. To prevent any abuse of this subject, we shall *guard* it.

The repetition of the name "Israel" distinctly marks the characters to whom the text is more immediately to be applied. It is the *praying, waiting*, and *depending* sinner that is exhorted to hope in God: and it is he alone who can expect redemption at the hands of God. Let such therefore see their duty and their privilege: but let those who live in the habitual neglect of God know, that their "hope is as a spider's web, that shall soon be swept away with the besom of destruction." Job viii. 13, 14.

2. To impress the subject more deeply on our minds, we shall *enforce* it.

The advice here given is the most *suitable* that can be given, and if followed, will be *productive* of the greatest *happiness*. Were any of us directed to indulge an hope from our own endeavors, we should soon perceive the folly of such advice. Every day and hour would bring us fresh occasion for despair. But in God there is nothing wanting: he has the *right*, the *power*, and the *will* to redeem us. Nor, if we trust in him, shall we ever be confounded. Isaiah xlv. 17.

Let us therefore not limit either the mercy or power of our God, but putting away all self-righteous hopes, Phil. iii. 3. or unbelieving fears, Ps. xlii. 11. let us repose an unlimited confidence in our merciful and faithful Redeemer.

THE DUTY OF THE CHURCH AS MARRIED TO CHRIST.

Ps. xlv. 10, 11.—Hearken, O daughter, and consider, and incline thine ear; forget also thine own people, and thy father's house. So shall the King greatly desire thy beauty: for he is thy Lord; and worship thou him. (S. S.)

EVERY change of situation brings with it many correspondent duties—
That of marriage in particular requires a sacrifice of other attachments—
It binds each party to renounce whatever habits or practices may be found inconsistent with their mutual happiness—
Such sacrifices are more eminently necessary for those united to Christ*—
To this effect God addresses the church in the words of our text—
We may consider,

I. THE DIRECTION GIVEN TO THE CHURCH.

The church is, by adoption, by regeneration, and especially by her union with the Lord Jesus Christ, become the "daughter" of God—2 Cor. vi. 18.
She is here addressed by him under that affectionate appellation—
Nor is it possible for a father to give more salutary advice—
Or to deliver it in more persuasive terms; "Hearken, consider, incline,"&c.
The direction itself is of a very peculiar nature.
The Jews were permitted to marry the heathen virgins whom they had taken in war—
But they were to allow them the space of a month to forget their own relations—Deut. xxi. 10—13.
Thus the captives, weaned from former habits, might become loving companions, and obedient wives—
In reference to this law, the church is exhorted to forget her friends—
She has been taken captive by Christ, who makes her the first overtures of marriage—
But his union with her is incompatible with carnal attachments—
She can never love and obey him as she ought, till her heart be weaned from all other lovers—
It is given to every individual in the church of God.
Every wife is to forsake her parents, and cleave to her husband—Gen ii. 24.
Much more is it needful for the soul to forsake all for Christ—
To him we are espoused by our own voluntary surrender—2 Cor. xi. 2.
Nor will he be satisfied with a divided heart—Hos. x. 2.
Ungodliness and worldly lusts must be entirely renounced—Tit. ii. 11. 12, and 1 Pet. iv. 2, 3.
The companions of our unregenerate state must be forsaken—2 Cor. vi. 14—17.
Our very parents, yea, even life itself, must be hated, when they stand in competition with him—Luke xiv. 26.
The change in our actions and effections must be entire—2 Cor. v. 17.
And we must subscribe from our hearts the terms proposed to us—Hos. iii. 3.
This injunction will not appear harsh, if we attend to,

* The psalm before us is a kind of nuptial hymn; the former part of which recites the excellencies and glories of the heavenly Bridegroom, and the latter celebrates the praises of the church, which is his bride.

II. THE ARGUMENTS WITH WHICH IT IS ENFORCED.

God deals with us in all things as intelligent beings—
And labors to persuade us by rational considerations.

1. It is our highest interest.

Though the church is vile in herself, she is complete in Christ—Col. ii. 10.

He has given orders for her thorough purification—Esther ii. 3.

When she is presented to him, she is cleansed from all the filthiness of her former state—Eph. v. 25—27.

Hence she is exceeding beautiful in his eyes—Song iv. 9—11.

And he feels a longing desire after communion with her—Song ii. 14.

No bridegroom ever so much rejoiced over his bride, as he over her—Isa. lxii. 5.

More especially is he delighted with her when he sees that her heart is whole with him. Prov. xi. 20.

How powerful an argument is this with an ingenuous soul!—

What can influence a wife more than to know that her conduct will conciliate the esteem of her husband?—

And what can delight a regenerate soul so much, as to please Christ?—

Let this hope then animate us to renounce all for him—

And to address him in the words of holy David—Ps. lxxiii. 25

2. It is our indispensable duty.

The husband is to be considered as a Lord over his wife—1 Pet. iii. 6.

To him she owes an humble obediental reverence—Eph. v. 33.

Christ also is the supreme head and Lord of his Church—

No limits whatever are to be set to his authority—

We must " worship" and serve him equally with God the Father—John —v. 23.

Let us then at least shew him that regard, which we ourselves expect from a fellow-creature—

A husband will not endure a rival in his wife's affections—

Shall we then " provoke the Lord himself to jealousy" by carnal attachments?—

Let us not dare in such a way to violate our nuptial engagements—

When any thing solicits a place in our hearts, let us utterly reject it—

And let us exercise that fidelity towards him, which we have ever experienced at his hands—

ADDRESS,

1. Those who are endeavoring to unite the love of the world with the ove of Christ.

The interests of the world, and of Christ, are altogether opposite—

Our Lord declares them to be absolutely irreconcilable—Matt. vi. 24.

St. James also represents even a wish to reconcile them, as an incontestible proof of enmity against God—Jam. iv. 4.

As Jesus deserves, so he demands our whole hearts—Prov. xxiii. 26.

Let us not then " mock him, and deceive ourselves"—

If the Lord be God, let us not serve Baal, but him—1 Kings xviii. 21.

And let us unite in imitating the repentant Jews—2 Chron. xv. 12.

2. Those who are desirous of uniting themselves to Christ.

It is a great honor indeed which ye aspire after—

Yet is it offered to the vilest of the human race—Ezek. xvi. 3, 4, 5, 8.

But you must get a change of raiment, that you may not dishonor your new station—Zech. iii. 3—5.

Labor then to " purge out all remains of the old leaven"—
Be on your guard, lest after having escaped the pollutions of the world, you be again entangled with them and overcome—2 Pet. ii. 20.
" Remember Lot's wife" that you may shun her example—
So shall you enjoy the sweetest fellowship with Jesus—
And live in the fruition of him to all eternity*—

THE DUTY OF WALKING IN THE LIGHT.

John xii. 35, 36. Yet a little while is the light with you. Walk while ye have the light, lest darkness come upon you: for he that walketh in darkness, knoweth not whither he goeth. While ye have light, believe in the light, that ye may be the children of light. (S. S.)

THE perverseness of men in resisting the means of conviction, is apt to beget an asperity in the minds of their instructors, and to make them cease from their labors of love. But we are required "in meekness to instruct them that oppose themselves." And our blessed Lord affords us in this respect an admirable example. He had plainly told the Jews, that he must be crucified: and their very answer shews that they understood his meaning. But, instead of receiving the information aright, they cavilled at it, and concluded from thence that he could not be the Messiah, ver. 32—34. Our Lord did not judge it proper at that time to afford them any farther means of conviction, when they had so abused those that were already afforded them: but he most affectionately warned them to improve their present advantages, before they should be finally withdrawn from them.

The words being equally applicable to us, we shall consider,

I. THE EXHORTATION.

Christ is here spoken of as "the light."

We might consider the term " light" *in general*, as referring to the gospel: but *here* it undoubtedly relates to Christ himself. John i. 9, and viii. 12, and xii. 46. He is justly characterized by this name, not only as being the eternal fountain of light, but as enlightening the world by his doctrines and life.

" In him," under this character, we are to " believe."

All that he has spoken respecting his person, work, and offices, together with all his promissory, or threatening declarations, should be received by us without gainsaying, and be relied upon without hesitation.

" In him" also we ought to " walk."

We view earthly things in the light of the material sun; and avail ourselves of its light, every step we take. Precisely thus should we act with respect to Christ, "the Sun of Righteousness." We should view sin and holiness, time and eternity, yea, every thing without exception, in the light that HE, by his word and conduct, reflects upon it. Nor should we take any one step in life, without a direct reference to his word as our rule, and his life as our example.—1 John ii. 6.

To render this exhortation more impressive, let us consider,

II. THE ARGUMENTS WITH WHICH IT IS ENFORCED.

* This subject, and all others of a similar nature, must be treated with extreme care and delicacy.

There are three topics mentioned in the text, from whence we may urge this important duty,

1. From the shortness of the time that we shall enjoy the light.

The Jews now had the light; but it was to be extinguished within the space of four days. Hence our Lord *repeatedly* urges this consideration. "Walk, *while ye have the light.*" And how strongly does this argument apply to us! You have the light at present, yea, even greater light than the Jews enjoyed under the ministry of Christ: (for there were many subjects, which he did not fully open; and the things he did utter, could not be perfectly understood, till the day of Pentecost; whereas you have Christ exhibited to you in all his glory; and the fulness, the freeness, the suitableness of his salvation constantly set before you.) But how soon may it be removed from you, or you from it! Rev. ii. 5. Amos viii. 11, 12. O then, "*while ye have the light,* believe, and walk, in the light."

2. From the danger we incur by disregarding the light.

If we will not attend to the voice of Christ, a "darkness will come upon us," even "darkness that may be felt." They who never have had Christ preached unto them, are indeed in an awful condition; but by no means so awful as that, of those who have despised the gospel, ver. 39, 40. The darkness of which the text speaks, is *judicial,* sent them by God as the punishment of their iniquity; and the very light that shines around them, serves only to increase their blindness, and to aggravate their guilt. 2 Cor. ii. 15, 16. 2 Thess. ii. 11, 12. In this state, "they stumble at the noonday," and wander, "not knowing whither they go;" till at last they fall into that pit of destruction, where is weeping, and wailing, and gnashing of teeth for evermore.

Should not then the dread of such a state lead us to a just improvement of our present privileges?

3. From the benefit arising to those who rightly improve the light.

By "children of light" we may understand either *children of God* (who is light) or, *truly enlightened persons.** In either sense the general import is the same, namely, that, by believing in Christ, we shall attain the knowledge and enjoyment of God. Compare this state with that of those who are in darkness; and how great will this benefit appear!

Shall not then this blessed prospect allure us to embrace the gospel? Or shall we still prefer sin and misery to holiness and glory?

APPLICATION.

Let us no longer withstand the solemn warnings, and affectionate exhortations of the Lord Jesus; but improve to the utmost this accepted time, this day of salvation.

* Thus υἱοὶ ἀ'πειθείας is used ; Eph. ii. 2, and τέκνα κατά'ρας, 2 Pet. ii. 14, is so translated, as υἱοὶ φωτὸς may be here.

345

DILIGENCE IN DUTY NECESSARY TO BE FOUND OF GOD IN PEACE.

2 Pet. iii. 14.—Wherefore, beloved, seeing ye look for such things, be diligent, that ye **may** be found of him in peace without spot and blameless. (H.)

THE Apostle is speaking, in the preceding verses, of the drowning of the world by water, the coming of the day of the Lord, the destruction of the world by fire, and of a better state of things, in answer to the scoffers of the last days, who said, "Where is the promise of his coming? Since the Fathers fell asleep all things continue as they were." Verse 4. The words are an inference, or conclusion, from these promises. "Wherefore, beloved, since ye looked for such things." I shall have occasion to consider the context, in speaking to the words; what I propose is, to draw forth the sense of them in the several parts of which they consist.

I. IT IS HERE SUPPOSED THAT WE MUST BE JUDGED, and that an inquiry will be made into the states of men. This is implied in the expression, "being found in him;" i. e. by him as judge, or before him, when he shall come. The apostle uses the same expression in the same sense. Phil. iii. 9. The term relates to the final judgment, when the great inquiry shall be made, and the states of men determined. The future judgment is particularly represented and described in Scripture; I shall give you a short view of it to engage and affect your minds.

1. The time of it is appointed. The apostle here speaks of the day of judgment, and the coming of the day of God; chap. ii. 9; iii. 12; the period is determinately fixed; Acts xvii. 31; but of that day and hour knoweth no man. When the period arrives, there will not be a moment's delay; and it will come too soon, come when it will, for those who scoff at the seeming delay.

2. The judge is ordained. This our Lord himself tells us. John v. 22, 27; and again, Rom, ii. 16; 2 Cor. v. 10. The Saviour of sinners is to be Judge of sinners. His appearance will be very glorious, and with great magnificence and grandeur. Luke ix. 26.

3. The rule of judgment is fixed, or the measure of proceeding at that day. We are to be tried by the gospel of Christ, and not by the law of innocence. If he were to enter into judgment with us, and to be strict to mark iniquity, no living creature could be justified, or stand before him. The whole world must be condemned at his bar, and upon the ground of rigorous justice. But we shall be judged by the gospel of Christ, and according to the gracious constitution of the new covenant; so the apostle says. Rom. ii. 16. The apostle James is more direct, chap. i. 25. where he calls the gospel the law of liberty; also, the perfect law of liberty. chap. ii. 12. And which the apostle calls the law of faith, Rom. iii. 27. in opposition to the law of works, which accepts of true believers in Christ, or sincerity of heart, without absolute perfection, and with many imperfections. This is included in the books which shall be opened; Rev. xx. 12. and according to which he will judge the world in righteousness.

4. The persons to be judged are the whole world or the whole race of sinful man. All who died in Adam, shall be judged by Christ, as well as made alive by him; for they are raised in order to be judged. All nations are to be gathered before him. Matt. xxv. 32. We are all to appear before him; 2 Cor. v. 10. the small and great, Rev. xx. 12.

5. The matter of judgment or the cause to be tried, is expressed in the most comprehensive terms; Eccl. xii. 14. and this is the constant language

of the gospel. 2 Cor. v. 10. So that every man shall be rewarded according to his deeds; Rom. ii. 6. being judged according to their works. Rev. xx. 13; xxii. 12. God will judge the secrets of men by Jesus Christ; the most retired transactions of their lives, and the workings of their thoughts and desires, which lie concealed in their own breast, and fall not under the notice of others; and every idle word which men shall speak, they shall give an account thereof, Matt. xii. 36; *i. e.* every evil word, which is either false or hurtful.

6. And then there is the final issue and event of judgment; *i. e.* rewards and punishments. To the righteous it will be, "well done good and faithful servant, enter thou into the joy of thy Lord; and come ye blessed." &c. Matt. xxv. 34. 41. To the wicked it will be, "thou wicked and slothful servant; cast the unprofitable servant into outer darkness, there shall be weeping and gnashing of teeth; and, go, ye cursed," &c. verse 46. The execution of the sentence will immediately follow, "for these shall go away into everlasting punishment, but the righteous into life eternal." They each shall go to their respective, final, and unchangeable state; and so, from the consequence of it, it is called the eternal judgment. Heb. vi. 2.

II. I OBSERVE, THAT A CHRISTIAN'S GREAT CONCERN is to be found of his judge in peace, and without spot and blameless. Here is a double expression used, which evidently refers to two different things, of the greatest importance.

1. It refers to our justification and acceptance with God, which is the state of every true believer. There can be no peace in the day of judgment to a fallen sinner, but in the way of forgiveness. We must be pardoned and justified through the blood of Christ; for that is the measure of our present acceptance with God, which will be the rule of the final judgment; so the apostle says; Phil. iii. 9, which is parallel to that of the apostle. Acts xiii. 39; also Gal. ii. 16. Thus we are brought into a state of friendship with God for being justified by faith; Rom. v. 1, we have peace with God.

The consequence of this is, peace of mind; a composed frame of mind, without the uneasiness of doubt, or torment of fear, or dread of divine displeasure. A blessed serenity of mind, arising from the testimony of conscience to their own sincerity, and the witness of the Spirit to their relation to God. They have that peace of God which passes all understanding; which none of the troubles of life, or fear of death, nor the presence of the Judge, or the terror of judgment, can disturb.

And this will appear in a peaceable frame of mind towards others: in good-will towards all men, fervent love to all the children of God. Heb. xii 14.

I shall only farther add, that although the believer is justified already, yet we are most properly justified at the final judgment, when it will be most solemn and most complete.

2. It refers to our sanctification and holiness. This is the import of the other expression, "without spot and blameless." This may refer to our present sanctification, which is called the sanctification of the Spirit, &c. Eph. i. 4. For this end God has chosen believers; Phil. ii. 15; and they are to keep themselves unspotted, &c. James i. 27. This was the character of Zachariah and Elizabeth. Luke i. 6. And as such Jesus Christ will present them to himself at last. Eph. v. 27; also 1 Thess. iii. 13. It is a great act of the mediation of Christ, towards his members, not only to " wash them in his own blood, but to present them pure and faultless at last." This certainly was the grand end of his whole undertaking; see Titus ii.

4; also 1 Peter iii. 18. Paul represents it as the highest ambition of the christian's heart; 2 Cor. v. 9, and the greatest blessing he could wish for others. Phil. i. 10.

III. THAT IN ORDER TO OUR BEING FOUND OF OUR JUDGE IN PEACE we must be diligent. It is a work of labor and care, and not to be done with idleness and sloth. Men may sit still and perish; but they must be diligent who would be saved. Consider this diligence according to the scripture account of it, in the following instances.

1. There must be the due exercise of our natural faculties and reasonable powers. Those, we readily admit, are weakened and disordered by sin; but divine assistance is promised by God, who is the God of nature as well as grace. We are reasonable creatures, when we are not holy creatures, and can act as men, when we cannot act as saints, and in order to being such, see Deut. xxxii. 29; Isa. xlvi. 8; Hos. v. 4; 1 Cor. xiv. 20; Phil. ii. 12.

2. The improvement of the talents and enjoyments of life. Every man has his proper talents, besides his natural powers, though in different degrees, for which he must account at last. Matt. xxv. 14; Luke xix. 13. Such are life and health, acquired knowledge and experience, liberty and opportunity, possessions and prosperity, interest and credit in the world. Those who improve therein shall be commended, Matt. xxv. 21, and those who do not improve them shall be punished, ver. 25. We are only stewards of our talents; Luke xvi. 2, and our Lord advises a proper use of them; ver. 9; also the apostle, 1 Tim. vi. 17.

3 We must perform the proper duties of our place and station. John ix. 4. In this sense our Lord pronounces his servants blessed; Matt. xxiv. 46, and this the apostle recommends. 2 Pet. i. 10. Faithfulness in the way of duty is a good preparation for the coming of the Lord 1 Cor. xv. 58.

4. There must be watchfulness against sin. So our Lord directs his disciples in this case: Luke xxi. 34, in this view he often requires watchfulness. Matt. xxvi. 41, 42; Mark xiii. 37. The apostle abounds with exhortations to sobriety and watchfulness. 1 Thess. v. 6, 8; Pet. iv. 7; Heb. xii. 15, 17. And the judge is represented saying, "Behold I come, blessed is he that watcheth and keepeth his garments." Rev. xvi. 15.

5. The use of appointed means, or institutions of worship. These are properly means of grace. Thus we must be found in the daily practice of prayer. Luke xviii. 1; also xxi. 36. We must converse with the word of God; Heb. ii. 1; 2 Pet. i. 19, and the apostle says, that "God is a rewarder of them who diligently seek him," or come to him in any way of worship or service. Particularly the Lord's Supper is a perpetual memorial, not only of the death, but of the coming of Christ. 1 Cor. xi. 26. Thus, by frequent converses with God in the ordinances of his worship, and receiving communications from him, we are formed to a more spiritual frame, and serious habit of mind, and in a nearer fitness for the coming of the Lord. Hereupon,

6. There must be the exercise and improvement of suitable graces, or proper dispositions of mind. 2 Pet. i. 5; iii. 18. Particularly faith; Heb. vi. 1; also hope; Heb. vi. 11; 1 Pet. i. 13; and looking; Tit. ii. 13; Heb. ix. 28; Jude 21, and in this chapter, ver. 12.

IV. I SHALL CONSIDER THE MOTIVES and reasons of this diligence here suggested and referred to. This is intimated in the words of connexion, " Wherefore, beloved, seeing ye look for such things; i. e. the things which he had been speaking of, or the arguments of his foregoing discourse. The great ideas in his mind at that time were,

1. The destruction of the present world, ver. 7, to be accomplished by a deluge of fire; also, ver. 10, the whole globe of the earth shall be set on fire, and whatever belongs to it, and has been infected with sin. All the works of nature and of art, the stately buildings and proud palaces, the monuments of vanity, ambition, and curiosity, which have endured for many ages, and stood the longest injuries of time; all the grandeur and glory of this world, the pageantry and show of it, will be then destroyed and consumed to ashes, and there will be no remainder or ruins of them left; "for the heavens shall pass away," &c., ver. 10.

There will be a universal conflagration; heaven and earth will be all on fire at once, and make one burning vault, one funeral pile: it will be the funeral of the world. What will be the terror of the affrighted inhabitants! no place of refuge! Yea, the fire which will consume the world, will destroy the wicked, ver. 7. Now, how forcible is the reason? Be diligent to be found of him in peace, when the great day of his wrath shall come.

2. The expectation of a better state, ver. 13. He represents it as the common expectation of christians, grounded on the promise of God; " we, according to his promise, look for it, a new heaven and a new earth." Isa. lxv. 17. Heaven and earth will be alike, at least for a limited time, and become a glorious state, in which only righteousness and righteous persons shall dwell. And the expectation of such a state of things should operate as a powerful motive, that we may not come short of the glory of God, but be fit to partake of it, and share in all the blessedness of it. Let us, therefore, according to our Lord's direction, " watch and pray, that we may be accounted worthy to escape all these things which shall come to pass, and to stand before the Son of man." And, in the words of the apostle, " Give diligence, so an entrance shall be ministered abundantly into the everlasting kingdom; and, let us labor to enter into that rest, lest any man fall after the same example of unbelief."

CONSTANCY CROWNED BY CHRIST.

Rev. ii. 10.—Be thou faithful, &c. (H.)

THESE are the words of our Saviour to the angel or pastor of the church of Smyrna; and they divide themselves into two parts, a precept and a promise. The precept is in these words— "Be thou faithful unto death." The promise in these—"And I will give," &c. There is the work in the one, and the reward in the other. I shall,

I. CONSIDER THE DUTY HERE RECOMMENDED. Faithfulness here, relates to the Lord Jesus Christ; our being true to our profession of his religion— to our repeated engagements with him to be his—our attachment to him, and our obedience to his commands—to continue therein to the end of our life. The necessity of this will appear, when we consider that,

1. Not to persevere, is a curtailed sacrifice, a maimed service, and such as God will not accept. No maimed beast was to be presented in sacrifice. Lev. xxii., 21, 22.

2. Inconstancy and instability is an argument of unsoundness and insincerity. Prov. xvii. 17

3. Christ persevered for us, and therefore we ought to persevere for him John xiii. 1. He is not only the beginning, but finisher of faith. Heb xii. 2. He held out to the last gasp. John xix. 30.

4. It is a rule in civil law, that it is as nothing that holdeth not. A will unfinished is no will; a deed, unless it be signed, sealed, and delivered, is no deed.

5. The former part of our life yieldeth to the latter; and the latter part of our life carrieth away from the former. Ezek. xviii. 21, 22. And so on the other side also, ver. 24.

6. The end of every thing is all in all. Ps. xxxvii. 37; lxxiii 17. The grand end of living should be, to make a good end, to be found in peace. 2 Pet. iii. 14.

7. It is perseverance alone that carries away the crown: unless we are faithful unto death, there is no crown of life for us. Christianity is compared to a race. Heb. xii. 1. It is not he that cometh first, but every one that holdeth out to the last is crowned. Matt. xxiv. 13; Mark xiii. 13.

8. God himself is eternal, from whom we expect our reward; and the reward we look for is everlasting. "What hath levity and inconstancy," saith Augustine, "to do with eternity?"

And if we would be faithful to Christ, our master, and hold out in our christian course to the end, we must,

1. Enter upon it with resolution: we must count the cost. Luke xiv. 28—30. Lay our accounts with the worst, and prepare for it. Luke xiv. 33. It is for want of this that many, who at first ran well, have been hindered.

2. Labor after sincerity. That which is counterfeit will not last long. Ps. lxxviii. 37; 1 Tim. iv. 1.

3. Be careful to keep a good conscience; 1 Tim. 1. 19; iii. 9, which some have cast away. 1 Tim. i. 19.

4. Slight no sin. Every sin, however small, comparatively speaking, is of a deadly nature. The mote must be cast out as well as the beam. Matt. vii. 3, 4.

5. Be jealous of thine own weakness; trust not too much to thine own strength. This was Peter's fault, and we know how foully he fell. Matt. xxvi. 33—35; John xiii. 37. And his fault is left upon record, as a warning to us.

6. Shun evil occasions. By unwatchfulness in this, thousands relapse into sin. 2 Pet. ii. 20. See David's case. Ps. cxlii. 3. Satan has his snares in our meat, drink, apparel, recreation, lawful delights, our trading, traffic, buying, and selling: we walk among snares, Job xxii. 10, and had need tread warily, Prov. iv. 25, 26, and walk wisely. Eph. v. 15.

7. Be much in prayer to God for support. Matt. xxvi. 41. It is from him that we must receive strength to stand. Eph. vi. 10, 11, 13. Thus prayed David. Ps. lxxxvi. 11.

8. Keep the fear of God alive in thy soul. Pray with David, Ps. lxxxvi. 11, and God will fulfil his promise. Jer. xxxii. 40.

9. Take heed of standing still; for he that begins to stand still, will soon draw back. 2 Pet. iii. 17. And to prevent it, grow in grace, ver. 18. If we be not growing, we are decaying.

10. Walk in humility. Take heed of pride. Remember Uzziah; 2 Chron. xxvi. 16, remember Hezekiah. 2 Chron. xxxii. 25, 26. It is a deadly poison, exceedingly displeasing to God, 1 Pet. v. 5, and destructive to the work of grace in the soul.

11. Consider the short time that this laborious course is required of us; it is only till death; and, as our life is short, that employment cannot be long that is to end with it. Not that our fidelity to Christ shall ever end, but our trials in consequence of it shall; they are but light and momentary. 2 Cor. iv. 17.

12. Be often surveying the royal reward promised in the text, as well as in other parts of the word of God. This was the case with Moses; Heb. xi. 25, 26, and the apostle. 2 Cor. iv. 8, 10, 16, 18. The reward is sure. Gal. vi. 9. It was the case with our Saviour, whose example we may safely imitate. Heb. xii. 2, 3. How important the apostle's advice. Heb x. 35.

II. The gracious promise here given—"I will give," &c.

1. He that promises is Christ, ver. 8, and he is well able to make it good. Matt. xxviii. 18; Rev. ii 16, 18; iii. 21. He is the Amen, true and faithful. Rev. iii. 14. Those who are faithful to Christ shall find him faithful to them. Heb. x. 23.

2. What he gives is a free gift. We owe him all that we do, or can do Rom. viii. 12. We can claim nothing of him as our right. Rom. xi. 35, 36. He does not owe us so much as thanks. Luke xvii. 9, 10. Of his mere bounty he will not suffer us to go unrewarded.

3. The gift promised is a crown; 2 Tim. iv. 8, it is a kingdom. Luke xii. 32; Matt. xxv. 34. Who would not strain hard for a crown?—Who would not endure much for a kingdom?

4. This crown is a crown of life; not like the crowns that earthly kings wear, that cannot save them from disease and death. They may die, and do die. Ps. lxxxii. 7; cxlvi. 3, 4. But this is a crown that giveth life to him that hath it, and keepeth him in life that weareth it.

5. The life that this crown giveth (though not expressed here) is an eternal, everlasting life. Matt. xxv. 46. It is an incorruptible crown. 1 Peter i. 4.

I shall now conclude with some improvement of the subject. And,

1. How ample shall be the recompense of the persevering christian! This crown of life—of eternal life, will indeed be a glorious compensation for all his sacrifices, services, and sufferings which he has performed and endured for the sake of Christ. Matt. ix. 27, 28; Mark x. 28—30; Luke xvi. 26, 33.

2. How deplorable the state of those who have forsaken their first love; Rev. ii. 4, 5, who run well for awhile, and then give over; Gal. v. 7, who begin in the Spirit, and end in the flesh; Gal. iii. 3, who put their hand to the plough, and then look back, Luke ix. 62, as Lot's wife did towards Sodom; Gen. xix. 26, that, like Demas, follow Paul awhile, Col. iv. 14, and return again to the world, 2 Tim. iv. 10, and turn away from the holy commandment. 2 Pet. ii. 20—22. Returning like the dog to his vomit, and the sow that was washed to its wallowing in the mire, ver. 22. Their last state is worse than the first. 2 Pet. ii. 20; Matt. xii. 45.

3. Let us consider what we lose if we give over, as well as what we gain, if we persevere. Hold fast, that no man take thy crown. Rev. iii. 11. And what a painful reflection will it be, to think that we have deprived ourselves of a crown, of a kingdom, of eternal felicity, for perhaps a mere trifle, the pleasures of sin, which are but for a season.

4. Be admonished then to hold fast, &c.; ver. 25, to cleave to God; Acts xi. 23, to give all diligence, &c. Heb. vi. 17. And seeing that we know these things, &c. 2 Pet. iii. 17, then may we be faithful unto death, and receive, at last, the crown of life.

PERSEVERANCE IN RELIGION THE CHRISTIAN'S DUTY.

Judges viii. 4.—Faint, yet pursuing. (H.)

FIT me to this for the arms of the Christian; descriptive of the fatigue he endureth, and of his resolution to persevere. Though the words relate to quite another matter, yet they may, without any impropriety, be accommodated to the great purpose of animating us to the duties of our christian profession

I. BRIEFLY DESCRIBE THE CHRISTIAN'S WARFARE.

The life of a real disciple of Jesus is frequently thus represented in scripture. 1 Tim. i. 13; vi. 12; 2 Tim. ii. 3. He is engaged in the cause of God and Christ; of truth and liberty. His enemies are, the devil; 1 Pet. v. 8, the world, evil passions and corruptions; enemies numerous, subtle, powerful who give no quarter. If they cannot conquer, will do their utmost to afflict, distress, torment; the conflict is often fierce and violent. Christ is the Captain under whom he fighteth; his weapons are, "the shield of faith," &c.; the object is the overthrow of sin.

A noble warfare this! and shall in the issue, be crowned with joy, &c.

II. THE VARIOUS TEMPER AND CONDUCT OF THE CHRISTIAN; the reason of his many discouragements on the one hand; and of his resolution to persevere on the other. "Faint, yet pursuing."

1. View him as he is, sometimes faint and spiritless. The most intrepid soldier may, on some occasions, tremble; and the man whose constitution is the most robust and healthful, cannot always boast an exemption from faintness. No wonder that such, at certain intervals, is the sad experience of the christian in regard to the concerns of religion. His hands are feeble and his soul melts like wax; his spirit languisheth, and his strength faileth; and this may, perhaps, be ascribed,

1. To the past toils and labors he has endured.

2. To the want of proper refreshment. 1 Sam. xiv. 31; Isa. i. 10. The apostle was just at the point of fainting. 2 Cor. xii. 9.

3. Through the dread of being overcome. 1 Sam. xxvii. 1.

2. Resuming his wonted courage, and, in the strength of divine grace, resolving to pursue. He will not ignominiously submit: no, he will keep the field, maintain the conflict, push the victory. A brave resolution. He considereth what will be the consequence of submitting, on the one hand, and of pursuing, on the other. In order to animate the timorous in the pursuit, reflect,

1. What will be the effect, should you throw down your arms, yield to the enemy, and apostatize from your profession.

1. You will lose the advantage you have already gained. 2 John 8; Gal. iii. 3, 4; iv. 15; v. 7.

2. Be overcome; and here shame and misery present themselves to your view. This ought to excite to action. Luke xiv. 29, 30; Matt. xii. 43—45; 2 Peter ii. 20, 21; Heb. x. 26—29.

2. In order to quicken and enliven, amidst the fatigues and dangers of this spiritual war, consider,

1. The goodness of the cause in which you are engaged; the cause of God. It is called, "A good fight of faith."

2. The seasonable and effectual support you may depend on receiving. 2 Kings vi. 15, 16; Isa. xli. 10; 2 Cor xii. 9; Isa. liv. 17; Heb xiii. 5, 6; Ps. lx. 12.

Christ is also your Captain; and in his character, conduct, and example, **you** have every possible encouragement. Matt. xii. 20.

You may also notice your weapons; you need not to meet the enemy naked. Eph. vi. 10—18.

3. The triumph that shall succeed; the prospect of this should animate you. Rev. xxi. 7.

Inferences.

1. That undisturbed rest and tranquility are not to be expected here.

2. That the Christian may be reduced very low, but not be overcome.

3. Let those who have as yet felt little faintness in their conflict; take heed how they presume. Isa. xl. 29, 30.

Lastly, Ever remember the encouragement you have to pursue. Clad in armor of proof, led by a Captain of unconquerable magnanimity, supported by a numerous body of saints, all shouting, "The sword of the Lord and his Christ;" angels waiting for the event, and a cloud of witnesses, on every side, marking your conduct; and you yourselves pouring out incessant cries to heaven to prosper the enterprize: thus advancing, relying on the power and faithfulness of God, what have you to fear? Victory, complete victory shall crown the day; be persuaded, therefore, "though faint, yet to pursue"

GOD'S CLAIM ON OUR OBEDIENCE.

Exod. v. 2.—Who is the Lord, that I shall obey his voice? (Sk.)

In the verse immediately preceding our text, we find Aaron delivering this message to Pharoah,—"Thus saith the Lord God of Israel, Let my people go, that they may hold a feast unto me in the wilderness." To this message, Pharaoh answers in the words before us, "Who is the Lord, that I should obey his voice, to let Israel go? I know not the Lord, neither will I let Israel go." The words imply, that as Jehovah was not an Egyptian Deity, and consequently not the professed object of Pharaoh's worship, he therefore concluded that he was under no obligation to obey Jehovah's voice. This conclusion teaches us, that ignorance of God is a most alarming evil, as it leads to daring rebellion against God; and this, if persisted in, must be attended with certain destruction, Prov. xxix. 1.

But the inquiry in our text, though at first employed in an avowed contempt of God, will admit of improvement favorable to piety. In attempting to make this improvement, under the divine blessing, let us consider some particulars relative to God's voice; and his claims on our obedience to it.

I. Some particulars relative to God's voice.

By the voice of God is meant the declaration of his will concerning man kind. Here therefore it may be proper to consider,

1. *The persons to whom he speaks—mankind.* "Unto you, O men," &c Prov. viii. 4.—He speaks to men as his *favorite* creatures, whose welfare he desires. This appears from his wish, Deut. v. 29. "O that there were," &c;—from his commands, Isa. xlv. 22; Acts xvii. 30.—his declaration, Ezek. xxxiii. 11.—his complaints, John v. 40; Matt. xxiii. 37,—and his threatenings, Prov. i. 24—26.—He speaks to men as *ignorant* creatures; who need his instruction in order that it may be well with them, Isa

lx. 2, and xlviii. 16, 17 ; Jer. x. 23, and xxxviii. 20.—He speaks to men as *improvable* creatures ; who are intrusted with a gracious talent, Luke xix 12, 13, and thereby capable of choosing the path of piety, Deut. xxx. 19. 20 ; Jer. vi. 16.

2. *The means by which he speaks.* These are his *works*, and his *word.* —God speaks to us by his *works*, His works of *creation*, Ps. xix. 1 These prove his existence, Heb. iii. 4, and display his perfections ;—his infinite power, goodness, and wisdom, Rom. i. 20. " The invisible things," &c.

> " The meanest pin in nature's frame,
> Marks out some letter of his name ;—
> Across the earth, around the sky,
> There's not a spot, or deep or high,
> Where the Creator hath not trod,
> And left the footsteps of a God."

And by his works of *providence.* His indulgences lead us to repentance, Rom. ii. 4 ; his corrections and judgments teach us lessons of righteousness, Isa. xxvi. 9. Micah vi. 9. God's works should therefore be attentively considered by us, Isa. v. 12, 13.—God speaks to us also by his *word*, Heb i. 1, 2. By this it is his purpose to judge us at the last day, John xii. 48, and by this our whole deportment should now be governed, James ii. 12 Taht we may thus conform to the will of God, let us consider,

3. *What he says to us.* He speaks to us variously, according to our various states, as sinful—submissive—and reclaimed creatures.—As *sinful creatures*, who transgress his laws, he speaks to us in the language of reproof ; charging us with rebellion, Isa. i. 1, 2, and ingratitude, Deut. xxxii. 6, and in the language of warning ; showing us that we are rejected by him, Prov. xv. 8, 26 ; under his curse, Gal. iii. 10 ; and under the sentence of eternal death, Ezek. xviii. 20 ; Rom. vi. 21.—As *submissive* creatures, who desire to obey him, he speaks to us in the language of kind authority, Isa. lv. 6, 7 ; Matt. xi. 28, 29 ; of encouragement, i. 16—18 ; and of caution against delay, Ps. xcv. 7, 8.—As *reclaimed* creatures, restored to his favor and service, he speaks to us in the language of instruction, Micah vi. 8 ; Tit. ii. 12 ; and in the language of consolation, Isa. xl. 1 ; Ps. lxxxiv. 11. Let us consider,

4. *With what design he speaks.* This is to engage our obedience.— His works teach us to glorify him as God, Rom. i. 21.—His word requires practical piety, as man's indispensible duty, 1 Sam. xv. 22 ; Matt, vii. 21 ; James i. 22, 25. The obedience thus required, must be *prompt*, without delay, Job xxii. 21. *Universal*, without defect, Ps. cxix. 6. *Persevering*, without intermission, Rom. ii. 7, and *humble*, without arrogance. It must be humbly ascribed to divine grace, Isaiah xxvi. 12 ; humbly presented through Christ, for acceptance, 1 Pet. ii. 5 ; and humbly acknowledged as unprofitable at best, Luke xvii. 10. Such being the obedience which God requires, let us consider,

II. HIS CLAIM ON OUR OBEDIENCE TO HIS VOICE. These will appear by answering the inquiry here instituted ; " Who is the Lord, " &c.

1. *He is our indisputable Proprietor.* He becomes thus—By right of *creation ;* he is the Lord our Maker, Ps. xcv. 6, 7, and c. 3.—And by right of *preservation ;* sustaining us by his constant agency on us, and care for us, Job x. 12 ; Acts xvii. 28 ; Ps. cxlv. 15. 16. Hence we are obliged to obey God on principles of *equity*, Ps. cxix. 73.

2. *He is our acknowledged Sovereign.* This he is by our baptismal covenant, and by open, deliberate profession of subjection to him, Deut xxvi. 17. Obedience to God is therefore due on principles of *fidelity*, 2 Tim. ii. 19; Eccl. v. 4.

3. *He is our best Friend, and kindest Benefactor.* This is evident—From his various *providential indulgences*, Ps. lxviii. 19.—From his *redeeming mercy*, by which eternal salvation is provided for a perishing world, John iii. 16; 2 Cor. viii. 9.—And from his *gracious influence*, which is freely givin to all who ask it, Luke xi. 13. Hence obedience to God is due on principles of *gratitude*, Rom. xii. 1.

4. *He is the Disposer of our eternal destiny.* As such,—he is *omniscient*, to observe all our deportment—all our actions, words, and thoughts, Ps. cxxxix. 1—4; Job xxxiv. 21, 22.—He is *just*, to recompense all characters, 2 Cor. v..10; John v. 28, 29.—He is *powerful*, to execute all his purposes; both of mercy and vengeance, James iv. 12. Hence we should obey God on principles of *prudence;* that we may secure the approbation of our Judge, 1 John ii. 18. Thr- 'ile God remains our Proprietor, our Sovereign, our Friend, and our Judg,, his claims must be admitted. And this admission, *justifies scriptural piety from reproach—demonstrates the evil of irreligion—and encourages the hope of penitents.*

1. *It justifies scriptural piety from reproach.* By scriptural piety is meant, that obedience which God requires in his word; obedience, seasonable in its commencement; universal in its extent; constant in its exercise; and humble in its pretensions. This is frequently reproached by the ungodly as irrational, disgraceful, injurious to our interests, and a source of melancholy.—But compliance with the demands of justice cannot be unreasonable; the exercise of fidelity and gratitude cannot be disgraceful; the acquisition of godliness cannot be injurious, 1 Tim. iv. 8; nor can melancholy arise from a smiling conscience, and cheerful hope, Matt. xi. 19; 1 Pet. ii. 15.

2. *It demonstrates the evil of irreligion,* or inattention and disobedience to God's voice. This is too common in all ages, Job xxi. 14, 15. It is an evil in itself, as all who are guilty of it are sacrilegious, treacherous, ungrateful, and mad self-destroyers, Eccles. ix. 3. It is an evil in its consequences; being attended with remorse here, and torment hereafter, Rom. iii. 16, 17, 18. Though kings set the dreadful example, and whole nations follow it, neither their dignity nor number can exempt them from vengeance, Isa. xxx. 33; Ps. ix. 17.

3. *It inspires penitence with hope.* God's voice encourages them to hope—for gracious illumination, Prov. i. 23; for redeeming mercy, **Ps. cxxx.** 7, 8; and for eternal life, Ezek. xviii. 27, 28; Rev. xxii. 14. "**Blessed,**" &c.

THE FATHER'S CHARGE.

Ephesians vi. 4.—And ye fathers, provoke not your children to wrath: but bring them
up in the nurture and admonition of the Lord. (Sk.)

IF we consider our state and circumstances in the world, we cannot fail
to be reminded, that we all stand in a twofold relation. We are related to
God in an absolute sense, as creatures are related to their Creator; and in a
subordinate sense, we are related to each other, as husbands and wives,
parents and children. And from every relation in life, there are duties and
obligations which necessarily arise, the performance of which is of the
utmost importance to the happiness of man, and the wellbeing of society.
From the indissoluble relation in which we stand to God, spring the duties
of love, reverence, and obedience: and from the connexion which we have
with each other, arise obligations, which though of minor importance, are
yet of essential utility. The text is addressed to fathers; a class of men
who fill most responsible stations in the world; and on whose conduct the
tone of morals through all the gradations of society most essentially depends. There can be, therefore, no impropriety in addressing such individuals from the pulpit.—Two things claim their attention,

I. THE DUTIES WHICH PARENTS OWE TO THEIR CHILDREN.

II. THE OBLIGATIONS THEY ARE UNDER TO PRACTICE THOSE DUTIES.

The duties which parents owe to their children, may be distinctly understood, by adverting to the circumstances in which children are placed, on
their introduction into the world.

1. *Children are weak and helpless, and totally incapable of caring for
themselves; and hence arises the first duty which parents owe them, that
of feeding and clothing them.* The weakness of infancy is proverbial.
See the helplessness of little children; oh, how mean and degraded is our
origin! There is scarcely an animal in existence, that has not, in this
sense, the advantage of man. Parents must feed their children.—How pitiable are the circumstances of those parents, whose extreme indigence precludes the possibility of their performing towards their offspring the first
duty in nature. Children should be fed, not pampered. The plainest food
is the most wholesome, and the most nutritious. The children of the poor,
who are fed on the coarsest food, and clothed with the coarsest raiment, or
scarcely clothed at all, are the very pictures of health; the rosy cheeks, the
sprighty features, the vigorous constitution, all unite to proclaim the utility
of plain food and fare.

2. *Children are ignorant, and without understanding; hence they should
not only be fed, but taught.* The mind of an infant is a perfect blank,
devoid of all intelligence, and even unconscious of its being; but in proportion as the capacities of children expand, and their minds are rendered
capable of receiving knowledge, they should be instructed; and who so
proper to teach children, as parents. This is the doctrine of the text;
nurture and *admonition*, signify, discipline and instruction.—Children
should be taught *early*; it is scarcely possible to begin too soon:—*familiarly*; according to their comprehension:—*affectionately*; show them by
your conduct how deeply you are interested in their welfare;—*extensively*;
whatever concerns their duty; such as propriety of conduct—consistency
of character—add the rules of moral conduct.

3. *Children are unruly, and therefore must be governed.* This duty
devolves upon parents. Children are fond of having their own will; and

356

nothing is more difficult than to conquer that headstrong obstinacy which is common to children. But they must be governed, and brought into subjection; and it is as much the duty of parents to govern their children, as it is to feed or clothe them. The dispositions of children vary exceedingly; some may be governed by love, others must be subdued by fear; this makes correction necessary, Prov. xix. 18; xxix. 15: Heb. xii. 9.

4. *Children are prone to evil, and therefore must be restrained.* Eli's sons made themselves vile, and he restrained them not; he mildly reproved them, when he ought to have effectually restrained them; and for this, God punished him with the extirpation of his whole race. Oh! if God were to deal thus with every parent, who treads in the steps of Eli, how many families would have their names cut off from the earth! There are many parents who encourage both by precept and example, the prectice of evil in their children; who let them go where they will, and do what they will, without control or restraint. Having briefly hinted at the duties which parents owe to their children, let us notice,

II. The obligations they are under to practice those duties.

1. *They should do it for their own sake.* For the credit of their *own charactars.* What greater disgrace can attach to a parent, than the neglect of his children? To take no pains to cultivate their minds, to improve their manners, or to save their souls. For their *personal comfort:*—how loud and bitter are the complaints uttered by parents against their children, and how deep the anguish endured on their account. Children may become sources of unspeakable pleasure, or occasions of grievous torment to their parents; but a vast proportion of the misery which they endure, originates in the criminal neglect of their offspring.

2. *They should do it for their children's sake.* We take it for granted that parents love their children, but how do they manifest that love? Perhaps by letting them have their way: that is, in other words, permitting them to go quietly to the devil.—Perhaps by leaving them large property; that is providing food for their pride, and poison for their souls. To bring up our children in the nurture and admonition of the Lord, is to do what we can to make them *wise,* to make them *good,* and to make them *happy.*

3. *They should do it for society's sake.* The children of the present age, will be the men and women of the future age; and the morals of society, half a century hence, will depend, as far as human calculations can go, on the manner in which parents now bring up their children. The seed which is now sown, will then be ripened for the harvest. Those who neglect to practice the advice in the text, not only accelerate the ruin of their children, but do their utmost to make them nuisances and pests to society, wherever their lot may be cast.

4. *They should do it for God's sake.* Children are a heritage of the Lord; they are his property; he is the father of their spirits; but he puts them under the care of their earthly parents, and they are to train them up for him, that they may know, love, and serve him all their days.

Conclusion.

1. Learn how careful the apostles were to instruct their converts, not only in the matters of faith, but rules of conduct descending even to the most particular duties of domestic life.

2. The practicability of a religious education. What is here enjoined is possible to be done. Children may be "brought up in the nurture and admonition of the Lord." There may be a thousand petty shifts, to which

ignorant and idle parents may resort to palliate their sins; but the inference from the text is plain.

3. How awful is the responsibility of parents, fathers especially.—*Ye fathers*, the text is God's voice to you; Oh hear it, reverence it, put it into practice!

~~~~~~~~~~~~~~~~

THE HAPPY RESULT OF WAITING PATIENTLY FOR THE LORD.

Ps. xl. 1—3.—I waited patiently for the Lord; and he inclined unto me, and heard my cry. He brought me up, &c. (Sk.)

By the prophet Hosea, we hear God complaining, "My people are destroyed for lack of knowledge." From this complaint it appears that *ignorance is destructive;* and numerous facts concur in attesting the same melancholy truth. Some through ignorance of their *state*, remain unconcerned about salvation; some, through ignorance of their *duty*, omit to use the means which are appointed and required by God for obtaining salvation; and others, through ignorance of their *privileges*, conclude there is no hope, and sink into inactive despair of salvation.

Our text is therefore of peculiar importance, as it is exactly calculated to prevent or remove that ignorance which is so fatal to the best interests of mankind. Here we behold a description of our state as sinners, and learn the *necessity* of salvation; a description of our duty, as subjects of a divine Redeemer, and learn the *way* of salvation; a description of our privileges, as gospel penitents, and learn the *attainableness* of salvation. "I waited patiently for the Lord," &c. These verses teach us,

I. Our state as sinners. This we learn from David's state as a sinner, which he describes by the simile of a man fallen into a deep sounding pit; with his feet stuck fast in the miry clay at the bottom of it. This striking figure teaches us that our state, as sinners, is a state of deep declension—of total defilement—of imminent danger—and of utter helplessness.

1. *It is a state of deep declension;* we are deeply fallen. *We are fallen* from the most desirable enjoyments. Man, as the creature of God, while he retained his original rectitude, was the subject of holiness, peace, and hope; but having all sinned, and come short of the glory of God, we have lost our peace and hope, with our purity—we know not the way of peace, Rom. iii. 17, 18;—and we are without hope, while without Christ, Eph. ii. 12;—" the crown is fallen from our head: wo to us that we have sinned." *We are deeply fallen*, into a pit of noise or sounding, as the words may be rendered, a pit that sounds by reason of its great depth. We are deeply sunk in *depravity*, or evil propensities—for we are at enmity against God, our parent, benefactor, and redeemer, Rom. viii. 7. We are deeply sunk in *transgression*; for we have expressed the enmity of our hearts against God, by wilful rebellion against him in our lives, Dan. ix. 9, 10. We are deeply sunk in *condemnation;* for we are under the curse of God, Gal. iii. 10; and the sentence of eternal death, Ezek. xviii. 20. We are deeply sunk in *misery*; for the pit into which we have fallen is a horrible one. The darkness of ignorance—the pangs of remorse—and the agitations of guilty fear—all concur to produce the most dreadful horror, Ps. cxix. 120.

2. *It is a state of total defilement.* The miry clay of sin defiles *all the*

faculties of the sinner's mind;—unto them that are defiled and unbelieving nothing is pure; but even their mind and conscience is defiled, Tit. i. 15;—their understandings, wills, and affections are corrupted—and out of the evil treasure of their hearts, they bring forth evil things. Consequently sin defiles—*all the powers of the 'sinner's body.* These also are yielded as instruments of unrighteousness unto sin, Rom. vi. 13; so that we are all as an unclean thing, Isa. lxiv. 6.

3. *It is a state of imminent danger.* While we remain in this horrible pit certain destruction awaits us. Destruction *awaits* us—for we have justly merited it by our sin, Rom. vi. 23—and it is justly threatened by a holy God, Prov. x. 20. And destruction is *certain* if we remain here, for the earnest of it is already given us, John iii. 36.

4. *It is a state of utter helplessness.* As, with respect to the perishing object here described, the pit into which he is sunk is so deep, that the top of it is far above his reach—the clay so confines his feet that he cannot climb —if help come to him it must be from above—and he cannot expect deliverance, unless he obtains it by earnest cries;—so it is with perishing sinners. Salvation is *above* the reach of human *efforts,* Ps. cxxx. 4, and cxli. 2;—our help can come only from *heaven,* Ps. cxxi. 1, 2; and we cannot obtain deliverance unless we cry for it, Ezek. xxxvi. 37. This we learn also from the words of our text, which teach us,

II. OUR DUTY AS THE SUBJECTS OF A DIVINE REDEEMER. This we learn from David's example, "I waited," &c. Like him,

1. *We must make " the Lord" the object of our pursuit* : for the salvation which we need consists in the enjoyment of God. Being exposed to destruction, we need his *delivering mercy,* Ps. xvi. 4.—Being defiled, we need his *purifying influence,* Ps. li. 10.—Being deeply fallen, we need his *restoring grace* to raise us, Ps. cxlii. 6, 7.—As it is from the Lord alone that salvation cometh, so like David,

2. *We must wait for the Lord.* This must be done,—By *penitent application* to him, like the prodigal, Luke xv. 18, 19.—By *earnest application;* we must cry to him, Jer. xxix. 13.—By *confident dependence,*—on the foundation laid by God, Isa. xxviii. 16,—and on the promises made by him, Heb. x. 19, 22. Like David,

3. *We must wait patiently for the Lord.* Patient waiting implies,- Humble *consciousness* and *acknowledgment* of our *demerit,* Gen. xxxii. 10. —*Entire resignation* to God's method of operation on our minds; that he may dispense his saving benefits and comforts as he pleases, Ps. lxxviii. 40, 41.—*Unfainting perseverance* in seeking him, Luke xi. 9, and xviii. 1—7. According to these promises, the words of our text teach us,

III. OUR PRIVILEGES AS GOSPEL PENITENTS. These we learn from David's success, " He inclined unto me," &c. As gospel penitents expect,

1. *An interest in God's gracious regards.* He will incline unto you.— He will incline his *ear* to your cry, Prov. xv. 8; Ps. cxlv. 18, 19.—He will incline his *heart* to compassionate your misery, Ps. ciii. 8, 13 —He will incline his *hand* to save and help you, Matt. xiv. 30, 31; Isa. xli. 10.

2. *Expect the enjoyment of most desirable favors.* Even—complete *deliverance* from danger and pollution; " He will bring you," &c., Ps. xci. 14—16 :—firm *establishment* on the rock, Christ, Ps. xvi. 8; 1 Peter v. 10 :—and sacred *consolation;* he will put the new song into your mouth; that which David sings, Ps. ciii. 2, 3;—and Isaiah predicts, Isa. xii. 1. 2.

3. *Expect a capacity for extensive usefulness.* " Many shall see it," &c.—When divine grace is enjoyed, it may and should be *seen,* Acts xi. 23;

Isa. lx. 1.—When the grace of God is seen in its effects and fruits, it leads those who behold it to glorify God, Matt. v. 16.

In applying this subject, recollect,

1. *The suitableness of gospel salvation to our natural state.* We are fallen, polluted, weak, and miserable; and by this salvation, we are raised, purified, strengthened, and comforted, 1 Cor. i. 30; Col. ii. 9, 10.

2. *The necessity of waiting for God,* in order that we may obtain his saving benefits. This he expressly requires of us, Ps. xxxvii. 34.

3. *The certain success of gospel penitents:* from God's declaration, Lam. iii. 26:—from his kindness to all such, Luke xi. 10; and from his perfections, Rom. x. 12; Ps. c. 5. "The Lord is good," &c.

SUBMISSION TO GOD

James iv. 7.—Submit yourselves therefore to God. (Sk.)

JAMES was accustomed to deliver his instructions in laconic sentences, where little was said, but much meant; the words few, but the sense comprehensive and important: a very cursory perusal of this epistle will sufficiently confirm the truth of this observation. The text however may be considered as a practical illustration of it; "Submit yourselves therefore to God." In order to profit by this highly important admonition we will endeavor to,

I. EXPLAIN THE NATURE OF THE SUBMISSION HERE ENJOINED
II. URGE THE REASONS FOR REDUCING IT TO PRACTICE.

I. EXPLAIN THE NATURE OF THE SUBMISSION HERE ENJOINED.

1. *We should submit to God in his authoritative sway.* God is a great King, "and his kingdom ruleth over all:" as a sovereign, he hath revealed laws, sanctioned by the highest authority, founded in immutable justice, and conducive to human happiness; to these laws we should submit, by forsaking sin, believing in Christ, reverencing God, loving our neighbor, &c.

2. *We should submit to God in his gracious influences.* God is the God of Grace. His Spirit strives with man, illuminates his understanding, convinces him of sin, subdues his will, and sanctifies his affections. "Submit yourselves therefore to God." His Spirit may be quenched, the light that is in you may become darkness, "I have called, and ye refused," &c. Prov. i. 24. In submitting to God, prize the teachings of his Spirit, cherish his holy influences, covet earnestly the best gifts, and shun whatever will wound your consciences, or vex the Holy One of Israel.

3 *Submit yourselves to God in his providential dispensations.* Your circumstances are various: some are afflicted in body—some are oppressed with poverty—others sustain painful bereavements. Here you are too frequently accustomed to murmur, to look at the situations of others with envy, and to entertain unworthy thoughts of God. But submission becomes you: it is God who afflicts, and he doeth it in mercy; cease therefore to complain, and humbly acquiesce in all his dispensations. This submission should be *voluntary.* There is a willing, and a forced submission. God will humble every man, either by his grace or justice; but we should willingly submit our understandings to his instructions, &c. It should be *universal;* there is a submission due to parents by children to masters by

servants, to princes by subjects, to husbands by wives, but these submissions are partial and temporary; but the submission in the text is universal; it admits of no exceptions, and knows no limits. It should be *constant*, at all times, in all circumstances, and in all situations.

II. URGE THE REASONS FOR REDUCING IT TO PRACTICE.

1. *We urge it from a consideration of the greatness and goodness of the Being to whom you are called to submit.* It is God, whose greatness is unsearchable, and whose power is infinite; who is above all and through all, and in you all; whose goodness is equal to his power, and whose will is holy, just and good.

2. *We urge it on the ground of relationship and obligation.* God is your Creator, you are his creatures; God is your Father, you are his children; God is the Sovereign, you are his subjects: submission therefore becomes you. In addition to this, you owe your all to God; your life, and clothes, and food; your personal and relative comforts all come from Him: gratitude therefore should bind you to submit to God.

3. *We urge it for the sake of your personal happiness.* Happiness supposes the removal of guilt from the conscience: submit to God's method of saving sinners, and you will be justified by faith. It supposes the regeneration of the nature; submit to the influences of the Holy Ghost, and you will be "born again of the Spirit," &c. It supposes internal tranquility: submit to God, and you will experience "the eternal sunshine of the spotless mind."

4. *We urge it from a consideration of the punishment which inevitably follows the crime of non-submission to God.* There is not one truth within the whole compass of religion more incontestably proved than this, that God will punish his enemies; and a refusing to submit to God, is the surest proof of personal enmity to him. The original sin of Adam, "that brought death into the world and all our wo," was non-submission; and the crime of apostate spirits was of the same description; and those who refuse to submit to God, must be punished by him, Luke xxi. 27.

The text should *suggest an inquiry*, Do we submit to God? Alas! how little submission there is to God in the world! Some violate his laws—others reject his counsel—others murmur at his providence. What is our character?—The text should *produce conviction.* We have all been found among the number of those who have neglected to submit to God; this should teach us our *folly*, our *ingratitude*, and our *danger;* and it should also excite deep remorse, genuine humility, &c. The text should *direct our conduct.* What else need we *know*, than how to submit to God? What *else* need we *do*, than practice this submission? What else need we covet to *enjoy*, than a consciousness of having submitted to God?

SUBMISSION TO BEREAVING PROVIDENCES.

Job i. 21.—The Lord gave, and the Lord hath taken away, blessed be the name of the Lord. (Pr.)

THE affliction and the patience of Job are set before us as an example, and there is scarcely any case that can occur, but something in his complicated trials will be found to correspond with it. His afflictions were sent, not so much in consequence of any particular sin, as for the trial of his faith. God is represented as glorying in him, and satan answers by alleging that his religion was all founded in self-interest. The Lord therefore consents that trial should be made : the trial was made, and it turned to the honor of Job.

However painful any affliction may be, while we are exercised by it, yet when it is over we often perceive that all was wise and good; at least we see it so in others. In Job's trials in particular, God was glorified, satan confounded, and the sufferer comes forth as gold.

That which supported him under all, was the power of religion, the value of which is never more known than in the day of adversity. This is the armor of God, which enables us to stand in the evil day ; and having done all, to stand. That which enabled Job to take every thing well at the hand of God, was the love he bore to his holy name ; and that name he blessed and adored, under all his bereavements.

There are two things in the text particularly worthy of notice :—The spirit of submission exemplified in the conduct of Job, and the principles on which that submission was founded.

I. THE SPIRIT OF SUBMISSION, UNDER BEREAVING PROVIDENCES, EXEMPLIFIED IN THE CONDUCT OF JOB.

There are several particulars in this case which serve to show the greatness and severity of Job's affliction, and the aboundings of the grace of God towards him, which enabled him to endure it all with so much meekness and submission.

1. The *Degree of his afflictions.* The objects taken away were more than were left, and seemed to leave him nothing to comfort him ; his whole substance, his whole family, excepting one who only served to increase his distress. After this he is grievously afflicted in his own person : still he is submissive and resigned : chap. ii. 10.— — —We may have had our losses, in property, in children, and in valuable friends ; but we have not lost our all. We have also had personal affliction, but it has been mixed with mercy ; not like Job's unattended with any alleviating circumstance.

2. His trouble came upon him *suddenly and unexpectedly,* and completely reversed his former circumstances.— — —It was all in one day, and that a day of feasting too, when every thing appeared promising around him. Prosperity and adversity are like two opposite climates : men can live in almost any temperature, if but inured to it ; but sudden reverses are insupportable. Hence it is we feel most for those who have seen better days when they fall into poverty and want.— — —Yet we see that Job calmly submitted to all his trials and bereavements, and even blessed the name of the Lord. And shall not we copy his example? We have never experienced his trials, nor does God usually deal thus with any of his people ; his strokes are more gradual, and less severe than in the present instance. We often witness the dying pains and sorrows of our friends, till they and we are made willing to part ; thus the load is gradually diminished, so that we are able to bear it. But it was not so with Job, and therefore his submission is the more remarkable.

3. Though Job was eminently pious, it is doubtful whether *his children were so* in any degree, and this would render the bereavement far more severe.— — —It is a great alleviation to our affliction, when those who are removed by death have given us reason to hope that they are now with God, and that they sleep in Jesus. But this consolation appears to have been denied to Job, who in the day of his calamity had manifested a godly jeal-

ousy over his children, which indicated his apprehension that all was not right, chap. i. 5: and how much this must have added to his affliction cannot be described. Yet we hear him say, The Lord gave, and the Lord hath taken away: blessed be the name of the Lord.

4. His submission also appears in a *holy moderation* which attended his griefs.— — —A man of no religion would have been distracted, or have sunk in sullen despair. A heathen would have cursed his gods, and perhaps have committed suicide, being filled with rage and disappointment.— — — But Job, fully sensible of his affliction, and feeling it in every point, still in patience possesses his soul. He rises from the earth, rends his mantle, shaves his head, and prostrates himself before the Lord.

5. Amidst all his sorrow and distress, he preserves a holy resolution *to think well of God*, and even blesses his holy name.— — —Losses and trials are sent to prove us, and we have no more religion than we actually possess and manifest in the day of affliction. If half that religion so generally professed were submitted to this test, it would be found lamentably deficient; and this probably is the reason why some towering professors feel so little for their brethren in adversity.

II. The principles on which job's submission was evidently founded.

There is something in the meek and humble resignation of a good man in the day of trouble, very different from that of other persons. Some sort of patience and submission is found amongst men in general, but not like that which real piety produces. There is the patience of despair, and a submission to fate; but Job's was of a very different description.

1. He considers *all that befel him as God's doing*, and this calms and quiets his spirit.— — —He overlooks instruments and second causes, which would have given to his losses the character of injuries, and have filled him with indignation; and therefore he does not say the Chaldeans and Sabeans had done him this injustice, but "the Lord gave, and the Lord hath taken away." Seeing and confessing his hand, answered every objection: and however trying to the dispensation, it is the Lord, let him do what seemeth him good.— — —This is true submission, to have no will of our own, but to have it lost and swallowed up in the will of God, even in those things that are most contrary to our natural inclination. "I opened not my mouth," said David, "because thou didst it."

2. He recollects that *all he had was from the hand of God*; that it was merely a gift, or rather lent for a time, to be employed for his glory.— — — "The Lord gave," says the patient sufferer. These cattle, these children were not mine, though I called them so: in taking them away the Lord has only resumed his own, and left me as I was before, naked as from the dust I came.

3. He feels thankful that they were *once given him to enjoy*, though now they are taken from him.— — —Supposing we are not allowed to enjoy our mercies for ever, or without interruption; were they not mercies while we did enjoy them? We may see reason to bless God that ever we had property, or children, or friends to enjoy, and that we possessed any of them so long as we did; though now, by the will of providence, we are deprived of them all.

4. Even when bereaved of every earthly comfort, he considers God as *worthy of his gratitude and adoration*.— — —Job could bless the hand that took away, as well as the hand that gave; and this must have been a special act of faith. We may not be able at present to see the mercy con-

tained in any of our bereavements, yet in the end we may see it, as was the case with Jacob, when Joseph was sold into Egypt. But Job already sees enough to assure him, that all his afflictions should be over.ruled for good, and should promote his spiritual and eternal welfare.

REFLECTIONS.

1. How wise then and how needful, to choose the better part which shall never be taken from us: to set our affections on things above, where all is durable and lasting; and not on things on the earth, which are all fading from our sight, and quickly passing away.

2. Afflictions, if not sanctified, will only tend to aggravate our guilt. They are the voice of God, calling us from earth and sense; the discipline which our heavenly Father employs, to make us partakers of his holiness; and if despised or disregarded, will leave us worse than we were before.

3. The example of Job teaches us that a spirit of despondency and discontent in a time of trial, is utterly inconsistent with true religion; yet how many there are that faint in the day of adversity, and who, instead of deriving consolation and support from the promises of the gospel, are utterly inconsolable, and sink into gloom and despondency.

4. While we admire the patience and submission of Job, we cannot but abhor the unfeeling conduct of his friends, who with only a small proportion of his piety could pass unwarrantable censures upon his character, and withhold from him those succors which humanity itself demanded. Job vi. 14.

PAUL'S PRAYER FOR HIS COUNTRYMEN.

Rom. x. 1.—Brethren, my heart's desire and prayer to God for Israel is, that they might be saved. (Pr.)

Paul's conversion subjected him to the suspicion that he was an enemy to his country, a disaffected man, and of a most uncharitable judgment concerning his brethren, the Jews. This is no uncommon thing, though it is somewhat strange that a man cannot embrace the gospel, and begin to love Christ supremely, but he must immediately be suspected of the want of love towards mankind. Paul however repels the charge with the most solemn attestation, appealing to the Searcher of hearts for the sincerity of his motives, and for the ardent love he bore to his countrymen. Rom. ix. 1—3. In return for all their unkindness towards him, he longs and prays for their salvation; and in this he imitates the example of his blessed Lord, who desired the forgiveness of his murderers. It is christianity alone that can inspire such sentiments, and give such an example to the world.

I. Enquire what it was that made the apostle so desirous of the salvation of his countrymen.

1. He considered *the danger they were in of perishing*, and being lost for ever — — —Had there been no danger, and religion were only a matter of opinion, there would have been no need for such anxious solicitude. But a good man beholds multitudes all around him going on in darkness, he foresees the consequences that must follow, and is anxious if possible to avert them.— — —Paul also knew the terrors of the Lord, he considered the import of the threatenings, was assured of their certainty, and that God was in real earnest, however poor thoughtless sinners might be disposed to trifle.

When Aaron saw men dying of the plague in the Israelitish camp, he ran in with a censer before the Lord, and stood between the living and the dead. Paul in like manner interposed his labors and his prayers to save his impenitent countrymen from eternal ruin, and every real christian will do the same.

2. *The love of Christ* constrained him to seek the salvation of souls, and to labor for their welfare.— — —He considered what Christ had done in giving himself for us ; what humiliation, what sufferings, and what an ignominious death he had endured for our sakes ; and the heart of this holy apostle was touched with the example, and stimulated to every exertion for the salvation of souls. 2 Cor. v. 14, 15.

3. The *magnitude of salvation itself*, is sufficient to justify all the anxiety which the apostle manifested.— — —Who can tell how great this salvation is, or what the soul is capable of suffering or enjoying in the eternal world ? A period may arrive when the suffering of one soul shall be greater than that of the whole creation, from the beginning to the end of time ; and who then can conceive of the unutterable importance of an interest in the salvation of the gospel ?— — —Something of it may be seen in the price paid for our redemption, and in the bitter agonies of Christ in the garden and on the cross ; but there is a depth in his sorrows which we cannot fathom, a dignity and a glory in his person which transcends our highest conceptions.

4. The apostle was influenced by a concern for *the glory of God*, which is inseparably connected with the salvation of sinners.— — —There is joy in heaven over a sinner that repenteth, and joy on earth ; and the father of the prodigal rejoices that his lost son is found. When a sinner is brought to submit to God's government, to bear his image and likeness, and is received into the bosom of his family, the riches of his grace are illustrated, and his glory revealed. The conversion and salvation of sinners are the reward of Christ's sufferings, the travail of his soul, which he was to see, to his joy and satisfaction. Paul therefore, and every other true believer, would long for the salvation of souls, that Christ might be glorified.

5. There were *some peculiar reasons* in the present case, that so powerfully awakened the apostle's sympathy, and which it will be proper briefly to notice—

1. It is natural for a christian to feel especially for the souls of *his own countrymen*, who have a more immediate claim upon his regard ; and this was the case with Paul. Persons who inhabit the same part of the world, or live in the same neighborhood, contract that sort of partiality which the love of country creates ; and it is not the office of religion to destroy, but to improve and elevate those sympathies, by imparting to them its own benevolent qualities. Hence our Lord felt for Jerusalem more than for any other city ; and Paul for " Israel," because they were his own people. Luke xix. 41, 42.

2. Among his countrymen he had *numerous acquaintances*, whom he saw to be in danger of perishing through unbelief, and it was natural he should feel much on their account. When we look around and see many of those with whom we spent our early days, and formed our earliest intimacies, still strangers to the gospel ; and walking according to the course of this world, we cannot but lament their unhappy condition, and long to see them brought home to God.

3. We are led to feel more still for our *near relations and friends*, if any of them are left in the gall of bitterness, and in the bonds of iniquity. This can never fail to be the case, where religion has its proper influence on the heart. Our brethren, our parents, our children, must necessarily lie near

our hearts, and the thoughts of an eternal separation is insupportable. Jeremiah was pained at his very heart, and his bowels were troubled within him, to think of the destruction of Jerusalem; but how much more, to think of the destruction of soul and body in hell. Moses could not endure to leave Hobab his father-in-law behind him in the wilderness; nor could David contemplate the destruction of his rebellious son, without being overwhelmed with grief. Neither could Paul view the state of many of "his kinsmen according to the flesh, without having great heaviness and continual sorrow of heart." Rom. ix. 1—3.

II. Briefly notice the means which the apostle employed for the conversion and salvation of his countrymen.

If we use no means, it is a proof, that our desire for the salvation of others is not sincere.

1. Paul labored incessantly *in word and doctrine*, to bring them to the knowledge of the truth; and he did this amidst reproaches, necessities, and persecutions; encountering every difficulty and discouragement, that he might win them to Christ. Acts xx. 19—21. And though we may not be called to public services, we are required to bear witness to the truth, and meekly to instruct those who oppose themselves, in the hope that repentance may be given to them. 2 Tim. ii. 25. An admonition seasonably and prudently administered, has in many instances been attended with good effect.

2. A holy and *exemplary life*, adorning the doctrine of God our Saviour in all things, is a blessed means of fixing the attention of others upon the reality and importance of religion; and Paul did not fail to exemplify the doctrine which he preached. 2 Cor. i. 12; 1 Thess. ii. 10. If we desire, therefore, the salvation of those around us, let them see our good works, and glorify our father who is in heaven. 1 Pet. iii. 1, 2.

3. Fervent and *importunate prayer*. Though we cannot command success, God can give it; and if we were more fervent in prayer, our labors would be more successful. Primitive christians abounded in this holy exercise, and Paul himself affords an illustrious example: "Brethren, my heart's desire and prayer for Israel is, that they might be saved."

LOVE TO THE BRETHREN.

John xv. 12.—This is my commandment, That ye love one another, as I have loved you. (H. H.)

The law and the gospel are in perfect unison with each other: the law, *as a covenant*, sends us to the gospel, that we may obtain mercy with God; and the gospel sends us back again to the law, *as a rule of life*, that, by obeying its commands, we may honor and glorify our God. The loving our neighbor as ourselves was enjoined by the law, and indeed was a summary of all the duties of the second table.* Our blessed Lord, enjoining the same duty from new considerations, calls it "a new commandment," and emphatically *his* commandment; that so we may be led to examine it with stricter attention, and to regard it with deeper reverence: he says, in effect, Labor constantly to fulfil that old commandment of the law; and,

* Compare Lev. xix. 18, with Rom xiii. 8—10, & Gal. v. 14.

that you may never want either a directory to guide, or a motive to animate, you in your exertions, take my love to you as the *reason* and *pattern* of your love to each other.

To elucidate his words, we shall shew,

I. How CHRIST HAS LOVED US—

We must, of course, content ourselves with a few hints only of a subject, which has a height and depth, and length and breadth that can never be comprehended, never explored. Consider then the love of Christ to us:

1. How free!

Who ever did any thing to it? It exerted itself towards us long before we had any existence in the world. Who can do any thing *now* to merit it? We deserve to forfeit it every day and hour; but to earn an interest in it is beyond the power of man. We have nothing of our own but sin; and that would be a poor price to pay for the love of Christ. Indeed, if we deny the freeness of his grace, we rob him of the brightest jewel in his crown.

2. How tender!

There is not one of his people, however weak and afflicted, whom he does not watch over with more than parental tenderness, "carrying the lambs in his bosom, and gently leading them that are with young." Yes; "we have not an High-priest who cannot be touched with the feeling of our infirmities:" "in all our afflictions He is afflicted:" if we are stricken by the hand of persecution, He feels the blow, Acts ix. 4: "he that toucheth us, toucheth the apple of His eye." In every possible state he sympathizes with us, as a head with the members, and never fails to succour us with "grace sufficient for us."

3. How abundant!

If We regarded only the temporal blessings we receive at his hands, we must confess his love to us to be very abundant. But who can contemplate his unwearied intercessions at the right hand of his Father, or the incessant communications of his Spirit to their souls, and not stand amazed at the exceeding riches of his grace and love? And besides all this, he is "preparing mansions for us in his Father's house," and training us up daily, that we may be counted worthy to inhabit them for ever and ever. Well is his love represented as "passing knowledge!" Eph. iii. 10.

4. How costly!

Free as his love was to us, it was not exercised by him but at an expense that exceeds all calculation. Before it could operate for our advantage, he must leave his heavenly glory, assume our fallen nature, endure the scoffs and insults of his own creatures, and "pour out his soul unto death" as a sacrifice for sin. And would he pay this amazing price, in order to redeem our souls from death and hell? Yes, he undertook and executed the mighty work; and never drew back till he could say, ' It is finished."

From contemplating this stupendous mystery, let us proceed to inquire,

II. IN WHAT RESPECTS HIS LOVE TO US IS A PATTERN FOR OUR LOVE TO EACH OTHER—

The love which the saints should bear to each other is of a sublime nature, very different from that which they owe to the world around them.*
To resemble that of Christ to us, it should be,

1. Disinterested—

Our love to the saints should not be confined to those of the same church

---

* The two are carefully distinguished from each other. Gal. vi. 10; 1 Pet. ii. 17.

or party, nor should it have respect to any pleasure or advantage that we expect to derive from them; for this is only a refined species of self-love, Matt. v. 46, 47: it should respect them only as children of our heavenly Father, as members of Christ our living Head, and as joint-heirs of the same eternal glory. It should be proportioned to their piety, rather than to any other endowments; and be occupied in advancing their happiness, not only as much as our own, but oftentimes in preference to our own. It was thus that the love of Christ operated towards us; and it is proposed for our imitation more especially in this point of view; "Mind not every one his own things, but every one also the things of others. Let this be in you which was also in Christ Jesus." Phil. ii. 4, 5.

2. Sympathizing—

We are all passing through a vale of tears, "born to trouble as the sparks fly upward." Hence we need each other's care and assistance through the whole of our lives. The kindness of friendship is a remedy which God has put within our reach, to enhance our joys and to alleviate our sorrows: we should therefore enter into the concerns of others, and feel them as our own; "weeping with them that weep, and rejoicing with them that rejoice." By this, we are told, we shall more especially comply with the injunction in the text; "Bear ye one another's burthens," says the Apostle, "and so fulfil the law of Christ." Gal. vi. 2.

3. Beneficent—

Love must not interest merely the feelings of the mind: it must exert itself in acts correspondent to the occasions on which it is exercised. Is our neighbor distressed? we must relieve him: Is he ignorant? we must instruct him: Is he weak? we must strengthen him: Is he fallen? we must raise him up: Has he shewn some infirmities? we must bear with him. Has he offended us? we must forgive him. Are there any opportunities whatever of doing him good? we must gladly and speedily embrace them. It is in this way also that the Apostle urges us to imitate our Lord and Saviour: "Put on, as the elect of God, holy and beloved, bowels of mercies, humbleness of mind, meekness, long-suffering; forbearing one another, and forgiving one another, *even as Christ forgave you*, so also do ye." Col. iii. 12, 13.

4. Self-denying—

That love which will exert itself only in things that are easy and pleasing to oneself, is not worthy the name of love. A truly christian affection will lead one to "condescend to men of low estate;" to visit the chambers of the sick; to enter into the dungeon of the prisoner; to cut off some of one's superfluities in order to supply the necessities of others; to do good in return for evil; to expose oneself to the derision of a thoughtless world, in order to be instrumental in turning some of them from the evil of their ways; and "to lay down, if need be, even our own lives for the brethren." This was the way in which St. Paul manifested his love, 1 John iii. 16; and in which we also after the example of our Lord, are called to manifest ours. Phil. ii. 17, 18.

This being the way in which our love may resemble his, we shall shew you,

III. THE OBLIGATION WE ARE UNDER TO FOLLOW THAT PATTERN—

Our blessed Lord has enjoined a conformity to him in these respects,

1. As an act of obedience to him—

He does not *recommend* such love as decorous and beneficial, but *commands* it as a duty which he will on no account dispense with. He stamps his own authority upon it; intimating thereby that he will make it a subject of particular inquiry in the day of judgment. Indeed the decision at the last day is represented as turning principally upon this point; they who for his sake have abounded in offices of love being made *exclusively* the objects of his favor, while they who have neglected them are marked as objects of his indignation and abhorrence. If therefore we have any regard to his authority, or any dread of his everlasting displeasure, we must see the importance of following the example of his love.

2. As an evidence of our love to him—

Having in another place enforced this duty in terms similar to the text, he adds, that the exercise of brotherly love is the distinctive badge of our profession, the habit whereby all his followers must be known. 1 John xiii. 34, 35. To the same effect his loving and beloved disciple also speaks, declaring that our profession of love to God is mere hypocrisy without this, 1 John iv. 20; and that without this we can have no assurance, no evidence, that we have passed from death unto life. 1 John iii. 14, 17, 19. Shall we then at once write "*Hypocrite*" upon our foreheads? Shall we be contented to be ranked with "murderers, who certainly have not eternal life abiding in them?" 1 John iii. 15. If not, we must see the necessity of imitating Christ, who "has left us an example that we should follow his steps."

INFER,

1. How little true religion is there in the world!

So far is love to the saints from being the common disposition of mankind, that almost all are rather filled with hatred against them: and where candor prevails over the enmity of the human heart so as to subdue its workings, there yet is a total want of that disinterested, sympathizing, beneficent, and self-denying love, which characterizes a true christian.————

2. What reason have even the saints themselves to be ashamed before God!

Let the most zealous and active christian compare his love with that of Christ: how poor and defective will his best efforts appear! Alas! alas! how often are things found among professing christians that are not only defective, but directly contrary to love! Beloved brethren, let us study more carefully St. Paul's description of love, 1 Cor. xiii: and above all, let us contemplate more the love of Christ to us; so shall we feel its constraining influence, and be stimulated to the exercise of this delightful duty

---

SUPERIOR IMPORTANCE OF RELIGIOUS ENGAGEMENTS. (Pr.)

Neh. vi. 3.—I am doing a great work, so that I cannot come down.

Nehemiah was truly engaged in a great work, and was chiefly employed in effecting the reformation of Israel, after their return from Babylon. Such also was his magnanimity, that he could not be content to live in a court, while Jerusalem lay waste. He comes to the holy city with the returning captives, and begins to rebuild its walls with all his might. The greatness of the work however did not consist merely in rebuilding the walls, but in the important ends to be answered by it; it was the city of the living God, and the seat of public worship. Yet no sooner had he commenced the un-

369

dertaking, than he meets with opposition. Some of the neighboring heathen tried to put him in fear; they also allured him, in the hope of diverting him from his purpose; but to all these he answered as in the text.

The conduct of Nehemiah on this occasion is worthy of example, and in this view we may apply it to ourselves.

I. CONSIDER THE CHRISTIAN AS ENGAGED IN A GREAT AND ARDUOUS WORK.

Though it is not in every respect like that of Nehemiah, it bears some relation to it. There are many great undertakings in the world, and many works of art which men call great; but they dwindle into insignificance, when compared with the work in which Christians are engaged. The cause of God in the world is of unspeakable importance, and the soul of man is of more consequence than the whole material creation.

More particularly—

1. Every christian is represented *as engaged in a race*, as running for an immortal prize, and this is an arduous undertaking.— — —It is no great thing indeed to enter upon the race; many do that who never win the prize. It is easy to set out in the ways of God, and to go on till we meet with some difficulty or some temptation: but it is a great matter " so to run as to obtain," and to " endure to the end." This requires no ordinary degree of zeal and fidelity. 1 Cor. ix. 24—27.

2. Christians are engaged in *an arduous contest with all the powers of darkness*, and wrestle not merely with flesh and blood.— — —It requires but little courage to begin the contest; many do that who are overcome at last Many put on the harness who do not put it off with honor, and endure for a time only, till overcome by some great temptation. But to fight the good fight of faith, and to lay hold on eternal life, is indeed an arduous enterprize. Here no success can be expected, unless we are made strong in the Lord, and in the power of his might. Oh to be faithful unto death, to finish our course with joy, and to be more than conquerors through him that loved us! Eph. vi. 10—13.

3. They are *engaged in the work of saving others*, as well as in seeking their own salvation.— — —Real christians do not wish to go to heaven alone; seeking the good of others is of the essence of true religion. No man is converted for his own sake, but that he may bring others to the knowledge of the truth; and when the Lord blesses his people, it is that they may become a blessing. Luke viii. 39. And what are all the works of men, compared with the salvation of an immortal soul, and seeking the everlasting welfare of those about us?

4. The proper employment of a christian is *the spread of the gospel*, and carrying on the cause of God in the world.— — —This is the work in which the prophets and apostles were engaged, in which Christ himself was engaged, and for the accomplishment of which the whole system of providence is directed. The work committed to Moses and Aaron was but a faint emblem of this, and the work in which Nehemiah and Ezra were engaged was all preparatory to it. The labors of the apostles and early christians were all employed in laying the foundation; it is for us to raise the superstructure, and to bring forth the topstone with shoutings, Grace, grace unto it.

II. THE WORK IN WHICH WE ARE ENGAGED IS SURE TO MEET WITH OPPOSITION, and it becomes us not to be diverted from it, but to say with Nehemiah, " I am doing a great work, and cannot come down."

God's work must be first and chiefly regarded, it must be our supreme end, and all others subordinated to it. Many are convinced that the concerns of the soul are of the greatest importance; they know that they must be converted, must be born again, must be brought to repentance, or perish everlastingly; and they fully intend to seek the Lord, but at present it is not convenient, for something hinders. Thus it is with many a thoughtless youth, who sees and feels his danger; and with many a busy tradesman, who would attend to the concerns of his soul, but urgent worldly calls prevent. Thus alas it is too frequently with the real christian, when tempted to the neglect of duty. But how much better is the answer of Nehemiah to all such impediments: I am doing a great work, and cannot come down.

1. In particular, *christians are engaged in seeking the Lord*, in waiting upon him in secret; and when they would draw near at the appointed season, something in the family, or in a way of business intervenes, and the work of God is suspended. But all these things should be regarded as an effort of the enemy to draw us aside from the path of duty, and cause the work of God to cease. Let us rather say with Abraham, " Tarry ye here, while I go up yonder to worship;" or answer like Nehemiah in the text.

3. Christians are employed *in relieving the distressed*, and in contributing to the support of the cause of God: but when they think of doing these things, some temptation is apt to present itself in order to prevent. We can do but little good without some self-denial, and if not prepared for this, the work of God must cease.

3. While engaged in doing good, *we are exposed to injuries from men*, as Ezra and Nehemiah were. There will always be some Tobiah or Sanballet, who will seek to hinder the work of God, but it behoves us to regard them not. When Whitfield was persecuted and abused for preaching in a seaport town, previous to his departure for Georgia, he was advised by his friends to stop and prosecute the offenders; but he replied that he had no time for such an undertaking, he must be about his Master's business.

4. The *enjoyments of life* too often call off our attention, or unfit us for religious duties. Of these we must beware; and if truly engaged for God, we shall have no time to lose in mere worldly amusements, but shall find enough in religion to engage all our time and all our thoughts. The work of God is great and large, and demands all our energies, and all our strength.

IMPROVEMENT.

1. Let christians be careful to guard against a light and trifling spirit, as totally incompatible with the solemn duties of christianity, and the right improvement of time.

2. Let the thoughtless sinner well consider the consequence of continuing to neglect the great concerns of his soul. How ready will such be another day to curse the vanities which led them to ruin and perdition. Seek the Lord while he may be found, and call upon him while he is near.

MOTIVES TO CHRISTIAN DILIGENCE.

Eccles. ix. 10.—Whatsoever thy hand findeth to do, do it with thy might; for there is no work, nor device, nor knowledge, nor wisdom, in the grave whither thou goest. (Pr.)

This counsel comes with the greater force, from a man who himself had not been idle in his day, and much of whose zeal had been expended in building a house for God. It is true, that on reviewing many of his own labors, he saw much vanity attached to them; yet he did not mean by this to encourage despondency or inactivity, or he would not have used the urgent and impressive language of the text.

I. Illustrate and explain the exhortation.

Many things are said in scripture, especially in the New Testament, which may seem to depreciate the works of men, yet true religion is far from being unfriendly to good works.

Properly to understand this language, three or four things require to be noticed—

1. Nothing must be done with a view of *superceding the work of Christ.* If we think to gain the favor of God, or the forgiveness of our sins, by any works or doings of our own, we deceive ourselves, and stumble at the stumbling-stone. Rom. ix. 32. x. 3.

2. Whatever is done *must be done in faith*, in order to its being acceptable to God. When it was asked, what shall we do that we may work the works of God; the answer was, This is the work of God, that ye believe on him whom he hath sent. John vi. 28, 29. Without faith it is impossible to please God. Heb. xi. 6.

3. Whatever is done *must accord with the revealed will of God*, or we cannot be his servants. Worldly men would take up the words of the text, and go into every kind of evil; power and not justice, being the only principle that gives law to their conduct. But we are not at liberty to do as we please, so long as there is one Lawgiver, who is able to save and to destroy.

4. In selecting the objects of our zeal and labor, we must have *a special regard to what providence places within our reach*, or "whatsoever our hands find to do." Many things may be within the reach of another, that come not within our sphere; and it is one of the vanities of human life to be always thinking of what we would do, if in other circumstances, while the good we might do is neglected or overlooked. Much depends on a proper selection of labor, according to the talents or opportunities we may enjoy. One may have wealth, and with that he may do much good. Another is poor, but he can pray, and give counsel. Another has wisdom or influence, and the liberal will devise liberal things. One can preach, and another can open a door tor the gospel, in his town and neighborhood. One may contrive, and another execute. Moses and Aaron did well together, neither of them would have done so well apart. Paul was a preacher, and left others to baptize, while he carried the gospel round about unto Illyricum. Let us consider also how much is left undone in the world, in the church, in the family, in the neighborhood where we dwell, and what labors our hands might find to do.

5. Having found what to do, *we are required to do it with all our might.* This includes at least two things.— — —1. That we do it *without delay.* Many things which our hands find to do at one time, may not be practicable at another; and therefore will not be done at all, if not done immediately. Opportunities are a call from God; they pass by, and return no more.— —

—2. That we do it in *good earnest.* If we look into the history of the church, we shall find that all the great things which have been done, were done by men who were in real earnest, and who labored with all their might. When God would redeem Israel, it was by one who was prepared to sacrifice a kingdom and a crown in his service, and who esteemed the reproach of Christ greater riches than the treasures of Egypt. And when he would bring his people into Canaan, it was by a man " who followed the Lord fully," and who nobly said, " We are well able to go up and possess the land. Also when Jerusalem was to be rebuilt, it was by a man who put not off his clothes, and by a people who had a mind to work. And by whom was the gospel at first diffused throughout the earth ? By men who counted not their lives dear unto them, that they might testify the gospel of the grace of God. By whom was the reformation undertaken in the sixteenth century ? By such men as Luther, whose zeal and whose labors were indefatigable. By whom has the gospel been carried into foreign parts, and bibles distributed in all languages ? By missionaries and by agents of a kindred spirit.

The motives by which the exhortation is enforced.

1. We are *hastening to the grave.* Every step we take, every hour we pass, we are going thither. Other things may be uncertain, as, whether we are going to heaven or hell; but this is certain nor do we know how soor we may reach the end of our journey.

2. When we come thither, *all our activity for God or man is at an end:* "for there is no work, nor device, nor knowledge, nor wisdom, in the grave whither thou goest." There is no more to be done for the souls of men, nor for their temporal interest, nor for the cause of Christ in the world.

What a loud call then is this to *sinners.* Life is the only time to escape the wrath to come; this time is now in your hand, if you have but a heart to improve it. A door is now open, but by and by it will be shut for ever The throne of grace is now accessible, but ere long it will be converted into a judgment seat. Christ is the way of life and salvation, but the way will be of no use when we have arrived at the end of our course, and the scene of life is closed for ever.

It is also a loud call to *chris'ians,* to redeem the time, and live wholly to the Lord. There is much to do, and the time is short; let us therefore labor with renewed diligence, and be as those who wait for their Lord

---

THE CHRISTIAN WARFARE.

Ephesians vi. 11—13.—Put on the whole armor of God, that ye may be able to stano against the wiles of the devil: for we wrestle not against flesh and blood, but against principalities, against powers, against the rulers of the darkness of this world, against spiritual wickedness in high places. Wherefore take unto you the whole armor of God, that ye may be able to withstand in the evil day, and having done all, to stand. (Pr.)

In the time of danger, when a powerful and malignant enemy is seeking our destruction, it would be natural to arm ourselves against him, that we may withstand the meditated attack. As christians we are engaged in a more important conflict than any pertaining to this world. " Wrestle not with flesh and blood," not with mortal men like ourselves, but with evil spirits and evil things. Hence we are called to be on our guard, to put on

373

the armor which is provided for us, and to take good heed to the direction given us.

I. CONSIDER THE DANGER TO WHICH WE ARE EXPOSED: ver. 12.

As it is in other cases, so it is in this; our greatest danger lies in not feeling our danger, and so not being prepared to meet it.

1, View *the enemy* we have to contend with. He is one who bears an *inveterate hatred* against us, and seeks nothing less than our destruction or eternal overthrow.— — —He hates us as God's creatures, but especially as those who have been rescued from his power, and taken up arms against him: nothing now will satisfy him but our eternal ruin.— — —It is therefore a struggle of life for life: if we do not overcome him he will overcome us. It is in vain to think of being neuter, or making peace with him.

2. He is *mightier* than we are; and unless we have help from above, we are no match for him.— — —We know but little of the power of wicked spirits, abstractly considered; but viewed as the god of this world, satan has all its temptations in alliance with him.— — —We know what power there is in these: with these he has cast down many mighty, yea many strong men have been slain by him.— — —With these he overcame our first parents, and with these also he attacked the second Adam, though in vain.

3. He is an *artful enemy.*— — —We are told of the "wiles of the devil," hiding his designs, and falling upon us when we least expect it. We are in his net before we are aware, and when providence seems to smile upon us. Deut. viii. 12.— — —He studies our propensities, and suits his temptations to them. Ephes. iv. 14.

4. He is *invisible.*— — —If he were "flesh and blood," like ourselves, we might beware: but his influence is like the nightly pestilence, which walks in darkness.— — —When least suspected, danger is nigh.

5. He is *near us*, as it were within our gates. The safety of a nation menaced by an enemy, often depends on his being kept at a distance, by walls or seas, of fortresses of defence. But here it is supposed that the enemy has entered into our borders, and that we have no other resource left but to struggle as it were for life.— — —It is not a contest with a distant enemy, but a kind of closing conflict: " we wrestle."

6. What is still worse, he has *a strong party within us.*— — —He was victorious with our first parents, when this was not the case, and when he had no party within: much greater therefore is the danger now.— — —If we do not obtain the victory, we shall ourselves be overcome, and perish in the conflict.

7. On *the issue* of this warfare depend all our hopes.— — —If we "stand" not in this, our loss when defeated can never be retrieved.

II. THE ARMOR PROVIDED FOR US: ver. 13.

Three things may here be observed—

1. In general, this armor is *the grace of the gospel*, believed and trusted in: this is opposed to human might or strength: ver. 10.— — —In common warfare it is usual for the commanders to persuade their enemies to think highly of their strength: but in this it is quite the reverse. We must go as Israel was always taught to do, as having no might of our own, but deriving all our strength from the Lord. 2 Tim. ii. 2.

2. It is described as *a whole or perfect armor*, sufficient to defend us in every part.— — —" Truth" is the girdle to strengthen us: " righteousness" a breastplate: the "gospel" of peace as shoes, by which we shall be able to trample upon the lion and the adder, the young lion and the dragon; " faith" is a shield; "salvation," or the hope of eternal life a helmet.—

374

— —All this armor is to be drawn from the truths of the everlasting gospel.

3. The *use to be made of it is*, that we may be able to "withstand," and to face the enemy. There is no armor for the back : he that fleeth is wholly defenceless, and must inevitably fall.

III. THE NECESSITY OF "PUTTING ON" THIS ARMOR, OR "TAKING" IT TO OURSELVES : ver. 11.

Armor is of no avail, unless it be used. The application of the gospel is that which proves our security.— — —Some persons make no use of it; and others a bad use : but it must be our concern to make a good use of it. — — —Use it in prayer, in other duties, in afflictions, in temptations : its truths, its promises and directions, will avail us in the whole of our warfare.

IV. THE INDUCEMENT TO DO SO ; "THAT WE MAY WITHSTAND IN THE EVIL DAY, AND HAVING DONE ALL, TO STAND."

It is here supposed that there are times of *special danger*, called "the evil day."— — —Times in which we are attacked with peculiar force ; such as seasons of persecution and temptation. It was an evil day to Joseph, when solicited by his faithless mistress ; but he successfully withstood.— — —It was an evil day to Nehemiah, when Sanballat and others came to hinder the work of the Lord ; to our Saviour, when the prince of this world came against him ; and to the martyrs when they had to resist even unto blood, striving against sin — —But they withstood in the evil day ; and having done all, they were enabled to keep their ground.

Some of God's servants, through neglecting their armor, have been *foiled* in the day of battle : of this there are many affecting examples.

The phrase, "having done all to stand," is very impressive : this is to keep the field at last. It is this which gives decision to a battle : we may be overcome, but if we overcome at last, it will be well.— — —We may obtain a victory now and then, and yet be finally conquered ; and "having done all," to fall at last.— — —Oh of what importance is it to be finally victorious !

These weapons are not only necessary in the spiritual warfare, but also in temporal dangers ; and though we may never be exposed to scenes of military conflict, we must all in some form or other have to encounter the king of terrors ; and for this, nothing can prepare us but "taking to ourselves the whole armor of God."

CHRISTIAN GENEROSITY.

Galatians vi. 2.—Bear ye one another's burdens ; and so fulfil the law of Christ. (Sk.)

"THE heart is deceitful above all things," as well as "desperately wicked," and is therefore to be watched over with the most scrupulous jealousy ; otherwise there is danger, lest under the semblance of piety and religious zeal, we should be led to indulge rancorous and unholy passions. Thus the apostle seems to have thought, or rather to have felt : whence the *caution*, chap. v. 13—16 : whence also the *exposure* of the fruits both of the flesh and the Spirit, ver. 19—23 ; and the *exhortation*, from chap. v. 25, to the text ; in which we have an important duty, enforced by a powerful motive.

I. THE DUTY ENJOINED ;—"Bear ye one another's burdens." The word "burden" denotes something which, by uneasy pressure, exhausts the strength and spirits of the person who is oppressed by it; and it may apply,

1. To *a weight of labor or bodily toil.* This is the effect of the original transgression, Gen. iii. 19. Thus were the Israelites *burdened,* Exod. i. 11. The pressure of this kind of burdens we may bear for " one another" by manual assistance, which even the poorest may give, by procuring the requisite help, or pecuniary aid, which would render the *excess of* labor unnecessary.

2. To *a weight of personal affliction;* in which " the corruptible body presseth down the soul," and, as in Job's case, the patient is a burden to himself, Job vii. 20. The pressure of this may be relieved by medical aid, (which a little experience and attention would enable many, who have not been bred to the profession, to afford,)—by kind attendance,—the soothing, sympathizing language of friendship,—or the considerations which religion affords, Heb. x. iii. 2; James i. 27.

3. To *a weight of domestic afflictions and cares.* This was a part of Job's overwhelming case, chap. i. 13—19. Here our text particularly applies to members of families, who should " bear one another's burdens," by manifesting a fellow feeling, in promptly and cheerfully lending a helping hand to lighten the common load of pain and trouble; and in suggesting those encouragements which affection, reason or religion may furnish. Not so Job's wife, who by endeavoring to deprive him of his only remaining support, contributed to make his " stroke heavier than his groaning," chap. ii. 9, and xxiii. 2.

4. To *a weight of providential losses, poverty, embarrassment, oppression, &c.* In reference to this, the Lord directs, Isa. lviii. 6, to " undo the heavy burdens," &c. This may be effected by public subscription, Acts xxiv. 17; 1 Cor. xiv. 1—3; by private contributions, James ii. 15, 16;— by furnishing materials for industry to work upon;—by judicious advice, suitable encouragement, remonstrance with oppressors, &c. Isa. lviii. 6, 7; Job xxix. 11—13; 1 John iii. 16, 17.

5. To *a weight of guilt and corruption.* So the Psalmist, Psa. xxxviii. 4, "For mine iniquities are gone over my head; as a heavy burden they are too strong for me." In this case christian sympathy is particularly demanded. "A wounded spirit who can bear?" 'Tis true every convinced sinner must bear this load for himself; yet it is often in the power of others materially to assist such. You find one of this character on the brink of despair: long has he been thus; and he fears he shall never obtain mercy:— *a relation of your own past experience* may serve to show him that his case is not desperate. Another may be painful because his distress has not been more distressing, and is therefore afraid that his repentance is not genuine. Here the experience of such as have had their hearts gently " opened" may be of vast benefit, Acts xvi. 14, 29—34. In every such case, we should point to " the Lamb of God," John i. 29; 1 John ii. 2; and bear their burdens in prayer *for* and *with* the humble penitents; and expound unto them the way of God more perfectly; Acts xviii. 26; showing, at once, the tenderness of the Saviour, Isa. xlii. 3, and the freeness and suitableness of his salvation, Isa. liii. 4—6; Rom. iv. 5.

6. To *a weight of temptation.* This may come *immediately* from satan, Matt. iv. 1; or, *mediately,* from persecuting men, from the world generally, from family connections, from the church, Matt. x. 36; Phil. iii. 18. In this case also, when the soul is " in heaviness through manifold temptations," the exercise of christian prudence and sympathy are requisite and beneficial. A friend, formed for adversity, may detect and expose the

devices of satan; may direct in affairs of difficulty; and, by advice and exhortation, support the soul of him that is ready to faint, and thus prove that "two are better than one," Eccl. iv. 9; Rom. xv. 1; 1 Thess. v. 14.

7. To *a weight of infirmities:* which is thought to be the apostle's more particular meaning in this place. These may belong to the *body,* worn down by labor, want, disease, or age, Eccl. xii. 3—5; or to the *mind,* wanting a clear and quick apprehension, a retentive memory, steady resolution, &c. By one or other of these infirmities your weak brother is *burdened;* therefore you should *pity* rather than upbraid him; and, as making his burden your own, *help* his *infirmities* rather than *punish* them as *crimes.* If. in addition to this, we *conceal the infirmities* of others, when, in consequence of such concealment, we expose ourselves to the blame which would otherwise fall on them, and thus take *the inconvenience on ourselves,* we then emphatically "bear one another's burdens," 2 Cor. xi. 29. In general we should have respect to circumstances, and administer our relief in the most proper *mode, measure, time.*

Propriety recommends this duty; we are children of the same family, members of the same body, &c.—*Personal advantage* recommends it; it improves the best and happiest feelings of the heart.—*Christianity* recommends it; "So fulfil the law of Christ." Thus we are brought to consider,

II. The enforcing motive. It is usual as well as proper in the apostles to enforce their advice and injunctions by a reference to the precepts and practice of Christ. Instance in liberality, 2 Cor. viii. 9; humility, Phil. ii. 4; generous sympathy, and mutual support; thus our text, "Bear," &c.. "*and so fulfil the law of Christ.*" We do not know of any law of Christ enjoining this duty in precisely these words, yet there is much in the teaching of our Redeemer to enforce both the principle and the practice. Hence we observe that the apostle's requirement is,

1. *Worthy of the character of Christ,* inasmuch as it is a *law of equity.* We who have so many burdens, of which a part must be borne by others, and of which we wish them to bear a part, ought to bear in return, Matt. vii. 12.—*A law of benevolence.* "Let every man seek another's wealth," Luke x. 37; 1 Cor. x. 24.—*A law of general utility,* by which society is benefited, the sum of evil being lessened, and that of happiness increased.

It is congenial with the spirit of Christ. "Let this *mind* be in you," &c. Phil. ii. 5. "He hath *loved* us." "Ye know the *grace* of our Lord Jesus Christ," &c. "Put on therefore, as the elect of God, *bowels of mercies, kindness, humbleness of mind,* " &c. Col. iii. 12, 13.

3. *It is agreeable to the example of Christ.* Mark the sacrifices he made for the welfare, the salvation, of the *poor* and the *unworthy;*—condescending to become man, to labor, to suffer, and to die, John xiii. 13; Phil. ii. 6—9; Heb ii. 14—16.

4. *It is deducible from the precepts of Christ.* "A new commandment give I unto you, that ye love one another: as I have loved you," &c. John xiii. 33, 34. Perhaps this is the very "law" to which the apostle refers. And Jesus calls it "*my* commandment," John xv. 12, 17. It comprehends and is the substance of every other, Gal. v. 14. Hence "love is the fulfilling of the law," Romans xiii. 10, and "the end of the commandment," 1 Tim. i. 5.

5. *It has and shall have the approbation of Christ.* As King and Law giver he has said, and in the day of judgment will say, "Blessed are the merciful, for they shall obtain mercy," Matt. v. 7, and xxv. 34—40.

INFER,

1. Seeing that our text expresses the peculiar genius of the religion by which we hope for salvation, the subject should awaken inquiry, 1 John iv. 19—21.

2. If examination should happen to lead us to humiliating views of past short-comings, &c. it should also lead to unreserved and constant obedience; which may be supported by a consideration of what we owe to *ourselves*—our *brethren*, Heb. xiii. 1, 2;—our *Saviour*, who regards what is done to his followers, as done unto himself, Matt. xxv. 40;—and to *our God*, who expects such return for his love, 1 John iv. 9—11.

~~~~~~~~~~~~~~

THE BEST EXERCISE.

1 Tim. iv. 7.—Exercise thyself rather unto godliness. (Sk.)

WHATSOEVER things were written aforetime, were written for our learning. The text therefore, though primarily addressed by St. Paul to Timothy, may be beneficial to us. There are exercises which belong exclusively to the ministerial character, but as godliness is designed to be a general blessing, and is the same in every clime, and through every age, the exercise recommended in the text is binding on us all. We will therefore notice,

I. THE OBJECT OF THE TEXT;—"godliness."

II. THE ATTENTION IT CLAIMS;—"Exercise thyself," &c.

III. THE MOTIVES THAT SHOULD EXCITE US TO A COMPLIANCE WITH THIS ADVICE.

I. THE OBJECT OF THE TEXT IS "GODLINESS." This is sometimes understood in a restricted sense, as having reference to one part of our duty only; hence it is mentioned in connection with other things, "Follow after righteousness, godliness, faith," &c. "Add to your faith virtue," &c., "and to patience godliness," &c.. 1 Tim. vi. 11; 2 Pet. i. 6. "Godliness," in its true etymological sense, signifies *right worship;*—worship *right in its object.* Some worship the work of their hands—others "the host of heaven,"—some worship they know not what,—others worship devils. "But thou shalt worship the Lord thy God." "Worship the Lord in the beauty of holiness." *Right in its subject.*—Forms of worship are necessary: Moses bowed his head and worshipped; Joshua fell on his face, and worshipped; but "God is a Spirit, and they that worship him must worship him in spirit and in truth." The homage of the heart is the only acceptable worship to God. *Right in its rule.*—Every thing relative to divine worship, must be regulated by the Divine precepts; the institutions of Christ, and not the inventions of men, must be the rules of our worship. The bowing to a crucifix, crossing with holy water, repeating Ave Marias, and all that ridiculous mummery peculiar to popery, is not right worship, because it has no sanction from the Bible. But *godliness* has been generally defined as being conformity to God: moral likeness to our Maker. Absolute resemblance to God is impossible; God is an infinite being; and eternity, immensity, and infinity, are incommunicable attributes. Likeness to God may be considered in having the understanding illuminated with his light, the heart renovated by his spirit, and the life regulated by his word.

378

II. The attention it claims;—"Exercise thyself," &c. We should exercise ourselves to *gain, retain, and recommend* godliness.

1. *Exercise thyself to gain godliness.* No man is naturally possessed of godliness; we are totally unlike God. Godliness is not to be gained by a few cold wishes, or languid desires. "*Exercise* thyself;" this is a word of great importance, it is borrowed from the practice of those who contended for the Olympic garland; who cast away every impediment, and strained every nerve to win the prize. There is much in godliness that demands the exercise of the human understanding, for "great is the mystery of godliness." Exercise yourselves to know all you can of godliness; its doctrines, its principles, and its practices. In order to this, give attention to reading—to hearing—to meditation—to prayer. Not only to gain the knowledge, but the enjoyment of godliness. It is a blessing to have a right judgment in all things, but knowledge of itself will not do; we must enjoy God, and dwell in God, and have God dwelling in us.

2. *Exercise thyself to retain godliness.* Some, after having sought it with many tears and much earnestness, seem unconcerned about retaining it. To hold it fast, *set a high value upon it.* To prize it too highly is impossible; there is no overrating it. *Seek for an increase of it.* The most advanced christian may yet advance; godliness possesses infinite attractions, and prospects interminable; and he who is not advancing is declining. *Stand aloof from the society of those who would rob you of your treasure.* If you possessed a large sum of money, or a rich collection of gems, pearls, and diamonds, you would not like to travel a road infested with robbers; and if you were obliged to, you would take heed to secure a guard, and get yourself well armed. Apply this to our subject, and exercise yourself unto godliness, to keep it in possession.

3. *Exercise thyself to recommend godliness.* Many are totally destitute of this invaluable treasure. They are ignorant of its vast advantages; and they are in extreme danger without it. Remember it is an important part of godliness, to love your neighbors as yourselves, and as you have been prompted under the influence of self-love, to seek this godliness for your own benefit; you are bound to recommend it to others. Do it by your conversation. Talk of it to your children, to your families, and to your neighbors. Do it by your holy lives. Exemplify in your conduct the purity of its principles. Let others see your good works, &c.—This exercise should be *spiritual;* all the powers of the immortal spirit should be engaged in it.—*Pre-eminent;* it should be our first and most important business.—*Habitual;* we should be always at it.—And, *Persevering;* we must be "faithful unto death."

III. The motives that should excite us to a compliance with this advice.

1. *Because this is the best exercise.* God is the best being; the participation of godliness, makes us resemble God; and every other exercise of which man is capable, is frivolous when held in competition with this. It is the best exercise; as it engages the best powers of man, and these powers are directed to the noblest object.

2. *It is the most honorable exercise.* Some think the exercise of godliness mean, and despicable; but who are they that draw this conclusion? Are they persons who have studied its character? No, they are men who hate godliness, because godliness condemns them. Is there no honor in treading in the footsteps of the most illustrious characters who have ever lived,—patriarchs, prophets, evangelists, apostles, and martyrs, "of whom the world was not worthy?" Is there no honor in that exercise which will

most effectually secure to us the possession of the divine nature? Which will "make us kings and priests unto God;" sons and daughters of the Lord Almighty?

3. *It is the most satisfactory exercise.* Bodily exercise is often irksome and laborious; and produces a weariness of the flesh; but the work of righteousness is peace, and the exercise of godliness yields secret satisfaction. What a comfort to have a conscience void of offence towards God and man! To know that we are working out our salvation! That we are walking in the narrow way that leadeth unto life; and returning to Zion with singing, and everlasting joy upon our heads.

4. *It is the most rational exercise.* There are many irrational exercises in the world, exercises that injure the constitution, ruin the health, and destroy the soul; but as godliness is profitable unto all things, that exercise must be most rational, which tends to secure this invaluable treasure.

5. *It is the most successful exercise.* How often are our exercises in this world unsuccessful; our labors frustrated; and our expectations blasted! but the exercise used in reference to godliness will be successful. They that ask shall receive, and they that seek shall find. We have the promises of an immutable Being to ensure success.

In conclusion we observe, there are in our congregations,

1. Some who have never begun the exercise recommended in the text. To such we say, You are capable, under the influence of Divine grace, of exercising yourselves unto godliness; you have means afforded you: you are very guilty in neglecting your salvation so long; if you procrastinate much more, your ruin will be inevitable; the longer you delay, the more difficult the work will be, and the less time you will have to accomplish it. Oh seize the present moment, and now begin this long neglected, but deeply important exercise.

2. Some who have begun, but have relaxed in the exercise; who have put their hand to the plough, but have looked back. Oh stir up the gift of God that is within you! Pray for the quickening influences of the Holy Ghost; and "give all diligence to make your calling and election sure."

3. Some who have begun, and continued to exercise themselves unto godliness. "Hold fast the beginning of your confidence steadfast unto the end, for in due season ye shall reap if ye faint not."

THE FIGHT OF FAITH

1 Timothy vi. 12.—Fight the good fight of faith. (Sk.)

THE apostle, in the chapter before us, after enjoining certain duties, and giving a caution against anti-christian teachers, proceeds to show the value of godliness with contentment: and he does this by contrasting it with the love of money, which is the root of all evil; "which, while some have coveted after, they have erred from the faith," ver 8, 9, 10. Covetousness being criminal and disgraceful in all, but especially in the ministers of religion; the apostle advised Timothy, as a man of God, to flee from it, and from all the vices which it occasions; and to pursue righteousness, godliness, faith, ove, patience, and meekness, ver. 11. He then adds "Fight the good fight of faith," or, as some read it, "agonize the good agony"—"Combat the good combat of faith;" which terms are quite agonistical, and refer to the eagerness with which those who entered in the Grecian games, struggled for, and laid hold on the prize. In impressing this subject, we may notice,

I. THE CHRISTIAN'S WARFARE.

II. ITS PECULIAR CHARACTER.

I. THE CHRISTIAN'S WARFARE.—It is *Defensive* and *Offensive.*

1. *Defensive.* He has to contend with, 1, *A depraved nature.* "The carnal mind is enmity against God," Rom. viii. 7. "The flesh lusteth against the spirit," Gal. v. 17. Pride, anger, envy, jealousy, hatred, malice, revenge, and all other dispositions contrary to the mind of Christ, must be opposed and overcome, Rom. xii. 21; Rev. iii. 12; xxi. 17. 2. *The temptations of satan.* These are various; hence he is styled "the accuser of the brethren," Rev. x. 12; "a roaring lion, seeking whom he may devour," 1 Peter v. 8; the "prince," and "the god of this world," "the prince of the power of the air," &c. John xii. 31; 2 Cor. iv. 4; Eph. ii. 2. These armies he commands, and varies his mode of operation, according to circumstances: hence he presented a Babylonish garment, &c. to Achan, Jos. vii. 21;—Bath-shebah to David, 2 Sam. xi. 2—4;—and thirty pieces of silver to Judas, Matt. xvi. 15. But whatever are his temptations, we are commanded to resist, steadfast in the faith, 1 Pet. v. 8; Jam. iv. 7.

3. *The allurements of the world.* Its spirit, maxims, and fashion, Rom. xii. 2; 1 Pet. iv. 2, 3. This warfare is also,

2. *Offensive.* Hence the christian has to attack satan's strong holds, 2 Cor. x. 4. These are, 1. *Ignorance.* Numbers are so deluded, as to imagine that ignorance will excuse them for neglecting religion; but this is their condemnation, they are ignorant, not of necessity but choice, John iii. 19. Others say, "Ignorance is the mother of devotion;" and use their utmost efforts to prevent the human family from being benefited by that book which was designed to be "a lamp unto our feet, and a light unto our path," Psa. cxix. 105. The duty of christians, is to combine their efforts to remove or prevent this evil. The means are—the circulation of the sacred scriptures—a living ministry—the instruction of youth—the distribution of tracts, &c.—2. *Prejudice.* Nothing more effectually fortifies the mind against truth than this; and to overcome it, you must exercise prudence, meekness, patience, and love. With these graces, connect scriptural and sound argumentation, associated with correctness of principle, and conduct. —3. *Pride.* To some religion is degrading—it will stain their honor—rob them of their reputation; and thus Christ is to some a stumbling block, and unto others foolishness, 1 Cor. i. 23; the pride of human reason will not suffer them to receive the doctrines of the cross. These you must combat with the hallowed weapons of truth, which will admit of no system of religion but that which God has revealed, 1 Cor. iii. 14.—4. *Love of the world,* ver. 10. To overcome this, you must show the importance of spiritual things compared with temporal things &c. Take care, however, to connect with your utmost exertions, unceasing and ardent prayer to God, for the convincing influence of the Holy Ghost, without whose aid nothing is wise, or strong, or good. Let us therefore notice,

II. ITS PECULIAR CHARACTER. It is designated,

First, *"A fight of faith."* It is a fight of faith as opposed,

1. *To physical exertion.* You are not to rally your forces, and combine your energies, to oppose an earthly power, or destroy the bodies of the

children of men; but rather to promote your own salvation, and that of others. It imports a mind determinately opposed to sin and satan, pursuing holiness and heaven, Eph. vi. 12.

2. *Mental speculation.* It is possible for a man to be well acquainted with the theory of christianity—to be a giant in literature—an able abettor of the truth—a wise disputant on theological subjects—a successful antagonist in the controversial field, and, after all, a stranger to inward religion. This was not the case with our apostle: he was not a mere theorist, 1 Cor. ix. 26, 27; Phil. iii. 14. This fight of faith imports a mind reconciled to God, Col. i. 21, 22;—a union with Christ by faith, Gal. ii. 20;—and the exercise of every grace, Eph. vi. 13—18.

3. *Doubtful uncertainty.* In an earthly campaign, a successful issue is uncertain. Troops may be well disciplined, under a judicious commander, and every thing ominious of success; but circumstances over which neither the commander nor his troops have any control, may determine the conflict, and place the victorious expectant in the hands of his enemies. But in this fight nothing can endanger those who are *immutably faithful;* " he that shall endure unto the end, the same shall be saved," Matt. xxiv. 13; Rev. ii. 10.

Secondly, " *A good fight of faith.*" This will appear when we consider,

1. *The authority by which it is sanctioned.*—" All scripture is given by inspiration of God," 2 Tim. iii. 16. This text therefore, considered in connection with other texts of equal import, proves that it is sanctioned by the highest authority, 1 Tim. i. 18, 19; Rev. iii. 11, 12, ii. 7.

2. *The aid afforded during the period of exercise.* In military operations, a sanguinary engagement protracted in its duration, induces debility, and exhaustion; and will not admit of those supplies necessary for recruiting strength and invigorating the spirit; but in this warfare the supplies are seasonable, and sufficient, Prov. iii. 6; Isa. xli. 10; 2 Cor. xii. 9.

3. *The security given.* In prosecuting this warfare, according to the rules laid down in the holy scriptures, you may say with an apostle, " Who shall separate us from the love of Christ?" &c. Rom. viii. 35—39. " No weapon that is formed against you shall prosper," Isa. liv. 17. " When the enemy shall come in like a flood, the Spirit of the Lord shall lift up a standard against him," Isa. lix. 19.

4. *The final triumph.* Instance the case of the apostle, " I have fought a good fight," &c. 2 Tim. iv. 7, 8, " Death shall be swallowed up in victory," 1 Cor. xv. 54—57. The conqueror shall be enthroned, Rev. iii. 21.

INFERENCES.

1. *This warfare will neither admit of substitution, nor cessation of arms.* The command is *personal* in its application, and *perpetual* in its obligation.

2. *This is the greatest encouragement.* Christ is your commander—the Holy Spirit your helper—the scriptures your directory—angels your guardians—saints your companions; and heaven the inheritance reserved for you, 1 Pet. i. 3—5.

3. *A refusal to fight is open rebellion against God.* Consider this ye sinners, and while the treaty of reconciliation is open, 2 Co.. v. 20, humble yourselves before God, and implore mercy.

REMEMBRANCE OF THE POOR RECOMMENDED

Galatians ii. 10.—We should remember the poor.   (Sk.)

THE leading topics of the christian ministry are frequently inculcated, and by judicious hearers, generally understood, and distinctly remembered. The fall of man, the redemption of the world, the necessity of regeneration, and the final rewards of virtue and vice, are subjects, which in a direct or indirect manner, breathe in every sermon you hear, in every prayer you offer, and in every hymn you sing. But there are other subjects of a subordinate character, clearly stated in the sacred volume, which though they may not form articles of your faith, yet stand as rules for your practice, and are too important to be discarded from the pulpit. Among those we may notice the reciprocal duties that arise from the various relations in which we stand to society ; and one of the least regarded. though not the least in importance, is the practice recommended in the text, " We should remember the poor." We will,

I. EXAMINE THE NATURE OF THE ASSERTION.

II. STATE THE OBLIGATIONS WE ARE UNDER TO COMPLY WITH IT.

III. ANSWER OBJECTIONS.

I. EXAMINE THE NATURE OF THE ASSERTION. We need not spend a moment in describing the poor: alas! they describe themselves. You daily witness the scantiness and poverty of their apparel, their pale and emaciated forms ; and you hear their piteous plaints, and the tale of their complicated woes. But we should,

1. *Remember the work of the poor.* On these the curse entailed by sin, daily rests ; in the sweat of their face they eat bread, till they return unto the ground. *Their work is irksome and laborious.* See their hands, worn hard with incessant toil ; their faces bathed in profuse sweat ; and their bodies bent, not so much with the weight of years, as with the pressure of ponderous burdens. *Their work is often destructive to health.* Many are plunged in mines ; view the confined situation in which they labor, the unnatural posture in which they pursue their work, the noxious damps that infect the air in which they breathe, and the incessant streams that distil upon their wearisome bodies. Huge masses of rocks often burst around them, and bury them alive in their subterraneous vaults ; and even if they escape these awful accidents, what multitudes go prematurely the grave. *But their work is chiefly beneficial.* They labor for the public benefit. Consider the labors of the mechanic, the husbandman, and the artizan.

2. *Remember the deprivations of the poor.* Here note, the means of instruction which are placed beyond their reach. The children of the poor are sent to work, as soon as they can earn a scanty pittance, with little or no learning, except what they get from Sunday schools. They read but little, partly for want of books, and partly for want of inclination. They are deprived in many instances of the common necessaries of life ; view the miserable huts and hovels in which they reside ; in low damp situations where the wintry winds howl through the broken casement: view their tattered vestments amid the rigors of winter, and their coarse food scantily administered, and scarcely sufficient to satisfy the demands of exhausted nature.

3. *Our remembrance of the poor should be founded on a personal acquaintance with their circumstances.* We should visit their abodes, and find out the retreats of wretchedness. It should be attended with a compassionate feeling towards them. "Indeed Sir," said a person of large prop-

erty, "I am a very compassionate man; but to tell you the truth, I do not know any person in want." The fact was he stood aloof from the poor, and kept out of their way.—And it should be accompanied by relief. Many say "Depart in peace, be ye warmed, and be ye filled;" but never administer the blessings which the poor need. We cannot do all we would, but let us do what we can. Cannot we retrench a little from our food? Or give them some garments? Or employ them in our farms, or at our merchandise?

II. STATE THE OBLIGATIONS WE ARE UNDER TO COMPLY WITH IT.

1. *The dictates of humanity require it.* There is a chord in human hearts, that vibrates to the touch of misery; hence all human beings occasionally remember mercy. The sufferings even of brutes excite compassion. The Jews had a law which required them to help an ox or an ass in distress, Deut. xxii. 4. And shall we show mercy to a brute, and neglect a man? The poor are our brethren, one God hath created us, one Saviour hath redeemed us, one heaven will receive us, if faithful unto death.

2. *The demands of duty require it.* The laws of God have made this imperative upon us. The texts that bear upon this point are numerous Deut. xv. 7—9; Dan. iv. 27; Luke vi. 36—38; Matt. vii. 12; 1 John iii. 17. Consider the connection of the text. The saints at Jerusalem were exceedingly oppressed by poverty. A contribution had been made for them in Macedonia, and in Achaia; St. Paul had written to the Romans concerning them; Peter, James, and John, wished to "remember the poor;" "the same, (said Paul) I also was forward to do."

3. *The rights of justice require it.* The common opinion is, that "the poor are solely dependent on the rich for a scanty pittance; and that men of affluence are independent; have independent fortunes," &c. But the reverse of this is the truth. Men who do nothing, are mere drones in the hive of society, who live upon the labors of others. To the poor we are most deeply indebted. Who erect our houses? Who form our clothes? Who procure our food? Do not the poor? therefore remember them. Justice requires this at your hands.

4. *The claims of interest require it.* Every man is obligated to pursue that course of conduct, which will most effectually subserve his present and final happiness. Is it not our interest to imitate God? God remembers the poor: his Son was poor; his disciples were poor; to the poor the gospel was preached; God hath chosen the poor. Angels are mindful of the poor; they visited poor shepherds—they conducted the soul of poor Lazarus to paradise. God will bless those who remember the poor, Psalm xli. 1, 2; Prov. iii. 9, xix 17; Isa. lviii. 10, 11.

III. ANSWER OBJECTIONS.

1. "*My circumstances are impoverished, and I have nothing to spare.*" What nothing?—Think of the poor widow, and her mites. Read the account of her to whom Elijah applied for a morsel of bread, 1 Kings xvii. 11, 12.

2. "*Charity must begin at home.*" But remember it should not *end* at home. The proper sphere of charity is abroad; the ties of relationship bind us to look at home; but benevolence looks abroad on all the suffering sons of humanity, and stretches forth her hands to relieve them.

3. "*I have a right to do what I will with my own.*" But what is your own? Are you not a steward? Is not God the universal proprietor of all things? Will he not call you to an account how you have spent his goods? It is not optional with you to give or not to give; God has made it imperative on you.

4 " *The poor do not deserve to be remembered.*" But their merit is not the ground or rule of our benevolence. We are to " be merciful, as our Father in heaven is merciful ;" and what if God had dealt with us according to our merit? How do we know, that the poor do not deserve what we give them? We do not know their value or their real characters.

Conclude with a *word of advice* to the *poor;* to excite them to economy, to submission to their superiors, and gratitude to their benefactors.—And a *word of comfort* to induce them to bear their lot of poverty, during the period of their mortal pilgrimage, with patience and resignation to God.

LIBERALITY TO THE POOR.

Luke iii. 10, 11.—And the people asked him, saying, What shall we do then? He answereth and saith unto them, He that hath two coats, let him impart to him that hath none ; and he that hath meat, let him do likewise. (H. H.)

In order to understand the true meaning of any part of scripture, the strictest attention must be paid to the context. If this rule be not observed, there is scarcely any thing which may not be sanctioned by the inspired volume ; and the most contradictory positions may appear to stand on equal authority. Suppose, for instance, the question in our text be taken, as other apparently similar questions must be taken, namely, as an inquiry into the way of salvation ; we shall make John the Baptist return an answer directly contrary to the whole tenor of the Gospel. When the gaoler asked Paul and Silas, "What he must do to be saved ?" they answered, " Believe in the Lord Jesus Christ, and thou shalt be saved." Acts xvi. 30, 31. *This is the only true answer that can be given to that question ;* for "there is no other name under heaven given among men whereby we can be saved." but the name of Jesus Christ. Acts. iv. 12. But if we look into the context, we find that John the Baptist had been "preaching the baptism of repentance for the remission of sins," ver 3 ; or, in other words had been preaching salvation by Jesus Christ, exactly as the apostle Peter, and indeed all the Apostles, did on the day of Pentecost.* Then, seeing multitudes coming to him for baptism, and apprehending that the great majority of them were taking up a profession of religion upon very light and erroneous grounds, he cautioned them strongly against a presumptuous confidence on the one hand, or an unproductive and hypocritical profession on the other ; and exhorted them, if they would not experience the fate of a barren tree, to "bring forth fruits worthy of repentance," ver. 7—9. In reply to this, the people ask, " What shall we *do?*" That is, *What fruits shall we bring forth,* in order to evince our sincerity ?† And the direction which John gives them, is an answer exactly suited to the occasion : it is to this effect ; " If you would approve yourselves sincere and upright in your profession of faith in the Promised Messiah, shew forth your faith by your works, and, above all, by an abounding exercise of love."

Having thus prepared our way by a view of the context, and having as-

---

* See the people's inquiry, and Peter's answer, Acts ii. 37, 38.

† See the Greek, ver. 8—10. This will remove all doubt : for they adobt the very same term as John had used.

certained what the Baptist's design was in giving the people the direction in our text, we shall proceed to the more distinct consideration of his answer, and shall open to you,

I. Its IMPORT—

It is manifest that the direction given by him is figurative, and therefore not to be taken in its strict and literal sense. But we must not therefore imagine, that we are at liberty to disregard it, as though it had no force at all. There can be no doubt but that the Baptist intended to inculcate a very tender compassion towards our indigent fellow-creatures, and a very enlarged exercise of liberality for their relief. To obtain, with as much precision as the subject is capable of, the true import of his words, we shall adduce from other parts of scripture, but especially from the writings of the same Evangelist.

1. Some other passages of similar tendency—

First, we shall notice one or two that are also figurative, Luke xii. 33, 34. & xiv. 12—14.— — —There can be no doubt but that these require a very high degree of liberality to the poor, since they were actually practiced *in their strictest sense* by the first christians, Acts ii. 44, 45, & iv. 32—37.— — —From these we may turn to others that are more plain, Luke vi. 38. & xi. 41.— — —What an accumulation of words is there in the former of these passages to encourage our compliance with the precept; and what a gracious benediction in the latter!———To *the rich* there is an especial charge given to be bountiful, 1 Tim. vi. 18, 19; but it is not to them only that this duty belongs; but to those also who gain a daily subsistence by their manual labor, Eph. iv. 28. To all, according to their ability, it equally appertains; for, on the foresight of a dearth in Judea, all the disciples of Antioch, every one according to his ability, contributed instantly to their relief, Acts xi. 28—30.

2. Some examples which are set forth for our imitation—

That of Zaccheus is particularly to our purpose, because he was just converted to the faith of Christ, and because our blessed Lord himself acknowledged this heavenly disposition to be an evidence of his having actually obtained acceptance with his God, Luke xix. 8, 9.— — —But the example of the Mecedonian churches is yet more pertinent; because it is an example, not of an individual, but of whole churches; and those, not in a state of ease and opulence, but of great affliction and deep poverty; and because it is expressly set forth for the imitation of others, who are called up to imitate it, *in order to prove the sincerity of their love to Christ*, 2 Cor. viii. 1—4, 8, 9. By carefully comparing these several passages, we see clearly what our duty is: we are not required to burthen ourselves in order to ease others, but so to participate their burthens that they may partake of our ease, ib. ver. 13, 14: thus to "bear one another's burthen is eminently to fulfil the law of Christ, Gal. vi. 2.

Having thus marked the import of the injunction in our text, we proceed to shew,

II. Its REASONABLENESS—

The whole of God's "law is good," and the service it requires is reasonable. But the duty enjoined in our text, though arduous to a selfish mind, is particularly reasonable. For consider,

1. What obligations we owe to God for the superior comforts which we enjoy—

It is God who assigns to all their lot, not only in respect to the situation in which they are born, Acts xvii. 26, 28, but in all the changes, whether prosperous or adverse, which they experience through life, 1 Sam. ii, 6, 7. Whatever therefore we have above others, " it is God alone who has made us to differ," 1 Cor. iv. 7. And how eminently is this the case with respect to the ravages of war which during these last twenty years have desolated almost the whole of Europe, but have never reached our happy land! Compare our state with that of a great part of Germany at this present moment,* and then say, whether a compassionate regard for our suffering fellow-creatures be not called for at our hands, and whether such an expression of it as our text requires, be at all unreasonable? Methinks, it is not possible to have even the most indistinct view of our obligations to God, without saying from our hearts, " What shall I render unto the Lord for all the benefits that he hath done unto me?"

2. What we ourselves should desire, if we were reduced to the state in which myriads of our fellow-creatures now are—

It is not easy to place ourselves in the situation of persons of whom we hear only by report: but yet we may conceive what we ourselves should desire, and what we should think reasonable, if we were perishing with cold and nakedness and hunger, whilst others, embarked in the same cause with ourselves, were exempt from those sufferings, and were enjoying comparative ease and affluence: Should we not wish them to stand forth for our relief? Should we not think it reasonable, that their exertions should rise in proportion to our necessities, and that they should almost literally fulfil the precept in our text, the man who had two coats imparting to us who had none, and that he who had meat should do likewise? Let us adopt for our principle the golden rule, and " Do unto others, as we would they should do unto us."

What our blessed Lord and Saviour has done for us—

This is the consideration which St. Paul himself suggests in reference to this very point, 2 Cor. viii. 9. O consider, " how rich he was" in the possession of his Father's glory; and how "poor he became," " not having so much as a place where to lay his head," but dying under the curse that was due to our sins. Consider too what his object was; namely, that we, who deserved to be in hell without a drop of water to cool our tongues, might through his poverty be rich, and possess all the glory of heaven. Does such love as this require no return? When this very Saviour tells us, that what we do unto the least of his brethren, he accepts as done to himself, shall we think any requisition hard, or any sacrifice too great? Truly, not only our property, but even our life itself, may well be sacrificed for him, 1 John iii. 16; and we should account ourselves happy in proportion as we have an opportunity to advance his glory in the world.

But instead of dwelling any longer on the general reasonableness of this precept, we will proceed to notice,

III. ITS SUITABLENESS TO THE PRESENT OCCASION—

Rarely, if ever, has greater occasion for charitable exertions existed than at present.†— — —Now therefore we might justly call upon you to comply with our text almost in the literal sense. But, waving that, we must urge you to adopt the *principle* that is there inculcated— — —and to bear in mind, that " he who soweth sparingly, shall reap also sparingly, and he who soweth bountifully shall reap also bountifully. Let every man do ac-

---

* This Sermon was preached in 1814, on occasion of a collection for the relief of the most grievous distresses in Germany.

† Here the particular occasion should be opened at considerable length.

cording as he is disposed in his heart, not grudgingly or of **necessity ; for** God loveth a cheerful giver," 2 Cor. ix. 6, 7. Do not however forget the important distinctions with which we began the subject. It is to glorify Christ, and to shew the sincerity of your love to him, that we invite you ;— not to purchase heaven by your alms. Bear that in mind ; and God will not forget it in the day of judgment.

A CALL TO WATCHFULNESS AND SOBRIETY.

1 Thess. v. 6.—Therefore let us not sleep as do others, but let us watch and be sober. (Sk.)

EVERY thing in this world is liable to degenerate. The richest soil would, if neglected, be soon overrun with weeds. The most laudable institutions, if not watched over, would be desecrated from their original purpose. The firmest and best constructed buildings, are subject to decay. Metals of the finest polish are liable to be tarnished, and Christians of the most exalted piety, may fall from their own steadfastness, and degenerate into lukewarmness and apostacy. On this principle, we justify all the cautions, warnings, and admonitory precepts found in the apostolic writings. In the last of these, we include the text; " Let us not sleep," &c. We have here.

I. A STATE ADVERTED TO ;—" *Sleep*, as do others."

II. A COURSE OF CONDUCT DESCRIBED ; " Watch, and be sober."

III. AN OBLIGATION TO PURSUE IT INTIMATED :—" Let us not sleep— but *let* us watch," &c.

I. A STATE ADVERTED TO ;—" *Sleep*." This is the state of sinners : their moral condition is variously described, as being a state of darkness— bondage—death, &c. Here, they are considered as being asleep, &c.

1. *Those who are asleep, are insensible of their state, and unconscious of all the objects that surround them.* They have eyes, but they perceive no objects; ears, but they hear no sound; hearts, but they feel no sensations. How descriptive is this of the state of sinners! To their worldly concerns, they are broad awake; all eye, all ear, all attention; but in reference to the interests of their souls, a deep sleep has fallen upon them. They are unconscious of the immediate presence of God with them—insensible of his amazing love—of their moral condition as sinners—of the duties that devolve upon them—of the dangers that await them—and the privileges they are called to realize.

2. *Those who are asleep, are motionless and inactive.* Powers the most vigorous may be in their possession ; blessings the most inestimable may be within their grasp, and business the most important may devolve upon them ; yet no efforts are called forth, no energies are roused—such is the state of sinners. For the accomplishment of worldly objects they are ever on the alert, but in reference to their spiritual interests, they are motionless and inactive ; a death-like torpor rests upon them : they hear of heaven, but make no efforts to enter in at the strait gate, and walk in the narrow way that leadeth to life ;—they hear of hell, but they give no diligence to escape its tremendous punishment ;—they are told of their duty, but to do it they manifest no concern.

388

3. *Those who are asleep, are often the subjects of illusion and deception* What senseless dreams delude them! How many airy nothings swim before their eyes! How many pleasing and painful thoughts occupy their minds as destitute of reason, as they are of reality! Nothing can be more characteristic of the condition of sinners. Their whole life is a dream. Delusions deep as hell bind them fast; and all their ideas of God, of themselves, of sin, and religion, misery, and happiness, are the phantoms of error, and the creatures of imagination.

4. *Those who are asleep, are frequently exposed to dangers which they have no power to escape.* Hence sleep is a defenceless state. Men may bolt their doors, yet thieves often enter and surprise them. But sinners are exposed to dangers infinitely more dreadful. They are taken already in the snare of the devil, and they are liable every moment to be arrested, and hurried down to perdition. Such is the state adverted to in the text. Let us notice,

II. THE COURSE OF CONDUCT EXPRESSED ;—" Let us watch and be sober."

1. *Watchfulness is opposed to sleep, therefore let us be wakeful.* Complying with the requisition of the apostle, "Awake thou that sleepest," &c. Rousing ourselves from that delusive slumber into which sin has thrown us. Let us awake, and keep awake.

2. *Watchfulness is opposed to thoughtlessness and stupidity, therefore let us be considerate and thoughtful.* Our worldly business claims our thoughts; but our souls, our God, our salvation, our duties, and privileges, possess higher claims. To these we should bend our thoughts, with deep concern and solicitude.

3. *Watchfulness is opposed to indolence and sloth, therefore we should be diligent.* "Slothfulness casteth into a deep sleep." We have much to do for our neighbors, ourselves, and our God, and we must work while it is day.

4. *Watchfulness has reference to danger, therefore we must be prepared to meet its attacks.* Our enemies are wakeful and vigilant, and always waiting to attack us to advantage. Let us always be on our guard, and watch as sentinels at the post of duty.

5. *To watchfulness we must add sobriety.* Be sober, that is temperate ; avoid gluttony and intoxication : eating and drinking are designed to nourish the body ; but we may make our table a snare, and convert our aliments into poisons. Be sober, that is calm and dispassionate : holding your tempers and passions in subjection, never suffering wrathful dispositions to surprise you.

III. AN OBLIGATION TO PURSUE IT INTIMATED ;—" *Let us* not sleep, but *let us* watch," &c We must regard this as an apostolic precept; an expression of this kind, in some cases, amounts to little more than advice or counsel ; but when a superior gives it to a dependent, and especially when God by the ministry of his servants, imparts it for our instruction, it is a law from which we dare not swerve.

1. *Our circumstances call us to comply with this requisition.* We need not sleep, but we may watch; the power and the obligation go together, we are not circumstanced as heathens are, nor as Jews, or Papists, or Mohammedans are. Our privileges are superior, therefore we should not sleep as do others.

2. *Our profession demands obedience to it.* Hear the apostle: " Ye are all the children of light, and the children of the day, "&c., ver. 5. " For they that sleep, sleep in the night," &c., ver. 7. We profess the christian

religion; this prohibits sin, therefore we should not sleep as others; **this prescribes** duties, therefore we should watch and be sober.

3. *Our personal security should bind us to observe it.* Sinners are in a state of dreadful danger; their imaginary peace is no security against its attacks, ver. 3. Safety and duty are inseparable, " Watch and be sober," this will insure protection.

4. *Our eternal happiness is connected with the performance of this duty.* —" Blessed are those servants whom the Lord when he cometh shall find watching."

Here then we discern,

1. The essential difference between the righteous and the wicked; the latter are asleep in their sins, the former are watching, &c.

2. That the christian religion binds us to the practice of a holy singularity; we must not do as others, but do what God has enjoined.

A CHARGE TO THE RICH.

1 Timothy vi. 17—19.—Charge them that are rich in this world, that they be not high-minded, nor trust in uncertain riches, but in the living God, who giveth us richly all things to enjoy; that they do good, that they be rich in good works, ready to distribute, willing to communicate: laying up in store for themselves a good foundation against the time to come, that they may lay hold on eternal life." (Sk.)

The holy scriptures contain advices and instructions suited to every sort and condition of men. And God's ministers are charged with messages to all;—some of these messages are mild and agreeable,—and others are the very reverse: so that in some cases, great and excellent messengers have shrunk from their duty, see Jer. xx. 7—18;—Jonah i. 3;—but they dare not refuse, Ezek. ii. 5—8, iii. 17; Jer. i. 8, 17. Allow me then to deliver the message contained in the text; by attending to the *subjects*, the *nature*, and the *execution* of the charge.

I. The subjects of this charge;—" the rich." Whatever difficulty may be found in the appropriation of the term *rich* to individuals; it is sufficiently obvious, that there are rich as well as poor. Riches are opposed to poverty;—and as poverty signifies scantiness, penury, want;—so riches imply abundance, a store, more than enough.

1 *There may be a thousand gradations of riches:* from the least superabundance, to the largest sum that a mortal ever possessed. But that man must be ranked among the rich, who can command the necessaries, conveniencies, and comforts of life, and still have something to spare.

2. *Riches are strongly desired by mankind.* And the rich are frequently envied by their inferiors. And if man might be viewed merely as an inhabitant of this world, such conduct would hardly be censurable But the word of God, which connects eternity with time, and man with eternity, shows that religion is a thing essential to the happiness of the present and of the future state. Speaking of riches and poverty, in a way suited to these momentous associations, declares advantages peculiar to the poor, and dangers peculiar to the rich. Some of the latter, with the way to avoid them, form,

II. The nature of this charge. Which comprehends,

The dangers specified.

1. *Highmindedness.* It is exceedingly difficult for a person to be rich and not to think the more highly of himself on *that* account. Solomon asserts, that the rich man is " wise in his own conceit," Prov. xxviii. 11; and Ezekiel, " that the heart is lifted up because of riches," chap. xxviii. 5. The manner in which such are honored, and the advantages which their riches give them, lead to ideas of superiority, and thus tend to generate and to nourish this ostentatious evil.

2. " *Trust in uncertain riches.*" Trust in riches, is mentioned in the scriptures as a very dangerous sin, see Mark x. 24; Prov. xi. 4, 28, xxiii. 5. And the rich are much exposed to *this* danger;—because riches may procure many worldly comforts;—they may banish many apparent evils. And to trust in any thing rather than in God, is the common fault of man. Let us now endeavor to understand from the apostle,

The way to avoid these dangers.

1. *Trust in the living God. Hold* your possessions as *uncertain*, but *depend* on God, who cannot fail. He gives even the riches: he gives all things ;—the enjoyment, the zest. He alone can enable us really to enjoy what we have. How few enjoy even riches! " Trust in the living God;" because, if riches fail, he can in the absence of riches, give sweet enjoyment. *Trust in God!* This is of more value than any quantity of riches; implicit dependence on God is greater security against want. than any extent of worldly property.

2. *Employ your riches in doing good.—Liberally ;—* " rich in good works." Be in good works what you are in worldly possessions, abounding.—*Promptly :—* " *ready* to distribute." Some people who are very *able*, are never *ready.—Extensively ;—* " ready to *distribute.*" We often hear of, what we may be allowed to call, home-charity; but the apostle here enforces distributive charity. So the Psalmist, " He hath dispersed, he hath given to the poor,". &c. Psa. cxii. 9.—*Freely—* " willing to communicate." How hardly are some persuaded to give, even a little!

Observe the different words which the apostle uses :—*Distributing*, appears to signify *general charity.* Give extensively; not to one or two persons or things, but to every laudable institution to which your means will extend.—*Communicate ;* be *socially benevolent.* Be willing to share your good things with your fellow creatures. Be *hospitably* benevolent, see 2 Cor. ix. 5: Rom. xii. 13; 1 Tim. iii. 2; Tit. i. 8; 1 Pet. iv. 9.

3. *Live for eternity ;—* " Laying up in store for themselves a good foundation against the time to come." *Laying up*, is a phrase which surely the rich understand. Laying up *for themselves.*—For whom are you *laying up?* see Psa. xxxix. 6; Matt. xxv. 40; Heb. vi. 20; 2 Cor. ix. 6—" That thay may lay hold on eternal life." *Riches* will not secure life. They permit their owners to perish; but a proper use of riches will end in everlasting life, see Luke xvi. 9. The apostle adapts his language and his ideas remarkably to the rich. They may still be *rich*,—thay may *lay up*,—they may still *trust in*,—and still aim at *high* things. Oh that the rich were wise, that they understood these things! Oh that their *riches*, their *trust*, their *laying up*, their *high views*, were all consecrated to God, But whether they will hear, or forbear to hear; *we* must not shrink from,

III. THE EXECUTION OF THIS CHARGE. It is easy to charge the *poor ;* but when the rich are the subjects, who will dare to say plain things to them? Their property, their dignity, their very appearance forbid. But the command is. " Charge *the rich.*" Allow us then, oh ye rich! not as "lords over God's heritage," but as messengers of the Most **High, to** charge you.

Recollect,—that though your riches give you great worldly advantages, they also expose you to very serious dangers ; " How hardly shall they that have riches enter into the kingdom of God !" Unsanctified riches always prove a curse to their owners. Would you enjoy any of their real advantages ? then, "Honor the Lord with your substance, and with the first-fruits of all your increase, Prov. iii. 9.

Beware of high-mindedness ; and remember, that though some rich men are wise and good ; yet riches *may* be associated with any thing, and almost every thing, that is mean, and low, and vile.

Recollect, too, that there is but one way of salvation, for the rich and the poor. Repentance towards God, and faith in the Lord Jesus Christ, are essential to your salvation.

Finally, remember that a great day of reckoning and of judgment will come, when God will judge every man according to his works.

THE CHRISTIAN'S DUTY AND HOPE.

1 Peter i. 13.—Wherefore gird up the loins of your mind, be sober, and hope to the end, for the grace that is to be brought unto you at the revelation of Jesus Christ. (Sk.)

One of the evidences of the truth and divinity of the christian religion is, that it obtained establishment in the world, not only without any assistance from human governments, or from the corrupt principles of human nature, but in opposition to both the one and the other. Nature loves sensual indulgence ; christianity requires self-denial. Nature shrinks from pain and persecution. But the early christians had, in consequence of their profession, to endure fiery trials, ch. iv. 12. Hence the encouragements and supports afforded them in the former part of the chapter ; and hence the exhortation to " a patient continuance in well doing," contained in our text itself ; which points attention to the christian's duty, and his expectation.

I. The christian's duty ;—"Gird up the loins of your mind, be sober, and hope to the end."

1. " *Gird up*," &c. Here is an allusion to the manner in which persons in eastern countries usually disposed of their long flowing garments, when circumstances would not admit of their wearing them at full length. This was the case ; that is, they confined what was loose and inconvenient by means of the girdle about the loins.

(1.) *In their journeying.* So Exod. xii. 11 ; 1 Kings xviii. 46 ; 2 Kings iv. 29. The advice, therefore, reminds us of our present state of *pilgrimage*, as ch. ii. 11. We are but too much disposed to call our lands our own, and to take up our rest here. But the text tells us that we should hold ourselves in readiness to leave the world. *Convinced,* like the Psalmist,—"I am a stranger," &c., Psa. xxxix. 12,—we should, like him and other ancient worthies, " *declare plainly*" our conviction and desires, Heb. xi. 13—16, by *acting* accordingly. " Gird up the loins ;" have all things, whether temporal or spiritual, in readiness, as Israel to leave Egypt, &c., 2 Kings xx. 1 ; 2 Tim. iv. 6—8.

(**2.**) *This "girding up," &c., was practised by servants, when they waited on their masters.* "*Gird* thyself and *serve* me." See Luke xii. **35, 37,** xvii. 8. In this view it may denote that *cheerful and ready devotion'* with which the christian, renouncing self-will and self-pleasing, should ever ask, "Lord, what wilt thou have me to do?" He should gird himself for any service, however mean, laborious, painful, or protracted, ch. ii. 13—21.

(**3.**) *Soldiers girded themselves for battle.* "Having your loins girt about with truth," Eph. vi. 14. This shows us the christian in his *militant state*, engaged in warfare with his three-fold enemy; and reminds us,—that opposition is to be expected, ch. iv. 12—14;—that we should be always prepared for resistance, ch. v. 8, 9;—and therefore should have all the accompaniments of the girdle of truth; namely, "the breastplate of righteousness," &c., Eph. vi. 10—17; and thus prepared, and praying always, verse 18, should *follow our captain*, and be led to certain victory.

2. "*Be sober*," (or vigilant, Parkhurst,) a state equally distant from stupidity and carelessness, on the one hand, and the rashness of intoxication on the other. The opposite of intoxication by *strong drink.* Drunkenness, a swinish, abominable, ruinous practice, Isa. xxviii. 1—8; Prov. xxiii. 31, 32; 1 Cor. vi. 10. The opposite of intoxication *by excessive passion*, whether fear, anger, love or any other, Prov. xvi. 32; James i. 19. And consequently the opposite of intoxication by *worldly cares*, compounded of unholy love, desire, fear, anxiety, &c., in fearful and fatal mixture; or by *carnal pleasure*, which enervates and destroys, Luke xxi. 34; Isa. v. 11, 12; 1 Tim. v. 6.—This wakeful sobriety is *valuable*, inasmuch as it enables a person to see his danger, and to provide against it; and to perceive his advantages, and avail himself of them. And it is *necessary;* because without this the mind must be so distracted, as to be a prey to every enemy; and especially to our vigilant and crafty spiritual foes.

3. "*Hope to the end.*" We speak here of the *duty* of hoping or trusting amidst difficulties and discouragements. God gives grace; it is our place to exercise it on proper grounds afforded. Here they had to repose on the *work of redemption performed*, ver. 3, 16; the *word of promise afforded*, ver. 10—12, 25; and the *blessed effects* already produced in their experience, ver. 7, 8. This leads us to

II. THE CHRISTIAN'S EXPECTATION;—"The grace that is to be brought," &c. The word "grace," means any favor or benefit; the *revelation* of Jesus Christ, his coming to judgment, called ver. 7, "his *appearing.*"

1. The word "*revelation*," seems to refer to his *appointment* by him who makes the revelation,—the eternal Father who has appointed the day, and committed all judgment to the Son, Acts xvii. 31; 1 Tim. vi. 15, 16.

2. And it would lead us to consider the *manner*, the *purposes*, and the *results* of this revelation.—The manner *awfully glorious:* in the Judge's announcement, attendants, equipage, &c. Not now as formerly, Isa. liii. 2; John i. 10, but with the trump of God, angels, flaming fire, &c., Luke ix. 26; 1 Thess. iv. 16, 17; 2 Thess. i. 7, 8; Rev. xx. 11—13.—The purposes *awfully righteous:* to manifest the holiness and equity of God's government;—to convince and confound the ungodly,—and to vindicate the righteous against the accusations of Satan and his sons, Matt. xxv. 1—40. Jude 15; Rev. xii. 9, 10.—The results *awfully transporting or terrific:* Matt. xiii. 41—50, xxv. 41—46. In the one case, all the bliss of heaven; in the other, all the woes of hell.

3. But this will be throughout to the saints, a revelation *of grace* Their bodies shall be *graciously* changed, Phil. iii. 12. In the separation, they

50

shall be *graciously* placed on the right. In *gracious* accents shall their **Redeemer** express his approval. Angels shall *graciously* conduct them; and Jesus graciously " present them before the presence of his glory ;" &c. And in every case the grace shall be heightened *by contrast.* We would therefore,

1. Propose the solemn questions, Rom. ii. 3—10.
2. Enforce the important advice, "Acquaint *now*," &c., Job xxii. 21. And then urge the apostle's exhortation in our text, and join in his prayer, chap. v. 10, 11.

THE SABBATH

Exodus xx. 8.—Remember the Sabbath day, to keep it holy. (Sk.

EVERY command of God is reasonable as it is divine ; and is enjoined no less from regard to human happiness, than to secure the glory of the great Lawgiver. Those generally termed the ten commandments, stand prominently conspicuous in the sacred volume; and from the manner in which they were announced, the frequency with which they are introduced, and their essential connection with all good conduct, they present the strongest claims on our attention. You are aware, that our text forms a part of this sacred code, that it stands among these commandments, and is found in a part of the divine records which gives an account of God's delivering his law to mortals ; and that it has the sanction which accompanies the mandates of heaven.

The institution of the Sabbath-day, and *the manner in which we should regard it*, are the topics which our text embraces ; and those which now demand our serious attention.

THE INSTITUTION OF THE SABBATH.

1. By the Sabbath, we understand, a day rendered sacred, on account of divine appointment, and comprising, successively, a seventh portion of our time.
2. The institution of such a day, is not only divine; but, in order of time, it is prior to all other institutions which have a moral bearing on human conduct. Indeed, we trace its origin to the highest possible date, for the first seventh day was a Sabbath ; blessed, sanctified, and kept: see Gen. ii. 2, 3.
3. No farther mention is made of the Sabbath-day, until Exod. xvi. 23 , where it is referred to in such a manner, as shows, that Moses, at least, was well acquainted with its sacred character. Renewed sanction was given to this ordinance, when, as in the account before us, it was announced among, and made one of the ten words, or commandments, delivered with such awful authority as the context records. It is observable, however, that this command, in its introduction, is referred to as a thing well known; so much the word " remember," naturally suggests.
4. Admitting that there were peculiarities connected with the observance of this day among the Jews, and that some other days were termed Sabbaths in the Jewish ritual ; suppose that some superstitious pretences respecting this day, when our Saviour was upon earth, were exploded by him ; see Matt. xii. 1 ; Luke vi. 1, and xiii. 10 ; and John v. 1 ; and that he who

is the Lord of the Sabbath, changed the day from the seventh to the first; the day on which he arose from the dead; see John xvi. 12; Acts i. 2, 3; Matt. xxviii. 1; Acts xx. 7; 1 Cor xiv. 1; Rev. i. 10; will any, or all of such circumstances, bear us out in the disregard of an institution, so sacredly enjoined by God, and so importantly useful to the man? As well might we reject the precepts of justice because the Author of our mild dispensation substituted "Resist not evil," in the place of, "An eye for an eye, and a tooth for a tooth;" or leave off divine worship, because an apostle said, "Let no man judge you, in respect of an holy day, or of the new moon, or of the Sabbath-days;" and abandon all christian ordinances, because the weak, or the wicked, blend superstition with observance, and are reproved by heaven for such conduct.

5. The manner in which a violation of this day was punished, Num. xv. 32—36; the reproofs given to those who treated it with inattention, Neh. xii. 17, 18; Ezek. xx. 21, xxii. 8, and xxiii. 38; and the promise made to such as should keep it holy, Isa. lvi. 2, 4, 6, 7, and lv. 13, 14; show, that the man who trifles with the sacredness of its appointment, exposes himself, in no small degree, to the divine displeasure. Let me, therefore, have your continued, and most serious attention, while I endeavor to show,

II. THE MANNER IN WHICH WE SHOULD REGARD IT. This is expressed in the text, by the words, "keep it holy;" which must signify—*that the day should be separated from all common uses; and that it should be dedicated to services of a religious nature.*

1. *The former of these ideas is minutely illustrated in the subsequent part of the commandment;* "In it thou shalt not do any work," &c. From which we learn, that the Sabbath is as much violated by us, if we employ our servants, or cattle, in ordinary purposes on that day, as if we were thus engaged ourselves. It is necessary, however, to observe, that works of real necessity were allowed: and that this is rendered evident—by the very nature of things;—by the conduct of those who were most strict in their attention to the Sabbath;—and by the sanction of the Lord Jesus himself; see Matt. xii. 11; Luke xiii. 15; John vii. 22.

2. *The dedication of the day to religious services,* is next to be considered. That such an idea is contained in the phrase, "keep it holy," appears evident from the following consideration:—As no common occupation was to engage the time or attention of individuals on this day, something religious must, or idleness would be the necessary consequence. *It appears demonstrable from Leviticus* xxiii. 2, 3, that on this day, the worship of God was to be publicly celebrated; and that such worship was to engage the attention of the people in their dwellings.—*The usages of the Jews,* as recorded by the evangelists, make it clear, that they did employ the Sabbath for such a purpose; see Luke iv. 16, and xiii. 10, and vi. 3.—And *the conduct of the apostles* shows, that under the christian dispensation, the seventh day, or the first, was regularly occupied in the worship of God: see Acts xiii. 14—42, and 44, and xvi. 13, xvii. 1, 2, xviii. 14, and xx. 7. *The custom of the church of Christ,* in all ages, might be adduced; but this appears unnecessary, as the most common reference to ecclesiastical history will satisfy any candid inquirer.

3. That works of mercy and of charity, whether they respect the bodies or the souls of men, are suitable exercises for some parts of the sacred day, none, I presume, will question. However, *to keep the Sabbath-day holy,* is not merely to abstain from common concerns, and to give regular attention to the externals of divine worship, but amidst all, to *worship God in*

spirit and in truth; and to consider the day and the services, as **peculiarly** belonging to God.

Let me exhort you, then " Remember the Sabbath-day, to keep it holy."

Do not *forget* the sacred day ; or merely remember it, to treat it with profanity.

Remember it—because God commands you to do it;—because it is a most salutary institution;—because the Sabbath is a day highly honored of God;—because awful judgments have arrested many in the profanation of it;—because it is a type of heaven's eternal rest.

OBSERVANCE OF THE SABBATH ENJOINED.

Isaiah lviii. 13, 14.—If thou turn away thy foot from the Sabbath, from doing thy pleasure on my holy day ; and call the Sabbath a delight, The holy of the Lord, Honorable ; and shalt honor him, not doing thine own ways, nor finding thine own pleasure, nor speaking thine own words : then shalt thou delight thyself in the Lord ; and I will cause thee to ride upon the high places of the earth, and feed thee with the heritage of Jacob thy father : for the mouth of the Lord hath spoken it. (H. H.)

THAT the observance of the Sabbath was intended to be of universal and perpetual obligation, does not admit of any reasonable doubt. It was enjoined to man in Paradise: and the commandment relating to it, when renewed to man at Mount Sinai, was, like all the other moral commandments, written by God himself on tables of stone. The Jewish prophets spake of it as to be continued under the gospel dispensation: see ch. lvi. 1, 4, 6 ; and the apostles evidently continued the observance of it, transferring it only from the last day of the week to the first, in commemoration of our Lord's resurrection from the dead, and of the work of redemption which was thereby completed. See John xx. 19, 26. Acts xx. 7. 1 Cor. xvi. 2. The ceremonial laws relating to it are abrogated ; but the moral part of it is as much in force as ever.

In the passage before us we may see,

I. IN WHAT LIGHT WE SHOULD VIEW THE SABBATH—

The estimation in which it should be held is here variously expressed: we are taught to account that day,

1. Holy—

Whatever was consecrated to God under the law was accounted holy : it was separated from all profane or common use, and was employed solely for the ends and purposes for which it had been thus set apart. Thus the Sabbath, being consecrated to the especial service of God, is called in our text " God's holy day ;" and, " The holy of the Lord." In the New Testament also it is called, " The Lord's day." Rev. i. 10. Hence it is obvious, that every part of it is to be regarded as the Lord's property, and to be improved for him alone. We should feel a veneration for it, precisely as we should for any thing else that had been dedicated to the Lord : and, as we shudder at the impiety of Belshazzar in using, at a feast, the sacred vessels which he had taken from Jerusalem, though he himself was not a worshipper of Jehovah ; much more must we, who acknowledge the sanctity of the Sabbath, shudder at the thought of alienating any portion of it from Him, to whom it exclusively belongs.

2. Honorable—

If any man, under the law, had regarded the temple, the sacrifices, and the vessels of the sanctuary, in no other light than as a common house, or common utensils, or common food, he would have been considered as greatly dishonoring God. Thus the very sanctity of the Sabbath should render it "honorable" in our estimation; and we should labor to "honor it" by every possible expression of our regard.

3. Delightful—

The arrival of that day should be greeted by us with holy joy: we should say, "This is the day that the Lord has made; we will rejoice and be glad in it." If we could suppose an angel sent down to this lower world to labor in some common occupation, and permitted every seventh day to return to his heavenly abodes, and spend that day in the employments suited to his taste, with what delight would he look forward to the stated returns of that day! So should it be with us; and so it *will* be, in proportion as we have attained to the views and dispositions of those blessed spirits. Not that we should delight in it merely as a day of rest to the body, but as a day wherein God calls us, like Moses, to come up and commune with him on his Holy Mount: and, instead of abridging it, or complaining of it as long and wearisome, we should rather say, with Peter, "It is good for us to be here:" and should almost regret the arrival of the period when we must descend from the Mount, to the less-pleasing occupations of time and sense.

But we will proceed to state more particularly,

II. In what manner we should employ it—

In what manner we should *not* employ it, is here distinctly told us—

Worldly business, and carnal pleasure, and unprofitable conversation, are all expressly proscribed: "we must not do our own ways, nor find our own pleasure, nor speak our own words." On all the other days of the week we may find time for these things; but on the Sabbath-day they are to be excluded altogether. It is a grievous mistake to imagine, that after the public services of the day we are at liberty to engage in vain pursuits, invented only to beguile the time, which otherwise would be a burthen upon our hands: there are pursuits proper to the day; and in them exclusively should our time be occupied. We do not mean to say, that such things as can neither be anticipated nor postponed may not be done with innocence: for even under the law, a latitude was allowed in relation to "what every man must eat." Exod. xii. 16. In reference to such things as are really necessary, we are authorized to say, that "God will have mercy, and not sacrifice:" but it becomes all to be on their guard, that they do not deceive their own souls; for God can easily distinguish the hidden motives of the heart; and will surely judge our actions as good or evil, according as their quality shall be found in his eyes. If the infringement of the Sabbath be reluctant, as in the extinguishing of a fire, or in the exercise of compassion to man or beast, it is well; but if we be actuated by considerations of ease, or interest, or pleasure, to alienate from God any of that time which ought to be consecrated to his service, we may be assured that we must answer for it in the day of judgment.

Our one aim on that day must be, to "honor God"—

The services which we are to render to our God on that day are various, and all compatible with each other. The first undoubtedly are *private:* we should give ourselves in a more peculiar manner to reading, to meditation, to prayer. On every day we should search the scriptures, but more especially on that day; applying them to our own hearts, examining ourselves by them,

397

and intreating God to make them effectual for the conversion and salvation of our souls. From our closets we should go to worship God in *public*, and to testify before all, our regard for his authority, and our delight in his service. Whilst engaged in the various offices of prayer, or hearing of the word, or of communicating at the table of the Lord, we should be particularly careful that the frame of our minds be suited to the employment in which we are engaged; lest, whilst we profess to be serving God, we be found only mocking and insulting him by hypocritical professions. In the intervals, when we are disengaged from private or public duties, we may relieve our minds, and improve our time, in such as are of a social nature. The visiting of the sick, the comforting of the afflicted, the instructing of the rising generation, and, above all, the endeavoring to teach our children and servants, and to "bring them up in the nurture and admonition of the Lord," are services well pleasing to God, and admirably suited to the sanctity of that holy day. It is much to be feared that this latter duty in particular is sadly neglected, even in religious families; and that the great predilection that has been manifested by the religious world for public services, has brought into disuse those more self-denying offices which formerly occupied a considerable portion of the Sabbath-day. But, in whichever of these duties we are occupied, our great aim must be, to "honor God;" demeaning ourselves as in his more immediate presence, and endeavoring to approve ourselves to him as faithful servants.

And shall the Sabbath, in this view of it, be accounted a day of gloom! No; we shall have far other sentiments of it, if we consider,

III. The benefits we may expect from a due observance of it—

Whatever reference there may be in our text to the return of the Jews from their captivity in Babylon, we cannot doubt but the promises here made have a higher and more spiritual import. In them we are assured, that, if we really keep the Sabbath as we ought, we shall be blessed with,

1. Delight in God—

There is not any thing which God more delights to honor than a due observance of the Sabbath. We may perform the outward duties of that day, and reap no material benefit: but if we truly and earnestly endeavor to honor God in the way before described, God will draw nigh to us, and reveal himself to us, and fill us with joy and peace in believing. And here we confidently make our appeal to all who have ever labored to spend a Sabbath to the Lord, whether they have not found such a measure of grace and peace flowing into their souls, as has abundantly recompensed their utmost exertions? Who must not acknowledge that one day thus spent in the courts and in the service of Jehovah, is better than a thousand passed amongst the vain delights of this world? Ps. lxxxiv. 4, 10. And where the Sabbath is thus habitually honored, we will venture to say, that such happiness will at times flow into the soul, as David experienced, when he said, "My soul shall be satisfied as with marrow and fatness, whilst my mouth praiseth thee with "joyful lips:" Ps. lxiii. 5; yes, "they shall be satisfied with the fatness of God's house; and he will make them drink of the river of his pleasures." Ps. xxxvi. 8.

2. Victory over our spiritual enemies—

This seems to be the import of that expression, "I will cause thee to ride upon the high places of the earth:" compare Deut. xxxii. 13, and xxxiii. 29; and it shall be fulfilled to all who conscientiously improve their Sabbaths to the glory of their God. Too many of those who profess religion, are, it must be confessed, scarcely, if at all, advancing in the divine life: their evil dispositions still retain such an ascendant over them, as to make them go on heavily all their days. But, if we were to inquire how they spent their Sabbaths, and what efforts they made to glorify God in their public, private, and social duties, we should soon find the reason of their slow progress. As our Lord said of some particular evil spirits, "These go not out, but by prayer and fasting," so we may say of the evils which are predominant in many professors of religion. They do not give way, because such slight efforts are made upon the Sabbath to subdue them. If that day were truly and entirely devoted to the Lord, Satan would no longer retain the ungodly as his vassals, nor be able to exert so much influence over those who have professedly cast off his yoke.

3. The full possession of the heavenly Canaan—

That land which was given to Jacob for his inheritance, was typical of the Canaan that is above, which truly "floweth with milk and honey." And it may be safely affirmed, that no person who conscientiously employed his Sabbaths here, ever did, or ever can, fall short of the heavenly rest. Thousands who have perished by the hand of the public executioner, have traced their shame and misery to a neglect of the Sabbath: but never was an instance known of one who duly improved his Sabbaths being left to die under the dominion of his sins. Indeed the services of the Sabbath cannot possibly consist with indulged and wilful sin: on the contrary, they are both a preparation for heaven, and a foretaste of it: on earth the saints behold their God by faith, but in heaven they will behold him face to face: on earth they, as it were, learn and rehearse their parts: and in heaven they will join the full chorus of saints and angels in everlasting hallelujahs to God and to the Lamb.

SEE hence,

1. How reasonable are the requirements of God in his gospel!

Had God required six days out of the seven to be spent in such exercises, it would have been highly reasonable that we should obey him: how much more when he gives us six for earthly business, and requires only one to be consecrated entirely unto him! If the services of that day were ever so painful, they might well be claimed by Him who has done such great things for us: and how much more when they are so delightful and so profitable! Grudge him not then that day, nor any portion of it: but let it be wholly and unreservedly devoted to his service.

2. How just will be the condemnation of those who disobey them!

A person who has attained to fifty years of age, has had *above seven years of Sabbaths.* O what blessings might not have been secured in that time, if all those Sabbaths had been sanctified to the Lord! and what judgments does not he merit, who has wasted all of them in a wilful neglect of God! Little as we think of Sabbaths now, we shall find ere long, that the profaning of them has greatly increased our guilt and misery. The Lord grant that this day may not pass away as so many others have done, unprofitably to our souls; but let it be to every one of us a preparation for our eternal rest!

CHILDREN INSTRUCTED TO FEAR GOD.

Psalm xxxi r. 11.—Come, ye children, hearken unto me; I will teach you the fear of the Lord. (B.)

SUCH was once the language of a king, a "man after God's own heart," and a prophet. What a commendation is contained in these words of all schools and institutions, the object of which is the religious instruction of children and young persons!

Inquire we,

I. WHAT WE ARE TO UNDERSTAND BY "THE FEAR OF THE LORD."

"Fear," like hope, desire, love, joy, or sorrow, is an affection of the human soul, and is good or bad, laudable, or the contrary, according as the object by which it is excited is good or bad, and according to the degree in which it is excited. The fear here spoken of has God for its object, and cannot be excessive, if it be of the right kind. For, we can no more *fear* than we can love, or desire, or rejoice in him too much, or expect too great things from him; supposing our fear of him be rational and scriptural.

It must not be a fear of terror or dread, unless we be going on in sin, and be under its guilt and power, in which case it is quite proper we should be afraid of his wrath.— — —

Nor is it a fear of timidity, dejection, and discouragement; unless that we must be discouraged from hoping for prosperity, protection, or happiness, while we continue in a state of enmity and disobedience to him.

Nor is it a fear of diffidence, distrust, or suspicion, as if he would not fulfil his promises, or make good his word.

But it is a fear of reverence; from a sense of his glory and majesty. Jer. x. 7; Heb. xii. 28.—Of awe and concern, from a sense of his power, wisdom, holiness, justice, and of our ignorance, sinfulness, and guilt. Jer. v. 21, 22. Matth. x. 28.—Of subjection; termed a "godly fear;" Heb. xii. 28; from a sense of his goodness, as well as power and wisdom, producing a disposition to obey him. Isa. l. 10.—Of watchfulness and circumspection; from a sense of his omnipresence and omniscience. Prov. xxviii. 14.

With respect to the properties of this fear, we may observe, it is awakening, alarming, humbling, restraining from evil, constraining to good.

The whole of religion is here meant by the fear of God. This is generally termed the "fear of God" in the Old Testament, Gen. xx. 11. xlii. 18. Ps. xix. 9, and the "love of God" in the New. Gal. v. 6. 1 Cor. xiii. 13.— — —

It is religion in the heart, and in experience; in opposition to that in the head, and in speculation merely.—In reality and in practice; in opposition to that in profession, and in pretence.—Internally, and in power; in opposition to that externally, and in form.—In its principle and source, therefore, steady and permanent; in opposition to that which is assumed, inconstant, and transitory.

II. HOW IT APPEARS THAT IT IS OF IMPORTANCE TO TEACH THIS TO CHILDREN AND OTHERS.

It is infinitely reasonable that we should reverence a Being so glorious, stand in awe of one so powerful and holy, be subject to one so good, be watchful under the eye of one so omniscient. All the divine perfections and the relations in which he stands to us, show the reasonableness of the particulars above mentioned, as comprehended in the fear of God.

It is in its beginning, the "beginning of wisdom;" in its progress, the progress of wisdom. Thus David, Ps. cxi. 10, Solomon, Prov. i. 7, ix. 10, and Job, ch. xxviii. 28.

This, and only this, raises man above the brute creatures. They reason, in a measure, as well as man, but are not capable of religion. It is this, above every thing, which ennobles, and perfects human nature.

It provides a remedy for the follies and actual misconduct, into which we naturally fall, in the government of our minds and actions, as also the irregularity and exorbitancy of the appetites and passions.— — —

It imparts a higher excellence and value to all human attainments, and directs us, in the employment of them, to regard the interest of our fellow creatures, and the glory of God.— —

It is the means of providing, most effectually, for our comfort in the present life, and for our everlasting felicity in the next.— — —

Hence it appears that it is our interest to possess this religion.—*Temporally;* "Godliness having the promise of the life that now is, as well as of that which is to come;" of the necessaries of life; Matt. vi. 33; of all things useful, Ps. lxxxiv. 11, xxxii. 9, 10; of deliverance from trouble, ver. 4—6, 19—*Spiritually;* It makes us partakers of the unsearchable riches of Christ; pardon, the divine favor, adoption, regeneration, progressive renovation, direction in our difficulties, protection in dangers, ver. 7, answers to prayer, deliverance from troubles, ver. 15—18.

Therefore, it is our happiness. We have thereby peace with God, peace of mind, hope of immortality, joy in the Holy Ghost, communion with God, the fellowship of saints, the moderate enjoyment of the creature.

Consider the honor of it. It may, indeed, be attended with reproach among the ignorant and wicked but it is truly to our honor, as it is so reasonable and excellent, and as we thus imitate the wisest and best men that ever lived, the angels of God, and even Christ himself; nay, and thus we become godlike. It will be our eternal glory. Hereby, and hereby only, is our nature advanced to the dignity of which it is capable.—

Consider its amiableness in all, especially in young persons.—

Now, if religion be thus reasonable, wise, advantageous, happy, honorable, we cannot have it too soon — And it is peculiarly for the honor of God, the good of society in general, and the comfort and advantage of their parents and friends in particular, and their own individual comfort, that children and young persons should be religious.

Hence piety towards God, benevolence to man, especially to the rising generation, and even self-interest, should induce us to say, with the royal Psalmist and Prophet, "Come, ye children, hearken unto me: I will teach you the fear of the Lord." I will do it myself, or I will do it by my substitute.—I will contribute from my fortune to have it done, or I will attend myself and see it done. I will promote it every way in my power.

III. How IT MAY BE TAUGHT THEM BEST, MOST SURELY, AND MOST LASTINGLY.

By instruction.—We must instruct them to know themselves, their ignorance, weakness, guilt, depravity.—To know God, his nature and attributes and the relations in which he stands to his creatures.—To know Christ, in his person, and offices, his love, and sufferings.—

We must instruct them to know the way of salvation, the will of God, their duty, and their happiness—To know the scriptures in order thereto.— To read and meditate. 2 Tim. iii. 15, 16.

By reproof, exhortation, corrections, rewards.—
By showing them a good example in all respects.—
By praying with and for them, and putting them on praying for themselves, and habituating them to public, social, family, and private worship.—

GLORIFYING GOD IN ALL THINGS.

l Cor. x. 31.—Whether therefore ye eat, or drink, or whatsoever ye do, do all to the glory of God. (P.)

THE word of God is of inestimable value, as it furnishes us with a comete directory how we may glorify God, and enjoy him for ever. The general rule contained in the text will afford particular direction to every lively christian who is anxious to know how he may best glorify him whose name he bears. The particular occasion of the words may be learned from the context; but they are fully applicable to us, and we may found upon them this grand maxim, that *it is the duty of christians, in all their actions, whether civil or religious, to aim at the glory of God.* It is impossible, indeed, to add to, or diminish from the essential glory of God. No mortal can, by any exertion, add to the splendor of the meridian sun; and it would be equally foolish for any mortal to imagine that he can add any thing to the glory of God. Yet it is not enough for us to be passive instruments here. The heavens, the animal, vegetable, and mineral tribes, display the glory of God *silently;* man is to do it *actively.* Christians are formed anew for this express purpose, that they may be a holy and peculiar people, zealous of good works. Let us apply the maxim I have stated.

I. To RELIGIOUS DUTIES. We are to glorify God,

1. By *believing in the Lord Jesus Christ*—" This is the work of God, that we believe in his Son Jesus Christ." Not to believe God, is to dishonor him—to make him a liar. The gospel is an authoritative system; it is revealed for the *obedience* of faith. Thus Abraham, by being strong in faith, glorified God: in how many instances he did this, his history will inform you. Like him, we must believe that God's promises are true, and that they shall be performed.

2. By *our repentance.* Impenitence dishonors God, by supposing that he winks at sin, or that he does not observe it. By making confession of sin, we give glory to God. We glorify his holiness, by which he hates sin; his omniscience, by which he discovers it. Thus the prodigal honored his father by his confession and his hopes; thus the publican glorified God, while the pharisee glorified himself; thus the thief on the cross honored Christ, and thus all true penitents honor him.

3. By *our obedience* in general. And here true faith is manifested, for faith works by love. God is pleased to esteem himself glorified by the *worship* of his people—" Give unto God the glory due unto his name worship before him in the beauty of holiness." God is dishonored in the world by idolatry, and by the homage rendered to the creature, and it becomes christians to be seen in public engaged in acts of solemn worship. *Prayer* is an act of homage, for in it we own that all our supplies are from him. *Praise*— " Whoso offereth praise, glorifieth me." In the ancient dispensation, all that

402

could excite to gratitude was employed, and it should be still more so in the christian church—*by a devout observance of his holy day*, Isa. lviii. 13,— by an *attentive hearing of his word*: thus Mary honored Christ more than Martha—by *reading* his word with simplicity—by making a *public profession* of our attachment to him—by *uniting with his people*—by *celebrating his dying love*.

4. By *our calm submission* to his chastening rod. None can hope to be exempt from these visitations. But if we "have had fathers of our flesh which corrected us, and we gave them reverence, shall we not much rather be in subjection to the Father of spirits, and live?" He is the ruler of the world, wise and good; it is our duty to glorify him in the fire, when we receive evil from his hand as well as when we receive good. Thus Job glorified him, and said, "The Lord gave, and the Lord hath taken away, blessed be the name of the Lord." Apply the maxim,

II. To CIVIL OR COMMON ACTIONS. Generally speaking, we are to glorify God in these actions, by doing all *in love;* for love is the fulfilling of the law—by our meekness, our patience, our usefulness. Thus we are to "let our light so shine before men, that they, seeing our good works, may glorify our Father which is in heaven."

But more particularly we are to glorify God,

1. In our *actions*. In order to this, they must be *lawful;* they must be pursued at *lawful times*—not performed on the Sabbath, for instance; and in a *lawful degree:* we shall not glorify God by destroying our health, by neglecting the private or public duties of religion, by inattention to our families, &c. We glorify God in the common actions of life.

By *aiming in them all at obedience to his will, and submission to his appointments*. Servants and masters are thus exhorted to serve the Lord Christ, and to do all in his name.

By *seeking for his blessing on all our endeavors*. "Go to now, ye that say we will go into such a city, and continue there a year, and buy and sell, and get gain; for that ye ought to say if the Lord will, we shall live, and do this or that."

By *ascribing all our success entirely to him*. We must not burn incense to our own net. Herod dishonored God when he was so elated with the people's shouting. So did Nebuchadnezzar when he said, "Is not this great Babylon that I have built by the might of my power, and for the honor of my majesty?" So all dishonor God who ascribe to themselves the contrivance, the execution, the completion of their works. We should glorify God,

2. In our *enjoyments*. "Whether ye eat or drink," &c. Not by *excess*, for this would dishonor God and ourselves too, but

By *humbly acknowledging our unworthiness*, as did the poor old woman, who, while eating her crust by the side of a brook of which she was about to drink, exclaimed, "All this and Christ too!" When we sit down to our tables, it becomes us to say, with David, "Who am I, O Lord God, and what is my house, that thou shouldst thus deal with me?"

By *adoring the bounty of God* in bestowing these things upon us. We are to regard them not as the purchase of our money, but as the gifts of his bounty, who as a parent supplies the wants of his children.

By *considering the love of Christ*, who was poor and destitute and self-denying, that we might have all things richly to enjoy.

By *aiming to employ our health* and strength and life to the service of God, that so in all things we may adorn the gospel of God our Saviour.

By *rising from the enjoyment of vanishing pleasures to the contemplation of heavenly satisfactions.* Looking up to Christ as the food of the soul, and longing for the day when we shall eat bread and drink wine in the kingdom of God. INFERENCES —

1. *How is man fallen?* If it be the duty of all to glorify God in all things, what a wretched being is man become! There are some who never perform one action to the glory of God. How displeasing, how dishonorable to God!

2. *How do we all stand in need of pardoning mercy!* We have not only committed *sinful* actions, but what has been *good*, has been done without proper motives, and with too much of self. When we read, when we pray, when we hear, when we give alms, we have often sought our own honor and advantage more than the glory of God. Let us seek forgiveness then.

3. *How necessary is regeneration!* If man by nature is indisposed to seek the glory of God, how important is it that he should be made a new creature, that new powers and dispositions should be infused into his soul, that the love of God should be shed abroad in his heart!

4. *How important is it to bear the rule of the text in mind continually.* Amidst the many things which present themselves to our notice, some are altogether unlawful, and others are inexpedient; but this maxim would always determine us, and set us right. Should two duties present themselves to us at the same time, we need only ask this plain, simple question, "By which of these actions shall I most glorify God?"

CHAPTER VI.

WARNINGS.

SINNERS ADMONISHED.

Prov. i. 23.—Turn you at my reproof: behold, I will pour out my Spirit unto you, I will make my words known unto you. (Sk.)

VARIOUS are the means which the Lord employs to convince the wicked of the error of their ways, and bring them to a knowledge of divine truth. He has not only sent his Son, to seek and to save that which was lost, but he also waits to be gracious; and is "long-suffering, not willing that any should perish, but that all should come to repentance." He, therefore, invites the most abandoned to participate the blessings of his salvation, and encourages them to believe, by the most powerful persuasions and captivating motives;—he mercifully pities the folly, and justly complains of the incorrigible obstinacy of the impenitent;—he frequently visits them with the tokens of his displeasure, and faithfully warns them of the danger to which they are exposed;—but as he is "good to all," he suspends the execution of his wrath, and gives them *space* to repent and believe the gospel; —and as he hath no pleasure in the destruction of sinners, he kindly admonishes them to escape the ruin of sin, and graciously promises the richest blessing to the truly penitent. Such is evidently the import of his affectionate address to mankind, in the language of the text, "Turn you at my reproof," &c. These words also describe the Lord's dealings with his sinful creatures in reference to—*the reproofs he administers—the submission he requires—and the encouragement he imparts.*

I. THE REPROOFS HE ADMINISTERS;—" Turn you at *my reproof.*" We are surrounded with faithful admonishers, who are all *arranged* and *employed* by God, to win the hearts of the disobedient to the wisdom of the just. He reproves us,

1. *By the scriptures.* His word contains the most *pointed* and *salutary* admonitions; it records the appropriate cautions and solemn warnings of Moses and the prophets—of Jesus Christ and his apostles, Rom. xv. 4; 2 Tim. iii. 16, 17.—It also repeatedly sends us for instruction and reproof to the works of creation—to admonitory examples of impiety—and the awful solemnities of death and the grave, Isaiah i. 2, 3; Prov. vi. 6; Matt. xi. 20—24; Deut. xxxii. 29; Eccl. ix. 10;—we are faithfully reproved in every part of the sacred writings. Let us hear and live.

2. *By ministers.* They are sent to warn the wicked of their danger, and show them the way of salvation.—They zealously persuade men by the terrors of the Lord, and encourage them by the promise of the Gospel; —as " ambassadors for Christ," they pray you, in his stead, to be reconciled to God. You have often heard their reproofs—witness their labors—and beheld their tears. But have you taken warning? Have you believed their report? Have you realized the truth of their message? Acts xxvi. 18; Col. i. 28.

3. *By conscience.* This in an *internal* and *universal* monitor—it is always with us, and cannot be silenced—it is a *witness* to all our proceedings, and irresistibly *arraigns* and *condemns* the guilty culprit, Rom. ii. 15. It speaks with *sovereign authority*, and its awful criminations fill the trembling sinner with inexpressible *anguish* and *bitterness* of soul, Prov. xviii. 14. Has it not often accused you of crimes, alarmed your fears, and warned you of approaching danger? Does it not frequently testify of your sinful state, and assure you that except you repent you must perish?

4. *By providence.* There is a perfect *harmony* between the purposes of God, and the arrangement of his works. "Day unto day uttereth speech, and night unto night showeth knowledge." The Lord often reproves us by pious parents—family connections—and godly neighbors. He also admonishes us, by afflictions and difficulties, to teach us the frailty of nature—the folly of sin—and the vanity of the world. The continual dissolution of our fellow-mortals, speaks loudly to survivors, and says to all, " prepare to meet your God—be ye also ready," &c. The *gracious design* of the Divine reprover will appear by considering,

II. THE SUBMISSION HE REQUIRES. "*Turn you* at my reproof." Through sin we have all forsaken the Lord, and " gone astray like lost sheep;" but he kindly *reproves* our folly, and *invites* us to return unto him,

1. *With penitent hearts.* We cannot come to him on the ground of *innocence* or personal worthiness; and as *guilty sinners* we ought to approach him " with broken and contrite hearts;" which are sacrifices highly becoming the creature, and always acceptable to the Creator, Ps. li. 17.—Genuine repentance includes—conviction of sin—humiliation of soul—compunction of spirit—holy indignation and shame—and humble confession to God, Luke xv. 17—19; 1 John i. 8, 9. " Repent ye, therefore, and be converted."

2. *With believing minds.* Jesus Christ is the *only way* to the Father, and the *medium* of all spiritual blessings;—through him, therefore, we

must return to God, *believing* in his name, and *trusting* in his merits;—it is by faith we credit the gospel—embrace the Saviour—and realize salvation, John iii. 18: Acts xvi. 31. " He that believeth shall be saved ;" for Christ is "able to save them to the uttermost that come unto God by him."

3. *With fervent devotion.* The Lord must be sought by earnest prayer, as the object of adoration and the source of blessedness ; though he knows our necessities, yet he will be inquired of for the communication of his blessings. We should call upon him sincerely—humbly—confidently—fervently—and diligently.—Prayer eminently distinguishes the character of every returning penitent, and God will assuredly hear and answer their requests, Luke xviii. 13 ; Acts ix. 11 ; Matt. vii. 7, 8.

4. *With prompt obedience.* The service of God, and the paths of sin, are *incompatible*, and can never be reconciled, Matt. vi. 24;—we must, therefore, cease to do evil, and learn to do well.—Religion requires a *universal* renunciation of the *principles* and *habits* of vice, and an entire devotedness to God, both of heart and life, Isa. lv. 6, 7 ; Titus ii. 12 ; Luke i. 74, 75. We should be induced thus to turn to God by,

III. THE ENCOURAGEMENT HE IMPARTS. " Behold I will pour out my Spirit," &c. This promise is highly important and comprehensive. The participation of the Holy Ghost is an inestimable privilege which includes every *holy principle* that he implants, and every *gracious disposition* which he inspires. The Spirit of God is,

1. *A convincing Spirit.* Under *this* character he is poured out upon all mankind, John xvi. 8—11. It is his special province to open the eyes of our understanding, that we may understand the scriptures ;—by him the Lord makes "known his *words* unto us ;"—he imparts a spiritual *discernment*, that we may discover our real state and character, and comprehend " the truth as it is in Jesus," 1 Cor. ii. 10—12.

2. *A quickening Spirit.* He removes the death of sin, and infuses the life of grace ;—he graciously dwells in his people, and by his *vital influence* they are born again, and become new creatures ;—he witnesses their adoption, and fills them with " the fruits of righteousness," Rom. viii. 15, 16; Gal. v. 22, 23. It is the Spirit *quickeneth* and *giveth life* and peace to the soul, Eph. ii. 1.

3. *A comforting Spirit.* All real consolation is *divine* in its author, and *spiritual* in its nature ;—it is the immediate *production* and fruit of the Holy Ghost, Rom. xiv. 17 ;—he communicates ample support and comfort in every time of need ;—he is. therefore, repeatedly styled "the Comforter." Through his sacred energy, we receive joy and peace in believing; and " rejoice evermore—pray without ceasing—and in every thing give thanks."

4. *A sanctifying Spirit.* He is justly denominated the " Spirit of holiness ;"—all his operations are *hallowing*, and productive of christian *purity ;*—he transforms the soul into the image and glory of God, Titus iii. 5 ; 2 Cor. iii. 18.—His baptismal fire *consumes* sin, and *purifies* the sinner, Matt. iii. 11, 12 ;—he sanctifies his people *wholly*, and preserves them *blameless*, unto the coming of our Lord Jesus Christ, 1 Thess. v. 23. Let us therefore now consider our ways, and turn unto the Lord, that we may receive the gift of the Holy Ghost, which he has promised to them that repent and call upon his name, Luke xi. 13.

A CAUTION AGAINST DECEPTION.

Deut. xi. 16.—Take heed to yourselves, that your heart be not deceived. (Sk)

IT is one essential characteristic in christian charity, that it "suffereth long and is kind." It not only suffers all the insults, provocations, and maliciousness of a persecuting world; but all the frailties, imperfections, and errors of the children of God. And never was there a more illustrious example of this long-suffering charity than Moses, who dictated the sentiment in the text. He had for a series of years borne with the insults of Israel. He had instructed them in their ignorance, he had reclaimed them in their wanderings, he had interceded for them in their dangers, and now, though about to be taken from them, and go up unto mount Nebo, over against Jericho, to die there; yet he is most tenderly concerned for their future welfare. In this chapter, after having reminded Israel of what God had done for them, ver. 4, 5, 6, 7, he directs them to consider what he was about to do, verse 10. And knowing the propensity which they had to neglect their immortal interests, and turn aside after other gods, he urges upon their attention the sentiment in the text, "Take heed to yourselves," &c. We notice here,

I. AN EVIL ANTICIPATED. That of having the heart deceived.

II. A CAUTION URGED AGAINST IT. "Take heed to yourselves," &c.

To be deceived is to be imposed upon, deluded, brought into error, so as to be led to entertain ideas and sentiments inconsistent with the truth. Men generally are liable to be deceived. We may be deceived *concerning ourselves;* we may think of ourselves more highly than we ought to think, and give ourselves credit for the possession of virtues to which we are total strangers: we may be vain in our imaginations, suppose that we are wise, when in God's sight we are fools; and think ourselves safe, when danger is at the very door. We may be deceived, *concerning God.* Concerning *his nature;* we may say in our hearts that there is no God, or imagine that God is altogether such a one as ourselves. Concerning *his laws;* we may think that they are not as pure, as spiritual, and as extensive as they really are. We may be deceived *concerning religion.* We may substitute mere morality, a sound creed, or a pompous profession, instead of a saving conversion to God, and a sanctification of the soul to his service. These, with a thousand other deceptive suggestions, and erroneous thoughts, may occupy our minds, and lead us astray. In proof of the possibility of deception in reference to the concerns of our souls, we observe,

1. *The scantiness and imperfection of human knowledge.* Absolute knowledge precludes the possibility of deception; if we knew every thing, and every thing perfectly, we could not be deceived. But what little we do know, we know very imperfectly. With the objects of sense we are most intimately acquainted, but our eyes, and ears, and palate, and feelings, have deceived us. Religion requires the exercise of the intellectual faculties, and as our knowledge is so limited and defective, we may be deceived. We infer it,

2. *From the deceitfulness of the heart.* "The heart is deceitful above all things." A deceived heart turns us aside. Hence we are in love with deception, and will not come to the light that our deeds might be manifest. When Elisha told Hazael of the horrible acts of cruelty that he would commit in after life, he so far thought it impossible that he should ever arrive at such a climax in crime, as to rip up women with child, that he said, "What!

Is thy servant a dog that he should do this great thing?" 2 Kings viii. 12 13. The possibility of being deceived, appears,

3. *From the deceitfulness of sin.* Sin is deceitful. It promises rewards, but pays punishment; and it would lose its power, could we strip it of its deceit. Hence it seldom appears in its own native character, or is designated by its own legitimate title. Revenge is called honor; covetousness, frugality; luxury and extravagance, good living; lust and obscenity, innocent liberties; and there is scarcely a crime committed, but what has some of its malignity softened down, to render it more fascinating and deceptive; and as proofs of the deceitfulness of sin, we might advert to the pleas and subterfuges to which men resort in order to conceal it from the public eye, or lessen its evil when detected. Because sin is so deceitful, we are liable to be deceived. We infer it also,

4. *From the deceitfulness of the world.* The great mass of mankind are involved in deception. Every sinner is a deceiver, he deceives himself, and labors to deceive others. He sports himself with his own deceivings. Would men deliberately prefer darkness to light, bondage to liberty, peril to safety, and misery to happiness, if they were not most awfully deceived? Would acts of sin, and crimes of the most heinous character be extolled, and idolized; and acts of piety be defamed and scandalized, if delusions deep as hell had not seized their unhappy subjects? How few men *appear* to be what they are in reality! How many would shudder at the thought of appearing in their true character! How much moral deformity is often concealed beneath a decent, and perhaps a religious exterior! How many whited walls and painted sepulchres present themselves to our view! We are also liable to be deceived,

5. *From the deceitfulness of the devil.* The devil is the most deceitful being in existence. All the deception upon earth owes its origin to his influence. He is the deceiver of the nations. He deceived Eve, the mother of us all, and he has been practicing the same infernal policy, in all climes and ages. And his success has been without a parallel. Such are the reasons we have for believing that our hearts may be deceived. But the text assumes that this deception is an evil pregnant with very pernicious consequences. And this appears from the consideration, that *those whose hearts are deceived are involved in a state of the most palpable error.* Error of any kind is to be deplored. What tradesman would wish to make errors in his accounts? What scholar that would not guard against error in his sums? But these errors are trivial, when compared to the grievous error in which those are involved whose hearts are deceived; who are deceived concerning their souls, their salvation, and their God. Nor is this all; those whose hearts are deceived, are exposed to extreme danger. "He that converteth a sinner from the error of his ways, shall save a soul from death." The death of the soul is a tremendous death; a double death, a second death; and to this death every sinner whose heart is deceived is constantly exposed: "Wo unto them that call evil good," &c.: "therefore as the fire devoureth the stubble," &c., Isa. v. 20—24. See the verse subsequent to the text. Let us examine,

II. THE CAUTION URGED AGAINST THIS DECEPTION. "Take heed to yourselves," &c.

1. *Be alive to a sense of your extreme danger.* No man will use caution where he suspects no danger. Our senses furnish us with intimations of the dangers to which the body is exposed; but alas! to the dangers of the soul, though infinitely more alarming, we are too frequently insensible

408

Who that surveys the mirth, and jollity, and merriment of the multitude would at all suspect that they were in any danger, or exposed to any peril? But who that reads the Bible with attention can fail to be convinced, that we are threatened with the most tremendous punishment? Now in order that we may take heed to ourselves, let us be broad awake to our danger. Let us consider what we are,—how deeply fallen! Let us weigh well our circumstances, dangers, and enemies; this will lay the foundation for caution and circumspection.

2. *Seek for the illuminating and sanctifying influences of the Holy Spirit.* The mind of man is so completely darkened by the deceitfulness of sin, that he has naturally no perceptions of his danger; but the Holy Ghost opens the eyes of our understanding, and we see the truth, and begin to know ourselves. But illumination alone is not sufficient; our powers must be renewed, we must become new creatures in Christ Jesus. Your danger may be perceived, but without the renewal of your hearts in righteousness, you will possess no mental energy to avoid it. The Holy Ghost will illuminate and sanctify you. O seek his influence by fervent, importunate prayer. "Take heed to yourselves."

3. *By the constant practice of self-examination.* Examine yourselves whether ye be in the faith. Whether you have the fruits of faith. Whether you are the followers of them who through faith and patience have inherited the promises Examine yourselves *faithfully :* self-love leads us to look partially on ourselves ;—*frequently :* never suffer a day to pass over your heads without an investigation of your conduct. It was the advice of an old heathen,

> " Let not the stealing god of sleep surprise,
> Nor creep in slumber o'er thy weary eyes,
> Ere every action of the former day,
> Strictly thou dost and righteously survey."

" Take heed to yourselves,"

4. *By watching over yourselves.* "Watch and pray." " Be ye therefore sober, and watch unto prayer." " Watch thou in all things." These are scriptural directions, and were addressed to the primitive saints. Watchfulness will lead you to keep a strict guard over your thoughts. Your thoughts will wander on forbidden objects, but by watchfulness you will detect them : vain, foolish, and lascivious thoughts will seek to obtrude on your attention. Take heed to yourselves in reference to your words and actions.

Conclude, by urging the text on the attention of hearers of all descriptions.

People of all ages, young and old.—Of all circumstances, rich and poor.—Of all relations, husbands and wives, parents and children, masters and servants.—Of all callings, preachers and people.—" Take heed to yourselves.'

THE FOLLY OF A FRUITLESS PROFESSION

Luke vi. 46.—Why call ye me Lord, Lord, and do not the things which I say? (S. S.)

THE honor of Christ and the salvation of our souls depend on our having right views of the gospel!—

We cannot therefore too earnestly insist on the doctrine of justification by faith in Christ—

Nevertheless we should constantly urge the practice of good works as the fruits and evidences of our faith in Christ—

The folly of expecting salvation while we neglect them is strongly represented by our Lord in the text—

I. SHEW WHO THEY ARE THAT DESERVE THE CENSURE IN THE TEXT—

The heathens have less to aggravate their sins than christians—

The greater part of those who live in countries that are evangelized are obnoxious to this censure—

1. Mere nominal christians deserve it.

Many are Christ's as having been devoted to him in baptism—

By the appellation of christians they profess to be his followers—

But they are in no respect subject to his will and word—

Christ commands them to "seek first the kingdom of God," &c. and they seek it last—

2. Formal, self-righteous persons deserve it.

Many will go far in the outward duties of religion—

They will profess too a veneration for the name of Christ—

But he calls them to regeneration, John iii. 3, and they deny their need of it—

He bids them live by faith on him, and it proves an hard saying—John vi. 53, 60.

They are satisfied with the form of godliness, without the power—

3. False professors deserve it.

None are so worthy of reproof as they—

They will talk much of their dependence on Christ—

They will profess perhaps to have experienced much of his power and grace—

They may even glory in the recollection of his truth and faithfulness—

But in the midst of all, they can be proud, covetous, passionate, censorious, unforgiving, deceitful and dishonest—

To such the text may be applied with peculiar energy—

Such persons ought to be addressed with all plainness of speech.

II. EXPOSTULATE WITH THEM ON THE FOLLY OF THEIR CONDUCT.

The service of God is justly called a "reasonable service"—

But a fruitless profession is most unreasonable—

No reason can be assigned "why" persons should rest in such a state.

1. Is not a conformity to Christ's precepts practicable?

Many allege that such strictness as he requires is unattainable—

We allow that absolute perfection is not to be expected in this world—

But an unreserved devotedness of ourselves to God is attainable—

Thousands of the saints of old have walked thus with God—

There is a cloud of living witnesses who exemplify this conduct—

God has promised grace to all who seek it diligently—

2. Is not obedience to him necessary?

We may be good citizens if we possess only the virtues of heathens.—

410

But an unfeigned regard to Christ is necessary to constitute us christians—
St. Paul has fully declared the inefficacy of outward religion—Rom. **ii.**
28, 29.

Judas and the foolish virgins awfully exemplified it—Matt. xxv. **3,**
11, 12.

Our Lord has warned us all respecting it—Matt. vii. 21—23.

3. Will not a feigned allegiance be discovered by him?

We may easily deceive our fellow-creatures—

But every motion of our hearts is visible to Christ—Heb. iv. 13.

Nor can the most specious appearances deceive him—John ii. 24, 25.

In his final judgment he will shew that he was privy to our most secret
thoughts and desires—1 Cor. iv. **5.**

4. Shall we not wish at last that we had been sincere and upright?

The reproach which attends the exercise of real religion, may make us
satisfied with the form of it at present—

But in the day of judgment we shall see our folly—Wisd. v. 1—9.

We shall not know what to reply to this question then—

The vain excuse we now make we shall not even dare to offer—

APPLICATION.

Let all then seek to become christians indeed—

Let us not be afraid to confess our Lord before men—

But let our lives be consistent with our professions—

Let us trust in the Lord as simply as if obedience were *not* required—

Let us obey the Lord as zealously as if obedience *only* were required—

THE EVIL AND DANGER OF BACKSLIDING.

Hos. iv. 16.   Israel slideth back, as a backsliding heifer.   (H. H.)

SUCH is the influence of bad example, that it is extremely difficult to
withstand its attractions, even at the time that we behold its fatal effects.
Israel, or the ten tribes, from their first apostacy under Jeroboam, were ir-
reclaimably addicted to idolatry.   The prophet finding his efforts vain with
respect to them, turns to Judah, and intreats that they would not tread in the
steps of Israel,* who, like an untamed and refractory bullock, had entirely
cast off the yoke, and refused all subjection to Jehovah.

Humiliating as this account of Israel is, it is but too just a representation
of the christian world, whose conduct is utterly unworthy of the name they
bear, and from whose ways we cannot stand at too great a distance.

To impress this awful truth upon your minds, we propose to shew,

I. WHEN WE MAY BE SAID TO RESEMBLE A BACKSLIDING HEIFER—

We owe submission to our heavenly Master; but give too much reason for
the comparison in the text.   This resemblance may be seen in us

1. When we will not draw in God's yoke at all—

Unconverted men in every age and place are rebels against God, Exod.
v. 2.   Ps. xii. 4.   Jer. ii. 31, & vii. 24; and, though all are not equally

---

* Ver 15.   At Gilgal and at Bethel, where God had formerly been worshipped, idols
were now set up.   The prophet, exhorting Judah not to go to those places, calls Beth-el,
(the house of God,) Beth-aven, (the house of vanity.)

profligate in their manners, all are equally averse to spiritual employments: the law of God is considered as imposing on them an intolerable yoke, to which they will not, they cannot submit. Rom. viii. 7. They are indeed subjected to it against their will; but neither chastisements nor encouragements can prevail upon them to draw in it: on the contrary, like a ferocious bullock, they are insensible of favors, and they fret at rebukes. Jer. xxxi. 18.

2. When we draw in it only by fits and starts—

Many appear willing to obey God in a time of sickness, Isa. xxvi. 16, or after some signal deliverance, Psa. cvi. 12, 13, or under an impressive sermon, Exod. xxiv. 3, 7, Jam. i. 24, or during a season of peace and tranquility: Matt. xiii. 21: but, as soon as ever the particular occasion that called forth their pious resolutions has ceased, or they find that they must suffer for Christ's sake, they forget the vows that are upon them, and return to their former state of carelessness and indifference. Psa. lxxviii. 34—37. They renew their resolutions perhaps at certain seasons; but "their goodness is as the morning dew, or as the early cloud that passeth away." Thus, like a heifer that will draw for one moment and will not the next, they are, in the strongest sense of the words, unprofitable servants.

3. When we grow weary of the yoke—

It is not uncommon for persons to go on well for a season, and yet draw back at last. They grow weary of *performing their duties*, of *exercising their graces*, of *mortifying their lusts*. If they maintain an observance of public duties, they become remiss in those of the family and the closet: their delight in the scriptures languishes; their meditations are cold; their devotions formal. Their faith, their hope, their love operate with less vital energy: and their besetting sins, whatever they were, regain their strength, and resume their ascendancy. These are like a horse or bullock, which, after having yielded to the yoke for a season, becomes restive and ungovernable, and disappoints thereby the expectations of its owner.

Lest the frequency of these characters should tempt us to think favorably of them, we proceed to shew,

II. THE EVIL AND DANGER OF SUCH A STATE—

We shall notice,

1. The evil of it—

A backslidden state, in whomsoever it is found, is exceeding sinful; but in those who have made some profession of religion, it is attended with peculiar aggravations.

It is a contemning of God; of his Majesty, which demands our subjection, and of his mercy, which would accept and reward our poor services. And it is in this light that God himself frequently complains of it. Numb. xi. 20; 1 Sam. ii. 30, and 2 Sam. xii. 10; Ps. x. 13.

It is a justifying of the wicked; for it says to them, in fact, "I was once as you are, and thought I should become happier by serving God: but I find by experience that there is no profit in serving him; and therefore I am returning to your state, which is, on the whole, the happier and more desirable."

It is a discouraging of the weak. Little do false professors think how much evil they do in this way. Mal. ii. 8. Many are induced to follow their example in some things, under the idea that they are innocent; and are thus drawn from one sin to another, till they make shipwreck of a good conscience, and utterly turn away from the faith.

And need we multiply words any further to shew the evil of backsliding from God? Well does God himself call it "a wonderful and a horrible thing." Jer. v. 30.

2. The danger of it—

This is an iniquity which God marks with peculiar indignation ; Jer. ii 19, 21, 22 ; and never fails to visit it, sooner or later, with some awful token of his displeasure.

The first symptoms of declension lead, if not speedily mourned over and resisted, *to utter apostacy.* Prov. xiv. 14. The disposition to backslide will soon increase, till it become inveterate, and, unless by a marvellous interposition of God himself, incurable.

The misery that will be incurred by means of it will far exceed all that have been endured, if no profession of religion had been ever made. " If any man draw back," says God, " my soul shall have no pleasure in him : he " draws back to certain and everlasting perdition:" Heb. x. 38, 39; and " it would have been better for him never to have known the way of righteousness, than, after having known it, to turn back from it." Matt. xii. 45. 2 Pet. ii. 21.

Let these consequences be duly weighed, and nothing need be added to shew us the importance of " holding fast our profession without wavering.'

To IMPROVE this subject, we shall,

1. Assist you in ascertaining your state before God—

Since all are " bent to backslide" more or less, it is of great importance to inquire of what kind our backslidings are, and to see whether they are merely the infirmities of an upright soul, or the revolt of an apostate. It is indeed difficult to determine this with precision ; yet something may be said to aid you in this inquiry.

Examine diligently the *cause,* the *duration,* and the *effects* of your backslidings. Those of the sincere arise from the weakness of their flesh, while yet their spirit is as willing as ever: but those of the hypocrite proceed from a radical disaffection to the ways of God. Those of the sincere continue but a little time, and are an occasion of greater diligence : those of the hypocrite remain, and become the habit of his soul. Those of the sincere humble him in the dust: those of the hypocrite produce a blindness of mind, a searedness of conscience, and a hardness of heart.

But though we thus discriminate for the information of your judgment, we recommend all to stand fast in the Lord, and to guard against the first risings of spiritual decay. Gal. vi. 9.

2. Give a word of counsel to those in different states—

Are you altogether backslidden from God? O return to him, and take upon you his " light and easy yoke !" He invites you with all the tenderness of a father ; Jer. iii. 12, 14, 22 ; he declares himself exceedingly averse to punish you according to your desert; Hos. xi. 7, 8 ; and he promises to " heal your backslidings, and love you freely." Hos. xiv. 4.

Are you drawing in his yoke? Bless and adore your God, who has inclined and enabled you to do so. It is his power, and his power alone, that has kept you hitherto: 1 Pet. i. 5; and therefore he must have all the praise. And in order to your continued stedfastness, reflect often on the evil and danger of backsliding; I may add too, on the comfort and benefit of serving God. Surely He is a good Master. Let but your hearts be right with him, and " none of his commandments will appear grievous to you :" 1 John v. 3; on the contrary, you will find that " *in* keeping his commandments there is great reward," Psa. xix. 11, and that your labor shall not be in vain with respect to the eternal world. " Be ye faithful unto death, and he will give you a crown of life." Rev. ii. 10

ADVICE TO BACKSLIDERS.

Rev. iii. 2.—Be watchful, and strengthen the things which remain, that are ready to die.
(S. S.)

THE epistles to the churches of Asia seem descriptive of the state of the
several churches at the time they were written—

But they are for the most part applicable also to other churches—

There are too many societies of christians that resemble that at Sardis—

There was much profession and but little life among them—

This our Lord signified to them in the letter he dictated to St. John—
ver. 1.

On account of it he gave them the salutary admonition in the text.

I. WHEN IT MAY BE SAID THAT THE THINGS WHICH REMAIN IN US ARE
READY TO DIE.

It is here supposed that there were some good things in the Sardian
church, though they were much on the decline—

What is said therefore of their being "dead" must be understood rather
in reference to their *frame* than their *state*—

The things which remain in us are ready to die, *when our graces
languish*—

The exercise of our graces is a sure test both of the reality and degree
of our spiritual life—

We may form a judgment by examining,

Our faith.

The office of faith is to realize invisible things—

When it is vigorous it discovers the comparative value of heaven and
earth—

It regards the promises and threatenings of God as certain—

Hence it stimulates the soul to an active pursuit of its chief good—

But many decline in their apprehension of divine things—

They neither see so clearly, nor feel so powerfully the truths of God as
they once did—

They consequently relax their diligence in the ways of God—

Such persons are evidently in the state of those at Sardis—

Our hope.

Faith sees the reality, and hope anticipates the enjoyment of heavenly
things—

When hope is lively it serves as an anchor of the soul—

It keeps us from fainting under the trials we meet with—

But oftentimes it is suffered to grow dead—

Then the future prospects are less valued—

Earthly things also rise in importance—

We are more discouraged with any difficulties—

We lose our enjoyment of heavenly things—

In this state the things that remain are ready to die—

Our love.

Love is as wings to the believing soul—

It carries us on with ardor and delight—

It makes us entertain low thoughts of all we do—

It excites us to still greater exertions—

But when it decays, we lose our fervor—

Duties become a burden and a task—

They are performed with less frequency and spirituality—
We endure with less concern the hidings of God's face—
We are more indifferent respecting his return to our souls—
What can more strongly indicate the dying state of a soul ?—
Moreover, the things which remain are ready to die, *when our corruptions increase.*
Graces and corruptions are as the scales of a balance—
The growth of corruption argues the decay of the divine life—
And such decay is manifest,
1. When our besetting sin resumes its ascendency.
It is the effect of grace to mortify and subdue our besetting sin—
But that sin is rarely if ever extinguished in this world—
It is generally the first that discovers our declensions—
When that regains its power, we are sure that it is ill with the soul—
2. When our natural hardness and obduracy of heart return
Divine grace brings a tenderness of spirit—
It shews itself by humiliation and contrition—
But sin will blind the eyes, and harden the heart—
In this state we shall feel less compunction *in* or *after* the commission of sin—
When conscience thus fails in its office we are in a dying state indeed—
3. When we are unwilling to be reclaimed
A heart duly impressed desires the light—
But persons in a backslidden state often feel averse to it—
They are backward to be told of their faults—
They are ready to palliate and excuse them—
They willingly expose themselves to the temptations of sin—
This is the worst symptom that a *living* soul can experience—
May God now accompany with his blessing,
II. OUR LORD'S ADVICE TO PERSONS IN SUCH A STATE.
None can more need advice for their bodies, than these for their souls.
1. Be watchful,
Against self-deception
There are many things which may hide our condition from us—
We may easily mistake gifts for graces—
We may attribute to God's Spirit what results from the operation of natural principles—
We may be less sensible of decay because it happens to be gradual—
The heart will suggest many plausible excuses—
It may satisfy itself also with hopes of a speedy revival—
But "be not deceived; God is not mocked"—
Against the occasions of sin.
Many fall by means of their excessive care about worldly business—
Others decline through mixing too much with worldly company—
Too free an use even of lawful things injures many—
But all decay through a neglect of sacred duties—
Be watchful then against occasions of sin—
See the effect which they have produced upon you—
Resist them in future on their first appearance—Prov. iv. 14, 15.
2. Strengthen the things that remain.
Go to Christ for his Spirit.

415

Christ is the only source of spiritual strength*
In vain will be all human endeavors without his aid—
Go then, and plead with him that promise—Jer. iii. 22.
"They that dwell under his shadow shall return," &c.—Hos. **xiv. 7.**
Exercise your graces more diligently.
Every thing improves by exercise—
Put forth therefore your faith, your hope, your love—
'Stir up the gift of God that is in you"—
You will then experience the truth of that promise—2 Pet. i. 10. 11.
Lay home upon your heart the most powerful considerations.
Think how uncomfortable a declining state is; how dishonorable to God, and dangerous to your own souls!
Consider that if God ever restore you, he may do it in such a way as shall be extremely terrible and distressing—
But what if he should "come at an unexpected hour ?"—
Let instant attention then be paid to the direction following the text—Rev. iii. 3.
ADDRESS,
1. To those who have no marks of life in them.
They who are in a declining state are in great danger—
If they be not restored "their last state will be worse than their beginning"—
What danger then must they be in who exercise no graces, and indulge numberless corruptions !—
Oh ! repent, ere it be too late—
2. To those who are enjoying the divine life.
" Be not high-minded, but fear," and be watchful—
"Work out your own salvation with fear and trembling"—
If it be difficult to proceed, it is still more so to recover lost ground—
Remember your strength consists in depending upon Christ—
When you are weak in yourselves then only are you truly strong—
Comfort yourselves with that description of your almighty Guardian—Jude 24.

ON EATING AND DRINKING OUR OWN DAMNATION.

1 Cor. xi. 27, 29.—Whosoever shall eat this bread, and drink this cup of the Lord unworthily, shall be guilty of the body and blood of the Lord...... For he that eateth and drinketh unworthily, eateth and drinketh damnation to himself, not discerning the Lord's body. (S. S.)

THE more excellent any thing is, the greater is the guilt contracted by the abuse of it—
A contempt of the law is not so bad as a contempt of the gospel—Heb. x. 28, 29
An irreverent attendance on divine ordinances is exceedingly sinful—
But to profane the Lord's supper is worse, inasmuch as that institution is more solemn and brings us nearer to God—

*Rev. iii. 1. "He hath the seven spirits of God," i. e. a fulness of all the gifts and graces of the Spirit, with a power to dispense them in all their perfection and variety.

Hence when St. Paul repr'ved the former, he spake mildly—1 Cor. **xiv** 33, 40.

But when he reproved the l:tter, he spake with great severity—

I. What it is to eat the bread, and drink the cup of the Lord unworthily.

To understand this, we should enquire how the Corinthians behaved—*

The abuses of which they were guilty are impracticable now—

Nevertheless we may imitate them in our spirit and temper—

Like them we shall eat and drink unworthily if we do it,

1. Ignorantly.

The Corinthians did not discriminate between the common and religious use of the consecrated elements—

Many at this time also partake without discerning the Lord's body—

They, not remembering his death, defeat the end for which the sacrament was instituted—

2. Irreverently.

The customs of our country do not admit of our meeting in the tumultuous way that was practiced at Corinth—1 Cor. xi. 21.

But many are altogether as destitute of reverence and sacred awe—

A light, worldly, impenitent heart is unbecoming that solemnity—

Such a frame, if habitual, makes us partake unworthily—

3. Uncharitably.

The rich did not impart of their provisions to the poor—1 Cor. xi. 22.

We also may be equally destitute of christian love—

We may be haughty, injurious, unforgiving, &c.—

Such a frame wholly unfits us for the Lord's table—Matt. v. 23, 24

4. Sensually.

The Corinthians made it an occasion for intemperance and excess—

Though we cannot imitate them in this, we may be as carnal as they—

A want of spirituality and affiance in Christ makes our service carnal—

Nor can such a service be acceptable to Him who will be worshipped in spirit and in truth—

To attend at the Lord's table in such a manner is no slight or venial offense.

II. The consequence of so doing.

The consequences mentioned in the text respect,

1. The guilt we contract.

They were "guilty of the body and blood of our Lord" who crucified him, as are they also who apostatize from his truth, Heb. vi. 6.

They too are involved in the same guilt who partake unworthily of the Lord's supper—

They manifest a contempt of this sacrifice, Heb. x. 29.

What dreadful iniquity is this!—

How carefully should we abstain from the commission of it!—

2. The punishment we incur.

The word "damnation" imports *temporal judgment*†—

Eternal damnation is by no means a necessary consequence of this sin, Matt. xii. 31.

---

*Ver. 20—22.—Their conduct seems at first sight to be absolutely inconsistent with a profession of christianity. But, having been accustomed to such behaviour in their feasts during their Gentile state, they were as yet too much addicted to their former habits.

†The apostle explains his meaning in the following verse; "for, for this cause," &c. and he tells us that it was a chastisement inflicted to *keep them from* eternal condemnation, ver. 32.

Yet if it be unrepented of, no doubt this punishment will follow—

And we may expect some spiritual or temporal judgments for it *here*—

We should therefore examine ourselves well before we attend the table of the Lord, ver. 28.

ADDRESS,

1. Those who urge this as an excuse for neglecting the Lord's supper.

There are many who under this pretext cover their own unwillingness to yield themselves up to God—

But God will not admit their vain excuses—

The habitual neglect of their duty insures the punishment which they desire to avoid—

Let all then devote themselves to the Lord in the use of all his instituted ordinances—

2. Those who are really kept away by a fear of incurring this punishment.

Many are kept from the table by a sense of their own unworthiness—

But to be unworthy, and to partake unworthily, are very different things*—

Yet if we have partaken unworthily in past times, let us humble ourselves for it; and then may we come again with joy—

This has been the experience of many, 2 Chron. xxx. 15—23, and may be ours also.

THE CONSEQUENCES OF NEGLECTING PRAYER.

Isai. lxiv. 7. There is none that called upon thy name, that stirreth up himself to take hold of thee: for thou hast hid thy face from us. (S. S.)

MAN is encompassed with dangers from which no human foresight can deliver him—

He is oppressed with wants which no creature can supply—

It is to God that he must look for the blessings which he needs—

But he is naturally so averse to prayer, that he will bear all his own burthens rather than apply to God for relief—

On this account it is that so many faint under their afflictions—

And this was the ground of God's controversy with his people,

I. THE NATURE OF PRAYER.

Prayer is represented in the scriptures by a variety of expressions—

It is here set forth under the idea of "calling upon God."

Petitions, either with or without a form, are not worthy the name of prayer, if they be unattended with a devout spirit—

Prayer is a work of the heart rather than of the lips—

It supposes that we feel our wants, desire to have them supplied, and believe that God is able and willing to relieve them—

It is also described as a "taking hold of God."

---

*A rebel against a mild and merciful prince is unworthy of pardon: but if he receive with gratitude the pardon offered him, and return to his allegiance, he receives it worthily. Thus we are *unworthy* of the smallest mercies, and much more of the children's bread: but if we receive this bread with humility, gratitude, and an increasing devotedness of heart to God, we receive it as we ought, that is, *worthily.*

God has set himself, as it were, before us in tne promises—
There we may lay hold on him by faith—
We may address him as the patriarch of old—Gen. xxxii. 26.
And this is the mean prescribed by God for the obtaining of his blessings—Isai xxvii. 5.
It is further called a "stirring up of oneself" to lay hold on God.
It is no easy thing to gain access to God in prayer—
We engage in it for the most part with much reluctance—
Our thoughts wander, ere we are aware, and in spite of our endeavors to fix them—
We seem to lose the accustomed energy of our minds—
We need again and again to stir up our sluggish hearts—
When we consider the duty in this light, we shall see reason to lament,

II. The general neglect of it.
Many live entirely without prayer.
They are wholly occupied with worldly concerns—
They are not sensible of any *spiritual* wants—
They rely on their own industry for *temporal* advancement—
They acknowledge not before God either their sins or their necessities—
Others only occasionally lift up their hearts to heaven.
They will cry under the pressure of some heavy affliction—Isai xxvi. 16.
But they resemble those spoken of by the prophet—Hos. vii. 14.
Like metal from the fire they soon return to their former hardness—Ps lxxviii. 34—37.
After some signal deliverance too they will praise God—
But, like the Israelites, they will soon forget his mercies—Ps. cvi. 11—13.
Some will maintain with constancy an external regard to this duty—
They will repeat their accustomed form at stated seasons—
Or they will offer a few general and cold petitions—
And with this outward act they will rest satisfied—
They feel no pleasure in the duty, but perform it as a task—
But there are few indeed who pray to God aright.
There is a remnant now, as there was in the prophet's days *—
There are some who "stir up their souls to lay hold on God"—
But these are few when compared with the bulk of mankind—
They may be said comparatively to be "none" at all—
To counteract this evil we proceed to set forth,

III. The consequences of this neglect.
The tokens of God's displeasure, which those in the text experienced, will be experienced by all who neglect prayer—
God will surely "hide his face from them."
He will not reveal to them his glory.
He reveals himself to his people as he does not unto the world—John xiv. 22.
He shines into their hearts to discover to them his glory—
But he will vouchsafe no such mercy to those who call not upon him—
His perfections are to them rather an object of terror than of admiration—
He will not manifest to them his love.
He often "sheds abroad his love in the hearts" of those who seek him—
But the neglecters of prayer "intermeddle not with their joy"—Prov xiv. 10.

---

* Isai. viii. 18. The prophet certainly did not mean to include them in his censure.

They are strangers to the Spirit of adoption—

They rather banish God from their thoughts, and wish like the fool*—

He will not communicate to them his blessings.

His faithful worshippers have all the blessings of grace and glory—

But others have no part or lot with them—

The blessings they do enjoy are turned into a curse unto them—

And to eternity must they ascribe their misery to their own neglect

APPLICATION.

They, who live without prayer, should consider these things,

This offense has been awfully marked by the indignation of God†—

How bitter must be the reflections of those who perish through this neglect!—

Surely all should seek the Lord while he *may* be found—

They also, who are formal in prayer, should lay them to heart.

These, as being more liable to deceive themselves, are in greater danger—

Our prayers must be fervent in order to be effectual—James v. 16.

If we would enter into heaven, we must press into it with violence—Matt. xi. 12.

Nor should this subject ever be forgotten by those who profess godliness.

Unless we stir up ourselves continually, we shall soon lose the divine presence—

We cannot guard too much against formality in prayer—

Let us be encouraged by God's gracious declaration ‖—

MEN'S PROUD CONTEMPT OF GOD.

Psalm, x. 4, 5.—The wicked, through the pride of his countenance, will not seek after God. God is not in all his thoughts: his ways are always grievous: thy judgments are far above out of his sight: as for all his enemies, he puffeth at them. (S. S.)

PRIDE, when manifested in a flagrant manner, universally excites disgust; so hateful is it, when divested of the specious garb in which it is generally clothed. But though all hate pride, when it appears in others, few are sensible how much it reigns within their own bosoms. In our converse with man, this evil disposition is ready to shew itself on every occasion: but in our conduct towards God, it is the fruitful parent of habitual neglect, and atheistical contempt. This is affirmed in the passage before us, in which we may notice,

I. THE STATE OF THE WICKED.

It is not easy to conceive a more humiliating description of their character than that given us by the Psalmist:

They "will not seek after God."

* Ps. xiv. 1. The words in Italics are not in the original.

† If all the souls that are banished from the divine presence were asked, "Wherefore has God hid his face from you?" they must assign the reason that is given in the text.

‡ Ps. lxxxi. 10—12. "God gave them up:" to what? to their enemies? to death? or to immediate and eternal condemnation? No; to what was worse than even that, "their own hearts lust," that they might "treasure up wrath against the day of wrath."

‖ Prov. xv. 8. God is not more pleased with the songs of angels than with the sighs and groans of a contrite soul.

God invites them to seek his face, and promises that he will be found of them; but they cannot be prevailed upon either by promises or threats: they will seek with eagerness an earthly object, that may make them happy; but they account God unworthy of any notice or regard, Job xxxv. 10.

" He is not even admitted into their thoughts."

It is astonishing to what a degree men often banish God from their minds. They will pass days, months, and even years, without one reverential thought of him, unless when they are alarmed by some awful providence, or awakened by some faithful discourse: and *then*, unless the grace of God prevent them, they will cast him out of their minds again as soon as possible, and drown their thoughts in business or dissipation, Job xxi. 14, 15.

They account " his ways," as far as they know them, "grievous."

When urged to devote themselves to God in sincerity and truth, they conceive that such a state is unattainable, or, at least, incompatible with the common duties and offices of life. They call the indulgence of their lusts, liberty; and the exercise of vital godliness, an intolerable bondage. Every part of the divine life is irksome to them, and *that* too, not occasionally, but "always," without any change or intermission.

The "judgments of God are far above out of their sight."

By the "judgments" of God we understand his word and works. Now these are not only out of their sight in some particulars (for they are incomprehensible in some respects even to the most enlightened saints) but they are altogether foolishness unto them, 1 Cor. ii. 14. When the mysteries of redemption are opened, they are esteemed by them as " cunningly devised fables:" and when the marvellous interpositions of Providence are insisted on, they are ready to exclaim, with Ezekiel's hearers, " Ah! Lord God, doth he not speak parables ?" Ezek. xx. 49.

"As for all their enemies, they puff at them."

If God himself threaten them as an enemy, they disregard his menaces. The denunciations of his wrath are deemed by them unworthy of any serious attention. They even puff at them with contempt and disdain. They quiet all their fears, saying, like them of old, " Tush, God shall not see; neither will the Almighty regard it:" Ps. xciv. 7. " I shall have peace, though I walk in the imagination of my heart," Deut. xxix. 19.

In order to account for this state of things, let us trace it to,

II. THE REAL SOURCE OF THEIR WICKEDNESS.

We might trace this practical atheism to men's ignorance and unbelief: but the Psalmist suggests to us the original ground and occasion of it: it all arises from the pride of their hearts.

Men are *too good*, in their own apprehension, *to need* God s *mercy*.

They will confess that they are not altogether so good as they might be; but they do not think they deserve God's wrath and indignation. Why then should they trouble themselves to ask for mercy at his hands, when they are in no danger of suffering his judgments ?

They are also *too strong to need his aid.*

They imagine, that they can repent when they please, and that, whensoever they resolve, they can easily carry their resolutions into effect. If they thought that "without God they could do nothing," and that " he must give them both to will and to do," then there were reason for imploring his assistance: but, when they acknowledge no such dependence upon God, wherefore should they seek his aid ?

Moreover, they are *too wise to need the teachings of his Spirit.*

They see perhaps their need of a revelation to discover to them the mind and will of God; but, when that is once given, they are not conscious that they need a spiritual illumination to discover the truths contained in it. They suppose their reason to be as sufficient for the investigation of spiritual, as of carnal things: and under that persuasion, they consider all application to God for the teachings of his Spirit, as enthusiastic and absurd.

Finally, they are *too happy to need the divine presence.*

They are occupied with carnal pleasure, and wish for nothing beyond it. If only they can have the undisturbed indulgence of their appetites, it is, to them, all the paradise they desire. As for the light of God's countenance, and the manifestations of his love, they know not what is meant by such things; they suppose that they exist only in the pretensions of hypocrites, and the conceits of fanatics.

In short, like those of Laodicea, they possess such an imaginary sufficiency within themselves, that they have no need of God at all, Rev. iii. 17. And hence it is that they care not to have God in all their thoughts.

INFER,

1. How astonishing is the depravity of human nature!

If all be not equally addicted to gross sins, all are equally " without God in the world," Eph. ii. 12: all have a " carnal mind that is enmity against God," Rom. viii. 7. Alas! What a picture of human nature! Let "every mouth then be stopped, and all the world become guilty before God," Rom. iii. 10, 11, 12, 19.

2. How great is the change that takes place in conversion!

The state of a converted soul forms a perfect contrast with that of the wicked. " Old things pass away, and all things become new." Let all then ask themselves, Am I now devoting myself to God, as once I did to the world; and despising the world, as once I despised God? This were indeed "a new creation," 2 Cor. v. 17.

3. How necessary is conversion in order to an enjoyment of heaven!

There must be within ourselves a meetness for heaven before we can enjoy it, Col. i. 12. Let not those then, who banish God from their thoughts, and cast off his yoke, suppose that they could be happy in heaven, even if they were admitted there. If they would delight themselves in God for ever, they must obtain in this world a conformity to his image, and a delight in his commandments.

THE CERTAINTY THAT SIN WILL FIND US OUT.

Numb. xxxii. 23.—Behold ye have sinned against the Lord: and be sure your sin will **find** you out. (S. S.)

THE fear of punishment, if not the best, is certainly the most common preservative from sin—

Under the Mosaic dispensation it was the principal motive with which the divine commands were enforced—

Nor did St. Paul, though so well acquainted with the liberal spirit of the gospel, think it wrong to " persuade men by the terrors of the Lord"—

The words before us, therefore may, not improperly, be addressed to us*—
We may take occasion from them to consider,

I. IN WHAT MANNER WE HAVE SINNED AGAINST THE LORD

It would be endless to attempt an enumeration of all the sins we have committed—

We shall confine ourselves to that view of them which the context suggests.

The sin against which Moses cautioned the two tribes was, unfaithfulness to their engagements—

And, a preferring of their present ease to the executing of the work which God had assigned them—

Now we promised at our baptism to renounce the world, the flesh, and the devil—†

These promises *then* made for us, we have renewed at our confirmation and at the Lord's table—

But how have we kept the covenant which we have thus solemnly entered into?—

Have we not maintained that friendship with the world which is enmity with God? James iv. 4.

Have we not rather sought to please than to mortify our carnal appetites? Tit. iii. 3.

Has not the god of this world led us captive at his will? Eph. ii. 2. 2 Tim. ii. 26.

And is not such a life one continued violation of our baptismal engagements?—

But the sin referred to in the text, will scarcely bear any comparison with ours.

The Israelites were to maintain a warfare with men; we with the devil, Eph. vi. 12.

They were to fight for an earthly portion; we, an heavenly, 1 Cor. ix. 25.

They might have urged that *their* aid was unnecessary, when *God* was engaged—

And that, after all, the prize was an inadequate reward for such fatigue and danger—

But, can we hope to conquer without exerting our own powers?—

Do we suppose that God will subdue our enemies without our concurrence?—

Or can we say that the prize held forth to us is not worth the contest?—

If our engagements be more solemn, our work more noble, and our reward more glorious than theirs, our sin in disregarding all must be proportionably greater—

Yet who amongst us must not confess that he has forgotten all his vows?—

Behold then, we may say to all, " Ye have sinned against the Lord"—
Nor are we to suppose that our sin will always pass unnoticed.

* The tribes of Reuben and Gad had solicited permission to have the land of Jazer and of Gilead for their portion instead of any inheritance in the land of Canaan. Upon their promising to fight in conjunction with the other tribes until the whole of Canaan should be subdued, Moses acceded to the proposal; but warned them withal, that if they receded from their engagement, they should assuredly meet with a due recompense from God.

† See the Church Catechism.

II. What assurance we have that our sin shall find us out.

Sin may be said to find us out when it brings down the divine judgments upon us.

Conscience, stupified or seared, often forgets to execute its office—

Nor speaks, till God, by his Providence or Grace, awaken it—

Sometimes years elapse before it reproves our iniquities—Gen. xlii. 21, 22

Sometimes it testifies to our face as soon as our sin is committed—Matt. xxvi. 74, 75, and xxvii. 3, 4.

Whenever it thus condemns us, our sins may be said to find us out—

But the expression in the text imports rather the visitation of God for sin—

There is a punishment annexed to every violation of God's law—Ezek xviii. 4.

And sin then finds us out effectually when it brings that punishment upon us—

That it will find us out, we have the fullest possible assurance.

The perfections of God's nature absolutely preclude all hope of impunity.

If he be omnipresent, he must see; if omniscient, remember; if holy, hate; and if just, punish the violations of his law—

If he be possessed of veracity and power, he must execute the judgments he has denounced—

The declarations of his Word abundantly confirm this awful truth—Isa iii. 11. Rom. ii. 9 : Ps. xxi. 8 ; Prov. xi. 21.

Sin leaves a track which can never be effaced; and evil, however slow-paced, will surely overtake it—Prov. xiii. 21 ; Ps. cxl. 11.

However scoffers may exult in their security, their ruin is fast approaching—2 Pet. ii. 3, and iii. 4, 9, and Deut. xxix. 19, 20.

The remarkable instances of sin being detected and punished in this world afford a strong additional testimony—

David and Gehazi, though so studious to conceal their guilt, had their iniquity marked in the punishment inflicted for it—2 Sam. xii. 9—12; 2 Kings v. 26, 27.

When according to human calculations, it was above two millions to one that Achan would escape, the lot fell on him by an infallible direction—Josh. vii. 14—18.

How much more then shall the most hidden things be brought to light hereafter!—

The appointment of a day of final retribution puts the matter beyond a possibility of doubt—

For what end can there be such a period fixed but that the actions of men may be judged—

And for what end can they be judged, but that every man may receive according to his deeds—Eccl. xii. 14.

We may then emphatically say to every sinner, *"Be sure, &c."*—

Infer,

1. How earnest should we be in searching out our own sins!

We think little of evils which have been committed by us long ago—

And imagine that they are effaced from God's memory as well as from our own—

But every action, word and thought is noted in the book of his remembrance—

He sees the transaction of former years as if they had this moment passed—

424

All our iniquities are viewed by him in one accumulated mass—

Nor does he abhor them less than in the very instant they were committed—

Let us not then pass them over, or palliate them, as youthful follies—

Let us remember how exactly the Lord's threatenings were executed on the Israelites in the wilderness—Numb. xxxii. 10—13.

And endeavor to avert his judgments while space for repentance is allowed us—

Let us mourn over our innumerable violations of our baptismal covenant—

Let us lament our solicitude about a present portion, our aversion to fight the Lord's battles, and our indifference about the heavenly Canaan—

We must repent of these things, or lie under the guilt of them for ever— Ps. l. 21 ; Luke xiii. 3.

2. How thankful should we be that a way of escape is provided for us !

It is not sin lamented, but sin unrepented of, which will find us out—

There is a city of refuge provided for those who will flee to it—Heb. vi. 18.

The man, Christ Jesus, is an hiding-place from the impending storm— Isa. xxxii. 2.

If we flee to him, we may be sure that sin shall NOT find us out—

Every perfection of the Deity is pledged to save a believing penitent— 1 John i. 9.

We are confirmed in this hope by the most *positive declarations of scripture*—Isa. vliv. 22 ; Mic. vii. 19 ; Heb. viii. 12.

We have most *authentic and astonishing instances* of sin forgiven— 2 Sam. xii. 13 ; Luke vii. 47, and xxiii. 43.

And *the day of judgment* is appointed no less for the complete justification of believers than for the condemnation of unbelievers—2 Thess. i. 9, 10.

Let this blessed assurance then dwell richly on our minds—

Let it encourage us to take refuge under the Saviour's wings—Matt. xxiii. 37.

Let an holy confidence inspire those who have committed their souls to him—2 Tim. i. 12.

And let all rejoice and glory in him as able to save them to the uttermost— Heb. vii. 25.

THE SIN OF MAKING LIGHT OF CHRIST.

Matt. xxii. 5.—But they made light of it. (S. S.)

WE are apt to condemn the Jews as blind and obstinate, because they rejected Christ in spite of the clearest evidence in his favor—but we ourselves are more guilty than they, because we enjoy much greater advantages for understanding the gospel than they did, and yet are as regardless of it as they were.

Our blessed Lord illustrated their conduct by a marriage-feast, to which they who were invited, refused to come. The same invitation is sent to us ; and we, no less than they, " make light of it "

To bring home a conviction of this upon our minds, we shall shew,

I. What are the blessings which we are invited to partake of God is here represented as having made a marriage for his Son.

The figure of a marriage union is often used to represent the connection that subsists between Christ and his church—Jer. iii. 14; Hos. ii. 19, 20. He is the bridegroom, and the church is his bride—Isa. liv. 5; Rev. xxi. 9. And the connexion is then formed, when the church gives up herself to Christ as her head and Lord, and by faith becomes so united to him as to be one flesh, Eph. v. 30—32, or to speak more properly, "one spirit with him"—1 Cor. vi. 17.

The feast prepared on the occasion contains all the blessings of grace and glory.

There is nothing that can nourish or delight the soul which God has not prepared for the bride on her union with Christ—Isa. xxv. 6. She instantly becomes related to him, and is considered in all things as his daughter, an object of his affections, and a partaker of his inheritance.—Let any one enquire, What is there that my soul can desire in time or eternity? and he shall find it all set before him, that he may freely and richly enjoy it.—

To a participation of this feast we are sent to invite you.

In one view, they to whom we are sent, are the bride; but in another view, they are the guests.—The commission God has given to his servants is to "go out into the highways and hedges, and to bring in as many as they can find."—To you therefore we come, declaring that no unworthiness on your parts shall exclude you, provided you put on the wedding garment, which the Master of the feast has prepared for you.—Accept the invitation; and all the blessings of salvation shall be yours.—Pardon, peace, strength, and whatever else can comfort the weary, and support the weak, shall become the daily, the everlasting food of your souls.—

To evince how much our message is disregarded, we proceed to shew,

II. Who are they that make light of the invitation.

Among the numberless classes that might be mentioned, two only shall be selected;

1. They who satisfy themselves with excuses for declining it.

The persons, mentioned in the context, excused themselves on account of "their farms or merchandize."—But their pleas, however satisfactory in their own eyes, were not admitted by God.—On the contrary, he declared them to be "unworthy ever to taste of his supper."—Now what excuses has any man more urgent than these?—And if these were of no avail in their case, what right have we to think, that the plea of worldly business will be admitted in our favor?—If the prosecuting of our worldly business were really incompatible with the enjoyment of God, there can be no doubt which we ought to prefer.—He was "a wise merchant, who having found a pearl of great price, sold all that he had and bought it."—But our duties to God and to the world are by no means irreconcilable with each other.— And therefore the resting in such vain excuses shews, that we make light of the salvation offered us—

2. They who do not accept it with all thankfulness.

Blessings, like those set before us in the gospel, ought to be regarded as of the first importance.—Indifference towards them is a positive contempt of them.—If a slave, whom we had ransomed at a great price, and to whom we offered liberty, and affluence, and honor, should express no gratitude, no joy on the occasion, should we not think that he "made light of" our proffered kindness?—But what bondage is so dreadful as that in which we are

426

held by sin and satan? or what liberty is like that of God's children? or what comparison is there between the riches and honors of this world, and those which are imparted to us on our union with Christ?—If then our joy and gratitude excited by the gospel salvation, be not in some measure proportioned to its value and importance, we cannot but be considered as making light of it—

Nor will this be thought a venial matter, if we duly consider,

III. THE FOLLY AND SINFULNESS OF THEIR CONDUCT.

But what words can sufficiently express this? for they make light of,

1. That which is of the greatest possible value.

Estimate the blessings of salvation either *positively* by the price paid for them, or *comparatively* by weighing them, as it were, in a balance against all other things, and then see what it is that they despise.—Only consider, that every one of those blessings was bought with blood, with the blood of God's co-equal, co-eternal Son, a price infinitely exceeding ten thousand worlds.—Is there no guilt, no folly in disregarding things of such inestimable value?—Bring into competition with them all that the world can give; and it will be found lighter than the dust upon the balance, yea, " altogether lighter than vanity itself."—Well therefore does the apostle put that unanswerable question, " How shall ye escape, if ye neglect so *great* salvation?—Heb. ii. 3.

2. That without which they can never be happy.

The creature, at best, is but as a " broken cistern : in vain shall any one go to it for solid happiness, Jer. ii. 13.—" There is not, there cannot be, any true peace to the wicked," Isa. xlviii. 22.—Let any man try to make himself happy, while the guilt of all his sins continues to lie upon him, and he is in awful suspense about his eternal state ; he may be thoughtless as a child, or stupid as a beast; but he cannot be happy.—And if this be the case in the midst of all his gaiety, what will be his situation in a dying hour?—At all events, supposing him ever so happy in life and in death, how will he feel himself on his first entrance into the invisible world?—Will he who made light of the marriage-feast on earth, sit down with boldness at " the marriage supper of the Lamb in heaven?"—Will all those employments to which he was averse in this world, be at once his joy and delight, as soon as he passes into the world above?—If he disregarded earthly things, he would have reason on his side ; because he might be happy in God, even though he were destitute of every thing else: but to hope for happiness without God is a desperate delusion; and consequently, to make light of the invitations of the gospel is nothing less than madness itself—

3. That which they are sure to value, when it will be gone beyond recovery.

Here men are of very different sentiments ; some accounting godliness the one thing needful, and others despising it as enthusiasm and needless singularity.—But in the eternal world there is no such diversity of opinion : the saints in glory are fully confirmed in the judgment they had formed on earth ; and the wicked in hell are fully convinced of their error; the one know by their enjoyments how good it was to obey the heavenly call; and the other know by their sufferings, what " a fearful thing it is to fall into the hands of the living God."—What then is it but madness to make light of that, which we are so sure to value when there remains to us no longer any possibility of attaining it?—Wisd. v. 4.

Let due weight be given to these considerations, and we shall need nothing more to convince us either of the folly or sinfulness of slighting the invitations of the gospel—

APPLICATION.

It is to be feared that, after all, many will persist in their infatuated conduct —But we would at least make one more effort to reclaim them; and beg of God to render his word effectual to their conversion.—

Know then that the marriage supper is now prepared; and we, as God's servants, come in his name to invite you to it.—We invite you *all:* the rich, the poor; the old, the young; the moral, the immoral.—We announce to you, that all things are ready. Are *ye* then not ready?—If ye say, "We have not a suitable garment; we declare to you, that the Master of the feast has provided garments for all his guests; and that ye need only to be clothed with the unspotted robe of Christ's righteousness, and ye shall instantly be acceptable in the sight of God.—Put away then your excuses: receive thankfully the invitation sent you: and begin to feast upon those spiritual provisions that shall nourish your souls unto life eternal.—

THE MANIFESTATION WHICH CHRIST HAS GIVEN OF THE FATHER.

John i. 18.—No man hath seen God at any time; the only begotten Son, which is in the bosom of the Father, he hath declared him. (S. S.)

THE knowledge of God is the great source of blessings to mankind
But the heathen world were altogether ignorant of him—
Nor were the Jews themselves fully instructed concerning him—
To make a full revelation of him to the world was a part of that work which was reserved for Christ himself—
And this office he performed, to the unspeakable comfort of this church and people—
The evangelist unites his testimony with that of John the Baptist in confirmation of this truth—
We shall enquire,

I. WHAT CHRIST HAS DECLARED OF THE FATHER.
God himself is invisible to the eye of sense—1 Tim. vi. 16.
Even Moses was permitted to see only his backparts—Exod. xxxiii. 23.
But Christ had a peculiar relation to the Father as "his only begotten son;" and a most intimate acquaintance with him, as being from all eternity, and at that very hour, "in his bosom"—
He has made known the Father to us, and declared,
1. His nature.
Mankind had gross conceptions of the Deity as a material being—
But Christ has assured us of his perfect *spirituality*—John iv. 24.
Nor was the *Unity* of God clearly ascertained among the Gentiles—
But Christ has left no room for doubt upon this subject—Mark xii. 29.
He has moreover revealed to us a *Trinity* of persons in the Godhead—
He has affirmed in the plainest terms his own Oneness with the Father—John x. 30.
He has spoken of the Holy Ghost as co-existing with himself and with the Father—John xv. 26.
And has joined the Three together as equal in authority and honor—Matt. xxviii. 19.
Thus has he enabled us by faith to "see him who is invisible"—
3. His perfections.

God had long since proclaimed his own name to Moses—Exod. xxxiv. 6, 7.

But Christ has afforded us more abundant discoveries of all his attributes—

He has clearly shewn us that his goodness is unbounded, Matt. v. 45 his sovereignty uncontrolled, Matt. xi. 25, 26, his power irresistible, Matt. xxvi. 53, his justice inflexible, ib. 42, his mercy infinite, John iii. 16, 17, and his truth inviolable—Luke xvi. 17.

There is not any thing relating to his Father, the knowledge of which could be at all serviceable to us, that he has not revealed—John xv. 15

He did not however merely utter these things like the prophets of old.

II. How he declared him.

Christ had formerly spoken of God in and by the prophets—1 Pet. i. 11 But now he declared the Father in a different manner.

1. By exhibiting a perfect pattern of him.

He was himself an exact resemblance of the Father—Heb. i. 3.

And in his conduct exhibited every perfection of the Deity—John viii. 29

Hence a sight of him was, in fact, a sight of the Father himself—John xiv. 7—9.

2. By making known his counsels.

Much of the Father's counsels had lain hid from the foundation of the world, or had been very imperfectly revealed—

Christ opened them to his hearers as they were able to bear them—John xvi. 12.

He made known God's intention to admit the Gentiles into his church—Matt. viii. 11, 12.

And assured us that the most abandoned of mankind should be cordially received the very instant he returned to God—Luke xv. 20.

But that none of whatever character could be saved, unless they sought acceptance with God through his mediation—John xiv. 6.

Thus by these declarations he has enabled us to attain a more perfect knowledge of the Father's mind and will—

3. By exerting a secret energy on the minds of men.

No man could know the Father unless Christ revealed him inwardly by his Spirit, as well as outwardly by the world—Matt. xi. 27.

His very disciples understood not until he opened their eyes—Luke xxiv. 45.

Nor can we attain to a true knowledge of God in any other way—

The " word must come to us in power and in the Holy Ghost," or it will come in vain—1 Thess. i. 5.

But when applied by his Spirit, it shall teach us plainly of the Father—Jn xvi. 25.

Infer,

1. How glorious a person must Christ be.

The description given of him shews his superiority above every created being—

He is not the Son of God by creation, as the angels are, nor by regeneration and adoption, as men; but by an inexplicable generation, his "only-begotten"—

And, as well in his incarnate as in his pre-existent state, was continually " in the bosom of the Father"—John iii. 13.

Nor was any other worthy to reveal the Father to us—

Let us then entertain just conceptions of his worth and dignity—

And manifest our delight in him as the saints in heaven did—Rev v. 5—9.

2. How precious ought the scriptures to be to us!

Job and David had but a small portion of the scriptures in their hands—

Yet did they value them above every thing in the world—Job xxviii. 12· Ps. cxix. 72.

How much more should we, who possess the sacred oracles entire!—

In these is recorded every thing that Christ has declared—

And by these we may be made wise unto salvation—2 Tim. iii. 15.

Let us then search them with diligence, and treasure them up in our hearts—

Nor let a day pass without digging into those invaluable mines—Prov ii. 4.

3 How inexcusable are they who are ignorant of God!

It is to our shame that many of us are still ignorant of God—1 Cor. xv. 34.

We have not that knowledge of him that produces correspondent affections towards him—

But what excuse can we offer in extenuation of our guilt?—

Has not Christ declared the Father in order that we might know him?—

And is he not willing also to reveal him in us by a powerful energy on our souls?—

Some, doubtless, are more guilty than others in proportion as they have possessed means of instruction—

But all will find the consequences of their ignorance most tremendous—2 Thess. 1. 8.

Let all begin then to enquire after God with their whole hearts—

Nor rest till they have attained that knowledge of him which is life eternal—John xvii. 3.

~~~~~~~~~~~~~~~~

CHRIST THE ONLY FOUNDATION.

1 Cor. iii. 11.—Other foundation can no man lay, than that is laid, which is Jesus Christ. (S. S.)

THERE is not any thing more injurious to the church of God than a party-spirit: yet even in the apostolic age did it begin to distract the Christian community. At Corinth it prevailed, and rose to an alarming height: and St. Paul was obliged to exert all his influence in order to counteract it. He reminded the partisans, that, as "God's building," they should be cemented together with brotherly love: that they should study to shew themselves worthy of the place they held in the church, in expectation of that day when all their works should be tried by fire; and that, instead of fomenting strifes and divisions, they should unite with each other in cleaving stedfastly to the one foundation, whereon they stood.

The declaration in the text is plain, and of infinite importance.

To enter more fully into it we shall consider,

1. WHAT FOUNDATIONS MEN LAY FOR THEMSELVES.

Every man has some foundation for his hope. Though there are many shades of difference in the sentiments of different men, yet their grounds of hope may be reduced to two;

1. Their own goodness.

Some think that nothing but gross sin can expose them to the wrath of God. They therefore congratulate themselves as having never done any thing to merit his displeasure. Others imagine that they may trust in the good works that they have done. They have, in their own apprehension, been regular in their duties to God and man: nor can they conceive that *they* should have reason to fear. Thus, like the Pharisee of old, they thank God that they are not as other men; and are filled with self-complacency, because they are punctual in the observance of certain duties, Luke xviii. 11, 12.

2. Their own works and Christ's merits united.

Many, who see, that their own works cannot justify them according to the strict tenor of the law, yet hope that they will, according to the milder demands of the gospel. If they see that these will not suffice, they will look to Christ to supply their deficiencies. If they see, that such an union is impracticable, and, that Jesus must be their only foundation, they hope, however, that he will save them for their works sake. Thus they either avowedly profess to participate with Christ the honor of their salvation; or, while they pretend to give the honor of it to him, they look for the original and moving cause of it within themselves. Like the Judaising christians, Acts. xv. 5, or the Gentiles whom Peter misled, Gal. ii. 12, 14, they unite the law to Christ; as though Christ needed to have something superadded to him, to render his death effectual. At all events, if they find their error in this respect, they will regard their works as *their warrant* to believe in Christ; and will expect mercy at his hands, not so much because his grace is free and all sufficient, as because they have something in themselves, which may deserve his notice and regard.

These plans of salvation however will be found very erroneous, if we enquire,

II. WHAT IS THAT FOUNDATION WHICH GOD HAS LAID?

Nothing can be more clear, than that he has not laid either of those, which have been before mentioned.

He often describes his people as performing good works: and often promises them, under that character, eternal life. But he always represents us as sinners, and as standing in need of his mercy. And he has sent his Son into the world for that very reason, because none could obtain mercy by any works of their own. Nor has he clearly shewn, that works are *wholly* to be excluded from the office of justifying. He has told us that salvation must be wholly of grace or wholly of works, Rom. xi. 6. That every degree of boasting is excluded from that salvation which he has revealed, Rom. iii. 27; Eph. ii. 8, 9. And that the persons, whom he justifies, are ungodly, and without any works whatever to recommend them, Rom. iv. 5.

Christ is the one foundation which he has laid in Zion.

He "has set forth his Son to be a propitiation for sin:" and every sinner is to build his hope on Christ alone. Christ is the foundation laid in the covenant of grace, Gen. xvii. 19; Heb. viii. 6. The same is laid in all the promises, Gen. iii. 15, and xxii. 18; 2 Cor. i. 20. The same was exhibited in all the types.* The same is laid also in the gospel, 1 Pet. ii. 4—6. We are expressly told that there is no other, Acts iv. 12. Nor indeed can there be any other to all eternity.

The necessity of building upon this will appear, while we consider,

* The Paschal Lamb, the Scape Goat, &c.

III. Why no other can be laid.

Many reasons might easily be assigned: but one or two may suffice.

1. Any other would be unworthy of the divine architect.

God himself is the architect, ver. 9; and must have all the glory of beginning and perfecting this building. But, if men were to found their hopes on any thing but the Lord Jesus Christ, they would have whereof to glory, Rom. iv. 2. So far as respect was had to any merit in them, so far might they ascribe the honor to themselves. Even in heaven their song must differ from that of the redeemed. Instead of giving *all* the glory to God and to the Lamb, Rev. v. 13, they must take a portion of it to themselves. But this would be utterly unworthy of God to suffer. Indeed he has told us that he never can nor will suffer it, 1 Cor. i. 29, 31; Eph. ii. 8, 9. We may be sure therefore that no such way of salvation shall ever be established, as leaves man at liberty to boast. We shall be rewarded *according to* our works, and in some respect *for* our works; but the only ground of acceptance, either for our persons or our services, is in Christ alone, Eph. i. 6.

2. No other would support the weight that is to be laid upon it.

Whatever our souls need in time or eternity must be derived from that, which is the foundation of our hope. Our pardon must be obtained by it; our peace flow from it; our strength and righteousness be given us on account of it; and eternal glory be bestowed on us, as the reward of it. And can we build our hope of such things in any degree on our own works? Can we, who, if we had done all that is commanded us, should be only unprofitable servants, imagine, that we can in any respect merit such things, when we have done nothing that is commanded us, at least, nothing perfectly, or as we ought to have done it? Surely such an hope would soon appear to be a foundation of sand; and would infallibly disappoint us to our eternal ruin. Yea, the very persons who build on such a foundation, almost invariably deny, that any man can be assured of his acceptance with God; they account such an assurance to be an enthusiastic delusion; which is a clear acknowledgment of the insufficiency of *their* foundation to bear this weight.

Infer,

1. How needful is it to enquire what foundation we are upon!

If we build but a common habitation, we are careful on what foundation we raise it. How much more care should we exercise, when we are building for eternity! Let us enquire, whether we have been deeply convinced of the insufficiency of our own goodness, and of the impossibility of uniting any works of ours with Christ's atoning sacrifice? And let us examine whether Christ's obedience unto death be our only hope, our only confidence? We never can be saved unless, with Paul, we utterly renounce the filthy rags of our own righteousness, and desire to be found clad in Christ's unspotted robe, Isa. lxiv. 6; Phil. iii. 9.

2. How secure are they who are built upon the Lord Jesus Christ!

Christ, on whom they stand, is jusly called "a *tried* stone, and a *sure* foundation," Isa. xxviii. 16. He never yet failed those who trusted in him. The vilest of mankind have found him able to save them to the uttermost. He is a Rock to those who trust in him; nor shall the gates of hell prevail against them, Matt. xvi. 18. Let all believers then rejoice in their security; and hold fast the profession of their faith without wavering, Heb. x. 23.

3. How careful should we be, what superstructure we raise upon him!

While Christ is the foundation of our hope, we are also to build upon him all our works. But our works will all be tried by fire. If they be not such as tend to his glory, they will be burnt up as hay, and wood, and stubble. If they be truly good, they will stand the trial, like gold, or silver, or precious stones, ver. 11—14. Let us then give diligent heed to our works. We may suffer loss *in* heaven, though we should not suffer the loss *of* heaven, ver. 15. Let us then seek "a full reward," 2 John 8. While we renounce good works *in point of dependence*, let us practice them *from love to our Redeemer*. Thus shall we put to silence our adversaries; and dorn the doctrine of God our Saviour

---

HATRED OF CHRIST IS HATRED OF THE FATHER.

John xv. 23.—He that hateth me, hateth my Father also. (S. S.)

MEN are ever disposed to palliate their sins, and, by representing them under some specious name, to conceal their real enormity—But God calls every sin by its proper name, and speaks of it with just abhorrence—Covetousness in his eyes is not prudence, but idolatry: Eph. v. 5; a disregard of his presence is not mere inadvertence, but a denial of his most essential attributes: Ps. x. 11, 13; and a contempt of his gospel is not a venial ignorance or inattention, but an absolute hatred both of Christ and of the Father—To confirm this truth we will endeavor to shew,

I. WHO THEY ARE THAT HATE CHRIST.

It may be thought that none but Jews can be guilty of hating Christ, and that the bearing of his name is a sufficient testimony of our regard for him.—But there are too many who, notwithstanding they have been baptized into his name, are yet "enemies to him in their minds."—Certainly we must number among his enemies,

1. Those who disregard his gospel.

The gospel of Christ ought to be universally received as "glad tidings of great joy."—But the greater part of mankind feel an aversion to it.—Some dislike its fundamental doctrine of salvation by faith, and represent it as injurious to the interests of morality.—Others hate the duties it enjoins, and traduce it as requiring a state of mind totally incompatible with the discharge of our offices in social and civil life.—Many even of those who approve of the gospel in their judgment, are yet very far from experiencing its power in their souls.—They enjoy not its promises, they fulfil not its precepts, they know not its renovating, sanctifying effects.—It may be asked, Are all these persons haters of Christ? Let Christ himself answer that question.—He states, that a practical renunciation of his authority is a proof, that they are enemies to him in their hearts, and will cause them to be treated as his enemies in the day that he shall judge the world—Luke xix. 14, 27.

2. Those who neglect his ordinances.

Our Lord has promised his peculiar presence to us while we seek him in the ordinances of his own appointment.—Should not then the hope of enjoying his presence endear the ordinances to us, and make us regard them as our most inestimable privilege?—But how are they regarded by the generality amongst us?—Does not worldly business or pleasure often detain us needlessly from the house of God! And when we are assembled for worship, do not our thoughts rove to the very ends of the earth, so that, though we "draw nigh to God with our lips, our hearts are far from him?"—Are not almost all persons cold and remiss in secret prayer?—And is not family religion either banished altogether, or conducted with such formality as to render it irksome and unprofitable?—Our Lord left it as his dying command that we should often partake of bread and wine in remembrance of his body broken and his blood shed for us—Yet is not his table either shamefully deserted, or else profaned by impenitent, unsanctified communicants?—And what construction must we put on such conduct? Our Lord plainly tells us, that he considers them as his enemies, and that none of those who thus despise his invitations, shall ever taste of his supper—Luke xiv. 18, 24.

3. Those who persecute his people.

Persecution is not carried now to the same extent that it has been in former ages—But has it ceased?—Experience proves that there is the same enmity in the hearts of men against the faithful servants of God as ever there was—There are many at this day who are true descendants of Cain and Ishmael—And, as long as there shall be an unconverted man upon earth, it will be found, that they, who are born after the flesh, will persecute those who are born after the Spirit—Gal. iv. 29. If they do not kill the saints, they will "revile them, and separate them from their company, and say all manner of evil against them falsely for Christ's sake"—And are not such persons enemies to Christ? Yes; he considers himself as the real butt of their malice—Saul thought that he was justly punishing some wild fanatics when he dragged the christians to prison and to death; but Jesus said to him, Saul, Saul, why persecutest thou *me?*—Acts ix. 4. And the prophet tells us that whosoever toucheth the Lord's people, toucheth the apple of his eye—Zech. ii. 8.

The extreme enormity of their conduct appears in this,

II. THAT THE HATRED OF CHRIST IS, IN FACT, A HATRED OF THE FATHER ALSO.

Christ is essentially "one with the Father;" and as "whosoever had seen Christ, had seen the Father," so, "whosoever hateth Christ must of necessity hate the Father also"—But it is evident in other points of view that they hate the Father; for they hate

1. His authority.

God commands all men to believe in his Son, to "kiss him" with holy reverence, and to honor him even as they honor the Father—Ps. ii. 12. John v. 23. But the unequivocal language of those who comply not with his command is, "We will not have this man to reign over us;" "Who is the Lord that we should obey him? we know not the Lord, neither will we obey his voice"—Whatever they may pretend, they are not deceived through unavoidable ignorance, or impelled by irresistible force to reject Christ: they do it from a rooted aversion to the Father himself, and evince by their conduct the truth of that declaration, "The carnal mind is enmity against God; for it is not subject to the law of God, neither indeed can be"—Rom. viii. 8, 7.

2. His image.

The word, the ordinances, and the people of God, all bear upon them the impression of God's holiness—And this is the very ground of that aversion which rises against them in the hearts of the ungodly—The gospel is disliked as requiring so much purity and self-denial—The worship of God could be easily tolerated, if an outward form would suffice; but the spirituality and devotion necessary to an acceptable performance of this duty, causes the carnal heart to revolt from it as irksome—If the saints too would countenance the world in its sinful practices, the offense of the cross would cease; but they "make their light to shine before men;" and on this accourt they, whose deeds are evil, hate, revile, and persecute them.—Now this clearly proves, that holiness itself is their aversion, and consequently that the image of God, which principally consists in holiness, is hateful to them—Will any say, it is hypocrisy that they hate, and not holiness? Wherefore then were Christ and his apostles so universally the objects of cruel persecution? Was there any guile in him? Was he not "the brightness of his Father's glory, and the express image of his person?" and walked not his disciples in his steps? It is certain, not only that the image of God is hated by the enemies of Christ, but that every thing that bears his image is hated by them *on that very account,* and *in proportion* as it exhibits a resemblance of him—

3. His very existence.

It is vain indeed to entertain the thought that God could be annihilated—But, if we could suppose for a moment that it were declared from heaven, "There is no God;" would not the tidings excite a general satisfaction?—Would not all the haters of Christ congratulate themselves that there was no God to call them to an account, none to punish them for their iniquities?—Would they not look forward to an unrestrained indulgence of their lusts with pleasure, instead of weeping for the loss of their best and dearest friend?—Yes; as the enemies of Christ exulting in his crucifixion, so would all who hate him rejoice, if the Father also were utterly extinct—That this is no fanciful idea will appear from the declaration of God himself, "The fool hath said in his heart, No God!"—Ps. xiv. 1.

INFER,

1. How desperate is the wickedness of the human heart!

Wherefore is it that men are so full of enmity against Christ and his Father? Is it for having given us his dear Son that they hate the Father; or do they hate Christ for laying down his life for us?—Many good things has he done; for which of them do we reject him?—O let the haters of God blush and be confounded; let them abhor themselves for all their iniquities, and abominations—

2. What a dreadful place must hell be!

Here the wickedness of men is restrained by the preventing grace of God—But in hell it will rage without control—How will all the miserable spirits then vent their malice! How will they gnaw their tongues and blaspheme their God?—Rev. xvi. 9. May *we* never know this by bitter experience—

3. How astonishing is the tender mercy of our God

One would suppose that God should feel nothing but indignation against such an ungrateful world—But behold! he "waiteth to be gracious unto them;" he sends them offers of pardon; he even entreats and "beseeches them to be reconciled to him"—2 Cor. v. 20. O let his goodness lead us to repentance—Let us cast away the weapons of our rebellion, and bow to the sceptre of his grace—So shall we yet be numbered among the friends of God, and be living monuments of his mercy to all eternity.

THE EVILS OF THE TONGUE.

James iii. 6.—The tongue is a fire, a world of iniquity. So is the tongue amongst our members, that it defileth the whole body, and setteth on fire the course of nature; and it is set on fire of hell. (S. S.)

AMONGST the most important of subjects must be reckoned the governmen of the tongue. The consideration of it is well calculated to convince the profane, to pluck off the mask from hypocrites, to humble the sincere, and to edify every description of persons. St. James, who intended his Epistle as a corrective to the abuse that prevailed in the christian church, insisted strongly upon this subject: and, in the words before us, has given us such a description of the tongue, as, if it had proceeded from any other than an inspired writer, would have been deemed a libel upon human nature. In order that the text may be fully understood, we shall shew,

I. THE TRUE CHARACTER OF THE HUMAN TONGUE.

The Apostle tells us "it is a fire."

Fire, in its original formation, was intended for the good of man; and, when subordinated to his wishes, is highly beneficial: but its tendency is to consume and to destroy. Thus the tongue was at first made for the Creator's praise; but through the introduction of sin, that member, which was, and, if well used, yet is, the glory of man, Ps. lvii. 8, is become "an instrument of unrighteousness" and all iniquity.

Fire also, even the smallest spark, is capable of producing incalculable mischief; such mischief as it may not be in the power of man to repair. Thus also will one single motion of the tongue, ver. 3, 4. It may so irritate and inflame a man, as to change him instantly into a savage beast, or an incarnate devil: and, if the whole world should labor to remedy the evil, it would mock their endeavors.

He further adds, that it is "a world of iniquity."

There is not any sin whatever, which does not stand in the nearest connexion with the tongue, and employ it in its service. Search the long catalogue of sins against God; then inspect those against our neighbor; and, lastly, those against ourselves; and there will not be found one, no, not one, that has not the tongue as its principal ally. See Rom. iii. 13, 14.— — — All iniquities whatever centre in it, and are fulfilled by it: so justly is it called. "A world of iniquity."

Its character will yet further appear by considering,

II. ITS EFFECTS.

1. These are defiling.

Sin, as soon as ever it is conceived in the heart, defiles the soul: but when it is uttered by the lips, "it defileth the whole body." Utterance gives solidity and permanency to that, which before existed in idea, and might have passed away: and, inasmuch as the tongue has every other member at its command to execute, according to their several powers, the things it has divulged, the whole man is become a partaker of its guilt and defilement, Eccl. v. 6; Mark vii. 20—23. And, though all its communications are not equally polluting, yet is there a stain left by means of them, a stain which nothing but the Redeemer's blood can ever wash away.

2. Destructive.

To such an astonishing degree has this fire gained the ascendant, that it has "inflamed the whole course of nature." Look at *individuals;* what malignant passions has it kindled in them! Visit *families;* what animosties, and inextinguishable feuds has it produced! Survey *churches;* and you will find the unhallowed fire burning even in the sanctuary of God;* and sometimes too, even in the very censers of his ministers, alluding to Lev. x. 1. Cast your eyes round upon whole *nations;* and you will perceive that, times without number it has kindled the flames of war, and spread desolation through the globe.†

To prove that this account is not exaggerated, we shall point out,

III. THE REASON OF ITS PRODUCING THESE EFFECTS

The tongue "itself is set on fire of hell."

Satan is the source and author of all the evils that proceed from the tongue. Does it falsify? behold, it does so at the instigation of that wicked fiend, "the father of lies," Acts v. 3; John viii. 44. Does it discourage men from the prosecution of their duty? It does so, as the devil's agent, Matt. xvi. 23. Does it accuse and scandalize the people of God? Who but satan is the author of such calumnies? Rev. xii. 10. Does it disseminate error? the propagator of that error is satan's minister, however he be transformed into an angel of light, 2 Cor. xi. 3, 13, 14, 15. Does it encourage any bad design? It is the devil himself who speaks by it, 1 Kings xxii. 21, 22. In every sin that it commits, it is actuated by "the prince of the power of the air, the spirit that now worketh in all the children of disobedience, Eph. ii. 2. Its whole "wisdom is earthly, sensual, *devilish*, ver. 15. It comes from hell, and leads to hell: and, if God were to withdraw his restraints here, as he does in hell, it would speedily produce a very hell upon earth.

This alone can account for the effects that proceed from it.

Doubtless the wickedness of the heart may account for much: but, if the flames were not fanned by satannic agency, we can scarcely conceive that they should rage with such an irresistible force, and to such a boundless extent.

INFER,

How great must be the evil of the human heart!

The heart is the fountain, in which "the evil treasure is;" Matt. xii. 35. the tongue is only the channel in which it flows. If the channel then be so vile, what must the fountain be? Yet every one of us has this tongue in his mouth, and this heart in his bosom: and, if God should leave us without restraint, there is not one of us but would proclaim all the evil of his heart, as the most loathsome sensualist, or most daring blasphemer.

2. How much do we need the influences of the Holy Spirit!

It is absolutely impossible for man to tame this unruly member, ver. 7, 8, Yet restrained it must be, if ever we would be saved, James i. 26. What then shall we do? shall we sit down in despair? God forbid. The Holy Spirit will help our infirmities, Rom. viii. 26, and Christ will give us his Spirit if we call upon him. Let us then look to Christ; and we shall prove by sweet experience, that his "grace is sufficient for us," 2 Cor. xii. 9, and that "through him strengthening us we can do all things." Phil. iv. 13.

3. How careful should we be of every word we utter!

Immense injury may we do by one unguarded word. We may take away a character which we can never restore, or inflict a wound which we can never heal. On this account we should "set a watch before the door of our

* By means of heretics, cavillers, and proud disputers, and others who cause divisions and dissensions.

† What has not been perpetrated under the influence of those two words, liberty and equalit-

437

lips," Ps. cxli. 3. Nor is this a matter of expediency merely, but of necessity; for God has warned us that we shall account of every idle word, and, that by our words we shall be justified, and by our words we shall be condemned, Matt. xii. 36, 37, and v. 22, last clause. Let us then be utterly purposed that our mouth shall not offend, Ps. xvii. 3. Let our tongue be as choice silver, or a tree of life, to enrich and comfort the Lord's people, Prov. x. 20, and xv. 4. Let our "speech be alway with grace seasoned with salt" for the honor of God, and the good of our fellow creatures, Col. iv. 6; Eph. iv. 29.

THE FOLLY OF VAIN EXCUSES.

Prov. xxiv. 11, 12.—If thou forbear to deliver them that are drawn unto death, and those that are ready to be slain; if thou sayest, Behold, we knew it not; doth not he that pondereth the heart consider it? and he that keepeth thy soul, doth not he know it? And shall not he render to every man according to his works? (H. H.)

OFFICIAL influence is a valuable talent: but to use it aright is often very difficult, and painful to the feelings. Hence those who are possessed of it, are apt to shrink back, when the exercise of it is likely to involve them in much trouble; and they will connive at abuses, which they cannot easily prevent. For such connivance they have excuses ever ready at hand; "They were not aware of the circumstances;" or, "They thought their interposition would be to no purpose." But power and responsibility are inseparable: and the magistrate who neglects his duty, must give an account of such neglect to God, and have his excuses weighed in the balance of the sanctuary. To succor the needy, and to relieve the oppressed, is a sacred duty, which no man can neglect, but at the peril of his soul: and to deceive ourselves with vain excuses is folly in the extreme.

We shall not however limit our views of this subject to magistrates, but shall extend them generally to all those excuses which men make for their neglect of acknowledged duties; and shall consider,

I. THE EXCUSES BY WHICH MEN DECEIVE THEIR OWN SOULS.

None are so hardy as to deny their obligation to serve God: yet the great mass of mankind will plead excuses for their neglect,

1. Of religious duties.

"They have not time to attend to their spiritual concerns." Not time? For what then is their time given them? and what other business have they in comparison of this? But, if they would speak the truth, is not their disregard of religion to be traced rather to their want of inclination to spiritual things— — —their want of faith in the divine records— — —their want of all fear of God, and all concern about their souls?— — —How vain then their plea of want of time, when their neglect arises from a total alienation of their hearts from God!

2. Of moral duties.

The duties of sympathy, of compassion, of activity in succoring the distressed, are mentioned in our text. Now for the neglect of these duties, such as the visiting of the sick, the instructing of the ignorant, the relieving of the needy, and the comforting of the afflicted, men will plead ignorance, inadvertence forgetfulness, inability. But is there not a great degree of criminality attaching to us, if we do not search out the poor and afflicted, on purpose to alleviate their distresses?— — —And is not the true cause of our supineness, that we have no love to our fellow-creatures, no zeal for God, no gratitude for redeeming love?— — —It is in vain to think that our neglects are venial under any circumstances, and more especially when they originate in cowardice, and sloth, and selfishness.

Seeing then that such excuses are vain, let us mark,

II. The folly of resting in them.

Were there no God to call us into judgment, our delusions would be of less consequence: but there is a God by whom all our excuses will be weighed; and he,

1. Will judge with truth.

He looketh not at the outward appearance; "He searcheth the heart and tries the reins," and is privy to the most secret workings of our minds. We may easily deceive ourselves; but him we cannot deceive. See how forcible is the appeal made to us in our text. Can we have any doubt whether he sees our conduct, or forms a correct estimate of it? Let us remember, that "he will bring to light the hidden things of darkness, and make manifest the counsels of the heart;" and that, whatever our judgment be, his will be according to truth.

2. Will award with equity.

Here again the appeal is strong, and carries conviction with it. We are sure that "God will judge the world in righteousness," and "give to every man according to his works." "Whatsoever we have sowed, that shall we also reap: if we have sowed to the flesh, we shall of the flesh reap corruption; but if we have sowed to the Spirit, we shall of the Spirit reap life everlasting."

Let this subject teach us,

1. To be jealous over ourselves with a godly jealousy.

We are apt to think that conscience is a safe guide, and that we may rest satisfied with its testimony; but conscience is corrupted by the fall, as well as all the other faculties of the soul. It is blinded, bribed, partial, and in many instances "seared as with an hot iron." Hence it is that "every man's way is right in his own eyes." Paul thought he ought to do many things contrary to the name of Jesus; and was applauded by his own conscience, whilst he was sinning against God with all his might. Be not therefore satisfied merely because you feel no condemnation in your own minds; but beg of God to enlighten your conscience, that it may guide you aright, and keep you from those delusions which would involve you in everlasting ruin.

2. To live in daily expectation of the future judgment.

Ask yourselves, not merely, What do I think of this or that conduct; but, What would God say to it, if I were instantly summoned to his tribunal? Such a question as this would often lead you to a very different estimate of yourselves from that which you have formed; and the consideration of his recording every thing in order to a future judgment would tend to keep you vigilant in all your conduct. Walk then as in his sight, and be satisfied with nothing which you are not well assured will satisfy him.

CAUTION AGAINST DECLENSION IN RELIGION.

Matt. xxiv. 12, 13.—Because iniquity shall abound, the love of many shall wax cold : **but** he that shall endure unto the end, the same shall be saved. (H. H.)

THESE words are a part of the discourse which our Lord held with four of his disciples in private, after he had retired from the temple to the Mount of Olives. Compare Mark xiii. 1—4 with Matt. xxiv. 1, 2. Being in full view of the temple, his disciples were struck with the magnificence of its appearance, and expressed to him their admiration of it: from whence he took occasion to foretell the speedy destruction of it, and to give them signs whereby they should ascertain the approach of the judgments which awaited their whole nation. At the same time he gave them instructions for their own support and comfort under all the trials which they themselves should endure previous to that time. He told them what evil treatment they should meet with from the enemies of his gospel ; and what difficulties they should encounter from his pretended friends. Their trials *from without* we considered in another discourse : * those *from within* we propose for our present consideration.

In the words before us our Lord suggests to his disciples,

I. THE DANGER OF SPIRITUAL DECLENSION.

Independent of the proneness of man at all times to backslide from God, there is a danger arising to us from the conduct of those with whom we stand connected. The bitterness of persecution, or abounding of corruption, may operate to abate our zeal in the service of our God ; but the falls and offenses of those who profess religion have a peculiar tendency to discourage the people of God ; and it is to this, we apprehend, our Lord more espe cially refers.

Such events must be expected in every age.

If we consult the holy scriptures, we shall find that, even in the apostolic age, multitudes who were once hopeful, declined from the ways of God, and made shipwreck both of faith and of a good conscience, 2 Tim. i. 15, and ii. 17, and iv. 10 — — —And what is there to prevent a recurrence of the same evils ? As long as the heart of man is so evil and so treacherous, it will ever be prone to start aside from God, even as a broken bow— — —

Whenever they do happen, they tend to quench the love even of the most established.

Great disappointment is felt by all the members of the christian church : and every one feels a portion of that disgrace which the instability of any member brings upon the whole body. From the frailty of some, the fidelity of others begins to be questioned : evil surmisings arise : a coolness and distance are occasioned among the brethren : the communion of the saints is interrupted ; and their associations for holy exercises are less frequented, or less enjoyed, Heb. x. 24, 25. Divisions then ensue : each leader endeavors to increase the number of his partisans : and thus all that union and harmony which should characterize the family of Christ is destroyed.

Hence arises also a coldness of heart towards God himself and a loss of fellowship with him— — —In a word, the almost inseparable effect of an irruption of iniquity into the church of God is, that "the love of many at least, if not of all, will wax cold." One single "root of bitterness springing up will trouble and defile many." Heb. xii. 15

* On Luke xxi. 17—19, which in Doddridge's Harmory of the Gospels, immediately precedes the text.

Such danger always existing, we proceed to suggest,

II. A PRESERVATIVE AGAINST IT.

Two things are certain, namely, that *on our continuance in well-doing our salvation depends;* and, that *by our continuance in well-doing our salvation is secured:* and the consideration of these two points will, under God, prove an excellent antidote against all the dangers to which we can be exposed.

Consider then, that,

1. *On* our continuance in well-doing our salvation *depends.*

To this truth the whole voice of scripture bears witness. We know full well that there are many promises made to the people of God; and that of those who have been given to Christ he will lose none. But it were a dreadful perversion of those promises, to think that we can be saved in any other way than that of "a patient continuance in well-doing." Rom. ii. 7. We must not attempt to make void the most positive declarations of holy writ, Ezek. xviii. 24, and xxxiii. 12, 13; Heb. x. 26, 27, 38, 39 ———— but must learn, like the apostle Paul himself, to make them an incentive to unwearied watchfulness and diligence, 1 Cor. ix. 27.————

2. *By* our continuance in well-doing our salvation *is secured.*

The promise in our text is absolute and universal: and throughout every part of scripture God says to us, "Be thou faithful unto death; and I will give thee a crown of life"———We need not disquiet ourselves about God's fulfillment of his promises: let us only attend to our own duties, and leave him to accomplish his own word in his own time and way. We shall find at last that "not a jot or tittle of his word has ever failed"———The words of our text were fulfilled literally to *every true disciple* at the destruction of Jerusalem, when *every apostate* perished. A refuge was provided for the whole body of christians, at Pella, and a way was opened for their escape thither: and so it shall be in the day of judgment, when Christ's faithful servants *universally*, and they *only*, shall be saved.

3. The consideration of these truths would be an effectual preservative against spiritual declension.

Suppose iniquity to abound ever so much, what is that to *us*, except as a matter of grief and lamentation for the persons who commit it? Let the iniquity shew itself in any *persons*, or in any *degree*, it is no reason that our love to God and man should wax cold: it should rather operate as a reason for us to stir up our love to a flame, in order to impede the progress of the corruption, or at least to prevent its assaults upon our own souls; as travellers in a wilderness kindle fires around them, in order to protect themselves from the assaults of ravenous and ferocious beasts. At all events, however much any persons may injure their own souls, and endanger their own salvation, it becomes us to take care that they do not destroy or injure us————

ADDRESS,

1. Let us above all things cultivate a spirit of love.

This is the characteristic feature of all God's children; and the want of it, whatever else we may possess, proves us to be only as sounding brass or as tinkling cymbals, 1 Cor. xiii. 1—3. A growth in this is the surest evidence of our growth in grace, 2 Thess. i. 3, 4.————and by this, more than by any thing else, is our establishment in the divine life secured, 1 Thess. iii. 12, 13.———Let us then "take care lest any root of bitterness spring up in our hearts;" and let us daily "put on charity, which is *the bond of perfectness.*" Col. iii. 14.

2. Let us beg of God the assistance of his Holy Spirit.

The consideration of our final happiness depending so entirely on our own continuance in well-doing, would be discouraging, if we did not know, that God has promised to us the aids of his Spirit; and that "the grace of Christ shall be sufficient for us." See how graciously the Lord supported Paul, when all his christian friends had forsaken him in his greatest extremity: "At my first answer no man stood with me, but all men forsook me: I pray God that it may not be laid to their charge: notwithstanding, the Lord stood with me, and strengthened me." 2 Tim. iv. 16. Thus shall you find him present with you in every hour of trial, and be made "more than conquerors through him that loved you."

THE SINFULNESS OF MURMURING AGAINST GOD.

Prov. xix. 3.—The foolishness of man perverteth his way, and his heart fretteth against the Lord. (S. S.)

THE wickedness of the heart is deep and unsearchable—
They who do not watch its motions, have no idea of its depravity—
But they who diligently examine it may discover many evils—
And by the light of God's word attain considerable knowledge—
The disposition mentioned in the text deserves special attention.

I. ILLUSTRATE THE DISPOSITION HERE SPOKEN OF.

The careless and ungodly world are ever ready to cast blame on God.

1. On account of their sins.

They give the rein to every evil thought and desire—
———expose themselves to every kind of temptation—
———lay innumerable stumbling-blocks in their own way—
And thus become enslaved by vicious lusts and appetites—
Against these iniquities God denounces his judgment—
But the slaves of sin continue hardened in their evil ways—
They condemn even God himself as the author of their sins—
This was the conduct of Adam immediately after the fall*—
And it is too often imitated by his guilty descendants—

2. On account of their sorrows.

Sorrow is entailed on all as the punishment of the first transgression—
But most of the afflictions which men suffer are brought on them by their own folly—
Some involve themselves in distress through sloth or intemperance—
Others ruin themselves by imprudence and extravagance—
But all under their calamities "fret against the Lord"—
They are full of invectives against those that have been the more immediate occasions of their trouble—Numb. xvi. 11, 41.
They consider their lot as hard and severe—
And thus do they reflect on Providence rather than on themselves—
Cain, the first-born of Adam, indulged this malignant spirit—Gen. iv 13, 14.
Nor are there any sons of sorrow who do not follow his example—
Nor are believers themselves wholly free from this disposition.

*Gen. iii. 12. He obliquely condemns God for giving the woman to him

442

They watch and pray against their besetting sin—
Yet are sometimes brought under the power of it—
On these occasions they are tempted to fret against the Lord—
They are ready to expostulate with him like those of old—Isa. lviii. 3.
They forget how justly they might have been eternally forsaken—
And that the remaining power of their sins is the consequence both of former habits, and of present neglects—
Under afflictions also they feel too much proneness to murmur—
What sinful impatience did the holy Elijah manifest!—1 Kings xix. 4.
Even Job himself preserved not wholly a becoming temper—Job vii. 15, 16.
This disposition however is most hateful in the sight of God.
II. THE EVIL OF IT.
It betrays the most *deplorable ignorance.*
God is not, nor can be, the author of sin—
He maintains in all things the character given of him—Deut. xxxii. 4.
Hence St. James shews the folly of casting blame on God—James i. 13, 14.
Nor can God punish any of us more than our iniquities deserve—
Hence the expostulation of the prophet is unanswerable—Lam. iii. 39.
Besides, to fret against God is not the way to interest him in our behalf—
Nor will it tend to the peace and composure of our own spirits—
It is as unprofitable to us as it is unjust towards him—
True wisdom would teach us to humble ourselves in his presence—
And to renew our supplications with greater earnestness—
This conduct is as sure to succeed, as the other is to fail of success—Prov. xxviii. 13.
It manifests the most *obstinate impenitence.*
Both sins and sorrows ought to produce humility—
When they increase our rebellion, our state is almost desperate—Isa. i. 5.
How awfully does such a temper characterize God's enemies!—Rev. xvi. 9.
And make us resemble those that are consigned over to perdition!—Matt viii. 12.
Surely nothing more heinous can be laid to our charge—
Nor any thing more speedily fit us for destruction—
It evinces the most *consummate arrogance.*
To fret and murmur is, in fact, to reprove God—
God himself considers it as a direct attack upon him—Mal. iii. 13, 14.
And can any thing be more presumptuous in such worms as we?
St. Paul reprobates this impiety with holy indignation—Rom. ix. 20.
And every one who allows himself in it, must answer it at his peril—
We conclude with suitable ADVICE.
1. Let us search into the occasions of our sins and sorrows
We may be surprised into sin by a sudden temptation—
But may trace our fall to preceding unwatchfulness—
Nor can we expect God to keep us, if we neglect to keep ourselves—
We are rarely earnest enough in using the means of safety—
We are too backward to meditation, prayer, and fasting—
Our afflictions also may have come without any misconduct on our part—
But who has not merited them by his sins?—
Men should only be considered as instruments in God's hands—Ps. xvii 13, 14

And the consideration of his will should silence every murmur—2 Sam. xvi. 10.

2. Let us always be careful to justify God.

We may not always be able to account for his dispensations—
But we should not on that account doubt the equity of them—
Whatever we suffer, we should not " charge God foolishly"—
Under the darkest dispensations we should say as the Psalmist—Ps. xxii. 2, 3.

If we wait we shall see the wisdom of many things which now seem utterly inexplicable—
We may rest assured that David's assertion shall be verified—Ps. li. 4.

3. Let us see what improvement may be made of our troubles.

There is no rod which has not a voice to us—
Our very sins may be permitted, in order to humble us—
And to make us more thankfully cleave to the Saviour—
Our trials, of whatever kind, are to purge away our dross—
And to fit us for eternal rest—
To view them in this light will greatly compose our minds—
Instead of fretting against the Lord, we shall be thankful to him—
And instead of increasing our misery, we shall make it a mean of joy.

THE FOLLY OF CREATURE-CONFIDENCE.

Hos. v. 13.—When Ephraim saw his sickness, and Judah saw his wound, then went Ephraim to the Assyrian, and sent to king Jareb: yet could he not heal you, nor cure you of your wound. (S. S.)

MEN continually provoke God to chastise them, but rarely make a due improvement of his chastisements. Instead of turning to God, they dishonor him more by applying to the creature under their distress rather than to him. The ten tribes, when punished for their willing compliance with Jeroboam's edicts,* sought repeatedly to the Assyrians for help instead of humbling themselves before God: but they found, as "Judah" also did on similar occasions, that their confidence in the creature served only to involve them in shame and disappointment.

Taking the text simply as an historical fact, we deduce from it two observations, which deserve our consideration.

I. MEN, IN TIMES OF TROUBLE, ARE PRONE TO LOOK TO THE CREATURE FOR HELP, RATHER THAN TO GOD.

This was one of the most common and heinous sins of the Jewish nation :† and it is universal also amongst ourselves.

1. In troubles of a temporal nature.

* Ver. 11, 12. God consumed them as moth does a garment, or as a rottenness the bones, secretly, slowly, gradually, effectually.

† Sometimes they relied on Egypt; Isaiah xxx. 1—3, and xxxi. 1. Sometimes on Assyria (as Manahem did on Paul, 2 Kings xv. 19, and Ahaz did on Tiglath-pileser, 2 Kings xvi. 7,) and sometimes on themselves, Isaiah xxii. 8—11. "Jareb" here certainly means the king of Assyria: but whether it was his proper name, or a name given him by the prophet, is uncertain. It means *Defender*, and might be applied to him in a taunting manner. In this view it would be a very severe sarcasm. See 2 Chron. xxviii. 20.

444

In *sickness of body*, we lean, like Asa, 2 Chron. xvi. 12, on the physician. In *distress of mind*, we complain and murmur; but forget to pray, Gen. iv. 13, 14. In *straitened circumstances*, we expect relief from friends. or our own exertions. God is invariably our *last* refuge.

2. In spiritual troubles.

Under *conviction of sin*, we betake ourselves to the observance of duties, and make resolutions to amend our lives, instead of fleeing to Christ as the refuge of lost sinners, Isaiah lv. 2. In *seasons* also *of temptation*, or *desertion*, we adopt a thousand expedients to remove our burthens, but will not cast them on the Lord, 1 Sam. xvi. 14—16. Though foiled ten thousand times, we cannot bring ourselves to lie as clay in the potter's hands; but will rest in the means, instead of looking simply to God in the use of means.

But the longer we persist in it the more we shall find, that,

II. THE CREATURE CANNOT AFFORD US ANY EFFECTUAL SUCCOR.

There are circumstances indeed wherein friends may be instrumental to our relief: but they can do,

1. Nothing *effectual*.

The consolations which are administered by man, or by the vanities of this world, are poor, empty, transient, Jer. ii. 13. Not the whole universe combined can ever bring a man to "glory in tribulations," Rom. v. 3, and to say with Paul. "I take pleasure in them for the sake of Christ:" 2 Cor. xii. 10, as soon might they enable him to stop the sun in its course, as to reduce to experience the paradoxes of that holy apostle, 2 Cor. vi. 10.

2. Nothing *of themselves*.

It is not a little humiliating to see how weak are man's endeavors to heal either the disorders of the body, or the troubles of the soul, when God is pleased to withhold his blessing. The best prescriptions, or the wisest counsels, are even lighter than vanity itself. Reasonings, however just and scriptural, have no weight: advice, however sweetened with love and sympathy, is rejected: the very grounds of consolation are turned into occasions of despair, Ps. lxxvii. 2, 3. When God says, "Let there be light," there is light: but till then, the soul is shut up in impenetrable darkness Job xxxiv. 29.

ADDRESS,

1. Let us guard against this sinful propensity, both in our national and personal concerns.

We cannot but see how prone we are, as a nation, to rest on human alli ances, and human efforts. Would to God we could correct this fatal error, and trust more entirely in the great disposer of all events!

As individuals at least we may, and must, correct it. If we would have the blessing of God, and not his curse, we must renounce all creature-confidence, and trust in him alone. Jer xvii. 5—8. See David's example, Ps. lx. 11, and cxxi. 1, 2.

2. Let us especially rely on Christ as the healer of our souls.

He is "the healer of the nations," Rev. xxii. 2, "Jehovah, who healeth us," Exod. x. 29; there is no physician besides him ; nor any balm, but his blood. We may use whatever means we will, either to pacify our conscience, or to purify the heart; but we shall find that they can "not heal us, nor cure us of our wound." But Christ is all-sufficient: he can in one moment purge us by his blood, and renovate us by his Spirit. To him then let us look with humble, uniform, unshaken affiance.

AGAINST SELF-CONFIDENCE.

1 Cor. x. 12.—Let him that thinketh he standeth, take heed lest he fall. (S. S.)

THE things which are recorded in the holy scriptures are written, not for the entertainment, but for the real improvement, of our minds, Doubtless, as gratifying our curiosity, there is no book under heaven so interesting as the Bible : but as exhibiting what must be realized in our own experience, as shewing us our duties and our difficulties, our helps and our remedies, our punishments and our rewards, it claims, infinitely beyond all other books, our unremitting attention. In this view the apostle, having mentioned the misconduct of the Israelites in the wilderness, and the destruction which they brought upon themselves by means of it, founds upon their history this solemn admonition; "*therefore* let him that thinketh he standeth, take heed lest he fall."

From these words we may learn,

I. THAT ALL, EVEN THE MOST EMINENT, ARE LIABLE TO FALL.

The most distinguished characters of antiquity have fallen*— — —They have betrayed their weakness in those very points, wherein their eminence chiefly consisted†— — —Who then amongst us will presume tosay, "I am in no danger of falling ?" ‡— — —

II. THAT THE MORE SELF-CONFIDENT WE ARE, THE MORE LIKELY WE ARE TO FALL.

Self-confidence naturally emboldens us to rush into temptation— — — And necessarily provokes God to leave us to ourselves— — — —By means of the former, our occasions of falling are greatly multiplied : by means of the latter, our ability to stand is utterly withdrawn‖— — —God, for his own honor's sake, is concerned to let us fall, in order that we may know and confess, that our sufficiency for any good thing is derived from him alone §— — —

III. THAT, IF WE WOULD BE KEPT FROM FALLING, WE MUST LOOK WELL TO OUR STEPS.

As in a slippery path peculiar caution is required, and an inattention to our steps will probably issue in some painful accident, so more especially is it necessary to use circumspection in the path of duty. Who can tell the snares and temptations that beset us ? Who can tell what may be the consequences of any step we take ? Who can reflect on all the circumstances that arose from one single glance of David's eye, and not feel himself exposed to continual danger ? The most important events of our lives may be traced to some trivial cause, some matter of pure indifference : and events,

* *Noah*, Gen. vi. 9, with ix. 21. *Lot*, 2 Pet. ii. 7, 8, with Gen. xix. 33—36. *David*, Acts xiii. 22, with 2 Sam. xi. 4, 5, 15. *Solomon*, (who was called Jedediah, the beloved of the Lord, 2 Sam. xii. 24, 25.) 1 Kings xi. 1—9.

† *Abraham*, Rom. iv. 20, with Gen. xii. 12, 13, and xx. 2. 11. *Job*, Jam. v. 11, with Job iii. 3. *Moses*, Numb. xii. 3, with xx. 10, 11. *Jeremiah*, Jer. ix. 1, with xx. 8, 9. *Paul*, Acts xx. 24, with xviii. 9. 10 ; when he seems to have been struck with a panic.

‡ John iv. 14, and 1 Pet. i. 23, shew the proper qualities and tendency of *grace ;* but do not at all affect what the scriptures elsewhere affirm to be the tendency of our inherent *corruption.*

‖ We have a striking example of this in Peter, who to gratify his curiosity went into the midst of his enemies, and was then left to experience his own weakness, Matt xxvi. 58, 74

§ Thus he acted towards the Israelites Deut. i. 42—44.

equally or more important, perhaps no less than the everlasting salvation of our souls, may depend on the very next step we take. Surely then we should in "all things be circumspect:" Exod. xxiii. 13; we should "take heed to our ways;" we should walk in an humble dependence on God for direction and support; we should cry to him continually "hold thou up my goings in thy paths, that my footsteps slip not." Ps. xvii. 5.

We shall conclude this subject with a few words of ADVICE.

1. To those who are offended at the falls of others.

Many, when they see a professor of religion act amiss, are ready to impute his misconduct to the gospel itself, as though christianity were only a cloak for hypocrites. But, considering the temptations that surround us, and the corruptions that are within us, it is rather a wonder that any stand, than that some should fall. We mean not to justify, or to extenuate, the sins of any: but we desire that religion should not be represented as promoting that, which it utterly condemns. Let the blame fall on those who merit it, and not be cast indiscriminately on all who profess godliness. Let Judas be branded as a traitor; but let not the odium of *his* offense attach to all the other apostles, and to their divine master.

2. To those who are endeavoring to walk uprightly before God.

It is of considerable use to persons when walking on slippery ground, to have hold of each other, that if one slip, the other may afford him immediate assistance. Many falls and bruises have been escaped by these means. Thus it is of great importance to christians to walk together in love, each helping to support his neighbor, and receiving help from others in the time of need. Eccl. iv. 9, 10. Let all then watch over one another with a godly jealousy. If one fall, let others endeavor instantly, in meekness, to raise him up. Gal. vi. 1. Above all, let every one know in whom his strength is; and pray continually, "hold thou me up and I shall be safe." Ps. cxix. 117.

"Now to him, who is able to keep us from falling, &c. be glory and majesty, dominion and power, both now and ever. Amen." Jude xxiv. 25

AGAINST HYPOCRISY.

Job xx. 4—7.—Knowest thou not this of old, since man was placed upon earth, that the triumphing of the wicked is short, and the joy of the hypocrite but for a moment; Though his excellency mount up to the heavens, and his head reach unto the clouds? yet he shall perish for ever, like his own dung: they which have seen him shall say, Where is he? (S. S.)

PREJUDICE or passion will miserably warp the judgment—

It will hide from us what we might know, and cause us to pervert what we do know—

Never was this more strongly exemplified than in the friends of Job—

Had they calmly considered, they might have comforted him in his affliction—

But, by a hasty misapplication of acknowledged truths, they most unjustly and cruelly condemned him—

Job had hinted to them the evil and danger of their conduct—Job xix 28, 29.

447

And Zophar, irritated at the caution, replies with great severity—

His words however, though misapplied, suggest to us two very important truths respecting sinners.

I. THEIR PROSPERITY IS TRANSIENT.

Of sinners, some *make no profession* of religion, and others *a false profession.*

Each of these characters may enjoy, for a while, great prosperity.

The *profane* are often exalted to places of dignity and power—

They prosper in all their labors for wealth and preferment—

They not only despise, but perhaps persecute the godly—

They " triumph," as though no evil should ever happen unto them—

This the Psalmist saw with deep regret—Ps. lxxiii. 3—12.

Hypocrites also frequently are held in estimation—Rev. iii. 1.

They are objects of envy to many an humble and contrite soul—

They will boast of experiences which might well be coveted—

And even attain considerable heights of joy—Matt. xiii. 20.

Their " excellency may mount up to the heavens, and their heads reach unto the clouds"—

But their prosperity will be of short duration.

Death will speedily seize upon the most stout-hearted sinner—

Then all, which he gloried in, shall come to an end—

None of his " pomp shall follow him," or his " wealth be carried with him"—

The hypocrite also shall have a period put to his dissimulation—

He shall soon appear in his proper character—

The all-seeing God will discover the secrets of his heart—

Nor is this time at any great distance—Deut. xxxii. 35.

In comparison of eternity, the duration of his joy will be " but a moment."

Then will they experience a sad reverse.

II. THEIR RUIN WILL BE TREMENDOUS.

The ungodly will in due time be visited for their offenses—

They will then " perish,"

1. To their own eternal shame.

Many portions of scripture appear to us indelicate—

But God's representations of sin are surely just—

And well calculated to make us nauseate and loathe it—

Such is his description of the *ways* of sinners—2 Pet. ii. 22.

And such his declaration respecting their *end*—Compare Rev. iii. 16, with the text.

They will perish under circumstances of disgrace and ignominy—

Christ will not deign to own them before his Father—Matt. x. 33.

The angels will come forth to execute the vengeance of God upon them—

The saints would even " thrust them out of heaven" if they should seek admittance there—Luke xiii. 28.

The damned themselves will insult them with bitter taunts—Isa. xiv. 9—16.

Nor shall they ever cease to be objects of contempt and abhorrence—

This is told us in the plainest terms—Prov. xiii. 5 ; Dan. xii. 2.

Nor while they retain, as they must, their character, is it possible that their situation ever should be changed—Rev. xxii. 11.

2. To the astonishment of all that knew them.

The question " Where is he?" refers primarily to the utter extinction of the ungodly—.

But it may well be considered also as an expression of surprise—

The *wicked* little think where their course will terminate—

If the rich man's request had been granted, Luke xvi. 23, 27. 28, what reply would his surviving brethren have made so soon as that in the text*—

The *hypocrites* also often escape detection in this world—

Perhaps they were celebrated, after their departure, as eminent saints—

We may conceive that their dearest friends, or their associates in holy exercise, may enquire after them in heaven—

What surprise and horror must seize them, when they hear of the doom which the heart-searching God has passed upon them !†—

ADDRESS—"KNOW YOU NOT THIS ?"

Know you not that this has been so from the beginning of the world ?

Does not the word of God assert, that " it shall be ill with the wicked ?" Isa. iii. 11 ; Ps. ix. 17.

Does not the most authentic history in the world prove it to have been so ?‡

Does not conscience itself testify that it shall be so still ?—

If you know, do you not *consider* this ?

Can any thing be more worthy of our consideration ?—

If we have " but a moment," should we not improve that moment ?—

Are we willing to perish in this ignominious and awful manner ?—

Let us live no longer in the neglect of religion.

The gratifications of sense can last but for a little time—

But the consequences of neglecting God will endure for ever—

Surely the care of the soul is the " one thing needful"—

Nor let us rest in a " form of godliness" without experiencing " its power."

It will avail us little to deceive our fellow-creatures—

The higher we have been in their estimation, the deeper will be our disgrace—

Let us then go to Christ for the remission of past sins—

Let us approve ourselves to him in future, as " servants that need not be ashamed."—

And labor to be " sincere and without offense until his coming again."

---

* They would most probably have exclaimed, " Where is he ! in hell! lifting up his eyes in torments ! Is it really so ? We never could have thought it : we had no doubt but that he was happy : he seemed to us as worthy and blameless a character as any : nor had he himself any doubts but that he was going to heaven."

† If a minister is to have those as his " joy and crown of rejoicing," who were truly converted by his ministry, we may, not improperly, suppose a degree of disappointment, if he miss those, concerning whom he had entertained the most sanguine hopes. We may suppose him, upon the first discovery, to say, " Where is he ! What, HE in hell! I often feared that I myself should go thither ; but who would have thought that HE should ?" The Lord grant that this may never be realized by any of us!

‡ Where are now the antediluvian scoffers, the haughty Pharaoh, the treacherous Judas, the worldly-minded Demas, the heretical Hymenous ? &c.

A CAUTION AGAINST DEPARTING FROM GOD.

Heb. iii. 12—14.—Take heed, brethren, lest there be in any of you an evil heart of unbelief, in departing from the living God. But exhort one another daily, while it is called
to-day lest any of you be hardened through the deceitfulness of sin. For we are made
partakers of Christ, if we hold the beginning of our confidence stedfast unto the end.
(S. S.)

THE consideration of the fullness and sufficiency of Christ, is that which
animates the believer in all his conflicts: yet it is on no account to supersede
our own care and watchfulness: on the contrary, it affords us the greatest
encouragement to watch, because it ensures success to us in our endeavors,
which without his almighty aid, would be of no avail—In this view it is
that the inspired writer calls us to "consider the Apostle and High-Priest
of our profession, Christ Jesus, who was not merely a servant, like Moses,
but a son, the heir and Lord of all, yea, the very builder of that spiritual
house, of which we profess ourselves to be a part"—On this truth he
grounds the exhortation in the text,* in which he suggests,

I. A SOLEMN CAUTION.

Difficult as it is to come to God, we find it easy enough to depart from
him—We should therefore be on our guard.

1. Against any departure from him.

While men are yielding to temptation, and turning aside from the ways
of God, they cherish an hope that they may still preserve their interest in
his favor, though they be not studious to do his will ·But a departure of
any kind, whether from the faith or practice of christianity, is nothing less
than a departure from him who is the only source of life and happiness—
We cannot therefore be too much on our guard against any secret declensions, which are so dishonorable to him whom we profess to love, and so
destructive of our present and eternal welfare—

2. Against that unbelief from whence all declensions arise.

As faith is that which brings us to God, and keeps us stedfast in our
adherence to him, so unbelief separates us from him, and, in proportion as
it is harbored, invariably alienates us from the life of God—Whatever be the
more immediate object of that unbelief, whether we attempt to lower the
strictness of God's precepts, or question the veracity of his promises or
threatenings, it proceeds equally from "an evil heart," and brings with it the
same pernicious consequences; it is a root of bitterness, which, if it be
permitted to spring up, will cause every devout affection to wither and decay
—We must therefore labor to eradicate it, if we would not eat for ever its
bitter fruits—

That his caution may have its due effect, the apostle prescribes,

II. THE MEANS OF IMPROVING IT.

Sin is of a deceitful and hardening nature.

When "a backslider in heart" commits a sin, many thoughts will arise in
his mind to palliate the evil, and to make him think that it will not be
attended with any important consequences—Soon he begins to doubt whether
the thing be evil at all; and, ere long, to justify it from the peculiarity of
his circumstances—At first he felt some remorse; but presently his conscience becomes less tender, till at last it is altogether seared and callous; so
that, notwithstanding he be miserably departed from God, he is regardless

* All the words between "Wherefore," in ver. 7, and the text, are a parenthesis: we
must therefore connect the text thus; "Wherefore" "take heed," &c.

of **his loss**, and insensible of his danger—Who that has ever noticed the workings of his own heart, has not found, what a bewitching and besotting thing sin is? yea, who has not often seen reason to bewail its deceitful, hardening effects?—

To guard effectually against it we should watch over each other.

Sin, from the foregoing qualities, naturally hides itself from our view, and renders us inattentive to the means of prevention—But ignorant as we often are of our own spirit, we see clearly enough the defects of others; yea, perhaps we condemn with severity in others the very things which we allow in ourselves—To watch over each other therefore, and to warn each other of those declensions which we either see or apprehend, is a most valuable service; and, if performed with discretion and love, it can scarcely fail of producing the happiest effects—This is a duty to which God has solemnly called us in his word; Lev. xix. 17, and it is to be a part of our "daily" work—Our time for it will be very short: either we or our brother may be speedily removed; and our opportunity of benefiting his soul may be lost for ever—We should exhort one another therefore "daily, while it is called to-day;" and, though it is often an unpleasant office, we should use all fidelity in the execution of it—By this means we may restore a brother before he has relapsed too far, and preserve him from that departure from God, which would otherwise terminate in his destruction—

Still further to enforce the caution given us, the apostle adds

III. A MOTIVE TO REGARD IT.

Our final participation of Christ's benefits depends on our stedfastness in the pursuit of them.

Without entering into the question, whether God has decreed the final perseverance of the saints, we may be fully assured, that none can obtain salvation but by persevering in the way of holiness to the end of life: the scriptures continually speak this language, "He that endureth unto the end, the same shall be saved:" "but if any man draw back, my soul shall have no pleasure in him"—Matt. xxiv. 13: Heb. x. 38. It is true that believers are already *in a measure* "partakers of Christ:" but the complete enjoyment of his benefits is reserved for the future life: and we must not only have a scriptural and well-founded confidence at first, but must keep it stedfast even to the end, in order to attain that full possession of our inheritance—

If any thing can stimulate us to caution, surely this must.

Eternity is at stake, and depends on our present condition: according as we approve ourselves to the heart-searching God, will our state be fixed for ever—Is it not madness to be remiss and careless under such circumstances? Would any one, who should have reason to think his house were on fire, sit still without endeavoring to find out the latent grounds of his alarm? And shall we know our proneness to unbelief, and not guard against its operation, lest it lead us to apostacy? Shall we acknowledge the deceitful, hardening nature of sin, and not exhort each other to mortify and subdue it?—Surely if we have the smallest concern for our souls, we shall not only regard the caution given us in the text, but labor to improve it in the way prescribed—

ADDRESS,

1. Those who have never come to God at all.

The foregoing subject is *in itself* applicable to those only who profess religion; but it may be accommodated to those also who make no such profession; for if they who have come to God are in danger of departing from him, and they who have enjoyed a scriptural confidence, may lose it; if they, who have believed may "make shipwreck of their faith," and they, who have "begun in the Spirit, may end in the flesh:" if they, who have "begun to run well, may be hindered," and they, who have "escaped the pollutions of the world, may again be entangled therein and overcome;" and, lastly, if they who "have been enlightened, and have tasted the good word of God and the powers of the world to come, may so fall away as never to be renewed unto repentance;" What must become of those who have never experienced any of these things? Can they be safe? Can they have any scriptural hope of heaven? If the strongest have so much need of caution, and the most circumspect such reason to fear the deceitful, hardening effects of sin, surely the careless have need to tremble, lest they "die in their sins," and "be driven away in their wickedness"—If all, except two, of those who came out of Egypt, perished in the wilderness, can they hope to enter into the land of Canaan, who have never once come forth from their spiritual bondage?—The point is clear; may God enable us to lay it to heart, and to consider it with the attention it deserves!—

2. Those who are conflicting with their spiritual enemies.

Much has already been spoken to you both in a way of caution and direction: we beg leave to add a word of encouragement—The thing, against which you are chiefly guarded, is unbelief; because *that* is the true source of all apostasy—We now would say, Be strong in faith giving glory to God—"Faith is the shield wherewith you are to quench the fiery darts" of your enemies—Only believe; and Omnipotence will come to your support—Only believe; and you shall experience "the mighty working of *his* power, who raised Christ from the dead"—Commit yourself to him "who is able to keep you from falling; and he will present you faultless before the presence of his glory with exceeding joy."

DANGER OF RELIGIOUS INDECISION.

Luke ix. 61.—Lord, I will follow thee; but let me first go bid them farewell which are at home at my house. (Pr.)

WHEN the marriage supper was provided, and the guests were invited, they all with one consent began to make excuse. And here, out of three that were invited to follow the Saviour, two are for pleading some delay; one wanted to go and bury his father, and the other to take leave of his friends. There is always something or another to hinder us in the path of duty, and to weaken our resolutions in following the Lord fully: it is therefore our wisdom to see the danger, and to guard against it. For this purpose let us

Consider the resolution mentioned in the text, and what are its principal defects.

1. He wished to follow Christ, but there was something of more urgent necessity that must first be attended to.—Thus the sick oftentimes resolve to reform their lives when they recover, but remain as before. The youth wishes to be religious but thinks that so grave a subject had better be deferred to old age. He must have a little more pleasure in his early days, and then he will attend to the concerns of his soul, will repent and obey the gospel. The servant must be free from his master, and then he thinks of becoming the servant of God. Some are for putting matters off for a few years, others only for a few days, when they shall be more at liberty from present diffi-

culties and engagements.— — —The folly of all this is very apparent: the concerns of the soul are of as much importance at this moment as they can be at any future time; life is uncertain, and every delay is a step towards final impenitence. Heb. iii. 8.

2. The person who formed the resolution in the text, evidently made it in his own strength.—Here is no reference whatever to divine assistance, no dependance upon the Lord, no seeking for grace to help in time of need, but an unqualified and self-confident resolution. "Lord, I will follow thee." How easy and how vain are such promises, yet how frequently do they meet our observation. The children of Israel said, "we will serve the Lord;" but considered not that his service requireth the renunciation of all their idols, and of all their sins. Josh. xxiv. 19. And in order to follow Christ we must deny ourselves and take up the cross, which grace only can enable us to do. John xv. 5.

3. The resolution when formed, seemed to depend on the consent of his friends, for though he speaks only of taking his leave, he probably wished to know whether they approved of the step he was about to take. Had he been influenced by proper motives, instead of leaving them behind, he would rather have endeavored to bring them with him, to follow Jesus in the way. Thus did Andrew and Philip, John i. 40—45; the woman of Samaria, John iv. 28—30; and others. Luke viii. 39.— — —But here was no seeking first the kingdom of God and his righteousness, no forsaking all for Christ, but a cleaving to worldly connexions rather than to him. Matt. x. 37.

4. Instead of following Christ cheerfully and with all his heart, he appeared somewhat dejected at the thought, and must go and take leave of his friends, as if he were about to die, and should see them no more. Such are the melancholy apprehensions which some persons entertain of true religion; they imagine it would be injurious to their worldly interest, and unfit them for the common duties and enjoyments of life, and that therefore they must take a final leave of the concerns of the present world.— — —Whereas, by cleaving to the Lord we should be better prepared to serve our generation, and to enjoy the blessings of providence. Religion improves all the relations, and heightens and endears to us all the comforts of life. Eccles. ix. 7.

5. By going home to his friends, he would expose himself to great temptation, and be in danger of breaking the resolution already formed. They would upbraid him with folly for attaching himself to a sect every where spoken against, and to a person so generally despised.— — —Paul consulted not with flesh and blood, neither must we, if we would follow the Lamb withersoever he goeth. Gal. i. 16. Those who are on the Lord's side must be as Levi, they must not know their own kindred. Deut. xxxiii. 9.

1 This subject may serve as a warning to those who trifle with the calls of the gospel. Here was a looking back, a lingering after the world, and Christ pronounces such to be unfit for the kingdom of God: verse 62.

2. Nothing but a decided attachment to Christ, and a determination to sacrifice all for his sake, can constitute us his disciples.

3. Let us beware of the ensnaring influence of worldly connexions, and of every inordinate affection; for these, rather than grosser evils, are the ordinary impediments to our salvation. Matt. xvi. 26.

UNGODLY PROFESSORS ADMONISHED.

James iv. 8.—Draw nigh to God, and he will draw nigh to you: cleanse your hands, ye sinners, and purify your hearts, ye doubled-minded. (Pr.)

In the early period of the christian church it was said, that "great grace was upon them all:" but as things proceeded, many were found amongst them who were mere professors, having nothing of religion but the form.

Such was the case in James' time.—His epistle is addressed to the believing Jews; but in writing to them, he at the same time addresses himself to unbelievers among them, as in the language of our text.— — —He supposes indeed that they did not live without prayer; but that when they prayed, they received not, because they asked amiss; ver. 3.— — —He also describes them as being of a worldly spirit, and double-minded in all their ways. Hence the pointed language now before us.

I. Consider the characters addressed.

1. Though they were professors of religion, they are considered as far from God.—In all their prayers and religious duties, they never "draw nigh to God," have no communion with him; and though belonging to the church, they are living without God in the world.— — —Characters of this description are still to be found in every christian society.

2. Their "hands" and their "hearts" are supposed to be defiled.—They had not laid aside all malice, and all guile, and hypocrisy, and envies, and all evil speakings, that as new-born babes they might desire the sincere milk of the word. 1 Pet. ii. 1, 2. They are still under the power of darkness, and the dominion of sin: their hands are full of oppression and fraud, and their hearts full of impurity.— — —They live after the flesh, and war after it; fulfilling the desires of the flesh and of the mind.

The apostle calls them "sinners," though they may profess to be saints, and be numbered with the people of God.

3. Under a profession of religion, they were nevertheless "double-minded;" halting between God and Baal, and were sometimes this, and sometimes that.— — —When conscience is awakened by the application of some powerful truth, or by the occurrence of some alarming providence, then they are on the Lord's side.— — —When in the company of pious people, they can be pious too: but when they are in the world, and mix with worldly company, they are on the side of the world. 1 Kings xxii. 4.

II. The counsel given them: "Draw nigh to God—cleanse your hands—purify your hearts."

And what does all this denote? Some may think it sufficient to answer,— pray to God, and reform what is amiss in your conduct.— — —This indeed is included, but this is not all; it includes repentance towards God, and faith in our Lord Jesus Christ.

1. The exhortation supposes that God is accessible through a mediator, for without this there would be no invitation to "draw nigh."— — —If no mediator were provided, we should be like the fallen angels, without hope: the name of the Lord could not have been invoked, with any assurance of success.— — —But the blood of Jesus Christ his Son cleanseth from all sin: we may therefore draw nigh to him, though we are "sinners," great sinners and have offended against light and knowledge.— — —The fountain is opened for sin and uncleanness, and we may wash and be clean.

2. Though exhorted to "cleanse our hands and purify our hearts," these acts are not preparatory to repentance and faith, but the very things them-

selves.————No other way of drawing nigh to God has the promise of acceptance: no other cleansing will purify the heart.————The influence of some inferior principle may be sufficient to cleanse the hands, but nor the heart; but the cleansing will only be partial, and not lasting.

Genuine repentance will both cleanse the hands and the heart.———— Weeping at the Saviour's feet, a Magdalene was made clean; and of the impure Corinthians it is said, but ye are sanctified, ye are justified, in the name of the Lord Jesus, and by the Spirit of our God. 1 Cor. vi. 11. Isai. xxx. 21, 22.

A sinner under the first conviction generally reforms his conduct, and casts away his open sins; but his heart can only be purified by faith; and without this, there can be no entering into the kingdom of God. Matt. v. 8.

III. THE ENCOURAGEMENT TO COMPLY WITH THIS ADVICE: "God will draw nigh to you."

This language does not imply that man is the first mover in the great affair of salvation: far from it. We are apprehended of Christ, before we apprehend him: he draws us, and we run after him. John vi. 44, xii. 32. Phil. iii 12.

But it does suppose that repentance precedes forgiveness, and believing in Jesus.————The Lord may draw near to us in his secret influence on the heart, and does so before we draw near to him; but not in a way of fellowship and communion————not as a God pardoning iniquity, and giving rest to the soul. We must come to Christ by faith, before that can be obtained. 2 Cor. vi. 17. 18.

How important are these words: "I will draw near to you"————what condescension, for the great God to draw near to a worm of the dust; yes, near to you; as a father, a friend, and a guide————near to you in death, when every other friend must take their leave. Ps. xlviii. 14.

Oh what a state, for a sinner to be called to die, when no one can help him but God, and for God to be afar off!

THE SCORNER REPROVED.

Proverbs xiv. 9.—Fools make a mock of sin. (Pr.)

IN the esteem of this pious philosopher, religion is the highest wisdom, and sin the greatest folly. Such is the general purport of his characteristics; but in the text especially, he has marked with the most degrading epithet a species of levity deserving of the severest rebuke. It is not enough for some men that they are sinners: they must add folly to their depravity, and treat the greatest of all evils as a light and trifling concern.

I. ENQUIRE WHO THEY ARE THAT MAY BE SAID TO "make a mock at sin."

1. They are those who excuse or palliate the evil of their own conduct, treating sin as a light matter, and saying of it as Lot did of Zoar, is it not a little one.————Some plead nature, some custom, some necessity, and others example: but as the prophet said, will ye plead for Baal? Is it possible to excuse or justify so great an abomination? Every attempt to conceal its enormity, to throw the blame on others, or on the circumstances in which

we are placed, is a fearful sign of impenitence, and of that inconsiderate levity which the wise man so severely reprehends. Proverbs xxviii. 13.

2. Those make a mock at sin who can commit it without regret, and glory in their shame, instead of being humbled for it. Phil. iii. 19.— — —There are scorners who turn sin into a jest, and even boast of their wickedness. Prov. x. 23.— - —Injuries done to fellow men, such as are adapted to fill the mind with horror and detestation, are too often made the subject of un-feeling ridicule. 2 Sam. ii. 14—16; Prov. xxvi. 18, 19.— — —Some will dare to sin for the diversion of others, and to commit acts of public injustice for the sake of a little popularity. Hos. vii. 3. Acts xii. 2, 3 ; xxiv. 27.

3. Those who rush into sin upon the slightest temptation, show how lightly they regard it, and with what contempt they treat the divine author-ity. The profane Esau could sell his birthright for a mess of pottage, and the covetous Judas betray his master for thirty pieces of silver Zech. xi. 13. From such mean and mercenary motives do men sacrifice their conscience and their souls ; and not only sell themselves to work wickedness, but sell themselves for nought.

4. Some make a mock at sin by scoffing at their reprovers, and treating them with utter disdain. Such was the conduct of Ahab towards Micaiah, and of Herod towards John the Baptist. 1 Kings xxii 8; Mark vi. 18, 19. On the same principle, parental authority is frequently despised, and minis-terial fidelity treated with levity and scorn. Prov. xiii. 1.

5. How lightly some men regard sin may be seen in their rejection of the atonement, and substituting in its stead their own endeavors to appease the divine anger, and to commend themselves to God. All self-righteousness is founded in light thoughts of sin, and leads to a rejection of the only way of salvation. Prov. vii. 36.

6. Some even go so far as to take pleasure in the sins of others, and turn into a scene of mirth what will issue in lamentation and woe. Hab. ii. 15. It is sufficiently evil to mock at human suffering, but inconceivably more so to mock at that which leads to endless perdition; first to tempt men to the commission of sin, and then to be diverted with their impiety.

II. THE FOLLY AND DANGER OF SUCH CONDUCT.

It is sufficiently to our shame that we are sinners ; but it is the height of folly to make a mock of sin.

1. Because of its intrinsically evil nature. Sin had its origin in the bot-tomless pit, 1 John iii. 8 ; whence it issued, and infected the nature of man, and is opprobiously termed "the filthiness" of the flesh and of the spirit. 2 Cor. vii. 1. It is the disgrace of our nature, and by it we have debased ourselves even unto hell. Isai. lvii. 9. It is the sum of all evil: from hence proceed evil thoughts, evil speaking, an evil conscience, and evil deeds. It is worse than death, for death would have no sting without it; and worse than hell, for it is sin that creates the never-dying worm, and the fire that cannot be quenched.

2. The present consequences of sin show the extreme folly of making light of it It is pregnant with all the evils that exist in the world, of what-ever kind or degree ; and who can calculate this mighty sum ? Whatever calamity befals a sinner in the present life, it may truly be said to him in the language of the prophet, "thy way and thy doings have procured these things unto thee." Jer. iv. 18. The ruin and distress brought upon the conscience has induced others, besides Judas, to cast themselves directly into hell, to get rid of their horror and despair. And even where sin is re-

pented of and pardoned, it brings unutterable distress upon the soul. **Ps. xxxviii. 3.**

3. The sufferings of Christ for sin, and the price paid for our redemption, awfully demonstrate the folly and madness of making light of sin. Behold the Son of God prostrate in Gethsemane, witness his agony and bloody sweat; see him on the cross, and hear his dying cries; and then say whether the cause of these sufferings can be regarded with indifference, or be made a matter of idle jest. No where does the evil of sin appear so great as in the sacrifice of the Son of God. Isai. liii. 4, 5.

4. The final ruin and destruction which sin will bring upon the soul in a future world. Could we descend into the dark and silent chambers of the grave, and behold the bodies of the wicked crumbling into dust, and becoming a prey to rottenness and worms; could we draw aside the veil that conceals from us the world of spirits, and plunge into all the thickest horrors of the bottomless pit, and see the justice of God pouring out a tempest of fire upon lost souls to all eternity; surely we could not be disposed to make a mock at sin, or live any longer in a state of impenitence and unbelief. A fire is kindled in his wrath, that shall burn to the lowest hell.

Let mockers beware then, lest their bands be made strong, and they be left to wonder and perish.—Be not deceived: God is not mocked: whatsoever a man soweth, that shall he also reap. Those who now deride religion, and make a mock at sin, will find that God also will laugh at their calamity, and mock when their fear cometh. Prov. i. 25—27.

FATAL ISSUE OF FINAL IMPENITENCE.

Job ix. 4.—Who hath hardened himself against him, and hath prospered. (Pr.)

Bildad, one of Job's friends, considered his complaints as amounting to a rebellion against God: ch. viii. 3. Job is greatly moved at this, and disowns the charge with abhorrence. "He is wise in heart, and mighty in strength; who hath hardened himself against him, and hath prospered?"

The words however imply, that there is such a thing as for a man so to harden himself as to contend with God: and that where this is the case it is certain to come to a dreadful issue.

I. Enquire wherein this hardness of heart consists.

1. The word signifies a spirit that is *obstinate and incorrigible;* full of perverseness, keeping up a contention with God.— — —In scripture language it is being stiff-necked, and uncircumcised in heart and ears. Neh. x. 16, 17; Acts vii. 51.

2. It is descriptive of that *rebellious spirit*, which discovers itself under the various dispensations of God, both in a way of mercy and of judgment. — — —Thus Pharaoh acted: sometimes he seemed humble and willing to submit: but when the judgment was withdrawn, he resumed his former resolution, and continued to harden himself against God.

3. There is also a *judicial hardness* to which sinners are liable, in a way of righteous judgment for their iniquities.— — —God is said to have hardened Pharaoh's heart; not that he produces evil in the mind of man, which is utterly impossible, James i. 13: but through man's perverseness, the divine dispensations make him worse instead of better.— — —If the

457

providences of God do not soften the human mind, it generally becomes thereby more hardened. Thus also the gospel produces a similar effect, where its influence is rejected : and instead of being a savor of life unto life, it becomes a savor of death unto death.   2 Cor. ii. 16

This is not owing to any defect in the gospel, or in the dispensations of God towards us ; but to the depravity of the human heart, wh ch perverts the means of salvation into those of destruction.— — —Hence this impenitent hardness is ascribed to man, as well as to God; to show that God has no influence in the matter, so as to affect man's free agency and accountability,

11 Notice some of the instances in which this sin is still committed.

Ineffectual and dangerous as it is for any one to harden himself against God, it is a sin no less prevalent than formerly ; and it will become us to notice the different ways in which it operates, that we may be warned against it.

1. It appears in indulging *hard thoughts of God*, of his government and of his holy law : in esteeming him as a hard master, and is considering sinful propensities as an excuse for sinful actions, though no one thinks of excusing the offense of others against himself on the ground of such a plea. — — —The indulgence of such thoughts lead on to final impenitence.

2. It manifests itself in a rejection or *dislike of God's way of salvation*. This impenitent aversion is directed against its freeness, as placing all men alike on a level.— — —Against its sovereignty, in that God should have mercy on whom he will have mercy : and its language is, " why doth he yet find fault?"— — —This was the stumbling block to the hardened and unbelieving Jews. Isa. vi. 9, 10 ; Rom. ix. 29—33.

3. Persisting in an evil course, *amidst many convictions and fears*, is another instance of this sort of depravity.— — —Pharaoh knew that he was wrong, and yet he dared to persist. Many have great light and strong convictions, yet they have loved idols, and after them they will go.— — —Some under threatening afflictions will do the same.

4. This hardness of heart appears in the *resistance that is offered to the hand of God in providence* instead of being humbled under it.— — — The great end of adverse providences is to make us willing to accept the punishment of our iniquity. Lev. xxvi. 41.— — —Instead of this, many are like Ephraim, a bullock unaccustomed to the yoke : and when their plans are frustrated, they still persevere in rebellion against God. Isa. ix. 10.— — —This is desperate wickedness, and braving the divine judgments. It is an evil thing to be haughty in the day of prosperity, but more so in a day of adversity : this is incorrigible wickedness.

5. *Presumptuously tempting God*, amidst the most affecting means of salvation, is another instance of this hardness of heart. It was thus with Israel in the wilderness. God spared them time after time, yet they rebelled against him. They were warned of this impenitence and unbelief, five hundred years afterwards, Ps. xcv. 8—11 : and after a thousand years more, the same warning was repeated, but without effect, for they perished in their unbelief. Heb. iii. 12.

III. The fatal issue of final impenitence: " Who hath hardened himself against him, and prospered ?

1. The longer you continue in this state, the *more hardened* you will become, till at last you will be past feeling. Ephes. iv. 19. This is the natural effect of unbelief, and sinning against God.

2. This also is the way in which God *punishes men* for their impenitence. Isa. vi. 8. And if God should give you up to this state, where
would you be at last!

3. *The end* of this impenitence and hardness of heart is fearfully
described by an apostle. and should warn us of our danger. Rom. ii. 5—9.

Let it be remarked however, that these awful consequences proceed on the
supposition that this impenitence is finally persisted in, and that mercy is
promised to the returning sinner, Isa. lv. 7.— — —Many have been brought
to drop the controversy with God, as Ephraim did, and have found mercy,
Jer. xxxi. 19, 20. And all other impenitent sinners are invited and encouraged to follow his example, Isa. xlvi. 12, 13.

DANGER OF SELF-DECEPTION.

Proverbs xiv. 12. There is a way which seemeth right unto a man, but the end thereof
are the ways of death. (Pr.)

However diversified the pursuits of men, all are in search of happiness.
Some seek it in the things of this life, and leave the concerns of futurity
unheeded. This their way seems wise to them, in making sure of what is,
though it can scarcely appear to themselves to be "right." Others are seeking the gratification of their depraved appetites in a way that is opposite to
their own consciences, and this therefore cannot seem to be right. The text
then must be understood of those who think well of their own way, but who
are under a gross deception. It is a painful thought, that there not only are
multitudes who know that they are in a wrong path, but many more who
think they are right even while "the end thereof are the ways of death."

The following considerations may account for this kind of self-deception,
or show how it is that men walking in a wrong way, may, nevertheless
think it to be right.

1. Much of this is to be attributed to the *influence of education.*— — —
We are not aware of the innumerable instances in which we are influenced
by the principles imbibed in early life, yet this first bias of the mind may
make things appear to be right, which in themselves are utterly wrong, and
lead to fatal consequences. How else could it be accounted for, that Saul
of Tarsus should not only be induced to persecute the church of God and
waste it, but to think that he ought verily to do it? Thus it is that many are
attached to certain forms and systems of religion, because they have been
brought up to them, and for no other reason. In different places, but from
a similar cause, paganism, mahomedanism, corrupted judaism, popery, and
other superstitions, are all thought to be right, though the end thereof are
the ways of death. Being the religion of their forefathers, it has altogether
the appearance of being right. It is the same where the truth is only partially received, and some of its leading doctrines rejected; and where they
teach for doctrines the commandments of men.

2. This kind of deception arises in part from *the power of example*, and
the countenance of the generality.— — —The example of those around us
has an inconceivable influence on our principles and conduct. A variety of
things positively evil, and which might easily be known to be so, appear
nevertheless to be right, because they are practiced and pursued by a large

portion of mankind. Setting our affections on things on the earth is a great evil, condemned in the scriptures; and yet this is the way of the world. The wicked boasteth of his heart's desire, and blesseth the covetous whom the Lord abhorreth. To a great majority of the Jewish nation it seemed right to be of the same religion as their rulers, though it included a rejection of Christ and his gospel; and it is much the same with the great bulk of other nations.

3. The *favorable opinion which good people may form of us*, may make our way seem to be right.— — —Our chief acquaintance may be with serious people, we may go with them to the house of God, and enjoy a portion of their esteem. They may hope that we are the followers of Jesus, and treat us as such; and so we may conclude that we are right, and that all is well. This seems to be the case with the foolish virgins, who in the parable are associated with the wise. But if we wish not to be deceived, we must not trust to the judgment or good opinion of any one, but desire that God would search us and set us right.

4. Many a way seems to be right, merely *because it is our own way.* — — —It is the way which we have chosen, and to which we have been accustomed. It is often seen in temporal things, that a man thinks his way to be right, because it is his way; and it is much more so in the concerns of religion. Hence many evils may cleave to us, and we see nothing of their sinfulness. We may even be altogether selfish and covetous, and not be aware of it; full of pride, and not perceive it; worldly-minded, vain and conceited, and yet think that all is right.

5. The *resemblance between real religion and what has only the appearance of it,* may be another cause of this deception.— — —In many instances this will make a way appear to be right, though it is leading us on to destruction. Self-righteousness has a seemly appearance, and promises fair for the kingdom of heaven; for it will be pleaded that we must be religious and devout, and do something towards our salvation. Yet it is certain, that by the works of the law shall no flesh living be justified.— — —Those who rest in a few delusive impressions and feelings, by which the heart is moved, but not changed, may flatter themselves with being the subjects of true religion; and those also who possess a mere speculative acquaintance with the gospel, are often very confident of being right, and of having truth on their side.— — —Those who rest in a partial reformation, and who comply with some of the duties of religion, may think that all is safe and right, while they are strangers to the love of God, and not renewed in the spirit of their mind.— — —Now the end of all these things is death; yet they seem to be right, and bear some resemblance to true religion. Thus, in innumerable ways are we in danger of being deceived, and falling into perdition.

Let us then look well to our way, and see that it be such as God has marked out for us in his holy word. Let us examine well our motives, and see that we are influenced by better principles than those of mere education, or example, or the good opinion of others. See that our hearts be truly right with God, and that we are walking in the way that is everlasting.

A CAUTION TO HEARERS.

Luke viii. 18.—Take heed, therefore, how ye hear. (B.)

THIS caution is an inference from the preceding parable of the Sower.—
In the parallel passage of St. Mark, iv. 24, it is, "Take heed *what ye*
hear." We shall explain and enforce the caution in both these senses.—
I. TAKE HEED WHAT YE HEAR.
This both concerns all ministers of the word, and all hearers.—
It is the indispensable duty of ministers to take heed what they preach.—
That their doctrine be *true*, that they may not deceive their hearers —That
it be *important*, that they may not trifle with them.—That it be *suitable* to
their state and character, that they may " rightly divide the word of truth,
and give to every description of hearers their portion of meat in due season.
Hearers should take heed what they hear. They must not take it for
granted that what they hear is *true, important, and suited to their state and
character;* but must bring it to the test of the holy scriptures, and examine
it thereby. For this purpose they should read the scriptures, and endeavor
to make themselves well acquainted with them, and understand them. And
if they find that, according to the divine oracles, the doctrines which they
hear answer the above description, they must so " take heed what they hear"
as to attend to it, and consider it maturely, that they may thoroughly understand and lay it to heart, and that it may have its designed effect upon their
spirit and conduct.—
Our Lord's caution, however, according to this Evangelist, implied another
thing, equally important:
II. TAKE HEED HOW YE HEAR.
Take heed, that you do not hear so inattentively, and in such a prayerless
state of mind, as not to understand, nor afterwards meditate on the word, and
so receive the seed as by the "way-side." Matt. xiii. 19. That having
heard and understood in a measure what you heard, and being affected
thereby, you do not rest in any ineffectual and transient impressions made on
your mind, and, therefore, be offended and fall away in time of trial and
temptation; but that the truth be deeply fixed in your mind, and that you
may have " root in yourself." Matt. xiii. 20, 21. That you guard against
the cares of the world, the love of deceitful riches, the vain pleasures of
life, and " desires after other things;" those pernicious weeds, which in so
many choke the springing blade, or forming ear, so that no fruit is brought
forth to perfection. Matt. xiii. 22.
But hear—in *simplicity of intention*, having a single eye to the glory of
God and your own salvation, present and eternal.—In *sincerity of heart*,
truly and earnestly desiring to discover and put away every error, and every
sin, and to know and do the whole will of God.—In *humility*, conscious
that you are unworthy to know the great and important things revealed in
the gospel, respecting the will of God, and the way of salvation from such
great misery to such great happiness; unworthy that God should speak to you
by his Son, and his inspired Prophets, Apostles, and Evangelists. We should
think ourselves undeserving that a nobleman, still more a king, or an angel,
should speak to us; how much more that Christ, or God, should make known
to us his will.—Hence you should hear with *reverence*, remembering it is
God's word, and that you are in God's presence, and under God's eye.—
With *seriousness*, persuaded the truth you hear is no light matter; but for your
life, your better and everlasting life. Would you not hear with seriousness

461

the advice of a skillful physician respecting your health, or of a lawyer concerning your property? And will you not hear with equal, nay with greater seriousness, what concerns you infinitely more?—With deep *attention*; let no sentence, or even word, that is uttered, escape you, and fail not afterwards seriously to consider what you have heard, and to examine yourself thereby. With *prayer*, while hearing, and before, and after you hear, " for the spirit of wisdom and revelation;" Eph. i. 17; persuaded " the things of God knoweth no man but by the Spirit of God." 1 Cor. ii. 11, 14. Hear with *faith*, firmly believing the certainty and importance of what is taught you from the oracles of God, always remembering the " word preached" does not profit those who hear it, in whom it is not " mixed with faith." Heb. iv. 2. With *love* to the truth, though searching and cutting, though disagreeable to your mind, like a bitter medicine to your taste, or giving pain like a lance which opens an imposthume.—With *meekness* with a calm, unruffled, peaceful mind, that what you hear, may prove an " ingrafted word, able to save your soul." Jam. i. 21. Above all, hear with a fixed *resolution*, formed in the strength of grace to be a " doer of the word and not a hearer only," to practice all you hear, as far as you see it to be agreeable to the word and will of God.

NONCONFORMITY TO THE WORLD.

Romans xii. 2.—And be not conformed to this world. (Sk.)

The christians at Rome, to whom St. Paul dedicated this epistle, had made considerable improvement in religion, and obtained great celebrity in their profession; they were the *beloved of God*, and their faith was *spoken of throughout the whole world.* To seek renown for personal beauty, or some exterior embellishment, is the genuine offspring of worldly vanity; but to be emulous to approve ourselves unto God, and obtain the *honor of all his saints*, is a principle which religion only inspires, and christians only enjoy. St. Paul had never seen the Roman in the flesh, but as he had the care of all the churches, he mentioned them always in his prayers—had often purposed to visit them; and to evince how deeply he was interested in their welfare, he sent them this epistle, which contains not only a statement of the sublime doctrines of christianity, but a clear view of experimental and practical godliness, together with the most affectionate exhortations to excite them to duty. St. Paul had *no dominion over their faith*, and therefore he begins his chapter thus, " I beseech you," &c, verse 1. The text is a part of this request, and therefore we will endeavor to show,

I. The nature of that conformity to the world which the text prohibits. By the phrase *this world*, we understand the ungodly part of mankind, all unregenerate persons, whether openly profane, or pharisaically moral. They are thus denominated either to show that worldly objects engross all their attention, or else to distinguish them from those who are not of this world, John xvii. 14. The prohibition against conformity to *this world*, is not be understood absolutely, or practiced rigorously; it is not *ceremonial*, consisting in " meats or drinks," or external forms and habits; nor is it *civil*, leading us to abandon all intercourse with the world; to retire from the haunts of men, and shut ourselves up in cloisters or nunneries. No; christians are to be the lights of the world; and they must go where their light will shine to the best advantage; they are the salt of the earth, and the salt must be diffused to preserve the mass from putrefaction. But the conformity here prohibited is *moral*, and may be reduced to the following points.

1. Be not conformed to the spirit and temper of the world; live not under the influence of carnal dispositions or ungodly tempers: what these are, the scriptures clearly state, Mark vii. 21—23; Gal. v. 19—21. Such are the genuine fruits produced by that "root that beareth gall and wormwood," and such the corrupt streams that flow from the impure fountain of the human heart.

2. Be not conformed to this world in the maxims by which you are governed, or the rules by which you are directed. The miser has his maxims of worldly prudence and carnal policy; the hero has his maxims of worldly honor; the pleasure-taker has his maxims of carnal gratification. Remember your actions are not to be directed by such rules, nor your characters formed by such models; if you study worldly maxims, it should be with a design to perceive their inconsistency with those rules you profess to follow.

3. Be not conformed to this world in your company. As men of business, you may and must resort to marts of trade and places of public merchandise, and as mechanics or husbandmen, you may be obliged to labor for the bread that perisheth, in company with the men of this world. But form no unnecessary alliance with them, make no choice of them for your companions, 2 Cor. vi. 17, 18; Eph. v. 11; James iv. 4, and,

4. Most of all, be not conformed to this world in your practices; all such as are inconsistent with your allegiance to God, your duty to your neighbor, and love to yourselves.

II. Assign some reasons for its prohibition.

1. *Duty prohibits it.* The text is the voice of God, it is the expression of his will. The same sovereign power that said "thou shalt do no murder," said "be not conformed to this world." You owe your all to God, his you are, and his will you are bound to obey; but by conformity to this world, you run counter to his will, and as much as lieth in you thwart his designs.

2. *Profession prohibits it.* The vows of God are upon you; your baptismal engagements bind you to renounce the pomps and vanities of this wicked world, &c. By the profession of christianity, you tacitly acknowledge that you are aiming to be like Christ; and how far he was from conforming to this world, the writings of the four evangelists sufficiently attest, John viii. 23, xviii. 36. By profession you engage to imitate the saints, and the stripes and tortures they endured from the world are indisputable evidences that conformity *to this world* was not their crime.

3. *Self-love prohibits it.* This is not such a world as we may safely imitate; it is a theatre of folly, a stage of vice, one great aceldama of blood and cruelty. The world lieth in wickedness; it is not merely sunk in the gulfs of wickedness, but lies there contentedly buried in sin, like the earth in the universal deluge; and by conforming to this world you take the most direct steps to plunge yourself into that condemnation which will be the portion of the ungodly.

4. *The love of your neighbor prohibits it.* By conforming to this world, you countenance crime, and strengthen the cause of wickedness; you give it settlement, succession, and perpetuity; you embolden others to sin, and

as sin and misery go together, you swell the aggregate of human wo, and people the regions of the damned.

5. *The interests of religion prohibit it.* By conforming to this world you stab your own peace, and wound your own conscience; you grieve the Spirit of God; you cause the friends of Zion to mourn; you turn the lame out of the way, and make the enemies of christianity triumph.

III. How may this conformity be prevented?

1. *By the regeneration of our natures;* read the close of the verse. This is a divine work, but prayer will secure the agency of that Being who effects it, John iii. 6; Matt. vi. 11.

2. *By the exercise of devout meditation* and daily prayer.

3. *By guarding against temptation*, keeping out of its way, being " all eye, all ear, all watchfulness."

4. *Above all, by a constant dependance on God.*

Conclusion.—1. The spirit of christianity is a totally distinct thing from the spirit of the world. 2. Our living in the world is no argument why we should be like the world; see Lot, Noah, Daniel, &c. 3. The charge of singularity should never frighten us from our duty. Let us not be fools for the sake of avoiding being called such, nor be damned for the sake of company.

AN ADDRESS TO THE FALLEN.

Rev. ii. 5.—Remember from whence thou art fallen, and repent, and do the first works; or else I will come unto thee quickly, and will remove thy candle-stick out of his place, except thou repent. (Sk.)

These words are a part of an epistle which was dictated by the Lord Jesus Christ, and addressed by the apostle John to the church of Ephesus; a church that had been formed by the apostles themselves, and that had advanced to a state of eminence under their particular inspection. See Acts xviii. 19—21, and xix. and xx. 16—38, and epistle to the Ephesians. Favored as this church had been, it became necessary, about forty years after its establishment, to address its minister and its members in the language which you have heard.

Falling from God has ever been man's prevalent fault;—in almost every part of the sacred volume we find cautions, admonitions, or threatenings respecting it;—our text refers to this evil,—it is an address to the *fallen;*—and from it we are led—*to consider their fall*, and *the means by which they may rise again.*

I. Their fall. The word *fall* is striking; it is that which is so frequently used to express man's first departure from God. In the text it is synonymous with the various expressions used by the sacred writers, to signify declension from God and his ways. Our departure from God may, in its nature and in its degree, be different. Let us therefore rather take a general view of the subject, than confine our ideas to the particular fault charged on this church, (in verse 4;) and rather connect our ideas with individuals, than refer them to whole communities; not forgetting that what describes the state of a fallen individual, may illustrate the condition of a fallen church.

It is a fall—*from the favor and the approbation of God ;*—where the soul lived under the smiles of the divine countenance ; into a state of guilt and condemnation. Compare Psalms xxvii. and li.

From the image of God ;—where knowledge, righteousness, and holiness adorned the mind, and rendered it peaceful and happy, into a state of inward depravity ; where evil principles—unholy passions—sinful dispositions—and bad tempers again darken, disturb and torment the soul.

From the love of God ;—where the best the strongest affections of the soul, were turned towards, and fixed on the greatest and best of beings ; into a state, where all these are drawn towards, and fixed on, the degraded creature, and the perishing world.

From a state of vigor, and holy zeal in the cause of God ;—where faith was active, love was warm, prayer and praise were fervent, and where efforts to do good were strong and constant : into a state of religious supineness ; where the soul is no longer vigorous towards God ; and where forms, sounds, and cold wishes, are substituted for prayer, praise and holy zeal.

It is *frequently* a fall *from rectitude of heart and life*, into the practice of immorality.

From having enjoyed the approbation, the respect, the love of the church, such persons become, to the people of God, mere objects of commiseration.

Oh, what a fall ! They *were ascending* toward heaven : but see ! they *now descend* towards hell.

Such a sight may gratify fiends. Bad men may say—"so would we have it." But over such the pious mourn ; and the gracious, the merciful God speaks to such in the language of paternal compassion, Hos. xi. 8 ; and in our text, Jesus, who would raise them again, addresses them thus, " Remember," &c.

Fallen as they are, they need not perish. Oh, that they may take heed to the things which they hear ! and from the following part of the subject, may they understand, and by the grace of God, use,

II. THE MEANS BY WHICH THEY MAY RISE AGAIN !

" *Remember—from whence thou art fallen.*" Strange as it may be, the fallen do forget, or seem to forget, their former situation. Sin dreadfully deceives and hardens. See 2 Sam. xii. 1—7 ; Heb. iii. 7—14 ; Rev. iii. 17. But it is essential to the rise of any fallen professor, that he remember *from whence* he hath fallen ; without this he can have no proper view of the nature and the extent of his fault.

Remember,—poor, fallen soul !—thou *once* wast a child of God, and couldst call God *thy* father. Thou *didst* live in a state of favor, of union, and of intimacy with thy God and Saviour.—Thou *wast* humble patient, meek, happy, loving, and beloved. Thy soul *did* aspire heavenward : and standing as on an eminence, thou couldst *look down* on created good, as perishable, trifling, diminutive, and mean ; and turning thine eyes upward, by faith thou couldst almost behold the glory of heaven ; while holy meditation, and spiritual desire really carried thee beyond the present life. Or, suppose that thou didst not rise quite so high ;—hast thou not left *so much* of what was great and good, that thy soul is filled with sorrow and regret for that which thou hast lost ? Dost thou not say, " Oh that it were with me as in days that are past !" We rejoice that thou art made thus sensible of thy present circumstances.—*Now*, take the following advice.

Repent—of thy fall. Falling is in itself a great sin, Jer. ii. 19. *Repent*, on account of the injury that thy fall hath done to thyself, to the people of God, to the cause of God. Repent *sincerely* and *deeply*. Read the fifty-first Psalm, and understand what deep and sincere repentance is. Many returning backsliders seem not to be affected, as they should be, on account of their fall. When fallen, there is no rising again without repentance.

"*Do thy first works.*" Leave off thy sins ; break from thy sinful associates. Have recourse to prayer, especially to private prayer. Use diligently the means of grace. Above all, go to Christ, the only Saviour, as thou didst first go. Cry mightily for salvation. Believe, *again* believe on the son of God. *Renew thy former zeal.*

Oh! how difficult it is to acknowledge the depth of one's fall ;—to begin anew. How many never effectually rise again, because they *will* be viewed as though they had never fallen.

The above advice is urged by the following awful threat ;—

"*Or else I will come.*" Such an intimation is always very weighty. See Luke xx. 19 ; Rev. xxii. 12.

"*I will come—quickly.*" Though the Lord Jesus is long suffering, having given time for repentance, and that time being nearly expired, he will *quickly* come. See ver. 21, 22 ; Isa. i. 5 ; Prov. xxix. 1.

"*I will remove thy candlestick out of his place, except thou repent;*" see chap. i. 12, 20, and ver. 1. I will withdraw divine light, divine influence, and leave the fallen church in its degraded state ; so that a lifeless ministry, and lifeless forms, shall be followed by darkness, and by death. See Isa. **v. 5, 6.** A threat long since executed on the Ephesian church :—a threat that will ere long be put in force against thee, poor fallen professor, "except thou repent." *O that thou mayest awake, and call upon God, that thou perish not!*

What a lesson is our text, for fallen professors, and for fallen churches!

But who are so backward to learn, as those that are thus fallen? The reason is obvious. See chap. iii. 17.

Yet *the fallen* are the most pitiable objects of commisseration in the world.

FOLLOWING THE MULTITUDE PROHIBITED.

Exodus xxiii. 2.—Thou shalt not follow a multitude to do evil. (Sk.)

WHATEVER was written aforetime was written for our instruction. But the most important parts of divine revelation, and those with which we ought to be most intimately acquainted, are the precepts ; which comprise the whole of a man's duty, and delineate with a critical exactness, a moral map of the road which he has to travel. The precepts of the Bible are of two kinds ; those which positively illustrate what we are obligated to do, and those which negatively describe what we are to leave undone : the text is of the latter description. which, though found in the Old Testament, and among the code of laws which God gave to the Jews, is not of less importance to us than it was to them ; we will therefore, in endeavoring to profit by it,

I. OFFER A FEW THOUGHTS FOR THE PURPOSE OF EXPLAINING ITS NATURE

II. URGE REASONS TO INDUCE US TO OBSERVE IT.

III. IMPART ADVICE FOR THE DIRECTION OF THOSE WHO WISH TO ESCAPE THE ENSNARING WILES OF THE MULTITUDE.

In explaining the text, there are two general observations which we have to make. First, something assumed. Secondly, something implied. It is assumed that the multitude do evil: it is implied that we are in danger of copying their example. First, *The multitude do evil.* Evil, is either moral or natural;—sin, or its consequences. The former is to be understood here; this is the most common import of the term, Gen. vi. 5; Isa. i. 16; Rom. xii. 9. That the multitude do evil, may be inferred, 1. *From the review of past ages.* Look at the example of the old world, when all flesh had corrupted its way; at Sodom and Gomorrah, when ten righteous persons could not be found amidst that vast population. God, indeed, in after ages, chose a people for himself, but even in reference to these, Isaiah said, "Except the Lord of Hosts had left unto us a very small remnant, we should have been as Sodom," Isa. i. 9. And if iniquity abounded among a people so highly distinguished, what could be expected from heathen nations, who were involved in the deepest darkness, and corrupted by the vilest idolatries? 2. *From the cruel persecutions which have been raised against the righteous in various ages of the world.* What these were in ancient times we learn from Heb. xi. 35—38. But why have the people of God been thus persecuted? because the multitude do evil. The reason why Cain slew his brother was, his works were evil, and his brother's righteous; and the prevalence of persecution has been a standing evidence of the truth we attempt to establish. 3. *From the common conduct of mankind.* Is not vice more general than virtue? Does not evil abound more than good? Is not the world followed with more avidity than religion? See how plays, and amusements, are sought after; what oaths are sworn, what lies are told, what thefts are committed, and what abominations are practiced?

Secondly, The precept in the text suppose, that *we are in danger of copying the example of the multitude.* We may infer this, 1. *From the innate tendencies which we have to evil.* The "imagination of man's heart is evil:" evil has its seat there; and if the fountain be evil will not the stream be evil? Loo kat little children, who have not been corrupted by the manners of th emultitude, yet what tendencies to evil are evinced, and dispositions to evil displayed in their conduct! 2. *From the prevalence of bad example.* Man is an imitative creature, and easily prevailed upon to imbibe the spirit, and copy the example of those with whom he may associate, and especially, when that example is in unison with his inclinations: hence we are not only disposed to evil, but have facilities to the practice of evil; we are like disordered people in a hospital, surrounded by the dying and the dead, breathing the very atmosphere of disease, putrescence, and death. The practice of the multitude renders vice familiar to our thoughts, and gradually wears off the abhorrence with which we once beheld it. 3. *From a variety of melancholy facts.* The multitude who now do evil, were not always such adepts in depravity; when they first entered into the broad way, their feet were not swift to do evil; they proceeded with hesitating steps, for none become completely wicked on a sudden, but by practice they became hardened in their crimes, and like the wicked whom they followed

II. Urge reasons to induce us to observe it.

The multitude doing evil are represented as guides, which men are accustomed to follow; but the reasons why we should not imitate them, are, 1. *They are unlawful and unconstituted guides.* The text itself sufficiently proves this. "Thou shalt not follow," &c. This is God's positive injunction to *thee;* it is personal, and absolute; and wilt thou not revere His authority? God's will is law, and should be regarded as an invariable rule of action; and to " follow a multitude," &c., is to act in direct opposition to God.

2. *They are bad guides.* The principles by which they are actuated are vile, vicious, and ungodly principles : pride, anger, malice, revenge, and all the bad passions that infest the mind: the practices they pursue are bad practices; the way they travel is a bad way. By following " a multitude to do evil," you will become like them, and by yielding to the current of vice, you render that current stronger, for carrying forward others to ruin.

3. *They are dishonorable guides.* For the credit of your characters, you ought not to follow " a multitude," &c. In all ages, the most honorable men have been those who have dared to be singular, and stood aloof from the degenerate crowd, unterrified by their frowns, and untempted by their smiles. Follow a multitude to do evil, and you will dishonor your character, stain your reputation, and involve yourselves in eternal disgrace.

4. *They are unprofitable guiles.* "What fruit had you in those things whereof ye are now ashamed?" Evil is a most unprofitable concern, Isa. xlviii. 22. We seldom embark in any enterprise without an eye to profit, but here you may calculate with moral certainty upon the loss of all that is valuable and profitable, for time and eternity.

5. *They are dangerous guides.* We all believe that there is a dreadful hell, a place and state of insufferable pain and punishment; and every evil doer is preparing himself for that punishment; treasuring up wrath against the day of wrath; his steps are taking hold on hell, and he is going down to the chambers of death. By following a multitude to do evil, you endanger your souls, and accelerate your ruin.

III. IMPART ADVICE FOR THE DIRECTION OF THOSE WHO WISH TO ESCAPE THE ENSNARING WILES OF THE MULTITUDE.

1. *Get your minds deeply and thoroughly impressed with the awfulness of your situation.* Dangers unseen will be unavoided. Consider your ways; reflect on your past conduct; converse with your own hearts; thoughtlessness is one of the greatest evils in existence, and nothing is more common. Without consideration, you will be irresistibly captivated to do evil.

2. *Seek the regenerating grace of God.* Our carnal natures are wholly inclined to evil; "that which is born of the flesh, is flesh."—Oh ! pray for the renewing influence of the Holy Ghost. The Ethiopian may as well attempt to change his skin, or the leopard his spots, as you can cease from doing evil without a change of heart.

3 *Be on your guard against the seductive wiles, and insinuating influence of the multi'ude.* Sinners will entice you; but come out from among them; have no communion with the unfruitful works of darkness, Ps. i. 1.

4. *Follow the happy few who strive to do good.* The church and the world form two societies, acting in direct opposition to each other; in one of these societies you *must* be; there is no standing neuter. On one side, be your allegiance, your honor, and your interest; on the other, your guilt, your shame, and your punishment. Can you hesitate for a moment where to take your stand? He that is not with Christ, is against him. Show that you are with Christ by being with his people. Oh, say, " This people shall be my people, and their God my God."—

INFER,

1. That the measures of right and wrong are not to be determined by the majority. Good and evil are fixed immutable principles; and their natures are unchangeable, whether many or few follow them.

2. What gratitude is due to God, for the revelation of his will, which marks the boundaries of right and wrong; and for the gift of his Son to redeem us from this present evil world: to whom be glory for ever and ever. Amen.

~~~~~~~~~~~~~~~~

THE REDEEMER'S COMPLAINT.

John v. 40.—And ye will not come unto me that ye may have life. (Sk.)

When we seriously contemplate a future state of existence, we are over-powered by the magnitude and awful grandeur of the important objects it presents. When in imagination we launch forth from the shore of time, into a boundless of eternity, we feel our need of some one, who shall be constantly present with us, to afford us support, and to make us happy. But to whom shall we turn? Our fellow men are as destitute and feeble as ourselves. Nor is there any being who can meet our necessities, but that God whose potent arm sustains the keys of death, and the invisible world. Against him we have sinned; and can we hope for so much favor at his hands? His word reveals him gracious and merciful. He has given his Son to be our Redeemer. Our Redeemer has procured for us all we need. He offers us what he has procured, " without money and without price;" and even complains " ye will not come unto me, that ye might have life." This complaint suggests several important considerations. Herein,

I. We have our natural state evidently implied;—the opposite of 'life;"—a state of death. This representation is frequently made by the scripture writers, who uniformly speak of the unregenerate, as being "dead in trespasses and sins." The representation applies,

1. To the sinner's *judicial state*. We are under the law to God, our rightful sovereign;—have broken his law by open rebellion, as well as by omissions of duty; of course, we are subject to the penalty which the law denounces; and that penalty is *death*. " The soul that sinneth shall die." Thus a condemned criminal, who has forfeited his life to justice, and now waits the time of execution, is *dead in law*. Hence ministers are said to be " the savor of death unto death;"—and the law is denominated the "min-istration of *death* and of *condemnation*," 2 Cor. ii. 16, and iii. 7—9. The term death, applies,

2. To the sinner's *spiritual state*. Accordingly the apostle says, " you hath he *quickened*, who were dead," &c, Eph. ii. 1—5. Here we find several points of agreement between a state of death, and that which it is employed to represent. We select two;—death is a state of *insensibility*, and *inaction*. A corpse is *insensible* to any *insult* or *indignity* that may be offered to it;—would be insensible if in the midst of a *conflagration*, nor does it feel any honors done it, or intended to be done. So a person spiritually dead, feels not the *vile insult* which satan, the "father of lies," and the *most deeply fallen*, offers to both his *understanding* and his heart, when he employs him in his *dirty* and *degrading* drudgery. He is insen-sible of his *danger* of that hell on the breaking brink of which he totters:—and of his *privileges* as a ransomed son of Adam, and the happiness and honor to which he is invited, both *here* and *hereafter*. He neither feels

469

shame and *regret* for his base rebellion, nor *love* and *gratitude* for what Jesus has done and suffered on his account. A corpse is totally *inactive;*— so the dead sinner makes no effort to escape misery, or to secure eternal bliss.

3. The word "death" applies remotely to the *eternal state* of the finally impenitent;—"the second death,—everlasting destruction from the presence of the Lord," Rev. xx. 6, and xxi. 8; 2 Thess. i. 7—9. But,

II. WE ARE POINTED TO THE SOURCE OF LIFE. "Ye will not come to ME."

1. Jesus is the source of *legal life ;*—of that pardon or justification, by which the sinner's sentence is reversed. "By him, all that believe are *justified from all things*," Acts xiii. 38, 39. "There is now *no condemnation;*" for "he was wounded *for our* transgressions;"—"died *for us :*"—"suffered, the just *for the unjust;*" therefore, "by his obedience many shall be *made righteous.*" See also Acts xxvi. 18; Eph. i. 7; Col. i. 14.

2. He is the source of *spiritual* life. "I am *the vine*, ye are *the branches.*" From him believers derive their *vitality*, their *feeling*, their *vigor*, their *fruitfulness* in good works. Hence the apostle, in one place says, "I live: yet not I; but *Christ liveth in me;*" and in another, reminds the pious christian, that when Christ, who *is our life*, shall appear, he also shall appear with him in glory," Gal. ii. 20; Col. iii. 3, 4. From this, it follows, that,

3. He is the source of *eternal life.* "Though he were as a Son, yet learned he obedience by the things which he suffered; and being made perfect, he became the *author of eternal salvation* unto all them that obey him, Heb. v. 8, 9. He *purchased* life eternal, John iii. 14, 15 ; Rom. v. 1, 2. He *teaches the way* to it, John vi. 68. He, by his Spirit, *qualifies for* it, Rom. viii. 9 : John xvii. 3 ; 2 Cor. v. 17. He will *dispense* it, John x. 27, 28 ; Matt. xxv. 31—46. In our text,

III. WE ARE INSTRUCTED HOW TO OBTAIN THE LIFE WE NEED. "Ye will not *come* unto *me.*" The "coming," thus recommended, implies,

1. *A change of situation.* The sinner, who was "*alienated*," and "*far off;*" now *forsakes* his way of wickedness—*approaches* the Saviour; "*draws nigh*" unto God through him ; and takes his station within the pale of the church, Prov. xv. 29 ; Col. i. 21; Eph. ii. 13.

2. It implies, also, *a change of object.* Formerly, he looked for *happiness*, to wealth, honor, worldly connections, &c; and for *salvation*, to a poor Pharisaic righteousness of his own ; but now, for both happiness here, and salvation hereafter, he is found "looking unto Jesus," Phil. iii. 7—9. Coming to Jesus may perhaps, require,

3. *A change of company.* If your companions will accompany you, well. If not, you must come out from among them, and be separate, 2 Cor. vi. 17. On the other hand, if we wanted to obtain an interview with an earthly prince, from whom we hoped for such favors as none but himself could bestow, we should most gladly avail ourselves of the company and advice of persons who had, in *circumstances similar* to ours, *sought*, and *found admittance* to his presence, and had *presented* their *petition*, and been *graciously accepted.* Apply this thought; and avail yourselves of the *experience* and *assistance* of those who have already come to Jesus, and found him able and willing to save, and who now say, "Come thou with us ; and we will do thee good," &c. This coming also supposes,

4. *Confidence* in the Redeemer's power and goodness.

5. *Earnest desire* of obtaining his salvation ; and, consequently, a *readi- ness* to make *every sacrifice,* and to use *every* necessary *means* in order to o' tain it. From our text,

IV. WE LEARN WHAT IS THE IMMEDIATE CAUSE OF MAN'S ETERNAL DESTRUCTION ;—"Ye WILL not come unto me." Concerning the freedom of the human will, there have been endless disputes. This is not a time and place to enter at length into the controversy ; yet we may offer a few remarks.

1. It is a settled point, that no man can come to Jesus, except the Father draw him, John vi. 44.

2. The question, therefore, is not whether a person may become con- verted without God's grace; but whether he may not so *reject* the counsel of God against himself, Luke vii. 30, and *resist* the Holy Ghost Acts vii. 51, as to *frustrate* the grace of God ? Gal. ii. 21.

3. In answer to this, it may be said, that the language of our text is that of *reproof.* Now, reproof supposes, that the reproved could have acted otherwise, and better than they have done : if they could not, then the blame rests, and the reproof should also rest, somewhere else. But,

4. This point is more fully determined, by Matt. xxiii. 37. "O Jerusalem, Jerusalem, how often *would* I have gathered thy children together, and *ye would not.*"

5. On this principle, God "is justified in his sayings;" and exonerated from the charge and suspicion of being the author of sin ; while man appears to be wholly chargeable with both that, and his own perdition.

Lastly. On this principle, and, indeed, even on the opposite one, every sincerely seeking soul may derive from the text the greatest encouragement If you *will* come, you have free liberty and pressing invitation to do so ; "Ho, *every one* that *thirsteth,* come ye to the waters." Isa. lv. 1. "The spirit and the bride say, come. And let him that heareth say, come. And let him that is athirst, come. And *whosoever will,* let him take the water of life freely," Rev. xxii. 17.

THE JUDGMENT.

Romans xiv. 10.—We shall all stand before the judgment seat of Christ. (P.)

Our church, during the present season of advent, commemorates our Lord Jesus Christ's first coming " in great humility," to " give his life a ransom" for sinners ; and I know not how to improve the present occasion better, that by directing your attention to his second advent, when He will come to be " glorified in his saints"—to be admired by all—and to pass the final and irrevocable sentence upon the whole family of man. To that awful time, the words of the text apply.—" For we must all stand before the judgment seat of Christ Lend me then your prayerful attention, whilst I consider,

I. THE CHARACTER OF THE JUDGE.

II. THE PERSONS TO BE JUDGED

III. THE EVIDENCE AND PROCESS BY WHICH THE JUDGMENT WILL BE CONDUCTED. And,

IV. THE SENTENCE ITSELF.

I. The character of the judge.

And here I would have every one bear in mind, that what we here say are not matters of trifling import, nor are they idle chimeras as some would have them ; neither are they the mere inventions of man ; but the verities of God's word : they are of eternal importance. The scene here portrayed, is one in which we must all bear a part ; in which the preacher before you must answer for a large share of responsibility committed to his charge, and you, his hearers, for what you hear.

Who will preside on the occasion ?—The Lord Jesus Christ—the Son of God—the Son of God in our nature—our "elder Brother," who came into the world to accomplish our redemption,—who took our nature upon him, and "gave his life a ransom for our sins."

We are informed by himself, that all judgment is committed to him,— "The Father judgeth no man, but hath committed all judgment to the Son." The same is the doctrine of the text,—"For we must all appear before the judgment seat of Christ." Our Saviour says, "When the Son of man shall come in his glory, and all his holy angels with him, then shall He sit on the throne of his glory—Matt. xxv. 31. And an inspired Apostle bears his testimony to this point, Acts xvii. 31. St. John says, in the close of the Apocalyptic vision, referring to the glorious appearance of the Son of God from heaven, Rev. xi. and xx.

Here we behold the Redeemer on his throne of glory, a throne which never had been sullied by impurity or wrong, but of which it may truly be said, 'Righteousness and judgment are the habitation of his throne."—There will be no place for sin after this solemn day, "For the heavens shall pass away with a great noise, and the elements shall melt with fervent heat ;" the glittering stars rush from their orbits, and all created matter be consumed.—

> "And like the baseless fabric of a vision,
> Leave not a wreck behind."

"Behold he cometh with clouds, and every eye shall see him, and they also which pierced him, and all the kindreds of the earth shall wail because of him."

What a wonderful change will then take place ! No longer we behold him the "man of sorrows, and acquainted with grief ;" his sufferings are over—the days of his humiliation past—the atoning blood has ceased to flow —he no longer stands a captive at Pilate's bar ; but now comes to pass sentence on Pilate himself. Then shall we see him "robed in dreadful majesty," making the "clouds his chariots," and riding upon the "wings of the wind."

Then let the Jews repeat their cry, "Crucify him, crucify him,"—let them bow the deriding knee before him and say, "If thou be the Son of God, come down from the cross."—Let the sensualist, and the scoffer at religion, come and meet their Judge—let the hypocritical professor of an holy and spiritual religion tell his idle creed, and show his piety ;—his heart fails him—he now first discovers religion to be a reality, and essential to the welfare of man, and comes from God—he will now be convinced that the Son of God was what he professed to be, "God blessed for ever."

We notice,

II. The persons to be judged.

The text says all. That Almighty Being, who first created all things by his power, now collects the scattered atoms of his creatures, that body and spirit may re-unite. The Apostle says, "For we must all appear before the judgment seat of Christ." What an assembly will that be !

Europeans and Asiatics, the swarthy sons of Africa, and the scattered tribes of America; the Jew, Turk, Pagan, Infidel, and Christian, will then stand on one common basis, and be judged according to the light which each has possessed, or the dispensation under which he has been privileged to live.—And each for himself, give " account of the deeds done in the body, whether they are good or bad."

In this assembly, we must all bear a part, and take our place; here all distinction but one solitary one, must for ever cease.

Let me, my brethren, call upon you here, to enquire what would be *your* feelings were you at this moment called upon to approach your God?

There is but one way for sinners, by which this dreadful disclosure may be avoided—by which those sins can be washed away; and that is by *now* fleeing to your Saviour, by covering them with his blood; otherwise you must eternally perish

Throw down then, I beseech you, the "arms of your rebellion"—turn to the Redeemer, who came " to seek and to save that which was lost." "Through Him, all your iniquities shall be blotted out," of the book of God's remembrance, and " be cast into the depths of the sea."

III. The evidence and process by which the judgment will be conducted.

" I saw the dead, small and great, stand before God; and the books were opened." The language is figurative, but plain. We are not to suppose that God, to whom the past, present, and future are alike, will require records or remembrances;—all things are open to him. But here he stoops to the capacities of our nature, and speaks " after the manner of men," according to the proceedings in earthly courts, where books are kept and evidences heard. At that awful day, many books will be opened. Time will not allow me to enlarge much on the subject, I will name but a few,

1. The book of *providence* will be clearly opened, and its mysteries explained.

2. The book of the *Moral Law*, and God's dealings towards all his intelligent creatures.

Such an one is not to be found. All have not received the gospel of Christ, and full salvation is alone revealed through that gospel. According to the privileges you have enjoyed, will your comparative guilt be weighed; and the wicked be eternally condemned.

The law demands perfect love to God and man;—consider what the law requires.

3. The book of *the scriptures*. God has given to the world these " treasures of wisdom and of knowledge," their object is to direct the sinner to the Saviour, to reveal a full and free salvation to all; none are excluded from its offers, all are invited to " throw down the arms of their rebellion," to believe and be saved.

4. The book of *conscience*. Conscience is a principle implanted in the mind, and is emphatically called " the Vicegerent of God."

IV. The sentence to be pronounced. The sentence will be short but decisive, and tremendous in its consequences. See Matt. xxv. and realize in your minds the scene before you.

The sentence is as decisive as it is awful.

Having now considered the subject before us, let me offer one or two remarkes by way of application; and,

1. The supreme importance of an interest in Christ.

2. The vast importance of good works, Matt. xxv. 41—45.

473

CHAPTER VII.

THE CONSEQUENCES OF SIN.

THE EVIL OF SIN.

Jeremiah ii. 19.—Know therefore and see, that it is an evil thing and bitter, that thou hast forsaken the Lord thy God, and that my fear is not in thee, saith the Lord God of hosts. (Pr.)

SIN has not only entered into the world, but is become universal. Every individual is the subject of it, every heart is tainted with it. Had it been otherwise, we should have been more sensible of its evil nature, and more shocked at its deformity. But seeing all are alike diseased, it is but little thought of, and we are not sufficiently aware of its evil tendency. And though it is universal, yet if we obtain not a cure, its malignity will prove no less fatal on that account.

I. ENQUIRE WHEREIN SIN CONSISTS, ACCORDING TO THE DESCRIPTION OF THE PROPHET.

It is here summed up in two things: "forsaking the Lord our God"—and "his fear not being in us."— — —We may see the difference between man's view of sin, and God's view of it. Man regards the evil of sin chiefly as it consists in outward conduct, and as it affects himself or his own interest. But God traces it to its source, as originating in the disposition of our hearts towards him.

1. Every sinner has *forsaken* God.— — —He does not desire him as his portion, but other things in preference.— — —He is not mindful of his favor, nor thinks it worth seeking after; but esteems the friendship of a fellow creature more than his. Like a prodigal son, he has no love to his father, nor concern about his honor. Every sinner says in his heart, "No God." He is nothing but enmity against him: the throne of heaven would not stand secure, if it depended on the sinner, whether God should reign or not. Such is the evil of having forsaken him.

2. As God is not loved, so *neither is he feared*, at least not in such a way as to depart from evil. "My fear is not in thee, saith the Lord God of hosts."— — — Because he forbears, and sentence is not executed speedily, the hearts of the sons of men are set in them to do evil. No evil is avoided, merely out of regard to his authority, but from selfish motives only.

3. From these two sources proceed *all the evils that are in the world.* — — —Forsaking God has been the cause of every abomination: hence all the wars, oppression, and injustice, between nations and individuals.— — — From the same source also arises a rejection of Christ and the gospel; a contempt of religion, and of religious people.— — —Hence also that hardness, and indifference to the gospel, in many who attend upon it.— — —Hence the most solemn warnings and tender expostulations are without effect, and all the mercy of the Saviour is neglected and despised.

II. CONSIDER THE EVIL AND BITTER NATURE OF SIN.

On some accounts, it is very difficult for us properly to understand and feel this part of the subject. The subject itself is incomprehensible, and we are too much blinded by our own depravity to see the evil there is in it.

However, there are a few mediums by which we may form some idea of its magnitude.

1. We may "know and see how evil and bitter a thing sin is," *by th*

precepts of God's holy law, which forbid it; and we must measure it by this rule to see what evil there is in it.— — —Men generally estimate the evil of sin by what is commonly esteemed in the world, or commonly practiced amongst men, and by what is allowed to be harmless and excusable. — — —But we must appeal to the law and to the testimony. The world is a poor judge of what is right, as well as of what is true: the word of God is the only criterion by which to judge. Rom. vii. 7.— — —What a pure and happy world would this be, if cemented by love. How much would it then resemble heaven.— — —how evil and how bitter is the reverse.

2. We may "know and see" *by the awful threatenings of God's word,* by which it stands condemned. Deut. xxviii. 15.— — —The Lawgiver of the world has connected punishment with every offense: and could a Being of infinite goodness curse the creatures he has made, if sin were not an evil of inconceivable magnitude!— — —Could a small evil raise such wrath, and kindle such a burning flame? God is displeased with nothing else but sin; and here his anger burns to the lowest hell.

3. We may know and see *by the bitter sorrows of true penitents.*— — —Oh what anguish of soul has it occasioned in those who have been brought to "know and see" its evil nature.— — —Hear the groans of David, see the tears of Peter, and the deep distress of many others. Psa. xxxviii. 1—6; li. 1—4; Zech. xii. 10.

4. Know by *the bitter fruits it has already produced.*— — —Great is the misery of man upon him; but sin is the cause of all.— — —What a catalogue of diseases, oppressions, hardships, and disappointments; the whole creation groaning under the load of human misery.— — —Yet all this is only some of the first effects of this evil and bitter thing.

5. By the still more bitter fruits *it would have produced,* if God had not restrained it.— — —Every city and town would then have been a Sodom. God's authority would be driven out of the world: all mankind would be hateful and hating one another.— — —But, with all that we see and know, we see not a thousandth part of the evil that would result, if God had not said to the waves of this mighty ocean, Hitherto shalt thou go, and no farther.

6. By the *bitter pains of eternal death.* There shall be weeping and wailing, and gnashing of teeth— — —the worm dieth not, and the fire is not quenched— — —the smoke of their torment ascendeth up for ever and ever.— — —This is the hell of fire which sin has kindled.

7. Know it also by the *bitter sufferings of the Son of God*— — —What means that bloody sweat in the garden.— — —What is the meaning of those awful words upon the cross, "My God! My God! why hast thou forsaken me!"— — —But who can estimate the full evil of sin by this comparison: the Saviour in sorrow drowned, but not in sorrow lost!

III. Enforce the exhortation: "Know therefore and see that it is an evil and bitter thing."

1. Unless we know and see this, we can *neither know nor see the salvation of God.*— — —This indeed is the reason why it is so little regarded: the whole need not a physician, but they that are sick.

2. Without a knowledge of the evil of sin, we shall *neither repent of it nor depart from it* to any good purpose.— — —It is only as we are impressed with this conviction that we can be kept from sinning against God, or be made to loathe ourselves in his sight.

3. If we know and see it not truly in this world, we shall be made to

know and see it to our cost in the world to come.— — —Sooner or later we must realise the nature and extent of this awful subject.

4. If we are brought to know and see it aright, *we shall come to Christ;* and herein will be the proof of our knowledge being in some measure what it ought to be. John vi. 45.

~~~~~~~~~~~~~~~

DREADFUL EFFECTS OF CARNALITY.

Romans viii. 6.—To be carnally minded is death. (Pr.)

WHILE the apostle exhibits in this chapter a brief view of the leading doctrines of the gospel, and the privileges of the godly, he is careful at the same time to show their holy nature, and practical effect.— — —If there be no condemnation, it is to those who " walk not after the flesh."— — —If all things work together for good, it is to them that " love God."— — — If the righteousness of the law is fulfilled in our justification, our sanctification is no less implied : and all carnality is inconsistent with the spirit and design of the gospel, yea, it is death itself.

That carnality has this tendency, may be seen in its effects. It destroys all activity for God, and so produces spiritual death. It fills the world with misery, and destroys all our hopes and happiness. It exposes us to the wrath to come, and so to death eternal.

Where carnality wholly prevails, it produces these effects totally : where it partially prevails, they exist in a partial degree.

I. CARNALITY, IN PROPORTION AS IT OPERATES, PRODUCES STUPIDITY, OR INACTIVITY FOR GOD.

1. The very *essence* of that spiritual death which pervades the heart of the unregenerate, consists in the prevalence of this carnality. To what else can we attribute insensibility under judgments— — —amidst so many mercies— — —unconcern about eternal things———unwillingness to come to Christ———living without God in the world.

2. Where carnality *partially* prevails it produces similar effects, only in a less degree. Its tendency is to render us inactive in holy duties, by weakening and destroying the principles of action : nothing can be done without it.

3. One of these principles is holy *love:* but carnality damps the sacred fire, cools and weakens our resolutions.

4. Another is *hope:* the hope of success in the Lord's service, and of heaven hereafter, is essential to holy activity.———But carnality beclouds our prospects, and hides the objects of hope from our view.

5. *Faith* is also a powerful spring of action : nothing makes us more alive to God than a realising view of invisible objects. Heb. xi.———But carnality weakens our hands, and destroys the energy of faith.

6. Conscious *integrity*, or walking before God, enlivens the christian in his course. Righteousness is the girdle of his reins, it strengthens him for action.———But carnality enervates the mind, produces pusilanimity, inaction and sloth.

7. Spiritual *joy* inspires the soul with courage, with holy ardor and delight in the ways of God.———But carnality is death : it weakens all the springs of action, and paralyzes the whole soul.

II CARNALITY, IN PROPORTION AS IT OPERATES, PRODUCES MISERY.

1. We need only consider the state of those who are *wholly* under the dominion of a carnal mind, and we shall see what are its effects.——— There we shall see men ever seeking after happiness, but never able to obtain it.———Men at war with themselves; conscience and inclination at perpetual variance; continual fear and suspense about futurity.———Every affliction gives alarm: they are afraid to know themselves, or their true state, or to think closely about the concerns of their souls. They are loaded with guilt, and are self-condemned.———Oh, to be carnally minded is death ———worse than death.

2. Where this principle only *partially* prevails, it operates in the same, and produces similar effects.———Guilt and darkness, misery and death, are its natural consequences. It causes distance from God, unfits us for communion with him, and casts us out of his sight; and this is the essence of all other misery.

What peace could Jonah have, when he had disobeyed the commandment of the Lord. What happiness could David find, after he had killed Uriah with the sword.———Whither can we go for comfort, apostate from our God!

III. CARNALITY TENDS TO RUIN IN THE WORLD TO COME, AND TO DEATH ETERNAL.

Left to pursue its course, this would be its final issue. Rom. vi. 23; James i. 15.———Eternal death is the just desert of sin, its proper wages, its natural effect, and penal reward.———It is enmity with God: it says to him, Depart from us: and he will say, Depart ye cursed.

Eternal death is the privation of all good, the endurance of all evil.——— Carnality leads to this: it rejects the only remedy, the only refuge, and plunges the soul into the gulf of perdition.

It has the same tendency wherever it exists, and in whatever degree ———If the issue be not the same, it is because that tendency is counteracted. Like poison in the blood, its fatal effects may be prevented; but if it take its course, it will end in death.

How dangerous to seek relief from misery in carnal pleasures. They are bought at the hazard of the soul: the end of these things is death.

***

THE DIFFICULTY OF SALVATION A JUST GROUND OF APPREHENSION TO THE UNGODLY.

1 Pet. iv. 18.—If the righteous scarcely be saved, where shall the ungodly and the sinner appear? (S. S.)

EARNESTNESS in the concerns of religion is often thought unnecessary— But the attainment of salvation is by no means easy—

This appears from the representations which the scriptures give of religion;—a race, a warfare, &c.

The difficulties implied in these metaphors may well alarm the careless— With this view St. Peter suggests the awful query in the text—

I. HIS ASSUMPTION.

The apostle did not mean to express a doubt, but rather to assume a position which he deemed incontrovertible—

The point he assumes is, that the righteous are saved with difficulty.

The truth of this position will appear, if it be considered that the righteous are not saved without,

Deep afflictions.

God's people in all ages have been afflicted—Zeph. iii. 12.

They have much to endure on account of their religion—2 Tim. iii. 12.

But their trials are beneficial to them—1 Pet. i. 7.

They scarcely ever make any great proficiency without them—Ps cxix. 67.

They always in the issue acknowledge them as blessings—Ps. cxix. 71.

Severe conflicts.

The christian finds much opposition from without and from within—Eph vi. 12.

No attainments whatever put him without the reach of trials—

St. Paul, long after he had been caught up into the third heavens, felt the severest conflicts in his soul—Rom. vii. 15, 23.

They are more or less, the lot of every christian—Gal. v. 17.

And, though painful, they are necessary for us all—1 Pet. i. 6.

None can attain salvation without them, Heb. xii. 8; yet all find it extremely difficult to bear them without fainting—

Powerful assistances.

Nothing less than almighty power can uphold the christian—

This the most righteous men have freely acknowledged—Ps. cxix. 117.

Hence the preservation of the saints is ascribed to God alone—1 Pet. i. 5.

How mistaken then are they who think the attainment of salvation easy !—

Surely if the righteous find the way to heaven so difficult, the ungodly have reason to tremble for their state.

II. THE INFERENCE HE DRAWS FROM IT.

The different characters in the text are the same as those mentioned in the preceding verse—

The question respecting the latter implies that their destruction must be.

1. Certain.

This is constantly affirmed throughout the holy scriptures.

The ungodly shall appear at the judgment-seat of Christ—2 Cor. v. 10.

But they shall not be united with the righteous—Ps. i. 5.

They shall be separated from them for ever—Matt. xxv. 46.

It is deducible also from the foregoing assumption.

The righteous are justified by the blood of Christ, renewed by the Spirit of God, and are striving with all their might, &c.—

The ungodly are unpardoned, unsanctified, unimpressed—

It is impossible that these should have the same end—Isai. iii. 10. 11.

We will appeal to the ungodly themselves, and leave them to say, "where they shall appear ?"—

The want also of many advantages for salvation is a further ground for it.

The righteous have sanctified afflictions, victorious conflicts, and all-sufficient assistances—

The ungodly remain unaltered by afflictions, unacquainted with spiritual conflicts, nor do they even seek God's assistance—

Surely if *those* be *scarcely* saved, *these* cannot be saved *at all*—

2. Dreadful.

St. Peter refers to the fiery trial of persecution in particular as rendering the christian's way to heaven so difficult—

He mentions it as permitted of God for the purging of his church—

He infers from it the dreadfulness of their destruction who oppose or re-ject the gospel—

This inference naturally follows—

If such be the *salutary purgations* of God's *friends*, what must be the *vindictive chastisements* of his *enemies?*

If such things come on his friends in this state of *probation*, what shall come on his enemies at the time appointed for final *retribution?*

If such be the visitations experienced by his friends *in the day of mercy,* what must his enemies expect *in the day of his wrath?*—

We may *improve* this subject,

1. For conviction.

Every one should inquire into his own character, state, and end *—

Let none rest till they can satisfy their consciences on scriptural grounds—

2. For consolation.

The difficulty of the salvation of the righteous implies however, that, though scarcely saved, they are saved at last—

This is a blessed and consolatory truth †—

Let all then under their difficulties commit themselves to God—1 Pet. iv. 19.

THE GREAT SIN OF REJECTING CHRIST.

John xv. 22.—If I had not come, and spoken unto them, they had not had sin: but new they have no cloak for their sin. (S. S.)

EVERY sin is committed against an infinitely good and gracious God—

Yet the stoical doctrine of the equality of sins is not therefore true—

Guilt may be aggravated or diminished by a variety of circumstances—

Hence our Lord denounced peculiar woe against Chorazin and Bethsaida—

To the same effect he speaks concerning the Jews in the text—

I. How GREATLY AGGRAVATED THE SIN OF THE JEWS WAS IN REJECTING CHRIST.

Sin admits of so many degrees of malignity, that one may be considered as no sin in comparison of another—

Not that any man can be absolutely without sin—1 John i. 8.

Nor is any man really excusable in the sight of God—Rom. i. 19—21.

But *comparatively* some may be said to " have no sin"—John ix. 41.

Thus it was with those whom our Lord spake—

If he had not come to them, they might have pleaded a want of the necessary means of salvation—

But our Lord's preaching rendered them wholly inexcusable—

* Am I righteous, that is, justified, sanctified, and striving for the heavenly prize? Am I improving afflictions, maintaining conflicts, and receiving assistances from God? Have I reason to hope that I shall appear at the right hand of the judge; or am I still unprepared to meet my God?

† John x. 28. This may be well illustrated by the narration of Paul's shipwreck, when all the crew, having been given to him, were, though with great difficulty, saved. Acts xxvii. 44.

They could not plead any want of
Instruction
Our Lord often spake in parables—
This was the means of inflicting judicial blindness on the proud—Luke vii. 10.
But it was well calculated for the instruction of the humble—
Besides, he delivered many things in the simplest terms—
Evidence.
Our Lord wrought many and stupendous miracles—
He performed them by a touch, a word, and even at a distance—
His miracles were as benevolent as they were open and undeniable—
Those who wished to descredit them, imputed them to the agency of satan—
Our Lord mentions them as aggravating the guilt of those who rejected him—ver. 24.
Warning.
There was no want of fidelity on our Lord's part—
He warned the people in the plainest and most awful manner—John viii. 21, 24.
Encouragement.
Every one that thirsted for his benefits was invited by him—John vii. 37, 38.
He offered to give *spiritual* life to all who would come to him—ibid.
He promised also to crown them with eternal happiness and glory—John xii. 26.
If *they* were thus without excuse, it becomes us to consider,
II. How much more inexcusable we are if we reject Christ.
Christ has come and preached to us by his word and ministers—
And many reject him after the example of the unbelieving Jews—
Though we be not avowed infidels, we *practically* reject Christ, when we do not receive him for all the ends and purposes for which he was sent—
And if we do so, our guilt is peculiarly aggravated—
We have not any Jewish prejudices to encounter.
The Jews had received their law from God—
They had been accustomed to expect a temporal Messiah—
Yet they saw a man altogether destitute and despised—
And beheld the law of Moses superseded by a new religion—
His works indeed should have obviated all these difficulties—
But we have not these difficulties to contend with—
We profess that the gospel is from God—
We profess that Christ's kingdom is of a spiritual nature—
We profess that his cross is his own glory, and his church's hope—
We see the whole design of God unfolded.
The Jews had only partial and contracted views—
They could not reconcile many seeming contrarieties—
The disciples, even after Christ's resurrection, were at a loss to account for the occurrences they had seen—Luke xxiv. 21.
But we behold the counsels of God completed—
The various prophecies are all accomplished—
The characters and offices of Christ are opened—
The great ends of his incarnation and death are effected—
The glory of God, as shining in his face, is fully displayed—
We have witnessed the success of the gospel.

Those to whom our Lord spake, saw his ministry despised—
The great and learned of their nation rejected him—
His followers were only a few, and those of the lowest class—
But we have seen the "grain of mustard become a large tree"—
The gospel has spread to the remotest corners of the earth—
It has triumphed over the prejudices and passions, the interests and pow-ers, of the world—
Its influence is yet daily exhibited before our eyes—
How heinous then must be our guilt if we reject him!
Surely our "sin must be of a crimson or a scarlet die"—
ADDRESS,
1. Those who make excuses for their neglect of Christ.
With what foolish and weak excuses do men deceive themselves*—
Surely God will not be deceived by these—
What cloak for your sin will you find when he shall call you to account?—
Will you plead a want of instruction, evidence, warning, or encourage-ment?—
Know that in that day you will be speechless—Matt. xxii. 12.
Your love of sin and hatred of the light are the true causes of your reject-ing Christ—John v. 40.
And this will be the ground of a more aggravated condemnation—John iii. 19.
2. Those who desire to attain the saving knowledge of him.
It is a great mercy to have such a desire formed in the heart—
But beware of cloaking or extenuating your sin—
Remember that awful yet encouraging declaration—Prov. xxviii. 13.
Confess your sin with all its aggravations—
There is a virtue in the blood of Jesus to cleanse you from it all—1 John i. 7.

THE SIN AND FOLLY OF GRIEVING THE HOLY SPIRIT.

Eph. iv. 30.—Grieve not the Holy Spirit of God, whereby ye are sealed unto the day of redemption. (B.)

THIS is one of the most necessary cautions, and most comprehensive and useful directions to be found in the oracles of God. None are of more general utility, or more needful to be inculcated and regarded. For all our saving knowledge in divine things, our holiness and happiness, depend on the Spirit of God, and a proper conduct towards him. The subject therefore is of the deepest importance, and deserves our most serious consideration. To set it in a just point of view, consider we,

* We may notice a few: "I have not time." For what is time given?—"I am not able." Do you do what you can?—"It is time enough yet." Shall you certainly live, and have the grace you now slight offered you again?—"I have the majority on my side." Are you not then in the broad road? and will associates mitigate your pain?—"Professors are hypocrites." Is that a reason you should not be sincere?--" God is merciful." To whom? the impenitent!

I. What is here meant by the "Holy Spirit of G d," and how he seals us to the day of redemption

By "the Holy Spirit of God," here, is meant that divine person or principle, to which every thing excellent is ascribed in scripture, or to his influence or inspiration.—All the life and motion in the universe, Gen. i. 2; particularly vegetable, animal, rational, and spiritual life.—Skill in arts. Exod. xxxi. 3.—Especially every gift, truly and durably good, and perfective of our nature, as illumination, the scriptures themselves, and the true knowledge of them, and of divine things, 1 Cor. ii. 11—14; Eph. i. 17; regeneration, John iii. 5, 6; including awakening, conviction, mourning, repentance, faith, an inward, universal, continued, and progressive change: direction, help, and succor, Rom. viii. 14, 26.—All our comfort and consolation, Rom. xv. 13.—Progressive and perfect sanctification, Tit. iii. 5; 2 Thess. ii. 13; 1 Pet. i. 2.—A knowledge of our title to, a preparation for, and an earnest of heaven.—For he "seals us to the day of redemption;" he marks us out for the Lord, stamps his image upon us, and preserves us to, and ensures to us, eternal and full redemption.—And yet men are wont to grieve this author of all good!

II. What is implied in grieving him, and how this is generally done.

Three expressions are used in scripture on this subject, which, though nearly related to each other, do not mean the same thing.—Doing "despite to the Spirit," Heb. x. 29; treating the Holy Spirit with contumely and affront: viz. blaspheming him, as by imputing the miracles wrought by his agency to the devil, calling his ordinary operations and grace a delusion of the devil, enthusiasm, &c.; persisting to sin wilfully in spite of all his remonstrances, Heb. x. 26.—"Quenching the Spirit." In allusion to fire, which is quenched or damped, by pouring water upon it, by heaping earth or ashes upon it, and whatever is not combustible; by withholding fuel from it, or by neglecting to stir it up. So may the Holy Spirit be quenched.—"Grieving the Spirit." By behaving unkindly towards him; as we grieve a friend, when he comes to warn us of danger, and urge us to flee to a place of safety, and we will not take warning and flee, Gen. xix. 12—14; when he comes to give us instruction and direction, and we refuse to receive it, as the Jews treated the prophets of old; to offer us help, and we reject the help offered, Matt. xxiii. 37; to invite us to partake of privileges and blessings, and we doat on trifling vanities, and disregard the invitation, John v. 40; Luke xiv. 16. To apply this. Our friend will be grieved and pained, not on his own account, but on ours; not merely or chiefly because we are enemies to him, but because we are enemies to ourselves; and the more he loves us, the more will he be grieved, and in the end will withdraw from us, and give us up.— —

But to proceed to the persons by whom, and the manner wherein, that is generally done.—We observe, it is done by the impenitent, when called to repentance by the word; the Spirit accompanies the word, and they feel relentings, but relapse into their besetting sins, fly into company, or plunge into business:—when visited by affliction; the Spirit of God works with his providence, and they are humbled, and form resolutions; they recover, and forget them, and "their goodness is like the morning cloud." Isai. vii. 13, lxiii. 9, 10.—By the penitent, when invited to come to Christ and believe in him: the Spirit draws them by the word and the advice and exhortations of the saints, but, through indolence, they rest in outward reformation, or through unbelief sink into despondency, and "reject the counsel of

God against themselves ;" how slow are we to believe unless we see signs and wonders !— —By believers. They have properly received the Spirit, and are sealed by him, as the text signifies ; but often grieve him, by yielding to unbelief, and slavish fears ; by pride and self-confidence, by the love of the world, by care and business, by evil tempers as discontentment or anger, by indulging in vain thoughts and trifling conversation, misemploying time and other talents, as health, and money, neglecting to do good, and so doing evil.— —

III. THE SIN, FOLLY, AND MISERABLE CONSEQUENCES OF GRIEVING THE HOLY SPIRIT.

The sin of it.—It is an act of undutifulness and injustice. It may be compared with the sin of grieving a kind and faithful friend, a loving and tender father, an affectionate husband.—An act of ingratitude. The Spirit is the author of all spiritual and eternal blessings to us, as we have seen: he is God's greatest and best gift, next to the gift of his Son. The gifts of God's providence, the scriptures, and the means of grace, and even our redemption by Christ, are all lost upon us without the Spirit, who alone can enlighten, quicken, regenerate, direct, comfort, and seal us to the day of redemption. What is the greatness of the sin of grieving this author of all good to us; the Spirit; the Holy Spirit: the Holy Spirit of God !— —

The folly of it.—It may be compared with the folly of grieving a friend, whose direction and help we continually want, a father, on whom we are dependant; a husband, without whom we cannot live happy. If we grieve the Spirit, we grieve our only guide to heaven, forsaken of whom, we shall miss our way and never arrive there ;—the only physician of our fallen souls, by whom being given up, we shall remain sick for ever; our only help against our enemies, being deserted of whom, we shall be overcome and destroyed ;—our only comforter in our troubles, without whom we shall certainly sink under them ;—the only one that can "seal us to the day of redemption ;" and not being sealed, we shall want the knowledge of our title, and our chief qualification for heaven. Ezek. ix. 4.— —

The miserable consequences of it.—So far as we grieve him, we remain ignorant, sinful, guilty, depraved, weak, and wretched.—Persisting to grieve him, we are doubly lost, as we should have been lost if the Spirit had not visited us at all ; we are in a superadded condemnation, because when "light is come into the world, we loved darkness rather than light," and rendered all God had done for our recovery vain : viz., the word of God, the means of grace, the death of Christ.— —

INFER,

The great goodness of God, whose Spirit is grieved, because man will resolve to sin and perish !—The amazing perverseness of man, to whom it is as natural to grieve the Spirit as to breathe !— —

Apply the whole to the impenitent, to mourners, to believers ; and **exhort from motives of gratitude and self-interest.**

THE CONSEQUENCES OF SIN.

Hos. viii. 7.—They have sown the wind, and they shall reap the whirlwind. (S. S.)

MISERY is attached to sin as its inevitable consequence—

This connection does not always appear to a superficial observer—

On the contrary transgression often seems productive of happiness—

And obedience, to be a source of much affliction and trouble—

But, whatever conclusions we may be led to draw from present appear-ances, we are sure that the wicked are not happy—

Nor have they any reasonable expectation of happiness in the eternal world—

The Israelites had forsaken the true God for idols—

And God warned them of the judgments which would ere long come upon them—

But the declaration in the text may be understood as a general position—

We shall take occasion from it to shew,

I. WHO MAY BE SAID TO SOW THE WIND.

To " sow the wind" is a proverbial expression for laboring in vain—

It is applied to idolaters, because the silver and gold lavished on idols was unprofitably spent—

And it may well be applied to all who seek happiness in a way of sin.

1. To sensualists. *immoral*

They expect to find much comfort in the indulgence of their lusts—

Hence they yield themselves up to all the gratifications of sense—

But they find that such pursuits can afford them no real happiness—

While they forsake the fountain of living waters they hew out to them-selves only broken cisterns that can hold no water—Jer. ii. 13.

Solomon, with the amplest means of enjoyment, confessed this—Eccl. ii. 1. 10, 11.

And we may address that appeal to all the votaries of pleasure—Rom, vi. 21.

2. To worldlings. *Materialist*

The lovers of this present world seem to follow something substantial—

They hope to obtain, not a momentary gratification, but solid and lasting benefits—

They promise to themselves the acquisition of ease, and affluence and respect—

But riches are justly, and on many accounts, termed "uncertain"— 1 Tim. vi. 17.

No dependence can be placed on their continuance with us—Proverbs xxxiii. 5.

Our cares are also generally multiplied by means of them—

But if they were more conducive to happiness now, what shall they profit in the day of wrath?—Prov. xi. 4.

What advantage has he now, who once took such delight in his stores— Luke xii. 19.

Or he, who placed his happiness in sumptuous fare, and magnificent apparel?—Luke xvi. 19, 23, 24.

Surely all such persons will find ere long, that they "sowed the wind"—

3. To formalists.

The performance of religious duties seems more calculated to make us happy—

It is certain that no one can be happy who disregards them—
But a mere round of services can never satisfy the conscience—
' The form of godliness without the power" will avail little—
It will leave the soul in a poor, empty, destitute condition—
Some indeed delude themselves with an idea that it will secure the divine favor—
And, under that delusion, they may be filled with self-complacency—Luke xviii. 11, 12.
But if God send a ray of light into the mind, these comforts vanish—
A sight of sin will speedily dissipate these self-righteous hopes—Rom. vii. 9.
Nor will any thing satisfy an enlightened conscience but that which satisfies God—
There was but one remedy for the wounded Israelites in the wilderness—John iii. 14, 15.
Nor can a wounded spirit ever be healed but by a sight of Christ—

4. To false professors.

Many wish to be thought religious, when they are destitute of spiritual life—
They perhaps are zealous for the doctrines of the gospel, and for their own particular form of church government—
But they are not solicitous to live nigh to God in holy duties—
Nor do they manifest the efficacy of religion in their spirit and con-duct—
Yet, because of their professing godliness, they think themselves possessed of it—
And buoy up themselves with expectations of happiness in the world to come—
Alas! what disappointment will they one day experience!—Matt. xxv. 11, 22.
What will it avail them to " have had a name to live while they were really dead ?"—
Or to have " cried, Lord, Lord, while they departed not from iniquity ?—
The pains they have taken to keep up a profession, will all be lost—
Nothing will remain to them but shame and confusion of face—
From the seed which they sow we may easily perceive,

II. WHAT THEY MAY EXPECT TO REAP.

"A whirlwind" is a figure used to represent extraordinary calamities—Prov. i. 27.
And such is the harvest which they will reap in due season—
Their calamities will be,

1. Sudden.

The corn ripens gradually for the sickle; and its fate is foreseen—
But the destruction of the ungodly cometh suddenly and at an instant.
They indeed have many warnings from all which they see around them—
But they put the evil day far from them, and think it will never come—2 Pet. iii. 4.
Thus it was with the whole world before the deluge—
Though Noah preached to them for many years, they would not regard him—
And were taken by surprise at last, as much as if no notice had been given them—Matt. xxiv. 38, 39.
Thus also it will be with all who reject the gospel salvation—

485

Solomon has expressly declared it in reference to those who sow discord—Prov. vi. 14.

And St. Paul has asserted it respecting all that live in a neglect of God. 1 Thess. v. 2, 3.

2. Irresistible.

Sinners of every description can withstand the word spoken by their fellow-creatures—Ezek. xx. 49.

But they will not be able to resist God when he shall call them into judgment—

Then, if the whole universe should enter into a confederacy to protect one sinner, they would fail in their attempt—Prov. xi. 21.

There is not any thing more irresistible to man, in some climates, than a whirlwind—

Yet far less power shall the ungodly have to avert the wrath of God—

They will be carried to destruction as the chaff before the wind—Ps. i. 4, 5.

And call in vain to the rocks to fall upon them, or the hills to cover them—Rev. vi. 15—17.

3. Tremendous.

Nothing can be conceived more dreadful than the desolation made by whirlwinds—

Yet this suggests a very inadequate idea of the ruin that will come on the ungodly—

The raining of fire and brimstone on Sodom and Gomorrah must have been exceeding terrible—

But even that was light, when compared with the vials of God's wrath which will be poured out upon the ungodly world—

Who can comprehend the full import of that threatening in the Psalms?—Ps. xi. 6.

Who can form a just idea of the judgment denounced by Isaiah—Isa. v. 24.

May we never experience such dreadful calamities!—

May we tremble at the apprehension of them, and seek shelter in Christ!—Isa. xxxii. 2.

INFER,

1. How earnest should we be in redeeming time.

The present hours are given us that we may sow for eternity—

Every action, word and thought is as seed that will spring up hereafter—

According to what we sow now, we shall reap at the last day—Gal. vi. 7, 8.

Every moment increases our "treasure of wrath," or our "weight" of glory"—

How should we be affected with this consideration!

Let us lay it to heart, and "walk not as fools, but as wise men"—Eph v. 15, 16.

And let that just expostulation shame us to a sense of duty—Isa. lv. 2

2. How blessed are they who are living to God!

There is not a work which they perform for him that will not be rewarded—

God would esteem himself unjust if he made them no recompense—Heb. vi. 10.

However small and insignificant the service be, it shall not be forgotten—Matt. x. 42.

Some perhaps may complain, that they cannot do any thing for God

And that they can only weep for their unprofitableness—

But the sighs and tears of the contrite are " precious seed"—
They will spring up to a glorious and abundant harvest—Ps. cxxvi. 6.
Let the humble then go on "sowing in tears till they reap in joy"—
Let them persist in their labor, assured that it shall not be in vain—1 Cor. xv. 58.

THE END OF UNBELIEVERS.

1 Pet. iv. 17.—What shall the end be of them that obey not the gospel of God.   (S. S.)

Many are the troubles of the righteous : and though their afflictions are not always penal, yet they are for the most part to be considered as paternal chastisements, and as the judgments which God inflicts on his own house-hold with a view to their advancement in faith and holiness—But though they are to be regarded in this favorable light by the sufferers them-selves, they have a very awful aspect upon the world at large ; for, as the Apostle intimates, if God's paternal chastisements be often so severe, what must his vindictive judgments be ? If judgment first begin at the house of God, what must the end be of them that obey not the gospel of God?—To impress this solemn consideration upon our minds, we shall shew,

I. Who they are that obey not the gospel.

To ascertain this, it will be proper to state briefly what the gospel requires.

The gospel supposes men to be in a state of guilt and misery, obnoxious to the wrath of God, and incapable of delivering themselves from it—It proposes to them a remedy of God's appointment : it sets forth Jesus as an all-sufficient Saviour ; and declares that sinners of every description may be washed in his blood, and renewed by his Spirit—But, if we will not apply to him by faith, and thankfully accept his proffered benefits, it dooms us to destruction under the aggravated guilt of despising, and trampling under foot the Son of God—The commission which our Lord gave to his disciples, Mar. xvi. 15, 26, and the answer given by Paul to the awakened jailor, Acts xvi. 30, 31, abundantly confirm this view of the gospel, and shew that a cordial acceptance of Christ as our only Lord and Saviour is the sum and substance of a christian's duty—

According to this statement, very many will be found disobedient to the gospel.

1. They who neglect Christ altogether.

This is so obvious a truth that the mention of it seems needless and absurd : but experience proves that the most abandoned sinners, and most avowed infidels, are often insensible of the guilt which they contract—Be it known however, that their excuses or objections will avail them nothing in the day of judgment : their whole lives were one continued act of disobedi-ence to the gospel ; and they will most assuredly be numbered amongst the enemies of their incarnate God—Their rejection of him, whether in prin-ciple or practice, will be a decisive evidence of their guilt—

2. They who unite something else with him as a foundation for their hope.

The gospel requires us to renounce all dependence on our own works—However good our works be, they must never for one moment be considered as justifying us before God, either in whole or in part—In Christ alone must be all our hope; and if we attempt to unite any thing of ours with his perfect righteousness, we shall not only not add to our security, but shall altogether invalidate all which Christ himself has done for us—St. Paul asserts this in the plainest terms, Gal. v. 2, 4; and from the fullest conviction of its truth desired to be found in Christ, clad with his righteousness and his only— Phil. iii. 9.

3. They who, while they profess to follow Christ, dishonor him by their conduct.

Many there are who with apparent zeal cry, Lord, Lord, who yet are far from doing the things which he commands—Many alas! "profess to know him, but in their works deny him:" they are observant of outward duties, but inattentive to their spirit and temper: instead of being meek and lowly, patient and forgiving, and solicitous only to honor God, they are proud and passionate, covetous and worldly, and studious rather to be thought christians than really to deserve the name—Let such know that they "amidst all their appearances of religion deceive themselves, and their religion is vain"— James i. 26. By neglecting to walk as Christ walked they disobey the gospel, as much as if they rejected him altogether—

To awaken such from their slumbers, we proceed to shew,

II. What their end shall be.

The peculiar manner, in which the apostle speaks of their "end," intimates that it will be dreadful,

1. Beyond expression.

In the text St. Peter infers from the trials, which God suffers to come upon believers *here*, the far greater miseries that shall be endured by unbelievers *hereafter*—But his very mode of suggesting this inference shews, that the two states could scarcely admit of any comparison: for what are any transient pains of body inflicted by the most ingenious cruelty of man, when compared with the eternal torments both of soul and body, which will be inflicted on the wicked by the hand of an incensed God?—St. Paul institutes a similar comparison, and, like St. Peter, leaves our imagination to supply what no language could possibly express—Heb. x. 29. There are indeed terms used in scripture to represent to us the misery of the damned—They are represented as "cast into a lake of fire and brimstone," "where the worm of an accusing conscience dieth not, and the fire of God's wrath is not quenched:" they "weep and wail and gnash their teeth;" and the "smoke of their torment ascendeth up for ever and ever:" But, awful as these expressions are, they convey no adequate idea of the misery sustained by those who have perished in unbelief: we must say of that, as St. Paul says of the things he heard and saw in the third heavens, that it is unutterable—2 Cor. xii. 4.

2. Beyond a doubt.

The apostle appeals to our own consciences for the truth of the inference which he suggests—He says, in effect, What must the state of unbelievers be? Can it be the same with that of obedient believers? Will God put no difference between those who serve him, and those who serve him not? Has not the scripture plainly declared the end of those who disobey the gospel? And are we not constrained to acknowledge the equity of that sentence, which the contemners of Christ are taught to expect?—Shall not an angel from heaven be accursed if he presume to preach any other gospel, Gal. i. 8, and can we hope to reject the gospel with impunity? Our wishes are doubtless in opposition to the declarations of God; but in our judgment we must approve of them; and we shall surely be silent in tl e day, that they shall be enforced, even though we ourselves be the unhappy monuments of God's displeasure—

We may *learn* from hence,

1. How to improve the dispensations of God's providence.

In God's providential dealings the most eminent christians are often involved in public calamities, or bowed down under a load of personal afflictions—On the other hand the enemies of God often triumph, and revel in a fullness of all earthly enjoyments—But the intelligent christian will see in these dispensations the certainty of a future day of retribution, when the wicked shall receive the just reward of their wickedness, and he himself be exalted to an inconceivable state of bliss—He will argue thus: If God so afflict his children in the day of his mercy, how will he punish his enemies in the day of his wrath? And if he so prosper his enemies and load them with benefits in this vale of tears, what prosperity and happiness must he have reserved for his friends in the regions of glory? If crowns and kingdoms be the portion of many who disregard and despise him, what shall be the inheritance of those who honor and obey him?—Such are the reflections suggested in the text; and such are the considerations which every dispensation, whether joyous or grievous, should excite in our minds.

2. How to judge of our state before God.

Mere morality is by no means a sufficient criterion whereby to judge of our state: we may be free from gross violations of God's law, and yet be far from yielding obedience to the gospel—Let us then enquire whether we be obeying the gospel by a simple dependence upon Christ, and by a spirit and temper suited to our profession? This is the test to wh:ch we must bring ourselves, since we shall be tried by it at the last day—In vain will be our morality, if Christ be not our only foundation; and in vain will be our professed adherence to Christ, if we do not adorn the gospel by an holy conversation—Let us then examine ourselves, that we may know beforehand what our end shall be—And let all earthly comforts or troubles be improved as means of exciting us to flee from the wrath to come, and to lay hold on eternal life.

THE CHARACTER AND END OF A SENSUALIST

Luke xii. 20, 21.—But God said unto him, thou fool! this night thy soul shall be required of thee: then whose shall those things be which thou hast provided? so is he that layeth up treasure for himself, and is not rich toward God. (Sk.)

How must these words have struck the ears, and have sunk into the soul of the person to whom they were addressed! Fancy to yourselves a man wholly engaged by the affairs of this life;—quite unconcerned about his situation as a dying mortal, and as a creature accountable to God;—his salvation—his immortal concerns—entirely neglected;—at night, and alone, ruminating and contriving thus,—"what shall 1 do," &c., ver. 17—19, when—sudden and unexpected—he hears that voice, from whose sentence there is no appeal, saying, "fool! this night thy soul shall be required of thee," &c. But why did I say, *fancy* all this? When all that was worldly and thoughtless in this man, it probably realized in the disposition and conduct of many present, who differ from him, not in character, but in situation.

489

against him the sentence of death had just been pronounced; against you it is not yet uttered. Thanks be to God that it is not! You are still in a land of hope. Oh! suffer me to expose the impropriety and danger of your conduct, by describing—*the folly of this person; and the manner in which God treated him.*

I. THE FOLLY OF THE PERSON MENTIONED IN THE TEXT: The meaning of the word " fool," as it is here applied, may be discovered by consulting the following passages; Deut. xxxii. 6; Psa. xciv. 8: Prov. xiv. 9; Rom. i. 21—25; Tit. iii. 3; Jer. xvii. 11. Thus understood, *folly* is wickedness; and the folly of this man consisted in,

1. *His making the things of this life his chief good.* That he did this, is manifest, from the whole of what is said respecting him.—The world was his god:—it had his heart;—all his wishes centred in it;—his thoughts were absorbed by its concerns:—he appears to have known no higher gratification than that which arose from eating, drinking, and making merry. How wicked was all this! It implies a total want of regard for God, Psa. lii. 7. If he were not a covetous man—one who is never satisfied—he was evidently a sensualist, who lived only for himself: see Rom. viii. 6, 13, and xiii. 14; Gal. vi. 7, 8. Besides, how foolish to depend on uncertain riches! Prov. xxiii. 5, and xi. 28; Jer. ix. 23. Can any measure of them keep off sickness, infirmities, or the ' thousand other ills that flesh is heir to?' Can they prolong life, or set death at defiance? Job xxxvi. 18, 19. Such conduct tends to sensualize the very spirit. Hence, another proof of this man's folly, is manifest in,

2. *His supposing that worldly goods would satisfy his soul.* Though he appears to have believed that he had a soul, his ideas of its nature must have been very gross; or could he have said " *soul,* thou hast much goods; eat, drink, be merry?" The folly of such conduct will appear, if we consider—*the nature of the soul.* It is a spiritual, and a rational principle, Gen. i. 27, and ii. 7; Job xxxii. 8. Can the gross materials that feed the body satisfy the soul?—*The capacities of the soul.* They, on account if its very nature, are so vast, that no measure of created good can possibly satisfy them.—*The duration of the soul.* It is immortal, everlasting, Eccl. xii. 7; Matt. x. 28. Can perishable things—such as earth affords—earth that will itself be destroyed, satisfy the immortal soul of man? Such foolish conduct, as that already described, naturally leads to another species of folly, that of,

3. *Presuming on continued, on long life.* He said, " soul, thou hast much goods laid up *for many years.*" How infatuated must that man have been, who could thus calculate! see Psa. xlix. 11—13. Do we not *see* mortals arrested, and borne to their graves, at every stage of life! How frequently do we *hear* the sighs and groans of the dying:—we *feel* pains, infirmities, and decays of nature, which are sure harbingers of death;—and in the death of relatives and friends, we almost *taste* the deadly draught; and yet men will, with confidence, calculate on long life!

4. *Thus one species of folly or of wickedness leads to another.* Men make created things their chief good; then persuade themselves that such things will satisfy even their souls: this is naturally followed by a wish to enjoy them for many years; and then they persuade themselves, that for many years they shall enjoy them. Persons of the above description do not always pass for wicked men, Psa. xlix. 18, but in the sight of God, their conduct is highly offensive, Jer. xvii. 5, as will appear from,

II. THE MANNER IN WHICH GOD TREATED THE SUBJECT OF THIS FOLLY. We have in the Bible such numerous intimations of the goodness, the mercy, and the longsuffering of God, as should correct the ideas of those, who, being penitent, would despair of his mercy; and of those whose severe dispositions would lead them to describe the blessed God only as a terrible sovereign. But we have, on the other hand, such intimations of God's justice, and of the exercise of the divine displeasure towards the impenitent, as should alarm the boldest offender; and correct the errors of those, who, by a species of humanity, would question the divine prerogative to punish, let the guilty escape, and even annihilate hell itself. The circumstance under consideration speaks awful things.

1. *This man was called away* SUDDENLY. "God said unto him, *this night* thy soul shall be required of thee." Sudden death—had been considered an evil; hence that petition in the liturgy, "from sudden death, good Lord, deliver us." In whatever light it may be viewed, as it respects the righteous, to the wicked it must be terrible. It finds them unprepared; it snatches them from all they love; it hurries them, in their sins, before the bar of God. See Prov. xiv. 32.

2. *He was called away* UNEXPECTEDLY. He had been calculating only on life and worldly enjoyments; on living long and enjoying much. What a terrible, and unexpected arrest! Even a good man cannot fail to be seriously affected by such a circumstance. See 2 Kings xx. 1—8; Isa xxxviii. 9.

3. *He was called away* AMIDST A PROFUSION OF WORLDLY GOODS. "Much goods laid up," was his language. Some in a state of wretchedness, misery, and want, without calculating on future consequences, have sought and have welcomed death, as a kind of deliverer from present wo. However dreadfully mistaken, such, though unprepared, have left the world without regret. But this man loved life: he had, to use a common phrase, "made his fortune," and was going to enjoy life. Ah! in what period, and in what circumstance could death be more unwelcome? See Job xx. 22, 23; Eccles. vi. 1, 2.

4. *He was called away* BY LANGUAGE THAT STRONGLY EXPRESSED THE DIVINE DISPLEASURE. The language is truly *cutting*. *He* had said, "*sou* thou hast," &c.; *God* said, "thy *soul* is required." *He* had calculated on "*many years;*" *God* said, "*this night* thy soul shall be required." *He* had said, "soul, *thou hast* much goods;" *God* said, "*whose* shall these things be?" *He had acted a part the most foolish;* and God addressed him by the cutting appellation, "*fool.*" He had passed through his day of grace, *totally neglecting salvation;* and *God summoned him away,* unrenewed and unforgiven. What a dreadful circumstance! and yet from the remainder of our text, we are led to fear that circumstances of this kind are not uncommon; for "*so is he that layeth up treasure for himself, and is not rich toward God.*"

The following reflections urge themselves on our attention:

1. Worldly prosperity is so far from being a proof of personal goodness, or of the divine favor, that the subjects of it may be so wicked as to incur sudden and severe destruction. See Psa. lxxiii. 2—12, 18, 19.

2. The proper enjoyment of life does not depend on large possessions, verse 15.

3. Rich men are, on account of their riches, in peculiar danger—of living without God—of indulging in sensual gratifications—of presuming on long life—and of neglecting their souls.

4. Life is uncertain.—It is therefore our highest wisdom to be living for eternity. Oh that men, instead of inquiring, as they too often do, in the

language of worldly concern, and of worldly anxiety, "what shall we do?" would thus inquire after salvation. Then would we gladly point them to Jesus the mighty Saviour, to religion the true riches, and to heaven the only sure depository, for what is truly valuable in time or in eternity.

A DESCRIPTION OF THE WICKED, AND THE HELL INTO WHICH THEY SHALL BE TURNED.

Psa. ix. 17.— The wicked shall be turned into hell, and all the nations that forget God. (Sk.)

THE authorized topics afforded to God's ministers, for instruction and reproof, are various and dissimilar. Revelation presents innumerable subjects to our view; all of which, though not of equal importance, are worthy of the deepest attention and the most implicit confidence; some of these are the themes of every gospel minister, and the delight of every christian congregation—the love of God to the world—the atonement of Christ for sinners—the invitations of the gospel to the most unworthy—and the heaven prepared for the saints, are truths of the most pleasing aspect, and the most encouraging character. Happy should we be in beholding all who sit under our ministry, charmed, converted, and drawn to God by the publication of these truths; but, alas! many are yet hardened through the deceitfulness of sin. These we must persuade by the terrors of the Lord, or "save with fear, pulling them out of the fire." Many are yet wicked; these must be told of the punishment which they are preparing for themselves—this is their "portion of meat" which must be administered "in due season,"—and this is the only apology we make for laying before you the awful affirmation chosen for the text; "The wicked shall be turned into hell," &c. Here observe,

I. THE CHARACTERS SPECIFIED:—"The wicked, and all the nations that forget God." Scripture is its own interpreter; and in describing the characters spoken of in the text, we will be guided by this rule, and compare spiritual things with spiritual. By the wicked, then, we understand,

1. All those who willfully violate the plain and positive precepts of God. Such as intemperate persons, who eat or drink to excess, Nah. i. 10; Joel i. 5; Luke xii. 34; Rom. xiii. 13; Eph. v. 18. Profane persons, whose mouths are full of cursing and bitterness, Exod. xx. 7; Matt. v. 34; James v. 12. Liars, Zech. viii. 16; Colos. iii. 9; Rev. xxii. 15. Profaners of the Sabbath, who prostitute that holy day in purposes of pleasure or business, Exod. xx. 8; Isaiah lvi. 2, and lviii. 13. Dishonest persons, who deprive their neighbors of their property, by acts of theft or extortion; taking advantage of their ignorance or necessity, to enhance the price of their goods, Exod. xx. 17; Matt. x. 19; 1 Thess. iv. 6.

2. Among the wicked we must include all the persecutors of the people of God. Such was Pharaoh, who said, "The Lord is righteous, and I and my people are wicked;"—such was Manasseh, who shed innocent blood very much, and "who wrought much wickedness," 2 Kings xxi. 6;—such was Haman, who meditated a plan for the destruction of all the Jews from India even unto Ethiopia, and who is designated as "this wicked Haman;"—and such were the Jews in the days of our Saviour, whom he denominated a "wicked generation," and concerning whom Peter said, "Ye have taken, and by wicked hands" &c., Acts ii. 23.

492

3. *In the list of wicked persons we also rank all hypocrites, and impos̄ tors in religion;* who profess to know God, but by works deny him. Such were the Pharisees, who came to our Lord, Matt. xxii. 15; but Jesus "perceived their wickedness," &c.; for though they made clean "the outside of the cup and platter, their inward part was full of ravening and wickedness," Luke xi. 39.

4. *All must be denominated wicked who are unregenerate.* Wickedness is not a superficial defect, but a profound radical principle, deeply rooted in the heart of man, which is said to be "desperately wicked:"—the crimes we have enumerated are a few only, of the fatal fruits produced by this root of bitterness. Man, considered as a fallen creature, is not merely inclined to wickedness, but his inward part is very wickedness: and this applies not only to a few individuals, but to all; for "the world lieth in wickedness:" and unless your hearts have been washed from wickedness, in the fountain opened for sin and uncleanness, you must be included in the characters specified in the text. But, in addition to the wicked, we have "all nations that forget God."—Perhaps this expression refers to heathen nations, whose gods were idols, Psa. xcvi. 5; but how far the whole inhabitants of any nation forget God we cannot determine. Nations are composed of individuals, and every man who forgets God (whatever be his country, clime, or language) must be included here. The latter part of the text may be considered as explanatory of the former—the wicked are they who forget God. David's description of a wicked man is, "God is not in all his thoughts," Psa. x. 4;—he forgets God in the character of a *Sovereign,* and refuses to walk in his law, Psa. xii. 4;—as a *Benefactor,* he renders not again according to the benefit done unto him, 2 Chron. xxxii. 25;—he forgets *the all-prevailing presence of God,* so as to have no consciousness that God seeth;—he forgets *the word of God*—to its precepts he never conforms—with its invitations he never complies—its promises he never embraces—and its threatenings he never fears. Having described the characters specified in the text, let us consider,

II. THE AFFIRMATION MADE CONCERNING THEM;—"They shall be turned into hell." Here we may remark three things—the *place* into which they shall be turned—the *manner* how it will be done—and the *certainty* of the affirmation. The place is *hell,* שאול a word used sometimes to describe the grave, or a separate state of departed spirits, Gen. xxxvii. 35; Psa. xvi. 10; but more commonly descriptive of that place of punishment into which the souls of the wicked shall be thrust, when discharged from the body, Luke xvi. 23. The holy scripture, which must be our sole guide in all things that relate to the eternal world, gives us various ideas concerning this awful state of being.

1. *It describes the place of punishment.* It is called "outer darkness," Matt. viii. 12;—a lake of fire, burning with brimstone, Rev. xix. 20, xx. 10;—a bottomless pit, Rev. ix. 1, 2, xx. 1, 2;—blackness, Jude 13;—the mist of darkness, 2 Pet. ii, 17, xx. 1, 2;—a furnace of fire, Matt. xiii. 42.

2. *The nature of the punishment.* It will be inflicted by fire—fire unquenchable, Matt. iii. 12; Luke iii. 17. The pain produced by fire, is the most intolerable that the body can sustain; even when it only touches a part of our flesh, how exquisite is the torment we feel! what then must the punishment of the damned be, who will be cast into a lake of fire? But there will be in hell, deep mental anguish; "there the worm dieth not," Mark ix. 43. This metaphor is used to describe the inward agonies, which the soul must sustain from the stings of conscience. Something of this kind is

493

intimated by Homer, who, in describing the sufferings of Tityus **in hell,** says,

> "Two rav'nous vultures, furious for their food
> Scream o'er the fiend, and riot in his blood,
> Incessant gore the liver in his breast,
> Th' immortal liver grows, and gives the immortal feast."
>
> *Odyss.* b. xi. 709.

The Roman poets, like the Grecian, describe furies as avengers of wickedness in hell. They represent these furies, as old, squalid, meagre, and pale they clothe their bodies with black garments; affix to their heads vipers in stead of hair, and arm their hands with scorpions, whips, and torches, &c. In hell, the wicked will also be punished by the just judgment of God. Who can read such texts as the following, without being struck with horror at the view of their punishment? Deut. xxxii. 23—41; Psa. xi. 6; Jer. xxiii. 19; 2 Thess. i. 7—9; Rev. xiv. 9—11.

3. *The exquisite sense of punishment which the wicked will feel.*— "There shall be weeping and gnashing of teeth, when ye shall see Abraham, and Isaac, and Jacob, and all the prophets in the kingdom of God; and you yourselves thrust out," Luke xiii. 28; Matt. xiii. 42, xxii. 13, and xxiv. 51. Weeping and wailing, in the view of that eternal loss which they had sustained, for they shall see Abraham, &c., in the kingdom of God;—and from a consciousness that they might have shared in the same blessedness;—and "gnashing of teeth," with undescribed agony, and inward vexation, for having plunged themselves into that place of torment; with envy at the saints, and every expression of rage and malice against God and goodness.

4. *The companions of their punishment.* Besides the fearful and unbelieving, the abominable, murderers, whoremongers, sorcerers, idolaters, liars, thieves, drunkards, and revilers, 1 Cor. vi. 10; Rev. xxi. 8, of which the wicked will be composed; they will be associated with "the devil and his angels," Matt. xxv. 41. The devil, who is described as an old serpent—an adversary—a dragon—and a roaring lion;—"his angels," his messengers:—these will be the tormentors of the wicked, Matt. xviii. 34. Their tempters here, will be their tormentors in hell; they will probably remind them of their folly—of their crimes—and of the heaven they have lost, and "toss their infamy from tongue to tongue."

5. *The perpetuity of their punishment.* The fire of hell is unquenchable, and the worm is deathless. The punishment is everlasting; the great gulf that intervenes between paradise and perdition, is impassable; and the crimes of the wicked, after death are unpardonable, Matt. xii. 32, xxv. 42, 2 Thess. i. 9; Rev. xiv. 11.

B—"The wicked shall be turned into hell;"—this shall be done,

1. *Unexpectedly.* A few indeed have presentiments of their approaching punishment, and forebodings of their impending doom; but the great mass of the wicked are lulled to sleep by the fascinating charms of sin, and the dreadful delusions of the devil;—are led on blindly towards destruction; and, contrary to all their expectations, are turned into hell.

2. *Suddenly.* How many are cut off in a moment! Death suddenly seizes upon them, and they go down *quick* into hell, Psa. lv. 23. And though many of the wicked may linger on to old age, yet the stroke of death is sudden, Psa. lxxiii. 19; Prov. xxix. 1; 1 Thess. v. 3.

3. *Irresistibly.* The expression in the text conveys an idea of violence and impetuosity; *turned*, or hurried headlong into hell; driven by death into

the territories of perdition. The destruction of the wicked will come upon them as a whirlwind, Prov. i. 27. They will be bound hand and foot, and taken away and *cast* into outer darkness, Matt. xxii. 13.

The certainty of the affirmation in the text, may be inferred,

1. *From the general consent of mankind.* The idea of future punish-ment has been almost universal, from the remotest periods of antiquity; and it cannot be supposed that men of different ages, and distant countries, would agree on this point, if the idea had not rested on grounds of wide extent, discernible to the understandings of men in general.

2. *From the justice of the moral Governor of the universe.* In the pres-ent state of things, evil goes unpunished in a thousand instances, either by human or divine justice; but the Judge of all the earth will do right, and will not suffer the eternal laws of right and wrong to be violated with impunity; and as the wicked are not punished here, the righteousness of God will in-duce him to turn them into hell.

3. *From the moral unfitness of the wicked for any other situation.* They must die, and heaven or hell must receive them; but they are totally unfit for the former, and completely prepared for the latter. Heaven is the region of holiness, and the habitation of the great King; but into his presence they cannot come, for evil shall not dwell with him; they cannot even *see* God; to hell they *must* go, this is the reward of their hands, the meed of their toil, and the wages of their iniquity.

4. *The certainty of the affirmation is incontestibly proved from the Bi-ble.* Psa. lxxv. 8; Matt. xxv. 41. We conclude by observing—How awful is the state of the wicked! Language fails to describe the horror and pun-ishment that await them; and what is most to be deplored, they have no knowledge of their danger. Oh how amazing is the infatuation that has seized them!—But what deep commiseration should christians feel in con-templating the circumstances of their wicked neighbors, and especially the awful state of heathen nations! Oh what efforts should they make to save souls from death!—and what praise should they offer to God, who has pluck-ed them as brands from the burning, and saved them from those things of which they are now ashamed.

CHAPTER VIII.

THE BLESSEDNESS OF RELIGION.

THE CITY OF GOD

Psalm lxxxvii. 3.—Glorious things are spoken of thee, O city of God. (Sk.)

ALTHOUGH the whole of this Psalm literally refers to the ancient city of David, it is undoubtedly an encomium on the glory and privileges of the gospel church, of which Jerusalem was a type. Jerusalem was exalted and fortified by its situation, but much more so by the favor and protection of Jehovah, ver. 1, 2. "He loved the gates of Zion more than all the dwell-ings of Jacob." What Jerusalem *was*, that the christian church now is—Built by God "upon the foundation," &c., Eph. ii. 20. He loves her beyond the kingdoms and empires of the earth, which rise and fall only to subserve his purposes concerning her. But although Jerusalem was eminently typical of the church on earth, it was no less so of the triumphant church above.—We shall therefore contemplate the words of our text,

I. IN THEIR LITERAL REFERENCE TO THE JEWISH METROPOLIS. Jerusalem was truly the "city of God:"—the city which he particularly chose—to which he paid especial regard. Hence "glorious things" were spoken of her. She was beautiful for situation, magnificent in her buildings, the delight of the nations, and the joy of the whole earth. She was the emporium of Jewish commerce, and the seat of oriental learning. Above all others, the following glorious things were spoken of this city :

1. *There was the seat of the civil government.* There were the splendid courts of the kings of Judah. "There," says the Psalmist, "are set the thrones of judgment," &c.—There the princes and nobles resided—thence issued the mandates by which the people were governed, &c.

2. *There the divine ordinances were celebrated.* There was the ark, the altar, the sacrifices, the stupendous temple of Solomon, and the testimony of Jehovah—There were the singers, the musicians, and the priests—Yea, there were the visible symbols of the divine glory, and the king of heaven dwelling in the midst of his people, 2 Chron. vii. 16; Ps. xlviii.

3. *There was the general rendezvous of all the Israelitish tribes.* Three times a year all the males came up to worship at Jerusalem. How interesting to see such multitudes all assembled to praise the Lord in the beauty of holiness, playing on sacred instruments, singing, making solemn processions, &c.

4. This city received a *glorious name,* " vision of peace ;" and was at length honored with *the presence of our Lord,* " the Prince of Peace."

II. IN THEIR SPIRITUAL APPLICATION TO THE CHURCH OF CHRIST. St. Paul styles this, " Jerusalem which is from above, which is the mother of us all"—of all believers, Gal. iv. 26. Hence Christians are represented as " fellow citizens," Eph. ii. 19. Now of this spiritual city, the antetype of Zion, glorious things are spoken :—

1. *That she is gloriously founded by the living God.* The church exists by his good pleasure and purpose. The plan was formed in the divine counsels, and fulfilled by the divine hand. (1.) She is built upon Jesus the sure foundation and precious corner stone. (2.) He purchased the church with his own blood. (3.) Instituted all her ordinances. (4.) Quickens every member by his own spirit. (5.) Protects and supports her by his power, and, (6.) Designs by all the wonders of his providence and grace to establish her for ever.

2. *That she possesses glorious privileges.* All ancient enfranchised cities had various immunities and privileges—but none ever had such as are enjoyed in the church. Some of these are, (1.) Spiritual illumination. The church is to the world as *Goshen to Egypt.* (2.) Justification by faith. (3.) The peace of God. (4.) Divine love. (5.) Joy in the Holy Ghost. (6.) Protection from danger. (7.) Triumph over enemies. (8.) Inestimable riches, and glorious dignities. (9.) The constant presence and favor of Christ.

3. *That she contains glorious inhabitants.* Suitable to the dignity of the founder, and the value of the privileges, is the character of the denizens. (1.) They are all *free,* Gal. iv. 31. (2.) They are a *heavenly race,* born of God, 1 John iii. 1. (3.) *A holy people.* (4.) *Priests and kings,* 1 Peter ii. 9; Rev. i. 6. (5.) *Heirs of God, and joint heirs with Christ,* Rom. viii. 17; Ps. xv.

4. *That glorious promises shall be accomplished in her.* See a summary of these, in that magnificent prophecy, Isa. lx.

III. IN THEIR GRANDEST TYPICAL REFERENCE TO HEAVEN ITSELF. Heaven is emphatically "the city of the Great King"—the "city which hath foundations"—"which is to come."—The city which the ancient patriarchs sought, and which St. John saw in vision, and afterwards described.

The future state of the saints is represented by various figures, calculated to convey the sublimest ideas of its perfection—a mansion—inheritance—crown, throne, &c.—But it is a *place* as well as a *state.* Though the essence of Deity pervades immensity, yet every other nature being finite, it is necessary there should be a *local* display of his glory, in some central point, where all the happy intelligences of the universe may be collected. That place is heaven; and glorious things are spoken thereof in the oracles of God. It is,

1. *Surpassingly grand in magnificence.* There the throne of the Supreme Glory is erected—and there the manifestations of Deity are witnessed—The sun is a splendid object here—the radiance of the stars, and the beauty of the firmament, impress our senses strongly—but these, and all other resplendent objects which glitter in mortal eyes, have no glory by reason of that which excelleth. See Rev. iv. and xxi. 9, to xxii. 5, where this glory is minutely described.

2. *Absolutely complete in its enjoyments.* This will clearly appear when we consider that it comprises,
1. The perfect exclusion of all evil—
2. The utmost perfection of body and soul—
3. The visions and fruition of God and Christ—
4. The most glorious and amicable society—
5. The most pleasing engagements.—

3. *Eternal in its duration.* Being built by Jehovah, it rests upon his own goodness, power, and truth—an immovable basis. "The saints shall reign for ever and ever."—Believers "shall not perish, but have everlasting life;" God "who had given us the hope of eternal life by Christ Jesus before the world began," cannot lie, or deny himself, Titus i. 2, 3.—This is the brightest gem in the crown of righteousness—the most radiant star in the constellation of future glory.

IMPROVEMENT. How important to be citizens of the spiritual Jerusalem, the gospel church! It was an honor and a privilege to be a denizen of ancient Jerusalem—how much greater to belong to this holy community; especially as this also qualifies us for the Jerusalem above.—

2 How cheerfully should christians welcome death! It will release them from earth and send them home to their Father's house! Purified by the blood of Jesus, they should hail the day of dissolution.

"O happy day—that breaks our iron chain!
That manumits,—that calls from exile home!
That leads to nature's great metropolis,
And re-admits us, through the guardian hand
Of elder brother, to our Father's throne!
Who hears our advocate, and through his wounds
Beholding man, allows that tender name."—"'Tis this," &c.

3. How foolish those who remain strangers to, and foreigners from the church, and thereby exclude themselves from heaven.

THE CHRISTIAN CONDUCTED TO GLORY

Psalm lxxiii. 24.—Thou shalt guide me with thy counsel, and afterward receive me to glory. (Sk.)

WHEN at the Divine command the Israelitish host forsook the land of Egypt, and entered upon the wilderness of the Red Sea, Jehovah was pleased to guide them as a flock by the hands of Moses and Aaron, but more especially by the mysterious pillar, which was as a cloud by day, and as a fire by night. By this instrument he safely led them through the sea—through the difficulties and perils of the wilderness—and conducted them to the frontiers of Canaan; then dividing Jordan before them, he received them into the land of rest, "the land flowing with milk and honey, which is the glory of all lands." These circumstances afford our text a striking illustration, as they form a beautiful emblem of the christian's journey through life, under the guiding and protecting hand of Jehovah, who at length divides the stream of death for his ransomed to pass over, and receives him into the Canaan of everlasting repose. The Psalmist had been tempted to envy the wicked, ver. 2, 15; but having vanquished the temptation, he labored to turn it to an advantage by increasing in humility, in love to God, and confidence in his care. In the text he beautifully opposes his own character and end to that of the wicked. 'Instead of following the devices of my own heart like the wicked, "thou shalt guide me with thy counsel." Instead of being like them cast down into destruction when life is ended, "thou shalt receive me to glory."' The text therefore expresses,

I. A GOOD MAN'S CONFIDENCE FOR THIS LIFE. "Thou shalt guide me with thy counsel." Counsel frequently means advice or instruction, frequently design or purpose. Either of these would apply here; but there is another signification, which embraces both the former, and extends much farther. Counsel is properly that which adapts means to the end. When we have an important design to accomplish, we have recourse to counsel, which provides suitable means to secure our object. Now the great end which God proposes concerning us is our salvation. To accomplish this, his counsel has provided means, viz. his providence, word, and Spirit. Hence, to be guided by his counsel, is to follow,

1. *The leadings of his providence.* God holds the reins of government in his own hands, and regulates human affairs. His various dispensations plainly mark out to attentive minds the path in which they should walk as to their earthly concerns, viz., their *employments, situations,* and *objects of pursuit.* No man can be guided by the Divine counsel who does not move in this providential road. When we get out of the way of God's appointment, we resemble a dislocated limb, for every motion gives us pain, Prov. iv. 26.

2. *The directions of his word.* The Bible explicitly reveals "the whole counsel of God." It affords ample information on every point relative to our duty, or interest; our present, or future felicity. It exhibits the way of life so luminously, that "the wayfaring man, though a fool, need not err therein." "Thy word is a lamp unto my feet, and a light unto my path." It is our only rule of faith, and of practice. It points *guilty* man to the atoning blood for *pardon.* It directs *polluted* man to seek the regenerating, purifying *influences of the Holy Spirit.* It opens to *miserable* man the richest source of *consolation;* and unfolds to *mortal* man an interminable prospect of "glory, honor, and immortality."

3. *The teaching of his Spirit*, John xvi. 13. This is always in perfect conformity with the written word, nor can it possibly be contradictory thereto. But the Spirit is sent to open our understandings, that we may comprehend the scriptures; to apply their doctrines and general rules to particular characters and cases; and to render the truth vital, penetrating, and efficacious. He emphatically speaks to the heart through the dispensations of providence, and the ministry of man, as well as by secret illuminations, impressions, and attractions. "Thou shalt guide me with thy counsel." The Psalmist's language pleasingly marks,

1. His *humility*. '"*Thou* shalt guide me," for I cannot guide myself.' See his humiliating confession, ver. 22. Equally convinced is the christian now, "that it is not in man who walketh to direct his steps;" he dares not trust his own understanding or heart; 'Whither,' he exclaims, 'my erring judgment, and my impetuous passions, whither, would you conduct me, if I were left to your guidance? Alas! experience returns a melancholy answer to this question. Oh my God! thou, thou only shalt guide me with thy counsel. I will trust in thee with all my heart, and not lean unto my own understanding. I will acknowledge thee in all my ways, that thou mayest direct my paths.'

2. His *submission and acquiescence*. 'However unpleasing to flesh and blood, I cheerfully follow thy guidance.' When a man is led or guided, he is not driven, dragged, or constrained: he voluntarily follows his conductor. The christian is not compelled to follow the divine counsel; he willingly consents and submits to it. This is a diposition essentially necessary, for God often conducts us through paths which cause every natural feeling to recoil.

3. His *strong assurance*. "Thou *shalt* guide me," &c. He had no doubt of being safely conducted, notwithstanding all his ignorance and weakness. Thus the christian, distrusting himself, is nevertheless fully assured that God will guide him securely through all vicissitudes of time, Isa. lxiii. 9; Deut. xxxii. 10, 11, 12.

II. A GOOD MAN'S CONFIDENCE FOR ETERNITY. Thou shalt "afterward receive me to glory." All the vast machinery of providence, and the still more wonderful economy of grace, tend to this grand purpose, to prepare the soul for glory. This is God's ultimate end in all. And when the christian arrives at the brink of that dark flood, which all must pass; his God is there, to bring him in safety through, and to receive him on the shore of everlasting deliverance, where he is crowned with unwithering honors, and filled with ineffable delight. He is received,

1. To a *glory of condition*. Contrast the meanness of his condition on earth, with the unsearchable riches, the immortal beauty, and the radiant majesty, to which he is the legitimate heir in the eternal state. Contrast also the imperfection of his intellectual powers, and the scantiness of his knowledge here, with the vigor of the former, and the immensity of the latter, in glory.

2. To a *glory of charity*. While here, the christian was regarded as base and mean. He was degraded, vilified, and slandered. Reproach and ignominy marked his career. But God renders his character glorious. In heaven all acknowledge him as a saint—a son of God—an heir of God—a priest—a king of glory.

3. To a *solid, substantial glory*. Earthly glory is an empty bubble, calculated only to glitter and deceive. But this is "a *weight* of glory," a

satisfying reality; the honor which comes from God, and which is suited to the dignity of man.

4. *To a permanent, unfading glory.* "An *eternal* weight of glory." When the sun shall lose his radiance, when the stars shall be extinguished, and all nature dissolved, then shall the christian shine with und?caying lustre, and be adorned with immortal splendors. His life and happiness, and glory, shall last forever, Matt. xiii. 43; Rom. ii. 7—10.

Such is the design of God. A design directly opposite to that of satan, who wishes to guide men by the counsels of the ungodly, the corruptions of their hearts, and his own suggestions, to everlasting perdition. Into which of these designs have we entered? Our tempers, conversation, and life, have already decided this question. Whose counsel shall guide us for the future? May we all reply,—' we will follow the counsel of the Lord!' Amen.

THE CHRISTIAN'S HAPPINESS.

1 Peter i. 8, 9.—Whom having not seen, ye love; in whom, though now ye see him not, yet believing, ye rejoice with joy unspeakable, and full of glory; receiving the end of your faith, even the salvation of your souls. (H. H.)

The world often wonder that christians do not conform to the vices of the age—1 Pet. iv. 4.

And are yet more surprised that any should be willing to suffer for the sake of their religion—

But every christian is actuated by a principle of love to Christ—

This principle even gathers strength from the opposition it meets with—

The apostle is writing to those who were in heaviness through manifold temptations—

He declares, however, that their trials were promoting their eternal good—

He then shews that they were supported under them by their attachment to Christ—

In his words we may see,

I. THE STATE OF TRUE CHRISTIANS—

Christians cannot be distinguished better by any thing, than by their regard to their divine Master:

1. They love Christ—

Once, like the ungodly around them, they were enemies to Christ and his cross—Phil. iii. 19.

They "saw no beauty in him, for which he is to be desired"—Isa. liii. 2.

But now he is truly precious to their souls—1 Pet. ii. 7.

They claim him as their best friend and portion—Cant. v. 10.

This is the character of every true christian—Eph. vi. 24.

If any answer not to this character, they are, and must be, accursed—1 Cor. xvi. 22.

2. They rejoice in Christ—

They have a good hope, if not a full assurance, of an interest in him—

They have access to him in their secret duties—

They receive strengthening and refreshing communications from him—

They rejoice in him, as their faithful and almighty Friend—Phil. iv. 4.

Their joy in him is " incapable of being fully declared"*—

It is a "glorified" joy, such as the saints in heaven possess†—

Every christian indeed does not experience the same measure of joy; nor is any one at all times alike joyful—

But no one is a christian, who does not esteem the light of the Redeemer's countenance above every other good—Ps. iv. 6, and lxxiii. 25.

That their felicity may be more generally experienced, we proceed to state,

II. THE MEANS BY WHICH THEY ATTAIN IT.

Paul was favored with a sight of Christ at the time of his conversion—

But this is not the way in which the christian's state is attained—

Many suppose, that if they could have a personal interview with Christ, they should love him, and rejoice in him—

But a sight of him with the bodily eyes only never produced this effect—

Many who even heard his discourses, and beheld his miracles, were amongst his bitterest enemies—

The christians to whom St. Peter wrote had never seen Christ—

The apostle *twice* mentions this circumstance, to shew that their regard for him did not arise from any personal acquaintance with him—

Faith is the only mean whereby we are brought to this love and joy—

It is only by faith that we can behold the excellency of Christ—

It is only by faith that we can apply his merits to ourselves—

It is only by faith that we can receive his gracious communications— Eph. iii. 17.

Repentance will lead to this state; and obedience spring from it—

But it is faith only that will prevail to bring us into it—Rom. xv. 13.

To increase our ardor in pressing forward to this state, let us consider,

III. THE BLESSEDNESS OF THOSE WHO HAVE ATTAINED IT—

The salvation of the soul is the great "end of our faith"—

Present comforts are desirable; but eternal happiness is that which the christian has principally in view—

It is to this that he looks forward, under his first convictions—

This is the end for which he cheerfully endures all his privations and conflicts—

In every possible state he has an eye to this, as the consummation of all his hopes and desires—

This blessed object is already attained by all true christians—

They do not wait for it till they arrive in heaven—

Their full reward indeed is reserved for another world—

But believers have the foretastes of heaven already communicated to them—

Yea, their love to Christ, and their joy in him, are an earnest, as well as pledge, of their eternal inheritance—

INFER,

1. What a rational character is the christian!

He is thought an enthusiast, for loving and rejoicing in Christ—

And they who have no such love or joy appropriate to themselves the name of *rational* christians—

But we are willing to meet our adversaries on this ground, and to submit our sentiments to this test—

If to admire supreme excellence, to love infinite amiableness, and to

---

* ἀνεκλαλήτω. † δεδοξασμένη.

501

rejoice in unbounded goodness, be a *rational* employment; yea, if the glorified saints and angels be rational; then the christian is a *rational* character; and the more so, in proportion as he loves and rejoices in Christ: and their adversaries are most *irrational*, in that they can love and rejoice in the things of time and sense, and yet feel no love to, nor any joy in, our adorable Lord and Saviour—

Let those who are now despised as enthusiasts, think who will be accounted *rational* in the day of judgment?

2. How clearly may we know, whether we be real christians, or not!

There are certainly different degrees of faith, love, and joy—

But every true christian experiences them in some measure—

This is decided by an authority that cannot be doubted—Phil. iii. 3.

Let us then examine what is the supreme object of our affections, and chief source of our joys—

Nor let us ever conclude well of our state, unless we can adopt from our hearts the language of St. Paul—Phil. iii. 8.

3. How highly should we value the ordinances of the gospel!

Faith, as has been shewn, is the mean of filling us with ardent love, and joy unspeakable—

And how is faith to be produced in our hearts, but by the preaching of the gospel?—Rom. x. 14.

Let us then love the ordinances of religion, and diligently attend them—

Let us come to them *with the express view* to have our faith, our love and our joy increased—

And let us judge of our improvement of them by the degree in which we experience these effects from them

---

EXTENT AND SOURCE OF THE CHRISTIAN'S POWER.

Phil. iv. 13.—I can do all things through Christ which strengtheneth me. (H. H.)

THERE are in the sacred writings many various, and apparently opposite, representations of the christian's state: he is mournful, yet happy; sinful, yet holy; weak, yet possessed of a derived omnipotence. These paradoxes are incomprehensible to the world at large: but the solution of them is easy to those who know what man is *by nature*, and what he is *by grace*, and what are the effects which flow from the contrary and contending principles of flesh and Spirit. Nothing can be more incredible, at first sight, than the assertion in the former part of our text: but, when qualified and explained by the latter part, it is both credible and certain: yea, it presents to our minds a most encouraging and consoling truth.

In elucidating this passage, we shall shew,

I. THE EXTENT OF A CHRISTIAN'S POWER.

Using only such a latitude of expression as is common in the holy scriptures, we may say concerning every true christian, that he can,

1. Endure all trials.

In following his divine Master, he may be called to suffer reproaches, privations, torments, and death itself. But "none of these can move him." When his heart is right with God, he can "rejoice that he is counted worthy to suffer shame for his Redeemer's sake:" Acts v. 41; he can "suffer the loss of all things, and yet count them but dung:" Phil. iii. 8; under extreme torture, he can refuse to accept deliverance, in the prospect of "a better resurrection:" Heb. xi. 35; he can say, "I am ready to die for the Lord's sake;" Acts xxi. 13; and when presented at the stake as a sacrifice to be slain, he can look upon his sufferings as a matter of self-congratulation and exceeding joy, Phil. ii. 17, 18; 1 Pet. iv. 12, 13.

2. Mortify all lusts.

Great are his inward corruptions; and many are the temptations to call them forth: but he is enabled to mortify and subdue them. Gal. v. 24. "The lust of the flesh, the lust of the eye, and the pride of life," are very fascinating: but "the grace of God, which has brought salvation to his soul, has taught him to deny them all, and to live righteously, soberly, and godly in this present world." 1 John ii. 15, 16, with Tit. ii. 13, 14. "By the great and precious promises of the gospel, he is made a partaker of the divine nature," 2 Pet. i. 4, and is stirred up to "cleanse himself from all filthiness, both of flesh and spirit, and to perfect holiness in the fear of God." 2 Cor. vii. 1.

3. Fulfill all duties.

Every different situation brings with it some correspondent duties: prosperity demands humility and vigilance; adversity calls for patience and contentment. Now the christian is "like a tree that is planted by the rivers of water, and bringeth forth its fruits *in its season.*" Psa. i 3. It is to this change of circumstances that the apostle more immediately refers in the text: "I have learned," says he, "in whatsoever state I am, therewith to be content. I know both how to be abased, and I know how to abound: everywhere, and in all things, I am instructed both to be full, and to be hungry, both to abound, and to suffer need. *I can do all things.*" Ver. 11—13. The christian knows that all his duties are summed up in love to God, and love to man: he is assured, that no changes in his condition can for one moment relax his obligation to approve himself to God in the execution of these duties: and he endeavors to avail himself of every wind that blows, to get forward in his christian course.

But in reference to all the foregoing points, we must acknowledge, that all christians are not equally advanced; nor does any christian so walk as not to shew, at some time or other, that "he has not yet attained, nor is altogether perfect." Phil. iii. 12. We must be understood therefore as having declared, rather what the christian "*can* do," than what he actually does in all instances. "In many things he still offends;" Jam. iii. 2; but he aspires after the full attainment of this proper character: in the performance of his duties, he aims at *universality in the matter, uniformity in the manner*, and *perfection in the measure* of them.

The christian's power being so extraordinary, we may well inquire after,

II. THE SOURCE FROM WHENCE HE DERIVES IT.

The christian *in himself* is altogether destitute of strength—

If we consult *the scripture representations* of him, we find that he is "without strength," Rom. v. 6, and even "dead in trespasses and sins." Eph ii. 1. Nor, after he is regenerate, has he any more power that he can call his own; for "in him, that is, in his flesh, dwelleth no good thing." Rom. vii. 15, 18, 19.

If *our Lord's assertion* may be credited, "without him we can do nothing;" we are like branches severed from the vine. John xv. 5.

If *the experience of the most eminent apostle* will serve as a criterion, he confessed, that he "had not *of himself* a sufficiency even to think a good thought; his sufficiency was entirely of God." 2 Cor. iii. 5.

His power even to do the smallest good is derived from Christ—

"It has pleased the Father, that in Christ should all fullness dwell," Col. i. 19, and that "out of his fullness all his people should receive." John i. 16. It is he who "strengthens us with all might by his Spirit in the inner man:" Eph. iii. 16; it is he who "gives us both to will and to do." Phil. ii. 13; Heb. xiii. 21. If we are "strong in any degree, it is in the Lord, and in the power of *his* might." Eph. vi. 10. Whatever we do, we must give him the glory of it, saying. "I live; yet not I, but Christ liveth in me:" Gal. ii. 20; "I have labored; yet not I, but the grace of God which was with me:" "by the grace of God I am, what I am." 1 Cor. xv. 10.

Nor is it by strength *once* communicated, that we are strong; but by continual communications of grace from the same overflowing fountain. It is not through Christ who *hath strengthened*, but who *doth strengthen* us, that we can do all things.* We need fresh life from him, in order to the production of good fruit; exactly as we need fresh light from the sun, in order to a prosecution of the common offices of life. One moment's intermission of either, would instantly produce a suspension of all effective industry.

From that source he receives all that he can stand in need of—

Christ is not so prodigal of his favors, as to confer them in needless profusion: he rather apportions our strength to the occasions that arise to call it forth. Deut. xxxiii. 25. He bids us to renew our applications to him; and, in answer to them, imparts "grace sufficient for us." 2 Cor. xii. 9. There are no limits to his communications: however "wide we open our mouth, he will fill it." Psa. lxxxi. 10. He is "able to make *all* grace abound towards us, that we, having *all-ways all*-sufficiency in *all* things, may abound unto *every* good work:" 2 Cor. ix 8; he is ready to "do for us exceeding abundantly above all that we can ask or think." Eph. iii. 20. "If only we believe, *all* things shall be possible unto us:" Mark ix. 23; we shall be "able to quench *all* the fiery darts of the devil," Eph. vi. 16, and "be more than conquerors over *all* the enemies of our souls." Rom. viii. 37

The uses to which we may apply this subject, are,

1. The conviction of the ignorant.

Many, when urged to devote themselves to God, reply, that we require more of them than they can do; and that it is impossible for them to live according to the scriptures. But what ground can there be for such an objection? Is not Christ ever ready to assist us? Is not omnipotence pledged for our support? Away with your excuses then, which have their foundation in ignorance, and their strength in sloth. Call upon your Saviour; and he will enable you to "stretch forth your withered hand:" at his command, the dead shall arise out of their graves; and the bond-slaves of sin and satan shall be "brought into the liberty of the children of God."

2. The encouragement of the weak.

A life of godliness cannot be maintained without constant watchfulness and strenuous exertion. And there are times when "even the youths faint and are weary, and the young men utterly fall." But "if we wait upon our God we shall certainly renew our strength, and mount up with wings as eagles." Isa. xl. 30, 31. If we look "to Him on whom our help is laid," Psa. lxxxix. 19, the experience of David shall be ours: "In the day when

* ἐνδυναμοῦντι.

504

I cried, thou answeredst me, and strengthenedst me with strength in my soul." Psa. cxxxviii. 3. Let not any difficulties then discourage us. "Let the weak say, I am strong;" Joel iii. 10; and the stripling go forth with confidence against Goliath. Let us "be strong in the grace that is in Christ Jesus," 2 Tim. ii. 1, and "his strength shall assuredly be perfected in our weakness." 2 Cor. xii. 9.

OUR TIMES IN GOD'S HAND.

Psalm xxxi. 15.—My times are in thy hand. (H. H.)

To the ungodly it is a satisfaction to deny the providence of God, and to cut him off, as it were, from any connection with his creatures. But the saints find a rich consolation in the thought that God reigneth. This it is which reconciles them to the evils they endure, and fortifies them against those which they have reason to apprehend. David, in the psalm before us, complains that there were many who "took counsel together against him, and devised to take away his life." But he comforted himself in the reflection, that, however *man* might be his enemy, *God* was "his God;" and that however bitterly his enemies might be enraged against him, "his times were not in *their* hands, but in *God's ;*" and, consequently, that they could do nothing against him but by his permission.

From this view of the text we are led to notice,

I. OUR DEPENDENCE ON GOD.

God is the Governor of the universe: he appoints the stars their courses; he makes the raging elements to fulfill his will, Ps. cxlviii. 8; he imposes a restraint upon the most savage beasts, causing them to suppress, 1 Kin. xiii. 28, or forget, Dan. vi. 22, their instinctive ferocity, or over-ruling the exercise of it, for the preservation, John i. 17, or destruction of men, 2 Kin. ii. 24, as he sees occasion. The affairs of men he more especially controls. In his hands are,

1. The occurrences of life

There is nothing really casual or contingent in the world. It is God that disposes of us from our earliest infancy to the latest hour of our lives. "He determines the bounds of our habitation, Acts xvii. 26. If we are called to the possession of wealth, or deprived of it by any untoward circumstances, it is "the Lord who gives, and the Lord who taketh it away, Job i. 21. If we enjoy health, or pine away in sickness, it is "the Lord who both wounds and heals, who kills and makes alive," 1 Sam. ii. 6, 7. "There is neither good nor evil in the city, but the Lord is the doer of it," Am. iii. 6. Even the falling of a hair of our head, trifling as it is, takes not place but by his appointment, Matt. x. 30.

2. The seasons of death.

To every man "there is an appointed time upon earth, Job vii. 1: there are "bounds which he cannot pass, Job xiv. 5. "God holdeth our souls in life, Ps. lxvi. 9: and "when he taketh away our breath, we die, and return to the dust," Ps. civ. 29. Youth and health are no security against the stroke of death: the most vigorous constitutions are soon broken, when God is pleased to afflict us, Job xxi. 23—25: the skill of physicians, however useful when attended with his blessing, is of no avail, Mark v. 26. So numerous are the occasions of death, that no caution can possibly avoid them: "a man may flee from a lion, and a bear meet him; or he may go into a house for safety, and a serpent bite him," Amos v. 19. When God "requires our souls," we must surrender them at his call," Luke xii. 20. Our days are protracted to an advanced age, if he be pleased to uphold us; if not, our course is finished as soon as ever it is commenced. It is "in God, and in God alone, that we live, and move, and have our being," Acts xvii. 28.

But though these ideas are certainly comprehended in the text, its more immediate scope is to declare,

II. OUR SECURITY IN GOD.

We have already observed, that the words of the text were introduced by David as a consolatory reflection, under the cruel treatment which he had received from friends and enemies. We are therefore taught by them to assure ourselves,

1. That none can destroy us before our time.

We appear to be, yea, we really are, in the midst of many and great dangers. But however we may be encompassed with enemies, they cannot prevail against us till the Lord's time for our removal is come. David was continually exposed to the rage and jealousy of Saul, who repeatedly cast a javelin at him, and hunted him incessantly with armed hosts "like a partridge upon the mountains." Yet though he was often in the most imminent danger, 1 Sam. xxiii. 26, and certainly would have been betrayed by the men of Keilah, ib. ver. 11, 12, yet God watched over him, and kept him in perfect safety. Many sought to apprehend our Lord; but "they could not lay hands on him till his hour was come," John vii. 30. & viii. 20; Luke xiii. 33: and even then Pilate "could have had no power against him, unless it had been given him from above," John xix. 11. Paul was in perils innumerable, "and in deaths oft," 2 Cor. xi. 23—27: once he was stoned, and even left for dead, Acts xiv. 19, 20; but none could take away his life, till he had finished the course marked out for him. Thus we also are immortal, till our work is done. We are surrounded with "chariots of fire and horses of fire," 2 Kin. vi. 17: yea, "God himself is a wall of fire round about us," Zech. ii. 5. And sooner shall successive bands of enemies be struck dead upon the spot by fire from heaven, 2 Kin. i. 10—12, than one of the Lord's little ones shall perish, Matt. xviii. 14.

2. That none shall hurt us without his permission.

As we depend on God for our happiness as well as for our existence, so are both our being and our well-being secured by him. Satan could not touch the person or the property of Job, till he had obtained leave of God to do so, Job i. 12, & ii. 6. "Nor can any weapon that is formed against us, prosper," Isa. liv. 17, any further than our God shall see good to permit it. "His angels encamp round about us," Ps. xxxiv. 7, and have an especial charge to "keep us in all our ways, that we dash not our foot against a stone," Ps. xci. 11, 12. "Neither the arrow that flieth by day, nor the pestilence that walketh in darkness, can hurt us. Thousands may fall at our side, and ten thousands at our right hand; but it shall not come nigh us," ib. ver. 5—7.

We are not indeed at liberty to rush needlessly into danger, from an expectation that God will deliver us; (this were to "tempt the Lord our God,") Matt. iv. 6, 7; but in the path of duty we have nothing to fear: we may "tread upon the lion, the adder, or the dragon;" Ps. xci. 13; Acts xxviii. 3—6: we may drink poison itself, Mark xvi. 18, or suffer ourselves to be committed to the flames, without experiencing the smallest injury, Dan. iii. 25—27: nothing in the whole universe can "harm us, if we be followers of that which is good," 1 Pet. iii. 13: if God see fit to keep us, we are as safe "in a den of lions" as in a house of friends.

From this subject we may *learn*,

1. To seek God without delay.

There is no period of life when we can call one day, or one hour, our own. We are altogether "in God's hands;" and, if he withdraw his support for one moment, we perish, as certainly as a stone gravitates to the earth. Shall we then, when so entirely dependent on our God, provoke him to cast us out of his hands? Shall we continue to despise his patience and forbearance, till he swear in his wrath that our "time shall be no longer?" Rev. x 6. Think, how many have lost the time afforded them, and how bitterly they now bewail their folly: and beg of God, that he would "so teach you to number your days, that you may apply your hearts unto wisdom." Ps. xc. 12.

2. To serve him without fear—

We are too apt to keep back from serving God through fear of the persecutions we may endure from man. But, if our times be in God's hands, all our concerns must be there too; and nothing can befall us but by his appointment. "Who art thou then, that thou shouldest be afraid of a man that shall die, and forgettest the Lord thy Maker?" Isa. li. 12, 13. Are we not told, that "the wrath of man shall praise him; and that the remainder of it he shall restrain?" Ps. lxxvi. 10. Be bold then for God; "set your face as a flint against the whole world," Isa. xlix. 7—9, and trust in him for protection. He will not indeed screen you from all trials; because it is on many accounts necessary that you should feel them, 1 Pet. i. 6: but he will suffer none to come upon you which he will not enable you to bear, none which he will not sanctify to your eternal good, 1 Cor. x. 13

3. To trust him without carefulness.

It is foolish as well as impious to distrust God, or to murmur at any of his dispensations. In whose hands could the disposal of all events be placed so much to our advantage, as in his, who possesses infinite wisdom to devise what is best, and infinite power to effect it? Would we be made the sport of chance or fortune? or would we have our present and everlasting concerns left wholly to our own management? If we are not fit to regulate our temporal affairs till we attain the age of manhood, how much less can we ever be competent to take the reins of God's government into our own hands, and to order the affairs of his kingdom. But our times will be in God's hands, whether we acquiese in it or not. Let us therefore contentedly leave ourselves to his all-wise disposal, assured, that "he doeth all things well," and will make "all things to work together for good to them that love him."

THE SECURITY OF THOSE WHO DWELL IN GOD.

Psalm xci. 9, 10.—Because thou hast made the Lord, which is my refuge, even the Most High, thy habitation, there shall no evil befall thee. (H. H.)

It is scarcely possible to conceive any terms more strong, or any images more lively, than those in which the scripture represents the privileges of believers. We need look no further than to the psalm before us for a confirmation of this truth. Indeed, according to the view given of this psalm by a learned Prelate, there is, in the first verses of it, an emphasis which cannot be surpassed. * And the whole may be considered as the believer's charter, in which all his privileges are contained, from his first acceptance with God to the consummation of his happiness in glory.

We have in the words of our text a just description of the believer:

I. His EXPERIENCE.

The true christian is one who has been "turned from darkness unto light, and from the power of satan unto God." Being once brought to God, he "makes the Most High his habitation." He regards God, not merely as reconciled to him, but as affording him what a dwelling-house affords to its possessor,

1. Free access.

A person goes familiarly to his house at all times, not doubting but that he shall gain a ready admission into it. He considers it as his own, and feels that it exists only for his accommodation. It is thus that the believer goes to God as his God: he has "access to him with boldness and confidence:" he is certain that, when he calls, he shall receive an answer; and "when he knocks, the door will be opened to him." In this precise view the Psalmist speaks of God; "be thou my strong habitation, whereunto I may continually resort." Ps. lxxi. 3.

2. Necessary provision.

Every man, whatever be his situation in life, expects to find in his own house the things suited to his necessities. He does not seek his meals at the houses of his neighbors, but in his own; and he returns home at stated seasons to partake of them. And whither does the believer go for daily supplies of bread for his soul? It is in Christ Jesus that his fullness is treasured up, and in him the believer expects to find the "grace that is sufficient for him." God invites him to come to him for the express purpose, that he may be filled and satisfied with good things: "Wherefore do ye spend your money for that which is not bread? Hearken diligently unto me, and eat ye that which is good, and let your soul delight itself in fatness." Isai. lv. 2.

3. Sure protection.

If storms descend, or dangers menace, we take refuge in our house, and find it a place of safety. Thus "the name of God also is a strong tower, to which the righteous runneth and is safe." Prov. xviii. 10. It is to himself that God invites us, when he says, "Come my people, enter thou into thy chambers, shut the door about thee, and hide thyself for a little moment, until the indignation be overpast." Isai. xxvi. 20. And that this was a primary idea in the mind of the Psalmist, appears from the very words of the text, wherein he calls God "his refuge," and from the whole scope of the psalm, from the beginning to the end. With this also agrees the beautiful description given of Jesus by the prophet, as "an hiding-place from the wind, and a covert from the tempest." Isai. xxxii. 2.

4. Sweet repose.

To this house a man retires from the noise and bustle of the world; and there he lays himself down to rest after the fatigues of the day. Home, though inferior in many respects to places of temporary residence, is to al-

* Bishop Horne reads the two first verses thus: " He that dwelleth &c. who abideth under &c who saith of the Lord," &c. Then at the end of ver. 2, he supposes the Psalmist to break off abruptly, and, instead of continuing his description, to address himself to the person before described; " Surely he shall deliver thee."

most all persons the most agreeable, because there they are most at ease. And such is God to the believer. "In every place, God is to him as a little sanctuary," Ezek. xi. 16; where he finds himself at rest. He carries his wants to God, and "casts all his care on him," and enjoys peace which passeth all understanding. In this sense he says *for his own encouragement,* "Return unto thy *rest,* O my soul:" and attests *for the glory of his God,* "Lord thou hast been our *dwelling-place* in all generations." Ps. xc. i.

In connexion with this experience of the believer, let us consider,

II. HIS PRIVILEGE.

The expression in the text seems to exceed the bounds of truth: but the more it is examined, the more will it be found to be strictly true. The man who makes God his habitation shall have no evil befall him:

1. None here.

No *casual* evil shall befall him. There is no such thing as chance: every thing, even to the falling of a sparrow, is ordered of the Lord. As for the children of God, "their heavenly Father hath given his angels charge over them, to keep them in all their ways;" see ver. 11, 12; and if any thing were to happen to them, *they* (the angels) would contract a fearful responsibility for their neglect. We must not however imagine that believers are at liberty to rush into needless dangers; for our Lord, when tempted by satan to cast himself from a pinnacle of the temple in expectation that the angels would preserve him from injury, replied, "Thou shalt not tempt the Lord thy God:" but nothing can happen to them except by the divine appointment: they are hid in the shadow of their Father's hand, and "their very hairs are all numbered."

But it may be thought that *penal* evil may come to them. This however we utterly deny. That they may be "visited with the rod," we readily acknowledge: but there is great difference between the vindictive arm of an incensed judge, and the gentle chastisements of an indulgent parent. The cup that may at any time be put into their hands may be bitter; but it has not in it one drop of wrath: it is altogether mixed by love; and not an ingredient can be found in it, which they themselves shall not one day confess to have been salutary and beneficial.

In short, no *real* evil shall befall them. That they may have troubles, is certain: that their troubles may be heavy and accumulated, is also certain. But who accounts even the amputation of a limb *evil,* if it be the only and infallible method of preserving life? Much less then are any sufferings to be accounted evil, which the believer can ever be called to sustain: for he shall never endure any, which shall not work for good to him in this life, and be the means of increasing his weight of glory in the next. Rom. viii. 28, and 2 Cor. iv. 17.

2. None hereafter.

It is in this life only that the believer can meet with even the semblance of evil: when he goes hence, he is instantly placed beyond the reach of harm. No sin, no sorrow, no pain, no temptation, no weariness, no want, can ever be felt by him in the mansions of bliss. He will there enjoy for ever one unclouded day; and his happiness will be without alloy, without intermission, without end. Rev. xxi. 4.

To render this subject more instructive, we shall add a word,

1. Of direction.

Christ, in reference to the sheepfold of his church, says, "I am the door; if any man enter in by me, he shall be saved, and shall go in and out, and find pasture." John x. 9. The same figure we may apply to the subject before us: "Christ is the door;" he is "the way to the Father;" and "no man cometh unto the Father, but by him." To those who come to God in any other way, he is not "a refuge," or "habitation," but "a consuming fire." Heb. xii. 29. But if we believe in Christ, then "will he dwell in us, and we shall dwell in him:" John vi. 56; yea, "he will be our house of defence, to save us for ever." Ps. xxxi. 2.

2. Of warning.

Who, except the believer, can apply to himself the promise in the text? As for the unbelieving and disobedient, they are in danger every hour: they know not but that God's wrath may break forth against them the very next moment to their destruction. Of this they are certain, (whether they will believe it or not,) that in a little time his judgments shall overtake them, and the greatest of all evils shall befall them, unless they repent. O that they would be prevailed upon to flee for refuge to the hope that it set before them! O that they would now seek to be "found in Christ!" Then should the destroying angel pass over them, and "they should dwell safely, and be quiet from the fear of evil." Prov. i. 33.

3. Of encouragement.

The weakness of men's faith often robs them of the comfort which it is their privilege to enjoy. Why should a believer be afraid of thunder and lightning? Were he but sensible what a protector he has, he would feel assured that no evil could come unto him. How varied are God's promises to him in the psalm before us! How diversified also are the assurances given him by Eliphaz in the book of Job! Job v. 19—24. Let him only commit himself to God, and he has nothing to fear. Let us then, beloved, have faith in God; and let those words of David be our song in this land of our pilgrimage; "God is our refuge, &c.; therefore will we not fear, though the earth be removed, and though the waters be carried into the midst of the sea: &c." Ps. xlvi. 1—4.

~~~~~~~~~~

THE TRIUMPHANT SONG OF THE REDEEMED.

Rev. i. 5, 6.—And from Jesus Christ, who is the faithful witness, and the first begotten ot the death, and the prince of the kings of the earth. Unto him that loved us, and washed us from our sins in his own blood, and hath made us kings and priests unto God and his Father; to him be glory and dominion for ever and ever. Amen.

THE Saviour having appeared in a vision to St. John, in "the isle of Patmos," he commanded him to write appropriate epistles to "the seven churches in Asia," to reprove their evils, correct their errors, and encourage their hopes. He therefore introduced the subjects of his addresses by an affectionate salutation in the name of the triune Jehovah; and having distinctly specified the Father and the Holy Spirit, he solemnly adds in the text, "and from Jesus Christ, who is the faithful witness," &c. These words strikingly illustrate the *mediatorial character* of Jesus Christ—the *exalted privilege* of his believing people—and the *personal influence* of redeeming grace. Let us observe,

I. THE MEDIATORIAL CHARACTER OF JESUS CHRIST. This is admirably described by the apostle, in the words before us; in which he faithfully re presents the various offices that he executes, as the mediator of the new covenant.

1. *He is the prophet of his church.* Hence he is denominated, "the faithful *witness.*" A *witness* is one who either *reveals* what was previously unknown, or *attests* what has been already announced. In both these respects Jesus Christ is "given to be a witness to the people." He has distinctly revealed the true character and will of God—the astonishing scheme and work of redemption—and the only way of salvation and eternal life, John iii. 16—18. The writings of Moses and the prophets were fully accomplished in him, for they "testified beforehand the sufferings of Christ, and the glory that should follow." The comparative darkness of the law is passed away, and the meridian light of the gospel now shineth. The sun of righteousness hath arisen on the moral world, to give light to them that sit in darkness and the shadow of death. As a teacher come from God, he "spake as never man spake;" and as an immutable witness, he still externally reveals and personally attests divine truth, both by the medium of his word, and the influence of his spirit, Rom. viii. 14—16; 2 Tim. iii. 16, 17. The testimony of Christ is invariably true, for he is the *faithful witness*, whose veracity is infinite, and fidelity infallible. He has brought life and immortality to light by the gospel; he guides his people into all truth, and makes them wise unto salvation, Isa. liv. 14.

2. *He is the high priest of our profession.* This is evidently intended, when he is called, "the first begotten of *the dead.*" His death and resurrection were important parts of his priesthood, and essentially connected with the salvation of sinners. An atonement was absolutely necessary, and therefore Jesus Christ in matchless love, "took upon him the seed of Abraham, to make reconciliation for the sins of the people." By his *sacrificial death*, he fully atoned for our iniquities, and opened a new and living way to the Father, Heb. x. 18—22. He also rose again for our justification, and is now "the resurrection and the life, having obtained eternal redemption for us." He is therefore emphatically, "the first begotten of the dead," because he is the first, who ever rose to die no more; and his resurrection clearly demonstrates the efficacy of his sacrifice, and is the strongest pledge of the blissful immortality which awaits his people in the world to come, Luke xxiv. 46, 47; 1 Cor. xv. 20. As the high priest over the house of God, Christ is our "advocate with the Father," and the altar which sanctifieth both the giver and the gift. Through him alone we have access to the throne of grace; and our persons and services are accepted by virtue of the life and death of him, who once suffered for our sins, and now "ever liveth to make intercession for us," John xiv. 6; Heb. iv. 14—16.

3. *He is the sovereign of the universe.* His dominion is supreme and unlimited, reaching through all space, and extending to all duration. He is therefore justly acknowledged "the prince of the kings of the earth;" for by him "kings reign, and princes decree justice." An *essential* God, his kingdom ruleth over all things, and he *only* sways the sceptre of universal empire, and sustains supremacy of character, as "the king of kings, and Lord of lords." And as "the mediator between God and man," he has founded a kingdom of grace, in which he triumphantly reigns for the salvation of mankind, Dan. ii. 44; Matt. iii. 2. This kingdom is spiritual in its character, and perpetual in its duration. All other empires are worldly and perishing; but the kingdom of Christ "is not of this world, and shall never be destroyed." The Almighty King of Zion reigns *universally* in the world—*mediatorially* in his church—*spiritually* in the hearts of his

people—and *eternally* in the glory of heaven, Heb. i. 8; Rom. xiv. 17; Matt. xxv. 34. His reign is infinitely wise, holy, just, merciful, and gracious. What a transcendently glorious and amiable Sovereign! Let us therefore consider.

II. THE EXALTED PRIVILEGE OF HIS BELIEVING PEOPLE;—" Unto him that loved us," &c. This inspired description of the nature and properties of Christian salvation, is highly appropriate and comprehensive; and distinctly specifies,

1. *The divinity of its origin;*—" Unto *him* that *loved us.*" God is unquestionably the source of all possible good, and from him every blessing descends. When he beheld the miserable and perishing state of mankind, he remembered us in infinite mercy, and graciously sent his Son to be the Saviour of the world, John iv. 9, 10. Jesus also loved us, and " gave himself a ransom for all, to be testified in due time." What unspeakable love has he manifested to fallen sinners! Consider his amazing incarnation, sufferings, crucifixion, resurrection, ascension, and intercession at the " right hand of the majesty on high," 2 Cor. v. 14, 15, viii. 9. His love contains unfathomable breadths, and lengths, and depths, and heights, which neither angels nor men can perfectly comprehend! This spontaneous and unparalleled love is the originating cause of all the ineffable blessings of present and eternal salvation, Eph. ii. 4—6.

2. *The excellency of its character;*—" And *washed* us from *our sins.*" All sin is moral contamination. It not only contracts guilt, but also defiles every power both of body and soul. Hence it is called, " uncleanness, corruption, defilement, the pollution of the world, and filthiness of flesh and spirit," Mark vii. 21—23. From these stains of guilt and depravity Christ saves all his faithful followers. The work of grace is *already begun* in their hearts. Their iniquities are freely and fully forgiven, and they believingly participate the cleansing efficacy of the blood of sprinkling, 1 John i. 7. Present salvation therefore includes both the justification of our *persons*, through the righteousness of Christ, and the sanctification of our *nature* by the spirit of holiness, Jer. xxiii. 6; Titus iii. 5. Pardon and purity are *equally* necessary, and are *actually* enjoyed by those who have " tasted that the Lord is gracious," and are saved " by the washing of regeneration, and the renewing of the Holy Ghost," 1 Cor. vi. 11; Tit. ii. 14.

3. *The efficacy of its medium;*—" And washed us in *his own blood.*" This is the only possible way in which sinners can be saved; " for without shedding of blood, there can be no remission." Every spiritual blessing is attributed to the blood of Christ. We are *redeemed, justified, adopted, washed*, and ultimately *glorified*, through " the *blood* of the everlasting covenant," Rom. iii. 24, 25; 1 Pet. i. 19; Rev. vii. 14. This medium of salvation was *typified* by the whole sacrificial dispensation of the Jews, which was a shadow of good things to come. But Jesus Christ has now *personally* " opened a fountain for sin and uncleanness," and saves his people not *ceremonially* by the blood of legal sacrifices, but *meritoriously* by his own " most precious blood," which was shed for them, Heb. xii. 14. This blood possesses not only an *atoning virtue*, for the expiation of sin, but also, a *cleansing efficacy*, which purifies the soul; for " the blood of Jesus Christ cleanseth from all unrighteousness."

4. *The dignity of its subjects;*—" And hath made us *kings* and *priests* unto God and his Father." Divine grace both saves and dignifies its possessors; it raises them from the ruin and misery of sin, to a state of glory and virtue. They are anointed spiritual *kings*, having already received a

kingdom of grace; and are the legitimate heirs of the kingdom of heaven, Col. i. 13; Heb. xii. 28. They are also consecrated *priests*, "to offer up spiritual sacrifices, acceptable to God through Jesus Christ." They receive this honor that cometh from God only, and participate all the inestimable dignities and privileges of the glorious gospel of peace, 1 Pet. ii. 9, 10. The believing recipients of salvation, are thus divinely honored and blessed; and are made by the blood and Spirit of Christ, "a royal and holy priesthood unto God and his Father." Surely, "happy art thou, O Israel; who is like unto thee, O people saved by the Lord!" This will lead us to notice,

III. THE PERSONAL INFLUENCE OF REDEEMING GRACE;—"To him be glory and dominion for ever and ever. Amen." This lively description of supreme majesty and power to the redeemer, may be regarded as,

1. *The language of admiration and love.* The believer discovers inexpressible perfection and glory, in the person and character of the Saviour: and therefore regards him, as the object of his intense desire and devout attachment. A *personal* apprehension of his infinite grandeur and goodness deeply affects the minds of Christians, and fills them with unutterable raptures of wonder, love and joy. The believing contemplation of his divine glories, redeeming works, and saving offices, powerfully attracts and captivates their hearts, and triumphantly subdues them to the sceptre of his kingdom. They gladly embrace him as an object altogether lovely and glorious; readily acknowledge the supremacy of his glory and dominion; and joyfully "count all things but loss, for the excellency of the knowledge of Christ Jesus the Lord," Gal. vi. 14; 1 John iv. 19.

2. *The language of gratitude and praise.* A participation of the unsearchable riches of Christ is invariably accompanied with grateful and affectionate dispositions of the heart. The doctrine of salvation by grace necessarily excludes boasting, and inspires the profoundest gratitude and thanksgiving. Though the obligations of believers to the redeemer are infinite and indescribable, they sensibly feel their overwhelming influence, and often gratefully exclaim, "bless the Lord, O my soul, and forget not all his benefits;" "unto him that loved us," &c. Their unfeigned gratitude is *practically* displayed, by their love to the Saviour's person,—obedience to his word,—zeal in his cause,—praise for his goodness,—and joyful anticipation of his kingdom, Ps. cxvi. 12—14; 1 Pet. i. 8, 9.

3. *The language of adoration and delight.* Jesus Christ is inexpressibly glorious and precious to them that believe. He is their "wisdom, righteousness and sanctification, and redemption." He is the object of their confidence,—the author of their salvation,—and the source of their happiness; they exultingly glory in his cross,—devoutly honor him as they honor the Father,—supremely adore the perfections of his character,—and greatly delight in the exercises of his worship, Prov. iii. 17; Phil. iii. 3. The text is their triumphant felicity and song in the house of their pilgrimage; and will ultimately constitute the blissful theme of their ceaseless hallelujahs, in the "house not made with hands, eternal in the heavens." Let all the redeemed therefore, believingly and piously add, *Amen.*

This subject displays the exalted dignity of the redeemer,—unfolds the nature and method of salvation,—and affords ample consolation to them, that "follow the Lamb whithersoever he goeth."

65

CHRIST THE BELIEVER'S LIFE, AND DEATH THE BELIEVER'S GAIN.

Philippians i. 21.—For me to live is Christ, and to die is gain. (Sk.)

WHEN St. Paul uttered this sentiment, he was a prisoner for Jesus Christ, deprived of his liberty, and under the control of his persecuting foes; but his soul was not bound: the Philippians were inexpressibly dear to him; he had them in his heart; they were his joy and his crown; and he longed after them all in the bowels of Jesus Christ: and their love to him, if less ardent, was not less sincere. Hearing of his deprivations, they voluntarily raised a contribution among themselves, and sent it to him by the hand of Epaphroditus their minister; in return, St. Paul sent them this admirable epistle. In the preceding verses to the text, he assures them that the things which had happened to him, were so far from impeding the progress of truth, that they had "fallen out," &c., ver. 12; and that his fellow helpers in the ministry were more confident by his bonds, ver. 14. He then, after expressing his confidence that all his sufferings would have a favorable issue, verse 19, 20, utters the devout and elevated sentiment in the text; "For me to live," &c. We have here two things:—

I. CHRIST THE BELIEVER'S LIFE.

II. DEATH THE BELIEVER'S GAIN.

"For me to live is Christ." This is in effect saying,

1. *Christ is the Author of my life.* 'Two kinds of life has double-natured man.' We all live as animal and rational beings, and have capacities for the performance of animal and rational actions. But believers live in a more exalted sense, and possess a higher life, a life of which Jesus Christ is the immediate Author. Once they were devoid of this, and even dead while they lived; they saw objects, heard sounds, tasted food, performed actions, and did all that was necessary as members of civil society and citizens of the world; but they had no spiritual senses, they saw not God, they heard not his voice, they tasted not his love, and they had no feeling of the powers of the world to come. But when they were dead in sin, Christ quickened them. "The hour is coming," &c., John v. 25. "I am the resurrection and the life," &c., xi. 25.

2. *Christ is the principle of my life.* Every kind of life, whether vegetable, animal, or spiritual, depends upon some principle from which it springs; for life is but the effects of some latent and operative cause. Christ not only lights up the lamp of spiritual life, but he feeds the flame, and supplies the oil by which it burns. Christ, dwelling in our hearts by faith, becomes the principle of our life. "I am the living bread," &c., John vi. 51. "Except ye eat the flesh," &c., ver. 53. "I live, yet not I, but Christ liveth in me," Gal. ii. 20. "When Christ, who is our life," &c., Col. iii. 4. "He that hath the Son," &c , 1 John v. 12. We are as much dependant on Christ for spiritual life, as plants are dependant on the earth for vegetable life, or the body is dependant on the soul for animal life.

3. *Christ is the model of my life.* Christians are not lawless beings who walk at random, or live according to the course of the world. No, they regard Christ as their pattern, and they study to be like him. They do this, because they know that the life of Christ was the most dignified and glorious life that was ever led upon earth, and that there is every thing great and good in the imitation of so illustrious a character.—Because the Spirit of Christ within them, excites them to follow the example of Christ without.—Because they love Christ, and love leads them to imitate the beloved object,—and they

know that the profession of christianity lays them under strong obligations to follow the Lord Jesus. " He that saith he abideth in him, ought himself also," &c., 1 John ii. 6.

4. *Christ is the end of my life.* Carnal men are most commonly selfish men ; they seek their own, and not another's wealth ; their own ease, or their own glory, or their own pleasure, engages all their attention, and occupies all their time ; and they live as fully to themselves, as if they were the authors of their own being, or the arbiters of their own fate. But believers consider Christ as the end of their life ; from a consciousness that they owe their being to Christ, and that he formed them for his glory, and redeemed them by his blood : they surrender themselves to his service ; whether they eat or drink, or whatever they do, the glory of Christ is their great object : they renounce their own ease, to sustain the cross of Christ : they sacrifice their own reputation for the reproach of Christ : and count not their lives dear unto themselves, so that they may advance the honor of Christ : with the apostle they can say, " None of us liveth unto himself," &c., Rom. xiv. 7, 8.

II. Death is the believer's gain. " To die is gain." We must distinguish here, between the act of dying and the consequences of death. There is every thing in death, considered in itself, that is appalling and dreadful. *Look at death in its deprivations.* Here the tenderest bonds of affection are dissolved ; the most endearing relations ended ; and the deepest pangs of parting endured. *Death in its agonies.* How inadequate is human language to describe the pains of the dying ; what deep waters go over them ! how hard the struggle they endure ! *Death in its degradations.* What can be more exquisitely beautiful than a human body adorned with youth, flushed with health, and fired with vigor, the eyes sparkling with joy, the heart dancing with gladness, the pulse beating high with expectation, and the cheeks glowing lovelier than the virgin rose. But in death all is changed ! all degraded ! a putrid mass of inanimate matter is all that is left ; a receptacle for worms, a prey for corruption, a heap of dust ! So that if there were nothing beyond death, it would be no gain to die ; for death in itself is a sore evil, and a most terrible curse inflicted upon mankind. But as it is gain to die, pronounced so by an inspired apostle, we must infer that there is another state of being to which death introduces us. In illustrating this subject, we consider the evils from which we are delivered,—and the blessings with which we shall be crowned.

First, The evils from which we are delivered.

1. *Death delivers us from the pains and miseries of the present life.* Man is born to trouble, and suffering is his lot upon earth. He suffers in his body ; what numerous ills life is heir to ! He suffers in his mind ; how many things would his spirit and put him to grief ! He suffers by commiseration ; his friends and fellow creatures suffer, and he weeps with those that weep. What a suffering man was St. Paul ! Hear his tale of wo : " Of the Jews, five times received I forty stripes save one," &c., 2 Cor. xi. 24. Nor was this all, he was a man of feeling ; " Who is weak, and I am not weak ? who is offended, and I burn not ?" " What mean ye, to weep, and break my heart ?" Acts xxi. 13. But in heaven there is no pain ; " sorrow and sighing shall flee away, and God shall wipe away all tears from our eyes."

2. *Death frees us from all the imperfections of our mortal state.* Our knowledge here is very imperfect and defective ; we know but in part : and the little knowledge of which we are possessed is frequently obtained by hard study and intense thought ; and this defective knowledge renders us liable to

mistake, to entertain wrong opinions of men and things; and a mistake in judgment frequently induces errors in practice. Paul withstood Peter to the face, because he was to be blamed. But to die is gain. "In heaven we shall know even also as we are known." 'There knowledge grows without decay.' That is the region of perfection, and there error can find no entrance.

3. *Death terminates the conflicts of our christian warfare.* Believers are now engaged in a most perilous contest. Their enemies are principalities and powers, &c., Eph. vi. 12. The issue of this conflict sometimes appears doubtful; "without are fightings and within are fears:" but when death comes, the fight is finished, the victory won, and the believer goes to his vast reward that awaits him in the skies.

Secondly, The gain to which the text refers, comprehends the acquisition of all possible good.

1. *It will be universal. In the situation;* we exchange houses of clay for everlasting habitations. *The society;* we leave behind our weeping companions, to greet he blood besprinkled bands on the eternal shore. *The enjoyments;* here the purest pleasures are often interrupted, and may be finally forfeited. There our enjoyments will flow on like a river, pure as the source from whence they spring. *In our capacities;* here we have blessings, but sometimes cannot enjoy them; there the body will be immortal, and the soul capacitated for enjoyments the most elevated and enlarged. *In employments;* the occupations of this world are sordid and laborious; there we shall sing the praises of God, contemplate the mysteries of his nature, the variety of his works, and the glory of his government.

2. *It will be incalculable.* There is no gain upon earth that may not be estimated. We have figures and numbers, and arithmeticians who can form estimates and make calculations to any amount. But who can calculate the value of heavenly joys! the worth of immortal pleasures!

3. *It will be eternal.* It is not the gain of a moment, or even an age, but the gain of eternity, and of all eternity can give. Gain that can never be forfeited, nor diminished in value. Earthly goods cease to give their possessors pleasure, in proportion to the duration of the period they possess them. Worldly joys cloy the appetite, and pleasures cease to please; but the happiness of heaven will increase in value to eternity.

In conclusion we observe,

First, *If Christ is the believer's life, how happy and desirable is his state!* 'What hath the world to equal this?' What life is so honorable, so profitable, and so glorious! How strange it is that we have so few candidates for such a life! Is this your life? Why should not the apostle's experience be yours? There is no state of christianity that belonged exclusively to any order of men. You may be as holy as apostles. If Christ is not your life, you are not christians; you may have been baptized into the christian name, and accustomed to attend christian ordinances; but in the benefits of christianity you have no share, and to the rewards of christianity you have no title. O what a miserable, worldly, sensual life is yours!

Secondly, *If death is the believer's gain, should not this more than reconcile us to the thoughts of dying?* Many look at death in the pains and agonies it inflicts, and tremble with fearful apprehensions. These we may never realize; many die as tranquilly as they sink into the arms of sleep: but should death be even as dreadful as we anticipate, 'tis useless ' to die a thousand deaths in fearing one.' Let us look at the promises of God, read the experience of dying saints, and especially "endure as seeing him who is invisible."

Thirdly, *If to die is gain, how selfish to indulge inconsolable grief for our departed friends, who have passed into the skies.* 'O the pain, the bliss of dying!' the bitterness of death is with them for ever passed, and the bliss of now dying is their unalienable portion.

THE HAPPINESS OF DYING IN THE LORD.

Revelation xiv. 13 —And I heard a voice from heaven, saying unto me, Write, Blessed are the dead, &c. (H)

THESE words are a voice from heaven, concerning the future state of those that die in Christ; and surely none are better qualified to comfort those who are left behind, than one of the heavenly company.

Our blessed Lord tells his disciples, when sinking into despondency at the idea of his leaving them, "If ye loved me, ye would rejoice, because I said, I go unto my Father," John xiv. 28; so when the believer dies, he goes to be with him : and, that we may not sorrow as those who have no hope, the text tells us, that they are not lost by ceasing to live in this world, but, are advanced to an infinitely better life than this : "Blessed are the dead," &c.

Consider,

I. WHAT IT IS TO DIE IN THE LORD, AND WHO MAY BE SAID TO DO SO.

This may be said of the martyrs who die for the Lord, and seal the truth of their profession with their blood. It is applicable also to all real christians, who are united to Christ, and die the members of his mystical body : these die in the Lord. And, in order to this,

Something is previously necessary.

1. That they be quickened and made alive by the Lord   John v. 20, 21; Eph. ii. 1.

2. That they be pardoned, justified, and sanctified.   1 Cor. vi. 11.

3. That they walk after him.   Heb. xii. 2; 1 Pet. ii. 21.

4. That they live to him, as they receive all from him.   2 Cor. v. 14, 15; Phil. i. 21.

Something is implied.

1. That we die in submission to his will, when, where, and how he pleases.   Rom. xiv. 7, 8.

2. In dependence upon him for life and immortality.

3. A sincere desire to be with him.   Phil. i. 23.

II. WHEREIN THEIR BLESSEDNESS CONSISTS ; and the text tells us, that,

"'They rest from their labors."

1. Arising from the evils to which they were subject in this world : disease, pain, want, &c.   "Many are the afflictions," &c.   Ps. xxxiv. 19. All shall be left behind at death.   Rev. xxi. 4.

2. From satan's temptations.   After death they shall be placed beyond the reach of his fiery darts.   2 Cor. iv. 4.   These they shall have left in the field of battle, and be "where the weary are at rest."   1 Pet. v. 8 Job iii. 17.

3. From the persecution of the ungodly.   John xv. 20.

4. From the remains of the carnal mind, wanderings in duty, and the im
perfections of the best of our religious services.

" Their works follow tl em."

All the works they have done for God and his Christ, to advance his glory,
prepare themselves for his kingdom, and serve his interest, and to help on
others to it. These works shall follow after, so as to enter with them, and
that in the most endearing manner.

1. In God's faithful remembrance of them all. Heb. vi. 10; Mal.
iii. 16.

2. In the recompense of reward, which God will bestow. 1 Cor.
xv. 58.

III. WHY THIS MESSAGE IS SO SOLEMNLY PROCLAIMED BY ".A VOICE
FROM HEAVEN."

1. To let an unthinking world know what becomes of the friends of
Christ when they die.

2. To assure believers that death is no hinderance to their happiness; but
the certain, though awful, way to it.

3. To leave it on record, to the end of time, for the assurance of every
christian, that their rest is not here, and to excite them to look after one
remaining.

APPLICATION.

1. Are the dead, who die in the Lord, blessed? how miserable are they
who die out of him : and if the former are blessed immediately, henceforth
from the time they die, so the latter must be wretched immediately upon
their dying.

2. How much better to a believer is the day of his death, than the day of
his birth; seeing he is born to labor, but dies to rest!

The Developing Person Through Childhood and Adolescence

Tenth Edition

Kathleen Stassen Berger

Bronx Community College
City University of New York

macmillan
education

Publisher: Rachel Losh

Associate Publisher: Jessica Bayne

Developmental Editors: Tom Churchill and Andrea Musick Page

Assistant Editor: Catherine Michaelsen

Executive Marketing Manager: Katherine Nurre

Supplements and Media Editor: Lauren Samuelson

Director, Content Management Enhancement: Tracey Kuehn

Managing Editor: Lisa Kinne

Production Editor: Betsy Draper, TSI evolve, Inc.

Project Liaison: Janice Stangel

Interior and Cover Design: Blake Logan

Photo Editors: Cecilia Varas and Bianca Moscatelli

Photo Researcher: Jacqui Wong

Art Manager: Matthew McAdams

Illustrations: Todd Buck Illustrations, MPS Limited, TSI evolve, Inc., Evelyn Pence

Production Managers: Stacey Alexander and Barbara Seixas

Composition: TSI evolve, Inc.

Printing and Binding: King Printing

Cover Photograph: Maria Abalos/Getty Images

Library of Congress Preassigned Control Number: 2015933599

ISBN: 978-1-319-15395-3

Manufactured in the United States of America

Second printing

Worth Publishers

41 Madison Avenue New York, NY 10010

www.worthpublishers.com

Credit is given to the following sources for permission to use the photos indicated:

Brief Contents and other Silhouettes in order of appearance

Lane Oatey/Getty Images

© John Lund/Annabelle Breakey/Blend Images/Corbis

George Doyle/Getty Images

© Vinicius Ramalho Tupinamba/Istockphoto

Mark Anderson/Getty Images

Lane Oatey/Blue Jean Images/Getty Images

Contents in order of appearance

Lane Oatey/Getty Images

©2016 Macmillan

Marilyn Nieves/Vetta/Getty Images

©2016 Macmillan

Zhang Bo/Getty Images

© John Lund/Annabelle Breakey/Blend Images/Corbis

©2016 Macmillan

Jose Luis Pelaez, Inc/Blend Images/Getty Images

©2016 Macmillan

© Vinicius Ramalho Tupinamba/Istockphoto

Claudia Dewald/Getty Images

©2016 Macmillan

Marcus Lindstrom/Getty Images

George Doyle/Getty Images

GM Visuals/Getty Images

©2016 Macmillan

WMay/Getty Images

Mark Anderson/Getty Images

Hola Images Rf/Getty Images

Aldo Murillo/Getty Images

Anna Wehmeyer-Germany/Getty Images

Lane Oatey/Blue Jean Images/Getty Images

©2016 Macmillan

About the Author

Kathleen Stassen Berger received her undergraduate education at Stanford University and Radcliffe College, then earned an MAT from Harvard University and an MS and PhD from Yeshiva University. Her broad experience as an educator includes directing a preschool, serving as chair of philosophy at the United Nations International School, and teaching child and adolescent development to graduate students at Fordham University in New York and undergraduates at Montclair State University in New Jersey and Quinnipiac University in Connecticut. She also taught social psychology to inmates at Sing Sing Prison who were earning their paralegal degrees.

Currently, and for most of her professional career, Berger is a professor at Bronx Community College of the City University of New York, where she began as an adjunct in English and for the past decades has been a full professor in the Social Sciences department, which includes sociology, economics, anthropology, political science, human services, and psychology. She has taught introduction to psychology, child and adolescent development, adulthood and aging, social psychology, abnormal psychology, and human motivation. Her students—who come from many ethnic, economic, and educational backgrounds and who have a wide range of ages and interests—consistently honor her with the highest teaching evaluations.

Berger is also the author of *The Developing Person Through the Life Span* and *Invitation to the Life Span.* Her developmental texts are currently being used at more than 700 colleges and universities worldwide and are available in Spanish, French, Italian, and Portuguese, as well as English. Her research interests include adolescent identity, immigration, bullying, and grandparents, and she has published articles on developmental topics in the *Wiley Encyclopedia of Psychology* and in publications of the American Association for Higher Education and the National Education Association for Higher Education. She continues teaching and learning from her students as well as from her four daughters and three grandsons.

Brief Contents

Contents

PART II

The First Two Years 135

PART V

Adolescence 443

My grandson, Asa, is in early childhood. He sees the world in opposites: male/female, child/grown-up, good guys/ bad guys. He considers himself one of the good guys, destroying the bad guys in his active imagination and in karate kicks in the air.

Oscar, his father, knows better. He asked me if Asa really believes there are good guys and bad guys, or is that just a cliché. I said that most young children believe in simple, straightforward opposites.

Undeterred, Oscar told Asa that he knows some adults who were once bad guys but became good guys.

"No," Asa insisted. "That never happens."

Asa is mistaken. As he matures, his body will grow taller and become better able to sit with feet on the floor, not kicking. His thoughts will include the idea that people change as they grow older, a theme throughout this book. What Asa says "never happens" occurs every day—none of us is a bad guy or a good guy, but all of us keep developing, ideally for the better.

Oscar is not alone in his awareness. Many folk sayings affirm development: People "turn over a new leaf," are "born-again"; parents are granted a "do-over" when they become grandparents; today is "the first day of the rest of your life." We recognize that the past never disappears and that parents always influence children, as in the saying "The apple does not fall far from the tree," but we also recognize many other genetic, biological, and social influences on each person, as detailed in the best-selling book *Far from the Tree* (Solomon, 2012).

The complexity, the twists and turns, the endless variety of the human experience at every age is fascinating to me, which is why I continue to study human development and revise this textbook, with new insights as well as new words and topics in every edition.

Pondering My grandson, Asa, looks thoughtfully at his father, Oscar.

We all have echoes of Asa in us: We want life to be simple, for people to be good guys. But life is not simple. Learning about human development helps everyone respond to life's variations and influences, not with imaginary kicks but with wise responses. Knowledge does that. In a vivid example, Stephen Pinker (2011) finds that humans kill each other less now than they did in previous centuries; he cites education as one reason.

Education occurs in many ways. This textbook is only one of them—an aid to understanding the complexity of your life, my life, and the lives of all the estimated 19 billion humans alive now or who once lived. Nonetheless, although life experiences and thousands of other books add to our education, writing this text is my contribution and studying it is yours. Together we might learn how to limit the bad and increase the good in each of us as time goes on.

New Material

Every year, scientists discover and explain more concepts and research. The best of these discoveries are integrated into the text, including hundreds of new references on many topics—among them epigenetics at conception, prenatal protections, infant nutrition, autism spectrum disorders, attachment over the life span, high-stakes testing, drug use and drug addiction, sex education, and diversity of all kinds (ethnic, economic, and cultural). Cognizant of the interdisciplinary nature of human development, I include recent research in biology, sociology, education, anthropology, political science, and more—as well as my home discipline, psychology.

Genetics and social contexts are noted throughout. The interaction of nature and nurture are discussed in many chapters, as neuroscience relates to research on family life. Among the many topics described with new research are the variations, benefits, and hazards of breast-feeding, infant day care, preschool education, single parenthood, and peer group pressures. Both my academic history and my human experience compel me to always note differences, deficits, and resilience.

New Pedagogical Aids

This edition incorporates learning objectives at the beginning of each chapter: The "What Will You Know?" questions indicate important ideas or provocative concepts—one for each major section of the chapter. After each major section, a medial summary repeats the main ideas of that section and then "What Have You Learned?" questions help students review what they have just read.

Learning Objectives

Much of what students learn from this course is a matter of attitude, approach, and perspective—all hard to quantify. Specific learning objectives arise from the

FUSE/GETTY IMAGES

"What Have You Learned?" questions, which now appear at the end of each major section rather than at the end of each chapter, as well as from the Key Terms that appear in bold in the text, defined in the margins, listed after each chapter and again in the glossary. You will notice that those Key Terms are repeated several times after they are defined, to reinforce learning and understanding.

Ideally, students will answer the learning objective questions in complete sentences, with specifics that demonstrate knowledge. Some items on the new lists are straightforward, requiring only close attention to the chapter content. Others require comparisons, implications, or evaluations. Cognitive psychology and research on pedagogy have shown that vocabulary, specific knowledge, and critical thinking are all part of learning. These features are designed to foster all three.

Healthy? Children have high energy but small stomachs, so they enjoy frequent snacks more than big meals. Yet snacks are typically poor sources of nutrition.

New *Opposing Perspectives* Boxed Feature and Updated *A View from Science* and *A Case to Study* Features

We all need critical thinking skills. Virtually every page of this book presents not only facts but also questions with divergent interpretations. A new boxed feature called *Opposing Perspectives* appears in this edition of *The Developing Person Through Childhood and Adolescence* for the first time. This box focuses on exciting and controversial topics—from prenatal sex selection to e-cigarettes. I have tried to present information and opinions on both sides of an issue so that students can practice weighing evidence, assessing arguments, and coming to their own conclusions.

In addition, the boxes titled *A View from Science,* which explain surprising insights from recent scientific research, and *A Case to Study,* which illustrate developmental issues through the story of specific individuals, have been extensively updated. All these new features are included in the Table of Contents.